Textbook of Forensic Science

Pankaj Shrivastava • Jose Antonio Lorente •
Ankit Srivastava • Ashish Badiye •
Neeti Kapoor
Editors

Textbook of Forensic Science

Springer

Editors
Pankaj Shrivastava
Biology and Serology Division
Regional Forensic Science Laboratory
Gwalior, Madhya Pradesh, India

Jose Antonio Lorente
University of Granada
Granada, Spain

Ankit Srivastava
School of Forensic Sciences
The West Bengal National University
of Juridical Sciences
Kolkata, West Bengal, India

Ashish Badiye
Department of Forensic Science
Government Institute of Forensic Science
Nagpur, Maharashtra, India

Neeti Kapoor
Department of Forensic Science
Government Institute of Forensic Science
Nagpur, Maharashtra, India

ISBN 978-981-99-1376-3 ISBN 978-981-99-1377-0 (eBook)
https://doi.org/10.1007/978-981-99-1377-0

This Springer imprint is published by the registered company Springer Nature Singapore Pte Ltd.
The registered company address is: 152 Beach Road, #21-01/04 Gateway East, Singapore 189721, Singapore

Preface

Forensic Science includes not only criminal investigative aspects but also civil investigations and preventive aspects as well. It is an interface between science, law, and justice. With the upsurge in crimes and criminal activities, understanding various aspects of forensic science is the need of the hour. Common man, young generation, newly recruited officers of law enforcement agencies, scientists in the forensic science laboratories, lawyers, healthcare professionals, as well as the students of forensic science, forensic medicine, science, as well as interdisciplinary researchers should acquire knowledge and basic understanding of the assorted aspects of "Forensic Science."

This book is written in a way to smoothen this journey of knowledge and to make it a more accessible text for graduate students in forensic science, officers of investigation agencies, various law enforcement agencies, as well as officers and analysts in forensic science laboratories. It is also useful for crime scene investigators, and new learners and researchers with an interest and inclination towards this fascinating field of "Forensic Science." This book consists of 26 chapters covering various aspects of "Forensic Science." This book is a balanced blend of basics and application part of the various arena of forensic science. It will help readers to understand the basic concepts with relative ease and without the need of reading complex literature presently available in the area. It will be an ideal reference material for forensic scientists and those without extensive forensic backgrounds. The book is written in uncomplicated and plain language that the interested community can easily understand. We have tried our best to share the available knowledge from around the globe in the field of forensic science with the aim of benefiting the numerous students pursuing their degrees in the field as well as those students who have a proclivity for forensic science.

Gwalior, Madhya Pradesh, India	Pankaj Shrivastava
Granada, Spain	Jose Antonio Lorente
Kolkata, West Bengal, India	Ankit Srivastava
Nagpur, Maharashtra, India	Ashish Badiye
Nagpur, Maharashtra, India	Neeti Kapoor

Contents

Editors and Contributors

About the Editors

Pankaj Shrivastava received his Ph.D. in Microbiology with a specialization in Biotechnology from the Department of Biological Science, Rani Durgavati University, Jabalpur, Madhya Pradesh, India. He is presently working with the Biology and Serology Facility of Govt. of Madhya Pradesh, India. He has more than 25 years of laboratory and research experience in the field of Forensic biological sciences including DNA. His research interests include population DNA database, improvement of methods in forensic DNA typing, finding rapid protocols for the technology, and microbial forensics. He is the recipient of the prestigious Pt. Govind Vallabh Pant Award from the Bureau of Police Research and Development, Ministry of Home Affairs, Govt. of India and Anusrajan Award from AISECT University, Bhopal for his authored books. He is also a recipient of the FICCI smart policing award for developing a fast DNA typing protocol. He has authored 13 books and published more than 100 research articles in the journals of repute in forensic science, 54 book chapters, 84 conference proceedings, and 15 popular science articles.

José A. Lorente is a Professor of Forensic Medicine at the University of Granada, Spain. After graduating at the Faculty of Medicine of Granada, he received Ph.D. Honors in Medicine and Surgery at the University of Granada. He has published over 140 peer-reviewed papers and several books and book chapters. He has a special focus on the use of DNA and its application to human rights; he also created and launched the DNA-PROKIDS Program in 2004. His areas of interest in forensics also deal with population variability and analysis of old and ancient DNA samples and databases expansion and control. He is also actively working in medical genomics and he is the scientific director of the Center for Genomics and Oncological Research (GENYO), where his team focuses on liquid biopsy and cancer interception. He is the founder and first president of the AICEF (Ibero-Latin American Network of Forensic Sciences) and an honorary member of the AFSN (Asian Forensic Sciences Network).

Ankit Srivastava is a well-known academician in the field of Forensic Science. Currently he is serving as Associate Professor and Coordinator in the School of Forensic Sciences, the W.B. National University of Juridical Sciences (WBNUJS), Kolkata. He also holds the post of Director, Centre for Studies & Research in Forensic Science, WBNUJS, Kolkata, India. He has more than 16 years of teaching and research experience in the field of forensic sciences. During his 16 years of journey, he authored several research articles and books published in different journals of national and international repute. He has visited and has been invited by various countries, namely Singapore, Thailand, China, USA, UK, Netherland, New Zealand, and Czech Republic, for lectures and presentations. In addition to this, he also associated as Editorial Board Member/Reviewer of different journals of national and international fame. He is also associated with internationally famed Rutgers University Camden, USA, as an external supervisor. Dr. Srivastava is associated with various reputed universities/institutions as a member of Advisory Board, Board of Studies, and external subject expert in Indian Universities. He also served as subject expert of Forensic Science in State Public Service Commissions of India.

Ashish Badiye is presently the Head of the Department and Assistant Professor (Senior Grade) at the Department of Forensic Science, Government Institute of Forensic Science, Nagpur, Maharashtra, India. He has completed his Ph.D., M.Sc. and B.Sc. (Honors) in Forensic Science. He has published over 55 research articles in journals of high repute and 18 book chapters. He has delivered invited talks, guest lectures, workshops, and demonstrations to Police officers, Public Prosecutors, and multiple colleges, institutes, and universities, across India on various aspects and topics related to Forensic Science. He is an expert Forensic Science trainer and assists the Maharashtra police in the various aspects of crime scene investigation. He has been awarded with "the Young Scientist Award" (2018) and "Special Recognition" (2017, 2018, 2019) for his services in "Scientific Aid to Investigation" to the Maharashtra Police. He is a member of the Board of Studies, Advisory Boards, Paper Setter, Examiner, and Evaluator, for various Universities in India. He also serves as a recognized reviewer for 30+ reputed journals.

Neeti Kapoor is presently working as an Assistant Professor (Senior Grade) at the Department of Forensic Science, Government Institute of Forensic Science, Nagpur, Maharashtra, India. She completed her Doctorate, Master's as well as Bachelor's degree in Forensic Science. She has teaching and research experience of more than 10 years in the field of Forensic Science and has published more than 50 research articles in journals of high repute and 15 book chapters in International publications. She serves as a recognized reviewer for more than 14 journals from reputed publishers. She is a member of the Board of Studies, Paper Setter, Examiner, and Evaluator, for various Universities in India. She has delivered several invited talks and practical demonstrations at various educational institutions and to the police officers on various topics including Forensic Dermatoglyphics, Crime Scene Investigation, Physical evidences, Forensic Chemistry and Toxicology, Narcotic Drugs and Psychotropic Substances, etc. Over the past decade, Dr. Neeti Kapoor have been instrumental in helping the police officers with the scientific collection, preservation, packaging and forwarding of the evidence, framing of the questionnaire, Crime Scene Analysis, Crime Scene Reconstruction, etc.

Contributors

Hema V. Acharya Forensic Psychology Division, Directorate of Forensic Science, Gandhinagar, Gujarat, India

Md. Alim Department of Forensic Science, Bareilly International University, Bareilly, Uttar Pradesh, India

Annapoorni Ammal Department of Forensic Science, Kristu Jayanti College (Autonomous), Bangalore, India

Ashish Badiye Department of Forensic Science, Government Institute of Forensic Science, Nagpur, Maharashtra, India

Hansi Bansal Department of Forensic Science, Government Institute of Forensic Science, Nagpur, Maharashtra, India

Manoj Bhandarkar Mini Forensic Science Laboratory, Home Department, Government of Maharashtra, Thane, Maharashtra, India

Vishwas Bharadwaj Cyber Division, State Forensic Science Laboratory, Jaipur, Rajasthan, India

Yash Baroniya Cyber Division, State Forensic Science Laboratory, Jaipur, Rajasthan, India

Tanurup Das School of Forensic Sciences, The West Bengal National University of Juridical Sciences, Kolkata, West Bengal, India

Kapil Dev Biology, Serology and DNA Division, Forensic Science Laboratory, Moradabad, Uttar Pradesh, India

Shivani Dixit Department of Forensic Science, DNA Division, UP State Institute of Forensic Sciences, Lucknow, UP, India

Rakesh Kumar Gorea Department of Forensic Medicine, Gian Sagar Medical College, Ram Nagar, Punjab, India

Abhimanyu Harshey Department of Anthropology, Lucknow University, Lucknow, Uttar Pradesh, India

Rasika Kakad Department of Forensic Science, Government Institute of Forensic Science, Nagpur, Maharashtra, India

Archana Kamble Karunya Institute of Technology and Sciences, Coimbatore, Tamil Nadu, India

Neeti Kapoor Department of Forensic Science, Government Institute of Forensic Science, Nagpur, Maharashtra, India

Akash Kumar Department of Anthropology, Lucknow University, Lucknow, Uttar Pradesh, India

Alok Kumar CSIR-IITR, Lucknow, Uttar Pradesh, India

Sachil Kumar Department of Forensic Sciences, College of Criminal Justice, Naif Arab University for Security Sciences, Riyadh, Saudi Arabia

R. K. Kumawat Serology and DNA Division, State Forensic Science Laboratory, Jaipur, Rajasthan, India

Pushpesh Kushwaha Serology and DNA Division, State Forensic Science Laboratory, Jaipur, Rajasthan, India

Samiksha Landge GH Raisoni University, Saikheda, Madhya Pradesh, India

Jitendra Mishra Deen Dayal Upadhyaya Gorakhpur University, Gorakhpur, Uttar Pradesh, India

Sandeep Mishra Dr Ram Manohar Lohiya National Law University, Lucknow, Uttar Pradesh, India

Vindresh Mishra Central Forensic Science Laboratory, Kolkata, West Bengal, India

Poonam Moon Karunya Institute of Technology and Sciences, Coimbatore, Tamil Nadu, India

Kriti Nigam Department of Forensic Science, Jharkhand Raksha Shakti University, Ranchi, Jharkhand, India

Muktikanta Panda Department of Anthropology, Dr. Harisingh Gour Vishwavidyalaya, Sagar, Madhya Pradesh, India

Kumar Askand Pandey Dr Ram Manohar Lohiya National Law University, Lucknow, Uttar Pradesh, India

Pankaj Kumar Pandey Ballistics Division, Forensic Science Laboratory, Govt. of NCT of Delhi, New Delhi, India

Pooja Pardeshi Department of Forensic Science, Government Institute of Forensic Science, Nagpur, Maharashtra, India

Rajendraprasad Pawar Institute of Excellence in Higher Education, Bhopal, Madhya Pradesh, India

Manisha Rana Biology Division, State Forensic Science Laboratory, Jaipur, Rajasthan, India

Mandar R. Sane Department of Forensic Medicine and Toxicology, All India Institute of Medical Sciences (AIIMS), Nagpur, Maharashtra, India

Shaesta Shahid Dr. APJ Abdul Kalam Institute of Forensic Science & Criminology, Bundelkhand University, Jhansi, Uttar Pradesh, India

A. N. Sharma Department of Anthropology, Dr. Harisingh Gour Vishwavidyalaya, Sagar, Madhya Pradesh, India

Harsh Sharma National Forensic Sciences University, Bhopal Campus, Bhopal, Madhya Pradesh, India

Karan Sharma Jaipur National University, Jaipur, Rajasthan, India

Pankaj Shrivastava Biology and Serology Division, Regional Forensic Science Laboratory, Gwalior, Madhya Pradesh, India

Ritesh K. Shukla Department of Biological and Life Sciences, Ahmedabad University, Ahmedabad, Gujarat, India

Rajesh Singh Biology Division, State Forensic Science Laboratory, Jaipur, Rajasthan, India

Ankit Srivastava School of Forensic Sciences, The West Bengal National University of Juridical Sciences, Kolkata, West Bengal, India

Pradnya Sulke Department of Forensic Science, Government Institute of Forensic Science, Nagpur, Maharashtra, India

Raju Tandan B.T. Institute of Excellence (affiliated to Dr. Harisingh Gour (Central) University), Sagar, Madhya Pradesh, India

Neelesh Tiwari Cyber Division, State Forensic Science Laboratory, Jaipur, Rajasthan, India

Murali Manohar Yadav Dr. APJ Abdul Kalam Institute of Forensic Science & Criminology, Bundelkhand University, Jhansi, Uttar Pradesh, India

Vijay Kumar Yadav Dr. APJ Abdul Kalam Institute of Forensic Science & Criminology, Bundelkhand University, Jhansi, Uttar Pradesh, India

Crime and Society: An Introduction to Criminology

1

Hansi Bansal, Ashish Badiye, Raju Tandan, and Neeti Kapoor

Abstract

Over centuries, criminality has been an integral part of societal structure and culture. Criminology is an amalgamation of different disciplines seeking to identify the causes of crime and criminal behavior. The primary focus of criminologists lies on the identification of the patterns, behavior, and sociological aspects of crime. Due to cultural, social, and political changes, society can deem certain behaviours criminal or decriminalize them. This directly impacts the crime rate and the allocation of resources within law enforcement agencies. Criminology is critically engaged in finding solutions to issues related to crime and justice. The cause of a crime is one of the significant areas of criminology, and criminologists identify various factors to explicate why a person commits a crime. This chapter discusses the various fields of criminology, factors responsible for crime and criminal behavior, theories of crime, and the criminal justice system. It also highlights the concepts of juvenile delinquency, punishment, victimology, and their impact on crime. The authors endeavored to present a holistic perspective on the multifaceted dimensions of Crime and Society in a single chapter, notwithstanding the complexity of the subject matter.

Keywords

Crime · Criminology · Punishment · Criminal Behavior · Criminal Justice System

H. Bansal · A. Badiye · N. Kapoor (✉)
Department of Forensic Science, Government Institute of Forensic Science, Nagpur, Maharashtra, India
e-mail: hansibansal@ifscnagpur.in; ashishbadiye@ifscnagpur.in; neetikapoor@ifscnagpur.in

R. Tandan
B.T. Institute of Excellence (affiliated to Dr. Harisingh Gour (Central) University), Sagar, Madhya Pradesh, India

P. Shrivastava et al. (eds.), *Textbook of Forensic Science*,
https://doi.org/10.1007/978-981-99-1377-0_1

1.1 Introduction

Crime is one of the most severe problems in society. It has existed in the world since the origin of humankind. Earlier, crimes might not have been earnest and organized, but their propensity and intensity have become grave in the present world. Crime is not limited to one class of society; it is prevalent in every stratum. It is usually not the result of a single factor; instead, multiple reasons or factors are responsible for the unlawful act. The outlook toward crime cannot remain constant when our society itself is dynamic. Thus, a crime is neither steady nor uniform. It varies from time to time, place to place, person to person, and society to society. Every nation plays its part in trying to curb its crimes and punish the criminals. As an academic discipline, criminology assumes pivotal roles in identifying the causes of crime, developing strategies to reduce it, and implementing preventive measures. It works for the protection of society. In 1885, Raffaele Garofalo first coined the term "criminology." It is broadly defined as the scientific study of crime to explore the reasons as to why people are engaged in criminal activities and the causes of such criminal behavior (Allen 1954).

Different authors and criminologists have given their versions of criminology, including the classification of crimes, offenders, and victims, and their interpretations vary accordingly. According to Edwin Sutherland and Donald Cressey, "Criminology is the body of knowledge regarding crime as a social phenomenon. It includes within its scope the processes of making laws, of breaking laws, and of reacting toward the breaking of laws." (Sutherland and Cressey 1960) This definition holds the concept that social factors are the root causes of crimes. However, other criminologists have a contradictory view, wherein they believe that individual traits and characteristics are responsible for criminal behavior. A logical and philosophical examination of crime is based on lucidity and deductive reasoning (Sutherland et al. 1992).

Criminology encompasses the study of different aspects of crime and law enforcement, the social setup of crime, the psychology of crime and the criminal, restriction on crime and its prevention, investigation of crime and detection, and punishment. Merriam-Webster's dictionary defines criminology as "the scientific study of crime as a social phenomenon of criminals and penal treatment." (Veeraraghavan 2019).

Criminology is similarly linked to the study of deviant behavior. However, crime and deviance should not be misjudged as synonyms. Deviant behavior is the action that contravenes the ideas, norms, and beliefs of a society. Criminology is named a subgroup of sociology that deals with the study of social behavior. It explores the origin, extent, and nature of crimes in a society, whereas criminologists identify a crime's nature, extent, and cause (Canter and Youngs 2016; Hood and Sparks 1970; Vito and Maahs 2015).

1.2 The Amalgamation of Criminology and Other Fields

Criminology incorporates broader knowledge about crime and criminals. Criminologists work to determine and understand the cause of crime and to know why some people are more inclined toward delinquent behavior. This field encompasses varied disciplines, working on techniques developed in social and natural sciences. The subdivision of criminology includes criminalistics, the study of crime detection, which is associated with the scope of forensic science. Other subdivisions of criminology include penology, the study of correctional systems and institutions, and biocriminology, the study of the biological factors affecting criminal behavior. The discipline of criminology utilizes the study of various other fields like biology, anthropology, statistics, psychology, statistics, psychiatry, cyber, etc. (Veeraraghavan 2019; Canter and Youngs 2016; Hood and Sparks 1970; Barlow and Kauzlarich 1984)

1.2.1 Criminology and Biology

Cesare Lombroso has carried out pioneering work in attributing crime and criminal behavior to biological factors. Two well-known fields of study influenced by Lombroso's biological explanation of crime are neuroscience and genetics. This clearly states the fact that a multidisciplinary approach can be used to study crime and criminal behavior. Data on crime are obtained from various sources, with behavioral genetics being one of them, and it demonstrates that biological factors are responsible for crime (Veeraraghavan 2019; Barlow and Kauzlarich 1984; Ahuja 2000).

1.2.2 Criminology and Anthropology

Anthropological criminology is a part of offender profiling based on the connection between a crime and the offender's personality, including physical features. Lombroso theorized the concept of born criminals. According to him, born criminals are anatomically identifiable based on characteristics like a sloping forehead, unusual size of ears, asymmetry of the face, excessive length of the arms, asymmetry of the arms, and other physical stigmata (Veeraraghavan 2019; Ahuja 2000).

1.2.3 Criminology and Psychology

In combination with psychology, criminology studies the intentions, thoughts, behavior, and feelings of criminals and certain mental disorders that cause an individual to commit a crime. This combination of the two disciplines also incorporates scientific methods, techniques, tools, and measurement scales, which help in deducing the profile of offenders (Veeraraghavan 2019; Ahuja 2000).

1.2.4 Criminology and Psychiatry

Criminology, along with psychiatry, studies the deviant behavior of individuals and their mental illness. Psychiatrists believe that criminal behavior can be understood by probing the personality of humans and the unconscious factors responsible for deviant and nondeviant behaviors (Veeraraghavan 2019).

1.2.5 Criminology and Criminalistics

Criminology and criminalistics collaborate closely withun the domain of law enforcement. Criminalistics deals with the collection of evidence, its analysis, its interpretation, and identification of the suspect. Criminology deals with assessing the nature of the crime, its cause, and strategies for crime prevention. Criminology also studies the mode of punishment and correction methods for the betterment of society. A mutual relationship exists between the two fields concerning why a crime is committed (criminology) and how it was committed (criminalistics) (Veeraraghavan 2019; Ahuja 2000).

1.2.6 Criminology and Victimology

Victimology is a subdiscipline of criminology, which deals with the study of victims of crimes. It examines the psychological effects of crimes on victims, the association between the victims and the criminal, and the interaction between the victims and the criminal justice system (Veeraraghavan 2019; Ahuja 2000).

1.2.7 Criminology and Penology

Penology is a subdiscipline of criminology, which deals with the social processes applied to prevent a crime via fear of punishment and suppression of criminal intent. It is the science of the origin and development of punishment, its significance, and its efficacy. Penology also deals with the treatment of convicted criminals and their rehabilitation (Veeraraghavan 2019; Ahuja 2000).

1.2.8 Criminology and Cyber Criminology

Cyber criminology is a field that encompasses the knowledge of criminology, victimology, social science, computer science, etc. It deals with the study of crimes that occur in cyberspace and their impact on the victims. This field is distinct from cyber forensics and explores the impact of cybercrimes from a social science perspective (Anon n.d.-a).

1.3 Crime and Its Definition

A crime is an illegal act committed, which is punishable by the authorities. Different criminologists have defined and interpreted crime in different ways. Legally, a crime is defined as an act or behavior committed in violation of the legal code. There are many perspectives from which we may understand the meaning of crime. Thinkers like Garofalo and Radcliff Brown have defined crime as a violation of customs, giving rise to penal action.

In order to convict a person of a crime, the two essential elements are "Actus reus" and "Mens rea" (Fig. 1.1). "Actus reus" refers to the "guilty act," i.e., the physical act involved in committing a crime as per criminal law. "Mens rea" means the "guilty mind," i.e., having a wrong intention to commit a crime or act against the law. These two elements must co-occur to constitute a crime.

According to Paul Tappan, crime can be defined as "an intentional act or omission in violation of criminal law committed without defence or justification and sanctioned by the state for punishment as a felony or a misdemeanour." (Anon n.d.-b) This definition highlights six different elements of a crime as follows:

- The crime or the act should have been committed, or the act must be an omission from a legal duty.
- The crime should be voluntary, where the person is well aware of his/her actions.
- The act should be intentional irrespective of whether it was general or specific.
- The act should be a violation of criminal law so that the state has the right to punish accordingly.
- The act should be committed without any justification. An act committed in self-defense or insanity will not constitute a crime.
- The act should be warranted as a felony or misdemeanor by the law (Anon n.d.-b).

According to Jerome Hall, crime can be defined as "legally forbidden and intentional action which has a harmful impact on social interests, which has criminal intent and which has legally prescribed punishment for it." (Hall 1960) He described the seven characteristics of crime:

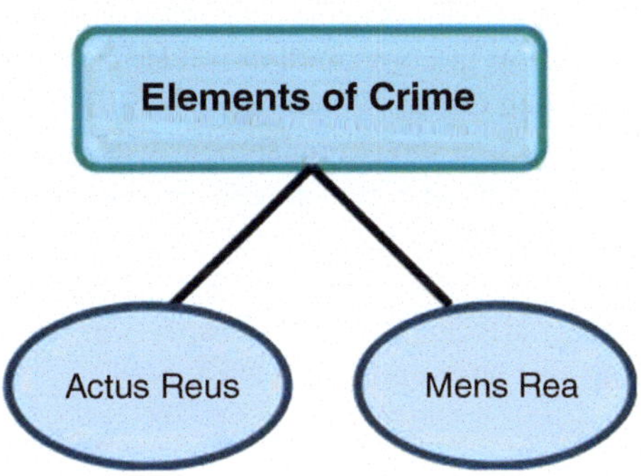

Fig. 1.1 Elements of crime

- The action must be harmful in terms of the interest of society.
- The harmful act should be legally forbidden.
- The act must bring out harmful outcomes that must be deliberate.
- The act must be deliberately motivated.
- The action must be the blend of criminal intention and conduct.
- There must be a formal relation between legally prohibited harm and conduct.
- The act must be discouraged by a given punishment prescribed by the law (Hall 1960).

According to psychological theory, crime can be explained as "behaviour due to defective or abnormal mental processes." This abnormality may be caused by a diseased mind, adjustment to inner conflicts, emulating incorrect role models, or inappropriate learning (Mischel 1969). According to a sociological concept, crime can be viewed as "deviant behaviour violating the existing norms and rules which prescribes the standards of how humans should behave normally." According to the Waverly encyclopedia, crime is defined as "an act forbidden by law and for performing which the perpetrator is liable to punishment." Halsbury defined crime as "an unlawful act or default, which is an offence against the public and which renders the perpetrator of the act or default liable to legal punishment" (Anon n.d.-c).

According to Hegger, the following seven characteristics should be included in action to be defined as a crime.

- The act should be actually committed; only intention is not adequate.
- The harm should be legally prohibited. Antisocial behavior does not come under crime unless it is not proscribed by the law.
- The conduct must bring about harmful consequence.
- The action should be the result of criminal intent.
- There must be a combination of Mens rea and conduct.
- The act caused must be the natural consequence of the intentional act.
- The action must have a legally prescribed punishment.

According to Russel, "criminal offences are the creation of criminal policies adopted by the stronger section of people from time to time and try to suppress the conduct which they feel may endanger their position." According to Sir William Blackstone, a crime is "an act committed or omitted in the violation of a law forbidding or commanding it." He has also observed crime as a violation of public rights and duties (Veeraraghavan 2019; Ahuja 2000).

In ancient days, punishment was a deterrent and was usually in the form of an exile or corporal punishment. However, in modern society, the concept of crime is quite different. Individuals often dissent from traditional beliefs, customs, and superstitions in the modern era. The progress of civilization and culture has enormously affected the various aspects of society. As a result of this effect, various legal concepts have come into existence.

1.4 Classification of Crime

Crime is any conduct that violates the law. Crimes are of different categories depending on the cause, people involved, motive, etc.. Some crimes are committed by an individual alone, whereas others involve a group of people. Some are committed within the geographical boundaries of a country, whereas international crimes occur worldwide. Crime is not a homogeneous type of behavior in any society. Therefore, an effort has been made to classify crime. Different criminologists have classified crime on a diversified basis.

Based on cruelty and seriousness, Sutherland classified crime as either a misdemeanor or a felony. The distinguishing factor between these two classifications lies in the punishment imposed on the offender. A misdemeanor is a less severe offence for which the criminal is imprisoned for a short period or a fine may be imposed for the act, whereas a felony is a severe offence for which the criminal is sentenced to long-term imprisonment or even death (Veeraraghavan 2019; Ahuja 2000).

Lemert classified crime as either situational or systematic. Situational crimes are committed by people due to the pressure or demand of the situation, whereas systematic crimes are planned before committing them and are systematic. An example of situational crime may be when a person leaves the keys in the vehicle and the criminal is presented with an opportunity to steal them. Loan sharking, burglary, etc., are a few examples of systematic crimes (Veeraraghavan 2019; Ahuja 2000).

Willem A. Bonger (a Dutch criminologist) classified crime into four types based on the motive behind the crime. They are economic crimes, sexual crimes, political crimes, and miscellaneous crimes (Bemmelen 1955).

- Economic crimes are those illegal acts committed by an individual or a group of individuals with a motive of financial gain. The sole purpose of such criminals is to gain an economic advantage. Money laundering, tax evasions, illicit capital heavens, etc., are a few examples of economic crimes.
- Sexual crimes are acts committed that generally involve illegal or coerced sexual conduct against another individual. Indecent exposure, sexual assault, rape, etc., are a few examples of sex crimes.
- Political crimes are crimes committed to cause damage/harm to the state, the state's government, or the political system of a state. Sedition, espionage, treason, etc., are a few examples of political crimes.
- Miscellaneous crimes are crimes with revenge as the chief motive. However, a crime can have more than one motive, i.e., a person may have both political and economic motives (Veeraraghavan 2019; Ahuja 2000).

Clinard and Quinney classified crime into six types. They are:

- Violent personal crimes: These involve using violence, and the offender usually does not hold an earlier criminal record (Fajnzylber et al. 2002). Examples include rape, assault, etc.

- Occasional property crimes: These are a violation of individual property rules. An example is shoplifting.
- Occupational crimes: An individual commits this type of crime during their occupation or job. The criminals accept the rules and regulations of society, except for honesty. Examples include misleading advertisements, black marketing, etc.
- Political crimes: Criminals of these types of crimes have a political and economic motive. Some examples are spying, treason, etc.
- Public order crimes: The regular conduct of society and its norms are disturbed by such crimes, causing harm. Examples include alcoholism, vandalism, breaking traffic rules, etc.
- Conventional crimes: Criminals offend the norms of individual property, and the money earned through these crimes is not their sole income. These types of crimes are committed on a part-time basis. Some examples are robbery, theft, dacoity, etc. (Ahuja 2000).

Crime can also be classified into four different groups, based on "against whom" it is committed:

- Against a person: A crime against a person includes those committed against a person's will and involves bodily harm or a threat to cause bodily harm. Kidnapping, domestic violence, stalking, battery, etc., are crimes against a person.
- Against property: Property crimes are usually committed with force or threat of force with the motive to obtain money, property, or others. Dacoity, robbery, larceny, etc., are some of the examples of property crimes.
- Against public decency: These types of crimes are committed with an intention to disturb the peace, cause public nuisance, and threaten the sense of public morality. Drunkenness, vandalism, bigamy, obscenity, etc., are a few examples of crimes against public decency.
- Against public justice: These types of crimes involve disorderly or disrespectful conduct, questioning the authority of the legal system. Contempt of court and perjury are a few examples of crimes against public justice (Ahuja 2000).

Individuals commit various other crimes. Some of them are mentioned in Fig. 1.2.

1.5 Crime and Criminal Behavior

Criminology is a diverse discipline that is characterized by different perspectives of theories laid down by different criminologists. Criminal behavior, also known as offending, can be generally defined as "any overt or covert law-breaking conduct in a given country or state, punishable upon conviction" (Morizot and Kazemian 2015).

According to the sociological process theories of crime, criminal behavior is learned while interacting with people during communication. The techniques of

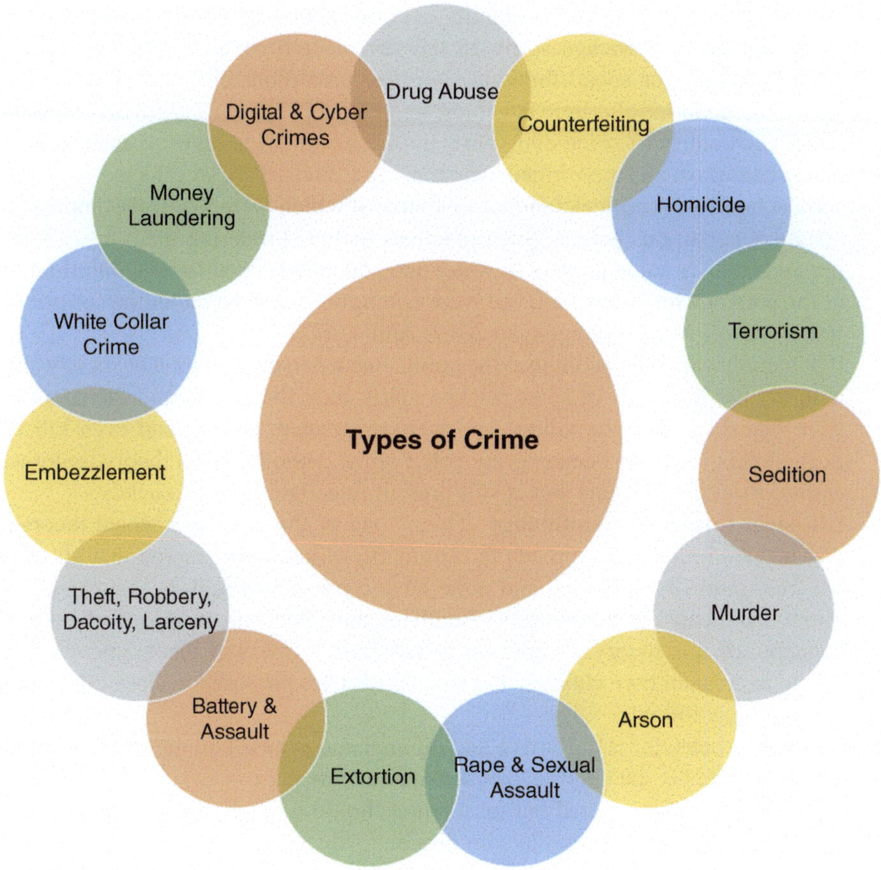

Fig. 1.2 Types of crimes

committing a crime, the specific direction of attitudes, motives, and rationalization are learned during this learning process. Different approaches have been studied to understand the concept and causes of crime and criminal behavior (Brown et al. 2010; Reid 2015; White et al. 2017).

Different theories to study criminal behavior and crime causation are explained as follows:

1. **Preclassical theory**: This is also known as the demonological theory and is based on religious beliefs and superstitions. In ancient times, people believed that evil spirits and some supernatural powers were responsible for a person's criminal tendency and that these instigated the person to commit crimes. According to this theory, people commit crimes not due to their free will but under the influence of some sinful spirit. The foundation of this theory is based on some unreal or mythical facts. The demonological theory is the oldest theory

that believes that a person commits a crime after capitulating to or for the blandishment of a wicked spirit. In the seventeenth century, religious values predominated over social thinking. A priest or a monarch, who acted as the leader or supporter of religious values, treated people who were perceived to be under the control of some evil spirit. In order to provide relief to such human beings, they usually performed worships and advised those affected to make certain types of sacrifices (animal or human), which were again the impact of certain superstitious beliefs. Such practices included ordering them to walk on fire and to offer some prayers in water and sometimes even terminating the life of the person whom they believed were committing a crime under the control of some evil spirits (Veeraraghavan 2019; Ahuja 2000).

If someone was able to convince the public that a person is a threat to society and is under the influence of some wicked spirit, then the person and their family were banished from the village and were mistreated, beaten, and even killed. Still, in the twenty-first century, the belief of the demonological theory is almost extinct from the judiciary but is still present in certain sects of society.

2. **Classical theory of criminology**: This is one of the widely accepted theories that takes a utilitarian approach to criminality. Classicists assume that all men are free, rational, and equal and none have a priority of rank or status and no initial handicaps or advantages. Bentham and Beccaria proposed the main concepts of this theory. According to Beccaria's free will theory, people are free to make their own choices. The main postulates proposed in classical school theory are as follows:
   (a) Man's behavior is purposive and rational and is based on the pleasure–pain principle, i.e., he chooses pleasure and avoids pain.
   (b) The punishment meted out for a crime should be such that it outweighs the benefits obtained from the commission of the crime.
   (c) The punishment imposed should not be highly deterrent and should be in proportion to the crime committed. Corporal punishment should be preferred in place of torture, and a fair trial should be ensured.
   (d) The court does not have the right to interpret the laws according to their ideas of justice. Only innocence or guilt should be proved, and punishment should be prescribed accordingly (Veeraraghavan 2019; Ahuja 2000; Morizot and Kazemian 2015; Brown et al. 2010).
3. **Neoclassical theory**: The classical theory was revised after criticism, and neoclassicist criminologists made changes. The neoclassical theory introduced the idea of maximum and minimum sentences. It described the concept of equal justice as unreal and suggested the importance of age, mental condition, and situations while prescribing punishment to criminals. Mentally diseased individuals and children below 7 years of age were exempted from the law. Neoclassical schools started dealing with the causation of crime, which was not included in classical theory (Veeraraghavan 2019; Ahuja 2000).
4. **Social disorganization theory**: This theory is also known as the Chicago School theory. It was proposed by Clifford R. Shaw and Henry D. McKay. The main principle of this theory is that location (place) is responsible for

deviant behavior and crime. According to this theory, a person's residential location is vital for predicting criminality compared to their characteristics. Criminality is directly related to the differences in ecological characteristics. Criminal tendencies are seen more in societies where social disequilibrium or disorganization is responsible for social issues (Morizot and Kazemian 2015).

5. **Differential association theory**: This theory was proposed by Sutherland in 1939 and was elaborated in 1947. According to this theory, criminal behavior is acquired through social interactions with others. This means that people tend to become delinquent or engage in unlawful activities when they associate with individuals who have pro-criminal attitudes, values, and behaviors, while lacking exposure to conventional norms and values. Differential association is possible because society is composed of various groups with varied cultures. According to this theory, cultural conflict is the underlying cause of differential association. These associations may vary in intensity, priority, duration, and frequency, i.e., the probability that a person will participate in criminal behavior is roughly determined by the frequency and consistency of his/her associations with patterns of criminal behavior (Brown et al. 2010).
6. **Biological theory**: Cesare Lombroso proposed the concept of heredity as a responsible factor for criminal behavior. He postulated that biological factors were more responsible for criminal behavior in comparison to environmental factors. He mentioned the concept of born criminals, i.e., individuals who suffer from physical, intellectual, and moral degeneration since birth. These born criminals could be identified by the typical facial features like asymmetry of the face, head, etc. (Siegel 2016).
   William Sheldon proposed another biological explanation for criminal behavior. He studied the photographs of individuals and categorized them into three somatotypes, viz., endomorphs, ectomorphs, and mesomorphs. Endomorphs are heavily built persons with outgoing and sociable personalities, mesomorphs are muscular and broad with aggressive personalities, and ectomorphs are lean and skinny with introverted personalities (Brown et al. 2010; Siegel 2016).
7. **Anomie strain theory**: In 1893, Emile Durkheim proposed the concept of anomie, which means a lack of usual ethical and social standards. Merton proposed that criminality and deviant behavior occurred due to the gap between cultural goals and social ways to achieve them. He stated that if the cultural goals of a society are status, wealth, etc., then the social means to achieve them are employment, education, etc. When a gap occurs between achieving these goals and the means to achieve them, frustration develops among the individuals and a strain is generated. As a result, people adopt illegal means to achieve their goals, which lead to crime causation. The main features of this theory are that specific stressors are caused due to the negative changes occurring in society, which increases the probability of crime. Thus, a crime is committed as a means to relieve those strains of society (Morizot and Kazemian 2015; Brown et al. 2010; Siegel 2016).
8. **Psychodynamic theory**: Sigmund Freud proposed this theory of criminality. According to this theory, the psyche has three components: "id, ego, and

superego." "Id" is the primitive part of the mental component of a person present since birth. It represents the unconscious drives of the body for different necessities of life. "Ego" is developed in the early life of a person. It satisfies the demands of the id and tries to keep it within the norms of society. "Superego" develops as an individual and integrates the moral standards of the society and the community. The central concept of this theory is that criminals develop a weaker ego due to negative happenings in their childhood. As a result, in their adulthood, they resort to criminal behaviors to satisfy their ego (Siegel 2016; Anckarsäter et al. 2009).

9. **Behavioral theory**: This is another psychological theory that explains the causes of criminal behavior. Behavior is learned through life's actions. Albert Bandura proposed that no individual is born with the ability to act violently. Violence and aggression are learned in the course of an individual's life from different sources, like family interactions, mass media, and environmental factors. Individuals residing in crime-prone areas are more likely to develop criminal tendencies and aggressive behavior. To an extent, the media is also responsible for criminal behavior and violence (Siegel 2016).
10. **Labeling theory**: Howard Becker proposed this theory in 1963. This theory deals with the reason why some people are labeled criminals or deviants by society. According to this theory, the social audience and not the person is vital for studying deviance. Deviance is not a quality of the act that a person commits but the consequence of the application by others of rules and sanctions to an offender (Becker 1963; Walklate 2007; Anon n.d.-d). It is the reaction of others that labels an individual in a specific manner. It is the society that brands some people as criminals and some as not. If a young individual from the lower strata of society steals a car, then he/she is labeled a "thief;" meanwhile, if someone from the upper strata of society does the same, he/she is described as a "mischievous pleasure-seeker" (Siegel 2016; Becker 1963).
11. **Self-concept and containment theory**: Walter Reckless introduced the concept of containment theory in 1967, addressing the question of why individuals choose either law-abiding or law-violating behavior when presented with alternatives. According to Reckless, the main factor influencing this choice is an individual's self-concept. He proposed that there are two critical aspects of control: inner and outer control. The balance between these control systems determines whether an individual will opt for a deviant path of crime or a conformist route. Reckless emphasized the significance of self-concept as the defining factor in making behavioral choices. Strong inner containment, including a positive self-concept, ego strength, a mature superego, high frustration tolerance, and a sense of responsibility, acts as a buffer against deviant behavior. It is also important to understand the external pushes, such as unemployment, discrimination, and poverty, as well as the external pulls, including negative peer pressure, that can influence individuals towards criminality. Moreover, internal pushes such as anger, anxiety, negative thoughts, and a rebellious attitude can directly impact a person's propensity to commit unlawful acts or break societal norms. By addressing these external and internal factors, and by

maintaining a balance between inner and outer containment, Reckless believed it was possible to prevent individuals from choosing a deviant path and encourage adherence to societal norms (Siegel 2016).

Criminology is the scientific study of the causes of criminal behavior. Criminal behavior has been explained by various theories proposed by different criminologists all over the world. The construction of social norms, which vary from society to society, depicts deviance as a social phenomenon. These theories are based on the assumptions and explanations proposed by criminologists. In the past, according to specific theories, criminal behavior was attributed to factors such as demons, skull traits, the inherent nature of individuals, and body types. These beliefs were discarded through scientific research. The explanations based on rational choice and biological perspectives were quite popular as the possible reasons for committing a crime. With the change of society and the norms, the possible explanations for criminal behavior also change. So, it is difficult to come to a universal conclusion about the cause of deviance and crime. No single theory is sufficient enough to explain all the probable causes of crime (Walklate 2007; Anon n.d.-d).

1.6 Factors in Crime

Several factors are responsible for the causation of crime. Understanding these causes helps in taking measures to reduce deviant behavior and criminal tendencies (Dutta and Husain 2009). Some of the factors responsible for crimes are as follows:

1.6.1 Peer Influence

Peer groups can indeed have a significant influence on the causation of crime, particularly among young individuals. When children and teenagers feel unable to meet the expectations set by their parents or are constantly compared to others, it can lead to feelings of frustration, inadequacy, and a desire for acceptance. In some cases, this can result in engaging in criminal behavior as a means to gain recognition or prove themselves.The pressure to conform to peer standards, especially in terms of material possessions like expensive clothing, can be a significant factor that pushes individuals towards criminal activities. Those who cannot afford such luxuries may feel compelled to resort to illegal means, such as theft or fraud, in order to meet the expectations and fit in with their peer group.Additionally, peer pressure can lead to the initiation of harmful behaviors such as drinking or smoking, which may then contribute to criminal acts. The desire to be accepted and included among their peers can lead young individuals to engage in activities that are illegal or violate societal norms. While peer influence is an important factor to consider in understanding the causation of crime, it is crucial to recognize that it is not the sole determinant. Other factors, such as individual characteristics, family dynamics, socio-economic conditions, and community influences, also play significant roles. A comprehensive understanding of crime causation requires examining the complex interactions among these various factors (Reid 2015; White et al. 2017).

1.6.2 Biological Factors

According to different criminologists, the biological characteristics of criminal behavior are said to be genetic and inherited. Criminologist Goring proposed that criminal behavior is inherited, much like physical, moral, and mental traits, based on statistical techniques. This perspective suggests a biological basis for criminal tendencies (Brown et al. 2010; Siegel 2016). Contrary to the biological determinism perspective, many criminologists emphasize the significance of environmental influences on criminal behavior. They argue that factors such as upbringing, socialization, economic conditions, peer associations, and community dynamics play crucial roles in shaping an individual's propensity towards criminal acts. These environmental factors can contribute to the development of criminal behavior by influencing social learning, attitudes, and opportunities for criminal involvement.

1.6.3 Economic Factors

The lack of access to basic needs and desires due to poverty and unemployment can indeed drive individuals to resort to illegal means to satisfy those needs. In many cases, the combination of these factors can lead to a heightened risk of engaging in criminal activities (Brown et al. 2010). Poverty and unemployment can create an environment of desperation and hopelessness where individuals might see criminal behavior as a way to secure their survival or improve their circumstances. The inability to provide for themselves and their families can push people towards crime as they seek to meet their basic needs.In areas with high population density and limited job opportunities, unemployment can exacerbate the situation. A growing population combined with insufficient employment opportunities can lead to increased competition for resources, which might, in turn, drive some individuals to criminal acts.

1.6.4 Lack of Education

While education does not guarantee that educated individuals will not commit crimes, it is observed that individuals with lower levels of education and weaker moral values may be more prone to resorting to illegal means for financial gain. Proper education, particularly in ethics and moral values, is crucial in enabling individuals to differentiate between good and evil. By instilling a strong sense of ethics and moral principles, education empowers individuals to make informed and ethical decisions, contributing to a lawful and harmonious society. While education alone cannot eliminate crime, integrating teachings of ethics and moral values into education equips individuals with the knowledge and tools to make ethical choices and understand the consequences of their actions. This helps in fostering empathy, compassion, and a greater sense of responsibility towards society (Brown et al. 2010).

1.6.5 An Ineffective Legal System

An inefficient legal system can contribute to an increase in crime and have negative consequences on deterrence, justice, and public trust. When a legal system is inefficient and judicial procedures are overly drawn out, potential offenders may perceive punishment as uncertain, thereby reducing the deterrent effect. Delays in justice can erode the effectiveness of punishment and fail to provide timely consequences for criminal behavior. Inconsistently or unfairly enforced rules, particularly those influenced by racial or social status, can create a sense of unfairness and resentment, undermining public trust in the legal system. Inadequate resources allocated to law enforcement, courts, and correctional facilities can result in backlogs, diminished investigative efforts, and overcrowded jails. These factors can impede the timely administration of justice and limit the capacity to effectively address crime. Furthermore, a poorly functioning legal system characterized by corruption and a lack of accountability can create an environment conducive to criminal activity. To prevent crime, ensure justice, and maintain societal order, it is essential to have an efficient and effective legal system that provides swift and fair outcomes, upholds the rule of law, and maintains public confidence. Adequate resources, proper training, streamlined procedures, and accountability mechanisms are crucial elements in achieving an efficient legal system. As a result of protracted court cases and the release of offenders, culprits often roam freely, and the wealthy find it easier to secure bail. After evading accountability in the past, offenders persist in engaging in unlawful behaviors, perpetuating criminal activities, and instilling a sense of terror within society (Veeraraghavan 2019; Ahuja 2000; Brown et al. 2010).

1.6.6 Cultural Factors

Cultural factors indeed play a significant role in shaping criminal behavior. Individuals who are raised in environments characterized by hopelessness, anxiety, and insecurity may develop a sense of mistrust towards themselves and others. The lack of self-confidence and unreal expectations about life can contribute to feelings of frustration and anger. When these negative emotions are not effectively managed or channeled, they can potentially manifest as deviant behavior.Cultural factors encompass a wide range of influences, including societal norms, values, beliefs, and the overall social environment. Cultural contexts that perpetuate a sense of despair, limited opportunities, and social inequalities can contribute to a higher prevalence of criminal behavior. In such environments, individuals may perceive crime as a means to address their frustrations or gain a sense of control or power.It is important to recognize that cultural factors interact with various other influences, such as economic conditions, educational opportunities, family dynamics, and peer associations. The complex interplay of these factors shapes an individual's perceptions, attitudes, and behavioral choices (Veeraraghavan 2019; Ahuja 2000).

1.6.7 Effect of the Media

The media undoubtedly wields a powerful influence on crime, although its impact is complex and hotly debated. Sensationalized reporting and a fixation on violent crimes can create a false impression of crime rates, inciting public fear and anxiety. Portrayals of criminal behavior in movies, TV shows, and video games may even inspire susceptible individuals to emulate such behavior. Additionally, high-profile crimes can serve as a blueprint for further criminal activity. However, it is crucial to recognize the multitude of other factors that can contribute to crime, such as personal tendencies, societal contexts, and economic circumstances. To fully comprehend the intricate relationship between media and crime, one must account for numerous variables and settings. Indeed, research has revealed a significant correlation between violence in the media and violent behavior among children, with those who watch more violent movies being more likely to engage in criminal behavior in adulthood. Violent content in video games, movies, and television programs can be potent triggers for deviant, illegal, and violent actions (Veeraraghavan 2019; Ahuja 2000).

1.6.8 Parental Factors

Parenting practices play a crucial role in shaping a child's development and can significantly influence their likelihood of engaging in criminal activities. When children do not receive adequate attention and guidance from their parents, they may become more susceptible to various negative influences, including criminal behavior (Brown et al. 2010). Lack of parental monitoring can lead to children being exposed to risky situations and unhealthy peer associations, increasing the possibility of engaging in deviant activities. Parents who are unable to provide proper attention and emotional support may contribute to feelings of neglect, which can impact a child's emotional well-being and decision-making.Furthermore, children from separated or divorced parents might face additional challenges. Disrupted family dynamics can contribute to emotional distress and instability, which can, in turn, influence behavioral choices. The absence of a stable and nurturing family environment may increase the likelihood of children seeking validation and belonging through negative peer groups or delinquent behaviors.

1.6.9 Mental Disorders

People suffering from mental disorders may commit a crime without even realizing it to be illegal. Mental disorders like delusion, psychosis, schizophrenia, bipolar disorders, etc., are related to different forms of crimes and criminal behaviors (Veeraraghavan 2019; Ahuja 2000; Anckarsäter et al. 2009). For instance, a person experiencing a psychotic episode might act on delusions or hallucinations that compel them to behave in ways that could be harmful to themselves or others. In some cases, these behaviors could lead to criminal acts, such as property damage or physical harm.It's important to recognize that the relationship between mental disorders and criminal behavior is complex and multifaceted. While some individuals with mental disorders might inadvertently engage in criminal activity due to their condition, it's also crucial to understand that the majority of people with mental illnesses are not prone to violence or criminal behavior.

1.6.10 Neurological Factors

Criminologists have studied the connection between injuries in some regions of the brain and criminality. Darby suggested that if a brain injury occurs in those areas of the brain responsible for decision-making and moral ethics, then those people have a higher probability of criminal tendencies or are more prone to committing a crime (Darby 2018). Neurotransmitters also play an essential role in determining criminal behavior to a certain extent (Siegel 2016).

1.7 Victimology

When a crime occurs, the main focus is usually on the criminal who has committed the crime and the modus operandi. Benjamin Mendelson coined the term "victimology" in 1947. In victimology, the main essence is the victim of the crime. Victimology can be defined as "the scientific study of the extent, nature, and causes of criminal victimization, its consequences for the persons involved and the reactions hereto by society, in particular, the police and the criminal justice system as well as voluntary workers and professional helpers" (Fattah 2000). Victimology is also a concept of importance that helps analyze the cause of crime and other vital facts and correlates of crime (Allen 1954; Albanese 2014).

Drapkin and Viano (1974) defined victimology as "the branch of criminology, which primarily studies the victims of crime and everything connected with the victim." Antilla (1975) defined victimology as "the logical, psychological, sociological, and criminological study of the victims which focuses the victim-offender relationship and the role played by the victim in the occurrence of the crime." (Porwal 2018).

Shinder (1982) defined victimology as "the relationship between the offender and the victim in crime causation." It deals with the process of victimization, becoming a victim, and the victim–offender problem and the sequence. The term "victim" was introduced in the Code of Criminal Procedure (CrPC) 1973 by the CrPC (Amendment) Act 2008 by introducing Section 2 (wa), which defines a victim as a "person, who has suffered any loss or injury caused by reason of the act or omission for which the accused person has been charged, and the expression "victim" includes his or her guardian or legal heir." (Anon n.d.-f).

1.7.1 Victim Precipitation Vs. Victim Facilitation Vs. Victim Provocation

These different concepts help understand the extent of a victim's role in a crime.

Victim precipitation: Marvin Wolfgang coined this term. This concept views the extent to which a victim is responsible for his or her victimization. This concept is based on two components, i.e., the victim is the first to act in the commission of a crime and the victim encourages the offender to commit the crime. However, this concept does not apply to all types of crimes, and it might hold for crimes such as assault, rape, etc. This concept explains how the victim's interaction may provoke the offender to commit a crime (Albanese 2014; Doerner 2017; Karmen 2015).

Victim facilitation: This concept states how a victim intentionally or unintentionally facilitates the offender to commit a crime, i.e., the victim's actions make it easier for the offender to commit a crime. For example, if a person leaves behind his/her car keys, this will facilitate the offender to steal the car (Albanese 2014; Doerner 2017; Karmen 2015).

Victim provocation: This concept says that the victim instigates or provokes the offender to commit a crime and due to the provocation by the victim, the offender commits the crime. This suggests that if the victim had not incited the offender, then the crime would not have occurred. The offender alone cannot be held responsible for the crime (Albanese 2014; Doerner 2017; Karmen 2015).

1.7.2 Types of Victims

Victims have been classified into different types on different bases by various criminologists. A few of them are explained below.

Benjamin Mendelsohn, also known as the father of victimology, classified victims based on the extent of their victimization. They are classified as:

- A completely innocent victim: A victim who has no role in his/her victimization (e.g., rape of small children and infants)
- A victim with minor guilt: A victim who is victimized due to his/her ignorance and falls prey to the offender (e.g., pregnant women who go to quacks for abortion)

- A voluntary victim: A victim who holds equal responsibility as that of an offender (e.g., consensual act of adultery)
- A victim more guilty than the offender: A victim who provokes or instigates the offender to commit a crime (e.g., a person instigating the opponent to kill him/her may be in an emotional state of mind.)
- The most guilty victim: A victim who is duped as a result of a crime (e.g., a rapist gets killed by his victim in the act of self-defense)
- A simulating victim: A pretending victim who gives evidence in courts to obtain a sentence against an accused person (e.g., hysterical, paranoids, or senile persons) (Veeraraghavan 2019; Ahuja 2000; Albanese 2014; Anon n.d.-e; Anon n.d.-f)

Walter Reckless classified victims into two types: reporting victims and non-reporting victims.

- Reporting victims: Reporting victims are the ones who report the crime without bothering about the consequences of reporting their victimization and are interested in getting the offender punished, and justice prevails.
- Non-reporting victims: Non-reporting victims are the ones who are unwilling to report the crime because of intimidation by the criminals or fear of the social consequences of reporting it (Anon n.d.-g).

Wolfgang described five categories of victimization. They are:

- Primary victimization: This type involves an individual or personalized victim.
- Secondary victimization: In this type, the victim is an impersonal target of the offender (e.g., a thief in a departmental store, a person traveling on a train without a ticket, etc.).
- Tertiary victimization: This type of victimization affects the public or the administration of the society.
- Mutual victimization: In this case, the victims are themselves offenders in a mutually consensual act (e.g., adultery, gambling).
- No victimization: This type of victimization is where the crime is of negligible significance, and there is no immediately recognizable victim (Veeraraghavan 2019; Ahuja 2000).

Von Hentig categorized victims into four types. They are as follows:

- Victims whose injury may be the price of more significant pain, e.g., in the case of abortion
- Victims who bring about detrimental results partly by their concurrent effort, e.g., prostitutes
- Victims who provoke or instigate the criminal to commit a crime, e.g., by challenging the criminal to kill him/her in an emotional state of mind
- Victims who desire to injure the offender (Veeraraghavan 2019; Ahuja 2000; Anon n.d.-h)

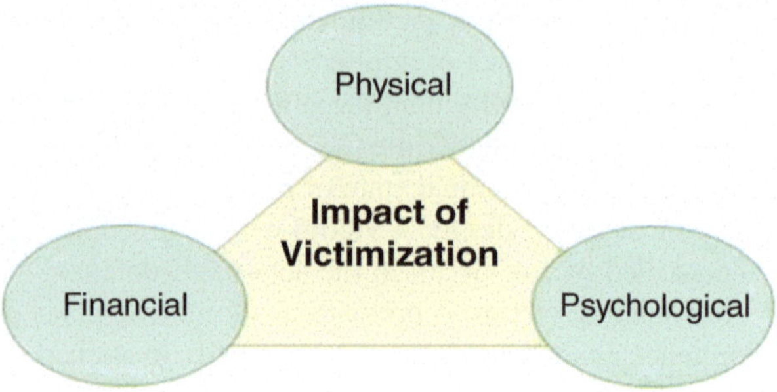

Fig. 1.3 Impact of victimization

1.7.3 Impact of Victimization

Every crime leaves a significant impact on the victim, which can be grouped into three categories (Fig. 1.3).

Physical impact: Victims are likely to experience numerous reactions after a crime. These reactions may include the physical injuries inflicted upon the them, increased heart rate, feeling frozen, shakiness, dryness of mouth, etc. These reactions may reoccur even after a while with the victim's memory of the crime's event (Skogan 1987; Finkelhor and Kendall-Tackett 1997).

Financial impact: This deals with the monetary loss incurred by the victim either due to robbery, burglary, or forced entry. The financial losses can be due to damage caused to the property by causing fire or other expenses. In many cases, the stolen money and prized possessions are never recovered. This may leave the victims distressed with feelings of anger, frustration, and guilt (Skogan 1987; Finkelhor and Kendall-Tackett 1997).

Psychological impact: This refers to the fear and anger that develop in the victim's mind. Victims may also develop post-traumatic stress disorder (PTSD). This may further manifest through the intake of alcohol and drugs, avoiding social meetings, etc. Other than the impacts mentioned earlier, post-victimization may have severe effects on the family and children of the victim and may hamper their future. It may also take several years to overcome the shock of the crime and return to normal (Skogan 1987; Finkelhor and Kendall-Tackett 1997).

1.7.4 Compensation to the Victim

The government has incorporated various compensation schemes and laws to provide aid to the victims post-crime. Compensation is provided to the victim by order of the court through set procedures. This compensation is for both material and non-material things. Laws governing compensation to the victims of a crime are mentioned in Sections 357, 357(1), 357 (2), 357 (3), 357A, 358, 359, and 250 of

CrPC 1973. Articles 14 and 21 of the Indian Constitution protect the rights of the victim.

Victim compensation, victim rehabilitation, and restorative justice are a few of the introduced measures, along with the laws and acts to help the victims. The government has put in place measures to rehabilitate victims, which cover their physical, mental, and psychological well-being. The victim is an inextricable part of a crime, and it is impossible to study crime entirely without understanding the importance of the victim (Anon n.d.-g; Anon n.d.-i).

1.8 Punishment

Since the origin of human civilization, crime and punishment have never ceased to exist. According to contemporary criminology, crime and punishment are interrelated terminologies. The severity of punishment depends upon the gravity of the crime that has occurred. The primary purpose of imposing punishment is crime prevention; it allows the offender to improve himself/herself and teach society to stay away from crimes (Garland 1991; Hirst 1984; Meyer 1968; Zaibert 2016).

Punishment can be stated as the immediate effect of a criminal act. It can be defined as "the imposition of an undesirable or unpleasant outcome upon a group or individual, meted out by an authority in contexts ranging from child discipline to criminal law as a response and deterrent to a particular action or behaviour that is deemed undesirable or unacceptable" (Anon n.d.-j).

1.8.1 Theories of Punishment

Different criminologists have proposed different theories for punishment. They are explained as follows:

Deterrent theory: According to this theory (Ellis, 2003), punishment for a crime should be severe enough such that it discourages the offender from repeating the crime in the future. This also sets an example for others so that they are discouraged from committing the same crime due to the severity of the punishment. This theory is considered to be inhuman without any moral foundation (Meyer 1968; Anon n.d.-j).

Retributive theory: According to this theory, punishment is decided based on the severity of the crime. Based on the principle of "an eye for an eye," retribution theory states that the criminal should be aware of the pain inflicted on the victim by him/her. It aims to avenge the victim's pain, harm, and injury by punishing the criminal, which is considered the most ancient form of justification for a crime. This theory is considered to be barbaric by many criminologists, sociologists, and penologists (Meyer 1968; Anon n.d.-j).

Preventive theory: The primary purpose of this theory is to prevent crime in the future. It believes in not taking revenge for the crime but instead keeping the antisocial elements away from society by imposing life imprisonment, death, incarceration, etc. The main objective of punishment is prevention, and the punishment also sets an example for other individuals of society to prevent them from indulging in criminal activities. Critics of this theory argue that it focuses solely on preventing other members of society from committing crimes, without providing opportunities for offenders to reform and improve their behavior (Meyer 1968; Anon n.d.-j).

Reformative theory: This is considered to be the most humane form of punishment. This theory aims to reform the criminal so that he/she abstains from committing crimes in the future. This theory believes that no criminal is a born criminal and that they are also to be treated as humans. Criminals should be reformed by educating them so that they refrain from indulging in criminal activities (Meyer 1968; Anon n.d.-j).

1.8.2 Forms of Punishment

Different forms of punishment are discussed below (Fig. 1.4):

1. Capital punishment: Also referred to as a death sentence, capital punishment is considered the most severe form of punishment for a serious offence like murder. This punishment is meted out for an extremely heinous crime with the objective that such grievous crimes will not be tolerated in society (Zaibert 2016).

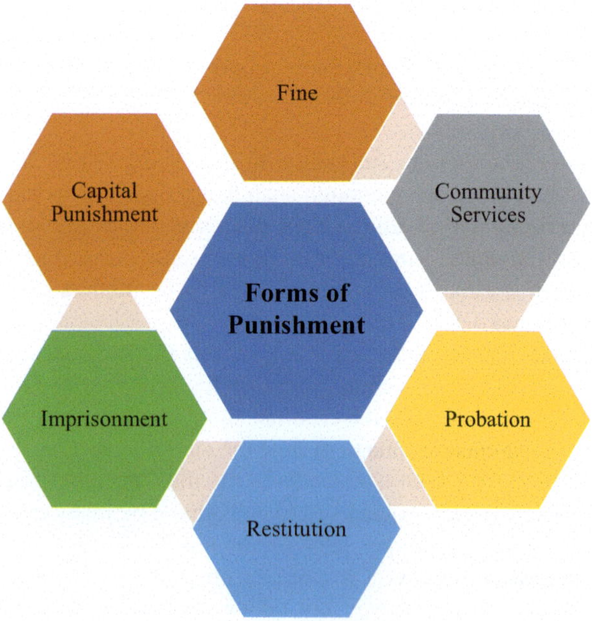

Fig. 1.4 Different forms of punishment

2. Probation: According to Feeley and Simons (1992), "probation is a form of low-cost surveillance for low-risk offenders." Any breach of the probation rules may result in him/her returning to prison. According to a few, probation is a form of punishment where individuals rehabilitate themselves and will mend their ways and lead an everyday life, whereas others believe that it is a "soft option" for criminals and that this punishment will have no effect on their thoughts of recommitting a crime.
3. Imprisonment: In this form of punishment, the individual is sent to prison/jail after being convicted by the court. The duration of imprisonment varies depending upon the severity of the crime. The two forms are simple and rigorous imprisonment.
4. Fines: This form of punishment is imposed when the crime is less severe. The court feels no threat to society from the criminal and spares him/her by imposing a fine. The court may impose a fine along with/without probation or imprisonment.
5. Restitution: This is replenishment of the loss or harm inflicted by the criminal on the victim. A fine is imposed, which is paid directly to the victim to compensate for the loss. If the criminal cannot pay the fine, then the court may order confiscation of his/her property in the form of restitution.
6. Community service: In this form of punishment, the court directs the criminal to work for society. The court may convict a criminal to work for the local community, like cleaning a wasteland, decorating public places and buildings, etc. The hours of work may vary depending upon the severity of the crime.

1.9 The Criminal Justice System in India

Every society, place, or country needs a set of norms, rules, and regulations to deal with the antisocial elements of society. A system is required to deal with people who cause harm to other individuals or the society as a whole, provide justice to the victims who have survived, and look after the survivors so that they do not face the same consequences again.

The criminal justice system is an instrument of social control. It is "the study and understanding of the deviations and the related sanctions necessary to ensure discipline among the diverse population in society and preventing the individuals and the society from being harmed by those who violate the existing norms, rules, and regulations." According to the Oxford English dictionary, the criminal justice system is defined as "the system of Law Enforcement, which is directly involved in apprehending, prosecuting, defending, sentencing, and punishing those who are suspected or convicted of criminal offences."

The criminal justice system is an essential tool to curb the antisocial behavior of a society. Some crimes are violent, whereas others are nonviolent crimes, and some crimes involve substance abuse and addiction. It is essential to keep in mind the role of the criminal and the cause for abnormal behavior, irrespective of the crime that is committed. A comprehensive approach is required to analyze the crime, the criminal, the situation behind the crime, and the criminal's behavior.

The criminal justice system acts as a law enforcement arm of a country, helps maintain social control, and mitigates crime. Its primary functions are to deal with criminal laws and trials in court, impose punishment, and work for the rehabilitation of both victims and criminals (Anon n.d.-k).

1.9.1 Objectives of the Criminal Justice System

The main objectives of the criminal justice system are as follows:

- To curb the occurrence of crime in society
- To punish the criminals for their antisocial activities
- To provide rehabilitation to the criminals for their improvement
- To maintain law and order in society
- To provide compensation to the victims for the loss suffered by them
- To dissuade the offenders from committing a crime in the future

1.9.2 The Structure of the Criminal Justice System

The judiciary is a branch of government that interprets the laws, sorts out disputes, and helps in administering justice to all the citizens of a country. The Indian judiciary is accountable to the Constitution of India. India has a single integrated judicial system. The structure of the Indian judiciary is pyramidal with the Supreme Court on the top, followed by the high courts. Subordinate to the high courts are the district courts and other lower courts.

India's criminal justice system consists of the Supreme Court at the helm (comprising 1 chief justice and 25 other judges). The Supreme Court is the highest court of the land located at New Delhi. Other judicial bodies at the union level take the form of tribunals whose members may be from the judiciary or the civil service. The Supreme Court of India is a court of records and hears appeals from any judgments of a high court. It has the power to issue prerogative writs like Habeas Corpus, Mandamus, Prohibition, Quo Warranto, and Certiorari to enforce fundamental rights (Sandhu and Choudhuri 1987). It has jurisdiction over all courts in India.

Following the Supreme Court are the high courts. These are located as one in number in each state and union territory. A high courts is also a court of records that hears appeals made by the district courts and has the power to grant writs. The judgments of the high courts are used as records by the lower courts in many deciding cases.

Below the high courts, there are session courts, where the judge handles civil cases in his/her capacity as a district judge. Following this are the district courts. These courts are presided over by a judge and are the principal courts of civil jurisdiction (Anon n.d.-k) (Figs. 1.5 and 1.6).

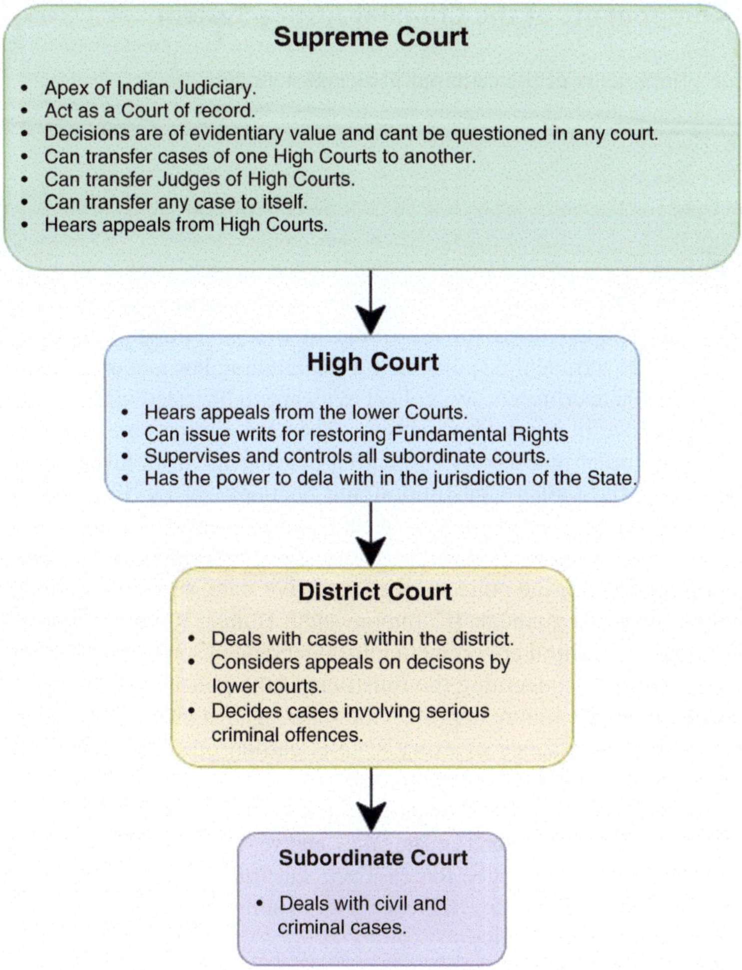

Fig. 1.5 Different courts in India

Fig. 1.6 Components of the criminal justice system

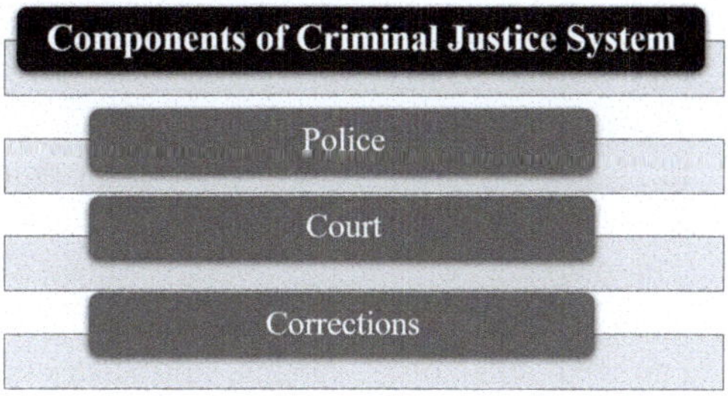

1.9.3 Components of the Criminal Justice System

The major components of the criminal justice system are:

- Police
- Courts
- Corrections

1.9.3.1 Police

According to the Oxford dictionary, the term "police" means a system of regulation to preserve order and to enforce the law of the internal government of a state. This is an agency of the government responsible for maintaining law and order in a society. The police investigate crime scenes, collect evidence to be tested in laboratories, and present the evidence in court after analysis. They have to enforce criminal law to maintain law and order in a society and help prevent crime from further occurrence.

Article 246 of the Indian Constitution and Section 3 of the Indian Police Act, 1861, states that the police force is a state subject and is not dealt with at the central government level. It is the responsibility of the state government to draft guidelines, rules, and regulations for the police of the respective state, and these regulations are found in the state police manuals (Commonwealth Human Rights Initiative Report, 2005). However, the central government must intervene in some special situations or play some unique role concerning the functions of the police. Article 355 specifies that "It is the duty of the Centre to protect the states against internal disturbances and to ensure that the governance of every state is carried on in accordance with the provisions of the Constitution" (Anon n.d.-l).

Organizational structure: The organizational structure of police is similar in almost all the states of the country. The rules and regulations are mentioned in the police manuals of the state police forces. Each state/union territory has its separate police force. Despite the diversity, there are a lot of similarities/commonness due to a few reasons. They are as follows:

- The working and administration of the police force are governed by the Police Act of 1861, which applies to most parts of the country.
- The majority of the criminal laws laid down in the Indian Penal Code (IPC), the Indian Evidence Act, and the Code of Criminal Procedure are chiefly applied to all the states of the country.
- The bulk of the senior state police officers is recruited, trained, and administered by central government, i.e., the Indian Police Service.

The state government has overall control over the police of the state. The director general of police is the head of the police force of a state. The state is further categorized into zones, ranges, and districts. A group of districts forms a range that is headed by the deputy inspector general of police. Furthermore, a superintendent of police is the head of the district force. In a few states, some zones comprise two or more ranges. The inspector general of police heads zones. The districts are further subdivided into subdivisions, circles, and police stations (Anon n.d.-k). The general organizational structure of the police force is described in the form of a flowchart, as depicted in Fig. 1.7.

1.9.3.1.1 The Roles and Functions of the Police

The police have an essential role to play in preserving the law and order of a society. The roles of the police are varied in nature. The police force plays a ubiquitous role as one of the most prominent organizations in society. In times of need, danger, and crisis, they are the ones who provide all types of necessary help. Pertaining to the duties of police officers, Section 23 of the Police Act, 1861, states that

> *It shall be the duty of every police- officer promptly to obey and execute all orders and warrants lawfully issued to him by any competent authority; to collect and communicate intelligence affecting the public peace; to prevent the commission of offences and public nuisances; to detect and bring offenders to justice and to apprehend all persons whom he is legally authorized to apprehend, and for whose apprehension sufficient ground exists; and it shall be lawful for every police- officer, for any of the purposes mentioned in this section, without a warrant, to enter and inspect any drinking- shop, gaming- house or other place of resort of loose and disorderly characters* (Anon n.d.-m).

1.9.3.2 Courts

Another vital component of the criminal justice system is the courts. The primary objectives of the courts are to discover the truth and impart justice. The hierarchy of the courts in India has been discussed in the earlier section. Here, we will deal with the different types of courts in India based on the nature of their jurisdiction.

According to the judiciary system of India, the courts have been broadly classified into three categories as per the hierarchy. They are the Supreme Court (the apex court), followed by the high courts and district courts. The hierarchical structure of the courts in India can be summarized as follows (Fig. 1.8):

Civil and criminal courts: Civil courts deal with disputes related to property, breach of contracts, illegal acts in money transactions, etc. The victim files a lawsuit against the offender in these courts, and judges administer justice by observing the nature of the act. The judge asks the offender to pay for the damages caused or compensate for the loss incurred by the victim. In criminal courts, justice is administered through district courts, followed by the high courts and the Supreme Court. The functioning of these courts is based on the laws laid down in the Indian Penal Code (1860) and the Code of Criminal Procedure (1974) (Anon n.d.-n).

Appellate and trial courts: An appellate court is any court that has the power to hear an appeal from the lower courts. For instance, the Supreme Court is an appellate court that hears the appeals from the high court and so on. The power to review the judgment of the lower courts varies according to the jurisdiction. Some appellate courts have limited powers for the review of the decision. In trial courts, both parties present their evidence and witnesses. Moreover, the judge then

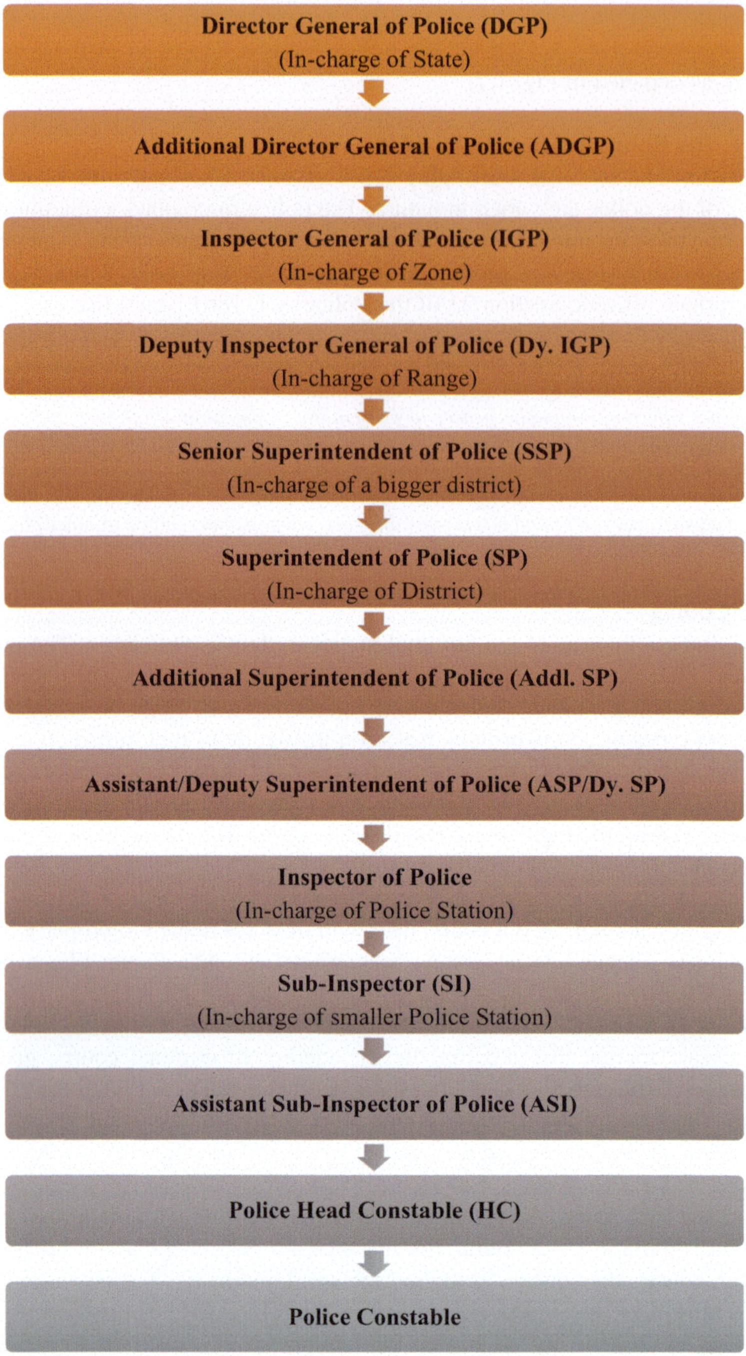

Fig. 1.7 Organizational structure of police (Adapted from CHRI, 2005) (Commonwealth Human Rights Initiative n.d.)

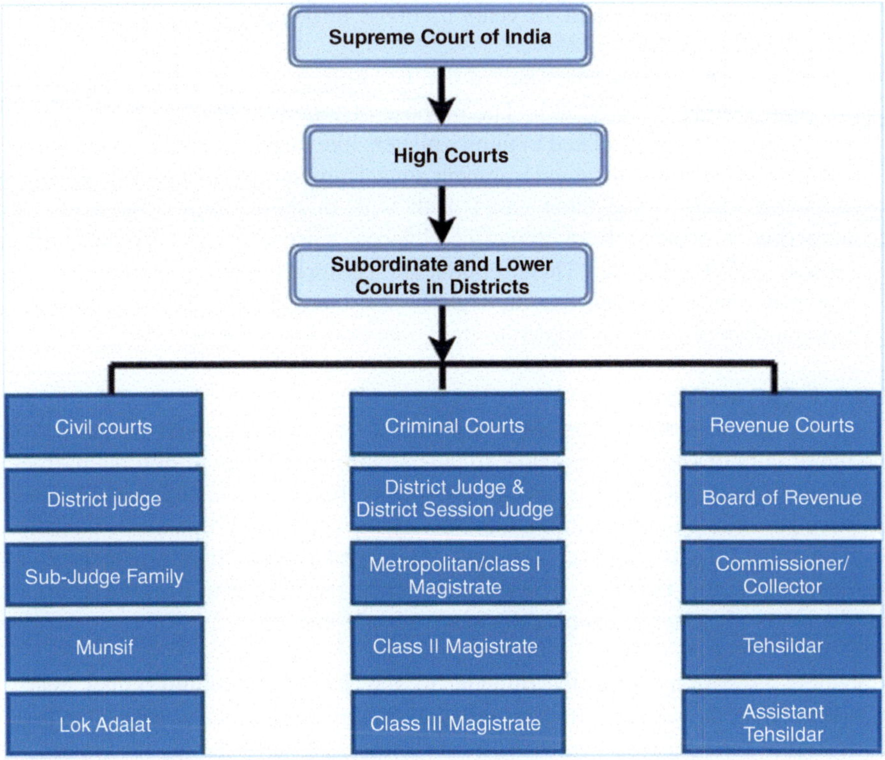

Fig. 1.8 Hierarchical structure of the courts in India

decides the outcome after hearing the case from both sides. The appellate court may overrule the decisions made in the trial court (Anon n.d.-n).

Juvenile courts: These are courts that deal with underage defendants charged with crimes, accused of some misconduct, who have been neglected or have been abused sexually, physically, and emotionally. The trials of children below 18 years of age are carried out by a particular judicial area handled by juvenile courts, now named the Juvenile Justice Boards. The purpose of these courts is social, legal rehabilitation and reformation of the individuals. Under the provisions of the Juvenile Justice Act, 1986, juvenile courts and special homes have the provisions to deal with the cases of delinquent children. Later on, after the amendment of the law as per the Juvenile Justice Act, 2000, the power to deal with such cases was handed over to the Juvenile Justice Boards. The functions of both remain the same, except that the Juvenile Justice Boards have more reformative and comprehensive powers. Furthermore, the Juvenile Justice (Care and Protection of Children) Act, 2015, has been passed by the Parliament of India, which replaced the Indian juvenile delinquency law, the Juvenile Justice (Care and Protection of Children) Act, 2000. According to the new law, juveniles between the age of 16 and 18 years involved in heinous crimes are treated as adults (Anon n.d.-n).

Family courts: The need for the setup of family courts in India was first proposed by late Smt. Durgabai Deshmukh. The purpose of establishing these family courts was to deal with cases related to family matters like marriage, divorce, custody of a child, alimony, etc., in an environment away from the regular courts to ensure a congenial setup. Some other cases dealt with in these family courts are the protection of women from domestic violence, misuse of Section 498A IPC, Section 125 CrPC, etc. These courts are equipped with psychologists and counselors because other than the legal issues, there are also psychological and humanitarian dimensions related to these matters (Anon n.d.-o).

1.9.3.3 Corrections

Another vital component of the criminal justice system is correctional measures. It is the moral duty of society to provide offenders with a chance to reform themselves. This correctional practice is a developing science based on maintaining a balance between punishment and rehabilitation. Society demands that criminals be punished for their unlawful acts; however, they should be given a chance to reform themselves and learn corrective behavior. The standard corrective measures include probation, parole, prison, restitution, community services, and fines.

Probation: Probation allows the offender to stay in the community rather than a prison under the supervision of a probation officer. It is a sanction granted to first- or second-time offenders with less severe crimes. The offender is asked to follow certain conditions imposed by the court (Ghosh 2008). The offender stays under the threat of being incarcerated if he/she is found to break the rules of the court or the probation officer. Some of the restrictions imposed by the court are that he/she will not be allowed to leave the place of his/her jurisdiction, will be asked to attend some educational or reformative program, will be asked to refrain from the use of a firearm, should be allowed to live at a directed place, etc. The court has the right to revoke or modify the probation (Criminal Procedure Code 1973).

Parole: Parole's provisions in India are regulated by the mandates made under the Prisons Act, 1894, and the Prisoner Act, 1900. It is defined as a prisoner's release on a temporary or permanent basis based on his/her good behavior. Although the parole rules are the same throughout the country, there are few alterations concerning each state. Parole can be further categorized into two types: custody parole and regular parole. In custody parole, the prisoner is allowed out of prison for a limited duration of a few hours escorted by the police. This is granted in case of the death of a family member, severe sickness, etc. Regular parole is granted for 1 month, but it may be extended maximum to a year under certain circumstances. Offenders convicted of rape and murder or similar charges are devoid of parole (Ghosh 2008).

Prison: Prison and its administration are governed by the Prisons Act, 1894, and the prison manuals of every state government. The state government has to draft the rules and regulations of a prison and modify them as per the need. The central government assists in maintaining and repairing prisons, medical facilities, vocational facilities, facilities for women offenders, etc.

Restitution: Restitution is a form of compensation given by the offender for the loss incurred by the victim. This loss can be in terms of money or may be some injury. It is the act of making up for the damage or harm caused to the victim. The judge may order the convict to make amends for the crime by paying for the losses incurred by the victim.

Community services: It is a punishment given to offenders that also serves to benefit the community. This punishment provides the offenders with an opportunity to see the injuries inflicted by his/her offence, which may help understand the limits of social tolerance of the offence. Community services include participation in substance abuse programs, counseling, painting, cleaning, etc.

Fines: It is a penalty of money paid by the offender to the victim to compensate for the crime, as decided by a court of law. It is an amount decided by a court of law or any other authority to settle a crime, especially minor crimes. Fines paid for the violation of traffic rules, loitering, etc., are some of the examples.

Correctional institutions: A correctional institution is a place designated by law to keep the persons held in custody under the process of law or lawful arrest. They may be institutional and noninstitutional.

Institutional corrections include jails, women jails, special jails, open jails, and Borstal schools. Jails are categorized as central jails, district jails, and sub-jails. Central jails have a larger capacity, and prisoners with imprisonment of more than 2 years are confined here. In states where there are no central jails, district jails serve as the main prisons. Sub-jails are further smaller institutions at the subdivisional level in states.

Women jails are prisons exclusively meant for female prisoners at the subdivisional, district, and central levels. Special jails are high-security prisons meant to confine particular types of criminals such as habitual offenders and those convicted of offences such as terrorism, violent crimes, and violations of prison discipline. Open jails are minimum-security prisons for offenders who are convicted and display good behavior by following the norms and discipline of the prison. Borstal schools are youth detention centers meant for the imprisonment of juveniles. These particular schools are made to ensure the young offenders' welfare, care, and rehabilitation in a proper environment, equipped with vocational training and education under the guidance of trained teachers.

Noninstitutional corrections refer to the correction of offenders without sending them behind bars. House arrest is a form of punishment, especially for nonviolent offenders who serve their sentences at their homes under close surveillance. It is also referred to as home confinement or home detention, where the mobility of the offender is restricted.

1.9.4 Steps of the Criminal Justice Process

Before the announcement of punishment by the judge in a court, there are several steps involved in criminal justice. These steps are (Fig. 1.9) as follows:

- Investigation: After a crime is reported, the police must investigate the scene of the crime. During this process, the investigator tries to collect evidence and other information from the crime scene, which will help identify the suspect and support an arrest.
- Arrest: When someone is suspected of committing a crime, they may be taken into custody as part of a legal process. This involves physically restraining them to ensure they appear in court or do not flee the area. It's a necessary measure to ensure public safety and justice. When the police apprehend a suspect based on probable cause and evidence found at the crime scene, it is known as an arrest. The arrested individual is then taken into custody and brought before a court of law. In order for an arrest to be made, there must be a reasonable connection between the suspect and the crime, known as probable cause.
- Prosecution: This is done by the district attorney (prosecution lawyer). During this step, the prosecution considers different factors like the robustness of the evidence and the offence's seriousness.
- Indictment: This refers to the accusation that a person has committed the crime. According to the CrPC, an indictment is an essential step. The prosecutor presents the information charging the criminal, and a preliminary inquiry is held to decide whether the evidence presented is enough for a trial. The criminal defendant and his/her attorney are allowed in such types of hearings.
- Arraignment: An arraignment is a formal court proceeding where the defendant is brought before a judge and informed of the charges against them. During the arraignment, the charges are read out to the accused person in a language they understand, and they are asked to enter their plea, which can be guilty, not guilty,

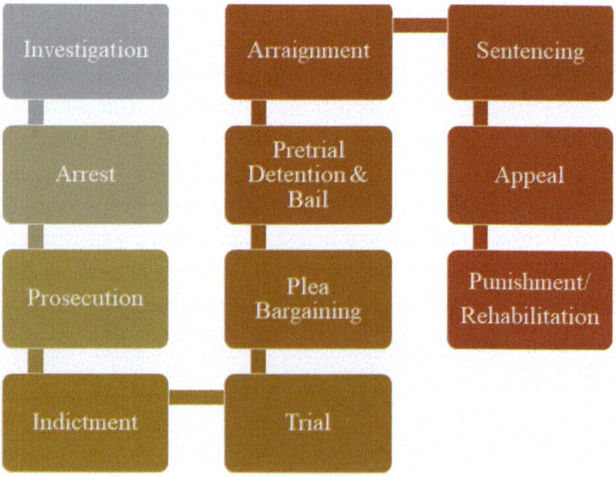

Fig. 1.9 Steps involved in the process of criminal justice administration

or, in some cases, no contest (also known as nolo contendere) claiming a lack of knowledge or denial of the charges. The accused person is also informed of their rights and the consequences of each plea option. The purpose of the arraignment is to ensure that the defendant is aware of the charges and to establish their plea before the trial proceedings commence.

- Pretrial detention and bail: Detention restricts the suspect in custody before the trial begins. When the crime committed is not very serious, the suspect can be released under certain conditions before the trial on bail. Bail is the amount paid by the defendant to be released, which ensures that he/she would turn up for the trial.
- Plea bargaining: This occurs between the prosecutor and the defendant's attorney. Here, the defendant pleads guilty to have a reduction of charge or sentence or asks to drop all the charges altogether.
- Trial: In this step, the prosecutor and the defendant's attorney present their evidence with a motive to prove or disprove guilt before a judge. Suppose the evidence suggests that the defendant has committed the crime beyond any reasonable doubt. He/she is pronounced guilty. If the charges turn out to be false based on evidence, then the person is acquitted of the charges and is released.
- Sentencing: The judge announces the sentence depending upon whether the suspect is found to be guilty or not guilty. The sentence may include imprisonment, fines, parole, correctional institution, or a combination of fines and imprisonment.
- Appeals: These are filed by the attorneys to an appellate court to review the sentence imposed by a lower court. An appeal is a request made (to a higher court) by the attorneys to reverse the decisions taken by the lower court. If these appeals are reversed, then they are sent back to trial courts for a reversal.
- Punishment/rehabilitation: Once a person is found guilty, punishment is imposed on him/her. It is administered by local, state, or correctional authorities. A person may be released before completing the full term based on moral grounds and sent to rehabilitation centers. The purpose of imposing punishment is to reform the criminals and set an example for society.

1.9.5 Administration of Criminal Justice

The process of the administration of justice is divided into three stages, and they are investigation, inquiry, and trial. In India, justice in criminal cases is administered under two main statutes, namely, the Criminal Procedure Code and the Indian Penal Code. These statutes provide the procedure to be followed during the different stages. Before getting into the details of the stages of criminal justice, let us understand a few basic terminologies.

- Cognizable offence: According to Section 2(c) of the CrPC, "Cognizable Offence means an offence in which, a police officer may, in accordance with the First

Schedule or under any other law for the time being in force, arrest without warrant." (Criminal Procedure Code 1973).

- Non-cognizable offence: Section 2(l) defines "non-cognizable offence means an offence in which a police officer has no authority to arrest without warrant." (Criminal Procedure Code 1973).
- First information report (FIR): A report pertaining to the occurrence of a cognizable offence received at the police station is called the first information report, popularly known as FIR. Since it is the first information about the cognizable offence, it is called the first information report (Anon n.d.-p). The police registers the report in an FIR register and begins the crime investigation on receipt of this information. A criminal case begins from filing a first information report (FIR), and it is the first stage in criminal proceedings.
- Bailable offence: In bailable offences, the accused can claim bail as a matter of right. The police are supposed to release such an accused on bail if he/she is prepared to pay the bail amount at any time while he/she is in the custody of a police officer (Criminal Procedure Code 1973).
- Non-bailable offence: In non-bailable offences, the accused is not entitled to bail as a matter of right, the police invariably do not grant bail in such cases, and only the court grants bail. The list of billable and non-billable offences is provided in the first schedule of the CrPC (Criminal Procedure Code 1973).
- Inquiry: Section 2 (g) defines "inquiry" as every inquiry, other than a trial, conducted under this code by a magistrate or a court. The primary aim of an inquiry is to determine the truth of the reported crime, i.e., to check whether the facts reported are true or false. It can be either judicial or nonjudicial (Criminal Procedure Code 1973).
- Investigation: According to Sec 2(h), "Investigation includes all the proceedings under this Code for the collection of evidence conducted by a police officer or by any person (other than a Magistrate) whom a Magistrate authorizes in this behalf" (Criminal Procedure Code 1973).
- Summons: This is a written document issued by the court that asks someone to be present in court. The person who is summoned can be the accused, a witness, or an expert.
- Warrant: Section 70 of the Criminal Procedure Code mentions the aspects of a warrant: "Every warrant of arrest that is issued by a Court under this section has to be in writing and signed by the presiding officer of the respective court. The warrant should also bear the seal of the same court that issued the warrant." (Criminal Procedure Code 1973).
- Preventive arrest: The police have the authority to make an arrest when it is deemed necessary to prevent a cognizable offence. This is the most common situation in which the police affect a preventive arrest. The police can also make preventive arrests under special laws such as the National Security Act, the Prevention of Illicit Traffic in Narcotic Drugs and Psychotropic Substances (PITNDPS) Act, etc., against dreaded criminals. It is also done under Section 151 of the CrPC, which states "(1) A Police Officer knowing of a design to commit any cognizable offence may arrest, without orders from a magistrate

and without a warrant, the person so designing, if it appears to such officer that the commission of the offence cannot be otherwise prevented" (Anon n.d.-q).

1.9.6 Stages of Criminal Justice

The three stages of criminal justice are described as follows:

1. Investigation: This is the preliminary stage of the criminal justice process. It begins after a crime is reported and the first information report is recorded. Section 154 of the CrPC. provides that "any information received in the police station in respect of a cognizable offence shall be reduced into writing, got signed by the informant and entered in the concerned register." Section 156(1) "requires the concerned officer to investigate the facts and circumstances of such a case without any order from the Magistrate in this behalf" (Criminal Procedure Code 1973).
2. Inquiry: The second stage is the inquiry stage, which is dealt with in Sections 177–189 of the CrPC and consists of a magistrate. This inquiry is made either on receiving a report by the police or upon a complaint made by another person (Anon n.d.-q).
3. Trial: This is the last stage in the process of criminal justice. It is the judicial adjudication of the innocence or guilt of an individual. Framing of charges or giving notice: Once the judge is satisfied that enough documents and evidence are available for a case, a trial may be ordered. If sufficient grounds of proceedings are not found after hearing the plea of the accused, then the judge may discharge the accused after recording the reasons for it. However, if the accused pleads guilty, then he/she will be convicted. Moreover, if he/she pleads not guilty, then the trial will begin (Anon n.d.-q).

   Following are the steps in a trial:

- Recording prosecution evidence: Once the charges are framed, the court asks the prosecution to present their side of evidence and witnesses. The witness takes an oath and testifies; this process is known as an examination in chief. The accused's lawyer cross-examines these witnesses.
- Statement of accused: The court has the power to examine the accused at any stage of inquiry or trial to obtain information regarding the case. With this, the accused gets a reasonable chance to explain the incriminating facts and situations of the case.
- Defense evidence: At this point, if no further evidence is found to be present stating that the accused has committed the crime, then the judge will order the acquittal of the accused. However, if the accused is not acquitted due to lack of evidence, then evidence is to be presented to support the defense.

- Final arguments: This is the final stage of the trial. After examining the witnesses for the defense, the prosecution is asked to sum up the case, and the accused is entitled to reply to it.
- Judgment: After the prosecution and the defense statements are complete; the judge makes his/her judgment.

Thus, the abovementioned steps sum up the whole process of the administration of criminal justice. There are many inherent lacunae in the process, which obstruct the speedy trial of cases and cause a delay in delivering justice.

1.10 Juvenile Delinquency

The deviant behavior of juveniles has increased to a great extent, thus hampering the stability of society. The criminality of a juvenile is born out of factors in his/her surroundings, lack of proper education, or may be even lack of discipline. It is considered that it is easy to repair the youth of a country rather than mend the adults. The countrymen have to bring these deviant youth on track (Anon n.d.-r; Anon n.d.-s).

Juvenile delinquency refers to crimes committed by minors. When a person deviates from the norms and regulations of a society, his/her behavior is termed as "delinquent behavior." When the actions committed by a juvenile are against the norms and are harmful to society, he/she is termed as a "juvenile delinquent." According to the Juvenile Justice Act, 2015 (India), Clause 15 states that "In case of the heinous offence alleged to have been committed by a child who has completed or is above the age of 16 years, the Board shall conduct a preliminary assessment with regard to his mental and physical capacity to commit such offence, ability to understand the consequences of the offence and the circumstances in which he has committed the offence." (Anon n.d.-t) Under the Juvenile Justice (Care and Protection) Act, 2015, a juvenile is defined under Section 2 (35) as "a child below the age of eighteen years."

Various theories have been proposed to explain the causes of juveniles indulging in crime. These theories of juvenile delinquency explain various factors that are responsible for their criminal behavior (Shaw and McKay 1942).

They are explained as follows:

1. Biological theory: As proposed by Lombroso, an individual is a born criminal if he/she is born with some inherited characters, which predispose him/her to indulge in criminal activities. However, modifications have been made in the concepts of biological theory. A combination of genetics and social environment holds the responsibility of deviant behavior. Children who have inherited genes and face stress in their surroundings are highly likely to commit a crime (Anon n.d.-s; Anon n.d.-t).
2. Social disorganization theory: Criminal behavior manifests in the developing brain when their growth is hindered due to a reduction in their scope of

advancement in society. The reasons may be poverty, a large number of school dropouts, and corruption. When their dreams are not fulfilled by legitimate means, they resort to illegal modes and commit crimes (Anon n.d.-s; Anon n.d.-t).

3. Cultural deviance theory: When children live in a surrounding of gangs and cults, they tend to join and get affected by their presence. They might experience isolation and frustration that impede them from achieving their goals and resort to criminal behavior (Anon n.d.-s; Anon n.d.-t).
4. Psychological theories: Criminal behavior is explained in terms of id, ego, and superego from the perspective of psychodynamic theory. This explains that if id is dominant and ego and superego tend to be weak, then there is a higher risk of criminal tendencies (Anon n.d.-s; Anon n.d.-t).

1.10.1 The Juvenile Justice System in India

The Juvenile Justice (Care and Protection of Children) Act, 2015 is a significant law in India that focuses on the care, protection and rehabilitation of juveniles in conflict with the law. The Act recognizes that due to their young age and susceptibility, children require specific attention and support when dealing with the justice system. Its primary aim is to uphold the rights and welfare of these children and ensure that they receive suitable care and rehabilitation.

Juveniles are not kept along with adult offenders, and they are reintegrated into society after finishing their sentence. The nature of punishments for a juvenile offender is proportionate to the seriousness of the offence committed by the juvenile. This may range from issuing warnings, releasing them on probation, or sending them to juvenile homes or special homes for a fixed duration. Juveniles should be protected and cared for, and all the necessary opportunities should be provided to them so that they may return to society as productive individuals. In India, the juvenile justice system is a benevolent institution that focuses on correcting the offenders and allowing them to assimilate into society with dignity (Anon n.d.-t).

1.10.2 Prevention of Juvenile Delinquency

It is crucial to prevent juveniles from committing crimes. If they are not prevented at an early stage, then they may soon turn into habitual offenders. Criminologists have suggested different methods for the prevention of juvenile delinquency. These may be classified as individual and environmental programs that deal with juvenile delinquency prevention through proper education, counseling sessions, or psychotherapy. Environmental programs may involve measures to improve the socioeconomic conditions of a society, which might be a factor for juvenile delinquency (Shaw and McKay 1942).

The government has also taken measures for the prevention of juvenile delinquency and protection of the youth from engaging in criminal activities. Prevention services provided by the government include imparting education, family counseling, sheltering of youth, providing education regarding substance abuse, and its treatment. The government plays a keen role in protecting the rights of these juveniles and adopts reformative methods to develop moral values in these children so that they can once again become a constructive part of the society and help in its upliftment (Anon n.d.-s; Anon n.d.-t; Shaw and McKay 1942).

1.11 Conclusion

Criminology has not only become a subject of interest for students but has also become the central topic of public interest because of the increasing rate of crime, the advanced techniques of crime, the varying attitudes of the liberal judges to crimes and criminals, and the changing laws over the period. Over time, the interest is shifting from the causes and theories of crime to enactment of laws, interpretation of laws, and law enforcement agencies. Thus, along with criminologists, police and judiciary also have a vital role in providing justice.

Whenever a crime is committed, the main focus is the criminal or perpetrator, and less attention is given to the harm caused to the victim or the person who has suffered because of the crime. Over the years, with some significant developments, "victimology" has become an area of interest for criminologists. There has been a transformation of attitudes and approaches toward the victims of a crime, and justice and compensation are provided to them.

As a whole, criminologists have an essential role to play in society. They study the different causes of criminal behavior while working with law enforcement agencies and researching which approaches are better for rehabilitation. Thus, their sole purpose is to make a society less susceptible to crime and criminal acts.

References

Ahuja R (2000) Criminology. Rawat Publications

Albanese JS (2014) The encyclopedia of criminology and criminal justice victim precipitation. Wiley-Blackwell, Malden, MA, pp 1–5. https://doi.org/10.1002/9781118517383

Allen FA (1954) Pioneers in criminology. J Crim Law Criminol Police Sci 45(4)

Anckarsäter H, Radovic S, Svennerlind C, Höglund P, Radovic F (2009) Mental disorder is a cause of crime: the cornerstone of forensic psychiatry. Int J Law Psychiatry 32(6):342–347

Anon (n.d.-a). https://london.northumbria.ac.uk/blog/what-is-cyber-crime-and-how-criminology-helps-to-reduce-victimisation/. Accessed 5 May 2021

Anon (n.d.-b). https://www.preservearticles.com/articles/what-is-the-legal-definition-of-crime/28807. Accessed 10 May 2021

Anon (n.d.-c). https://www.legalserviceindia.com/legal/article-4357-criminal-liability-crime-stages-of-crime-and-inchoate-crime.html. Accessed 12 May 2021

Anon (n.d.-d). http://criminal-justice.iresearchnet.com/criminology/theories/psychological-theories-of-crime/3/. Accessed 15 June 2021

Anon (n.d.-e). https://blog.ipleaders.in/compensation-victim-crime-india/. Accessed 18 June 2021

Anon (n.d.-f). http://www.dppodisha.nic.in/?q=node/17. Accessed 21 June 2021

Anon (n.d.-g). https://www.legalserviceindia.com/legal/article-6103-a-critical-study-on-victim-compensation-under-various-laws-of-india.html. Accessed 21 June 2021

Anon (n.d.-h). https://openoregon.pressbooks.pub/ccj230/chapter/1-14-victims-in-the-cj-system/. Accessed 25 June 2021

Anon (n.d.-i). https://www.legalserviceindia.com/legal/article-332-victim-compensation-scheme-an-aspect-of-modern-criminology.html. Accessed 25 June 2021

Anon (n.d.-j). https://www.unodc.org/e4j/en/crime-prevention-criminal-justice/module-7/key-issues/2%2D%2Djustifying-punishment-in-the-community.html. Accessed 30 June 2021

Anon (n.d.-k). http://cbseacademic.nic.in/web_material/doc/Legal_Studies/XI_U4_Legal_Studies.pdf. Accessed 30 June 2021

Anon (n.d.-l). https://www.latestlaws.com/bare-acts/central-acts-rules/article-355-constitution-of-india-duty-of-the-union-to-protect-states-against-external-aggression-and-internal-disturbance/. Accessed 30 June 2021

Anon (n.d.-m). https://www.indianlawsinfo.com/home/section/4951/section-23-in-the-police-act-1861/duties-of-police-officers. Accessed 30 June 2021

Anon (n.d.-n). https://blog.ipleaders.in/courts-justice-system-india/. Accessed: 3 July 2021

Anon (n.d.-o). http://www.legalserviceindia.com/article/l356-Family-Courts-in-India.html. Accessed 3 July 2021

Anon (n.d.-p). https://lawtimesjournal.in/first-information-report-fir-under-crpc/. Accessed 12 July 2021

Anon (n.d.-q). https://bprd.nic.in/WriteReadData/userfiles/file/6798203243-Volume%202.pdf. Accessed 3 July 2021

Anon (n.d.-r). http://www.legalserviceindia.com/legal/article-1724-juvenile-delinquency-in-india-causes-and-prevention-.html. Accessed 15 June 2021

Anon (n.d.-s). http://www.legalservicesindia.com/article/626/Juvenile-delinquency.html. Accessed 18 June 2021

Anon (n.d.-t). https://www.lawfinderlive.com/Articles1/Article92.htm?AspxAutoDetectCookieSupport=1. Accessed 15 June 2021

Barlow HD, Kauzlarich D (1984) Introduction to criminology. Little, Brown, Boston, pp 135–147

Becker HS (1963) Outsiders: studies in the sociology of deviance. The Free Press, New York

Bemmelen JMV (1955) Pioneers in criminology. J Crim Law Criminol Police Sci 46(3):293

Brown SE, Esbensen FA, Geis G (2010) Criminology explaining crime and its context, 7th edn. Anderson Publishing

Canter D, Youngs D (2016) Crime and society. Contemp Social Sci 11(4):283–288. https://doi.org/10.1080/21582041.2016.1259495

Commonwealth Human Rights Initiative (n.d.). https://www.humanrightsinitiative.org/publications/police/police_organisations.pdf. Accessed 21 June 2021

Criminal Procedure Code (1973) https://www.indiacode.nic.in/bitstream/123456789/15272/1/the_code_of_criminal_procedure%2C_1973.pdf

Darby RR (2018) Neuroimaging abnormalities in neurological patients with criminal behavior. Curr Neurol Neurosci Rep 18:1–7

Doerner WG (2017) Victimology. Routledge

Drapkin IE, Viano E (eds) (1974) Victimology. D.C. Heath, Lexington, MA

Dutta M, Husain Z (2009) Determinants of crime rates: crime deterrence and growth in post-liberalized India

Fajnzylber P, Lederman D, Loayza N (2002) What causes violent crime? Eur Econ Rev 46(7):1323–1357

Fattah EA (2000) Victimology: past, present and future. Criminologie 33(1):17–46. http://www.jstor.org/stable/42745214

Feeley MM, Simon J (1992) The new penology: notes on the emerging strategy of corrections and its implications. Criminology 30(4):449–474

Finkelhor D, Kendall-Tackett K (1997) A developmental perspective on the childhood impact of crime, abuse, and violent victimization

Garland D (1991) Sociological perspectives on punishment. Crime Justice 14:115–165
Ghosh S (2008) Probation and parole as methods of mainstraiming criminals: a socio-legal analysis from Indian perspective. https://doi.org/10.2139/ssrn.1151026
Hall J (1960) General principles of criminal law, 2d edn. Bobbs-Merrill, Indianapolis, IN
Hirst P (1984) The concept of punishment. Law Context A Socio-Legal J 2:73
Hood R, Sparks R (1970) Key issues in criminology. Weidenfeld and Nicolson, London
Karmen A (2015) Crime victims: an introduction to victimology. Cengage Learning
Meyer J (1968) Reflections on some theories of punishment. J Crim Law Criminol Police Sci 59(4): 595–599
Mischel W (1969) Continuity and change in personality. Am Psychol 24(11):1012–1018. https://doi.org/10.1037/h0028886
Morizot J, Kazemian L (2015) The development of criminal and antisocial behaviour theory research and practical applications. Springer Publications
Porwal R (2018) Victimology: victimization and emerging trends under current justice system. South Asian Law Rev J 4:83–102
Reid ST (2015) Crime and criminology. Wolters Kluwer
Shaw CR, McKay HD (1942) Juvenile delinquency and urban areas. University of Chicago Press, Chicago
Shinder (1982) https://www.lawctopus.com/academike/victimology-emerging-trends-compensation/
Siegel LJ (2016) Criminology-theories, patterns & typologies, 12th edn. Cengage Learning
Skogan WG (1987) The impact of victimization on fear. Crime Delinq 33(1):135–154
Sutherland E, Cressey DR (1960) Principles of criminology, 6th edn. Lippincott
Sutherland EH, Cressey DR, Luckenbill DF (1992) Principles of criminology. Altamira Press
Veeraraghavan V (2019) Textbook of criminology, 1st edn. Selective & Scientific Books, New Delhi
Vito GF, Maahs JR (2015) Criminology. Jones & Bartlett Publishers
Walklate S (2007) Understanding criminology current theoretical debates, 3rd edn. Open University Press, McGraw Hill
White R, Haines F, Asquith NL (2017) Crime and criminology. Oxford University Press, Melbourne, VIC
Zaibert L (2016) Punishment and retribution. Routledge

Introduction to Forensic Science

2

Neeti Kapoor, Pradnya Sulke, Pooja Pardeshi, Rasika Kakad, and Ashish Badiye

Abstract

The chapter "Introduction to Forensic Science" provides an overview of the diverse fields encompassed within forensic science, common types of evidence encountered at crime scenes, the seven principles of forensic science, and significant contributors to the field from around the world. The chapter begins by outlining the multidisciplinary nature of forensic science, including its subdivisions such as forensic chemistry, forensic biology, forensic anthropology, and digital forensics. It emphasizes the importance of integrating various scientific disciplines in the investigation of crimes and the analysis of evidence. Additionally, the chapter discusses common types of evidence encountered in forensic investigations, including fingerprints, DNA, trace evidence, firearms and ballistics, and digital evidence. The seven principles of forensic science, including the Locard's Exchange Principle and the Principle of Individuality, are presented to highlight the foundational principles guiding forensic investigations. Furthermore, the chapter recognizes major contributors in the field of forensic science from around the world, showcasing their significant contributions and advancements in forensic techniques and methodologies. By providing an overview, this chapter serves as a foundation for understanding the principles and applications of forensic science.

Keywords

Forensic science · Forensic fields · Evidence · Seven principles · Significant contributors

N. Kapoor · P. Sulke · P. Pardeshi · R. Kakad · A. Badiye (✉)
Department of Forensic Science, Government Institute of Forensic Science, Nagpur, Maharashtra, India
e-mail: neetikapoor@ifscnagpur.in; ashishbadiye@ifscnagpur.in

P. Shrivastava et al. (eds.), *Textbook of Forensic Science*,
https://doi.org/10.1007/978-981-99-1377-0_2

2.1 Introduction

Professor Prasanta Kumar Chattopadhyay defines Forensic science as the application of various scientific methods and techniques for the purposes of justice. As is evident from the meticulously chosen words, the focus is on the use of "scientific methods and techniques" rather than just methods to ensure replicability and reliability or results. Forensic Science is an integral part of the justice administration system, as it provides a way to analyze and interpret evidence in criminal as well as civil investigations. This evidence can be used to identify suspects, support a conviction, or exonerate suspects. The word "forensic" is derived from the Latin word "forensis," which translates to "forum." It is defined in several ways by different scientists and authors. "Forensic science is the application of science to the criminal and civil laws that are enforced by police agencies in a criminal justice system" (Saferstein 2015). "Forensic science is a scientific discipline directed to recognition, identification, individualisation and evaluation of physical evidence by the application of methods and principles of natural sciences for the purpose of administration of criminal justice" (Nabar 2002).

Forensic analysis and examination of physical evidence, such as fingerprints and DNA, and nonphysical evidence, such as witness statements and video recordings, is used to draw conclusions about criminal events and help identify suspects. It is also used to support convictions, as forensic analysis is considered more definitive than other forms of analyses. In addition, forensic science has been instrumental in exonerating innocent suspects, as it may conclusively prove that someone is innocent.

Forensic scientists and experts must understand the legal system well, as their testimony is often the deciding factor in a case. As such, they must be familiar with the rules of evidence and procedures for handling, analyzing, and presenting evidence in a court of law. They must be updated with the latest developments in the field and attend relevant conferences, seminars, trainings, and workshops to stay informed.

2.2 The Role of Forensic Science in the Criminal Justice System

Forensic science is a rapidly growing field in many countries across the globe. With the advancement of technology, criminals are also becoming more innovative in devising sophisticated methods to commit crimes, and forensic science is playing an essential role in helping apprehend them. It uses scientific methods, such as DNA analysis, toxicology, biometrics, ballistics, and other technologies, to identify suspects in illegal activities. Forensic science is a vital part of the criminal justice system, as it helps provide evidence to either support or refute a suspect's and/or a witness's claims during a trial.

Forensic science encompasses various disciplines and scientific techniques used to analyze physical evidence collected from a crime scene. These evidence include fingerprints, bodily fluids, weapon and tool marks, bloodstains, and fibers. Forensic science is also used to identify victims of a crime or disaster, such as missing persons or mass disasters. Forensic experts can use DNA analysis or other methods to match a victim to a known individual, often a family member. Forensic scientists use various scientific methods to study the evidence and draw conclusions about its significance in a case. They use techniques such as DNA analysis, trace evidence analysis, and ballistic analysis to examine evidence and compare it to other pieces of evidence or known suspects or victims. By doing so, they can establish a link between an individual and a crime.

Forensic scientists also play a vital role in civil cases, such as in personal injury or defamation cases. Forensic experts may be asked to provide expert testimony or analysis to support one side of the case. They may also be asked to testify as expert witnesses in criminal trials. Finally, forensic science can be used to help solve cold cases. This involves reviewing evidence that may have been missed or overlooked during the original investigation. By studying cold cases, investigators can identify new leads or uncover new evidence to help solve the case and assist in the delivery of justice.

2.3 Fields of Forensic Science

Forensic science is essentially used by law enforcement to provide crucial, evidence-based solutions to criminal cases. It is an incredibly complex field of science that requires specialized knowledge and skills to understand and can often be the key to a successful investigation. However, this area is vast and complex, and most people are unaware of the different branches of forensic science and how they can be applied to solve criminal cases. In this section, we discuss the various branches of forensic science, how they are used in criminal investigations, and how understanding them can help further an investigation.

Forensic science is a rapidly growing field of research and practice that can be broken down into many branches. Some are depicted in the figure below (Fig. 2.1), i.e., fingerprints, questioned documents, forensic chemistry, forensic toxicology, forensic biology, forensic serology, forensic anthropology, forensic odontology, forensic physics, forensic ballistics, forensic psychology, forensic biotechnology, digital and cyber forensics, forensic engineering, forensic nanotechnology, forensic entomology, forensic geology, and crime scene investigation. Apart from the ones mentioned in the figure, some other areas include humanitarian forensics, forensic meteorology, forensic metrology, forensic linguistics, forensic stylistics, forensic epidemiology, sports forensics, corporate forensics, forensic accounting, forensic auditing, forensic microscopy, underwater forensics, forensic archeology, drone forensics, cell phone forensics, forensic graphology, wildlife forensics, etc.

There are numerous subdisciplines of forensic science, of which some are briefed in the following sections.

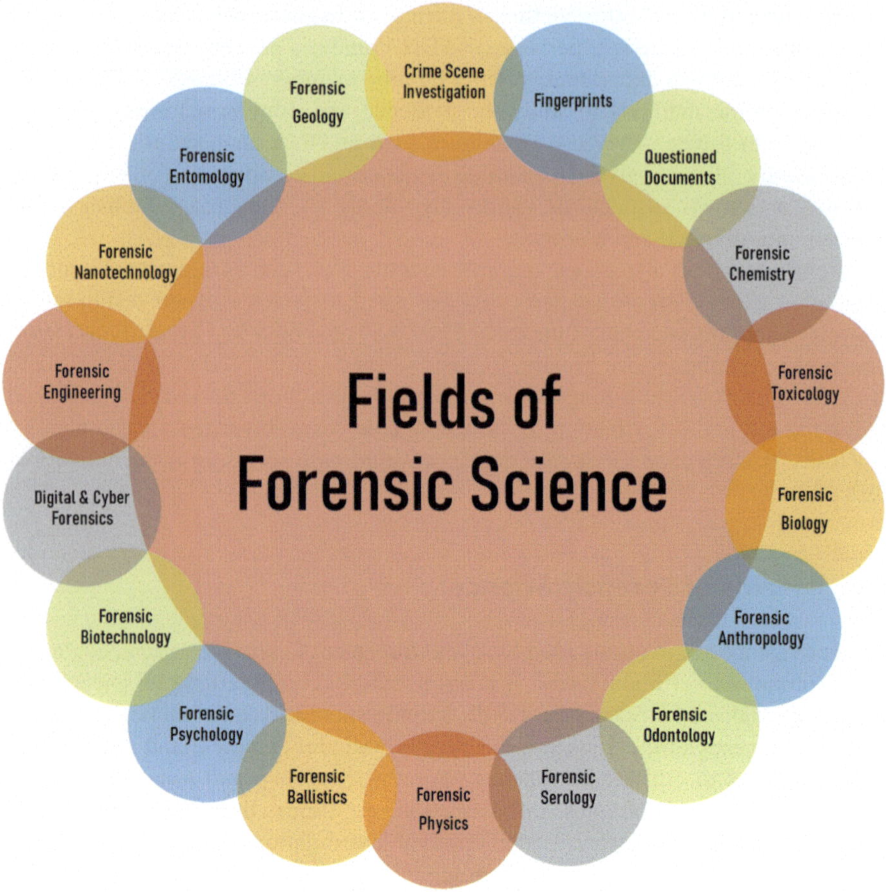

Fig. 2.1 Some of the fields of forensic science

2.3.1 Fingerprints

Fingerprint analysis is one of forensic science's most common and oldest branches. Fingerprint evidence has been used to identify individuals since the nineteenth century. This section is concerned with fingerprint examination and comparison. An expert develops and collects latent fingerprints from crime scenes and compares them to control samples collected from suspects. Various physical, chemical, and instrumental methods are available to aid in developing latent fingerprints. Even if individual identification is impossible, the information obtained can narrow the suspect pool. Apart from fingerprints, palmprints and footprints are also studied as sources of potential information for investigating civil and criminal cases (Saferstein 2015; James and Nordby 2009; Badiye et al. 2019; Yamashita and French 2010; Eckert 1992; Daluz 2015; Bansal et al. 2014; Kapoor et al. 2019a, 2020a; Kapoor and Badiye 2015a,b).

2.3.2 Questioned Documents

This section includes the examination of documents such as sale deeds, personal diaries, suicide notes, threatening letters, property papers, etc. "A questioned document is one that in its entirety or in part is suspect as to authenticity or origin" (James and Nordby 2009). The field of questioned document examination is also one of the oldest subdisciplines of forensic science. The area of questioned document examination is known after the evolving work of Albert S. Osborn, and the principles he established are still used by experts today. A questioned document examiner has to deal with the examination of handwriting, inks, papers, typewritten documents, typewriters, printed matter, printers, security documents, etc. (Saferstein 2015; James and Nordby 2009; Eckert 1992).

2.3.3 Forensic Chemistry

Forensic chemistry is a specialized field within forensic science that focuses on applying chemical analysis techniques to investigate and solve crimes. Forensic chemistry incorporates the analysis of physical evidence such as dyes, pigments, and petroleum products, blood alcohol determination, arson and explosive analysis, gunshot residue (GSR) analysis, etc. The analyses includes both organic and inorganic analyses using different analytical techniques. The various instrumental techniques that forensic chemists widely utilize include gas chromatography coupled with mass spectroscopy (GC-MS), Fourier transform infrared spectroscopy (FTIR), high-performance liquid chromatography (HPLC), atomic absorption spectroscopy (AAS), etc. A forensic chemist is dedicated to examining the composition and nature of substances, determining the source of the evidence, and matching the evidence collected from the crime scene with control samples (Saferstein 2015; James and Nordby 2009; Eckert 1992; Mishra 2021).

2.3.4 Forensic Toxicology

Forensic toxicology is a specialized branch of forensic science that deals with the analysis of biological samples to determine the presence of drugs, alcohol, poisons, and other toxic substances. Forensic toxicology is also used in workplace drug testing, poisoning cases, postmortem testing, investigation of contraband materials, dope testing, etc., and other such toxicological analyses. This field deals with the isolation, identification, and quantification of drugs, poisons, and other toxic substances with the help of modern instrumental techniques. A forensic toxicologist is also asked to analyze different biological fluid samples from victims of accidental or homicidal poisoning cases. Through their analyses and interpretations, forensic toxicologists contribute to the accurate determination of cause of death, the identification of illicit drug use, and the establishment of a comprehensive understanding of the circumstances surrounding various types of cases.

2.3.5 Forensic Biology

Forensic biology is a specialized branch of forensic science that focuses on the analysis of biological evidence to aid in criminal investigations. This field involves the examination of biological evidence such as hair, fibers, blood, diatoms, bones, pollen grains, etc. The prime work that a forensic biologist does is performing DNA profiling on different types of biological evidence such as blood and other body fluids. This also incorporates several other areas such as forensic botany, forensic taphonomy, wildlife forensics, etc. Wildlife forensics deals with the use of scientific principles and techniques in legal concerns entailing wildlife (Saferstein 2015; James and Nordby 2009; Eckert 1992; Gefrides and Welch 2011).

2.3.6 Forensic Anthropology

Forensic anthropology can be defined as application of the theory and methods of anthropology for forensic purposes. This study provides an insight into sex, age, race, and time of death from skeletal remains. A forensic anthropologist examines human remains for three purposes: (1) for identifying the victim or at least providing a biological profile (age, sex, stature, ancestry, anomalies, pathology, individual features); (2) for reconstructing the postmortem period based on the condition of the remains and the recovery context; and (3) for providing data regarding the death event, including evidence of trauma occurring during the perimortem period. Forensic anthropologists can be extremely helpful in mass disasters with significant skeletal remains or in cases of mass burials (James and Nordby 2009; Eckert 1992; Byers 2011; Klepinger 2006).

2.3.7 Forensic Odontology

Forensic odontology refers to the use of the science of dentistry to administer law and justice. Comparing their dental charts and X-rays to the dental evidence from victims can help identify victims of a disaster or homicide. This field also involves the examination of bite marks, lip prints, and rugoscopy on various surfaces, which may assist in cases such as sexual assault, murder, burglary, etc. (James and Nordby 2009; Eckert 1992; Kapoor et al. 2020b; Smitha et al. 2019).

2.3.8 Forensic Serology

Forensic serology is a specialized field within forensic science that focuses on the analysis of body fluids and the identification of blood-related evidence in criminal investigations. This deals with the examination of various bodily fluids such as blood, sperm, saliva, urine, vomit, and so on. Forensic serologists are involved in identifying body fluids using various presumptive and confirmatory tests, which are then sent to DNA analysis. Aside from these common body fluids, some cases may necessitate the examination of other fluids, such as menstrual blood, vaginal secretions, fecal matter, and so on. The evidence is examined following the presumptive and confirmatory tests to determine its origin among other parameters (Saferstein 2015; James and Nordby 2009; Eckert 1992; Gefrides and Welch 2011; Li 2012; Badiye et al. 2020).

2.3.9 Forensic Physics

Forensic physics is a specialized field within forensic science that applies principles of physics to investigate and analyze physical evidence in criminal investigations. This section examines evidence such as paint, glass, soil, and metals. It plays a significant role in investigating minute trace evidence and accident cases in a major crime laboratory. Various instrumental analyses are carried out, including neutron activation analysis, a nondestructive testing method, X-ray diffraction, etc. (James and Nordby 2009; Eckert 1992).

2.3.10 Forensic Ballistics

Ballistics is defined as the study of a projectile in motion. Forensic ballistics is a specialized field within forensic science that focuses on the analysis of firearms, ammunition, and the effects of projectiles in criminal investigations. It involves the examination of firearms, bullets, casings, and other ballistic evidence to determine their connections to crimes, such as shootings and homicides. Forensic ballistics experts study the unique markings left on bullets and cartridge casings by the firearm's barrel, known as "ballistic fingerprints," to match them to specific weapons. Forensic ballistics is classified into three categories: internal ballistics, external ballistics, and terminal or wound ballistics. Internal ballistics studies what happens inside the barrel when a shot is fired. External ballistics studies a projectile after it has left the barrel. Terminal ballistics investigates the projectile after it strikes the target, and wound ballistics investigates the projectile after it strikes a living target. In this section, laboratory examination entails examining bullets, cartridge cases, firearms, and other evidence from the crime scene and comparing it to control samples collected from suspected firearms. This examination is typically performed using a comparison microscope (Saferstein 2015; James and Nordby 2009; Eckert 1992; DiMaio 1999; Karger 2008). By analyzing trajectories, impact patterns, and other characteristics, these experts can reconstruct shooting incidents, identify firearms used, assess gunshot wounds, and provide crucial evidence in court proceedings. Forensic ballistics plays a vital role in connecting weapons to crimes, identifying suspects, and ensuring accurate and unbiased criminal investigations.

2.3.11 Forensic Psychology

Forensic psychology refers to the application of psychological methods, theories, and concepts in legal processes. Forensic psychologists may assist as expert witnesses, criminal profilers, and trial consultants, conduct competence evaluations, and assist litigants and fact finders in other ways. Psychological reports are frequently used to determine what happens to a client in the criminal and civil justice systems, whether through trial, prison terms, remuneration, or prison release plans. Moreover, a significant portion of forensic psychologists' employment pertains to specific populations, often including sexual offenders, violent offenders, drug- and alcohol-related crimes, and child custody work, which they should be aware of (James and Nordby 2009; Eckert 1992; Wrightsman 2001). In addition to identifying the presence of body fluids, forensic serologists often work closely with DNA analysts to extract DNA from these fluids for further genetic analysis.

2.3.12 Forensic Biotechnology

This subdiscipline uses biotechnology-based methods to carry out forensic analysis of evidence. Biotechnology is widely used in DNA forensics, but it has also demonstrated its potential use in forensic medicine and many other fields of forensic science. A forensic biotechnologist can link a suspect to the crime scene or identify an unknown individual by identifying DNA recovered from biological evidence, such as biological fluids, hair, or tissues collected at the crime scene. Using DNA fingerprinting to identify and monitor nonhuman organisms, such as an endangered species, is also one such application of biotechnology in forensics. Forensic biotechnologists use DNA degradation-based methods to determine postmortem intervals in forensic medicine (Shukla 2016; Francoeur 1989; Giuffrida et al. 2018). In addition to DNA analysis, forensic biotechnology also encompasses areas like Forensic Genomics, Microbial Forensics, etc.

2.3.13 Digital and Cyber Forensics

Digital forensics and cyber forensics are closely related disciplines that both involve the investigation and analysis of digital evidence to uncover information related to cybercrimes, computer security incidents, and digital misconduct. While the terms are often used interchangeably, they can sometimes refer to slightly different aspects of the field. While both digital forensics and cyber forensics deal with the analysis of digital evidence, cyber forensics is a more specialized field that centers on investigating cybercrimes and security incidents. Digital forensics encompasses a broader range of cases that involve digital evidence, regardless of whether they are specifically related to cybercrimes. Both disciplines are critical in uncovering the truth behind digital incidents, supporting legal proceedings, and ensuring the integrity of digital evidence in a wide array of contexts. It gathers data from computer systems, mobile phones, networks, wireless communication, storage devices, etc., in a way acceptable in a court of law. Cyber forensic investigation comprises identification, collection or extraction, preservation, interpretation or analysis, and communication as its significant steps. This stream comes into play when any type of cybercrime crops up, such as cyberterrorism, data spoofing, denial of service attacks, hacking, data breaches, phishing, ransomware, malware attacks, cyberstalking, credit card frauds, etc. (Saferstein 2015; James and Nordby 2009; Marcella Jr and Menendez 2002; Shrivastava et al. 2018). Digital forensics focuses on the broader scope of investigating digital devices and electronic systems to gather evidence related to various types of cases, including cybercrimes. This can encompass a wide range of scenarios, such as data breaches, intellectual property theft, fraud, cyberbullying, and more. Digital forensics includes the analysis of digital evidence from computers, smartphones, servers, storage media, and other electronic devices. It involves techniques for data recovery, file analysis, metadata examination, and the reconstruction of events. Digital forensics experts also play a role in traditional investigations where digital evidence is relevant.

2.3.14 Forensic Engineering

Forensic engineering is generally defined as "The application of engineering principles and methodology to answer questions of fact that may have legal ramifications" (Noon 2020). Forensic engineering is a branch of forensic science that focuses on investigating and analyzing engineering failures, accidents, and disasters to determine their causes, contributing factors, and potential legal implications. The key aspects of forensic engineering includes, the investigations of industrial accidents and accidents involving vehicles, recreational vehicles, failure analysis, material analysis, structural analysis, fires, explosions, storm surges, slips and falls, arson, water pipe damage, and more. Thus, forensic engineering has been added to the growing fields of forensic science (Saferstein 2015; James and Nordby 2009; Noon 2020; Cobb 2000). Forensic engineering helps establish liability, allocate responsibility, and inform safety improvements to prevent future accidents. It is used in a variety of contexts, including construction accidents, product liability cases, transportation incidents, and industrial accidents.

2.3.15 Forensic Nanotechnology

Forensic nanotechnology can be defined as utilization of nanotechnology in forensic investigations. Nanotechnology assists forensic science in two ways: one by easily detecting and analyzing nanoscale samples because of which essential evidence that could previously not be collected and analyzed due to the instruments' detection limits can now be explored and two through the use of nanomaterials that have novel properties that allow the collection and preservation of trace prime evidence that could previously not be acquired. Nanotechnology has applications in several forensic science streams, including toxicology, serology, biology, pathology, fingerprinting, questioned document examination, etc. (Chen 2011; Kapoor et al. 2019b, 2021; Lodha et al. 2016; Pandya and Shukla 2018; Shukla et al. 2021).

2.3.16 Forensic Entomology

"Forensic entomology is the branch of forensic science in which information about insects is used to conclude when investigating legal cases relating to both humans and wildlife, although on occasion the term may be expanded to include other arthropods." A forensic entomologist is mainly asked to recognize and identify insects at various phases of their life cycle, collect and preserve insects as evidence, estimate the postmortem interval (PMI) based on factors such as insect evidence, weather conditions, and so on, to provide testimony in a court to demonstrate insect-related evidence discovered at a crime scene. Thus, forensic entomology plays a key role in death investigation (Gennard 2007; Wolff et al. 2001; Goff 2009).

2.3.17 Forensic Geology

Geology is the study of the earth's origin, history, processes, and materials. Forensic geology is a specialized field within forensic science that focuses on using geological principles and techniques to investigate and solve criminal cases and legal investigations. This branch of forensic science involves analyzing various earth materials, such as soil, sediments, minerals, rocks, and other geological features, to provide insights into crime scene reconstruction, victim identification, and suspect profiling. A forensic geologist acts as an expert witness in providing expert testimony about geological activities or circumstances. In addition, sometimes forensic geologists are asked to answer questions about evidence such as the material. Where did the material come from? Is it unique to the crime scene? etc. (Lindemann 2011; Ruffell 2010; Di Maggio et al. 2017).

2.3.18 Forensic Meteorology

Forensic meteorology is "the science of using historic weather records, atmospheric data, eyewitness accounts, and re-enactment simulations to determine the weather conditions at a specific time and location" (Badiye et al. 2016). Nowadays, intensifying climate change has led to an increase in natural calamities and cataclysmic-related phenomena worldwide. Forensic meteorologists work on cases such as murders, car accidents, floods, aviation accidents, pollution, noise abatement, winds, snow, avalanches, lightning storms, and even sonic booms all over the world (Badiye et al. 2016; Scala and Wallace 2009). Forensic meteorology helps provide a scientific understanding of how weather conditions can influence various types of incidents and legal cases.

2.4 Some Common Evidence

Forensic science is critical, as it helps collect and analyze evidence to solve criminal cases. To ensure the best outcome in any given case, it is essential to understand the different types of potential evidence that can be collected during an investigation. Numerous types of evidence can be used in a forensic science case, from physical to digital evidence. The chapters up ahead present the different types of evidence encountered in forensic science investigations to help the readers gain a grasp of how each type of evidence can be used (Fig. 2.2). The advantages and disadvantages of each type of evidence and the importance of properly collecting, preserving, and analyzing the evidence are also discussed. By the end of this book, you will have a greater understanding of the types of evidence that can be used in forensic science and their critical role in solving criminal cases.

Every crime scene is unique and may present unique objects or materials as evidence. However, it is imperative to be aware of the list of potential evidence that

Fig. 2.2 Some evidence that may be encountered at an offence scene

is quite common. This may include fingerprints, palmprints, thumbprints, lip prints, footprints, footwear impressions, bones, dental remains, blood, saliva, semen, epithelial cells, vaginal fluid, urine, fecal matter, mutilated body parts, body organs, firearms, ammunitions, spent cartridges, explosives, glass, tapes, knives, bottles, hammers, swords, rods, soil, fibers, hair, feathers, pug marks, nails, teeth, ligatures, thread, paints, tool marks, photographs, negatives, drugs, toxins, poisonous substances, pollens, diatoms, questioned documents, handwriting samples, security documents, fake currency notes, digital evidence, mobile phones, laptops, computers, and digital storage devices, to name a few.

2.5 The Principles of Forensic Science

Forensic science relies on some basic guiding principles like any other scientific discipline. The seven main principles include the principle of exchange, the principle of individuality, the principle of progressive change, the principle of comparison, the principle of analysis, the principle of circumstantial facts, and the principle of probability (Fig. 2.3).

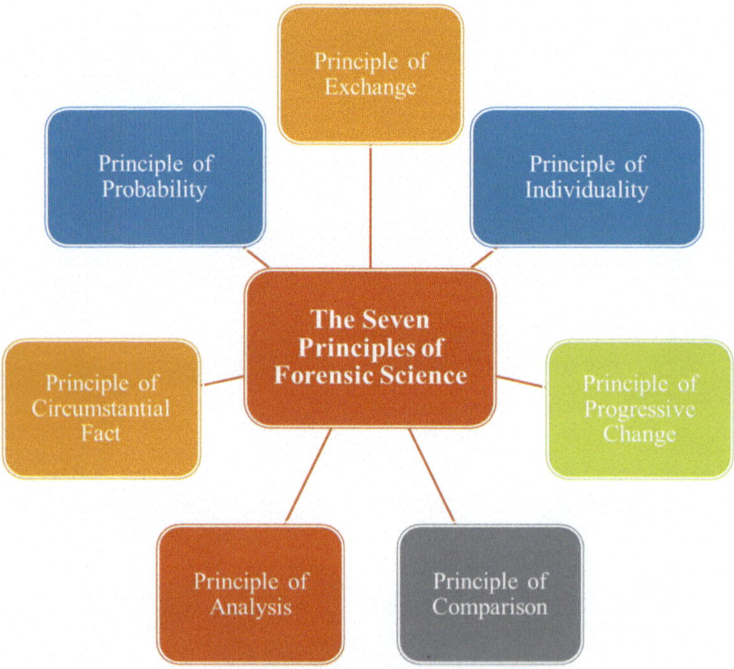

Fig. 2.3 The seven principles of forensic science

2.5.1 The Principle of Exchange

Locard's principle of exchange, often referred to as the principle of transfer, is a fundamental concept in forensic science. Dr. Edmond Locard first proposed it in the early 1900s, and it states that whenever two objects or entities come into contact with each other, there will always be an exchange of material. This material can be anything from fibers to DNA, and it can provide investigators with invaluable evidence for solving crimes. By analyzing the material exchange between two objects, investigators can build a profile of what happened during the crime and who may have been involved. This simple yet powerful idea has helped revolutionize criminal investigations, enabling forensic experts to identify and analyze evidence from crime scenes.

For example, imagine that a suspect touches the door handle of a crime scene; they will leave behind fingerprints, skin cells, sweat, and other materials. By examining this material, investigators can determine who was present at the scene, the probable path followed by that person, and how the crime was committed. This can be used to establish the person's presence at the offence's location. The chance impressions found on the weapon of an offence may also link the suspect to the crime and crime scene. This evidence can then be used to corroborate witness statements and help piece together the crime.

2.5.2 The Principle of Individuality

One of the most critical principles in forensic science is the principle of individuality. This principle acknowledges that every human being is unique and that every criminal act can be linked to a specific individual. It states that "Every object, natural or man-made, has unique quality or characteristics that are not duplicated in any other object." In other words, it may be said that no two things in the world are exactly alike. The principle of individuality is one of the core tenets of forensic science.

The principle of individuality is also vital for evaluating evidence from a crime scene. For example, a fingerprint left at a crime scene can help determine the identity of a suspect or victim (Bansal et al. 2014; Kapoor and Badiye 2015a). In addition, DNA analysis can be used to determine a person's identity (Badiye et al. 2020). For example, if a lip print from a suspect is found at the crime scene, it can be compared to the suspect's lip print sample in order to determine its origin (Badiye and Kapoor 2016; Kapoor and Tiwari 2013). This type of evidence can be used to connect a suspect to a crime scene and eliminate other potential suspects.

By understanding the individual characteristics of the suspect or victim, investigators can more effectively identify the person responsible for the crime. This knowledge can also help eliminate suspects who do not match the individual characteristics identified in the evidence.

2.5.3 The Principle of Progressive Change

The Principle of progressive change states that "Everything changes with the passage of time and nothing remains constant." This principle holds that all living and nonliving things, including humans, are constantly in a state of change from their birth to their death. The degree of this change can be measured by various factors, including age, environment, and lifestyle. In forensic science, this principle is important for understanding how materials and evidence are affected over time and how they can be used to reconstruct crime scenes and other events.

The first application of the principle of progressive change in forensic science is its use in the analysis of physical evidence. This can include fibers, hair, blood, and other bodily fluids. In this process, examining these materials over time can help identify the age of the material as well as any changes that may have occurred due to environmental factors, such as temperature or humidity.

The principle of progressive change can also be used to analyze trace evidence. Minute changes in the composition and characteristics of these materials can be studied over time to determine the material's age and any changes caused by environmental factors. This can be especially useful in reconstructing crime scenes and other events.

This principle is also utilized in document examination. Dating of documents is one of the challenging areas in document examination. It uses chronological changes that the components of a document, i.e., ink and paper, undergo with time to estimate the age of records. It encompasses the changes in ink when it is placed on paper, such as drying of ink, color change, solvent evaporation, etc., and changes in paper, such as color change, changes in fibers, etc., with the due course of time and estimates the absolute and relative ages of the document (Kapoor et al. 2021).

2.5.4 The Principle of Comparison

The principle of comparison states that "Only the likes can be compared." This technique is used to compare fingerprints, handwriting, fabrics, metals, fibers, and other physical evidence that may be found at a crime scene. It compares physical evidence collected from a crime scene to determine whether they match or share a common origin. The comparison of fingerprints can be done with fingerprints and that of footprints can be done with footprints. This principle is often used during forensic investigations to link physical evidence from a crime scene to a suspect or a particular event. For example, if a fingerprint is found on evidence, then the investigator can compare it with a known sample of the suspect's fingerprints to determine whether the two match.

2.5.5 The Principle of Analysis

The principle of analysis is one of the most important concepts in forensic science. This principle deals with examining and evaluating physical evidence to draw valid conclusions upon which a reliable opinion can be based. This principle states that "The analysis can be no better than the sample analysed."

The principle of analysis is an integral part of forensic investigations. By appropriately and scientifically analyzing the evidence collected during the study, forensic scientists can draw meaningful conclusions that can be used to solve the case. Analysis techniques such as DNA analysis, fingerprint and ballistic comparison, document examination, and toxicology are all important components of the analysis process.

2.5.6 The Principle of Circumstantial Facts

The principle of circumstantial facts states that "Facts do not lie, humans can, and they do." Facts cannot be false. They can neither be entirely missing nor can they lie. The significance of circumstantial facts is thus advantageous for oral testimony. Applying circumstantial facts in forensic science is a complex process, requiring proper evaluation to adequately determine a person's guilt or innocence. Although it is true that circumstantial evidence can be used to make a strong case, it is essential to understand that circumstantial evidence can be easily manipulated to fit different scenarios, making it difficult to draw a definitive conclusion. The suspect or the witnesses may lie intentionally; however, if the evidence pertaining to that particular incident is present at the spot or their analysis reveals otherwise, then the truth would come out. Circumstantial evidence can help corroborate a person's testimony or another type of evidence. This type of evidence can be invaluable in criminal investigations and trials.

2.5.7 The Principle of Probability

The principle of probability states that "All identifications, definite or indefinite, made consciously or unconsciously are based on probability." This has become essential for forensic science. This principle is based on the idea that an event has a certain chance of occurring and that these probabilities can be estimated and used to make decisions. It is used to help determine the likelihood that an individual is responsible for a crime, whether a piece of evidence is reliable, or even to predict the outcome of a trial. In recent years, probability has been used in several forensic applications, including DNA testing, drug analysis, fingerprint examination, and court proceedings.

The use of probability in forensic science is based on the notion that events can be assigned a probability of occurrence. For example, the likelihood that a particular type of DNA will be present in a sample from a crime scene can be estimated by comparing the DNA from the sample to that from a known individual. If the DNA from the sample is found to match the DNA from the known individual, then it is likely that the individual was present at the scene of the crime. Similarly, the probability that a fingerprint will match one from a suspect can be determined by comparing the fingerprints and analyzing the similarity between the two. The use of probability in forensic science has helped improve the accuracy of investigations and the chances of obtaining a conviction.

2.6 Some of the Major Contributors

Forensic science has become an important tool in criminal justice, allowing law enforcement to analyze physical evidence to track criminals and solve cases. It has been used to solve mysteries and crimes since ancient times. Ancient civilizations had their own forms of forensic science, employing techniques such as fingerprinting, handwriting analysis, and analyzing skeletal remains to identify suspects and determine the cause of death. Ancient historians often relied on forensic science to determine the facts about past events, including the identity of those involved and the circumstances surrounding the incidents. In more recent centuries, forensic science has developed into a sophisticated discipline, with scientists utilizing sophisticated tools and techniques to analyze evidence in criminal cases.

In ancient Egypt, forensic science was used to identify the perpetrators of crimes. Fingerprinting was used to help determine whether a document was authentic and to identify an individual who had touched an object. A form of handwriting analysis was also used to identify authors of written documents. In addition, ancient Egyptians utilized skeletal remains to determine the age and sex of murder victims and to help formulate theories about the cause of death.

One of the most interesting uses of forensic science in the ancient world was its application in courtrooms. In ancient Greece, forensic experts would examine the evidence presented at a trial, such as clothing or weapons, to determine the case's truth. Forensic scientists would sometimes even be called to testify as expert witnesses.

The development of more sophisticated laboratory techniques has also allowed forensic scientists to uncover more evidence from a crime scene than ever before. These methods include trace evidence analysis, which looks for microscopic particles of evidence such as soil, blood, and other bodily fluids, and chemical analysis, which looks for the presence of certain chemicals that may indicate a presence at the scene of a crime or a link between a suspect and a crime scene. The following is the list of some of the pioneers who contributed to the growth and development of the field of forensic science.

2.6.1 Mathieu Orfila (1787–1853)

Mathieu Orfila is a pioneer in forensic science and is widely credited with laying the foundations of modern forensic toxicology. He is known as the father of modern toxicology (Saferstein 2015; Nabar 2002; Pyrek 2018). He was a French chemist and toxicologist credited with bringing a scientific approach to the study of toxicology and developing the concept of legal medicine. His work helped revolutionize the criminal justice system by introducing an evidence-based approach to understanding and determining the effects of toxic substances on humans.

Orfila is best known for his seminal work on the effects of poisons and their detection in the human body. He was the first to recognize and document the impact of exposure to toxins that could be used to commit murder and other violent crimes. His book, *Toxicologie Generale*, published in 1814, is one of the earliest texts on the subject and is considered a foundational work in forensic toxicology (Saferstein 2015; Nabar 2002; Pyrek 2018; Wielbo 2000).

In addition to his work on the effects of poisons, Orfila made significant contributions to the study of medical jurisprudence. He was the first to recognize the importance of an autopsy in determining the cause of death and developed the concept of postmortem examination. He also recognized the need for modern approaches to interpreting evidence in criminal cases and developed the idea of using circumstantial evidence in court.

Orfila's work revolutionized the field of forensic science, and his contributions are still used in modern criminal investigations. He was a pioneer in the field, and his work was instrumental in developing modern forensic toxicology and establishing the current criminal justice system.

2.6.2 Alphonse Bertillon (1853–1914)

Alphonse Bertillon was the first to devise a systematic technique for criminal identification based on body measurements, known as the science of anthropometry. This technique employs a series of body measurements to distinguish one individual from another. Bertillon's work has been instrumental in developing forensic anthropology techniques and strategies. He has published several papers on using bone analysis and skeletal reconstruction in criminal investigations. He has also developed techniques for accurately identifying individuals from skeletal remains (Saferstein 2015; Nabar 2002; Pyrek 2018; Wielbo 2000; Hebrard and Daust 2013). His work provided a much-needed foundation for using these techniques in criminal investigations.

2.6.3 Sir Francis Galton (1822–1911)

Francis Galton is the pioneer of modern forensic science. His contribution to forensic fingerprinting has been immeasurable, and he is recognized as the father of the discipline. He is widely credited for introducing fingerprints as a form of identification in the late nineteenth century. His book, *Finger Prints* (1892), was the first to discuss the use of fingerprints in criminal investigations. Galton's research and ideas have been at the heart of fingerprint analysis ever since.

Galton's research into fingerprint analysis involved studying the ridge patterns of fingerprints. He explored the uniqueness of fingerprints and developed the critical techniques used in fingerprint identification and classification. He divided fingerprints into three categories: arch, loop, and whorl. Galton also identified methods for measuring and comparing fingerprints and techniques for collecting and preserving prints.

Galton was also the first to use fingerprints in a court to identify a suspect. He demonstrated that the prints found on the glass were those of a suspect in a murder case. His success, in this case, ushered in a new era of crime-solving and forensics based on fingerprints (Saferstein 2015; Nabar 2002; Yamashita and French 2010; Pyrek 2018; Wielbo 2000; Hebrard and Daust 2013).

2.6.4 Sir Edmond Locard

Sir Edmond Locard was one of the earliest pioneers of forensic science. He is credited for laying the foundation for the development of modern forensic science. He revolutionized how evidence was collected and analyzed, and his work was instrumental in helping law enforcement officials solve crimes. He was a French criminalist and criminologist from the early twentieth century credited with developing the first systematic methods for using physical evidence in criminal investigations. He was the founder of the world's first crime laboratory, which was established in Lyons, France, in 1910.

Locard's exchange principle is the cornerstone of forensic science, and it states that whenever two objects come into contact with each other, a cross-transfer of materials occurs between them. This means that any two items in touch with each other leave behind trace evidence that can be used to identify the source of the material. For example, if a piece of clothing was worn by someone in contact with a murder weapon, then microscopic particles of that weapon could be found on the clothing (Saferstein 2015; Nabar 2002; James and Nordby 2009; Pyrek 2018; Hebrard and Daust 2013).

2.6.5 Dr. Karl Landsteiner (1868–1943)

Dr. Karl Landsteiner was an Austrian physician and immunologist who made significant contributions to the field of medical science, particularly in the area of blood typing and the discovery of blood groups. His groundbreaking research laid the foundation for modern transfusion medicine and earned him the Nobel Prize in Physiology or Medicine in 1930. Landsteiner's contributions to forensic science include developing the classification system to identify different blood types.

Landsteiner's most notable accomplishment was his discovery and classification of human blood groups. In 1900, he identified and categorized blood into four major groups—A, B, AB, and O—based on the presence or absence of specific antigens on the surface of red blood cells. He found that people with type A blood were incompatible with people with type B blood, and vice versa. He also discovered that type O blood could be transfused into any type of blood. This discovery revolutionized blood transfusion practices, ensuring safe and compatible blood transfusions. It was the first step toward establishing a reliable system for identifying blood types in forensic science (Saferstein 2015; Nabar 2002; James and Nordby 2009; Pyrek 2018).

2.6.6 Dr. Leon Lattes (1887–1954)

Forensic serology has been used in solving crime cases since the early twentieth century. In more recent years, the contribution of Leon Lattes to the field has been immeasurable. Leon Lattes was an Italian biologist who developed the first blood typing test. In the year 1915, he instrumented a method for determining the blood group from dried bloodstains. The test was based on the principle of agglutination, which is the clumping together of red blood cells in response to the presence of an antibody. Lattes also developed a method of isolating and identifying the genetic material, or DNA, of blood samples. This technique was also used to identify individuals and to compare bloodstains found at crime scenes. This advancement in forensic serology greatly impacted the criminal justice system, as it allowed for quicker and more accurate case resolution.

2.6.7 Dr. Calvin Goddard (1891–1955)

When it comes to the history of forensic ballistics, Calvin Goddard's name will always be at the top of the list. As one of the earliest pioneers in the field, Goddard was instrumental in establishing the practice of matching bullets and other projectiles to firearms to link suspects to crime scenes. His work on the science of ballistics was the foundation of modern ballistic tests used in criminal investigations.

Goddard's work in forensic ballistics began in 1923 when he was a captain in the US Army Reserve. Goddard and his team successfully matched the bullets from the crime scene to the machine gun and linked the suspects to the crime. This case was one of the earliest examples of using ballistic evidence to solve a crime. However, Goddard's work in forensic ballistics did not stop there. He developed the first handheld comparison microscope, which is still used today to compare bullets with firearm marks. Goddard also wrote several influential books on the topic, including *The Science of Ballistics*. Throughout his career, Goddard advocated for the scientific use of ballistic evidence in criminal investigations.

2.6.8 Albert Osborn (1858–1946)

Albert Osborn is widely regarded as the father of forensic questioned document examination. Osborn's contributions to this field are significant, and his methods remain in use even today. In his book, *Questioned Documents*, Osborn lays the groundwork for developing a scientific approach to document examination.

Osborn was the first to determine that forgery could be identified by analyzing handwriting and other documents. He developed a system for analyzing records that included comparing the handwriting of a questioned document to known handwriting samples, looking for discrepancies in the paper, ink, and writing tools used, and analyzing the text for inconsistencies. Osborn's system was a breakthrough in the field, allowing for a more scientific approach to document analysis.

Osborn also developed a classification system for handwriting types, which is used today. Osborn could identify similarities between documents and make conclusions about their authenticity by categorizing handwriting into various categories, such as looped, angular, and connected.

In addition to his work in the field of forensic questioned document examination, Osborn also wrote many books on the subject, including *The Questioned Document* (1910), *Identification of Handwriting* (1917), and *The Problem of the Questioned Document* (1924). These books have become standard reference works for forensic document examiners (Saferstein 2015; Nabar 2002; Pyrek 2018; Lewis 2014; Osborn 1910).

2.6.9 Hans Gross (1847–1915)

Hans Gross is considered one of the most influential figures in modern forensic criminal investigations. Born in 1847 in the Austrian Empire, Gross was a lawyer and judge who later became the founding figure of criminology, the scientific study of crime and criminal behavior. He was the first to recognize the importance of forensic science in criminal investigations and wrote various influential works on the subject.

One of Gross's most important contributions to the field of criminal investigation was the establishment of the "criminalistics" system, a comprehensive system of collecting, preserving, and analyzing evidence. This system enabled investigators to identify, classify, and analyze relevant evidence, which was then used to build a case against a suspect. It also provided a legal framework for evaluating evidence and its admissibility in court. Gross wrote extensively on the need for strict adherence to the principles of criminalistics, and his work strongly influenced the development of modern forensic science.

2.6.10 Henry Faulds (1843–1930)

Henry Faulds is widely credited with revolutionizing the field of forensic fingerprint analysis. He was a noted British physician and scientist who played a significant role in developing fingerprint identification in the late nineteenth century. Faulds developed the world's first automated fingerprinting system and published the first scientific paper about the use of fingerprints for identification in 1880. He was also one of the first to suggest that fingerprints could be used as a form of personal identification in criminal investigations.

Faulds believed that fingerprints could be used to identify individuals with certainty, as they were unique to everyone. He was also an advocate of using fingerprint analysis to detect criminal activity. He developed a number of techniques for fingerprint analysis, such as dusting for prints and photographically enlarging them. He also developed a method of comparing fingerprints, known as the Henry System, which is still used today (Yamashita and French 2010; Pyrek 2018; Wielbo 2000; Hebrard and Daust 2013).

2.6.11 Sir Edward Richard Henry, Khan Bahadur Azizul Haque, and Rai Bahadur Hem Chandra Bose

Edward Richard Henry, Azizul Haque and Hem Chandra Bose are key figures in the history of the forensic fingerprint science. Assisted by two Indian police officers, sub-inspectors Azizul Haque and Hem Chandra Bose, Henry is credited with developing the fingerprint classification system, which is still used today. This system laid the foundation for modern forensic fingerprint analysis and revolutionized criminal identification worldwide. With their efforts, the world's first fingerprint bureau was set up in Calcutta in 1897 (Sodhi and Kaur 2005). The mathematical formula and the single-digit classification system devised by Azizul Haque and Hem Chandra Bose added a level of sophistication to the fingerprint identification process. These innovations allowed for more efficient organization and retrieval of fingerprint records, making it easier to identify individuals accurately and quickly. The concept of sub-classification further improved the accuracy and speed of identification, facilitating the adoption of fingerprinting as a standard method in law enforcement. Fingerprint analysis remains a cornerstone of criminal investigations and forensic identification, and their efforts have had a lasting impact on law enforcement practices worldwide.

The system was a major breakthrough in the field of forensic fingerprinting. Before this system, law enforcement agencies had little to no way of accurately identifying a person by their fingerprints. The classification system, however, allowed for much more accurate personal identification. In addition, the system allowed for the easy comparison of two fingerprints, which made it easier for investigators to determine whether two sets of prints belonged to the same person. Their work in forensic fingerprinting also helped establish it as an accepted form of identification (Saferstein 2015; Nabar 2002; James and Nordby 2009; Yamashita and French 2010; Sodhi and Kaur 2005).

2.6.12 William Herschel (1833–1917)

William Herschel is widely regarded as one of the pioneers of forensic fingerprinting. He began researching fingermarks in the late nineteenth century, and his work was crucial for the development of fingerprint identification systems. His work laid the foundation for the development of modern forensic fingerprinting techniques.

Herschel's most significant contribution to forensic fingerprinting was discovering the "persistent ridge pattern," which is the basis of modern fingerprinting. He developed a method of fingerprinting based on the idea of measuring the ridge patterns and comparing them to existing prints (Nabar 2002; James and Nordby 2009; Yamashita and French 2010). He noticed that each finger has its own pattern of ridges and furrows, which remain consistent over time.

2.6.13 Paul Kirk (1902–1970)

Paul Kirk was an influential American forensic scientist and biochemist who made significant contributions to the field of forensic science. He played a crucial role in the development and advancement of forensic techniques and methodologies, particularly in the areas of crime scene investigation, bloodstain pattern analysis, and forensic anthropology. He primarily focused on analyzing and identifying trace evidence using microscopic techniques. Kirk developed several techniques to identify the source of trace evidence, such as soil particles, hair, fibers, and glass fragments. He also worked to develop methods to determine the presence of gunshot residue and other residues from firearms (Pyrek 2018; Wielbo 2000; Hebrard and Daust 2013).

2.6.14 Henry C. Lee (1938-Till Present)

Henry Lee is credited as one of the pioneers of forensic science, having made groundbreaking contributions to the discipline. His research and findings have been essential for advancing the study of forensic science, and his work has had a lasting impact on the field. One of Lee's most important contributions was the development of a system of forensic field investigations. He developed a methodology that combined scientific analysis with an understanding of the physical evidence and the crime scene. This system allowed investigators to systematically collect, analyze, and interpret evidence and to conduct an adequate investigation. Lee's approach to forensic field investigation has been widely adopted and is still used today.

2.6.15 Dr. Lalji Singh (1947–2017)

Dr. Lalji Singh was a renowned scientist known as the "Father of DNA Fingerprinting in India." He was a molecular biologist and was critical in introducing DNA fingerprinting technology to the country's legal and investigative processes. Dr. Singh was instrumental in setting up the Centre for Cellular and Molecular Biology (CCMB) in Hyderabad, India, and he also played a key role in the establishment of the Centre for DNA Fingerprinting and Diagnostics (CDFD), which became a center of excellence for DNA profiling and forensic applications. His work on DNA fingerprinting had far-reaching implications for criminal investigations, paternity disputes, identification of victims, and missing persons. His contributions were especially significant in high-profile criminal cases, where DNA evidence played a crucial role in solving crimes and providing justice. Dr. Singh's efforts were not only limited to research but also extended to education and outreach. He was passionate about training forensic experts and promoting the understanding and application of DNA technology in various fields. His work has left a lasting impact on forensic science in India and has paved the way for advancements in DNA analysis techniques.

2.6.16 Sir Alec Jeffreys (1950-Till Present)

Sir Alec Jeffreys is a British geneticist who is widely recognized for his groundbreaking discovery of DNA fingerprinting, a technique that has revolutionized forensic science and has had significant applications in criminal investigations, paternity testing, and more. It provided a highly accurate method for identifying individuals based on their DNA, which was crucial in criminal investigations for linking suspects to crime scenes or victims. The technique has been used to solve countless criminal cases and has also been employed in exonerating innocent individuals who were wrongly convicted. In recognition of his groundbreaking work on DNA fingerprinting, Sir Alec Jeffreys was awarded the Nobel Prize in Chemistry in 1993 "for the discovery of the polymorphic DNA probes, which led to the development of DNA fingerprinting." He was awarded the prize jointly with Michael Smith, who developed site-directed mutagenesis, a technique used to alter specific genes within organisms. Overall, Sir Alec Jeffreys' discovery of DNA fingerprinting and his subsequent Nobel Prize have left an indelible mark on forensic science, shaping the way criminal investigations are conducted and enhancing the accuracy and reliability of genetic identification techniques.

2.7 Conclusion

Forensic science has continued to evolve over the centuries, with the development of more advanced tools and techniques for analyzing evidence. Today, forensic experts have access to sophisticated technologies, such as DNA analysis, to help solve crimes. Nonetheless, the basic principles of forensic science have remained unchanged from ancient times, and it continues to be an invaluable tool for crime solving.

Accurate and reliable evidence is essential for criminal cases. Forensic science has come a long way in recent decades and is vital in modern investigations and criminal cases. It is a powerful tool to help solve crimes, and its use has become increasingly prevalent in the legal system. As technology and understanding of the law continue to improve, forensic science will remain a critical tool. The upcoming chapters explain the forensic aspects of different types of evidence in detail.

References

Badiye A, Kapoor N (2016) Morphologic variations of lip-print patterns in a central Indian population: a preliminary study. Med Sci Law 56:200–204

Badiye A, Rahatgaonkar A, Kapoor N, Yadav M, Ahmed S (2016) Forensic meteorology: tip of the iceberg. J Indian Acad Forensic Med 38:77–79

Badiye A, Kapoor N, Mishra SD (2019) A novel approach for sex determination using palmar tri-radii: a pilot study. J Forensic Legal Med 65:22–26

Badiye A, Kapoor N, Shrivastava P (2020) Forensic DNA evidence: from crime scene to conviction. In: Shrivastava P, Dash HR, Lorente JA, Imam J (eds) Forensic DNA typing: principles, applications and advancements. Springer, Singapore. https://doi.org/10.1007/978-981-15-6655-4_4

Bansal HD, Badiye AD, Kapoor NS (2014) Distribution of fingerprint patterns in an Indian population. Malaysian J Forensic Sci 5:18–21

Byers SN (2011) Introduction to forensic anthropology, 4th edn. Routledge Taylor and Francis group

Chen Y (2011) Forensic applications of nanotechnology. J Chin Chem Soc 58:828–835

Cobb F (2000) Forensic engineering. CRC Press. https://doi.org/10.1201/9781420037029

Daluz HM (2015) Fundamentals of fingerprint analysis. CPC press

Di Maggio RM et al (2017) Global developments in forensic geology. Episodes 40:120–131

DiMaio VJM (1999) Gunshot wounds practical aspects of firearms, ballistics, and forensic techniques, 2nd edn. CRC Press

Eckert WG (1992) Introduction to forensic sciences, 2nd edn. CRC Press

Francoeur A-M (1989) Biotechnology in forensic medicine: new ways of fingerprinting. J Biotechnol 10:203–208

Gefrides L, Welch K (2011) Forensic biology: serology and DNA. In: The forensic laboratory handbook procedures and practice. Humana Press, pp 15–50. https://doi.org/10.1007/978-1-60761-872-0_2

Gennard DE (2007) Forensic entomology an introduction. Wiley

Giuffrida MG, Mazzoli R, Pessione E (2018) Back to the past: deciphering cultural heritage secrets by protein identification. Appl Microbiol Biotechnol 102:5445–5455

Goff ML (2009) Forensic entomology. In: Encyclopedia of insects. Elsevier, pp 381–386. https://doi.org/10.1016/B978-0-12-374144-8.00112-0

Hebrard J, Daust F (2013) History of forensic sciences. In: Encyclopedia of forensic sciences, 2nd edn. Elsevier Ltd. https://doi.org/10.1016/B978-0-12-382165-2.00191-4

James SH, Nordby JJ (2009) Forensic science an introduction to scientific and INvestigative techniques. CRC Press Taylor and Francis Group

Kapoor N, Badiye A (2015a) Sex differences in the thumbprint ridge density in a central Indian population. Egypt J Forensic Sci 5:23–29

Kapoor N, Badiye A (2015b) An analysis of whorl patterns for determination of hand. J Forensic Legal Med 32:42–46
Kapoor N, Tiwari P (2013) Study of lip prints among the population of Marathi community. Int J Sci Res Publ 3
Kapoor N, Ahmed S, Shukla R, Badiye A (2019a) Development of submerged and successive latent fingerprints: a comparative study. Egypt J Forensic Sci 9:44
Kapoor N, Badiye A, Shukla RK, Mishra SD, Srivastava A (2019b) Integration of nanotechnology in forensic sciences. In: Shukla R, Pandya A (eds) Introduction of forensic nanotechnology: as future armor. Nova Science Publisher, pp 33–48
Kapoor N, Mishra SD, Badiye A (2020a) Single-digit fingerprint analysis for hand determination: a study of twinned loops. Med Sci Law 60:182–187
Kapoor N, Kothari P, Shukla RK, Mishra SD, Badiye A (2020b) Age estimation from tooth-pulp area ratio: a preliminary study. Rev Med Leg 11:11
Kapoor N et al (2021) Forensic analytical approaches to the dating of documents: an overview. Microchem J 170:106722
Karger B (2008) Forensic ballistics. In: Tsokos M (ed) Forensic pathology reviews. Humana Press, Totowa, NJ, pp 139–172. https://doi.org/10.1007/978-1-59745-110-9_9
Klepinger LL (2006) Fundamentals of forensic anthropology. Wiley
Lewis JA (2014) Forensic document examination fundamentals and current trends. Academic Press
Li R (2012) Forensic serology. In: Kobilinsky L (ed) Forensic chemistry handbook. Wiley
Lindemann JW (2011) Forensic geology. In: Environmental and engineering geology, vol 3. EOLSS Publications
Lodha AS, Pandya A, Shukla RK (2016) Nanotechnology: an applied and robust approach for forensic investigation. Foresic Res Criminol Int J 2:35–37
Marcella A Jr, Menendez D (2002) Cyber forensics a field manual for collecting, examining, and preserving evidence of computer crimes. Auerbach Publications, New York. https://doi.org/10.1201/9781420000115
Mishra A (2021) Forensic chemistry and toxicology. In: Erkrkoglu P, Oguwa T (eds) Medical toxicology. InTechOpen
Nabar BS (2002) Forensic science in crime investigation. Asia Law House, Hyderabad
Noon R (2020) Introduction to forensic engineering. CRC Press. https://doi.org/10.4324/9781003068877
Osborn AS (1910) Questioned document, vol 16. The Genese Press, p 558
Pandya A, Shukla RK (2018) New perspective of nanotechnology: role in preventive forensic. Egypt J Forensic Sci 8:57
Pyrek KM (2018) Pioneers in forensic science innovations and issues in Practise. CRC Press Taylor and Francis Group
Ruffell A (2010) Forensic pedology, forensic geology, forensic geoscience, geoforensics and soil forensics. Forensic Sci Int 202:9–12
Saferstein R (2015) A review of criminalistics: an introduction to forensic science. Pearson 22
Scala J, Wallace J (2009) Forensic meteorology. In: Forensic entomology. CRC Press, pp 519–538. https://doi.org/10.1201/NOE0849392153.ch17
Shrivastava G, Sharma K, Khari M, Zohora SE (2018) Role of cyber security and cyber forensics in India. IGI Global, pp 143–161. https://doi.org/10.4018/978-1-5225-4100-4.ch009
Shukla RK (2016) Forensic biotechnology: application of flow cytometry in legal medicine. Int J Forensic Sci 1(1). https://doi.org/10.23880/IJFSC-16000103
Shukla RK, Badiye A, Vajpayee K, Kapoor N (2021) Genotoxic potential of nanoparticles: structural and functional modifications in DNA. Front Genet 12:728250
Smitha T, Sheethal HS, Hema KN, Franklin R (2019) Forensic odontology as a humanitarian tool. J Oral Maxillofac Pathol 23:164
Sodhi G, Kaur J (2005) The forgotten Indian pioneers of fingerprint science. Curr Sci 88:185–191

Wielbo D (2000) Forensic sciences. In: History. pp 1070–1075. https://doi.org/10.1006/rwfs.2000.0564
Wolff M, Uribe A, Ortiz A, Duque P (2001) A preliminary study of forensic entomology in Medellín, Colombia. Forensic Sci Int 120:53–59
Wrightsman LS (2001) Forensic psychology. Wadsworth Thomson Learning, Belmont, CA
Yamashita B, French M (2010) The fingerprint source book. U. S. Department of Justice, Office of Justice Programs, pp 157–158, 199–201

Forensic Science Laboratories in India

3

Ashish Badiye, Pradnya Sulke, Manoj Bhandarkar, and Neeti Kapoor

Abstract

Forensic science is an integral part of investigating and solving criminal cases, providing scientific analysis and expert testimony to aid the legal system. In this chapter, we will explore the essential functions and services of forensic science laboratories in the criminal justice system. Our focus will be on the current state of forensic science laboratories in India, including their organisational structure, challenges, and significant contributions to the pursuit of justice. We will also examine the establishment and evolution of forensic laboratories in India. It is noteworthy that these laboratories exist to ensure that the legal system has access to reliable scientific evidence that can help in the administration of justice. The role of forensic science laboratories in India is vital, and their contributions are invaluable to the pursuit of justice. The advancements made in technology, infrastructure, and expertise should be celebrated and utilised to ensure that the legal system has access to the most credible scientific evidence possible.

A. Badiye · P. Sulke · N. Kapoor (✉)
Department of Forensic Science, Government Institute of Forensic Science, Nagpur, Maharashtra, India
e-mail: ashishbadiye@ifscnagpur.in; neetikapoor@ifscnagpur.in

M. Bhandarkar
Mini Forensic Science Laboratory, Home Department, Government of Maharashtra, Thane, Maharashtra, India

P. Shrivastava et al. (eds.), *Textbook of Forensic Science*,
https://doi.org/10.1007/978-981-99-1377-0_3

3.1 Introduction

Forensic science laboratories play a crucial role in India's criminal justice system, providing vital assistance in investigating and resolving criminal cases. These labs are responsible for analysing various types of evidence, ranging from biological samples to digital media and trace evidence. Forensic scientists use a range of specialised techniques, including DNA analysis, fingerprint identification, ballistics, document examination, and toxicology, to name a few.

In recent years, India has placed a significant focus on technological advancements in forensic science. DNA profiling has emerged as a powerful tool in identifying suspects, connecting crime scenes, and establishing relationships between individuals. Forensic laboratories in India have made notable progress in DNA analysis, contributing to the resolution of numerous challenging cases and exonerating the innocent.

With the proliferation of digital technology, forensic science laboratories are facing new challenges and opportunities. Cybercrime investigations, digital forensics, and the analysis of electronic evidence have become increasingly essential in combatting cyber offenses and fraud. Forensic scientists use specialised techniques and tools to extract, preserve, and analyse digital evidence, which helps identify perpetrators and present robust evidence in court.

Recognising the importance of forensic science in the criminal justice system, the Indian government has taken steps to address various challenges being faced. Funding has been increased, infrastructure has been upgraded, and the quality and efficiency of forensic analysis have been improved. Specialised forensic laboratories have been established, and advanced forensic techniques have been introduced to enhance the capabilities of forensic science in India. Ongoing efforts aim to strengthen these laboratories and improve their capacity to meet the growing demands of the justice system.

3.2 Brief Historical Overview

Forensic science is the application of scientific techniques for the administration of justice. During the nineteenth century, as the number of deaths due poisoning increased, the need arose for fully equipped laboratories capable of isolating, detecting, and estimating various poisons from human body organs. In response to this, the first Chemical Examiner's laboratory was established in Madras Presidency in 1849, under the control of the Department of Health. Initially, it operated under the authority of a civil surgeon or a professor of some medical college, which meant it would relocate with the surgeon's transfer. However, the government and the court recognised the limitations of managing this laboratory on a part-time basis, leading to the appointment of a full-time permanent chemical examiner and the establishment of a permanent laboratory. Subsequently, additional Chemical Examiner's laboratories were set up in Calcutta in 1853, Agra in 1864 and Bombay in 1870. These laboratories were fully equipped to conduct toxicological analyses of human viscera and biological analyses of stains from human body fluid such as semen, blood, saliva, etc. Furthermore, these facilities extended their services to neighbouring states and Union Territories.

While the identification of poisons was being addressed, the identification of individuals, particularly criminals, was done using conventional methods. Police officials would rely on memory to recognise individuals based on their facial and physical features if they committed another crime. With the introduction of photography, CID started recording photographs of criminals with a complete elucidation of their appearance. However, one flaw in this system was that criminals could easily evade capture by just changing their appearance. Globally and in India, Bertillon's Anthropometric system gained widespread acceptance as a method for identifying individuals based on body measurements. Consequently, an Anthropometric Bureau was established at Calcutta in 1892. The bureau assisted police officials in identifying criminals based on anthropometric measurements until the use of fingerprint identification emerged as an alternative for individualisation.

After recognising the limitations of the Anthropometric system, a more superior personal identification system was needed. British civil servant William Herschel had started studying papillary ridges on the fingertips. He established that fingerprints never change during one's lifetime. He designed a technique for registration of thumb impressions of native contractors to shelter the government's interests so that contractors could not reject it. Then he extended his recording system to register the thumbprints of criminals. However, Herschel failed to implement this idea effectively. In 1891, Sir Edward Richard Henry was appointed as Inspector General of Police in Bengal. Henry, in 1897 included thumb impressions and anthropometric measurements as well in record slips to circumvent false identification of criminals. He also introduced a duplicate criminal record containing finger impressions of ten fingers, which later substituted the whole identification system with fingerprints. Henry appointed a couple of Indian police officials, Azizul Haque and Hem Chandra Bose, to work on this system. It was these two police officials who devised a mathematical formula in addition to Henry's sorting slips into 1024 pigeon holes. This mathematical formula met the practicality of his idea of an identification system based on fingerprints. Later, they also designed the extended sub-classification system, termed a single-digit classification system. Henry then approached the government about his idea to replace anthropometric data with fingerprint slips to identify habitual criminals. The government consented to it, and hence the first fingerprint bureau was set up at Calcutta in July 1897. Following India, many other countries started using fingerprints as the primary means of identifying habitual criminals.

When the explosion cases started to increase, the need to detect the cause of the explosion also increased. This led to the First Chief Inspector of Explosives appointment at the Department of Explosives in 1898, with Nagpur as his headquarters. After this, five regional offices were established at Calcutta, Bombay, Agra, Madras and Gwalior and three sub-offices at Shivakshi, Gomia and Asansol.

Meanwhile, the British Government of Bengal needed the expertise to analyse handwriting present on secret documents related to the Indian Independence

Movement. This led to the foundation of another post of Government Handwriting Expert of Bengal. Mr. CR Hardless, the then Superintended in accountant's General's office in Bengal, was designated for this post in 1904. This set-up was soon shifted to Shimla and was then put under the control of Director CID. Soon, Mr. F Brewster, a police officer of West Bengal CID, was then nominated for this post, and soon he became the Government Examiner of Questioned Documents (GEQD). Initially, the work of this laboratory was limited to the examination of writings of secret documents. Following this, utilisation of this branch was then extended to criminal and civil court cases. When this laboratory's duties and tasks increased, Mr. R Stott was appointed as Assistant Government Examiner of Questioned Documents in 1920. In 1925, Mr. R Stott took over the charge as Government Examiner of Questioned Documents (GEQD) after the retirement of Mr. Brewster. Mr. VOJ Hodgson soon replaced Mr. R Stott in 1944 and Mr. SN Sen, the first Indian to be appointed for this post. This branch then took the charges of secret censorship, detecting secret writing, and providing training to military personnel about the subject. After recognising the need for more such laboratories, two other organisations were established in Kolkata in 1964 and Hyderabad in 1968.

Forensic Serology Institute entitled 'Serology Department' was started in 1910 at Calcutta. Imperial Serologist to the Government of India headed this institute. Dr. Hankin had a significant role in the establishment of this laboratory. This institute provided its services in analysing various biological evidence from the crime scene. After independence, this was soon re-labelled as the 'Office of the Serologist and Chemical Examiner to the Government of India'.

In 1905, India's first Central Finger Print Bureau (CFPB) was established at Shimla but was soon abolished in 1922. At the conference of DIGs of Police, CID proposed the establishment of CFPB, and thus a committee was formed to submit a scheme. The Government of India approved the scheme, and soon a CFPB started functioning in Delhi in 1955. It was headed by the Superintendent of Police and was under the administrative control of the Intelligence Bureau (I.B.). It was the central authority to coordinate the activities of all State FPBs. In August 1956, CFPB was shifted to Calcutta. Recognising the need to standardise fingerprint experts' level in India, an All-India Board of Examination for Fingerprint Experts was formed by the Ministry of Home Affairs, Government of India, in 1958 at CFPB. This board conducted an annual examination for accrediting fingerprint experts from India. Then in the year 1973, the administrative control of the CFPB was shifted to the Central Bureau of Investigation CBI, and in the year 1986, it was again moved to the National Crime Records Bureau (NCRB) and was then again shifted to New Delhi.

Meanwhile, in 1915, a footprint section was established under CID, Government of Bengal. It assisted investigative authorities in identifying criminals based on the examination of footprints found on the crime scene. Later in 1917, a Note Forgery Section was established under CID, Government of Bengal, to analyse forged currency notes. In 1930, an Arms Expert was appointed, and thus a small ballistics laboratory was established under Calcutta Police to examine firearms.

A unique Institute to conduct training in the scientific investigation of crime against women, road accidents, explosion cases, drug abuse cases, etc., was formed and named Central Detective Training School (CDTS) in 1956 at Calcutta. Soon, four more CDTS was established at Hyderabad in 1964, Ghaziabad in 1970, Chandigarh in 1973 and Jaipur in 2012 (Table 3.1).

Table 3.1 Summary

Sr No.	Name of the laboratory/institute/school	Controlling agency/post	Year of establishment
1.	Chemical Examiner's Laboratory (Madras Presidency)	Department of Health in 1849. Initially, it was under the control of a civil surgeon or a professor of some medical college. Later, full-time chemical examiners were appointed and these laboratories were established under their authority	1849
2.	Chemical Examiner's Laboratory, Calcutta	Same as above	1853
3.	Chemical Examiner's Laboratory, Agra	Same as above	1864
4.	Chemical Examiner's Laboratory, Bombay	Same as above	1870
5.	Anthropometric Bureau, Calcutta	–	1892
6.	Fingerprint Bureau, Calcutta	–	1897
7.	Department of Explosives, Nagpur	Chief Inspector of Explosives	1898
8.	Government Examiner of Questioned Document (GEQD), Shimla (This was initially set up in Bengal in 1904)	Director, CID	1906
9.	Government Examiner of Questioned Document (GEQD), Kolkata	Director, CID	1964
10.	Government Examiner of Questioned Document (GEQD), Hyderabad	Director, CID	1968
11.	Serology Department, Kolkata	Imperial Serologist the Government of India	1910
12.	Footprint Section of Criminal Investigation Department	CID, Government of Bengal	1915
13.	Note Forgery Section in Criminal Investigation Department	CID, Government of Bengal	1917
14.	Ballistics Laboratory	Calcutta Police	1930
15.	Scientific Sections in the Criminal Investigation Department	CID, Government of Bengal	1936
16.	Central Fingerprint Bureau (CFPB), Shimla	–	1905 was soon abolished in 1922

(continued)

Table 3.1 (continued)

Sr No.	Name of the laboratory/institute/school	Controlling agency/post	Year of establishment
17.	Central Fingerprint Bureau (CFPB), Delhi	Headed by Superintendent of Police (SP) under the control of Intelligence Bureau (IB). In the year of 1986, the administrative control of the CFPB was transferred to National Crime Records Bureau (NCRB)	1955
18.	Central Detective Training School, Calcutta	This was initially ideated by Shri B.N. Mallick, the then Director, Intelligence Bureau. Later, it was brought under the control of BPRD	1956
19.	Central Detective Training School, Hyderabad	Now under the supervision of BPRD	1964
20.	Central Detective Training School, Ghaziabad	Now under the supervision of BPRD	1970
21.	Central Detective Training School, Chandigarh	Now under the supervision of BPRD	1973
22.	Indian Academy of Forensic Science	–	1960

3.3 Forensic Science Laboratories in India

Post-independence, in 1952, the first Forensic Science Laboratory in India at Kolkata was established, the *State Forensic Science Laboratory,* West Bengal. The Chemical Examiner's Laboratory in Kolkata was converted into State Forensic Science Laboratory, West Bengal, becoming the first FSL in India. When forensic science began to develop in India, the forensic scientists across India felt a need for an academy of their own which would be a platform for all forensic researchers to come together and carry out research in the field. Thus, the Indian Academy of Forensic Sciences was established in 1960.

3.3.1 Central Forensic Science Laboratries

Cognisance of the capability of forensic science in solving criminal and civil cases inspired the government of India to plan to set up five CFSLs, one of which was intended to be established at a central place and the remaining at four corners of the country. In 1957, the first Central Forensic Science Laboratory was established in Kolkata.

Second, CFSL was established in Hyderabad in 1967. Then in 1968, another CFSL was established in Delhi under the control of the Central Bureau of Investigation (CBI). CFSL Chandigarh was initially started as CID Scientific Section in 1933, under the Police Department of United Punjab in Lahore before independence. In

1961, it was named Forensic Science Laboratory Punjab, Chandigarh. In 1966, it was taken over by the Union Territory of Chandigarh. In 1970, the Bureau of Police Research and Development (BPR & D) was formed. It was created to modernise the Indian Police, assist the systematic study of police problems, and initiate the usage of science and technology in crime investigation methods in the country. Subsequently, in 1978, the Bureau of Police Research and Development (BPR & D) took over the control of FSL Chandigarh and then was named CFSL Chandigarh. In the year 2011, three new CFSLs were set up at Bhopal, Guwahati, and Pune.

Earlier, all CFSLs, excluding CFSL Delhi, were under the control of BPR & D. In the year 2002, the Directorate of Forensic Science Services (DFSS) was carved out from BPR & D, New Delhi to propagate and carry out the most acceptable forensic science practices in the country to assist the Criminal Justice System. The organisational setup of DFSS is shown in Fig. 3.1. Thus, All CFSLs were then put under the control of DFSS from the year 2002; however, CFSL Delhi is hitherto under the control of CBI. The list of CFSLs in India along with their controlling agencies, year of establishment, scientific Forensic divisions and their jurisdiction are shown in Table 3.2. The organisational setup of different CFSLs is shown in Figs. 3.2, 3.3, 3.4, 3.5, 3.6, 3.7, and 3.8. The jurisdiction of various CFSLs is shown in Fig. 3.9.

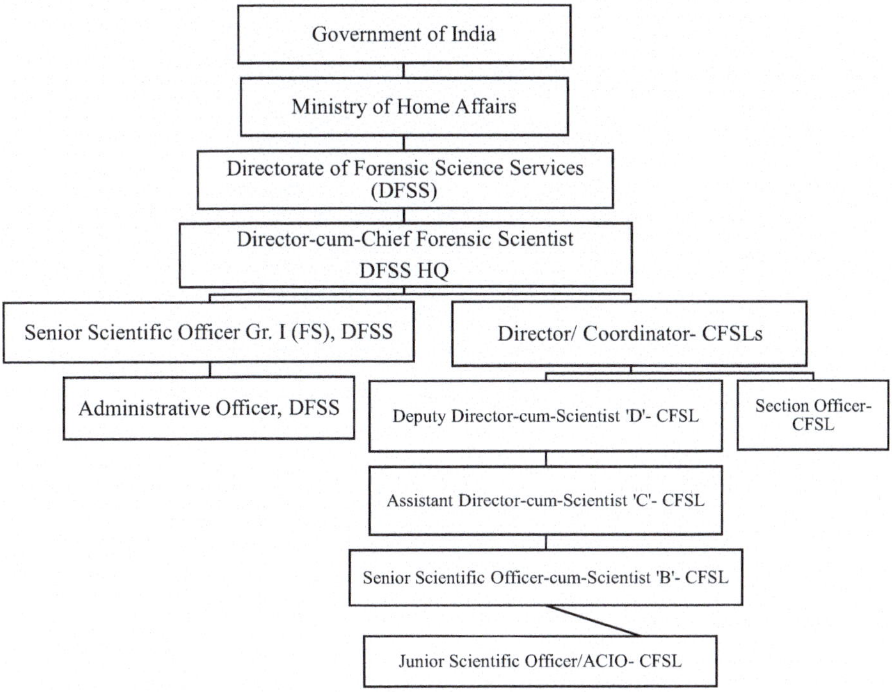

Fig. 3.1 Organisational structure of DFSS

Table 3.2 Central forensic science laboratories (CFSLs) in India

Sr. no.	Central forensic science laboratories	Controlling agency (current)	Year of establishment	Scientific forensic divisions	Jurisdiction
1.	Central Forensic Science Laboratory, Kolkata http://cfslkol.in/	Directorate of Forensic Science Services (DFSS), Ministry of Home Affairs, Government of India	1957	– Ballistics – Biology – Chemistry – DNA – Documents – Forensic Electronic Unit – Explosives – Narcotics – Physics – Toxicology	(a) Orissa (b) Bihar (c) Jharkhand (d) West Bengal (e) Andaman & Nicobar Islands
2.	Central Forensic Science Laboratory, Hyderabad http://cfslhyd.gov.in/	Directorate of Forensic Science Services (DFSS), Ministry of Home Affairs, Government of India	1967	– Ballistics – Biology – Chemistry – DNA – Documents – Explosives – Narcotics – Digital Forensics – Toxicology – Physics – Psychology	(a) Andhra Pradesh (b) Tamil Nadu (c) Kerala (d) Lakshadweep (e) Karnataka (f) Puducherry
3.	Central Forensic Science Laboratory, New Delhi https://cbi.gov.in/cfsl	Central Bureau of Investigation (CBI), Government of India	1968	– Ballistics and Explosive – Biology Division and DNA Profiling Unit – Chemistry – Computer Forensics – Document – Fingerprint – Forensic Psychology – Physics – Photo and Scientific Aid – Serology – A Scientific Aid Unit of CFSL at Chennai and Mumbai	CBI
4.	Central Forensic Science Laboratory, Chandigarh	Directorate of Forensic Science Services (DFSS),	1978	– Ballistics – Biology – Chemistry – Questioned Documents	(a) Jammu & Kashmir (b) Punjab (c) Himachal Pradesh

(continued)

Table 3.2 (continued)

Sr. no.	Central forensic science laboratories	Controlling agency (current)	Year of establishment	Scientific forensic divisions	Jurisdiction
	http://www.cfslchandigarh.gov.in/	Ministry of Home Affairs, Government of India		– Explosives – Physics – Toxicology – CFSL Unit Shimla-Questioned Documents	(d) Chandigarh (UT) (e) Uttarakhand (f) Delhi (g) NCR & Haryana
5.	Central Forensic Science Laboratory, Bhopal https://www.cfslbpl.gov.in/	Directorate of Forensic Science Services (DFSS), Ministry of Home Affairs, Government of India	2011	– Biology/Serology – Questioned Document and Photography – Chemistry/Narcotics – Ballistics – Computer Forensic – Speaker Identification and Audio-video Tape Authentication	(a) Madhya Pradesh (b) Uttar Pradesh (c) Rajasthan (d) Chhattisgarh
6.	Central Forensic Science Laboratory, Kamrup, Guwahati https://cfslghy.gov.in/	Directorate of Forensic Science Services (DFSS), Ministry of Home Affairs, Government of India	2011	– Ballistics – Biology – Chemistry – DNA – Digital – Documents – Explosive – Narcotics – Physics – Toxicology	(a) Assam (b) Manipur (c) Mizoram (d) Meghalaya (e) Sikkim (f) Nagaland (g) Arunachal Pradesh (h) Tripura
7.	Central Forensic Science Laboratory, Pune http://cfslpune.gov.in/	Directorate of Forensic Science Services (DFSS), Ministry of Home Affairs, Government of India	2011	– Ballistics – Biology – Chemistry – Documents – DNA Fingerprinting – Digital Forensics – Explosives – Narcotics – Physics	(a) Maharashtra (b) Gujarat (c) Goa (d) Daman & Diu (e) Dadar & Nagar Haveli

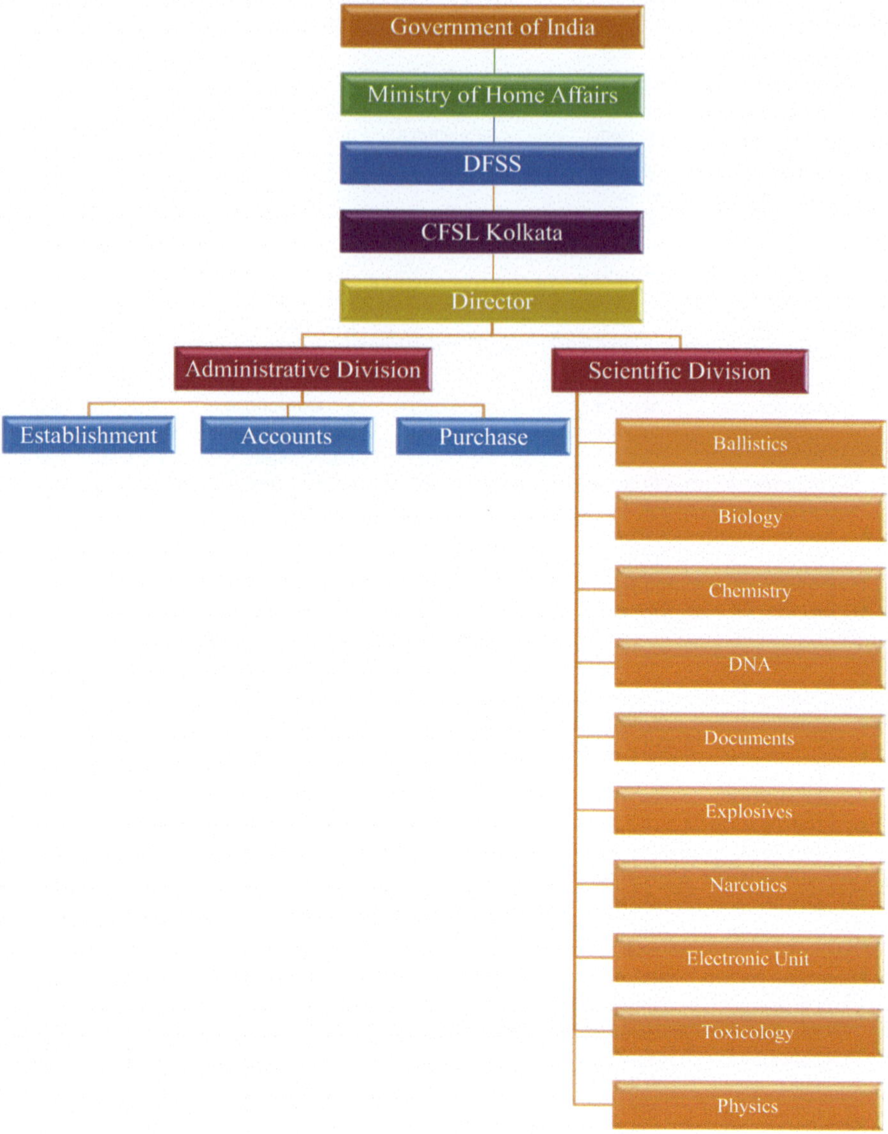

Fig. 3.2 Organisational setup of CFSL Kolkata

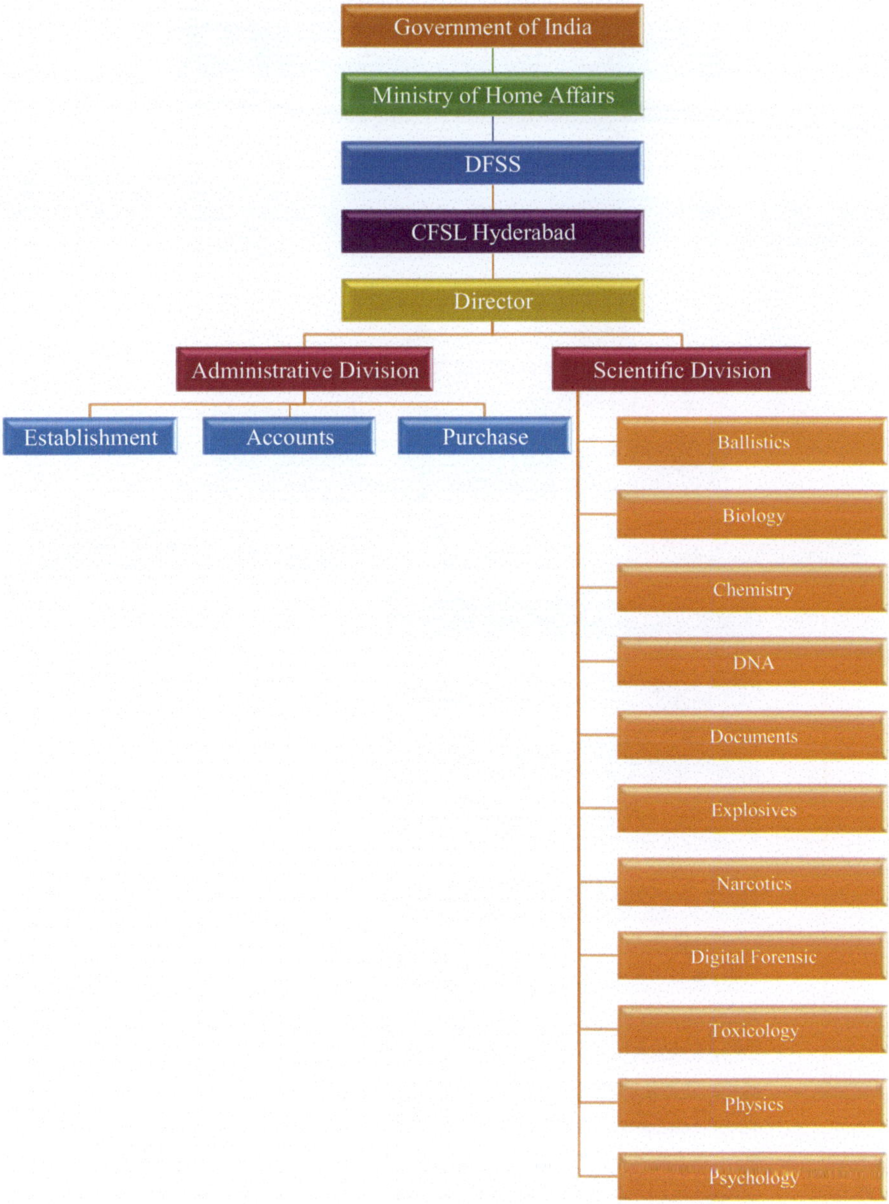

Fig. 3.3 Organisational setup of CFSL Hyderabad

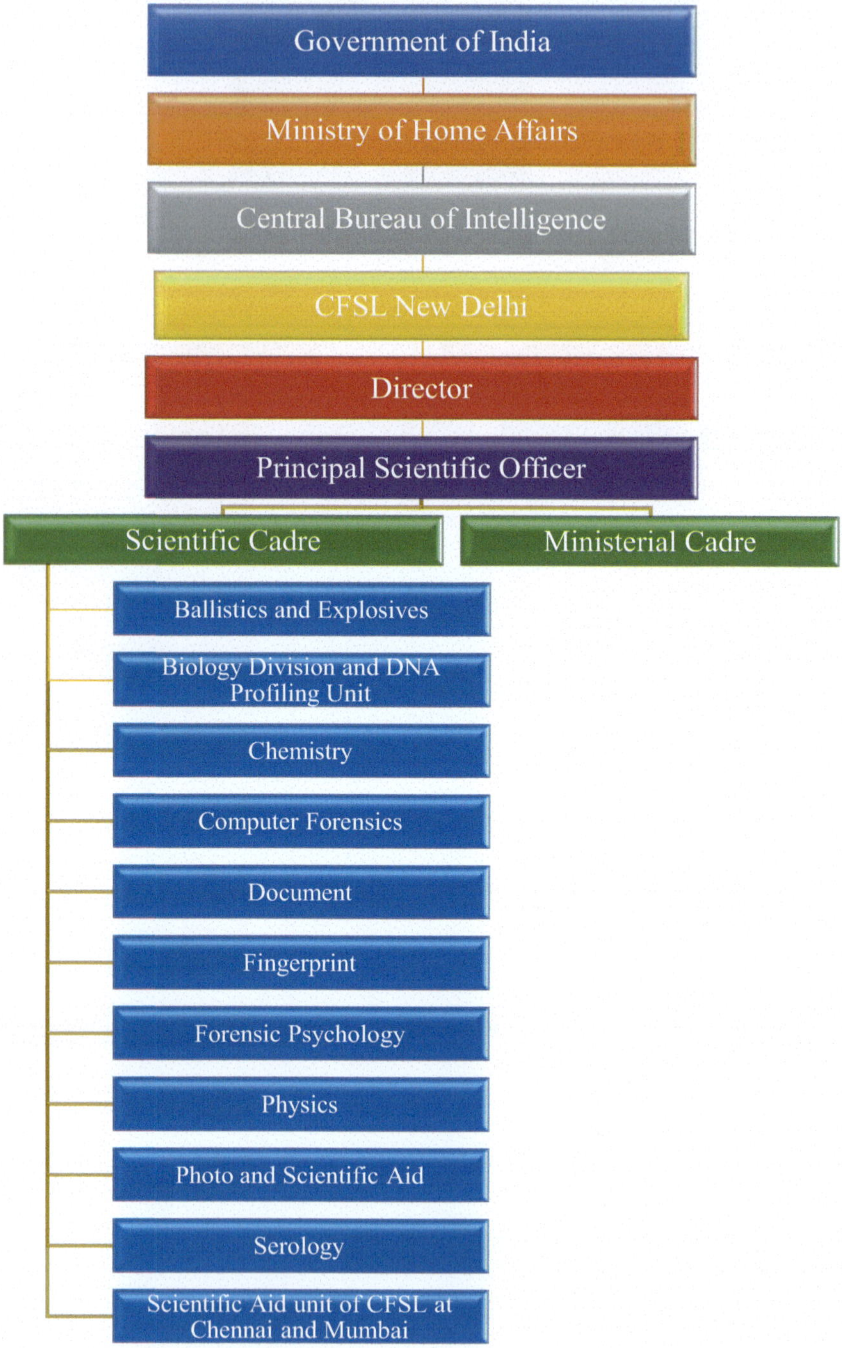

Fig. 3.4 Organisational setup of CFSL New Delhi

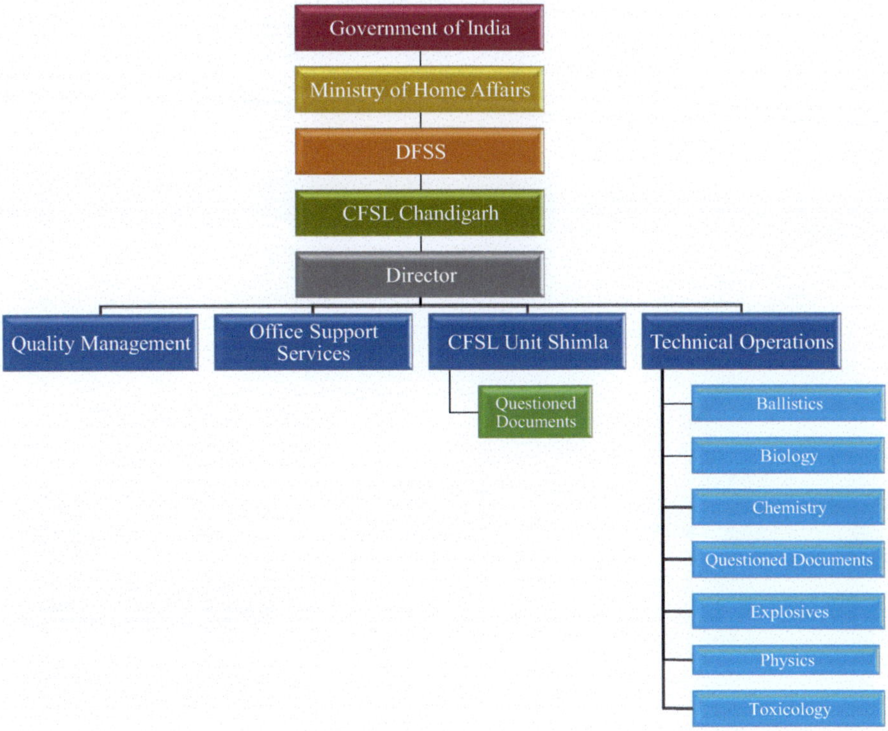

Fig. 3.5 Organisational setup of CFSL Chandigarh

3.3.2 State Forensic Science Laboratories

After the SFSL West Bengal (Kolkata) was established, many such SFSLs began to be set up in different states of India. In 1958, SFSL Maharashtra (Mumbai) was started up, then SFSL Rajasthan (Jaipur) and FSL Tamil Nadu (Chennai) in 1959, SFSL Bihar (Patna) in 1960, SFSL Kerala (Thiruvananthapuram) in 1961, SFSL Orissa (Bhubaneshwar) in 1962 (first setup in Cuttack and in 1971 shifted to Bhubaneshwar), SFSL MP (Sagar) in 1964, FSL Jammu and Kashmir in 1964, and SFSL Karnataka (Bengaluru) in 1967. The Directorate of Forensic Science, Assam (Guwahati), was set up in 1967. It was first established as Forensic Science Laboratory Assam in Shillong (capital of undivided Assam) in 1967. Later after two years, it was shifted to Guwahati under the control of the Director-General of Police Assam, and then a separate Directorate of Forensic Science was created in 2005. In 1969, Scientific section of CID, U.P. was converted into Forensic Science Laboratory. A Government order was issued in the year 1979 for the merger of the Chemical Examiner's Laboratory, Agra and the Forensic Science Laboratory, Lucknow and to develop these two laboratories as full-fledged Forensic Science Laboratories. Initially SFSL Haryana was established at Rohtak in 1973 and then was shifted to Madhuban (Karnal) in 1976. In 1974, SFSL Andhra Pradesh was set

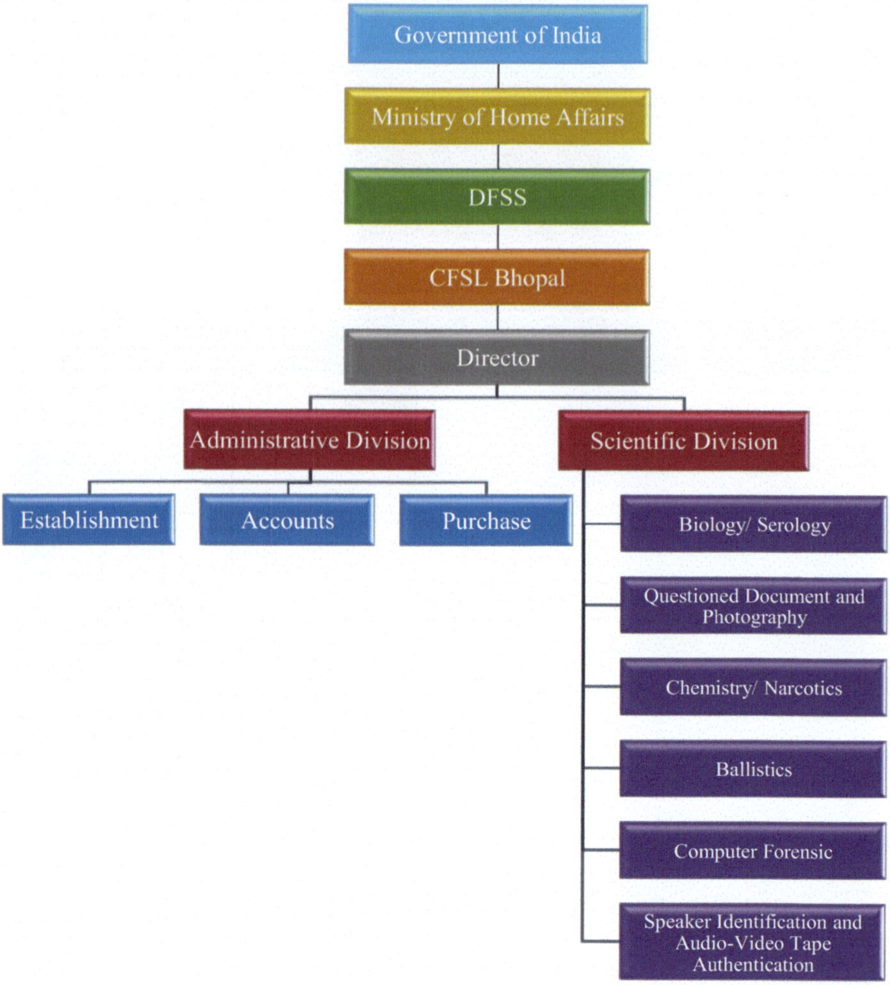

Fig. 3.6 Organisational setup of CFSL Bhopal

up at Hyderabad, which became SFSL Telangana after Telangana separated from Andhra Pradesh, and the new SFSL Andhra Pradesh is recently established at Mangalagiri. Forensic Science Laboratory at Ahmedabad, Gujarat was established in 1974 but has now shifted to Gandhinagar as Directorate of Forensic Science. FSL Punjab (Chandigarh) was set up in 1980, SFSL Meghalaya (Shillong) in 1987, SFSL Manipur (Pangel, Imphal) in 1987–88. In 1988, SFSL Himachal Pradesh was established in Shimla but was shifted to Junga in 1996. FSL Delhi (Rohini) was setup in 1995. Thereafter, in 2000, FSL Mizoram was set up at Aizawl. In 2002, SFSL Chhattisgarh (Raipur) was set up. It was initially a Regional Forensic Science Laboratory in Raipur in Madhya Pradesh. Later, when Chhattisgarh was established as a different state, this RFSL was converted into SFSL Chhattisgarh. In the same

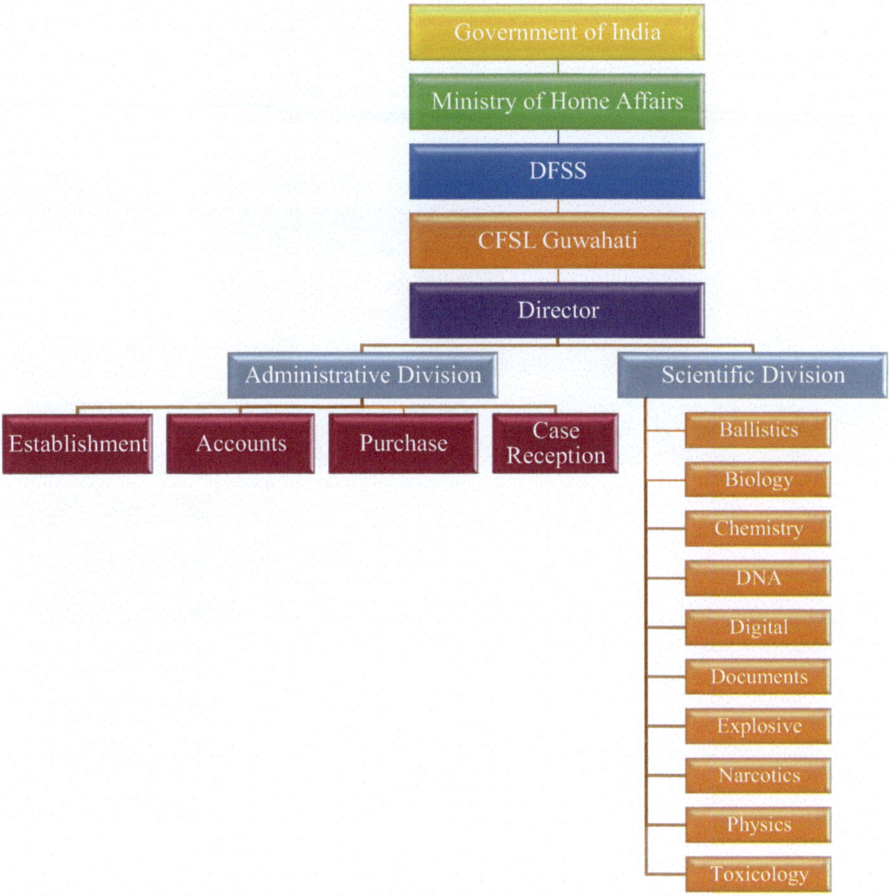

Fig. 3.7 Organisational setup of CFSL Guwahati

year, SFSL Tripura was established at Agartala. In 2003, FSL Andaman and the Nicobar Islands was set up at Port Blair. The foundation stone of SFSL Arunachal Pradesh building was laid in 2004 and the construction of building was completed by 2006 in the premises of Police Training Centre, Banderdewa. In 2005, SFSL Jharkhand was established at Ranchi; in the past, it was started as RFSL Ranchi before the separation of Jharkhand. Later it was converted into SFSL after the formation of Jharkhand state.

There are seven Central FSLs (Table 3.2) and 32 State FSLs (Table 3.3) in India.

Apart from CFSLs and SFSLs, different states in India have Regional FSLs, District FSLs, Mini FSLs and Mobile FSLs. As per the official record available on the official website of DFSS, there are total 80 Regional FSLs (plus 10 more are approved and under process of being established) and 529 Mobile Forensic Units (MFUs)/District Mobile Forensic Units (DMFUs). A representative image is shown

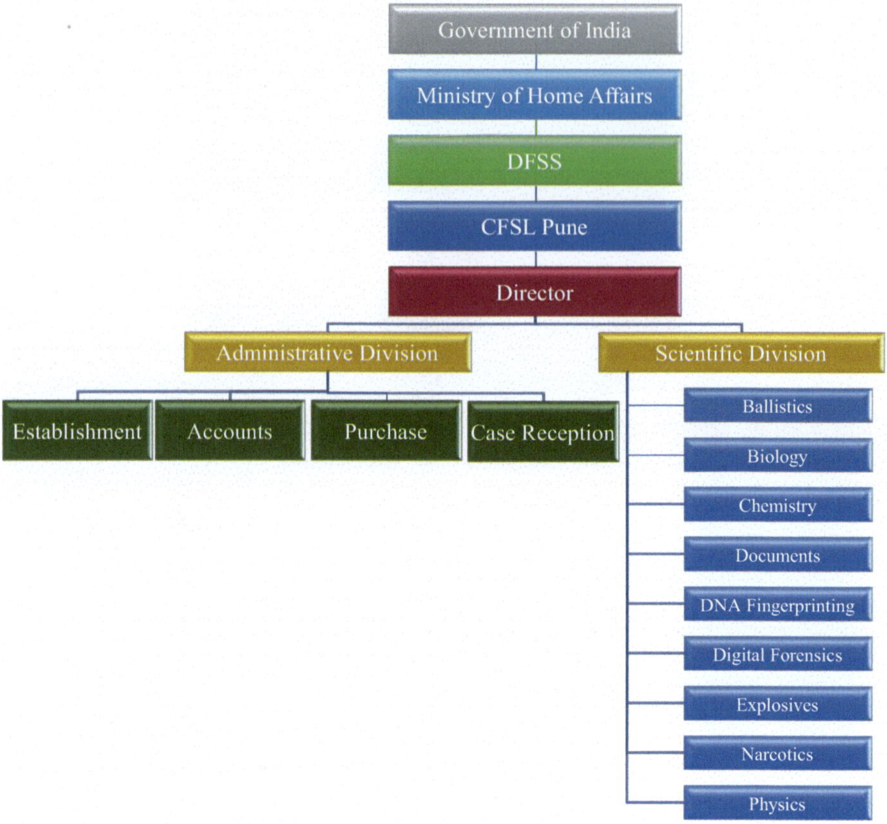

Fig. 3.8 Organisational setup of CFSL Pune

in Map 3.1. These are under the control of the State Forensic Science Directorate under the State Home departments.

3.4 Role and Functions of FSLs

The role and functions of forensic science laboratories in India are significant in the criminal justice system and encompass a wide range of activities. These laboratories serve as specialised centres for scientific analysis and examination of evidence, playing a pivotal role in assisting law enforcement agencies, prosecutors, and the judiciary. Overall, FSLs in India have multifaceted roles and functions, ranging from evidence analysis and crime scene support to expert testimony and research. Their work is crucial in ensuring the fair administration of justice. Below are some of the key roles and functions performed by forensic science laboratories in India:

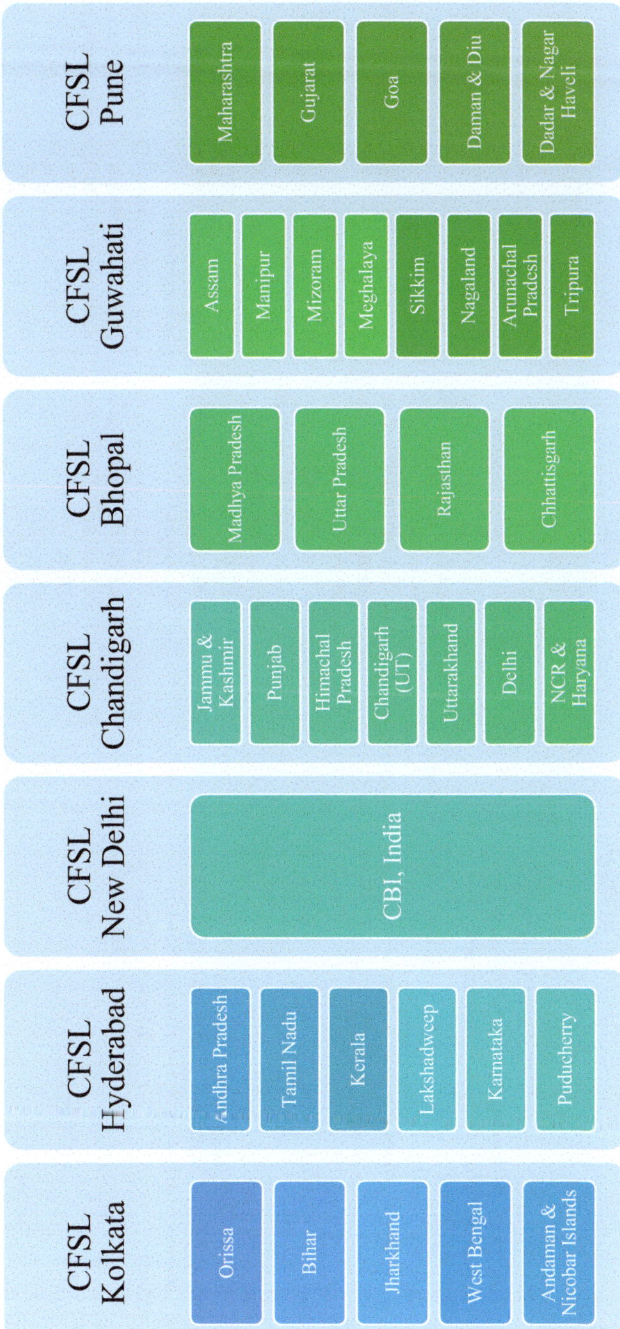

Fig. 3.9 Jurisdiction of CFSLs

Table 3.3 State forensic science laboratories in India

Sr. no.	State FSL	Controlling agency/ authority (present)	Establishment year	Forensic divisions (and/or units)	Website
1.	State Forensic Science Laboratory, West Bengal (Kolkata)	Department of Home and Hill Affairs, Police Establishment Branch, Govt. of West Bengal	1952	– Ballistics – Biology – Chemistry – Physics – Questioned Document – Toxicology	http://www.wbfsl.gov.in/
2.	State Forensic Science Laboratory, Maharashtra (Kalina, Mumbai) (Now Directorate of Forensic Science Laboratories, Mumbai)	Home Department, Government of Maharashtra	1958	– Toxicology – Biology & Serology – DNA – General Analytical and Instrumentation – Prohibition and Excise – Ballistics – Physics – Cyber Forensic – Tape Authentication and Speaker Identification – Psychology	https://dfsl.maharashtra.gov.in/en
3.	State Forensic Science Laboratory, Rajasthan (Jaipur)	Directorate of State Forensic Science Laboratory Rajasthan, Govt. of Rajasthan	1959	– Arson and Explosive – Ballistics – Biology – Cyber Forensic – Chemistry – DNA – Document – Physics – Polygraph – Photo – Narcotics	https://home.rajasthan.gov.in/content/homeportal/en/stateforensicsciencelaboratorydepartment/forensiclaboratories/stateforensicsciencelaboratoryjaipur.html

				– Serology – Toxicology	
4.	Forensic Sciences Department, Tamil Nadu (Chennai) (The foundation of Forensic Science Department can be traced back to a small laboratory known as the 'Chemical Examiner's Laboratory' in the year 1849. The first integrated 'Forensic Science Laboratory' was established in 1959 by combining three Laboratories, namely the 'Chemical Examiner's Laboratory', 'Police Laboratory', and 'Prohibition and Excise Laboratory'.)	Home Department, Govt. of Tamil Nadu .	1959	– Anthropology – Ballistics – Biology – Chemistry – Computer Forensics – DNA – Document – Excise – Explosives – Instruments – Narcotics – Photography – Physics – Prohibition – Serology – Toxicology – R&D	https://www.tn.gov.in/tamilforensic/history.htm
5.	State Forensic Science Laboratory, Bihar (Patna)	CID, Government of Bihar	1960	– Physics – Ballistics – Narcotics – General Chemistry – Explosives – Toxicology – DNA – Serology – Biology – Cyber	https://police.bihar.gov.in/CID.aspx

(continued)

Table 3.3 (continued)

Sr. no.	State FSL	Controlling agency/ authority (present)	Establishment year	Forensic divisions (and/or units)	Website
6.	State Forensic Science Laboratory, Kerala (Thiruvananthapuram)	Kerala State Police	1961	– Ballistics – Biology – Chemistry – Cyber – DNA – Documents – Document-Civil – Explosives – Physics – Polygraph – Serology	https://keralapolice.gov.in/page/forensic-science-lab
7.	State Forensic Science Laboratory, Orissa (Bhubaneshwar) (It was first set up in Cuttack in 1962 and was later shifted to Bhubaneshwar in the year 1971)	Odisha Police	1962	– Ballistics – Biology – Chemistry – Cyber Forensic – DNA – Lie Detection – Physics – Serology – Toxicology	https://www.odishapolice.gov.in/?q=Forensic
8.	State Forensic Science Laboratory, Madhya Pradesh (Sagar)	CID, Madhya Pradesh Police Department	1964	– Biology – Serology – Ballistics – Physics – Chemistry – Toxicology – Explosives – DNA Fingerprinting – Toxicology – Voice Analysis	https://www.mppolice.gov.in/sites/default/files/FSL_FInal/FSLHomePage.html

9.	Forensic Science Laboratory, Jammu and Kashmir (The FSL has two complexes—Jammu and Srinagar)	Home Department, Govt. of Jammu and Kashmir	1964	– Narcotic and Chemical – Biology/Serology – DNA – Documents – Fingerprint – Cyber	https://www.jkfsl.gov.in/
10.	State Forensic Science Laboratory, Karnataka (Madiwala, Bengaluru)	Karnataka State Police (Directorate of Forensic Science Laboratories Karnataka)	1967	– Audio-Video Forensic – Biology – Chemistry – Computer Forensics – DNA – Narcotic – Mobile Forensic – Firearms – Physics – Photography – Psychology – Questioned Document	https://dfsl.karnataka.gov.in/en
11.	Directorate of Forensic Science, Assam (Guwahati) (It was first established as Forensic Science Laboratory Assam in Shillong (capital of undivided Assam) in 1967. Later after 2 years it was shifted to Guwahati under the control of Director General of Police Assam and then a separate Directorate of Forensic	Home Department, Govt. of Assam	1967	– Ballistics – Biology – Chemistry – Drugs and Narcotics – Explosives – Instrumentation – Photography – Physics – Questioned Document – Serology – Toxicology	https://forensic.assam.gov.in/

(continued)

Table 3.3 (continued)

Sr. no.	State FSL	Controlling agency/ authority (present)	Establishment year	Forensic divisions (and/or units)	Website
	Science was created in 2005)				
12.	Forensic Science Laboratory, Uttar Pradesh (Lucknow) (In 1969, Scientific section of CID, U.P. was converted into Forensic Science Laboratory. A Govt. order was issued in the year 1979 for the merger of the Chemical Examiner's Laboratory, Agra, and the Forensic Science Laboratory, Lucknow, and to develop these two laboratories as full-fledged Forensic Science Laboratories)	Uttar Pradesh Police	1969	– Ballistics – Biology – Chemistry – Documents – Physics – Serology – Toxicology – Lie Detection – Medicolegal Instrumental Analysis	https://uppolice.gov.in/pages/en/topmenu/police-units/technical-services-(ts)/about-us/en-forensic-laboratory
13.	State Forensic Science Laboratory, Haryana (Madhuban, Karnal) (Initially it was established at Rohtak in 1973 and then was shifted to Madhuban in 1976)	Haryana Police Department	1973	– Ballistics – Biology – Chemistry – Document – Instrumentation – Lie Detection – Physics – Serology – General Section – Photo Section	https://haryanapolice.gov.in/AboutUs#Forensic%20Science%20Lab

14.	State Forensic Science Laboratory, Telangana (Hyderabad) (Prior to division of Andhra Pradesh into two states, i.e. Andhra Pradesh and Telangana, this laboratory used to be the SFSL of Andhra Pradesh)	Telangana State Police Department	1974	– Ballistics – Biology – Biomedical – Chemistry – Computer Forensics – DNA – Document – Forensic Engineering – Narcotics – Polygraph – Physics – Serology – Toxicology	https://www.tspolice.gov.in/jsp/userunits?method=viewUnits
15.	Directorate of Forensic Science, Gujarat (Gandhinagar) (Initially it started as Forensic Science Laboratory, Ahmedabad)	Home Department, Government of Gujarat	1974	– Forensic Toxicology – Forensic Physical – Forensic Ballistics – Forensic Photography – Question document – Forensic Chemicals/ Explosives/ – Narcotics – Blood Alcohol – Biology – Serology – DNA – Psychology – Fingerprint – Department of Computer Forensics – Mobile Forensic Services – Prohibition Possession	https://dfs.gujarat.gov.in/dfsl/CMS.aspx?content_id=147

(continued)

Table 3.3 (continued)

Sr. no.	State FSL	Controlling agency/ authority (present)	Establishment year	Forensic divisions (and/or units)	Website
16.	Forensic Science Laboratory, Punjab (Chandigarh)	Punjab Police	1980	– Ballistics – Biology – Chemistry – Document – Photography – Physics – Serology – Toxicology	http://punjabpolice.gov.in/(S(lul4 cdvxutsbyaq0exlgkr45))/tech_wings.aspx
17.	State Forensic Science Laboratory, Manipur (Pangei, Imphal) (Now re-designated as Directorate of Forensic Science)	Home Department, Government of Manipur	1987–1988		http://www.manipurpolice.gov.in/?page_id=4
18.	State Forensic Science Laboratory, Meghalaya (Shillong)	Meghalaya police, Government of Meghalaya	1987	– Biology – Chemical division – Physical division – Questioned Documents	https://megpolice.gov.in/forensic-science-laboratory-meghalaya
19.	State Forensic Science Laboratory, Himachal Pradesh (At first SFSL Himachal Pradesh was set up in Shimla in 1988. In the year 1996 it was shifted to Junga)	Home and Vigilance Department, Govt. of Himachal Pradesh	1988	– Biology and Serology – Chemistry and Toxicology – Document and Photography – Physics and Ballistics – DNA – NDPS	https://himachal.nic.in/index.php?lang=1&dpt_id=174
20.	Forensic Science Laboratory, Rohini, Delhi		1995	– Ballistics – Biology/DNA	https://fsl.delhi.gov.in/fsl/forensic-science-laboratory

	(Initially it was under the administrative control of Delhi Police but later in 1995, the control was transferred to Home Dept., Government of NCT of Delhi)	Home Department, Government of NCT of Delhi		Fingerprinting – Chemistry (Including Toxicology, Narcotics, General Chemistry & Explosives) – Documents (including Computer Forensic Unit & Fingerprint Unit) – Forensic Psychology – Physics – Photo – Crime Scene Management – Quality Management	
21.	Forensic Science Laboratory, Mizoram (Aizwal) (Mizoram Forensic Science Laboratory was first created as a branch under CID (Crime) in the year 1998. Later, in 2000 it was shifted under the administrative control of Police Hqrs)	Department of Forensic Science Laboratory Mizoram, Govt. of Mizoram	2000	– Ballistics and Toolmarks – DNA/Serology – Chemistry – Fingerprint – Photography – Toxicology – Questioned Documents – Cyber Forensics	https://forensic.mizoram.gov.in/
22.	State Forensic Science Laboratory, Chhattisgarh (Raipur) (It was initially a Regional Forensic Science Laboratory, Raipur, in	Chhattisgarh Government	2002	– Biology – Chemistry – Physics – DNA – Toxicology – Ballistics	http://fsl.cg.nic.in/

(continued)

Table 3.3 (continued)

Sr. no.	State FSL	Controlling agency/ authority (present)	Establishment year	Forensic divisions (and/or units)	Website
	Madhya Pradesh. Later when Chhattisgarh was established as a different state, this RFSL was converted into SFSL Chhattisgarh)			– Serology – Narcotics – Diatom – Excise	
23.	State Forensic Science Laboratory, Tripura (Agartala)	Home Department, Govt. of Tripura	2002	– Biology/Serology – Chemistry – Cyber Forensics – DNA Typing – Document – Physics/Ballistics – Polygraph – Toxicology	https://sfsl.tripura.gov.in/
24.	Forensic Science Laboratory, Andaman and Nicobar Islands (Port Blair)	Crime Investigation Department	2003	– Chemical Science (Provision type cases, Arson, NDPS, Toxicological analysis)	https://police.andaman.gov.in/index.php/en/support-units/criminal-investigation-department.html
25.	State Forensic Science Laboratory, Arunachal Pradesh (Banderdewa) (The foundation stone of FSL building was laid on 14th May 2004 and the construction of building was completed by Feb' 2006 in the premises of Police Training Centre, Banderdewa)	Arunachal Pradesh Police	2004	– Narcotics – Questioned Documents – Photography – Ballistics – Biology/Serology – Cyber Forensic	https://ptcbanderdewa.in/fsl.html

26.	State Forensic Science Laboratory, Jharkhand (Ranchi) (In past it was started as RFSL Ranchi, before the separation of Jharkhand. Later it was converted into SFSL after the formation of state)	Jharkhand Police Department	2005	– Ballistics – Biology – Serology – Explosives – Physics – Toxicology – General Chemistry (including NDPS) – DNA Profiling Unit	https://jhpolice.gov.in/sfsl/history
27.	State Forensic Science Laboratory, Uttarakhand (Dehradun)	Uttarakhand Police	2006	– Chemistry – Biology & DNA – Toxicology – Questioned Documents – Ballistics	https://uttarakhandpolice.uk.gov.in/dpages/forensic-science-laboratory-dehradun
28.	Forensic Science Laboratory, Nagaland (Dimapur)	Nagaland Police		– Fingerprints – Narcotics – Photography – Questioned Documents	https://police.nagaland.gov.in/forensic-science-lab/
29.	Forensic Science Laboratory, Goa (Verna)	Goa Police		– Biology and Serology – Chemistry and Toxicology	https://citizen.goapolice.gov.in/web/guest/forensic-science-lab
30.	Forensic Science Laboratory, Puducherry	Home Department, Government of Puducherry		– Biology and Serology – Crime Scene unit	https://police.py.gov.in/Contact%20us/Forensic%20Science%20Laboratory%20Puducherry.pdf
31.	Forensic Science Laboratory, Andhra Pradesh (Mangalagiri) (After the division of Andhra Pradesh into 2 states Telangana and Andhra Pradesh, SFSL Hyderabad became the	Andhra Pradesh Police			

(continued)

Table 3.3 (continued)

Sr. no.	State FSL	Controlling agency/ authority (present)	Establishment year	Forensic divisions (and/or units)	Website
	State FSL for Telangana and a new SFSL was set up at Mangalagiri)				
32.	Regional Forensic Science Laboratory, Sikkim (Ranipool, Gangtok)				

- Evidence Examination and Analysis: Forensic laboratories in India are responsible for the examination, analysis, and interpretation of various types of evidence collected from crime scenes. This includes biological evidence such as DNA samples, fingerprints, ballistics, trace evidence, questioned documents, digital evidence, and more. The laboratories employ sophisticated techniques and scientific methods to extract information, identify patterns, and draw conclusions from the evidence.
- Crime Scene Investigation Support: Forensic science laboratories provide vital support to crime scene investigators. They offer expertise and guidance in the proper collection, preservation, and documentation of evidence to ensure its integrity and admissibility in court. This includes providing training and assistance in evidence handling, evidence packaging, and maintaining chain of custody.
- Scientific Analysis and Examination: Forensic scientists in these laboratories perform scientific analysis and examination of evidence using specialised techniques and equipment. They employ a wide range of forensic disciplines such as DNA profiling, fingerprint analysis, ballistics, toolmark examination, drug analysis, toxicology, questioned document examination, forensic anthropology, digital forensics, and more. These examinations help establish connections, identify suspects, determine causes of death, and provide scientific evidence in criminal cases.
- Expert Testimony and Court Proceedings: Forensic science laboratories in India provide expert testimony in court proceedings. Forensic experts, based on their analysis and findings, present their conclusions and opinions to assist the judge and jury in understanding complex scientific evidence. Their testimony can play a vital role in supporting or refuting allegations and helping the court arrive at a just and informed decision.
- Research and Development: Forensic laboratories also engage in research and development activities to advance forensic science techniques and methodologies. They explore emerging technologies, and contribute to the scientific knowledge base in the field. This helps in improving the accuracy, reliability, and efficiency of forensic analysis, leading to better outcomes in criminal investigations.

3.5 Conclusion

Forensic science laboratories in India play a vital role in the criminal justice system by providing scientific analysis and evidence that aid investigations, court proceedings, and the pursuit of justice. They are responsible for the examination and analysis of various types of evidence, ranging from DNA profiling to fingerprint identification, ballistics, toxicology, and digital forensics. The services offered and divisions available also vary. Despite their significance, forensic science laboratories in India face challenges such as limited resources, outdated equipment, and a shortage of skilled forensic professionals. However, the Government of India and

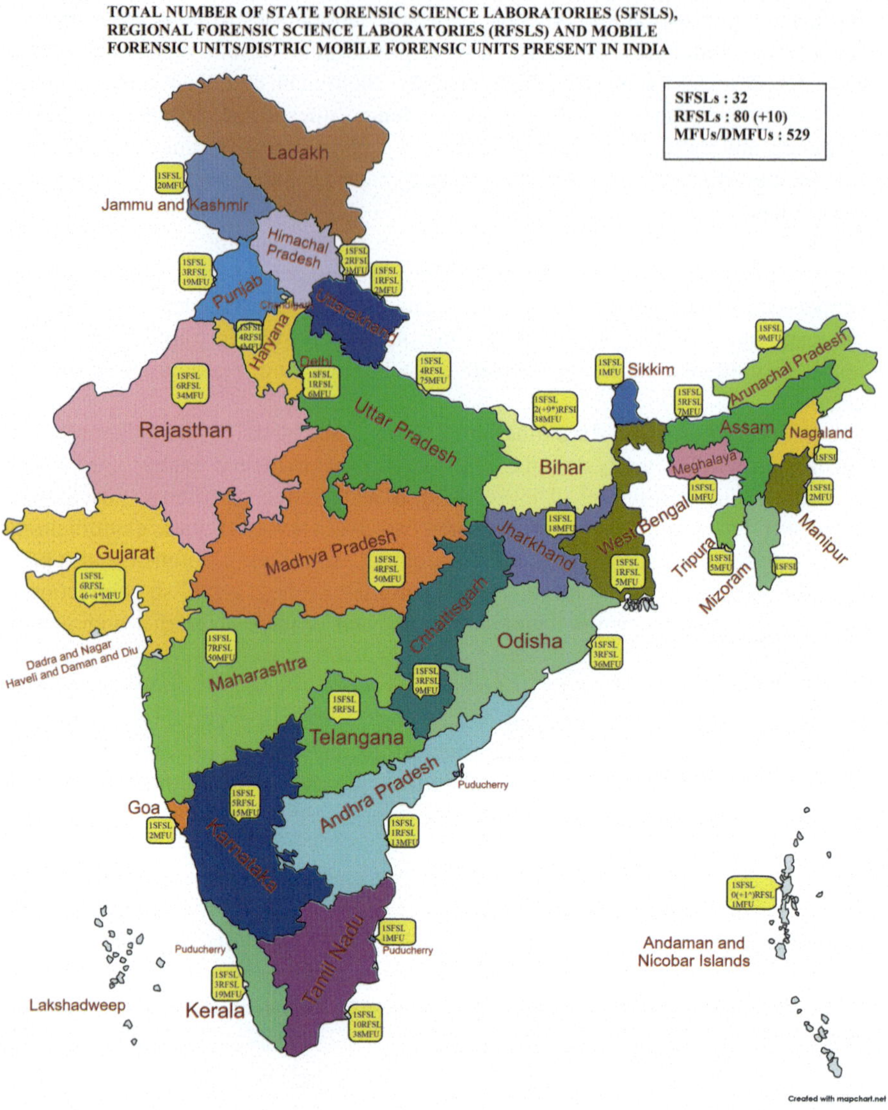

Map. 3.1 Representative map of India showing the number of State FSLs (SFSLs), Regional FSLs (RFSLs), Mobile Forensic Units (MFUs)/ District Mobile Forensic Units (DMFUs) (Till 2022)

other state governments have taken several steps to address these challenges, including increased funding, infrastructure development, and capacity building initiatives. Efforts have been made to improve the quality and efficiency of forensic analysis and enhance collaboration with law enforcement agencies and other stakeholders.

Over the last few decades, there has been constant up gradation in the infrastructure, facilities, and instrumentation available in the FSLs. Many FSLs now offer state-of-the-art facilities for analysing a wide range of evidence. The time taken for analysis has also reduced significantly. This, in turn, has resulted in quick turn-around time and hence reduced time taken by the honourable courts to deliver verdicts. Realising the need and increased scope of forensic science over the last few years, many universities, institutes and colleges have started offering several traditional and modern courses in the subject. The subject, Forensic Science, is predicted to grow manifolds in the next few years.

Bibliography

Tewari RK, Ravikumar KV (2000) History and development of forensic science in India. J Postgrad Med 46(4):303–308. Available from: http://www.bioline.org.br/request?jp00100 (last accessed on 15.07.2023)

Web References

http://dfs.nic.in/index.html (last accessed on 15.07.2023)
http://cfslkol.in/ (last accessed on 15.07.2023)
http://cfslhyd.gov.in/ (last accessed on 15.07.2023)
https://cbi.gov.in/cfsl (last accessed on 15.07.2023)
http://www.cfslchandigarh.gov.in/ (last accessed on 15.07.2023)
https://www.cfslbpl.gov.in/ (last accessed on 15.07.2023)
http://cfslpune.gov.in/ (last accessed on 15.07.2023)
https://cfslghy.gov.in/ (last accessed on 15.07.2023)
http://www.wbfsl.gov.in/ (last accessed on 15.07.2023)
https://dfsl.maharashtra.gov.in/en (last accessed on 15.07.2023)
https://home.rajasthan.gov.in/content/homeportal/en/stateforensicsciencelaboratorydepartment/forensiclaboratories/stateforensicsciencelaboratoryjaipur.html (last accessed on 15.07.2023)
https://www.tn.gov.in/tamilforensic/history.htm (last accessed on 15.07.2023)
https://police.bihar.gov.in/CID.aspx (last accessed on 15.07.2023)
https://keralapolice.gov.in/page/forensic-science-lab (last accessed on 15.07.2023)
https://www.odishapolice.gov.in/?q=Forensic (last accessed on 15.07.2023)
https://www.mppolice.gov.in/sites/default/files/FSL_FInal/FSLHomePage.html (last accessed on 15.07.2023)
https://www.jkfsl.gov.in/ (last accessed on 15.07.2023)
https://dfsl.karnataka.gov.in/en (last accessed on 15.07.2023)
https://forensic.assam.gov.in/ (last accessed on 15.07.2023)
https://uppolice.gov.in/pages/en/topmenu/police-units/technical-services-(ts)/about-us/en-forensic-laboratory (last accessed on 15.07.2023)
https://haryanapolice.gov.in/AboutUs#Forensic%20Science%20Lab (last accessed on 15.07.2023)
https://www.tspolice.gov.in/jsp/userunits?method=viewUnits (last accessed on 15.07.2023)
https://dfs.gujarat.gov.in/dfsl/CMS.aspx?content_id=147 (last accessed on 15.07.2023)
http://punjabpolice.gov.in/(S(lul4cdvxutsbyaq0exlgkr45))/tech_wings.aspx (last accessed on 15.07.2023)
http://www.manipurpolice.gov.in/?page_id=4 (last accessed on 15.07.2023)
https://megpolice.gov.in/forensic-science-laboratory-meghalaya (last accessed on 15.07.2023)

https://himachal.nic.in/index.php?lang=1&dpt_id=174 (last accessed on 15.07.2023)
https://fsl.delhi.gov.in/fsl/forensic-science-laboratory (last accessed on 15.07.2023)
https://forensic.mizoram.gov.in/ (last accessed on 15.07.2023)
http://fsl.cg.nic.in/ (last accessed on 15.07.2023)
https://sfsl.tripura.gov.in/ (last accessed on 15.07.2023)
https://police.andaman.gov.in/index.php/en/support-units/criminal-investigation-department.html (last accessed on 15.07.2023)
https://ptcbanderdewa.in/fsl.html (last accessed on 15.07.2023)
https://jhpolice.gov.in/sfsl/history (last accessed on 15.07.2023)
https://uttarakhandpolice.uk.gov.in/dpages/forensic-science-laboratory-dehradun (last accessed on 15.07.2023)
https://police.nagaland.gov.in/forensic-science-lab/ (last accessed on 15.07.2023)
https://citizen.goapolice.gov.in/web/guest/forensic-science-lab (last accessed on 15.07.2023)
https://police.py.gov.in/Contact%20us/Forensic%20Science%20Laboratory%20Puducherry.pdf (last accessed on 15.07.2023)

4 Legal Aspects of Forensic Science: A Bird's Eye View

Jitendra Mishra, Sandeep Mishra, Ankit Srivastava,
and Kumar Askand Pandey

Abstract

Forensic science is the blend of science with law having multidisciplinary dimensions. Forensic analysis not only provides the information of evidential value but also enhances the support to the justice delivery system. The technological advances have introduced new investigative methods. Here, the admissibility of the evidence extracted from this scientific practice is a germane question that is frequently asked in the court of law. Further, before the evidence is considered, it is necessary to ensure that the technique has not violated any legal rights of an individual. This chapter reviews the status of legal frame work and issues related to the assessment of the admissibility and the probative value of the forensic evidence in the court of law.

J. Mishra
Department of Law, Deen Dayal Upadhyaya Gorakhpur University, Gorakhpur, Uttar Pradesh, India

S. Mishra
Department of Legal Studies, Dr Ram Manohar Lohiya National Law University, Lucknow, Uttar Pradesh, India

Amity Law School, Amity University Uttar Pradesh, Lucknow, Uttar Pradesh, India

A. Srivastava
School of Forensic Sciences, The West Bengal National University of Juridical Sciences, Kolkata, West Bengal, India
e-mail: ankitsrivastava@nujs.edu

K. A. Pandey (✉)
Department of Legal Studies, Dr Ram Manohar Lohiya National Law University, Lucknow, Uttar Pradesh, India
e-mail: ka_pandey@rmlnlu.ac.in

P. Shrivastava et al. (eds.), *Textbook of Forensic Science*,
https://doi.org/10.1007/978-981-99-1377-0_4

Keywords

Forensics · Criminal Justice System · Evidence · Fundamental rights · Admissibility of evidence

4.1 Introduction

The relationship between law and science has been a curious one and the law has traditionally tried to keep pace with the advances in science and technology, often failing at that and more often than not the former has followed the latter. The advances in science and technology have often facilitated wrongful activities with greater precision but at the same time, science and technology has also helped in better detection, investigation and prosecution of such wrongs. A better interface between the law and science and technology leads to better dispensation of justice. Law and forensic science have had a long cherished symbiotic relationship and the law as administered in the courts often derives strength and greater acceptability by looking up to forensic science. Proof of legal claims that the courts of law insist on can be made in many cases only by invoking what we call the principles of forensic science, i.e. by application of scientific methods and techniques. While, forensic science has greater application in detection and proof of crimes, its role is equally important in many other legal disputes such as paternity disputes, etc.

The role of forensic evidence such as DNA, Polygraph, Ballistics, Fingerprints and Toxicology in the process of administration of justice has often proved that scientific investigation of crime with the aid of forensic science has more probative value than direct evidence in deciding cases. In majority of cases where forensic evidence has been used, greater rate of conviction is witnessed.

4.2 Forensic Science: Role and Importance

The word 'forensic' is derived from a Latin word *forensis* which means relating to 'court of law' or of 'public debate or discussion'. According to the Oxford companion of law, forensic science means '... branch of science concerned with the application of scientific knowledge for legal purposes'. According to the Oxford Dictionary, the forensics means, 'scientific tests or techniques used in connection with the detection of crime'. The Cambridge dictionary defines it as 'scientific methods of solving crimes that involve examining objects or substances related to a crime'. In other words, we can say that forensic science is a scientific discipline for identification and evaluation of physical evidence by the application of the methods and principle of natural science for the purpose of administration of justice. In legal terminology it may mean the science which deals with the principles and practice of different branches of science which help to clear the doubtful question before the courts. It is a science composing of those matters which may be considered as common ground to both the scientist and legal practitioners. Use of science to detect truth is not new, it is as old as the society; but with the changing of society's behaviour the methods of scientific uses are also transformed. The help of science to discover the truth is available and used across the globe.

Forensic science has remarkable contribution in administering justice in criminal investigation and others serious violations. Evidence which is used in courts and which is arrived at by scientific or technical means is called forensic evidence. Forensics deals with the recovery and analysis of latent evidence. Latent evidence can take many forms, from fingerprints left on a window to DNA evidence recovered from blood stains to the files on a hard drive.

The carefully collected scientific information and test results establish a fact or truth at or before trial. The purpose of the scientific evidence is to help the court for arriving at a correct decision. It must be remembered that in criminal matters, the ultimate goal of all forensic science is to link the accused to a particular crime based on the physical sample obtained from the place of incidence with the help of scientific methods and analysis. Available scientific evidence can always link the culprit with crime, victim and place, etc. with certainty; it is free from feelings, bias, emotions, memory lapse, etc. The main purpose of scientific evidence is to provide the information based on scientific result which is not capable of being interpreted by ordinary people or judges. In many cases, forensic science processes identify and compare the materials. They establish the presence or absence of a link between the crime and criminals. In the scientific investigation the investigator is most important person among all. In fact, his works determines the success or failure of the application of forensic evidence in the processing of a criminal case. If he fails to collect the relevant evidence correctly or is unable to provide accurate sample for comparisons the findings of a forensic scientist will not only be useless; but they will be misleading and even may help the culprit. Forensic science is not only useful in the conviction of accused but by the use of proper technique in evidence collection we can save an innocent who is falsely alleged in a criminal activity.

Forensic evidence can mainly help in two ways: first, in specific terms which is related to the presence of suspect or accused; second, one which is of general nature and does not associate with a particular person. For example, if a shoe is recovered from the place of incident, the scientific test will demonstrate type of footmarks; but the recovery of semen-stained cloths from the place of incident may point towards a particular person present on the crime scene.

4.3 Expert Evidence and Forensic Science

The closest interaction between forensic science and law is to be found in the Indian Evidence Act, 1872 (hereinafter IEA) which recognises an expert's testimony on certain facts on which the court must form an opinion. Interestingly, generally, the law of evidence does not allow any person to give his or her opinion on facts under consideration by the court of law. Every witness is a witness of fact and not allowed to give opinion upon it. However, it may be that on certain facts of scientific nature, the presiding judge is not experienced in the concerned area and needs assistance to form an opinion on it. The law, therefore, as an exception to the general rule against admissibility of opinion evidence, allows an expert to proffer their opinion on technical and scientific matters. But how do we know that a person is an expert and qualified to give evidence on a fact related to the area of their expertise? Most experts are professionally qualified with years of experience in their field, and so their expertise will not be questioned.[1] But there may be cases where expertise may be acquired unconventionally.[2] The law does not insist on a professional qualification for an expert and anyone who has acquired special skills and knowledge through education, training or practise may be called as an expert. In *R* v. *Silverlock*[3] the solicitor of the prosecution was permitted to give evidence as a handwriting expert because he had acquired the expertise by giving considerable attention and studying handwriting over a period of more than a decade, although it was not his professional work. Similarly, in *R* v. *Stockwell*[4] an artist working in the field of medicine and life sciences whose job was to compare photographs and prepare pictorial illustrations of the essentials of anatomical features and surgical operations, was allowed to give expert opinion as a facial mapping expert. His evidence was declared admissible as he had gained sufficient experience in the field and the expert opinion was crucial for arriving at a conclusion which would not have otherwise been possible. The Indian law has not deviated from the English practice and no 'formal qualification' is required for an expert to testify in a particular field of knowledge where he has gained sufficient experience.

That opinion of an expert is relevant and the answer to the question 'who is an expert' is to be found in Section 45 of the IEA.[5] Indian Supreme Court has also said

---

[1] Alan Taylor, Principles of Evidence, (Cavendish Publishing Limited, London, 2nd ed., 2000) at 396.

[2] Ibid.

[3] [1894] 2QB 766.

[4] (1993) 97 Cr App R 260.

[5] Opinions of experts. – When the Court has to form an opinion upon a point of foreign law or of science, or art, or as to identity of handwriting, or finger impressions, the opinions upon that point of persons specially skilled in such foreign law, science or art, or in questions as to identity of handwriting or finger impressions are relevant facts.

Such persons are called experts.

Illustrations

(a) The question is, whether the death of A was caused by poison.

The opinions of experts as to the symptoms produced by the poison by which A is supposed to have died, are relevant.

(b) The question is, whether A, at the time of doing a certain act, was, by reason of unsoundness of mind, incapable of knowing the nature of the act, or that he was doing what was either wrong or contrary to law.

The opinions of experts upon the question whether the symptoms exhibited by A commonly show unsoundness of mind, and whether such unsoundness of mind usually renders persons incapable of knowing the nature of the acts which they do, or of knowing that what they do is either wrong or contrary to law, are relevant.

that no formal qualification is required for an expert. Obviously, a person who throws light on complex issues relating to science is called an expert. A person may be an expert in medical science, forensic science or ballistic science or any other branch of science or art. An expert is a person who by his experience, training and education has obtained superior knowledge about the subject in which he/she is testifying. The expert has peculiar knowledge or skill in a particular subject and such knowledge or skill is not common to all. The court of law, before admitting any of the opinions made by an expert, needs to ensure that the person is an expert according to the said provision of law.

The requirements for the admissibility of expert evidence are:

- The expert must be from within a recognised field of expertise;
- The expert's evidence must be based on reliable principles; and
- The expert must be qualified in that discipline.[6]

4.4 Forensic Science As a Tool in Administration of Justice

Under the IEA, 'evidence can be given only of relevant facts and facts in issue'.[7] A fact may be relevant but not necessarily admissible; also, a document may be relevant but not necessarily admissible. It may also be possible that a document or an expert report may be admissible but it will not be accepted by the court. Therefore, owing to its relevancy, the principles of relevancy and admissibility are equally applicable to the forensic evidence in India.[8]

The admissibility of scientific evidence is governed by several other Indian legislations as well such as the Code of Criminal Procedure, 1973 (CrPC),[9] the Identification of Prisoner Act, 1920. These legislations have some provision on admissibility and relevancy of scientific evidence. As mentioned earlier, the scientific evidence must pass the relevancy and admissibility test under the IEA. Therefore, generally, admissible and acceptable scientific evidence form part of the study of forensic science. Facts relating to forensic medicine and forensic science may be relevant, inter alia, under:

(c) The question is, whether a certain document was written by A. Another document is produced which is proved or admitted to have been written by A.

The opinions of experts on the question whether the two documents were written by the same person or by different persons, are relevant.

[6] *Ramesh Chandra Agrawal* v. *Regency Hospital Ltd.*, (2009) 9 SCC 709.

[7] Section 5, IEA.

[8] For a detailed discussion on relevancy and admissibility of facts, meaning of facts and facts in issue, see Kumar Askand Pandey, Vepa P. Sarathi's Law of Evidence, (Eastern Book Co., Lucknow, 8th ed. 2021).

[9] See Sections 291-293, 311A.

- Section 7 of the IEA as to 'cause or effect' of a relevant fact. This may include effects of poison, asphyxia, gunshot wounds, rigor mortis, etc.
- Section 9 of the IEA, i.e. 'identity of anything or person' or 'fixing the time or place in which any relevant fact happened'. Fingerprints, footprints, handwriting, polygraph test, narco-analysis test, DNA test, blood test, ballistics, cause and time of death, autopsy and fixing the age, etc. come under this provision.
- Section 14 of the IEA as to 'state of mind or bodily feeling'.[10]

The primarily requirement for an expert evidence to be admissible is that the evidence must be rendered by the expert himself. The test is that the matter is outside the knowledge and experience of the lay person. Thus, there is a need to hear an expert opinion where there is a scientific issue to be settled. The scientific question involved is assumed to be not within the court's knowledge. Thus, cases where the science involved is highly specialised and perhaps even mysterious, central role of expert cannot be disputed. Therefore, the expert opinion performs an important role in arriving at legitimate conclusion. The reliability of the opinion of expert depends on the facts upon which it is based and the validity of the process by which the conclusion is reached. Thus, the importance of an opinion is decided based on the credibility of the expert and the relevant facts supporting the opinion, so that its accuracy can be cross checked. Therefore, the emphasis has been on the data on the basis of which opinion is formed and the same is clear from following inference: Mere assertion without mentioning the data or basis is not evidence, even if it is produced by expert. Where the experts give no real data in support of their opinion, the evidence although admissible, may be excluded from consideration as affording no assistance in arriving at the correct value.[11]

Section 67 of the IEA provides, inter alia, that if a document is alleged to be signed by any person, the signature must be proved to be in his handwriting. Sections 45 and 47 of the said Act, prescribe a method in which such signature can be proved. Under Section 45, the opinion of the handwriting expert is relevant while under Section 47 the opinion of any person acquainted with the handwriting of the person who is alleged to have signed the document is admissible. Section 73 of the IEA provides for ascertainment of the disputed seal and signature through the process of comparison. Under this section, the court has the power to compare the writings and adjudicate the matter accordingly.

Expert opinion on any technical matter may be considered, but it is purely discretionary. The court, if it deems fit, may not require any expert opinion for arriving at a conclusion. For example, in the matter of pollution control, it is not necessary that for determination of the question of forest land, any latest technology should be used when the technology already in use is adequate to make an accurate

[10] V. Nageswara Rao, The Indian Evidence Act, (LexisNexis, Gurgaon, 2nd ed. 2015).

[11] *Ramesh Chandra Agrawal* v. *Regency Hospital Ltd.*, (2009) 9 SCC 709.

assessment. It has been observed that expert opinion affirming infringement of the copyright in a musical composition was relevant and admissible in evidence.[12]

Let us now look into some specific instances where forensic scientist's or medical expert's opinion is often resorted to and the jurisprudence thereof.

4.4.1 Opinion of Handwriting Expert

In connection with the ascertainment of hand writing, it is stated that if the court must form an opinion as to the person by whom any document was written or signed, the opinion of any person acquainted with the handwriting of the person by whom it is supposed to be written or signed that it was or was not written or signed by that person, is a relevant fact.[13]

Under both the Sections 45 and 47, the evidence of expert is an opinion; in the former, it can be proved by scientific method with the help of experts; and in the latter, it can be proved based on third person opinion bestowing to their familiarity resulting from frequent observations and experience. A Witness is said to be acquainted with the handwriting of accused if he has much familiarity with the writings of accused, one who had not seen the accused person's writing so much or in such a way as to become familiar with their writings could not be said to be really acquainted with the handwritings of the accused.

4.4.2 Evidence of Seal and Signature

When the signature, writing or seal of a person is in dispute, to find out the fact whether a signature, writing or seal is that of the person by whom it purports to have been written or made, any signature, writing or seal admitted or proved to the satisfaction of the court to have been written or made by that person may be compared with the one which is to be proved, although that signature, writing or seal has not been produced or proved for any other purpose. The court may direct any person present in the court to write any words or figures for the purpose of enabling the court to compare the words or figures so written with any words or figures alleged to have been written by such person.[14] Under Section 73 of the IEA, a court can satisfy itself about the handwriting of the accused either by asking the accused to write the words in the court, or to obtain a fresh opinion of the expert. Under Section 67 of the IEA, 'If a document is alleged to be signed or to have been written wholly or in part by any person, the signature or the handwriting of so much

[12] *Ram Sampath* v. *Rajesh Roshan*, 2008 SCC Online Bom. 370.

[13] Section 47, IEA.

[14] Section 73, IEA.

of the document as is alleged to be in that person's handwriting must be proved to be in his handwriting'.[15]

It is important to note that Section 311 A of the CrPC empowers a magistrate to direct any person to give specimen of signature or handwriting for the purpose of investigation and proceeding.

4.4.3 Evidence of Fingerprint and Footprint Impression

With necessary modifications Section 45 of IEA applies also, to the identity of finger impressions. The IEA provides several modes of proving a finger-impression, such as:

1. By the opinion of a person especially skilled in the science/study of finger impressions, like an expert under Section 45 of IEA.
2. By the evidence of a person who has actually seen the person thumb-marking on a document, which then become relevant under Section 60 of IEA.
3. By the court comparing the finger impression of a person with his admitted or proved finger-impressions under Section 73, IEA.

Under Section 4 of the Identification of Prisoner Act, 1920, a police officer is competent to take fingerprints of the accused. Section 5 of the said Act lays down that if a Magistrate is satisfied that for the purposes of any investigation or proceeding it is expedient to direct any person to allow his measurements or photograph to be taken, he may make an order to that effect, and in that case the person to whom the order relates shall be produced or shall attend at the time and place specified in the order and shall allow his measurements or photograph to be taken, as the case may be, by a police officer. The above provision of said section is not mandatory but is directory and to eliminate the possibility of fabrication of evidence it was eminently desirable that they were taken before or under the order of a Magistrate.[16] However, the mere absence of magisterial order authorising the collection of fingerprint evidence will not be termed illegal.[17] Thus, there cannot be any hard and fast rule that in every case, there should be a magisterial order for lifting the fingerprints of the accused.[18]

Under the now repealed Prevention of Terrorism Act, 2002, the Chief Metropolitan Magistrate or the Chief Judicial Magistrate was authorised to record the statement, if any, made by the person produced before it and get his signature or finger-impression.[19]

---

[15] Section 67, IEA.

[16] Section 5, Identification of Prisoner Act, 1920.

[17] *Mohd.Aman* v. *State of Rajasthan*, (1997) 10 SCC 44.

[18] *Sonvir* v. *State (NCT) of Delhi*, (2018) 8 SCC 24.

[19] Section 32 (5), Prevention of Terrorism Act, 2002.

It must be noted that with some modification Section 45, IEA applies to footprints as well. Obviously, the word 'measurement' in Identification of Prisoners Act, 1920 also includes footprints. The evidence of footprint is quite relevant to investigation and can help in tracing the offender as in almost every crime offender must leave some impressions of footprint or shoeprint at the crime scene. These impressions should be collected by investigator very cautiously and these impressions can be examined by a forensic analyst and used to identify the culprit. Just like fingerprints, the footprint of every individual is unique due to the difference in ridges and patterns and can be used for identification. However, there are some obvious drawbacks in footprints impressions' analysis viz. when a footprint is made by a person with dirty shoes who walked on the dirty floor; they are not visible to the naked eye. Footprint analysis itself is a difficult and time-consuming task and the available database on the footprints may not provide a match. The accuracy of these results is debated and therefore, there are apprehensions in relying on the evidence in the courts. The science of identification of the footprints or sole print has not yet reached the stage of an exact science. The fact that the foot marks tallied with those of the accused means no more than that these marks were made by shoes of a size corresponding to the size of the shoes of the accused. There may be a large number of shoes of the size of the shoes of the accused in the area.[20] Further, the science of identification of footprint is not a fully developed science and, therefore the conclusions as to the identity of a culprit may not be arrived at based on such evidence.[21]

As the biological constitution of every person is distinct so the fingerprint impression of everyone has a distinct character. Opinion of a fingerprint expert has been held to be more reliable than a handwriting expert. Unlike the science of comparison of handwriting, the science of fingerprint expert is almost perfect. It cannot be laid down as a rule of law that it is unsafe to have the conviction on the sole ground of uncorroborated testimony of fingerprint expert; however, caution is the best rule. The value of opinion of fingerprint expert has same value as any other expert. In the *Jaspal Singh case*[22] the Supreme Court has held that the science of identifying thumb impression is an exact science and does not admit of any mistake or doubt and a conviction can be based on the opinion of thumb-impression expert. It was also held that as a prudent rule a court of law must not play the role of a fingerprint expert. In every case where the fingerprint is a crucial piece of circumstantial evidence, the court must take the help of fingerprint expert. To ascertain whether a finger-impression is that of the person it is said to be, any finger-impression of that person may be compared with the former impression, although that impression has not been produced or proved for any other purpose. The court may also direct any person to be present in court and to make a finger impression for

[20] *Bharat Bhandari* v. *State (Govt. of NCT of Delhi)*, Crl.A.227/2011, decided on 3 August 2012.

[21] *Mohd.Aman Babu Khan* v. *State of Rajasthan*, AIR 1997 SC 2960.

[22] *Jaspal Singh* v. *State of Punjab*, AIR 1979 SC 1708.

the purpose of enabling the court to compare the impression so made, with any impression alleged to be finger impression of such person.[23]

The IEA makes facts, not otherwise relevant, relevant if they support or are inconsistent with the opinions of experts, when such opinions are relevant.[24] When there was no clarity in the process adopted by the investigating agency for lifting fingerprints from the scene of crime and further analysis made thereafter, the Supreme Court said that no reliance can be placed on report that the lifted fingerprints from the glasses matched with the sample fingerprints of the accused.[25]

4.4.4 Medical Evidence

The medical opinion of an expert has great bearing on and is of great assistance in the trial of criminal cases. It greatly helps the prosecution in establishing its case by soliciting corroboration from it by showing that the injuries could have been caused by the alleged weapon of offence by the accused person in the manner alleged. It may also help the accused to prove his innocence in the alleged case. The accused persons with the assistance of medical evidence try to demolish the prosecution story by showing that the offence could not have been caused by the alleged weapon of offence or the death could not have occurred in the manner alleged by the prosecution. The medical evidence play a huge part in proving the guilt of the accused and lead the investigating authorities to the truth. 'Medical evidence' means a proof given by medical expert, which is based on his scientific knowledge skill and personal experience. These evidence are corroborative in nature and do not necessarily prevail over testimony of an eye-witness, unless such testimony is invalidated.

With the aid of medical examination through the process of scientific evaluation, the courts can take the help of experts to form an opinion on issues such as identification of person, examination of cause of death, type of assaults, wound, injuries, ascertaining sexual matters, state of poisoning, rape, age, consent, etc. A medical professional witness who performs a post-mortem examination or examination of the injuries is also a 'witness of fact' although he also 'gives an opinion' on certain aspects of the case. Whether the injuries are anti-mortem or post-mortem, the probable weapon used in causing injuries, the effect of injuries, consequences of injuries, whether they are sufficient in the ordinary course of nature to cause death, the duration of injuries and the probable time of death, cause of death, plea of unsoundness of mind, determination of age, etc. may be proved and done with the help of scientific evidence. On these aspects, the court may not have any expertise and must rely on the opinion of the scientific expert.

Collection of medical evidence may be crucial and critical in many cases under the IPC, e.g. to determine the case of murder, to prove rape or to prove acid attack or

[23] *State of Uttar Pradesh* v. *Ram Babu Mishra,* AIR 1980 SC 791.

[24] Section 46, IEA.

[25] *Hari Om* v. *State of Uttar Pradesh*, (2021) 4 SCC 345.

causing of grievous hurt with a corrosive substance, etc. Chemical examination and the consequent result may be crucial under the Narcotic Drugs and Psychotropic Substances Act, 1985; state of pregnancy for the purpose of termination under the Medical Termination of Pregnancy Act, 1971. The CrPC contains several provisions related to the medical examination of accused and victim. These are only few illustrative legislations under which the scientific evidence assumes great importance in determination of rights and liabilities.

However, it is to be noted that any medical evidence does not itself prove the case; its value is only corroborative. It can only prove that the injuries could or could not have been caused in the manner alleged and the death could or could not have been caused by the injuries. It is well settled that the medical jurisprudence is not an exact science and it is indeed difficult for any doctor to say with precision and exactitude as to when a particular injury was caused and the time when sexual intercourse took place. The evidence of an expert is merely an opinion which may lend corroboration to the direct evidence. It is well settled that medical evidence is only opinion evidence.[26] If the opinions of two competent experts conflict on a particular point, the court ought to accept that opinion which is not in conflict with the direct evidence. Since witnesses are the eyes and ears of justice a court is not entitled to discard the direct evidence of credible witnesses deposing to thing observed by their own eyes, merely on the opinion of medical evidence.[27] Where the opinion of a medical witness is contradicted by another medical witness both of whom are equally competent to form an opinion, the court should normally accept the evidence of the medical witness whose evidence is corroborated by direct evidence.[28]

4.4.5 Medical Examination of Accused

Under the scheme of CrPC, an emphatic recognition of medical evidence is to be found in Sect. 53. The law says that if an offence is committed and the medical examination of the accused is likely to bring out evidence of commission of the offence or its nature, it is lawful for a registered medical practitioner or anyone acting in his aid and in good faith to conduct medical examination of the accused upon a request made by a police officer, not below the rank of a sub-inspector. This section specifies and explains that that the medical examination so conducted shall include examination of biological material collected from the person of the accused by using modern and scientific techniques including DNA profiling o any other test deemed necessary by the examining medical practitioner. It has been held that the import of the expression 'examination of the person' cannot be confined only to external

[26] *Ram Dev* v. *State of Uttar Pradesh,* 1995 Supp. (1) SCC 547.

[27] *Piara Singh* v. *State of Punjab*, AIR 1977 SC 2274.

[28] Ibid.

examination of the body of the person.[29] It has been a practice of the police to subject an accused of rape to potency test. However, it may be noted that enlarging the definition of rape after the Criminal Law (Amendment) Act, 2013 has rendered such test unnecessary as the present definition of rape is not confined to mere peno-vaginal intercourse. Even inserting any body part or a foreign object in the vagina, anus, urethra or inserting penis in the mouth of the victim shall constitute the offence of rape.

Interestingly, medical examination of the accused who is arrested by the police is now mandatory after substitution of Section 54 of CrPC with a new provision through the Code of Criminal Procedure (Amendment) Act, 2008.[30] The object of the earlier provision was to enable the accused to dissociate him from the alleged offence or to show that some other person may have committed the offence in question. The provision in its present form does not explicitly spell out these objectives, however, even under the present provision, a medical examination may help the accused the way earlier provision did.

4.4.6 Medical Examination in Sexual Assault Cases

We have seen that medical examination of an accused for the purposes of effective investigation of a criminal charge has received a wider meaning by the Criminal Law (Amendment) Act, 2005 whereby numerous provisions were added in the CrPC for the medical examination of accused. Section 53 A of the CrPC provides for the procedure for medical examination of accused of rape: 'When a person is arrested on a charge of committing an offence of rape or an attempt to commit rape and there are reasonable grounds for believing that an examination of arrested person will afford evidence as to the commission of such offence, it shall be lawful for a registered medical practitioner employed in a hospital run by the Government or by a local authority and in the absence of such a practitioner within the radius of 16 kms. from the place where the offence has been committed by any other registered medical practitioner, acting at the request of a police officer not below the rank of a sub-inspector, and for any person acting in good faith in his aid and under his direction, to make such an examination of the arrested person and to use such force as is reasonably necessary for that purpose'.

By way of Criminal Law (Amendment) Act, 2005,[31] provisions have been made for medical examination of a rape victim within 24 hours of the report of the incident. Medical examination so conducted may afford crucial piece of scientific evidence that shall be irrefutable in connecting the accused to the crime. The doctor conducting the medical examination shall be an important prosecution witness and the result of the medical examination will invariably be relied upon by the

[29] *Anil Anantrao* v. *State*, 1981 Cri LJ 125.

[30] Act 5 of 2009.

[31] Act 25 of 2005.

prosecution in proving its case. For the medical examination of such woman, it is necessary that her consent should be taken. Without the consent of the woman or any other person competent to give consent on her behalf, the medical examination shall be rendered unlawful.[32]

The medical examination of both the accused and the victim under Sections 53 A and 164 A of CrPC, respectively, shall include the examination of blood, blood stains, semen, swabs in case of sexual offences, sputum and sweat, hair samples and finger nail clippings using modern and scientific techniques including DNA profiling and such other tests which the registered medical practitioner thinks necessary in a particular case.

It should be noted that in a primitive practice, the rape survivors were subjected to what is known as 'two-finger test'. This test, it was believed, would lead to an inference whether the survivor was sexually active or not. In a land mark judgment *Lillu* v. *State of Haryana*[33] the Supreme Court deprecated the practice of subjecting the rape victims to 'two-finger test', holding that 'rape survivors are entitled to legal recourse that does not re-traumatize them or violate their physical or mental integrity and dignity' and declared the 'two-finger test' inhuman, cruel and degrading and thereby outlawed the same.

4.4.7 Identification of Persons Through DNA

In many legal disputes, identification of a person assumes great importance and in some other, identity of a corpse may be a controverted fact. The discovery of deoxyribonucleic acid (DNA) has made the most significant contribution in the identification process. DNA is unique in every individual and therefore, the DNA technology is widely resorted to and legally recognised across jurisdictions for establishing identity. DNA profiling not only assists in identifying the victims but also establishes the identity of the perpetrators mainly by the recovered biological substance from the person of the victim or accused or from the crime scene.

The identification of individuals by the aid of DNA test is considered to be an errorless process, provided that the samples are collected in the scientific manner and a proper chain of custody is maintained. It has been pointed out by the Supreme Court that after the incorporation of Section 53A in the CrPC, it has become necessary for the prosecution to go for DNA test in appropriate cases which would facilitate the prosecution to prove its case against the accused.[34]

To make DNA based forensic evidence more reliable and helpful in the justice delivery system of the country the government of India has proposed DNA Technology (Use and Application) Regulation Bill, 2019 for the purpose of establishing identity of missing persons, victims, offenders, under trials and unknown deceased

[32] Section 164 A, CrPC.

[33] (2013) 14 SCC 643.

[34] *State of Gujarat* v. *Kishanbhai*, (2014) 5 SCC 108.

persons. The primary intended purpose of Bill is for expanding the application of DNA based forensic technologies to solving crime. The Bill seeks to ensure that there is also the assurance that the DNA test result is reliable and furthermore that the data remain protected from misuse or abuse in terms of the privacy right of the citizens. Establishment of national and regional DNA data banks and DNA regulatory board will assist in forensic investigation.[35]

4.4.8 The Deception Detection Tests

Scientific advancements have led to discovery of many tests which are widely used during investigation of offences and their result are sought to be made part of the charge-sheet filed by the police after completing investigation. It is beyond the scope of this chapter to discuss the scientific and technical aspects of these tests commonly known as Deception Detection Tests (DDTs) which include brain mapping, polygraph and narco-analysis tests. However, subjecting the accused or a suspect to these DDTs often raise questions of legal and constitutional importance.[36] The results obtained by conducting brain mapping, polygraph, narco-analysis or similar other tests have no substantial evidentiary value, i.e. the test results cannot be acted on by the court in drawing an inference about the guilt or innocence of the accused except for corroboration.

4.4.9 Ballistic Science

In criminal cases, the main purpose of the science of fire arms is to establish the distance from where the shot was fired, the direction from which it was fired, the approximate time since when the weapon was last fired, and whether the wounds caused were accidental, suicidal or homicidal and whether a given bullet or cartridge was used in a particular weapon. The range from which a shot has been fired is usually of the utmost value to the investigating officer and to the courts. It may assist in verifying a statement made by the accused or a witness, or may be of value in deciding whether a wound could be self-inflicted. In *Santokh Singh* v. *State of Punjab*[37] the Supreme Court ruled out suicide where the ballistic report pointed out that the shot was not fired from point-blank range.

Firearms identification is now a well-known subject of expert testimony. It is of immense help to the court in adjudicating that a certain bullet was fired from specified gun and with the approximate distance and side. Such testimony is based on an established scientific principle that each arms has its own impact and they

[35] https://pib.gov.in/Pressreleaseshare.aspx?PRID=1577738 (last visited on 12 July 2021).

[36] Math, Suresh Bada. 'Supreme Court judgment on polygraph, narco-analysis & brain-mapping: a boon or a bane'. The Indian journal of medical research vol. 134,1 (2011): 4-7.

[37] (2010) 8 SCC 784.

leave different marks and pattern. Firearms identification is subject of scientific research, and a proper field of expert testimony. In a leading case underlying the importance of ballistic expert's evidence and acquitting the accused, the Court said that 'In cases where injuries are caused by firearms, the opinion of the ballistic expert is of a considerable importance where both the firearm and the crime cartridge were recovered during investigation to connect an accused with the crime. Failure to produce the expert opinion before the trial court in such cases affects the creditworthiness of the prosecution case to a great extent'.[38]

It is necessary that in the collection process of articles the police officer investigating the case must be cautious of all facts, circumstances and recovery of physical things. Seal and seizure of cartridge and firearms should be done with proper prudence. Delay in sending articles for examination of recovered substances diminishes the value of opinion. In a case court acquitted the accused and stated that it was not safe to place reliance on the report of the ballistic expert because it was an admitted fact that the empty cartridges which were sent to the ballistic expert after six months were not sealed at the time of seizure.[39] Interestingly, when there is no other evidence to convict the accused, acquittal may be recorded based on the ballistic expert's report. Normally, when the evidence of the eyewitnesses is in contradiction with medical evidence and ballistic expert's report, the accused would be acquitted.

4.5 Cyber Forensics

In an era when criminal activities in cyber space are on a rise, cyber forensics has assumed great significance and importance in detection and prosecution of crime.

Conventional crimes are also committed in more sophisticated manner through computers in which case traditional methods of investigation may not be of any help in bringing the accused to book. Cyber criminals who are tech savvy and well versed with the technological knowhow may evade detection and identification if subjected to traditional investigative methods. New age crimes require new age methods for their detection and investigation and development of cyber forensics has provided powerful tool in the hands of the law enforcement agencies and the judiciary.

The cyber forensics or computer forensics focuses on digital evidence by involving data acquisition, preservation and recovery of potential data related to a particular case. Digital evidence is defined as information and data of value to an investigation that is stored on, received or transmitted by an electronic device and this valuable evidence can be acquired when electronic devices are seized and secured with care, for examination. The computer forensics works to find out digital evidence, such evidence required to establish whether a crime has been committed and by whom. It may be defined as the discipline that combines elements of law and

[38] *Sukhwant Singh* v. *State of Punjab*, (1995) 3 SCC 367.

[39] *State of M.P.* v. *Ghudan*, (2003) 12 SCC 485.

computer science to collect and analyse data from computer systems, networks, wireless communications, and storage devices in a way that is admissible as evidence in a court of law.[40] In other words, computer forensics is the collection of tool and techniques used to find evidence in a computer.[41] From a technical standpoint, the main goal of computer forensics is to identify, collect, preserve, and analyse data in a way that preserves the integrity of the evidence collected so that it can be used effectively in a legal case. Cyber forensics involves the procedure of preservation, collection, validation, identification, analysis, interpretation, documentation, presentation of computer evidence stored in a computer.

There are some typical aspects of a computer forensics investigation such as those who investigate computers must understand the kind of potential evidence they are looking for to structure their search. Second, the investigator must pick the appropriate tools to use. Files may have been deleted, damaged, or encrypted, and the investigator must be familiar with an array of methods and software to prevent further damage in the recovery process. Two basic types of data are collected in computer forensics known as Persistent data and Volatile data. Persistent data is the data that is stored on a hard drive (or another medium) and is preserved when the computer is turned off. Volatile data is any data, which is stored in memory, or exists in transit, that will be lost when the computer loses power or is turned off. Volatile data resides in registries, cache, and random-access memory (RAM). Since volatile data is ephemeral, it is essential an investigator knows reliable ways to capture it.

Proof of electronic record is a special provision introduced by the IT Act that amended various provisions under the IEA. The Sections 65 A and 65 B of IEA prescribe the rule of admissibility of the electronic record in the court. The electronic records may be proved by producing the original computer resource as primary evidence or as secondary evidence in accordance with Section 65 B of the IEA. The special provisions on admissibility of evidence relating to electronic record shall that as prescribed in Section 65 B of the IEA. It is also provided in Section 45 A of the IEA that when in a proceeding, the court has to form an opinion on any matter relating to any information transmitted or stored in any computer resource or any other electronic or digital form, the opinion of the 'examiner of electronic evidence' is a relevant fact. An examiner of electronic record shall be an expert within the meaning of Section 45 of the IEA.

The most crucial questions that have come up for consideration before the courts in India relate to the condition of admissibility of electronic evidence. For more than a decade, it seems, even the Supreme Court did not give any weigh to the special provisions of the IEA exclusively dealing with admissibility of electronic evidence. For example, in the *Parliament attack case*[42] the Supreme Court held that call details record (CDR) are admissible as secondary evidence even without compliance with

[40] https://us-cert.cisa.gov/sites/default/files/publications/forensics.pdf (last visited on 15 July 2021).

[41] https://www.certconf.org/presentations/2006/files/WD4.pdf (last visited on 15 July 2021).

[42] *State (NCT of Delhi)* v. *Navjot Sandhu*, (2005) 11 SCC 600.

Section 65 B of the IEA as the applicability of general provisions in the IEA to electronic records is not excluded.[43]

However, it is to be noted that the IEA prescribes procedural conditions for making electronic evidence admissible. The admissibility of a digital document, i.e. electronic record alternatively called a computer output, depends on the satisfaction of the four conditions as follows:[44]

1. The electronic record containing the information should have been produced by the computer during the period over which the same was regularly used to store or process information for the purpose of any activity regularly carried on over that period by the person having lawful control over the use of that computer;
2. The information of the kind contained in electronic record or of the kind from which the information is derived was regularly fed into the computer in the ordinary course of the said activity;
3. During the material part of the said period, the computer was operating properly and that even if it was not operating properly for some time, the break or breaks had not affected either the record or the accuracy of its contents; and
4. The information contained in the record should be a reproduction or derivation from the information fed into the computer in the ordinary course of the said activity.

Interestingly, when the original electronic record itself is produced before the court it is treated as a primary evidence and there is no need of any certificate but when any electronic record which is only a copy of the original digital document[45] is produced before the court as relevant, it is mandatory for the person in whose control the computer/communication device was, at the time data was fed/recorded in the computer/communication device or any other electronic storage medium, to produce a certificate as envisaged under Section 65 B of the IEA.

That a certificate is mandatory for admissibility of an electronic record was finally settled by the Supreme Court in *Arjun Panditrao Gorantyal* v. *Kailash Kushanrao Gorantyal*,[46] endorsing the earlier decision of the Supreme Court in *Anvar P.V.* v. *P. K. Basheer*[47] and disagreeing with the decision in *Shafhi Mohammad* v. *State of Himachal Pradesh*,[48] where it was held that as the requirement of certificate pertains to only a procedural aspect of admissibility, it shall not be insisted upon if the device from which the secondary electronic data has been produced was not under the

---

[43] See Kumar Askand Pandey, 'Appreciation of Electronic Evidence: A Critique of Judicial Approach', 6 RMLNLUJ (2014) 24.

[44] Section 65 B (2), IEA.

[45] Any information originally recorded in a computer that has been copied on an optical or magnetic media is secondary electronic record.

[46] (2020) 7 SCC 1.

[47] (2014) 10 SCC 734.

[48] (2018) 2 SCC 801.

control of the party intending to produce it in the court. The certificate, said the Supreme Court in *Anvar P.V.* v. *P.K. Basheer*[49]:

(a) Must describe the manner in which the electronic record was produced;
(b) Must furnish the particulars of the device involved in the production of that record;
(c) Must deal with the applicable conditions mentioned under Section 65B (2) of the IEA; and
(d) Must be signed by a person occupying a responsible official position in relation to the operation of the relevant device.

The Supreme Court further clarified that the person issuing a certificate need only say that the statement in the certificate is 'true to the best of his knowledge'. The Supreme Court has interpreted Sections 22A, 45A, 59, 65A & 65B of the IEA to hold that data in CD/DVD/Pen Drives or similar devices are not admissible without a certificate under Section 65B (4) of the IEA. It is now absolutely clear that in case of computer output without such a certificate, neither there can be oral evidence to prove the contents of the electronic evidence nor the opinion of the expert under Section 45A of the IEA could be resorted to prove the genuineness of the electronic evidence.[50]

4.6 Forensic Evidence and Rule Against Self Incrimination

The Indian Constitution contains an invaluable right against self-incrimination which prohibits testimonial compulsion.[51] In simple terms this right means that no one can be compelled to be a witness against himself. It is often argued that the procedure of conducting DDTs is violation of right against self-incrimination. It is quite possible that a person suspected or accused of a crime may have been compelled to testify through methods involving coercion, threats or inducements during the investigative stage. Also, involuntary statements are more likely to mislead the judge and the prosecutor, thereby resulting in miscarriage of justice. However, it must be noted that compelling an accused person to give his specimen handwriting or signature, or impressions of his fingers, palm or foot to the investigating officer or under orders of a court for the purpose of comparison do not incriminate the accused person, or even tend to do so. It has been held by

[49] (2014) 10 SCC 734.

[50] Kumar Askand Pandey, 'Appreciation of Electronic Evidence: A Critique of Judicial Approach', 6 RMLNLUJ (2014) 24, 38.

[51] See Article 20 (3): 'No person accused of any offence shall be compelled to be a witness against himself'. International Covenant on Civil and Political Rights (ICCPR) in Article 14 (3) (g) enumerates the minimum guarantees that are to be accorded during a trial and states that 'everyone has a right not to be compelled to testify against himself or to confess guilt'.

11-judge Constitution Bench of the Supreme Court that by giving these impressions or specimen handwriting, the accused person does not furnish evidence against him and the scope of right against self-incrimination is limited to 'personal testimony', i.e. conveying of information based on personal knowledge.[52] In a recent decision, the Supreme Court has said that a Judicial Magistrate can direct an accused to provide his voice samples for investigation even without his consent.[53] It must also be remembered that the right against self-incrimination applies only and exclusively to criminal cases and in a civil case, e.g. for establishing paternity, a person may be compelled by to provide his biological material for DNA test.[54]

In *Selvi* v. *State of Karnataka,*[55] the Supreme Court had an opportunity to look into the question of right against self-incrimination vis-à-vis DDTs and observed: 'Even though the actual process of undergoing a polygraph examination or a BEAP test is not the same as that of making an oral or written statement, the consequences are similar. By making inferences from the results of these tests, the examiner is able to derive knowledge from the subject's mind which otherwise would not have become available to the investigators. These two tests are different from medical examination and the analysis of bodily substances such as blood, semen and hair samples since the test subject's physiological responses are directly correlated to mental faculties. Through lie-detection or gauging a subject's familiarity with the stimuli, personal knowledge is conveyed in respect of a relevant fact. It is also significant that unlike the case of documents, the investigators cannot possibly have any prior knowledge of the test subject's thoughts and memories, either in the actual or constructive sense. Therefore, even if a highly-strained analogy were to be made between the results obtained from the impugned tests and the production of documents, the weight of precedents leans towards restrictions on the extraction of 'personal knowledge' through such means. In any case, the compulsory administration of the impugned tests impedes the subject's right to choose between remaining silent and offering substantive information. The requirement of a "positive volitional act" becomes irrelevant since the subject is compelled to convey personal knowledge irrespective of his/her own volition'. The Supreme Court also found the narco-analysis test to be intrusive and held that DDTs cannot be conducted without the consent of the accused or a suspect and such consent must be obtained before a Judicial Magistrate in the presence of their lawyer. Interestingly, considering the inherent invasive nature of polygraph tests and their likely misuse by the investigating agencies, the National Human Rights Commission (NHRC) had published 'Guidelines for the Administration of Polygraph Test (Lie Detector Test) on an Accused' in 2000. The Supreme Court has said that these guidelines

[52] *State of Bombay* v. *Kathi Kalu Oghad,* AIR 1961 SC 1808.

[53] *Ritesh Sinha* v. *State of U.P.,* (2019) 8 SCC 1.

[54] *Narayan Dutt Tiwari* v. *Rohit Shekhar,* (2012) 12 SCC 554.

[55] (2010) 7 SCC 263.

must be strictly followed and other DDTs should also comply with them. The salient features of the said guidelines are:

1. No Lie Detector Tests should be administered except when consented by the accused. An option should be given to the accused whether he wishes to avail such test.
2. If the accused volunteers for a Lie Detector Test, he should be given access to a lawyer and the physical, emotional and legal implication of such a test should be explained to him by the police and his lawyer.
3. The consent should be recorded before a Judicial Magistrate.
4. During the hearing before the Magistrate, the person alleged to have agreed should be duly represented by a lawyer.
5. At the hearing, the person in question should also be told in clear terms that the statement that is made shall not be a 'confessional' statement to the Magistrate but will have the status of a statement made to the police.
6. The Magistrate shall consider all factors relating to the detention including the length of detention and the nature of the interrogation.
7. The actual recording of the Lie Detector Test shall be done by an independent agency (such as a hospital) and conducted in the presence of a lawyer.
8. A full medical and factual narration of the manner of the information received must be taken on record.

4.7 Evidentiary Value of Expert's Opinion

The report given by a forensic expert is not substantive evidence and is inadmissible in evidence unless the expert is examined. If, however, the expert is dead or is not available for examination in court, under the circumstances mentioned in Section 32 of the IEA, the report is admissible and relevant. Where the expert who conducted the examination is not examined in court nor the report of expert is tendered in evidence, the same cannot be used as substantive evidence. Being an expert witness, his testimony has to be assigned great importance. However, there is no irrebuttable presumption that an expert is always a witness of truth; his testimony has to be evaluated and appreciated like the testimony of any other ordinary witness. The opinion of expert has only corroborative value. It has been held that a handwriting expert's evidence under Section 45 of IEA is only opinion evidence and it can rarely, if ever, take the place of substantive evidence. Before acting upon such evidence, it is usual to see if it is corroborated either by clear, direct evidence or by circumstantial evidence.[56] Similarly, opinion of a fingerprint expert is not substantive evidence and such opinion can only be used to corroborate some items of substantive evidence which are otherwise on record.[57]

[56] *Sashi Kumar Banerjee* v. *Subodh Kumar Banerjee*, AIR 1964 SC 529.

[57] *Hari Om* v. *State of Uttar Pradesh*, (2021) 4 SCC 345.

In *Palani* v. *State of T.N.*,[58] the Supreme Court has recently reiterated that oral evidence of an eye witness has to get primacy, and the medical evidence is basically opinionated and that the medical evidence states that the injury could have been caused in the manner alleged and nothing more. 'The opinion given by a medical witness need not be the last word on the subject', said the Supreme Court in *State of Haryana* v. *Bhagirath.*[59] It further added that 'Such an opinion shall be tested by the court. If the opinion is bereft of logic or objectivity, the court is not obliged to go by that opinion. After all opinion is what is formed in the mind of a person regarding a fact situation'.

However, corroboration may not invariably be insisted upon before acting on the opinion of a handwriting expert and there need be no initial suspicion. But, on the facts of a particular case, a court may require corroboration of a varying degree. There can be no hard and fast rule, but nothing will justify the rejection of the opinion of an expert supported by unchallenged reasons on the sole ground that it is not corroborated. The approach of a court while dealing with the opinion of a handwriting expert should be to proceed cautiously, probe the reasons for the opinion, consider all other relevant evidence and decide finally to accept or reject it.[60]

4.8 Conclusion

The scientific expert is a competent, reliable and dependable witness whose evidence inspires confidence. The scientific evidence is not an infallible one and cannot be placed on a higher pedestal than other evidence found credible by the court. Mere forensic evidence will not be sufficient to warrant conviction in criminal cases and at best such evidence may be used to test the veracity of the eyewitness. If the ocular evidence and forensic evidence are at variance, it is settled that the former shall be preferred provided that it inspires confidence.

There is no absolute rule of law or even of prudence which has developed into a rule of law that in no case can the court base its findings solely on the opinion of an expert; but the imperfect nature of the forensic evidence places onerous responsibility on the courts to exercise extra care and caution before acting on expert opinion. Before a court can place reliance on the opinion of an expert, it must be shown that he has not betrayed any bias and the reasons on which he has based his opinion are convincing and satisfactory. Reasons for the opinion must be carefully probed and examined. All other relevant evidence must be considered. In appropriate cases, corroboration must be sought. The sophistication with which crimes are committed nowadays and the primitive methods of investigation result in a very high rate of acquittal. Forensic science is a promising field of knowledge and its judicious uses in

[58] (2020) 16 SCC 401.

[59] (1999) 5 SCC 96.

[60] *Murari Lal* v. *State of M.P*, (1980) 1 SCC 704.

investigation shall certainly ensure qualitatively better justice dispensation. Utility of forensic science in administration of justice cannot be overemphasised but in a country governed by rule of law and constitutional principles, the forensic science has to conform to the legal norms for its acceptability.

Instruments and Techniques in Forensic Science

5

Annapoorni Ammal, Vijay Kumar Yadav, Kriti Nigam,
and Ankit Srivastava

Abstract

Instruments and techniques hold an immeasurable importance in the field of forensic science. Each branch of forensic science depends on various instruments and techniques to extract information of extreme value. This includes instruments that have been in use since ages to the recent advancements that enable to surpass the previous drawbacks. Techniques relevant in various fields are adopted and adapted to forensic science which until today has served many purposes. The basic building block of instrumentation and techniques includes chromatography, spectroscopy, and microscopy. Each of these techniques includes basic models as well as advanced models. Starting from column and (or) paper chromatography to recent advancements associated with gas chromatography, each of them uplifts the importance of the technique. By applying the basic principles of spectroscopy, a wide variety of instruments have been introduced into the arena, which enable to extract even the subtle information from evidence collected. This includes atomic spectroscopy and molecular spectroscopic techniques. Ultraviolet-visible spectroscopy, infrared spectroscopy, Raman spectroscopy, and nuclear magnetic

A. Ammal
Department of Forensic Science, Kristu Jayanti College (Autonomous), Bangalore, India

V. K. Yadav
Dr. APJ Abdul Kalam Institute of Forensic Science & Criminology, Bundelkhand University, Jhansi, India

K. Nigam
Department of Forensic Science, Jharkhand Raksha Shakti University, Ranchi, India

A. Srivastava (✉)
School of Forensic Sciences, The West Bengal National University of Juridical Sciences, Kolkata, West Bengal, India
e-mail: ankitsrivastava@nujs.edu

P. Shrivastava et al. (eds.), *Textbook of Forensic Science*,
https://doi.org/10.1007/978-981-99-1377-0_5

resonance spectroscopy has been covered deep in the chapter. Microscopic techniques such as compound, comparison, polarizing, fluorescence, stereo and electron microscopy will provide a clear idea about the technique as well as its application in forensic science. Apart from these three techniques, electrophoresis which holds its unique position in forensic investigation has been dealt in the end of the chapter. The chapter will provide a detailed insight into various tools and techniques used in forensic science at the same time their detailed application and future developmental possibilities.

Keywords

Chromatography · Gas chromatography · UV-visible spectroscopy · NMR spectroscopy · Raman spectroscopy · Electron microscopy · Electrophoresis · PAGE · Immunoelectrophoresis

5.1 Introduction

The heart of forensic science is the evidence we collect from various crime scenes and nearby regions. Any such evidence obtained plays a major role in drawing a conclusion about what really occurred during a crime. Every evidence whether seems relevant or irrelevant contributes to this conclusion. Once such evidence are collected by the forensic scientist, each and every part of it needs careful study and analysis. To seek out all the relevant information from evidence we bring in various instruments and method into our arena. They facilitate the comparison of our evidence as well as individualize them. It also backs us up in the court of testimony when questions related to our findings arise. Since the dawn of forensic science up to now, various developments have enabled us to analyze evidence with greater accuracy and is continuing to do so. A thorough knowledge about the principles and working of each instrument is adequate as the result of an analysis depends on the method employed to a greater extend. When it comes to the examination of those evidence in trace quantities, the method selected is of prime importance. Precise, more accurate and mainly non-destructive techniques should be used for the analysis of evidence since once destroyed it cannot be regained. Countless techniques and methods are adopted in this field for the study of diverse evidence. Before moving onto the world of these diverse techniques it is important to know the prime difference between a technique and a method. A technique is a scientific process that provides valuable information on the composition of a substance while a method applies the technique to solve a particular problem. Off the diverse techniques and methods used prime importance is given to four namely chromatography, microscopy, spectroscopy, and electrophoresis. This chapter will take you through the fundamental principles, instrumentation, and application of the above said techniques in the field of forensic science.

5.2 Chromatography

Chromatography can be considered a universal technique for separation which is extensively used now a day in the field of forensic science. When chemical evidence are obtained in trace or minor amount, it is the preferred method for the separation of the individual components of the system. The chemical as well as physical properties of various components in a sample vary which serves the basis for the separation. The accuracy with which the method separates the fractions from a multi-component mixture implies the reason for its wide use in the field. During the 1900, Mikhail Tsvet a Russian-Italian botanist combined the then existing practice of column fractionating with a paper filter technique to separate various plant pigments. As a result of his finding, he named the technique chromatography where "chroma" and "graphy" meant "color" and "writing," respectively, in Greek. Knowledge of certain terminology such as those mentioned below provides better understanding of the technique.

An analyte is the mixture that has been taken for separation and the colored band that appears as a result of chromatography is the chromatogram (Heftmann 2004). Chromatographic techniques make use of two types of phases namely the stationary phase and the mobile phase. The phase which is immobile and adhered to a support material or towards the walls of a column is called the stationary phase. The analyte to be separated get adsorbed onto the surface of this stationary phase and hence it is also called adsorbent, while a mobile phase moves over the stationary phase and in many cases carries the analyte along with it. Depending on various criteria, chromatography can be classified into different categories. Figure 5.1 clearly shows the classification of the technique on various basis. Based on the purpose of carrying out chromatography, it can be classified into preparative and analytical chromatography.

In preparative chromatography the components are separated and are employed for further purposes. Hence, the components purified by the method undergoes certain quantification process and (or) alternative procedures or applications. This requires the introduction of large amount of sample into the chromatographic system. Analytical chromatography aims at the separation of the analyte to identify

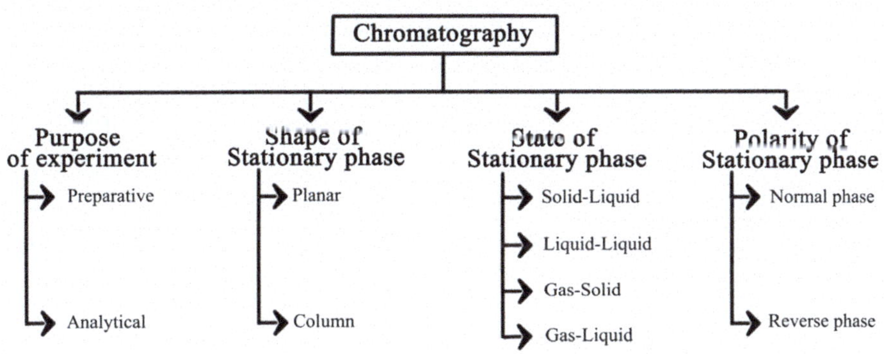

Fig. 5.1 Classification of chromatography

and quantify them. Hence, relatively small quantity of sample is required. Depending on the shape of the stationary phase it is either planar or column chromatography. Planar chromatography is when the stationary phase used is planar as in paper and thin layer chromatography. Column chromatography incorporates methods in which the stationary phase is packed within a tube or column and separation is achieved by making use of the variation in retention time of each component of the analyte as in HPLC and GC. When the physical state of the stationary phase is considered, chromatography can be divided into four main classes such as solid-liquid chromatography, liquid-liquid chromatography, gas-solid chromatography and gas-liquid chromatography as given in the table below.

Based on the polarity of the stationary phase the classification done is as normal phase and reverse phase chromatography. When the stationary phase is polar and mobile phase is non-polar the chromatography is called normal-phase chromatography. The component of the analyte which is polar in nature shows greater affinity towards the stationary phase and gets eluted slowly, while the non-polar component elutes out at a faster rate.

Stationary phase	Mobile phase	Chromatography
Solid	Liquid	Solid-liquid chromatography
Liquid	Liquid	Liquid-liquid chromatography
Gas	Solid	Gas-solid chromatography
Gas	Liquid	Gas-liquid chromatography

Reverse phase chromatography is when the polarity of the two phases is reversed such that mobile phase is polar, while the stationary phase is not.

The principle behind chromatography is that of selective distribution (Braithwaite and Smith 1999). When the mixture to be separated is distributed between the stationary phase and the mobile phase, the various components of the analyte get adsorbed onto the surface of the adsorbent in varying degrees depending on its affinity. Hence, component with greater affinity will be in an adsorbed state and those with less affinity are present in the mobile phase or is said to be in free state. Once the components are separated the time taken by each component to reach the detector is measured. This indicated the "retention time." By considering the retention time and the compound that reaches a detector corresponding peaks, patterns are generated and are plotted as the chromatogram. Once various components are separated, qualitative as well as quantitative analysis can be performed. The major classes of chromatography include:

1. Column chromatography
2. Thin layer chromatography
3. Paper chromatography
4. Gas chromatography
5. High performance liquid chromatography
6. High performance thin layer chromatography

5.2.1 Column Chromatography

Column chromatography is a separation technique developed by the American Petroleum Chemist D T Day in 1900 and by M S Tswelt in 1901. The technique is based on the principle of selective adsorption. It makes use of a chromatographic column where the stationary phase is packed intact. A mobile phase carries the analyte which then passes through the adsorbent in the column. Due to the interaction between the two phases separation of the components of the mixture takes place. During the process equilibrium is maintained in the concentration of the component of the analyte component in the mobile and stationary phase. This equilibrium constant called the partition coefficient is defined as the molar concentration of a substance in the stationary phase to that in the mobile phase. This can be expressed as:

$$\text{Partition Coefficient, } K = \frac{\text{Molar concentration of analyte in stationary phase}}{\text{Molar concentration of analyte in mobile phase}}$$

The sample to be separated is dissolved in a suitable solvent and is allowed to pass through a column packed. The widely used solvent includes light petroleum, cyclohexane, carbon disulfide, etc. The component that has the higher affinity towards the adsorbent is adsorbed in the upper part of the column. Depending on the decrease in affinity of components the individual fractions get adsorbed down the column. As a result, a band called the chromatogram is developed. Each portion occupies a well-defined region in the column known as the zone. The adsorbent is filled within a glass tube tapered at the bottom end called as the chromatographic column (Fig. 5.2). Depending on the complexity of the sample to be separated either successive elution or gradient elution is employed. If the sample is complex in nature a series of solutions are used to separate each component and is called successive elution. In successive elution, a component is dissolved in one solvent and the next solvent is introduced afterwards; while in gradient elution, a compound which is present at the interface of two separated components are eluted out. For these two, completely miscible liquids are used. After the separation of individual components, they can be detected by using various detectors including optical detectors, differential refractometers, flame ionization detectors, conductivity detectors and detectors based on heat of adsorption.

Column chromatography can be used for the separation of various drugs. Toxins from blood and tissue can be separated out by adopting this method. When two or more geometrical isomers are present within a sample, the technique helps in separating them. When the presence of steroids is detected in urine, they can be easily separated out using column chromatography. All different kinds of mixtures that are complex in nature can be separated as it provides a wide range of mobile phase to be used in the technique. A certain limit of sample for analysis is not decided for column chromatography as any amount of mixtures can be employed. It is considered one of the robust chromatographic methods and the solvents used for separation can be reused for the next round of chromatography.

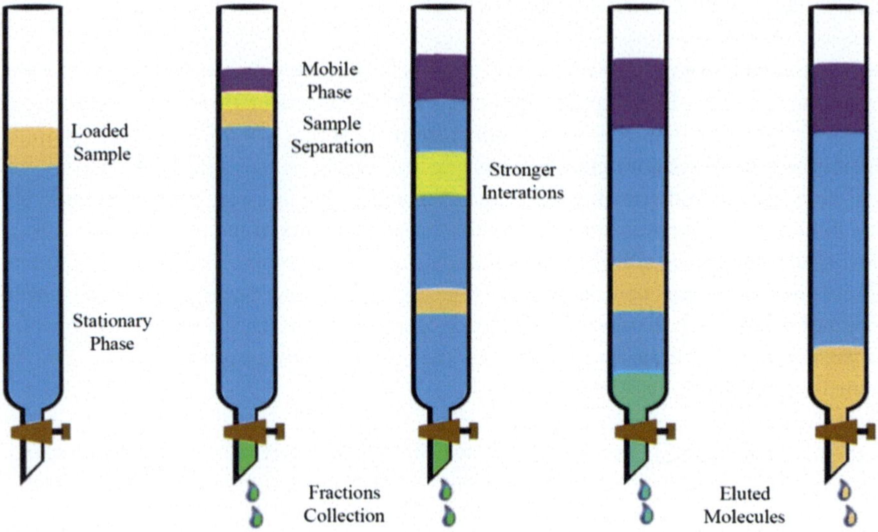

Fig. 5.2 Representation of column chromatography

5.2.2 Paper Chromatography

Paper chromatography is a type of partition chromatography. The stationary phase used is a paper either a cellulose filter paper or Whatman filter paper between the fibers of which a stationary liquid generally water is held which adsorbs the materials. The mobile phase employed is the developing solvent in the liquid state in which the analyte is dissolved. The rate of migration is calculated based on a factor called retention factor. Retention factor or generally Rf value is the ratio of distance travelled by the component from the baseline to that of the distance moved by the solvent from the base line. Therefore, it can be formulated as:

$$\mathrm{Rf} = \frac{\text{Distance moved by sample from baseline}}{\text{Distance moved by solvent from baseline}}$$

While performing paper chromatography the type of paper to be used is selected based on whether qualitative or quantitative analysis is to be done. A Whatman filter paper is the one which is generally used. At about 1 cm from the bottom end of the paper a line is marked with the help of a pencil (usage of pen leads to the separation of components of the ink along with sample). This line is called the base line. The sample to be separated is dissolved in a suitable solvent or applied directly as a spot. The sample in which the analyte is dissolved is selected based on certain criteria. The solvent should not chemically interact with the analyte and hence chloroform, benzene, cyclohexane, etc. are used depending on the nature of the stationary phase.

The paper is then place inside a container where mobile phase is placed. The paper is inserted such that the lower end of the paper just touched the solvent.

Fig. 5.3 The picture shows the separation of three samples A, B, and C by paper chromatography

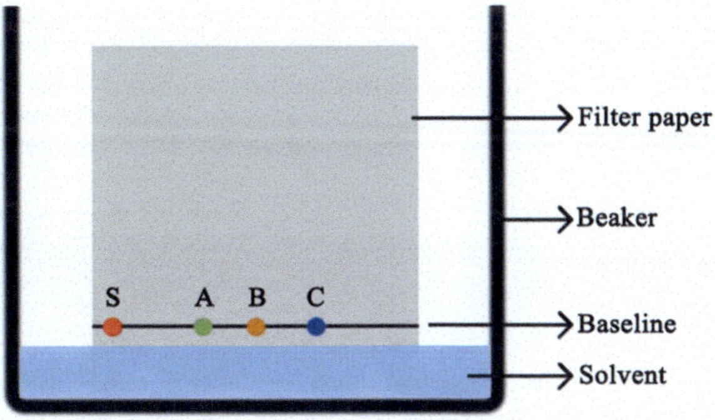

Figure 5.3 depicts the general arrangement of a paper chromatography. The mobile phase gradually moves upwards by capillary action. Along with the mobile phase the mixture is also carried towards the upward direction. Based on its affinity towards the liquid in the filter paper the components of the sample get adsorbed. As the mobile phase reaches the other end of the paper, various component gets separated leaving behind a chromatogram where colored individual components occupy a particular zone. In case of colorless fractions, chemical as well as physical methods can be employed for the process of visualization. For the quantitative analysis the separated components can be isolated by a process called elution. For this the part of the spot to be isolated is cut out and soaked in a minimum amount of solvent and can further be analyzed using methods such as gravimetric analysis, UV spectrophotometry, etc.

Paper chromatography can be used for the analysis of blood in the crime scene as well as for the analysis of fibers obtained from the body of the victim or suspect. In cases when two ink samples have to be analyzed to see whether they are same, paper chromatography can be used (Curry 1953–1954). It is used to separate certain proteins and amino acids in their pure form from mixtures where impurities are present. The use of paper chromatography is best exploited by forensic chemist for process including the general separation of alkaloids. It is also used to investigate sterols such as natural estrogens and sapogenins and presence of antibodies. For simple separation paper chromatography is used as it is easy to carry out the procedure anywhere.

5.2.3 Thin Layer Chromatography

Thin layer chromatography (TLC) is a chromatographic technique similar to paper chromatography. Here, a thin layer of magnesium oxide, aluminum oxide or silica gel is coated over a flat glass plate. The technique was first introduced by Izmailov and Shraiber and was later developed by Stahl in 1958. Thin layer chromatography is also called as drop chromatography, strip chromatography, spread chromatography, surface chromatography, and open column chromatography. The principle of TLC is similar to that of paper chromatography. As in paper chromatography, the

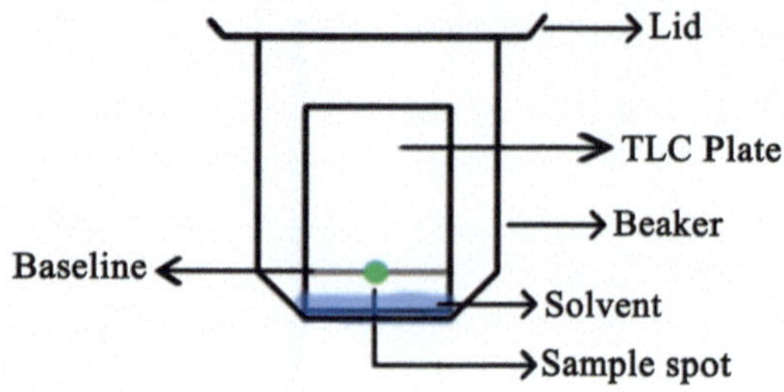

Fig 5.4 Diagrammatic representation of TLC

rate of migration is determined by using the Rf value. When the value of retention factor is zero, the solute remains in the stationary phase while a component is still within the mobile phase when it is one and does not possess any affinity towards the stationary phase. A variety of coating material is used for the process of analysis in TLC. The coating material used is generally called thin layer adsorbent along with which certain substances are added which adhere them properly onto the surface of the glass plate. These substances are called binders. Inert fluorescent indicators are added to the adsorbent which helps in visualizing the components after separation. By exposing the plates under UV, the separated fractions can be distinguished as it appears as dark spots. The sample to be analyzed is dissolved in a suitable solvent which is volatile and non-polar in nature. The sample application is done depending on whether the analysis to be performed is quantitative or qualitative in nature. A glass tank similar to the one used in paper chromatography is used which is made saturated with the vapor of the mobile phase.

A baseline is drawn within the glass plate and samples are applied as spot as represented in Fig. 5.4. The plate is then placed within the tank at an angle of 45°. As the mobile phase moves upward by the process of capillary action, the components of the mixture get separated. Once the process is completed the plate is taken out for visualization. Evaluation of the chromatogram can be done directly by visual assessment, spot area determination or by indirect methods such as gravimetric analysis and UV Spectrophotometry once the fraction is eluted out of the plate.

TLC can be employed for the separation of alcohols by using kieselguhr as the stationary phase and cyclohexane as the developing solvent. By using silica gel as stationary phase, bile alcohol can also be separated. In toxicological studies, TLC enables the isolation and determination of alkaloids while antibiotics can be separated with accuracy. This method of separation also serves a good tool in the analysis of drugs such as Barbiturates and tranquilizers. The major advantages of TLC over other methods include its fewer equipment requirement and easiness in separation. When it comes to non-volatile components TLC has proved to be an efficient technique where components are separated successfully. Separation of samples in micro-liter volume facilitates this to be a simple yet widely used chromatographic technique.

5.2.4 Gas Chromatography

Gas chromatography is a technique used for the separation of compounds that can be vaporized without decomposing. This technique is dependent on the boiling point and polarity of the analyte. The mobile phase is an inert gas (helium, hydrogen, nitrogen, argon) which carries the sample to be separated. The flow rate of the carrier gas is controlled by pressure regulators, gauges, and flow meters (Fig. 5.5). The stationary phase used is a low volatile, thermally stable and chemically inert substance. The stationary phase is held onto the surface of a support (diatomaceous earth) which holds the liquid and thereby facilitates the liquid molecules to get exposed to the mobile phase. The separation of a component is enabled when the analyte in gaseous form interacts with the stationary phase coated over the walls of the chromatographic column. Depending on the retention time of each component they elute out at a different rate. During the process of separation those components that are of high volatility elutes out first, followed by components that are least volatile. Since the mobile phase is a gas and stationary phase a liquid, GC can also be called as gas-liquid chromatography (Zadora and Zuba 2009).

The column used in GC can either be a packed column or an open tubular column (McNair and Miller 2009). A packed column consists of a thin layer of a liquid adsorbed onto the surface of a chemically inert solid support and a capillary column consists of a thin layer of liquid coated over the walls of the column in few tenths of a micrometer in thickness providing flexibility for bending them into coils. The sample to be separated is either injected manually or by autosamplers as commonly seen in the modern devices. Manual injection is done with a syringe where the sample gets converted to gaseous form within the instrument. Autosamplers are more precise than manual injection. The sample is placed inside a sealed vial within a tray where the device injects the sample automatically. When the mobile phase along with the sample pass through the column containing the stationary phase, the individual fractions are separated. This can be detected with the help of detectors

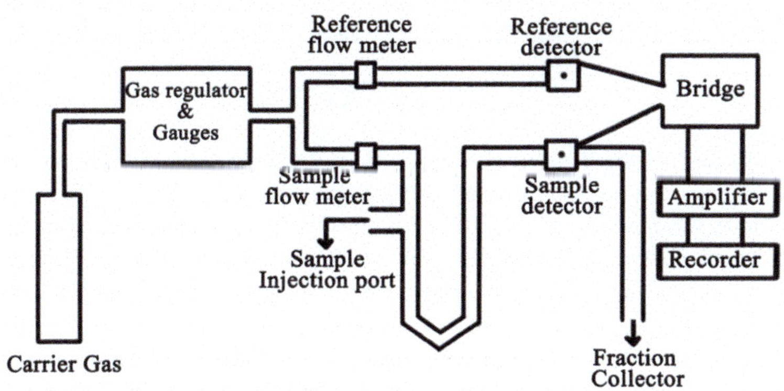

Fig. 5.5 Block diagram of gas chromatography

including the flame ionization detector, thermal conductivity detector, electron capture detector, thermionic detector, hall electrolytic conductivity detector, etc.

Most of the GC used in forensic science laboratories is outfitted with mass spectrometry to detect the compound being separated. In forensic pathology it enables to determine various fluids and their components. It also facilitates the analysis of pollutants in water collected from various sources. In toxicology, GC enable in the identification of toxic products by analyzing various biological fluids, and alcohol content in blood and urine with greater precision. Certain volatile organic compounds which are present in paints, glues, correction fluids, gasoline, etc. can now be analyzed with GC. When a GC is run for blood samples, from the graph obtained the presence of carbon monoxide can be detected along with other gases (Kunsman and Levine 2003). This method also enables to detect the presence of cyanide in blood. In cases where drugs of abuse such as the Gamma-hydroxybutyrate (GHB) and its derivatives, barbiturates, benzodiazepines, antidepressants, and narcotics are involved, GC acts as a powerful tool of detection. When compared with other such techniques, GC provides greater accuracy in separation while the column length enables the separation of components with greater resolution.

5.2.5 High Performance Liquid Chromatography

HPLC is the most versatile as well as widely used elution chromatography. The process is based on the separation of various components of an analyte between the mobile phase and the stationary phase packed within a column. While the analyte passes over the surface of the adsorbent motion of various components get retarded depending on their structure (Hanai 1999). The intermolecular interaction between the molecule of the analyte and that of the adsorbent leads to the adsorption and separation of each component. Various criteria measured in HPLC include its retention factor, capacity factor and column efficiency. Retention factor (R_t) is the measure of speed at which a substance moves within the chromatographic system. If the retention volume is V_r, volume of the stationary phase is V_s, V_m the volume of mobile phase and K the partition coefficient then:

$$V_r = V_m + KV_s$$

The concept of theoretical plates is of prime importance in HPLC. As the name suggests they are not physical plates but imaginary regions within the column. When the column is imagined to be divided into a number of sections each component of the analyte spends a fixed time in each of the sections or plates. Hence, while the analyte moves through the column it in turn moves from one plate to other. The theoretical plates can be considered a measuring tool in column efficiency. When the number of theoretical plate is high the efficiency of separation is high and vice versa. If N is the number of theoretical plates, H the height of the plate and L the length of the column, then:

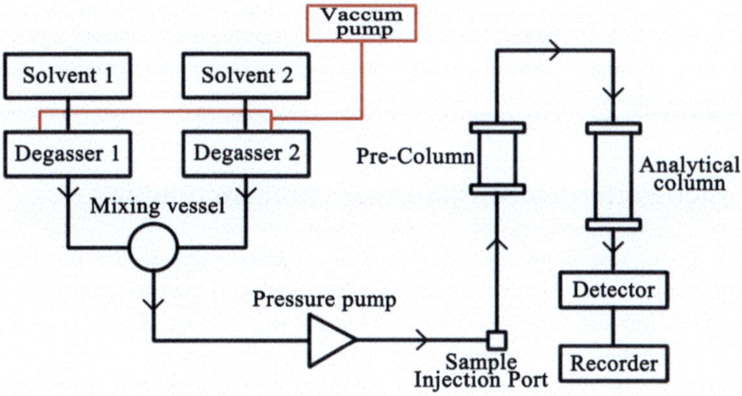

Fig. 5.6 Block diagram of high-performance liquid chromatography

$$N = \frac{L}{H}$$

"H" which is the height of the plate is also referred to as the height equivalent of theoretical plates (HEPT). Smaller the value of H greater will be the efficiency. The chromatographic column used in HPLC is equipped with steel jacket to withstand high pressure. The instrumentation includes container for one or more mobile phase, degasser, mixing vessels, high pressure pump, a sample injection port, a pre-column, an analytical column, a detector, and recorders as shown in Fig. 5.6. The solvent reservoir passes the solvent into the degasser which removes any dissolved gases present. After the completion of this process, the solvent moves into the mixing system which uniformly mixes the mobile phase. This is then passed to the pumping system and thereby towards the column. While the mobile phase passes towards the column the sample is injected through the injection port. The modern HPLC make use of autosamplers where the user only has to keep the sample in a vial which is then taken automatically by the device. The sample along with the mobile phase passes through the stationary phase held inside the steel jacketed column. The mobile phase initially passes through a short column called the pre-column or guard column and then moves through the analytical column. The detectors (UV-visible absorption detector, fluorescent detectors, refractive index detector, and photodiode array detector) detect the compounds that have been separated within the column.

HPLC can be widely used to separate and detect drugs and toxins present within body fluids such as blood and urine. It also serves the best tool in analyzing the post blast residues and its traces on hand and cloth. Various components used in explosives have various retention time and hence these substances can be detected and separated by the method. It has been used widely for the determination of post mortem intervals by analyzing the vitreous humor. Detection of certain drugs and isolation of various inks and dyes can also be done with this technique. It is preferred over other methods of chromatography due to its increased accuracy, speed, and precision. The technique is extremely efficient and quick as it uses a pump system to push the solvent through the stationary phase. The recovery of sample is possible in an improved manner which enables it to be used under the category of non-destructive techniques.

5.2.6 High Performance Thin Layer Chromatography

HPTLC is an advanced form of thin layer chromatography where the separation efficiency is increased by providing an optimized coating material, improvised sample application and developed procedures for the feeding of mobile phase. The principle behind high performance thin layer chromatography is same as that of TLC. Depending on the affinity of a component towards the stationary phase the analyte gets separated and those with more affinity travels slower thorough the adsorbent than component having lesser affinity. The stationary phase is coated over a plate made of particles having narrow size distribution. The plate is pre-coated with a layer of aluminum oxide, magnesium silicate, magnesium oxide, polyamide, cellulose, kieselguhr, etc. The major characteristics of the plate are its high resolution and high selectivity for detection. The mobile phase used in HPTLC is selected based on the adsorbent used and the physical as well as chemical property of the analyte. The solvent used as mobile phase includes diethyl ether, methylene chloride, chloroform, and hexane. The sample to be analyzed is completely dissolved in a suitable solvent which is non-polar and volatile in nature. A very little amount of highly concentrated sample is applied for the analysis. The sample is applied onto the stationary phase as a spot similar to that in TLC. Development of the chromatogram can be done in a flat-bottom chamber, horizontal development chamber or a twin trough chamber. The chamber is filled with mobile phase solvent to the appropriate volume and the plate is kept in it. This enables the separation of individual fractions with greater accuracy. Once the process is completed the plate can be removed from the trough where the chromatogram is developed by heating the plate.

HPTLC is widely used in forensics lab to detect the insecticides present in human serum in cases of acute poisoning. In pharmaceuticals it serves as a valid tool in quality control, uniformity test and purity checks. When aflatoxins are present within food materials even in submicron levels HPTLC facilitates their separation. One of the major challenges faced by forensic scientists is the identification of unknown drugs on intoxication cases. HPTLC enable both the quantitative as well as qualitative analysis of such toxic substances even when present in minute amounts. In clinical practices, it serves best for metabolic studies, drug screening as well as stability testing. Adulteration in food materials are easy to identify as HPTLC provides a risk free and economical way of analysis. It also serves the best method for the analysis of certain intermediates and dyes as well. The increased separation efficiency of the multi component system in less time enables HPTLC to be widely used as a forensic tool. It is cost effective at the same time numerous samples can be analyzed in less time with greater accuracy. Due to these advantages, it has emerged a powerful tool among the other chromatographic techniques especially when it comes to forensic science.

5.3 Microscopy

Microscope is an optical instrument that enables the observer to see details that are not visible while observed under a naked eye. The word microscope comes from the Greek words *micros* and *skopeo* which mean "small" and "looks at," respectively. Microscopes enable to see through minute details of the evidence with which we can relate the evidence to a reference or standard material. As it is a non-destructive technique, various types of microscopes are widely used in the field of forensic science (Wheeler and Wilson 2008). Dating back to the late 1300s, the most primitive form of microscope consisting of only two lenses fitted within a tube was prevalent. This paved a way for the later developments towards the modern-day microscopes. In 1590, Hans and Zacharias Jennsen developed the first microscope which was followed by Galileo Galilee (1609) who perfected it into a compound microscope. Giovanni Faber named this device as microscope on behalf of a scientific society "Academia deihince." When Anthony van Leeuwenhoek started his experimentation using microscope in the mid-17th century, a new sophisticated model of microscope was developed. In 1874, Ernst Abbe formulated a mathematical equation connecting the resolving power and wavelength which enabled him to theoretically maximize the resolution of microscopes (Bell and Morris 2010). When the history dealt with using light as a source of illumination to observe microscopic world, Max Knoll and Ernst Ruska pioneered in developing the first microscope that used electron to illuminate the specimen. This led to the invention of Transmission Electron Microscope in 1931 and later to Scanning Electron Microscope by Ruska in 1942. The development in the field of microscopy is still going on and various microscopic techniques incorporates the digital technology to visualize and examine the finest details of the specimen.

The two main criteria of microscopes include their magnification and resolution power. In laymen's language magnification is explained as how much bigger an object will appear when observed under a microscope (Fig. 5.7). Hence, magnification can be defined as the measure of the ability of the lens system to enlarge the image and is denoted by "X." It can be expressed as:

$$\text{Total Magnification} = \text{Magnification of eyepiece} \times \text{Magnification of objective}$$

$$M = M_e \times M_o$$

Resolution of an optical instrument indicates the shortest distance between two points in a specimen that can still be distinguished. Or it is the ability of the microscope to distinguish two closely spaced objects from each other. The resolution of a microscope is always greater than that of the human eye. When "d" is the

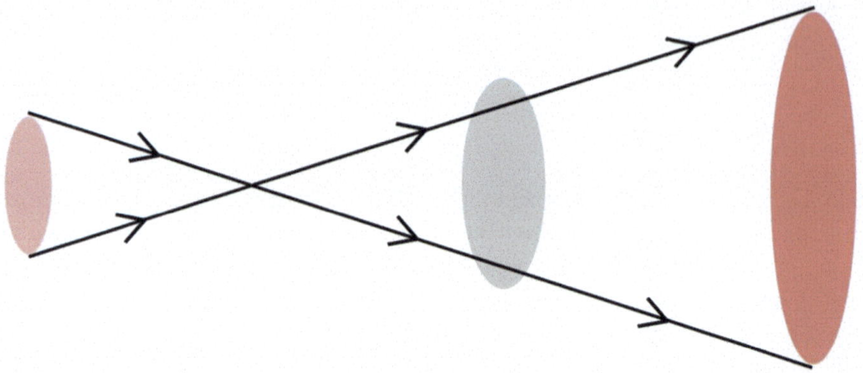

Fig. 5.7 Diagram showing how a lens magnifies an image

distance between two points, "λ" the wavelength of the light used for illumination and N.A the numerical aperture then:

$$d = \frac{\lambda}{\text{NA}}$$

The ability of a microscope to capture the light once it has passed through the specimen determines the extent to which the specimen could be resolved. The light leaving the specimen forms a cone of light which is gathered by an objective lens. Larger the cone greater will be the angle at which light enters the objective lens. This cone is termed as the numerical aperture of the lens. Numerical aperture can be explained as the limit of the angle of light entering the objective (Fig. 5.8). Numerical aperture can be denoted by the equation:

$$\text{NA} = n\text{Sin}\alpha$$

where α is half the angle at the apex of the cone. Hence: $d = \frac{\lambda}{n\ \text{Sin}\alpha.}$

Typically, when magnification increases resolution also increases. But after a certain limit increase in magnification result no higher increase in resolution. That is, image will be more magnified but poorly resolved. This phenomenon is called empty magnification.

Microscopes can be classified based on the source of illumination as light microscopes and electron microscopes (Fig. 5.9). Light microscopes make use of visible light while a beam of electron from an electron gun serves as the illuminating source in an electron microscope. Light microscope includes compound light microscopes, comparison microscopes, polarizing microscopes, fluorescence microscopes and stereo microscopes (Wilson and Wheeler 2009). Transmission

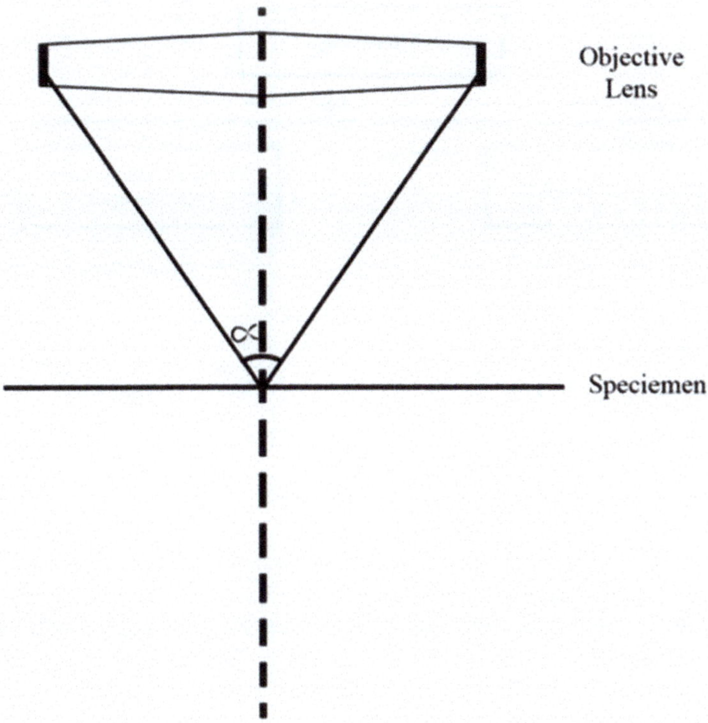

Fig. 5.8 Numerical aperture

electron microscope (TEM) and scanning electron microscope (SEM) fall under electron microscopes.

5.3.1 Compound Light Microscope

An optical instrument consisting of two convex lenses which when combined produces a magnified image of an object under visible light is called a compound light microscope. In most of the compound light microscopes the light source is provided internally which enable the observer to view the object anywhere without depending on the external lighting. A typical compound microscope uses two lenses namely ocular or eyepiece lens and objective lens. A variety of choices are available for both ocular and eyepiece lens magnification. The ocular lens used generally has 10× magnification while the objective may have magnification ranging from 4× to 100× magnification. The object to be studied is placed just outside the focus of the objective lens (F_0) as in Fig. 5.10. When the object is illuminated by the light, they pass through them and are gathered by the objective lens. A ray passing parallel to the principal axis will pass through the focus of the lens and rays passing through the

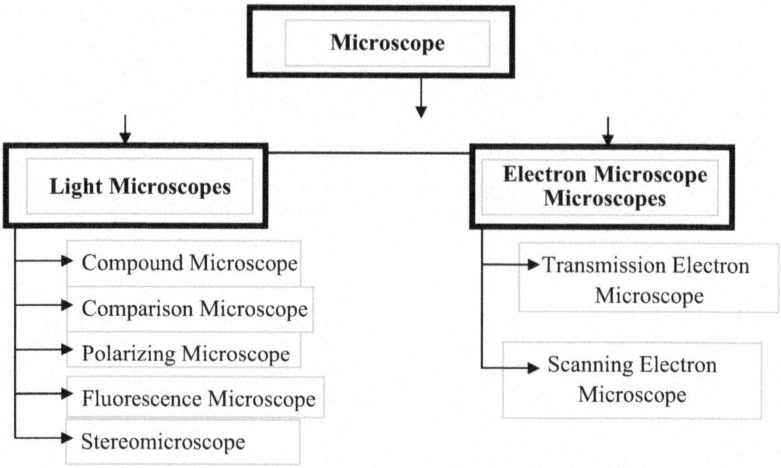

Fig. 5.9 Classification of Microscopes based on Illumination

principal point or optic center pass without any deviation and are converged to form a real image I_1. This image is formed between the focus of the eyepiece (F_e) and the eyepiece lens and acts as an object to the eyepiece. Ray passing through the object gets refracted and hence do not converge. Therefore, they are extended back to meet at a point to produce a final image I_2 which is inverted and enlarged.

The major parts of the compound microscope can be categorized into mechanical and optical parts. The mechanical part includes base, pillar, inclination joints, body tube, Coarse and fine adjustment, the stage, and the nosepiece. The optical part includes the light source, the condenser, objectives, and eyepiece. The light source can be a mirror or an inbuilt electric light source. The light from the source reaches a condenser which provides a cone of light. A diaphragm which is generally placed below the condenser regulates the amount of light entering the condenser. On the stage above the condenser the specimen to be observed is placed. The light passes through the specimen and reaches the objective lens. The light then passes to the eyepiece which magnifies the real image produced by the objective lens and produces a virtual image that can be observed by the eyes of an observer.

A compound microscope can be used in a forensic lab to observe minute details of collected evidence. Examination of soft and hard wood can be performed which enable the clear visualization of their internal structures. When the sample collected include hair of various animals, compound microscopic examination helps in distinguishing them. Determining the shape of the root of hair enable to identify the species to which the hair belongs. Microscopic examination also helps to identifying the somatic region to which a hair is associated with as of head, pubic, facial, limb, chest, axillary, and eyebrow and eyelash hairs. As in many modern compound microscopes, certain software enables the calculation of medullary index directly while observing the sample. General characteristics of hair acquired from various activities such as insect bite, crushing, bleaching, presence of blood, etc. can

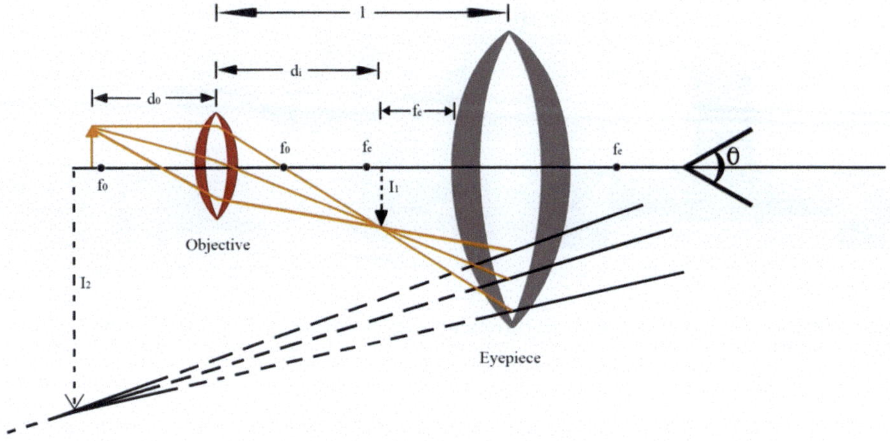

Fig. 5.10 Image formation in a compound microscope

be examined with the compound microscope and thereby provide relevant information in relation to the nature of a crime. Examining hair under microscope therefore provides information about their physical, variable, phenotypic, as well as quality. Observing a glass fragment under microscope enable to study the point of impact which helps in determining the order of the impact made on the glass. Biological samples such as blood, semen, vaginal discharge, etc. can be made clear by staining them properly and viewing them under these microscopes. Primary observation of bullets and fiber analysis can be carried out by using a compound light microscope. Compound microscopes are widely used because of the easiness in viewing a specimen under proper magnification. Whenever evidence is obtained it is observed under a microscope as part of the routine procedure.

5.3.2 Comparison Microscope

Comparison microscope is the combination of two compound microscopes invented by Calvin H Goddard. The two compound microscopes are connected to each other by an optical bridge which enables a split view window (Fig. 5.11a) and hence two separate objects can be viewed and analyzed at a time. The optical bridge with which the two compound microscopes are connected comprises of lenses and mirrors (Fig. 5.11b). They bring the two images back together at a single eyepiece. Certain software connected along with comparison microscope enable us to view the two specimens side by side separated by a line on a computer screen.

The microscope connected to the computer system visualizes the samples observed which enable the viewers to compare each and every point of the two specimens. The specimen placed at the left stage will appear on the left side of the screen, while that at the right stage appears on the right side. The parts and working of each part are similar to that of a compound microscope. The exact same

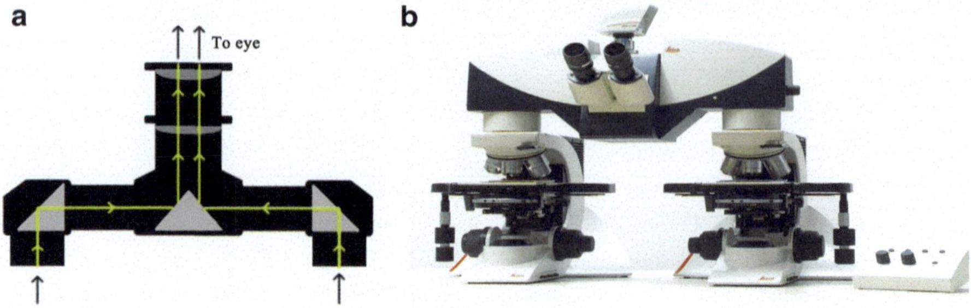

Fig. 5.11 (**a**) The optical path in a comparison microscope; (**b**) Forensic Comparison Microscope Leica FS CB

illumination and intensity conditions are employed for comparison microscope also. This provides the viewer a clear image of two samples which enable point-by-point side-by-side comparison.

Comparison microscope has proved to be an invaluable tool for forensic examination. The comparison of hair, fibers, soil, torn items, bullets, and cartridge cases has been successfully carried out by the using a comparison microscope. This tool has served an appropriate role in examination of various materials in forensic ballistics. Comparing two bullets enable the prediction of whether they have been fired from a single firearm. At the same time, it also helps us in identifying the gun from which it has been fired. The valid role it plays in comparing two fingerprints side by side not only saves our time but also improves the efficiency. When two specimens are to be compared under a normal compound microscope, it must be done one after the other independently. This requires us to keep in memory the features of each specimen to compare them. Since this method lacks scientific precision, invention of a comparison microscope had helped in overcoming this difficulty and thereby enables comparison of two specimens with high precision.

5.3.3 Polarizing Microscope

The technique of illuminating a sample using polarized light is implemented in polarization light microscope. Examination of anisotropic material in detail can be facilitated when a microscope is equipped with polarizer and analyzer. Generally, materials will have a single refractive index and hence they show same optical properties in all directions. But in certain substances, light gets refracted multiple times as they possess two refractive indexes. Such substances are called birefringent material. Birefringent materials are anisotropic in nature and possess a crystalline structure. When a material is anisotropic in nature it indicates that the material is made of not just one type of material and hence the optical properties of light changes depending on the orientation of incident light. Examination of birefringent materials is possible using a polarizing microscope (Elkins 2019). This technique is also called petrographic microscope. Light from almost every source including the

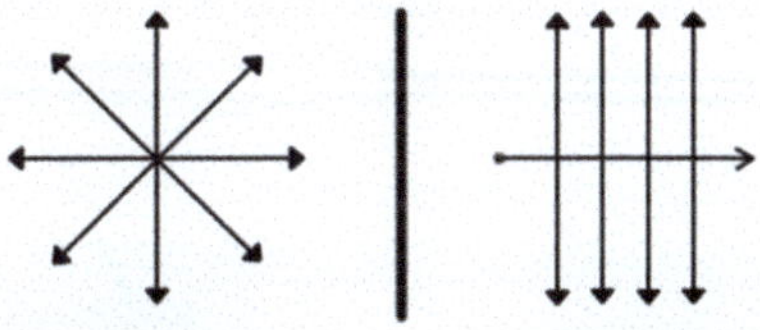

Fig. 5.12 Polarization of light

sun is unpolarized in nature indicating that the electric vector oscillates in all possible direction of vibrations. When an un-polarized light is passed through a Polaroid, a single plane of vibration is obtained by filtering out all other possible vibration which results in a change in intensity. Such a light having a single direction of vibration is called a polarized light (Fig. 5.12). The process of generating polarized light is made possible by certain polarizing filters (Patzelt 1974).

A polarizing microscope uses two polarizing filters the polarizer and analyzer which are placed 90° to each other (crossed position). The polarizer is placed above the light source while the analyzer occupies a position above the sample. The polarizer polarizes the light emitted from the light source and passes through the sample as in Fig. 5.13. When a birefringent sample is placed the polarized light passing through them generate two waves right angle to each other. Of these two waves one is filtered out by the analyzer thereby allowing waves in a single direction to reach the eye. This enables the visualization of sample in a dark background. The structural formation and dynamics of macromolecules of chemicals, drugs and environmental samples can be analyzed under polarization microscope. Placing a compensator enables the measurement of retardation of light passing through them.

Samples such as soil, crystals, minerals, fibers, etc. can be examined under polarization microscope and their birefringence can be determined. This enables in distinguishing materials that are not birefringent in nature. The property of a material to exhibit different colors on exposure to polarizing light is called dichroism and materials such as rayon fiber that shows dichroism can be distinguished by polarized light. Evaluation of trace elements such as hair, fiber, glass, soil, explosives, etc. under a polarized microscope facilitates the study of their nature as well as their structural details

The micro-crystallization of components of various explosives can be identified using polarizing rays. Examination of rocks enables to determine their structure as well as in studying their optical characters. This marks the major reason for use of polarized microscope geological studies. Presence of impurities in food items such as butter, cream, etc. can be analyzed due to its anisotropic nature. Glass and ceramics can be observed to study their defects which can be identified by considering certain criteria such as their color, shape, refractive index, and impurities in

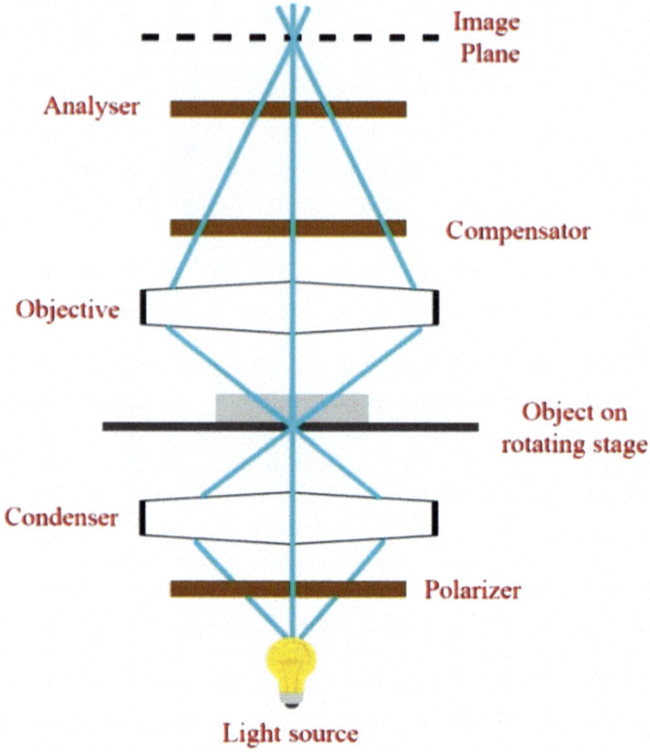

Fig. 5.13 The optical path in a polarization microscope

crystal. The composition of metals is also studied by using a polarized microscope in a wide variety of cases.

5.3.4 Fluorescence Microscopy

Fluorescent microscope explores and enables visualization of the fluorescent properties of a microscopic specimen. Fluorescence is a type of luminescence, where an electron absorbs the energy of a photon, get excited and transit to the vibrational level of the first excited state. From there the electron moves to the lower vibrational levels by a process called non-radiative relaxation. The electrons fall back into the ground level emitting radiation as fluorescence. The wavelength of the emitted light is greater than that of the incident light (Strokes effect). Certain molecules are fluorescent in nature while non-fluorescent molecules or proteins can be made fluorescent by adding certain chemical groups called fluorochrome or fluorophores. When fluorescent or fluorescent imparted sample is illuminated by light, they emit fluorescence with which visualization is made possible. A typical fluorescent microscope consists of an illuminating source, collecting lens, condenser

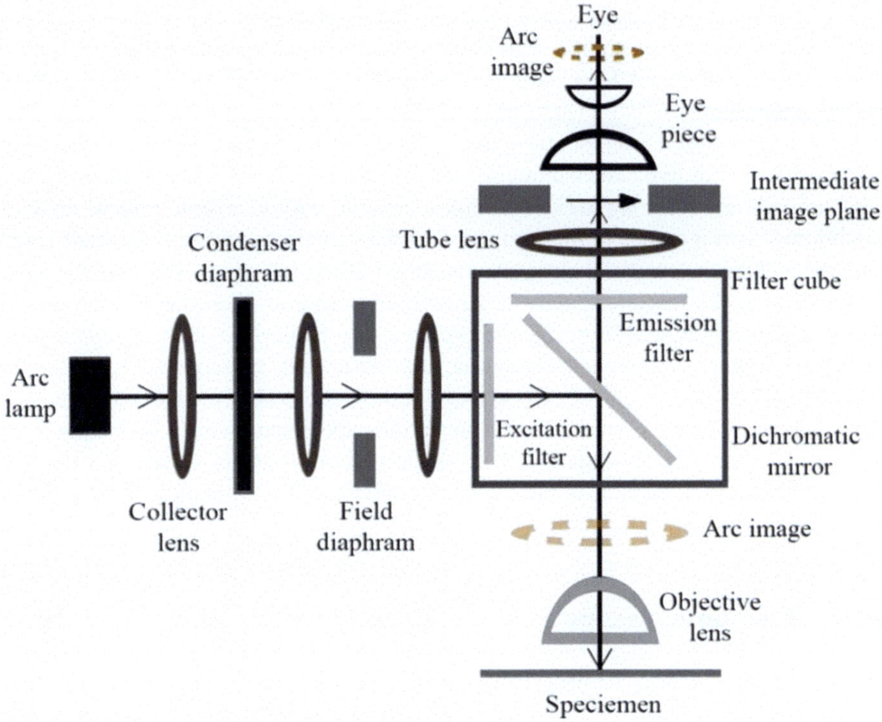

Fig. 5.14 The optical path in a fluorescent microscope

diaphragm, field diaphragm, excitation filter and emission filter, dichromatic mirror, objective, and eye piece (Fig. 5.14). The radiation source emits either UV or visible radiations and therefore Xenon arc lamp, Mercury Vapor lamp, High power LEDs and Lasers are employed. The light from the source passes through the collector lens, condenser, and field diaphragm to reach the filter cube. The collector lens enables the travel of all the rays parallel to each other. The filter cube comprises of an excitation and emission filter and a dichromatic mirror. Both excitation and emission filters are made by coating a thin dielectric material over the surface of an optically flat glass plate (Elkins 2019).

The nature of their coating determines the range of wavelength to be transmitted and that to be reflected. The excitation filter filters out all light except that is required for illumination and is reflected towards the specimen after hitting the mirror. The specimen is either fluorescent by nature or is treated with fluorochrome. The specimen absorbs the light and undergoes the process of electronic transition to emit fluorescent light. The lenses used are coated with an anti-reflection coating which minimizes the background fluorescence. The emission filter only allows the fluorescence to pass through thereby blocking any stray radiations. This makes sure that no ultraviolet radiation used for illumination falls on the observer's eye. The light then passes towards the eyepiece to reach the observer's eye which enables to view the image in fluorescence. The fluorescence emitted can also be detected by a camera either with a CCD (Charge Coupled Device) or CMOS (Complementary Metal Oxide Semiconductor) sensors.

When a compound microscope is used to study cells, the process of staining kills the cells as a result live cells cannot be studied. In case of a fluorescent microscope, cells as well as other biological samples can be studied keeping them in live condition. When it comes to the study of complex structures within cells, multicolor staining enables the easy and clear visualization of their structures. Proteins showing the property of fluorescence can be distinguished from non-fluorescence proteins by applying the technique. Fluorescent microscope can be used to analyze fibers, soils and dyed cellular components. The humic and fulvic acids present in the soil can be detected with the technique. Compared with other methods of microscopy, fluorescent microscopes enable visualization of various specimens with a high degree of specificity. Cells can be maintained in viable condition at the same time various stains can be used to track different molecules and hence multiple molecules within a specimen can be distinguished.

5.3.5 Stereomicroscope

When samples are not to be observed under high magnification, a stereomicroscope acts as an adequate tool. At the same time, it provides a 3D view of the specimen being observed. Opaque objects that do not allow light to pass through can be observed with stereo microscopes, since visualizing such samples under normal microscope requires ultrathin sectioning. Stereo microscopes possess an eyepiece system comprising of the optional eyepiece with varying magnification, an eyepiece tube that keeps the eyepiece intact in its position and a diopter adjustment ring which help to avoid inconsistencies that may arise while viewing the specimen using one or both the eyes. The mechanical parts of the microscope include the focus, working stage, stage clips and an inbuilt LED illuminator (Fig. 5.15).

Stereomicroscopes consist of two separate eyepieces. The path of light in each eyepiece is different which provides two different angles for viewing. A top light and a bottom light is provided to the microscope, where the top is illuminated for placing the specimen and the bottom for properly viewing the image. The change in angle of the light reflected from the specimen surface enable a three-dimensional view of the sample. The microscope enables the forensic scientists to perform preliminary evaluation of the evidence and thereby helps in deciding the tests to be performed further. Stereo microscopes are used for the analysis of plant and animal materials, crystals, circuits, coins, jewelry, textiles, paint chips, glass fragments and watches. Analysis of the color and number of layers in a paint chip is facilitated by stereo microscope as it provides a clear 3D view of the sample. In document examination, overwriting is identified with stereomicroscopes. In cases where lamp filaments are involved, the technique determines whether a it was illuminated while an incident or not. Examining the tire prints and shoe prints also provide valuable information in

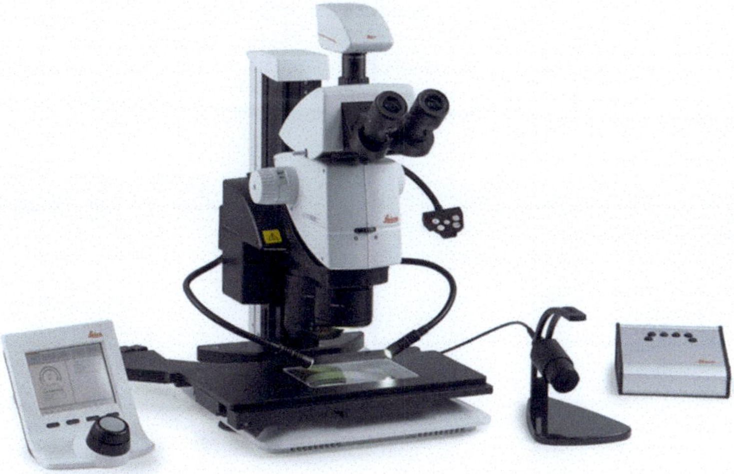

Fig. 5.15 Leica M125 C stereo microscope

solving cases. The characteristics of the biological specimen can be studied easily with the help of a stereomicroscope. Physical examination of materials like fibers enable in determining features related to its construction. Ropes, carpets, threads, etc. are observed under a stereomicroscope before applying any other techniques. The major reason stereomicroscopes are preferred over a normal compound microscope is that it provides a three-dimensional view of the specimen. Along with that, it also possesses a zoom lens which enable to view the specimen under various magnifications.

5.3.6 Electron Microscope

When a beam of electron is used for illuminating the sample a high-resolution image is obtained. The technique of microscopy which enables the process is called an electron microscopy. Two classes of electron microscopy are used widely including the transmission electron microscopy (TEM) and scanning electron microscopy (SEM). When a beam of electron incident on the surface of a specimen auger electrons, backscattered electrons, X-ray photons, secondary electrons, visible photons, etc. are produced by the interaction of electron with the sample as shown in Fig. 5.16. These signals are collected by various detectors which produced a high-resolution image of the specimen.

The limit of resolution of an electron microscope is determined by the equation:

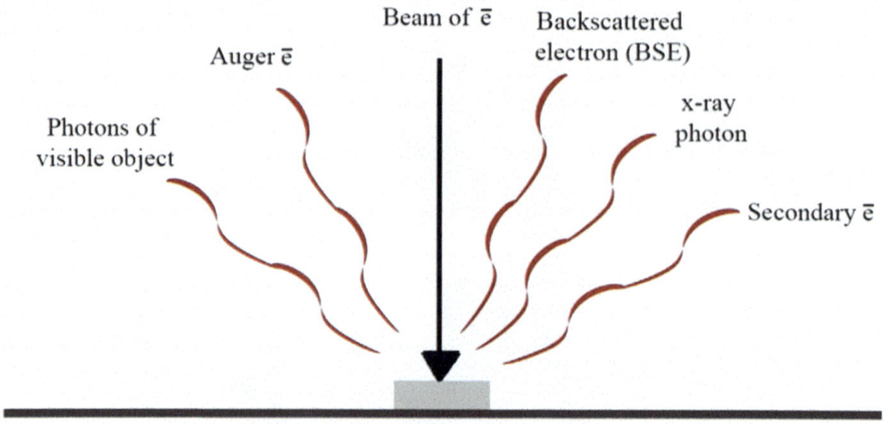

Fig. 5.16 Interaction of electron with a specimen

$$d = \frac{1.2\lambda}{\mathrm{Sin}\theta}$$

Where λ is the wavelength of the electron and θ is the angle at which the electrons are collected. The range of "d" falls between 1.5A^o to 3A^o. When the resolution obtained in light microscopy is compared with that of an electron microscope it is clear that due to the increased wavelength of electrons, the limit of resolution is greater for the later than the former. This enables the electron microscope to resolve at an atomic level.

The main difference an electron microscope possesses from a light microscope is the difference in the method of illumination. When a light microscope used radiation of the electromagnetic spectrum, electron microscopes make use of a beam of electron. The beam of electron is generated with the help of an electron gun made of tungsten wire or lanthanum hexaboride (LaB_6). The wire inside the electron gun is heated by applying a voltage and thereby emits electrons. A cylinder called Whenolt cylinder is placed outside the wire which focuses the beam towards the accelerator stack which accelerates the beam. The whole system is constructed under vacuum. The wire is kept at a very low voltage (−30 V) while the ground or the bottom of the microscope is kept at a relatively high voltage (0 V) which enable the flow of electron down the microscope towards the specimen.

The beam then passes through an electromagnetic lens (EM lens) system which consists of a lens, deflector, stigmators, cooling channel and aperture. EM lens are coiled wire around which a magnetic field passes through. When electrons reach the lens, the deflectors align them properly along the optical axis and pass them through the lens (Mikkelsen and Corton 2004). The stigmators compensate the field associated with the lens thereby strengthens the field. A cooling channel reduces the temperature increased due to the continuous flow of current. The aperture having a hole in its center blocks certain beams and allows others to pass through. This is projected towards the sample in the holder and detectors are used to collect the signals from the sample which is then viewed on the screen.

5.3.6.1 Transmission Electron Microscope

TEM is a technique developed by Knoll and Ernst Ruska in 1931 that collects the electron being transmitted through the sample which carries details about them. Since the electron beam is allowed to transmit through the sample, a thin section of the sample is taken. Instrumentation of a normal TEM comprises of the electron gun, electromagnetic lenses, vacuum chamber, condensers, sample stage, phosphor screen, detectors, and computer system (Figs. 5.17 and 5.18). When an electron is incident on a specimen, it is scattered which generates secondary as well as backscattered electrons along with X-rays and auger electron. The part of the electron beam that are not scattered gets transmitted and are collected by lenses thereby producing an image the fluorescent screen. Various detectors such as semiconductor detector, scintillator-photomultiplier system, charged coupled devices, and faraday cup are used to collect the signals which are then converted into an image on the computer screen (Elkins 2019).

Before viewing the sample, it needs to be treated in a specific way to make sure we get a perfect image. The specimen is initially fixation to prevent any damage by

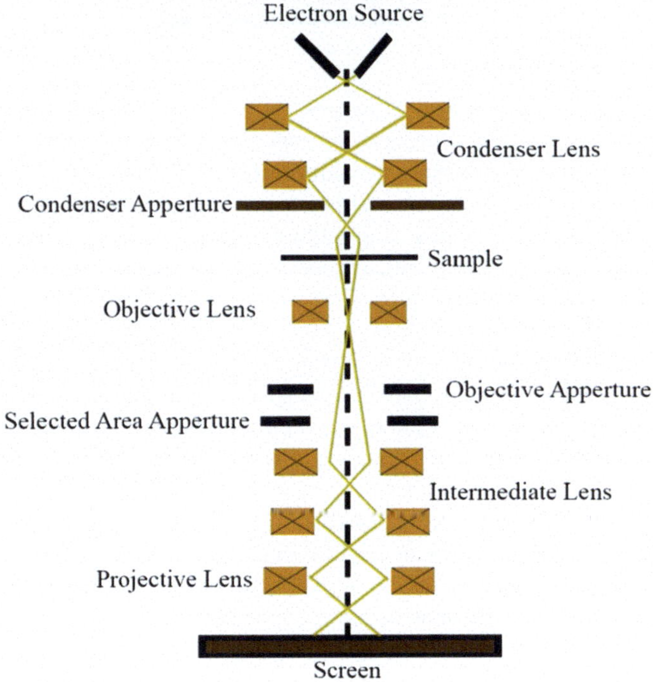

Fig. 5.17 Ray diagram of TEM

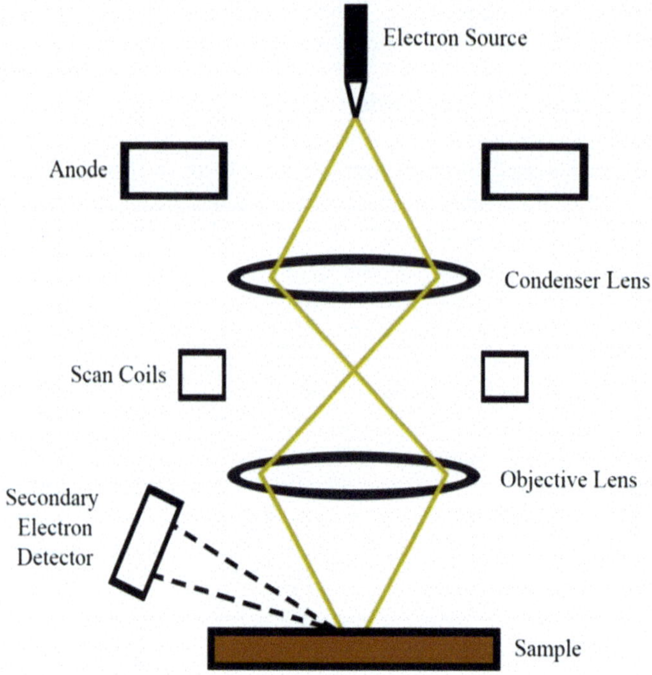

Fig. 5.18 Ray diagram of SEM

using glutaraldehyde or liquid nitrogen (cryogenized). It is then rinsed in a buffer solution and treated with osmium tetroxide (OsO_4). This increases the contrast of minute details within the specimen and is termed as secondary fixation. Once this process is completed the specimen is dried by freezing to remove the water content and is treated with an organic solvent, a process called dehydration. This specimen is presented with epoxy resin and kept in an oven at 60 °C overnight. This is then polished with certain ultra fine abrasives and stained using certain heavy metals (uranium, lead, and tungsten) and thereby thin sections are generated. TEM is widely used in forensic science for the analysis and study of internal structures of various biological and non-biological specimens as well as for material analysis. The image is two dimensional and obtained as black and white (David and Barry 2009).

5.3.6.2 Scanning Electron Microscope

SEM is when the electrons from an electron gun is equipped to scan the surface of the specimen and thereby provides a high-resolution three-dimensional image. In SEM the image is not generated as whole at a time rather as pixel by pixel. A part of the surface of the specimen is scanned at a time and the corresponding image is produced. This process continues until the whole surface is scanned thereby accumulating pixels of each scan to construct a whole image. SEM is comparatively larger in size and hence needs more space as compared with other microscopic techniques. The electron beam from the gun passes down the vacuum chamber where an electromagnetic lens system is arranged. On its way the beam of electron is accelerated by the accelerator stack, deflected by the magnetic field of the lens, and thereby follows a path along the circumference of the coil to reach the specimen through the objective lens at the end of the column (Elkins 2019). The specimen is placed inside the specimen holder within a specimen chamber and is swept with the electron beams using scan coils. Organisms cannot be studied in live conditions as the technique requires the sample to be cryogenized before viewing.

When a beam of electron strikes the surface of a specimen various signals including backscattered electron and secondary electrons are generated which are then collected by various detectors. The signals collected are converted into electrical pulse and are processed to be displayed as a SEM image. The detectors used can be Everhart-Thornley (ET) detector, Through-The-Lens (TTL) detector and Backscattered Electron detector. The ET detector is generally used to collect secondary electrons as well as backscattered electrons. It is placed in the chamber at the end of the objective near the specimen (Ul-Hamid 2018). A through-the-lens detector collects secondary electrons and is placed above the objective lens. The backscattered electron detector is placed below the pole piece and above the specimen in such an angle is suitable for electron collection. A backscattered electron detector is used as an ET detector will not collect all the backscattered electrons. SEM can be used in forensic entomology to view various parts of insects under high resolution. SEM provides the better platform for the analysis of pollen grains, broken cuticle of hair and broken filaments in light bulb (to determine whether the light was on or off during an incident). When SEM is coupled with EDS and X-ray analyzer, the chemical composition of trace elements such as gunshot residues can be determined. The surface morphology can be very well studied by using the technique.

5.4 Spectroscopy

Spectroscopy is a method that enables the forensic scientists to identify the evidence, analyze its structural features including their functional group and quantitate them. Spectroscopy works on the principle of how electromagnetic radiation interacts with matter. The instruments which are used for spectroscopy are called spectrophotometer, spectrometer, and spectrograph. A radiation that propagates through space has an electric as well as magnetic field associated with them. Such radiations are called electromagnetic radiations. They propagate in form of waves due to the vibrating electric and magnetic field. These waves generally called electromagnetic waves are of different types. They may be gamma rays, X-rays, ultraviolet rays, visible rays, infrared rays, microwaves, or radio waves as depicted by Fig. 5.19. Each of these radiations has a range of wavelength and frequency. When these radiations are arranged according to the increasing or decreasing order of their wavelength or frequency an electromagnetic spectrum is formed. It possesses dual nature, i.e., both wave and particle (Vo-dinh and Gauglitz 2003). According to the particle nature,

	GAMMA RAYS	X-RAYS	ULTRAVIOLET	VISIBLE	INFRARED	MICROWAVES	RADIO WAVES	
WAVELENGTH (nm)	10^{-4}	10^{-2}	10^{0}	10^{2}	10^{4}	10^{6}	10^{8}	10^{10}
FREQUENCY (Hz)	10^{21}	10^{19}	10^{17}	10^{15}	10^{13}	10^{11}	10^{9}	10^{7}

Fig. 5.19 Electromagnetic spectrum

radiation is comprised of discrete packets of energy called photons. Each photon is associated with a particular amount of energy. This energy is directly proportional to the frequency of the radiation. The way a radiation interacts with matter also varies with different radiations.

The energy associated with an electromagnetic radiation can be formulated as:

$$E = h\vartheta = h\frac{c}{\lambda}$$

Where “h” is Planck’s constant (60,626 × 10^{-34} $m^2Kg\ s^{-1}$), "ϑ" the frequency of radiation, “c” is velocity of light and "λ" is the wavelength of radiation. Of the regions in an electromagnetic spectrum, those radiation that are visible to the human eye fall between 400–800 nm wavelengths. When light is passed through a prism, it undergoes dispersion to produce radiations of different wavelengths. This arrangement of various colors or wavelengths is termed as a spectrum. Hence, a spectrum shows the arrangements of wavelength of various radiations. Various types of spectrum are obtained namely Absorption spectrum, emission spectrum and continuous spectrum. The spectrum obtained by passing sunlight through a prism is the continuous spectrum. Hot solids generally produce continuous spectrum. If a spectrum shows a series of alterative bright and dark lines, and the bright lines are present on a dark background it is an emission spectrum, while a spectrum with dark lines of a bright background is an absorption spectrum.

Depending on the how an electromagnetic radiation interacts with matter, processes such as absorption, transmission, fluorescence, or phosphorescence can take place. When a material absorbs the radiation that falls on it, the phenomena is termed as absorption, while when the radiation is passed through the material without being absorbed it is transmission.

The basic components of a spectroscopic system consist of an energy source, wavelength selector, sample holders, detectors, and signal processors. The source of energy is a major requirement in case of any spectroscopic instrument. A source is selected based in the intensity and stability of the beam that it produces. When thermal energy is to be supplied either a plasma source or flame is used. When the method requires using a narrow band of radiation, a wavelength selector is employed. A filter, monochromator or interferometer is used to obtain a narrow band of radiation. Filters are used when a fixed nominal wavelength is required for the analysis. When the sample is to be analyzed by adjusting the nominal wavelength band, a monochromator is preferred over filters. To produce a simultaneous flow of radiation towards the detector, an interferometer is used. Once the radiation interacts with the matter in the sample, the detector enable the detection of the analyte and it is sent to the signal processing system which plots graphs for analysis. The science of spectroscopy was developed by the German chemist Robert Wilhelm Bunsen and German physicist Gustav Robert Kirchhoff. The modern spectrometry began to improve by the work of Albert Abraham Michelson which is the optical interferometer. The discovery of Raman Effect by Sir CV Raman made a significant advancement in the field of spectroscopy.

Spectroscopy can be classified into two as atomic and molecular spectroscopy. They are dealt in detail in the chapter.

5.4.1 Atomic Spectroscopy

When an electromagnetic radiation is allowed to pass through an atom, they absorb and emit the radiations which enables us to study the properties of atoms based on the spectrum obtained. This method is called as atomic spectroscopy (Chatwal and Anand 2019). The way a chemical element interacts with radiation generates a unique spectrum, which when used properly helps in the analysis of the composition of these elements in the sample. Moving down to the atomic world shows that the electrons in an atom are concentrated to certain energy levels. These energy levels called as the atomic orbitals which are quantized rather than continuous. Electrons in an atom always tend to stay in an energy level where they are stable. When an electron absorbs or emit radiation, they tend to move from one energy level to the other. While moving they either absorb or release certain amount of energy. The amount of energy absorbed or released is equal to the difference in the energy of the two energy levels (Pavia et al. 2013).

If by absorbing a radiation an electron transit from E_1 to E_2, then:

$$\text{The amount of energy absorbed} = \Delta E = E_2 - E_1$$

Every chemical element present has a unique number of electrons in their ground level and hence the amount of energy absorbed or released by them will also show a unique pattern. This enables the determination of the composition of a sample.

5.4.1.1 Atomic Absorption Spectroscopy

The commonly used spectroscopic technique to detect the presence of metals and metalloids in a sample is the atomic absorption spectroscopy (AAS). AAS can be used to detect almost 62 elements. Apart from detecting the metal in the sample, AAS can also be used to study the concentration of metals present in a sample. The foundation stone for the development of AAS was laid by the discovery of dark lines in the continuous emission spectrum of the sun. This breakthrough discovery was contributed in 1802 by Wollaston. This work was later continued by Fraunhofer in 1814. In 1955, the first paper describing AAS was published by Alan Walsh. It was in the mid-1960s, the instrumentation gathered acceptance and was commercialized.

The sample to be analyzed is dissolved in a suitable solvent and introduced into an atomizer. This converts the sample into vapor in which atoms will be present. Of these certain atoms are in excited state and some in ground state. AAS makes use of the atoms in their ground state to carry out the process of analysis. When a radiation is allowed to pass through the sample in the vapor state, those atoms in the ground state absorbs the energy and get excited into higher energy levels. This absorption reduces the intensity of radiation. The decrease in the intensity of radiation is directly proportional to the amount of atom present in the ground state. This indicates that the greater the rate of absorption, more number of atoms are in the ground state. This absorption of radiation by the sample is measured by AAS. This serves as the basic principle behind AAS. The total amount of radiation absorbed by an atom can be expressed as follows:

$$\nu = \frac{\pi e^2}{mc} Nf$$

where, e is the electronic charge, c the velocity of electromagnetic radiation, m the mass of the atom, N the number of atom and f the frequency of oscillation.

The instrumentation of AAS includes a radiation source, an atomizer and sample holder, a wavelength selector, detector and a signal processor and read out as depicted in Fig. 5.20. The most common radiation source employed includes the hollow cathode lamp, electrodeless discharge lamp or a diode laser source. Hollow cathode lamp uses the metal to be analyzed as an electrode. A tunable dye laser which produces radiation ranging between 213 and 900 nm acts as a good source as the beam possess greater intensity. The source is followed by a chopper which performs the process of production of intermittent light that is broken light. The major criterion for the analysis of a sample with AAS is that the species under investigation be in gaseous or atomic state. This enables the free atom to absorb the radiation. To convert the sample to vapor state either a flame atomizer or electro thermal atomizer is used. In flame atomizer, the sample is first converted into mist by introducing it into a nebulizer. The droplets or aerosols are then mixed with a fuel

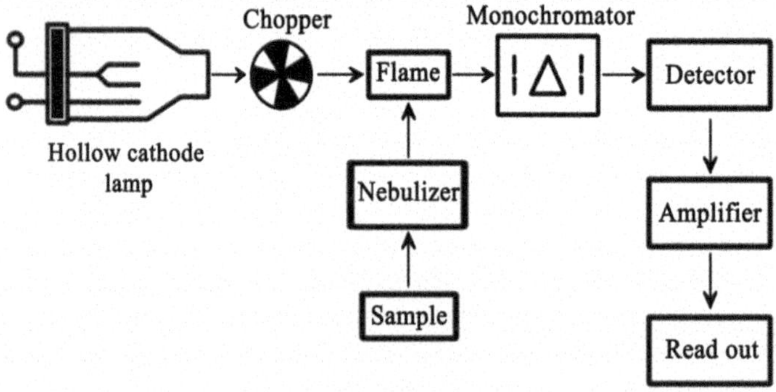

Fig. 5.20 Block diagram of AAS

gas and oxidant which carries the aerosol towards the burner head. By process such as vaporization, dissociation, reduction or oxidation, the sample is converted to free atom. In electro thermal atomizer, a graphite furnace is used. The sample is introduced initially into the graphite furnace. This leads to the evaporation of solvents. The sample is ashed later and temperature is drastically increased to 2000–3000°C. This vaporizes and atomizes the sample to produce free atom.

The radiation from the source is absorbed by the sample in gaseous state (Willard et al. 1986). Since the radiation produced is from the metal under analysis, similar atoms in the sample absorb this radiation. A part of the incident beam is also transmitted. The radiation is then passed through a monochromator. The transmitted rays fall on the photocells of the detector.

Depending on the light incident on the photocathode a current is produced, which is read out. Atomic absorption spectroscopy has been used for the analysis of a wide variety of elements in various solutions. In clinical analysis it serves one of the best techniques in analysis of metal content in biological fluids such as blood and urine. In food analysis, it enables to identify the presence of contaminants and impurities. When water from various sources are obtained such as river, pond, sea, etc., the level of various elements can be evaluated by AAS. It also serves the best tool in pesticide analysis, drug analysis, and purity test and to examine the level of certain toxic substances in samples. Its simple and easy to operate principle is what makes it suitable for the analysis. The major advantage of AAS is that presence elements even in little concentration can be detected.

5.4.1.2 Atomic Emission Spectroscopy

Atomic emission spectroscopy is a technique used to analyze an element and to estimate its concentration in a sample. The intensity of light is considered the criterion for the estimation of quantity or concentration of a particular element in the sample. The principle behind AES is the examination of the wavelength of photons emitted from an atom or molecule when they transit from a state of higher energy to a state of lower energy.

When an electron is excited by a radiation of particular energy, the electron transit to higher level and emits energy to fall back to lower energy level. Atomic emission spectroscopy studies the energy emitted by an electron, as each element emits photon of a characteristic wavelength. A thorough analysis of the emission enables us to identify the atoms present in a sample at the same time to quantify them. Hence, both quantitative and qualitative analysis can be performed.

The major instrumentation of atomic emission spectroscopy includes a sample holder, atomizer, monochromator, detector, amplifier and a read out. When the sample is in liquid state, it is first nebulized and then a stream of gas carries the sample towards the source of excitation. For solid samples, introduction to the source is done in the form of slurry. Solid samples can be converted to atomic state with the help of a laser pulse or spark or arc excitation source. The flame heats the sample in form of the aerosol which provides the atom with energy. The atom undergoes electronic transition to release energy as photons. The energy emitted as photon then passes through the monochromator and reaches the detector. The

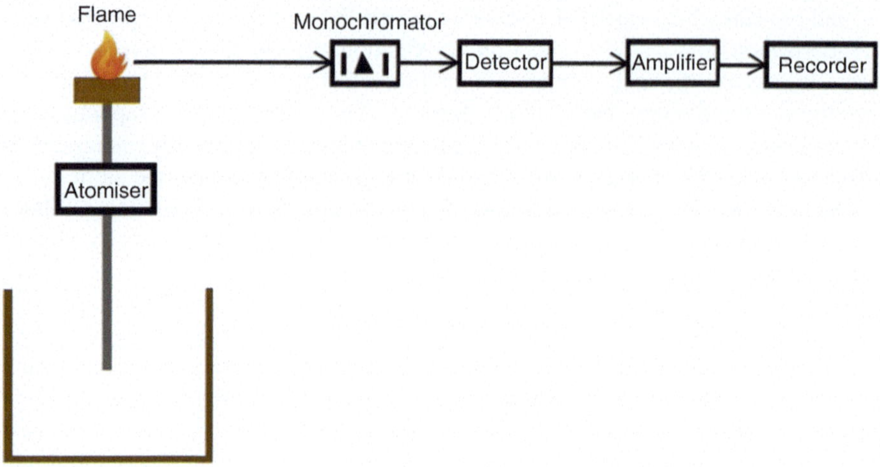

Fig. 5.21 Block diagram of AES

detector employed can be a photomultiplier tube or a photographic film or plate. The signals are amplified and sent to the read out. Hear a plot of emission intensity versus wavelength is constructed. Based on the limited wavelength, atom is identified and emission intensity is used as a measurement to analyze the concentration of the atom in the sample. Inductively coupled plasma atomic emission spectroscopy uses plasma as a source to break down the sample into their atomic form (Fig. 5.21).

Atomic emission spectroscopy can be used to identify the metal content in tissues. In cases related to poisoning, elements such as manganese, copper, zinc, cadmium, etc. can be detected. It can also be used to detect the traces of lead in human liver. To analyze the elemental concentration of glass, atomic emission spectroscopy is widely used. Analysis of the elements in the glass enables the chemist to identify as to whether it is from window, bottle, vehicle, or any other source. Determination of the presence and concentration of arsenic in food supplements and bromate and bromide in baked goods are also possible. One of the several advantages of AES is that elements present even in parts per million quantities can be detected. AES enable multi-elemental analysis even from a very little amount of sample. When plasma source is utilized, the sample can be analyzed even for detecting non-metals. The method is preferred due to its low chemical interference and production of a stable and reproducible signal.

5.4.1.3 X-Ray Spectroscopy

The electromagnetic radiation which falls under the wavelength of 10^{-5} to $100A^o$ is called X-ray region. They are radiation of shorter wavelength and are produced by inner electronic transition of electron or by the deceleration of electrons. Region from $0.1A^o$ to $20A^o$ is generally used for the process of spectroscopy. The use of X-rays to identify various substances was discovered in 1908 by Charles Barkla, a

British physicist. He discovered that the X-ray from a material is characteristic to that individual substance. Later William Henry Bragg and William Lawrence Bragg used spectroscopy to study how these radiations interact with matter.

Generation of X-rays can be done in various ways. This includes generation of X-ray by synchrotron sources, or by hitting a metal surface with electrons of high energy, or by allowing a primary beam of X-rays to strike a material to generate a secondary X-ray which is called as X-ray fluorescence (XRF), or by the radioactive decay of elements which emits X-ray. When X-ray interacts with a material processes such as absorption, emission, fluorescence, and diffraction occur. Based on these processes, spectrum can be generated.

When a beam of X-ray is allowed to pass through a thin sample, a part of the radiation is absorbed and scattered. The amount of radiation scattered is negligible when compared to that absorbed. When the material absorbs X-ray an electron from the innermost orbital gets ejected. When the energy of the X-ray is suitable enough for the electron in an innermost orbital to get ejected more number of such electrons are emitted. Using this absorption spectrum is generated which enable to identify the material.

When an electron is ejected, the atom behaves as ions. During the process of excitation, they transform to higher energy levels. Due to its instability in the higher levels, they emit radiations. The radiation so emitted is called X-ray fluorescence. By using this principle XRF enable one in the identification of a substance. The instrumentation of X-ray spectrometer includes an X-ray source, wavelength selector, sample holder, detector, signal processor and recorder (Fig. 5.22) The X-ray sources employed in the technique can be an X-ray tube, secondary fluorescence source or a radioisotope. The X-ray tube is an evacuated glass tube consisting of an anode and a cathode. When electricity is supplied to the tube electrons are emitted from the cathode and bombards with the metal within the anode. This results in the decrease of power of the electron and an X-ray photon is generated.

The X-ray produced by the radiation source will have rays belonging to a wide wavelength. While examining a sample it is proffered to use a narrow wavelength radiation. Hence, a monochromator or filter is added to the instrumentation of X-ray spectrometer. Once the radiation is passed through the sample it moves towards the detector. Spectrometer generally uses either a solid-state detector or a scintillator detector. The signals generated are then send to the signal processor which processes

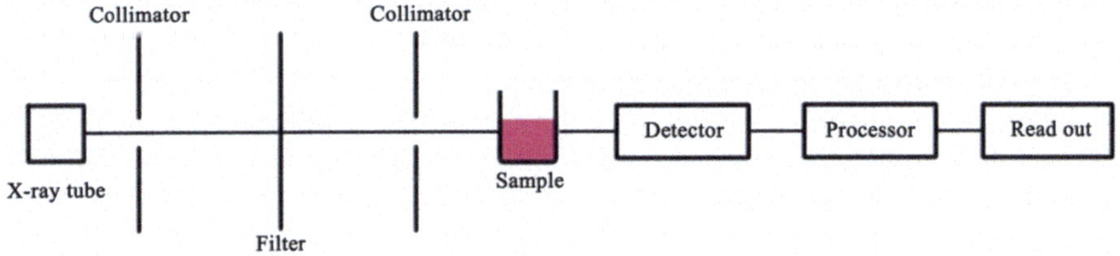

Fig. 5.22 Block diagram of X-ray spectrometer

the signal. Within the processor the signals are amplified and reach readout where the spectrum is generated. Analyzing the spectrum provides the chemist to identify the substance under analysis.

X-ray spectroscopy can be used for the analysis and comparison of samples such as rocks, soils, minerals, etc. Hence, when samples of soils are under question the answer to whether they are from the same region can be determined. XRF can be employed when it comes to the analysis of gunshot residues. It also serves the best in analyzing the counterfeit coins by comparing the composition of various elements with a genuine one. Ink and paints can be studied and analyzed by using XRF. When a document is under question, X-ray spectrometers can be used to study the composition of the ink which enables to distinguish samples under observation. In certain cases where other techniques fail to distinguish paint samples from hit and run cases, energy dispersive X-ray fluorescence (EDXRF) have proved to be very useful. X-ray spectroscopy also serves best in determining the structure of a compound. When other spectroscopic methods fail in the identification of a particular compound, this method is utilized. It is preferred as it is a non-destructive technique which enables the recovery of the sample after analysis. In case when the amount of sample to be detected is little as well as further analysis is required, X-ray spectroscopy is preferred. When compared to other techniques this has the advantage of producing the result as fast as possible with little or no sample preparation. In certain cases, the sample can be analyzed as it is. The development of portable devices of XRF also enables instant identification of sample within the crime scene itself.

5.4.2 Molecular Spectroscopy

When a spectroscopic study is conducted based on the amount of radiation absorbed or emitted by a molecule, it is termed as molecular spectroscopy. When an electromagnetic radiation of particular wavelength is allowed to pass through a molecule, they move from a lower energy level to a higher one. The transition between energy level and the amount of radiation absorbed depends on the chemical composition of the sample (Hollas 2002). In this case, a molecule does not absorb radiation of any wavelength but only that in particular range. Hence, those radiations are not absorbed by the molecule hence passing through them. Gathering the information about the structure of a molecule is possible by analyzing the nature of the electronic transition through which a molecule passes through.

5.4.2.1 Ultraviolet-Visible Spectroscopy

UV-visible spectroscopy is a widely used spectroscopic method for the qualitative and quantitative analysis of organic and biological molecules. The UV radiation falls in the wavelength range of 190–400 nm and region from 400–800 nm is considered to be visible region. The principle behind this spectroscopic technique is the Beer Lambert Law (Chatwal and Anand 2019). The law states that the amount of light absorbed by a substance dissolved in a solution is directly proportional to the concentration of the substance in that solution and the path length of light through the solution.

According to Beer Lambert law,

$$A = \log\left[\frac{I_0}{I}\right] = \varepsilon cl$$

A = absorbance
I_0 = intensity of incident light
I = intensity of light leaving from the sample
c = molar concentration of solute
l = length of sample cell
ε = molar absorptivity

When UV or visible radiation is passed through a material, energy of the radiation is absorbed by the electrons. This results in the transition of electrons from lower electronic states to higher electronic state by excitation. The degree of absorption of radiation is recorded by using a UV-visible spectrophotometer. This is plotted as absorbance versus wavelength. This plot obtained is known as UV-visible spectrum. Analysis both quantitative and qualitative can be done using this spectrum.

To conduct the analysis, the sample whether solid or liquid is dissolved in a suitable solvent. The condition to be followed while selecting the solvent is that it should not absorb the radiation of wavelength that is used for study. After preparing the sample, it is placed in a cell made of substance which does not absorb the radiation under study. Quartz cells are generally used as sample holders a general spectrophotometer consists of a radiation source, monochromator, detector, and recorder (Fig. 5.23). The radiation source should provide radiations in the wavelength range of UV and visible. Hence, a hydrogen lamp or deuterium discharge lamp is preferred for UV, while a tungsten filament lamp for visible. Since the radiation emerging from the source carries various wavelengths it is preferred to use a monochromator to select a particular wavelength for study. The radiations of specific wavelength pass through the sample kept in the cell. A part of the radiation gets transmitted which reaches the detector. The detector detects the intensity of transmitted radiation which enables the recorder to plot a graph of absorbance versus wavelength. A general spectrophotometer uses photomultiplier tube as the detector, while in modern instruments photodiode is employed.

A UV-visible spectrophotometer can be either a single beam or double beam instrument. In a single beam spectrophotometer, a single optical path is allowed between the source and the detector. It consists of a single sample holding cell. Hence, before running the instrument with the sample, it should be calibrated with the blank solution. Blank solution is the solution in which the sample is dissolved. A Double beam spectrophotometer will have two optical pathways between the source and the detector. It consists of two sample holders, one each for reference or blank solution and the sample solution. In the routine test for narcotic and in general drug

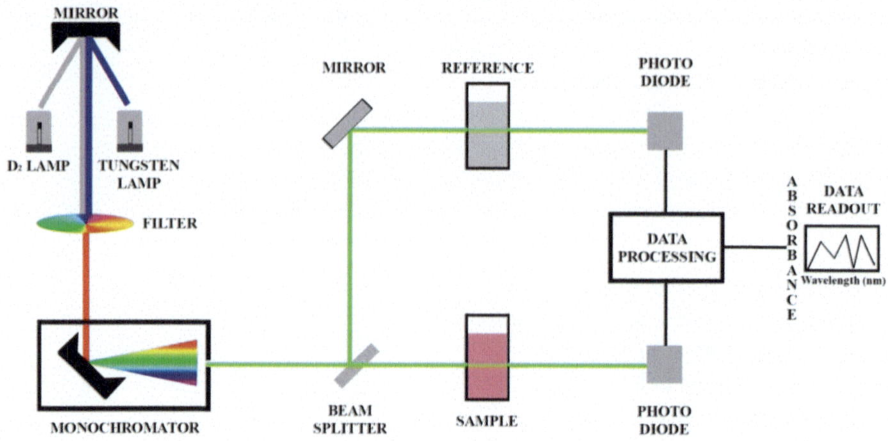

Fig. 5.23 Block diagram of double beam UV-visible spectrophotometer

testing, this technique serves best as various drugs possess a fixed range of absorption. In case of death due to drug overdose various bodily fluids can be analyzed by this technique. During the breathalyzer test, concentration of alcohol is measured by the same technique. In forensic document analysis, the technique enables the identification, examination, and characterization of ink. This method of ink analysis is preferred over other techniques due to its simplicity. UV-visible spectroscopy can also be used to analyze the amount of oxygen present in the hemoglobin and to detect the presence and concentration of salicylates in samples such as urine and in drugs obtained from various body fluids. In cases related to carbon monoxide poisoning, the detection of the presence of carboxy-hemoglobin formed by the combination of hemoglobin with carbon monoxide can be made possible by this method. It also serves the best in detecting whether blood stain is present on an object by detecting the presence of certain enzymatic activity.

Components that are separated by various chromatographic methods such as HPLC can be passed through UV-visible spectrophotometer to perform qualitative analysis. In cases where fibers are involved, this method of spectroscopy enables to determine the combinations of dyes used in them as well as enable their identification. It can also be used to analyze the presence of metals such as iron, copper, aluminum, lead, arsenic, etc. in evidence and at the same time quantify them. The major reason UV-visible spectrophotometer is preferred over other methods of spectroscopy is its quick analysis capability. The instrument is simple to operate and easy to use. The accuracy in analysis enables the method to be preferred during the evaluation.

5.4.2.2 Fluorescence and Phosphorescence Spectroscopy

Another frequently used technique in the field of forensic science is the fluorescence spectroscopy. The method of fluorescence and phosphorescence spectroscopy can be together considered as luminescence spectrometry. The principle of fluorescence and phosphorescence is used in analyzing a sample in this method. Electrons present in an atom revolve around the nucleus at the same time spin on its own axis. Hence, each electron has a specific spin associated with them. Normally an electron pairs with another electron of spin opposite. Hence, the net spin is zero. Such a state where an electron pairs with another electron of opposite spin is called a singlet state. In certain cases, an electron pairs with another electron of the same spin. Such a state is called a triplet state and here the net spin is not zero (Fig. 5.24).

There are different energy states associated with a molecule. This can be the ground singlet state, the first electronic singlet state, second electronic singlet state, excited triplet state, etc. When a radiation of particular wavelength is allowed to fall on the molecule, it absorbs the energy and gets excited to undergo a transition to higher electronic state. This can be the first or the second electronic singlet state. Only certain molecules undergo transition if bombarded with a radiation of specific wavelength.

As the figure suggests, a radiation of λ_1 wavelength enables the transition from ground state to second electronic singlet state while that of λ_2 enable the transition from ground to first electronic state. Since the electron is unstable in the higher levels, they emit the energy in forms of photons and falls back to lower levels. When the electron falls back to the lower level, they emit radiation of specific wavelength. This is called fluorescence. When the transition between the excited singlet state and the ground state include crossing to an excited triplet state, the radiation emitted is called phosphorescence. The transition of electrons from the excited singlet state to an excited triplet state is called an intersystem crossing. This does not result in the emission of photons; therefore, the process is termed as non-radiative relaxation. The instrumentation of a fluorescence spectrometer consists of a source that emits UV-visible radiation, an excitation monochromator, a sample holder, an emission monochromator, and a detector (Fig. 5.25). The source for UV-visible radiation can be xenon arc lamp, high pressure mercury arc lamp or lasers. The radiation from the source passes through the excitation monochromator which can be either a grating or a filter. Since laser emits a narrow beam of radiation of required wavelength, filters are not used while laser is the source of light. This filters out the required wavelength which excites the electrons in the sample. The electron on absorbing the energy emits light which we generally called fluorescence. This radiation of higher wavelength then passes through an emission monochromator which is placed 90° from the excitation monochromator. The radiations are detected by the detector which is generally a photomultiplier tube.

Fluorescence and phosphorescence spectroscopy can generally be used to detect carbon monoxide, carbon dioxide, cyanide and nitrogen poisoning by using probes of hemoglobin and myoglobin. Arsenic poisoning, lead poisoning, etc. can also be detected using this technique. It also serves the best for the characterization of ink in document analysis and in the analysis of drug, glass, petroleum as well as biological samples. The use of fluorescence spectroscopy in the study of marine petroleum pollutants has been accepted widely. It enables the determination of petroleum contaminants in water and to determine a particular petroleum derivative component

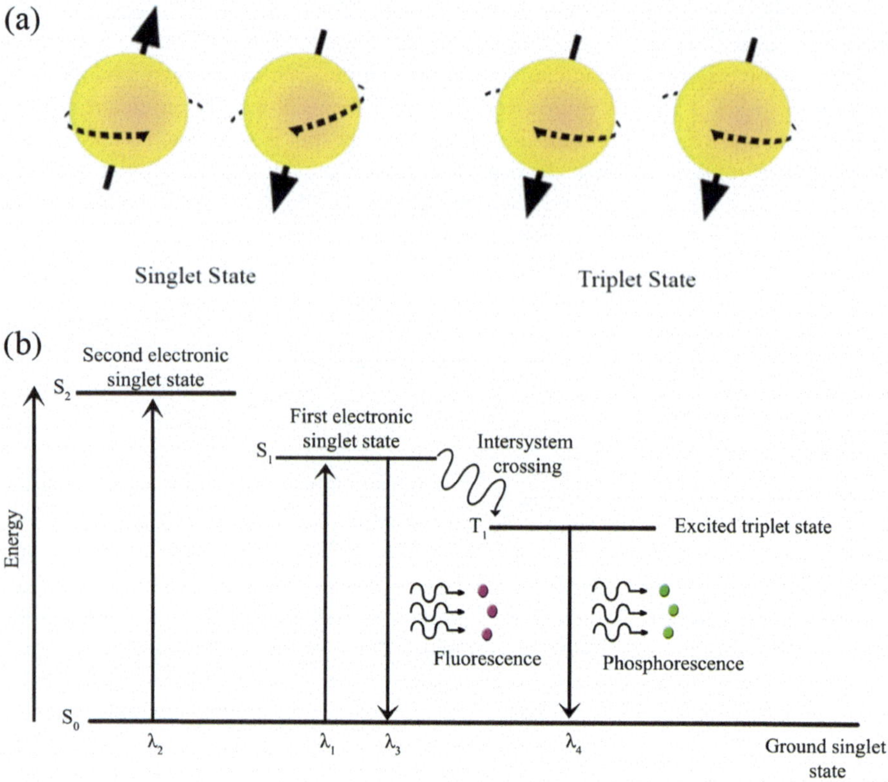

Fig. 5.24 (**a**) Spin of electron in singlet and triplet state; (**b**) Mechanism of luminescence

which enables the identification of the pollution source. Determination of glucose content in blood is also done by fluorescence and phosphorescence spectroscopy. Apart from this fluorescence spectroscopy is widely used in environmental, industrial, medical, DNA sequencing, forensic genetics, and biotechnological fields. The high sensitivity and specificity is what makes the method distinctive from other spectroscopic methods. At the same time, the analysis of a substance which possesses natural fluorescence can be done with greater specificity with fluorescence spectroscopy.

5.4.2.3 Infrared Spectroscopy

The region of the electromagnetic spectrum ranging from 800 nm to 1 mm in wavelength is termed as infrared region. This region is again divided into three. Region from 800 nm to 2.5 μm is called as the near infrared region (NIR), 2.5 μm to 25 μm is mid infrared region (MIR) and from 25 μm to 1 mm is far infrared region (FIR). When it comes to infrared spectroscopy wavenumber is considered. For near infrared radiation it extends from 12,500 cm $^{-1}$ to 4000 cm $^{-1}$, for mid infrared

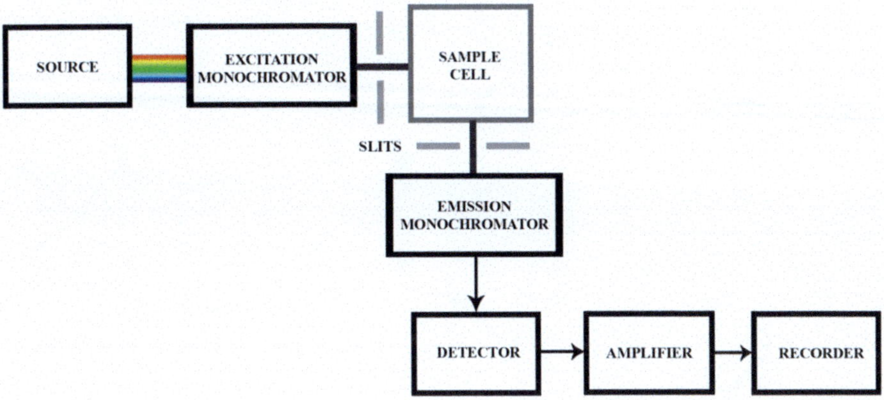

Fig. 5.25 Block Diagram showing the instrumentation of fluorescence spectroscopy

region it extends from 4000 cm $^{-1}$ to 400 cm $^{-1}$ and from 400 cm $^{-1}$ to 10 cm $^{-1}$for far infrared. The region of infrared radiation that is employed fir spectroscopy is its vibrational part which extends from 2.5 μm to 25 μm.

Vibrations within a molecule can be of two types stretching or deformation vibration. Stretching vibration is the result of a change of bond length while a change in bond angle results in the formation vibration. Defamation vibration can be bending, twisting, wagging, and rocking (Fig. 5.26). When an infrared radiation falls on a molecule as with other radiation molecules get excited to higher energy levels (Skoog et al. 1988). Not all molecules absorb infrared radiation. The absorption depends on the frequency of the radiation. A molecule absorbs infrared radiation when the frequency of vibration of infrared radiation matches the natural vibration frequency of that molecule. Even if the molecule's natural vibration frequency matches the frequency of infrared radiation if the molecule does not have dipole moment, absorption does not take place. Therefore, a compound having dipole moment is IR active where as a compound without a dipole moment is IR inactive. Once an IR spectrum of a molecule is obtained it can be called as a molecular fingerprint. No other molecule will show a spectrum identical to that particular molecule except for enantiomers. Hence, if the peak of a spectrum coincides with that of another it indicates that the two molecules are identical.

A normal IR spectrophotometer uses a monochromator to select a particular frequency of radiation. In case of FT-IR (Fourier transformation infrared spectroscopy) an interferometer is used instead of a monochromator. Hence, the spectrum is called an interferogram.

IR spectrophotometers can be either dispersive infrared spectrophotometers or Fourier transformation infrared spectrophotometers (FT-IR). In dispersive infrared spectrophotometer an IR source, mirror, sample cell, chopper, monochromator, detector, and readout are employed. Dispersive infrared spectrometer uses two sample holders, one for the reference and one for the actual sample to be analyzed. The beam after passing through the sample reaches a chopper and then to the

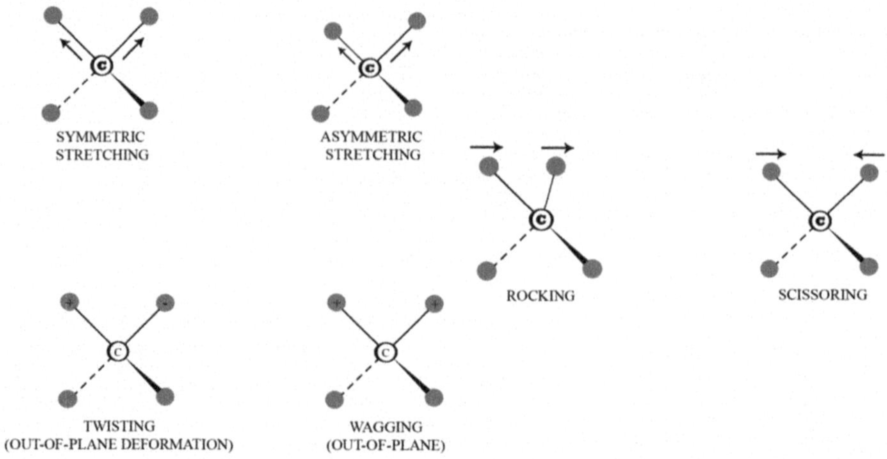

Fig. 5.26 The types of infrared vibrations

monochromator. The monochromator separates the radiation into individual wavelengths and then passes it on to the detector. The detector is capable of sensing the variation in the intensity of the reference beam and the sample beam. The signals obtained by the detector are amplified and sent to the recorder which provides the IR spectrum of the compound.

The FT- IR spectrophotometers are modern infrared spectrometers which make use of interferogram. Interferogram is a plot of intensity versus time. Since the plot of intensity versus frequency is preferred for spectral analysis, a mathematical operation known as Fourier Transform is used to obtain the individual frequency of absorption from an interferogram. Such an instrument is called an FT-IR. The main advantage of FT-IR over other instruments is that it takes only less than a second to obtain an interferogram. Figure 5.27 shows the diagram of an FT-IR instrument. FTIR spectrometer makes use of an interferometer. In the interferometer the radiation from the source passes through a mirror which is placed at an angle of 45° with the incoming IR radiation. This mirror is called the beam splitter. When the two reflected from the splitter recombine at the beam splitter, due to a change in the path length they undergo both constructive and destructive interference. This is then directed towards the sample. The signal from the sample is passed to the detector which then produces an interferogram. This interferogram cannot be read by humans and hence Fourier transform operation is implemented by using a computer which constructs a plot similar to an IR spectrum.

FT-IR spectroscopy is the most commonly used IR spectroscopy when it comes to crime laboratories. The FT-IR spectrum of each compound is unique which serves it the major instrument for analysis. Infrared spectroscopy can be used in the identification of paint, ink, sweat, fuel, hair, etc. It can also be employed in the identification of forged or altered documents by examining the ink, without even extracting it from the paper.

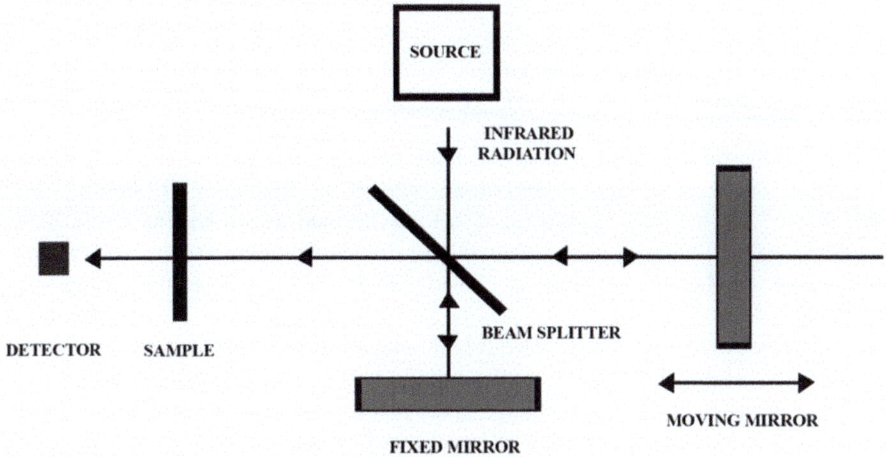

Fig. 5.27 Instrumentation of Fourier Transformation Infrared Spectroscopy

To study the origin of a fiber whether it is human, animal, synthetic or others, IR spectroscopy can be used. The examination of improvised explosive devices (IED) can also be made possible by IR spectrophotometer. Biological samples such as blood, cerumen (earwax), fingernails, feces, fingerprints, hair, vaginal mucus, nasal mucus, saliva, semen, and urine can be analyzed using IR spectrophotometer. Infrared spectroscopy acts as a powerful tool in the analysis of organic materials. The development of FT-IT made it to be used as a popular tool in the analysis of complex mixtures. The major advantage of using IR spectroscopy is that the sample after analysis can be regained intact and hence the method is non-destructive.

5.4.2.4 Raman Spectroscopy

When radiations in the visible region are allowed to pass through a sample a part of it is absorbed and transmitted by the sample. Along with this process a minute part of the radiation is scattered in all possible directions by the sample. If the frequency of incident light is taken as υ_i and that of scattered light as υ_s, then: If $\upsilon_i = \upsilon_s$, then the scattering is termed as Rayleigh scattering. Of the total scattered radiation, 1% shows a varied frequency. This is expressed as $\upsilon_i \neq \upsilon_s$. This is termed as Raman scattering.

When an electron is excited by absorbing the energy of an incident radiation, they transit to a virtual energy level. This electron then emits its energy and falls back to a lower level. If the energy emitted is equivalent to the energy of the incident Photon, hence:

$$h\upsilon_i = h\upsilon_s$$

This phenomenon is Rayleigh scattering and the electron fall back to its initial vibration level. When using the energy if the electron falls back into a different vibrational level, then it is called Raman scattering. This is indicated as follow:

$$h\upsilon_i \neq h\upsilon_s$$

$$\text{Hence}: \upsilon_i \neq \upsilon_s$$

Depending on the final energy or final vibrational level of electron Raman scattering can be stokes line or anti-stokes line. If the frequency of photon is less than that of the incident photon ($\upsilon_s < \upsilon_i$) it is termed as stroke line while if the frequency of the photon is greater than that of the incident photon ($\upsilon_s > \upsilon_i$) it is anti-stokes line. A Raman spectrum is considered as the molecular fingerprint of a molecule.

Raman spectroscopy is the method of analyzing the spectrum based on the inelastic scattering of monochromatic radiation. When a photon is incident on a molecule, process of energy exchange takes place. This results in the formation of scattered photon with either higher or lower energy than that of the incident photon. This energy difference that takes place within the molecule is compensated by changing the rotational and vibrational energy of the molecule. This provides the information about the energy levels (Fig. 5.28).

The instrumentation of Raman spectrophotometer consists of a laser, which projects the light towards the sample. The lasers of wavelength 532 nm, 785 nm, 830 nm, and 1064 nm are commonly used. This radiation passes onto a sample through fiber optic cables. Before reaching the sample, the light bends at an angle of 90° through a turning prism. This light then passes through a beam splitter, focusing lens and monochromator and finally reaches the analyte. The energy of the radiation is absorbed by the electrons and hence a transit from lower rotational and vibrational energy levels to a virtual energy state occurs. The radiation emitted is collected with the help of focusing lens to the entrance slit. The radiation emerging from the analyte possesses both Rayleigh and Raman scattered radiation. A filter removes the Rayleigh scattered light as well as the anti-strokes line. The entrance slit directs the light towards the grating where dispersion occurs. This produces various wavelengths and is detected by a detector. The detector used earlier was a charged

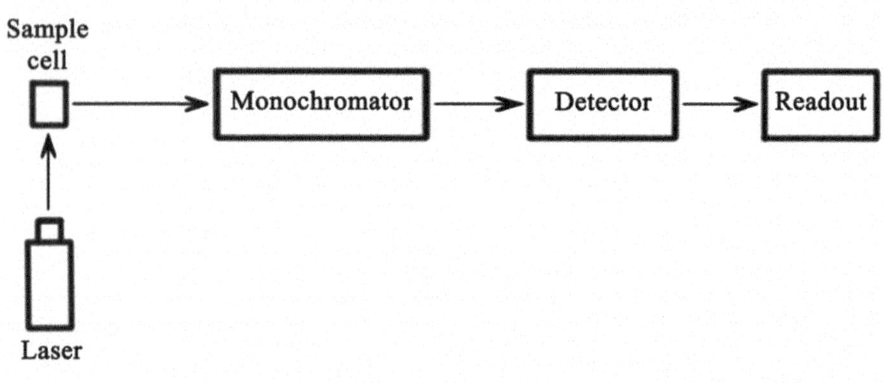

Fig. 5.28 Instrumentation of Raman Spectroscopy

coupled device (CCD) and is currently replaced by a photomultiplier tube (PMT) or photo-detectors.

Raman spectroscopy can be used to analyze bodily fluids. It also serves a good tool to differentiate between various bodily fluids. Apart from this human blood can be differentiated from animal blood and menstrual blood from peripheral blood. When a bodily fluid is contaminated by dust, soil and sand Raman spectroscopy helps in the identification of these contaminants. Raman spectroscopy is also used extensively in Forensic Chemistry to identify as well as differentiate various drugs, art objects, fibers, ink, paint, pigments, and body fluids. It can be used to detect almost eight barbiturates and sodium salt analogs in the analysis of drug of abuse (Bumbrah and Sharma 2015). Study of the mineralogical, chemical as well as physical properties of soil is also possible with the technique. Materials both organic and inorganic devoid of their nature as solid, liquid, vapor, polymer, etc. can be analyzed using Raman spectroscopy. Samples can be directly analyzed without any preparation. Obtaining Raman spectra takes only few seconds and it keeps the sample intact. Hence, this non-destructive can be applied even when the volume of sample is low.

5.4.2.5 Nuclear Magnetic Resonance Spectroscopy

NMR spectroscopy is a nondestructive technique which enables the forensic scientist to determine the chemical structure of toxin (protein), metabolites, drugs and even explosives. GC-MS and FT-IR which are other methods to identify a chemical substance has their own library which enable the identification of an unknown substance. When a previously unseen compound is to be detected and any record of it is not present in either GC-MS or FT-IR, NMR spectroscopy emerges as a useful technique in the laboratory.

Atom contains a nucleus and is surrounded by electrons. The nucleus houses the proton which can spin on its own axis as a result of which it creates a magnetic field around them. This magnetic field enables the atom to behave like a whole magnet. Since atoms can act as a magnet when two atoms are placed close to each other due to attractive and repulsive forces the atoms rearrange themselves and attain a stable state (Fig. 5.29).

When an atom is placed in an external magnetic field, the atom rearranges itself in such a way that the direction of the magnetic field of the atom coincides with that of the applied field. In this state the atom is said to be highly stable. Hence, an atom which is present in any orientation aligns itself in an external magnetic field to match the spin. Spin so achieved is called Alpha (α) spin.

If a particular amount of energy is supplied to the atom which is oriented towards the external field, it reverses its spin such that the atom turns a 180°. Such a spin is called Beta (β) spin. In Beta spin, the atom aligns opposite to that of the external magnetic field. Since there are electrons revolving around the nucleus, they tend to shield the magnetic field provided by the protons. The phenomenon by which electrons of the atom shield the magnetic field is called magnetic shielding. Magnetic shielding varies for different atoms because of the variation in the number of electrons present within an atom or nearby the atom. When a sample is taken in a

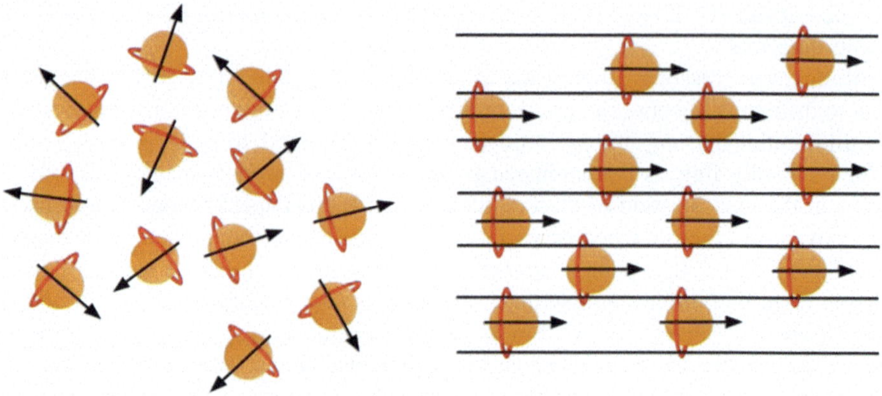

Fig. 5.29 Alignment of electrons while external field is applied

test tube and placed between the two poles of a magnet the nucleus of all the molecules in the sample align in the direction of the external magnetic field. This leads to the decrease in energy of the nucleus. When radiation of a particular energy is allowed to pass through the nucleus, it absorbs the energy and reverses its spin in such a way that the spin is opposite to that of the external magnetic field. The energy required by a nucleus to reverse its spin is individual to each nucleus. Most of the nucleus requires energy in the range of radio waves. The wavelength of the radio wave absorbed by each nucleus is different. The radiation after passing through the sample strikes the detector. The nucleus only absorbs radiation of that energy with which it could reverse its spin. Hence, when a plot is recorded the detector detects the radiation transmitted by the sample. NMR spectroscopy enables the identification of a particular atom or element in various locations as each atom produces a unique NMR signal depending on the location.

The instrumentation of NMR consists of permanent magnet, radio frequency generator, radio frequency detector, sample holder, magnetic coil recorder and read out system (Fig. 5.30). The sample holder is placed between the magnets. A glass tube is used to keep the sample. The magnetic coil generates a magnetic field when current flows through them. Once the radiation passes through the sample, energy released is detected and spectrum generated. Due to the high cost of the instruments most of the forensic laboratories lack NMR spectroscope and hence samples are analyzed privately in NMR spectroscopic labs.

The use of NMR in forensic science is of prime importance when it comes to the identification of drugs. Drugs both natural and synthetic in origin can be analyzed with the help of NMR. Drugs that are generally analyzed using the technique includes amphetamines and their derivatives, opiate alkaloids, cocaine, cannabinoids, anabolic steroids, etc. when it comes to forensic toxicology cases when poisons are involved in murder, sexual assault or other crimes are so common. The use of this technique helps the toxicologist to identify the poison. For this body

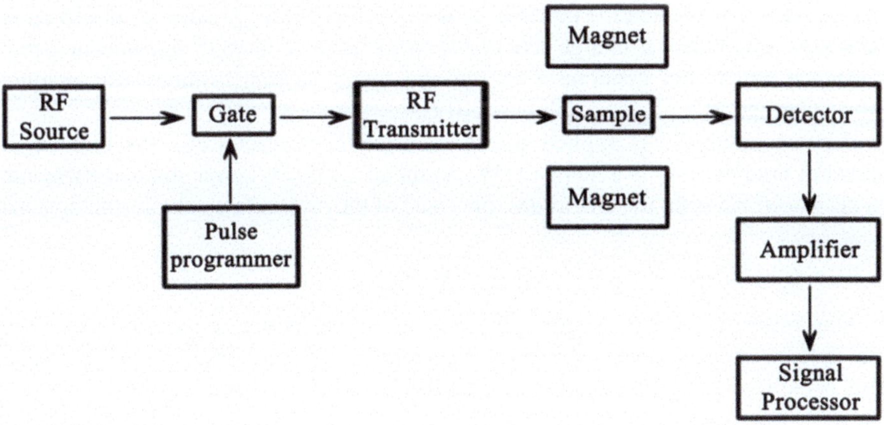

Fig. 5.30 Instrumentation of NMR

fluids and tissues are analyzed. In arson cases where hydrocarbon liquids are encountered and in the analysis of fossil fuels NMR plays a major role. Analyzing the post-explosion residues in cases of explosion helps to identify the type of explosion that occurred. When the amount of sample is in bulk amount, this technique enables its identification. NMR spectroscopy can be used to obtain valuable information about the structure of proteins and enzymes. It also enables to visualize the three-dimensional structure of proteins when a suitable software is used along with NMR. It possesses high data analysis and acquisition speed. By using this non-destructive technique precious samples can be recovered after analysis.

5.5 Electrophoresis

One of the highly efficient methods of separation frequently used in the field of forensic science is the electrophoresis. Electrophoresis is a separation technique which enables the migration of charged particles under the influence of an electric field. The method was first discovered in 1809 by Ferdinand Friedrich Reuss when he observed that the soil particles dispersed in water gets separated when an electric field was applied. When a charged particle is allowed to pass through an external electric field, the particle tends to exhibit differential motion. This is dependent on the charge and size or length of the particle. When such an electric field is applied to a colloidal particle (solid particles suspended in a fluid medium), the particles migrate towards the oppositely charged electrode because of the Electrostatic Coulomb force acting on the particle. As a result, the charged particle always moves towards the opposite charge. A molecule with a positive charge moves towards the cathode and that with a negative charge moves towards the anode. One of the major criterions of electrophoresis is that the molecules to be separated should possess a charge. This implies that the material be ionic or ionogenic (Mosher et al. 1992). A substance which has a charge associated with them is termed as ionic and that substance which can generate a charge and could be transformed into an ionic form is termed as ionogenic (Ghowsi 2012).

When a voltage V is applied across two electrodes placed at a distance "d" a potential gradient "E" is generated (Weatermeier 2005). When a charged molecule "q" is placed between the electrodes, the force of the molecule can be formulated as:

$$F = E \times q$$

This force drives the molecule towards the oppositely charged electrode. The principle behind electrophoresis is the differential rate of migration based on weight. This is expressed by the equation given below:

$$\text{Mobility of a molecule} = \frac{\text{Appplied voltage} \times \text{Net charge on the molecule}}{\text{Friction of the molecule}}$$

Certain factors both internal and external affect the process of electrophoresis. The inherent or internal factors include the magnitude of charge on the molecule and its weight and shape. External environment such as the pH, type and concentration of the buffer, electric field, viscosity of the solution, and temperature also affects the process of electrophoresis. Rate of migration of a molecule is inversely proportional to the size of the molecule and directly proportional to the charge. This means that when the size of a molecule is larger, then the rate at which it migrates under the applied electric field is less when compared to that of a molecule smaller in its size. The movement of the charged molecule when an electric field is applied is expressed in terms of Electrophoretic mobility, which is the velocity per unit of the electric field. Electrophoretic mobility is expressed as:

$$\mu = \frac{Eq}{f}$$

Where "E" is the applied voltage "q" the net charge on the molecule and "f" the frictional coefficient. The current between the two electrodes are conducted mainly by the ions of the buffer and partly by the ions of the sample. The sample to be separated may contain either solely positive charged or negative charges particle. In such cases it is easy to run the sample. For proteins, amino acids, peptides, and enzymes both positive as well as negative charges will be present within the same molecule and their charge is dependent on the pH of the buffer used for electrophoresis (Consden et al. 1946). Such molecules are said to be amphoteric. The buffer used in electrophoresis will have a constant ionic strength and pH.

The medium used in electrophoresis or the equipment used for separation such as glass plates or tubes, capillary, etc. carries a charged group within them. These may be the presence of carboxylic groups in gel such as starch or agarose or the silicium oxide present on the glass surface. When subjected to a buffer of particular pH they get ionized and attain a negative charge. Hence, they are attracted towards the anode.

Since these negative charges are fixed within the matrix, their migration is restricted. This result in the counter flow of water ions (H_3O^+) towards the cathode and thereby leads to the formation of blurred pattern in the band. This process is called electro-endosmosis. When the fixed groups carry a positive charge, the electro-osmotic flow gets directed towards the anode. This results not only in the blurring of bands but also causes the gel to dry.

Various types of electrophoresis are used widely in forensic science. This includes the gel electrophoresis, capillary electrophoresis, immunoelectrophoresis, moving boundary electrophoresis and immune electro focusing.

5.5.1 Gel Electrophoresis

When electrophoresis is performed on a network of hydrated gel as its matrix, the technique is termed as gel electrophoresis. The matrix which acts as a physical support medium consists of pores which enable it to act as a molecular sieve. Depending on the charge and size of the various molecules within a mixture they get separated by these sieves when an electric field is applied. When the molecule to be separated falls under the category of protein or nucleic acids, length is considered instead of their molecular weight. On performing electrophoresis, those molecules with large mass and length are said to stay on the upper region of the matrix, while those with mass and length lesser gets separated near the lower portion of the matrix. When it comes to gel electrophoresis, various types of gels are used depending on the type of molecule to be separated. The gel types include starch, agarose, and polyacrylamide (Magdeldin 2012). Agarose gel electrophoresis makes use of a natural linear polymer "agarose" which is obtained from seaweeds such as Gelidium and Gracilaria. It is a polysaccharide made of disaccharide units called agarobiose (Fig. 5.31) which is linked together by glycosidic linkage. Agarose is dissolved in a suitable buffer which introduces certain pores. Greater the concentration of agarose smaller will be the pore size. After dissolving agarose in the buffer, it is poured into the casting unit after placing the comb which serves in creating the wells for sample application is placed.

Once the support is ready the tank is filled with buffer solutions such as tris-acetic acid EDTA (TAE) or tris-borate EDTA (TBE), which are generally called as electrode buffer. Before adding the DNA sample, a ladder DNA whose molecular weight is known is added which act as a reference. Adding a ladder DNA enables in determining the length or molecular weight of the sample whose electrophoresis has been performed.

Once this process is done the sample to be separated is mixed with the loading buffer. If the sample alone is added into the wells, due to the decreased density they float over the matrix which prevents them from undergoing the process of separation. Addition the loading buffer increases the density of the sample and thereby prevent running away of samples from the well. The increased density enables the sample to sink into the pockets of the wells. To trace the process of separation and to prevent the running away of the separated sample from the bottom end of the matrix, certain

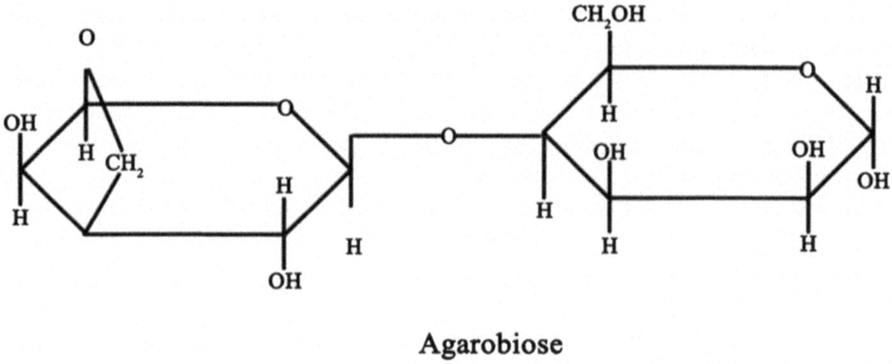

Fig. 5.31 Structure of Agarobiose

dyes such as bromophenol blue or xylene cyanol is added along with the loading buffer. Once the sample is applied, the chamber is covered with a lid and voltage is applied which initiates the process of separation. Once the process is completed the slab is taken out and visualized with the help of visualizing agents. Various visualizing methods includes ethidium bromide staining method, silver staining technique, etc. In the presence of UV light ethidium bromide fluoresce which enable the visualization of the separated fragments or molecules (Southern 1975).

Agarose gel electrophoresis has been widely used in the field of forensic science. It has even been used to measure the size of STR (Short Tandem Repeats) products.

5.5.2 Polyacrylamide Gel Electrophoresis (SDS-PAGE)

When electrophoresis is performed on a matrix made of polyacrylamide gel, the technique is termed as polyacrylamide gel electrophoresis. Polyacrylamide is made of monomers called acrylamide. When acrylamide is polymerized in the presence of ammonium persulfate (APS) and N,N,N′,N′-tetramethylene diamine (TEMED), a linear chain of polyacrylamide is formed which in turn undergoes cross linking to form cross-linked polyacrylamide. Sodium dodecyl sulphate is an anionic detergent which is added to polyacrylamide to eliminate the influence of structure and charge of protein in the process of separation. The protein which is folded with both positive and negative charge and having disulfide linkage unfolds when SDS (negatively charged) is added in the presence of reducing agents such as 2-mercaptoethanol. While the protein unfolds, they possess negative charge proportional to their length (Mikkelsen and Corton 2004).

To prepare the matrix, the acrylamide along with tris-HCl buffer is poured into the casting mold and is over layered with water to prevent direct contact between the gel and air. Once the acrylamide polymerizes, the water is removed. This layer of acrylamide acts as a separating gel. Over the separating gel, another layer of acrylamide with less concentration than the first is poured. This acts as a stacking gel layer. The comb is placed here to create wells for sample application. Once this process is completed, the sample is prepared. This is then mixed with twice the amount of sampling buffer and boiled for about 3–5 min. Before the sample is applied to the wells, the chamber is filled with electrode buffer. This is followed by sample application and the lid of the chamber is closed. When an electric voltage of 50 V is applied, the process of electrophoresis is initiated. Once the process is completed the matrix is taken out and placed in a tray which contains Coomassie brilliant blue and shake with an orbital shaker in room temperature. After the process is completed, the matrix is transferred into a destaining solution and the separated bands are visualized.

5.5.3 Capillary Electrophoresis

Capillary electrophoresis is an Electrophoretic method which is widely used in the separation of solvents with characteristic features such as thermal liability, high polarity, and non-volatility. This Electrophoretic method which works on the same basic principle of electrophoresis is widely applied in the field of forensic science due to its high efficiency and greater selectivity. Capillary electrophoresis uses a capillary which houses the matrix over which the process of separation takes place. The modern developments in the field of capillary electrophoresis as contributed by Jorgenson and Lucas in 1981 enabled the technique to be considered a mature as well as versatile method of separation. The analyte gets separated based on its Electrophoretic mobility which varies with the charge, size, and viscosity of the solvent.

The technique makes use of a thin hollow capillary tube filled with an electrolyte which enables the electro osmotic flow. The instrument is maintained such that the inlet possesses a positive charge while the detector end or the outlet a negative charge (Fig. 5.32). The capillary is connected to a buffer reservoir which is in turn connected to the electrodes. The characteristic property of the capillary is its efficient heat dissipation due to which high voltage can be applied during separation which enhances the rapidity of the process (Database 2020). The sample is introduced into the capillary through the sample injection system. Of the various types of capillary electrophoresis, Capillary Zone Electrophoresis, Capillary Gel Electrophoresis (CGE), and Micellar Electrokinetic Capillary Electrophoresis (MEKE) are widely used in forensic science. In case of Capillary Zone Electrophoresis, an open capillary column is used with a buffer low in viscosity (Jorgenson and Lukacs 1981). For Capillary Gel Electrophoresis, the capillary is filled with gel or any similar viscous solution as its matrix. For Micellar Electrokinetic Capillary, a charge detergent is added to the separation buffer that enables analyte devoid of charge to be transported through the capillary. When the concentration of the detergent is sufficiently high, micelles are formed. These micelles which are formed will break apart and thereby associate with the analyte thereby resulting in the migration of the analyte along with the micelle (Voeten et al. 2018).

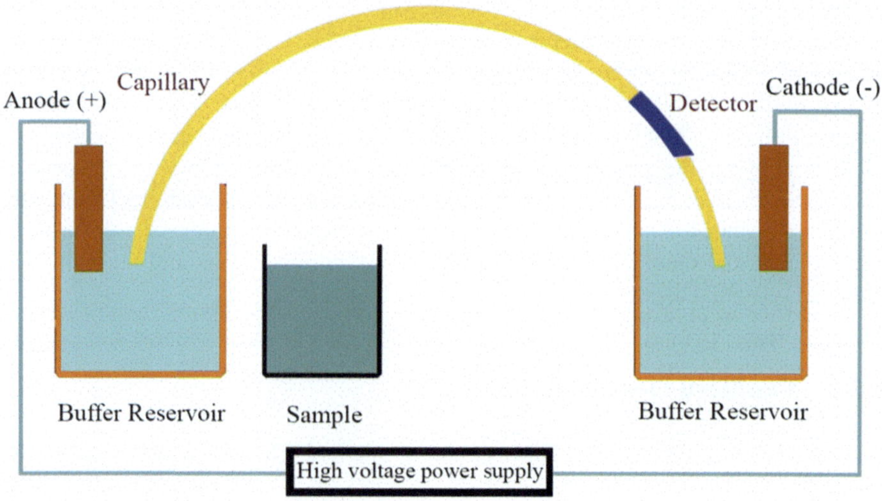

Fig. 5.32 Representation of capillary electrophoresis

Capillary Electrophoresis enables the separation of samples even in nanoscales quantities with few micro liters of reagents (Piette and Parmentier 2002). CE can be used to estimate the time since death by analyzing the amount of potassium in vitreous humor (Henssge and Madea 2004). Micellar Electrokinetic Capillary Electrophoresis facilitates the analysis of gunshot residues (Northrop 2001) and has also been used to detect the smokeless powder residue in pipe bombs (Smith et al. 1999). Screening for drugs using hair sample has been evidently possible when capillary electrophoresis is done (Petersen and Mohammad 2001). When urine contains drugs and other metabolites CE can be used to detect their presence with minimal sample (Lurie 1998).

5.5.4 Immunoelectrophoresis

Immunoelectrophoresis is a two-stage process where electrophoresis is applied to separate proteins followed by immunoprecipitation. The process of immunoprecipitation is attained with the help of antibodies against specific proteins. This has proved to be a suitable method to identify as well as quantify proteins by evaluating the differences in their antigenic composition and charge. The method was first devised in 1953 by Graber and Williams. The process is made possible by separating the proteins using electrophoresis using agar as the matrix. Once the proteins are separated suitable antiserum will be added which results in precipitation reaction when suitable antigen reacts with serum antibodies and thereby forms a line of precipitation (Levinson 2009).

By applying immunoelectrophoresis, a number of proteins present in serum can be identified (Laurell 1998). Various divisions of immunoelectrophoresis include counter-current immunoelectrophoresis, rocket immunoelectrophoresis, direct immunoelectrophoresis, etc. In counter immunoelectrophoresis the sample to be separated and the antibodies are places in respective wells and the antigen moves towards the anode and antibody moves towards the cathode when an electric field is applied on the agar matrix. The antigen having a charge moves electrophoretically and the antibodies are carried by the process of electro-osmotic flow. Electrophoresis can be performed on a glass slide where wells are punched out. Antigen and antibody are filled in the wells after which electric current is applied. After 30–60 min, the line of precipitation appears.

In immunodiffusion, a zone electrophoresis is done followed by diffusing the antigens towards the antibodies (Nowontny 1969). Rocket electrophoresis is a variant of radial immunoelectrophoresis developed by Laurell (1998). The bands formed after precipitation appears to be in shape of a cone or in a broader sense like a rocket. To perform rocket electrophoresis, antibodies are incorporated into the gel and antigens into the wells. Once electric field is passed, migration of antigens towards the agar gets facilitated. Quantitative estimation of antigen in serum can be easily determined by this process. The process of immunoelectrophoresis which is generally called as immunodiffusion is applied widely in clinical laboratories (Parija 2012).

5.5.5 Isoelectric Focussing

Electrophoretic method used to separate ampholytic molecules that act as weak acids and bases based on their isoelectric point is termed as Isoelectric Focusing (IEF).

Off the 20 amino acids present in a biological system 7 are having side chain groups that can be readily ionized. This indicates that at a certain value of pH they are neutral, while in certain other pH they become ionizable. Since a protein is composed of combination of amino acids including the ionizable one, the net charge on them varies with various physiological pH. Every protein has a pH value unique to themselves at which the overall net charge on them will be zero. This pH is called the isoelectric point (Brasher and Thrope 1998). This specific point is the property of a specific protein. Hence, if two proteins have the same composition of ionizable amino acids, they will have the same isoelectric point (Righetti et al. 1989).

This property can be made use to purify proteins. Hence, from a mixture of proteins various proteins can be separated as depicted in Fig. 5.33. Th e method which separates proteins based on their isoelectric point is called isoelectric focusing.

The IEF was developed by the works carried out by A J P Martin. To carry out the process we create a gel with a pH gradient by placing them on a special apparatus. The gel with a pH gradient will have low pH (acidic) at one end and high pH at the other (basic) whose ends are connected to a voltage source. The pH gradient is generated with the help of carrier ampholytes (Egen et al. 2019). The proteins mixture to be separated is placed on the gel. When two proteins which possess various isoelectric point is allowed to migrate in the presence of such an applied

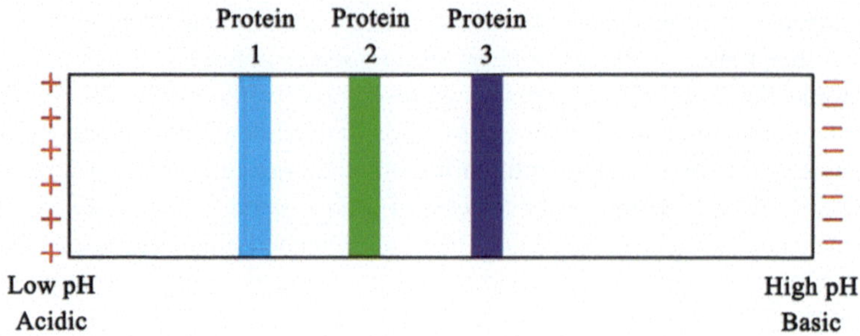

Fig. 5.33 Separation of proteins in IEF

electric field and pH gradient, they start to migrate towards the electrode having charge opposite to that of the proteins. As they move through the gel having a pH gradient, a point is reached where the pH reaches a value for which that protein becomes chargeless. Protein migration gets ceased at this point which is in turn their isoelectric point. This enables the separation of various proteins in a mixture (Righetti et al. 1990).

Contrary to other electrophoresis techniques where migration continues until the electric field is removed, IEF enable the separated proteins to cease migrating once the isoelectric point is reached even if the field continues to be applied. IEF can be performed in a number of formats including capillary IEF, IEF performed using large format devices, etc. When the carrier ampholyte is provided as a solution, a capillary can be used for the process of separation. Both gel and capillary has been widely used to perform IEF. Apart from them certain larger format devices enable the large-scale separation of molecules based on their isoelectric point. This includes the IsoPrime which was developed by Righetti and the Rotofor (Righetti et al. 1989). A typical IEF is shown in Fig. 5.34.

IEF has extensively been used to study post translational modification and for the identification of proteins. When proteins have to be identified from complex samples such as cell, tissue, or even plasma, IEF can be used (Pergande and Cologna 2017). Depending on the sample to be separated, steps prior to electrophoresis is employed including selection of the suitable buffer. The reason IEF is extensively used is its ability to separate large amount of sample with high resolution.

5.6 Conclusion

The importance of instruments and techniques in solving cases of forensic significant is well evident. Forensic science utilizes techniques and instruments allied with other pure fields of science. By adapting and adopting such techniques, many samples that are fragile in nature can be examined. The information collected from such examination serves for the better investigation process. The basic instrumentation and principles of major instruments discussed in the chapter also serves as the building

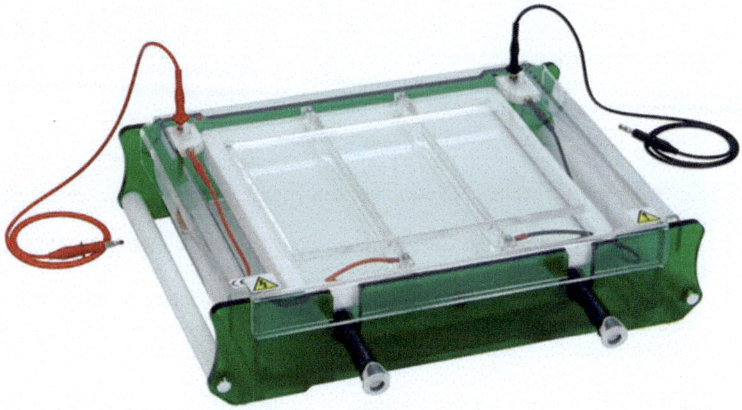

Fig. 5.34 Isoelectric Focusing Unit (Source: Alpha Matrix Biotech)

block for advanced techniques related to respective instrumentation. Various advancements have been introduced in the field of chromatography including ultra high-performance supercritical fluid chromatography. The above-mentioned technique has shown to serve the purpose of drug analysis. Vibrational spectroscopy is being analyzed more and advancements are being made to involve the instrument in forensic applications. Raman spectroscopy as well as attenuated reflectance spectroscopy is widely used now-a-days in sample analysis especially related to biological specimens. Microscopy can also be added to the list of instruments that are being innovated. Various inventions such as serial block-face SEM and focused ion beam SEM have proved to be better analytical tool in life science. Such techniques have high scope to be incorporated into forensic science for better sample analysis. The field has seen profuse advancements with capillary electrophoresis. This includes the microchip-capillary electrophoresis (ME) (Blanes et al. 2021). Each of the recent advancements in the field of instrumentation serves a high purpose in examining sample of forensic importance. Each advanced techniques and instrumentation are yet to be experimented with samples of forensic relevance. Hence, the scope and future of instrumentation and techniques in forensic science is wide.

References

Bell S, Morris K (2010) An introduction to microscopy. CRC Press, Boca Raton

Blanes L, Gabriel E, Saito R, Tomazelli W, Cole N, Doble P, Roux C, Santos R (2021) Capillary and microchip electrophoresis. In: Analytical techniques in forensic science. Wiley, pp 407–423. https://doi.org/10.1002/9781119373421.ch15

Braithwaite A, Smith FJ (1999) Chromatographic methods, 5th edn. Kluwer Academic Publisher

Brasher D, Thrope R (1998) Isoelectric focussing. In: Encyclopedia of immunology, 2nd edn. Academic press, pp 1510–1514

Bumbrah G, Sharma R (2015) Raman spectroscopy—basic principles, instrumentation and selected application for the characterization of drugs of abuse. Egypt J Forensic Sci 6(3):209–215. https://doi.org/10.1016/j.ejfs.2012.06.001
Chatwal G, Anand S (2019) Instrumental methods of chemical analysis, 5th edn. Himalaya Publishing House
Consden R, Gordon A, Martin A (1946) Ionophoresis in silica jelly; a method for the separation of amino-acids and peptides. Biochem J 40:33–41
Curry A (1953–1954) The application of paper chromatography to forensic chemistry. J Crim Law Criminol 44:787
David B, Barry C (2009) Transmission electron microscopy- a textbook for material science, 2nd edn. Springer, New York, NY
Egen N, Thromann W, Twitty G, Bier M (2019) New preparative isoelectric focusing apparatus. In: Electrophoresis. Electrophoresis '83. International Electrophoresis Society, Berlin, pp 547–550
Elkins KM (2019) Introduction to forensic chemistry. CRC Press/Taylor & Francis group, Boca Raton, FL
Ghowsi K (2012) Electrophoresis. InTech, Croatia
Hanai T (1999) HPLC: a practical guide. Royal Society of Chemistry, Cambridge
Heftmann E (2004) Chromatography, Journal of chromatography Library, vol 69B, 6th edn. Elsevier, pp 519–1156
Henssge C, Madea B (2004) Estimation of the time since death in the early postmortem period. Forensic Sci Int 144:167–175
Hollas JM (2002) Basic atomic and molecular spectroscopy. Royal Society of Chemistry
Jorgensen J, Lukacs K (1981) Zone electrophoresis is open-tubular glass capillaries. Anal Chem 53: 1298–1302
JoVE Science Education Database (2020) Capillary electrophoresis. In: Analytical chemistry. JoVE, Cambridge, MA
Kunsman G, Levine B (2003) Carbon monoxide/cyanide. In: Levine B (ed) Principles of forensic toxicology. American Association of Clinical Chemistry, Washington DC
Laurell A (1998) Immunoelectrophoresis. In: Encyclopedia of immunology, 2nd edn. Academic press, pp 1292–1297
Levinson S (2009) Immunoelectrophoresis. In: Encyclopedia of life science. Wiley, Chichester. https://doi.org/10.1002/9780470015902.a0001136.pub2
Lurie IS (1998) Capillary electrophoresis of illicit drug seizures. Forensic Sci Int 92:125–136
Magdeldin S (2012) Gel electrophoresis- principles and basics. InTech, Croatia
McNair HM, Miller JM (2009) Basic gas chromatography, 2nd edn. Wiley, pp 53–103
Mikkelsen S, Corton E (2004) Bioanalytical chemistry. Wiley, Hoboken, pp 213–224
Mosher R, Saville D, Thormann W (1992) The dynamics of electrophoresis. S.l. Wiley
Northrop DM (2001) Gunshot residue analysis by micellar electrokinetic capillary electrophoresis: assessment for application in casework part II. 3. J Forensic Sci 46:560–572
Nowontny A (1969) Basic exercises in immunochemistry: a laboratory manual. Springer, Berlin, pp 235–237
Parija S (2012) Textbook of microbiology & immunology, 2nd edn. Elsevier
Patzelt WJ (1974) Polarized light microscopy- principles, instruments, application, 3rd edn. Leitz, Wetzlar
Pavia D, Lampman G, Kriz G, Vyvyan J (2013) Introduction to spectroscopy, 5th edn. Cengage Learning
Pergande R, Cologna S (2017) Isoelectric point separation of peptides and proteins. Proteomes 5:4. https://doi.org/10.3390/proteomes5010004
Petersen J, Mohammad A (2001) Clinical and forensic application of capillary electrophoresis. Humana press, Totowa, NJ
Piette V, Parmentier F (2002) Analysis of illicit amphetamine seizures by capillary zone electrophoresis. J Chromatogr 979:345–352

Righetti P, Wenisch E, Faupel M (1989) Preparative protein-purification in a multi-compartment electrolyzer with immobiline membranes. J Chromatogr 475:293–309

Righetti P, Wenisch E, Jungbauer A, Katinger H, Faupel M, Faupel M, Preparative purification of human monoclonal-antibody isoforms in a multicompartment electrolyzer with immobiline membranes (1990) J Chromatogr 500:681–696

Skoog D, Holler F, Crouch S (1988) Principles of instrumental methods of analysis, 7th edn. CBS Publisher & Distributors, New Delhi

Smith K, McCord B, McCrehan W, Mount K, Rowe W (1999) Detection of smokeless powder residue on pipe bombs by micellar electrokinetic capillary electrophoresis. J Forensic Sci 44: 789–794

Southern E (1975) Detection of specific sequences among DNA fragments separated by gel electrophoresis. J Mol Biol 98:503–517

Ul-Hamid A (2018) A beginners' guide to scanning electron microscopy. Springer, Cham

Vo-dinh T, Gauglitz G (2003) Handbook of spectroscopy. Wiley-VCH, Weinheim

Voeten R, Ventouri I, Haselberg R, Somsen G (2018) Capillary electrophoresis: trends and recent advances. Anal Chem 90:1464–1481. https://doi.org/10.1021/acs.analchem.8b00015

Weatermeier R (2005) Electrophoresis in practice, 4th edn. Wiley-VCH, Weinheim

Wheeler P, Wilson J (2008) Practical foresic microscopy—a laboratory manual. Wiley-Blackwell

Willard H, Merrit L, Dean A, Settle. (1986) Instrumental methods of analysis, 7th edn. CBS Publications

Wilson LJ, Wheeler B (2009) Optical microscopy in forensic science. In: Encyclopedia of analytical chemistry. Wiley

Zadora G, Zuba D (2009) Gas chromatography in forensic science. In: Encyclopedia of analytical chemistry. Wiley

Crime Scene Investigation: An Introduction 6

Ashish Badiye, Pradnya Sulke, Harsh Sharma, and Neeti Kapoor

Abstract

Forensic science is a multidimensional field consisting of various subfields in it. Some of them are fingerprints, questioned documents, forensic toxicology, forensic biology, forensic ballistics, digital and cyber forensics, preventive forensics, etc. Crime scene investigation is an integral and fundamental part of forensic science. A proper investigation of a crime scene to establish its association with the suspect/s subsequently assists in proving or disproving the crime. An undisturbed crime scene may act as the most vital source of potential information. It is imperative to understand that every crime scene is unique. Crime scene investigation includes a chain of steps that a forensic expert must perform. It starts with securing the crime scene and providing medical assistance to a victim if required and ends with presenting evidence in the court following several different intervening steps. It also includes crime scene management which refers to managing different tools, techniques, expertise and other components for a successful scene investigation. This chapter provides an overview of several different aspects of crime scene investigation, the steps involved in it, crime scene management and crime scene reconstruction.

Keywords

Crime Scene · Management · Reconstruction · Documentation · Physical evidence

A. Badiye · P. Sulke · N. Kapoor (✉)
Department of Forensic Science, Government Institute of Forensic Science, Nagpur, Maharashtra, India
e-mail: ashishbadiye@ifscnagpur.in; neetikapoor@ifscnagpur.in

H. Sharma
National Forensic Sciences University, Bhopal Campus, Bhopal, Madhya Pradesh, India

P. Shrivastava et al. (eds.), *Textbook of Forensic Science*,
https://doi.org/10.1007/978-981-99-1377-0_6

6.1 Introduction

Crime can be defined as any unlawful act that is punishable by law. In the sociological aspect, crime is defined as the deviant behaviour of a person about the established or accepted standards of behaviour of a society (Sharma 2003). However, the Indian Penal Code defines crime as an act or omission that offends against an existing land law, is harmful to an individual or society, and is punishable by law.

Forensic science is a vast area consisting of several different subfields; some of these subfields are listed down. However, this is not an exhaustive list; many other subfields exist (Fig. 6.1).

A person who can recognize, identify, analyze, and classify the given physical evidence in reference to criminal and civil cases due to their education &/or experience is designated as a Forensic expert or forensic scientist. They have a set of roles to perform (Fig. 6.2).

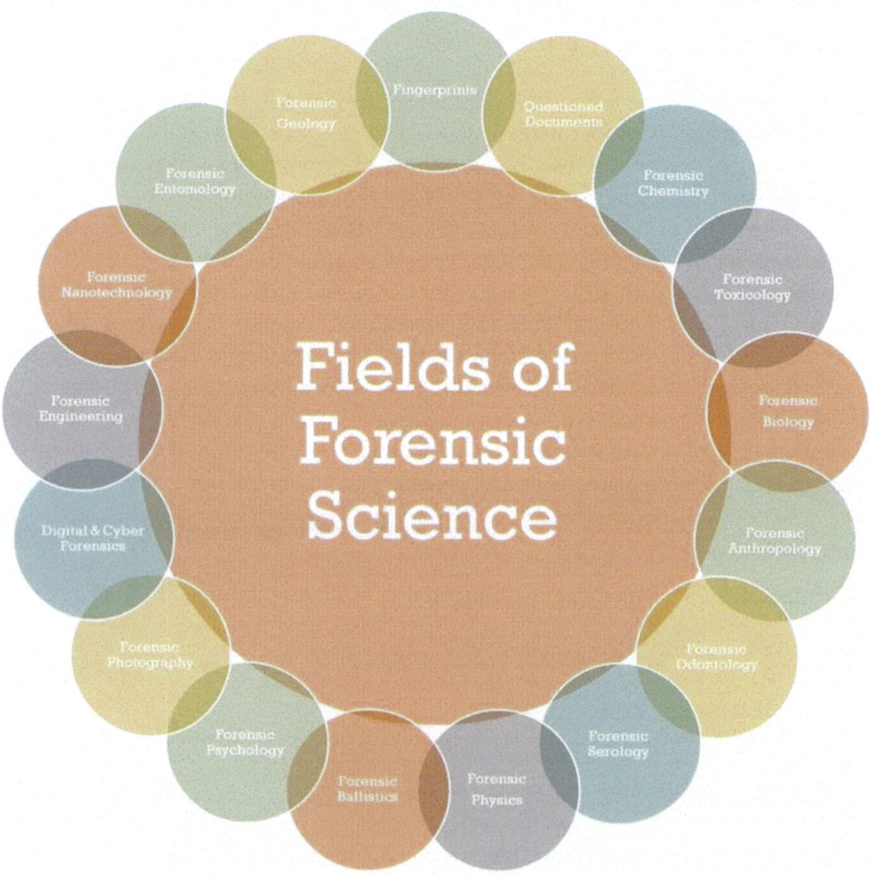

Fig. 6.1 Fields of Forensic Science

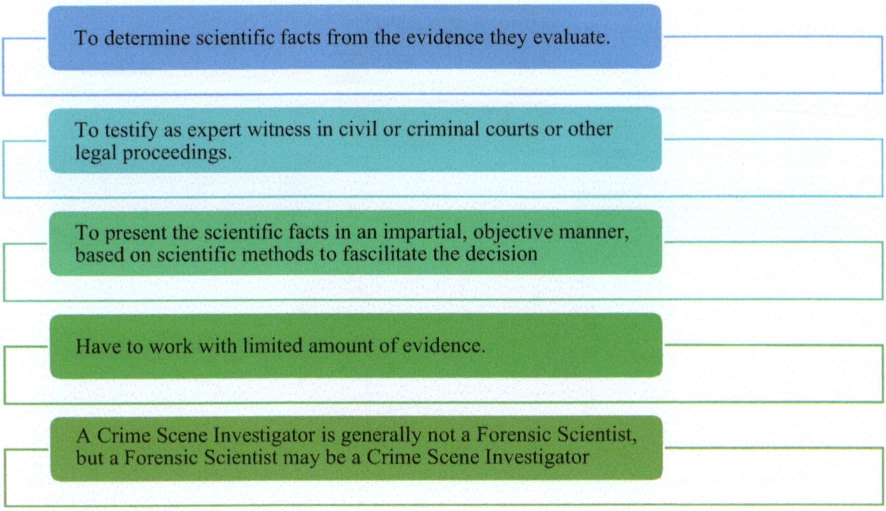

Fig. 6.2 Roles and Responsibilities of Forensic Expert

As the above figure depicts the different roles of a forensic expert, it suggests that proving facts in court primarily depends on the analysis of evidence encountered at the crime scene. Every crime scene is unique in itself. Hence, a thorough investigation of crime scenes is vital in solving criminal cases.

Like any other scientific discipline, Forensic Science also relies on a set of established principles and laws shown in Fig. 6.3.

6.2 Crime Scene Investigation

Forensic examination commences at the crime scene. A crime scene can be defined as a scene of the occurrence of a crime or the nearby and adjoining area where the crime was committed. It is the richest source of physical evidence relating to the crime, so it becomes of prime importance to investigate crime scenes thoroughly. If the investigator cannot correctly recognize, identify, collect, and preserve the evidence from the crime scene, it will undoubtedly hinder further laboratory examinations and the complete investigation procedure. Consequently, this makes crime scene investigation a foundation for investigating any criminal case to prove or disprove facts. Crime scene investigation is a systematic step-by-step process involving crime scene examination, which requires a blend of scientific knowledge, logical reasoning, systematic outlook, and investigative experience (Harris and Lee 2019). Crime scene investigation is believed to provide crucial information about the crime that are: (a) Information about corpus delicti; (b) Information about modus operandi; (c) Information about the link between a criminal, victim, scene and its objects; (d) Information about patterns of events. Crime scene investigation is

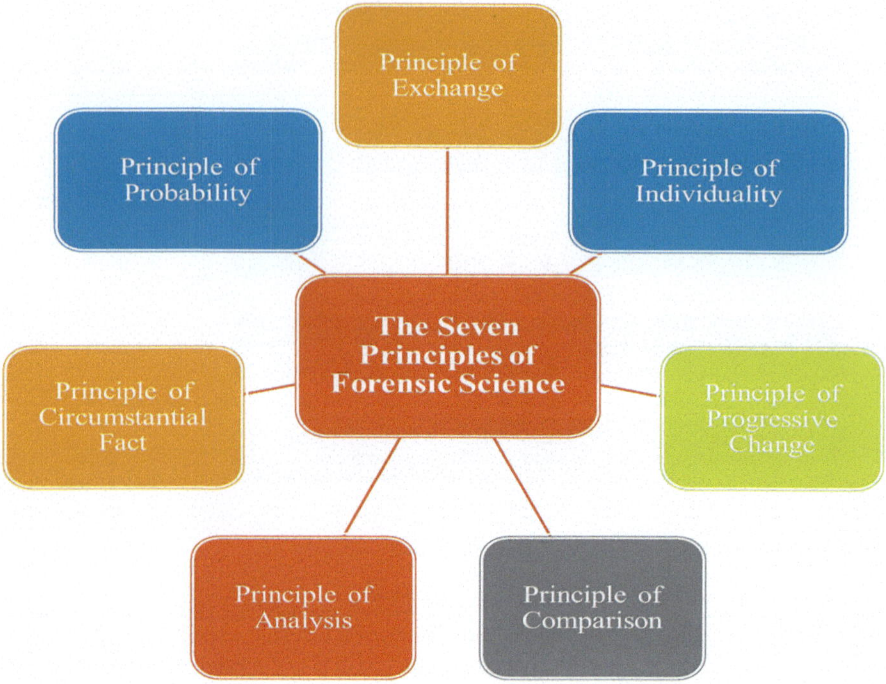

Fig. 6.3 The Seven Principles of Forensic Science

generally advised to carry out by an investigating team. Detailed steps of Crime Scene Investigation are discussed in other sections.

6.3 Types of Crime Scenes

There are several different ways in which crime scenes can be classified. Few classifications of crime scenes are (Harris and Lee 2019; Miller 2019; Lee and Pagliaro 2013) briefed below. In practice, crime scenes can exhibit characteristics of multiple size categories, and the classification may not always be clear-cut. Investigators and forensic experts assess each crime scene on a case-by-case basis, considering factors such as the nature of the crime, the location, and the extent of the area affected. Ultimately, the primary goal is to thoroughly process and analyze the crime scene, regardless of its size, to gather evidence and information that can aid in the investigation and the pursuit of justice.

Classification based on physical location: Based on where the crime was committed, crime scenes can be classified as indoor, outdoor and mobile crime scenes. Crimes committed within any built-in properties such as hotels, houses, gyms, auditoriums, etc., are known to have an indoor crime scene. In contrast, these crimes committed in the external environment, such as gardens, roads, forests, farms, etc., are known to have outdoor crime scenes. Moreover, the crime scene for a crime committed in any moving transportation medium such as a car, bus, auto, etc., is called a mobile crime scene.

Classification based on the original location of the crime: Crime scenes can be categorized as primary and secondary. A primary crime scene is an original location where the crime has been committed. It is the initial site where the illegal activity occurred, such as a murder, robbery, or assault. The primary crime scene holds significant evidentiary value, as it can provide crucial clues about the nature of the crime, the sequence of events, and the individuals involved. In contrast, the secondary crime scene refers to a location or locations that are related to the primary crime scene but are not the actual site where the crime occurred. Secondary crime scenes can include areas where the perpetrator disposed of evidence, attempted to create an alibi, or attempted to cover up the crime. Examples of secondary crime scenes include a site where a body was dumped, a vehicle used in the crime, or a location where stolen goods were hidden.

Classification based on the size of a crime scene: They can be classified as macroscopic and microscopic crime scenes based on the size of the crime scene. Macroscopic crime scenes are typically large-scale crime scenes that encompass a wide area. These crime scenes often involve outdoor locations such as parks, fields, or entire buildings. Examples of macroscopic crime scenes include homicide scenes in public spaces, large-scale arson incidents, or complex crime scenes involving multiple rooms or outdoor areas. The scene focused on particular evidence from the extensive crime scene is referred to as a microscopic crime scene. Contrary to this, Microscopic crime scenes are small-scale crime scenes that involve highly focused areas. Examples of microscopic crime scenes include cases involving trace evidence analysis, such as fiber or hair analysis, or scenes involving the recovery of microscopic biological samples.

Classification based on the type of crime committed: Crime scenes can be widely classified depending on the type of crime committed, such as homicide crime scene, robbery crime scene, etc. It is not the case with every type of crime that it shall have the physical location or the scene for the crime. Crimes such as cybercrimes, corporate frauds, forgeries, etc. need not have physical crime scenes. With the rise in the use and abuse of technology, the crimes are now being committed in virtual space. Virtual crime scenes refer to crimes committed in the digital realm, such as cybercrimes, online fraud, or hacking incidents.

Classification based on the scene's appearance. Depending on the condition and the appearance of the crime scene, it is categorized as organized and disorganized crime scenes. An organized crime scene is characterized by a deliberate and planned approach by the perpetrator. It typically indicates a higher level of control, premeditation, and sophistication in the commission of the crime. In organized crime scenes, there is often evidence of careful staging, concealment of the crime, and attempts to minimize the chances of detection. The scene may appear orderly, with a lack of obvious signs of struggle or chaos. The perpetrator may have taken measures to clean up or remove evidence, such as wiping away fingerprints or disposing of incriminating materials. Organized crime scenes can be more challenging for investigators due to the calculated efforts made to leave minimal traceable evidence. A disorganized crime scene, on the other hand, is characterized by a spontaneous, chaotic, and unplanned nature. It suggests a lack of control and forethought on the part of the perpetrator. Disorganized crime scenes often exhibit signs of violence, struggle, and disorder. Evidence may be scattered, and there may be indications of impulsive actions by the offender. The scene may contain disarray, overturned furniture, broken items, and signs of a hasty exit. Investigators typically encounter a wider range of evidence in disorganized crime scenes, including bloodstains, torn clothing, or items left behind by the perpetrator.

Classification based on criminal activity: Crime scenes can be labelled as active and passive depending on the offender's activity. An active crime scene refers to a situation where the criminal activity is currently ongoing or has recently occurred. It implies that the perpetrator is still present or may return to the scene. Active crime scenes require immediate response from law enforcement and emergency services to ensure public safety and apprehend the offender. Examples of active crime scenes include an ongoing hostage situation, a bank robbery in progress, or an assault occurring at the scene. The primary focus in active crime scenes is to mitigate the immediate threat and secure the area for the safety of individuals involved. A passive crime scene, in contrast, refers to a location where the criminal activity has already taken place and is no longer ongoing. It is a crime scene that investigators arrive at after the incident has occurred, and there is no immediate danger to individuals present. Examples of passive crime scenes include a burglarized home, a homicide scene where the perpetrator has left, or a site where a robbery has already taken place. In passive crime scenes, the focus shifts to the collection of evidence, documenting the scene, and conducting a thorough investigation to determine what happened and identify the responsible party.

6.3.1 First Responding Officer

The crime scene is a dynamic system that changes by adding or removing traces. It changes soon after the arrival of the first responders; thus, they have the authority not to contaminate the crime scene and work appropriately. First responders are the only persons who have a view of the crime scene in its original state. Thus, actions and steps taken by first responders have a significant impact on crime scene investigation. First responders are generally police officers, emergency service officials, etc. They have several key responsibilities that form the extent of further investigation success. The recommended actions for the first responding officer are (Saferstein 2015; Miller 2019; Fisher 2004; Ogle and Plotkin 2018; U.S. Department of Justice Office of Justice Programs 2000);

- Assist the victim(s) with any signs of life and provide instant medical assistance.
- Call the medical emergency.
- Guide medical personnel to not hamper the other physical evidence while assessing the victim(s).
- Document statements of the victim(s) if at death's door.
- Search for the suspect if still present near the scene.
- Define the boundaries of the crime scene, and secure it using crime scene control tape.
- Protect the scene from outsiders, media and other personnel.
- Call the crime scene investigator and other experts required for the examination.
- Interview witnesses (if present) and nearby persons.
- Maintain the log of persons entering the crime scene.
- Scan the crime scene, and look for any vehicle or persons leaving the crime scene or any other that may be related to the crime.

6.4 Steps in Crime Scene Investigation (Fig. 6.4)

6.4.1 Securing and Isolating Crime Scene

Protecting the crime scene is the first and foremost step in crime scene investigation. The first responding officer is responsible for protecting and securing the crime scene. Locard's principle of exchange suggests that every contact leaves traces, the same way every person entering the crime scene will transfer some traces to the crime scene and also take some traces from the scene (Miller 2019). Thus, the entry of persons to the scene should be restricted to maintain the originality of the crime

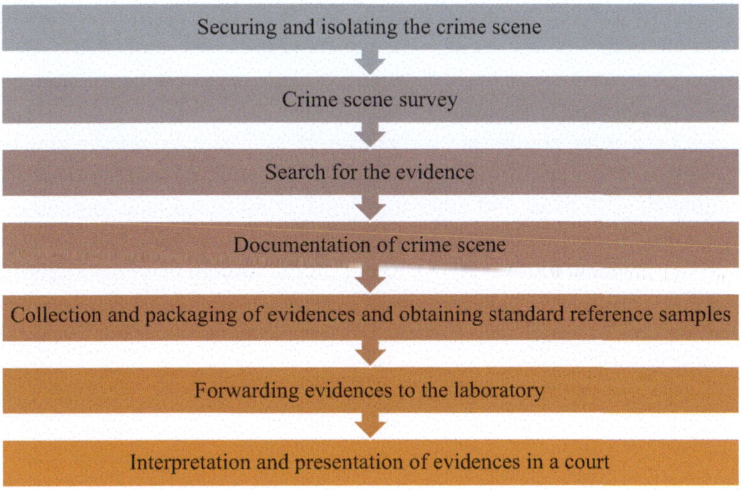

Fig. 6.4 Steps in Crime Scene Investigation

scene. Once the victim is provided with medical assistance (if required), the scene's boundaries are set and barricaded using a crime scene control tape (Saferstein 2015; Harris and Lee 2019; Miller 2019; Ogle and Plotkin 2018; U.S. Department of Justice Office of Justice Programs 2000). If this is not available, the crime scene can be secured using any other things readily available at the crime scene, such as wooden sticks, ropes, bricks, stones, etc. Crime scene securing appears to be an uncomplicated step, but in real-life scenarios, it may be proved to be strenuous, especially for outdoor crime scenes and thus require logical and practical command of the investigator. Once the scene is barricaded, it is guarded against unauthorized personnel from entering the crime scene. Subsequently, the lead investigator can enter the scene and evaluate the area. Other experts are also called to the scene, for instance, fingerprint expert, autopsy technician, etc., if required. An entry log for every person entering the crime scene is maintained (Harris and Lee 2019). The first responding official shares crucial information about the crime and the scene with the crime scene investigator. The body is maintained undisturbed if the victim is dead, rather than hastily sending it for autopsy. Observing the body's external appearance, position, etc. is recommended. Since, after removal of the body, the documentation of all these aspects would not be possible.

6.4.2 Crime Scene Survey

Once the crime scene is secured and protected, the initial survey of the scene begins. The primary 'walk-through' provides a vital overview of the scene, threats to the scene's integrity, and recognition and protection of potential physical evidence (U.S. Department of Justice Office of Justice Programs 2000). Generally, it is recommended that the scene survey is performed by the crime scene investigator and the first responder officer together (Miller 2019). Scene survey includes determination of entry and exit points of the suspect. With this, preliminary documentation is also conducted. Note-making while surveying is recommended to document the condition of the crime, such as the condition of electric switches, displacement of any furniture, prediction of any violent acts, etc.

Along with the crime condition, 'walk through' assists in recognizing the possible evidence. Any evidence requiring immediate preservation, pattern evidence that may get contaminated with time, and other transients, conditional, and transfer evidence should be identified as soon as possible in this survey (Harris and Lee 2019; Lee and Pagliaro 2013; Ogle and Plotkin 2018). Recognition, though becomes slightly tricky, as this depends on the practical experience of the investigator. Lastly, the scene survey also includes formulating the possible crime theory to assist further investigation (Miller 2019).

6.4.3 Search for Evidence

Searching of evidence is the systematic and orderly search for possible physical evidence on the crime scene (Lee and Pagliaro 2013). This is the critical stage of crime scene investigation. After the scene survey, the potential pieces of evidence might be overlooked, and this is the step where the crime scene investigator performs a detailed search for the possible potential evidence for the crime. As mentioned in the earlier section, evidence recognition is not easy as it requires the practical experience of the crime scene investigator. The crime scene search should be thorough and systematic to avoid missing evidence. This becomes the integral step as the case is solely proved based on analysis of the evidence; thus, if the single piece of evidence goes out of hand while scene investigation, further there will be no privilege to recover this evidence, which may hamper the investigation.

Crime scene search being the spine of the entire crime scene investigation can be done using five different search patterns that are as follows (Saferstein 2015; Ogle and Plotkin 2018; U.S. Department of Justice Office of Justice Programs 2000):

Strip or line method: In this pattern, the crime scene is set into parallel rectangular strips, and each strip is searched by an investigator moving along the strip in the same direction. The size of the strips depends on the size of the crime scene. This method is suitable for outdoor crime scenes with defined boundaries for searching for small to medium-sized evidence.

Grid method: In this method, the investigator first moves along the strips as in the strip method and then searches the strips that are angled at a right angle to the initial strips. This is more thorough than the strip method, as each site is searched twice. This method is also preferred for the crime scene that has defined boundaries.

Zone or quadrant method: In this search pattern, the scene is divided into different zones or quadrants, and different investigators then search each quadrant. These zones can be then again subdivided into smaller zones for detailed zones.

Spiral method: In searching crime scenes using spiral methods, the investigator could either start searching from an innermost point or the periphery and then move in a spiral fashion. Nevertheless, depending upon the crime, the search is recommended to be started from the periphery, as starting from the innermost point may destroy evidence when the investigator moves inside, to begin with.

Wheel method: In this method, multiple investigators move from the boundaries of the crime scene to the inner centre point or vice versa.

Selecting an appropriate search method is the investigator's job, and depending on the scene size and complexity, the investigator may choose any of the above methods. Sometimes, the combination of two methods can also be used. Moreover, sometimes the scene is such that any method may not be proved very useful. During the search, every piece of evidence is marked for future reference.

6.4.4 Documentation of the Crime Scene

After the evidence is located, the next step is to document the crime scene. Documentation is also significant as it would assist the expert in testifying the facts in court with proper proof of the crime scene. The main aim of documentation is to record the crime scene's condition and preserve the crime scene for future analysis if required. Documentation is believed to be the most time-consuming step of crime scene investigation. Crime scene documentation is traditionally done using four different sequential methods that are discussed below;

6.4.4.1 Note Making

This process begins with the arrival of the first responding officer. This is usually the handwritten documentation of the crime scene. Notes can be an effective way of documenting the scene items that cannot be photographed or videotaped (Harris and Lee 2019). Notes should contain all the necessary information that is (Saferstein 2015; Harris and Lee 2019; Miller 2019; U.S. Department of Justice Office of Justice Programs 2000):

- Date and time at which the first responding officer was informed about the crime and at which the first responder arrived.
- Who informed about the crime?
- All the information of other persons contacted about the crime along with their arrival and departure times.
- Scene description includes major structures present on the crime scene, condition of the crime scene, presence of conditional evidence, etc.
- Victim description about the condition of the victim, position, presence of wounds, jewellery, identification information, etc.
- Any unusual thing or change on the scene should also be noted down.

These are some vital information that should be noted down to ensure proper scene documentation. The first responding officer is the first to arrive at the scene; thus, he has the job of making proper notes and documenting the original crime scene. Voice notes may also be used in place of or along with written notes.

6.4.4.2 Photography

The primary purpose of crime scene photography is to provide an accurate and unaltered record of the crime scene. Digital photography is preferred these days over film photography. Three types of photographs are taken at the scene of a crime, as shown in the Figure below. The overview or overall or bird's eye view photographs are usually taken from a ground higher up, from corners, to cover the entisre crime scene and maximum evidence in a single shot. The next set of photographs is mid-range photographs. These cover the closely located evidence along with a fixed point of reference. The next in the sequence are close-up photographs of the individual evidence without a scale of reference and then a scale of reference. A log must be maintained (Fig. 6.5).

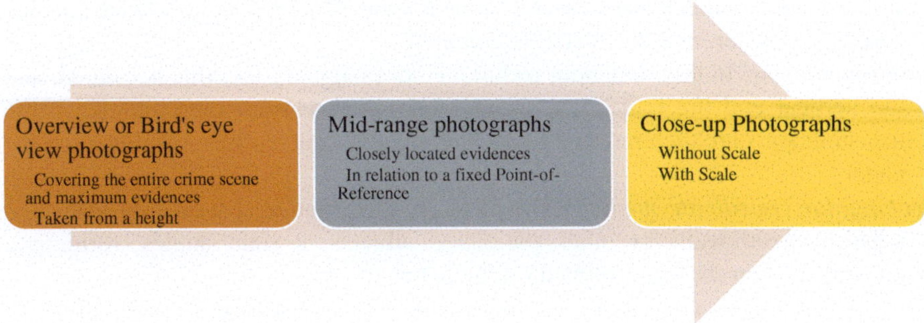

Fig. 6.5 Crime Scene Photography

Fig. 6.6 Crime Scene Sketching Types

6.4.4.3 Sketching

This is a way to document the crime scene so that the position of every piece of evidence and other items can be recorded. The investigator does crime scene sketching. Sketch provides the best two-dimensional representation of located evidence and the interspaces between two other pieces of evidence (Saferstein 2015). Thus, sketches are the permanent record of the size and distance of the crime scene and its physical evidence (Ogle and Plotkin 2018). There are two types of sketches: (a) rough or preliminary sketch: This is the rough representation of position of the evidence without any measurement. This sketch is drawn on the crime scene itself. Moreover, while investigating the scene, the investigator takes measurements for every piece of evidence to prepare a fair sketch. (b) Fair or finished sketch: This is prepared in the laboratory using measurements taken during crime scene investigation, using any of the methods described below. Whether rough or fair, sketch should consist of the date, name and signature of investigating officers, legends, case number, etc. (Fig. 6.6).

Sketching can be done using one of the following methods (Miller 2019; Ogle and Plotkin 2018; U.S. Department of Justice Office of Justice Programs 2000);

Triangulation method: Two reference points are chosen at the crime scene, which are immovable from the crime scene, such as two ends of a wall, etc. The distance of evidence is measured from these two points subsequently. Distance between the two reference points is also measured. These measurements are then converted into smaller units using a suitable scale. The pieces of evidence are then marked on paper, and the sketch is prepared.

Baseline method: In this sketching technique, an imaginary baseline is created, and the vertical and the horizontal distance of evidence from the baseline. These measurements are then reduced to smaller values using a scale and plotted on the paper.

Rectangular coordinate method: The distance of evidence is measured from two adjacent fixed walls or other stationary subjects at right angles, forming a rectangle. Then these are plotted on the paper.

Polar coordinate method: This method measures the distance from a fixed reference point and the angle from the fixed line originating from the reference point. This method is best suited for large outdoor crime scenes with less availability of fixed points. This method requires a compass and protractor to determine the direction and angle of the evidence from the point.

Computer-based software: With the increase in the use of technology for every aspect, Forensic scientists are also making great use of modern technologies. Advanced computer software is now available to provide two- and three-dimensional sketch (Harris and Lee 2019; Fisher 2004). These computer-aided programmes have a library of different already drawn objects such as furniture, building, vehicles, etc. These software provide more accurate scene drawings than handmade sketches as the former are more subjected to human errors. This method assists in crime scene reconstruction and is the best tool for reconstructing shooting scenes, blood spatters, arson cases etc.

6.4.4.4 Video-recording

This is also another potential method of recording a crime scene. The investigator moves through the crime scene recording all the scene aspects on a camera. This method has advantages over photography as it records the scene live and provides a tour of the crime scene (Saferstein 2015; Fisher 2004; Ogle and Plotkin 2018). However, it also has some disadvantages over conventional photography; one such is, as it records everything in the video, it may capture the extra background noise. Also, cameras' stabilization and zooming power may affect the recording (Saferstein 2015; Ogle and Plotkin 2018). While videotaping the scene some cautions must be excercised (Saferstein 2015; Harris and Lee 2019; Fisher 2004; Ogle and Plotkin 2018; U.S. Department of Justice Office of Justice Programs 2000); The date, time and day should be accurately adjusted before starting the video recording; The videotaping should be done very slowly; Recording should incorporate every aspect of the crime scene including the entry and the exit point of the scene and also the located evidences; The overview, mid-range and close-up section for the located evidences are advised to be included; Usage of appropriate front and side lighting and also there should be an arrangement for removal of flash; The investigator is recommended to narrate the scene accurately while recording including time, date location and case number, to avoid future confusions but this remains controversial whether to include audiotape or not, as some authorities suggest a big no to include audio tapes; The filming should not include needless equipments used during investigation and other scene personnel; These were some necessary precautions that are needed to be advocated while recording the crime scene.

6.4.5 Collection and Packaging of Evidence

After crime scene documentation, the next step is collecting and packaging evidence. Evidence being an integral part of the case investigation must be collected and packed to avoid contamination and cross-contamination (Kleypas and Badiye 2023). The collection and packaging of evidence should be done in a considerate manner, and some precautions to be considered that are listed below;

- Transient and fragile evidence should be collected first and carefully to exclude its damage.
- If there are multiple objects in evidence, each object should be separately packed.
- Every packed evidence should be labelled with its evidence number.
- If some packages have biologically hazardous material or any other hazardous material such as inflammable liquids, they should be labelled with their respective tags for such hazardous materials.
- Evidence such as blood spatter, gait pattern, etc., must be photographed as soon as possible to maintain its authenticity.
- The collection should be done such that any addition by the investigator should be strictly avoided, and to do this, the investigator is advised to wear safety gear.
- Handpicking of evidence should be done cautiously, and the investigator should try to touch the evidence such that a minimum area remains in contact.

These primary guidelines must be kept in mind while collecting evidence from the scene. Besides these general precautions, there are no uniformly proposed guidelines for collecting evidence (Fig. 6.7).

Different type of evidence requires different techniques of collection. Collection and packaging principles for a few pieces of evidence are discussed below;

Collection of biological and serological evidence such as blood, hair, fibres, and other body fluids: Blood, if wet, should be collected using dry swabs and if pool is available, it is recommended to collect using syringes and store it in appropriate vials. If dry (dry blood stains), blood can be collected using wet swabs or scrapping. Other body fluids can be collected in the same way as blood. Evidence such as hair, fibres, etc., should be collected using rubber tip forceps or vacuumed and packed in Ziplock bags or can be wrapped in paper using the druggist fold method. Other biological evidence, such as nails, tissue samples, etc., should be handpicked (wearing gloves) or using rubber tip forceps.

Collection of clothing having biological stains: Clothing items are handpicked, and if wet, they are recommended to be air-dried before packaging. They should be packed so that stains are not altered, folded carefully, and packed in paper, a cardboard box, or an envelope. If collective clothes are found, they are advised to

Fig. 6.7 Some of the physical evidence encountered at the crime scene

pack separately (Fisher 2004; U.S. Department of Justice Office of Justice Programs 2000).

Collection of fingerprints: Visible fingerprints should be immediately photographed to preserve them. If feasible, tape lifting should be used to collect these. Latent fingerprints are first developed using any suitable method, and then tape lifting and photography can be used to collect and preserve these fingerprints. Care should be taken that some development methods render temporary prints; they should be quickly preserved or processed to make them permanent. Plastic prints are collected using casting and preserved as such or by photography.

Collection of documents: Documents are handpicked and stored in cotton-bedded airtight containers. If damaged or charred documents are encountered, they have a specialized collection method as the investigator is first advised to stabilize the charred documents and then store them in a cotton-bedded container or any other preferred method for storage can be used.

Collection of firearms and ammunition: If a firearm as a whole is found, it is handpicked and is packed in a wooden or cardboard container and fixed to the bottom of the box. If live cartridges, an empty cartridge case, or a bullet are recovered from the scene, they should be cautiously collected and packed in cushioned or cotton-bedded boxes to prevent damage (Fisher 2004; U.-S. Department of Justice Office of Justice Programs 2000).

Collection of soil, drug, powders: If soil is transferred to the crime scene through shoeprints, tyre marks, etc. then the pattern evidence should be first documented and preserved. The soil can be collected using a spatula and stored in vials or, if entirely dried, packed in a paper using the druggist fold method. If the dried soil is found on objects that cannot be transported to the laboratory, then this soil can be scrapped from that item and packed in vials. The dried drug or suspected powders can be collected using a spatula and packed in vials, ziplock bags or paper.

Collection of tools such as knife, hammer, axe, etc.: Tools are excellent value evidence as they may have fingerprints of the perpetrator. Thus, they should be checked for other trace evidence and collected. They can be handpicked; if blood stains are seen, it is recommended to collect the blood sample from it and then air dry it first before packing; they can be packed in paper, cardboard or a plastic bag depending on the size of the evidence.

These were collection and packaging methods for some of the common evidence on the crime scene. Though there is no limitation for the type of evidence that may occur on the crime scene, these guidelines would assist in collecting and packaging unknown evidence found on the scene. *Control or reference samples* are that piece of a sample that does not have the value of the evidence, and the sample is well known to the investigator. These are also collected the same way and are packed and labelled separately. Once the evidence and control or reference sample are collected and packed, they are labelled with evidence number, case number, and other necessary details.

6.4.6 Forwarding Evidence to the Laboratory

Following the evidence collection and packaging, they are forwarded to the laboratory for analysis. Evidence is either submitted to the laboratory by personal delivery or by couriers. The evidences are transported such that there should be no damage to them. Care should be taken while forwarding that the evidence is sealed correctly to avoid contamination. Evidences should be submitted to the laboratory as soon as possible. This ensures that analysis can be carried out soon as biological and serological evidence are prone to degradation. Contamination and cross-contamination is to be avoided at all stages. A forwarding letter is attached to each package with the necessary details such as case number, date, police station, the seal, description of the evidence in the package, the type of analysis sought and authorization.

6.4.7 Interpretation and Presentation of Evidence in a Court

After submission of evidence to the laboratory, the evidence is analyzed using different tools and techniques, and after analysis, the laboratory hands over the scientific report of analysis and the left-over samples back to the investigator/investigation agency. The investigator then has the job of interpreting the analysis results and connecting them with the facts of the crime with which the investigator is well acquainted. Also, the investigator must maintain the chain of custody for each piece of evidence. All evidence from the point of collection to forwarding it to the laboratory should meet the legal requirement of the court, and hence the chain of custody is maintained. The chain of custody record has the entry of every person to whom the possession of evidence is handed. Maintaining a chain of custody also assists in maintaining the authenticity of the evidence presented in court. Any lacunae in the chain of custody of the evidence may make the evidence inadmissible in court (Badiye et al. 2023). Presentation of analysis results in the court plays a vital role in the judgement of the criminal case. Thus, the expert must testify the evidence in the court in such mode that it proves the fact in question. Also, with this, the expert should be able to answer all the questions relating to his testimony. This is the final step in an investigation where the judge concludes the case with a judgement considering all the evidence and facts.

6.5 Crime Scene Management

A single investigator does not generally carry out a crime scene investigation; instead, a team is deployed to carry out a crime scene investigation. In the same way, they utilizes many tools, techniques, and procedures for investigation. Thus, there is also a need to manage these components to ensure a successful crime investigation; hence, crime scene management also becomes essential along with crime scene investigation. Four elements of crime scene management are (Miller 2019; Lee et al. 2001);

6.5.1 Information Management

As mentioned in earlier sections, crime scenes provide vital information about the crime, suspect, victim, and their interrelation. Hence, this information becomes the prime source of linking the suspect with the victim and crime. Other information sources include information from a witness, information from the victim, information from the first responding officer, information from records and databases, information from suspects, information about the victim's background, etc. (Lee et al. 2001). These facts obtained from different sources travel in different directions with different theories of crime committed; thus, proper information management is one aspect one should positively look for. This duty goes to the crime scene investigator to correctly line these facts to prove the case. Also, there are variations in the form of information, as it may be in written, oral or recorded form; thus, the investigator has the charge to manage these information sources in a way that does not destroy the authenticity of the information and subsequently could be potentially used for investigation.

6.5.2 Workforce Management

Crime scene investigation should be carried out by a team of a few members, although there is no fixed number. With the increase in the number of members of investigating team, the threat to the crime scene and its investigation increases. Thus, administrating this workforce becomes essential. Many other elements may have a positive effect or may be proved disadvantageous for the crime scene investigation. One of these is the availability of well-trained personnel; crime scene investigation requires tedious training as one wrong step may hinder the whole investigation (Lee et al. 2001). Another is that different jobs are done by their experts or they are randomly assigned their duties on the crime scene (Lee et al. 2001). Other elements could be the personnel's experience, which will undoubtedly assist the investigation. The last element could be the personnel's working capacity, whether they are assigned the right amount of duties and can efficiently work for them. Looking up upon all these elements will ensure proper workforce management.

6.5.3 Technology Management

Crime scene investigation utilizes multiple tools and techniques. Thus, there should be an appropriate supply of tools and equipment to the scene for its proper investigation. The crime scene may require fingerprint kits, drug testing kits, other hand tools, cameras, collection and packaging tools, some portable equipment, etc. (Lee et al. 2001). This is the duty of the crime scene investigator to ensure that there is favourable availability of these tools and technology, to ensure on-time analysis of the scene as the absence of any one critical tool may hamper further investigation.

6.5.4 Logistic Management

This includes administering planning and resource allocation concerns. As mentioned earlier, the crime scene is a rich source of information and thus needs to be processed using appropriate investigation plans and proper management of other logistics. This is the duty of a crime scene investigator to design a proper investigating plan. This includes finalizing the crime scene investigation model, searching method, making possible use of all innovative available resources, keeping the crime scene safe from outsiders, etc. These are the problems that are needed to be addressed under logistic management. Also, sometimes the case is that the investigation may involve a few different organizations or agencies. One of the significant problems in such cases is the mutual cooperation of these multiple agencies; thus, this is to be looked upon for proper management. This all needs to be addressed to render triumphant crime scene investigation.

6.6 Crime Scene Reconstruction

Crime scene reconstruction can be defined as "The process of determining or eliminating the events that occurred at the crime scene by analysis of scene appearance, the locations and positions of physical evidence, and the forensic laboratory examination of the physical evidence" (Miller 2019). Another definition says, "As the determination of what events occurred (and often the sequence of those events) during the commission of a crime through the analysis and interpretation of the physical evidence at the scene" (Ogle and Plotkin 2018). The definition depicts that reconstruction is primely based on crime scene investigation, laboratory analysis and result interpretation. Reconstruction is a complex procedure involving the interlinking of physical evidence, stain pattern evidence on the crime scene, laboratory results, information obtained from different sources, and other evidence (Lee et al. 2001). Computer-aided reconstruction software can also be used to reconstruct the crime scene (Lee et al. 2001).

6.6.1 Stages in Crime Scene Reconstruction

Crime scene reconstruction is a very complex process requiring inductive and deductive logic, statistical data, information from the scene, stain pattern analysis, and laboratory analysis results. The steps are shown below (Lee et al. 2001) (Fig. 6.8).

Data Collection: As the name suggests, this step includes gathering data from different sources. Information is collected from witnesses, victims, and other sources. Information about the condition of the victim, information about pattern and impression evidence on the scene, information about the other physical evidence from the scene, etc. is obtained in this step and is then reviewed and compiled and examined (Miller 2019; Lee et al. 2001).

Conjecture: This stage includes forming a preliminary opinion or conclusion about what events must have occurred during the commission of a crime. It should always be kept in mind that this is not the conclusion but the rough explanation of the crime, which may be the opposite of the actual theory of crime (Miller 2019;

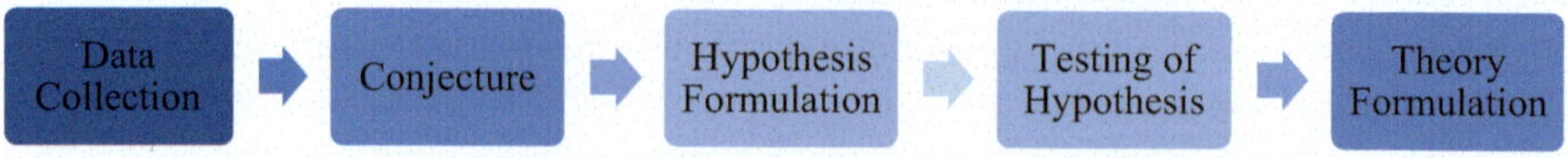

Fig. 6.8 Stages in Crime Scene Investigation

Lee et al. 2001). Conjecture formation is done before sending the evidence to the laboratory for analysis.

Hypothesis formulation: Subsequent addition of data based on crime scene analysis and analysis of other patterns and impression evidence leads to the formation of the most probable and educated hypothesis. This step is done after analyzing and inspecting the whole crime scene and the other information obtained from witnesses and victims (Miller 2019; Lee et al. 2001).

Testing of hypothesis: After the hypothesis formulation, this hypothesis is tested using laboratory testing. This can be done by sending the physical evidence encountered at the scene for analysis and comparison with the controlled or reference samples. This stage finally proves or rebuts the hypothesis (Miller 2019; Lee et al. 2001).

Theory formulation: This is the last step which includes compiling and analyzing all the obtained information from the victim, witness, information from pattern and impression evidence, condition of the victim, information about other persons involved in the case, results obtained from the laboratory, and further investigation leads to the formation of a theory about what must have been occurred on the crime scene (Miller 2019; Lee et al. 2001).

If the reconstruction process is conducted thoroughly, it will yield an appropriate theory for the crime.

6.7 Conclusion

It is evident that the crime scene as well as crime scene investigation is of utmost importance in solving crimes and providing justice. The investigator should follow all the processes and procedures meticulously, scientifically and within the ambit of the law. The investigator must not undermine any evidence. The opportunities to appropriately identify and appreciate the importance of various evidences at the scene must be grabbed by the Forensic experts in the first instance itself. As it is almost never possible to revisit the crime scene over and over for the collection of evidences. It is important to avoid contamination and cross-contamination at all stages. Chain of custody should be maintained at all costs. It is important to have appropriate knowledge, experience and understanding of various aspects of crime scene investigation to achieve good results.

References

Badiye A, Kapoor N, Menezes RG (2023) Chain of custody. [Updated 2023 Feb 13]. In: StatPearls [Internet]. StatPearls Publishing, Treasure Island (FL). https://www.ncbi.nlm.nih.gov/books/NBK551677/

Fisher BAJ (2004) Techniques of crime scene investigation, 7th edn. CRC Press, Boca Raton

Harris HA, Lee HC (2019) Introduction to forensic science and criminalistics, 2nd edn. CRC Press, Boca Raton, FL

Kleypas DA, Badiye A (2023) Evidence collection. [Updated 2023 May 8]. In: StatPearls [Internet]. StatPearls Publishing, Treasure Island (FL). https://www.ncbi.nlm.nih.gov/books/NBK441852/

Lee HC, Pagliaro EM (2013) Forensic evidence and crime scene investigation. J Forensic Investigation 1(1):5

Lee HC, Palmbach T, Miller MT (2001) Henry Lee's crime scene handbook. Elsevier, London

Miller MT (2019) Crime scene investigation. In: Forensic science: an introduction to scientific and investigative techniques. CRC Press, Boca Raton

Ogle RR, Plotkin SL (2018) Crime scene investigation and reconstruction. 4th edition, Pearson

Saferstein R (2015) Criminalistics: an introduction to forensic science, 11th edn. Pearson Education, New York

Sharma BR (2003) Forensic science in criminal investigation and trials, 5th edn. Universal Law publishing, New Delhi

U.S. Department of Justice Office of Justice Programs (2000) Crime scene investigation: a guide for law enforcement

Correlation of Postmortem Changes with Time Since Death

7

Sachil Kumar and Rakesh Kumar Gorea

Abstract

This chapter explores in detail all the changes occurring after death in a dead body and how and why such changes take place, and what are the causes that can influence these changes. Many such changes occur immediately after death, which helps to clinically declare a person dead, although, where there is any uncertainty, some tests have been proposed that may eliminate doubts. Some changes occur within hours, which are called early changes, and these signs confirm the death of a person and usually the person is buried or cremated after the onset of these changes. Late signs are the parts of nature's way to dispose of all the body's tissue so that all the complex tissue of the body changes to simpler forms, resulting in the destruction of the whole body, including the bones. Knowing the different changes in a dead body time since death can be estimated, which can help the police investigators to plan their future investigations for the successful prosecution of the cases. Other methods which can be also used for the estimation of postmortem intervals such as radio-carbon dating, decomposition-^{1}H magnetic resonance spectroscopies, DNA degradation, strontium90, gastric emptying, the activity of enzymes, the uterus cycle, brain RNA and protein degradation are also discussed.

When the investigating team arrives at the crime scene, there are clues on the body which point towards the time of occurrence of death. If the investigators are well conversant with the postmortem changes in the body they can have an

S. Kumar (✉)
Department of Forensic Sciences, College of Criminal Justice, Naif Arab University for Security Sciences, Riyadh, Saudi Arabia
e-mail: SKumar@nauss.edu.sa

R. K. Gorea
Department of Forensic Medicine, Gian Sagar Medical College, Ram Nagar, Punjab, India

P. Shrivastava et al. (eds.), *Textbook of Forensic Science*,
https://doi.org/10.1007/978-981-99-1377-0_7

accurate guess when the death has taken place. This guess is scientific which will be of immense help to rule out/include persons in the criminal investigations.

Keywords

Time since death · Postmortem changes · Algor mortis · Lividity · Rigor mortis · Decomposition · Mummification · Forensic entomology · DNA · Enzymes

7.1 Introduction

For hundreds of years, time since death TSD or postmortem interval (PMI) has been a crucial factor in the forensic arena in the investigation of homicides and in certain civil cases (Kumar et al. 2013a, b). It has been pointed out by Schleyer that the time of death is important in instances of unwitnessed fatal traffic accidents, homicides, and suicides (Schleyer 1963). Many cases involving criminal investigations revolve around the time of death and the potential alibi of a suspect. An erroneous time of death can lead investigators down the wrong path or perhaps concentrate a case on an innocent suspect.

In spite of the fact that there has been an enormous literature published on the subject of PMI estimation, its determination remains challenging, even for skilled pathologists (Henssge and Madea 2004, 2007). All methods currently used for estimating TSD remain relatively unreliable. Most of the methods come up with a mere approximation, as there are many variables, both extrinsic and intrinsic, which can influence the process of the postmortem changes.

Researchers in this area, dating back to the eighteenth century, paid much attention on postmortem temperature measurements and potential algorithms to model the body cooling behavior. Primary muscular flaccidity, muscular stiffening or 'rigor mortis', supravital reactions, lividity, and putrefaction have additionally been used for PMI determination (Madea 2015; Noriko 1995). The different life stages of insects, infesting the dead body have also been used for the estimation of an extended PMI, but this varies in different environmental conditions (Amendt et al. 2004; Day and Wallman 2006; Bourel et al. 2003; Schroeder et al. 2003). Chemical and immune-histochemical techniques consisting of using biochemical markers for PMI estimation have been studied. These approaches involve analyzing the concentration of plasma chloride and determining the ratio of sodium ion to potassium ions in vitreous humor (VH), cerebrospinal fluid (CSF) and blood. In addition to these methods, ^{1}H magnetic resonance spectroscopies (Yang et al. 2008), DNA degradation, Strontium-90 Calcium analog levels, enzymes, gastric contents and uterine cycles have also been explored as feasible methods of PMI identification (Schnabel et al. 1997).

To more accurately assess the TSD, the investigators first needed to have complete information regarding the sequence of postmortem changes starting within the decedent's body. These are unpreventable, irreversible, and progressive changes, and have a greater variability with circumstantial and environmental factors. However, conversely, they also have a degree of steadiness in their progression.

7.1.1 Death (Thanatology)

The thanatology also known as deathlore derived from the "Greek Dialect" deals in all its perspectives with the scientific study of death, types of death and suffering. In Greek mythology, thanatos (***θάνατος: "death"***) is the embodiment of death (Oxford Dictionaries n.d.). The English suffix *-ology* comes from the Greek suffix *-logia* (***-λογια: "speaking"***).

Death is not an event but it's a continuous cycle. Death is defined as "*complete, permanent and irreversible stoppage of three interlinked vital systems of the body, called tripod of life, namely—the respiration, circulation and nervoussystems*" (Laureys 2005).

There are two death phases (Bardale 2011):

1. Somatic Death/Clinical/Systemic Death
   (Within minutes of death)
   It is due to the irreversible and complete stoppage of one of the vital functions of the body (e.g. brain) followed by the cessation of functions of the other two vital organs (e.g. heart and lungs), the so called "tripod of life" (Fig. 7.1).
2. Molecular/Cellular Death
   (Short time to hours)

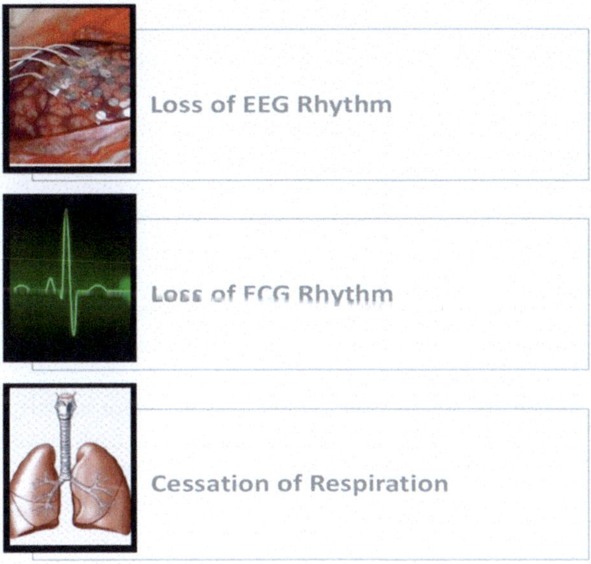

Fig. 7.1 Signs of somatic death

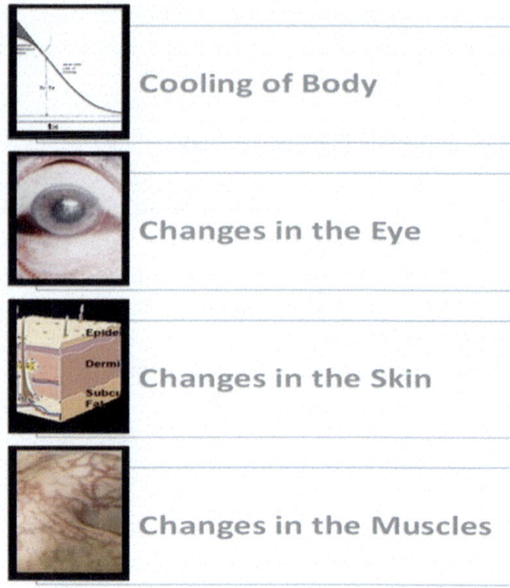

Fig. 7.2 Signs of molecular death

The death of individual cells and tissues usually occurs within 1–2 h of the cessation of vital functions. It is generally complete within 3–4 h of somatic death. The necessary signs are shown in Fig. 7.2, which are of legal importance, in particular in the estimation of the TSD.

7.1.2 Postmortem Changes

After one's death, chemical and physical changes occur, resulting in the disintegration of the body. These changes can be divided into instant, early and late(Tsokos and Byard 2016). The significance of these changes primarily depends on their sequential nature, which can be used to calculate the PMI. Although they are affected by numerous variables, certain postmortem changes remain rooted in the misdiagnosis of PMI. The changes are as stated underneath:

1. Immediate Postmortem Changes
   Permanent cessation of brain functions, complete cessation of circulatory functions, entire and permanent cessation of respiratory functions
2. Early Postmortem Changes
   Changes in the eyes, pallor mortis, algor mortis, livor mortis, rigor mortis, supravital reactions, chemical changes in bodily fluids
3. Late Postmortem Changes
   Decomposition, adipocere, mummification, skeletization, forensic entomology

7.2 Immediate Postmortem Changes

7.2.1 Permanent Cessation of Brain Functions

All functions of the nervous system cease with somatic death. With the loss of sensory and motor functions, the subject is insensible. There is absence of brainstem reflexes (light, corneal, cilospinal, oculocephalic, vestibular, laryngeal and cough reflex) with flaccid muscles. The pupils are widely dilated by 4 mm or more and fixed, and they no longer react to bright light (Wijdicks 2001).

The criteria used to determine the cessation of brain functions are referred to below:

1. **Deep unresponsive coma**—The diagnosis of deep unresponsive coma requires a comatose-affected person who shows a lack of spontaneous movement as well as a lack of motor responses in the cranial nerve. CNS-mediated motor pain response, seizures, decortications and de-cerebration impede brain death (BD) diagnosis. Some BD individuals may have spinal reflexes or motor responses confined to spinal distribution that do not preclude the diagnosis of BD.
2. **Irreversible and irreparable brain injury**—There should be a history of severe brain trauma, a vascular accident or a primitive nervous system tumor or another condition diagnosed with clinical or supplementary tests. Reversible forms of coma, including poisoning, drug abuse, hypothermia and shock, should be excluded.
3. **Absence of brainstem and spinal integrated reflexes**—Twelve pairs of cranial nerves form the afferent and efferent channels of local reflexes within the brainstem. These reflections emphasize the integrity of the brain stem and their lack is a synonym for the functional loss of these structures. The reflexes are pupillary light reflex, vestibulo-ocular reflexes, the "doll's eye and ice water calorics", corneal reflex and the gag & cough reflex (Fig. 7.3).
4. **Tests**—the tests are as follows:
   - **Atropine Test**—The atropine test evaluates the heart activity of bulbar parasympathetic in BD patients. The method consists of 2 mg of atropine sulphate injection intravenously, and monitoring the pulse for a period of 15 s, and after 5, 10 and 15 min. Atropine dramatically increases the patient's heart rate in the patient with an intact brain. In a brain-dead patient, atropine will not influence heart rate.
   - **Apnoea**—A patient who undergoes machine controlled ventilation and does not make any effort against the ventilator for a period of 15 min may be considered brain dead. Further evidence comes with apnoeic oxygen testing. This final test should only be carried out when all the established criteria are observed, and minimal ventilation movement excludes the diagnosis of BD.
   - **Electroencephalogram (EEG)**—It is a non-obligatory test which evaluates electrical brain activity. Some experts argue that electrical brain silence needs to be verified in order to diagnose BD. However, the standards set by the Harvard Committee include this test as the fifth. In the U.K. and elsewhere, the

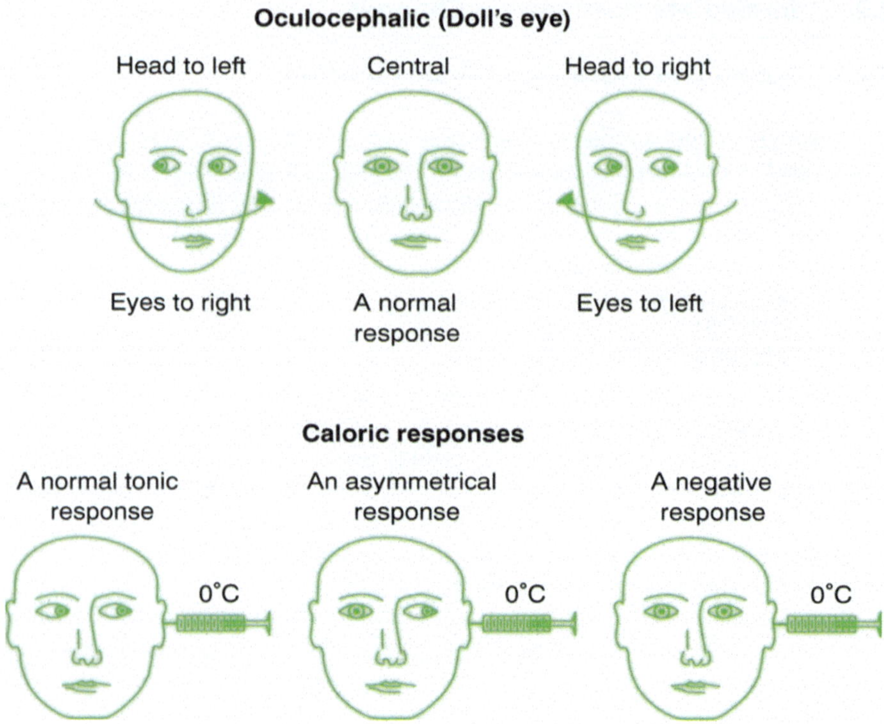

Fig. 7.3 Doll's eye and ice water calorics (Bateman 2001). In Doll's eye, mechanical/gravitational forces stimulate vestibular responses while in ice water calorics thermal energy stimulates vestibular responses

diagnosis of irreversible BD is considered to be sufficient to infer brain death and, consequently, death of clinical procedures without the need for instrumental techniques.

- **Observation period**—BD criteria should be present during a 30-min observation period and 6 h later in a second examination.

7.2.2 Permanent and Complete Cessation of Circulatory Functions

With somatic death, the function of the heart stops with consequent cessation of circulation (Bernat 2010). The clinical procedures and tests used to assess the cessation of cardiac activity are referred to as:

1. **Palpation**—radial, brachial, femoral and carotid pulsation may be absent.
2. **Auscultation**—The whole pericardial area is auscultated for the presence or absence of heart sounds. The auscultation must be achieved for a minimum period of one min and repeated at quick intervals if important.
3. **Tests**—the tests are as follows:
   - **Magnus's Test**—tying a ligature tightly at the base of a finger, sufficient to cut off the venous channels without occluding the arteries. The finger remains white, if circulation has stopped, otherwise the area beyond the ligature becomes blue and swollen.
   - **Diaphanous Test**—the hand is to be held against a strong source of light. It appears red and translucent during life. But it is yellow and opaque after death.
   - **Icard's Test**—The hypodermic injection of a solution of fluorescein does not produce any discoloration of the skin, if circulation has stopped; however, it renders the neighboring skin yellowish-green, if circulation is still going on. The substance will also be detected inside the blood drawn by pricking the skin at some distance from the seat of injection. If a few white silkthreads are immersed within the blood, and then boiled in test-tube containing distilled water, the threads will turn out to be greenish in color. The solution of fluorescein is acquired by dissolving 1 g of resorcin-pththalein, and 1 g of sodium bicarbonate in 8 cc. of water.
   - **Pressure Test**—If the circulation continues, if pressure is exerted on the finger nail, the nail surface is translucent but then red as the pressure is relaxed. There is no such occurrence among deceased people.
   - **Heat Test**—The application of heat, e.g. a burning match or melted sealing-wax to the skin will not produce a true blister with a red line of demarcation if circulation has stopped.
   - **Artery Incision Test**—When a small artery is cut, there is no jerky flow of blood, if circulation has stopped.

7.2.3 Entire and Permanent Cessation of Respiratory Function

With somatic death, there may be an entire and permanent stoppage of respiration (Illes 2017). The clinical examination and tests to set up the cessation of breathing are stated underneath.

1. **Inspection**—no respiration movements will be seen
2. **Palpation**—breathing actions can't be appreciated
3. **Auscultation**—no sound of breath can be heard from any part of the lungs
4. **Tests**—the tests are as follows:
   - **Feather Test**—There might be no motion of a feather or cotton fibers held in front of the mouth and nostrils if respiration has stopped, however, this isn't a dependable test as the slightest draught of air or anxiety at a part of an observer will pass the feather or cotton fibers.

- **Mirror test**—No haziness is evident on the reflective surface of the mirror in front of the mouth and nose.
- **Winslow's test**—This test was proposed by ***Jacques-Benigne Winslow***, a Danish physician (1669–1760). If breathing has stopped, no image movement is formed by reflecting artificial or solar light on the surface of mercury or water contained in a small pot and placed over a thoraco-abdominal area. Furthermore, water is not spilt out of a vessel filled to the edge and placed in the chest or stomach if the breath stops.

7.3 Early Postmortem Changes

7.3.1 Postmortem Changes in the Eyes

A victim's eyes can also contain answers to the PMI, because a thin, cloudy film is developed in 3 h after death (Prasad 2003). Due to the lower fluid pressure behind the eye, the eyeballs become softer and the extent to which this occurred can be used as a measurement of the TSD.

7.3.1.1 Loss of Corneal Reflex

- Corneal reflex is caused by the abolition of brain functions; corneal reflex loss is not a sure sign of death as it is found in instances of deep insensibility, i.e. with general anesthesia, epilepsy, and narcotic poisoning.

7.3.1.2 Corneal Opacity

- Clouding of the cornea, which becomes dull and opaque, wrinkled and brown in about 6 h after death (Fig. 7.4); may even be dimmed before death in narcotic

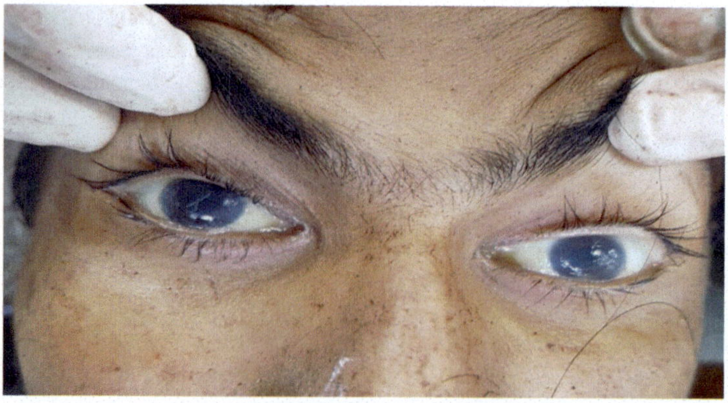

Fig. 7.4 Opacity of cornea (loses glistening appearance, becomes dull and opaque)

poisoning, cholera, uraemia, and wasting diseases. Sometimes in cases like CO / HCN poisoning after death, glistening may be maintained.

7.3.1.3 Flaccidity of the Eyeball

- **Tache NoirDe La Sclerotique**—Normally the eyelids close after death because of primary flaccidity of the muscle, but fail to produce complete occlusion and, consequently, where the sclera remains exposed, a cellular debris, dust, and mucus film forms two yellow triangles on the sclera on either side of the iris with a base to the corneal margin and apex towards the medial or lateral eye canthus, which within 3–4 h becomes reddish brown or black (Fig. 7.5).
- Intraocular pressure (IOP) falls quickly because it depends upon arterial pressure.
- After death, the eyes look pulpy and sunken into the orbital fossa due to IOP fall within mins. **Normal IOP during life varies between 12 and 22 mmHg.**
  - 1 h following death: <12 mmHg
  - 2 h following death: <10 mmHg
  - 3 h following death: <8.5 mmHg
  - 8 h following death: <5 mmHg

For more than 4 days, it becomes nil.

7.3.1.4 Pupils Condition

- Loss of light reflex and iris is relaxed into the equilibrium state assuming the pupil's dilated position; dilated pupil as rigor mortis develops due to loss of muscle tone in the iris and later on constricts.

7.3.1.5 Changes in Retinal Vessels

- Segmentation or trucking in retinal blood vessels (Kevorkian Sign, rail roading, or cattle trucking) within hours of death as loss of blood pressure causes the blood flow to divide or break down into segments (Fig. 7.6). It becomes pale in color for the first 2 h; the disk outline becomes hazy in about 6 h and blurs in 7–10 h.

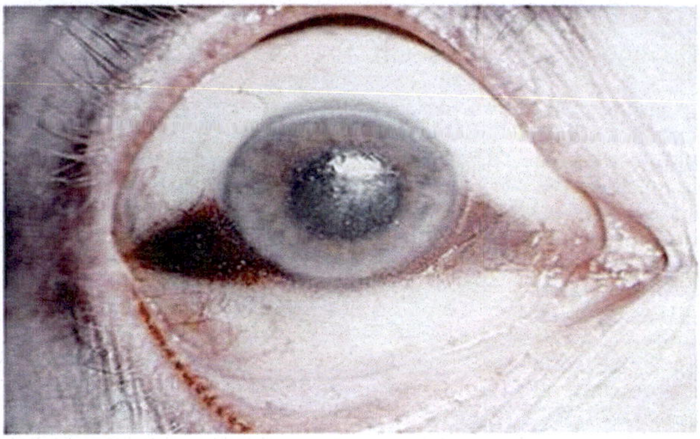

Fig. 7.5 Tache Noire de la sclerotique (French for Black spot of the sclera) is a drying artifact along with brownish discoloration of sclera in exposed parts when eyelids are not closed at death and left open for two to a few hours

Fig. 7.6 Kevorkian sign

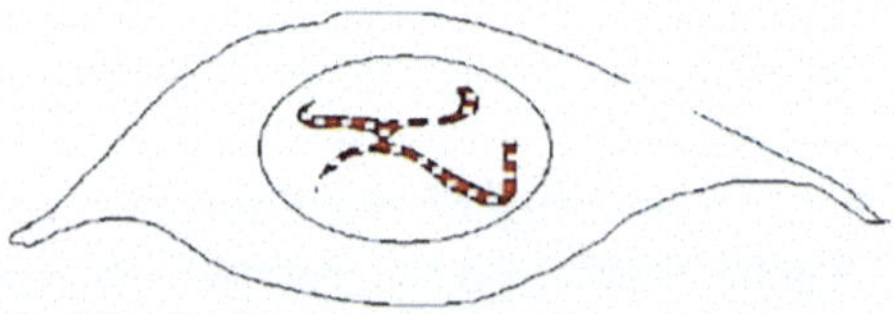

Fig. 7.7 Pallor mortis. (Adopted from https://www.ranker.com/list/eight-stages-of-death/inigo-gonzalez)

7.3.1.6 Chemical Changes

- Potassium levels in vitreous humor (fluid inside eye) can be measured at various rates.

7.3.2 Pallor Mortis (Postmortem Paleness)

Pallor mortis (Latin: *pallor* "paleness", *mortis* "of death"), the first level of death, is a postmortem paleness which appear nearly immediately after death in those with light / white skin (Fig. 7.7) (Schäfer 2000). It exists in dark-skinned people, but the effect is much more subtle than in fairy-skinned people. It results from the cessation of the whole body's capillary circulation. Gravity then allows the blood to sink into lower sections of the body and develop lividity. The upper parts of a body that are free of blood develop pallor mortis. There is little interest in this phenomenon due to the fact that similar paleness of the skin can be present in the living and therefore belong to the dubious signs of death.

7.3.2.1 Timing and Applicability

Pallor mortis occurs very early after death (within 15–20 min); paleness develops after death so quickly that it has little or no use in calculating the PMI, apart from saying that it occurred less than half an hour ago or more earlier, which might aid if the corpse was discovered immediately after death (within 30 min or less) (Bartle 2018).

Schafer used an optoelectronic color measurement tool to inspect postmortem paleness in 126 dead bodies and compared those findings with 72 living Caucasian volunteers' common skin colors (Schäfer 2000). They noted that the result is influenced by hairy skin, so all hair should be eliminated by shaving before color determination.

7.3.2.2 Conditions Simulating Pallor Mortis

A living individual might appear fatally pale. It can happen if the blood flees from the surface of the skin like in a profound shock. In addition, coronary heart failure (insufficientia cordis) can render the face appear grey; the individual has blue lips. In cold conditions, skin can often appear fatally pale due to vasoconstriction as part of the body's homeostatic processes, or if the skin is vitamin D deficient, as seen in individuals who spend the maximum period of time inside, off from daylight (Causes of skin paleness in dark and light skin n.d.).

7.4 Algor Mortis or Postmortem Body Temperature Reduction

Algor mortis (Latin: *Algor*—"coldness"; *mortis*—"of death"), refers to the second stage of death, is characterized by the cooling of the body after dying until the environmental temperature is matched (Chisiu 2018). A balance between heat loss and heat production is maintained throughout life. Human beings and other mammals are homoeothermic, capable of maintaining a relatively constant body temperature despite wide ambient temperatures. However, after life loss, the heat production stops and the body heat is lost to the environment. The temperature of the body drops slowly till the ambient temperature is matched. The temperature of the dead body at any given time may be used to determine the PMI keeping in view the rate of fall of body temperature.

7.4.1 Calculation of TSD

There are several formulas for estimating the postmortem cooling rate; however, with all these formulas, it is assumed that death occurs in temperate conditions and that the deceased has a normal antemortem body temperature (i.e. the preceding body temperature, which actually varies from 93.74 °F to 100.04 °F, as determined rectally). Glaister Equation is the general equation used to measure PMI (body temperature based) (What is algor mortis 2020):

$$\text{TSD} = 98.6\,^{\circ}\text{F} - \text{Rectal Temp}\ (^{\circ}\text{F})/1.5''/\text{Rate of Temp Drop}$$

This drop in temp per hour after death highly depends on the surroundings temperature and roughly ranges from 0.75 to 1.5 °F/h.

Thumb Rules (Henssge and Madea 2007): PMI = 37 °C − Rectal Temp (°C) + 3

7.4.2 Background

The term was first used by Dowler in 1849. For figuring out the PMI, core body temperature reading was the earliest known method, as outlined by Dr. John Davey in the mid-nineteenth century in his book, "***Physiological and Anatomical***" and this procedure was focused on experiments with thermometry carried out in 1828 on British soldiers in Malta and even in the British Isles (Davy 1839). Davey confirmed a time-dependent rise in body temperature of 108 °F and sometimes 113 °F; this change was attributed was due to a humid climate and an infectious disorder. Davey claimed that where the time of death is a concern, by taking the temperature in deep tissue with consideration to the affecting circumstances, "*probably in most instances an answer may be given approximating to the truth and which may be of considerable use in evidence*". Various researches were done, such as that of Davey, which included Dr. Bennett Dowler in 1845 and Dr. Benjamin Hensley in 1846; but, it was not until 1868 that any significant breakthrough was made. Harry Rainy was the one to apply mathematical principles to figure out PMI (Boahene 2015). According to his report "*having obtained these data, we cannot precisely calculate the period which has passed since death, but we can almost always determine a minimum and maximum of time within which that period will be included*". In addition, he suggested a formula for calculating the midpoint of this range; but, as the body's cooling proceeded more gradually than expected under Newton's Rule, the measured PMI ultimately reflected the minimum PMI.

7.4.2.1 Newton's Law of Cooling

This cooling law is called after Isaac Newton, an English physicist. Newton's "***Law of Cooling***" was first published in a paper entitled "***ScalaGraduumCaloris***" published in the Royal Society of London's philosophical transactions in 1701 (Hubig et al. 2015). A coroner used a formula based on the "***Newton's Law of Cooling***", to determine the PMI.

The formula is: "**t = −10 ln (*T* − Rt)/98.6 − Rt**" *where T* = the body's measured temperature (°F); Rt = the constant room temperature (Rt); *t* = elapsed TSD (h).

7.4.3 Henssge's Nomogram for PMI Determination (Fig. 7.8) (Henssge and Madea 2004)

- Straight line is drawn across the space separating ambient t° and rectal t° (15 and 27)
- Corrective factor for various deviations from the standard' (naked extended body, still air) in this case 1.3 due to three layers of clothes
- The body weight is increased/multiplied by 1.3 (70 × 1.3 = 91 kg)

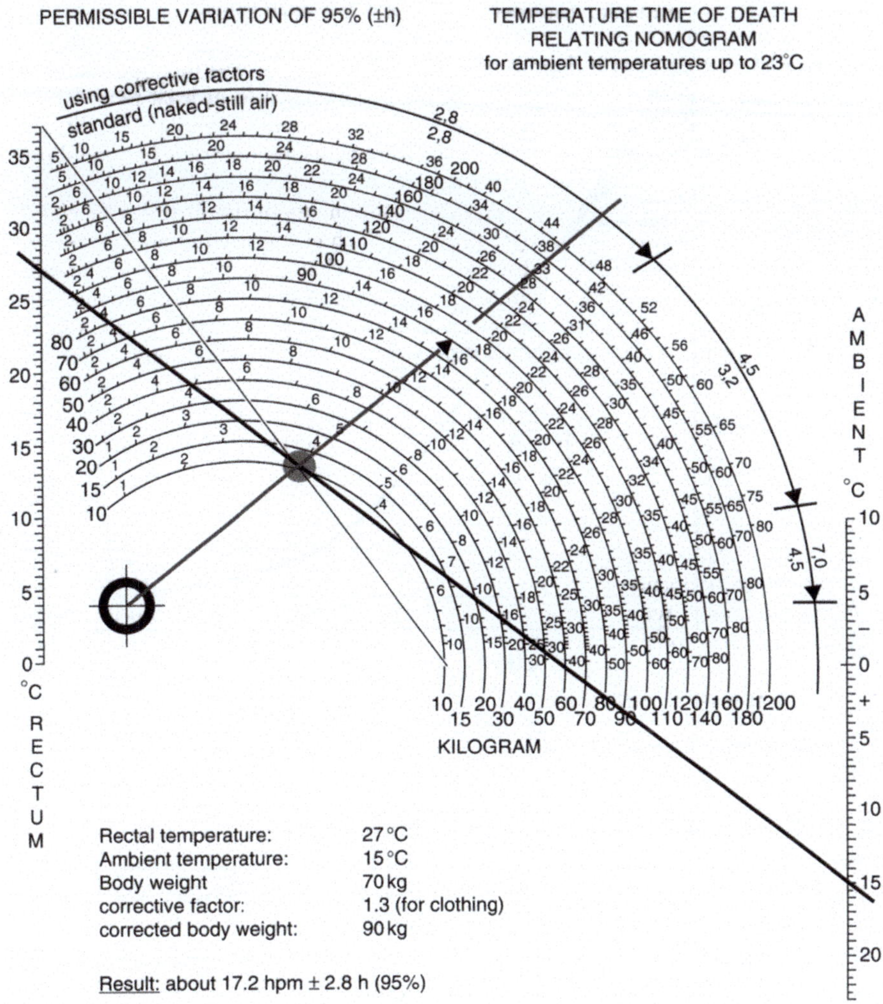

Fig. 7.8 Henssge temperature nomogram up to 23 °C (upper) (Henssge and Madea 2004)

- Second line is drawn from the center of the circle through the crossing with the diagonal line of the nomogram all the way to the outer circle (95% confidence) and read the number ate intersection with 90 kg line)

One of the mathematical PMI estimation algorithms was invented in 1962 by T. K. Marshall and F. E. Hoare (Fig. 7.9). They used a two-exponential equation to account for a sudden rise in the ambient temperature of 15 °C, which would be suitable for mathematically describing the cooling of the body.

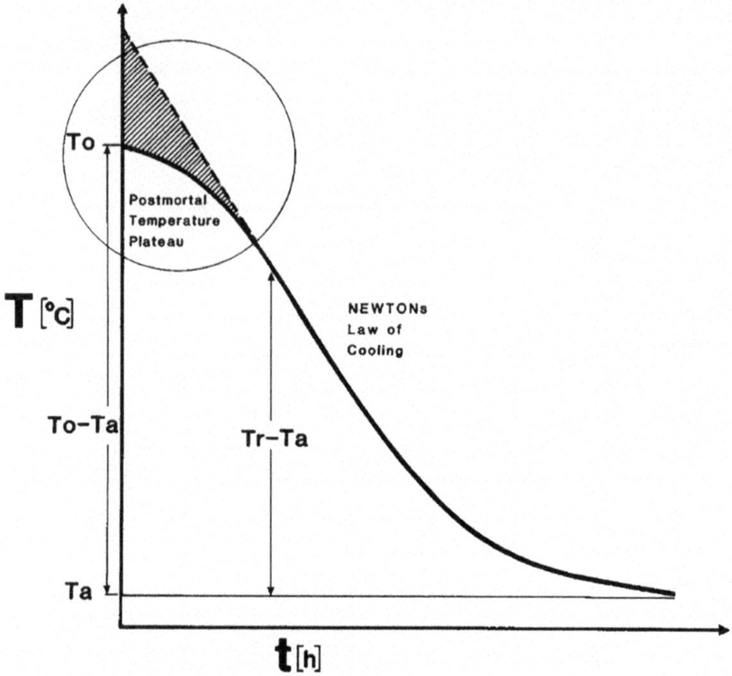

Fig. 7.9 Sigmoidal cooling curve shape. Mathematical description of Marshall and Hoare's two exponential models (Henssge and Madea 2004)

7.4.3.1 Factors Affecting the Body's Cooling Rate

- **Environmental temperature (predominant factor):** The rate of body temperature drop is simultaneously comparable to the disparity between the deceased body temperature and the ambient temperature.
- **Air movement:** Air movement over the surface of the dead body causes a quick fall of temperature because of increased evaporation of body fluids. The body in a very well-ventilated room cools more quicker than that one in a room with zero ventilation.
- **Humidity:** Cooling is speedier in a humid than in a dry atmosphere due to the fact that moist air is a better heat conductor.
- **Medium of disposal:** Cooling is earliest in water, and delayed in buried bodies. The ratio of the rates of fall in temperature inside the three media, water: air: soil = 4:2:1. The rate is thus maximum in water, slight in air and minimum in a buried body.
- **Built of cadaver:** Obese bodies cool slowly, and lean bodies swiftly, seeing that fat is a bad conductor of heat.
- **Age and sex:** Rate of loss of heat is more in children and the aged, in comparison to adults due to the fact the surface area of the body is more in relation to the body

volume. Females retain body heat for a comparatively longer period due to their subcutaneous fatty tissue.

- **Clothing or coverings of the body:** A well-protected body retains heat for an extended duration in comparison to a bare or thinly clothed body, as clothes are bad heat conductors.
- **Position and posture of the body:** If the body lies in supine and extended position, the loss of heat is rapid due to the fact the greater surface area of the body is exposed; whereas in a curled fetal position, the loss will be gradual.
- **Mode of death:** In the case of sudden death in a healthy individual, the body tends to cool slowly, whereas in death because of a long and wasting illness, the body cools unexpectedly.
- **Postmortem caloricity**
  It's far a phenomenon in which the body temperature of a corpse rises or remains surprisingly high sometimes after the loss of life as opposed to falling. **This happens in:** sun stroke and pontine hemorrhage; tetanus and strychnine poisoning; acute infection with bacteria or viruses, lobar pneumonia, typhoid fever, encephalitis, etc.; intense asphyxia deaths—temperature rise by 2–3 °c at death (Dowler 1845).

7.4.4 Rigidity (Rigor Mortis)

After death, the muscle relaxes completely—a condition called "primary relaxation or flaccidity"—succeeded in a condition characterized by muscles stiffening and shortening-rigor mortis,—and superseded into the complete relaxation of muscles—Secondary relaxation or flaccidity (Tsokos and Byard 2016). Rigor mortis is a temporary stiffening of the muscles, with very little shortening of fibers, that occurs soon after loss of life (Latin: rigor "stiffness", mortis "of death") (Fig. 7.10).

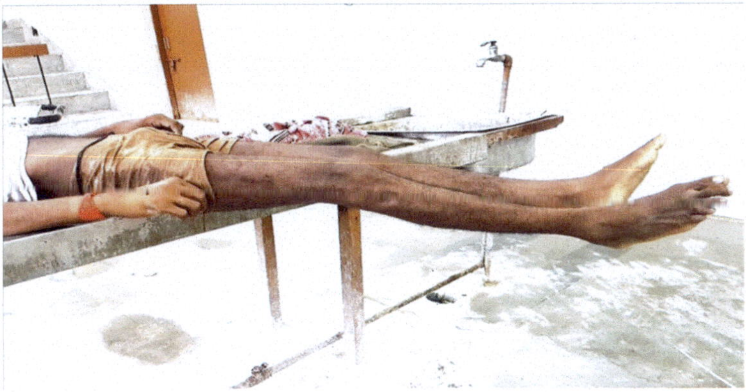

Fig. 7.10 Rigor mortis (stiffening of muscles). Few hours after death the body's joints are stiffened and locked in place. The phenomenon is caused by the skeletal muscles stiffening

Individual cell death takes place at this stage. It's far one of the recognizable signs and symptoms of death.

7.4.4.1 Physiological Mechanism

The sequence of muscle tissue stiffening can be caused by different levels of lactic acid in different muscles, which is directly linked to the difference in glycogen levels and different types of muscle fibers. Owing to the loss of integrity of the sarcoplasmic reticulum of muscle cells, calcium ions flood into the contractile unit or sarcomere containing alternating actin and parallel protein filaments. Calcium unblocks the binding sites on actin, causing the two molecules to bind from myosin through a cross-arm. Since the cross-arm is retracted, the actin is pulled along the thick fiber of myosin.

The sarcomeres are joined end-to-end so that once this action is summed over the length of the muscle, the tissue shortens and will become rigid. Commonly, ATP-driven active transport pumps the calcium back into the sarcoplasmic reticulum, thus allowing detachment of the actin-myosin complex and inducing relaxation in live bodies. The development of rigor mortis has been closely linked to the depletion of ATP; the onset of rigor happens when the ATP content of the muscle decreases below a critical level. In the absence of ATP, the state of contraction persists as rigor, in which the actomyosin complex stays irreversibly bound. Resolution of rigor involves structural changes in the myofibrils. Electron microscopic analysis of the contractile unit shows that actin molecules are isolated from the end of the sarcomere, enabling the contractile unit to be prolonged again. Muscle cells consist of proteolytic enzymes called cathespins, which may also facilitate the dissociation of actin from the ends of sarcomeres and hence reverse rigor (Krause and Zett 1973).

7.4.4.2 Order of Apparition (Table 7.1)

- Nysten's Rule: Rigor mortis does not start simultaneously in all muscles.
- Shapiro (1950): Rigor mortis most likely to develop simultaneously in all muscles. Smaller muscles > Larger
- Involuntary muscles (myocardium = 1/2 h) > voluntary muscles (Eyelids > Necks > Lower Jaw > Face > Chest > Upper Limb > Abdomen > Lower Limbs > Fingers and Toes)

Table 7.1 Rule of 12

Time	Event	Appearance
Within 2 h	Rigor begins	Eyelids, jaws stiffen
After 2 h		Center of body stiffens
12 h	Complete rigor	Entire body
15–36 h	Slow loss of rigor, small muscles first	Lost in head and neck, last is bigger leg muscles
36–48 h	Rigor disappears, muscles become relaxed	

The disappearance of rigor mortis follows the same fashion as it comes on. However, it may be observed that while being well established in the upper limbs, it may not be seen in the lower limbs while it has already disappeared from the upper limbs depending upon the TSD. It has been noted that the lower limbs are the last to be affected by rigor and last to exhibit disappearance too.

7.4.4.3 Resolution (Secondary Flaccidity)

- Rigor decreases and eventually disappears as the actin-myosin links are denaturated with early decomposition. Disappearance follows the same pattern as the beginning. The interval is 24–192 h (mean = 76 ± 32 h).

7.4.4.4 Conditions That Influence Rigor Mortis Onset and Duration

- Age, nature of death, poisoning, muscular state, atmospheric conditions etc.

Four phases of rigor mortis are another problem that renders rigor mortis an inaccurate proxy for PMI:

1. the "delay period" soon after death, in which the muscle remains relaxed due to the availability of ATP;
2. the "onset period," where the ATP level drop below a threshold level and relies on Type I (red) versus Type II (white) muscle;
3. the "rigor" period, when rigidity is completely formed and becomes irreversible, and
4. the "resolution" period, the stage when rigidity fades, and the muscle becomes limp.

The timing of rigor mortis is therefore a circular event that moves from relaxed to stiff and back to the relaxed.

7.4.4.5 Conditions Simulating Rigor Mortis

- Heat Stiffening
  Protein coagulation occurs in muscles, especially in burning deaths or at very high temperatures (≥65 °C), this stiffening is known as a pugilistic or boxing attitude (Fig. 7.11). Muscles on the surface are contracted, dried up or even carbonized. A zone of brownish-pink 'cooked meat' exceeds normal red muscle. Stiffness remains until the ligaments and muscles are degraded and there is no normal rigor mortis (Modi 2013).
- Cold Stiffening
  When a body is exposed to freezing temperatures (−5 °C), the tissue becomes frozen and rigid, because of the freezing of body fluids and the solidification of subcutaneous fat that simulates rigor. The body is very cold and significantly stiff. When the joints are forced to bend, the ice cracking takes place in the synovial fluid. If the body is put in a warm atmosphere, the stiffness disappears and after a time, the normal rigor mortis occurs. Subcutaneous fat hardening, peculiarly in

Fig. 7.11 Pugilistic or boxer attitude

children, often renders the skin fold's rigid, that can be confused with the ligature mark.

- Cadaveric Spasm
  Cadaveric spasm, frequently mentioned as postmortem spasm, and instantaneous or cataleptic rigidity, is an uncommon type of muscular stiffening that happens at the moment of death and continues in the rigor mortis period and may be confused with genuine rigor mortis (Postmortem Changes and Time of Death 2012). It is seen in instances of drowning victims when grass, weeds, roots or other materials are clutched, and provides evidence of life at the time of entry into the water and also in deaths that occur with great excitement of tension. Occasionally, in instances of sudden death after extreme and prolonged muscular tension and excitement, it has been found that the body becomes instantaneous rigid in position or the last activity that was done before death, e.g. tightly clutching a knife (Fig. 7.12).
- Controversy
  Five requirements were laid down by ***Matthias Pfaffli and Dau Wyler***, Legal Medicine Professors, University of Bern, Switzerland, for a death to be examined and listed as having a cadaveric spasm (Pirch et al. 2013):
  - The body part assumed to undergo cadaveric spasm must be free from the force of gravity;
  - the dead body should be observed before the development of rigidity;
  - postmortem changes with respect to the lividity of the deceased must be adequately and continuously documented;
  - before the crime scene is examined, the death scene must be undisturbed;
  - no third party may be present at death to prevent manipulation of the body.

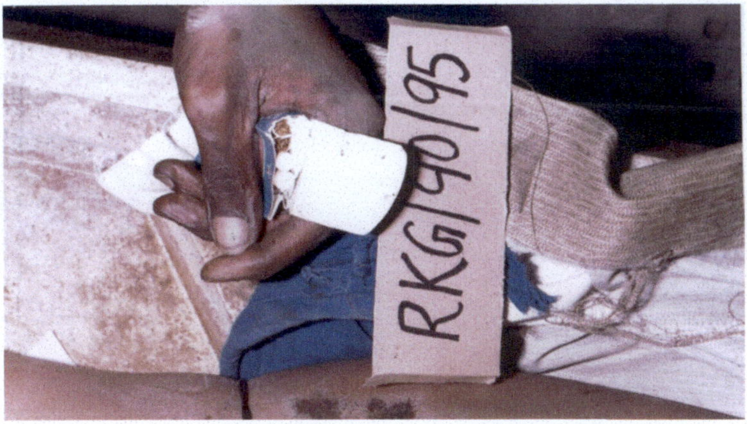

Fig. 7.12 Cadaveric spasm in the hand with a pack of cigarettes grasped in the hand

Due to the improbability of all these requirements being examined in one subject, it is unlikely that cadaveric spasms will be consistently documented and therefore proven to exist.

There is very little or no pathophysiological or scientific basis for supporting the validity of postmortem spasms. This phenomenon cannot chemically be explained to be analogous to "true" rigor mortis. Several other factors have therefore been examined and investigated in an attempt to alternatively account for the reported cases of alleged cataleptic rigidity. In a research, no consistent evidence of postmortem spasm was found even in deaths of the same kind (Bedford and Tsokos 2013) (Table 7.2).

7.4.4.6 Medico-Legal Importance

Rigor mortis is one of the certain death signs; helps to estimate the PMI; and it establishes the corpse position at the moment of death. The posture of the body in which the rigor mortis is established indicates its position unless external forces or putrefaction disturb the position.

7.4.5 Supravital Reactions

Tissue reactions to post-mortem stimulation are supravital reactions. Upon the cessation of the circulation, ischemia in organs and tissues results in reversible, then irreversible changes affecting their shape and function. However, the length of time of these phenomena depends very much on the tissue; for example, brain cortex structures undergo definitive changes after a few mins, while other tissues (the kidney, the skeleton muscle) can tolerate prolonged ischemia for up to several hours. This intermediate period, which begins with BD and lasts until cell activity has stopped within the entire organism, is sometimes referred to as the 'supravital

Table 7.2 Differences between cadaveric spasm and rigor mortis (Knüsel et al. 1996)

Character	Cadaveric spasm	Rigor mortis
Time of Onset	At the time of Death	Within 1–2 h of death
Occurrence	Predisposed by sudden violent death	Occurs in all deaths
Muscle	Local Voluntary Muscle e.g. Hand with knife in suicide	Both Voluntary and involuntary Muscle
		Heart is the first to be involved
		Small muscle of digits develop it last
Muscle Stiffening	Great Force is required to break it	Moderate force is required to break it
Primary flaccidity	Does not occur	Occurs
Mechanism of Production	Still Obscure	Known
Response of Electrical Stimuli	Present	Absent
Medico-Legal Importance	Gives idea about Mode of Death	Gives an insight of TSD

period', because external stimuli applied to the body can lead to life-mimicking, observable responses.

The supravital reactions figuring out the PMI (Madea 1994):

- Skeletal muscle mechanical excitability
- Skeletal muscles electrical excitability, especially the facial mimic muscles
- Iris smooth muscles Pharmacological excitability

7.4.5.1 Mechanical Excitability of Skeletal Muscle Postmortem

Zsako's Phenomena, a propagated excitation of muscle fibers, and Idiomuscular contraction, a local contraction of the muscle is two, one of a kind phases of postmortem skeletal muscle mechanical excitability (Madea and Henssge 1990).

1. **Tendon reaction (Zsako's phenomenon),** a contraction of the whole muscle due to propagated excitation following mechanical stimulation. This can be obtained, for instance, by striking the lower third of the thigh 4–5 fingerbreadths above the patella with a reflex hammer, resulting in an upward movement of the patella due to contraction of the whole quadriceps muscle. The phenomenon of Zsako is especially transient, as it cannot normally be noticed after 2–3 h postmortem.
2. **Idiomuscular contraction,** a localized muscular contraction (bulge) at the stimulation point, showed, e.g., by striking a reflex hammer on the biceps muscle of the arm. This can be determined several hours after the Zsako phenomenon has been stopped.

Studies of these phenomena were done by means of hitting with the hand, back of the hand, back of a knife, or a chisel and by pinching different muscles including the limb, neck, and right thigh muscles; and M. pectoralis; M. deltoideus; and M. biceps brachii. These studies pronounced different values for the duration of mechanical excitability for the muscles of each different type, which made the comparability of the outcomes difficult and puzzling.

For the very early PMI, the mechanical excitability of the Zsako muscle phenomena was indicated with three different phases of whole muscle contraction:

1. First-degreeIdiomuscular contraction (propagated excitation) may be visible up to at least 1.5–2.5 h postmortem.
2. Within the second phase a strong and typical reversible Idiomuscular spasm develops and can be noticed as late as 4–5 h postmortem.
3. A weak Idiomuscular spasm develops in the last stage. This could present for an extended length (up to 24 h). The weak idiomuscular spasm may be visible within the time interval of up to 8–12 h postmortem.

These data show a time limit and inaccuracy that makes mechanical excitability an unreliable PMI estimation method.

7.4.5.2 Electrical Excitability of Skeletal Muscle Postmortem

This is usually investigated on the face muscles. Needle electrodes are inserted through the skin (at the upper eyelid's nasal part or on both sides of the mouth) and electrical impulses are applied provided by a portable generator. The reaction—a contraction of one or more muscles—can be quoted semi-quantitatively depending on the strength of the contraction and its extension to areas far from the electrodes, both decreasing as time increases since death (Madea and Henssge 1990).

In the 1780s, during frog leg experiments, Luigi Galvani first established the ability of isolated muscle groups to contract under external electric stimulation. By subjectively evaluating the degree of contraction of specific muscle groups during electrical stimulation, rough estimates of the PMI have been suggested.

7.4.5.3 Pharmacological Excitability of the Iris Musculature

The iris muscle is even longer reactive to electrical and pharmacological stimulation than the skeletal muscle. For practical purposes, the pharmacology excitability of the iris is examined after subconjunctival injection of drugs (no injection must take place into the anterior chamber). The pupil's initial diameter should be recorded accurately with a transparent multi-diameter template. Approximately, 0.5 ml of a solution of norepinephrine, tropicamide, atropine or acetylcholine should then be injected. A positive reaction can be seen within 5–30 min, with the diameter becoming larger (norepinephrine, tropicamide, atropine) or smaller (acetylcholine) and lasts for a minimum of 1 h (Dettmeyer et al. 2013).

If at this time no change is visible, the reaction is considered to be −ve.

Supravital reactivity might be worthy for the determination of PMI, but only in the first few hours after death (not any of the choices listed above has been observed after 12–15 h postmortem). Since only semi-quantitatively the muscular responses obtained can be calculated, their investigation requires highly experienced operators. The equipment required for electrical stimulation also restricts the application of this method to perform death scene investigations.

7.4.6 Lividity

Man is the most cunning of all animals. Chameleon changes its color during lifetime but the man changes his color even after his death.

Livor mortis (Latin: livor—"bluish color", mortis—"of death"), postmortem lividity (Latin: postmortem—"after death", lividity—"black and blue"), hypostasis (Greek: hypo, meaning "under, beneath"; stasis, meaning "a standing") or suggillation, is one of the death signs(Fig. 7.13) (Mayer 2012; Rayamane et al. 2014).

7.4.6.1 Site of Appearance

This relies on the body's original pose upon death. Most deaths occur in the supine position and hence hypostasis occurs on the back of the cadaver (Dorsal distribution). Livor mortis always follows the gravitational rule until it gets fixed. In case of drowning, lividity is found in the region of head, forearms, lower legs, ear lobules and external genitalia. Hypostasis does not appear in the areas subjected to pressure either by the body weight (area of contact flattening), tight clothing e.g. tight waist band and also not seen in skin folds. The slightest pressure by these agents will prevent capillary filling with blood. Due to livor mortis, the lung is dark purple in the rear-dependent areas and can simulate congestion.

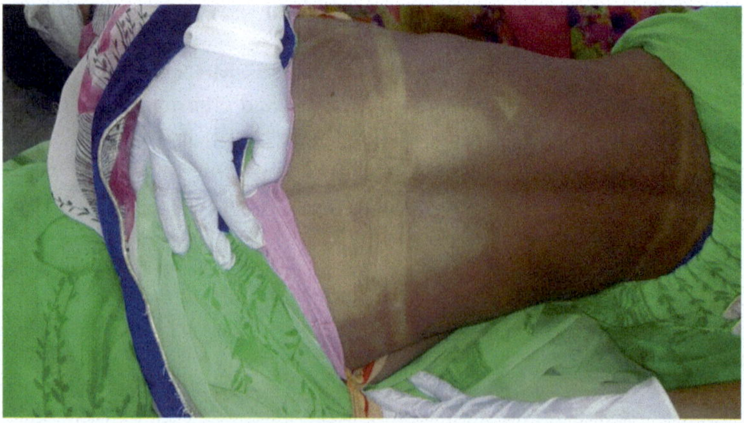

Fig. 7.13 Livor mortis with pallor areas of contact flattening in a corpse

7.4.6.2 Time of Appearance

Immediately after the cessation of circulation and being noticeable in 0.5–2 h after death as a consequence of blood settling in dependent areas of the body i.e. the lowest part of the body because of the gravity or hydrostatic pressure. Initially, it takes the form of a series of mottled patches, which increases gradually in size and then coalesces for 3–6 h and is fully developed and fixed in 6–8 h of death (Bertino 2012). Normally, it's far said that if pressure applied by a thumb blanches the area, the lividity is not fixed, and PMI is less than 8 h. If the area is not blanched, lividity is fixed, and the PMI is over 8 h (Modi 2013).

7.4.6.3 Mechanism

Fixation is permanent due to the diffusion of hemoglobin through capillary walls and tissue staining. According to Knight B, the fixation of lividity is untrue, as 'secondary gravitation' can occur and if left in a new position for a few hours, some or all hypostasis can fall to the most dependent areas. ***Noriko et al.*** supported the hypothesis that lividity fixation is not due to the spread of Hb in skin tissue but to hemo-concentration in blood vessels. The overall result of his work becomes most appropriate up to 24 h. Clotting of blood and collapsing of capillaries network are also some suggesting theories behind the fixation of PM lividity (Modi 2013).

7.4.6.4 Medico-Legal Importance

It's a certain death sign. Lividity has been used in estimation of time of death, but some forensic practitioners use it as a tool in death scenario reconstruction.

7.4.7 Electrolyte Concentration in Vitreous Humor, Blood, and Cerebrospinal Fluid (CSF)

When the ATP content of the cell fall below a critical level, autolysis begins inside the cell and causes suspension of the chemical, physical, and morphological reliability of the body. One of the direct effects of the energy breakdown is the loss of selective membrane permeability, which ends up in diffusion of ions based totally on their concentration gradient. The extent of autolytic processes, mainly the rise in potassium concentration and the decrease in sodium and chloride concentrations, depends on the TSD and was used as a way to estimate PMI (Garland et al. 2019; Garg et al. 2004).

7.4.7.1 Influencing Factors

Changes in electrolyte concentration are affected by many factors, including sample collection location, tissue and cell-specific characteristics, glycolysis rate, ambient temperature, pH and disease, cause of death, urea retention, and agonal period duration. The majority of measurements of the electrolyte concentration method are based on the changes in potassium, sodium and chloride concentrations. Blood, cerebrospinal fluid (CSF) and vitreous humor (VH) were used in the fluid. Autolysis takes place more slowly in VH compared to blood and CSF, and the selective permeability disappears after a long time of about 120 h PMI for VH compared to 15–20 h for CSF and only a few hours for blood autolysis. The potassium concentration increases with TSD and the slope increases with increased ambient temperature. Another reported factor causing a change in potassium concentration is the pre-death status of health or chronic disease. Another factor that influences the reproducibility of vitreous electrolyte measurements is the high viscosity of the VH fluid; numerous attempts to reduce the viscosity through heating or enzymatic digestion have been reported to improve reproducibility. In maximum cases of linear PMI and K+ regression analysis, the K+ concentration was used as a dependent and the PMI was used as independent variable, but ***Munoz et al.*** supported the use of PMI as a dependent variable in linear regression analysis (Muñoz et al. 2001). ***Madea et al.*** have reassessed data from previous research to better estimate TSD using PMI as a dependent and [K+] as an independent variable. They also studied the method proposed by ***Lange et al. (1994)*** and the non-linear approach of using the 'Loess smooth curve' model for its precision in PMI estimation (Lange et al. 1994). There were only 153 cases in the predicted PMI, 339 with a systematic overestimation of the TSD. The end result showed that ***Munoz et al.'s*** recommendation to use the [K^+] as an independent variable and the PMI as a dependent variable would increase the accuracy of the PMI estimate (Muñoz et al. 2001), but ***Lange et al. (1994)*** recommended non-linear approach leads to an overestimation of the PMI, failing to increase the accuracy of the PMI (Lange et al. 1994). In order to estimate PMI, ***Zhou et al. (2007)*** studied, only selected medical-legal bodies to limit the effects of ambient temperature, putrefaction status, analytical technique, sampling method, sampling storage and sampling from left eye to right eye (Zhou et al. 2007). ***Singh et al. (2006)*** mentioned a significant correlation with a double logarithmic linear relationship with the determination of PMI between 2.5 and 58 h for 311 subjects, 112 of which were at an average RT of 40.4 °C in summer and 199 subjects at a mean temperature of 14.3 °C in the winter season (Singh et al. 2006).

7.4.7.2 CSF

PMI estimates in CSF (cerebrospinal fluid) from sodium and potassium ion concentrations were determined by Yadav et al. utilizing flame photometry in a hundred medicolegal autopsies with a known PMI. They noted that CSF electrolyte changes are an important parameter for the PMI calculation. They also stated that the temperature and hospitalization factors in which intravenous saline infusion is performed may influence the estimation of PMI; at the same time, the sodium/potassium ion concentration ratio was reported to be a better parameter than the use of sodium or potassium concentration alone to predict PMI. ***Singh et al. (2003)*** confirmed a linear double logarithmic association between PMI concentration and plasma chloride concentration in humans, where chloride concentration was used as an independent value and concluded that the link between changes in plasma chloride log concentration and PMI log is very significant (Singh et al. 2003). Yet the relationship has become relatively reliant on other variables, like age, cause of death, gender, and ambient temperature.

7.5 Late Postmortem Changes

7.5.1 Decomposition

Decomposition (sometimes referred to as postmortem decay) is the biological process that reduces organic material to simpler forms. It takes place systematically in all biological organisms with the stoppage of normal life functions and begins immediately following death. Degradation occurs through two major processes of chemistry: autolysis and putrefaction.

7.5.1.1 Autolysis

Autolysis (or "self-digestion") is the destruction of the cells by the action of their own enzymes. It may also refer to the enzyme's digestion by another molecule of the same enzyme. As soon as the blood circulation and breathing stop, the body has no way to get oxygen or waste disposal. Excess carbon dioxide causes an acidic environment and causes the cell membranes to break. The membranes release enzymes which start to eat inside the cells. Autolysis usually occurs most quickly in the stomach and pancreas and can be the predominant process of decomposition in arid climate. The warmer the tissue is, the faster the autolysis progresses. Therefore, animals that die on a hot day and are left outside will have more autolysis. Additionally, if an animal dies with a fever, autolysis will progress more rapidly. Large animals generally tend to autolyze quicker as well because, in large carcasses, the innermost tissues stay warm long after the loss of life (just takes longer for a large body to cool than a small body).

7.5.1.2 Putrefaction

Putrefaction refers to the destruction of the body's soft tissue through bacteria and enzymes. Color changes, the evolution of gasses and liquefaction are the main changes that can be seen in tissues that are putrefied. Many scholars distinguish phases of the putrefaction process, some based on the analysis of the decomposition of animal carcasses. For e.g., ***Shean et al. (1993)*** discern four phases (soft tissue decomposition, bone exposure, remains only with connective tissue and bone only) which are divided into 15 phases (Shean et al. 1993), while ***Galloway et al. (1989)*** analyzed the process of decomposition using a longitudinal analysis of forensic cases in the Sonoran Desert and established a five-stage model that is now widely used (Galloway et al. 1989)

Its evolution can be divided into five stages:

- **Initial decay (up to 36–72 h postmortem):** however, the corpse remains fresh externally, but internally it begins to decompose, because of the combination of enzymatic autolysis and bacterial proliferation from the intestine. Individual cells break down, releasing cell contents and enzymes into the body.
- **Early putrefaction or green putrefaction or Discoloration (up to 1 week postmortem):** hemolysis and generation of hydrogen sulfide gas by anaerobic bacteria, including *Clostridium welchii,* result in the early decomposition change,

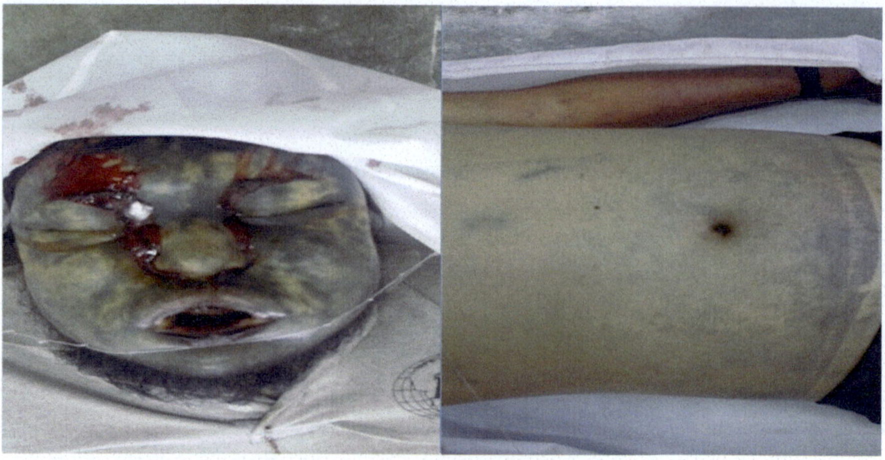

Fig. 7.14 Putrefactive greenish discoloration had spread across the face, chest and abdomen

i.e., blue-dark green discoloration. Internally first appear under the surface of the liver while externally in the lower abdominal quadrants (start from right iliac fossa due to the proximity of cecum to the skin). In the end, the entire abdomen becomes discolored, accompanied by the rest of the body. Seepage of hemoglobin pigments from hemolysed blood and gaseous rupture of blood vessels contributes to localized skin discoloration (green, purple, black), mimicking contusions (Fig. 7.14).

Other signs include skin blisters; abdominal/scrotal swelling with gas; oozing of putrefactive fluids by mouth and nostrils (not to be mistaken for blood); and the typical odor of decaying flesh. Approximately 2–4 days after death, the skin becomes marble-like, as the veins in the body are closer to the surface and thus easier to see. "Marbling" refers to an arborescent discoloration pattern caused by vascular distribution hemolysis. It appears with a reddish and later green color on the thighs and sidewalls of the abdomen, chest and shoulders.

- **Black putrefaction (up to 1-month postmortem):** The corpse shows a creamy flesh with exposed parts turning black, especially on the head and face. Skin decomposition leads to generalized epidermal separation and the nails fall off. As gases escape, the abdomen collapses. The odor of degradation is maximum.
- **Butyric fermentation (up to 2 months' postmortem):** this stage is marked by a progressive drying of the cadaver and the occurrence and proliferation of mold. It has a cheesy odor caused by butyric acid, and this odor attracts a new suite of corpse organisms. When the body ferments, the surface of the body that is in contact with the soil is covered with mold. The reduction of soft food makes the body less appealing to the maggot's mouth hooks and more suitable for the beetle's mouth chewing.

- **Dry decay, then skeletonization (months to years):** Final corpse drying and gradual disappearance of the remaining soft tissue.

This timeline of putrefactive events is unfortunately only indicative of what can happen, since there is an enormous and generally unpredictable intersubjective variability. Ambient temperature always affects the rate of putrefaction to some extent, but many other factors may also interfere, such as fatness or stoutness of the body(obese subjects putrefy faster than slender subjects), ante-mortem diseases or circumstances of death (sepsis or edema in the pre-death period may precipitate decay). In addition, there are some variants of the 'classical' sequence of decomposition stages, depending on environmental conditions: adipocere formation (in warm, humid, preferably anaerobic conditions) and mummification (in hot and dry environments, especially when air is moving). Despite these factors, and however great the forensic investigator's experience, the putrefactive phenomena affecting a corpse cannot be presented to be reliable TSD markers.

7.5.1.3 Variants of Putrefaction

- Adipocere
- Mummification

7.5.2 Adipocere or Saponification

Adipocere also called "***grave wax***" or saponification is a wax-like organic substance formed by the process of putrefaction wherein the fatty tissues of the dead body change into a grayish-white postmortem matter by anaerobic bacterial hydrolysis (Adipocere 2016). Therefore, it is seen more often in submerged corpses in water or in damp, warm environment (Fig. 7.15). Its name, ascribed to Fourcroy in 1789, comes from the Latin adipo (***fat***) and cera (***wax***) combinations.

Fig. 7.15 Adipocere formation throughout a female's body

7.5.2.1 History

Hydriotaphia, Urn Burial (1658), is a work reported by ***Sir Thomas Browne*** where he first described Adipocere (Murad 2008). In this work, a hydropicall body that was buried in a church yard for 10 years, authors found a fat concretion in which the earth's niter and the body's salt and liquor coagulated into massive lumps of fat into the consistency of the hardest castle soap. The chemical process of adipocere formation, saponification, was understood during the seventeenth century when microscopes were widely accessible. In 1825, health practitioner and lecturer Augustus Granville is thought to have (somewhat unwittingly) made candles from the adipocere of a mummy and used them to light the public lecture he gave to report on the mummy's dissection. Granville apparently thought that the waxy material belongs to the substance that had been used to preserve the mummy, instead of its being a product of the saponification of the mummified body (Pain 2009).

7.5.2.2 Formation

This process is marked by the hydrolysis and degeneration of unsaturated body fat (adipose tissue) into a yellowish-white waxy substance made up of saturated fatty acids. Essentially, hydrolysis and hydrogenation of body fat is a form of adipocyte-specific decomposition (fat cells) and its lipids.

Adipocytes are rich in glycerol molecules and triglycerides (or triglycerides). Once these cells are subjected to a humid, warm and anaerobic environment that has been invaded by Clostridium *welchii* presently known as C. *perfringens*, the process of adipocere formation begins. Previously, it was believed that adipocere formation require either damp conditions or the body immersion in the water, but it is now known that the body's water content in itself can be adequate to induce adipocere, including in bodies buried in well-sealed coffins.

In the process of adipocere formation, C *welchii* produces and enzymes lecithinase that breaks triglycerides into saturated and unsaturated free fatty acids through hydrolysis. Triglycerol hydrolysis takes place in the presence of sufficient water and enzymes until all molecules are reduced to free fatty acids. The non-decomposed body normally contains about 0.5% free fatty acid. However, the percentage of free fatty acids can reach up to 70% or higher with adipocere formation. Unsaturated free fatty acids, such as palmitoleic and linoleic acids, react with hydrogen to form hydroxystearic, hydroxypalmic acids and other stearic compounds. This final product is referred to as adipocere because its substantial resistance to bacterial action is stable for long periods of time. In addition, adipocere formation due to increased tissue acidity and dehydration due to water loss in hydrolysis inhibits endogenous bacteria, which slowdowns the cycle of putrefaction (Decomposition: what is grave wax? 2009).

Adipocere usually develops first in the subcutaneous fat of the orbits, cheeks, breasts, abdominal walls and buttocks. There are also occasions when internal organs are involved, in particular the liver, the kidney and the heart. The change is generally irregular and partial but rarely affects the entire body (Murad 2008). Adipocere can be observed within 2 weeks, but it usually takes 1–2 months to be substantial and 5–6 months to be completed. It can persist in a closed vault for years or decades.

7.5.2.3 Medico-Legal Importance

Preserves the body, which can permit identification after death; it may give conclusions about the cause of death; it indicates that the TSD was at least weeks to several months.

7.5.3 Mummification

Mummification is a modified form of putrefaction characterized by the dehydration and exsiccation (the drying process) of the tissues (Fig. 7.16). It can be partial and coexist with different forms of conservation and/or putrefaction. It extends to the entire body more easily than other processes like adipocere. Once the changes are complete, the body remains in that condition indefinitely (Modi 2013; Postmortem Changes and Time of Death 2012).

7.5.3.1 How Does Mummification Occur?

The mummification process usually takes place in a hot, extremely dry environment, one with air circulation, which as well as can take place in freezing conditions. This is commonly due to the low humidity that allows rapid tissue dehydration, which simultaneously slows down or inhibits bacterial and other microorganism-related decomposition. There is, however, a form of peripheral mummification, typically seen in the early stages of human decomposition, in which the trunk begins to show in early green color in the lower right abdominal quadrant. Examination of the distal extremities, especially the fingers and the toes, shows a brownish coloration with proof of tissue desiccation and a parchment-like appearance in the skin. This drying effect can also be seen in the skin of the scrotum, in which it appears like brown parchment. These changes are commonly seen in temperate climates between 48 and

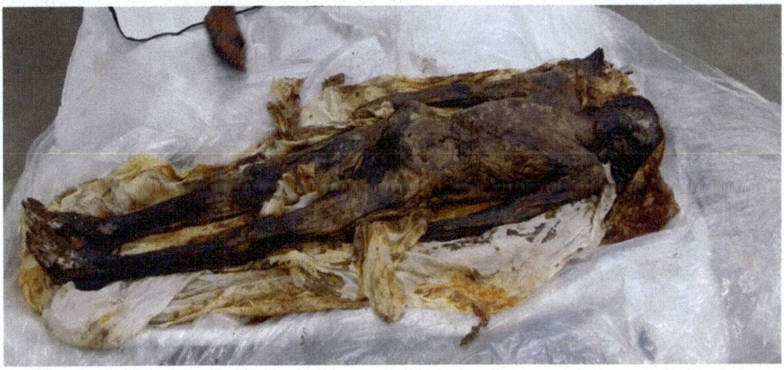

Fig. 7.16 Mummification–The body can dehydrate in a hot, dry climate, inhibiting bacterial decay; the skin dries into a dark, leathery look

72 h at a temperature of approximately 70 °F. Mummification may occur naturally or may be achieved through artificial means (Modi 2013; Postmortem Changes and Time of Death 2012).

The required time for complete mummification cannot be precisely specified, but depending on the size of the body and the atmospheric conditions it takes several weeks to months.

7.5.3.2 Conditions Simulating Mummification

There may be an essential point to consider because the shrinkage of the skin can certainly lead to linear skin defects that can imitate lacerations or incised wounds. They are commonly found across the groin, armpits and neck. The internal organs also show evidence of mummification in prominent shrinking conditions. It can usually have a black color and a parchment-like quality.

7.5.3.3 Medico-Legal Importance

Mummification may have significant medico-legal relevance for the four main goals of forensic anthropology, body identification, PMI, the cause of death and abnormal pathology within deep organs. For the former, mummies are often found in a surprising state of preservation and in these situations, it is much easier to find out the identity of the victim than with adipocere. Last but not least, large lesions can be preserved. However, it can be difficult or impossible to detect ecchymosis or wounds due to discoloration, artifacts and fungal action.

7.5.4 Skeletonization

Skeletonization is the last stage of death in which the last remains of the soft tissues of a body or carcass have declined or dried to the point of exposure of the skeleton (Fig. 7.17) (The Australian Museum 2018). In a temperate climate, it usually takes 3 to several weeks for a body to decompose wholly into a skeleton, depending on

Fig. 7.17 Skeletonization, the last stage of death, during which the last remains of the soft tissues of a body or carcass have decayed or dried to the point of exposure of the skeleton

factors such as temperature, insect presence and submergence in a substratum such as water. In tropical climates, skeletonization may occur in weeks, while in tundra areas, if subzero temperatures persist, it may take years to skeletonize or may never happen. Natural embalming processes in tourist bogs or salt deserts can indefinitely delay the process, leading to natural mummification, sometimes.

The skeletonization rate and the current corpse or carcass condition can be used to determine the PMI. The average time for complete skeletonization in a subtropical climate buried body is 1 year (Dix and Graham 1999). After skeletonization, if scavenging animals do not destroy or remove bones, it takes about 20 years for acids in many fertile soils to completely dissolve the skeleton of medium to large mammals, such as humans, leaving no trace of the body. The skeleton may persist in neutral pH soil or sand for hundreds of years before it eventually disintegrates. Alternatively, bones can be fossilized, converting into minerals that can persist indefinitely, especially in very fine, dry, salty, anoxic or slightly alkaline soils. In addition, organic components, unlike inorganic salts in bone, can be converted to petroleum (Byrd and Tomberlin 2019).

7.5.5 Forensic Entomology

Forensic entomology is the scientific study of the use of bugs and their arthropods relatives (succession pattern, larval weight, larval length and accumulated degree hour) that inhabit decomposing remains to aidlegal issues, especially in a court of law (Fig. 7.18). Entomologyis derived from the Greek term *entomon* (insect) + *logos* (word, reason) which means insect study (Gupta and Setia 2004). Since insects are usually the first one to become active in deteriorating human remains, sometimes drawn to the body within minutes of death, the use of insects to determine TSD may be highly effective (Aggarwal et al. 2003).

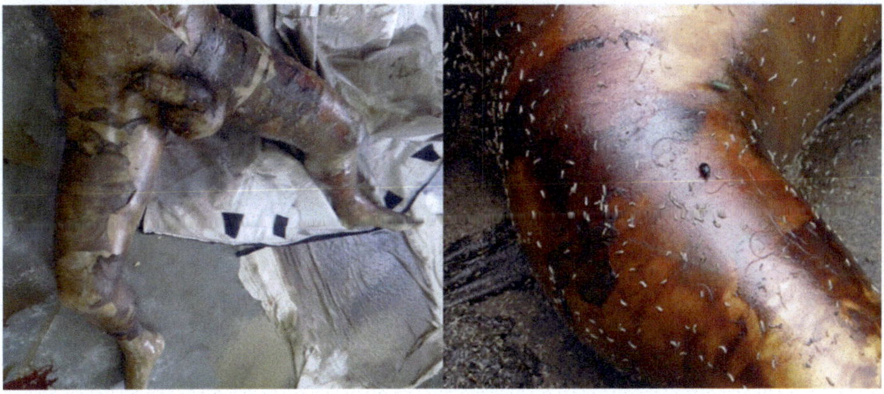

Fig. 7.18 The invasion of Arthropod's succession patterns with their developmental stages of various species found on decomposed carcasses during legal investigations

Determining the TSD from insect activity is a complex job involving a lot of steps. As the decomposition of human remains continues, the corpse progresses through multiple phases of deterioration, each of which becomes desirable to specific types of insects. When such 'waves' of insect colonization are established for a certain geographical region and the timing of each wave is well recognized, an overview of the arthropod fauna on the body may be used to measure the PMI. In order for this dating approach to be reliable, a database must be built for each geographical zone, because the species of insects identified in connection with human remains and the timing of their colonization differ by geographical location.

7.5.5.1 Ecological Roles of Insects in Decomposition

- Necrophages—species that feed on body tissue; mostly true flies and beetles; important age determination (larval instar) for PMI
- Omnivores—insects that feed on both the corpse and related fauna; ants, wasps and certain beetles; may alter the decomposition rate.
- Parasites and Predators—lots of beetles, true flies and wasps attacking immature flies
- Use the corpse as an extension of the resource; springtails, spiders, centipedes, some mites.

7.5.5.2 Stages of Insect-Aided Decomposition (Ramayah 2014; Rodriguez III 1982)

1. The "Fresh" Stage (Days 1–2):
   (a) body temperature falls to match the environment,
   (b) insects land on body, feed on body fluids, lay eggs in body cavities.
   (c) eggs take 12–18 h to hatch,
   (d) maggots feed on body.
   (e) predators and parasites arrive next.
2. The "Bloated" Stage (Days 2–6):
   (a) putrefaction begins,
   (b) anaerobic bacteria inside body release gases,
   (c) abdomen and then the whole body blows up like a balloon,
   (d) body becomes very hot,
   (e) housefly arrives and lay eggs,
   (f) eggs hatch and maggots feed on body tissue,
   (g) more predatory insects are attracted to the scene,
   (h) Body fluids seeping from the body.
3. The "Active Decay" Stage (Days 5–11):
   (a) Skin cracks open as maggots feed
   (b) gases escape body
   (c) strong foul odor is released
   (d) increasing number and types of insects, flies begin to pupate.
   (e) Predatory beetles like rove beets and histerids come to feed other insects
4. The "Advanced or Post-Decay" Stage:

   (a) Bones, cartilage, skin and hair are mostly left
   (b) different beetle types arrive
   (c) mites become used to inhabit soil under the body as they feed on body decomposition by-products
   (d) site for adult and immature moth flies, sphaerocerid and muscid flies, rove beetles.
5. The "Skeletal" Stage
   (a) All that remains is only bones and hair
   (b) Odor is mainly that of normal litter and soil.
   (c) some dermestid beetles, histerids, fly pupae, adult and immature rove beetles, normal soil fauna (mites) begin to return.
   (d) can last even several months.

7.5.5.3 History

In medieval China, the first documented incident in which insects were used in a forensic context. In 1325, Sung Tz'u, a Chinese lawyer, wrote a medico-legal textbook called "Hsiyüan chi lu" which can be translated as "The Washing Away of Wrongs" (van Gulik 2004). The book possibly mentioned the first case in which insects led to the murderer. A farmer "Aman" was murdered by repeatedly slashing near a rice field, apparently by a sickle assailant; all suspects were told to bring their sickles to one place and lay them on the ground. Blowflies were presumably drawn to one of the sickles due to the translucent traces of tissue already left on it, and the perpetrator eventually broke down and admitted to his offence.

The first application of forensic entomology in a contemporary court was in France in the eighteenth century, where Dr. Bergeretd'Arbois used insect succession as a tool to identify the PMI (incorrectly) for clearing a case. A couple who restructured their home in Paris uncovered the mummified remains of a child behind a fireplace. Suspicion fell on the couple immediately, although they moved into the house only recently (Benecke 2001). Bergeret, who autopsied the victim, observed on the corpse evidence of insect populations. He concluded that the body was placed behind the wall years earlier in 1849 using methods similar to those used by forensic entomologists today. To reach this date, Bergeret used what was known about the life cycles of insects and the successive colonization of a corpse. His report persuaded the police to charge the former home tenants, who were later convicted of the murder (Benecke 2001).

Flowler (1888) studied human remains insects in the United States, and later, in 1898, Motter collected insect fauna statistics from 150 serious disinterests in Washington, DC. Canine remains were also exhumed and insects were examined. Notes were made later on the differences between human and canine cadavers in the carrion species (Joseph et al. 2011).

Jean Pierre Megnin, a French veterinarian, documented the predictability of insect colonization in corpses for years. In 1894 La Faune des Cadavres was published, the culmination of his medical-legal experience. He described eight waves of insect succession that could be used to investigate suspicious deaths.

Megnin also noted that buried bodies were not susceptible to colonization in the same series. Only two colonial stages invaded these corpses (Benecke 2001; Klotzbach et al. 2004).

In the twentieth century, insects were found to be valuable in court cases involving insect colonization of body parts recovered from the water and not only whole bodies found on land. In 1935, a number of body parts were recovered from the Scottish river near Edinburgh, which were later identified as originating from two women. The identities of the deceased were determined and the names of the women in the family were Mrs. Ruxton and Mary Rogerson. The presence of Calliphoravicina Robineau-Desvoidy larvae in their third larval instar showed that the eggs were laid before the bodies were dumped in the river. Together with other evidence, this information led to Dr. Ruxton's husband being convicted of the murder.

7.5.5.4 Influencing Factors

Insects or arthropods are found in a decomposing body or carion of the vertebrates. While the activity of insects varies depending on the season, temperature, precipitation amount and habitat (i.e., shaded or open, buried or exposed), these variables have been thoroughly studied in certain specific areas and can therefore be taken into account when determining the PMI. The presence of hydrogen sulphide and ammonia-rich compounds, humidity and certain pheromones are influential stimulants for insect oviposition. Several factors limit the colonization of a corpse, such as its burial, climate, geographical region, blanket cover or tight wrapping, indoor placement, plastic bag wrapping, seasonal influences such as cold and rainy weather and daytime. ***Campobasso et al. (2001)*** stated that the majority of Diptera cannot colonize deeply buried bodies of more than 30 cm (Campobasso et al. 2001). Research by Anderson and several others has shown that the succession of insects and the composition of species on a corpse vary in various geographical regions and by season, so data collected for a particular region or area cannot be used without reservation to estimate PMIs in another region (Schroeder et al. 2003; Sharma and Singh 2015; Smith 1986; Campobasso et al. 2001). ***Bourel et al. (2003)*** stated that the PMI estimate depends on the location of the eggs, whether in the mouth or on the body surface of the mouse; thus, the calculation method should be different in human cases if the eggs are placed in warm natural openings such as the nose or on the body surface (Bourel et al. 2003). ***Wells et al. (2001)*** mentioned that fertilized eggs can be retained before oviposition in the oviduct of some female flies until they have completed the embryonic development in cases where an appropriate oviposition site is not available. As a result, the larvae would erupt immediately after oviposition and complicate the estimate of PMI (Wells and King 2001).

7.5.5.5 Medico-Legal Importance

The primary use of insects that answer questions during death investigations is to estimate the TSD of the victim. This option exists because the insects are the first to colonize dead animals. Another application of entomology is the use of the geographical distribution of a specific insect species (where it lives) to determine the movement of the body. Also, it is used to find the cause and manner of death and to detect toxins, drugs or even the victim's DNA through insect larvae analysis. For carrion blood-feeding insect specimen, which would possibly have fed on the cadaver, human DNA can be successfully extracted. The presence of DNA of suspects in the insects at a known location may establish a link between the victim and the crime within a definable period of time.

7.6 Other Methods Used in the Calculation of PMI

7.6.1 Radio-Carbon Dating

Since the 1940s, dating techniques for radiocarbon (^{14}C) have been widely used in environmental and archeological studies. The date of radiocarbon started as a means to date objects from the geological record based on the carbon-14 decline rate. After the death of an organism, the carbon 14 accumulated from the atmosphere in the body begins to decrease at a known rate, e.g., half of the radiocarbon in an organism decays after 5730 years. The amount of decay is therefore used to measure how long has passed since the organism died (Hodgins 2009).

The technique was used in archeology when the potential of archeological materials containing the same chemical elements as geological materials was recognized to date. Due to the half-life of radiocarbon (5730 years), it is typically relevant for objects that are considerably older (at least 300 years) than those considered to be of forensic significance as a dating technique based on decay rate. However, materials that do not show decay can also be found to date by comparing the carbon 14 level in the tissue with the atmospheric levels and finding the year in which the atmospheric levels match the carbon 14 most closely in the tissue.

There are various variables affecting radiocarbon levels in the atmosphere and in various tissue types. Consequently, the radiocarbon age calibration must be carried out to convert it to calendar age and to adjust for the variables that influence the date (Hodgins 2009).

7.6.2 Decomposition-^{1}H Magnetic Resonance Spectroscopies

Radiology methods such as ^{1}H magnetic resonance spectroscopy (MRS) were used to identify the metabolites that emerged during brain tissue decomposition as a step towards the quantitative calculation of PMIs in putrefaction. This procedure was intended to offer a non-invasive chemical examination of organ metabolites shielded by the skull from environmental conditions, so it is assumed that decay and appearance of metabolites are following a reproducible time frame. Sheep heads were put in closed plastic containers and held at a steady temperature of 21 ± 3 °C for 18 days and were analyzed everyday up to 18 days' postmortem. The samples were analyzed using high-resolution NMR and the presence and degree of combination of the five metabolites, acetate; alanine; trimethylamine; butyrate; and proportionate; were used to calculate PMI. A correlation coefficient between the predicted time and the true time is $r = 0.93$ for the entire period up to 300 h postmortem. The values are displayed with two standard deviations in the error range. In this system, PMIs > 250 are systemically underestimated. ***Yang et al. (2008)*** utilized H-MRS techniques to analyze the developmental changes of *N*-acetyl aspartate (Naa), a neuron marker; total choline (Cho), a cell membrane marker; and total creatine (Cr), an energy marker, in concentration and ratio relation for Naa/Cr, Naa/Cho, Cho/Cr at two different temperatures of 10 °C and 30 °C in rabbits' brains between 0 and 24 h postmortem (Yang et al. 2008).

7.6.3 DNA Degradation

In addition to the incorporation of DNA as biochemical or immunohistochemical methods for calculating the PMI, the degradation of DNA was published over 30 years ago. Using a cytophotometric scanning method, a non-linear decline in DNA was defined in human liver and testis samples. Due to the wide range of values, however, DNA degradation in the determination of the PMI is of no practical value.

The degradation of DNA as a PMI predictor has again been studied by flow cytometric evaluation. Initial statistics showed a correlation between DNA and PMI degradation with tissue decomposition at Rt in ten cases. The author pointed out the possible influence of body temperature and environmental conditions, clothing, etc. ***Di Nunno et al. (1999)*** reported that the degradation of DNA is not influenced by external factors such as temperature but by biological differences resulting from the disease and the putrefaction process of the intestinal contents (Di Nunno et al. 1998).

The analysis of postmortem DNA degradation using single-cell gel electrophoresis was used to measure PMI more precisely. Johnson et al. (2002) utilized single-cell gel electrophoresis, followed by staining and quantitative analysis of fragments. These researchers identified an approximately linear association between DNA fragmentation and PMI with $R2 = 0.8934$ and $R2 = 0.5244$ for the two forms of assays, comet-tail-length and comet-tail-moment, respectively, used in their study for up to 56 h postmortem (Johnson and Ferris 2002). ***Miki et al. (2011)*** found that quantifying the amplified DNA in the liver and brain at the same time may become a useful tool for the forensic diagnosis of PMI in the cold season. ***Chen et al. (2005)*** display a good relationship between the degradation of DNA and human tissues with PMI, especially within the spleen (Chen et al. 2005).

7.6.4 Strontium^{90}

In recent times, a number of radiometric methods have been introduced to confirm TSD. For instance, ^{14}C and ^{90}Sr bomb pulse dating covers the last 60 years and gives reliable TSD when teeth or bones are available. ^{90}Sr is an artificial nuclear fission product of the atmospheric A-bomb testing that took place between 1945 and

1979.^{90}Sr has a physical half-life of 28.1 years and a biological half-life between 7.5 and 18 years. ^{90}Sr is an analog to calcium and is therefore deposited in human bones. During life, ^{90}Sr is continuously held in the body, but after death, it degrades continuously. The analytical technique using ^{90}Sr is simpler than for bomb pulse ^{14}C but leads to larger uncertainties related to β counting. ***Neis et al. (1999)*** used ^{90}Sr to determine TSD using nine bone samples, three from 1931/1932 and six from 1989 to 1994 (Neis et al. 1999). The samples from 1931/1932 did not show any ^{90}Sr activity. All the samples from 1989 later showed ^{90}Sr activity, but the intensity was very variable. ***Neis et al. (1999)*** also reported that ^{90}Sr was above the detection limit on archeological bones. The presence of diagenetic ^{90}Sr is therefore a serious disadvantage in the application of the TSD calculation method (Neis et al. 1999). ***Schrag et al. (2014)*** reported on the use of ^{90}Sr and ^{210}Pb dating and anthropological investigations to calculate the TSD (Schrag et al. 2014). The author also mentioned that diagenesis and the inter-individual difference in radionuclide uptake represent the main sources of uncertainty in radiometric methods for TSD calculation (Schrag et al. 2014).

^{232}Th series dating has also been suggested for the determination of TSD but requires a large number of bones (at least 300 g), which can be a major limitation to the use of the method in forensic sciences. In fact, the counting time of α and γ spectrometry involved in the measurement to achieve the desired detection limit is at least 15 days. In comparison, ^{210}Pb dating is promising but is submitted to diagenesis and human behaviors such as smoking, factors that need to be carefully considered.

7.6.5 Gastric Emptying

Meticulous autopsy provides not only information about the cause and circumstances leading to death but also helps to estimate the TSD. The gastric content inspection must be part of every postmortem examination since the approximate TSD can be calculated indirectly if the time of the last meal is known.

It has been determined through extensive research, light meals take about 2 h to pass through the stomach under normal circumstances. A heavy meal takes about 6 h to pass through the stomach.

- Carbohydrate-rich meals empty in 2–4 h.
- Protein-rich meals empty in 2–4 h.
- High-fat content meals empty in 2–4 h.

Meal reaches to ileocaecal valve within 6 and 8 h.

Food movement distal to stomach
- Hepatic flexure-6 h
- Splenic flexure-9–12 h
- Pelvic colone-12–18 h

Emptying rate changes due to

- Type of food eaten
- Parsons's rate of metabolism
- Sickness
- Drug or medication intake
- Prior medical and emotional conditions

7.6.6 Activity of Enzymes

Attempt to estimate PMI using the measurement of postmortem enzyme activity started out within the late 50s and early 60s.

7.6.6.1 Transaminases/Aminotransferases

Various scholars and scientists have suggested a particular and progressive increase in transaminase levels in the dead body serum as the TSD increases, but ***Hall (1958)***, ***Enticknap (1960)*** and ***Coe (1974)*** have done the most comprehensive study. They indicated a definite increase in these enzyme levels after death, but no more details on the estimation of PMI from these results (Hall 1958; Enticknap 1960; Coe 1974). ***Mukherjee (1994) and Nandy (2010)***, however, document the increasing trend in serum aminotransferase levels up to the second to the third day of death and believe that such calculations are too erratic and asymmetrical to help in anything like "postmortem clocking" (Mukherjee 1994; Nandy 2010). ***Evans (1963)*** establishes the initial increase of transaminase activity from 3 to 4 h after the loss of life and a fairly steady rise to high levels was observed until about 60 h after death when diminution activity commenced (also reported by ***B Knight***) (Evans 1963). ***Hall (1958)*** found a significant, rapid rise in SGOT in intra-cardiac blood, but found a low level in femoral blood in patients who died unexpectedly in clinically good patients (Hall 1958).

7.6.6.2 Acid Phosphatase-Within 48 h, Levels Increase 20 Times

Parikh (1992), ***Modi*** (2013), and ***Biswas*** (2012) mentioned a definite increase in the levels of these enzymes after the loss of life. ***Nandy (2010)*** reported a peak level between 36 and 48 h after the loss of life (Nandy 2010), at the same time as ***Mukherjee*** noted in the first 2–3 days after death, the rising titer (Mukherjee 1994). ***Enticknap (1960)*** stated arise of serum Acid Phosphatase level from just more than nil just after death to 2.5 kA unit at 18-h postmortem then there was a transient fall up to 30 h after death (15 kA Units). Again, the enzyme levels increased so that the peak was reached at 40 kA unit level at 40 h and finally the levels fell at 25 kA units up to 50 h and remained at the same level well beyond 60 h after the loss of life (Enticknap 1960).

7.6.6.3 Alkaline Phosphatase: Increase with PMI

- Normal antemortem range-1.5–4 BU
- 10 h after death-5.3 BU

- 18 h after death-9 BU
- 48 h after death-30 BU

Naumann (1950) pointed out that the average concentration of alkaline phosphatase was 5.3 BU in 14 cases 101/2 h after death (normal antemortem range 1.5–4 BU). ***Coe (1974)*** opined that the concentration almost doubled and tripled 8 and 18 h after the death (Coe 1974).

7.6.6.4 Amylase-After 2 Days the Levels Are 3–4 Times the Normal Levels of Antemortem

Enticknap (1960) confirmed that the amylase levels show double peaks or a biphasic increase after the loss of life. It rose sharply from 100 Somoghi units immediately after death to 350 units 6 h after death, after which it decreased to 150 units after 30 h and 40 h after death, recorded a peak of over 350 units (Enticknap 1960).

7.6.6.5 Lactate Dehydrogenase

For the first 60 h after death, ***Enticknap (1960)*** showed a patterned increase in activity [Lactate Dehydrogenase (LDH)] (Enticknap 1960). He proposed the following equation for predicting the number of LDH units in Wroblewski: ***"Wroblewski units of LDH/1000 = 2.69 + 0.24 (time in hours after death)"***. He discovered that LDH accumulated in cadaver sera in three phases, starting with a rapid increase within several hours. Next, the next 2–3 days saw a slower, usually linear increase, and the levels finally peaked around the fourth day.

Enticknap (1960) work was further carried out by ***Schleyer*** (1963), who added that his postmortem increase should be attributed to autolysis of red blood cells because red blood cells are the main source of serum LDH. There has been no significant difference in activity due to the cause of death. ***Lythgoe (1980)*** no longer found a linear relationship in increasing activity of the enzyme(Lythgoe 1980). ***Gos et al. (1993)*** measured LDH and malate dehydrogenase (MDH) enzyme activity in the human liver to calculate PMI at various storage temperatures from −3 to 17 °C using 25 bodies between 6 and 69 years of age. Although the activity of each enzyme was stated to be temperature dependent, they defined statistical discrepancies between LDH and MDH at all different temperatures. Therefore, it is necessary to estimate which regression line and which enzyme should be used in each case to calculate PMI (Gos and Raszeja 1993). ***Singh and Prasad (2009)*** observed that the rate of activity of creatinine phosphokinase, gamma-glutamyl transferase, LDH and amylase has a statistically important association with PMI of up to 36 h (Singh and Prasad 2009).

7.6.6.6 Esterase Including Cholinesterase

Petty et al. (1958) stated that there was no substantial variation in true blood cholinesterase levels between refrigerated and unrefrigerated samples and no noticeable decline in activity in periodically analyzed samples up to a few weeks after death (Petty et al. 1958). ***Arnason and Biarnason (1972)*** reported 1/4 h to 720 h after death total starch gel electrophoresis serum esterase on the postmortem sera (Arnason and Bjarnason 1972).

7.6.6.7 Phosphoglutamutase

Dixit (2007) studied the association of phosphoglutamutase in postmortem blood with time and cause of death and also reported many factors, along with environmental conditions, depending on the estimation of PMI (Dixit 2007).

7.6.6.8 Creatine Kinase

Bollinger and Carrodus in 1938 reported a postmortem increase in creatine serum levels (Bolliger and Carrodus 1938). The results were subsequently supported by ***Naumann*** (1950) and ***Karkela*** (1993) with similar CSF studies.

7.6.7 The Uterus Cycles

Various stages of uterine mucous membrane growth and decrease depend on time; the histological reputation of the mucous membrane of the uterus could therefore be used to determine the PMI in female subjects. To estimate PMI, ***Schnabel et al. (1997)*** studied the cycles of the mucous membranes of the uterus of 27 years old prostitute by comparing the menstrual period and assuming regular cycles that cannot be used for women before menarche or menopause. Oral contraception medications may also be tormented by this method (Schnabel et al. 1997).

7.6.8 Brain RNA

Brain RNA degrades linearly after death, 18S rRNA in the postmortem period is more stable than beta-actin mRNA. To predict TSD, their ratio can be used (Zhu et al. 2011).

7.6.9 Protein Degradation

Emerging advances in the field of molecular techniques give more sensitive and precise results in comparison to traditional observational methods and due to these advancement proteins degradation analysis is new target which may use as biomarker for the estimation of PMI. Protein molecules are exactly regulated throughout life and frequently predictably deteriorated after loss of life. Researchers have searched specific protein in mammalian brain, skeletal muscle, myocardium and lung which can be changed in time-dependent postmortem.

An exhaustive study considering 40 femur bones from 40 different cadavers ranging from 5 to 20 years was done by ***Prieto-Bonete et al.*** (2019). They selected 32 proteins for evaluating late PMI estimation (5–20 year) and observed that based on protein profile present in bone can be used for approximate evaluation of TSD.

Pittner et al. (2017) in a case report of murder-suicide used muscle protein to estimate PMI using protein degradation analysis and observed it a valuable tool however they were unable to sensibly convert data to respective times of death. Protein degradation analysis of brain tissue samples (cadaver specimen = 18) showed that Talin-1 protein has a significant correlation with time lapse therefore useful marker for PMI estimation (Pittner et al. 2017). ***Lee et al. (2016)*** found a significant association of Glyceraldeyde 3-phosphate dehydrogenase (GAPDH) protein in a concentration and time-dependent manner by using lateral flow assay and can be used to estimate PMI (Lee et al. 2016). ***Fountoulakis et al. (2001)*** contemplated changes in the protein level of the rat brain kept at 23 °C for several postmortem times up to 72 h. The changes mostly related to structural proteins and enzymes (Fountoulakis et al. 2001). ***Lametsch et al. (2002)*** identified 18 proteins and peptides in Longissimus dorsi from pig muscle that were found to change postmortem (Lametsch et al. 2002). ***Wang (2011)*** noted postmortem proteolytic degradation of the heavy myosin chain in the Atlantic cod skeletal muscle (Wang 2011). ***Sabucedo and Furton (2003)*** investigated the degradation of cardiac Troponin I (cTnI) in the bovine model and identified a characteristic banding pattern, a pseudo-linear relationship between the cTnI breakdown percentage and the log of the PMI ($r > 0.95$). This degradation-banding pattern of tissue cTnI is helpful in the early determination of PMI (0–5 days) (Sabucedo and Furton 2003). ***Kumar et al. (2016)*** centered on temperature-dependent PM degradation of cardiac Troponin-T (cTnT) and its relation with PMI in human. The data indicated that its degradation can provide an extended time window (0–10 days) during which PMI can be more accurately and precisely determined (Kumar et al. 2016). ***Kikuchi et al. (2010)*** found that TSD is related to HMGB1 concentration in a time-dependent manner (Kikuchi et al. 2010). Postmortem pathological changes of actin in skeletal muscles of rats were studied by ***Liu et al***. (2008) by making use of laser scanning confocal microscope (LSCM) and transmission electron microscope (TEM) (Liu et al. 2008). Through the TEM, they observed that actin filament deteriorated with the lapse of PMI. The LSCM revealed a reduction in the extent of anti-actin antibody staining in the skeletal muscles in correlation with increased PMI. ***Xiao and Chen (2005)*** concluded that actin can be detected 8 days PM and that βeta-tubulin instead of α-tubulin can be detected 2 days PM (Xiao and Chen 2005). ***Li et al. (2003)*** studied the phosphorylation of signaling proteins in relation to TSD and concluded that phosphorylated proteins and other proteins decreased rapidly according to PMI. They also observed PMI effects on each frontal cortex and hippocampus at room temperature (RT) and 4 ^{0}C. This suggests that two-dimensional gel electrophoresis and functional assays that depend upon the phosphorylation state of proteins are highly sensitive to time lapses (Li et al. 2003). ***Kang et al. (2003)*** supported CaMKII and CNA as possible markers for short and long-term PMI calculations (Kang et al. 2003). ***Pittner et al. (2015)*** found that cTnT, SERCA1, titin, desmin and nebulin showed regular and predictable degradation, which may be utilized as substrates for future molecular-based means of PMI estimation (Pittner et al. 2015). ***Foditsch et al. (2015)*** observed that nebulin, desmin, SERCA 1, and titin exhibited time-specific protein patterns. The degradation patterns they defined suggest that porcine skeletal muscle may be used as a forensic model tissue (Foditsch et al. 2015).

7.7 Conclusion

After death, due to autolysis and bacterial action, different changes are taking place in the body which, if observed properly can help to find the PMI. If the environmental and body factors are stable, speed of appearance of these changes can give a fairly accurate PMI but these factors are rarely constant and so are the postmortem changes; that is why we rarely say determination of the PMI and it is always stressed that it is the estimation of the TSD. Accurate estimation of PMI is very important during investigation for unwitnessed deaths and in controversial witnessed deaths too.

Cooling of the body is a very important observation and can give us a fairly accurate idea during the early hours of death when the environmental variations of temperature are known, but due to lack of awareness, it is not commonly utilized in most of the situations. Changes in the eyes and postmortem staining strengthen this estimation. It is postmortem staining, rigor mortis and decomposition changes that are commonly employed by forensic pathologists to determine TSD, as in majority of the situations it gives a fairly accurate estimation of the PMI. These changes are easy to observe and are less time-consuming, which is why to base the TSD in these changes is most popular. Up to 36–48 postmortem interval these changes gives us a very good idea of TSD but using these methods give us a wide range of time since death. Different researches have been done to narrow these ranges but have not proved much useful.

While determining the PMI, one should not rely on a single method or single change but all the different changes should be given due importance. Usually, different postmortem changes in the dead bodies are overlapping. As the duration of the TSD increases, the range which can be estimated also widens. Biochemical changes in blood, CSF and vitreous fluid prove helpful during this phase of estimation of PMI. Out of these biochemical changes potassium levels in the vitreous fluid are more sensitive and reliable for up to 4 days. During this phase and time following after this H Magnetic Resonance Spectroscopy help to reach at right conclusions up to 10–15 days. But the facilities for this are limited and it prevents wide usage of this technique. After this interval, forensic entomology helps us to reach a conclusion for many weeks to months depending upon the environmental conditions. Mummification or Adipocere formation if observed, also help us to find out the PMI up to 1 year. Changes in the ligaments and different changes to skeletonization also help to find out the TSD but the range of estimation of time since death is further widened. Protein degradation of the bones can also help in finding out the PMI up to 20 years after death sometimes. If we have to deal with forensic archeology specimens, Carbon dating and Strontium levels further assist to find out the PMI which can be done up to thousands of years.

The arena of estimation of PMI is a very important question and is a neglected field of research, but it requires substantial research so that estimation may turn to the determination of TSD.

References

Adipocere. Oxford Dictionaries UK Dictionary. Oxford University Press. Accessed 23 Jan 2016

Aggarwal AD, Gorea RK, Aggarwal OP, Singh D (2003) Forensic entomology–a guide to post-mortem interval. J Punjab Acad Forensic Med Toxicol 3(3):7–10

Amendt J, Krettek R, Zehner R (2004) Forensic entomology. Naturwissenschaften 91(2):51–65

Arnason A, Bjarnason O (1972) Post mortem changes of human serum esterases. APMIS 80 (6):841–846

Bardale R (2011) Principles of forensic medicine & toxicology. JP Medical Ltd., New Delhi

Bartle J (2018, Dec 16) Every corpse has a story: How experts find clues in the dead. https://www.news.com.au/technology/science/human-body/every-corpse-has-a-story-how-forensic-experts-find-clues-in-the-dead/news-story/ad68d794f1e8af2fefe8a9edfc4e24b5

Bateman DE (2001) Neurological assessment of coma. J Neurol Neurosurg Psychiatry 71(suppl 1): i13–i17

Bedford PJ, Tsokos M (2013) The occurrence of cadaveric spasm is a myth. Forensic Sci Med Pathol 9(2):244–248

Benecke M (2001) A brief history of forensic entomology. Forensic Sci Int 120(1-2):2–14

Bernat JL (2010) How the distinction between "irreversible" and "permanent" illuminates circulatory–respiratory death determination. J Med Philos 35(3):242–255

Bertino AJ (2012) Forensic science: fundamentals and investigations 2012 update. Nelson Education, Delhi

Biswas G (2012) Review of forensic medicine and toxicology. JP Medical Ltd., New Delhi

Boahene A (2015) Forensic estimation of time since death: a comparative study of polynomial regression and modified Newton's models. Doctoral dissertation

Bolliger A, Carrodus AL (1938) Creatine retention in blood and cerebro-spinal fluid. Med J Aust 1 (2):69–72

Bourel B, Callet B, Hédouin V, Gosset D (2003) Flies eggs: a new method for the estimation of short-term post-mortem interval? Forensic Sci Int 135(1):27–34

Byrd JH, Tomberlin JK (eds) (2019) Forensic entomology: the utility of arthropods in legal investigations. CRC Press, Boca Raton

Campobasso CP, Di Vella G, Introna F (2001) Factors affecting decomposition and Diptera colonization. Forensic Sci Int 120(1–2):18–27

Causes of skin paleness in dark and light skin (n.d.). https://www.medicalnewstoday.com/articles/325562

Chen X, Shen YW, Gu YJ (2005) The research of relationship between DNA degradation and postmortem interval. Fa Yi Xue Za Zhi 21(2):115–117

Chisiu I (2018, Sept 24) Home. http://lawyr.it/index.php/articles/reflections/1272-estimating-the-time-of-death-algor-mortis

Coe JI (1974) Postmortem chemistry: practical considerations and a review of the literature. J Forensic Sci 19(1):13–32

Davy J (1839) Researches: physiological and anatomical, vol 2. Smith, Elder and Company, London

Day DM, Wallman JF (2006) Width as an alternative measurement to length for post-mortem interval estimations using Calliphora augur (Diptera: Calliphoridae) larvae. Forensic Sci Int 159 (2–3):158–167

Decomposition: what is grave wax? Archived from the original on 15 Feb 2009. Accessed 6 Nov 2011

Dettmeyer RB, Verhoff MA, Schütz HF (2013) Forensic medicine: fundamentals and perspectives. Springer, New York

Di Nunno NR, Costantinides F, Bernasconi P, Bottin C, Melato M (1998) Is flow cytometric evaluation of DNA degradation a reliable method to investigate the early postmortem period? Am J Forensic Med Pathol 19(1):50–53

Dix J, Graham M (1999) Time of death, decomposition and identification: an atlas. CRC Press, Boca Raton

Dixit PC (2007) Text book of forensic medicine & toxicology, 1st edn. Peepe Publishers, New Delhi, p 110

Dowler B (1845) Post-mortem caloricity of yellow fever. Boston Med Surg J 33(1):14–17. https://doi.org/10.1056/nejm184508060330104. ISSN 0096-6762

Enticknap JB (1960) Biochemical changes in cadaver sera. J Forensic Med 7:135–146

Evans WED (1963) The chemistry of death. Charles C. Thomas, IL, pp 40–62

Foditsch EE, Saenger AM, Monticelli FC (2015) Skeletal muscle proteins: a new approach to delimitate the time since death. Int J Leg Med 130(2):433–440

Fountoulakis M, Hardmeier R, Hoger H, Lubec G (2001) Postmortem changes in the level of brain protein. Exp Neurol 167:86–91

Galloway A, Birkby WH, Jones AM, Henry TE, Parks BO (1989) Decay rates of human remains in an arid environment. J Forensic Sci 34(3):607–616

Garg V, Oberoi SS, Gorea RK, Kaur K (2004) Changes in the levels of vitreous potassium with increasing time since death. J Indian Acad Forensic Med 26(4):136–139

Garland J, Olds K, Rousseau G, Palmiere C, Ondruschka B, Kesha K et al (2019) Using vitreous humour and cerebrospinal fluid electrolytes in estimating post-mortem interval-an exploratory study. Aust J Forensic Sci 52(6):1–8

Gos T, Raszeja S (1993) Postmortem activity of lactate and malate dehydrogenase in human liver in relation to time after death. Int J Leg Med 106(1):25–29

van Gulik RH (2004 [1956]) T'ang-Yin-Pi-Shih: parallel cases from under the pear-tree, reprint edn. Gibson Press, p 18. ISBN 978-0-88355-908-6

Gupta A, Setia P (2004) Forensic entomology–past, present and future. Anil Aggrawals Internet J Forensic Med Toxicol 5(1):50–53

Hall WEB (1958) The medico-legal application of the serum transaminase test. J Forensic Sci 3:117–122

Henssge C, Madea B (2004) Estimation of the TSD in the early post-mortem period. Forensic Sci Int 144(2–3):167–175

Henssge C, Madea B (2007) Estimation of the TSD. Forensic Sci Int 165(2–3):182–184

Hodgins GW (2009) Measuring atomic bomb-derived 14C levels in human remains to determine Year of Birth and/or Year of Death. US Department of Justice, p 98. http://muttermuseum.org/exhibitions/the-soap-lady/

Hubig M, Muggenthaler H, Sinicina I, Mall G (2015) Temperature based forensic death time estimation: the standard model in experimental test. Leg Med 17(5):381–387

Illes J (ed) (2017) Neuroethics: anticipating the future. Oxford University Press, Oxford

Johnson LA, Ferris JA (2002) Analysis of postmortem DNA degradation by single-cell gel electrophoresis. Forensic Sci Int 126(1):43–47

Joseph I, Mathew DG, Sathyan P, Vargheese G (2011) The use of insects in forensic investigations: an overview on the scope of forensic entomology. J Forensic Dent Sci 3(2):89

Kang S, Kassam N, Gauthier ML, O'Day DH (2003) Post-mortem changes in calmodulin binding proteins in muscle and lung. Forensic Sci Int 131:140–147

Kärkelä JT (1993) Critical evaluation of postmortem changes in human autopsy cisternal fluid. Enzymes, electrolytes, acid-base balance, glucose and glycolysis, free amino acids and ammonia. Correlation to total brain ischemia. J Forensic Sci 38(3):603–616

Kikuchi K, Kawahara KI, Biswas KK, Ito T, Tancharoen S, Shiomi N, Koda Y, Matsuda F, Morimoto Y, Oyama Y, Takenouchi K (2010) HMGB1: a new marker for estimation of the postmortem interval. Exp Ther Med 1(1):109–111

Klotzbach H, Krettek R, Bratzke H, Püschel K, Zehner R, Amendt J (2004) The history of forensic entomology in German-speaking countries. Forensic Sci Int 144(2–3):259–263

Knüsel CJ, Janaway RC, King SE (1996) Death, decay, and ritual reconstruction: archaeological evidence of cadaveric spasm. Oxford J Archaeol 15(2):121–128

Krause D, Zett L (1973) Physiological and morphological studies of the mechanism and development of rigor mortis (author's transl). Z Rechtsmed 72(4):245–254

Kumar S, Verma AK, Ali W, Pandey A, Ahmad I, Singh US (2013a) A study of unnatural female death profile in Lucknow, India. Am J Forensic Med Pathol 34(4):352–356

Kumar S, Verma AK, Ahmad I, Ali W, Singh US (2013b) Profile of unnatural deaths-a study of autopsies at mortuary of King George's Medical University, Lucknow, India. Med Leg Update 13(2):113

Kumar S, Ali W, Singh US, Kumar A, Bhattacharya S, Verma AK, Rupani R (2016) Temperature-dependent postmortem changes in human cardiac troponin-T (cTnT): an approach in estimation of time since death. J Forensic Sci 61:S241–S245

Lametsch R, Roepstorff P, Bendixen E (2002) Identification of protein degradation during post-mortem storage of pig meat. J Agric Food Chem 50(20):5508–5512

Lange N, Swearer S, Sturner WQ (1994) Human postmortem interval estimation from vitreous potassium: an analysis of original data from six different studies. Forensic Sci Int 66(3):159–174

Laureys S (2005) Death, unconsciousness and the brain. Nat Rev Neurosci 6(11):899–909

Lee D-G, Yang KE, Hwang JW et al (2016) Degradation of kidney and psoas muscle proteins as indicators of post-mortem interval in a rat model, with use of lateral flow technology. PLoS One 11(8):e0160557

Li J, Gould TD, Yuan P, Manji HK, Chen G (2003) Post-mortem interval effects on the phosphorylation of signaling proteins. Neuropsychopharmacology 28(6):1017–1025

Liu Y, Kuai J-X, Zhang Y-W, Wang Y-Y (2008) The relationship between the degradation of actin and the postmortem interval in rats. J Forensic Med 24:165–167

Lythgoe AS (1980) The activity of lactate dehydrogenase in cadaver sera: a comparison of different sampling sites. Med Sci Law 20(1):48–53

Madea B (1994) Importance of supravitality in forensic medicine. Forensic Sci Int 69(3):221–241

Madea B (ed) (2015) Estimation of the time since death. CRC Press, Boca Raton

Madea B, Henssge C (1990) Electrical excitability of skeletal muscle postmortem in casework. Forensic Sci Int 47(3):207–227

Mayer RG (2012) Embalming: history, theory, and practice, 5th edn. McGraw-Hill Medical, New York

Modi, R. B. J. P. (2013). A textbook of medical jurisprudence and toxicology. Elsevier Amsterdam.

Mukherjee JB (1994) Personal identification. Forensic medicine and toxicology, 2nd edn. Arnold Associates, New Delhi, pp 128–129

Muñoz JI, Suárez-Peñaranda JM, Otero XL, Rodríguez-Calvo MS, Costas E, Miguéns X, Concheiro L (2001) A new perspective in the estimation of postmortem interval (PMI) based on vitreous [K+]. J Forensic Sci 46(2):209–214

Murad TA (2008) Adipocere. In: Embar-Seddon A, Pass AD (eds) Forensic science. Salem Press, Hackensack, p 11. ISBN 978-1-58765-423-7

Nandy A (2010) Principles of forensic medicine including toxicology. New Central Book Agency, Kolkata

Naumann HN (1950) Studies on postmortem chemistry. Am J Clin Pathol 20(4):314–324

Neis P, Hille R, Paschke M, Pilwat G, Schnabel A, Niess C, Bratzke H (1999) Strontium90 for determination of TSD. Forensic Sci Int 99(1):47–51

Noriko T (1995) Immunohistochemical studies on postmortem lividity. Forensic Sci Int 72(3):179–189

English Dictionary, Thesaurus, & grammar help - Oxford Dictionaries. Oxford Dictionaries - English

Pain S (2008) What killed Dr Granville's mummy. New Scientist 200(2687):72–73

Parikh CK (1992) Identification. Parikh's text book of medical jurisprudence and toxicology, 5th edn. CBS Publishers and Distributors, New Delhi, pp 30–49

Petty CS, Lovel MP, Moore F (1958) Organophosphorus insecticides and postmortem blood cholinesterase levels. J Forensic Sci 3:226–237

Pirch J, Schulz Y, Klintschar M (2013) A case of instantaneous rigor? Int J Leg Med 127(5):971–974

Pittner S, Monticelli FC, Pfisterer A, Zissler A, Sänger AM, Stoiber W, Steinbacher P (2015) Postmortem degradation of skeletal muscle proteins: a novel approach to determine the time since death. Int J Leg Med 130(2):421–431

Pittner S, Ehrenfellner B, Zissler A, Racher V, Trutschnig W, Bathke AC et al (2017) First application of a protein-based approach for time since death estimation. Int J Leg Med 131 (2):479–483

Postmortem Changes and Time of Death (PDF). Dundee.ac.uk. Archived from the original (PDF) on 2012-09-05. Accessed 22 Aug 2012

Prasad BK (2003) Post-mortem ocular changes: a study on autopsy cases in Bharatpur Hospital. Kathmandu Univ Med J 1(4):276–277

Prieto-Bonete G, Pérez-Cárceles MD, Maurandi-López A, Pérez-Martínez C, Luna A (2019) Association between protein profile and postmortem interval in human bone remains. J Proteomics 192:54–63

Ramayah S (2014) Decomposition and insect succession pattern on monkey carcasses placed indoor and outdoor with notes on the life table of Chrysomya ruffifacies (Diptera: Calliphoridae). Doctoral dissertation, Universiti Sains Malaysia

Rayamane AP, Kumar MP, Nanandkar SD, Chavan GS, Bhise SS, Dayananda R (2014) Medicolegal significance of postmortem lividity in determination of time since death. J Forensic Med Toxicol 31(1):12–17

Rodriguez III WC (1982) Insect activity and its relationship to decay rates of human cadavers in East Tennessee. Master's Thesis, University of Tennessee.https://trace.tennessee.edu/utk_gradthes/4146

Sabucedo AJ, Furton KG (2003) Estimation of postmortem interval using the protein cardiac troponin I. Forensic Sci Int 134:11–16

Schäfer AT (2000) Colour measurements of pallor mortis. Int J Leg Med 113(2):81–83

Schleyer F (1963) Determination of the time of death in the early postmortem interval. Methods Forensic Sci 2:253–293

Schnabel A, Neis P, Bratzke H (1997) Cycles of the uterus mucous membranes and estimation of time of death. Int J Leg Med 110(1):31–32

Schrag B, Uldin T, Mangin P, Bochud F, Froidevaux P (2014) Dating human skeletal remains using 90Sr and 210Pb: case studies. Forensic Sci Int 234:190–1e1

Schroeder H, Klotzbach H, Püschel K (2003) Insects' colonization of human corpses in warm and cold season. Leg Med 5:S372–S374

Sharma M, Singh D (2015) Historical approach of forensic entomology: a review. Int J Adv Res Sci Eng Technol 9:838–845

Shean BS, Messinger L, Papworth M (1993) Observations of differential decomposition on sun exposed v. shaded pig carrion in coastal Washington State. J Forensic Sci 38(4):938–949

Singh D, Prasad R (2009) Relationship between the postmortem intervals and the pericardial enzyme activities in subjects of Chandigarh zone of India–a preliminary study. J Indian Acad Forensic Med 31(1):30–36

Singh D, Prashad R, Parkash C, Sharma SK, Pandey AN (2003) Double logarithmic, linear relationship between plasma chloride concentration and TSD in humans in Chandigarh Zone of North-West India. Leg Med 5(1):49–54

Singh D, Prashad R, Sharma SK, Pandey AN (2006) Estimation of postmortem interval from human pericardial fluid electrolytes concentrations in Chandigarh zone of India: log transformed linear regression model. Leg Med 8(5):279–287

Smith KG (1986) A manual of forensic entomology. Trustees of the British Museum (Natural History)
The Australian Museum (2018) Decomposition-body changes. https://australianmuseum.net.au/about/history/exhibitions/death-the-last-taboo/decomposition-body-changes/
Tsokos M, Byard RW (2016) Post mortem changes - overview. In: Payne-James J, Byard RW (eds) Encyclopaedia of forensic and legal medicine, 2nd edn. Vol. 4, Oxford, AcademicPress, pp 10–31
Wang PA (2011) Post mortem proteolytic degradation of myosin heavy chain in skeletal muscle of Atlantic cod. Doctoral thesis, Universitetet i Tromsø.https://hdl.handle.net/10037/3337
Wells JD, King J (2001) Flies of forensic importance (Calliphoridae). Pan-Pac Entomol 77(4):235–239
What is algor mortis? How to calculate time of death using Algor Mortis (2020, May 28). https://www.scienceabc.com/pure-sciences/what-is-algor-mortis-definition-stage-of-death.html
Wijdicks EF (2001) The diagnosis of brain death. N Engl J Med 344(16):1215–1221
Xiao JH, Chen YC (2005) A study on the postmortem relationship between the degradation of protein and the postmortem interval. Fa Yi Xue Za Zhi 21:110–112
Yang TT, Li ZW, Liu L, Zhen N (2008) Estimation of postmortem interval with single-voxel proton 1H-MR spectroscopy at different temperature. Fa Yi Xue Za Zhi 24(2):85–89
Zhou B, Zhang L, Zhang G, Zhang X, Jiang X (2007) The determination of potassium concentration in vitreous humor by low pressure ion chromatography and its application in the estimation of postmortem interval. J Chromatogr B 852(1–2):278–281
Zhu Y, Dong YC, Liang WB, Zhang L (2011) Relationship between RNA degradation and postmortem interval in mice. Fa Yi Xue Za Zhi 27(3):161–163

Introduction to Fingerprints

8

Neeti Kapoor, Poonam Moon, Pooja Pardeshi, and Ashish Badiye

Abstract

Fingerprints are an individual's unique characteristic that remains identical throughout an individual's lifetime. No two individuals can have the same fingerprints, not even the identical twins. Therefore, fingerprints are the most widely adopted method for the biometric purpose. Also, fingerprints, both visible and invisible, are one of the most common pieces of evidence encountered at crime scenes. Researchers have developed different physical, chemical and analytical methods for developing latent fingerprints. The present chapter includes a basic introduction to fingerprints, including history, fingerprint laws, classification, types, collection and preservation methods. Various development methods such as physical, chemical, optical and sophisticated instrumental analytical methods for latent fingerprints are also included.

Keywords

Dermatoglyphics · Fingermarks · Fingerprint classification · Fingerprint pattern

N. Kapoor · P. Pardeshi · A. Badiye (✉)
Department of Forensic Science, Government Institute of Forensic Science, Nagpur, Maharashtra, India
e-mail: neetikapoor@ifscnagpur.in; ashishbadiye@ifscnagpur.in

P. Moon
Karunya Institute of Technology and Sciences, Coimbatore, Tamil Nadu, India

P. Shrivastava et al. (eds.), *Textbook of Forensic Science*,
https://doi.org/10.1007/978-981-99-1377-0_8

8.1 Introduction

Fingerprints, palm prints and footprints are the impressions of friction ridges. Friction ridges are defined by the Scientific Working Group on Friction Ridge Analysis, Study and Technology (SWGFAST) as "a raised portion of the epidermis on the palmar or plantar skin, consisting of one or more connected ridge units". The palmer surface refers to the hand, consisting of the palm, finger joints and fingertips, whereas the plantar surface refers to the lower portion of the foot and toes. The friction ridges are the minute raised portions of the skin on the palmer and planter surface. Just like the mountains are formed when they are pushed up from the earth's crust to the surface, in a similar way, friction ridges are formed when they are pushed up from the epidermis layer to the surface of the skin. They are unique characteristics of an individual and remain unchanged throughout their lives. These friction ridges are found in humans and primates. Due to their rough and textured surface, the friction ridges provide resistance between our hands and anything touched or held (Daluz 2015).

Fingerprints are proved to be valuable evidence in the field of forensic science. The fingerprint examiners compare the fingerprints collected from the crime scene with the known fingerprints to ascertain their source. Thus, the fingerprint comparison is the process of comparing two friction ridge impressions to determine if they have come from the same source or not (Kapoor et al. 2020a, b; Kapoor and Badiye 2015a, b).

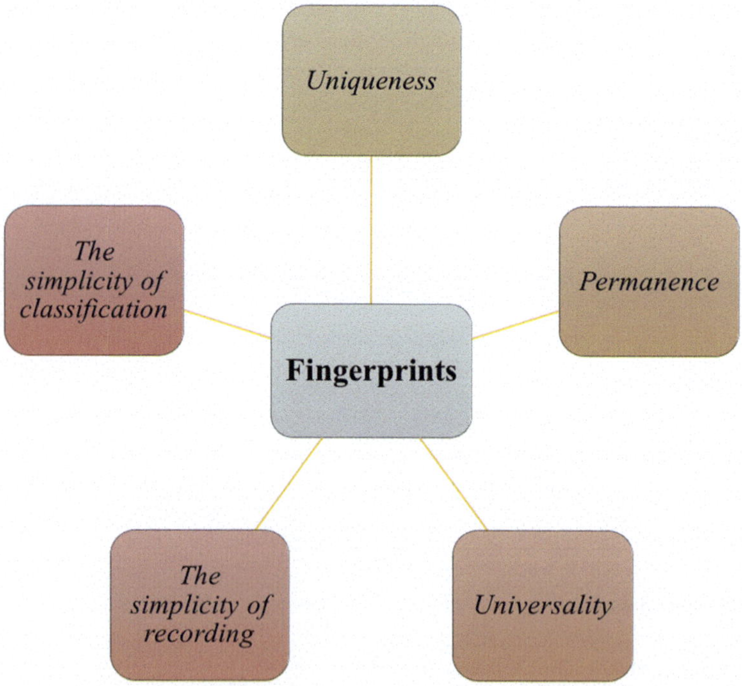

Fingerprints can be compared based on two structural characteristics: pattern types and minutiae. These are not unique and are class characteristics of an individual. Class characteristics are those features that place an individual or object in a group or subcategory. In comparison, minutiae are unique individual characteristics of a person. Fingerprint examiners compare the class and individual characteristics and then conclude (Bridges 1942; Daluz 2015).

8.2 Fundamental Principles of Fingerprints

First principle: "*A fingerprint is an individual characteristic: no two fingers have yet been observed to possess identical ridge characteristics*".

According to this principle, fingerprints are the unique characteristics of an individual. Even after examining millions of fingerprints, no two fingerprints have ever been found identical. Neither two different individuals can have identical fingerprints, nor can the two different fingers of the same individual have the same fingerprints. Even identical twins do not have the same fingerprints—all of these points towards the fact that fingerprints are unique to each individual.

Second principle: "*A fingerprint will remain unchanged during an individual's lifetime.*"

The ridge patterns on the palmer and plantar surface remain unchanged throughout an individual's life. These ridge patterns form between the third and sixth months of fetal life. They grow and expand from childhood to maturity, but the arrangement and the number of friction ridges remain unchanged throughout life. An adult individual's fingerprint would be an enlarged copy of their childhood fingerprint. Rare mutilations, diseases, or injuries on the epidermis can affect the ridge patterns. However, changes in the pattern do not occur. Also, grafting of new ridge patterns has been found impossible.

Third principle: "*Fingerprints have general ridge patterns that permit them to be systematically classified.*"

The third principle states that fingerprints can be easily classified based on ridge patterns. The classification systems thus developed can be used methodically. Many fingerprint slips can be classified to give each individual an almost unique position in the files. This helps in easy retrieval as well. Computerized fingerprint records are more accessible and fast to retrieve (Nabar 2013; Nath 1991, 2006; Sharma 2014).

8.3 Importance of Fingerprints

Fingerprints are the impressions of the ridges on the digital phalanges of hands. The ridges are also present on the palms, soles and toes. These are generally called papillary or friction ridges. These ridges have a definite shape and appear in different patterns. Each pattern possesses specific details which can be used to identify an individual. These ridge characteristics are formed in the early stages of foetal life.

Fig. 8.1 Uses of fingerprints

The development of fingerprints starts in the intrauterine life of the foetus from the third or fourth month and remains unchanged throughout an individual's life and even after the death till the decomposition of skin starts (Bansal et al. 2014). Fingerprints are not affected by any temporary impairment to the skin, such as warts or blisters, resulting from occupations such as manual labour, carpentry and bricklaying. The ridge characteristics return to their natural alignment once the skin conditions have been healed. Law enforcement officers and other agencies can use fingerprints for personal identification. The fingerprints found on the crime scene can be compared with the fingerprints of the known criminals. They are also used for maintaining identification records. They can be used to identify missing persons, unconscious persons and unknown deceased persons and correctly identify the individual in kidnapping cases. Fingerprints can be used to prevent the wrong identification of infants in hospitals. They are also used in place of signatures in India (Kapoor and Badiye 2015a, b) (Fig. 8.1).

8.4 History of Fingerprints

To date, it is mysterious who first used fingerprints for identification. However, the evidence of using fingerprints can be traced back to the earliest forms of civilization. Evidence has been recorded of unintentional fingerprint impressions on the ancient bricks and pottery unearthed in China. The archaeologists wonder if these impressions on earthenware are intentional, unintentional, decorative or tool marks. Archaeologists have found recorded evidence from the Middle East, where the potters used to sign their work with the fingerprint impressions on clay. These impressions may merely be identifying marks rather than impressions linked to a specific person. Scholars have found fingerprint impressions on Babylon and clay seals bearing thumb impressions of ancient Chinese origin. Clay slabs bearing fingermarks have also been found in Tutankhamen's Tomb in Egypt, approximately 3000 years old. In ancient Assyria, fingerprints were used as a seal to give authenticity to essential documents. Later in 240 BC, Chinese emperors started using thumbprints as an official seal on essential documents. The use of fingerprints as seals continued in China up to 1278 AD during the Sung period.

Dr. Nehamiah Grew, 1684 and Govard Bidloo, 1685 gave scientific descriptions of dermatoglyphics in their works. Grew observed the patterning of the fingers and palm and described the sweat pores and the arrangement of epidermal ridges. Bidloo wrote a book on Human Anatomy where he also described the arrangement of ridges in detail. Marcello Malpighi, in 1686, described the elevated ridges on the fingerprints and referred to multiple fingers on palmer surfaces. He observed that the ridges are drawn into loops and spirals at the end of the fingers, but he did not follow these observations further. Later during the eighteenth century, many studies appeared mentioning dermatoglyphics. In his study, J.C.A. Mayer suggested that the skin ridges' arrangements are never duplicated in two persons, but they may have similarities that may be closer in some individuals. Whereas, in others, the differences are quite marked, yet in spite of their peculiarities of arrangement, they all have a certain likeness.

Schroter, 1814, in his study, explained the arrangement of ridges and pores while describing the morphology of palmer skin. In 1823, Johannas E. Purkinje systematically classified the fingerprint patterns for the first time, forming an important landmark in the history of fingerprint science. He published a treatise mentioning the diversity of ridge patterns on the fingers. He classified them into nine categories. His work had no practical application for the identification problem and was only intended for scholarly treatise. He has suggested the probability of utilizing fingerprints for personal identification.

In India, fingerprints have been used for authentication and signing documents for hundreds of years. In 1858, W. J. Herschel was the first to use fingerprints for official use on a large scale in India. He was an administrator for the East India Company in the province of Bengal. He used fingerprints to prevent the fraudulent collection of army pay accounts and identity on other documents. William Herschel continued this practice, as documents containing fingerprints had more significance than those with signatures alone. He was credited as the first British man to acknowledge the power of the individuality of fingerprints.

Another pioneer in the history of fingerprint analysis is Dr. Henry Faulds. He studied fingerprint structure in detail and became the first European to publish an article that stated that visible fingerprints such as bloody, greasy and sooty fingerprints could solve crimes. This article was published in the journal "Nature" in 1880. The article's title was "On the Skin-Furrows of the Hand". He had performed experiments that established that fingerprints remain unchanged throughout an individual's lifetime. He also suggested that chance prints found on the crime scene can be used to identify the criminal. Henry Faulds wrote a letter to Charles Darwin and shared his observation. Darwin referred Faulds to his cousin, Sir Francis Galton.

Sir Francis Galton started his observations on fingerprints around 1890 and wrote his first book in 1892 entitled "Fingerprints". His research was based on his contemporaries and the historical use of fingerprints in Asian cultures. He found that fingerprints are the individual characters and remain unchanged throughout an individual's lifetime. He also devised a scientific method of fingerprint classification. He also described the minute characteristic structure in the fingerprints called minutiae or Galton details used to compare the fingerprints.

Juan Vucetich was a statistician from Argentina. He read Galton's research in 1891, realized fingerprints' superiority over Bertillonage, and installed fingerprint files as an official means of criminal identification. He developed the first classification system for fingerprints based on the pattern identified by Galton. His system is still used in Spanish-speaking countries of Central and South America. He is the first person to identify the criminal based on fingerprints left at the crime scene.

Edward Richard Henry, an Inspector general of police in Bengal, and officers Azizul Haque and Rai Bahadur Hem Chandra Bose started a fingerprint study. They developed a ten-digit classification system for classifying fingerprints, which soon took over Bertillon's anthropometric card system. This system was adopted as a means of identification of habitual criminals in the year 1897. The first-ever fingerprint bureau in the world was established in Calcutta (India) in June 1897. For their earnest contributions, Azizul Haque was given the honorary title of "Khan Bahadur", and Hem Chandra Bose was given the honorary title "Rai Bahadur."

Fingerprinting for criminal identification was officially introduced in England and Wales in 1901. In the United States, the first systematic use of fingerprints was started by Henry P. de Forest in 1902. The classification systems of Henry and Vucetich formed the basis of the modern ten-digit fingerprint identification.

In 1903, New York became the first state in the US to use fingerprinting for criminal record purposes. Later in 1904, a display about criminal fingerprinting at the World's Fair in St. Louis, Missouri, was presented by New York in partnership with Scotland Yard. There they shared their knowledge with the police officers from across the country as well as from Canada. New methodologies of fingerprint and the science of fingerprint were described and refined throughout the 1900s. The International Association for Criminal Identification was formed in Oakland, California, in 1915. It was the first professional fingerprint organization, and also it is the oldest active international forensic association. It has been renamed the International Association for Identification. The first Identification Division of the Federal Bureau of Investigation was established by J. Edgar Hoover in 1924 and followed by the FBI laboratory in 1932.

Due to the increase in crime rate and the consistency of population growth, there was a need to develop a new method for searching and sorting criminal fingerprint records. The old classification method was not feasible for the organization and storage of the records. The invention of computers in the 1960s and 1970s was most likely considered feasible for digitizing and searching large volumes of data such as fingerprint records. With this realization, an Automated Fingerprint Identification System (AFIS) was developed, also known as the "fingerprint computer". It was utilized in Europe, Asia and North America (Daluz 2019; Swanson 2013).

8.5 Levels of Fingerprint Identification

There are three levels of fingerprint identification based on the features seen in the developed print. The first level (pattern) refers to the pattern details that can be seen in the print, such as ridge line flow and pattern type (e.g. loop, arch, whorl, etc.). The second level (points) refers to the presence of minutiae points such as bifurcations, spur, inner terminus, outer terminus, etc., and the third level (shape) includes all the dimensional characteristics of a ridge such as sweat pores, incipient ridges, edge contour and creases.

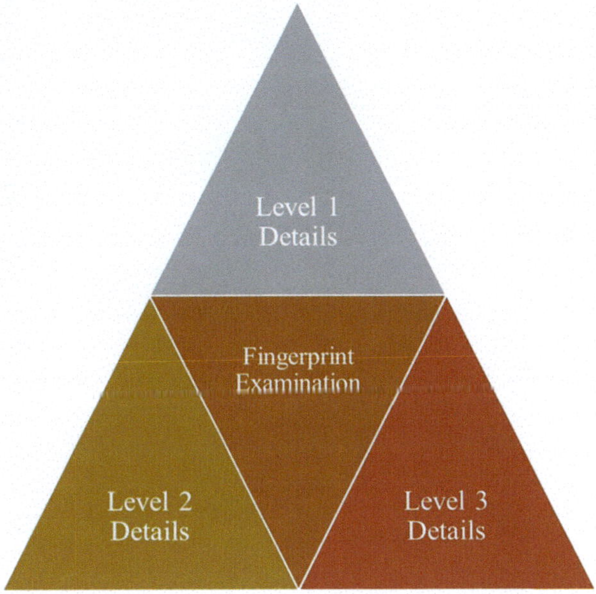

The first-level features in the developed fingerprints are not unique for an individual but can be used for classification. At the same time, the second-level features can be used to individualize fingerprints. The third-level characteristics are more minor details concerning the ridges and pores, i.e. pore size, shape and inter distances. They are also unique but are challenging to obtain in latent fingerprints. The pores are divided into two types based on their position in the print, viz., open and closed pores. If the pore is entirely closed by a ridge, then it is called as closed pore. If the pore is intersecting with the valley lying between the two ridges, then it is an open pore (Yassin et al. 2012).

8.6 Types of Patterns of Fingerprints

The main types of fingerprint patterns are Arches, Loops, Whorls, and Composites. Arches may be Plain (A) or Tented (T); Loops may be Radial (R) or Ulnar (U); Whorls may be Spiral (SW) or Concentric (CW); and Composites may be Central Pocket (CP), Lateral Pocket (LP), Twinned Loop (TL) or Accidental (X) (Kapoor 2020). See Fig. 8.2. These patterns are categorised by the presence or absence of tri-radii or delta.

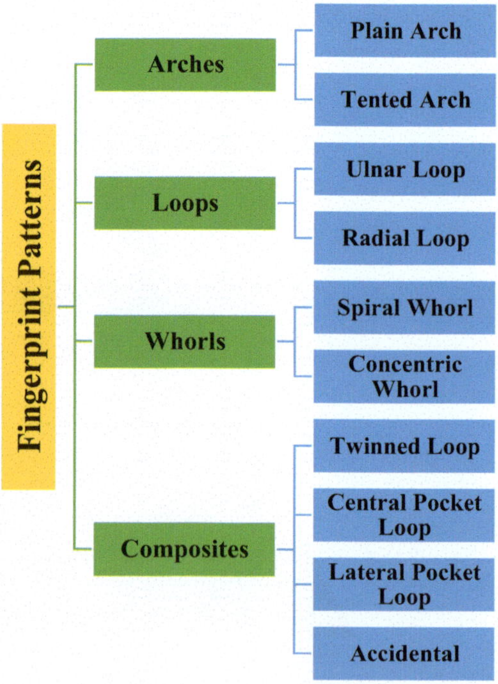

Fig. 8.2 Patterns of fingerprints

8.6.1 Arch Pattern

Arches are the least common fingerprint pattern found in the population. In an arch pattern, the ridges enter from one side of the impression and flow or tend to flow to the other side with a rise in the centre. The highest point of the rising ridge is known as the "crest", which is often found in the middle of the pattern.

Arches are also sub-divided into two categories: Plain arch and tented arch. The plain arch consists of a smooth arching pattern in which all the ridges rise and fall relatively uniformly through the pattern. They have no looping ridges, recurves or ridges angular to the wave pattern. A tented arch is a pattern that consists of one or more ridges at an angle to the flow of the arch, which is often perpendicular to the ridges at the base of the print. In another way, we can describe a tented arch as a pattern consisting of either an angle, an upthrust or two of the three primary characteristics of a loop pattern.

8.6.2 Loop Pattern

A loop is a pattern of fingerprint in which one or more ridge enter from one side of the finger, recurve around the core and exit out from the same side of the finger. A loop pattern must have at least one recurving ridge, one delta, and one or more ridge counts. The "Fingerprint Training Manual" of the Federal Bureau of Investigation (FBI) defines a loop pattern as "A loop is that type of pattern in which one or more ridges enter upon either side, recurve, touch or pass an imaginary line between delta and core and pass out or tend to pass out upon the same side the ridges entered". It is the most commonly found fingerprint impression among the population.

The loop pattern is classified into two types: ulnar and radial loops. The *radial loop* refers to the loop pattern that flows towards the arm's radius bone, i.e. towards the inner side of the arm. In contrast, the *ulnar loop* refers to the loop pattern that flows towards the arm's ulnar bone of the arm, i.e. towards the outer side. When the latent fingerprints collected from the crime scene consist of a loop pattern, one may not tell which hand has made the print. In such cases, loop patterns are referred to as right-slanted or left-slanted loops.

8.6.3 Whorl Pattern

Whorls are the second most commonly found fingerprint impressions in the general population. It is a circular type of pattern. In a whorl pattern, one or more ridges make complete circuits around a central core, which can be a spiral, oval, circular or any other circle variant. The whorl pattern must have at least two deltas, and a sufficient recurve must be present before each delta.

8.6.4 Composite Pattern

A composite pattern is a type of fingerprint that combines any of the two or more fingerprint patterns mentioned above. It is the least found fingerprint pattern. They are further sub-divided into four types as follows:

Central pocket loop It consists of features of both loop and whorl. The pattern looks like a loop but consists of a small whorl inside the loop, which looks like a pocket. It consists of two deltas: one is located at the edge of the pattern area, and another is located at the inside of the pattern area. It also fulfils the requirement of the loop, i.e. having one or more whorl ridges around the core. Because of its appearance, this pattern is also sometimes known as a bulb or a flower.

Lateral pocket loop It is a double loop pattern. Two loops are either overlapping or surrounding each other, and the ridges surrounding the cores of the loops terminate to the opposite side of the delta. In this pattern, both loops flow in the same direction with the core lines without being divided by either delta.

Twinned loop This pattern also consists of two loops, which are either overlapping or surrounding each other and the termination of the ridges representing the core of each loop separated by one of the deltas.

Accidental It consists of the fingerprint patterns which cannot be placed in any of the above categories of fingerprints. They are made up of the combination of any two different patterns except a combination in which one of the patterns is an arch. This pattern consists of at least two deltas, but it may have four in some cases. When a pattern is formed by a combination of loop and plain arch, it is interpreted as a *nascent loop* and as accidental (Kapoor 2020; Nabar 2019; Bridges 1942; Daluz 2019; Hawthorne 2009).

8.7 Ridge Tracing and Ridge Counting

Ridge counting is performed in a loop pattern of fingerprints. It refers to the number of friction ridges crossing the imaginary line between the core and the delta. The counting of the ridges begins from the delta. Deltas are often not adequately defined but are ambiguous areas of ridge flow. The delta is defined as "that point on a ridge at or nearest to the point of divergence of two type lines and located at or directly in front of the point of divergence" in the FBI manual. To find the point of origin to start counting, one must find the type lines. Type lines are defined as the two friction ridges, either continuous or broken, that diverge from the delta in opposite directions and surround the main pattern. The core of the print can be an obvious point at the centre of the patterns, or it might be more uncertain. If the innermost ridge is a loop, then the ridge counting should be done to the point just past the print centre. Once the delta and core are found, the ridge counting is done.

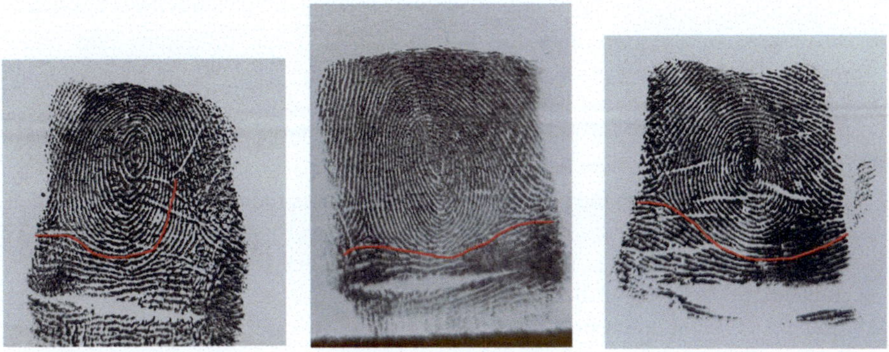

Fig. 8.3 (**a**) Inner ridge tracing; (**b**) meeting ridge tracing; (**c**) outer ridge tracing

Ridge Tracing is done in the case of the whorl pattern. It follows the friction ridge path from the left delta to the right delta. With the help of ridge tracing, the whorls can be classified into inner (I), meeting (M) and outer (O). According to the FBI fingerprint manual, the process of fingerprint tracing is described as follows:

- If three or more ridges are inside the right delta, the tracing is an—I—inner.
- If three or more ridges are outside the right delta, the tracing is an—O—outer.
- If there are one or two ridges either inside or outside the right delta, or if the tracing stops on the right delta itself, the tracing is a—M—meeting (Daluz 2015) (Fig. 8.3).

Ridge characteristics The individuality and the uniqueness of fingerprints are determined by their unique ridge characteristics and not only based on the shape or pattern of the print. These ridge characteristics are also known as minutiae. The different ridge characteristics are ridge endings, bifurcations or forks, dots, enclosures, short ridge, convergence, divergence, etc. On an average nearly 150 ridge characteristics can be located on individual fingerprints. Two fingerprints are said to be matched when they have identical ridge characteristics and the same relative position on the prints (Nabar 2013; Saferstein 1983).

Minutiae are the significant features of fingerprint patterns which can be used for the identification and individualization of a person. These are used for the matching of fingerprints and is used to determine the uniqueness of a fingerprint pattern. Up to 25–80 minutiae can be found in a fingerprint pattern depending on the resolution of the fingerprint scanner and also on the placement of the finger on the scanner. Minutiae is the point where the ridge lines end or fork. The minutiae points are the local ridge discontinuities and can be of many different types. Some of the commonly occurring types are given below:

1. Ridge ending: it is the point in the pattern where the ridge ends suddenly.
2. Ridge bifurcation: it is the point where a single ridge divides into two branches.

3. Ridge trifurcation: it is the point where a single ridge divides into three branches.
4. Successive bifurcation: it is the point where a ridge bifurcates two times successively.
5. Ridge dots: these are tiny ridges which appear as a dot.
6. Ridge islands: these are the patterns enclosed patterns formed by two ridges having middle space between them.
7. Ridge divergence: it is the point where the two ridges moving parallel diverge in two different directions.
8. Ridge convergence: it is the point where two ridges from different directions converge and move parallel to each other.
9. Spurs: it is like a notch protruding from a ridge.
10. Bridges: these are the small ridges which join two adjacent parallel ridges.
11. Crossovers: these are formed when two ridges cross each other.
12. Short ridges: there are numerous small-size ridges, larger than dots.

8.8 Recording of Fingerprints

Fingerprints from suspects are recorded by fingerprint ink, roller and slab. The recording procedure of fingerprints is as follows: firstly, the ink is applied to the slab using a roller. Then suspects' fingers are inked by rolling the fingers on the inked slab and then placing them gently on the fingerprint form. The equipment required for this process is a polished glass or metal slab, rubber roller, ink tube, fingerprint form, cotton or rag to clean the roller and a suitable solvent for cleaning the slab.

1. Clean the slab and the roller, so that it is free from dust or other material.
2. The suspect's palm and fingers should not have perspiration. If perspiration is present, they are asked to wash their hands with soap and water and wipe with a towel.
3. Apply ink to the slab and spread it evenly with the help of a roller. Do not apply too much ink to the slab.
4. Place the slab at a sufficient height to allow the suspect's forearm to assume a horizontal position when the fingers are inked.
5. Roll the suspect's fingers on the slab gently. Avoid applying too much pressure.
6. Avoid rolling fingers on the slab's same place until the ink is applied again.
7. Now roll the fingers on the fingerprint form gently without applying much pressure.
8. Avoid taking fingerprints of the person suffering from any contagious or infectious disease until they are fully recovered.
9. Avoid taking fingerprints of lepers (Nabar 2013).

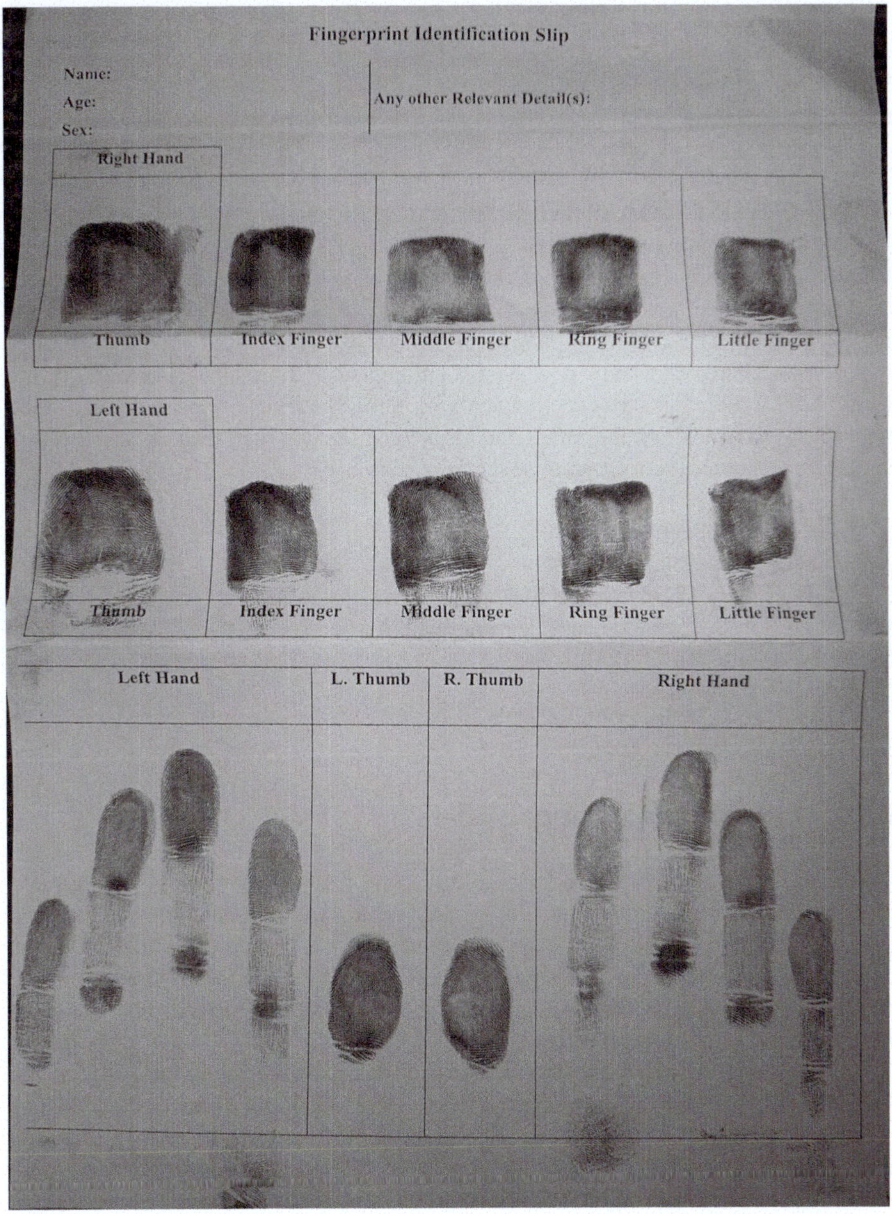
Fingerprint Identification Slip
Name:
Age:
Sex:
Any other Relevant Detail(s):
Right Hand
Thumb
Index Finger
Middle Finger
Ring Finger
Little Finger
Left Hand
Thumb
Index Finger
Middle Finger
Ring Finger
Little Finger
Left Hand
L. Thumb
R. Thumb
Right Hand

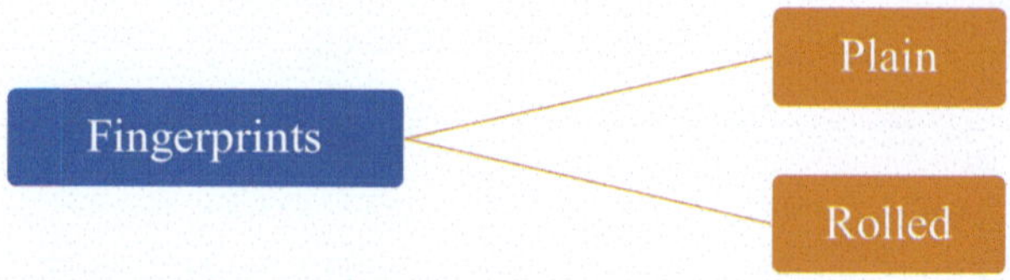

8.9 Classification of Fingerprints

Classification of fingerprints is a systematic process by which a large set of fingerprints can be suitably arranged and filed for easy retrieval whenever needed for comparison. The classification system that is most widely used in many countries is based on Henry's system. It consists of numbers and alphabets arranged in the form of a fraction. It is based on the study of ten fingerprints of an individual. Each fingerprint pattern is first identified and marked on the slip then further classification is performed under the following seven systems:

1. Primary Classification System
2. Secondary Classification System
3. Sub-secondary Classification System
4. Second Sub-Secondary Classification System
5. Final Classification System
6. Key Classification System
7. Major Division System

8.9.1 Primary Classification System

The patterns are divided into numerical and non-numerical patterns in the primary classification system. Out of the four basic types, whorl and composite are the numerical patterns, whereas loop and arches are the non-numerical patterns. All the rolled fingerprints taken on the fingerprint slip are numbered from one to ten in the following order: right thumb—1, right index—2, right middle—3, right ring—4, right little—5, left thumb—6, left index—7, left middle—8, left ring—9, left little 10.

Then numerical values are assigned to the fingers in the following order as the fingers numbered 1 and 2 are assigned values 16 each; 3 and 4 are assigned values 8 each; 5 and 6 are assigned values 4 each; 7 and 8 are assigned values 2 each and 9 and 10 are assigned value 1 each.

If the pattern on the finger is a numerical pattern, i.e. whorl or composite, then a numerical value is assigned as mentioned above. If the pattern is non-numerical, i.e. loop or arch, then a 0 value is assigned. After that, the values of all the even number of fingers are added and placed in the numerator, and the values of odd fingers are added and placed in the denominator. To obtain the primary classification number, "1" is added to the numerator and denominator. The reason for adding 1 to both numerator and denominator is to obtain the formula of at least 1/1 instead of 0/0.

$$\text{Primary Classification} = \frac{\text{Sum of all even numbered fingers} + 1}{\text{Sum of all odd-numbered fingers} + 1}$$

One can obtain the least, and the highest possible classification from the primary classification is 1/1 and 32/32, respectively.

8.9.2 Secondary Classification

If a large group of people have the same primary classification, one can go for secondary classification. It consists of capital letter symbols of the patterns of the two index fingers with the right index in the numerator and the left index in the denominator. The symbols assigned to different fingerprint patterns are as follows: Arch (A), Tented Arch (T), Radial loop (R), Ulnar loop (U), Whorl (W), Central Pocket Loop (C), Lateral Pocket (S), Twin loop (S) and Accidental (X).

$$\text{Secondary Classification} = \frac{\text{Pattern on right index}}{\text{Pattern on left index}}$$

8.9.3 Sub-secondary Classification

The sub-secondary classification is divided into three different methods depending on the occurrence of patterns on the index, middle and ring fingers which are as follows:

1. **Lettered Group Method**: Prints are classified under lettered group when plain arch, tented arch and radial loop pattern occurs on any fingers other than the index finger. The patterns are given small alphabetical symbols in the sequence of their appearance. Then, to get the lettered classification, the right-hand patterns are written in the numerator, and the left-hand patterns are written in the denominator.

$$\text{Lettered Group Method} = \frac{\text{Patterns on right hand}}{\text{Patterns on left hand}}$$

2. **Henry's Method of Ridge Counting and Tracing**: This classification method is performed when patterns like the plain arch, tented arch and radial loop are present on the index finger. Loops are divided into two types based on the three fingers' ridge count between the core and delta.
   Index finger
   (a) If loops have a ridge count between 1 and 9, they are taken as "I" type.
   (b) If loops have a ridge count of 10 and above, they are taken as "O" type.
      Middle finger:

(a) If loops have a ridge count between 1 and 10, they are taken as "I" type.
(b) If loops have ridge count 11 and above, they are taken as "O" type.

Ring finger:

(a) If loops have a ridge count between 1 and 11, they are taken as "I" type.
(b) If loops have ridge count 12 and above, they are taken as "O" type.

According to this method, classification is obtained by putting the patterns on right-hand fingers in the numerator and left-hand fingers in the denominator.

$$\text{Henry's Method of Ridge Counting and Tracing} = \frac{\text{Right Index, Middle and Ring}}{\text{Left Index, Middle and Ring}}$$

3. **New Method of Ridge Counting and Ridge Tracing:** According to this method, the loops are divided into three types based on ridge count between the core and delta of the three fingers.

Index Finger

(a) If loops have ridge count between 1 and 5, they are taken as "I" type.
(b) If loops have ridge count between 6 and 12, they are taken as "M" type.
(c) If loops have ridge count 13 or above, they are taken as "O" type.

Middle Finger:

(a) If loops have ridge count between 1 and 6, they are taken as "I" type.
(b) If loops have ridge count between 7 and 13, they are taken as "M" type.
(c) If loops have ridge count 14 or above, they are taken as "O" type.

Ring Finger:

(a) If loops have ridge count between 1 and 7, they are taken as "I" type.
(b) If loops have ridge count between 8 and 14, they are taken as "M" type.
(c) If loops have ridge count 15 or above, they are taken as "O" type.

Their ridge tracing shows that the whorls patterns are divided into I, M and O types. Plain arches, tented arches and radial loops existing on the index finger are taken as "I" types for classification.

For the sub-secondary classification using the new ridge counting and tracing method, the right-hand index, middle and ring fingers are taken as the numerator and the left-hand index, middle and ring fingers in the denominator.

$$\text{New Method of Ridge Counting and Tracing} = \frac{\text{Right Index, Middle and Ring}}{\text{Left Index, Middle and Ring}}$$

4. **Second Sub-Secondary Classification:**

This method of classification considers only the middle and ring fingers. Small alphabetical letters represent all the patterns except plain arch, tented arch, and radial loop. This classification is not used in the middle and ring fingers consist of a plain arch, tented arch or radial loop patterns. For the second sub-secondary classification, the patterns on the right index, middle and ring fingers are written in the numerator and the patterns on the left index, middle and ring fingers are written in the denominator.

$$\text{Second Sub} - \text{Secondary Classification} = \frac{\text{Right Index, Middle and Ring}}{\text{Left Index, Middle and Ring}}$$

5. **Final Classification:**
The final classification system is done by recording the ridge count of loops and whorl patterns present on the little fingers of both hands. In the case of whorls, the ridge counting is done from the left delta to the core in the case of the right little finger and from the right delta to the core in the case of the left little finger. If a double loop pattern is present on the right little finger, ridge counting is done between the left delta and the core of ascending loop. Whereas in the case of the left little finger, ridge counting is done between the right delta and the core of the ascending loop. The ridge count of the right little finger is taken as the numerator and the left little finger is taken as the denominator to get the final classification.

$$\text{Final Classification} = \frac{\text{Ridge Count on Right Little Finger}}{\text{Ridge Count on Left Little Finger}}$$

6. **Key Classification System:**
This classification system only considers ridge counts of loop and whorl patterns on the right thumb. The ridge counting in case of whorl and double loop present on the right thumb is done in the same way as the final classification. For the whorl pattern, ridge counting is done from left delta to the core, and in the case of the double loop pattern, the ridge counting is done from left delta to the core of the ascending loop.

$$\text{Key Classification System} = \text{Ridge Count on Right Thumb}$$

7. **Major Division System:**
Major division system include right and left thumb. It is done by ridge counting in case of loop pattern and ridge tracing in a whorl pattern. The loop pattern is divided into three types depending on the ridge count as follows:
   (a) If loops on the thumb have a ridge count between 1 and 12, they are identified as "I" type.
   (b) If loops on the thumb have a ridge count between 13 and 19, they are identified as "M" type.
   (c) If loops on the thumb have a ridge count of 20 and above, they are identified as "O" type.

   The whorl and composite pattern are traced as listed under tracing of whorl and "I", "M" and "O" grouping obtained. Then for obtaining the major division, the pattern on the right thumb is taken as the numerator, and the pattern on the left thumb is taken as the denominator.

$$\text{Major Division System} = \frac{\text{Pattern on Right Thumb}}{\text{Pattern on Left Thumb}}$$

8.10 Other Classifications

8.10.1 Single-Digit Classification System

Usually, the chance prints are encountered at the scene of a crime. They are scarce and often not in a fixed sequence. In such cases, we cannot use the aforementioned ten-digit classification to search a single fingerprint. For classifying the single-digit chance prints, different classification methods have been devised. One of the most commonly used single-digit classifications is the Battley's system developed by Chief Inspector Henry Battley of the New York State fingerprint bureau.

Along with the ten-digit fingerprint bureau, single-digit bureaus are also present in most states that use Battley's single-digit classification system. This method is the most practical and accurate handling of a single fingerprint.

In this classification, all the pints from one particular finger are filed together, containing one finger per drawer on a 3″ * 5″ card size that contains a rolled print of one finger. According to the general classification, the cards are sub-divided within the drawer. Then, with a magnifying lens provided with a reticle in the centre and that the centre of the reticle is a dot, they can be further sub-divided. Around the dot, seven circles are drawn having radii of 3, 5, 7, 9, 11, 13 and 15 mm, respectively. The area of each circle is represented by the alphabet starting from the letter "A" reading outwards. This system uses a "special core" for interpreting the pattern of fingerprint. This special core is located in the innermost recurving ridge, in the case of loops and whorls. To obtain the delta readings in loops and whorls, the central dot of the reticle is placed on the special core and the letter of the circle in which the delta lies is noted (Fig. 8.4).

8.10.2 Automated Fingerprint System

Fingerprint Analysis Criminal Training System (FACTS) is an automated fingerprint system that uses image processing and pattern recognition techniques to automatically capture, encode, store and match fingerprints. The NCRB's Central Fingerprint Bureau uses this technique in New Delhi. This technique can integrate fingerprint data with the crime and criminal information system. For matching fingerprints, ridge minutiae characteristics are considered. They are further characterized by the direction of ridge flow and ridge counting.

To identify minutiae, high-speed processors extract features from the digitized image of the fingerprint obtained through a charge-coupled device (CCD) camera. These data are stored in high-capacity optical disc cartilage in a compressed form of 2000 bytes of memory. A jukebox helps to access any particular disc automatically.

The fingerprints are first photographed by using a digital camera. The camera enhances the image for the expert, who identifies the core and delta of the fingerprint. The minutiae are then identified by the processor and compared with the fingerprints in the database record to establish the fingerprint's identity. The matching speed of

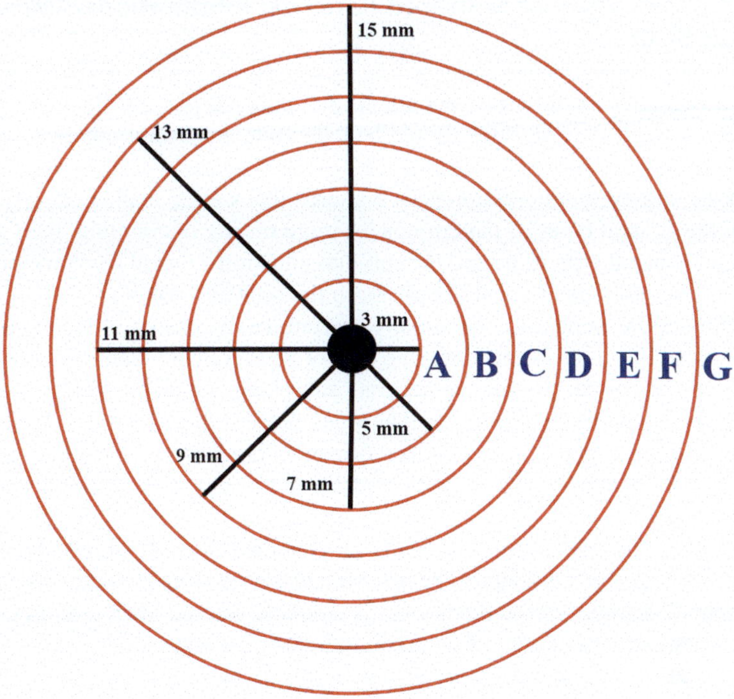

Fig. 8.4 Battley's Single Digit Classification system

FACTS is claimed to be as high as 500 fingerprints per second of data in a database record.

Automated fingerprint identification system (AFIS) AFIS is a biometric system developed in the 1960s to identify individuals based on fingerprints and palm prints. Its main aim was to classify, search and consolidate ten-digit print records in an automated manner. This technique was first used for the Federal Bureau of Investigation (FBI) fingerprint database. Later, Minneapolis-St. Paul became the first city in the United States to install this system. At the same time, other nations also started working to make similar systems. France developed Sagem Morpho Inc. for automated latent print searches. It recently merged with Motorola's company Printrak and established a new system Morphotrak in the United States. NEC in Japan also developed their AFIS system after visiting various AFIS sites. They worked on the issue of matching the inked prints (Loll and Police 2013).

8.10.3 Classification of Scattered Patterns: Amputations—Missing at Birth

There is a necessity for fully referencing all the scattered patterns. For their proper classification, the following rules should be taken into consideration:

- When the fingerprint impression is so scattered that we can neither classify it into any of the general types of pattern nor for ridge tracing or counting, then in such cases, the general type value and the sub-classification value of the corresponding finger of the other hand should be given to the scattered pattern.
- If the fingerprint impression is partially scarred, i.e. it consists of significant scar marks about the core, the general type cannot be accurately identified. However, we can reasonably determine the accurate sub-classification by performing ridge tracing and counting by observing the ridges. Such impressions should be given the primary value of the pattern of the corresponding finger of the other hand and the sub-classification value as indicated by the ridges of the partially scarred impressions.
- If the fingerprint impression is so scarred that neither the general type pattern nor the ridge tracing or counting can be determined with reasonable accuracy, and the corresponding finger of the other hand is similarly scarred, then both the fingers are given an arbitrary value of whorls with meeting tracing.
- If the finger of one hand is amputated, then it is given the classification identical as that of the corresponding finger of the other hand, including the pattern and ridge count or tracing.
- If two or more fingers are amputated, they are given classifications identical to the fingers of the opposite hand, with no additional references.
- If the two or more amputated fingers are opposite, they are given the classification of whorls with meeting tracing.
- If all ten fingers are amputated or missing at birth, the classification will be

  $$\frac{\text{M 32W MMM}}{\text{M 32W MMM}}.$$
- If both hands of the individual are amputated, the footprints should be recorded, as they also bear friction ridges with definite patterns. The FBI maintains a footprint file for identification purposes in cases where the subject has all fingers amputated or missing by birth.

8.10.4 Classification of Bandaged or Imprinted Fingers

Fingerprint cards bearing notations cannot be appropriately classified for injured or bandaged fingers. If the injury of the fingers is temporary, then the prints should be taken after the complete healing of the fingers. If the injuries are to the extent that it is impossible to take inked impressions by any inking devices, then the fingers are given the classification same as that of the finger of the other hand. If only one finger is missing, reference searches should be conducted in every possible classification. If more than one finger is lacking, they should be given the classifications of the opposite fingers, but no reference searches should be conducted. If two lackings are opposite each other, they should be classified as whorls with meeting tracings (Nabar 2019).

8.11 Collection of Fingerprints

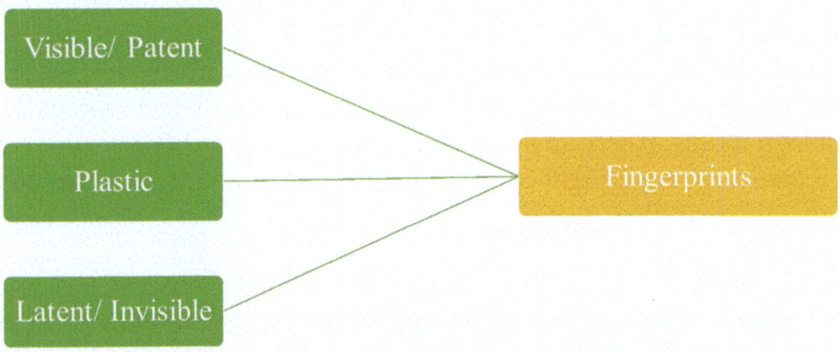

1. **Patent prints:** Patent fingerprints are also known as visible fingerprints. These prints are contaminated with any coloured substance such as dust, blood and grease; therefore, they are easily visible to the naked eyes. For multicoloured flashlight or forensic light sources can help detect patent impressions. They are collected by using the photography method. There is no need to develop the patent prints to be directly photographed in high resolution with a forensic measurement scale. The image quality can be improved by using low-angle or alternate light sources and/or certain chemicals or dyes during the photography, but this is usually unnecessary.
2. **Plastic prints:** Plastic prints are created only if the surface is pliable enough to record prints at the time of contact. Thus, the prints created are three dimensional. The impressions are created when the friction ridges of the fingers are pressed against the surface, creating a mould of the friction ridges. These impressions are found on surfaces like clay, putty, soft wax, melted plastic, tacky paints, etc. Plastic prints do not need any development. They can be easily visualized using oblique lighting and photographed for further analysis. They can also be preserved by using silicon-type casting material (Yamashita et al. 2014).
3. **Latent Prints:** Latent prints are the most abundantly found prints on the scene of crime out of the three. Latent is known as invisible or hidden. They are created due to the secretions left by our fingers onto the surface when a person touches any object. Our finger and palm consists of friction ridges, and these friction ridges consist of sweat pores. Sweat continuously oozes out of these pores. Thus, when an individual touches any surface, an impression is left behind due to the secretion of sweat and these impressions are exactly the same to the pattern of

ridges on the fingers (Kapoor et al. 2019; Sodhi and Kaur 2019). The ultimate goal of the latent fingerprint examiners is the successful development or enhancement of the latent prints and identification or elimination of the individuals based upon the developed latent print (Lee and Gaensselen 2001).

The most common method for collecting latent prints is to develop the prints on porous and non-porous surfaces by dusting fingerprint powders and then lifting the prints using adhesive fingerprint tape. The tape containing the print is then placed on a latent lift card to preserve the print for further analysis. The investigators may use an alternate light source or cyanoacrylate method before using the powder method and then photograph the print.

Alternate light sources are becoming more common in the investigation for examining the surfaces such as doors, doorknobs, windows and railings to check for latent fingerprints. Alternate light sources are the laser or LED devices that emit light of a particular wavelength or spectrum of light. Some devices also consist of spectra and different filters that can be photographed or processed further with the help of powders and dyes.

Cyanoacrylate (also known as superglue) fuming is sometimes used by the investigators on the surfaces before using the powder methods for collecting the latent prints. This method is used for non-porous surfaces. The object containing the prints are exposed to cyanoacrylate fumes. The fumes adhere to the prints and can be viewed by oblique lighting or a white light source. The developed prints are further enhanced by using fingerprint development powders to get better contrast (*Fingerprint Analysis: How It's done* 2013).

8.11.1 Composition of Fingerprint Residues

There are three major sweat glands responsible for the secretion of sweat: the eccrine, apocrine and sebaceous glands. Out of the three eccrine glands are found throughout the body, and they are present in more numbers at palms and soles. The regions containing hair follicles usually contain sebaceous glands. These glands are also localized at the face and scalp. In comparison, the apocrine glands are primarily found in the axillary regions such as armpits and genital areas. Generally, eccrine and sebaceous glands contribute to the formation of latent fingerprint residues (Girod et al. 2012; Ramotowskithird 2012). Sweat contains water (>98%), minerals (0.5%) and organic components (0.5%). Sweat secreted by eccrine glands generally consist of proteins, urea, amino acids, uric acid, lactic acid, sugars, creatinine and choline. The sweat secreted by sebaceous glands consists of glycerides, fatty acids, wax esters, squalene and sterol esters. The chemical composition of the fingerprint residue may be affected by several factors such as age, sex, diet, type of disease, medication and the presence of contaminants on the surface such as oil, dust, dirt, blood and grease.

8.12 Methods of Visualization/Development

Different methods are used to develop and visualize latent prints, such as powder dusting, chemical, optical, fuming and instrumental. Optical methods use electromagnetic radiations of appropriate wavelengths to visualize latent fingerprints. The powder physically sticks to the latent fingerprint residues in the power method. Appropriate powders are used to create contrast with the background. Chemical methods develop latent prints by converting one or more sweat residue constituents into a coloured derivative. In fuming methods, the fumes of the reagent get adsorbed to the residues to visualize the print. Post-treatment can be used to further enhance the prints.

The selection of the method of development depends on the nature of the surface (porous, non-porous or semi-porous), texture (smooth or rough), condition of the surface (dry or wet) and also the colour of the surface on which the latent prints are present. The successful development of the prints also depends on the ageing of the prints (Bumbrah et al. 2016).

8.12.1 Powder Dusting Method

The powder dusting method for developing or visualizing latent fingerprints is one of the oldest and most commonly used methods. This method involves finely divided particles that physically adhere to the oily and greasy secretions present on the latent fingerprints. The early practitioners used a variety of locally available ingredients for making the powders, such as charcoal, cigar ashes, soot, talc and powdered iron. It is a physical method of development that relies on the principle that powder particles get adhered to the latent fingerprint residues because of their affinity to the moisture of the residues. In this method, the size and shape of powder particles, relative surface area and charge play a significant role (Badiye and Kapoor 2015; Yamashita et al. 2014) (Fig. 8.5).

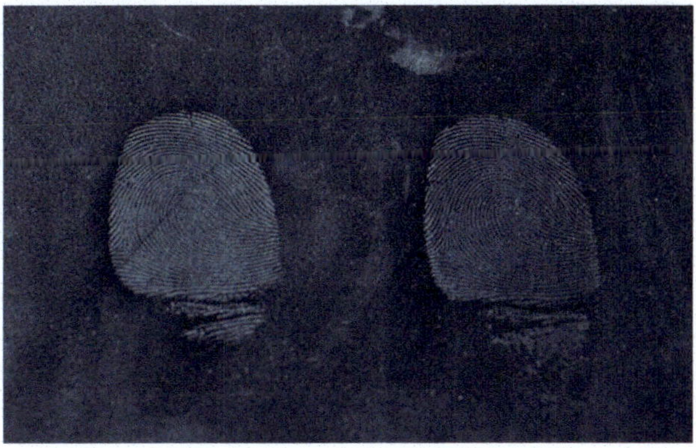

Fig. 8.5 Latent fingerprint developed using powder dusting method

Different powders are used for latent fingerprint development, such as regular powders, metallic powders, and luminescent powders, depending on the type of surface on which print is present.

Regular fingerprint powders consist of resinous polymer, which helps in adhesion and a colourant that gives contrast. Over the years, many different powder formulas have been developed. Some of the most common fingerprint powder formulas are as follows:

Black Fingerprint Powder Formulas:	
Ferric oxide powder	
Black ferric oxide	50%
Rosin	25%
Lampblack	25%
Manganese dioxide powder	
Manganese dioxide	45%
Black ferric oxide	25%
Lampblack	25%
Rosin	5%
Lampblack powder	
Lampblack	60%
Rosin	25%
Fuller's earth	15%
White Fingerprint Powder Formulas	
Titanium oxide powder	
Titanium oxide	60%
Talc	20%
Kaolin lenis	20%
Chalk-titanium oxide powder	
Chalk	15%
Kaolin lenis	15%
Titanium oxide	70%
Grey Fingerprint Powder Formulas	
Chemist grey powder	
Chemist grey	80%
Aluminium powder	20%
Lead carbonate powder	
Lead carbonate	80%
Gum arabic	15%
Aluminium powder	3%
Lampblack	2%

Luminescent (fluorescent and phosphorescent) fingerprint powders consist of natural or synthetic compounds that fluoresce or phosphoresce when exposed to ultraviolet light, laser light or any other light source. Such powders develop latent fingerprints on multicoloured surfaces where regular powders cannot be used

a
b

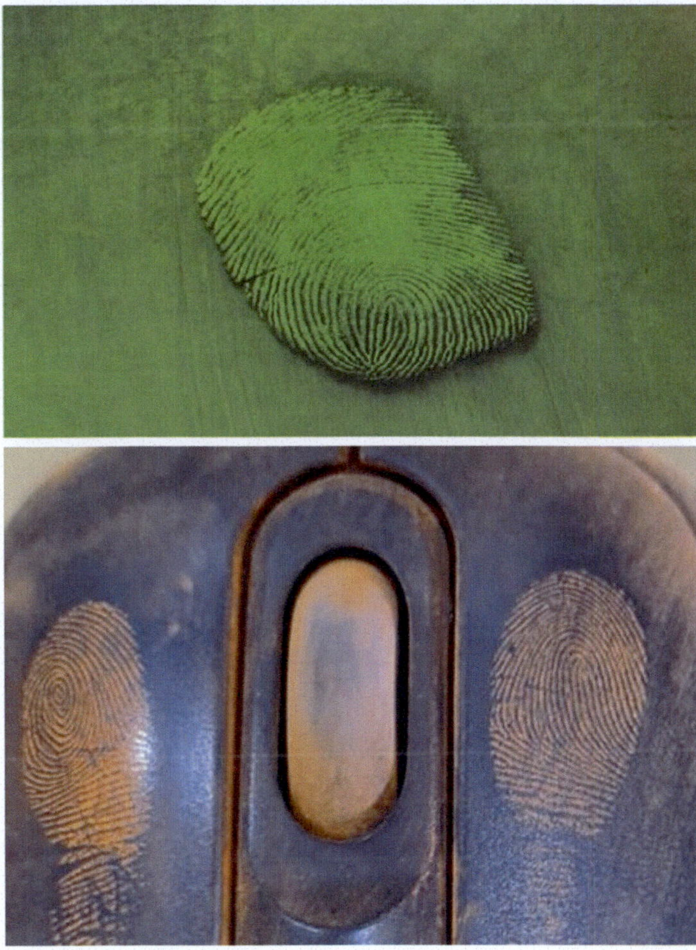

Fig. 8.6 (**a**, **b**) Latent fingerprints developed using fluorescent powders

because of a lack of contrast with the background. These types of powders are rarely used in the field. However, with the advent of laser detection, fluorescent or phosphorescence powders have been greatly enhanced. Some of the most common luminescent powders used for fingerprint development are acridine yellow, acridine orange, coumarin 6, crystal violet, *p*,*p*′-dichlorodiphenylmethyl carbinol, 3,3′--diethyloxadicarbocyanine iodide, 3,3′-diethylthiotricarbocyanine iodide, merocyanine 540, Nile Blue perchlorate, Rhodamine B, Rhodamine 6G, phenothiazine and many more (Girod et al. 2012; Ramotowskithird 2012) (Fig. 8.6).

Metallic fingerprint powders consist of fine ferromagnetic powders, which are applied on the surface using a magnetic applicator (Yamashita et al. 2014). These powders can successfully develop latent fingerprints on surfaces like leather, plastic, walls and human skin. They can also be used for developing prints on vertical surfaces. The components of magnetic powders are iron oxide and iron powder dust, and some colouring components to give contrast (Girod et al. 2012; Ramotowskithird 2012).

8.12.2 Chemical Method

Ninhydrin Ninhydrin is used to develop latent prints on porous surfaces such as paper. It reacts with the amino acids in the latent fingerprints' residues and gives purple colour prints (Ruhemann's Purple). Visualization of prints by using ninhydrin may take several days or even weeks. This drawback can be overcome by heat and moisture (Lee and Gaensselen 2001). Factors such as temperature, humidity, the pressure exerted by the fingers/palm on the surface of contact, time of contact and the amount of sweat transferred can affect the development of prints. Ninhydrin reacts with different amino acids because it is a non-specific amino acid reagent. Thus, each amino acid present in the fingerprint residue contributes to the development of the print. Also, amino acids are very stable compounds due to their affinity towards cellulose. Due to this, very old latent prints on porous surfaces can be developed by this method (Champod et al. 2004; Jasuja et al. 2009).

The method involves using ninhydrin powder in a volatile substance such as ethyl alcohol, acetone and ether, and 1.5% of ninhydrin is the most frequently used proportion (1.5 g ninhydrin in 100 mL of acetone or ether or ethyl alcohol) (Fig. 8.7).

Silver Nitrate Method The silver nitrate method is one of the oldest methods used for latent fingerprint development on porous surfaces such as documents, currency and unpainted wood. It has been used since the nineteenth century. In this method,

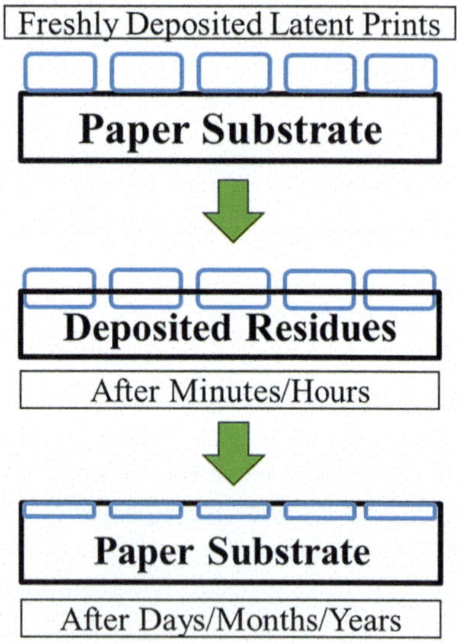

Fig. 8.7 Schematic cross section of a latent fingermark on a paper substrate at various stages after deposition (Adapted from Frick et al. 2015)

silver nitrate reacts with sodium chloride in the latent fingerprint residue to form silver chloride. Then after the irradiation of light, the prints become black. This is because the silver ions present in the silver chloride are reduced to elemental silver and visualize the latent prints. Initially, this method was used to develop prints on porous surfaces such as paper and wood. Later, ethanol-based 3% silver nitrate solution was used to develop latent fingerprints on water-repelling surfaces such as waxed papers (Trozzi et al.). The prints developed by this method are reddish brown against the background. It is a simple and effective method for developing latent prints on standard porous surfaces and some water-repelling surfaces. The major drawback of this technique is a decrease in contrast due to background stains.

$$AgNO_3 + NaCl \rightarrow AgCl + NaNO_3,$$

$$2AgCl \text{ exposed to light} \rightarrow 2Ag + Cl_2.$$

The developed print should be photographed before the paper gets darkened. If the print does not develop, but the document gets dark due to the silver nitrate treatment, then the original colour of the document can be restored by treating it with mercuric chloride solution and then drying. Both the products of this reaction are white and can be removed by rinsing in water (Nath 1991; Sodhi and Kaur 2019).

$$Ag + HgCl_2 \rightarrow AgCl + HgCl.$$

Oil Red O Oil red O (ORO), historically used for the staining technique, is a lipophilic dye. It is related to the Sudan group. Since the late 1920s, ORO has been used for staining lipids in biological tissue sections. Later in 2004, it was used to detect latent fingerprints for the first time. It is a fat-soluble diazo dye that dissolves in lipids and stains them red. This method detects fingermarks on porous surfaces that are wet, exposed to high humidity and contain fewer amino acids. ORO has the empirical formula $C_{26}H_{24}N_4O$, and its molecular weight is 408.510. It contains two azo groups (–N=N–), four methyl groups ($-CH_3$) which are attached to two benzene rings and one hydroxyl group (–OH), which is attached to one naphthalene ring. The staining procedure of ORO includes three steps: colouration, neutralization and drying. Two test solutions are required to develop latent fingerprints on dry or wet porous surfaces: stain and buffer solutions. Stain solution is used to stain the print, while buffer solution is used to maintain the pH. The buffer solution neutralizes the basic nature of the ORO solution. It also neutralizes the alkaline content of the colouring solution to make the treated objects stable and secure. This method is simple, fast, cost-effective and non-destructive (Bumbrah et al. 2019).

Nile Red Nile red, having the chemical name 9-diethylamino-5H-benzo[α]-phenoxazine-5-one, is a neutral phenoxazone dye used as a fluorescent probe for staining neutral lipids. Nile red's absorption and emission vary with solvents of different properties. This phenomenon is known as solvent chromism. Saunders, in 1993, first reported the use of Nile red for the development of latent fingerprints (Frick et al. 2015).

Nile red can effectively develop latent fingermarks on various paper substrates that have been wet before treatment (Braasch et al. 2013). Nile red is found to develop prints aged up to 5 years. Nile red produced luminescent ridge details in fresh and aged prints; still, it cannot replace the physical developer method for developing lipid-rich prints. However, it can be used as a sequel to enhance the latent prints, either partially developed or undeveloped, using the physical developer method.

Osmium tetroxide Osmium tetroxide can be used to develop freshly deposited latent fingerprints. It can be used as a liquid or as vapors. Osmium tetroxide is highly poisonous, and therefore, it should be very carefully used. A small quantity of 1% solution is needed for the development. It is more effective when used in a vapour form than in liquid. For this purpose, a fuming chamber can be used, and the solution is kept in a small dish and heated. The object should be exposed to the vapours for up to an hour or more. For convenience, the object may be kept exposed to the fumes overnight. Since the prints developed are not fugitive and need not be fixed. As soon as the prints are developed, a photograph should be taken. The osmium tetroxide reacts with the fatty substances present in the fingerprint residues. In the presence of fatty substances, it gets reduced to free osmium, which is dark in colour like most finely divided metals. This method is not helpful for prints that are several months old (Nath 1991).

Small Particle Reagent Method The small particle reagent method can develop latent fingerprints on non-porous and wet surfaces. Conventional SPR consists of a suspension of molybdenum disulfide particles in an aqueous medium containing a surfactant. The molybdenum disulfide particles adhere to the fingerprint residues and give a grey print. SPR based on charcoal powder, zinc carbonate and titanium dioxide is also reported (Jasuja et al. 2008).

Phase transfer catalyst method This method is used for developing latent fingerprints on the sticky side of adhesive tape. Fresh prints developed by this method show the third level of ridge details. It can also develop old prints for up to 11 days. The phase transfer catalyst method can be used to develop prints from various absorbent and non-absorbent surfaces. Phase transfer catalyst formulations give better quality prints than cyanoacrylate fuming, small particle reagent or gentian violet (Bumbrah et al. 2016).

Nanoparticle method Various types of nanoparticles have been used for the development of latent fingerprints, which include silver, gold, titanium dioxide, zinc oxide, iron oxide and europium oxide.

Multi-metal deposition method (MMD) This method is used for the development of fingerprints on porous (surfaces masking tape, cardboard, fabric tape), semi-porous (expanded polystyrene, latex gloves, waxed paper) and non-porous (metals and plastics). It is a two-step process. The first step involves the deposition of gold metal and the second step involves the deposition of silver metal over the latent fingerprint. Various modifications of this technique have been developed to achieve better contrast (Sodhi and Kaur 2017).

Single-metal deposition method (SMD) The single-metal deposition method is an alternative to the MMD technique to develop latent fingerprints on non-porous and porous surfaces. MMD method gives good results, but the process is very time consuming. SMD method utilizes a gold enhancement procedure instead of silver enhancement of gold colloids. Due to this, the number of baths is reduced by one, the number of reagents used is reduced and the cost is reduced. The most important benefit of SMD over MMD is that it reduces the procedure's labour intensity and gives better results (Stauffer et al. 2007).

8.12.3 Fuming Method

Iodine fuming Iodine fuming is another technique used to visualize latent fingerprints for many years. Initially, it was thought that the mechanism of iodine fuming involves a reversible addition of iodine to the double bonds of the unsaturated fatty acids present in the fingerprint residues by halogenation. Later, a study done by Almog, Sasson and Anah suggested that the mechanism of iodine fuming involves physical adsorption of the iodine fumes to the residues and no chemical reaction involved in this process. By sublimation, iodine crystals produce violet colour vapours which get adsorbed to the print residues. The latent prints are then visualized as yellowish-brown prints. This colour of iodine is not stable. Soon the colour of prints gets faded unless the iodine is chemically fixed. Therefore, developed prints should be preserved by photography for further analysis. Iodine can be used to develop latent prints in four different ways, viz., iodine fuming gun method, iodine fuming cabinet method, iodine dusting method and iodine solution method (Lee and Gaensselen 2001).

Prints developed by iodine fuming need immediate post-treatment to stabilize them before disappearing. A reagent based on the aqueous solution of brucine alkaloids can be used to fix prints developed by iodine fuming. They have used dipping and vapour methods to fix the prints on various porous and non-porous surfaces. It was found that the dipping method is more suitable for the non-porous surfaces, whereas for porous surfaces vapour method is more effective. In the case of non-porous, pH was found to be affecting the development of latent fingerprints. No such variations were found in the case of porous surfaces. This reagent also has a good shelf life. It gave similar results even after 2 months. Also, the method is straightforward to perform, and it does not give any background colouration.

Iodine fuming is also helpful in developing latent fingermarks on thermal paper. Thermal papers are extensively used in modern day-to-day life, and in some cases, they can act as a vital piece of physical evidence for the presence of latent fingerprints. Different methods have been suggested for the development of prints on thermal paper. However, each has some drawbacks such as pre- and post-treatment, background colouration and complex and cumbersome procedure. In order to overcome such drawbacks, the use of iodine fuming was suggested (Jasuja and Singh 2009). This method can be used to develop both fresh and aged prints present on thermal paper without any background colouration. In standard cases, prints developed by iodine fuming are not permanent and need a post-treatment method for fixing the prints. Nevertheless, in thermal paper, the developed prints are permanent and do not fade away. The reason behind this is the oxidation of leuco dyes present in the thermal paper by the iodine. Prints developed on different thermal papers give different colours depending on the substituents present in the paper. Also, there was no difference in the visualization of fresh eccrine and sebaceous marks. However, in the case of aged prints, there was a marked difference in eccrine and sebaceous marks concerning the intensity and permanency of fingermarks (Jasuja and Singh 2009).

Cyanoacrylate (Superglue) Fuming The cyanoacrylate fuming method was first introduced by the latent fingerprint examiners working at the US Army Criminal Investigation Laboratory in Japan (USACIL-Pacific) and in the Bureau of Alcohol, Tobacco and Firearms (BATF) laboratory in 1982. This method is helpful for visualizing prints on non-porous surfaces such as plastics, electrical tape, garbage bags, styrofoam, carbon paper, aluminium foil, finished and unfinished wood, rubber, cellophane, and rubber bands, smooth rocks and copper. The prints developed by this method lack contrast and are difficult to visualize as they are white in colour. Therefore a post-treatment is necessary for the enhancement of the developed prints. One of the simple procedures is to dust the regular fingerprint powder. Other methods include staining the developed prints using any historical dye solutions that can provide contrast with the background. Gentian violet solution, Coumarin 540, Ardrox, Rhodamine 6G, basic yellow 40, etc., are some of the dyes that can enhance the prints (Lee and Gaensselen 2001).

The latent prints undergo natural dehydration with time due to their exposure to severe environmental conditions such as humidity, UV light and heat. This makes it difficult for the development of latent fingerprints. Therefore, before applying any method to visualize latent prints, a pre-treatment procedure should be performed. Pre-treatment procedures include treating the prints with acetic acid vapour, ammonia vapour and heated water vapour (Bumbrah 2017). This helps reintroduce moisture to the dehydrated prints and gives better results after visualization.

8.12.4 Optical Method

Optical methods for latent fingerprint development are new advances in the area. They are non-destructive, and as a result, they do not influence the later procedure of fingerprint development. Visible fingerprints can be detected by observing the object bearing the print under white light and then photographed. It does not need any further treatment. Also, the prints contaminated with any coloured substance, such as blood, can be enhanced by selective absorption techniques. The invisible prints or latent prints that can be developed using other methods can also be enhanced using more complex optical methods. Optical detection techniques can be used in four different methods as follows:

Absorption The absorption mode is used for the enhancement of visible fingerprints. In this method, consideration is given to the print's colour and the surface's colour.

Luminescence Different lasers have been used to detect latent fingerprints for many years. The four principal lasers employed are argon ion, copper vapour, Nd: YAG and tunable dye laser. Good results have been found on many surfaces, including human skin, metals and polystyrene foam (Menzel 1980, 1985). Studies have shown that this technique produces good results mainly when the fingerprint samples are contaminated with luminescent products from the environment (Salares et al. 1979). This technique has a relatively low success rate, but it is always suggested that the search for inherently luminescent fingerprints should always be done before using destructive development methods. The object suspected of bearing latent fingerprints should be observed under a suitable high-intensity light source. Appropriate filter goggles must be used while using this method.

Diffused reflection When light falls on the latent fingerprint on the smooth surface, it is diffusely reflected. This property of light is used to detect prints on non-porous, smooth and shiny surfaces such as glass and plastic polished metals. Oblique lighting is proven to help detect latent fingerprints on shiny surfaces and the prints contaminated with dust or developed using any other method.

Ultraviolet Imaging This technique works on the principle that the surface may or may not absorb the UV radiation, but the fingerprint on the surface absorbs some of the UV radiation and diffusely reflects the remaining. This creates a contrast between the surface and the print. The ridges may be observed as dark against the light background or light against the dark background, depending on the nature of the surface. To get satisfactory results, the type of UV lamp used and the angle of incidence of the UV illumination is very important (Champod et al. 2004).

8.12.5 Instrumental Method

Latent fingerprints are one of the most important and potential evidence found on the crime scene. The processing techniques for latent fingerprints include using various chemicals, powders, and light sources that can damage the print and the object on which print the found. Thus, there is a need to develop a non-invasive technique for detecting and visualizing latent prints on various surfaces without damaging the print and the evidence substrate. Lasers can be used for the detection of latent fingerprints. They have good direction and high intensity and are monochromatic compared to the multi-band light source. UV photography, a non-invasive detection method without any preprocessing to detect latent fingerprints on various surfaces, is suggested (Li et al. 2011). The results showed clear images of the fingerprints using two lasers, He-Ne and diode. This method of latent fingerprint detection is non-invasive and uses a low level of lasers without using chemicals. It also gives results in a short period.

8.13 Conclusion

The study of fingerprints is a testament to the intricate and awe-inspiring nature of human identification. The fundamental principles that underlie the uniqueness and permanence of fingerprints have propelled them into the forefront of forensic science, making them an indispensable tool for both law enforcement and various fields of research. The multi-layered approach to fingerprint identification, encompassing levels of analysis, various pattern types, and recording methods, underscores the complexity and precision required in this discipline. Equally crucial are the innovative development methods employed to unveil latent prints, shedding light on once-hidden evidence. In essence, the study of fingerprints is not merely a forensic endeavor; it is a testament to the precision and persistence of nature's design, providing law enforcement with an indispensable tool to solve crimes and bring justice to the forefront. This chapter has unraveled the intricate world of fingerprint science, revealing its multifaceted importance and the ongoing quest to harness its potential in the service of justice.

References

A simplified guide to Fingerprint Analysis (2013). https://www.forensicsciencesimplified.org/prints/how.html

Badiye A, Kapoor N (2015) Efficacy of Robin® powder blue for latent fingerprint development on various surfaces. Egypt J Forensic Sci 5(4):166–173. https://doi.org/10.1016/j.ejfs.2015.01.001

Bansal HD, Badiye AD, Kapoor NS (2014) Distribution of fingerprint patterns in an Indian population. Malaysian J Forensic Sci 5(2):18–21. http://forensics.org.my/pdf/fssmVol.5No.2/Article04.pdf

Braasch K, de la Hunty M, Deppe J, Spindler X, Cantu AA, Maynard P, Lennard C, Roux C (2013) Nile red: alternative to physical developer for the detection of latent fingermarks on wet porous surfaces? Forensic Sci Int 230(1–3):74–80. https://doi.org/10.1016/j.forsciint.2013.03.041

Bridges BC (1942) Practical fingerprinting. Funk & Wagnalis Company

Bumbrah GS (2017) Cyanoacrylate fuming method for detection of latent fingermarks: a review. Egypt J Forensic Sci 7(1). https://doi.org/10.1186/s41935-017-0009-7

Bumbrah GS, Sharma RM, Jasuja OP (2016) Emerging latent fingerprint technologies: a review. Res Rep Forensic Med Sci 6:39–50

Bumbrah GS, Sodhi GS, Kaur J (2019) Oil red O (ORO) reagent for detection of latent fingermarks: a review. Egypt J Forensic Sci 9(1):3–9. https://doi.org/10.1186/s41935-018-0107-1

Champod C, Lennard CJ, Margot P, Stoilovic M (2004) Fingerprints and other ridge skin impressions. In: Fingerprints and other ridge skin impressions. CRC Press, Boca Raton. https://doi.org/10.1201/9780203485040

Daluz HM (2015) Fundamentals of fingerprint analysis. CPC press, Boca Raton

Daluz HM (2019) Fundamentals of fingerprint analysis (second edition). CRC Press, Boca Raton

Frick AA, Fritz P, Lewis SW (2015) Chemical methods for the detection of latent fingermarks. In: Forensic chemistry: fundamentals and applications. Wiley, New York, pp 354–399. https://doi.org/10.1002/9781118897768.ch9

Girod A, Ramotowski R, Weyermann C (2012) Composition of fingermark residue: a qualitative and quantitative review. Forensic Sci Int 223(1–3):10–24. https://doi.org/10.1016/j.forsciint.2012.05.018

Hawthorne MR (2009) Fingerprint: analysis and understanding. CRC Press, Boca Raton

Jasuja OP, Singh G (2009) Development of latent fingermarks on thermal paper: preliminary investigation into use of iodine fuming. Forensic Sci Int 192(1–3):11–16. https://doi.org/10.1016/j.forsciint.2009.08.005

Jasuja OP, Singh GD, Sodhi GS (2008) Small particle reagents: development of fluorescent variants. Sci Justice 48(3):141–145. https://doi.org/10.1016/j.scijus.2008.04.002

Jasuja OP, Toofany MA, Singh G, Sodhi GS (2009) Dynamics of latent fingerprints: the effect of physical factors on quality of ninhydrin developed prints—a preliminary study. Sci Justice 49(1):8–11. https://doi.org/10.1016/j.scijus.2008.08.001

Kapoor N (2020) An analysis of single digit fingerprints for determination of hand using various types of fingerprint patterns. http://hdl.handle.net/10603/330631

Kapoor N, Badiye A (2015a) Sex differences in the thumbprint ridge density in a central Indian population. Egypt J Forensic Sci 5(1):23–29. https://doi.org/10.1016/j.ejfs.2014.05.001

Kapoor N, Badiye A (2015b) Digital dermatoglyphics: a study on Muslim population from India. Egypt J Forensic Sci 5(3):90–95

Kapoor N, Ahmed S, Shukla RKRK, Badiye A (2019) Development of submerged and successive latent fingerprints: a comparative study. Egypt J Forensic Sci 9(1):44. https://doi.org/10.1186/s41935-019-0147-1

Kapoor N, Badiye A, Mishra SD (2020a) Fingerprint analysis for the determination of hand origin (right/left) using the axis slant in whorl patterns. Forensic Sci Res 7(2):285–289. https://doi.org/10.1080/20961790.2020.1794362

Kapoor N, Mishra SD, Badiye A (2020b) Single-digit fingerprint analysis for hand determination: a study of twinned loops. Med Sci Law 60(3):182–187

Lee HC, Gaensslen RE (2001) Advances in fingerprint technology (second edition). CRC Press, Boca Raton

Li H, Cao J, Niu J, Huang Y, Mao L, Chen J (2011) Study of non-invasive detection of latent fingerprints using UV laser. In: International symposium on photoelectronic detection and imaging 2011: laser sensing and imaging; and biological and medical applications of photonics sensing and imaging, 8192, 81921V. https://doi.org/10.1117/12.900235

Loll A, Police P (2013) Automated fingerprint identification systems (AFIS). In: Encyclopedia of forensic sciences, 2nd edn. Elsevier, New York. https://doi.org/10.1016/B978-0-12-382165-2.00261-0

Menzel ER (1980) Fingerprint Detection With Lasers | U.S. Department of Justice Office of Justice Programs. NCJ Number 78311

Menzel ER (1985) Comparison of argon-ion, copper-vapor, and frequency-doubled neodymium: yttrium aluminum garnet (ND:YAG) lasers for latent fingerprint development. J Forensic Sci 30(2):11817J. https://doi.org/10.1520/jfs11817j

Nabar BS (2013) Forensic science in crime investigation, 3rd edn. Asia Law House, Hyderabad

Nabar BS (2019) Forensic science in crime investigation. Asia Law House, Hyderabad. ISBN: 978-9388437691

Nath S (1991) Fingerprint identification in crime detection. Reliance Publishing House, New Delhi

Nath S (2006) Personal identification through fingerprints, 1st ed. Shree Publishers and Distributors, New Delhi. ISBN: 9788183291170

Ramotowskithird RS (2012) Lee and gaensslen's advances in fingerprint technology. In: Lee and Gaensslen's Advances in fingerprint technology. Routledge, Oxfordshire. https://doi.org/10.1201/b12882

Saferstein R (1983) Criminalistics: an introduction to forensic science, 1st edn. McGraw-Hill College, New York

Salares VR, Eves CR, Carey PR (1979) On the detection of fingerprints by laser excited luminescence. Forensic Sci Int 14(3):229. https://doi.org/10.1016/0379-0738(79)90142-7

Sharma BR (2014) Forensic science in criminal investigation & trial, 5th edn. Universal Law Publishing, New Delhi

Sodhi GS, Kaur J (2017) Multimetal deposition method for detection of latent fingerprints: a review. Egypt J Forensic Sci 7(1):1–7. https://doi.org/10.1186/S41935-017-0017-7/FIGURES/9

Sodhi GS, Kaur J (2019) Application of metals and metal salts in latent fingerprint detection: a review. Int J Forensic Sci 2(2):71–77

Stauffer E, Becue A, Singh KV, Thampi KR, Champod C, Margot P (2007) Single-metal deposition (SMD) as a latent fingermark enhancement technique: an alternative to multimetal deposition (MMD). Forensic Sci Int 168(1):e5. https://doi.org/10.1016/J.FORSCIINT.2006.12.009

Swanson CL (2013) Pattern evidence/history fingerprint sciences. In: Encyclopedia of forensic sciences, 2nd edn. Elsevier, New York. https://doi.org/10.1016/B978-0-12-382165-2.00272-5

Yamashita B, French M, Bleay S, Cantu A, Inlow V, Ramotowski R, Sears V, Wakefield M (2014) Latent print development. In: Latent fingerprint examination: elements, human factors and recommendations. Nova Science Publishers, Hauppauge, pp 225–320. https://doi.org/10.4324/9780429454530-12

Yassin AA, Jin H, Ibrahim A, Zou D (2012) "Anonymous Password Authentication Scheme by Using Digital Signature and Fingerprint in Cloud Computing," 2012 Second International Conference on Cloud and Green Computing. Xiangtan, China, pp 282–289. https://doi.org/10.1109/CGC.2012.91

Palmprints: An Introduction

9

Ashish Badiye, Archana Kamble, and Neeti Kapoor

Abstract

Palmprints are the prints formed due to the friction ridges in the middle portion of the ventral part of the hand. These are equally important as fingerprints because of their uniqueness and persistence. However, as the palmprints have a larger surface area, they can provide more number of ridge details than fingerprints. Palmprints are often found at the crime scenes like sexual offences, burglary, kidnapping, murder, rape, theft, and forgery. Apart from normal ridge details, palmprints also have unique characteristic features, including principal lines, tri-radii, and vestiges; some ridge characteristics are specific to a particular palm region. This chapter presents various aspects and classifications of the palmprint. Considering the actual scene of crime, the investigating officer may not get a complete palmprint; thus, in such cases, the unique ridge details and the palmprint classification system may serve the purpose of comparing and identifying the unknown print with the suspect's palmprint.

Keywords

Hand prints · Palm prints · Palmprint classification · Interdigital · Thenar · Hypothenar

A. Badiye · N. Kapoor (✉)
Department of Forensic Science, Government Institute of Forensic Science, Nagpur, Maharashtra, India
e-mail: ashishbadiye@ifscnagpur.in; neetikapoor@ifscnagpur.in

A. Kamble
Karunya Institute of Technology and Sciences, Coimbatore, Tamil Nadu, India

P. Shrivastava et al. (eds.), *Textbook of Forensic Science*,
https://doi.org/10.1007/978-981-99-1377-0_9

9.1 Introduction

'Palm' refers to the inner surface of the hand, and 'palmprints' are the prints formed by the inner surface of the hand. The terms 'palmprint' and 'handprint' cannot be used interchangeably as the handprint includes the print of the whole hand, including the print of the fingers and thumb phalanges, while the palmprint is a portion of the ventral part of the hand (Gopal et al. 2016). Handprints and palmprints are often encountered at the crime scene. Handprints can provide information such as the stature of the person (Krishan et al. 2015), sex (Kapoor and Badiye 2015a; Jerković et al. 2021; Dayarathne et al. 2021), determination of hand (Kapoor and Badiye 2015b; Kapoor et al. 2020), and personal identification. Palmprints can also play a significant role in differentiation between left and right hands, determination of sex (Badiye et al. 2019), personal identification, and presence of any abnormalities in the palm. Handprints and palmprints can be encountered in crimes like burglary, theft, kidnapping, sexual assaults, etc., on various surfaces. Just like fingerprints, palmprints can be used for the identification of suspects, as palmprints are also unique and persistent (Fig. 9.1).

Generally, the palmprint is divided into three groups: interdigital area (area below the fingers), thenar area (area near thumb), and hypothenar area (area near little finger). Palmprints have some characteristic features; thus, even when partial prints are collected from the crime scene, they may provide helpful information (Fig. 9.2).

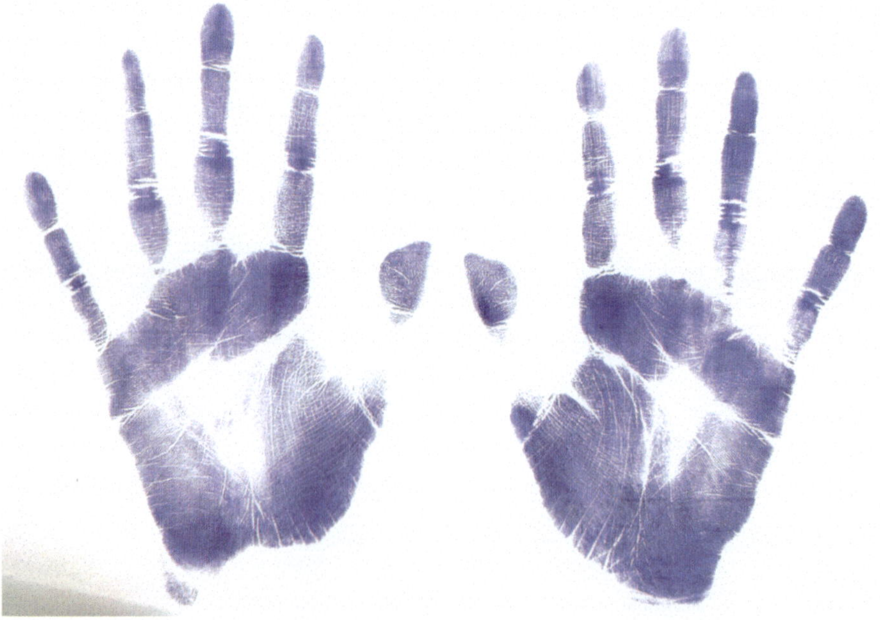

Fig. 9.1 Inked handprints of left and right hand

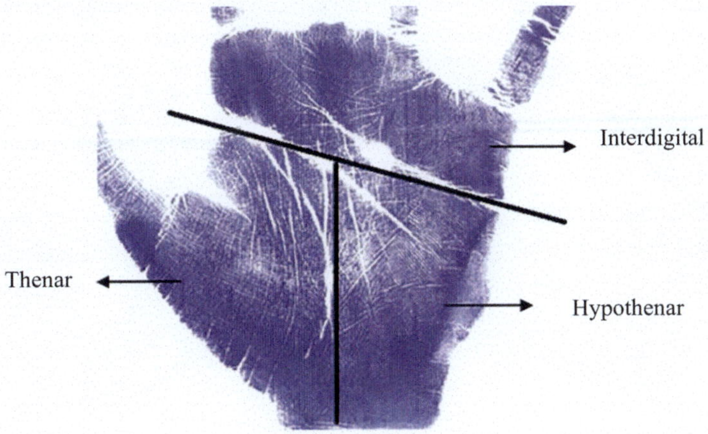

Fig. 9.2 Three palmar regions: interdigital, hypothenar, and thenar

9.2 The Emphasis on Palmprints over Fingerprints

Palmprints are similar to fingerprints as they are unique for every individual; even monozygotic twin does not have the same palmprints. They are persistent throughout human life and have ridge details similar to fingerprints. Fingerprints are smaller in size and thus may have more probability of getting smudged prints. However, palmprints have a larger surface area than fingerprints; thus, the ridge details are better appreciated. Palmprint also has unique characteristics like principal lines, tri-radii, etc., which can be used for classification and identification purposes.

9.3 Regions of Palm

- Interdigital Region
  The interdigital region shows many ridge details. The primary ridge flow starts from the bottom of the index or middle finger, runs in the interdigital region, and exits the palm from the ulnar side. This characteristic feature is called a "waterfall" (Fig. 9.3). Usually, the interdigital areas have four deltas located below each finger. However, palmprints may have less or more than four deltas (Maceo et al. 2013). The delta below the index finger is termed "clean delta," the delta below the middle finger is termed "snow cone delta," the delta below the ring finger is called "double snow cone right/left," and the delta below the little finger is known as "side cone" (Horton 2018). The most common patterns found in the interdigital region are loop and whorl; other than that, patterns like column and tented arch are also observed (Horton 2018). The interdigital region can be divided into VP regions: the region between the index and middle fingers, the region between the middle and ring fingers, and the region between the ring and little fingers as II, III, and IV, respectively (Maceo et al. 2013) (Fig. 9.4).

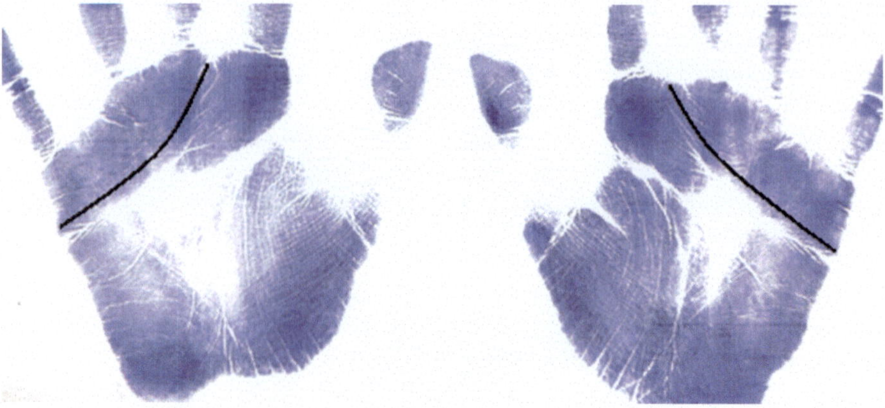

Fig. 9.3 Waterfall region of interdigital region of left and right hand

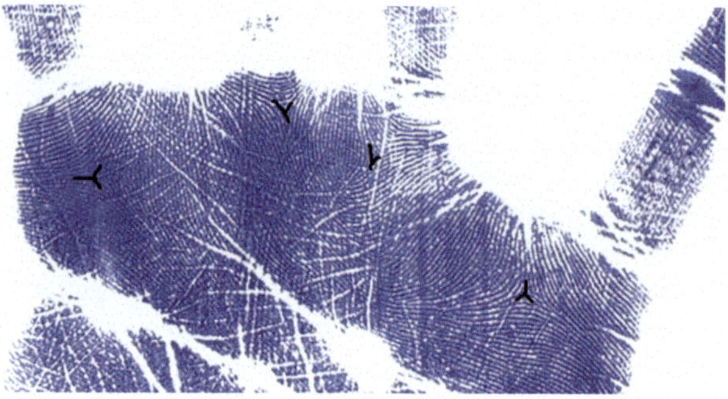

Fig. 9.4 Interdigital region of right palm showing the index (I), middle (M), ring (R), and little (L) deltas

- Thenar

  The thenar region is the area below the thumb of the palm. The thenar region has two characteristic features, namely, half-moon and vestiges. The ridges entering the palm through the middle of the index finger and the thumb and leaving from the bottom of the print give rise to a semi-circle formation around the thumb and is called a "half-moon." Another characteristic feature of the thenar area is the vestige. The vestiges run perpendicular to the pattern's normal ridge flow and are usually found at the base of the thumb. Vestiges are only found in thenar region; thus, it can be very helpful in partial palmprint examination to understand the orientation of the hand as well as differentiation between right and left hand. Vestiges are also called "thenar area clues" (Horton 2018). Vestiges may be small and independent. However, this region may also show patterns such as loop, column, and whorl (Maceo et al. 2013). Another region called the flip area is located in the web area. These ridges change the flow direction as they flip up, thus termed as "flip area" (Horton 2018) (Fig. 9.5).

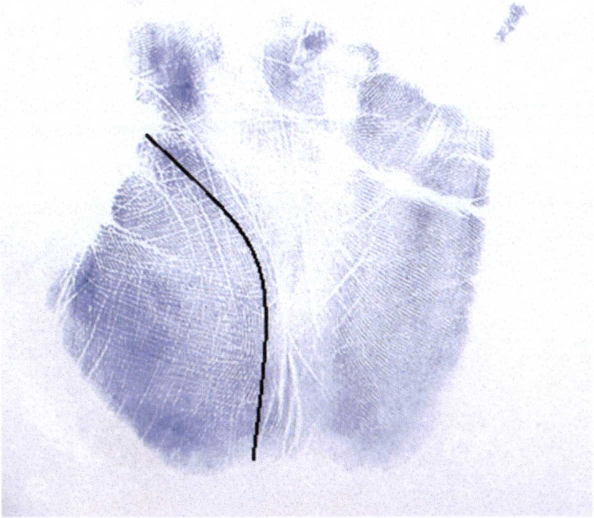

Fig. 9.5 Thenar area of right hand

- Hypothenar Region
  The hypothenar area covers the most significant part of the palm, and thus, it is primarily present in most partial palmprints. The ridges show a downward movement and exit from the side of the hand. The portion of the ridges in the hypothenar region tends to converge and appears as a funnel, thus termed as "funnel area." "Belly out" regions are at the bottom of the hypothenar area, where the ridges running down the pattern make a turn and exit the palm through the side of the hypothenar region. The ridges flowing in the vertical direction form a delta at the lower portion of the palm. It is termed the "carpal delta" and is mainly formed between the thenar and hypothenar regions. A slight arch below the carpel delta is called a "hump." The most common pattern found in the hypothenar region is a loop. The loop pointing towards the outer edge of the palm is called the "ulnar loop," while the "radial loop" points towards the center of the palm. The loop pointing toward the bottom of the palm is called a "proximal loop" (Maceo et al. 2013; Horton 2018) (Figs. 9.6, 9.7, and 9.8).

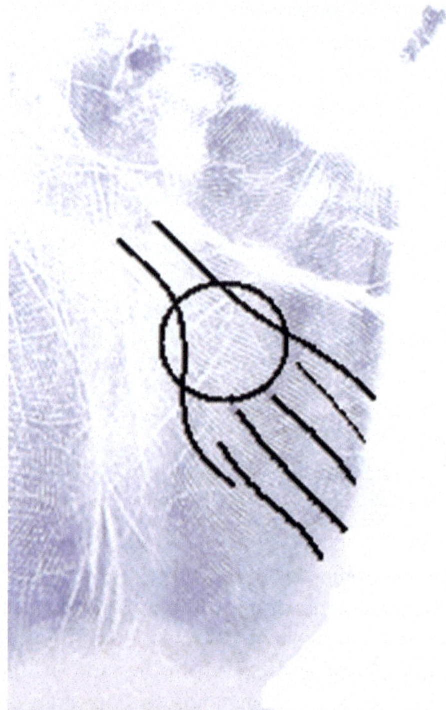

Fig. 9.6 Funnel area of the right hand

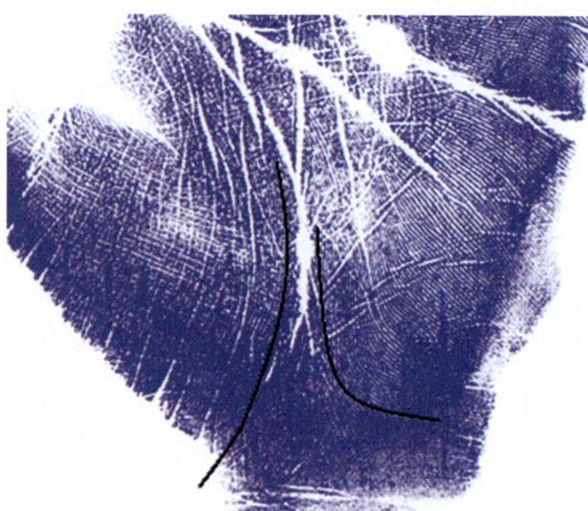

Fig. 9.7 Outline of the belly out portion of the right hand

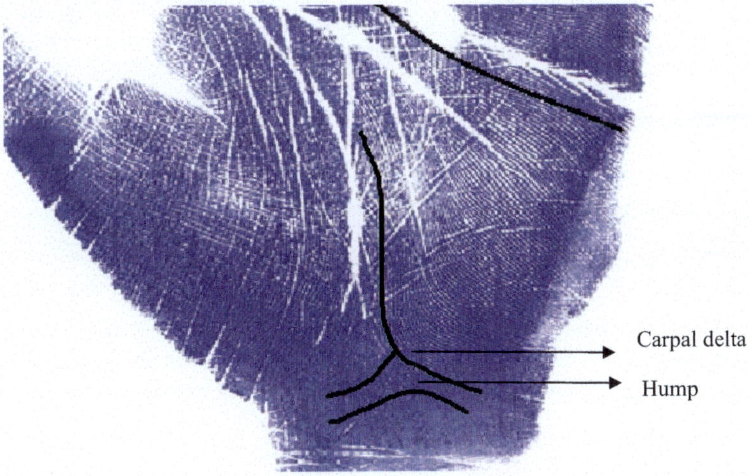

Fig. 9.8 The carpal delta and hump areas of the palm of the right hand

9.4 Classification of Palmprints

Classification of palmprints is very helpful for documenting and comparing complete and partial prints. Some palmprint classification systems are given below.

9.4.1 Western Australian Palmprint Classification

- Primary Classification
  The primary classification is based upon the ridge flow in the palm's three regions, i.e., interdigital, thenar, and hypothenar regions. The values assented to the areas are similar to the Henry classification, but this classification provides numerical values irrespective of the type of pattern present. Furthermore, in the end, one is added to the total score (Table 9.1).
- Secondary Classification
  The secondary classification has two divisions. The first division is based on the patterns present in the thenar and hypothenar areas. And the values are expressed in the form of fractions with thenar values in the numerator and hypothenar values in the denominator. The second division (secondary subclassification) deals with

Table 9.1 Primary value determination (Baird 1959, pp 21–24)

Area of consideration		Value
Interdigital	Delta near fifth finger	1
	Delta between third and fourth finger	2
	Delta between third finger to radial edge	4
Thenar		8
Hypothenar		16
No pattern in the area		0

the area between the thumb, index finger, and interdigital area (Holder et al. 2011). Therefore, the classification formula becomes

$$(\text{primary}) = (\text{thenar})\ (\text{thumb to index area})/(\text{hypothenar})\ (\text{interdigital}).$$

9.4.2 Liverpool Palmprint Classification System

The Liverpool classification system is based on three divisions of palm, similar to the Western Australian Palmprint Classification system; however, the Liverpool classification system has four parts and is represented in alpha numeric symbols.

1. Primary Division
   The primary division has three parts thenar, hypothenar, and interdigital. In cases when more than one pattern is present in the palmer area, it is considered as one pattern. While in cases when the patterns are present in different palmer areas, all the values are added together. Value pattern indications are represented in Table 9.2.
2. Secondary Division
   The secondary classification is based upon the ridge patterns present in the hypothenar region of the palm. Table 9.3 represents the symbols for each pattern observed in the hypothenar region. In the secondary subclassification, the ridge characteristics are recorded when a single loop is present in the hypothenar area. And in case of absence of any pattern, type of delta is recorded.
3. Tertiary Division
   Tertiary division is considered for the patterns in the thenar area. If two patterns are present in the thenar region, the coding box is divided into two parts by a diagonal line from the lower-left corner to the upper right corner of the box. Moreover, the pattern present near the interdigital area is represented by an alphabetical symbol in the upper left triangle. The pattern near the thenar region is represented by an alphabetical symbol in the lower-left triangular box of the coding box.

Table 9.2 Pattern indication from primary value

Primary	Value pattern indication
1	None
2	Thenar only
3	Interdigital only
4	Hypothenar only
5	Thenar and interdigital only
6	Thenar and hypothenar only
7	Interdigital and hypothenar only
9	Patterns in all three areas

Table 9.3 Symbols used in the secondary classification in the Liverpool Palmprint Classification System

Pattern	Symbol
Whorl A (circular)	A
Whorl B (elliptical)	B
Twinned loop	TL
Lateral pocket loop	LP
Central pocket loop	CP
Accidental/composite	ACC
Tented arch	T
Loop core inward	I
Loop core outward	O
Loop core downward	D
Loop core upward	U
Loop core nutant	K
Nondescript	N
Plain arch	N
No pattern	
High carpal delta	H
Low carpal delta	L

Table 9.4 Pattern value for part 2 of the quaternary division

Position of pattern	Value
Under index finger	8
Under middle finger	4
Under ring finger	2
Under little finger	1

4. Quaternary Division
   The quaternary division is based on the patterns observed in the interdigital region of the palm. It sub-divided into three parts. Part 1 represents the pattern present in the interdigital area. Part 2 provides a numerical value to the pattern in relation to the fingers (Table 9.4). Part 3 involves recording the ridge count for arch and loop patterns.

The complete classification system of the Liverpool palmprint classification is represented within a coding box, and the patterns are mentioned in the coding box as alphanumeric symbols (Table 9.5).

9.4.3 The Brogger Moller Palmprint Classification System

The Brogger Moller Palmprint Classification System employs a special measuring glass with four separate measuring areas. Each area has three concentric circles with 2, 4, and 6 cm radii. This classification system involved patterns present in three regions of palm and primary, secondary, and tertiary values (Tables 9.6, 9.7, and 9.8). And the measuring glass was used to determine some values as represented in the table below (Holder et al. 2011).

Table 9.5 Coding box for Liverpool Palmprint Classification System

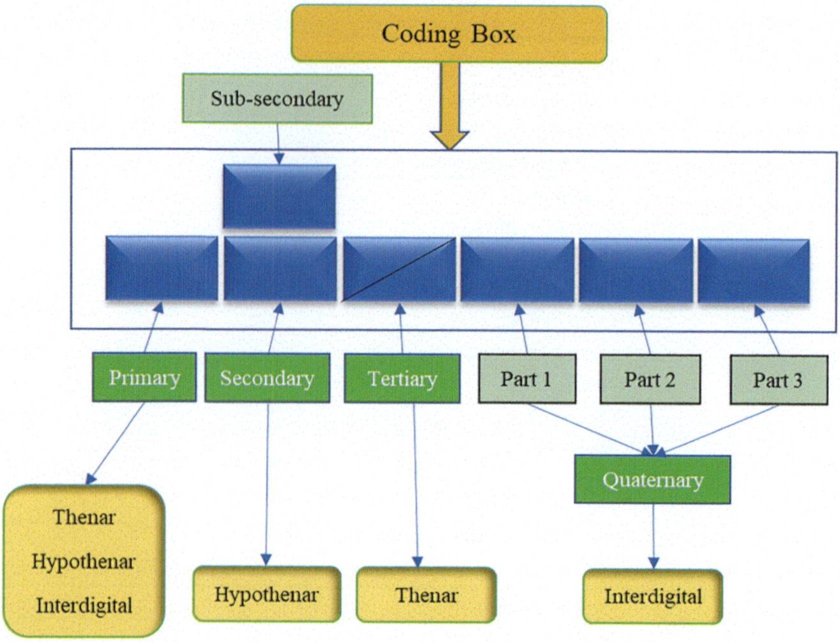

9.4.4 Palmprint Classification Using Principal Lines

The principal lines have been used to classify a palmprint. The print can be classified into six categories based on the principal lines and intersections. To classify the print, the principal lines are defined, and the number of principal lines and intersections are counted (Wu et al. 2004) (Table 9.9).

9.4.5 Automated Palmprint Classification Systems

Some authors have worked in the area of automated palmprint identification systems (Chen et al. 2001; Duta et al. 2002; Funada et al. 1998; Li et al. 2002; Sowmiya Manoj and Arulselvi 2021; Wu et al. 2002; Zhang and Shu 1999). Sakdanupab and Covavisaruch (2008) provided an automated palmprint classification system based on extraction of the heart line, head line, and life line. Scanned palmprints were overlaid in the computer system and compared by automated tools (Connie et al. 2005). The FBI has initiated a process to collect and convert into digital format to maintain a digital library (Holder et al. 2011).

Table 9.6 Classification for the hypothenar (Moenssens 1971, pp 200–205)

Ridge pattern	Primary	Secondary	Tertiary
No design (carpal delta only)	1	Using circle measurement, dot at carpal delta and read circle where the lowest ridge of the carpal area falls	None
Distal loop opening toward interdigital, with core pointing to ulnar side	2	Using 0–9 scale, measure the distance between the carpal delta and core of the loop	8 = only when the core has a distinct inclination toward the carpal/radial area
Outward loop opening toward ulnar side, with core pointing toward thenar	3	Using a 0–9 scale, measure the distance between the carpal delta and core of the loop	None
Whorls	4	Using a 0–9 scale, measure the distance between carpal delta and core (for double whorls, using core closest to carpal delta)	None
Double loops	5	Using a 0–9 scale, measure the distance between two cores	None
Arches	6	1 = arches	None
		2 = tented arches	
Loops opening toward the wrist, with the core pointing toward the ulnar side of the palm	7	Using a 0–9 scale, measure the distance between core and delta above it	None
Composite patterns (any pattern not conforming to the above patterns)	8	None	None

Case Study: Automated systems aid in comparing the unknown print with the database and finding the matching print. AFIS has helped in solving many crimes. A case was reported of a break-in into a business, and lateral palmprints were found on the entrance lock. The prints were developed using magnetic powder, and a scanned copy was run in the AFIS to find the match. However, no result was found. A few months later, fingerprints and palmprints of a suspect were collected and compared with the unknown lateral palmprint, and it was found to be a positive match. It was found that the suspect's record already exists but due to lack of sufficient amount of ridge details of lateral palmprints, it was not detected (Hefetz et al. 2021).

Table 9.7 Classification for the interdigital (Moenssens, pp 206–207)

Ridge pattern	Primary	Secondary	Tertiary
One loop in the base area	1	2 = if the loop is between index and middle fingers 3 = if loop is between middle and ring fingers 4 = if the loop is between the ring and little fingers	Using 1–6 scale, measure the height of the loop (from deltas to core)
Tented arch	2	1 = arch below index finger 2 = arch below middle finger 3 = arch below ring finger 4 = arch below little finger	Using a 1–6 scale, measure height of the arch (from the base of the arch to the summit)
Double loops	3	2 = if the loop is between the index and middle fingers 3 = if a loop is between middle and ring fingers 4 = if a loop is between the ring and little fingers	Using 1–6 scale, measure the height of the ulnar loop (from deltas to core)
Two loops in the same interdigital area and tented arches and loops in other areas	4	2 = if a two-loop combination is between the index and middle fingers 3 = if a two-loop combination is between the middle and ring fingers 4 = if a two-loop combination is between the ring and little fingers	None
Plain arches	5	None	None
One loop and one tented arch	6	2 = if a loop is between the index and middle fingers 3 = if a loop is between middle and ring fingers 4 = if a loop is between the ring and little finger	Using 1–6 scale, measure the height of loop (from deltas to core)
Three loops or combinations of three loops and tented arches	7	Three loops = height of loop between the ring and middle fingers. Combination of three loops and tented arches = height of pattern located next to the ulnar side of palm	None 2
Long transversal loop below one or several digital deltas	8	None	None
One or several whorls appear alone or in combinations with loops and tented arches	9	2 = if whorl is between the index and middle fingers 3 = if whorl is between middle and ring fingers 4 = if whorl is between the ring and little fingers	None

Table 9.8 Classification for the thenar (Moenssens, pp 207–209)

Ridge pattern	Primary	Secondary	Tertiary
No pattern (or plain arch)	1	None	None
Various patterns	2	1 = one proximal loop opens toward the radial side with the core pointing to the web of the thumb or center of the palm	Using a 0–9 scale, measure distance between the core and the nearest delta
		2 = one proximal loop and one distal loop	Using a 0–9 scale, measure the distance between the core of the proximal loop and nearest delta
		3 = one proximal loop and one whorl	None
		4 = one proximal loop and one double loop	None
Patterns with peculiar ridge formations	3	None	None
One distal loop opening toward the web of the thumb with the core pointing downward	4	Using a 0–9 scale, measure the distance between core and delta (not carpal delta)	None
Three different patterns	5	1 = one single whorl	None
		2 = one whorl and one distal loop	None
		3 = two whorls	None
Four different patterns	6	1 = one double loop	None
		2 = one double loop and one distal loop	None
		3 = one double loop and one whorl	None
		4 = two double loops	None
Two collateral distal loops both opening toward the web of the thumb	7	None	None
Two proximal loops, either both opening toward the carpal area or one toward the radial area and one toward the carpal area	8	None	None
Any pattern not discussed	9	None	None

Table 9.9 Palmprint classification system based on principal lines and intersections

Category	Number of principal lines	Number intersections	Symbol
1	1	0	(a)
2	2	0	(b)
3	2	1	(c)
4	3	0	(d)
5	3	1	(e)
6	3	>1	(f)

9.5 Conclusion

The study of palmprints holds immense potential in identifying individuals and assisting in criminal investigations. Palmprints, with their intricate patterns and distinctive features, offer a wealth of information for forensic analysis. The subsequent exploration of the regions of the palm highlights the complex nature of palmprints. The various parts, including the thenar, hypothenar, and interdigital areas, each possess distinct characteristics that contribute to the overall identification process. Understanding these regions' specific details and patterns is vital for accurate palmprint analysis.

Overall, the chapter emphasizes the unique nature of palmprints as a valuable forensic tool. Forensic experts can extract crucial information for individual identification and crime scene analysis by examining the handprints' regions and employing classification systems. As technology advances, palmprint analysis promises to play an increasingly integral role in forensic investigations, enhancing our ability to solve complex cases and bring justice to those affected.

References

Badiye A, Kapoor N, Mishra SD (2019) A novel approach for sex determination using palmar tri-radii: a pilot study. J Forensic Leg Med 65:22–26. https://doi.org/10.1016/j.jflm.2019.04.005

Baird AJ (1959) System used by the Western Australian police force for the classification and filing of palmprints (unpublished)

Chen J, Zhang C, Rong G (2001) Palmprint recognition using crease. In: Proceedings 2001 international conference on image processing (Cat. No. 01CH37205), vol 3, pp 234–237

Connie T, Jin ATB, Ong MGK, Ling DNC (2005) An automated palmprint recognition system. Image Vis Comput 23(5):501–515. https://doi.org/10.1016/j.imavis.2005.01.002

Dayarathne S, Nawarathna LS, Nanayakkara D (2021) Determination gender using foot, footprint, hand and hand print measurements in a Sinhalese population in Sri Lanka using supervised learning techniques. Comput Methods Programs Biomed 1:100017. https://doi.org/10.1016/j.cmpbup.2021.100017

Duta N, Jain AK, Mardia KV (2002) Matching of palmprints. Pattern Recogn Lett 23(4):477–485

Funada J, Ohta N, Mizoguchi M, Temma T, Nakanishi K, Murai A, Sugiuchi T, Wakabayashi T, Yamada Y (1998) Feature extraction method for palmprint considering elimination of creases. In: Proceedings. Fourteenth international conference on pattern recognition (Cat. No. 98EX170), vol 2, pp 1849–1854

Gopal, Srivastava S, Bhardwaj S, Bhargava S (2016) Fusion of palm-phalanges print with palmprint and dorsal hand vein. Appl Soft Comput 47:12–20. https://doi.org/10.1016/j.asoc.2016.05.039

Hefetz I, Liptz Y, Oz K (2021) The benefit of AFIS searches of lateral palm and non-distal phalanges prints in criminal investigation. Forensic Sci Int 328:111024. https://doi.org/10.1016/j.forsciint.2021.111024

Holder EH, Robinson LO, Laub JH (2011) The fingerprint sourcebook. U.S. Dept. of Justice, Office of Justice Programs, National Institute of Justice

Horton A (2018) Using pattern area ridge flow in the three areas of the palm to determine classification trends. The University of Southern Mississippi

Jerković I, Kolić A, Kružić I, Anđelinović Š, Bašić Ž (2021) Adjusted binary classification (ABC) model in forensic science: an example on sex classification from handprint dimensions. Forensic Sci Int 320:110709. https://doi.org/10.1016/j.forsciint.2021.110709

Kapoor N, Badiye A (2015a) Sex differences in the thumbprint ridge density in a central Indian population. Egypt J Forensic Sci 5(1):23–29. https://doi.org/10.1016/j.ejfs.2014.05.001

Kapoor N, Badiye A (2015b) An analysis of whorl patterns for determination of hand. J Forensic Leg Med 32:42–46. https://doi.org/10.1016/j.jflm.2015.02.015

Kapoor N, Badiye A, Mishra SD (2020) Fingerprint analysis for the determination of hand origin (right/left) using the axis slant in whorl patterns. Forensic Sci Res 7(2):285–289. https://doi.org/10.1080/20961790.2020.1794362

Krishan K, Kanchan T, Kharoshah MA (2015) Estimation of stature from handprint dimensions – positional variations in real crime scene situations. Egypt J Forensic Sci 5(4):129–131. https://doi.org/10.1016/j.ejfs.2015.10.002

Li W, Zhang D, Xu Z (2002) Palmprint identification by Fourier transform. Int J Pattern Recogn Artif Intell 16(04):417–432

Maceo A, Carter M, Stromback B, Vegas L, Police M, Vegas L (2013) Palm prints. In: Encyclopedia of forensic sciences, vol 4, 2nd edn. Elsevier, Amsterdam. https://doi.org/10.1016/B978-0-12-382165-2.00277-4

Moenssens AA (1971) Fingerprint techniques. Chilton Book

Sakdanupab M, Covavisaruch N (2008) An efficient approach for automatic palmprint classification. In: 2008 IEEE International conference on signal image technology and internet based systems, pp 229–234. https://doi.org/10.1109/SITIS.2008.22

Sowmiya Manoj M, Arulselvi S (2021) Palm print identification and classification using KNN algorithm. Materials Today Proc. https://doi.org/10.1016/j.matpr.2021.01.804

Wu X, Wang K, Zhang D (2002) Fuzzy directional element energy feature (FDEEF) based palmprint identification. In: 2002 International conference on pattern recognition, vol 1, pp 95–98

Wu X, Zhang D, Wang K, Huang B (2004) Palmprint classification using principal lines. Pattern Recognit 37(10):1987–1998. https://doi.org/10.1016/j.patcog.2004.02.015

Zhang D, Shu W (1999) Two novel characteristics in palmprint verification: datum point invariance and line feature matching. Pattern Recogn 32(4):691–702

Forensic Podiatry: An Introduction 10

Neeti Kapoor, Archana Kamble, and Ashish Badiye

Abstract

Forensic podiatry is an application of podiatric knowledge in forensic investigation. Footprints/impressions can be found at crime scenes like burglary, theft, murder, sexual assaults, and kidnapping. In such cases, footprint analysis can provide a wealth of information about the criminal, including details about their gender, height, age, weight, and any foot anomalies that may aid in narrowing the pool of suspects. Moreover, in some cases, personal identification can also be done by footprint classification and ridge detail analysis. The present chapter presents an overview of the various aspects of footprints including the various classification systems used to compare footprints collected from the crime scene and the samples collected from the suspects and the forensic significance of the same. Classification systems can also be very helpful even when the examiner does not have the suspect's sample, as they make it possible to record information for future use more concisely.

Keywords

Footprint · Footwear · Impressions · Marks · Footprint classification

N. Kapoor · A. Badiye (✉)
Department of Forensic Science, Government Institute of Forensic Science, Nagpur, Maharashtra, India
e-mail: ashishbadiye@ifscnagpur.in

A. Kamble
Karunya Institute of Technology and Sciences, Coimbatore, Tamil Nadu, India

P. Shrivastava et al. (eds.), *Textbook of Forensic Science*,
https://doi.org/10.1007/978-981-99-1377-0_10

10.1 Introduction

Forensic podiatry was defined by Vernon and McCourt in 1999 as the "application of sound and researched podiatric knowledge in the context of forensic and mass disaster investigations. This may be for personal identification, to show an individual's association with the crime scene, or to answer any other legal question concerning the foot or footwear that requires knowledge of the functioning foot" (Dimaggio 2005). Podiatry experts analyze the footwear found at the crime scene, footprints, inked footprints, gait patterns, etc. Vernon, in 2006, enlisted the work of forensic podiatrists, which included analysis of barefoot impressions, footprint sequencing, footwear analysis, and analysis of the CCTV footage for gait patterns (Badiye et al. 2020; Vernon 2006).

The first case in which the culprit was identified based on the uniqueness of the barefoot impression was in early 1888 in France. A study conducted in 1989 revealed that the foot impressions show a high degree of variability and persistency over the years. However, the friction ridges present on the flat surface of the foot still provide individualizing characteristics (Massey and Kennedy 2019). Footprints also have similar ridge patterns as fingerprints; thus, they are equally unique and can be used for personal identification. Ridge patterns help in gender differentiation (Badiye et al. 2019; Kapoor and Badiye 2015; Krishan et al. 2010; Nithin et al. 2009; Souza et al. 2022) as well as personal identification (Caplan 1990; NarayanMohanty and Sikka 2021; Rivaldería et al. 2017).

Footprints/impressions are vital evidence as they can provide information about the person's stature (Moorthy et al. 2014; Reel et al. 2012; Švábová et al. 2022; Verma et al. 2020), gender (Basu and Bandyopadhyay 2017; Dayarathne et al. 2021; Kanchan et al. 2014), weight (Švábová et al. 2022), state of motion (Howsam and Bridgen 2018; Mukhra et al. 2020; Neves et al. 2018), individualization (Moorthy and Sulaiman 2015), etc. Analysis of ghost footprints helps in differentiating between static and dynamic footprints. Ghosting can be defined as the lighter portion of the bare footprint which has an extended portion with each toe and the heel (Nirenberg et al. 2020).

10.2 Foot Anatomy

Human foot has a complex anatomy, some researchers have demonstrated a detailed study of foot anatomy (Vazquez-zorrilla et al. 2020). The skin of the foot has three layers superficial layer, epidermis, and dermis layer. The thickness of the foot and palm's epidermis layer differs from the rest of the body. On the foot and palm, its thickness is between 0.8 and 1.4 mm, whereas the rest of the body has 0.07–0.12 mm thick layer of the epidermis. The foot includes a total of 26 bones with sesamoid bones. The bones are categorized into the heel, arch, and forefoot.

Morphological classification of the foot (based on structure and form of the foot) is as follows:

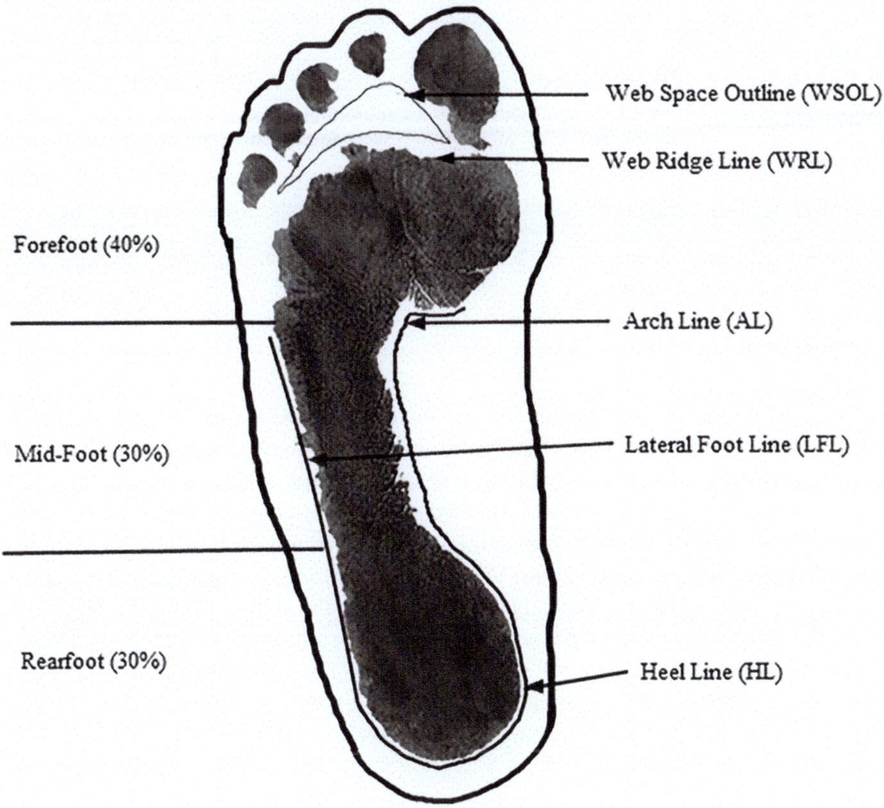

Fig. 10.1 Bare inked footprint with foot outline

- Ectomorph: tall, slender, long-boned, slim-muscled
- Mesomorph: stocky, muscular, heavy-boned
- Endomorph: fleshy, plump, small-boned, fatty

The bare footprint represents the skeletal structure pressing against the soft tissue beneath it. However, using the foot outline whenever possible to provide the complete morphological picture is crucial because noncontact areas are not visible (Dimaggio 2005) (Fig. 10.1).

10.3 Footprints as Evidence at the Crime Scene

Like fingerprints, each person's unique footprint is different, and even monozygotic twins have different prints (Lin et al. 1982; Vanderkolk 2013). Fingerprints are mostly found at the crime scene; however, there may be a chance that the perpetrator has taken precautionary measures by wearing gloves or cleaning the contact

Table 10.1 References of estimation of biological characteristics from footprint analysis

Biological characteristics	Work done by
Estimation of stature	Verma et al. (2020), Švábová et al. (2022), Moorthy et al. (2014), Reel et al. (2012), Hemy et al. (2013), Robbins (1986), Krishan (2008b), Caplova et al. (2018)
Estimation of sex	Basu and Bandyopadhyay 2017, Dayarathne et al. (2021), Krishan et al. (2011), Kanchan et al. (2014)
Estimation of body weight	Švábová et al. (2022), Robbins (1986), Krishan (2008a), Caplova et al. (2018)
Personal identification	Moorthy and Sulaiman (2015), Mukhra et al. (2018)

surfaces. Nevertheless, entering or leaving the crime scene is impossible without his feet touching the ground. Thus, bare footprints and footwear impressions should be appropriately documented and lifted whenever found at the crime scene. The footprints are compared with the suspected sample but can also aid in crime scene reconstruction and personal identification (Basu and Bandyopadhyay 2017; Mukhra et al. 2018; Pizzamiglio et al. 2006). A series of footprints found at the crime scenes can be used for gait pattern analysis. Gait analysis is the study of human movement. It can reveal information like the sex of the person, walking style, age, body weight, and any abnormalities in walking, which may help narrow down the pool of suspects (Badiye et al. 2020). Various parameters like step length, stride length, and footprint length are used for gait pattern analysis on the surface (Table 10.1).

10.4 Types of Footprints

1. Visible Foot/Footwear Prints
   The visible prints are formed due to material transfer from the shoe to the surface. Such prints are usually visible through the naked eye. Imagine the shoe/foot smeared with mud in contact with the floor. Thus, the print created would be a visible foot/footwear print.
2. Latent Foot/Footwear Prints
   These are not visible to the naked eye. Such prints are formed by static charges between the sole and the surface. Powder treatment, chemical, and electrostatic methods are required to develop and lift such latent foot/footwear prints.
3. Plastic Foot/Footwear Prints
   Plastic prints are also called 3D prints. These prints are formed when the foot comes in contact with a soft surface creating a 3D impression of the foot. Imagine stepping onto the ground with wet soil.

10.5 Classifications of Footprints

10.5.1 The FBI's Footprint Classification System

The classification system used by the FBI was a significantly modified version of the one created by Wentworth and Wilder in their book. The observation of the foot's ball, located just below the big toe, served as the foundation for the FBI's classification system. Arch, loop, and whorl pattern groups are the most common types of pattern groups seen in this region. Each group has a letter designation and is further broken down into types and ridge counts (for loop and whorl patterns only) (Table 10.2) (FBI 1985, p. 24). This classification is represented in fractions as the right foot values in the numerator and the left foot values in the denominator. The fraction contains values as given below (FBI 1985, p. 24).

$$\frac{\text{Primary-pattern Subdivision Final}}{\text{Key Primary-pattern Subdivision}}.$$

The "Primary-pattern" is in capital letters, and then the "Subdivision" of the pattern is written in small letters. "Final" represents the total number of ridge counts in the loop or whorl of the right foot, and its value is placed on the right side of the subdivision. Whereas the term "Key" represents the total number of ridge count in the loop or whorl of the left foot, its value is placed at the left side of the subdivision.

Illustration Example: If a pair of footprints has a "double-loop whorl with ridge count 23" of the right foot and left foot has a "loop with ridge flow entering and exiting toward the toes having ridge count as 26," then it can be represented in fraction form according to the FBI's Footprint Classification System as

Table 10.2 The FBI's Footprint Classification System (Holder et al. 2011)

Sr. no.	Pattern	Letter
1.	Arch	"O"
Subdivisions	Vertical ridge flow	O1
	Horizontal ridge flow	O2
2.	Loop	"L"
Subdivisions	Ridge flow entering and exiting toward the toes	La
	Ridge flow entering and exiting the big toe side of the foot	Lb (right foot) and Lc (left foot)
	Ridge flow entering and exiting toward the heel of the foot.	Ld
3.	Whorl	"W"
Subdivisions	Whorl pattern either with a plain whorl or a central pocket loop whorl	Ww
	Double loop whorl	Wd
	Accidental whorl	Wx

$$\frac{\text{Wd}23}{\text{La}26}.$$

10.5.2 Chatterjee Footprint Classification System

The footprint was divided into six areas by Sri Salil Kumar Chatterjee based on areas of the foot. In this classification, the patterns present in area 1 are represented using alphabets, while the patterns present in the rest are represented numerically (Chatterjee 1953, pp. 179–183). The final classification can be represented as a fraction. The numerator consists of the values of the right foot, and the denominator has values of the left foot (Holder et al. 2011) (Tables 10.3 and 10.4, Fig. 10.2).

Table 10.3 Division of foot areas by Chatterjee Footprint Classification System

Area	Region on the foot
Area 1	Ball of the foot, below the big toe
Areas 2–4	Interspaces below the toes
Area 5	Center of the foot
Area 6	Heel

Table 10.4 Alpha and numeric pattern representations (Moenssens 1971, p. 212)

None	O	0
Arch	A	1
Tented arch	T	2
Right slope loop	R	3
Upward slope loop	U	4
Left slope loop	L	5
Loop with downward slope	D	6
Whorl	W	7
Central pocket loop	C	7
Lateral pocket loop	S	8
Twin loop	S	8
Accidental	X	9

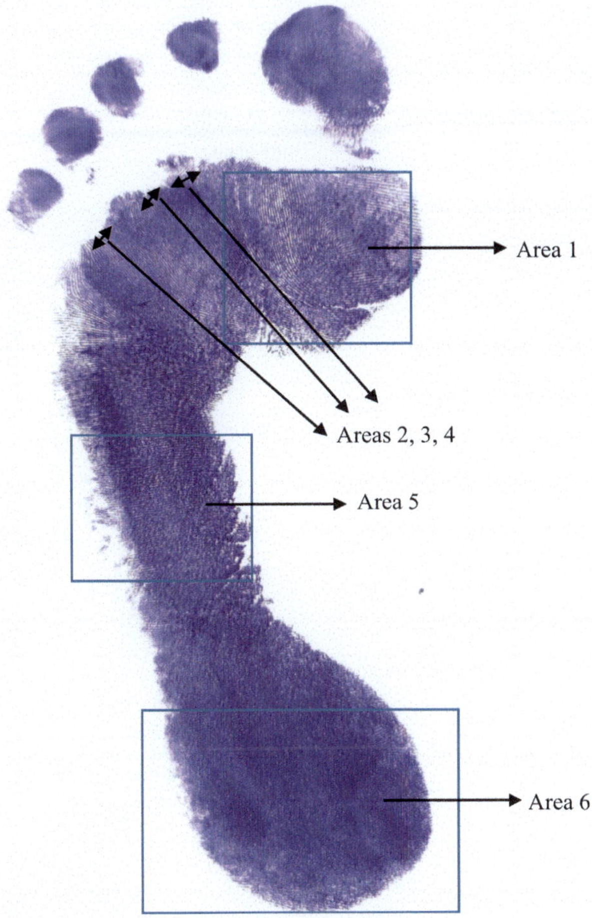

Fig. 10.2 Divisions of foot areas based on the Chatterjee Footprint Classification System

10.5.3 Classification of Footprints by Robert B. Montgomery

Two researchers have developed different footprint classification systems: Cummins and Wilder. Meanwhile, the Cummins classification system was very complicated for practical use; on the other hand, the classification given by Wilder had only 17,60,000 possibilities. Thus, for practical use, Robert B. Montgomery developed a more straightforward footprint classification system, including some features of both researchers and adding Montgomery's points (Montgomery 1927). This classification included a total of nine divisions.

First Division The ball of the foot bears five patterns. One is present on the hallucal, three are below small toes, and one is at the hypothenar region of the foot. These areas are found with patterns like Arch, Loop and Whorl are represented as "A," "U," and "W," respectively. When the footprint has no pattern in the designated areas, it is shown by "O." Loop can be an upright loop opening distally or the inverted loop opening proximally. Depending upon the presence of the pattern

Table 10.5 Numerical values for First Division classification of the foot

Footprint regions	Numerical values
Hallucal area	16
First plantar	8
Second plantar	4
Third plantar	2
Hypothenar	1

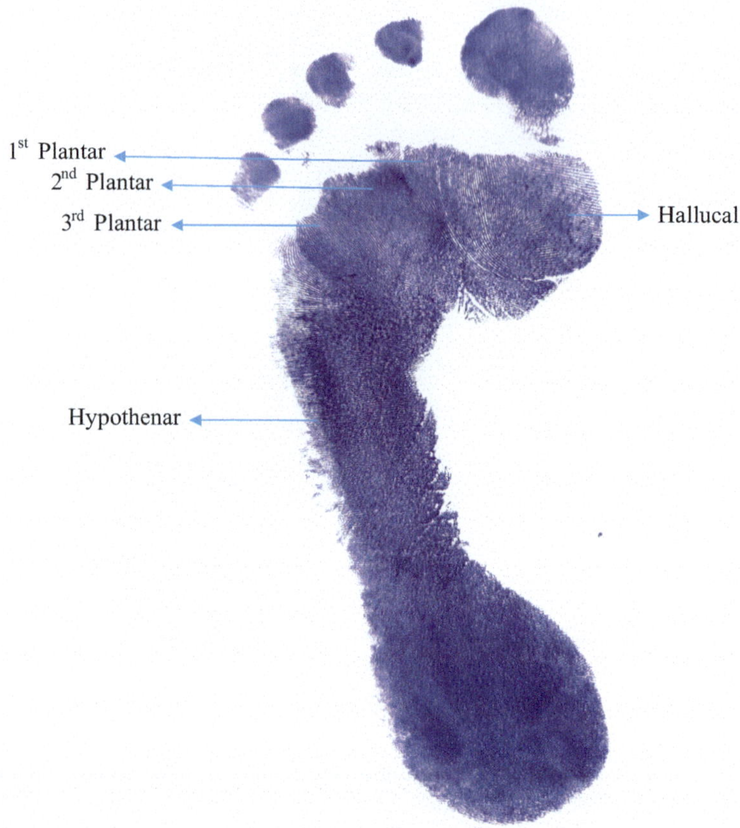

Fig. 10.3 Areas of the foot for the Montgomery classification system

in the footprint, values are given as represented in Table 10.5. The classification is expressed in the fraction, i.e., values of the right foot in the numerator and values of the left foot in the denominator. And value one is added to the numerator and denominator to get the final fraction. This classification can have 1024 possible combinations. The first division of the footprint classification is similar to Henry 10-digit classification system. However, Robert B. Montgomery's classification system also includes the values for the whorl (Fig. 10.3).

Illustration For example, Suppose the right footprint has a whorl pattern in the hallucal region, a loop in the first plantar region, no pattern in the second and third plantar regions, and a loop pattern in the hypothenar region. Whereas, the left footprint has an arch pattern in the hallucal region, no pattern in the first and second plantar regions, a loop in the third plantar region, and a whorl in the hypothenar region. So according to the Montgomery classification system the prints will be classified as represented below. Once the patterns are represented in fraction form, their respective values are inserted in place of the alphabets, as shown in table 10.5. After addition of the values of the fraction, 1 is added to the numerator and denominator. After addition of 1 in the numerator and the denominator, we get the first division classification.

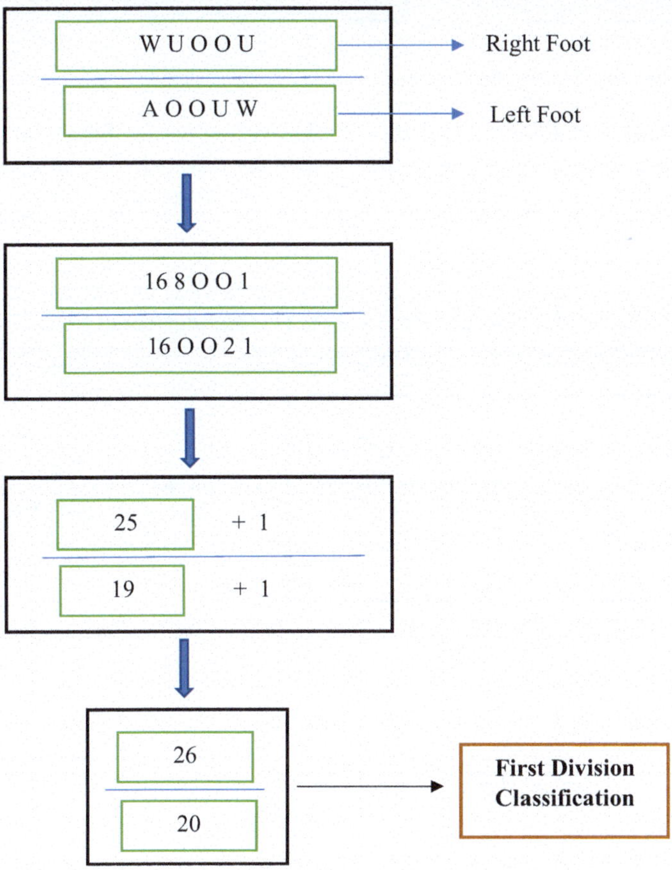

Second Division Capital letters are used to write the symbols for the hallucal patterns. The symbols are written in capital letters on the right side of the fraction of the first division classification (Table 10.6).

Table 10.6 Symbols used in Second Division classification

Sr. no.	Patterns	Symbol
1	Arch	A
2	Whorl	W
3	Loop	U

Illustration For example, hallucal regions of the right and the left foot bear whorl and arch, respectively; then, the second division classification of the footprint is represented by denoting "W" and "A" on the right side of the fraction of the first division classification.

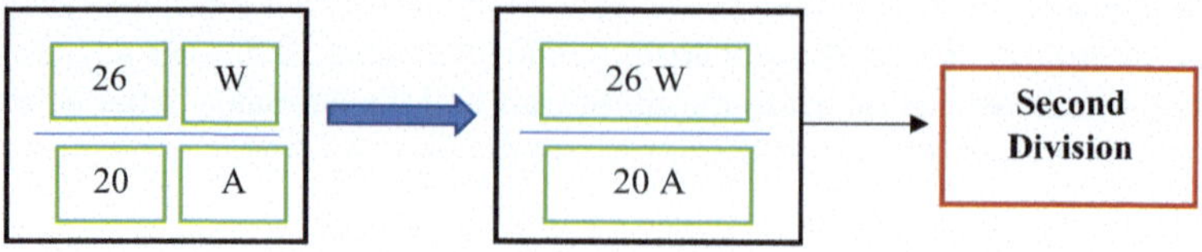

Third Division The third division involves keen observation of the loop patterns in which the inner-most free ridges within the loop are counted. The count above nine is considered as nine only (Fig. 10.4). Whorl and no pattern regions have zero counts.

Illustration For example, the right foot has patterns W U O O U with ridge count 6 2 0 0 3, and the left foot has pattern A O O U U with ridge count 5 0 0 1 2, and then the ridge counts are represented as fractions.

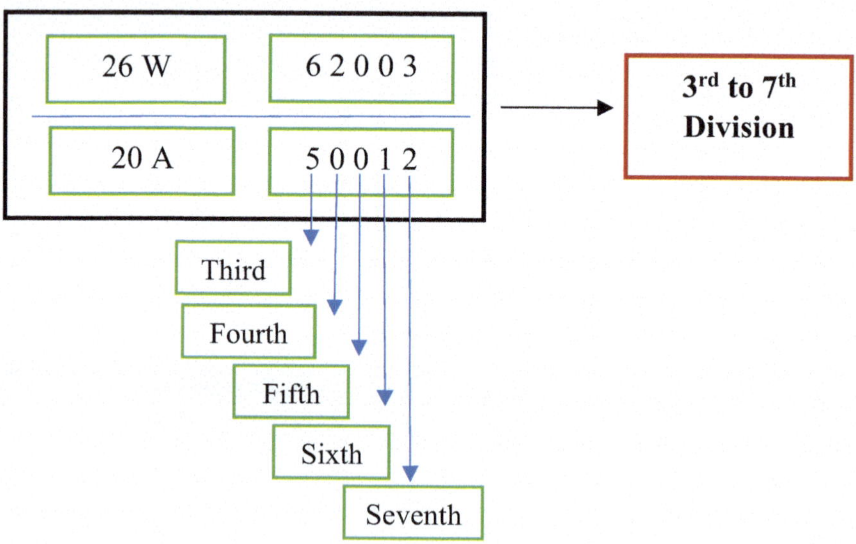

The **Fourth, Fifth, Sixth, and Seventh Divisions** are classified similar to the third division.

Eighth Division It represents the hallucal whorls with small letters "c" for clockwise and "cc" for counterclockwise.

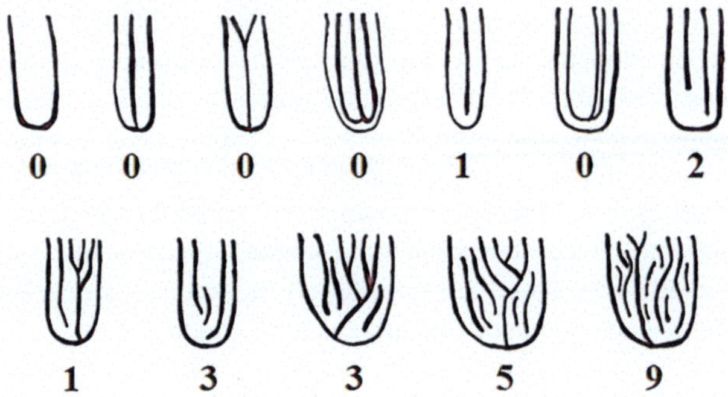

Fig. 10.4 Examples of ridge count in a loop pattern

Table 10.7 Ninth division classification system

Sr. no.	Hallucal whorl	Symbol
1.	Seam	sm
2.	Central pocket	cp
3.	Lateral pocket	lp
4.	Twin loop	tl

Ninth Division This deals with the type of hallucal whorls other than the regular whorl. There are 25 subdivisions possible here (Table 10.7) (Montgomery 1927).

10.6 Documentation of Footprints

If there are any barefoot impressions at the crime scene, they must be photographed and gathered for subsequent analysis by a barefoot morphology examiner. It is recommended that all impressions visible be photographed before enhancement and after enhancement using proper forensic photography principles and protocols. The charge-coupled device (CCD) of the camera must be parallel to the captured impression for taking high-quality pictures of the barefoot impression evidence (Massey and Kennedy 2019). When there is impression evidence, high-resolution pictures of the individual imprints or impressions, as well as general photographs of the evidence's location in relation to the surrounding area, are taken. Examiners may employ alternative light sources or chemical enhancers to obtain as much information as possible, particularly with latent impressions.

10.7 Collection Methods of Footprints

10.7.1 Collection Methods of the Footprint from the Crime Scene

Casting is the most widely used method to collect footprints from soft materials like snow, mud, and other surfaces. Plaster is used frequently for casting (McGraw 1984). To collect the prints from the snowy surface, the examiner can use Snow-

Print-Wax on the surface, allow it to dry, and then put a mixture of plaster and water to develop the cast (Carlsson 1981). Examiners frequently attempt to collect the complete object that bears the impression, such as the entire piece of cardboard or paper with a shoe print. However, a proper lifting technique should be used to collect the print for surfaces that cannot be collected entirely, like counter tables, slabs in the kitchen, etc. Fingerprint powders can enhance the print, and adhesive lifters can be used to collect the prints from smooth surfaces like wood, tile, metal surface, etc. Gelatin lifters are used on rough or textured surfaces. Electrostatic dust print lifting devices can be used on surfaces such as carpets.

10.7.2 Collection of the Footprints from the Subject

Firstly, High-quality photographs of the subject's feet are taken from various angles and positions. This includes capturing the sole, toes, and any distinguishing features or marks. The photographs serve as a visual record of the footprints and provide a reference for further analysis. The photography is followed by casting the foot. To create three-dimensional replicas of the subject's feet, casting materials such as foam or dental stone are used. The subject's foot is carefully placed into a prepared mold, and the casting material is poured in. After sufficient hardening time, the cast is removed, resulting in a detailed representation of the foot's surface and contours. Inked impressions are collected to capture the individual characteristics of the subject's feet. This involves applying ink or a similar substance to the soles of the subject's feet and having them make impressions on a suitable surface (Massey and Kennedy 2019). Different positions, such as standing, walking, or various weight distributions, may be utilized to capture a range of footprints.

10.8 Footprint Analysis

The comparison of barefoot impressions is conducted in the same manner as any other physical match, using the same scientific principles. While comparing the unknown sample with the known, the examiner shall first compare the class characteristics, including the size of the foot, number of toes, width of the ball, and heel of the foot. If class characteristics are similar, the finer details are observed, including the shape, size, and length of each toe, ball, and heel area. The examiner must also make a note of the transient alterations in footprint caused due to any injury. When used in combination, all these characteristics can help compare and differentiate foot impressions (Massey and Kennedy 2019). Once the examiner writes the report, and it is sent to another examiner along with all the documents, the report is considered the final if their observations are similar.

10.9 Futuristic Approach: Recovery of DNA from Footprints

The field of DNA profiling is evolving continuously. DNA profiling has become a gold standard for personal identification in forensic science (Oosthuizen and Howes 2022). Every person has a unique DNA profile just as fingerprints thus widely used for personal identification. Some researchers have proposed a method to recover trace amounts of DNA from footprints, proposing that fingerprints and footprints of humans and animals have some shed skin cells which can serve as a source of Genetic material (DNA) (Dalén et al. 2007). Extraction of DNA from footprints can have broad applications in wild-life forensics to identify the specific animal, and at a crime scene, it can provide a linkage between the suspect and the scene of a crime.

10.10 Case Study

In a village, a woman (25 years) was found dead in her house due to partial hanging. The rope was tied around her neck, and another end was tied to the wooden roof. A nearby chair was found to bear a footprint formed by dust lifted by an electrostatic dust print lifter. With crime scene reconstruction, autopsy report, and comparison of the footprint, it was found to be a case of suicide (Moorthy 2019).

10.11 Conclusion

In conclusion, the chapter provides an overview of the fundamental aspects of footprints as valuable evidence in forensic investigations. It highlights the unique characteristics and intricacies of foot anatomy, emphasizing the importance of footprints in identifying individuals and reconstructing events. Footprints can provide vital information such as the size, shape, and gait pattern of the perpetrator, aiding in suspect identification and linking individuals to the crime scene. The classifications of footprints discussed in the chapter highlight the systematic approach to analyzing and interpreting footprints. Understanding the class characteristics, such as arch type, toe shape, and wear patterns, enables investigators to narrow down potential matches and draw essential conclusions from the collected footprints. Detailed documentation, including precise measurements, photographs, and written descriptions, ensures accuracy and reliability in analysing and comparing footprints.

References

Badiye A, Kapoor N, Mishra SD (2019) A novel approach for sex determination using palmar tri-radii: a pilot study. J Forensic Legal Med 65:22–26. https://doi.org/10.1016/j.jflm.2019.04.005

Badiye A, Kathane P, Krishan K (2020) Forensic gait analysis. In: StatPearls. StatPearls Publishing, Treasure Island

Basu N, Bandyopadhyay SK (2017) Crime scene reconstruction—sex prediction from blood stained foot sole impressions. Forensic Sci Int 278:156–172. https://doi.org/10.1016/j.forsciint.2017.06.017

Caplan RM (1990) How fingerprints came into use for personal identification. J Am Acad Dermatol 23(1):109–114. https://doi.org/10.1016/0190-9622(90)70194-M

Caplova Z, Švábová P, Fuchsová M, Masnicová S, Neščáková E, Bodoriková S, Dörnhöferová M, Beňuš R (2018) Estimation of stature and body weight in Slovak adults using static footprints: a preliminary study. Leg Med 34:7–16. https://doi.org/10.1016/j.legalmed.2018.07.002

Carlsson K (1981) A new method for securing impressions in snow. Am J Forensic Med Pathol 2(3):277–278. https://doi.org/10.1097/00000433-198109000-00018

Chatterjee SK (1953) Finger, Palm and Sole Prints. Artine Press, Calcutta

Dalén L, Götherström A, Meijer T, Shapiro B (2007) Recovery of DNA from footprints in the snow. Can Field Naturalist 121(3):321–324

Dayarathne S, Nawarathna LS, Nanayakkara D (2021) Determination gender using foot, footprint, hand and hand print measurements in a Sinhalese population in Sri Lanka using supervised learning techniques. Comput Methods Prog Biomed Update 1:100017. https://doi.org/10.1016/j.cmpbup.2021.100017

Dimaggio JA (2005) The role of feet and footwear in medicolegal investigations. In: Forensic medicine of the lower extremity. Forensic science and medicine. Humana Press, Totowa, pp 375–400

Federal Bureau of Investigation (1985) Classification of Footprints. U.S. Department of Justice, U.S. Government Printing Office: Washington DC (Revised and reprinted from Law Enforcement Bulletin, September 1971).

Hemy N, Flavel A, Ishak N-I, Franklin D (2013) Estimation of stature using anthropometry of feet and footprints in a Western Australian population. J Forensic Leg Med 20(5):435–441. https://doi.org/10.1016/j.jflm.2012.12.008

Holder, E. H., Robinson, L. O., & Laub, J. H. (2011). The fingerprint sourcebook. U.S. Dept. of Justice, Office of Justice Programs, National Institute of Justice.

Howsam N, Bridgen A (2018) A comparative study of standing fleshed foot and walking and jumping bare footprint measurements. Sci Justice 58(5):346–354. https://doi.org/10.1016/j.scijus.2018.06.003

Kanchan T, Krishan K, Prusty D, Machado M (2014) Heel–Ball index: an analysis of footprint dimensions for determination of sex. Egypt J Forensic Sci 4(2):29–33. https://doi.org/10.1016/j.ejfs.2014.02.002

Kapoor N, Badiye A (2015) Sex differences in the thumbprint ridge density in a central Indian population. Egypt J Forensic Sci 5(1):23–29. https://doi.org/10.1016/j.ejfs.2014.05.001

Krishan K (2008a) Establishing correlation of footprints with body weight—forensic aspects. Forensic Sci Int 179(1):63–69. https://doi.org/10.1016/j.forsciint.2008.04.015

Krishan K (2008b) Estimation of stature from footprint and foot outline dimensions in Gujjars of North India. Forensic Sci Int 175(2):93–101. https://doi.org/10.1016/j.forsciint.2007.05.014

Krishan K, Ghosh A, Kanchan T, Ngangom C, Sen J (2010) Sex differences in fingerprint ridge density—causes and further observations. J Forensic Leg Med 17(3):172–173. https://doi.org/10.1016/j.jflm.2009.12.003

Krishan K, Kanchan T, Sharma A (2011) Sex determination from hand and foot dimensions in a North Indian population. J Forensic Sci 56(2):453–459. https://doi.org/10.1111/j.1556-4029.2010.01652.x

Lin CH, Liu JH, Osterburg JW, Nicol JD (1982) Fingerprint comparison. I: similarity of fingerprints. J Forensic Sci 27(2):11484J. https://doi.org/10.1520/JFS11484J

Massey SL, Kennedy RB (2019) Bare footprint marks. In: Encyclopedia of forensic sciences, 2nd edn. Elsevier, New York. https://doi.org/10.1016/B978-0-12-382165-2.00275-0

McGraw AC (1984) Casting, another means of identification. J Forensic Sci 29(4):11791J. https://doi.org/10.1520/JFS11791J

Moenssens AA (1971) Fingerprint Techniques. Chilton Book Company, Philadelphia

Montgomery RB (1927) Classification of foot-prints. J Am Inst Criminal Law Criminol 18(1): 105–110

Moorthy TN (2019) Footprint evidence solved the mystery in a suspicious death: A rare case report. Peer Rev J Forensic Gen Sci 3(2):183–185. https://doi.org/10.32474/PRJFGS.2019.03.000156

Moorthy TN, Sulaiman SFB (2015) Individualizing characteristics of footprints in Malaysian Malays for person identification from a forensic perspective. Egypt J Forensic Sci 5(1):13–22. https://doi.org/10.1016/j.ejfs.2014.04.003

Moorthy TN, Raman N, Mustaqqim A, Mostapa B, Boominathan R (2014) Stature estimation from footprint measurements in Indian Tamils by regression analysis. Egypt J Forensic Sci 4(1):7–16. https://doi.org/10.1016/j.ejfs.2013.10.002

Mukhra R, Krishan K, Kanchan T (2018) Bare footprint metric analysis methods for comparison and identification in forensic examinations: a review of literature. J Forensic Leg Med 58:101–112. https://doi.org/10.1016/j.jflm.2018.05.006

Mukhra R, Krishan K, Nirenberg MS, Ansert E (2020) Comparative analysis of static and dynamic bare footprint dimensions in a north Indian population. Forensic Sci Int 308:110169. https://doi.org/10.1016/j.forsciint.2020.110169

NarayanMohanty M, Sikka R (2021) oReview on fingerprint-based identification system. Mater Today Proc. https://doi.org/10.1016/j.matpr.2021.03.414

Neves FB, Arnold GP, Nasir S, Wang W, Macdonald C, Christie I, Abboud RJ (2018) Establishing state of motion through two-dimensional foot and shoe print analysis: a pilot study. Forensic Sci Int 284:176–183. https://doi.org/10.1016/j.forsciint.2018.01.008

Nirenberg M, Ansert E, Campbell J, Curran M (2020) Chasing ghosts: an investigation of the ghosting phenomenon in footprints. Sci Justice 60(5):432–437. https://doi.org/10.1016/j.scijus.2020.06.006

Nithin MD, Balaraj BM, Manjunatha B, Mestri SC (2009) Study of fingerprint classification and their gender distribution among South Indian population. J Forensic Leg Med 16(8):460–463. https://doi.org/10.1016/j.jflm.2009.07.001

Oosthuizen T, Howes LM (2022) The development of forensic DNA analysis: New debates on the issue of fundamental human rights. Forensic Sci Int Gen 56:102606. https://doi.org/10.1016/j.fsigen.2021.102606

Pizzamiglio M, Fratini P, Floris T, Cappiello P, Matassa A, Festuccia N, Garofano L (2006) BPA analysis as a useful tool to reconstruct crime dynamics. Part II. Int Congress Ser 1288:538–540. https://doi.org/10.1016/j.ics.2005.10.050

Reel S, Rouse S, Vernon W, Doherty P (2012) Estimation of stature from static and dynamic footprints. Forensic Sci Int 219(1–3):283.e1–283.e5. https://doi.org/10.1016/j.forsciint.2011.11.018

Rivaldería N, Gutiérrez-Redomero E, Alonso-Rodríguez C, Dipierri JE, Martín LM (2017) Study of fingerprints in Argentina population for application in personal identification. Sci Justice 57(3): 199–208. https://doi.org/10.1016/j.scijus.2017.02.004

Robbins LM (1986) Estimating height and weight from size of footprints. J Forensic Sci 31(1): 143–152

Souza MA, Santos AS, da Silva SW, Braga JWB, Sousa MH (2022) Raman spectroscopy of fingerprints and chemometric analysis for forensic sex determination in humans. Forensic Chem 27:100395. https://doi.org/10.1016/j.forc.2021.100395

Švábová P, Caplova Z, Benus R, Chovancová M, Sona M (2022) Estimation of stature and body weight from static and dynamic footprints—forensic implications and validity of non-colouring cream method. Forensic Sci Int J 330:111105. https://doi.org/10.1016/j.forsciint.2021.111105

Vanderkolk JR (2013) Identical twins don't share fingerprints. Nature 499(7456):29. https://doi.org/10.1038/499029d

Vazquez-Zorrilla D, Millan-Alanis JM, Alvarez-Villalobos NA, Elizondo-Oma E, Guzman-Lopez-S, Vilchez-Cavazos JF, Fernandez-Rodarte BA (2020) Anatomy anatomy of foot compartments: a systematic review. Ann Anat 229:151465. https://doi.org/10.1016/j.aanat.2020.151465

Verma R, Krishan K, Rani D, Kumar A, Sharma V (2020) Stature estimation in forensic examinations using regression analysis: a likelihood ratio perspective. Forensic Sci Int Rep 2:100069. https://doi.org/10.1016/j.fsir.2020.100069

Vernon W (2006) The development and practice of forensic podiatry. J Clin Forensic Med 13(6–8):284–287. https://doi.org/10.1016/j.jcfm.2006.06.012

Ear Prints in Forensic Science: An Introduction

11

Archana Kamble, Ashish Badiye, and Neeti Kapoor

Abstract

Earmarks or ear prints are considered an additional tool for the personal identification of suspects. Due to its characteristic morphology, it can be easily differentiated from other prints like lip prints, palm prints, fingerprints, footprints, etc. Every person has a different ear morphology. Therefore, ear prints discovered at a crime scene can help identify the offender and narrow the pool of suspects. Ear prints can be observed at the crime scenes like burglary, theft, HBT, etc. Anthropometric measurements and biometric tools are widely applied to ear print classification and identification. The present chapter incorporates the classification system, feature of the ear, ear print collection methods and forensic significance of ear prints. The forensic investigator can use ear prints in conjunction with other evidence to positively identify the offender. However, additional research is necessary for partial ear print analysis.

Keywords

Ear Print Identification · Ear Print Classifications · Ear Morphology · Biometric Identification · Latent Prints

A. Kamble
Karunya Institute of Technology and Sciences, Coimbatore, India

A. Badiye · N. Kapoor (✉)
Department of Forensic Science, Government Institute of Forensic Science, Nagpur, Maharashtra, India
e-mail: neetikapoor@ifscnagpur.in

P. Shrivastava et al. (eds.), *Textbook of Forensic Science*,
https://doi.org/10.1007/978-981-99-1377-0_11

11.1 Introduction

The human face has many characteristic features like eyes, eyebrows, nose, lips, chin, cheeks, and ears. Biometric systems have been employed to identify the eye by extracting the characteristic features of the iris (Czajka 2021; Marra et al. 2018). Lip prints have also been used for personal identification (Agarwal and Raman 2022; Ahmed et al. 2018; Doroz et al. 2022; Karim and Gupta 2014; Wrobel et al. 2018). Physiognomy helps in facial reconstruction (Davy-Jow 2013; Aulsebrook et al. 1995; Tedeschi-Oliveira et al. 2016), which may serve in a personal identification of the suspect and identification of dead bodies in the cases of mass disaster, arson, and burns.

Human skin, including the facial skin, secrets sweat. Furthermore, whenever skin comes in contact with any surface, it tends to exchange its mark/print on that surface. Similarly, the external human ear forms a print whenever it comes in contact with a surface. The human ear has a typical morphology; however, the structure is highly variable from person to person and thus can be used to identify the suspect. Ear print can be observed on surfaces like doors, windows, glass, or walls in theft and burglary cases. They are also found in sexual assaults, sexual abuse, or physical assault cases. Usually, these prints are latent, i.e. not visible through the naked eye and therefore overlooked by the culprit while leaving the crime scene. However, in some situations, when a person is physically injured, we may also find bloody ear prints. Ear prints may not be as unique as fingerprints but are also not common. Human ears do have morphological features which can help in personal identification. Unknown ear prints can be compared with the sample ear print collected from the suspect as well as ear prints can also be advantageous in identifying the suspect with the CCTV footage. Ear identification can be made using surveillance camera images (Hoogstrate et al. 2001). Ear examination also aids in the personal identification of deceased individuals whose dead body has been mutilated (Krishan et al. 2019; Verma et al. 2014). The uniqueness of the ear was studied in the central Indian population with 1404 adult male and 1257 female subjects, confirming that every ear has a unique morphology and can be used for personal identification (Purkait 2016).

"Earology" is also known as "otomorphology", which means the study of the external ear. "Earology" was first reported by Johann Casper Lavater. Later, Haken Jorgensen developed a method to record the morphology of ears using measurements of ear and ear moulds collected from criminals in Denmark. Alphonse Bertillon devised a system to record different parts of the human body and described this system as "*Portrait Parle*", meaning "speaking picture". Bertillon considered the ear as the most specific part of the body. In the 1940s, Alfred Iannarelli devised a classification system for ears. Van der Lugt also attempted to classify the ears based on the different ear measurements and morphological features (Verma et al. 2014).

11.2 Application of Ear/Ear Print Examination in Forensic Science

The ear's general structures were examined in various populations (Alexander et al. 2011; Bozkır et al. 2006; Chattopadhyay and Bhatia 2009; Singh and Purkait 2009; Rubio et al. 2015). The ear lobe is used for personal identification and shows characteristic differences in identical twins (Feenstra and Van der Lugt 2000). Sex identification based on the ear dimension is also possible (Ahmed and Omer 2015; Kaushal and Kaushal 2011; Murgod et al. 2013; Sforza et al. 2009). Earmark and ear print recognition and comparison were demonstrated by researchers (Dhanda et al. 2011; Junod et al. 2012).

Ear biometrics: Biometric identification serves as a non-invasive method for identification. Dinkar and Sambyal (2012) demonstrated a method for identification using the biometric method. The external ear was studied and classified based on the weighted scoring system and pattern recognition with neural networks. Using the biometric system, ten features of the external ear could further be divided into 37 sub-features. In the study, they included 400 Indian Goans people as subjects. The photographs of both right and left ears were taken. Out of the total of 800 ear photographs, only 80 showed visual similarities, and by analysing these visually similar ears with the biometric tools, it was found that none of the individuals had identical weighted scores in different individuals as well as in the left and right ear of the same individual (Dinkar and Sambyal 2012). Mussi et al. (2021) developed an image processing algorithm to identify the auricular elements of the ears with its application in identifying and recognizing the suspects. This method was based on two parts: image contrast enhancement and identification of four anatomical regions, namely, helix, anti-helix, concha region, and tragus region (Mussi et al. 2021). Canny edge detection method has also been used for personal identification (Kavipriya et al. 2021). 2D ear imaging is used for automated human identification (Kumar and Wu 2012). Kumar and Chan (2013) have demonstrated the application of Radon transform and local curvature encoding system. Fusion of tragus with ear was also used for identification (Annapurani et al. 2015). Abaza and Bourlai (2013) demonstrated real-time human identification based on ear morphology. This method had the advantage that it could be utilized during the day as well as night time. The complete system was based upon two steps: the first step was to collect the thermal imprints of the human skin using the high-definition mid-wave IR camera, and in the second step, a fully automated ear recognition system was developed (Abaza and Bourlai 2013).

11.3 Ear Morphology

In order to compare ear prints/marks or examine the ear through photographs or videos, the examiner needs to understand various parts of the ear clearly. The ear has different parts; the external ear is called the pinna or auricle. The external ear comprises skin, cartilage, connective tissues, and ligaments (Krishan and Kanchan 2015) (Fig. 11.1).

Various parts of the ear are discussed below (Tables 11.1 and 11.2):

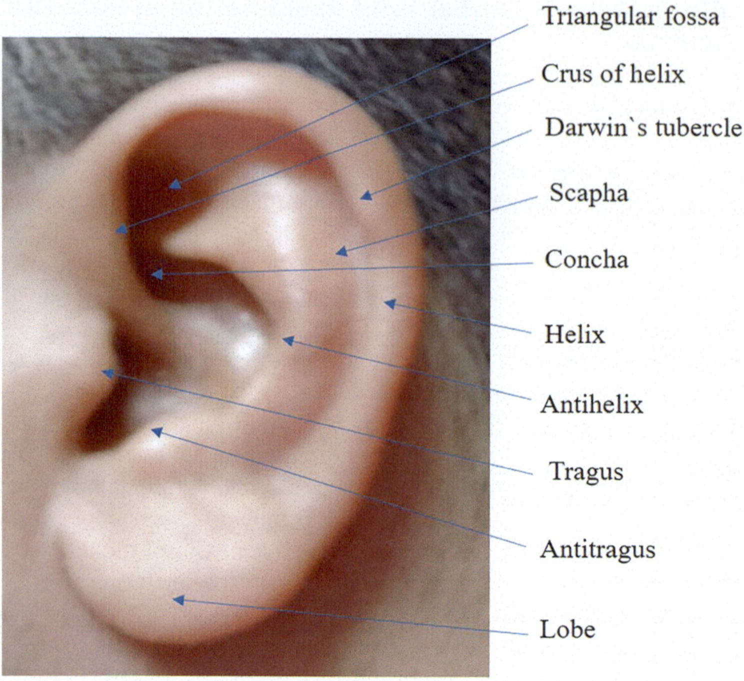

Fig. 11.1 General anatomy of the external ear

Table 11.1 Various parts of the external ear with their description (https://elementsofmorphology.nih.gov/anatomy-ear.shtml)

Sr. No.	Name of part of the ear	Description
1.	Helix	The outer rim of the ear forms the "helix". Helix can be divided into three parts: (1) ascending helix, (2) superior helix, and (3) descending helix
2.	Crus of Helix	The anteroinferior ascending helix's continuation, which protrudes posteriorly into the concha cavity over the external auditory meatus
3.	Scapha	The channel running through the helix and anti-helix
4.	Tragus	A posterior, slightly inferior, protrusion on the inner side of the external ear of skin-covered cartilage, anterior to the auditory meatus
5.	Concha	The fossa bounded by the tragus, incisura, antitragus, anti-helix, inferior crus of the anti-helix, and root of the helix, into which opens the external auditory canal
6.	Antitragus	The cartilaginous protrusion between the incisura and the anti-helix's origin that protrudes anterosuperiorly
7.	Anti-helix	The separation of the concha, triangular fossa, and scapha from the antitragus results in the creation of a curving cartilaginous ridge in the Y-shape is the anti-helix
8.	Triangular fossa	The concavity enclosed by the ascending part of the helix and the superior and inferior crura of the anti-helix
9.	Lobe/lobule of auricle	Lobe is present at the bottom of the external ear. It is the soft, fleshy structure lacking firmness as compared to the rest of the auricle

Table 11.2 Somatoscopic characteristics describing the form of the external ear (Purkait 2015)

Sr. No.	Features	Characteristics	Classification
1.	External ear	Shape	Triangular
			Round
			Oval
			Rectangular
2.	Darwin's tubercle	Shape	Absent
			Nodosity
			Enlargement
			Projection
			Tubercle
3.	Helical fold	Form	Flat
			Curved
			Normally rolled
			Wide covering scapha
		Shape of upper helix	Upper directed angle
			Obtuse medial angle
			Obtuse lateral angle
			Obtuse acute angle
			Double right angle
			Obtuse angle
			Circular
4.	Tragus	Shape	Long
			Round
			Knob shaped
5.	Antitragus	Shape	Prominent
			Medium
			Flat
6.	Lobule	Shape	Tongue
			Triangular
			Rectangular
			Arched
			Round
		Attachment to cheek	Attached
			Partially attached
			Free
7.	Concha	Shape	Narrow
			Proportionate
			Broad
8.	Anti-helix concha border	Shape	Straight
			Curved
			Round
			Laterally protruding

11.4 Classification of Ear Based on the Shape of the Auricle

The shape of the auricle can be oval, round, rectangular, or triangular.

1. Oval ear: The length of the ear is more than its width. Furthermore, the width is observed to be maximum at the centre.
2. Round ear: The ear's length and width are nearly the same, with a rounded top and bottom.
3. Rectangular ear: The length of the ear is more as compared to the width, but it shows a rectangular top and bottom, i.e. the width of the ear is uniform throughout the top, middle, and bottom.
4. Triangular ear: The length of the ear is more than its width, and the width is maximum at the rounded top (Kaushal and Kaushal 2011).

Measurement of the ear: Length—The length of the ear is measured as a distance between the uppermost point of the helix and lowermost point of the ear lobe parallel to the ear base (the base attached to the head); Width—The width of the ear is measured as a distance between the base of the ear and the outermost part of helix, which is perpendicular to the ear base (Kaushal and Kaushal 2011).

11.5 Iannarelli System of Ear Classification

Alfred Iannarelli is considered a pioneer in using ear measurements for personal identification. In 1949, he developed a forensic method for personal identification based upon the ear examination. He collected a large number of ear images and then divided each image into 12 different parts and developed a database which included more than 10,000 ear images. However, Iannarelli's method could only be applied to a population of less than 16.7 million (4^{12}).

The Iannarelli system is based upon 12 measurements of the ear (Bhanu and Chen 2008). Iannarelli used photographs to classify ears based on these measurements. To take the measurements of the ear, a transparent compass with eight spokes, each separated by 45° angles, is placed over the image of the ear. The compass is placed so that the first reference line should touch the crux of helix at the top and the innermost point of the tragus at the bottom. In the next step, the second reference line is focused on meeting the concha from top to bottom. Once both reference lines are placed, the ear measurements are noted.

11.6 Polish Otoscopic Identification System

Otoscopy involves classifying and examining ear auricle print for human identification. Habil and Kasprzak (2005) have briefly described the Polish otoscopic identification system in three levels.

Level I: Type of Ear Auricle	Level II: General Identification Characteristics	Level III: Detailed Identification Characteristics
1. Oval type 2. Round type 3. Triangular type 4. Rhomboidal type 5. Polygonal type	These characteristics are observed and compared with a catalogue which consists of 1- 24 fields.	1. Scars 2. Marks of ear piercing 3. Elongated pierced hole due to heavy jewellery 4. Traces of worn jewellery 5. Creases

This method is very effective and has been included in Poland's forensic expert training curriculum (Habil and Kasprzak 2005). The Polish methodology described six steps for ear print examination.

Step 1: Assessment of the print recovered from the crime scene and the print collected from the suspect to check the suitability of the prints for identification.

Step 2: Elimination of false suspects. The suspect prints are eliminated based on the ear auricle type and the ear print's measurement.

Step 3: Coding of characteristics. If the comparative prints collected from the suspects have not been excluded in steps 1 and 2, then the general characteristics of the prints are examined on the evidential and comparative prints. To make this step user-friendly, a catalogue has different fields from 1 to 24. Any characteristic feature present in the evidential print but absent in the comparative prints can be excluded.

Step 4: Contour technique. In this step, a clean, transparent sheet is placed on the evidential print, and the contour of the print is traced with dotted lines. Then this transparent sheet is placed over the print under comparison, and the dotted lines are matched.

Step 5: Determination of common identification characteristics. In this step, the photographs of the evidential and comparative prints are compared using the 24 fields. Similar characteristics observed in different areas of both prints are highlighted in photographs. 10–15 details are usually marked.

Step 6: The final step includes the analysis of results with a record of course examination and statistical evaluations. Furthermore, a conclusion is formulated based on the results, and an expert report is written.

11.7 Development and Collection of Latent Ear Prints from Crime Scene

The following methods can be used to develop ear prints:

1. Powder method

   Latent ear prints can be found on surfaces like door knobs, tables, screens of mobile phones, etc. Such prints can be developed using fingerprint powder. If the surface is light-coloured, then the examiner shall use a dark-coloured powder, whereas when the suspected prints are likely to be present on the darker or multi-coloured surface, they must use white powder/light-coloured powder. Excess powder is removed with the help of an ostrich feather brush and fixed with cellophane tape. When the whole article bearing the print cannot be collected, the print is lifted using cellophane tape.

2. Ninhydrin method
   It is a chemical method that involves the application of a chemical reagent over the surface to develop the latent print. To prepare the reagent, 1 g of ninhydrin is dissolved in 100 ml acetone, and 1 ml of acetic acid is added to this solution. This reagent can be sprayed or applied using a brush over the surface. The article bearing the print may be heated in an oven at 60 °C for 10 min to increase the reaction rate and develop the prints faster. Purple-coloured prints are observed. This method is more suitable for porous surfaces.
3. Iodine fuming method
   The article bearing the ear prints is placed in the fuming iodine chamber for 4–5 min to develop the latent prints. However, the prints developed by iodine fuming are temporary and shall be fixed using cellophane tape.

With these methods, the ear prints can be developed and compared with the ear print samples collected from the suspects. The procedure to collect the ear print from suspects is given below:

1. Take a photograph of the ear.
2. Take a thermographic picture of the ear with the help of a thermal camera.
3. The earmark/ear print is collected by pressing the ear against a flat glass surface. Several prints shall be collected at varying pressure. The prints are then developed with fingerprint powder and fixed by cellophane tape (Dhanda et al. 2011).

The prints are then examined for the presence of various morphological characteristics of ear. These features can be used for comparison. Only clear and readable prints are considered for positive identification; else, it is deemed inconclusive (Fig. 11.2).

11.8 Forensic Significance of Ear Print

The human external ear has many characteristic features. All individuals, including the monozygotic twins, show variation in ear morphology. Even the left and right ears of the same person are not identical; thus, ear prints are unique and can be used for personal identification. Ear prints are formed due to the deposition of sweat present on the skin; thus, they are typically not visible by the naked eye and have a high probability of being overlooked by the perpetrator while leaving the crime scene. Developed latent prints help in the exclusion of a large number of suspects. The presence of an ear print of a suspect at the crime scene links the suspect to the

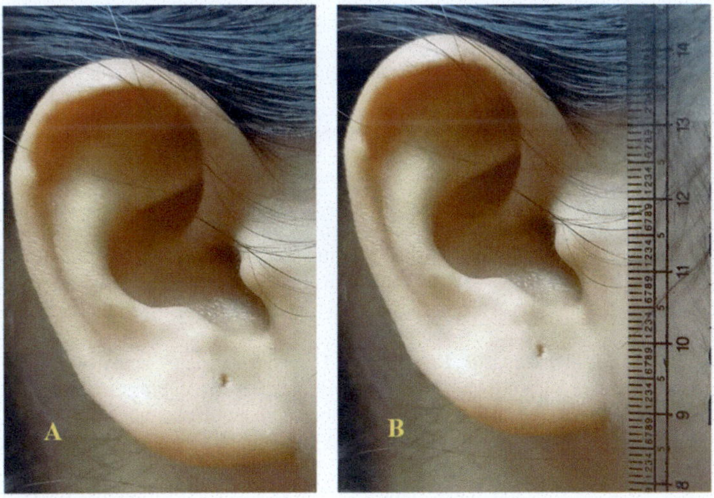

Fig. 11.2 Photograph of ear without scale (**a**) and with scale (**b**)

crime scene; thus, such print should be carefully handled and preserved. Ear prints can be compared with the available database to identify the suspect when there is no suspect. The ear is used to identify people in cases like mass disasters, arson, drowning, etc. A mutilated body can also be identified with the help of an ear examination. Studies conducted on the Indian population reveal that the ears of the male are considerably more significant than the females. The women also wear artefacts like earrings, tops, danglers, loops, etc. These features can also be used for sex identification. Biometric systems have wide applications in the ear, earmark, and ear print examination. Various biometric systems record the ear's image, which can be used to compare the evidential ear print. Recent advancement in research also facilitates real-time image analysis from CCTV. Thermal image analysis helps analyse and compare the prints with real samples.

11.9 Conclusion

In conclusion, the chapter has provided a brief overview of the application of ear/ear print examination in forensic science. The discussion explored various aspects, including the significance of ear prints as forensic evidence, the morphological characteristics of ears, and the classification systems used to categorize ears based on auricle shape. The Iannarelli and Polish Otoscopic Identification systems were examined as prominent classification methodologies. Additionally, the chapter addressed the development and collection of latent ear prints from crime scenes, emphasizing the forensic value of such evidence. This chapter sheds light on the diverse aspects surrounding the application of ear prints in forensic investigations.

References

Abaza A, Bourlai T (2013) On ear-based human identification in the mid-wave infrared spectrum. Image Vis Comput 31(9):640–648. https://doi.org/10.1016/j.imavis.2013.06.001

Agarwal V, Raman R (2022) Chapter 4 - A cognitive system for lip identification using convolution neural networks. In: Zhang Y-D, Sangaiah AK (eds) Cognitive data science in sustainable computing. Academic, London, pp 83–99. https://doi.org/10.1016/B978-0-12-824410-4.00013-1

Ahmed AA, Omer N (2015) Estimation of sex from the anthropometric ear measurements of a Sudanese population. Leg Med 17(5):313–319. https://doi.org/10.1016/j.legalmed.2015.03.002

Ahmed SA, Salem HE, Fawzy MM (2018) Forensic dissection of lip print as an investigative tool in a mixed Egyptian population. Alexandria J Med 54(3):235–239. https://doi.org/10.1016/j.ajme.2017.08.002

Alexander KS, Stott DJ, Sivakumar B, Kang N (2011) A morphometric study of the human ear. J Plast Reconstr Aesthet Surg 64(1):41–47. https://doi.org/10.1016/j.bjps.2010.04.005

Annapurani K, Sadiq MAK, Malathy C (2015) Fusion of shape of the ear and tragus – a unique feature extraction method for ear authentication system. Expert Syst Appl 42(1):649–656. https://doi.org/10.1016/j.eswa.2014.08.009

Aulsebrook WA, İşcan MY, Slabbert JH, Becker P (1995) Superimposition and reconstruction in forensic facial identification: a survey. Forensic Sci Int 75(2):101–120. https://doi.org/10.1016/0379-0738(95)01770-4

Bhanu B, Chen H (2008) Ear Detection and Recognition in 2D and 3D BT. In: Human Ear Recognition by Computer. (Eds.) Springer London. pp. 11–19. https://doi.org/10.1007/978-1-84800-129-9_2

Bozkır MG, Karakaş P, Yavuz M, Dere F (2006) Morphometry of the external ear in our adult population. Aesthetic Plast Surg 30(1):81–85. https://doi.org/10.1007/s00266-005-6095-1

Chattopadhyay PK, Bhatia S (2009) Morphological examination of ear: a study of an Indian population. Leg Med 11(suppl 1):S190–S193. https://doi.org/10.1016/j.legalmed.2009.02.057

Czajka A (2021) Is that eye dead or alive? Detecting new iris biometrics attacks. Biometric Technol Today 2021(5):9–12. https://doi.org/10.1016/S0969-4765(21)00060-6

Davy-Jow S (2013) The devil is in the details: a synthesis of psychology of facial perception and its applications in forensic facial reconstruction. Sci Justice 53(2):230–235. https://doi.org/10.1016/j.scijus.2013.01.004

Dhanda V, Badhan JS, Garg RK (2011) Studies on the development of latent ear prints and their significance in personal identification. Prob Forensic Sci LXXXVIII:285–295

Dinkar AD, Sambyal SS (2012) Person identification in Ethnic Indian Goans using ear biometrics and neural networks. Forensic Sci Int 223(1):373.e1–373.e13. https://doi.org/10.1016/j.forsciint.2012.08.032

Doroz R, Wrobel K, Orczyk T, Porwik P, Cholewa M (2022) Multidimensional nearest neighbors classification based system for incomplete lip print identification. Expert Syst Appl 202:117137. https://doi.org/10.1016/j.eswa.2022.117137

Feenstra L, Van der Lugt C (2000) Personal identification from the ear lobe. Nederlands Tijdschrift Voor Keel- Neus- Oorheelkunde 6(2):53–55

Habil P, Kasprzak J (2005) Forensic Otoscopy – New Method of Human Identification. Jurisprudencija 66(58):106–109

Hoogstrate AJ, Van Den Heuvel H, Huyben E (2001) Ear identification based on surveillance camera images. Sci Justice 41(3):167–172

Junod S, Pasquier J, Champod C (2012) The development of an automatic recognition system for earmark and earprint comparisons. Forensic Sci Int 222(1–3):170–178

Karim B, Gupta D (2014) Cheiloscopy and blood groups: aid in forensic identification. Saudi Dent J 26(4):176–180. https://doi.org/10.1016/j.sdentj.2014.05.005

Kaushal N, Kaushal P (2011) Human earprints: a review. J Biom Biostat 2(5). https://doi.org/10.4172/2155-6180.1000129

Kavipriya P, Ebenezar Jebarani MR, Vino T, Jegan G (2021) Ear biometric for personal identification using canny edge detection algorithm and contour tracking method. Mater Today Proc. https://doi.org/10.1016/j.matpr.2021.03.351

Krishan K, Kanchan T (2015) Identification: Prints - Ear. In Encyclopedia of Forensic and Legal Medicine: Second Edition (pp. 74–80). Elsevier Inc. https://doi.org/10.1016/B978-0-12-800034-2.00210-X

Krishan K, Kanchan T, Thakur S (2019) A study of morphological variations of the human ear for its applications in personal identification. Egypt J Forensic Sci 9(1):6. https://doi.org/10.1186/s41935-019-0111-0

Kumar A, Chan T-ST (2013) Robust ear identification using sparse representation of local texture descriptors. Pattern Recogn 46(1):73–85. https://doi.org/10.1016/j.patcog.2012.06.020

Kumar A, Wu C (2012) Automated human identification using ear imaging. Pattern Recogn 45(3): 956–968. https://doi.org/10.1016/j.patcog.2011.06.005

Marra F, Poggi G, Sansone C, Verdoliva L (2018) A deep learning approach for iris sensor model identification. Pattern Recogn Lett 113:46–53. https://doi.org/10.1016/j.patrec.2017.04.010

Murgod V, Angadi P, Hallikerimath S (2013) Anthropometric study of the external ear and its applicability in sex identification: assessed in an Indian sample. Aust J Forensic Sci 41(4): 431–444

Mussi E, Servi M, Facchini F, Furferi R, Governi L, Volpe Y (2021) A novel ear elements segmentation algorithm on depth map images. Comput Biol Med 129:104157. https://doi.org/10.1016/j.compbiomed.2020.104157

Purkait R (2015) Application of external ear in personal identification: a somatoscopic study in families. Ann Forensic Res Anal 2:9

Purkait R (2016) External ear: an analysis of its uniqueness. Egypt J Forensic Sci 6(2):99–107. https://doi.org/10.1016/j.ejfs.2016.03.002

Rubio O, Galera V, Alonso MC (2015) Anthropological study of ear tubercles in a Spanish sample. Homo 66(4):343–356. https://doi.org/10.1016/j.jchb.2015.02.005

Sforza C, Grandi G, Binelli M, Tommasi DG, Rosati R, Ferrario VF (2009) Age- and sex-related changes in the normal human ear. Forensic Sci Int 187(1):110.e1–110.e7. https://doi.org/10.1016/j.forsciint.2009.02.019

Singh P, Purkait R (2009) Observations of external ear—an Indian study. Homo 60(5):461–472. https://doi.org/10.1016/j.jchb.2009.08.002

Tedeschi-Oliveira SV, Beaini TL, Melani RFH (2016) Forensic facial reconstruction: nasal projection in Brazilian adults. Forensic Sci Int 266:123–129. https://doi.org/10.1016/j.forsciint.2016.05.004

Verma K, Joshi B, Vikas K (2014) Morphological variation of ear for individual identification in forensic cases: a study of an Indian population. Res J Forensic Sci 2(1):1–8. http://www.isca.in/FORENSIC_SCI/Archive/v2/i1/1.ISCA-RJFS-2013-010.php

Wrobel K, Doroz R, Porwik P, Bernas M (2018) Personal identification utilizing lip print furrow based patterns. A new approach. Pattern Recogn 81:585–600. https://doi.org/10.1016/j.patcog.2018.04.030

An Introduction to Questioned Documents 12

Samiksha Landge, Rajendraprasad Pawar, Rasika Kakad, Ashish Badiye, and Neeti Kapoor

Abstract

Documents are frequently discovered at crime scenes and serve as crucial evidence. They convey information through letters, symbols, figures, or other methods. This chapter provides an overview of various aspects related to documents, including handwriting analysis, forgery detection, identification of alterations and obliterations, and more. The chapter commences with an exploration of unique identifiers of individuals through their handwriting characteristics, such as letter formations, spacing, slant, pressure, and rhythm. Furthermore, the chapter scrutinizes the various alterations and obliterations that are frequently encountered in questioned documents. It highlights contemporary techniques utilized to remove or modify content, such as erasures, chemical treatments, and overwriting. The chapter also covers various methods for detecting these alterations, such as utilizing different light sources, electrostatic detection, infrared imaging, and more.

Keywords

Class characteristics · Questioned document · Forgery · Handwriting · Individual characteristics

S. Landge
GH Raisoni University, Saikheda, Madhya Pradesh, India

R. Pawar
Institute of Excellence in Higher Education, Bhopal, Madhya Pradesh, India

R. Kakad · A. Badiye · N. Kapoor (✉)
Department of Forensic Science, Government Institute of Forensic Science, Nagpur, Maharashtra, India
e-mail: neetikapoor@ifscnagpur.in

P. Shrivastava et al. (eds.), *Textbook of Forensic Science*,
https://doi.org/10.1007/978-981-99-1377-0_12

12.1 Introduction

Questioned documents play a vital role in forensic investigations, legal proceedings, and historical research, as they often hold critical information that can either support or challenge the authenticity, authorship, or integrity of various types of documents. This chapter serves as a foundational guide, introducing the fundamental concepts, techniques, and methodologies used in the examination of questioned documents. From handwriting analysis and forgery detection to ink analysis and paper examination, this chapter explores the wide range of disciplines and practices involved in unraveling the secrets hidden within documents. Whether investigating fraudulent documents, deciphering mysterious writings, or determining the origin of a document, the knowledge and skills presented in this chapter are essential tools for forensic document examiners and anyone intrigued by the intricacies of uncovering the truth concealed within the written word.

The term "Document" is defined in the Indian Evidence Act, 1872 (IEA) and the Indian Penal Code, 1860 (IPC). According to **Section 3 of IEA and Section 29 of IPC** —"*Document means any matter expressed or described upon any substance by means of letters, figures or marks or by more than one of those means, indented to be used or which may be used for purpose or recording that matter*" (Indian Evidence Act 1872), (Indian Penal Code 1860).

The documents found at crime scenes or encountered in various contexts can be categorized based on their purpose and nature as historical documents, administrative documents, educational documents, financial documents, letters, legal documents, electronic documents and security documents. Historical documents provide glimpses into the past, shedding light on significant events and people. Administrative documents serve as records for organizational or governmental purposes, documenting transactions, decisions, and policies. Educational documents encompass a wide range of materials used for teaching and learning, such as textbooks, worksheets, and academic certificates. Financial documents are crucial for managing and tracking monetary transactions and assets. Letters, a form of personal correspondence, hold sentimental and informational value, capturing individual thoughts and emotions. Legal documents are legally binding papers that establish rights, obligations, and agreements. Electronic documents, in today's digital age, encompass various digital file formats and electronic records stored on computers or devices. Lastly, security documents are designed with specific security features to prevent counterfeiting or tampering.

While handwriting is commonly understood as the act of writing with one's hand, it goes beyond mere manual dexterity. Handwriting is often referred to as the mind writing or the brain writing as it reflects the subconscious mind at work. When individuals write, their subconscious thoughts, attitudes, and personality traits are manifested through their handwriting. Each letter or symbol impression made on a writing surface carries meaning in a particular language, forming what we know as handwriting (Lindblom and Jan 2006). In essence, handwriting can be considered a visible form of speech or a talking paper, as it encapsulates thousands of unique characteristics that combine to create a highly personal and individualistic form of expression (Bunker 1979).

12.2 Principles of Handwriting and Signature

1. A person's handwriting also follows one of the principles of forensic science: the **principle of individuality**. No two people in this world can write precisely alike. This is because handwriting is a subconscious act, and every individual attains different training in learning how to write. Writing also differs with mental and emotional changes and the experiences in life, hence the writing of a person has a slight variation with time which cannot be copied because no other person can experience the same things as the original writer.
2. Handwriting and signatures show natural variations. The same word or a signature cannot be written precisely alike, even when written one after another by the same person; there will be a slight variation. These natural variations are seen

because of fatigue, age, illness, drugs or alcohol, writing position, emotional disturbances, etc. These characteristics of natural variation allow the examiner to distinguish between the forges and genuine writing.
3. A person can be identified by analysing the handwriting. Some people may show similarities in handwriting due to similar instruction or influences, closer examination reveals fundamental differences that allow for identification.
4. Handwriting changes along with time and skill because of the influences. External factors and personal development can contribute to an individual's unique writing style.
5. During the time of forgery, the forger tries to imitate those characteristics of the handwriting which are more appealing and ignores other features which are less conspicuous and difficult to copy. Successful imitation requires matching the original writer's skill and speed.
6. Every person's writing undergoes gradual life changes; however, the changes are prolonged and may not be discernible in most cases.
7. A writer cannot surpass his writing skill and ability unless he makes strenuous efforts and practice.
8. A person cannot adopt different writing styles at different times, as to change one's regular style of writing is an exceedingly difficult task (Huber and Headrick 1999; Sharma 2014; Koppenhaver 2007).

12.3 Characteristics

The handwriting of an individual possesses distinct characteristics that contribute to their uniqueness. These characteristics can be categorised as class and individual, with a primary focus on how a person writes. While characteristics may be shared by multiple individuals, over time, these learned traits become personalized and serve as distinguishing elements in one's writing style. These modifications and idiosyncrasies in the writing of the individual aid in identifying the original author of the handwritten document. Some of the class and individual characteristics are as follows:

12.3.1 Class Characteristics

Class characteristics can be particularly compelling in forensic document examination because they provide evidence of similarities within a defined group. These shared features can help establish a commonality among individuals who have received similar education or have been influenced by the same cultural or linguistic factors. When these class characteristics are identified in a questioned document, it can provide supporting evidence for attributing the document to a specific group or category. They contribute to the overall analysis and evaluation of a document's authenticity and can assist forensic document examiners in narrowing down potential sources or authors.

Style: The handwriting style primarily depends upon the training given to the individual during the learning days. The style generally depends upon the early teaching and practice, which is common in a group of people. With time and experience in writing, the individual adapts his writing style. The style may be creative or simple. The figures or symbols used by the individual can be round, angular or a mixture of both. Typical stylistic features found in handwriting are margins, date format, length of sentence, headings and subheadings, grammar, punctuations, etc. (Huber and Headrick 1999; Sharma 2014; Koppenhaver 2007; Choudhary and Vaya 2016).

Movement: To produce writing on a surface, the writer uses his fingers, arms, wrist or a combination of these to produce the necessary movements. These movements to produce writing are either the writer uses his fingers, arms, wrist or a combination of these. These movements are called writing movements or movements of writing. Different movements or combinations also show different features in writing, such as speed and pictorial effect. Speed of writing, the rhythm of writing, slant, etc., are also related to the movement of writing (Huber and Headrick 1999; Sharma 2014; Koppenhaver 2007; Ellen 2006).

Pen position: The pen position refers to the way a person holds and grips the writing instrument, which can leave distinct marks on the page. The pen position can provide valuable insights into a writer's habits, style, and overall technique. Different individuals may hold the pen in various ways, such as using a tripod grip, an overhand grip, or an underhand grip. These variations in pen position can result in observable differences in letter formations, slant, spacing, and overall writing style. The writing instrument is usually held at an angle between 15 and 90°, and commonly, people are found to hold it at 60°. Because of the angle at which the it is held, the pressure applied also differs, and the wear and tear are also different for different individuals (Sharma 2014; Koppenhaver 2007).

Line quality: Line quality determines the skill of a person when writing. A person with higher skills and who frequently writes has smooth and uniform writing. Line quality also helps in identifying the speed of writing. On the other hand, individuals with poor line quality often display slower writing speed, which can be indicative when assessing the authenticity of a document. The line quality can also help identify if the person is weak (physical condition), illiterate, writing in an unnatural position, etc., and all these things are observed in the person exhibiting poor line quality while writing (Lindblom and Jan 2006; Sharma 2014; Koppenhaver 2007; Koppenhaver 2002; Nickell 2014). These observations can be valuable in the analysis of handwriting and contribute to determining the genuineness of a document or identifying potential discrepancies. Therefore, line quality serves as an important characteristic in assessing the skill, speed, and potential authenticity of a person's writing.

Rhythm: To write rhythmically, a person should be highly skilled. The skill is acquired by writing experience and other factors like physical, emotional and intellectual personality. When observed, poor rhythm can be a potential indicator of the handwriting being copied or forged. A person with poor skill cannot copy the rhythm and skill of an experienced writer and thus may help narrow down the suspect pool. Other factors need to be considered in conjunction with rhythm to make a conclusive determination. Furthermore, it is subjective to assume that a person with poor skill cannot copy the rhythm and skill of an experienced writer. Some individuals may be adept at mimicking or imitating handwriting styles, regardless of their own level of skill. Therefore, solely relying on rhythm as a determining factor may not be sufficient in identifying a suspect. Rhythm in writing may also provide an idea about an individual's mental and physical makeup (Lindblom and Jan 2006; Huber and Headrick 1999; Koppenhaver 2007; Ellen 2006; Morris 2020). Drawing concrete conclusions about someone's personality solely based on handwriting rhythm is not scientifically supported and can lead to unreliable assessments. It is imperative to follow a caution approach.

Tremors: Tremors in the handwriting are seen because of certain factors like sickness, illiteracy and even old age. Tremors are also seen in writing when a person is suffering from any kind of disease and does have an ability to write, like Parkinson's disease. When someone attempts forgery, they may intentionally incorporate these tremors into their writing, but they often place them incorrectly or in a manner that does not align with the natural charactericties of the original writer's tremors. This discrepancy can raise suspicions and indicate the fraudulent nature of the document (Lindblom and Jan 2006; Sharma 2014; Koppenhaver 2007; Hilton 1993). It is important to consider that tremors alone may not definitively prove forgery, as some individuals may naturally have slight tremors or variations in their handwriting that are not related to fraudulent intent. However, when combined with other handwriting inconsistencies and discrepancies, the presence of unnatural or inaccurately placed tremors can contribute to the assessment of a document's authenticity.

Speed: Speed is one of the characteristics which is examined in handwriting analysis. The speed of the writer differs because of various factors. Some writers have a fast thought process or are naturally impatient, resulting in faster writing. On the other hand, slow writers tend to write in a more systematic and legible manner. Fast writing individuals usually have smooth lines indicating a good line quality, while the slow writers may show tremors in their writing and have poor line quality, such as inconsistencies or shakiness (Huber and Headrick 1999; Koppenhaver 2007; Morris 2020).

Size: The size of the person's writing can vary significantly from one individual to another. It is seen that children usually write with larger strokes, and as they grow older and gain more control over their motor skills, the size of the writing gradually decreases, becoming smaller and more refined compared to their earlier writing. Variations in the size of writing are also observed based on different conditions (Lindblom and Jan 2006; Koppenhaver 2007; Morris 2020). Factors such as the writing instrument used, the writing surface, the individual's mood or state of mind, and even physical or environmental conditions can influence the size of handwriting. For example, someone may write larger when using a marker on a whiteboard compared to writing with a pen on paper.

12.3.2 Individual Characteristics

Individual characteristics of the handwriting are those which identify the author of the handwritten document. Some of the characteristics examined are as follows:

Pen pressure: The force the writer applies upon the pen or any other writing instrument on the writing surface (paper) is referred to as the pen pressure. The pressure applied is also different for every individual. The pressure has also been classified as heavy, medium, light and graduated. Pressure applied can also give insight into other aspects like speed, skill and sometimes even the writer's literacy (Lindblom and Jan 2006; Sharma 2014; Morris 2020).

Shading: Shading is observed in the writing of skilled writers and comes out naturally because of the practice. The shading is seen mainly on the upper and lower zone letters, i.e. there is a difference between the widths of these strokes. Shading also depends upon how the pen was held and at what angle (Lindblom and Jan 2006; Huber and Headrick 1999). Different pen grips and angles can produce varying levels of shading, further contributing to the uniqueness of the handwriting. The shading effect adds depth and dimension to the handwriting, making it visually appealing and distinctive.

Pen pause: Pen pause can be defined as the frequency at which a writer stops or pauses while writing. Experienced and skilled writers usually have a smooth and continuous flow in their writing, without noticeable pauses. However, occasional pauses may occur when they are distracted, or have a particular habit of pausing at specific places in their writing. When forgery is attempted, the forger may unknowingly replicate the pen pause patterns of the original writer. This becomes evident upon close examination, as the forgery will exhibit pauses and hesitations that are inconsistent with the genuine writing style. One common mistake made by forgers is the presence of a pen pause at the beginning stroke, which is not observed in the authentic writing of the original writer (Sharma 2014).

Pen lifts: The number of times a writer lifts the pen while writing is known as pen lifts. Pen lifts can be seen in the writing at specific locations and varied frequency. For some writers, pen lifts can be seen in a continuous rhythmic fashion or at only some specific places, such as when transitioning between letters or words. (Lindblom and Jan 2006; Sharma 2014). The specific pen lift patterns are often unique to each individual and can serve as a distinguishing characteristic in the identification of a particular writer.

Starting and ending strokes: A skilled writer's starting and ending strokes are smooth, and no hesitation marks are seen. When the original writer writes, the width of these starting and ending strokes is thin. However, when writing is forged, these initial and ending strokes show hesitation marks or tremors, and the width tends to be thicker, as the forger may exert more pressure or struggle to replicate the natural finesse of the genuine writer. In forgery, these strokes are more drawn rather than written (Lindblom and Jan 2006; Huber and Headrick 1999; Sharma 2014; Koppenhaver 2007; Morris 2020). It is important for forensic document examiners to carefully examine the quality, smoothness, and width of the starting and ending strokes to identify potential signs of forgery.

Spacing: Spacing is considered one of the important characteristics while examining a handwriting document. Spacing refers to the gaps observed between two words, between two lines and the margins on the right and left sides of the page. Each individual has their own unique spacing pattern in their writing, making it a valuable factor for identification. This factor while writing is challenging to forge because the forger will subconsciously write with the spacing he is habitual to, which can differ from those of the original writer (Lindblom and Jan 2006; Sharma 2014; Koppenhaver 2007; Morris 2020).

Alignment: While writing on a blank sheet of paper with no ruled lines, the writer assumes an imaginary baseline and writes according to it. This is a highly characteristic feature. Alignment is most commonly observed in three main directions: ascending or upward direction, descending or downward direction or a straight line (Huber and Headrick 1999; Sharma 2014; Koppenhaver 2007). Some writers tend to have a natural inclination to write with an upward slant, while others may have a downward slant or prefer to write in a straight and level manner.

Hesitations: Hesitation marks are also examined in the handwriting. Hesitation marks are observed in various parts of the writing, including the starting and ending strokes, vertical lines, curvatures, and loops. These marks occur due to the writer's hesitation or uncertainty while replicating the original author's style as closely as possible (Sharma 2014; Koppenhaver 2007). During forgery attempts, the forger often tries to mimic the characteristics of the original writer's handwriting. However, the subconscious fear of detection or the lack of familiarity with the author's natural writing tendencies can result in hesitation marks. These marks may manifest as slight pauses, tremors, or irregularities in the strokes, indicating the forger's struggle to reproduce the writing accurately.

Retouching: Retouching in handwriting refers to the act of making corrections or alterations to letters or words while writing. Retouching while writing is done more commonly when the pen does not work correctly and a letter or word is rewritten. This retouching is a natural occurrence and is not habitual for most writers. However, when forgery is done, the forger misunderstand it as deliberate shading technique and applies retouching while writing in order to imitate the original author. Another aspect is that the forger may be in a habit of lifting the pen while writing or pausing the pen while writing; retouching is done to hide this (Huber and Headrick 1999; Koppenhaver 2007; Sharma 2014).

Placings: Every individual has a habit of placing the dot over an "i" or crossover "t" differently; even the punctuation marks used by an individual differs. The placement of the dot or cross can vary in terms of its shape, size, and position. Some may have a habit of placing a circle or dot or dash over "i" also with a different location like some may place it in the right or left or up direction, which is difficult to copy throughout the document. It is also said that the placing pattern may also change even in genuine writing (Sharma 2014; Koppenhaver 2007). These placement patterns can be difficult to replicate consistently throughout a document, making it challenging for forgers to imitate. It's important to note that even in genuine writing, the placing pattern may change to some extent. Factors such as writing speed, context, and personal variations can influence the precise placement of these elements. This further reinforces the individuality of a person's handwriting and adds to the uniqueness of their writing style.

Embellishments: Embellishments in handwriting refer to decorative or ornamental elements that skilled writers incorporate into their writing. Embellishments are seen in the writing of skilled writers. These are mainly found in the starting and ending strokes, but skilled writers may show embellishments throughout the writing at specific locations or with specific letters (Sharma 2014; Koppenhaver 2007). These embellishments can take various forms, such as loops, curls, swirls, or other decorative additions that enhance the overall aesthetic appeal of the writing. Embellishments are considered a characteristic feature of skilled writers, as they demonstrate a level of control, creativity, and attention to detail in their handwriting. These decorative elements are typically consistent and show a certain level of artistry.

12.4 Factors Affecting the Handwriting

Educational background, language, employment, type of writing materials, writing surfaces and writing instruments used, support, posture, time, emotions, mental abnormalities, mood, intoxication, drugs and medication, intake of abusive substances like alcohol, cocaine, heroin etc., diseases and disorders, neurological abnormalities, surroundings, noise, etc., are some of the factors which directly or indirectly affects the handwriting of an individual. Apart from these factors, some mechanical factors such as intensity of light, cold, heat and accidental strokes significantly affect handwriting. The handedness of the writer, whether right handed or left handed, is also considered one of the important factors affecting the writer's handwriting (Ellen 2006; Richard 2007; Rao and Maithil 2013).

- *Educational background*: The level of education and training received can have an impact on handwriting style and legibility.
- *Language*: Different languages may have unique writing systems and letterforms that can influence handwriting characteristics.
- *Employment*: The nature of a person's occupation or profession may influence their handwriting due to specific writing demands or habits associated with their work.
- *Writing materials, surfaces, and instruments*: The type of pens, pencils, paper, or digital devices used for writing can affect the handwriting style and quality.
- *Support and posture*: The stability and support provided to the writer while writing, as well as their posture, can impact the handwriting.
- *Time*: The speed and efficiency with which a person writes may vary depending on the time available or the urgency of the task.

- *Emotions, mood, and mental abnormalities*: Psychological factors such as emotions, mood swings, and mental health conditions can influence handwriting characteristics.
- *Substance abuse and medication*: Intoxication or the use of certain medications and substances can affect motor control and coordination, thereby impacting handwriting.
- *Diseases, disorders, and neurological abnormalities*: Certain medical conditions, neurological disorders, or physical disabilities can result in changes in handwriting.
- *Surroundings and environmental factors*: External factors like noise, lighting conditions, temperature, or distractions in the surroundings can influence handwriting.
- *Handedness*: Whether an individual is right-handed or left-handed can affect the formation and execution of handwriting strokes.
- *Age*: Handwriting can change over time as individuals mature and develop their writing skills. Children's handwriting may differ from that of adults, and older individuals may experience changes in their handwriting due to natural ageing processes.
- *Fatigue*: Tiredness or physical fatigue can affect handwriting, leading to changes in letter formation, line quality, or overall legibility.
- *Writing speed*: The pace at which a person writes can impact the appearance of their handwriting. Faster writing may result in less attention to detail, while slower writing can allow for more precise and deliberate strokes.
- *Cultural and societal influences*: Cultural norms, writing conventions, and handwriting instruction can vary across different societies and cultures, leading to distinct handwriting styles and variations.
- *Personal preferences*: Each individual has their own preferences when it comes to handwriting, such as letter shapes, slants, or spacing. These personal choices can contribute to the uniqueness of their handwriting.
- *Muscle memory*: Regular practice and repetition of specific writing movements can create muscle memory, affecting the consistency and fluidity of handwriting.
- *Handwriting habits*: Personal habits or idiosyncrasies in writing, such as looping certain letters, crossing t's, or forming specific connections between letters, can become ingrained in an individual's handwriting.
- *Fine motor skills*: The development and coordination of fine motor skills, including hand and finger dexterity, can impact the precision and control of handwriting.
- *Writing style influences*: Exposure to different handwriting styles, calligraphy, or artistic influences can shape an individual's handwriting preferences and techniques.
- *Writing instrument characteristics*: The type of writing instrument used, such as a pen, pencil, or marker, can impact handwriting. Each writing instrument has its own weight, grip, and smoothness, which can affect letter formation and overall handwriting style.

- *Writing surface*: The surface on which a person writes, such as a smooth desk, textured paper, or a digital device, can influence handwriting. Different surfaces may require adjustments in pressure or grip, leading to variations in handwriting.
- *Hand injuries or conditions*: Any injuries or conditions affecting the hands, such as fractures, arthritis, or neurological disorders, can have an impact on handwriting. These factors may cause pain, limited mobility, or involuntary movements that can affect writing abilities.
- *Psychological or emotional state*: A person's emotional state, stress levels, or psychological factors can manifest in their handwriting. Intense emotions or mental health conditions may influence the pressure, size, or overall appearance of handwriting.
- *Writing purpose and context*: The purpose and context of writing, such as taking notes, writing a formal letter, or creating artwork, can influence the style and presentation of handwriting. Different writing tasks may require specific adjustments in handwriting techniques.
- *Language proficiency*: Individuals who are bilingual or multilingual may exhibit variations in their handwriting due to the influence of different language writing systems or script styles.

Additionally, mechanical factors such as intensity of light, temperature (cold or heat), and accidental strokes can also have a noticeable impact on the quality and appearance of handwriting. Handwriting analysis is a complex process that involves considering multiple factors and comparing various aspects of a person's writing to make informed assessments. These factors can collectively contribute to the uniqueness and variability of an individual's handwriting.

12.5 Examination of Handwriting

12.5.1 Specimen or Requested Writing

A specimen or requested writing is obtained from a person to compare and individualize their handwriting with the questioned handwriting. It is crucial to collect the specimen writing when the person is feeling comfortable and at ease. When collecting specimen writing samples, it is important to keep the following considerations in mind. By adhering to these guidelines, the collection of specimen writing samples can be conducted in a standardized and comprehensive manner, allowing for effective comparison and analysis in handwriting examinations.

- Create a comfortable environment for the person before collecting the specimen writing. Initially, ask them to write their name, address, hobbies, favorite film, food items, and destinations.
- Ensure that all the writings and signatures are collected using the same or similar writing instrument, material and surfaces.

- During the collection process, dictate at a slow, normal, and fast pace. Use separate sheets for each speed of dictation.
- The dictation should include a variety of words, symbols, signs and digits to cover a wide range of writing characteristics.
- The specimen writing should be obtained in the same language or medium as the questioned writing.
- Avoid providing specific instructions or guidance regarding punctuations, language, abbreviations, symbols, etc.
- These samples should also be collected at different intervals, such as on alternate days or alternate weeks, to observe any natural variations in the person's handwriting.

12.5.2 Natural Writing/Admitted Writings/Collected Writings

Natural writing is considered ideal for comparison because a person writes it for obvious purposes in normal life. It is also known as collected writing, admitted writing, or contemporaneous writing. It can be obtained from personal belongings such as diaries, notes, letters, etc., or from the school or colleges where the person has completed his/her education. It can also be obtained from the employment offices, banks, utility services, insurance agencies, hospitals, courts, etc., if the person is associated with these places. Answer sheets, agreements, contracts, cheques, financial records, drafts, orders, communication letters and bills can be considered important specimens to obtain the natural writings for comparison and identification in any handwriting related disputes. It's important to note that the freshness of the samples is also significant. Ideally, the natural writing samples used for comparison should not be too old, as handwriting can evolve and change over time. Fresh or recent samples provide a more accurate representation of an individual's current writing characteristics. The principle of comparison states that "only likes can be compared"; therefore, the comparison is made with the same or nearly the same type of samples in similar conditions and writing surfaces, instruments or material used (Ellen 2006; Richard 2007; Rao and Maithil 2013).

12.6 Collection and Packaging of the Documents

Like the other physical evidence, document as evidence must be collected, preserved and packaged with utmost care and sincerity. Samples of the documents examination and comparison can be collected from various sources, either from the house of the victim, suspect or criminal or from the locker, school, college, working place, office, etc. Dump yards, dustbins, waste paper baskets or boxes installed at the house, offices or workplace can be critical sources where a complete document or pieces of a document may be found. These suspected places or sources should be adequately searched during the investigation.

The documents found on the crime scene should be picked up carefully and placed on a clean sheet of paper. The document then should be examined for the presence of any extraneous material like pollen grains, dust, soil, hair or blood. All these extraneous materials should be collected appropriately. The document should be packed in an envelope larger than the document. Questioned documents should be handled carefully to preserve the latent fingerprints. Rubber-tipped forceps or handpicking of the document is recommended. Fingerprints should not be developed before submitting the document for examination as they may interfere with the examination of the document.

Do not write over documents or make any markings with a pen or pencil. Do not mutilate by erasing, repeated refolding, cutting or tearing. Avoid excessive handling. Keep documents in envelopes or protective folders. Do not allow anyone except a qualified expert to carry out chemical or other types of tests. Take documents to the laboratory or expert at the earliest convenience. Every document should be handled carefully, and photography should be done before and after the collection, especially for charred documents or documents found in the arson cases. In the case of charred documents, they should be stabilized before collection to prevent damage during lifting, handling, packaging and transportation.

The documents should be protected from extreme environmental conditions like heat, moisture, contaminants, etc. Documents should not be treated unnecessarily with any kind of solvents or chemicals. The documents should not be damaged, folded, torn, punched, tagged, twisted or stapled. During the evidence collection, the identification mark should be placed on the backside of the document or where no typed, printed or handwritten information is present (Hilton 1940).

12.7 Forgery: Types and Detection

According to section 464 IPC, "Whoever makes any false document or part of the document with an intent to cause damage or injury to the public or any person, property or with an intent to commit fraud or that fraud may be committed, commits forgery". There are four main types of forgery:

1. Simulated forgery
2. Traced forgery
3. Forgery by memory
4. Forgery without model

1. **Simulated forgery:** Simulated forgery is generally the imitation or copying of actual writing or signature. This is also known as "freehand forgery", "imitation forgery" or "copying forgery". In this type of forgery the forger keeps a model in front of him and tries to imitate or copy the pictorial effect of the handwriting as similar as possible with his observation and skills. While imitating the signature, the simulator tries to draw it pictorially similar to the original signature. However, even after the signature might look precisely similar, it lacks some details that can

be identified during examination (Lindblom and Jan 2006; Sharma 2014; Ellen 2006; Nickell 2014; Mohammed 2019; Harrison 2008).

2. **Traced forgery**: Traced forgery is when the forger reproduces an exact replica of the original or genuine writing using different methods. This type of forgery, when committed, has a close resemblance to the model. Some ways in which traced forgery is executed are as follows:
   (a) **Direct tracing**: The most common and straightforward method for tracing forgery is a direct forgery. More often, the paper bearing the genuine signature is held against a window, and then after proper adjustment, the signature is traced or outlined on the required paper as the outline of the signature can be seen through the window glass (Sharma 2014; Ellen 2006; Nickell 2014; Harrison 2008).
   (b) **Projection tracing**: Projection tracing is considered to be an easy method for doing forgery. In this method, the document consisting of the genuine is placed over the document where it is to be forged. The genuine signature is then traced with a pointed instrument with pressure to see indentation marks on the following paper. The document consisting of the indentations is then traced with an ink pen; thus, a forged signature is done (Sharma 2014; Ellen 2006; Nickell 2014; Harrison 2008).
   (c) **Use of Carbon paper:** This type of tracing forgery is akin to projection tracing. In this method, a carbon paper is placed over the document where forgery is to be done, and then the original document is kept over the carbon paper. With the help of any sharp writing instrument like a pen or pencil, the signature is traced and imprinted on the paper kept underneath. The signature is then inked with a pen (Sharma 2014; Ellen 2006; Nickell 2014; Harrison 2008).
   (d) **Use of tracing paper:** In this method, a model signature is kept over a tracing paper and traced with the writing instrument. The tracing paper is then kept over the document, then again traced with the writing instrument, and finally inked with a pen (Lindblom and Jan 2006; Sharma 2014; Ellen 2006; Nickell 2014; Harrison 2008).
3. **Forgery by Memory:** Forgery by memory is very similar to freehand forgery. In this method of forgery, the forger uses his memory to copy the original writer's forms, letters and style to write or for doing a signature. A model is not present in this method of forgery (Harrison 2008).
4. **Forgery without model:** Forgery without a model is also known as a forgery by impersonation. It refers to the writing or a signature made by a person representing himself to be another person to whom the writing or the signature may either be made bonafide by the person. Such types are also called allograph signatures or writings (Harrison 2008).

12.7.1 Detection of Forgery

Forgery can be detected by a minute examination of the writing on the questioned document. The first examination step includes observing and noting the class and individual characteristics. Characteristics include placing the dot over "i" or the cross over "t", spacing, style of writing, pressure applied, angle of the writing and alignment.

In case of a forged signature, a superimposition technique can be employed for comparison. If the genuine signature matches/overlaps with the forged signature, it indicates that the signature is forged. This can be said because there is a slight variation in signature even when done consecutively.

Hesitation marks in the starting and ending stroke also account for an attempt of doing forgery. Apart from this, pen stops and lifts at the unusual site also indicate forgery. Abrupt changes in the strokes and the direction of writing, and non-continuous strokes are also signs that can be seen when forgery is done. Other factors through which forgery can be detected are observing any overwriting, crowded writing, pen blobs, abrasion over the paper, misplaced shading, variation in pen pressure, change in slant, etc. Marginal spacing, defective line quality, retouching, tremors, indentations, and the presence of more than two types of pen inks indicate forgery.

Speed of writing is one of the features of handwriting, which also plays a vital role while detecting forgery. In genuine writings, the written material will have uniform writing, whereas if the speed is either fast or slow, variations in the writing are visible during an examination.

Tremors, which manifest as irregularities or shakiness in handwriting or signatures, are generally seen in forged writings or signatures. These tremors are naturally present in handwriting because of age, illness, disease, etc., but when someone tries to copy a signature, uniformity in writing is not seen, along with hesitations in the wrong place (Sharma 2014; Ellen 2006; Nickell 2014).

12.8 Alterations

The term "alteration" refers to any intentional modification, change, or manipulation made to a document with the purpose of deceiving or misleading others. In the context of document examination and forensic analysis, alterations can take various forms and may involve additions, deletions, erasures, or modifications to the content, appearance, or structure of a document. Generally, it is a modification made to a document by physical, chemical or mechanical means such as erasures, addition and obliterations of the words, or employing electronic means to digitally modify electronic documents. It can also be done by charring and indentations. The intention behind alterations is often to conceal or manipulate information, forge signatures or endorsements, create false records, or perpetrate fraud.

If the changes are made in a document without the concerned person's or other parties consent, then such changes are called "deceitful alterations". Identifying and detecting alterations in documents is a crucial task in forensic investigations and legal proceedings. Document examiners utilize a range of specialized techniques and tools to uncover hidden alterations and restore the original content whenever possible. These methods can include visual examination under different lighting conditions, use of magnification devices, infrared imaging, chemical tests, and even the application of computer software for digital document analysis. Detection of alterations depends on good training and available equipment. By meticulously examining the physical and visual characteristics of a document, experts can detect signs of alterations such as variations in ink color or texture, inconsistencies in handwriting or printing, misalignments, or disruptions in the sequence of content. Through these analytical processes, the detection of alterations helps to ensure the integrity and accuracy of documents presented as evidence and aids in determining the truthfulness of the information contained within them. The various types of alterations are as follows:

Abrasion: Abrading the paper generally means using any destructive means to erase something. Abrasion is also known as erasure or removal of writing, typewriting, or printing from paper by means of rubber erasures or by using a sharp instrument like a knife, blade, glass piece, etc. Because of using a sharp object on the paper, the erasure area gets damaged; the fibres present get disturbed, and the area becomes thinner than the other part of the paper where erasure is not executed, leaving the paper to become more porous. When a pen is used to write over erasures, the ink is readily absorbed by the paper. If pencil is used to write, bumps are seen because of the unevenness in the paper (Lindblom and Jan 2006; Koppenhaver 2007; Richard 2007).

Detection: Physical erasures can be detected using different methods or, more commonly, different light sources. The document can be exposed to infrared or ultraviolet light to detect fluorescence or luminescence changes. The erasure area becomes thin, which can be detected by using transmitted light. Indentations left by the erasure are also detected by holding the paper at eye level and an angle so that the light can pass through. Other means of detecting erasure are oblique lighting and Electrostatic detection apparatus. Various powders are also used to detect erasures, including the mixture of methylene blue and starch; another powder that can be used is bicarbonate of soda (baking soda) and toner powder (Lindblom and Jan 2006).

Chemical Erasure: Chemical fluids or solvents are used to erase the ink from the paper. Different types of inks need different chemicals to erase them. However, a complete removal is not always possible, and these chemical eradicators leave stains on the paper and cause the paper to expand. The paper, after drying, does not go back to its original size but leaves wrinkles at the location of the fluid (Lindblom and Jan 2006; Sharma 2014; Ellen 2006; Richard 2007).

Detection: Erasure with chemical treatment can be detected with the help of UV light, IR light, oblique light or transmitted light. Indentations can be deciphered by ESDA and by the use of oblique lighting because indentations are not altered by the chemical erasures and thus can be restored. Inks with carbon composition can be restored when erased chemically with sulphocyanic acid fumes. The fumes react with iron, and the red colour after reactions reveal the writing. Iodine fuming also accounts for one of the methods of deciphering the alteration. The iodine crystals are kept in a glass or dish, and the paper is then exposed to fumes. Sublimation takes place, which reveals the writing. The process can be fastened by warming the glass with a candle. Nowadays, iodine fuming is not recommended as the fumes are toxic, and when used, a photograph is suggested because the deciphered portion fades away quickly (Lindblom and Jan 2006; Huber and Headrick 1999; Sharma 2014; Koppenhaver 2007).

Obliteration: Overwriting a sample of handwriting or any printed matter with the help of any pen, pencil, correction fluid or opaque material is obliteration. These obliterations are made either accidentally or purposely to hide something essential or any mistake. The method used to detect the obliteration depends on the original writing and the means used (Lindblom and Jan 2006; Huber and Headrick 1999; Sharma 2014; Koppenhaver 2007; Richard 2007).

Detection: The obliterated writing can be deciphered using transmitted light and then captured by photography. In this method, the document is placed on a light box or a transmitted light machine; then, photography is done. If correction fluid is used to obliterate in some cases, it leaves the underneath shape seen on the opaque material, which can also be deciphered with the help of transmitted light. A non-destructive technique uses acetate sheets and a photocopier to decipher the opaque material. This method consists of placing the document on the photocopier where the opaque material is faced up, then it is covered with black paper and the toner level is adjusted to full dark. A transparent sheet is then inserted into the tray, and a transparent copy is produced. The copy will then contain the obscured material read through the paper.

Another method includes spraying a solvent consisting of acetone on the document. This will remove the opaque material and decipher the writing. As this is a non-destructive method, photography should be done before starting and after completing the process. When a document is obliterated using a black marker, it can be soaked in methyl alcohol or ethyl alcohol for its decipherment as it removes the marker ink without damaging the written or printed matter underneath. Infrared or ultraviolet light is also suggested to be used as it may cause the writing to fluoresce and thus decipher it (Lindblom and Jan 2006; Sharma 2014; Koppenhaver 2007).

Insertions: Insertions are generally the addition of any word, digit, symbol, sign, etc., into the original document to commit deceitful activity. It is fraudulent in most cases. The addition is commonly made in the space between the letters, words or sentences. For example—**eight thousand** can be converted into **eighty thousand** by adding the letter **"y"**. In a similar case, adding the number "0" is required to convert the "8" into 80 (Lindblom and Jan 2006; Sharma 2014; Richard 2007). Additions or insertions are most of the time found in crowded places. These additions are more challenging to be detected than the erasures. The methods to detect insertions are as follows.

Detection: When a handwritten document is altered by addition, the most common way to decipher it is by observing the misalignment as it is probably in crowded places. The addition made in any document can be detected by examining handwriting features such as the spacing between the words and numbers, pen pause and pen lift, connecting or intersecting lines, line qualities and differences in the appearance of inks or shapes and size of the letters or numbers. The writing will usually have a different style if written by another person rather than the original writer. The size and shape of the alphabets will also differ, which helps identify the insertions committed. A typewritten document can be deciphered by observing the misalignment, as it is difficult to align the document perfectly vertically or horizontally. When a grid is placed over the document, it will eventually reveal the text that has been added to the document or not. The typeface will help identify the alteration if a different typewriter is used. Inks used to alter the document are often different; hence, the ink difference can help detect the addition. Exposing the document to different light sources like infrared light or ultraviolet light will help decipher.

The composition of ink can be determined by using Thin Layer Chromatography, High-Performance Liquid Chromatography or UV–visible spectrophotometer. Video Spectral Comparator (VSC) and stereo microscopes are also helpful in determining the differences in inks. Both the techniques are non-destructive and very sensitive by which the intersecting lines or sequence of strokes can be determined in case alteration is done in a document through addition. Sometimes an examination with UV rays, IR rays and colour filters may also be helpful for this purpose (Lindblom and Jan 2006; Koppenhaver 2007).

Page substitution: Adding paper to a multi-page document is page substitution. This addition to the page can be identified by observing some minute details. The first method which can be used to identify the addition of a page is to expose them to different light sources like IR light, UV light and even the transmitted light. These lights will make the paper fluoresce, and different papers will fluoresce differently, thus aiding identification. Another method of identification includes measuring the size and width of the paper, observing the colour of the paper, see any stains or marks present on the paper like the punch hole marks, staple marks or presence of any indentation marks, etc. (Lindblom and Jan 2006; Koppenhaver 2007).

Cutting: Cutting is the most frequently used type of alteration where a small portion of one document is cut and then pasted onto another, or something else is pasted onto the respective document which had been cut. These alterations are detected, but the original material present before alteration cannot be detected (Lindblom and Jan 2006; Koppenhaver 2007).

The Sequence of Writing/Intersecting Lines: One of the most practised alteration types is adding writing into the original or already written matter. The forensic expert can distinguish if the material was present before or added afterwards. These writing sequences can be detected using a stereomicroscope, handheld microscope, linen counter or microscope equipped with UV light (Shukla et al. 2022; Badiye et al. 2022; Sharma et al. 2022; Kapoor et al. 2022). This can be detected because the ink used speaks for itself. When ink is used to write over already written matter, the ink spreads at the intersection detected using the above-listed instruments (Lindblom and Jan 2006; Huber and Headrick 1999; Sharma 2014; Koppenhaver 2007). The most efficient way to assess the sequence of strokes is to use a Video Spectral Comparator with various features such as UV illumination, side lighting, high magnification, and so on.

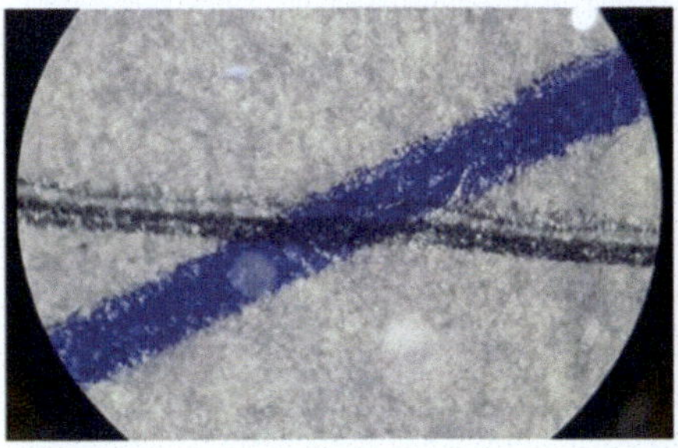

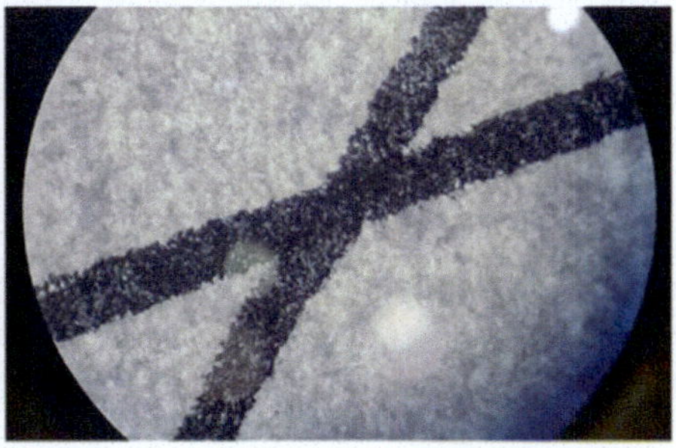

Folds and Creases: Alteration of this type is often done without any intention and knowledge that it may act as potential altered evidence. When a paper has folded, the folding lines break the topmost layer of paper and damage it. Because of this damage, when a pen is moved over the area of those folds or creases absorbs more ink which spreads a little more than the undamaged part of the paper. This alteration is then detected using a stereomicroscope, handheld microscope, etc. (Shukla et al. 2022; Lindblom and Jan 2006; Sharma 2014; Koppenhaver 2007; Ellen 2006).

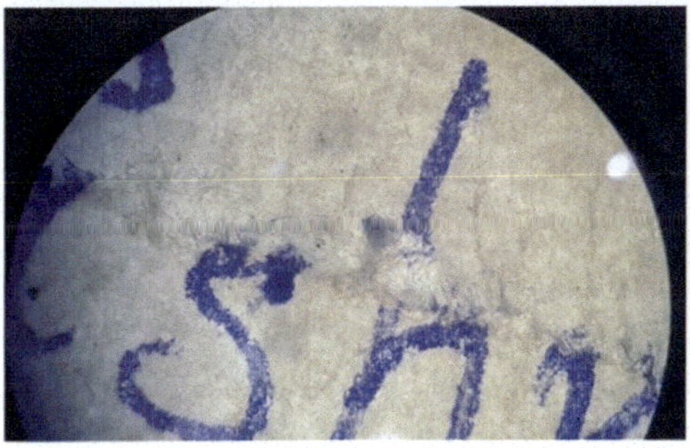

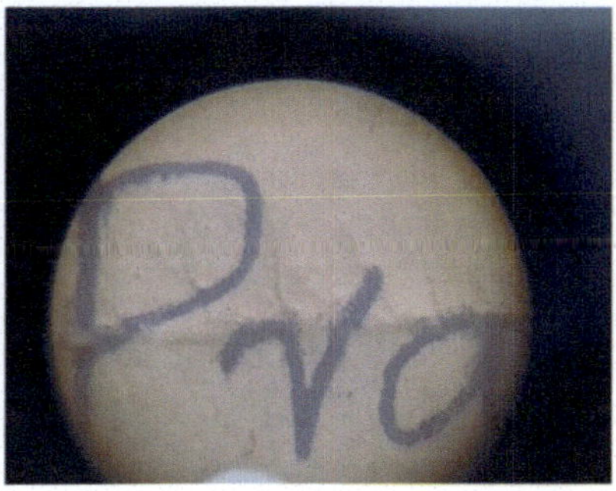

12.9 Examination of Typewritten Document

Printers have largely replaced typewriters. Typewritten documents are less often encountered nowadays because typewriters are not used by people as widely as printers nowadays. However, different make and model of typewriters are still observed, and the examination of these typewritten document is common particularly for personal use or legal purposes.

Typewritten documents are examined for their authenticity and to determine whether any alteration is present. Some of the following points considered for examining typewritten documents are discussed herein.

Typeface: The typeface is considered the style of how the alphabets should be written and even the numerals. Every machine has a particular typeface which can be different on a large or small scale from other manufacturers of the typewriter. Differences can be observed with letters and numerals like the cross bar over "t", to observe if "3" has a curve or a straight line, etc. these letters also have a difference in size which is also an essential factor during the examination.

Letter Spacing: Another characteristic is letter spacing. Every machine ensures that the letters are adequately spaced. In this, the characters are counted to an inch, i.e. the length occupied by 100 characters in inches. The two most common spacing, ten or 12, are seen in typewriting: 10 characters to the inch are known as pica and have a spacing of 254 mm per 100 characters and 12 characters to an inch are referred to as elite which has a spacing of 212 mm per 100 characters.

Comparison with the typewriter: A typewritten document is not necessarily always compared with a typewritten document only. Many times the typewriter is also examined to determine if the document is produced by the machine only or not. With time and use of the machine, wear and tear are observed, which aid in the examination.

Alignment of letters: One of the key points which can be considered during the examination is the alignment or misalignment of the letters. This is important because the letter may be either placed a little upward, downward, close or far from the residing letter during the manufacturing. This defect will be seen on the document and often helps identify the machine.

Ribbon characteristics: The examination may involve analysing the ribbon used in the typewriter. Different typewriters can have variations in ribbon characteristics such as ink colour, density, and fading patterns. These can provide valuable information for identification.

Impressions and indentations: The examination may focus on identifying impressions or indentations on the document that may have been left by the typewriter keys or other parts of the machine. These can help determine the specific typewriter used.

Line spacing and margins: The spacing between lines and margins on the document can be examined for consistency and specific measurements. Variations in line spacing or margins may indicate different typewriters or tampering.

Mechanical defects: The examination may involve assessing any mechanical defects or unique quirks associated with a particular typewriter model. This can include irregularities in key strikes, misalignments, or other mechanical inconsistencies that may leave identifiable marks on the document.

Typewriter identification marks: Some typewriters may have identification marks or serial numbers that are unique to a specific model or manufacturer. These marks can be examined for authenticity and compared with known typewriter records.

Anachronisms: When examining a typewritten document, it is important to consider the date of the document and determine if the typewriter used to produce it was available or in use during that time period. Anachronisms may suggest forgery or tampering.

Temporary Defects: Temporary defect that can be useful in identification is the presence of dust or dirt. When dust or dirt accumulates on the typewriter's typeface, it can cause the letters to be printed with a more solid appearance than they were originally intended to be. When two keys are pressed together, it can result in an effect where both keys or either of them are affected. This impact can be visible in subsequent printing impressions, indicating the occurrence of simultaneous key depression. Sometimes, after pressing certain letters, the ink printed on the paper may appear darker or lighter. This discrepancy in ink intensity can be attributed to factors such as ink saturation, ink ribbon condition, or variations in typing pressure. Occasionally, typewritten letters may appear broken or incomplete on the paper. This defect provides a crucial clue about the condition of the typewriter, potentially indicating mechanical issues or irregularities in the typing process. Defects related to the spacebar can also be observed. For instance, the spacebar may provide excessive or insufficient space while typing letters, which can indicate abnormalities or malfunctions in the typewriter mechanism. The absence of a character from the typescript can be an important clue for identifying the make and model of the typewriter. This can occur if a letter key is not fixed correctly during manufacturing or becomes detached due to operational failure. double impression of a key can hold significance during examination. Continuous use and wear and tear can prevent a key from returning to its original position after being pressed, resulting in a double impression on the subsequent printing (Lindblom and Jan 2006; Huber and Headrick 1999; Sharma 2014; Koppenhaver 2007; Ellen 2006; James et al. 2014; Harris and Lee 2019; Houck 2018; Esther 2009). These defects and anomalies provide forensic experts with valuable information about the condition, usage, and potential characteristics of the typewriter used to create the document. By carefully examining these observations, along with other aspects of the typewritten document, analysts can make informed assessments and draw conclusions regarding the identification and potential implications of the typewriter involved.

12.10 Examination of Photocopied Documents

With the more usage of the photocopy machine, it has become essential to examine photocopied documents. This examination is commonly practised due to the involvement of crimes such as fraud, terrorism and passing on the secrets or confidential materials. Photocopies are used because the perpetrators often believe that it may not be helpful as the original documents for identification purposes.

One aspect of examination involves analyzing the toners used in the photocopier machines. Toners are used to print images onto the paper that is only partially absorbed. The chemical composition of the toner can be determined by using an instrumental technique like the scanning electron microscope. Dry toners' composition includes a higher percentage of resin which can be determined by pyrolysis mass spectroscopy and infrared spectroscopy for identification and comparison. Toners also contain a specific amount of iron which can be identified using a non-destructive technique like magnetization. Toners are also specific for the particular make and model of a machine; this information may aid in identifying the machine.

Extraneous marks made on the paper account for additional important information. The grippers, grabbers and rollers in the photocopier machine leave certain marks on the paper, which are unique for the machine. The photocopy-generated documents differ in size and dimension from the printed matter by around 1%. Most of the time, there is a slight enlargement in size, although reduction may also be seen, and this too varies for different brands and models of machines.

Marks on the photocopied document are also ubiquitous because of damage to the machine. Damage to the platens, lids, glass plates and even the scratches and dirt over it leads to printing those marks onto the paper. Trash marks are one of the significant ones produced over the document. These marks are formed by the dust and dirt present in the machine and appear on the paper in the form of small dots at random places, further identifying the machine that causes it. Some marks that may not be recognized but are important as those of others are the staple marks, holes, folds, tears, stains and any other extraneous material (Lindblom and Jan 2006; Koppenhaver 2007; Ellen 2006; Houck 2018).

12.11 Examination of Secret Writing

Examination of secret writing is done to analyse the hidden messages that have been concealed by using various types of invisible inks. The invisible inks cannot be seen until they are revealed using different unveiling methods (Andharmule et al. 2013). Initially, physical methods are applied to preserve the document. The physical method that can aid in detecting the secret writing is using different light sources such as UV light, IR radiation and different filters available to visualize the writing better. A household cloth iron that evenly distribute heat in all directions can be used to decipher secret writing. The secret ink containing any type of body or vegetable fluid will often disclose the writing when ironed. This can also be achieved by keeping the document over a burner flame, but it is not recommended as it can destroy the evidence.

In addition, an IR lamp can also be used by exposing the document to radiations through a small opening. While doing this, any powder can also be dusted to see if it adheres to the surface of the paper where the message is secretly written. The iodine fuming method, more commonly used to develop the latent fingerprint, can also be used to decipher secret writing. This method is also non-destructive because, after some time, the colour starts to fade away (Huber and Headrick 1999; Ellen 2006).

12.12 Document Dating

Determining the age of a document is an intricate and challenging task that requires expertise in the field of questioned document examination. To date a document, there are various methods that can be employed, including examining its paper, ink, handwriting, and intersecting lines. The dating process can be achieved through static, dynamic, or supplementary approaches, or a combination of these (Kapoor et al. 2021).

Static methods employ time tags, chemical composition analysis, and elemental profiling to determine the age of the document. Dynamic methods include ink, paper, and toner ageing, which involve examining the changes in the chemical and physical properties of the materials used in the document over time. Supplementary methods include accelerated ageing techniques, chemometric approaches, analysing luminescent components, constructing a chronology of documents, radiocarbon dating, and nanotechnology-based approaches (Kapoor et al. 2021).

In static dating methods, the time tags used are usually watermarks, manufacturer logos, and other markings that indicate the date of manufacture of the paper. Chemical composition analysis involves determining the presence and concentration of specific chemical elements in the document. Elemental profiling, on the other hand, involves comparing the elemental composition of the document with that of other documents of known age (Kapoor et al. 2021).

Dynamic dating methods rely on the changes in the physical and chemical properties of the ink, paper, or toner used in the document. Ink ageing involves analysing the changes in the chemical properties of the ink, such as the loss of volatile solvents or the oxidation of the ink. Paper ageing involves analysing the changes in the physical properties of the paper, such as the loss of strength or the yellowing of the paper due to ageing. Toner ageing involves analysing the changes in the physical and chemical properties of the toner used in the document over time (Kapoor et al. 2021).

Supplementary methods, such as accelerated ageing techniques and chemometric approaches, involve subjecting the document to specific conditions to simulate the ageing process and analysing the changes that occur. Analysing luminescent components involves examining the fluorescence and phosphorescence properties of the document to determine its age. Constructing a chronology of documents involves comparing the document with other documents of known age to establish a timeline of the document's creation. Radiocarbon dating involves analysing the carbon content of the document to determine its age.

Nanotechnology-based approaches involve using nanoparticles to analyse the document's physical and chemical properties (Kapoor et al. 2021).

12.13 Conclusion

The examination of documents is a key component in forensic investigations, as it provides valuable insights and contributes to understanding a case. Document examination involves a meticulous process of collecting and preserving physical evidence, detecting hidden messages, and analysing different types of forgery, including handwriting, typewritten documents, photocopies, and secret writing. Forensic experts employ a combination of scientific methods, specialized equipment, and expert analysis to identify unique characteristics, detect alterations, and decipher concealed messages. Their work enhances the understanding of document authenticity, aids in identifying individuals involved in fraudulent activities, and helps resolve complex cases. The field of document examination is constantly evolving with technological advancements and the development of new forgery techniques, providing invaluable support to the legal system and ensuring the integrity of documentary evidence. While this introductory chapter cannot cover all aspects of questioned documents, readers are encouraged to refer to other books for a more detailed account of the various aspects.

References

Andharmule D, Kapoor N, Badiye A (2013) An evaluation of some commonly used methods for visualization of secret writing. Res J Forensic Sci 1:1–4

Badiye A, Landge S, Thakare S, Kushwaha SS, Kapoor N (2022) Forensic Applications of Simple (Handheld) Microscope. In book: Forensic Microscopy: Truth Under the Lenses, 1st edn. CRC Press

Bunker MN (1979) Handwriting analysis. Nelson-Hall Co., Chicago

Choudhary SK, Vaya SL (2016) Identification & characterization of the type of tremors in handwriting: a review. Int J Latest Technol Eng Manag Appl Sci (IJLTEMAS) 5(2):67–69

Ellen D (2006) Scientific examination of documents: methods and techniques. Taylor & Francis, Routledge

Esther B (2009) Cool written records: the proof is in the paper. Abdo Publishing, Minneapolis

Harris HA, Lee HC (2019) Introduction to forensic science and criminalistics. CRC Press

Harrison W (2008) Suspect documents their scientific examination. Universal Law Publishing Co. Pvt. Ltd

Hilton O (1940) The care and preservation of documents in criminal investigation. J Crim Law Criminol (1931–1951) 31(1):103–110. https://doi.org/10.2307/1137276

Hilton O (1993) Scientific examination of questioned documents. CRC Press, Boca Raton

Houck MM (ed) (2018) Digital and document examination. Elsevier

Huber RA, Headrick AM (1999) Handwriting identification: facts and fundamentals. CRC Press, Boca Raton

Indian Evidence Act, 1872

Indian Penal Code, 1860
James SH, Nordby JJ, Bell S (2014) Forensic science: an introduction to scientific and investigative techniques, 4th edn. Taylor and Francis, Routledge. https://doi.org/10.1201/b16445
Kapoor N, Sulke P, Shukla RK, Kakad R, Pardeshi P, Badiye A (2021) Forensic analytical approaches to the dating of documents: an overview. Microchem J 170:106722
Kapoor N, Shukla RK, Badiye A (2022) Introduction to Simple (Handheld) Microscope. In: Forensic Microscopy. CRC Press, pp 41–56
Koppenhaver K (2002) Attorney's guide to document examination. Quorum Books, Westport
Koppenhaver K (2007) Forensic document examination : principles and practice. Humana Press, Totowa
Lindblom BS, Jan KS (2006) Scientific examination of questioned documents. Taylor & Francis, Boca Raton
Mohammed LA (2019) Forensic examination of signatures. Academic Press
Morris RN (2020) Forensic handwriting identification: fundamental concepts and principles. Academic Press
Nickell J (2014) Detecting forgery: forensic investigation of documents. University Press of Kentucky, United States
Rao DMS, Maithil DBP (2013) Crime scene management a forensic approach. Selective & Scientific Books, Delhi
Richard S (2007) Criminalistics an introduction to forensic science. Pearson Prentice Hall, Hoboken
Sharma BR (2014) Forensic science in criminal investigation & trial. Universal Law Publishing Company, New Delhi
Sharma P, Aneja P, Choudhary SK, Mathur S (2022) Forensic Applications of Stereo Microscope. In: Forensic Microscopy. CRC Press, pp 156–181
Shukla RK, Kapoor N, Badiye, A. (Eds.). (2022) Forensic Microscopy: Truth Under the Lenses, 1st edn. CRC Press. https://doi.org/10.4324/9781003120995

Introduction to Forensic Psychology 13

Hema V. Acharya, Neeti Kapoor, and Ashish Badiye

Abstract

The chapter "Introduction to Forensic Psychology" provides an overview of various techniques and methods utilized in forensic psychology, specifically focusing on interview techniques and analysis tools. The chapter begins by exploring the fundamentals of forensic psychology and its application within legal and criminal justice systems. It then delves into the examination of key interview techniques, including the Morgan Interview Technique, FAINT Interview, and Statement Analysis. Additionally, it highlights the significance of systematic content analysis techniques in assessing written or verbal statements for potential deception indicators. The chapter further discusses the use of specialized tools such as the Polygraph, Narco analysis, Brain Electrical Oscillation Signature Profiling (BEOSP) test, Suspect Detection System, and Layered Voice Analysis in forensic investigations. Finally, it emphasizes the importance of integrating these techniques within forensic psychology practice to enhance the accuracy and reliability of investigative procedures.

Keywords

Interview techniques · Detection of deception · Polygraph · Narco-analysis · BEOSP test · Suspect Detection System · Layered Voice Analysis

H. V. Acharya
Forensic Psychology Division, Directorate of Forensic Science, Gandhinagar, Gujarat, India

N. Kapoor · A. Badiye (✉)
Department of Forensic Science, Government Institute of Forensic Science, Nagpur, Maharashtra, India
e-mail: neetikapoor@ifscnagpur.in; ashishbadiye@ifscnagpur.in

P. Shrivastava et al. (eds.), *Textbook of Forensic Science*,
https://doi.org/10.1007/978-981-99-1377-0_13

13.1 Introduction

Psychology is an enthralling realm that captivates us all. It beckons us to delve into the depths of our unconscious and subconscious thoughts, unraveling the enigma behind our preferences and aversions. Furthermore, it awakens our curiosity to discern the inner workings of others' minds and unravel the intricacies of their very being. This is the essence of psychology—an awe-inspiring subject that never fails to mesmerize. Its roots span from the earliest moments of gestation to the twilight years of old age, permeating every stage of human existence. The vast tapestry of the psychology fraternity encompasses child and adolescent, adult, educational, clinical, and geriatric psychology, each branch shedding light on a unique facet of our complex nature. Through interviews, psychological tests, and the application of therapeutic techniques, psychology seeks to unravel the mysteries of human behavior. And in the realm of forensic psychology, it delves even deeper, scrutinizing the motives, psychopathology, and unfulfilled desires that lead to criminal acts, shedding light on the darkest corners of the human psyche.

Historically speaking, the word 'forensic' has come from '*forensis*'. In ancient Rome, the forum was a central public space where legal proceedings, discussions, and debates took place. Based on debate, the jury used to make decision.

Informal use of psychology was done by the well-known character Sherlock Holmes, who, with his acumen in the human psyche, understood the motive, modus operandi and act of the accused.

13.2 Brief Contributions in the Field

The origins of forensic psychology can be attributed to figures like Wilhelm Wundt, often referred to as the father of experimental psychology. Wundt's emphasis on understanding human behavior through scientific observation laid a foundation for the application of psychological concepts in legal contexts. However, it was not until the early 20th century that the field truly took shape. In 1895, J. McKeen Cattell conduct research on the accuracy and confidence of individuals' responses to a series of questions. He developed a method of rating the degree of confidence in participants' answers. Alfred Binet was a French psychologist and is known as a pioneer in intelligence testing. In the early 20th century, Binet, along with his collaborator Théodore Simon, developed the Binet-Simon Scale, which was one of the earliest intelligence tests. The test aimed to assess cognitive abilities and identify children who might need additional educational support. Lewis Terman adapted and standardized Binet's intelligence test for use in the United States. Terman developed the Stanford-Binet Intelligence Scale in 1916. This test has been widely used in assessing intellectual abilities, including in forensic settings.

After World War II, the scope of forensic psychology expanded from witness testimony to cross-examining the accused and the defendant.

William Stern was a German psychologist, and is known for his work in the field of intelligence testing and the development of the concept of the Intelligence

Quotient (IQ). Albert von Schrenck-Notzing, a German psychiatrist and para psychologist, is known for his research on suggestibility and the effects of suggestion on witness testimony. However, his work primarily focused on the study of hypnosis and its potential influence on memory. Schrenck-Notzing conducted research on the phenomenon of "posthypnotic suggestion" and explored the impact of suggestion on memory recall. He believed that hypnosis could enhance recall abilities and aid in the retrieval of repressed or forgotten memories. While Schrenck-Notzing's work on suggestibility and memory has implications for forensic psychology, his contributions to the field were primarily theoretical and related to the study of hypnosis rather than directly applied to forensic contexts.

In 1895, Cesare Lombroso invented an instrument to measure changes in volumetric displacement to measure emotional changes and detect deception. He is considered to be the father of Modern Criminology. Lombroso's instrument, often referred to as the "plethysmograph," aimed to capture physiological responses associated with emotional states and potential deception. By measuring changes in volumetric displacement, the device provided a means to assess variations in blood flow, which Lombroso believed could shed light on an individual's emotional reactions. In 1908, Hugo Münsterberg wrote a book titled 'On the witness stand' which gave a forensic perspective to psychology. It marked a significant milestone in the development of forensic psychology. Münsterberg explored topics such as eyewitness testimony, suggestibility, and the reliability of memory, highlighting the potential for psychological insights in legal proceedings.

In 1917, the psychologist William Marston found that systolic blood pressure strongly correlated to lying. This led him to the design of the modern polygraph detector. Earlier, polygraph detection was considered the only scientific tool for detecting deception. Though controversial, the polygraph opened doors to using physiological responses as indicators of deception, influencing the practice of forensic psychology in areas such as criminal investigations and interrogation techniques. Solomon Asch conducted research on social conformity, shedding light on how individuals can be influenced by others' opinions and behaviors. His work has relevance to understanding witness testimony and the dynamics of group influence in forensic contexts. Elizabeth Loftus is renowned for her research on eyewitness testimony and the malleability of memory. Her work has challenged assumptions about the reliability of eyewitness accounts and has influenced the field of forensic psychology by emphasizing the importance of accurate and unbiased witness testimony. Robert Hare developed the Psychopathy Checklist, a widely used tool for assessing psychopathic traits. His work has been instrumental in understanding and identifying psychopathy in forensic contexts. In 2001, the American Psychological Association recognized Forensic Psychology as an independent field of Psychology. This recognition was a significant milestone in establishing forensic psychology as an independent and distinct discipline.

13.3 Role of Forensic Psychologist

The forensic psychologist studies the psyche of offenders and examines various factors to provide insights for investigations. They gather the facts, the police records, post-mortem reports, forensic reports, legal aspects and the history of the victim/survivor and the accused. The interview conducted is non-clinical in nature, involving legal and investigative questions. It requires a deep understanding of the criminal psychology and behaviour. During the interview, the forensic psychologist may employ psychological tests and techniques to gather additional information and then present their findings in a language that can be understood by the court and investigators.

In western countries, forensic psychologists are employed by a range of entities including private detective agencies, self-employment, and government sectors. The court also appoints the forensic psychologist. Meanwhile, in India, generally speaking, the facility of a forensic psychologist is used in the government sector like forensic laboratories. However, it can be used in other government sectors like correctional homes, juvenile homes and remand homes where the expertise of forensic psychologists can be utilized. Generally, graduates in Sociology or Psychology are recruited in India for these positions. They may undergo additional training to handle the issues related to antisocial behaviour and psychopathology. They are trained to identify signs of manipulation or exaggerated fake non-clinical symptoms during the interview session. It involves particular skills to handle criminals, witnesses and complainants. Additionally, forensic psychologist may also be involved in training and evaluating police or other law enforcement personnel, providing them with the personality profile of the accused.

The court often engages the services of a forensic psychologist to assess the accused's competency to stand trial. If the individual is incompetent, the psychologist's report will include recommendations for the interim period during which efforts are made to restore the person's competency to understand the court proceedings and participate appropriately in their defence. Additionally, the court may appoint a forensic psychologist to evaluate the accused's state of mind at the time, the crime was committed. It is to ascertain if the accused has a history of mental illness, has experienced any traumatic illness in the early days resulting in psychopathology, or has been a victim of physical/sexual abuse or has a criminal history in the family, personality disorder etc. Based on the collected information, the psychologist provides an expert opinion about the possible cause or motive of the crime and may make recommendations for rehabilitation if necessary. The court takes their services for future risk assessment and evaluation of witness creditability.

Forensic psychologists can also be used in civil cases like insurance claims related to accidents, or determining the responsibilities of child custody and visitation. The court may appoint the forensic psychologist to evaluate the child's allegation of physical and sexual abuse and to evaluate the parenting capabilities of each part, and make recommendations regarding custody arrangements. In cases where serious crimes has been committed by a juvenile, the court request an assessment of the juvenile's mental age and maturity level before taking up the case for trial. The forensic psychologist will also evaluate the potential for appropriate interventions and rehabilitation of such juveniles. Furthermore, Forensic psychologists can contribute to enhance the capabilities of the state and national law enforcement agencies and the criminal justice system, by training them and imparting their knowledge and expertise.

13.4 Interview Techniques

An interview is a technique in which two people i.e., the interviewer and interviewee (subject), preferably engage in face-to-face conversation to gather detailed information about the crime. The primary goal of the interview is to get factual information by establishing rapport with the interviewee. Alongside the interview, the observation of the subject is equally important as it helps assess their current thought process, emotions and interpersonal qualities. It is an important aspect that will give clues to the areas that need further evaluation and assessment. The subject should feel comfortable with the interview and the testing process. The interviewer allows the subject to narrate their story, which forms the basis of a structured interview. The interviewer should have a good insight into the psyche of human behaviour and logical thinking, enabling them to differentiate between nervousness resulting from the forensic investigation and attempts to hide the truth. They should be able to identify signs of being caught, emotional dilemma and evasiveness. Preliminary information about the subject, his hobbies, habits and family life, may often prove successful in breaking the ice. In the forensic setup, it is advisable to establish the rapport in first few hours of the subject's presence. The interview should be conducted without bias against any religion, caste, occupation or habit. The interviewer should be accepting and mature to understand the reason and motive behind the subject's statements.

The interview should progress by asking the open-ended questions and encouraging the subject to give detailed answers in an unrestricted manner. If required, silent pauses should also be utilized. The interviewer poses the questions, and the interviewee/subject provides the answers. The information given by the subject may not always be accurate; therefore, the interviewer needs to verify the veracity of the available police documents like the subject's statement, FIR and other medical and forensic reports. During the interview, the interviewer must consider both the legal and psychological aspects of the case. The interviewer will evaluate the subject's mental processes like attention/concentration, memory, orientation, mood, intellectual functioning, thought and perceptual processes and decide the probable psychological tests to be administered. The purpose of the interview is not to get the confession but to gather relevant details about the crime.

13.4.1 Interview Room

The interview room should be well ventilated and well illuminated so that the subject's expression and postures can be easily observed. It should be free of visual distractions and noise free. The room should provide a minimum of one table and two chairs. Giving a revolving chair to the subject should be avoided so that the observation of their posture and action can be appropriately noted. The interviewer's chair should be positioned higher than the subject's chair, giving the subject a psychological sense of the interviewer's authority. A spatial distance of approximately 4 ft away between the interviewers' chair and the subject's chair should be maintained.

The room should have a one-way mirror facility or video camera to monitor and record the interview and the subject's emotions and behaviour. It is important to refrain from displaying any religious or saint pictures in the room to allow the subject to speak freely and avoid potential biases. It will also help the examiner safeguard themself against any accusation, whether verbal or non-verbal, made by the subject. The subject should be instructed to keep their mobile outside the interview room, and the interviewer should keep their mobile on silent mode to avoid disruptions.

Ideally, the duration of the interview should range from 30 to 45 minutes, depending on the nature and severity of the crime and the subject's attention span. Moreover, a notepad with a pen, pencil and eraser should be made available to take notes and for the subject to explain the location of the offence. The interviewer can take notes during an interview as long as their writing skills are consistent. It is important for the interviewer to empathize with the subject's feelings, motivations and fears, as this will help foster a sense of comfort and a supportive environment. The interviewer should speak in a language that is simple and easily understandable. His voice should be audible and clear. A translator is mandatory, if the subject speaks a different language. The translator should be a government gazetted officer or an equivalent person from the academic field, capable of maintaining the confidentiality of the case and the subject being interviewed.

13.4.1.1 Characteristics of Interviewer

- Should possess at least a post-graduate degree in Psychology, especially Clinical Psychology, Criminology, Forensic Psychology, Forensic Science or as prescribed by the relevant authority.
- Should be observant.
- Should be able to use non-accusatory questions.
- Should be able to establish rapport with the subject easily.
- Should be objective and non-judgemental interview.
- Should not be biased or prejudiced towards any cultural or societal norm.
- Should have active listening skills and the ability to raise effective questions.
- Should probe and ensure the information.
- Should use the language which the subject understands.
- Should adhere to ethical guidelines and professional standards.
- Should use mild, audible and clear tone (and avoid a loud and blaming tone).

- Should have the maturity to understand the subject's lifestyle, criminal history and/or psychopathology.
- Should maximum the use of open-ended questions and encourage the subject to give more information.
- Should avoid moralizing, preaching and patronizing the subject.
- Should avoid unwarranted assurance to the subject.

13.4.1.2 Non-Verbal Characteristics

- Should maintain suitable conversational distance.
- Should maintain the eye contact.
- Should have calm and attentive body posture.
- Should show empathy.
- Should use 'silence' appropriately.

13.4.2 Morgan Interview Theme Technique (MITT)

The Thematic Apperception Test (TAT) was developed by Henry A. Murray and Christiana D. Morgan at Harvard University in the late 1930s. This projective test was initially developed for clinical patients to explore unresolved conflicts, motivations and attitudes. The TAT consists of 20 drawing cards, each containing an ambigous stimulus that prompts the subject to create a story encompassing their past, present and future. These stories reveals the hidden emotions and internal conflicts. While working with law enforcement agencies, Raymond Morgan applied the TAT to the criminals and found that the TAT test was very effective in detecting deception. On getting success on the TAT, Morgan developed his own set of sketches that resembled various types of crime scenes. He called this technique the Morgan Interview Theme Technique (MITT) (Gordon & Fleisher, 2010, 2019). The test has 42 sketches comprising 5 irrelevant, 18 relevant non-violent, 8 relevant violent, 6 relevant sexual, 3 apprehension and 2 guilt and remorse sketches. The ambiguous nature of the sketches allows the subject to project their anxiety, worry, fear and security. This test can also reduce the subject's anxiety and creates a comfortable environment for a forensic interview. It was observed that MITT techniques helped the interviewer gain insight and determined his truth or deception. Morgan made few observations for the truthful and deceptive subjects:

1. Truthful subjects were able to relate the sketch to the crime scene and were able to create a story related to it. Deceptive subjects, on the other hand, tend to avoid any association between the sketches and the crime scene. When pressed, the deceptive individuals would give a story that lacked any reference to the crime.
2. Truthful subjects gave more positive and upbeat stories, while deceptive subjects often conveyed more negative and downbeat stories.
3. There is logic in the story of truthful subjects, while the deceptive subjects displayed inconsistencies and illogical elements. Deceptive individuals would try to find relevance in sketches that were actually irrelevant to the crime.

4. Truthful subjects were adept at providing a satisfactory conclusion to their stories, while deceptive subjects struggled to bring their narratives to a satisfactory ending. They often appeared perplexed and unsure about how to conclude the story.

13.4.3 FAINT

The Forensic Assessment Interview (FAINT) is an interview technique used to quantify the qualitative response of the subject. It attempts to interpret non-verbal behaviour into non-verbal cues. The FAINT interview is scored on following:

1. Posture
   Paul Ekman is a well-known psychologist who has extensively studied facial expressions and non-verbal behavior. According to Ekman, a truthful subject will show the signs of good eye contact, appear composed, relaxed and talkative. They will maintain face-to-face body alignment and use more illustrative language. Their answers tend to be direct and in alignment with the asked questions. On the other hand, a deceptive person will show nervousness and will try to evade the answers. They will appear tense for no apparent reason and will be defensive in his answers. Non-verbal clues like restlessness and increased body movements will be seen.
2. MITT
   Raymond Morgan has developed 42 sketches with ambiguous stimuli in which the subject is asked to respond to the pictures by telling the picture's past, present and future. The purpose of using these ambiguous stimuli is to elicit the subject's interpretations, thoughts, and emotions, which can provide insights into their psychological state, motivations, and conflicts. The stories they create in response to the sketches can reveal hidden emotions and internal conflicts. It's important to note that the MITT technique is a projective test and should be administered and interpreted by trained professionals in the field of forensic psychology.
3. Projective/Relevant/Comparison questions
   During the interview, different types of structured questions should be asked to the subject to get full information from them. The irrelevant questions are informal questions that help establish rapport with the subject. These questions will establish a neutral atmosphere. It will minimize resistance by structuring a strategy used by tricky subjects to avoid answering sensitive questions by answering the interviewer's questions with a question. The relevant questions are closed-ended questions that directly inquire about the subject's involvement or knowledge regarding the crime. Relevant questions are formulated so that the truthful will have no resistance to answering, and the deceptive person will be forced to lie to them. The comparison questions are relative, creating the mental environment for correctly identifying truthful subjects. These questions are often broad in scope, and are devised in a way that truthful subjects are expected to answer affirmatively. These questions are designed to create a contrast between

the relevant and irrelevant questions. The interviewer can observe patterns or inconsistencies that may indicate deception.

4. The suspect's written statement

   The suspect/subject's written statement refers to a document in which an individual who is suspected or accused of a crime provides a written account of their involvement or knowledge of the incident in question. The purpose is to obtain the individual's perspective on the events under investigation and allows the suspect/subject to present their side of the story and provide details that may be relevant to the case.

   After the completion of the interview with the subject, it is common practice to provide them with paper and a pen to write their own version of the crime incident. This allows the subject to provide a written account of their perspective, including details about their relationship with the deceased (if applicable) and their presence at the time of the incident.

   The subject should be instructed to include preliminary details, such as their personal information and any relevant background information that may help in understanding their involvement or knowledge of the crime. They should be given sufficient time and space to write their version of the incident in their own words. This written statement serves as an additional source of information and can provide insights into the subject's understanding of the events, their level of detail, and any inconsistencies with their previous statements or the evidence collected during the investigation.

13.4.4 Content-Based Statement Analysis (CBSA)

Content-Based Statement Analysis (CBSA): In 1902, William Stern defined statement analysis as a technique in which a person's statement depends on their cognitive ability as well as on the interviewing process used to obtain the statement. The content of a statement can provide insights into the individual's cognitive processes, personality characteristics, and potential deception. Stern conducted experiments involving children who had made statements alleging sexual abuse. He told the children to write down about the incidents. He observed that children's statements could be influenced by external factors, such as the presence of other people during the writing process.

When analyzing a statement, cognitive ability, creativity and self-control play significant roles. A truthful statement based on genuine recollection of events tends to be less elaborate compared to a fabricated statement. In order to maintain the illusion of truth, deceptive statements often require a greater degree of creativity to ensure coherence and avoid contradictions.

CBSA has 19 criteria to analyse the following:

1. Logical structure: The statement will be relevant to the incident, though not necessarily chronological. The content will be concrete, original, precise and evident.

2. Unstructured production: The content will be unstructured and not chronological.
3. Quantity of details: The information given by the subject is more creditable since it is difficult for a person with no experience to describe the incident in detail.
4. Contextual Embedding: The time and space during the narration will be more specific than the fabricated one. The explanation regarding the incident in context to time and space will be relevant to what the subject speaks in the interview.
5. Description of interactions: The subject will give sequential details of the actions and interactions with other people before and after the incident. He will be sequential and be able to give the details of the interactions when the crime happened.
6. Reproduction of the conversation: The subject will be able to give the complexity of conversation sequences referring to the relevant act.
7. Unexpected complications during the incident.
8. Unusual details: The subject will give unusual details instead of the stereotyped statement. It depends on how the interview extracts the minute information from the subject.
9. Superfluous details: The subject will give the details outlining the incident, which would help relate to the major incident. This information is mainly given by the subject who has witnessed the criminal act. A person who has not experienced any act will be unable to give the peripheral details.
10. Accurately reported details misunderstood: The subject gives meaning or interpretation to the details.
11. Related external exposure: When the accused is making the statement referring to the conversations or incidents in comparison with the criminal act.
12. Accounts of subjective mental state: When the subject adds the emotional content or expresses his psychological state about the criminal act.
13. Attribution to perpetrator's mental state: The subject describes the accused's mental state. This has to be more free will than the response to the question.
14. Motivation related contents: The subject will try to convince the interviewer by making automatic corrections. This will indicate the subject's attempt to convince the examiner.
15. Admitting lack of memory: The subject will readily accept the forgetfulness in retrieving a specific memory, though it has to be checked whether the subject is saying in response to the question or otherwise
16. Raising doubts about his own testimony: This will be a subtle sign of the subject telling the truth to the examiner. He will often show mistrust in his narration. This will also show that the person unconsciously does not accept his narration.
17. Self-deprecation 'Self Accusation': When the subject accepts his fault or mistake in the statement, it reinforces that the information given by the subject is accurate to their knowledge.

18. Pardoning the perpetrator—'discharging the accused person': When the subject considers or wants to give another chance to the perpetrator. This statement will be incompatible in case of motivation for a false allegation.
19. Offence Specific elements: The subject will include detailed elementary information about the crime. This could be the detail regarding the grooming behaviour of the accused.

The examiner considers the 19 criteria mentioned above, which determine the statement's credibility, though not all the criteria need to be met to establish the subject's credibility. There is no numerical or cut-off scoring method in this technique. The opinion derived from this interview will be an element of the whole process. The interview analysis will indicate the subject's genuineness, which correlates with further interview sessions and evidence.

13.4.5 Systematic Content Analysis (SCAN) Technique

Avinoam Sapir is a well-known Israeli expert in the field of statement analysis, linguistic profiling, and forensic psycholingustics. Avinoam Sapir developed the SCAN technique, which analyses verbal and written statements to detect deception and infer psychological traits. Sapir has divided a statement into three parts: *Pre-incidence*, *Incidence* and *Post-incidence*. He has observed that the truthful subject will give 20% of pre-incident information, 50% of information will depict the incidence that took place and the rest 30% of information will be comprised of post-incidence. Especially in the case of rape and molestation, the truthful subject will elaborate on what happened after the incident and how they had to face the shame and humiliation. The subject who writes the statement will be rich in information and would be able to relate to the incident, e.g. My husband, My daughter, etc. There will be more use of singular tense instead of the third person. If the person does not use 'I' in his statement, it calls for further inquiry. The subject may start his statement in singular tense; 'I had gone to the office in my car, I was getting late, punched in at 9.30 and worked till noon'. It is seen that where the subject does the actual act, he uses singular tense, and when he enters the office, the singular tense is missed, giving a sign of deceptive narration. Although the subject might not present the events in chronological order, the relevance to the sequence will be maintained. The statement given will be spontaneous and lengthy without many interruptions. There will be creditability and flow in the statement.

13.5 Polygraph

In 1895, Cesare Lombroso experimented with the medical instrument, hydrosphygmograph, which the doctors medically used to check the patient's blood pressure. Lombroso used this instrument to detect the deception or truthfulness of the accused by measuring the changes in the blood pressure—the pulse of the accused. In 1897, Georg Sticker became the first person to use the galvanometer application to detect deception (Widacki 2015). He further suggested that using GSR together without asking questions would stimulate the emotional response that could be reliably measured physiologically (Gordon 2016). Although different experiments were done, the polygraph was not officially implemented in a criminal investigation. William Marston, known for his work on the polygraph, expanded upon these early efforts by adding the periodic discontinuous measurements of blood pressure and respiration as additional parameters to determine the subject's truthfulness. He used the word association test, which showed promising results. Vittorio Benussi, an Italian psychologist, contributed to the understanding of respiration patterns in relation to truthfulness. He explained that 'if the length of inhalation were divided by the length of expiration, the ratio was greater before telling the truth than afterwards and greater after lying than before lying' (Benussi & Antonelli 2002). Benussi's work highlighted the potential physiological indicators of deception. However, the scoring method for measuring respiration was inaccurate compared to blood pressure.

In 1921, John A Larson combined the Mackenzie ink polygraph instrument, which had three parameters; blood pressure, pulse and respiration which continuously recorded complex physiological changes such as arterial and venous pulses during the entire test period. Larson combined the Mackenzie ink polygraph to record and monitor changes based on the research of Benussi and Marston. The polygraph first came into significant contact with the legal system in 1923, when Marston attempted to have the results of a polygraph test admitted as evidence (Fyre v/s United states, 1923). In 1926, Leonarde Keeler, known as the 'father of modern polygraph', improved the polygraph instrument of Larson by introducing metal tambours and a synchronized chart drive mechanism that used roller paper, enhancing the functionality and reliability of the instrument. In 1938, Keeler collaborated with Charles Wilson to add Galvanic Skin Response (GSR) as the third component of the polygraph instrument. In 1942, Keeler and Larson developed relevant/irrelevant testing techniques, that require responses in Yes/No format, aimed at distinguishing truthful and deceptive responses (Matte 1996). In 1945, John E. Reid observed that the changes in the muscular activity of the subject are controlled by the parasympathetic system and are not readily observable. Consequently, in 1947, Reid added the measurement of muscular activity to polygraph instruments. The "control question technique" developed by Reid involves the use of specific types of questions to establish a baseline for comparison and to gauge the subject's physiological responses. This technique typically includes relevant questions related to the specific incident being investigated and control questions that are designed to elicit a stronger physiological response from deceptive individuals. He also developed a combination of the card test and the confirmatory 'yes' test to check the subject's cooperation. He also gave a 'silent answer test' in which the subject does not have to give any verbal answers to the questions, and the veracity is concluded based on the recordings of the non-verbal physiological responses.

A polygraph examination includes a series of yes/no questions to which the examinee responds while being connected to sensors that transmit data on these physiological phenomena such as blood pressure, pulse rate, respiration, and GSR. The instrument uses analog or digital technology to record the data. Because the original analog instruments recorded the data with several pens writing lines on a moving sheet of paper/chart, the record of the physiological responses during the polygraph test is known as a 'polygraph chart'.

13.5.1 The Polygraph Instrument

The conventional polygraph instrument is modified with the advancement of technology and now is known as a computerized polygraph instrument. The computerized polygraph no longer rely on pens attached to tambours to write in ink onto a roll of paper-driven clockwise (Mackenzie 1908) in the way original Keeler polygraph modes used to work. The computerized polygraph produces digital outputs directly from the measuring instruments into a computer with the appropriate polygraph software (Hirota et al. 2005). There are three primary purposes of polygraphs, i.e. event-specific investigation, employee screening and pre-employment screening.

There are two broad categories of sensors used in polygraphs, i.e. *Pneumatic* and *Electrical*

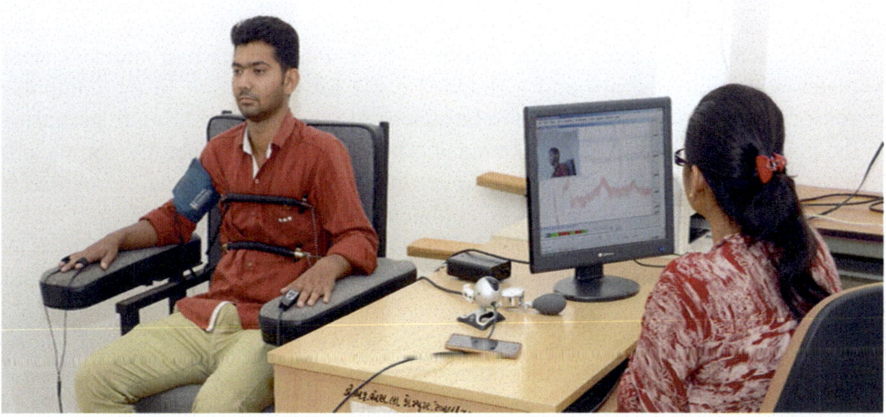

1. Pneumatic sensors
   (a) Pneumograph (Chest assembly)
   This sensor measures changes in respiration. It consists of a convoluted tube, anti-roll bars, beaded chain or Velcro strips and rubber tubing to connect to the computer sensor box. One pneumography chest assembly will be placed around the examinee's upper body area to record the thoracic breathing pattern. A second pneumography chest assembly will be placed around the lower abdomen area to record the abdominal breathing pattern. When the muscle expands, the air inside the tube gets displaced. It is the expansion and contraction of the muscles that form a wave. The transducer converts this wave into an electrical pattern on the computer.
   (b) Sphygmograph (blood pressure cuff assembly)
   This sensor measures blood pressure. The polygraph system records the systolic stroke, diastolic stroke and a dicrotic notch. This sensor consists of a rubber bladder covered with a cloth sleeve and Velcro wrap, pump bulb assembly, which includes a sphygmomanometer and associated rubber tubing for connecting the sensor to the computer sensor box. It is placed over the brachial artery.
2. Electrical sensors
   (a) Plethysmograph
   This sensor measures blood pulse volume. It uses a light source and a photosensitive cell to measure light changes that pass through the tissues. The amount of light reaching the photosensitive cell is related to the amount of blood it passes before reaching the sensor. The amount of blood absorbed is proportionate to the amount of haemoglobin (Hb) in the blood vessel. The change in Hb is due to sympathetic nervous system fluctuation.
   (b) Electro Dermal Activity (EDA) Galvanograph
   This sensor measures sweat conductivity. It consists of two stainless steel plates with Velcro straps and a shielded cable for connection to the computer sensor box. The finger plates are to be attached to the index and ring fingertips of the non-dominant hand of the examinee. The fingertips are generally porous and have lots of sweat. Hence, hydrated fingertips have maximum signal strength as it conducts electrical activity. Skin conductance is generally considered more efficient and reliable (Wynn et al. 2000). This sensor has been long regarded as the most sensitive and reliable of all the channels of the polygraph (Kircher and Raskin 2002).

   Another sensor called the Piezoelectric Sensor pad or the 'P gauze'—also known as 'activity sensor' is a countermeasure. It detects any form of physical movement. It is placed on the seat, arms and feet of the examinee.

13.5.2 Procedure

There are five significant steps in administering the polygraph to an examinee.

1. Pre-test interview
   The pre-test interview is detailed. It is done with the subject/examinee/witness and the investigating officer (I.O.). After taking the detailed information regarding the examinee, his role and relation with the case, the examinee will be briefed about the instrument and is shown the instrument and how it works. The examinee is allowed to ask the questions, and the examiner will also give an explanation. The pre-test interview shapes the expectations and emotional state of the examinee during the test. During the interview, the examiner will provide the examinee with an atmosphere that makes him mentally accessible and less anxious about the whole ordeal. The examiner will likely form impressions of the examinee's truthfulness based on the examinee's demeanor and response in the pre-test interview. These impressions can inform the examiner's approach during the examination and guide the interpretation of the results.
2. Court Order and Informed consent
   This is the most vital part of the test as the polygraph cannot be administered on an individual without a prior court order and the examinee's informed consent. The Investigating Officer should produce the subject in front of the court and take permission of the subject to be taken for a polygraph test (Selvi Ors V/s State of Karnataka). The examinee must provide written consent for the test and be informed of their right to refuse. The test cannot proceed without the examinee's consent (as per NHRC guidelines 2000).
3. Question Formulation
   Based on all the information gathered during the pre-test interview, a series of Yes/No questions are developed, which are short, simple and easy to understand. Each question should be close-ended and based on a single/specific issue. The questions should not consist of any legal jargon. The questionnaire should consist of relevant, irrelevant and control questions.
4. Test administration
   Before administering the polygraph test, the examinee should be familiarized with the examination room, instrument and the questions that he/she will be asked. The examiner provides proper instructions to the examinee on how to sit and respond to the questions and may give a demonstration to make things more transparent. A baseline recording of the examinee's physiological responses is obtained for comparison purposes. Initial buffer items are also intended to reduce the situational effects on the examinee's physiological responses. Hence, a card or coin sorting test creates a baseline.

   Each question of the questionnaire should be administered three times. This ensures that the examinee produces the same or similar physiological responses to the same questions all three times. A 15–20 seconds pause should follow each question allowing the time for the previous response to fade and the physiological measure to return to their baseline. This procedure is followed throughout the test, with the examiner noting when the test began when the questions were asked and when it ended. The examiner should also make notes of any extraneous behaviour, such as coughing and sneezing, and their timings. After the initial completion of the questionnaire, the examiner may ask for any clarifications on specific questions or make other refinements before repeating the test twice for comparison. After the test is completed, a post-test interview will be done.

5. Post-test interview

   As the name suggests, the post-test interview is conducted after the test is administered to the examinee. This is an interview that the examiner conducts with the examinee based on the test results. New information can also be gathered from the examinee during this phase and should be cross-checked before being included in the report or reaching a conclusion.

13.6 Brain Electrical Oscillation Signature (BEOS) Profiling Test

The application of neurophysiology is applied in the Brain Electrical Oscillation signature profiling (BEOSP) test (Zachariah et al. 2017). This test detects the subject's involvement in the crime by bringing out evidence of his intention and participation. The crime investigation has two dimensions: one to identify the criminal and the second to identify and direct the other probable criminal in the crime. This test can indicate the potential source of crime. The criminal cannot deny his involvement as this test has intuitive awareness, which is result oriented and beyond the scope of intentional masking. The electrical phenomena of the brain reveal highly sensitive and specific indicators of the various cognitive states. Psychoneurological studies have proved that when a person has experience with specific events, definite changes are observed in functional neuroimaging and cognitive electrophysiology. The two such electrical activities are those related to recognition by knowing and remembering the experience. For extracting the electrical activation associated with the awareness of recalled experience or remembrance, the multichannel electrical activity of the brain is recorded, while 'knowing' is the cognitive process of recognition with or without familiarity.

In contrast, remembrance is the recall of episodic and autobiographic details from a person's life. Awareness of the transcoded detail and the remembrance of the mental imageries of the different experience components constitutes Experiential knowledge in the individual (Mukundan 2007). George Mandler has introduced the dual theory of memory, which differentiated recognition between knowing and remembrance (Mandler 1980). All life experiences have their own context; remembering that context is equally important while remembering an experience. A context may refer to aspects more than what is referred to by time and place, while the source is found to have independent localization, as recall of an episode does not necessarily result in the recall of the source information. What makes an event in life an autobiographical episode is the experiential aspect of the event.

Experiential knowledge is acquired through participation in an activity and stored with its temporal and spatial (time and space) reference in the brain. Conceptual knowledge is based on awareness and devoid of any self-experience and projects only 'knowing' in the brain.

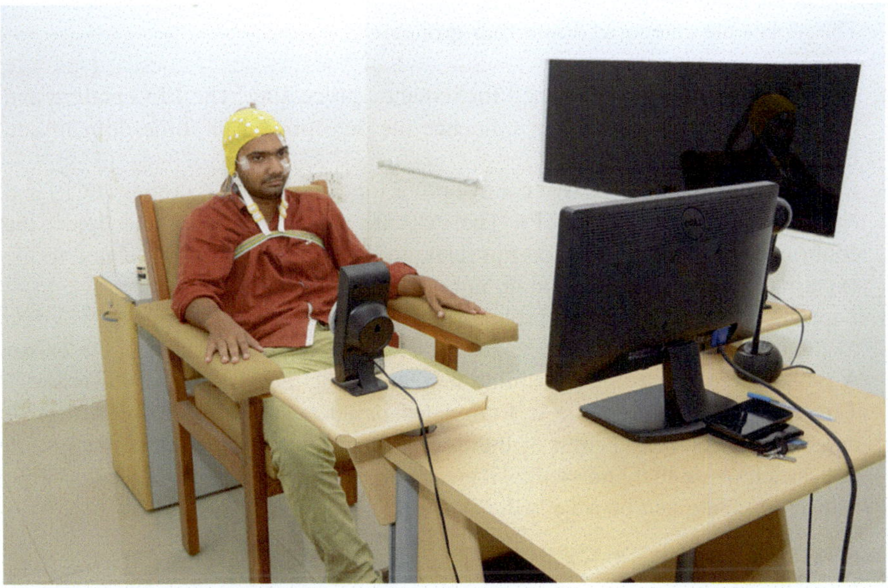

The Brain Electrical Oscillation Signature Profiling test, widely known as the BEOS test, projects the signature of remembrance of experience using a frequency-time domain analysis program.

For the administration of the BEOS test on the examinee, the pre-test interview, court order and examinee's informed consent are taken similarly during the administration of the polygraph test.

13.6.1 Formulation of Scenario and Probes

After taking detailed information about the crime and the subject under investigation, the forensic expert prepares the scenario and probes. As a procedure, the scenario is prepared on specific sequential detail given by the I.O. The more minute details are given from the I.O., the better the formulation of probes will be. Based on the details given by I.O and the interview with the subject, the scenario is formulated comprising intention, motive, conspiracy, act and disposal of evidence. The probes in the scenario are formulated sequentially and are interlinked with the events and characters. The probe is given an I.D. mark based on the type of awareness/memory of the subject and the hypothesis of the police.

The probe is very crucial as it should be formulated in such a way that it triggers the neurocognitive process of the subject. The probe's words and phrases should be formulated so that the subject understands its semantic process and, thereby, its interpretation. Similarly, when probes are recorded on the BEOS test, the speaker should not use any emotions or add expression to the probe. The subject should be able to understand the recorder's voice and dialect.

The probes are categorized into four groups:

1. Neutral probes: They are formed for semantic processing. The EEG pattern and fluctuation in the baseline can influence the detection of the time domain and frequency domain.
2. Control probes: There are two control probes: positive control probes (PCP) and Negative control probes (NCP). The PCP are not controversial and depict the confirmed facts, while NCP do not relate to the subject. They are related to the experimenter's hypotheses and do not necessarily relate to the subject.
3. Target A probe: The target A probe is formulated based on the information given by the I.O. If the subject's test results show Experiential knowledge of the Target A probe, there is a strong possibility that the subject is suspected of the crime.
4. Target B probe: This probe is formulated based on the subject's narration. It reflects the subject's version of the incident and his alleged role. If the system indicates Experiential knowledge, it means there is a probability that whatever the subject is saying can be accepted.

5. The procedure for the BEOS test: The BEOS instrument should be kept in a soundproof room with a one-way mirror facility. The chair should be placed in the middle of the examination room with a computer monitor a meter away from the chair to present visual probes. The speakers are placed in the room to hear the auditory probes and instruct the subject at every stage of a new session of BEOS recording. The recording and proceeding of the BEOS test are monitored from the examiner's room. The subject sits with his legs resting on a leg rest on the floor of the examination room, while the examiner sits on the other side of the one-way mirror room. The examiner maintains the subject's privacy and confidentiality. The first requirement before BEOS administration is to record the auditory probes and store the visual probes for a display to the subject. The visual and auditory stimulation presentation (VASP) is used for recording auditory probes. Each probe is read out in a uniform and steady tone when recorded digitally on the computer—a list of probes assembled in the VASP system and event markers attached to each probe. The main data acquisition system controls the probe presentation, which monitors the incoming EEG signals online and sends the probe presentation signal to the VASP system if the incoming EEG is in predefined conditions. The probe presentation is delayed until such a predefined condition is restored.

   The electrical activity from the scalp is recorded on a multichannel amplifier using 30-channel electro-cap and two channels for eye movements. The electrodes positions used are FP1, Fp2, AF4, F7, F3, Fz, F4, F8, FT7, FC3, FCz, FC4, FT8, T3, C3, Cz, C4, TP7, CPz, CP4, TP8, T5, P3, P4, T6, O1 and O2 along with the electrodes attached below and above right eye and above left eye for calibration. The subject's scalp has to be clean and non-oily so that the electro-cap can be easily attached to the cap with the help of gel. The chest strap is attached to the subject's chest so that the electro-cap does not move and the easy recording. The subject is allowed to read the probes before the examination to avoid a startle reaction during the test. If the subject is sleeping or distracting his mind, the probes are not further presented, which makes the examiner alert and guides the subject to retake the test. After set I is completed, the subject is given a break and after that, set II is retaken, and the same procedure applies.

   The BEOS is started by asking the subject to sit relaxedly. As a part of calibration, the subject's eyes close and eyes open recording is taken. After that, the Target B probes are presented to the subject. The subject is instructed not to give verbal answers or non-verbal reactions to the probes heard. In between break is given to the subject which requires. After Target B probes (Set I) is over, the subject takes Set II, and the procedure is repeated. After the test is completed, the BEOS system generates the result. The result will indicate the subject's 'Experiential Knowledge' regarding the crime and his involvement in the crime.

13.7 Narco Analysis

The application of **Clinical hypnosis** was started to treat psychosomatic and mental disorders. Progressively the use of clinical hypnosis is done by other medical fraternities also for various purposes. The subjects having earlier traumatic experiences which are suppressed and later manifested in the form of psychological illness/problems are treated by clinical hypnosis. It removes the psychological blockage, inhibitions and fixations which disrupt the subject's daily life. Depending upon the severity, duration and individuals' personality make up the sessions of the hypnosis are scheduled. The hypnotherapy sessions are undertaken at intervals stretching from 30 to 45 min. Considering the subject's mental state, the therapist decides the interval and duration of the session. The hypnotherapy technique helps the therapist reach out to the root cause of the problem and thereby achieves catharsis. A sense of self-worth and well-being is generated in the subject through this technique. If the subject is overstressed or reluctant to take a suggestion or is non-cooperative, the therapist resorts to a technique in which the subject is taken to a trance with the help of the sodium pentothal drug. This method is commonly known as drug-induced hypnosis or Narco analysis. The first case of drug hypnosis was done in 1845. It is used in the high-profile Boston Strangler, Ted Bundy and Sam Shepherd cases. It is a valuable investigation tool with other evidence and aids the investigating agency in their quest to find the guilty.

The phrase 'truth serum' was given by Robert House in 1922, also known as the Father of Truth Serum. He experimented with Scopolamine on two criminals who were suspected of doing a crime. Under the influence of Scopolamine, the criminals denied the charges levied upon them; later, during the case trial, these suspects were released, which made House believe that Scopolamine cannot create a lie. After that, Blackwena, 1929, used sodium amytal to produce a hypnotic effect on patients. It was observed by Lindemann 1932, that sodium amytal injected slowly and intravenously produced a marked effect in psychiatric patients. After that, sodium pentothal (thiopental), was used widely by the soldiers of World War II to overcome their traumatic experiences. The drugs commonly used in the context of narcoanalysis or truth serum tests are sodium amytal (amobarbital), pentothal sodium (thiopental) and seconal (seconbarbital).

The use of narcoanalysis as a technique gained attention in 1987 when it was first used in Gujarat, India, specifically in the Sabarmati jail for accused individuals. It received further attention after the Godhra carnage. The Narco analysis after that was used in cases where the suspects/criminals are suspected of withholding the information, misleading the investigation or falsely confessing the crime. The lack of scientific interrogation methods and alternatives to coercive tactics led the investigating agencies to use Narco analysis as a tool. Drug-induced hypnosis, or Narco analysis is used for investigative purposes, when agencies reach a dead end and are clueless. This technique aims to provide the missing gaps in the investigation and provide leads for further investigation. It can help the reveal the plans of the accused and eliminate the innocent from the case. In the past, Scopolamine was used on prisoners who denied the charges of murder and eventually were found not guilty.

Subsequently, the drugs, viz., sodium pentothal and ketamine, are used for invasive procedures. Sodium pentothal, commonly used by anesthetists for surgical procedures and is considered safe to administer to subjects in forensic work.

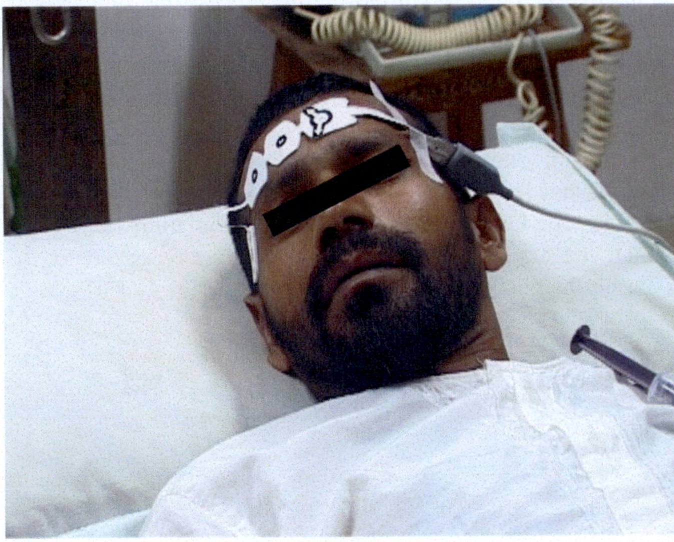

13.7.1 Procedure for Narco Analysis Test

As a procedure for the Narco test, the subject's pre-test interview and court permission for the Narco analysis should be taken. Before conducting the test, the subject is explained the procedure and the possible outcome of the test and the right to refuse the test (Indian Constitution Article, 20 (3)). The government doctor checks the subject's physical and mental fitness. Once the subject is certified physical and mentally fit by the medical authority, the post-test Narco analysis test is done to assess the physical and mental state of the subject.

The Narco analysis requires an environment with medical equipment and tools. Because it is an invasive technique, emergency medical kits and backup are a must to deal with medical emergencies. The test is conducted by a team comprising forensic experts and includes the anesthetist responsible for giving the drug to the subject, psychiatrist and nursing staff. The role of a psychiatrist is to monitor the mental abrasion or trauma during the narco interview. The nursing staff must take care of the subject during and after the test. The whole Narco interview should be videographed. If the lawyer is required to witness the test, they are given the option to watch their client through a one-way mirror. No one except the team members is allowed during the Narco interview to maintain the suspect's privacy and confidentiality. During the Narco interview, free association techniques are used to make the subject stress free and comfortable. The subject is not pursued but is encouraged to unload their negative feelings, anxiety and fear. As the drug proceeds, the subject's body will be loose, and their speech will be slurred. In this process, the subject is asked about the incident, and the missing relevant information regarding the incident is revealed. The information given by the subject during the Narco interview should be carefully analysed, as the subject has said things in between his state of wakefulness and trance.

After the Narco interview, the post-test interview is conducted to assess the physical condition and based on clues gathered during the Narco interview; the subject is interviewed. Often the subject reveals the truth during the post-test interview, which the expert records. The subject is also asked to write further information during the post-test interview.

13.8 Suspect Detection System

The suspect detection system, also known as the 'SDS' test, is a technology applied to interrogation and screening systems for identifying potential criminals at much earlier stages of the investigation. It is a technology capable of collecting and analyzing psycho-physiological indications and cross-referencing these indications with additional objective information. It is effective in counter-terrorism and crime prevention behaviour pattern recognition. SDS develops an intent detection system using behavioural pattern recognition algorithms and business intelligence. The software uses the 'Guilty knowledge' and 'Stimulated Reaction' methods with advanced sensors like P300, GSR, BVP and Thermal Imaging analysis. The system is portable and easy to administer at any given place. The test administration is less time consuming, and results are auto-generated, making the system objective and reliable. The system performs the test with a high level of accuracy and reliability. The SDS system enjoys the status of the only established technology which has proved to be able to differentiate between 'guilty' and 'innocent' within 5 min with a low rate of false alarm.

This system works on a Stimulated Psycho Physical Reaction (SPPR) where the postulate is that a criminal and a non-criminal will show different levels of arousal and psycho-physical reactions to the same set of words or questions. Such reactions are uncontrollable since the words or questions can only evoke reactions in people with the necessary knowledge and intent to harm. The SDS uses the guilty knowledge test to identify an individual's guilt.

The theoretical basis of this instrument is that visual and audio stimuli will increase the subject's physiological arousal. The psycho-physiological uncontrolled responses (parasympathetic system) of the criminal intent or guilty knowledge-related questions or statements.

The significant advantages of the SDS system are as follows:

1. Automated Decision-making tool: It enables screening and investigation to isolate terrorists, criminals and hostile employees at checkpoints, border crossings, interrogation facilities, crime scenes, combat zone and field operations.
2. Self-learning system: Analyse the historical data and study behavioural patterns
3. One-stop intelligence collection: Document authentication, biometric I.D. (fingerprint, voice, video) data collection for future tracking
4. Easy to operate: It is a fully automated system that does not require an expert human operation.

13.8.1 The Procedure for the SDS Test

The SDS system consists of hardware; a laptop attached to the case, the sensors are alongside the laptop, which is responsible for electrodermal tracing, as well as some supporting devices like a scanner (to scan the subject's I.D.), camera (to record and save the facial movements of the subject) and biometric (for data collection) are also available in this system. The software includes essential system management, signal processing and decision algorithm, which are inbuilt to provide the algorithms for detecting physiological responses. This system, with the help of these parameters, detects the person who has the knowledge or gives the response related to malicious intent.

The examinee is seated comfortably in front of the instrument. The examinee's biometric and digital photo is taken with the camera attached to the system. The examiner first logs into the system and fills in the details of the examinee in the 'enter examinee' section, like filling up the name of the examinee, date of birth, gender, photo and fingerprint. After that, the questions are prepared, typed and recorded in the system based on the investigating officer's and subject's interview. The examinee's left hand on the palm sensor is placed on the system. The questionnaire comprises multiple-choice type questions about the crime. One of these questions contains information only the examiner and the suspect/criminal would know about. The examinee's reaction to a specific event-related stimulation will differ from that of an uninvolved individual. Using the Guilty knowledge method enables the SDS to build and use an algorithm that can significantly reduce the levels of false alarms. The GSR in the system checks the examinee's blood volume pressure. This is used as it has higher accuracy in detecting blood pressure.

A total of 4 +2 sets of questions are presented to the examinee. After four sets of questions, another two sets from the earlier four sets are repeated, which are most relevant to the situation. The benefit of the system is that only if the system suspects the examinee will the fifth and sixth sets of questions be repeated. The questions will be presented on the screen of the examinee. The questions are recorded and can be simultaneously heard through headphones by the examinee. The questions are usually in the language the examinee understands and can comprehend. The examinee's GSR is simultaneously measured through a sensor case while he/she answers the questions. The whole procedure takes about 5–7 min. The test results are automatically generated by the system and given to the examiner. The results is a statistically calculated algorithm based on the SDS database. It conducts analysis and weighs the strongest reaction to the relevant stimulus. Validity of each reaction is done by comparing all the reactions, and the results are given as to whether the examinee is a 'Suspect' or 'Non-Suspect'.

13.9 Layered Voice Analysis (LVA)

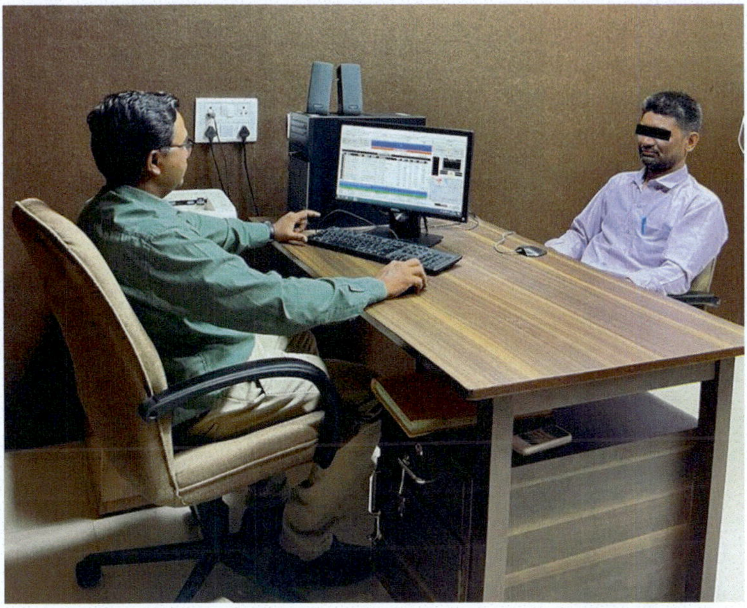

This technique focuses on the emotions conveyed through the speech. It recognizes and identifies emotions based on the analysis of vocal characteristics and patterns. It analyses the conversation of the subject in real time, which will help the examiner to probe further into the doubtful conversation and may help the examiner to understand the direction of the criminal. The technique leads to hidden and concealed information just by conversation. The subject is required to speak into the microphone during the LVA test. The interview with the subject should be conducted in a noise-free environment so that the voice of the subject is audible and clear. LVA provides quick analysis in real time, which helps the examiner to answer specific questions related to the subject's role in the offence. In case involving multiple suspects, this test may help in narrowing down the suspect pool within a short period. LVA generates automated result that summarizes the overall emotional behaviour of the subject. The interview taken can also be used as offline analysis and further investigation. The result is displayed in the form of a graph, segment and bar display, making it user-friendly and easy to understand.

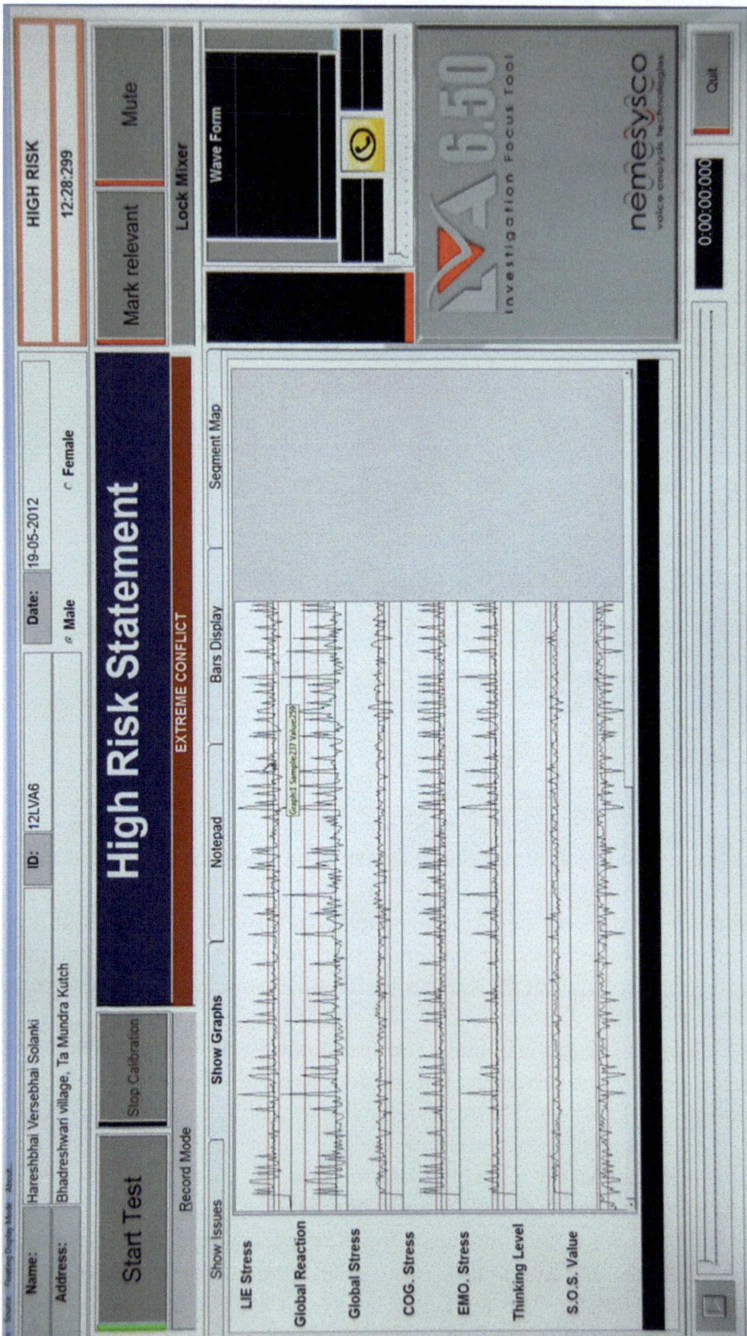

Online analysis of LVA test

13.10 Conclusion

In conclusion, the chapter sheds light on the essential elements of forensic psychology in relation to investigative techniques and tools. Forensic psychologists can gather valuable information and assess the veracity of statements by employing a range of interview techniques, including the Morgan Interview Technique, FAINT Interview, and Statement Analysis. Moreover, specialized tools like the polygraph, narco analysis, BEOSP test, Suspect Detection System, and layered voice analysis provide additional means for extracting crucial insights and detecting potential deception cues. By leveraging these techniques and incorporating them into forensic investigations, practitioners can contribute to more accurate and reliable outcomes, ensuring the criminal justice system's integrity. Understanding forensic psychology's diverse methodologies and tools equips professionals with valuable resources to enhance their ability to investigate, analyze, and understand complex criminal cases.

References

Bartol CR, Bartol AM (2006) History of forensic psychology. In: Weiner IB, Hess AK (eds) . The handbook of forensic psychology, John Wiley & Sons Inc., pp 3–27

Benussi V, Antonelli M (2002) Psychologische Schriften: Psychologische Aufsätze (1904–1914). Brill, Netherlands

Gordon NJ, Fleisher WL (2010) Effective interviewing and interrogation techniques. Elsevier Science, Netherlands

Gordon NJ (2016) Essentials of polygraph and polygraph testing, 1st edn. CRC Press. https://doi.org/10.1201/9781315438641

Gordon NJ, Fleisher WL (2019) Effective interviewing and interrogation techniques, 4th edn. Academic Press Elsevier, London

Hirota A, Matsuda I, Kobayashi K, Takasawa N (2005) Development of a portable digital polygraph system. Jpn J Forensic Sci Technol 10(1):37–44

Kircher JC, Raskin, DC (2002) Computer methods for the psychophysiological detection of deception

Mackenzie J (1908) The ink polygraph. Br Med J 1(2476):1411

Mandler G (1980) Recognizing: the judgment of previous occurrence. Psychol Rev 87(3):252–271. https://doi.org/10.1037/0033-295X.87.3.252

Matte JA (1996) Forensic psychophysiology using the polygraph: scientific truth verification, lie detection. JAM Publications

Mukundan CR (2007) Brain experience: neuroexperiential perspectives of brain-mind. Atlantic Publications, New Delhi

Stern W (1936) The metaphysical foundations of critical personalism. Personalist 17(3):238–248

Widacki J (2015) Discoverers of the galvanic skin response. Eur Polygraph 9(4):209–220. https://doi.org/10.1515/ep-2015-0008

Wynn JK, Dawson ME, Schell AM (2000) Discrete and continuous prepulses have differential effects on startle prepulse inhibition and skin conductance orienting. Psychophysiology 37(2): 224–230

Zachariah BA, Vaya DS, Zachariah BT (2017) Brain fingerprinting technology (BFP) and brain electrical oscillation signature (BEOS): which unique technique is best. Glob J Res Anal 6(12)

Essentials of Forensic Physics 14

Abhimanyu Harshey, Tanurup Das, Vindresh Mishra,
Ritesh K. Shukla, and Ankit Srivastava

Abstract

Forensic Physics is the branch of Criminalistics that utilizes the principles of physics and lays the foundation for the analysis of physical evidences. Scientific examination of physical evidence provides the information of investigative significance. Glass, soil, paint, fiber, tool marks, serial numbers, etc., are the most common types of physical evidences that are often encountered at various types of scenes of occurrence. Investigation and adequate interpretation of the analytical results ensure the way fair justice. In the connection with the interpretation of results, the role of statistics and standards has been discussed also. This chapter is dedicated to the forensic analytical perspective of the different physical evidence, namely, glass, soil, paint, fiber, tool marks, and serial numbers. For the ease of understanding and complexities of the subject, scientific fundamentals and principles have also been discussed. Analytical procedures for the forensic examination of physical evidence are discussed in consonance with the current research trends.

A. Harshey
Department of Anthropology, Lucknow University, Lucknow, Uttar Pradesh, India

T. Das · A. Srivastava (✉)
School of Forensic Sciences, The West Bengal National University of Juridical Sciences, Kolkata, West Bengal, India
e-mail: ankitsrivastava@nujs.edu

V. Mishra
Central Forensic Science Laboratory, Kolkata, India

R. K. Shukla
Department of Biological and Life Sciences, Ahmedabad University, Ahmedabad, India

P. Shrivastava et al. (eds.), *Textbook of Forensic Science*,
https://doi.org/10.1007/978-981-99-1377-0_14

Keywords

Forensics · Criminalistics · Glass · Soil · Paint · Fiber · Tool marks · Serial number

14.1 Introduction

Forensic Science is the blend of science with law. Obviously, Forensic Science is multidisciplinary in nature that includes a plethora of scientific disciplines for the analysis and investigation of physical evidences and thereby provides the scientific grounds to the criminal justice system. The term "*Physical evidence*" is frequently used in Forensic Science. Any tangible object is termed as physical evidence in legal context when it enters to the court of law as evidence. However, the scientific perspective of physical evidence connotes the objects collected from the scene of occurrence and having potential investigative significance. A scene of occurrence is generally referred to as a rich source of physical evidences. The interaction of the living beings or any physical entity with each other or with the surroundings are recorded as the change in the immediate environment. These changes, caused due to the mutual exchange of traces, follow the law of nature and, therefore, can be studied scientifically. Locard's principle of exchange defines the origin of the physical evidence and its role as a mute witness (Mistek et al. 2019).

Additionally, the term "*trace evidence*" is a frequently used term in Forensic Science that defines a specific category of physical evidence. Here, the term trace is representative of two means, i.e., size or amount, and residues. Materials of small size or in small amounts are often present at the scene of crime. However, size may not be referred to as a defining characteristic as materials may also be present at the crime scene in large amounts. The later notion defines the residues or traces left as a consequence of any event. This notion seems to be reflecting the idea of transfer or exchange of the traces. Dr. Paul L. Kirk quotes that anything can be physical evidence but all physical evidences are not essentially trace evidence. The term trace evidence also reflects the idea of transfer evidence (Kirk 1953). The identification of evidence and its analysis is a challenging task and essentially requires the appropriate scientific temperament, knowledge, skill, and experience. Forensic examination of the physical evidence provides the investigative aids by linking culprit, victim, and other elements with crime, establishing the sequence of the events. In other words, the physical or trace evidence contributes to the reconstruction of the crime scene as well as offers associative evidence (Stoney and Stoney 2015; Buzzini et al. 2019; Trejos et al. 2020). The forensic investigation extracts the information, from the exhibits, of evidential significance and beyond the shadow of reasonable doubt and thus strengthens the pathway of unbiased and fair justice (Fig. 14.1).

Forensic Physics is the branch of Forensic Science that utilizes the principles of Physics for the purpose of physical evidence analysis. Forensic Physics dominantly undertakes the study and the analysis of physical properties of the evidence in account. Physical properties such as density, refractive index, and birefringence are principally analyzed. This chapter is focused on the forensic examination of

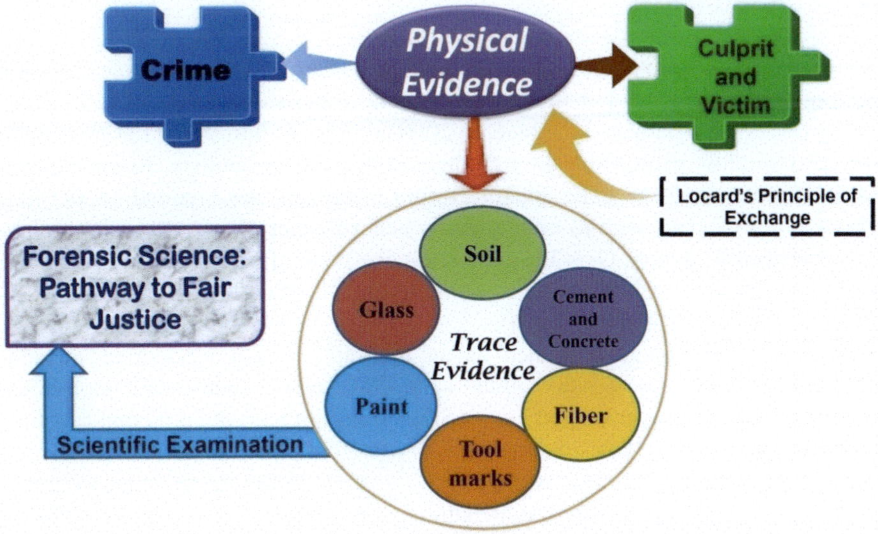

Fig. 14.1 Concept of physical and trace evidence: linking crime with culprit and victim and scientific examination of evidence ensuring the way for fair justice

glass, soil, paint, fiber, ropes and cables, tool marks, and serial numbers. These are most commonly used in daily life as well as often supposed to be present at the crime scene. Indeed, these have their own narration that needs adequate forensic interpretation. It is very interesting to know how the fundamentals and techniques of basic science are used to decode the silence of the evidence. Basic fundamental and relevant phenomenon have been discussed also for the ease of understanding of complexities.

14.2 Glass

Glass is one of the frequently appearing evidences at the scenes of hit and run, burglary, shooting incidents, etc. Glass is well-explored topic in basic sciences. Glass examination efficaciously contributes to the reconstruction of the crime scene. It involves the application of principles and techniques of various subject areas of physics and its branches, i.e., mechanics, optics, etc. Examination of physical properties, fracture analysis, and physical match dominantly contributes to the forensic analysis of glass. Since compositional variations affects the properties of the glass, the chemistry of glass is another significant aspect that needs to be understood before moving toward the forensics. Careful observation of physical and chemical properties provides sufficient grounds for the classification of glass; however, it requires experience and adequate knowledge. In this section we will discuss and explore the glass in terms of nature, composition, and forensic examination.

14.2.1 Introduction

The word Glass is derived from a late-Latin term "*Gloesum,*" which denotes lustrous and transparent material. The first manufacturing of glass is reported in 1500 BC by the Egyptians for ornamental purpose. In 2000 BC, Syrians introduced flat glass to be used as a window pane. With the introduction of oven technology, Romans made major improvements to glass manufacturing. Germans are credited to develop various types of glass such as optical glass, heat resistant glass, and cooking glass in the nineteenth century. Over the period, the glass manufacturing process has been undergone various technological developments for enhanced quality and cost-effective products (Varshneya 1994).

Glass is conventionally defined as an inorganic fusion product of metallic silicates that has cooled to rigid state. Therefore, glass is amorphous, non-crystalline, and super-cooled liquid. Silica sand (SiO_2) is the principal constituent of all commercial glasses. Silica is basic glass former, while other materials are added to meet the purpose. For example, lime stone and alumina are added to impart durability to the glass. Different metallic compositions are added as coloring substances to impart specific color to the product. The component and thereby resulting color is summarized in Table 14.1 (Copley 2001).

Glass manufacturing is a multistep process, as illustrated in Fig. 14.2, that initiates with the formation of the batch that is weighing and mixing of raw materials,

Table 14.1 Coloring chemical components imparting specific color to the glass

Color	Component
Blue	Cobalt oxide; cupric salt; iron, vanadium
Purple	Gold chlorides (Purple of Cassius); manganese; nickel; titanium; neodymium
Green	Ferrous oxide; sodium chromate; potassium di chromate; chromium; cupric salt; cobalt; vanadium
Yellow	Sodium arsenite; nickel; cadmium sulfide; cerium; uranium; chromium
Red	Selenium; gold; antimony sulfide; copper
Pink	Selenium; chromium; cobalt
Amber	Carbon; sulfur
Brown	Carbon; sulfur; titanium; iron
Black	Ferric oxide; cupric oxides; excess of nickel and manganese

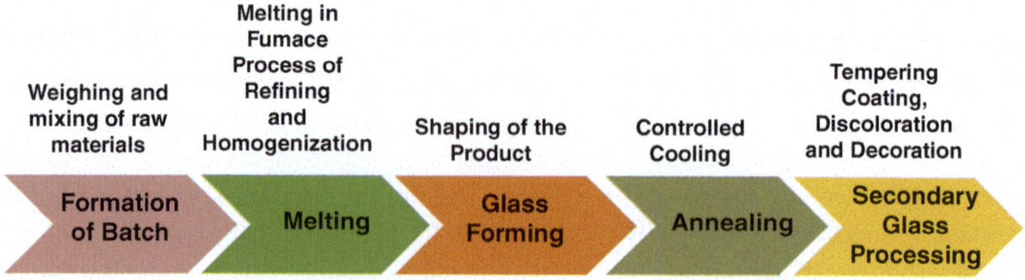

Fig. 14.2 Schematic representation of glass manufacturing process

i.e., acidic oxides, basic oxides, coloring substance (to provide specific color to the glass), and cullets (waste glass). The batch is placed at high temperature (approximately 1500 °C) in a furnace. CO_2 and water gases are emitted as the raw material melts and thereby produces the bubbles on the surface. The refining process eliminates these bubbles. However, homogenization ensures the removal of small localized variations in composition that may lead to variations in the refractive index, therefore causing some visual defects. Molten glass forms a wide range of products from flat glass and containers to a filament of small diameter. Viscosity changes with temperature. Therefore, the range of viscosity change rate and glass forming method must be appropriate with each other. The cooling of glass is not a uniform process that may cause uncontrolled stress. Annealing is controlled cooling which imparts the stress resistivity to the glass and thus makes it durable. Secondary glass processing involves tempering (reheating and rapid cooling), coating, discoloring (removal of color sheds naturally imparted by raw materials), and decoration of the glass product (Copley 2001).

14.2.2 Composition and Variety of Glass

Routine life meets with the variety of glass products with distinguished compositional differences to serve specific purpose. Fused Silica (SiO_2), after cooling, forms glass which is good thermal shock resistant and chemically durable. Soda-lime glasses have a wide spectrum of products having much involvement in daily life of a common man such as bottles (containers), flat glass (window pan), and other domestic glassware. Silica is fused at 1700 °C; therefore, sodium carbonate is used as an additive which converts into sodium oxide and lowers the melting temperature ranging between 1500 and 1650 °C. Lime imparts durability to the glass. The presence of impurities or other components (whether accidental or intentional) offers a means for discrimination among glass pieces in a forensic context (Almirall et al. 2000).

On the other hand, kitchenware, laboratory glassware, etc., are borosilicate glasses that possess high thermal stability and chemical durability. Boron oxide (B_2O_3) is added principally with silica to improve performance against thermal shock. Additionally, smaller quantities of alumina (Al_2O_3) may also be there. To deal with the temperature higher than the melting point of borosilicate glass, aluminosilicate glass offers good deal. It typically includes 20% alumina with other oxides of calcium, magnesium, and small amounts of boron oxide. Steam boiler, gauge glass, combustion tube, etc., are major applications of aluminosilicate glass. Lead oxide (PbO) is a dominant constituent of optical glass. A glass with at least 24% PbO is generally referred to as crystal glass. PbO accounts for the high refractive index and thus useful for the formation of flint glass (high dispersive glass). Other optical purposes such as optical filter may be achieved by the addition of other elements, e.g., Cu, Ni, Mn, Fe, etc. However, incorporation of the heavy metallic oxides contents in silicate glass yields radiation shielding effects. Lead glasses with different compositions are also useful for electrical applications. Borate glass contains PbO (60–90%) and offers soldering applications. Vanadium oxide (V_2O_5) and phosphorus pentaoxide (P_2O_5) are used in phosphate glasses that are semiconducting oxide glasses. Chalcogenide glass is non-oxide in nature and represents a particular class of semiconductor glass. It is used in the manufacturing of infrared transmitting materials, optical components of thermal imaging devices, etc. General quantitative compositional details for different types of glass are summarized in Table 14.2 (Copley 2001).

14.2.3 Considering Glass as Evidence

Interpretation of glass evidence in forensics has been practiced for a long time. Various researchers have contributed to the different investigative dimensions of glass evidence. In fact, glass is one of the most obvious types of evidence that is frequently present at various scenes of occurrence, namely, hit and run, arson, burglary, shooting incidence, etc. Glass may be present either as shattered pieces or as a fractured entity (Stoney and Thornton 1985). Glass, as evidence, is principally investigated to explore the origin of the source (whether two or more pieces belong to the same source?) and fractography. Fracture analysis is often referred to as fractography that deals with an understanding of fracture mechanism to interpret the fractures. Fracture analysis assists the investigator to explore a wide spectrum of queries such as cause of the fracture, nature of the impact, the direction of impact, and angle of impact. Analysis of the physical properties of glass helps an investigator to identify or to discriminate the glass panes (Jauhari et al. 1974; Stoney and Thornton 1985; Gogotsi and Mudrik 2010). In this section analytical perspectives of glass are discussed from forensic stand point.

14.2.4 Forensic Examination of Glass Evidence

14.2.4.1 Examination of Physical Properties

As mentioned previously, refractive index and density are the targeted physical properties for forensic analysis. In this section we will come across with the experimental procedure followed for the determination of the refractive index and density.

14.2.4.1.1 Refractive Index Assessment

As a basic rule, a ratio of the speed of light in vacuum and any other medium is referred to as refractive index. Due to the greater speed of light in vacuum than that of in any medium, the value of the refractive index is essentially greater than one. Refractive index of any medium depends upon the temperature and the wavelength of light in inverse relation. However, contrary to liquid and gases, temperature negligibly affects the refractive index of any solid. Different types of glasses possess different refractive indexes and thus provide a valuable mean for the comparison of glass pieces. Forensic Science laboratories apply Becke Line Immersion Method for the assessment of refractive index of glass. The Becke line method involves the

Table 14.2 Quantitative cescription of glass composition (in %)

	SiO_2	Al_2O_3	Fe_2O_3	Na_2O_3	K_2O	CaO	MgO	PbO	B_2O_3	As_2O_5
Flat glass	71	2.14	–	16	–	9	3	–	–	–
Domestic glassware	71	3	2	16	1	5	3	–	1	–
Borosilicate glass	80	4.5	–	4.5	–	–	–	–	11	–
Lead crystal	54.9	0.1	0.02	0.2	12.3	–	–	31.9	0.5	0.5
Optical glass	38	0.2	–	5.2	1.2	0.3	–	45.1	–	–
Insulating lead	63	3.5	–	7.6	6	0.2	–	21	–	–
Container	72.7	1.9	0.22	13.8	1	10	–	–	–	–

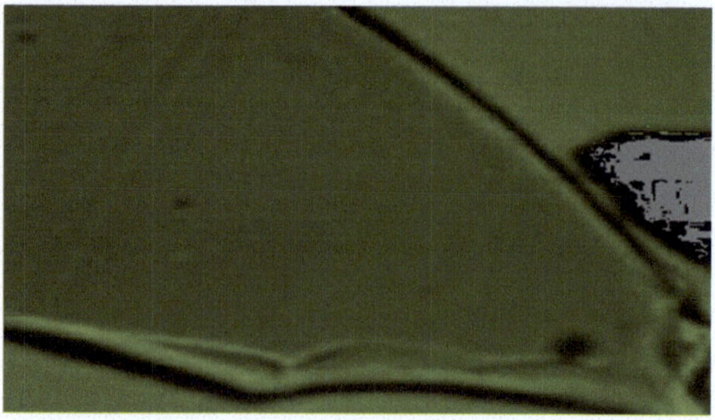

Fig. 14.3 Appearance of a bright halo around the glass in Becke line method

phenomenon of the refraction for the refractive index measurement. The deviation in the path of light beam occurs as the medium changes. As per Snell's rule, the ratio of sine values of angle of incidence and refraction is also referred as refractive index. When any light beam travels through any transparent object, namely glass, it bends or deviates due to refraction and this is the reason that glass becomes visible. Similarly, if the glass is immersed in the liquid of same refractive index as that of glass, no refraction will take place and glass will become indistinguishable to the eyes. This forms the conceptual foundation for the refractive index measurement.

Practically, the immersion of glass in liquid of different refractive index causes a bright halo due to the difference in the refraction by the liquid and the glass. This bright halo is technically referred to as Becke line (Fig. 14.3). It is notable that, on the immersion of glass in the liquid of same refractive index, Becke line disappears irrespectively from complete disappearing of the glass. It has been observed that glass, especially thick glass, does not disappear completely. For this purpose, a hot stage with a thermocouple is attached to a compound microscope. This instrumental sophistication is commercially termed as Glass Refractive Index Measurement (GRIM). To ensure robust interpretation of the results as well as to reduce the probability of error, experiments should be performed at various wavelengths. Found values of refractive index must be plotted versus different temperatures (the plot is also known as dispersion plot) to measure the variation of refractive index with the temperature (Munger et al. 2014).

It is interesting to know that microscope intervened in the refractive index assessment of small glass pieces in the year 1972. In this series of consecutive developments, GRIM came into existence in 1980. Further, GRIM 2 enhanced the sensitivity by including a phase contrast microscope with a CCD detector coupled video camera attached to the hot stage (Locke and Underhill 1985; Hamer 2001). GRIM 3 has eased the process of RI measurement due to its compatibility for automation.

14.2.4.1.2 Density Assessment

Conceptually, density is the distribution of mass per unit volume (i.e., D= m/v). Density determination of glass fragment involves the immersion of glass piece in any liquid. If the glass pieces are regularly shaped, a direct method may be used for the same. However, irregularly shaped glass piece needs indirect assessment method. Direct method lies on the foundation of the concept that each object, when immersed in any liquid, removes equal volume of liquid. Recall the basic experiment of immersion of the ice cube in a glass filled with water. If a regularly shaped glass piece is immersed in any liquid, it will displace the liquid and increase the volume. The volume of displaced liquid will be equal to the volume of the glass piece.

Glass pieces present at the scene of occurrence are most frequently irregularly shaped. Therefore, indirect methods are more common. This method is known as sink and float method. This method involves the immersion of glass pieces into a mixture of two miscible liquid, such as bromobenzene and bromoform, filled in a tube. One liquid should have lower density, and the others should be of higher density than that of glass. The settlement of the glass pieces at different liquid levels depends upon their respective density. The movement of these pieces in variable density is caused due to the decrease in density by heating the tube. It is a sensitive method; however, repeated experiments are recommended for the elimination of error (Houck and Siegel 2010).

14.2.4.2 Interpretation of Glass Fracture

Fractography has been discussed over the decades by various researchers across the globe. Fracture analysis lays on the foundation of principles of mechanics. The strength of inter atomic force theoretically governs the strength of material. However, the tensile stress is associated with number of variables such as physical properties of the surface (namely, size and shape) and amount of load and its duration. Loading on the glass causes production of tension on the opposite side to the impact and thereby glass breaks. Interestingly, tensile stress of the glass is much lower than compressive strength; therefore, under the loading or any impact, tensile stress crosses its limit followed by the breaking of the glass. The stress is released in the form of cracks. It is worthy to note that crack propagates through the path of least resistance (Overend et al. 2007; Bradt 2011). In this regard, Griffith explained the static crack as reversible thermodynamic system and identified the need of preexisting flaws for the propagation of cracks (Griffith 1920).

However, another model identified a normal equilibrium between the rate of formation and rupture of atomic bonds. Applied stress disturbs this equilibrium and crack initiates as the consequence of exceeding the rate of rupture than that of formation. Further, Irwin introduced the stress intensity factor, representing the intensity of elastic stress near the crack tip, as a measure of brittleness or fracture toughness of the material (Irwin 1957). Glass failure under the unbalanced force does not follow the notions of Griffith and Irwin theory. Dynamic fracture mechanism undertakes such situations. In this regard, Mott took the kinetic energy of cracks into account to explain the behavior of cracks in terms of kinetic energy and crack velocity as a function of crack depth (Mott 1948).

As a crux of the above discussion, it may be referred that under the force, elastic bending of glass occurs. The stress and energy are transferred to the glass and

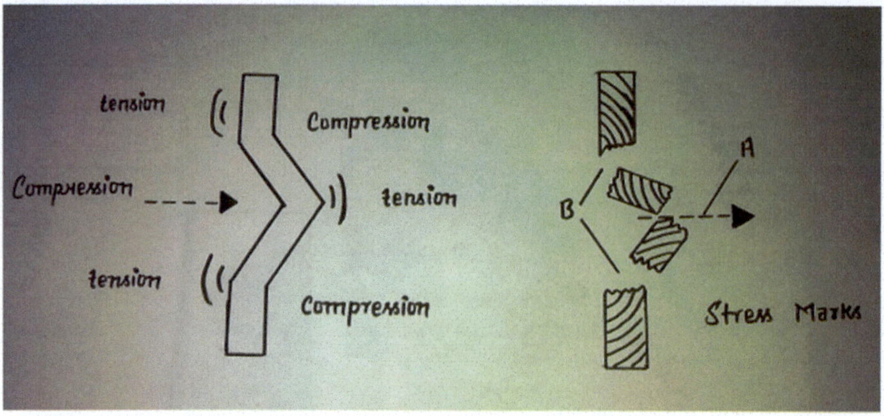

Fig. 14.4 Mechanism of glass fracture. (Source: Harshey et al. 2017)

produce tension on the opposite side of the surface facing the force. At this moment, stress releases outwards from the point of impact and thereby causes radial fractures. If the stress is still there, it will produce compression on the opposite side and subsequent tension on the forward side. It leads to the formation of fracture propagating between the radial cracks in spiral form, and therefore referred to as concentric fractures or spiral fractures. Additionally, high velocity projectile striking on the glass pane causes propagation of a shock wave, also known as compressive or stress wave, from the point of impact to the opposite side. Stress wave behaves like a tension wave and causes tension on the opposite side. Subsequently, it reflects as a compressive wave and produces compression on the front side. Interestingly, these consecutively reflected waves cause constructive interference and enhance the amplitude of resultant stress wave followed by the ejection of the scabs or flakes (also called chips). It results as formation of crater or cone fracture on the opposite surface. These cone fractures are also known as Hertzian fracture or Hopkinson fracture (Thornton 2001; Overend et al. 2007). Figure 14.4 presents the fracture mechanism followed in flat glass.

Alike to the flat glass, fracture of glass container due to impact is governed by the mechanism of hinge and flexure stress mechanism. The impact is followed by the outside bending of glass walls under flexure stress. This bending produces hinge stress. Notably, as a result of impact on the exterior surface of the glass container, flexure and hinge fractures originate on the inner and outer surfaces, respectively. In this thread, one more significant point is there to be discussed, i.e., fracture due to heat. Excessive exposure to the heat is another reason for the glass failure. Failure of flat glass due to thermal shock appears as wavy pattern of cracks. Alike to the fracture due to impact, the point of origin for the cracks is not observed. However, in the container, fractures originate from the bottom and do not show the fan-shaped branching of the cracks (Thornton 2001). Figure 14.5 presents some patterns of fracture due to various causes.

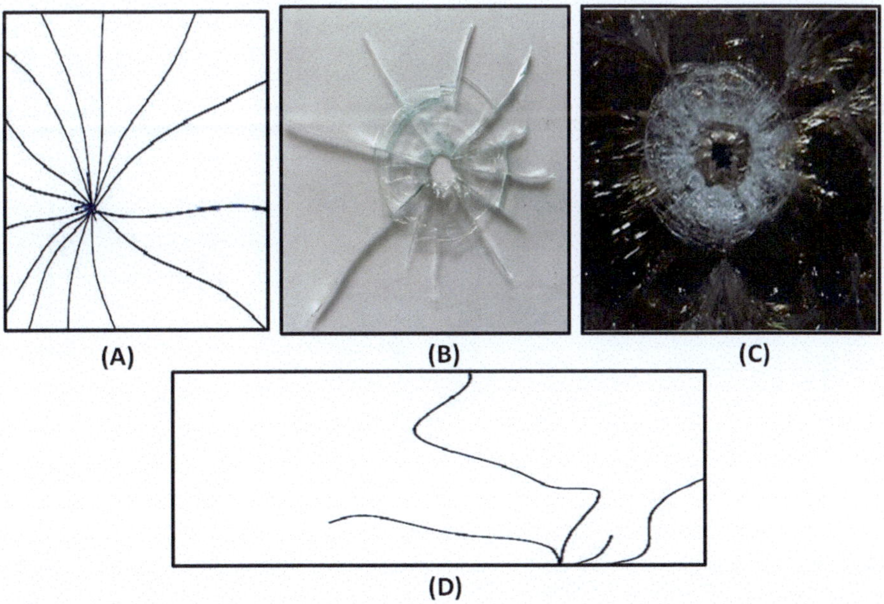

Fig. 14.5 Fracture pattern on glass due to various causes (**a**) fracture due to blunt impact; (**b**) projectile impact (fired through air rifle); (**c**) projectile impact (bullet fired through standard firearm); (**d**) fracture due to heat exposure

Understanding of fracture mechanisms provides the grounds to assess cause of the fracture as well as the direction of impact. Obviously, high velocity projectile impact will cause a regular shaped small hole with low flaking. Additionally, low velocity projectile will produce a comparatively large hole with irregularities in shape and more flaking. Diameter of fracture hole or crater is the function of crack propagation velocity rather than firearm caliber. Radial cracks create rib marks on the edge of the glass pane. It helps determine the direction of impact. As a rule of thumb, rib marks are produced as a consequence of radial cracks forming right angle on the reverse side to the direction of applied force. This observation is generally referred to as 3R rule. Set of curved lines, observed on the broken edge of the glass pane, is referred to as rib marks. A fractured glass pane possesses various features. Readers are suggested to refer Byous (2013) for more details about these marks and features. Shape of crater indicates the probable direction of impact. The impact perpendicular to the surface causes a symmetrical crater while greater flaking in the crater may be observed in the opposite direction of the impact if projectile hits on angle (Fig. 14.6).

Determination of the sequence of fracture is another important aspect of forensic fractography. Especially in the case of gunshot, as a basic rule, cracks do not cross the existing fractures. Radial cracks originating from later shot will not intersect the radial cracks caused by previous fractures as shown in figure. This approach provides significant aids to reconstruct the crime scene.

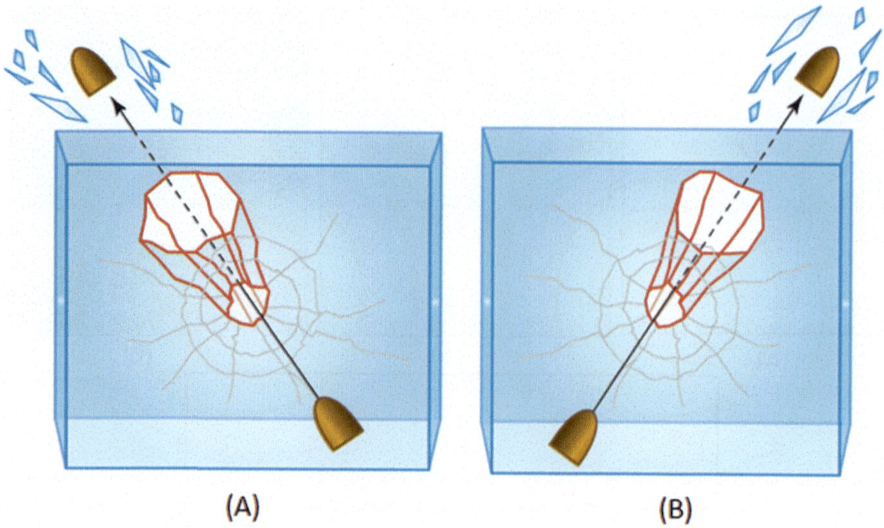

Fig. 14.6 Pattern of glass fracture due to bullet impacted at angle (**a**) gunshot from right side; (**b**) gunshot from left side. (Courtesy: Girard 2018)

Recently, many fracture studies have been reported. Harshey et al. (2017) analyzed the pattern of the fracture on a window pane made by air rifle. Further, Tiwari et al. (2019) studied the characteristics of multiple fractures due to the impact of air rifle pellet. Additionally, Abhyankar et al. (2018) investigated the impact of different pellet shapes on the glass fracture pattern. A terminal ballistics experiment was performed by Hsiao and Meng (2018) in order to estimate the impact velocity through the analysis of glass fracture patterns and deformed pellets. They found good correlation between the deformed pellet features and impact velocity. Waghmare et al. (2019) reported distinctive patterns of bullet after the interaction with the windowpane glasses. Since glass is brittle, several polymer sheets have offered a suffice substitute for the glass products. Alim et al. (2020) analyzed the fracture pattern on the polymethylmethacrylate sheet (PMMA). Authors found a statistical consistency in the features of the fractures. The absence of the concentric fractures was observed in the PMMA sheets.

Physical fit is another approach that significantly aids the forensic investigation and well reported in the literature. The exact matching or fitting of glass pieces through their broken edges is called as establishment of physical fit. Puzzle game may be referred to as a crude analogy for the same. It is comparatively easy to achieve physical fit in pieces with irregular margins. Over the year various methodologies, such as oblique light photography and superimposition of fracture surfaces, have been reported to analyze the physical fit. Recently Brooks et al. (2020) have reviewed the trend of physical fit studies in trace evidence analysis. In recent years, a shift has been observed towards more performance-based, objective, and statistically treated (assessing error rates to increase the probative value of the evidence), application of automated analysis using algorithms.

14.2.4.3 Elemental Analysis of the Glass

Elemental profiling of the glass is one of the routine analyses in forensic laboratories. It provides the means to classify the glass into possible categories. Classification may provide the link between the questioned and standard glass sample. Different studies show that discrimination based on physical properties such as refractive index and density may provide erroneous results. Several instrumental methods have been reported for the chemical compositional profiling of the glass samples. Spectroscopic methods have majorly contributed toward the same. Atomic spectroscopy methods, viz., Atomic Absorption Spectroscopy (AAS), Atomic Emission Spectroscopy with inductively coupled plasma (ICP-AES); X-ray fluorescence (XRF), and Scanning Electron microscope with energy or wavelength dispersive detectors (SEM-EDX/WDX), offer effective analytical approach for the same. Inductively Coupled Plasma Mass Spectroscopy (ICP-MS) is sophisticated technique that provides sensitive analysis with lower detection limits and has appeared as an effective alternative to the neutron activation analysis (NAA) (Akmeemana et al. 2020).

14.3 Soil

Soil is important trace evidence that appears at most of the scene of occurrence. As a general observation, it appears that different disciplines look toward the soil with different points of view. In the agriculture and engineering domain, soil is subjected as an important factor for cultivation, farming, and structural component, respectively. Additionally, chemical properties of soil are targeted in soil chemistry. From a forensic stand point, it is noteworthy that soil is supposed to be consist of natural earth materials (i.e., minerals, etc.) and disintegrated surfaces (both natural and artificial) that lie on earths' surface and may be transported by human interventions such as shoes and vehicles. Soil is class evidence that provides associative links between the suspect and crime scene. Forensic analysis of soil is multidisciplinary and method oriented in nature. It majorly involves the principles and techniques of pedology, mineralogy, geophysics, geochemistry, and molecular biology. Anthropological and archeological considerations have also been added to the soil forensics. Under or over rating of soil evidence may lead to confusing and misleading information. Therefore, while assessing the evidential value of a soil sample, utmost care is needed as well as expert advice is also advised. In this chapter, we will get familiar with the basic fundamentals of soil science that are essential for the understanding of forensic analytical concerns (Wiltshire 2009; Ruffell 2010).

14.3.1 Introduction and Morphology

Conventionally, the soil is referred to as a mixture of organic materials, minerals, liquid, etc., that supports life. In the terms of pedology, soil is attributed as medium for plant growth, a mean of water storage. The organic fraction of soil includes the decaying flora and fauna that is collectively known as humus. Minerals, that are crystalline solids possessing metal and non-metal atoms in regular geometry and compose the rocks, are inorganic constituents of soil. Factors like climate, relief, parent rock, vegetation, time, organism, etc., influence the formation of soil by various physical, chemical, and biological processes that ultimately contribute to the properties of the soil. An overview of the soil profile is depicted in Fig. 14.7.

Sand, clay, and silt are inorganic mineral constituents of soil that form quantitative background to define the soil texture. Properties such as porosity, permeability, infiltration, shrink–swell rate, water-holding capacity, and susceptibility to erosion essentially depend upon the soil texture. The size of a sand particle is greater than that of silt and clay. Clay particles are the smallest. United States Department of

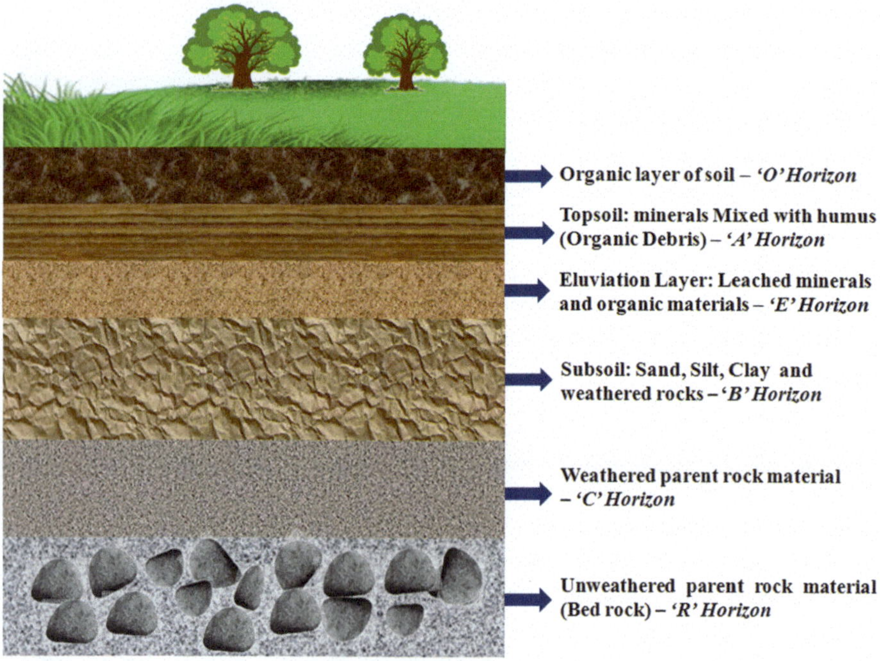

Fig. 14.7 Different layers of soil profile: at a glance

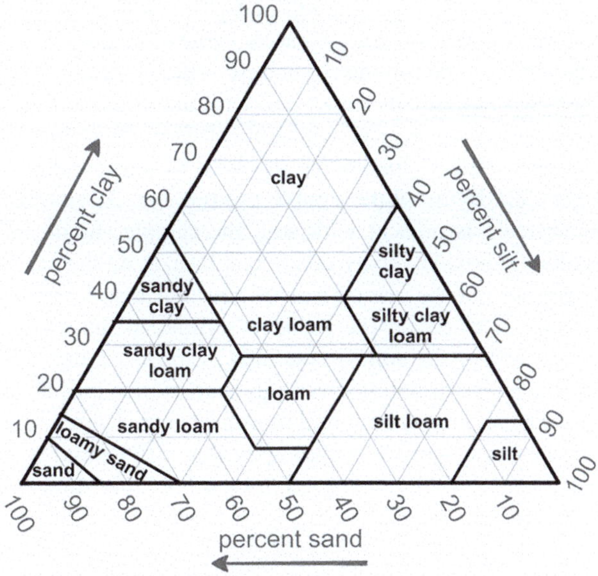

Fig. 14.8 USDA Soil textural triangle (Groenendyk et al. 2015)

Agriculture (USDA)[1] attributed the term "loam" to the specific category of soil that is categorized neither as sand nor as clay and silt (Fig. 14.8).

14.3.2 Considering Soil as Trace Evidence

The abundance of soil in the environment as well as good ability of its fine particles to transfer and stick increases the probability of its presence as trace evidence. Trace evidences are supposed to essentially possessing few characteristics such as unique, classifiable, easily transferable, and collectible. Forensic perspectives of soil science is majorly dedicated to determining the type of soil and to locating the source of origin. Soil examination aids the investigation of various criminal and civil cases such as hit and run, abduction, sexual assault, murder, theft, and drug shipment. Diversity of soil samples (that depends upon aforementioned factors) enables the forensic examiner to distinguish among the soil sample, although it requires a good experience. Urban soils are anthropogenic that possess various contaminants (ashes, bricks, glass, other metallic residues corresponding to different professions) associated with local human actives and thus increase the degree of discrimination power (Morrisson et al. 2009; Petrisor 2014; Spikmans 2019).

[1]United States Department of Agriculture (USDA) (1987) Soil mechanics level 1 Module 3. USDA textural classification study guide. Retrieved from https://www.nrcs.usda.gov/Internet/FSE_DOCUMENTS/stelprdb1044818.pdf.

The collection, packaging, and processing of soil samples is one of the crucial tasks that determine the probative value of analysis and evidence. Soil transfers and adheres to the belongings (such as vehicles, clothes, shoes, etc.) of the perpetrator and other individuals associated with the offense. The questioned samples must be collected in plastic jars with utmost care. Plastic and paper bags are not usually recommended. If the soil is in moist or wet condition and found adhered to the object, air drying of the sample is advisable. Additionally, if any biological fluid or tissue, etc., is present with soil, the sample should be packed in a paper bag or cardboard box. Diversity of soil emphasizes on the need for a representative sample. Therefore, for the comparison of questioned soil, samples should be collected from various distances at the scene of crime. In this regard, particle size distribution assessment of the soil sample aids in to assure that whether the sample is enough representative or not. Interestingly, variation in profile and horizon of soil with depth at one location may be found most probably. Therefore, need for the development of surface and subsurface mapping databases of natural and anthropogenic soils felt and many countries have moved forward in this direction (Fitzpatrick et al. 2009; Fitzpatrick 2013).

14.3.3 Forensic Analysis of Soil

Soil is analyzed with objectives of identification and discrimination of soil samples. Subsequently, it will lead to determination of the spot to which the soil sample corresponds. The analysis of soil is majorly based on the characterization of physical and chemical properties by means of different analytical methods.

14.3.3.1 Screening and Assessing Physical Properties

Color, particle size distribution, and density are major and targeted physical properties on the course of forensic soil analysis. The side-by-side visual comparison helps differentiate the soil samples by their color, texture, and gross appearance. Soil color is a joint function of moisture content, location, and the presence of minerals. It is obvious that fertile soils form agricultural land appears as dark brown while the whitish appearance of soil corresponds to the lack of moisture. Plant and animal residue, i.e., humus, is likely to be present in agricultural soils in higher quantity as compared to other types of soil. A stereomicroscope helps visualize the inorganic and organic (including man-made debris) constituents. A polarizing microscope enables the identification and characterization of soil components. It also provides the information about the color and particle size distribution.

Particle size distribution is a well-established parameter to characterize the soil. Standardized protocols for the same are available. Sieving offers an easy and effective approach for the assessment of particle size. A weighed quantity of the soil is passed with sieve nest, and the processed fraction is weighed and percentage distribution of particle size may be assessed. Additionally, particle size analyzer also provides the particle size distribution analysis (Di Maggio 2017).

Density is another property of interest in forensic investigation. The density gradient method is the conventional and accepted method for the density assessment of the soil. Experimental setup consists of glass tubes with diameters of 6 to 10 mm filled with liquids of different densities. Liquids such as ethanol and bromobenzene are usually used as low-density liquids that get settled at the top of tube. However, bromoform, tetrabromoethane, etc., are the liquids of choice to be used as high-density liquid. Generally, 6–10 liquids are placed there in a gradient tube. On the addition of soil sample to the density gradient tube, soil particles settle in the layer of equal density to that of soil. This helps compare the densities as well as assess the origin of questioned and controlled soil samples. In the light of diversity of the soil evidence, this test must be interpreted carefully as well as performed in combination with other methods to enhance the power of discrimination (Houck and Siegel 2010).

14.3.3.2 Assessment of Chemical Properties

Chemical perspectives of soil include morphology, pH, characterization of inorganic content (mineralogical aspect), identification of organic constituents, and foreign additives. Due to variability in the chemical profile of soil from the same area or location, chemical analysis also requires a careful interpretation of the results to distinguish or to associate the soil samples.

X-ray diffraction (XRD) is a very important and frequently used technique in the material science domain. It is based on the Bragg's rule. This is majorly used to study and reveal the structural geometry of crystals. Since minerals possess a distinct crystalline structure, XRD offers an effective approach for mineralogical study facilitating forensic analysis. It may also help characterize the foreign inorganic deposits such as metals in soil. XRD technique has gone several developments with time. Quantitative XRD analysis has been found to be a potential and effective approach for the forensic soil analysis. Additionally, XRF is a non-destructive and efficient approach for the elemental profiling of soil. Inductively coupled plasma optical emission spectroscopy (ICP-OES), ICP-MS, laser-induced ICP-MS (LA-ICP-MS), laser-induced breakdown spectroscopy (LIBS), and ICP-AES have also been applied for the elemental profiling of the soil. In addition to the elemental identification, these techniques have also been found to be efficient for the detection of toxic components, metallic deposits, and contaminants that may help characterize and differentiate the soil samples originated from different sites. In this thread of inorganic analysis, SEM-EDX is generally used analytical technique that offers visualization of soil components along with their profiling. SEM analysis reveals fine details of morphological characters, color, texture, and particle size at very high magnification. SEM-EDX results are useful for the discrimination and screening of the soil samples (Keaney et al. 2009; Woods et al. 2014a, b, 2016).

As marked previously, animal and plant residues, microbes, etc., are complex organic substance that constitutes the organic fraction of soil. Organic components also serve as markers for the identification and characterization of the soil. Humic acid, that is the product of an animal, plant, or bacterial decomposition, has been found to be an effective marker for the comparison of soil samples. Assessment of carbon and nitrogen content is the foundation for the organic analysis (Mulani and Deshpande 2018). Vibrational spectroscopy techniques, namely, Infrared (IR) and

Raman spectroscopy, have been found to be efficient non-destructive approaches for the forensic analysis of soil evidences. The geometric arrangement, bond strength, and atomic mass influence the vibrational spectra of any substance. The range of 400 cm^{-1} to 1500 cm^{-1} in the IR spectrum is referred to as the fingerprint region. Generally, IR spectroscopy includes a mathematical operation, namely, Fourier transform to measure the transmission or absorption of IR by the sample and the method is termed as Fourier transform IR spectroscopy (FTIR). Conventional FTIR involves the sampling with the KBr pellet. However, the inclusion of attenuated total reflectance (ATR) and diffused reflectance with FTIR has eliminated the sample preparation process. Soil samples can be analyzed either by bulk samples, extracted organic fractions or by comparing pre- and post-combustion IR spectra. In the current scenario, handheld IR spectrometers are gaining attention as it offers cost-effective, sensitive, and rapid onsite screening of the soil samples. Different soil samples collected from surface and depth were analyzed by ATR-FTIR (Fig. 14.9). Chemometric modeling of soil samples analyzed with ATR-FTIR has been found to be providing a good discrimination (Chauhan et al. 2018). Additionally, Raman spectroscopy also provides an effective approach for the soil analysis (Cardell and Guerra 2016).

Along with spectroscopic methods, chromatography has also been contributed to the forensic soil examination. GC-MS, pyrolysis GC-MS, and HPLC have been applied for the detection of organic constituents of soil samples (Mazzetto et al. 2019). Prior to the analysis, the sample is extracted in organic solvents such as acetonitrile, etc. Along with aforesaid spectroscopy methods, NMR spectroscopy, chromatography, thermal analysis, and isotope analysis are the some methods of choice that have been applied for the detection or analysis of humic acid for the characterization of soil collected from different sites (Francioso et al. 2005; Li et al. 2020). At this juncture it is also worthy to note that despite the separate inorganic and organic analyses, two-tier analysis of inorganic and organic contents has been found to be enhancing the effectiveness and robustness of analysis. For the tandem analysis of inorganic and organic fractions of soil, LIBS and ATR-FTIR jointly offers enhanced sensitivity and selectivity of the soil analysis (Xu et al. 2020). Additionally, DNA analysis of organisms in the soil such as bacteria provides a substantial aid to forensics (Sensabaugh 2009).

Different analytical techniques from domains such as ecology, botany, palynology, and taphonomy have also been applied and used in forensics for soil examination. Examination of burial remains, microbes, pollens, plant spores, and fungal entities have provided significant aid in forensic soil testing. As mentioned previously, the soil is also referred to as an ecosystem supporting different organisms. As a general observation, an ecosystem is majorly affected by the human interventions. Examination results provide important leads regarding the mutual link or connection between objects and places, estimate time science body deposition, and thus ultimately help reconstruct the crime scene. Sangwan et al. (2020) have recently reviewed research progresses along with all the relevant information associated with forensic soil sciences. A compendium edited by Ritz et al. (2009) has included a practical and research-based perspective of soil forensics. The investigative

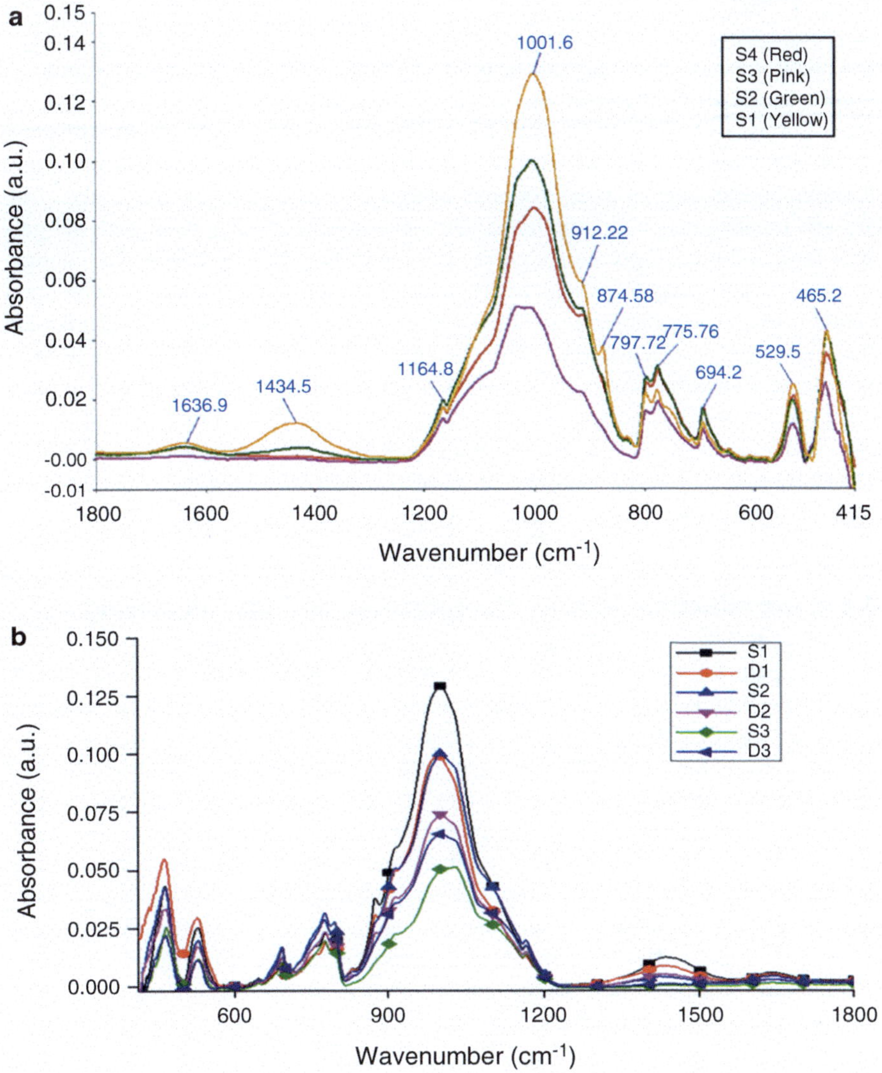

Fig. 14.9 ATR-FTIR spectra of soil samples (**a**) FTIR spectra of four surface soil samples along with their peaks in fingerprint region; (**b**) ATR FTIR spectra of surface and depth soil samples. (Reprinted from Chauhan et al. 2018 with permission from Elsevier)

perspective of soil sciences in forensics and different research endeavors are discussed in detail in a proceeding edited by Kars and van den Eijkel (2016). Another publication that is specifically dedicated to the soil forensics is edited by Di Maggio and Barone (2017). For more specific and research-based approaches in soil forensics, readers are suggested to refer these dedicated collections of works.

14.4 Paint

Paint meets decorative and protective proposes in the daily life of a common man. A common use of different paints also enhances the probability of its appearance at the scene of crime especially burglaries, hit and run, forced entry, etc. As that of glass and soil, paint analysis is also majorly focused to determine the source of origin and discrimination among samples. Forensic analysis of paint is one of the challenging tasks and requires care and experience. On the course of contact, paint material gets transferred, and thus, it presents a good example of Locard's principle of exchange. A variety of paints may be present in different forms at the crime scene. Examination of paint provides associative leads to link the persons (e.g., victim and culprit) and objects involved in offence and offers the significant aids for the reconstruction of crime scene. Class characteristics are often targeted and variety and variation in paint lay the foundation for the specific categorization of the paint. Forensic analysis of paint needs a better understanding of the chemistry and properties of paint. In this section, we will go through nature, composition, properties, and forensic analytical perspectives of paint.

14.4.1 Introduction: Nature, Composition, and Manufacturing

Typically, paint is referred to as a viscous, opaque, colored, or colorless suspension of pigments, additives, and fillers that is applied on any surface for decorative and protective purposes. Binder, pigments, and solvent are principal constituents of paint. Binder, as the name indicates, provides the adhesion on the surface as well as also aid as a medium for pigments and fillers to be dispersed through. Acrylic resins (e.g., acrylic acid, styrene, etc.), alkyd resins (e.g., fatty acid, polysols, etc.), epoxy resins (e.g., epichlorohydrin), urethane resins (e.g., isocyanate), vinyl resins (e.g., poly vinyl chloride, poly vinyl acetate, etc.), phenolic resins (e.g., phenol), amino resins (e.g., melamine, benzoguanamine, etc.), and cellulose resins (cellulose acetate) are often used as binders. Pigments may be inorganic or organic in nature and intended to impart the opacity and color. It is noteworthy that pigments are insoluble in binder and distributed evenly. Pigments possess a different refractive index than that of binder or resin and thus provide opacity by the means of scattering of light. Usually pigment particles are crystalline in nature and possess specific geometry. Different properties of inorganic and organic substances found the basis for the selection of substances as a pigment. Organic pigments are usually used more because of their intense color and high tinting capacity. Phthalocyanine blues, toluidine reds, phthalocyanine greens, and hansa yellows are some common organic pigments often used in decorative paints. However, automotive and refinish coating preferably use inorganic colorants. Flavanthrone, anthrapyrimidine, phthalocyanine blues, phthalocyanine greens, perylene, thioindigo reds, quinacridone reds, and dioxazine violets or quinacridone violets are some other examples of organic pigments. Inorganic pigments are comparatively inexpensive and are anticorrosive in nature. The purest black and white color may be obtained by inorganic pigments

Table 14.3 Coloring chemical components imparting specific color to the paint

Color	Pigment
White	Titanium oxide
Black	Carbon (Lam Black)
Yellow	Lead chromate, barium chromate, calcium chromate, cadmium sulfide, nickel titanate, strontium chromate, iron oxide, zinc chromate
Orange	Lead chromate, zinc chromate, silicon chromate, cadmium sulfide
Red	Iron oxide, lead oxide
Green	Lead chromate, chromium oxide
Maroon	Copper ferrocyanide
Blue	Iron ferrocyanide

Table 14.4 Fillers or extenders

Filler/extender	Property imparts
Calcium carbonate	Glaze, fire retardant
Calcium sulfate	Whiteness (in combination with titanium oxide)
Silica	Hardness/resistance to abrasions
Potassium-aluminum silicate	Reinforcement of film
Calcium metasilicate	Stabilize the system

rather than organic ones. Table 14.3 summarizes some common inorganic substances and the resultant color (Bentley 2001).

Automotive and refinish paints involves chromium-, cadmium-, and lead-based pigments. It appears that lead- and chromium-based pigments possess anticorrosive properties. Due to environmental concerns, these are not involved for decorative purposes. The use of zinc phosphate-based anticorrosive pigments is on increase in place of the heavy and toxic metal-based pigments. The presence of pigments and other additives, i.e., fillers and extenders, significantly affect the mechanical properties. Table 14.4 presents some properties of paint and responsible filler.

Solvents are usually volatile in nature that aids ease for the application of paint coating on the surface. Regulation of evaporation rate, flow properties, and viscosity are some primary functions of solvents. Since the properties of the solvent affect the consistency of coating and application, the choice of solvent must be determined in accordance with the method of paint application. Water, hydrocarbon, terpenes and other oxygenated organic liquids are often used as solvents. Paints generally recovered from the scene of occurrence or other articles of interest such as vehicles and cloths in the dry state, i.e., in form of chips. Notwithstanding, it evaporates after coating, and the probability of solvent traces detection is small though measurable cannot be ignored completely. As the paint is coated on surface, it eventually dries forms a film. Film formation is a complex chemical process that is needed to be understood. Basically, there are four basic phenomena, namely, evaporation, polymerization, oxidation, and coagulation, that explain the mechanism of film formation. Solvents evaporate with time as they come in contact with air. Evaporation is

Table 14.5 Terminologies: *at a glance*

Term	Explanation
Architectural paints	Typical household coatings
Curing	A process that includes external agents (e.g., heat, light, etc.) to affect the chemical process
Dye	A coloring substance that is soluble in a medium
Drying	All the mechanism of film formation that is not limited to evaporation only
Enamel	A pigmented coating produces glossy and reflective effects after drying
Lacquer	Quickly drying clear pigmented coating. It represents the coating that form after the solvent evaporation
Latex	A water-based emulsion of resin contains suspended pigments
Paint	A colored or colorless coating is applied to the surface for decorative or protective purposes
Pigment	Medium-insoluble coloring agent (usually fine powder)
Shellac	Generally used as an insulating varnish, sealing agent, adhesive. Technically, it is a resinous product that yields from the extraction of Lac insect
Stain	A coloring substance that is used for coloring purpose rather than the protective objectives
Varnish	An un-pigmented coating that is a solution of oils and resins (organic or synthetic) in an organic solvent

governed by general principles of physics. Monomers are cross-linked together and yield chains of polymers. The phenomenon of polymerization occurs due to the exposure to the heat. Oxidation is a complex mechanism that is generally referred to as a type of cross-linking. It can be observed in oily resins or fatty acids such as polyester, alkyds, and varnishes. Emulsion-based systems include coagulation for film formation. Film formation in common latex domestic paints is based on this mechanism.

After this general introduction to the paint, we have come to various technical terms. Before moving ahead toward the forensics standpoint as well as to avoid any confusion and a better understanding of the facts, at this juncture it is germane to look sharply toward some technical terminologies. Terminological definitions are provided in Table 14.5 (Houck and Siegel 2010).

Technically, resins and cross-linking processes define the paint systems. Paint manufacturing is a multistep process that initiates with the physical dispersion of pigments. Extenders and pigments are used in dry powder form. Mixing, testing, and specification adjustment are preceding step of the former. A number of mechanical processes and instruments (e.g., grind stage, high-speed dispersion device) are used in mixing and preparing the pigment concentrate (Bentley 2001).

Multilayer paint system is responsible for various paint properties such as adhesion to the surface, anticorrosion character, and atmospheric degradation resistant. Automobile paints are usually encountered as evidence. Automotive coatings consist of four coatings. Pretreatment involves electroplating with zinc to protect the surface from rust. Further, epoxy resin, containing pigments, is coated as primer over the surface. Topcoat supersedes the primer. It is single color or multicolor or metallic color coat. The topcoat is representative of vehicle color. The un-pigmented coats are finally applied to impart gloss, robustness, and durability to the coating.

14.4.2 Considering Paint as Evidence

Paint is generally found in form of chips and flakes. A person's clothing, shoes, vehicle, and tools are the most probable site where paint may be present. The investigator should search for establishment of the point of contact. It may significantly help trace the location of paint evidence. Collection and processing of paint evidence is very diverse as well as important task. A paint smear may pose some challenges to the investigator since it produces due to the strike of the coated objects on any object or surface, and therefore, it may contain the components from different layers of the paint. In this connection it is advisable that the entire object should be sent to the laboratory if possible.

Like other physical evidence, the paint may also vary because of manufacturing variations, and thus, it emphasizes over the need for control or known samples. While collecting control, it must be ensured that the sample must be enough representative. Collection of control within the proximity of the damaged area is therefore recommended rather than directly from damaged area. Known sample must contain all the layers of paints. Observation of layer and thickness must be given proper consideration because the surface may have been repainted or damaged. It readily outlines the necessity of control sample collection from various places and proper labeling and documentation (De Forest 2001).

14.4.3 Forensic Examination of Paint

Forensic investigator analyzes paint to fix number of queries such as the origin of paint flake and comparison and discrimination among samples. Like other afore-discussed evidences, paint analysis also requires careful study of its physical and chemical properties. It is noteworthy that examination of paint is not new for the forensic domain although it was initiated for a long period. Over the period several technological advancements have been aided to support and strengthen the paint analysis. Preliminary visual examination involves the recording of general details such as condition, size, shape, color, and layers in smear. At this stage, proper documentation of the evidence and proceedings are of utmost importance. In this section several aspects of paint examination are discussed.

14.4.3.1 Microscopic Examination

Microscopic analysis reveals minute detail at a fine level. This is usually performed in order to analyze the paint layers. Appropriate magnification (2×–10×) is achieved by stereomicroscopes and polarizing microscopes. For a detailed analysis of layer, paint chips are cut into very thin cross sections by using a microtome. Microscopic analysis of cross sections revels the structure, any irregularities, pigment appearance and distribution, layer defects, and any other specific peculiarities. A polarized microscope not only identifies pigments but also aids the identification of other components such as extenders. On the literature survey, it appears that polarized microscope offers a good deal for the paint analysis. While interpreting the results of paint examination, correlation of six layers plays a significant role on the assessment of source of origin. In many intense, the physical fit has been found to be an effective approach. However, this practice requires adequate experience (Houck and Siegel 2010; Stoecklein 2001).

14.4.3.2 Chemical Tests and Instrumental Methods

Discrimination of different layers of pigment and binder composition may also be done by chemical tests. Different constituents of paint react differently to oxidizing and reducing chemicals. Chemical tests are destructive in nature. In the current scenario of advanced instrumental methodologies, chemical tests are of very limited use. Instrumental analysis not only provides sensitivity but also imparts robustness to the analysis. In this regard, FTIR and pyrolysis GC analyses have been found to be contributed enormously. In this section analytical insights have been discussed (Challinor 2001).

IR spectroscopy provides information of analytical significance about both inorganic and organic species or at the molecular level. IR spectroscopy involves the interaction of IR radiation with a chemical substance. Consequent absorbance or transmittance of IR is measured by plotting frequency or wavelength and intensity of absorbed or transmitted IR by chemical substance as X and Y axes. This plot then may be compared with standard/ known sample data to determine functional group and establish the identity, similarity, and differences. Fundamentals of IR spectroscopy may be found elsewhere in this book or other relevant publications.

Interestingly, for the forensic analysis of paint, dispersive IR and FTIR appear in the literature. In dispersive instruments, the interaction of IR radiation with the sample is followed by the dispersion of radiation caused by monochromators into constituent wavelengths. Experimental findings reveal the superiority of diffraction gratings over conventional prisms in terms of resolution. FTIR successfully superseded dispersion-based instrument and consequently benefited from the enhanced resolution and shorter analysis time. Further, FTIR coupled with the microscope visualizes minute details along with chemical details. FTIR analysis provides a non-destructive as well as sensitive and rapid approach for paint analysis especially when the sample is in very small amount. 4000–2000 cm^{-1} range is generally taken. For more detail about forensic analysis of paint by IR spectroscopy, readers are suggested to refer "An Infrared Spectroscopy Atlas for the Coatings Industry" published by the Federation of Societies for Coatings Technology which provides extensive reference stuff for the paint analysis. Table 14.6 provides peaks that are significant in paint analysis with their attribution. These spectral data are useful to compare the test result for the interpretation (Beveridge et al. 2001; Mistek et al. 2019).

Table 14.6 Peaks of interest in IR spectra of paint

Chemical species	Spectral band (cm^{-1})	Attribution
Alkyd resin	2900	Aliphatic C–H stretching
	1730	C=O absorption
	1285	C–O stretching
	1122	
	1376	Methyl and Methylene stretching
	1467	
	743	Out-of-plane bending of four hydrogen on aromatic ring
	706	Aromatic ring bending
Amino resins	1550	In-plane deformation of triazine ring
	1450	
	815	Out-of-plane triazine ring vibration
Acrylic resins	2958	Aliphatic C–H stretching
	2875	
	1732	Carbonyl peak
	1451	Methylene C–H bending
	1387	Methyl C–H bending
	1293	C–O–C stretching of aliphatic ester
	1169	
Epoxy resins	2800	C–H stretching (contributed by oil and epoxy)
	3000	
	1736	Carbonyl absorption
	1607	C = C stretching aromatic bisphenol ring
	1582	
	1510	
	1245	C_6H_4–O stretching
	1042	C–O stretching
	829	Out-of-plane bending of two adjacent hydrogens on the para-substituted aromatic ring
	560	C–O–C stretching and bending vibration
Polyurethane resins	3380	N–H stretching
	2936	C–H stretching
	2861	
	1729	Carbonyl stretching
	1691	
	1522	N–H bending
	1468	Methylene bending
	1380	Methyl bending absorption
	1254	C–N–H stretching
Vinyl resins	2900	C–H stretching
	1738	Carbonyl stretching
	1434	Methylene bending
	1373	Methyl bending

(continued)

Table 14.6 (continued)

Chemical species	Spectral band (cm^{-1})	Attribution
	1240	C–O stretching from O=C–O
	1021	O–CH_3
	605	Bending of acetate group

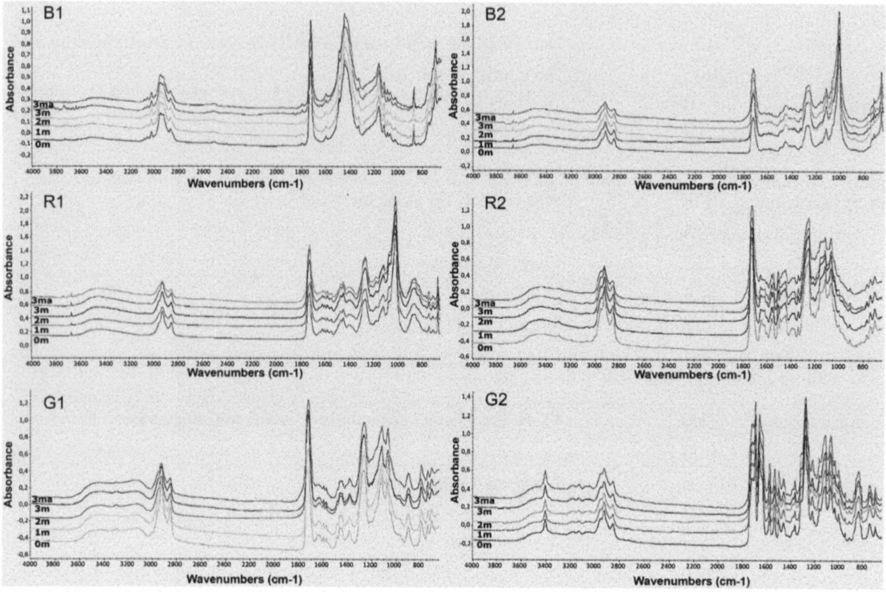

Fig. 14.10 (**a**) FTIR Spectra and (**b**) Raman Spectra for 6 spray paints after, respectively 0, 1, 2, 3 months of natural weathering and 2 months of artificial exposition in a climate chamber. (Reprinted from Jost et al. 2016 with permission from Elsevier)

Raman spectroscopy is another promising non-destructive approach for many evidence analyses. It is based on the principle of scattering of light rather than transmittance or absorbance and produces vibrational spectra of the compound. The application of Raman spectroscopy in forensic evidence analysis is trending nowadays Bell et al. 2005a, b). Raman, IR, and Optical spectroscopy may also be applied for the aging and weathering effects of paints. Jost et al. (2016) studied weathering and aging effects on spray paints using FTIR and Raman spectroscopy in combination with chemometrics. Figure 14.10 shows the IR and Raman spectra, for this study, diagnosing the weathering effects.

Pyrolysis GC-MS is another instrumental method of expert's choice for paint analysis. Thermal degradation of chemical species in an inert atmosphere is technically called pyrolysis. It yields characteristic compositional molecular fragments. Pyrolysis unit is coupled with GC-MS for the identification purpose. Pyrolysis results are function of final temperature, size and shape of the sample, rate of heating, gas flow rate, type of column, etc. Known samples should be run carefully followed by the questioned samples. Pyrograms of control and questioned samples are compared for interpretation. Microspectrophotometer also facilitates color analysis. The control samples are also needed for color comparison.

Additionally, SEM-EDX analysis provides structural details at a magnified scale along with elemental composition. In SEM, secondary electrons provide the surface details and atomic number and elemental information is determined by backscattered electrons and X-rays. SEM-EDX analysis provides a fruitful assistance in distinguishing paint layers by structural features (e.g., layer thickness, number of layers), elemental composition, identification of contaminants, and pigment particle distribution. For better analysis and interpretation, a need of paint analysis database has been outlined. It is worthy to note that a database of layer structures, primer colors, binders, pigment chemistry, and topcoat chemistry is developed by Scientific Working Group for Materials Analysis Paint Subgroup and an FBI-sponsored group of subject matter experts. This database was developed under project and involves the data from various countries (Houck and Siegel 2010).

14.5 Fiber and Fabric

The use of textiles is associated with the evolution of humans. Textiles and clothing have distinguished social, cultural, and economical notions and significance. It has been used for a long time for protective purposes by humans. Clothes, damaged textiles, and fibers frequently appear at the scene of occurrence that essentially involves the physical contact. Clothing and fiber may provide investigative leads if explored properly. Forensic examination of the fibers and textile is not new although it has extended over the years. Forensic examination of fiber often provides class characteristics. Individualizing with a high degree of discrimination requires adequate experience of the expert. Over the period, varieties of fibers have been introduced as well as are being used. In this section, we will explore the fundamental of textiles and fibers along with forensic analytical context.

14.5.1 Introduction and Classification

Fiber is defined as the smallest unit of a textile possessing greater length than width. For a very long period, natural sources such as animals and plants were the only sole sources of fibers. Technological advancements in textile sciences led to the development of artificial fiber in the early 1900s. Rayon was the first manufactured fiber. Fibers may be classified into two major categories, i.e., natural and man-made fibers as presented in Fig. 14.11.

Natural fibers are essentially originating either from the animals, plants, or minerals. Animal hairs covering usually serve as fiber and may be further classified into three classes on the basis of protein composition. However, plant fibers are

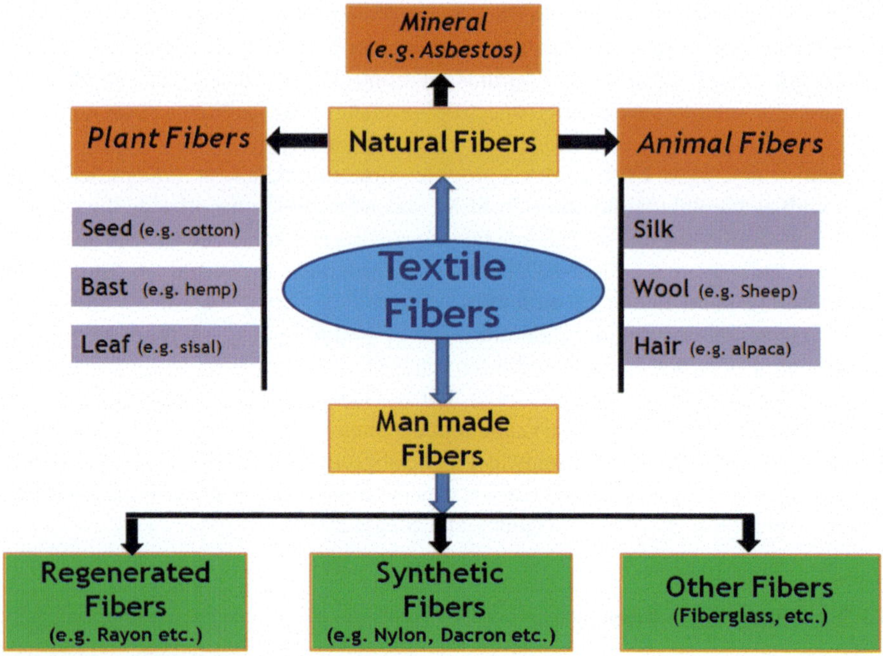

Fig. 14.11 Classification of fiber: at a glance

classified on the source part of the plant. Man-made or artificial fibers are categorized as synthetic polymer fibers, natural polymer fibers, and others. Fiber-forming polymers are supposed to be having linear chains of molecules that may be attributed to the longitudinal and transverse structure of fiber. High molecular weight of polymer causes a high melting point and low solubility while the flexibility of the chains imparts stretchability to the fibers. Fibers are converted into yarns (also called thread). A product that possesses small cross section of fibers with or without twists is technically called yarn. In the textile industry, yarns are usually classified as simple yarn (one fiber), blend (two or more fibers), and fancy yarns (decorative in nature consisting irregular structures at regular intervals). On the basis of twisting, yarns are categorized as single yarn, folded yarn (also called ply yarn), and cord yarns (also called cabled yarn). Plied yarn is a twisted assembly of the two or more single yarns. Two or more plied yarns are twisted and the assembly is referred to as cabled yarn that may be further twisted to yield a rope. The liner density is the measure of mass per unit length. Yarns are described in terms of "Tex" that is a SI unit of the linear density (gram per 1000 m length). Weight of 9000 m fiber is represented in terms of "Denier" (Carr 2017).

Additionally, fabric is the manufactured assembly of the yarns. Yarns are woven, or knitted together, providing a surface area and mechanical strength. Technically woven, non-woven, and knitted fabrics denote major categories of fabrics. Plain woven fabrics involve over and under the interlacing of yarn at right angles. One

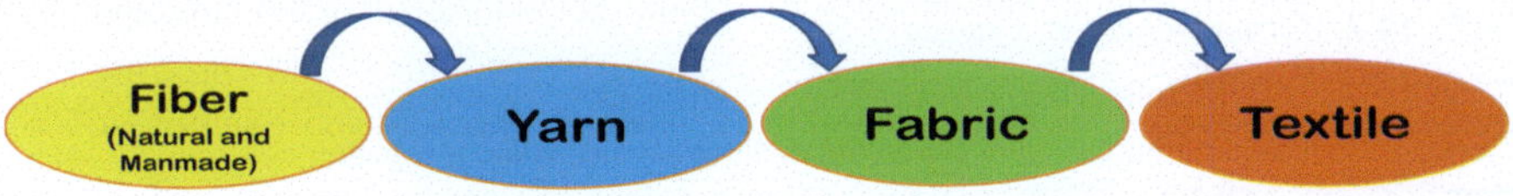

Fig. 14.12 Hierarchy of textile

yarn is usually interlaced with two yarns in twill weaving. Strength, mass, stability, abrasion resistivity, and stability are the dependent function of number of yarns in per 10 mm. The interlocking of stitches is a characteristics feature of knitted fabrics. Across the width knitting is done by the same yarn in weft knit fabrics. Besides this, vertical distribution of the knits with formation of a vertical loop is observed in the wrapped knits. Non-woven fabrics include web-like structure of yarns made by mechanical, physical, or chemical methods. Fabrics can be assessed technically by means of density and thickness of the fabric. Manufacturing of textile is a systematic process. The word "textile" usually denotes the woven fabrics. Elements of a textile are presented hierarchically in Fig. 14.12 (Robertson et al. 2017).

14.5.1.1 Rope and Cordages

Archeological studies have detected the use of ropes thousands of years ago. Initially, plant (e.g., hemp, cotton, sisal, etc.) and animal fibers were used to construct the ropes. Later polyester-, polypropylene-, and polyethylene-based artificial fibers were came into introduction for the rope manufacturing. Widespread use increases the probability of appearance of ropes at the scene of occurrence. Traditionally, rope structure includes the twisting of strands together. The forensic investigator is usually asked to compare and discriminate the samples. Analytical procedure for rope examination lays on the foundation of the fiber examination. Techniques for the fiber examination are usually applied for the rope examination. Microscopic examination revels the structural details of the rope. While conducting forensic examination, documentation of the details is must. Type of rope, structure, color, adhesion of any foreign body, structure, and color of foreign body must be noted carefully. Edges of the rope must be observed carefully while dealing with damaged rope. Nature of damage may indicate the nature and direction of the implied force. Regular and sharply cut edges are usually apparent in sharp cutting. Irregular edges result due to the use of blunt object. However, before moving toward the forensic considerations, lets overview few terminologies associated with rope as summarized in Table 14.7 (Wiggins 2017).

14.5.2 Considering Fiber and Textile as Evidence

Fiber evidence is present in great variety at the scene of occurrence. Fiber evidence is microscopic in nature; however, some macroscopic evidences such as end product may also be encountered. Fiber evidence is subjected to microscopic and instrumental analysis for the assessment of physical and chemical properties. Tremendous

Table 14.7 Terminologies: at a glance

Term	Explanation
Rope	Structure has a minimum of three strands twisted together
Twin	A balanced twisted structure (diameter < 4 mm) having two or more strands
Strand	Assembly of twisted yarns
Core	Fiber(s) running across the length through the center of the rope
Lay	Direction of strand twist that is denoted as "S" and "Z"
Angle of Lay	Angle between the axis of rope and strand
Length of Lay	Length of the path through the strand completes one turn of the twist

expansion in the variety of fibers as well as advances in fiber manufacturing technology has underlined the need for basic knowledge to the forensic examiner regarding the type, structure, and manufacturing of fibers. In forensics, fiber evidence is majorly diagnosed for the identification, comparison, and discrimination of the evidence. Forensic examination of fiber provides the quantitative and qualitative grounds for the comparison. Damaged textiles due to blunt or any sharp impact are also analyzed to determine the nature of force, impact, and assault. Handling, collection, and packaging of fiber evidence is an important perspective in forensics. Concerning cloth items can be carefully packed in paper bags. Clean forceps should be used to collect the fibers. Carpet, bedding, etc., should be folded in a protective manner to avoid the cross-contamination. Collected samples are sent to the forensic laboratory for the analysis. We will explore the forensic analytical dimensions in the next section.

14.5.3 Forensic Examination

Forensic examination of fiber is a complex task and the evidential value depends upon the expertise of the analyst. Color, refractive index, and birefringence are the physical properties of interest that provides the grounds for the identification and comparison of the samples. In this segment, we will look toward the different analytical procedures and another associated phenomenon for the forensic analysis of fiber.

14.5.3.1 Assessment of Physical Properties

Microscopic examination is one of the preliminary tasks on the course of fiber examination. Microscopic analysis by means of a polarized light microscope and comparison microscope provides the structural details and offers the means of discrimination. Cross-sectional details may also be revealed by the microscopic analysis and aid the comparison of fibers. In Wayne William case, cross-sectional details offered the mean of comparison and linked the culprit with the crime. Cross section of fiber may be of different shapes such as round (or single-lobed), bi-lobed, tri-lobed, multi-lobed, and flat. Microscopic examination also reveals the structural

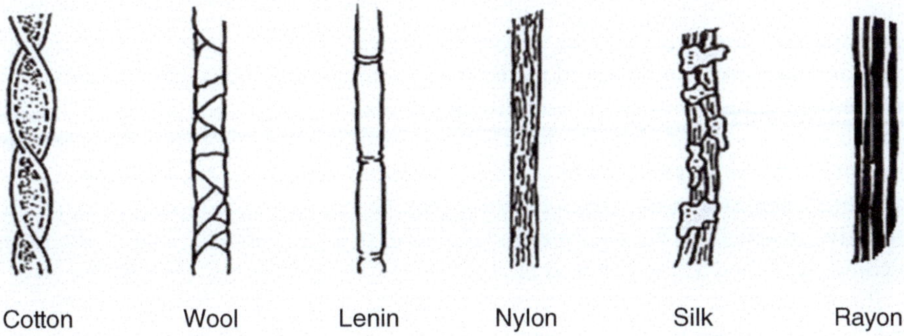

Fig. 14.13 Microscopic appearance of fibers

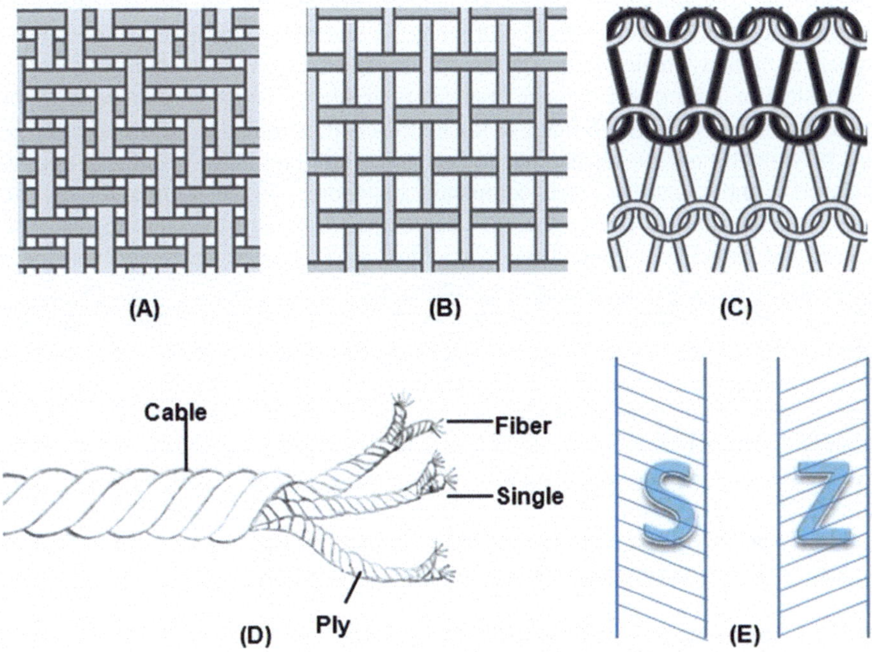

Fig. 14.14 Structural details (**a**) Twill weaving; (**b**) Plain weaving; (**c**) Knitting; (**d**) Structure of a yarn; (**e**) twist

details of the fabric such as weaving and knitting patterns as depicted in Figs. 14.13 and 14.14 (Carr 2017).

Refractive index and birefringence are also determined. The examination procedure follows the fundamentals of optics. Due to the thickness of fiber in the center than that of edges, fiber reacts like a crude lens. If the refractive index of fiber is greater than the mounting medium, fiber will react like a converging lens, while fiber may produce concave lens-like effects if it has refractive index less than the mounting medium. Movement of the Becke line may be observed under microscope for the determination of the relative refractive index of the fiber. Friedrich Becke introduced the concept of Becke line. Further, there is another direct method for the assessment of the refractive index that is comparatively simple than the previously mentioned method. In this method, fibers may be placed in the liquids of different refractive indexes. As the fiber meets with liquid of equal refractive index, the fiber becomes invisible. These methods require repetitive experiments to reduce the error.

Birefringence is generally referred to as double refraction of light in transparent and crystalline substances. Birefringence causes the splitting of light in two beams, i.e., ordinary and extraordinary. Both the waves propagate in the medium with some phase difference. This phenomenon is also observed in polarized light microscopes. Birefringence is the optical property of a material having a refractive index as a function of polarization and direction of light propagation. On the course of the birefringence study, interference colors may be seen that correspond to the fiber's properties, namely, material, crystalline nature, and structural orientation.

Physical matching and damage analysis is another practice associated with the forensic analysis of fiber. Damage to the textiles is most likely to be occurred in the case of violent incident. Damage analysis is subjective in nature because it may be analyzed visually, and therefore, completely depends upon the skills of the investigator. Careful analysis of the damage characteristics reflects the cause of damage, nature, and direction of the force. Over the years, several practices have been reported in the scientific literature (Smith and Thompson 2017; Taupin et al. 2017). Terminal ballistics of fibers has been investigated for a very long time. Examination of the bullet holes on the various textiles may help determine the shooting range (Wightman et al. 2015; Hinrichs et al. 2017; Kemp 2017). In forensic science laboratory, while dealing with such cases of textile damage analysis, simulation of experiment is recommended for the testing of hypothesis as it may assist an investigator to form an opinion. Physical fit may suffer from material loss due to damage. Tearing and wearing of the edges may help assess the nature of force when explored under the microscope. Physical fit and damage analysis offer a high associative link between two objects (Brooks et al. 2020).

14.5.3.2 Assessment of Chemical Properties

Color significantly contributes to the forensic examination. Colors are imparted specifically to the end product. A particular product range is generally supposed to have specific range of colors. Color is referred to as a potential parameter for the discrimination. Several natural and synthetic dyes and pigments are known for the coloring of fibers. Dye is an organic chemical species that reflects or absorbs a wavelength in the visible range. Dyes are used in accordance with the desired color effects and the type substrate (fiber). Pigment is a water-soluble microscopic particle that is applied at the time of production. Dying of fiber/fabric is a complex and multistep process. Variations in color provide the means of discrimination. Visual examination, chemical analysis, and instrumental analysis are usually performed for

Table 14.8 Solubility of fibers

	Acetone	Formic acid	Dil. HCl	Con. H_2SO_4	NaCl
Cotton	✗	✗	✗	✗	✗
Hair	✗	✗	✗	✗	✓
Hemp	✗	✗	✗	✓	✗
Silk	✗	[a]	[a]	✓	✓
Wool	✗	✗	✗	✗	✓
Ramie	✗	✗	✗	✓	✗
Linen	✗	✗	✗	✓	✗
Acetate	✓	✓	✗	✓	✗
Acrylic	✗	✗	✗	✗	✗
Nylon	✗	✓	✓	✓	✗
Rayon	✗	✗	✗	✓	✗
Polyester	✗	✗	✗	✗	✗

[a]Is representation of partially soluble

the color examination. Comparison microscope and microspectrophotometer may effectively aid the color comparison. Solubility test is another approach to assess the behavior of fiber in any solution. Solubility of the different fibers in different solution is provided in Table 14.8.

In addition to the physical properties and microscopic analysis, chemical examination of the fiber provides more detailed information regarding the composition. TLC for the dye analysis has been the method of choice for a long period. Additionally, pyrolysis GC and FTIR are generally used for the structure determination of the fiber polymer. Pyrolyzer coupled with IR also provides good deal for the fiber analysis. Pyrolysis GC is the most widely used technique for the analysis of fibers since it provides good discrimination and reproducible results. Raman and FTIR offer more advantages over any other technique because of non-destructive and rapid analysis. SEM-EDX as an imaging tool effectively assists the fiber investigation by providing very minute morphological details with high magnification. Several studies are available in this context. In addition to these techniques, XRF, NAA, ICP-MS, ICP-AES, ICP-MS, and XRD are also used for the fiber analysis (Lepot et al. 2008; Kirkbride 2017). Lepot et al. (2020) have recently reviewed all the research endeavors in the forensic textile and fiber analysis domain.

14.6 Tool Marks

The importance of tool marks in the domain of forensic science holds a unique position. The use of tools usually leaves an impression on the substrate upon which it is acted. This impression which is, in turn, the mark made by the tool has helped scientists identify the weapon used during the commission of a crime. The prime role of tool marks examination in the field of forensic science is to identify whether a bullet has been fired from a particular firearm under question. This is made possible by using the principles of microscopy. Identification is done when marking made by the weapon on the substrate resembles that of the weapon. Apart from the instruments used, a forensic scientist should keenly observe the minute orientations and marking of the tool to properly analyze them.

14.6.1 Introduction and Types of Tool Marks

The markings made by any tool on substrates that results from surface to surface contact are termed tool marks. The major classes to which tool marks can be divided include the impression type of tool marks and the friction or abrasion types of marks (Burd and Greene 1948). The former includes the compression or indented tool marks and the latter includes the sliding tool marks. Compression marks generated by pry bars and screwdrivers are examples of impression tool marks. The impressions left by such tools on the windows, doors, and lockers are generally encountered at the crime scene. Compression tool mark can be defined as the tool mark which reflects the working surface of the tool as a result of compression formed against any softer substrate or material. When sliding of a tool takes place along the surface of any substrate, striations that are parallel to each other are generated. Such marking is called sliding tool marks. Sliding tool marks are generated by screwdrivers, pry bars, and chisels and often look similar in appearance.

Apart from the two broad classifications, a third type of tool mark is also prominent. These are the cutting tool marks that possess' characteristics of both impression and friction marks. When the tool cuts material and at the same time slides along the surface, sliding tool marks are generated. This is observed in cases where hammers and pry bars are involved. Hasp locks, lock chains, and chain-link fences generally contain cutting tool marks especially in cases of burglary and trespassing. The use of cutting torches is common in cases where safes are being broken. Even though cutting torches leave no direct mark on the crime scene, the hoses used for connecting the acetylene and oxygen tanks leave certain marks.

Sliding and compression tool marks show difficulty in the identification of their class and individual characters, respectively. The accuracy with which tool marks are identified also depends on the nature of the material upon which the mark is generated (James et al. 2014).

14.6.2 Considering Tool Marks as Evidence

The location where tool marks are found may vary from one scene to another. The mark left behind by the use of a tool can be either two dimensional or three dimensional. A series of events are followed for the testimony of tool marks as evidence in the court of law. This includes the discovery of tool marks in the crime scene, their proper and scientific documentation, collection, transportation, and analysis by a forensic expert. A standard operating procedure is followed systematically from the collection of evidence from the crime scene to the examination. The

SOP (Standard Operating Protocol) for tool marks has been clearly defined and explained by Baiker et al. (2016).

Certain common areas where tool marks are obtained in high probability includes possible entry points such as windows, doors, cabinets, and even on the safe's doors. Once a tool mark is found to be present at the crime scene proper care must be given to prevent any alterations of the obtained mark. The orientation at which the tool has created the mark should also be noticed for proper analysis of the tool mark with that of the questioned weapon or tool. Certain situations allow the direct comparison of the tool mark with the questioned tool. In certain other cases a cast is to be generated which holds the characteristics of the tool mark. The primary method followed during the collection of tool marks evidence is photography. A proper photograph of the tool mark, along with proper orientation enables the forensic scientist to effectively carry out the process of analysis. Close-up and macro photographs of the tool mark on the substrate are taken following the standard procedure.

The cast is made in such a way that it makes the comparison process easy (Houck and Siegel 2010). The casts are generally light and easy for handling and storing. They are made with polymeric materials grounded to fine powders. One such example of the material is the dental stone. Apart from this, metal alloys having a relatively low melting point, and silicone rubber are also preferred for the same. Silicone material has been used as casting substances along with certain catalyst (tin or platinum catalysts) which completes the process of polymerization leading to the formation of a perfect cast with minute features. The material also makes use of pigments either gray or red. The major advantage of casting is the proper replication of microscopic features that are prominent in the tool. Before the casting, it is made sure that the tool marks are photographed properly and the characteristics of the tool mark and its location is properly documented. The suspected tool obtained from the crime scene is also collected and sent to the forensic lab along with the casting.

For proper comparison of the tool marks generated, control tool mark impressions are also generated. The substrate upon which the control marks are to be generated is decided depending on the surface upon which tool marks are found at the crime scene. If the marks are obtained on surfaces like wood, plastic, or any soft material, control marks are also generated upon similar material to ease the process of comparison. Substrates generally used to generate clean and clear marks include soft lead sheets, modeling clays, or leather (Petraco and Petraco 2016). Lead is preferred for obtaining tool marks due to its unique ability to project the finer details of the tool under analysis. Since lead is a soft metal, it does not create any drastic alteration to the tool whose impression is being obtained (Baiker-Sorensen et al. 2020). An alternative to lead is wax which is non-toxic at the same time cheap. When tool marks are obtained in wax at room temperature, it creates similar impression as that on lead (Baiker et al. 2015). Other similar surfaces which are good recipients of tool marks includes painted surfaces, plastics, and soft metals such as brass and copper. Raw wood and hard metals prevent the formation of a clean marking by the tool due to its structural features. This makes them poor recipients of tool marks.

14.6.3 Forensic Examination of Tool Marks

The proper examination of the tool mark is done in the forensic laboratory by comparing the tool mark obtained from the crime scene with the control tool mark generated on a similar surface. Microscopic characteristics of the tool are observed with the help of stereomicroscope and comparison microscope. The preliminary examination is done with the help of a stereomicroscope in case the evidence mark is large in size. Final comparison is ensured with a comparison microscope. The side-by-side comparison of the questioned mark with the control helps determine the involvement of a tool in a crime. Class as well as individual characters of the tools are noted by microscopic examination. The presence of similar pattern within the tool mark from the microscopic features of the tool leads to identification. When the examination makes sure that the mark obtained from a tool does not possess similar class characteristics, the identification is termed to be negative. In certain cases certain class characteristic matches but adequate individual characters will not be present to ensure a proper positive match. Hence, the result is framed to be inconclusive.

In cases related to burglary when safes are involved, microscopic examination of certain substances that insulate the safe holds a major value. Substances like diatomaceous earth, gypsum, vermiculite, and sawdust are used for insulating the safes. When a tool is used to break open such safes, a transfer of insulating material takes place. Hence, examination of presence of such materials on the tool under question helps in the proper investigation.

Advances made in the field of tool mark examination include the automated mark comparison system. Algorithms are developed to compare two marks in such automated systems. One such system made to carry out the bullet and impression comparison is the multi-feature score-based algorithm (Hare et al. 2017). The system initially compares the peaks and valleys found on the striation marks and later predicts the matching-based certain feature vectors. Along with multi-feature vector system single similarity metric system is also used for tool mark comparison. The efficiency of the former has shown to outstand the later. Such automated systems works well when presented with a database of tool marks. Adequate databases of tool marks are relatively less which creates challenges in the identification of tool marks. One such database is the FORMS-Locks database generated by Keglevic and Sablatnig (2017). FORMS-Lock contains the comparison microscopic images of tool marks obtained from real-life crime scenes. Another digital database has been generated by the Netherlands Forensic Institute which contains three hundred sets of data on 55 flat-head screwdrivers.[2]

The conventional method used to date for the comparison of tool marks is the comparison microscope. Recent advancement in the field has led to the development of a technique that enables the comparison of 3D features of data (Duez et al. 2018).

---

[2]National Institute of Standards and Technology (NIST), NIST Ballistics toolmark database. Available at https://www.nist.gov/programs-projects/nist-ballistics-toolmark-database.

The Virtual Comparison Microscope (VCM) enables such examination. The software was initially developed to compare firearm marks and was later extended for comparing tool marks. The 3D data of the tool marks are loaded on to the system and can be translated side by side. It also allows the examiner to zoom in and out of the data without damaging the original resolution.

MANTIS (Mark and Tool Inspection Suite) is yet software that enables the comparison of tool marks. This software is coupled with a mobile system having an optical 3D topography scanner (Chumbley et al. 2017). The current researches going on in the field of tool mark examination eventually leads the forensic examiner to properly analyze and interpret the relevance of a tool in the crime scene. The involvement of software and algorithms increases the accuracy of comparison making tool mark more relevant forensic evidence in the court of law.

14.7 Serial Number

We all come through the serial numbers in our daily life. All products have their own batch number (serial number) that attributes the unique identity. Serial number is mandatory for some objects especially firearm, vehicle, etc., in legal context as it associates with the identity of the user. Obliterated serial numbers (either intentionally or accidentally) poses complex challenges to the forensic investigator. Forensic investigator attempts to restore the obliterated marks or number. In this section we will explore the scientific grounds behind the restoration.

14.7.1 Introduction

Serial numbers are generally referred to as an alphanumeric unique combination that may help identify and distinguish the items or objects. There are three methods (i.e., casting, engraving, and punching) that are often used for the marking of the serial numbers. Cast marks are raised on the metallic object. These are produced in mold. Further, engraving is another method for the marking. An electric engraver or a chisel is used for the marking. Punching of the metal surface the die possessing marks yields the production of punched marks. Objects are punched in majority for the production of marks. Cast, engraved, and punched marks are shown in Fig. 14.15.

For unauthentic, illicit, illegal use, offenders usually remove markings form the object with intent to destroy the unique identity of the object. An over-stamping is an easy method used by the perpetrator. In this method, numbers are over written e.g., numbers like 2, 3, 5, 6, 9, and 0 are stamped and made to 8 while 1 and 7 may be modified to 4. Therefore, each number should be observed carefully to detect the traces of over-stamping. Obliteration of entire marked surface by a pointed object is usually referred to as center punching. Peening and drilling also disturb the surface and thereby remove serial numbers. Grinding is supposed to be the most common

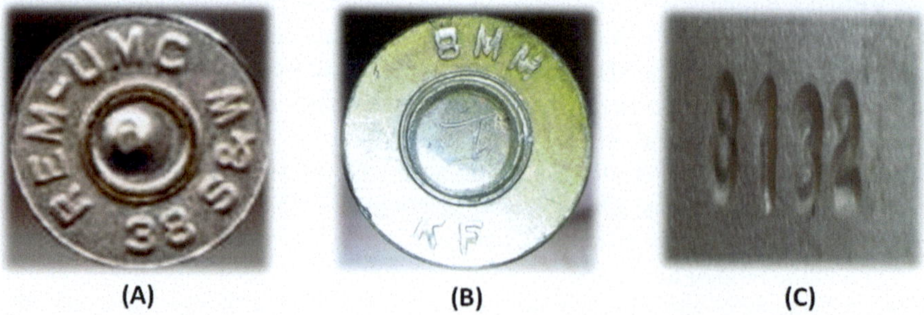

Fig. 14.15 Types of marks (**a**) Cast marks; (**b**) Engraved marks; (**c**) Punched marks

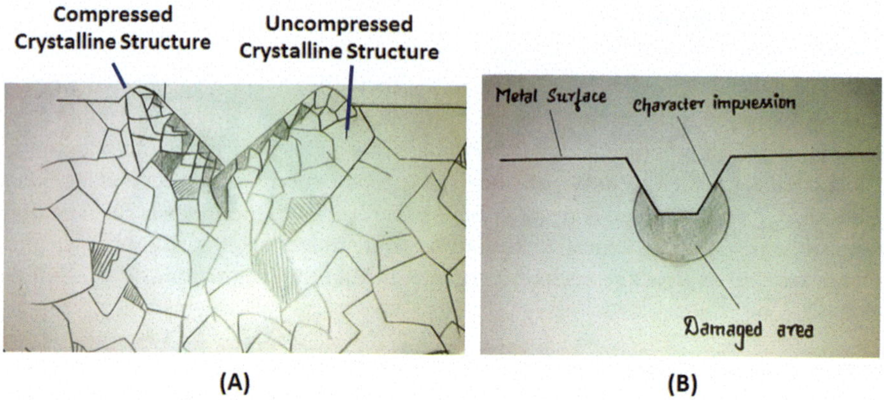

Fig. 14.16 Principle of restoration: (**a**) Cross-sectional view of deformation of crystalline structure of metal by stamping; (**b**) Damaged area underneath a stamped character considering forensic sigificance of restoration

method. In these method, marks bearing surface is polished by the grinder followed by the re-stamping of marks.

Now we look toward the fundamental principle of restoration. Metals possess polycrystalline structure that also defines the mechanical properties of the metal. Stamping or punching of marks or numbers on the metal surface cause disturbance to the surface and compression of the crystalline structure. Therefore, immediate vicinity of the stamped area exhibits altered hardness and strength. Depth of punching effect (disturbance) depends upon the type of metal as well as the applied force (Fig. 14.16). Even after the removal of marks, the surface may contain an altered crystalline structure that may reveal the outline of the stamped marks or serial number if treated properly (Heard 2008).

Serial numbers are the object identifers. It may provide the information such as batch number and make and model that may help establish the identity of the object. Forensic investigator often confronts with the objects with obliterated serial numbers or identification marks. From an investgative perspective, the establishment of the object identity is must. Restoration is the process followed to reveal the obliterated marks or serial number. In forensic science laboratories, restoration is usually practiced in the case of vehicle chasis number identifiaction, stolen objects, and firearm serial number restoration. Restaration is a complex process that requires patience and care. Number of methods are reproted for the restoration in the forensic context. In the upcoming section, we will go through the different practices and procedures usually followed for the restoration.

14.7.2 Restoration

Restoration of the obliterated marks needs sufficient knowledge of material science and material chemistry. In Forensics, stamped or punched marks are commonly subjected for restoration. Chemical etching and heating methods are generally applied for the same. Restoration methods require prior preparation of the surface. A fine emery paper may be used to polish the surface by removing the scratch and gross marks. Further, the surface is treated for cleaning with the acetone or chloroform.

14.7.2.1 Chemical Etchcing

The procedure of chemical etching is almost the same for all the metal surfaces although it involves different chemical compositions according to the metal. As the name indicates, procedure includes the rubbing of metal surfaces with an appropriate reagent. After some time (approximately 1 min) numbers or marks may be visible. Chemical etching may be continued for 2 h with various intervals, i.e., 2, 5, and 10 min. Numbers may be visualized under obilique light for the best view. In order to increase the speed to restoration and result enhancement, heating of metal surface also practiced. Different chemical cominations are used for different metals. Chemical schemes are provided in Table 14.9.

Contrary to metals, wood, leather, rubber, and polymer surface are amorphous in nature and therefore require a different approach of chemical etching for the restoration of punched marks. Wooden articles are punched or stamped with identification marks or numbers that may be obliterated by disturbing the marks bearing surface. Exposure of steam to the erased surface causes softening of the wood followed by swelling of fibers that have broken and bent during the punching and thus projects the impression over the surfaces. Pretreatment with the solution of potash or caustic soda is recommended for the acceleration of the process of restoration in the case of hard wood. As far as restoration on leather is concerned, it initiates with the cleaning of the surface with a cotton swab soaked in chloroform. The surface is observed under UV light. If the marks are filled with oil to hide, chloroform dissolve the oil and outlines the letters or marks as a bright fluorescence. Additionally, swabbing of the surface with cotton swab soaked in 2N caustic soda causes the decipherment of marks on the basis of differential adsorption. Embosed area of the leather surface absorbs the solution slowly as compared to the rest surface and thus solution

Table 14.9 Chemical compositions for restoration on metallic surfaces

Metal	Chemical compostion
Iron and steel	*Fry's reagent* (Most efficient)
	90 g cupric chloride; 120 ml hydrochloric acid; 100 ml water (surface area is then washed with acetone and subsequently treated with 15% HNO_3)
	5 g cupric chloride; 40 ml hydrochloric acid; 25 ml ethyl alcohol; 30 ml water
	5 g ferric chloride; 50 ml hydrochloric acid; 100 ml water
	Saturated solution of picric acid in ethyl alcohol
	40 g chromic acid; 50 ml water
	1% nitric acid in water
Aluminium	*Villela's reagent* (Efficient but dangerous)
	30 ml glycerine; 20 ml hydrofl uoric acid; nitric acid
	Hume-Rothery reagent (less efficient but comparatively safe)
	200 g cupric chloride; 5 ml hydrochloric acid; 1000 ml water
Zinc and Zn-Al alloys	50% hydrochloric acid followed by 50% nitric acid
Copper, German Silver, Brass, and other Copper Alloys	40 g cupric chloride
	150 ml hydrochloric acid
	50 ml water
	19 g ferric chloride
	6 ml hydrochloric acid
	100 ml water
Stainless Steel	Swabbing with Dil. H_2SO_4 or 10% solution of HCl in alcohol
Cast iron and cast steel	10% Solution of H_2SO_4 and potassium dichromate
Tin	10% Solution of HCl
Gold and platinum	HNO_3; HCl; water in ratio of 1:5:6

absorbed surfaces softens and darkens. While in the case of rubber, light swabbing with petrol, carbon disulfide is advantegeous; however, it requires caution.

Restoration on the polymer surface requires basic knowledge of polymer chemistry. Polymers do not bear particular molecular geometry and therefore no structural alteration results, and therefore, marks can be restored by the chemical treatment. Laser drilling and heating stamp are commonly used to produce the marks on the polymeric surfaces. Heat treatment and swelling with different reagents, according to the surface as summarized in the table, are useful for the restoration of obliterated marks.

14.7.2.2 Electrochemical Method

Electrochemical method offers another efficient approach for the restoration of serial numbers developed in the early 1950s. A cotton swab with an electrolytic solution and metal (subjected for restoration) are used as cathode and anode, respectively.

Application of voltage results in the dissolution of metal in the solution. Interestingly, the compressed area behaves differently than the uncompressed area. The value of applied voltage should be greater than the crticle voltage (minimum voltage necessary for the current flow). The value of criticle voltage depends upon the metal, e.g., Steel: 6V; Brass: 7V; Aluminium: 7.5V (Heard 2008).

14.7.2.3 Magnetic Particle Method

The magnetic particle method offers a non-destructive approach for the restoration. Magnetic particle dust that may be available as suspension or dry powder is spread over the metal surface. Since compression causes changes in crystalline structure, magnetic properties are also changed. Any crack or surface flaw may be characterized by the deposition of the magnetic powder. The utility of this method is majorly limited to the ferromagnetic materials.

Besides the above-metioned techniques, heat etching, hardness profile measurement, relief polishing, transsmission and reflection X-ray, SEM, electron channeling contrast, etc., are some other methods that are also applicable for the restoration purpose (White and Keller 2015). Among all the afore-mentioned chemical etching is a very simple, cost-effective, and effective technique. It does not require sophisticated instrumentation; therefore, it may also aid on-field application. Over the years different approaches are reported in order to formulate more efficient chemical composition for the chemical etching on various metallic surfaces (Kumar et al. 2020). Restoration on plastic surfaces has also been practiced for a very long time. Research progresses in polymer surface restoration have been recently reviewed by Uysal et al. (2020).

14.8 Standards and Statistics

14.8.1 Standards

For the reference of readers, various standards for the different physical evidence analysis published by the American Society for Testing and Materials are appended in Table 14.10.

14.8.2 Statistics

Internationally, to determine the relevancy and admissibility of scientific evidence, there are various standards or protocols, e.g., Frye test (test for general acceptance), Daubert test, prejudicial effect test, usefulness standard, etc. Here, validity is measured in terms that whether the evidence is producing misleading or confusing impressions or not. The report of the National Academy of Science (NAS) identified many challenges associated with forensic practice. Report found the absence of standards and uniform methodology. Further, variation in result interpretation, absence of error assessment, certification of experts, lack of fundamentals of uniqueness, and reproducibilty of the method were outlined as main concerns of the

Table 14.10 ASTM standards for the forensic purpose

Standard	Description
1732-19e1	Standard Terminology Relating to Forensic Science
E2927-16e1	Standard Test Method for Determination of Trace Elements in Soda-Lime Glass Samples Using Laser Ablation Inductively Coupled Plasma Mass Spectrometry for Forensic Comparisons
E2926-17	Standard Test Method for Forensic Comparison of Glass Using Micro X-ray Fluorescence (μ-XRF) Spectrometry
E1967-19	Standard Test Method for the Automated Determination of Refractive Index of Glass Samples Using the Oil Immersion Method and a Phase Contrast Microscope
E3272-21	Standard Guide for Collection of Soils and Other Geological Evidence for Criminal Forensic Applications
E1610-18	Standard Guide for Forensic Paint Analysis and Comparison
E2224-19	Standard Guide for Forensic Analysis of Fibers by Infrared Spectroscopy
E2808-21	Standard Guide for Microspectrophotometry in Forensic Paint Analysis
E2809-13	Standard Guide for Using Scanning Electron Microscopy/X-Ray Spectrometry in Forensic Paint Examinations
E2228-19	Standard Guide for Microscopical Examination of Textile Fibers

academy and therefore emphasized over the statistical interpretation of the analytical results of trace evidence examination. Report tagged the DNA evidence as a gold standard and remarked various concerns regarding the subjective nature of physical evidnce analysis (Srivastava et al. 2020). Academy observed the need for statistical operations for forensic analysis results to reduce the erroneous interpretation and false-positive and -negative interpretation of the results.

Statistics have been applied in forensic science in wide sepctrum of its operations. Inferential statistics, correlation, regression, and central tendency measure are most common types of operations used in forensic research. Recently, application of chemometrics has offered an enormous contribution to the forensic analysis of physical evidences (Muehlethaler et al. 2011; Kafadar 2015; Stern 2017; Sauzier et al. 2021;). Kumar and Sharma (2018) have discussed the potential of chemometrics in forensic analysis in detail. Chemoemtrics enables significant analysis and interpretation for characterization/ identification, classification/ discrimination, detection of adulterants, porpuses utlizing spectroscopic, chromatographic, thermo-gravimetric, microscopic, and X-ray-based techniques. Understanding of statistics is extremely necessary for adequate interpretation of the results.

14.9 Conclusion

Scientific examination of different physical evidences provides the information of evidential significance. Glass, soil, paint, fibers, and tool marks are most common types of evidences that helps reconstruction of the scene of occurrence. Basic information in terms of the composition and physical as well as chemical properties of the physical evidence are essentially required for better analysis. Forensic examination should be in accordance with the standard protocols to increase the probative value of the evidences. It is always recommended to take a control sample for better comparison. Interpretation of results is of distinguished importance, and on this course, statistical validation of the results should be done to access the power of analysis and probability of error and to eliminate the possibility of false-positive or -negative interpretation of the results.

References

Abhyankar S, Srivastava A, Yadav VK, Nigam K, Harshey A (2018) Glass fractures made from different pellet shapes-a preliminary study. J Forensic Sci Crim Investig 8(3):1–17

Akmeemana A, Weis P, Corzo R, Ramos D, Zoon P, Trejos T, Ernst T, Pollock C, Bakowska E, Neumann C, Almirall J (2020) Interpretation of chemical data from glass analysis for forensic purposes. J Chemometr 35(1):e3267

Alim M, Negi KS, Abhyankar S, Tiwari N, Harshey A, Srivastava A (2020) Towards the investigation of the shooting incidents: evaluation of the fracture pattern on the polymethylmethacrylate sheet made by .22″ and .177″ caliber air rifle. Heliyon 6(5):e04088

Almirall J, Buckleton J, Curran J, Hicks T (2000) Examination of glass. In: Curran JM, Hicks T, Buckleton JS (eds) Forensic interpretation of glass evidence. CRC Press, Boca Raton

Baiker M, Pieterman R, Zoon P (2015) Toolmark variability and quality depending on the fundamental parameters: angle of attack, toolmark depth and substrate material. Forensic Sci Int 251:40–49

Baiker M, Petraco NDK, Gambino C, Pieterman R, Shenkin P, Zoon P (2016) Virtual and simulated striated toolmarks for forensic applications. Forensic Sci Int 261:43–52. https://doi.org/10.1016/j.forsciint.2016.01.035

Baiker-Sorensen M, Herlaar K, Keereweer I, Pauw-Vugts P, Visser R (2020) Interpol review of shoe and tool marks 2016-2019. Forensic Sci Int Synergy 2:521–539

Bell SE, Fido LA, Speers SJ, Armstrong WJ, Spratt S (2005a) Forensic analysis of architectural finishes using Fourier transform infrared and Raman spectroscopy, Part I: the resin bases. Appl Spectrosc 59(11):1333–1339

Bell SE, Fido LA, Speers SJ, Armstrong WJ, Spratt S (2005b) Forensic analysis of architectural finishes using Fourier transform infrared and Raman spectroscopy, Part II: White paint. Appl Spectrosc 59(11):1340–1346

Bentley J (2001) Composition, manufacture and use of paint. In: Caddy B (ed) Forensic examination of glass and paint. Taylor & Francis, New York

Beveridge A, Fung T, MacDougall D (2001) Use of infrared spectroscopy for the characterisation of paint fragments. In: Caddy B (ed) Forensic examination of glass and paint. Taylor & Francis, New York

Bradt RC (2011) The fractography and crack patterns of broken glass. Fail Anal Prev 11:79–96

Brooks E, Prusinowski M, Gross S, Trejos T (2020) Forensic physical fits in the trace evidence discipline: a review. Forensic Sci Int 313:110349. https://doi.org/10.1016/j.forsciint.2020.110349

Burd DQ, Greene RS (1948) Tool mark comparisons in criminal investigations. J Crim Law Criminol 39:379

Buzzini P, Kammrath BW, De Forest P (2019) Trace evidence? The term trace from adjective to noun. Wiley Interdiscip Rev Forensic Sci 1(5):e1342

Byous J (2013) Hertzian fractures and related terms-a glossary. AAtR Publ, Savannah

Cardell C, Guerra I (2016) An overview of emerging hyphenated SEM-EDX and Raman spectroscopy systems: applications in life, environmental and materials sciences. Trends Anal Chem 77: 156–166

Carr D (ed) (2017) Forensic textile science. Woodhead Publishing, New Delhi

Challinor JM (2001) Pyrolysis techniques for the characterisation and discrimination of paint. In: Caddy B (ed) Forensic examination of glass and paint. Taylor & Francis, New York

Chauhan R, Kumar R, Sharma V (2018) Soil forensics: a spectroscopic examination of trace evidence. Microchem J 139:74–84

Chumbley S, Zhang S, Morris M, Spotts R, Macziewski C (2017) Development of a mobile toolmark characterization/comparison system. J Forensic Sci 62:83–91

Copley GJ (2001) The composition and manufacture of glass and its domestic and industrial applications. In: Caddy B (ed) Forensic examination of glass and paint. Taylor & Francis, New York, pp 27–46

De Forest PR (2001) What is trace evidence. In: Caddy B (ed) Forensic examination of glass and paint. Taylor & Francis, New York

Di Maggio RM (2017) Pedology applied to forensics. In: Di Maggio RM, Barone PM (eds) Geoscientists at crime scenes: a companion to forensic geoscience. Springer, New York, pp 31–51

Di Maggio RM, Barone PM (eds) (2017) Geoscientists at crime scenes: a companion to forensic geoscience. Springer, New York

Duez P, Weller T, Brubaker M, Hockensmith RE, Lilien R (2018) Development and validation of a virtual examination tool for firearm forensics. J Forensic Sci 63(4):1069–1084

Fitzpatrick RW (2013) Soil: forensic analysis. In: Jamieson A, Moenssens AA (eds) Wiley encyclopedia of forensic science. Wiley, Chichester

Fitzpatrick RW, Raven MD, Forrester ST, Ritz K, Dawson L, Miller D (2009) Criminal and environmental soil forensics a systematic approach to soil forensics: criminal case studies involving transference from crime scene to forensic evidence. Springer, Netherlands Dordrecht, pp 105–127

Francioso O, Montecchio D, Gioacchini P, Ciavatta C (2005) Thermal analysis (TG-DTA) and isotopic characterization (13C–15N) of humic acids from different origins. J Appl Geochem 20(3):537–544

Girard JE (2018) Forensic analysis of glass. In: Girard JE (ed) Criminalistics: forensic science, crime, and terrorism, 4th edn. Jone and Bartlett Learning, Burlington

Gogotsi GA, Mudrik SP (2010) Fracture resistance of technical and optical glasses: edge flaking of specimens. Strength Mater 42(3):280–286. https://doi.org/10.1007/s11223-010-9216-2

Griffith AA (1920) The phenomena of rupture and flow in solids. Philos Trans R Soc Lond 221: 163–198

Groenendyk DG, Ferré TP, Thorp KR, Rice AK (2015) Hydrologic-process-based soil texture classifications for improved visualization of landscape function. PLoS One 10(6):e0131299

Hamer PS (2001) Microscopic techniques for glass examination. In: Caddy B (ed) Forensic examination of glass and paint. Taylor & Francis, New York

Hare E, Hofmann H, Carriquiry A (2017) Algorithmic approaches to match degraded land impressions. Law Probab Risk 16(4):203–221

Harshey A, Srivastava A, Yadav VK, Nigam K, Kumar A, Das T (2017) Analysis of glass fracture pattern made by 4.5 mm (.177″) caliber air rifle. Egypt J Forensic Sci 7:20

Heard BJ (2008) Handbook of firearms and ballistics: examining and interpreting forensic evidence, 2nd edn. Wiley, Chichester

Hinrichs R, Frank PRO, Vasconcellos MAZ (2017) Short range shooting distance estimation using variable pressure SEM images of the surroundings of bullet holes in textiles. Forensic Sci Int 272:28–36

Houck M, Siegel J (2010) Fundamentals of forensic science, 2nd edn. Academic Press, London

Hsiao YT, Meng HH (2018) Estimating the impact velocity of airgun pellet via terminal ballistics experiments. Forensic sci J 17(1):27–36

Irwin GR (1957) Analysis of stresses and strains near the end of a crack traversing a plate. J Appl Mech 24:361–364
James HS, Norby J, Bell S (2014) Forensic science: an introduction to scientific and investigative techniques. CRC Press, Boca Raton
Jauhari M, Chatterjee SM, Gosh PK (1974) Remaining velocity of bullets fired through glass plates. J Forensic Sci Soc 14:3–7
Jost C, Muehlethaler C, Massonnet G (2016) Forensic aspects of the weathering and ageing of spray paints. Forensic Sci Int 258:32–40
Kafadar K (2015) Statistical issues in assessing forensic evidence. Int Stat Rev 83(1):111–134
Kars H, van den Eijkel L (2016) Soil in criminal and environmental forensics. In: Proceedings of the soil forensics special, 6th European Academy of Forensic Science Conference, pp 163–183
Keaney A, Ruffell A, McKinley J (2009) Geological trace evidence: forensic and legal perspectives. In: Ritz K, Dawson L, Miller D (eds) Criminal and environmental soil forensics. Springer, New York
Keglevic M, Sablatnig R (2017) FORMS-locks: a dataset for the evaluation of similarity measures for forensic toolmark images. In: CVPR Workshops, pp 1890–1897
Kemp SE (2017) Forensic analysis of sharp weapon damage to textile products. In: Carr D (ed) Forensic textile science. Woodhead Publishing, Duxford
Kirk PL (1953) Crime investigation. Interscience Publishers, New York
Kirkbride KP (2017) Infrared microspectroscopy of fibres. In: Robertson J, Roux C, Wiggins KG (eds) Forensic examination of fibres. CRC Press, Boca Raton
Kumar R, Sharma V (2018) Chemometrics in forensic science. Trends Anal Chem 105:191–201
Kumar A, Srivastava A, Das T, Harshey A, Saini VR, Kumar A, Alim M, Nigam K, Yadav VK (2020) Restoration of obliterated stamped marks on aluminium surfaces by metallographic etching technique. Orient J Chem 36(6):1212–1217
Lepot L, De Wael K, Gason F, Gilbert B (2008) Application of Raman spectroscopy to forensic fibre cases. Sci Justice 48(3):109–117
Lepot L, Lunstroot K, De Wael K (2020) Interpol review of fibres and textiles 2016–2019. Forensic Sci Int Synergy 2:107
Li T, Song F, Zhang J, Liu S, Xing B, Bai Y (2020) Pyrolysis characteristics of soil humic substances using TG-FTIR-MS combined with kinetic models. Sci Total Environ 698:134237
Locke J, Underhill M (1985) Automatic refractive index measurement of glass particles. Forensic Sci Int 27:247–260
Mazzetto JM, Bonfleur EJ, Vidal-Torrado P, Dieckow J (2019) Potential of soil organic matter molecular chemistry determined by pyrolysis – gas chromatography/mass spectrometry for forensic investigations. Sci Justice 59(6):635–642
Mistek E, Fikiet MA, Khandasammy SR, Lednev IK (2019) Toward Locard's exchange principle: recent developments in forensic trace evidence analysis. Anal Chem 91(1):637–654
Morrisson AR, McColl SM, Dawson LA, Brewer MJ (2009) Characterisation and discrimination of urban soils: preliminary results from the soil forensics university network. In: Ritz K, Dawson L, Miller D (eds) Criminal and environmental soil forensics. Springer, New York
Mott NF (1948) Brittle fracture in mild steel plates. Engineering 165:16–18
Muehlethaler C, Massonnet G, Esseiva P (2011) The application of chemometrics on Infrared and Raman spectra as a tool for the forensic analysis of paints. Forensic Sci Int 209(1–3):173–182
Mulani K, Deshpande H (2018) Humic acid analysis for comparison of soil samples: a forensic perspective. Nucl Magn Reson 11:12
Munger C, Gates KM, Hamburg C (2014) Determining the refractive index variation within panes of vehicle windshield glass. J Forensic Sci 59(5):1351–1357
Overend M, Gaetano SD, Haldimann M (2007) Diagnostic interpretation of glass failure. Struct Eng Int 2:151–158
Petraco N, Petraco NDK (2016) Impression evidence: footwear and tool marks cases from the crime scene to the courtroom. In: Forensic science handbook, vol II. CRC Press, Boca Raton

Petrisor IG (2014) Environmental forensics fundamentals: a practical guide. CRC Press, Boca Raton

Ritz K, Dawson L, Miller D (eds) (2009) Criminal and environmental soil forensics. Springer, New York

Robertson J, Roux C, Wiggins KG (2017) Forensic examination of fibres. CRC Press, Boca Raton

Ruffell A (2010) Forensic pedology, forensic geology, forensic geoscience, geoforensics and soil forensics. Forensic Sci Int 202(1–3):9–12

Sangwan P, Nain T, Singal K, Hooda N, Sharma N (2020) Soil as a tool of revelation in forensic science: a review. Anal Methods 12(43):5150–5159

Sauzier G, van Bronswijk W, Lewis SW (2021) Chemometrics in forensic science: approaches and applications. Analyst 146:2415–2448

Sensabaugh GF (2009) Microbial community profiling for the characterisation of soil evidence: forensic considerations. In: Ritz K, Dawson L, Miller D (eds) Criminal and environmental soil forensics. Springer, New York

Smith MJ, Thompson K (2017) Forensic analysis of textile degradation and natural damage. In: Carr D (ed) Forensic textile science. Woodhead Publishing, Duxford, pp 41–69

Spikmans V (2019) The evolution of environmental forensics: from laboratory to field analysis. Wiley Interdiscip Rev Forensic Sci 1(3):e1334

Srivastava A, Harshey A, Shrivastava P (2020) Legal aspects of forensic DNA typing. In: Shrivastava P, Dash HR, Lorente JA, Imam J (eds) Forensic DNA typing: principles, applications and advancements. Springer, Singapore, pp 607–628

Stern HS (2017) Statistical issues in forensic science. Annu Rev Stat Appl 4:225–244

Stoecklein W (2001) The role of colour and microscopic techniques for the characterisation of paint fragments. In: Caddy B (ed) Forensic examination of glass and paint. Taylor & Francis, New York

Stoney DA, Stoney PL (2015) Critical review of forensic trace evidence analysis and the need for a new approach. Forensic Sci Int 251:159–170

Stoney DA, Thornton JI (1985) The forensic significance of the correlation of density and refractive index in glass evidence. Forensic Sci Int 29(3):147–157

Taupin JM, Adolf FP, Robertson J (2017) Examination of damage to textiles. In: Robertson J, Roux C, Wiggins KG (eds) Forensic examination of fibres. CRC Press, Boca Raton

Thornton JI (2001) Physical examination of glass evidence. In: Caddy B (ed) Forensic examination of glass and paint. Taylor & Francis, New York

Tiwari N, Harshey A, Das T, Abhyankar S, Yadav VK, Nigam K, Srivastava A (2019) Evidential significance of multiple fracture patterns on the glass in forensic ballistics. Egypt J Forensic Sci 9(1):1–5

Trejos T, Koch S, Mehltretter A (2020) Scientific foundations and current state of trace evidence—a review. Forensic Chem 18:100223

Uysal S, Mercan M, Uzun L (2020) Serial number restoration on polymer surfaces: a survey of recent literature. Forensic Chem 20:100267

Varshneya AK (1994) Fundamentals of inorganic glasses. Academic Press Elsevier, Cambridge

Waghmare NP, Gupta K, Naik J (2019) Toothpaste pattern: a distinctive feature of an 8 mm bullet fired through a glass target. Arab J Forensic Sci Forensic Med 1(10):1427–1432

White RM, Keller RR (2015) Restoration of firearm serial numbers with electron backscatter diffraction (EBSD). Forensic Sci Int 249:266–270

Wiggins KG (2017) Ropes and cordages. In: Forensic examination of fibres, 3rd edn. CRC Press, Boca Raton, pp 89–98

Wightman G, Wark K, Thomson J (2015) The interaction between clothing and air weapon pellets. Forensic Sci Int 246:6–16

Wiltshire PE (2009) Forensic ecology, botany, and palynology: some aspects of their role in criminal investigation. In: Ritz K, Dawson L, Miller D (eds) Criminal and environmental soil forensics. Springer, New York

Woods B, Lennard C, Kirkbride KP, Robertson J (2014a) Soil examination for a forensic trace evidence laboratory—Part 1: Spectroscopic techniques. Forensic Sci Int 245:187–194

Woods B, Lennard C, Kirkbride KP, Robertson J (2014b) Soil examination for a forensic trace evidence laboratory–part 2: elemental analysis. Forensic Sci Int 245:195–201

Woods B, Lennard C, Kirkbride KP, Robertson J (2016) Soil examination for a forensic trace evidence laboratory–Part 3: A proposed protocol for the effective triage and management of soil examinations. Forensic Sci Int 262:46–55. https://doi.org/10.1016/j.forsciint.2016.02.034

Xu X, Du C, Ma F, Shen Y, Zhou J (2020) Forensic soil analysis using laser-induced breakdown spectroscopy (LIBS) and Fourier transform infrared total attenuated reflectance spectroscopy (FTIR-ATR): principles and case studies. Forensic Sci Int 310:110222

Essentials of Forensic Ballistics 15

Pankaj Kumar Pandey, Abhimanyu Harshey, Murali Manohar Yadav, and Ankit Srivastava

Abstract

Forensic ballistics is one of the most fascinating scientific disciplines. It has great potential in the criminal justice system in resolving crimes, particularly, in the reconstruction of events produced in a shooting incident and firearm identification. It is therefore essential for the forensic experts to acquire basic knowledge of firearms and ammunitions. In this prospect, the current chapter elaborately explains the various types of firearms and ammunitions. The various forensic aspects of resulting phenomena while a firearm is discharged are also discussed relating it to the range of fire estimation. This chapter further talks about firearm identification, gunshot residue examination, and automated firearm identification system.

Keywords

Ballistics · Forensic ballistics · Firearm identification · Gunshot residue · Range of fire · Automated firearm identification

P. K. Pandey
Ballistics Division, State Forensic Science Laboratory, Govt. of NCT of Delhi, New Delhi, India

A. Harshey
Department of Anthropology, Lucknow University, Lucknow, Uttar Pradesh, India

M. M. Yadav
Dr. APJ Abdul Kalam Institute of Forensic Sciences & Criminology, Bundelkhand University, Jhansi, India

A. Srivastava (✉)
School of Forensic Sciences, The West Bengal National University of Juridical Sciences, Kolkata, West Bengal, India
e-mail: ankitsrivastava@nujs.edu

P. Shrivastava et al. (eds.), *Textbook of Forensic Science*,
https://doi.org/10.1007/978-981-99-1377-0_15

15.1 Introduction

The word "forensic" originated from the Latin word forensis, which means public, to the forum, or public discussion. The use of Forensic with something suggests that it is related with legal system or suitable to the court of law. Forensic Ballistics is the discipline mainly concerned with the science of firearm and ammunition examination in any criminal investigation. Forensic Ballistics mainly relies on evidence such as fired bullets, fired shell casings, gunpowder/propellant residues, firearms, etc., recovered from the scene of the crime and from the suspect. The term "Forensic Ballistics" was first used by Colonel Calvin H. Goddard in the year 1925 and working with a chemist Philip Gravelle, Judge C. E. Waite, and Capt. E. C. Crossman, developed the comparison technique for identifying characteristic markings of firearm tool marks on fired bullets and cartridge cases. It was an important advance in the forensic science of firearm identification.

Ballistics is the science that utilizes the principles of mechanics and deals with the motion, behavior, and effect of a projectile. Forensic Ballistics involves the principles of Ballistics to investigate shooting incidences involving firearms. Forensic Ballistics examination and investigation of the scene of shooting is one of the most challenging tasks for the investigator. For the efficient processing of a crime scene, a perfect blend of knowledge and experience is required. It can be broadly classified into four disciplines: internal ballistics, intermediate ballistics, external ballistics, and terminal ballistics (Heard 2008).

Internal ballistics deals with the motion and associated phenomenon that happens within the barrel of a firearm from the moment the firing pin strikes the percussion cap of the cartridge and the primer starts the propellant's ignition until the projectile/projectiles exit from the barrel. The basic study includes the primer ignition time, ignition, and burning of the propellant, the pressure due to the created gases, temperature, muzzle velocity, and acceleration of the projectile inside the barrel, recoil, and the muzzle velocity when the projectile/projectiles leaves the muzzle of the firearm. Intermediate ballistics also known as Transitional ballistics deals with the motion of the projectile/projectiles just in the vicinity of the muzzle immediately after the exit of the projectile until it is under the influence of out coming gases.

External ballistics is the study of motion/factors affecting the motion of projectile/projectiles in the air when it leaves the muzzle of a barrel to the moment it hits the target. It includes muzzle velocity, angle of exit, shape and weight of the projectile, gravity, rotation of the earth, spin of the projectile, air resistance etc.

Terminal ballistics is the study of motion/behavior of the projectile/projectiles when it reaches the target. There are many factors which affect the performance of the projectile depending upon the type of target. The factors include basically the weight and shape of the material used in the projectile, explosive charge, terminal velocity etc. When the target is human or animal, it is called wound ballistics which addresses the effects of projectiles on living tissues. Wound ballistics is a term originally used by Callender and French as a special branch of terminal ballistics (Di Maio 1998; Maiden 2009).

15.2 Nature and Scope of Forensic Ballistics

Forensic Ballistics essentially deals with the firearm-related investigation and therefore, suitably includes the principles of physical and chemical scenes to evaluate the evidential value of the entities associated with the crime. A Forensic Ballistics expert conducts various examinations to answer the queries raised during the investigation and may assist in the reconstruction of the crime scene. Forensic Ballistics investigation provides investigative leads about:

1. Whether a gun is fired or not?
2. Which type of firearm was used in firing?
3. Whether the cartridge case or bullet was fired with a particular suspected firearm? (Firearm-Ammunition linkage)
4. Whether an individual fired a weapon or was present at the scene during the firing?
5. What was the range of fire? What was the angle and direction of fire?
6. Was the shooting incident of suicidal, homicidal or accidental in nature?

In the criminal and antisocial activities, firearms are being extensively employed for a variety of purposes by criminals and anti-social elements. Firearms become the choice for crime activity as it is being an effective tool to propel a projectile from a large distance with high velocity and wounding capability. These firearms are used to commit suicide, homicide, dacoity, robbery and in terrorist activity (Chapman and Milroy 1992; Singh and Singh 2005). Firearms are also used in police firing and military operations. Moreover, accidental incidents also do happen such as firing during mishandling of a firearm, killing of a person due to a stray bullet which hits an unintended target in celebratory gunfire or ricochet of the bullet from any object also proven dangerous if it hits any person (Cherry et al. 2001; Waghmare et al. 2012; Gabor 2016; Yong 2017).

Several studies analyzing the trends in the use of firearms in criminal activities across the globe have been reported in the literature. In India, annual reports of the National Crime Record Bureau (NCRB)[1] shows an increase in the involvement of firearm in illegal activities. Especially, country-made and improvised firearms are being used at a very large scale and posing various complications to police and forensic investigator. Generally, factory-made standard firearms and ammunitions are used for a variety of purposes. However, the modern era has also witnessed extensive use of illegal non-standard firearms known as country-made firearms/homemade firearms/improvised firearms or unusual firearms worldwide owing to the low-cost and easy availability (Thejaswi et al. 2013; Sinha 2015). Additionally, the use of air-gun, which involves mechanical action (either pressurized air or compressed spring) rather than a chemical reaction (burning of propellant) to propel a projectile, in criminal activities

[1] "Crime in India" published by NCRB, Ministry of Home Affairs, Govt. of India. Available at: https://ncrb.gov.in/en/crime-india.

have also been reported. Therefore in this regard, several airgun-based terminal and wound ballistics studies enriching the research literature of forensic ballistics have been published in the recent past (Harshey et al. 2017).

This chapter is constituted to describe the nature of Forensic Ballistics investigations. Fundamentals, principles, methods of firearm investigation, and existing analytical procedures are also discussed.

15.3 Firearm

Firearm is defined as "A machine or a device designed to discharge a projectile or projectiles of any kind by the action of any explosion or other form of the energy such as an expansion of compressed air". Firearm can also be defined as "A thermodynamic device that converts thermal energy stored in a propellant into kinetic energy of projectile or projectiles".

In the process of discharge of a cartridge; first, a firing pin of the firearm strikes the percussion cap of the cartridge which has primers in it. Primer being a very sensitive compound generates a flame which ignites the propellant. Burning of the propellant generates huge amount of gases which create tremendous pressure inside the case and this pressure pushes the projectile or projectiles out of the barrel of firearm with very high velocity ranges from about 200–3000 ft/s.

15.3.1 Parts of Firearm

All Firearms mainly consists of three basic group of parts: Barrel, Action, and the Butt Stock or Grip as presented in Fig. 15.1.

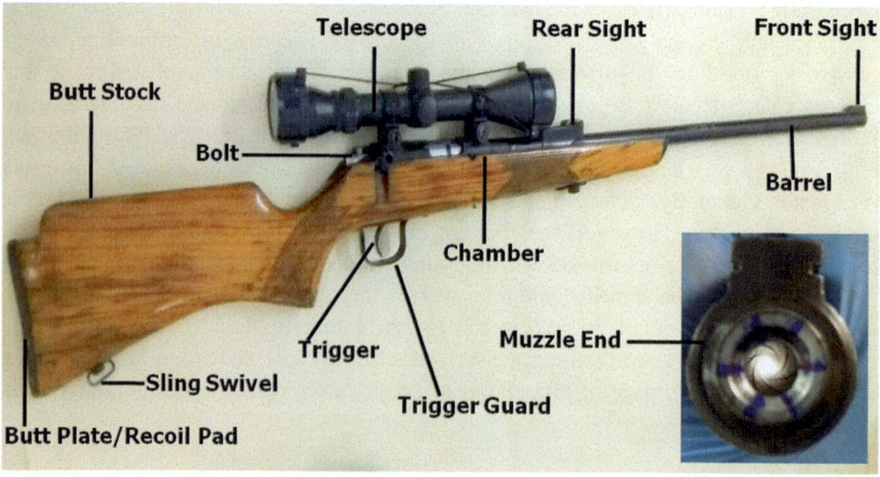

Fig. 15.1 Bolt action rifle of 0.22″ caliber. Inset shows the muzzle end and rifling in the bore

15.3.1.1 Barrel

A gun barrel is a long hollow metal tube having one end open at the front side called the muzzle end. The back end of the tube connected with the action part of the firearm is called breech end. The part near the breech end in which the cartridge is loaded is known as the chamber. The inner surface of the barrel is either smooth or rifled. Once the cartridge is fired, expanding gas force pushes out the projectile/ projectiles through the barrel with very high velocity. The barrel also has front sight and rear sight at the muzzle and breech end respectively which are used to accurately hit the projectile at the target. The hollow interior of the barrel is called the bore which is usually measured in millimeters or inches.

15.3.1.2 Action

It includes the arrangement of all the moving parts of the firearm that loads, locks, fires, eject, and extract a cartridge. The action mechanism of firearm can be categorized in several ways: single action, double action, break action, pump action, lever action, bolt action, semi-automatic action, automatic action etc.

15.3.1.3 Butt Stock or Grip

It is the part of firearm to which the barrel and action mechanism are attached. The Butt stock of the gun in composed of two pieces the Butt and the fore-end.

15.3.2 Classification of Firearms

Firearms may be classified on the number of parameters or characteristics i.e. loading characteristics (Breech loading, Muzzle loading); Bore Characteristics (Smooth bore and rifled bore); Handling Characteristics (Hand gun, shoulder arm); Action Characteristics (Bolt action, Lever action, Pump action, Semi-automatic, and Automatic action). Figure 15.2 presents the classification scheme of firearms.

15.3.2.1 On the Basis of Size

Firearms can be divided into two categories: handguns and long guns or shoulder arms. Handguns are designed to be fired by one hand without support from the body. Long guns or shoulder arms are designed to be fired while being supported by the shoulder.

15.3.2.1.1 Handguns

There are three basic types of Handguns i.e. single-shot pistols, semiautomatic pistols and revolvers.

15.3.2.1.1.1 Pistols

Single-shot handguns/pistols can fire only one shot or one round, at a time. Since these handguns hold only a single round of ammunition, and hence must be reloaded for the next fire manually. In order to fire, the action mechanism of single-shot

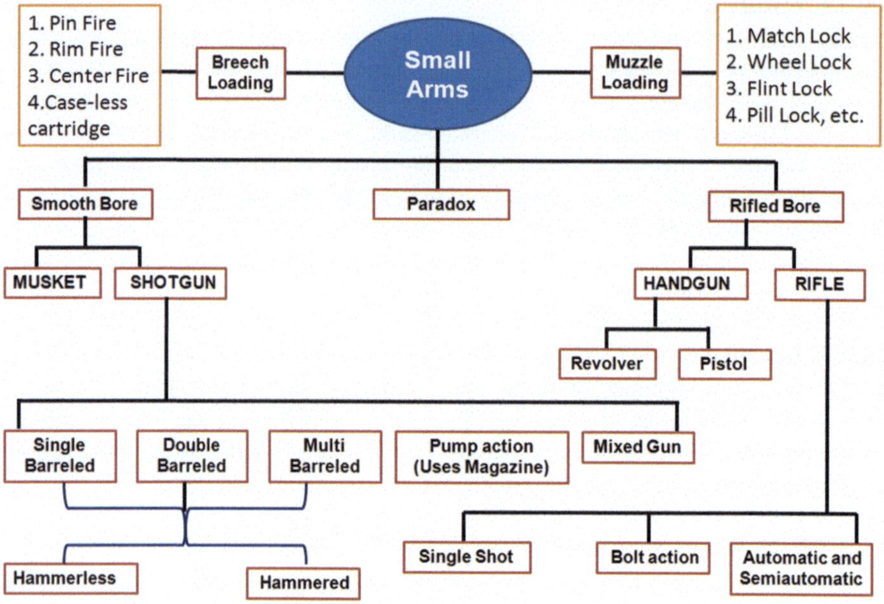

Fig. 15.2 Classification scheme of firearm

handguns generally requires the hammer to be manually cocked backwards before the trigger is pulled.

In self-loading pistols/handguns or semiautomatic pistols/handguns, a magazine slot is designed in the grip in which a magazine with loaded live rounds can be fitted. These firearms do not need ammunition to be reloaded for the next fire. They only need a separate pull of the trigger for each fire and use energy from the discharge to perform a portion of the operation such as extraction and ejection of the fired shell and reloading of the new round from the magazine to the chamber of the pistol. The smallest semiautomatic handgun/pistol ever made is known as the Liliput pistol having the caliber of 4.25 mm (Heard 2008).

15.3.2.1.1.2 Revolver

A revolver is a handgun that has a revolving cylinder having a number of firing chambers which rotates and aligns with the single barrel during successive firing. Each chamber in the revolving cylinder holds one cartridge only. In this way, the revolver allows to fire multiple rounds loaded in its different chambers. The cartridge cases have to be ejected manually from the chambers before reloading it with a new round.

Revolvers can be single-action or double-action handguns. In single-action revolvers, in order to fire, the hammer manually cocked backward each time before the trigger is pulled. Whereas, in double action revolvers, in order to fire, the hammer need not be manually cocked but the trigger is need to be pulled only. When the trigger is pulled, the hammer gets cocked, the cylinder automatically rotates and the

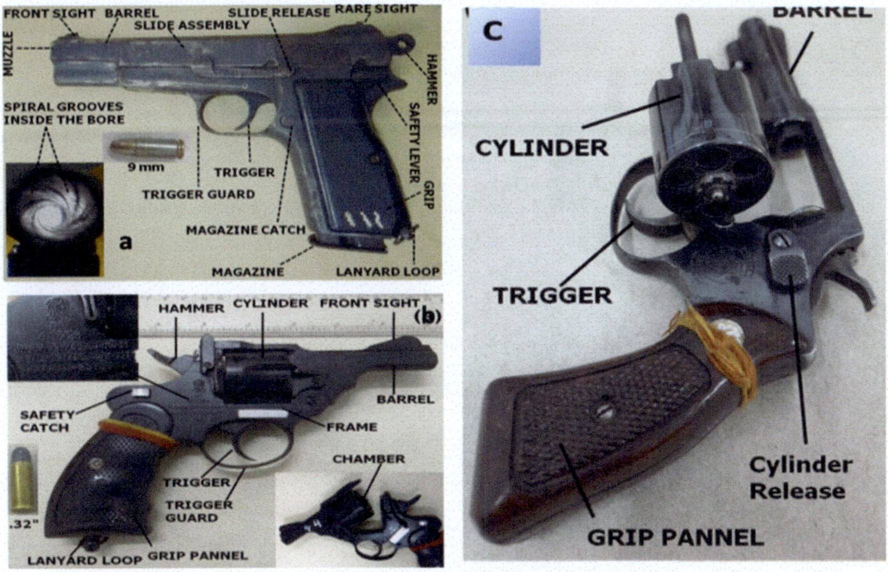

Fig. 15.3 (**a**) 9 mm semi-automatic pistol (manufactured by RFI India). Inset shows the spiral rifling of right-handed twist inside the bore of the barrel; (**b**) 0.32″ caliber break-top revolver of Indian Ordnance Factories. Lower inset shows the six chambers when the cylinder is open while the upper inset shows the enlarged view of the details in the frame; (**c**): 0.32″ caliber In Swing-out revolver of Smith & Wesson

next chamber line up with the barrel for firing. Depending upon how the revolving cylinder is attached, revolvers can be categorized into three categories: Break-top revolvers, Swing-out revolvers, and solid frame revolvers.

In Break-top revolvers the frame is hinged at the rear such that on the release of a top catch, both the barrel and the cylinder flip downward for loading the cartridges or ejecting cartridge cases. In Swing-out revolvers the frame is hinged at the rear such that on pressing the latch the cylinder swings out to the side of the revolver for loading or ejecting cartridge cases. While, solid frame revolvers the cylinder is held in the frame by a central pin, around which it rotates. There is no way to uncover all the chambers in the cylinder at once and the chambers in the cylinder are loaded separately through a loading gate by manually rotating the cylinder. Figure 15.3 depicts the pistol and revolvers as discussed.

15.3.2.1.2 Long Guns or Shoulder Arms

There are two basic types of long guns: shotguns and rifles.

15.3.2.1.2.1 Shotguns

These are the firearms having smooth bore barrel and designed to fire shot shells that either contain numerous shots/pellets or a single projectile like a slug. A shotgun can be single-barreled or double-barreled. In a double-barreled shotgun, the two barrels

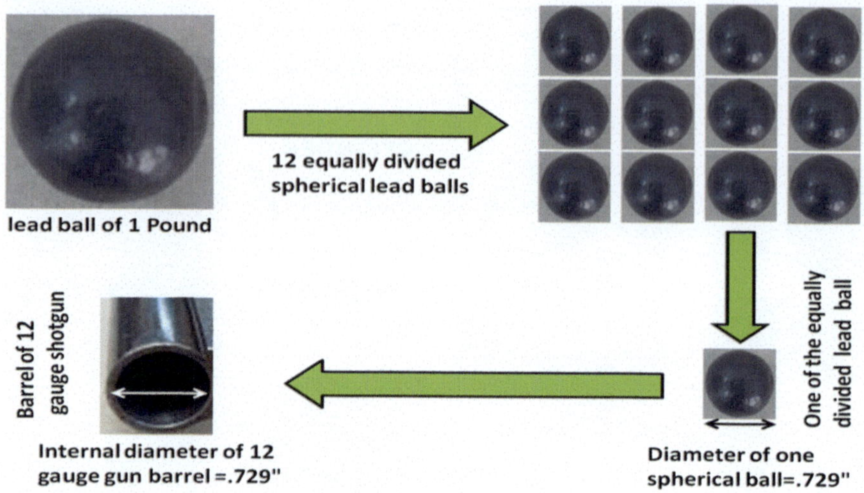

Fig. 15.4 Schematic illustration of the 12 bore/gauge

either arranged horizontally (side by side) or vertically (one over another). The hollow interior of the barrel is called the bore.

Smooth-bore shotguns are further classified based on the internal cross-sectional diameter of the barrel and designated by a number such as 12 bore/gauge shotgun. The '12' in 12 bore is not a unit of length but a division of weight. The 12 refers to a 12th of 1 lb of lead and specify internal cross-sectional diameter of the barrel such that 12 equal spherical balls of 1 lb of pure lead, each exactly fitting the barrel; diameter of what we know as a 12-bore (0.729″) as depicted graphically in Fig. 15.4.

There are many other shotguns of various bores such as 8, 10, 16, 20, 28 and 32 gauge but 12 bore is by far the most popular shotgun. The bore of all other shot guns is also defined in a similar way as that of 12 gauge shotgun. In general, the diameter of the barrel of *N*-bore gun is equal to the diameter of a spherical lead ball weighing 1/*N* lb. Basically, the Gauge of shotgun is equal to 1 lb divided by the weight of lead sphere.

The diameter of the internal cross-section of the barrel of shotgun related with the bore number by the following relation (Sharma 2002).

$$Nd^3 \approx 4.657$$

where, '*N*' is the bore number and '*d*' is the diameter of the bore of barrel in inches.

It is evident that if the bore number is less the bore diameter will be more. This can be understood from the values of bore diameter for various bore numbers as provided in Table 15.1.

It is to be noted that when the cross-sectional bore diameter is more than 0.500″, the smooth bore firearms are known by their bore number. While the bore diameter is less than 0.500″, the firearm is designated by its bore diameter in inches. For

Table 15.1 Diameter of bore for different bore sizes

Bore size (Gauge)	Bore diameter (Inch)
8	0.835
10	0.775
12	0.729
16	0.662
20	0.615
28	0.550
32	0.526

example 0.410″-musket which is a smooth bore firearm of cross-sectional bore diameter 0.410″.

15.3.2.1.2.2 Choke

In shotguns, when a cartridge loaded with pellets is discharged, the pellets start to spread after exiting from the muzzle end. In order to reduce the dispersion of the pellets and increase the number of pellets striking at a given area, the barrel is narrowed toward the muzzle. This narrowing of the barrel is referred as the *choke* of the shotgun (Mattoo and Nabar 1969; Burrard 1960; Nag and Sinha 1992; Arslan et al. 2011). Its purpose is to shape the spread of the pellets in order to gain accuracy as well as better range. In double-barreled shotgun the barrels may also have different choke diameters.

There is a lot of science and mathematics involved in creating the perfect choke for a particular shotgun. In the case of 12 gauge shotgun, where there is no choke, there are only 40% of the pellets hit in the 30″. circle at a distance of 40 yards from the muzzle of the shotgun. There are various factors for instance the length of the shotgun barrel, the material of the choke, the geometry of the choke and the finish of the choke that plays important role in making good chokes.

There are generally five choke types used in the shotguns: Quarter choke, half choke, three-quarter choke, full choke and improved cylinder. The more the degree of restriction in the barrel, the more will be the density of pellets at the given area of target. The following table shows the amount of constriction and its effect of that on the pallet spread pattern measured by app. percentage of the total pellets in a cartridge in a 30″ circle at the range of 30 and 40 yards (Sharma 2002; Heard 2008; Arslan et al. 2011). Table 15.2 shows the distribution of pellets and it is very evident that choking of shotgun barrel leads to an increased number of striking pellets at the given area of the target (Heard 2008).

15.3.2.1.2.3 Rifles

Rifles are the firearm that has a ‘rifled’ bore barrel i.e. the bore of the barrel consists of a number of spiral grooves cut longitudinally having a uniform twist. Rifles are shoulder firearm designed to hit the target beyond the range of shotgun firearms. Rifling is provided in the barrels of rifled firearms, in order to exert a torque and hence impart a spin to the bullet that travels through it. A spinning bullet is gyroscopically stable in its trajectory, and hence the rifling enhances accuracy and

Table 15.2 Distribution of pellets according to choke

S. No.	Barrel choke	Amount of constriction in muzzle diameter	Muzzle diameter of 12 gauge shotgun after choke	Percentage of total pellets in a 30″ circle at the range of 30 yards	Percentage of total pellets in a 30″ circle at the range of 40 yards
1.	True cylinder	No constriction	0.729″	60%	40%
2.	Improved cylinder	0.003–0.005″	0.724–0.726″	72%	50%
3.	Quarter choke	0.01″	0.719″	77%	55%
4.	Half choke	0.02″	0.709″	83%	60%
5.	Three quarter choke	0.03″	0.699″	91%	65%
6.	Full choke	0.04″	0.689″	100%	70%

Table 15.3 Various firearms, their muzzle velocity and firing range

S. No.	Firearm	Approximate muzzle velocity	Approximate effective range	Approximate maximum range
1.	Country made firearms	200–500 ft/s	–	200 yards
2.	Air-gun/Air-rifle	300–700 ft/s	50–150 yards	400 yards
3.	Revolver	600–800 ft/s	75 yards	2200 yards
4.	Pistol	800–1300 ft/s	100 yards	2500 yards
5.	Shotgun	1200–1600 ft/s	40–250 yards	1400 yards
6.	Rifle	1200–3900 ft/s	1400 yards	5700 yards

range of the rifled firearm. Most of the modern pistols, revolvers and rifles have rifling in their barrels. The cartridges of such firearms are loaded with single projectile known as bullet. In the rifled barrel, the raised portions of the bore are known as "lands" and grooved portions are known as "grooves". The "lands" are the raised portions (actually are the portions of the barrel not touched by the rifling cutter) between the "grooves" such that the number of lands and grooves in any particular rifled barrel are always the same (Fig. 15.5). The number of spiral grooves cut into a barrel can range from 1 to 24 or even more; but generally it varies from 4 to 7. There are rifles comprising 12, 16 and 20 or even more grooves in its barrel. Such rifles are known to have micro-grooved barrels.

Rifling is often described by its twist rate and pitch. The distance the rifling takes to complete one revolution/turn is called twist such as "1 turn in 12″" (1:12″) and the term pitch refers to the angle at which the rifling is cut in the barrel. A shorter distance means faster twist and bullet will rotate at a higher spin rate. The actual twist

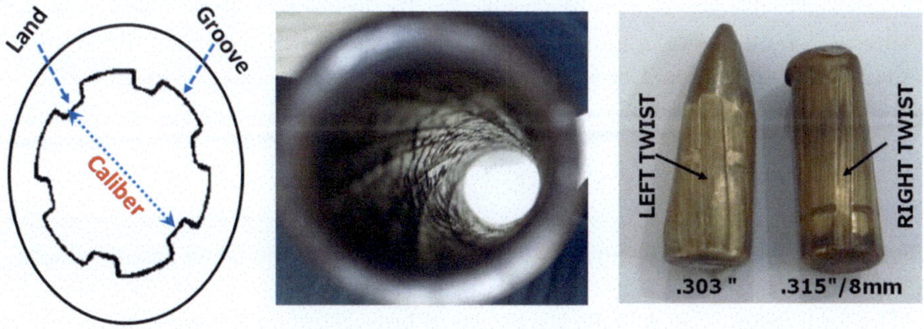

Fig. 15.5 From the left, Cross-sectional view of a rifled barrel showing lands, grooves and caliber. Spiral grooves having right twist inside the barrel of 9 mm pistol and Fired bullets carrying left-handed twist and right-handed twist of rifling

rate is calculated very carefully in relation to the bore of the firearm, the muzzle velocity, the weight, density and length of the intended bullet. The twist/direction of rifling can be either clockwise (right) or counterclockwise (left).

In rifled barrel, the distance measured between two opposing lands is known as *caliber* of the firearm. It is measured in hundredths or thousandths of an inch (0.22 cal, 0.315 cal) or in millimeters (9 mm). In order to properly identify the cartridge, it is usual, particularly in rifle calibers, to add the cartridge case length along with the caliber such as 8 × 57 mm (8 mm is the caliber and 57 mm is the case length), 7.62 × 39 mm, 7.62 × 51 mm and 7.62 × 25 mm (pistol round). In another nomenclature, sometimes the year of introduction of a particular caliber of ammunition is added, e.g. 0.30–06 is a 0.30″ caliber rifle round introduced in 1906. Similarly, 0.30–3 is the same caliber of 0.30″ but was introduced in the year 1903 (Heard 2008).

It is to be noted that the caliber is not an exact measurement of the bore diameter and most of the bullet have a somewhat larger diameter than the caliber of a firearm. For example, 0.45″ pistol has land diameter of 0.444″, whereas the bullet diameter is 0.451–0.454″ (usually, 0.451″ for full metal jacket bullets and 0.454″ for lead bullets). A 0.303″ British cartridge has a bullet diameter up to 0.312″ (Di Maio 1998; Sharma 2002; Heard 2008).

Once a projectile exited from the barrel of the firearm it begins its trajectory. Generally, a projectile does not travel with its axis aligned to the direction of flight and the angle between the projectile axis and the direction of the flight is called yaw angel. The trajectory of projectile in the air is influenced by many factors—some are associated with the projectile itself, some are related to the earth's gravitational forces and some factors are associated with the surrounding in which the projectile travel. The overall effect is a force acting upon the side of the projectile leads to drag. The total drag is the sum of all the component drags and a dimensionless quantity called drag coefficient is used to measure the efficiency of projectile during its flight. On the other hand, a quantity called *ballistic coefficient* is a measure of the ability of a projectile to overcome air resistance in flight (Heard 2008). It is inversely proportional to the deceleration of a projectile. The larger the ballistic coefficient, the smaller will be the deceleration and hence better the bullet will retain its velocity while cut through the air. The value of ballistic coefficient C can vary from 0.12 and as high as 1.00 for commonly used bullets and is calculated by using the formula;

$$C = \frac{w}{i \cdot d^2}$$

where, $C =$ ballistic coefficient; $w =$ weight of bullet; $i =$ form factor and $d =$ diameter of the bullet.

The form factor '*i*' is actually a measure of how streamlined a bullet is e.g. for a highly streamlined pointed bullet form factor of 0.55 is reported whereas for a wadcutter bullet the form factor has value of about 2.0. The aerodynamics of the shape of bullet e.g. flat base bullet, or boat-tailed bullet is crucial in deciding its ballistics coefficient.

15.3.2.2 On the Basis of Loading

15.3.2.2.1 Muzzle Loading Firearms

In muzzle-loading firearms the propellant charge and the projectile/projectiles are loaded from the muzzle end (Fig. 15.6). In these firearms the barrel is closed at the breech end and opens at the muzzle end only. In these firearms, underneath the barrel a metallic '*Ram rod*' is attached which is used to push the powder propellant and projectiles from the muzzle end. The barrel carries a nipple on its side near the breech end. The percussion cap is placed on the nipple and the hammer is attached there in such a way that after cocking it when the trigger is pressed the hammer strike at the percussion cap placed at the nipple. The composition in a percussion cap causes a flame which through the nipple ignites the propellant charge inside the barrel and generates gases; the pressure of which causes the loaded projectile/projectiles to propel out from the barrel with high velocity. In such firearms the range of fire will

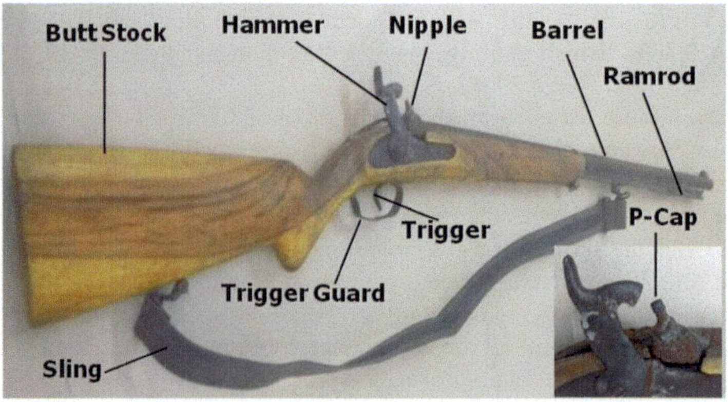

Fig. 15.6 Muzzle loading gun

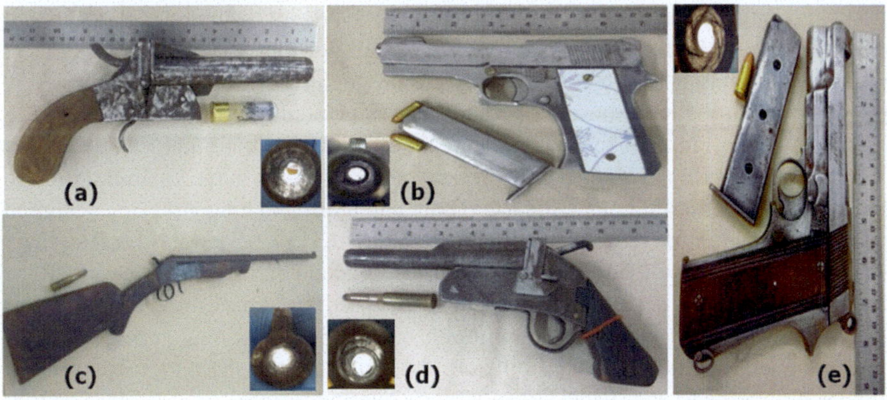

Fig. 15.7 Country-made/improvised non-standard (**a**) 12 bore pistol (**b**) 7.65 mm semiautomatic pistol (**c**) 0.315″ single barrel gun (**d**) 0.315″ pistol, along with the corresponding ammunition and inset shows the bore of the barrel of the respective firearm. Even the bore of the firearm designed to fire bullet does not have any rifling. (**e**) Improvised non-standard 9 mm semiautomatic pistol

depend upon the quantity and manner of loading (denser or loosely filled) of the propellant charge. In muzzle-loading firearms, anything like pieces of lead, iron, pieces of glass, stones etc can be used as a projectile. At present these types of firearms are rarely used.

15.3.2.2.2 Breech Loading Firearms

In such firearms, the cartridge is loaded from the breech end into the chamber either directly or through the magazine. Most of the modern firearms are breech loaders (Figs. 15.1, 15.3, and 15.7).

15.3.3 Country Made Firearms or Improvised Firearms

These are illegally made firearms of substandard material either homemade or in clandestine firearm factories in various countries worldwide (Thejaswi et al. 2013; Sinha 2015). In the crime activity, the use of these illegally modified legal firearms, replicas of popular branded firearms, crude homemade firearms etc. has increased exponentially worldwide. Since these non-standard illegal firearms differ in forensic point of view and appearance-wise/design as well from standard legal firearms, hence, are also known as unusual firearms. These firearms are often made of inexpensive and substandard material owing to which sometimes the barrel or other parts of such firearms even get damaged during the fire. Some of the improvised firearms are also termed as *Zip Guns* (Koffler 1969). Usually, these illegal firearms are designed in such a way to chamber a particular type of standard ammunition already available legally. The bore of the barrel of such firearms is often very rough and sometimes crude non-spiral rifling is also made in the bore of the barrel which is not regular. The fired bullet when travel through such barrels does not carry any regular rifling marks on it. Sometimes, the bore of the barrel is so loose that the bullet carries barrel striations only at the small portion which strikes the barrel surface. If the barrel length is not proper the propellant could not burn completely and even due to the loose bore of the barrel the generated gases leaks which lead to reduced striking range of the bullet. Sometimes the barrel bore diameter is so less that due to the extensive generated pressure the barrel got burst. In India, a large number of illegal country made firearms (both handguns and long guns) are designed to fire the cartridges of 12 bore and 7.65 mm, 9 mm, 0.315″, 0.32″ (revolver) and few 0.22″ caliber. Muzzle loading firearms are also encountered in crime cases. Since these firearms are illegal, cheap and non-licensed firearms, many times these firearms are thrown away after committing crime and sometimes during fire they get damaged too which poses a problem in investigating the shooting incident or to link such firearms to any suspect even after recovering it from crime scene. The tool marks identification of such firearms is also tedious sometimes as the marks present on fired cartridge case and fired bullet do not follow any defined class. The forensic experts may give erroneous opinion if the expert does not have proper understanding and experience of various tool marks in case of such non-standard firearms (Fig. 15.7).

15.3.3.1 Paradox Gun

These are smooth bore firearms with a partially rifled barrel towards the muzzle end. This provision enables it to fire both single projectile (spherical ball/slug/rifled slug) and shots with reasonable accuracy as it provides some spin which helps to provide better stability and accuracy to the projectile during its flight in the air.

15.3.4 Air-Guns and Air-Rifles

These are the pneumatic firearms which on discharge, propel out the projectile from the barrel by utilizing the pressure of pressurized air. Such firearm does not involve the use of any kind of propellant/gun-powder to generate the required pressure to push the projectile out of the barrel (Heard 2008; Harshey et al. 2017). There are two basic mechanisms used to generate pressure either by compressing the air and then releasing it which causes the projectile to propel out or by compressing spring in a chamber and the sudden release of spring leads to air release with high-pressure which push the projectile towards muzzle end of the firearm. Air gun (long gun) and Air pistol (hand gun) have smooth barrel bore whereas Air-rifles have rifling in its barrel bore (Abhyankar et al. 2018; Tiwari et al. 2019). Typically, metallic pellets are used as a projectile in such firearms. The two most common sizes of projectiles is 0.177″ and 0.22″ caliber lead pellet (Alim et al. 2020). Other less common traditional calibers include 0.20″, 0.25″ and 0.30″. Fig. 15.8 shows an air rifle of 0.177″.

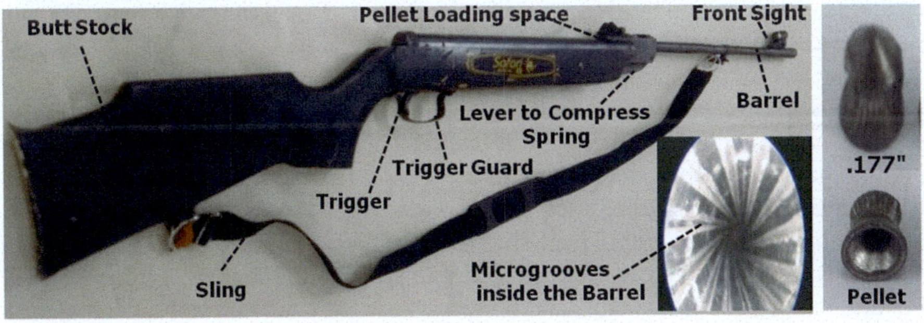

Fig. 15.8 Air rifle of 0.177″ caliber along with pellet of 0.177″

15.3.5 Action Mechanism of Modern Firearms

The loading and firing mechanism of firearms is called actions. Based on the type of the firearm and its design there are various types of action mechanisms. The common forms are hammer action, hammerless action, lever action, pump action, revolving action, bolt actions, semiautomatic and automatic action.

15.3.5.1 Hammer Action

In firearms possessing such action, hammer is featured outside in the rear action part. Hammer must be cocked before the trigger is pulled. As trigger is pulled; the hammer is released, causing the cartridge in the chamber to fire.

15.3.5.2 Hammerless Action

In firearms possessing such action, usually firing hammer do not expose and is attached inside in the action part. The user can not pull it to cock the firearm.

Firearms having an exposed firing hammer were many times subjected to accidental firing owing to the exposed firing pin whereas in hammerless firearms an internal firing pin reduced the risk of accidental firing.

15.3.5.3 Lever Action

Firearms having Lever action uses an external lever in order to cycle breech mechanism. Lever is generally located below the receiver often either around trigger guard or trigger guard itself.

15.3.5.4 Pump Action

Firearms having pump action uses a movable fore-end that can be moved forward and backward in line with the barrel by the user in order to eject a fired cartridge case of ammunition and to chamber a new cartridge.

15.3.5.5 Revolving Action

As the name suggests, such action mechanism is posses by revolvers. Such firearm has a revolving cylinder having a number of chambers. In successive firing, cylinder rotates and new chamber aligns with the barrel. Revolving action is further categorized as single action and double action as explained above.

15.3.5.6 Bolt Action

Firearms having bolt action uses a bolt that is manually operated to load cartridges into the chamber, to cock the firearm, to eject and to extract the cartridge case from the chamber. The bolt is commonly placed on the right-hand side of the firearm and the firing pin is attached within the bolt. When the bolt is pulled back, the chamber is exposed and a cartridge can be loaded in the chamber. When the bolt is pushed forward, the firearm gets cocked and breech is closed by the bolt re-locking against receiver. When the trigger is pulled, the firing pin moves forward and firearm gets discharged. Now, on pulling the bolt backward, the fired case extracted and ejected. Bolt-action firearms can be single-shot firearms or often repeating rifles which has magazine in it containing number of live cartridges. In repeating rifles, repeated pull and push of the bolt is required for the successive fire of the available cartridges in the magazine.

15.3.5.7 Semi-Automatic Action

Firearms having semiautomatic action mechanism requires just a separate pull of the trigger to fire the next round. The firing cycle of extraction, ejection of fired case and reloading of the new cartridge from the magazine takes place automatically by utilizing energy from the discharge. In 5.56 mm INSAS (Indian Small Arms System) assault rifle there is a selector lever/switch on the left side of the receiver which can be adjusted to fire the rifle either in semi-automatic mode or three-round burst firing mode. In burst mode, with a one pull of trigger, the firearm discharges three cartridges together.

15.3.5.8 Automatic Action

Firearms having automatic action mechanism requires just a long press of the trigger for continuously fire the cartridges. The extraction, ejection of fired case and reloading of the new cartridge from the magazine take place automatically. Automatic and semi-automatic firearms have the three basic types of the actions for extraction, ejection of fired cartridge case and reloading of new cartridge from the magazine into the chamber: (1) Blow-back action, (2) Recoil operated action (short recoil-operated action and long recoil-operated action) and (3) Gas-operated action.

15.4 Muzzle Velocity and Various Ranges of Firearms

Muzzle velocity is defined as the velocity with which a projectile leaves the muzzle of a firearm and it depends upon the type of ammunition and firearm used to discharge the ammunition. Handguns are low-velocity firearms whereas rifles are high-velocity firearms. However, the muzzle velocity of country-made non-standard handguns and long guns is very less as compared to regular standard firearms used to discharge using the same ammunition.

There are basically two important ranges associated with firearms namely; maximum range and effective range. Maximum range is the distance up to which the projectile can travel and effective range is the maximum distance up to which a projectile is expected to hit the target accurately and damages the target. Table 15.3 shows the common range of values of muzzle velocity and firing range for various firearms based on available literature which may change up to some extent as per change in ammunition and firearm parameters (Di Maio 1998; Sharma 2002; Heard 2008).

15.5 Types of Ammunition

Ammunition for any firearm is an assembly that can be discharged from a firearm and generally the various components of ammunition are brought together in the form of a cartridge that consists of a (1) cartridge case, (2) primer, (3) propellant (gunpowder), (4) projectile (bullet/slug/spherical ball) or projectiles (pellets or shots) and some sort of wads (in shotgun cartridges). In shotgun cartridges the projectile can be single ball/slug or multiple pellets/shots, however, rifled cartridges (meant to fire from a rifled bore) always consist of single projectile i.e. bullet. Based on the location of the primer and exploding the priming mixture; there are mainly three types of ammunition used in firearms: pin-fire, rim-fire, and center-fire (Heard 2008; Wallace 2018).

Pin Fire Cartridges In such cartridges, a small cylindrical cup contains the primer mixture located in the cavity formed inside of the head of cartridge case. In these cartridges the firing pin is the part of the cartridge which extends radially into the primer. The priming mixture is ignited by striking a hammer on the pin attached with the cartridge. Now, these types of cartridges are obsolete.

Rim Fire Cartridges In such cartridges, the cavity containing the primer mixture is placed in the rim of the head of the cartridge case. The primer mixture is ignited when either the hammer or the firing pin strike and crush the rim of the cartridge (Fig. 15.9).

Center Fire Cartridges In such cartridges, the primer mixture is placed in the center of the cartridge head in a small circular metal cup known as percussion-cap. The primer mixture is ignited by striking the firing pin on the percussion cup. Most of the modern firearms are designed to discharge center-fire cartridges. Center-fire cartridges are basically of the following types.

1. **Rimmed cartridges:** In these types of cartridges there is an extractor flange also known as "Rim" which slightly projects outside just ahead of the cartridge head. Hence the diameter of the cartridge at the head i.e. rim diameter is larger than the diameter of the cartridge body. The rim helps in holding the cartridge in the

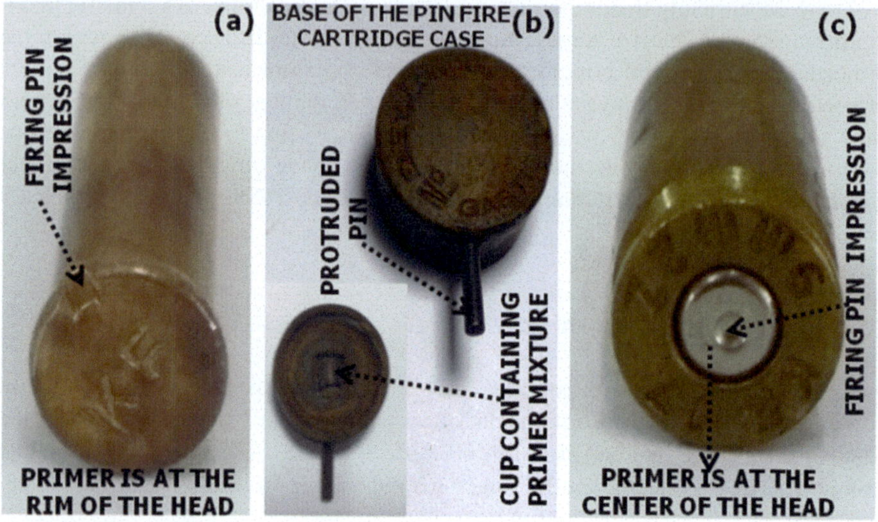

Fig. 15.9 (**a**) Rim fire cartridge case (**b**) Base of the pin fire cartridge case and (**c**) Center Fire cartridge case

chamber of the firearm and also facilitates the extraction of the cartridge from the chamber.

2. **Rimless cartridges:** In these types of cartridges the diameter of the cartridge rim is equal to the diameter of the cartridge body. There is a groove around the body of the case just in front of the flange.
3. **Semi-Rimmed cartridges:** In these types of cartridges, the diameter of extractor flange/rim is larger than the diameter of the cartridge body but not as much as in the rimmed cartridges. Moreover, like Rimless cartridges these cartridges also have a groove around the body of the case just in front of the flange.
4. **Rebated cartridges:** In these types of the cartridges, the diameter of extractor flange/rim is smaller than the diameter of the cartridge body. These cartridges also have a groove around the body of the case just in front of the flange.
5. **Belted cartridges:** In these types of cartridges, there is a raised belt around the cartridge case body in front of the groove. The addition of the belt allows proper headspace and prevents over-insertion of the cartridge in the chamber hence now the diameter of the rim does not matter.

Other than the above, blank and dummy cartridges are also used. Blank cartridges have either a crimped neck or are sealed with paper disks. A blank cartridge has primer and propellant but no projectile. On discharge, it produces flash and noise usually employed for training purposes. In close range sometimes it may even cause casualty. A dummy cartridge however does not have any primer, propellant or projectile and used for teaching purpose particularly for training in loading and unloading a firearm.

Cartridge cases of metallic ammunition are usually made of brass, a composition of 70% copper and 30% zinc. However, Shotgun cartridge cases are usually made of plastic or multilayered paper with brass heads. When a cartridge is discharged from a firearm, cartridge case expands and seals the chamber against rearward escape of gases, hence the hardness of brass is made in such a way that it return to its original dimensions and make the case easy to extract. There are basically three general shapes for cartridge cases: straight, bottleneck, and tapered. Almost all pistol and revolver cartridges are usually straight (some pistol uses bottlenecked cartridges), rifle cartridges are bottle-necked and shotgun cartridges are straight (though, the cartridge cases of 0.410 muskets are tapered).

15.5.1 Primer, Propellants and Projectiles

When the firing pin of the firearm strikes the base of the cartridge, it is the primer compound in the percussion-cap which initiates the burning of the propellant gunpowder.

15.5.1.1 Primers

The primer mixture consists of a sensitive explosive compound. There are two types of primers for metallic cartridges viz. Boxer and Berdan primer. Boxer primer contains an assembled external anvil (anvil is a small metal block which resists the blow of the firing pin and hence primer is crushed) and a single flash hole whereas in Berdan primer the anvil is built into the cartridge case itself as an integral part and there are usually two flash holes. Initially, the primer was made of largely mercury fulminate and lead azide which is later replaced by a composition of lead styphnate, barium nitrate, and antimony sulfide and is most commonly used primer composition. The detection of elemental constitutes (lead, barium and antimony as the gunshot residues) of the priming mixture in the hand swab forms the basis to determine whether an individual has fired a firearm. Nowadays, lead-free priming mixture which is basically the salt of zinc and titanium called SINTOX is also used (Wallace 2018; Harshey et al. 2020).

15.5.1.2 Propellants

In the firing process, the burning of propellant is essential in order to eject the projectile from fired cartridge to outside target through the barrel. In a cartridge, the combustion and burning of propellant produces a huge amount of pressure of gases inside the cartridge shell to propel the projectile out of the barrel of firearm. The typically used propellants are of three types: (1) Black gun powder, (2) Smokeless powder and (3) Semi-Smokeless powder.

15.5.1.2.1 Black Gun Powder

Until the end of the nineteenth century, most of the cartridges were loaded with black gun powder. The black powder mixture consists of 75% potassium nitrate, 15% charcoal and 10% sulfur. In this mixture, the potassium nitrate acts as an oxidizer (the oxygen supplier), charcoal as a fuel and the sulfur provides more density and makes the mixture more readily ignitable. The burning of black gun powder produces a large amount of solid residue and only about 44% of the powder converts into gases. Black gun powders are rarely used nowadays. It is however; used in muzzle-loading firearms, blank cartridges, country made/homemade ammunitions and refilled ammunitions. Nowadays, mostly smokeless powders are used as propellant owing to their higher efficiency of combustion as compared to that of black gun powders. The rate of burning depends on the size of the powder grain and based on the size it is classified as FG, FFG, FFFG and FFFFG. The 'F' refers to how fine the powder grains are. More number of 'F' indicates finer powder particle grains and finer grain size implies more effective burning of the propellant. However, there is a limit beyond which effective burning cannot be increased by reducing the powder grain size.

15.5.1.2.2 Smokeless Powder

At present, it is the most used propellant due to its high efficiency of combustion as compared to that of black gunpowder. Theoretically, it is converted completely into gaseous products. It produces very little smoke as compared to black gun powder. This powder falls into three categories: single-base smokeless powder, double-base smokeless powder and triple-base smokeless powder. Single-base smokeless powder consists of nitrocellulose alone while double-base smokeless powder consists of nitrocellulose dissolved in nitroglycerine and triple-base smokeless powder consists of nitrocellulose, nitroglycerin, and nitroguanidine. In general, triple-base smokeless propellants are used in large caliber ammunition such as used in artillery and tank guns. The powder grains have various shapes such as small sphere, disk, flakes, cylindrical etc and the diameter of individual powder grains varies from several tenths of a millimeter up to more than 1 mm. To improve the effectiveness, prevent undesirable ignition and minimize the generation of static electricity the powder granules are further coated with conductive graphite. The graphite coating also reduces the effect of moisture and hence the powder can be stored for a long time.

15.5.1.2.3 Semi-Smokeless Powder

This powder is a mixture of nitrocellulose, potassium nitrate, charcoal, and sulfur. Generally, the ratio is 80% of black gun powder and 20% of smokeless powder. It is more useful than black powder in that it develops less smoke and left less solid residue in the bore of a firearm. Semi-smokeless powder was used long back such as LESMOK powder; however, in modern ammunitions this powder is not used.

15.5.2 Projectiles

It is the very important component of ammunition. Shotgun cartridges either contain numerous shots/pellets or a single projectile such as slug while rifled cartridge/ metallic cartridge always have a single projectile known as bullet. Shots or pellets are designed to fire from smooth bore firearms while bullets are designed to fire from a rifled barrel. The power of a projectile depends upon its weight, design and velocity. To achieve better momentum the mass of the projectile should be larger and to increase penetrating power the size of the projectile should not be large. Hence, high-density metal is required to make projectile. Lead is a soft, dense and the cost-effective metal that makes it appropriate material for making projectiles.

In shotgun ammunition, the shots/pellets or slug usually been made of lead (containing addition of some other metals such as arsenic, antimony, tin in a small amount to make it a bit harder which helps to provide the shots with a uniform pattern and less possibility of getting fused), but owing to the restrictions on lead some other metals such as steel, tungsten or bismuth are also used. Shotgun pellets usually fall into two categories: birdshots and buckshots. The British system for designating shot size is based on the number of shot per ounce. Larger size shots usually having diameter of about 5.16–9.14 mm are called 'buckshots' while smaller ones are called 'birdshots'. The smallest lead birdshot diameter is about 1.22 mm (Heard 2008; Sharma 2002; Tom 2004).

The various sizes of the shots loaded in shotgun cartridges usually vary from LG, MG to number 12 and dust. Table 15.4 gives the number of shots per ounce, designation of shot sizes, weight measurement (in gram) and diameter (in millimeter and inch) of each type of individual shots.

The following formula relates the diameter of a particular size of shot with the total number of shots of that size in 1 oz.

$$Nd^3 \approx 0.291$$

where, N = total no. of shots, d = diameter of an individual shot in inches.

From the Table 15.4 it is clear that smaller the shot number, the larger will be the pellet diameter. It is believed that the notation LG, MG, SG, SSG refers to long goose, medium goose, small goose and special short goose respectively. It is to mention here that there are various bores with different cartridge lengths. The most common cartridge of 12 bore shotgun is of 2.5″ length. In these cartridges the shot load is about 30.12 g and therefore the number of shots/pellets will vary from that given in Table 15.4 which is basically for 1 oz or 28.35 g, e.g. the number of pellets of 1 number size will be about 107 and 2 number size will be 128 and so on (Fig. 15.10).

Usually, Projectiles are made of lead metal but due to high velocity and high temperature during firing such lead bullets are sometimes damaged and get skidded in the rifling of the bore. In high-power rifled cartridges such lead bullets cannot be used. To overcome this it is covered by the jacket of hard metal usually made of gilding metal (copper/zinc alloy) or cupro-nickel (copper/nickel alloy). In addition, the hardness due to jacket provides the bullet deeper penetration into the target. Jacketed bullets can be fully jacketed or semi-jacketed. In fully metal jacketed bullets the jacket covers the whole bullet with opened base exposing the lead core, while in semi-jacketed bullet the jacket is open at the nose to reveal the lead core. There are varieties of bullets with different calibers, and sizes viz. lead bullet, full metal jacketed, metal point/nose, soft point, hollow point, flat point, etc. The base

Table 15.4 Measurements of pellets according to the designation

S. No.	Designation/ size of the shots	No. of shots in 1 oz (≈28.35 g)	Weight of each shot in grams	Diameter of each shot in inches	Diameter of each shot in millimeters
1.	LG	6	4.730	0.360	9.14
2.	MG	7	4.050	0.347	8.61
3.	SG	8	3.540	0.332	8.43
4.	SSG	15	1.890	0.269	6.83
5.	AAAA	30	0.950	0.214	5.24
6.	AAA	35	0.810	0.203	5.16
7.	AA	40	0.710	0.194	4.84
8.	A	50	0.570	0.180	4.57
9.	BBB	60	0.470	0.170	4.32
10.	BB	70	0.410	0.161	4.09
11.	B	80	0.350	0.154	3.90
12.	1	100	0.280	0.143	3.63
13.	2	120	0.240	0.135	3.41
14.	3	140	0.200	0.127	3.25
15.	4	170	0.170	0.120	3.05
16.	5	220	0.130	0.110	2.79
17.	6	270	0.110	0.102	2.59
18.	7	340	0.080	0.095	2.41
19.	8	450	0.060	0.087	2.21
20.	9	580	0.050	0.080	2.03
21.	10	850	0.030	0.070	1.79
22.	11	1040	0.026	0.068	1.73
23.	12	1250	0.020	0.062	1.57
24.	Dust	2600	0.010	0.048	1.22

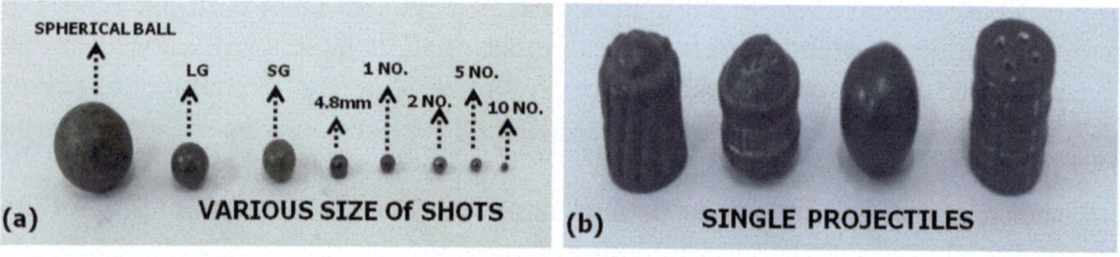

Fig. 15.10 (**a**) Various sizes of shots/pellets and (**b**) spherical ball/slugs

portion of a bullet is generally provided with circumferential grooves called cannelure which is used to hold the lubricant and for the proper crimping with the cartridge case. There are some famous names used for bullets are: Wadcutter bullet, Hollow point bullet, soft-nosed bullet and dum-dum bullet.

A *wadcutter-bullet* is a flat-nosed bullet with a sharp shoulder particularly designed for shooting paper or cardboard targets, usually at close range. It is designed specifically for competitive shooting; the flat nose of the bullet ensures that it cuts clean into the target.

A *hollow point bullet* is a semi-jacketed bullet having the hollow point/nose which on striking at the target expands and causes more damage, particularly at soft targets like human tissues.

A *soft-nosed bullet* is a semi-jacketed bullet with an exposed lead tip that is partially covered in a metal jacket. The exposed soft nose creates more reliable expansion and causes more damage. Unlike, the hollow point bullet there is no loading issue in these bullets and hence ideal for firearms that have loading issues with hollow point bullets.

Dum-dum bullet is derived from the Dumdum Arsenal, near Calcutta, India in 1894. Initially, it was designed from a standard 0.303″ rifle bullet by cutting the metal jacket from the nose side to expose the lead core. By cutting away the tip of the metal jacket, it became very effective and causes more damage on impact at the target particularly at human body.

15.5.2.1 Tandem Bullets or Piggyback Bullets

Tandem Bullets refer to the phenomenon of simultaneous discharge of multiple bullets in a single fire (Jentzen et al. 1995; Ersoy et al. 2012; du Toit-Prinsloo et al. 2014). This phenomenon occurs rarely and is different than multiple bullets fired from a single entrance in multiple fires. Tandem bullet phenomenon occurs when one bullet is lodged inside the barrel of the firearm prior to discharge, and on the firing of a cartridge the lodged bullet exited along with the discharged bullet. These two bullets travel together only up to a short distance and they hit the target before separation a single entry hole may be created. However, if they separate out before to hit the target two entry holes may be created at the target. In Tandem bullet scenario the so-called “bullet rule” is broken wherein the sum of number of recovered bullet from the body and exit wounds in the body should be equal to number of entry wounds in the body (Fig. 15.11).

$$\text{Entry wounds} = \text{Exit wounds} + \text{the number of projectiles recovered from the body}$$

A typical feature of tandem bullets is “piggyback structure” in which the base of the lodged bullet (front bullet) gets widens and the nose of the striking bullet is flattened. The Tandem bullet phenomenon is associated with poor quality of cartridge (could be due to ageing or contamination of the propellant powder which leads to prevention of powder ignition and hence sufficient pressure doe not generated to propel out the bullet from the barrel) or improper caliber cartridge. There are few case reports available in literature in one of which more than two projectiles were found in a single entrance gunshot wound. We have seen in our experiments that the features of Tandem bullets are more complicated in the country made non-standard firearms. Identification of tandem bullets plays a crucial role in the investigation and subsequent legal proceedings and therefore its identification and effect on target must be carefully analyzed otherwise the erroneous interpretation may misguides the investigation.

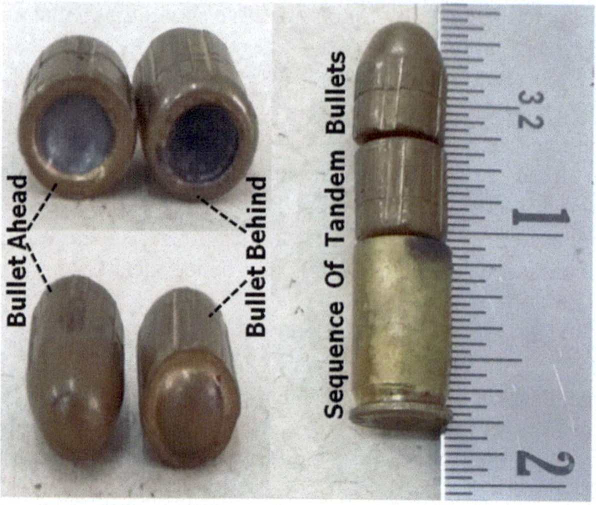

Fig. 15.11 Typical demonstration of a tandem bullet phenomenon of 7.65 mm caliber projectiles fired from a standard pistol of 7.65 mm caliber. The flattening of the nose of the bullet behind and widening of the base of the bullet ahead (lodged bullet) is clearly evident

15.5.2.2 Stray Bullet or Falling Bullets

Stray bullets are termed for those bullets which hits an unintended target in celebratory aerial firing (Ordog et al. 1994). On many occasions such as new year celebrations, marriage celebrations, rallies, gatherings, victory celebrations, etc., the aerial firing proven dangerous when hits any person. Even, deaths are reported in the literature due to such practices. Although, vertical shooting is less lethal than angulated shooting; still, the terminal velocity of falling bullet is sufficient to penetrate human skin. Sometimes, the stray bullet hit an unintended target at a significant distance from the scene of firing and it becomes difficult to reconstruct the shooting incident. In such situations, at times, identification/(possibility) of stray bullet may lead the investigation in the right direction.

15.5.2.3 Ricochet Bullets

These are the projectiles which continue to flight after an impact/deviation with any object or surface (Haag and Haag 2011). In general, these projectiles or fragments of the projectile deflect from any surface or object without penetration. It is a low-angle phenomenon and the angle above which the particular projectile no longer ricochets is called critical angle. Hence, the incident angle of any particular projectile must be less than the critical angle for ricochet to take place. There are many factors which affect the projectile ricochet such as incident angle, type of impact surface, shape, weight and velocity of the projectile etc. Understanding the effect of ricochet bullets on various targets can provide crucial information such as determination of direction of travel of the causative bullet.

15.5.2.4 Hang Fire

A typical time of interval of fire from striking the firing pin to percussion-cap, ignition of propellant and exiting of bullet is about 4 ms. However, sometimes on pressing trigger, and striking of firing pin to the percussion cap gives a click sound but the gun discharges after a delay. Such delay discharges are termed as "Hang fires". It was Haag, L. C. who succeeded to perform hang fire in his experiments by Contaminating the propellant with oil or alcohol/water solutions and the time interval of the hang fires was estimated at 200–250 ms. Haag also observed that in hang fires the velocity of the projectile gets reduced and a significant amount of unburnt propellant particles remain inside the fired case and in the bore of the barrel (Haag 1991).

15.5.3 Wads

In shotgun shell/cartridges, different types of wads are used for special purposes. A circular disc of cardboard or plastic loaded on the top of the cartridge is known as an overshot wad. Overshot wad is generally meant to seal the mouth of shotgun cartridge, the edges of the cartridge are turned down to crimp at the mouth of the shell. In general, there is marking on overshot wad which indicates the size of the shots loaded in the shell. Similarly, one wad is loaded just below the shots inside the cartridge known as undershot wad. There is another wad usually made of plastic or cardboard which mainly separates the projectiles from the propellant is called air-cushion wad or filler wad that basically provides a seal that prevents the escape of gases generated from burning of the propellant. In addition, air–cushion wad also saves the shots from deformation by preventing the direct contact of the hot gases with shots. Nowadays, in most of the ammunitions undershot wad and air-cushion wads are combining as a single wad. There is another circular wad usually made of paper or cardboard is over-powder wad placed on the top of the powder charge separates powder charge from the filler wad. The base wad placed inside the shotgun shell at its base in order to fill up the space in the shell not occupied by the propellant powder. After firing this wad is not ejected out while the other wads expelled along with the projectiles and also acts as projectile. Many times, in close-range fire, air-cushion wad enters inside the target along with the shots. Unlike the shotgun cartridges, in metallic ammunition, there is no wad used. The components of the metallic cartridges are metallic cartridge case, percussion cap having primer, propellant and bullet. The shape of the bullet is generally conical. Figure 15.12 presents a typical shotgun and rifle ammunition. Different wads are presented in Fig. 15.13.

15.6 Firearm Identification: Various Tool Marks on Fired Cartridge Case and Bullet

The unique microscopic tool marks are left on the various parts of firearms during the manufacturing and machining process (such as cutting, hammering, filing, polishing etc) and on firing these marks transferred to the fired cartridge casing and bullets. The various tool marks of the firearm which imprints on fired cartridge case and fired bullet are created during the machining process of the firearm

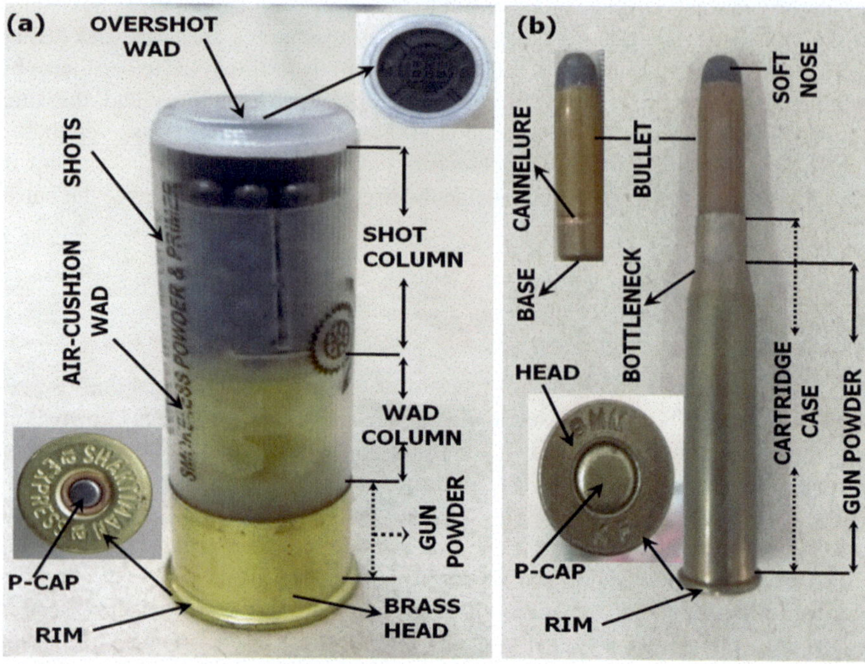

Fig. 15.12 (**a**) A transparent 12-bore shotgun cartridge; (**b**) 8 mm/0.315″ caliber metallic cartridge

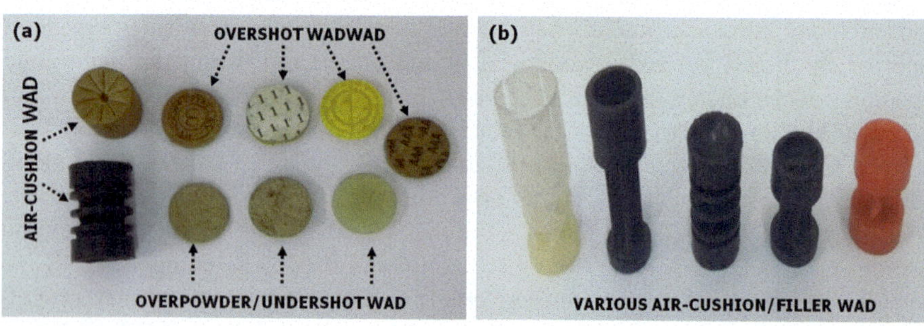

Fig. 15.13 (**a**) Various types of wads (**b**) Various types of air-cushion/filler wads

manufacturing and also from normal wear and tear. The randomly distributed imperfections in the surface profile of various parts of the firearm created accidentally either during manufacturing or by the normal use of the firearm are unique and individualistic. These marks are not duplicated in any other firearm even in those manufactured in succession. This is the basis of firearm identification. Just like the fingerprint and DNA analysis used for human identification, the scientific analysis of unique tool marks is used in firearm identification which plays a crucial role in the criminal justice system (Thompson 2010; Gunther and Gunther 2015).

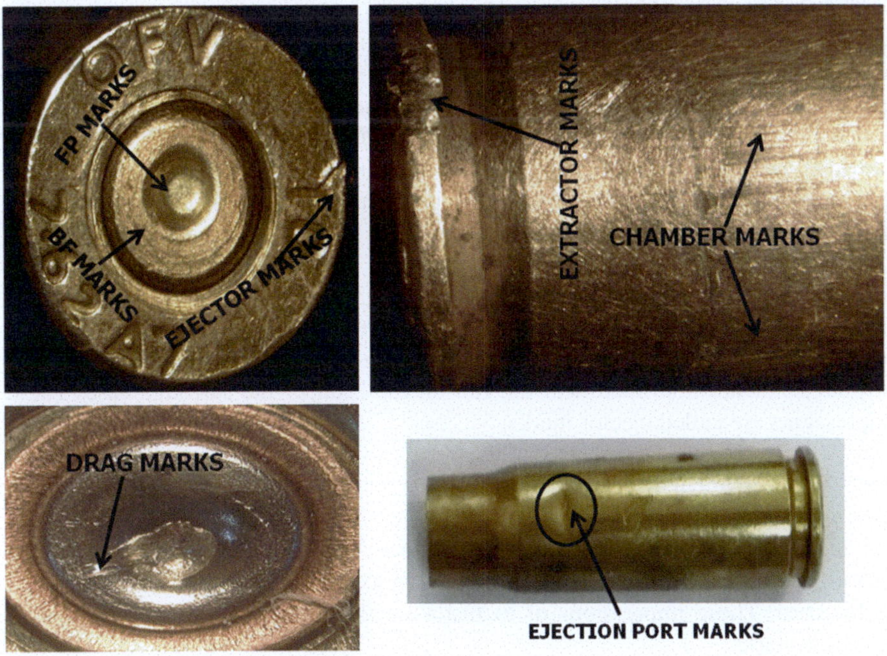

Fig. 15.14 Various types of firearm tool marks on a fired cartridge case

15.6.1 Marks on Fired Cartridge Casing

On discharging of a firearm, the fired cartridge case can carry firing pin marks, breech face marks, chamber marks, ejector marks, and extractor marks of the firearm as shown in Fig. 15.14.

15.6.1.1 Firing Pin Marks

During a fire, when a firing pin of the firearm strike on percussion-cap of the cartridge, the firing pin which is made of metals (usually steel, aluminium and titanium) harder than the metal of percussion-cap leaves its impression on percussion-cap. This impression is called firing pin marks.

15.6.1.2 Breech Face Marks

During a fire, on burning of the propellant powder the various gases create tremendous pressure of the order of 2–20 tons/square-inch inside the cartridge which forces the projectile to propel out of the barrel. At the same moment, as a result of recoil the cartridge case is forced back with high pressure against the breech face of the firearm. As a result the impressions surrounding the firing pin area imprinted on the head of the cartridge case. These impressions are called breech face marks.

15.6.1.3 Chamber Marks

The chamber of a firearm is the part of the firearm in the barrel in which the cartridge is loaded before firing. During a fire, owing to the tremendous pressure of propellant gases the walls of the cartridge case expand and tightly seal the walls of the chamber which resulted in the transfer of chamber impressions on the outer walls of the cartridge case. These impressions are called chamber marks. It has been observed that chamber marks are more prominent in homemade/country-made firearms due to crude/irregular walls of the chamber.

15.6.1.4 Ejector Marks

In semiautomatic and automatic firearms, after firing the cartridge case is ejected out by the ejector from the action of a firearm. During the ejection process, impressions of the ejector are imprinted near the rim on the head of the cartridge case. These impressions are called ejector marks.

15.6.1.5 Extractor Marks

The extractor is a part of firearm which after fire employed to remove a fired cartridge case from the chamber of a firearm. The interaction of extractor and cartridge case leaves the impression usually on extracting groove side near the rim of the case. These impressions of extractor on the fired cartridge case are called extractor marks.

15.6.1.6 Ejection Port Marks

These are the impressions created by hard contact of rapidly moving ejected cartridge case with the ejection port of a firearm.

15.6.1.7 Drag Marks

In some firearms, particularly in hammerless shotguns (in which hammer is unexposed) and in some country-made firearms, after firing the firing pin does not return to its original position. After firing when the chamber is opened, the firing pin returns to its original position leaving the drag marks on the percussion-cap.

15.6.2 Marks on Fired Projectile/Bullet

On discharge of a firearm, the fired bullet travels through the barrel and carries the marks of the interior surface of the barrel over the bullet surface. Bullets are made to fire from a rifled barrel. Rifling is provided in the barrels to impart a spin to the bullet that travels through it. Hence a bullet carries rifling impressions (i.e. grooves of barrel imprinted as lands in the bullet and lands of the barrel appears as grooves in the bullet) of the barrel. But most of non-standard country made/home made firearms does not have standard rifling in its barrel and the bullets fired from such firearms either carry crude rifling marks or simply the barrel striations (Fig. 15.15). Unlike rifled firearm, shotgun has a smooth barrel and the projectile (mostly the lead balls/ slug or pellets) emerges through the barrel generally does not carry any peculiar

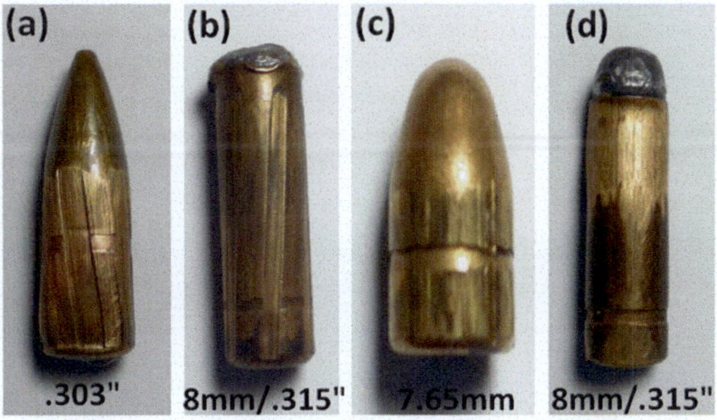

Fig. 15.15 A fired bullet showing (**a**, **b**) Regular rifling marks with left and right twist (**c**) Crude rifling (**d**) Barrel striations

characteristic markings to relate them with the firearm. Sometimes, shotgun projectile/projectiles (lead balls/slug or buckshot) may also carry the irregularities of the bore surface of the shotgun which may be useful in firearm identification.

15.6.3 Comparative Matching of Cartridges and Bullets: Firearm Identification

This is one of the most important aspects of forensic ballistics and is employed in deciding whether a particular cartridge case or a bullet is fired from the firearm of interest or not (Hatcher et al. 1957; Heard 2008; Gunther and Gunther 2015). In linking the criminal with the crime it plays a crucial role and has great evidentiary value in the criminal justice system. As discussed in the earlier section, after fire each firearm leaves various unique individual marks on the fired cartridge cases and fired bullets. The comparison of these individual tool marks in various fired cartridge cases and bullets forms the basis of firearm identification. The firearm tool marks are classified as class characteristics tool marks and individual characteristic tool marks. Class characteristic tool marks are exhibited by group or class of firearms while individual characteristic tool marks are unique to an individual firearm and used to exclude all other firearms of similar class. On the basis of class characteristic marks the number of potential firearm sources can be limited and when sufficient agreement in individual characteristics marks is found, firearm identification can be established. The shape, size, position of the various marks such as firing pin, breech face, extractor, ejector and chamber marks imprinted on fired cartridge case are the class characteristic of firearm toolmarks whereas the microscopic finer details of these impressions are the individual characteristics of any particular firearm. Similarly, in fired bullets the direction, number, width, depth and pitch of the rifling marks (grooves and lands) specify the class characteristics tool marks whereas microscopic finer details of the grooves and lands signify individual characteristics of any particular firearm.

The comparison microscope is the scientific instrument used by the firearm examiner in the comparison of tool marks for the firearm identification. This

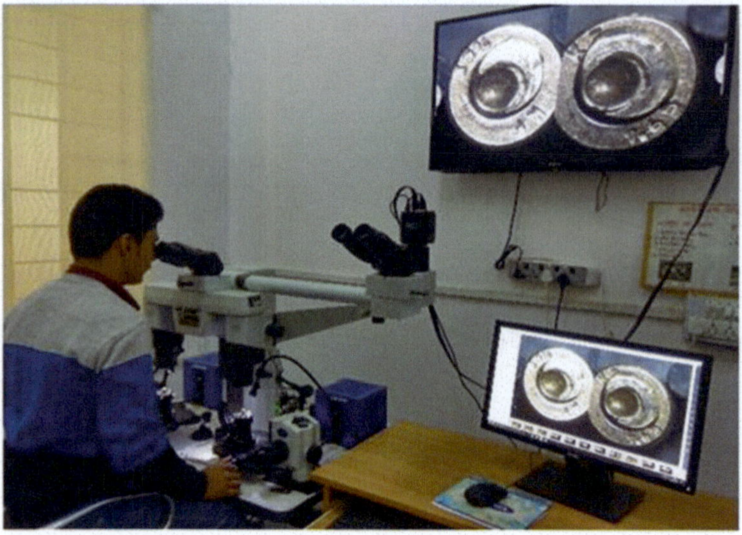

Fig. 15.16 Comparison microscope setup showing comparative matching of firing pin and breech face marks of two cartridge cases in a split view window

instrument firearm examiner compares and analyzes various tool marks imprinted on two objects of interest such as two cartridge cases or two bullets. The objects placed side by side on the given object holders and the magnified image of which can be viewed simultaneously in a split view window. The magnification can be adjusted as per the requirement (Fig. 15.16).

The underlying principle in comparison is that like must be compared to like. The cartridge case recovered from the scene of crime or from the accused/suspects is known as evidence cartridge case and the fired bullet recovered from the scene of crime or from the body of the disease/victim is called evidence bullet. Now to establish the firearm identity i.e. to answer whether the recovered cartridge case and bullet are fired from the same firearm which is recovered from the accused/ suspect, the live cartridge of the same make and caliber as that of the evidence cartridge case is fired from the questioned/suspected firearm. In this way test fired cartridge case and test fired bullet are recovered. The evidence cartridge case and evidence bullet were compared in comparison microscope with the test-fired cartridge case and test-fired bullet respectively for the various firearm tool marks.

In order to analyze firearm/tool marks evidence, an examiner must have wide experience and knowledge about the various class characteristics, individual characteristics of firearm tool marks and about manufacturing procedure of firearms. The positive matching establishes the linkage between the cartridge case/bullet and firearm while the negative matching excludes the questioned/suspected firearm (Figs. 15.17 and 15.18).

It is to be noted that (1) Sometimes, the recovered evidence bullets are almost completely deformed (2) sometimes, bullet carries very few striations, particularly in

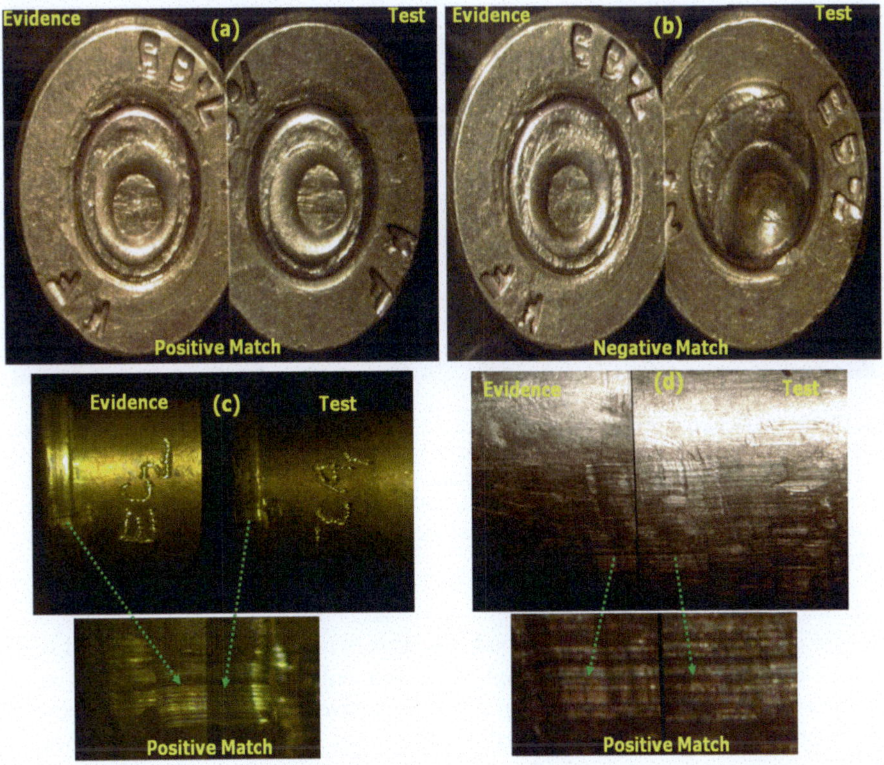

Fig. 15.17 Comparison photomicrograph showing (**a**) Positive match for firing pin and breech face marks (**b**) Negative match for firing pin and breech marks as the class itself (viz. shape, size, position of firing pin marks and breech face pattern) of the two fired cases is different (**c**) Positive match for extractor marks and (**d**) Positive match for chamber marks

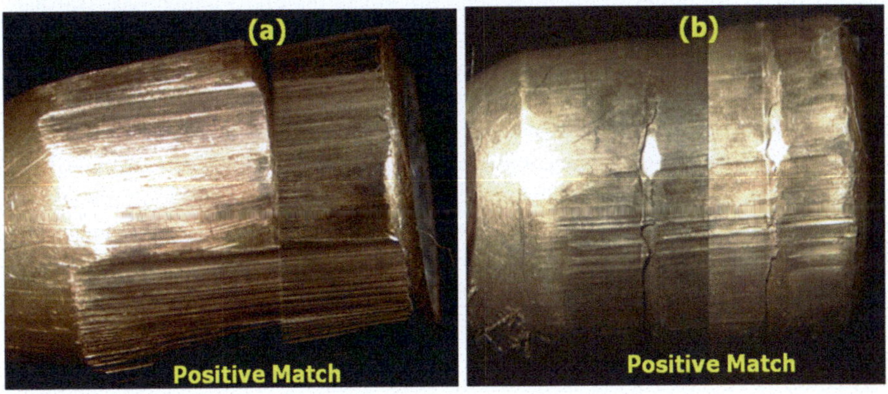

Fig. 15.18 Comparison photomicrographs showing positive match of (**a**) two fired bullets of 9 mm caliber for rifling marks (**b**) two fired bullets of 7.65 mm caliber for barrel striation marks

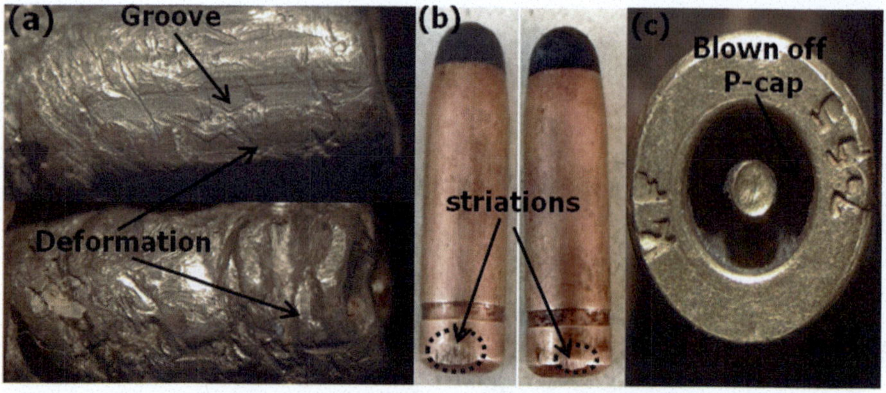

Fig. 15.19 (**a**) Deformed evidence lead bullet of 0.32″ caliber recovered from the body of decease. Only a single groove is identifiable the striations of which are also wiped out by extraneous marks (**b**) Fired bullet of 0.315″/8 mm caliber from a loose bore country-made firearm having only a few barrel striations at its base, insufficient to provide any conclusive opinion based on its matching (**c**) A cartridge case of 7.65 mm caliber with blown off percussion-cap and no firing pin and breech face impressions available to match

the case of the country made/homemade firearms, when the bore of the barrel is so loose that the bullet traveling through it contact only a very small area. In such situations, it becomes difficult to provide a conclusive opinion regarding whether a particular bullet fired from questioned firearm or not. A similar situation comes up when a percussion-cap of the fired cartridge case is blown off/absent/punctured and other tool marks impressions such as that of chamber, ejector and extractor are also not sufficient to furnish any definite opinion. In such situations, even after the thorough microscopic examinations of various marks if the firearm examiner/expert is not convinced about the conclusive matching then the opinion resulted as indefinite which does not means the negative match. Although, the examiner is not able to link the fired case/bullet to the individual firearm in the above situations, still he/s can give some important information such as whether a particular cartridge case or bullet is fired from a regular standard firearm or country-made firearm. For example, if the percussion-cap of the cartridge case is blown off/absence and no other impressions are sufficient to provide a definite opinion then on the basis of its blown off percussion-cap and irregular bulging expert can opine that it is fired from a loose chambered/country made firearm. Similarly, based on the barrel striations on the bullet/absence of regular rifling on the bullet, it can be opined that this bullet is fired from smooth bore non-standard firearm (Fig. 15.19).

In the case of the pellets/shots, in practical, it is very difficult to furnish any opinion on whether the particular shot was fired from the barrel of a particular firearm. There are a number of shots in a shotgun shell and few of the outer shots only come into contact of the surface of the bore. Since the contact area of shots with the bore is very small and it is not necessary that the test shots also touch exactly the same surface as the evidence shots contacted. However, attempts are made by passing a single lead ball of diameter a bit larger than the bore diameter of the barrel. The striations of the bore appear on its surface which can be compared with the striations on the surface of the shots. But it also does not work much in practical. However, in case of larger size shots such as LG size shots or a single spherical ball/slug in which the contact area with bore surface is comparatively more the chances of transfer of bore irregularities/striations are more. If these irregularities on evidence pellet/ball and test pellets/ball are found peculiar and convincing in microscopic comparison then the linkage of evidence shots/ball with the questioned firearm can be established.

15.6.3.1 Automated Firearms Identification

In forensic ballistics, one of the most important evidence is to link a particular crime to a firearm with the help of microscopic matching of the recovered cartridge casings and bullets. By utilizing computerized imaging technology the characteristics firearm toolmarks over the surface of cartridge casings and bullet can be stored. In order to match a particular cartridge casing and bullet recovered in a crime case this stored image database can be very useful to select potential candidates until they find a positive match. If multiple crimes were committed with the same firearm the imaging of recovered bullet or cartridge casing stored in database files can be correlated. Hence, even in the absence of the recovery of firearm involved in the commission of crime it can be concluded that the same firearm is involved in multiple crimes and in future if one case is traced another will also be solved. This computerized imaging technology is useful in order to link multiple crimes to a single firearm or to use tool marks information of the firearms of prior investigations that have been used in the commission of crime but not recovered.

Automated Firearms Identification systems utilize database to automate the process of matching. These systems are specialized computer hardware/software combinations which basically capture and store the toolmarks data that can be later used when required to compare with the characteristic images of fired bullets and cartridge casings recovered in any crime investigation.

In 1993, the Federal Bureau of Investigation (FBI) and the Bureau of Alcohol, Tobacco and Firearms (ATF) developed separately their own automated ballistics identification system namely Drugfire, and Integrated Ballistics Identification System (IBIS) respectively.

Initially, Drugfire facilitated image capturing and storage in the database and enable law enforcement community to compare the stored images of cartridge casings with suspect cartridge when required. This identification system was later upgraded to store the bullet imaging as well in the database and perform an automated comparison to suggest the potential candidate matching from the existing images. IBIS, on the other hand, at first imaged only bullet and was later upgraded to image cartridge casings as well, and was then subsequently renamed as the Integrated Ballistics Identification System (IBIS). In 1999, FBI and ATF jointly incorporate both DRUGFIRE and IBIS technologies into new unified single program called National Integrated Ballistics Information Network (NIBIN) which is standardize on the IBIS platform.

There also exist other ballistic identification systems. The IBIS is the very popular automated ballistics identification system worldwide. It is important to note that the IBIS system can assists in the searching and identifying potential candidate matches but it does not conclude whether or not a particular bullet or casing fired from the same weapon. The firearm identifications must be done by firearm examiner by visually comparing the characteristic marks of the bullet or casings retrieved from the crime scene with the potential candidates screened by the system from the database. In the present scenario, various law enforcement agencies producing firearm toolmarks database of fired bullets and cartridge casings and sharing the information in crime fighting.[2]

15.7 Various Close Range Phenomenon and Range of Fire Estimation

The distance of the target from the muzzle end of the firearm is called range of fire. To estimate range of fire is one of the important aspects in forensic ballistics. In shooting incident it plays crucial role in investigations particularly, to differentiate suicidal and homicidal nature of the case. For example if in any case investigation it is proved that the distance of fire is more than the length of arm of the deceased, then usually, it suggests that the possibility of suicidal and struggle is very less and understanding of this helps the investigator to investigate into the right direction. Sometimes, the accused try to fabricate the case by the wrong narrative viz during the self-defense the firearm discharged in the struggle over a firearm without intending to fire. In such situation if the distance of fire is determined to be a distant range then it negates the narrative of the accused and helps to find out the truth. At times, it happens that the homicide cases are simulated as suicidal and accidental. Usually, in the suicidal cases of gunshot the range of fire tended to be contact or near contact.

In the process of firing, the gun powder burn and produce huge amount of gas pressure which forced the projectile to eject out from the barrel of the firearm. Theoretically, all the gun powder in the cartridge should be burn out within the barrel but in actual it does not happen. When a firearm is discharged, along with the bullet/projectile the hot gases, smoke (soot), partially burnt or unburnt propellant particles, primer discharge residue some other residues are also ejected out. The low weight and poor ballistics coefficient of these various residues limit their travel up to a short distance in the air and different types of residues travel different distances from the muzzle end. Based on the presence or absence of the various phenomena in the target around the gunshot hole due to these residues, the distance of fire can be estimated.

Burning and Scorching When a firearm is discharged, the hot gases which mainly consist of carbon monoxide and hydrogen also emerge with the projectile from the

[2]For more information: https://afte.org/about-us/what-is-afte/what-is-firearm-and-tool-mark-identification.

muzzle end of the firearm. As these gases come into contact with environmental oxygen they generate a flame. This flame extends only up to a few inches from the muzzle of the firearm and causes a burning, scorching or singing effect at the target around the gunshot hole. Usually, the burning effect is not visible on the skin, however; in hair, woolen clothes, silk material etc this effect become clear and visible. The burning effect also appears as globule (bead formation) at the margins of some fibers due to melting effect. For long guns the flame effect can extend up to 6″ and for handguns it can be seen only up to 2–3″ distance from the muzzle end of the firearm around the gunshot hole. Hence, if in any target burning or singing due to flame is present then the range of fire may not have been more than few inches. The burning effect of flame is also known as charring. Unlike the blackening, it cannot be removed easily.

Blackening or Smudging It results from a deposit of smoke moving behind the projectile. Smoke is mostly a group of carbon particles deposited as a blackish area around the gunshot hole in clothes, skin or in any other target. The blackening effect is more prominent in black gun powder as compared to modern smokeless powders. In modern ammunitions, for long guns blackening effect usually can extend up to 12″ and for handguns it can be seen only up to 6–8″ distance from the muzzle end of the firearm around the gunshot hole. The intensity of the blackening will depend upon the range of fire, type of firearm and quantity of propellant/gunpowder used. It is to be noted that blackening can be wiped off with water, rubbing with some material or even due to hemorrhage.

Tattooing or Stippling or Peppering It results due to partially-burnt or unburnt gunpowder particles around the gunshot hole. If the target is skin then tattooing can clearly be seen as number of small discrete spots around the gunshot hole. Unlike, blackening it cannot be wiped off. This effect is more with black powder than with modern smokeless propellants due to more unburnt/partially burnt particles. Like blackening the density of the tattooing marks also depends upon the range of fire, type of firearm and propellant/gunpowder used. The distribution pattern of these gun powder marks around gunshot hole depends upon the angle of the firearm with the hole at which the fire is shot. For long guns tattooing/gunpowder marks can be seen up to 4 ft and for handguns this effect can be seen usually up to the distance of about 2–3 ft from the muzzle end of the firearm around the gunshot hole. Sometimes, when the garments are dark-colored or heavily blood-stained, the powder marks around the gunshot hole may not be visible, particularly in the case when very fine size of the gunpowder/propellant is used. In such situation, “Walker test” is performed to detect the presence of tattooing/gunpowder present around the gunshot hole (Fig. 15.20).

Bullet Wipe It is the dark area/ring around the margins of a gunshot hole. The bullet lubricant (generally grease is used in the bullet cannelure for proper grip of the case mouth on the bullet), barrel lubricant, dirt in the bore of the firearm (which get deposited on the fired bullet), lead (of bullet or primer) and other discharge residues deposited on the bullet surface when it passes through the barrel. When bullet is rubbed with the target (such as garment or skin) this black material is transferred and

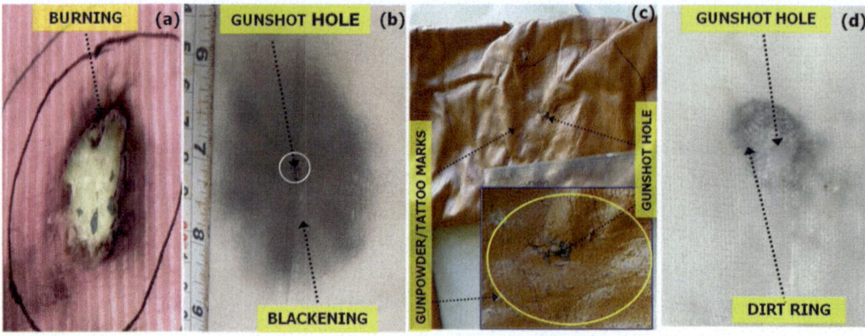

Fig. 15.20 Appearance of (**a**) Burning effect (**b**) Blackening (**c**) Powder marks/tattooing and (**d**) Dirt ring in a target after firing

deposited on the periphery of the bullet entry hole usually in the form of a ring. Bullet wipe can be seen around the gunshot entry hole at any range of fire and when there are no discharge residues like blackening or tattooing around the margins of the gunshot hole, bullet wipe/dirt ring is useful to identify the gunshot entry hole.

Abrasion Collar When spinning bullet penetrates the skin, the immediate surroundings/edges of the gunshot wound are abraded in the form of collar known as an abrasion collar. The shape and width of the abrasion collar depend upon the angle of fire. Initially, it appears reddish and when dries it becomes brownish-black in appearance. Usually, in rifled firearm which propel spinning bullet with high velocity, the appearance of abrasion collar is very common. When bullet hits the skin perpendicularly the shape of abrasion collar is appear generally in circular and regular shape while when it strike the skin at oblique angle its shape become non-circular and irregular. The distribution of abrasion collar around the margins of the gunshot wound provides the direction of fire but it cannot provide information about the range of fire.

It is important to note that all the phenomena discussed above appears around gunshot entry hole only and not in the exit hole. If the first target is garment then burning, blackening or tattooing may be absent around the gunshot wound in the skin. In such situations, careful examination of clothing as a first target is important.

Range of fire is generally classified as contact range, near contact range, intermediate range and distant range.

Hard/pressed contact range In this range, the firearm is pressed firmly against the skin surface. This prevents the escape of the various gases and smoke generated during the discharge of the firearm and the gunshot residue enters into the wound. Hence the various effects due to firearm discharge may be absent around the entry wound in hard/pressed contact wound. In such gunshot wounds if there is any rigid tissue such as bone then the combustion gases which entered into the wound collides with the rigid tissue, forced back and resulted in tearing of the gunshot hole/wound in a typical stellate/star shape pattern. In hard/pressed contact gunshot if the skin is forced against the muzzle due to the backward expanding gases the wounds often show muzzle impression of the firearm around the hole. This star shape pattern often appears in the garment also that covers the wound.

Near contact range In this range, there is a gap between the muzzle of the firearm and the body/target and therefore the gunshot residues appear around the gunshot hole. Usually, in these types of gunshot hole/wound the burning/singeing due to flame effect and blackening are seen. However, powder tattooing/stippling around the wound is absent as there is not enough space between muzzle of firearm and target to allow the powder particles deposition.

Intermediate-range This is the range at which gunshot hole/wound does not possess burning/singeing effect due to flame but shows blackening effect due to smoke and powder tattooing effect due to unburnt/partially-burnt gunpowder particles.

Distant-range This is the range of fire at which the gunshot hole/wound does not have any burning, blackening or tattooing effect i.e. the range beyond the reach of flame, smoke and powder particles. Only the projectile from the muzzle of firearm reaches the target. Bullet wipe/dirt ring and abrasion collar can be present even at distant-range shots.

The range of firing can be estimated based on the presence or absence of the above-discussed phenomena viz. burning/singeing, blackening and tattooing around the gunshot hole/wound. Beyond the range of tatooing effect, the range of fire is considered as distant range and distance of fire cannot be estimated accurately. However, in the case of shotguns, the distance of fire can also be estimated by the pellets/shots dispersion patterns on the target beyond the range of powder tattooing. The forensic aspects of gunshot entry hole/wound are shown in Fig. 15.21.

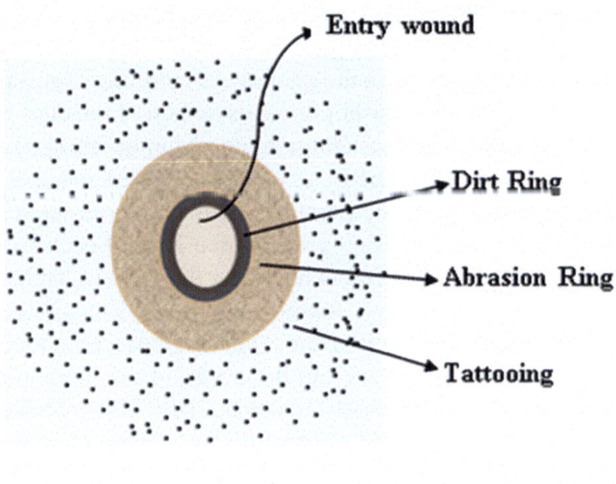

Fig. 15.21 Forensic aspects of a gunshot entry hole/wound

15.7.1 Dispersion of Pellets/Shots at the Target

When a shotgun cartridge loaded with pellets is discharged, the pellets spread after leaving the muzzle and spreading increases with increasing distance from the muzzle of the firearm. The distance of fire can be estimated by measuring the distribution of this spread of pellets/shots at the target. The pellets leaving the muzzle of the firearm entered into the target en-mass up to a distance of about 2 m. The size of the resulting gunshot hole is usually larger than the muzzle diameter of the shotgun. As the distance increases small holes due to few of the individual pellets surrounding the main hole become visible. This individualization of the pellets surrounding the main hole at about 2 m is such that the overall appearance of the main hole at the center looks like a rat hole. Further increasing the distance, usually, about 2–7 m this rat hole is then surrounded by individual holes of pellets. For larger distances usually more than 8 m the central main hole becomes absent and complete individual pattern of holes due to pellets appear at the target. Even though, there are some formulae in literature to calculate the range of fire based on pellet spread (Heard 2008; Sharma 2002); however, pellet dispersion patterns are variable and depend upon various parameters such as barrel length, diameter/choke of the barrel of the shotgun, type of ammunition and size of the fired pellets (Fig. 15.22).

Usually, It is observed that, up to the distance of 10 m, in full choke barrel the dispersion of the pellets at the target in inches is approximately equal to the distance of fire in meters whereas, for a true cylinder (no choke) barrel, the dispersion of the pellets at the target in inches is approximately double of the distance of fire in meters. The dispersion of pellets decreases with increasing choke of the barrel for a particular distance of fire. In practical, the accurate distance of fire can be estimated only by the test firing from the same firearm and similar ammunition at various ranges and then by comparing the effects at the test target to the evidence target.

15.8 Gunshot Residue Examination

To know whether a person has fired the firearm, the detection of Gunshot Residues (GSR) in his hands is of great importance. In the process of firing, the combustion products produced from the gunpowder, priming materials, vaporized particles of the projectile form the gunshot residues and these residues are expected to be deposited on the hands of the firer (Romolo and Margot 2001). By swabbing the hands of the suspect the deposited particles can be collected and analyzed for the presence of the GSR. Starting from the paraffin test to the more modern techniques like scanning electron microscope energy dispersive X-ray Spectroscopy (SEM-EDX), there are many methods employed in detecting the GSR in the hand of the suspect. There are basically two types of components in GSR namely: Organic components and inorganic/metallic components. The organic compounds are produced due to the burning of the propellant and the origin of the inorganic components is mainly the priming compound (Goudsmits et al. 2015; Brożek-Mucha 2017). Identifications of organic components of GSR mainly include the identification of nitrites and nitrates

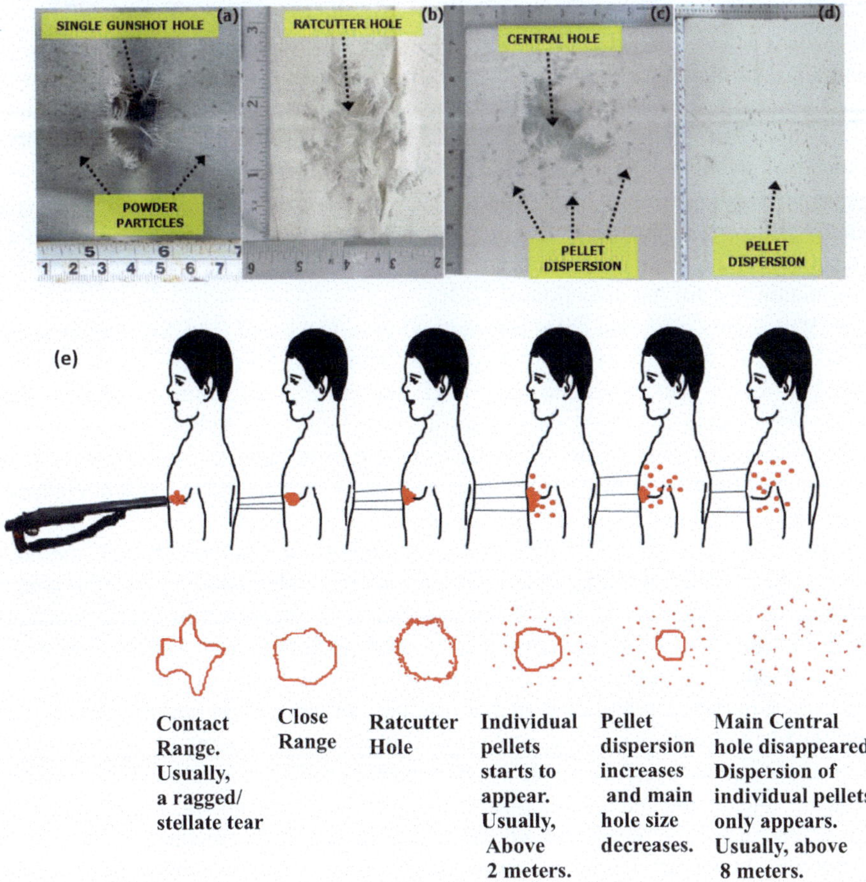

Fig. 15.22 (**a**) A single gunshot hole from a distance of (**a**) 1 m (**b**) Rat-cutter hole from a distance of 2 m and (**c**) The dispersion of pellets in a distant range fire of about 5 m (**d**) The dispersion of pellets in a distant range fire of about 9.5 m. A shotgun shell was loaded with B.B. size pellets and the shotgun barrel was half choked. (**e**) Appearance of shotgun hole/wound at different ranges of fire

using chemical spot tests whereas for the identification of inorganic components (viz. Pb, Ba, Sb) chemical tests and various instrumental methods were employed. The modern and most successful instrumental technique for GSR analysis is Scanning Electron Microscopy with Energy Dispersive X-ray spectrometry (SEM-EDX) (Maitre et al. 2017). Following are some of the methods used for GSR analysis.

In "**paraffin test**" of GSR analysis, the residues were removed from the hands using the paraffin cast technique. In general, the melted paraffin wax is applied on the hands of the suspect. The gunpowder residue particles are removed by the paraffin cast. In this method, the presence of nitrate residues produced from the propellant is detected. A color test in the removed cast is performed with a reagent either diphenylamine or diphenyl benzidine. A dark blue spot formation is an indication of the presence of nitrate residues. Another test for GSR is the "**Greiss test**" which detects the presence of nitrite ion in the hand swabs. In the hand swabs (generally, the swabbing is done by the cotton or Whatman filter paper 42 moistened with 5% nitric acid solution) upon treatment of Greiss reagent resulted in red pink color if the nitrite is present in the sample. These tests give the indication of the presence of nitrite as a GSR. However, the source of these residues cannot be determined in these tests which pose problem because there are many substances such as fertilizers, urine, cigarette, some cosmetics etc which can give false positive results for nitrate residues. Hence, these are just corroborative evidence, not the confirmation test for the detection of GSR.

In 1959, a new chemical color test method was developed for GSR detection by Harold Harrison and Robert Gilroy, known as "**Harrison-Gilroy test**". This method is used to detect primer residues e.g. lead, antimony and barium rather than the gunpowder residues as in the case of paraffin and Greiss test. Although, this test has comparatively less false positive results, yet, due to its inadequate sensitivity and other drawbacks such as non-determination of the source of the individual element this method is also not used widely.

In 1966, for the analysis of GSR, "**Neutron Activation Analysis (NAA)**" method was developed. The sampling is done by various methods including swabbing and washing. In this method sample is bombarded with the neutrons in the nuclear reactor and through the energy distribution analysis presence of barium and antimony element is determined. The analysis of GSR is based on the detection of greater an amount of population of barium and antimony than which is normally found in blank hands. This is a qualitative and quantitative method for elemental determination. However, the main disadvantage of this technique is that it cannot determine one of the main components of GSR i.e. lead and the requirement of nuclear reactor for the measurement also limits the use of this method.

"**Atomic Absorption Spectroscopy (AAS)**" and "**Flameless Atomic Absorption Spectroscopy (FAAS)**" are another instrumental techniques used for detecting the GSR elements lead, barium and antimony. In this method, the sampling is done by swabbing palm and back of the hands with cotton moistened with diluted hydrochloric acid. The basic principle is based on the absorption of the incident radiation at a specific wavelength. The absorbed light is proportional to the quantity of that particular element present in the sample. In FAAS heated graphite tube is used instead of a flame as in AAS which makes FAAS more sensitive. This method is comparatively more sensitive and accurate, however, it cannot rule out the possibility of the identified particles as environmental contamination.

"**Scanning Electron Microscopy with Energy Dispersive X-ray spectrometry (SEM-EDX)**" is the modern and most powerful instrumental tool for the GSR particle analysis. Sampling is done using adhesive lifts such as double-sided adhesive tape on a strip. The best way of sampling is in SEM stubs which are easily placed to the SEM stub holder in the SEM chamber for direct GSR examination. In this technique, both morphological and elemental characteristics of the individual GSR particles can be identified. In SEM, a beam of high energy electrons is focused into the sample. As a result, characteristic X-ray is produced that corresponds to a particular element. SEM has an extremely high resolution of ~1–2 nm and magnification up to ~1,000,000×. In SEM, GSR particles can be identified by their characteristic morphology. The size of GSR particle varies in the range of 0.1–5 μ and is mostly spheroidal and sometimes spherical in shape. The elemental composition of that individual particle can be determined through energy-dispersive X-ray analysis i.e. EDX. So, this technique even can analyze if the GSR elements Pb, Ba and Sb are present in the same particle. In the standard primer composition which contain lead styphnate, barium nitrate, and antimony sulfide other than the unique three-component particles combination the GSR particles can also be the combination of Pb/Ba, Pb/Sb and Ba/Sb. In this way "unique" GSR particles which originate only as a result of primer explosion can be identified by SEM-EDX method (Heard 2008; Gassner et al. 2016).

Since GSR particles are very small and hence trapped in the microscopic folds of the skin. It is to be noted that these GSR particles can easily be removed in various daily activities from the hands e.g. by washing the hands. The probability of removal of GSR from the hands of the deceased is very less until it is disturbed externally. With time the GSR particles may remove or redistribute. Hence, the sample for the GSR examination should take as soon as possible. Environmental conditions such as raining and sweating can also lead to negative result even in the hands of the firer. It also matters in which part of the hands the GSR results were found positive. If some person handled the recently fired firearm the GSR can be positive in the palm of his hands. If a suspect fired a firearm then GSR can be positive on the back of his firing and supporting hand. Similarly, the GSR particles can be found on the palm and back of the hands of a victim standing in front of the firer. Therefore, care must be taken while collecting the GSR samples and also while interpreting the results (Feeney et al. 2020). Recently, Harshey et al. (2020) reviewed the contribution of Metallic-Organic Frameworks (MOFs) for the detection of GSR originating from non-toxic ammunition.In addition, toward the development of handheld devices for onsite detection of GSR, Electrochemical sensors have been utilized for more than three decades. They have found an effective approach towards the presumptive detection of IGSR and OGSR components (O'Mahony and Wang 2013; Harshey et al. 2021).

15.9 Gunshot Entry Vs. Exit Wounds and Gunshot Homicidal Vs. Suicidal Cases

In shooting incident cases, it is very important to identify gunshot entry and exit holes/wounds. Many times, homicidal cases are staged as suicidal or accidental and suicidal or accidental cases as homicidal to falsely accuse others. Therefore, to know the truth or manner of death in the shooting cases, the basic features of gunshot entry wound, exit wound, and knowledge of distinctive features of gunshot homicidal and suicidal cases is very crucial. The various distinctive features are given in Tables 15.5 and 15.6:

Table 15.5 Distinctive features of gunshot entry and exit wounds

Characteristics	Entry wound	Exit wound
Edges	Usually inverted. Sometime deviation may appear in contact wounds	Everted
Size	Usually smaller except the close range shot	Usually bigger than corresponding entry
Dirt ring/Bullet wipe	May present	Not present
Abrasion collar	Present	Not present except in shored exit wound
Burning, Blackening, tattooing	Presence depends upon the range of fire	Not present
Muzzle imprint	May be present in pressed contact fire	Not present
Garment fiber	The garments may be turned towards inside and thread of garments may driven into the wound.	The garments may be turned towards outside
Presence of Carbon monoxide	Due to the presence of the carbon monoxide the track of the entry wound may appear as bright pink	No carbon monoxide present

Table 15.6 Distinctive features of gunshot homicidal and suicidal cases

Characteristics	Homicide	Suicide
Presence and position of the firearm	One or more firearms may be used. Firearm usually not found at crime scene.	One firearm is used and found at crime scene usually near or on the body. Many times, handguns remain in the hand of the decease particularly if the person was lying or sitting.
Site of gunshot entry	Any part of the body	Usually head, submental space, chest or abdomen. It is rare in suicide the entry wound found back side of the body.
Number of fire	Can be one or many	Typically one.
Gunshot residues and location	Generally not found in the hands of the decease. However, in close range shot GSR may be found but the location of particles can be anywhere.	GSR particles usually found on the back of the hands and supporting hand.
Direction of fire	Can be upward, downward, forward or backward	Usually upward
Eyewitness	Usually present	Usually there is no eyewitness present.
Range of fire	Can be any range	Usually contact or near contact range

15.10 Conclusion

In this chapter, a brief overview of forensic ballistics has been outlined. Various types of firearms, ammunitions, their parts and action mechanism are discussed. Forensic ballistics basically relies on the comparison of various tool marks imprinted on the cartridge casing and bullets while a cartridge is discharged. Tool marks examination leads to possible inclusion or exclusion of questioned firearms in a particular crime and it carries a great evidential value to serve the criminal justice system. So, various marks that a fired cartridge case and fired bullet carries are discussed along with comparative matching of those marks for the firearm identification. Various close-range phenomena in shooting incidents and range of fire estimation are explained. Moreover, different methods or techniques used for gun-shot shot residue examination are discussed. We also talked about automated firearm identification systems popularly known as IBIS. Distinctive features of gunshot entry and exit wounds/holes along with the characteristics of suicidal and homicidal cases are also tabulated which are very useful to decide the nature/manner of death in cases of shooting incidents.

References

Abhyankar S, Srivastava A, Yadav VK, Nigam K, Harshey A (2018) Glass fractures made from different pellet shapes - a preliminary study. J Forens Sci Crim Investig 8(3):1

Alim M, Negi KS, Abhyankar S, Tiwari N, Harshey A, Srivastava A (2020) Towards the investigation of the shooting incidents: evaluation of the fracture pattern on the polymethylmethacrylate sheet made by .22″ and .177″ caliber air rifle. Heliyon 6(5):e04088

Arslan MM, Kar H, Üner B, Çetin G (2011) Firing distance estimates with pellet dispersion from shotgun with various chokes: an experimental, comparative study. J Forensic Sci 56(4):988–992

Brożek-Mucha Z (2017) Trends in analysis of gunshot residue for forensic purposes. Anal Bioanal Chem 409(25):5803–5811

Burrard G (1960) The modern shotgun, vol I. Herbert Jenkins, London

Chapman J, Milroy CM (1992) Firearm deaths in Yorkshire and Humberside. Forensic Sci Int 57: 181–191

Cherry D, Runyon C, Butts J (2001) A population based study of unintentional firearm fatalities. Injury Prev 7:62–65

Di Maio VJM (1998) Gunshot wounds: practical aspects of firearms, ballistics, and forensic techniques. CRC Press, New York, NY

Ersoy G, Gurler AS, Ozbay M (2012) Upon a failure to equal entry and exit wounds: a possible case of tandem bullets in view of the literature. J Forensic Sci 57(4):1129–1133

Feeney W, Pyl CV, Bell S, Trejos T (2020) Trends in composition, collection, persistence, and analysis of IGSR and OGSR: a review. Forens Chem 19:100250

Gabor T (2016) Confronting gun violence in America. Springer, Cham

Gassner AL, Ribeiro C, Kobylinska J, Zeichner A, Weyermann C (2016) Organic gunshot residues: observations about sampling and transfer mechanisms. Forensic Sci Int 266:369–378

Goudsmits E, Sharples GP, Birkett JW (2015) Recent trends in organic gunshot residue analysis. Trends Anal Chem 74:46–57

Gunther JK, Gunther CO (2015) The identification of firearms from ammunition fired therein with an analysis of legal authorities. Skyhorse Publishing, New York, NY

Haag LC (1991) To create a hangfire. AFTE J 23(2):660–667

Haag MG, Haag LC (2011) Shooting incident reconstruction, 2nd edn. Academic Press, Elsevier Inc, London

Harshey A, Srivastava A, Yadav VK, Nigam K, Kumar A, Das T (2017) Analysis of glass fracture pattern made by 4.5 mm (.177″) caliber air rifle. Egypt J Forensic Sci 7:20

Harshey A, Das T, Srivastava A (2020) Analytical contributions of lanthanide based metal-organic frame works as luminescent markers: recent trends in gunshot residue analysis. Microchem J 154:104597

Harshey A, Srivastava A, Das T, Nigam K, Shrivastava R, Yadav VK (2021) Trends in gunshot residue detection by electrochemical methods for forensic purpose. J Anal Test 5:258–269

Hatcher JS, Jury FJ, Weller J (1957) Firearms investigation, identification and evidence. The Stackpole Co, Harrisburg, PA

Heard BJ (2008) Handbook of firearms and ballistics: examining and interpreting forensic evidence, 2nd edn. John Wiley & Sons, New York, NY

Jentzen JM, Lutz M, Templin R (1995) Tandem bullet versus multiple gunshot wounds. J Forensic Sci 40(5):893–895

Koffler BB (1969) Zip guns and crude conversions–identifying characteristics and problems. J Crim Law Criminol 60(4):520–531

Maiden N (2009) Historical overview of wound ballistics research. Forens Sci Med Pathol 5:85–89

Maitre M, Kirkbride KP, Horder M, Roux C, Beavis A (2017) Current perspectives in the interpretation of gunshot residues in forensic science: a review. Forensic Sci Int 270:1–11

Mattoo BN, Nabar BS (1969) Evaluation of effective shot dispersion in buckshot patterns. J Forensic Sci 14:263–269

Nag NK, Sinha P (1992) An investigation into pellet dispersion ballistics. Forensic Sci Int 55(2): 105–130

O'Mahony AM, Wang J (2013) Electrochemical detection of gunshot residue for forensic analysis: a review. Electroanalysis 25(6):1341

Ordog GJ, Dornhoffer P, Ackroyd G, Wasserberger J, Bishop M, Shoemaker W, Balasubramanium S (1994) Spent bullets and their injuries: the result of firing weapons into the sky. J Trauma 37(6):1003–1006

Romolo FS, Margot P (2001) Identification of gunshot residue: a critical review. Forensic Sci Int 119(2):195–211

Sharma BR (2002) Firearms in criminal investigation and trials. Universal Law Publishing Co. Pvt. Ltd, New Delhi

Singh BP, Singh RP (2005) Shotgun shooting in northern India-a review (1980–1990). Forensic Sci Int 150:103–111

Sinha JK (2015) Forensic investigation of unusual firearms ballistic and medico-legal evidence. CRC Press, New York, NY

Thejaswi HT, Kumar A, Jegadheeshwaraj (2013) Desi-Kutta (country made Firearm) and wound ballistics. A review. J Indian Acad Forens Med 35:165–169

Thompson RM (2010) Firearm identification in the forensic science laboratory. Gun violence prosecution program. The National District Attorney Association, Arlington, VA

Tiwari N, Harshey A, Das T, Abhyankar S, Yadav VK, Nigam K, Srivastava A (2019) Evidential significance of multiple fracture patterns on the glass in forensic ballistics. Egypt J Forensic Sci 9(1):1–5

du Toit-Prinsloo L, Morris NK, Saayman G (2014) Tandem bullet injury: an unusual variant of an unusual injury. Forens Sci Med Pathol 10(2):262–265

Tom W (2004) Firearms, the law, and forensic ballistics, 2nd edn. CRC Press, New York, NY

Waghmare NP, Suresh R, Puri P, Varshney KC, Anand V et al (2012) Modern trend of country made/improvized pistols used in the capital of India. J Forens Res S1:1–7

Wallace JS (2018) Chemical analysis of firearms, ammunition, and gunshot residue. CRC Press, Boca Raton, FL

Yong YE (2017) A systematic review on ricochet gunshot injuries. Legal Med 26:45–51

Road Accident Investigation

16

Md. Alim, Tanurup Das, Vijay Kumar Yadav, Kapil Dev,
Ankit Srivastava, and Kriti Nigam

Abstract

As the world witnessed, the motor vehicle, a mode of transport, is one of the most significant inventions for humans. At the same time, rapid urbanization, steady increase in the number of vehicles, speeding, and negligence on the road increase accident risk. According to the "Global Status Report on Road Safety" published by the World Health Organization (WHO), road/vehicle accident is the eighth leading cause of death for people, that is approximately 1.35 million every year in the world. Accident cases are rapidly increasing. This chapter explains the key elements of the systematic and scientific methods for road accident investigation. Determination of vehicle direction, the velocity at pre-crash, during a crash, post-crash, and change in the velocity are the primary queries for the investigating officer to the way of accident reconstruction. Despite significant usage of conventional scientific methods such as theory, empirical formula, and performing a crash test, there are few limitations for reconstructing the accident scene. The

M. Alim
Department of Forensic Science, Bareilly International University, Bareilly, Uttar Pradesh, India

T. Das · A. Srivastava
School of Forensic Sciences, The West Bengal National University of Juridical Sciences, Kolkata, West Bengal, India

V. K. Yadav
Dr. APJ Abdul Kalam Institute of Forensic Science & Criminology, Bundelkhand University, Jhansi, Uttar Pradesh, India

K. Dev
Biology, Serology and DNA Division, Forensic Science Laboratory, Moradabad, Uttar Pradesh, India

K. Nigam (✉)
Department of Forensic Science, Jharkhand Raksha Shakti University, Ranchi, Jharkhand, India

P. Shrivastava et al. (eds.), *Textbook of Forensic Science*,
https://doi.org/10.1007/978-981-99-1377-0_16

results based on conventional methods require knowledge and expertise; therefore, small errors may cause damage in all the perspectives for reconstruction. However, advancements in reconstruction techniques, i.e., accident database, computer simulation software, and event data recorder (EDR), provide great accuracy and significant results.

Keywords

Accident · Forensic investigation · Road accident · Air crashes · Accident investigation

16.1 Introduction

The word accident is typically derived from the Latin verb *accidere,* which means the unfortunate occurrence, happening, falls upon, or by reasonable chance. "Accident" can be defined as a tragic event or action that may not return the result as originally intended but routinely experiences an unfavorable impact on the overall affair (Vincoli 1994). "Road accident" is a term that describes the accident with people and property by the involvement of at least one vehicle on the road. Meanwhile, road accidents, traffic accidents, vehicle accidents, and vehicle collisions are used as synonyms in this chapter.

Contrary to the commonly encountered misshape as arson, beating, stabbing, murder, theft, etc., motorized vehicle accidents or road accidents are proportionately new that are subject to forensic investigation. Vehicular accidents veered to new mayhem instruments as the motorized vehicle was introduced to humans.

Firstly, the concept of an automobile, based on the steam engine, began in Europe. In 1769 Nicolas Cugnot, inventor of the first vehicle, tested the first tractor energized by a steam engine. Cugnot was the first person reported to get into a motor vehicle accident (Nyamwange and Nyamwange 2014). At almost the closing of the nineteenth century, the first gasoline-based motor vehicles were introduced. In 1891, the first automobile accident undoubtedly occurred in American history was in Ohio City. James William Lambert, a successful American automobile inventor, was the first reasonable person undoubtedly involved in the gasoline-powered, single-cylinder automobile accident (Fig. 16.1). His vehicle received careens out of control after hitting the tree root and then smashed into a hitching post (Bailey 1960). During the first and mid-twentieth century, except the years during World War II, motor vehicle industries went through rapid growth and made vehicles globally. The commercialization of vehicles adapted by people is same as other technologies that compress time and distance and promote personal independence (James and Nordby 2009).

There were no vehicular mishaps before the innovation of self-propelled vehicles. From the early year of the invention of motor vehicles, death in vehicular accidents and property loss is relatively low. For example, in Great Britain during the year 1896, two people were killed in a vehicle accident, while in 1899 in the USA, it was only a case registered. Nevertheless, during the mid of the twentieth century, the production of vehicles increases promptly that equally elevates people's death and

Fig. 16.1 John W. Lambert (Bailey 1960)

injury due to vehicle accidents. For instance, by the end of 1965, only in the USA, 49,000 and 3,500,000 people were killed and injured in vehicle accidents. In the very next year, in 1966, more than 12,000 and 14,000 people in France and the Federal Republic of Germany lost their lives in vehicle accidents (Nogayeva et al. 2020). However, the statistics of death and injuries in a vehicle accident are sobering and recorded by different national and international organizations worldwide.

Organizations like National Crime Record Bureau (NCRB, India), National Highway Traffic Safety Administration (NHTSA, USA), and World Health Organization (WHO) produce data on road accidents and losses every year. For example, WHO statistics say vehicles collision is responsible for the leading cause of death of 1.35 million lives every year, which is the eighth leading cause of death globally in 2016. The severity of vehicle accident injury that leads to death in the world can be seen in Table 16.1.

It is evident from the day the self-propelled vehicle was invented that it had sufficient mass and velocity to cause severe injury and property loss. Apparently, in the earlier history of motorized vehicles, forensic investigation of the vehicular accident was not intricate. However, the development and commercialization of vehicles propel the frequency of vehicle accidents. The frequent collisions of cars, trucks, bicycles, and motorcycles make vehicle accident is most prone and indulges nearly 20–50 million people in getting injured globally make to be forensically examined. The significant factors for road accidents are improper driving, excessive speed, intoxication (alcohol and drugs), right of way, failure of vehicular yield, evident failure to stop at the signal, disregard of signals, bad road conditions, improper turn and maneuver, improper passing, inexperienced driver, too close following, distracted driving, overloading of vehicles, and poor vision (e.g., Dazzling sun) (Rolison 2020; Mahata et al. 2019; Naurois et al. 2017).

Table 16.1 WHO's estimates of death related to vehicle accident (per 1M population) in 2013 and 2016

Country	2013	2016	Country	2013	2016	Country	2013	2016	Country	2013	2016
Afghanistan	15.5	15.1	Denmark	3.5	4	Lesotho	28.2	28.9	Saint Vincent and the Grenadines	8.2	
Albania	15.1	13.6	Djibouti	24.7		Liberia	33.7	35.9	Samoa	15.8	11.3
Algeria	23.8		Dominica	15.3	10.9	Libya	23.8	26.1	San Marino	3.2	0
Andorra	7.6		Dominican Republic	29.3	34.6	Lithuania	10.6	8	Sao Tome and Principe	31.1	27.5
Angola	26.9	23.6	Ecuador	20.1	21.3	Luxembourg	8.7	6.3	Saudi Arabia	27.4	28.8
Antigua and Barbuda	6.7	7.9	Egypt	12.8	9.7	Madagascar	28.4	28.6	Senegal	27.2	23.4
Argentina	13.6	14	El Salvador	21.1	22.2	Malawi	35	31	Serbia	7.7	7.4
Armenia	18.3	17.1	Equatorial Guinea	22.9	24.6	Malaysia	24	23.6	Seychelles	8.6	15.9
Australia	5.4	5.6	Eritrea	24.1	25.3	Maldives	3.5	0.9	Sierra Leone	27.3	
Austria	5.4	5.2	Estonia	7	6.1	Mali	25.6	23.1	Singapore	3.6	2.8
Azerbaijan	10	8.7	Eswatini	24.2	26.9	Malta	5.1	6.1	Slovakia	6.6	6.1
Bahamas	13.8		Ethiopia	25.3	26.7	Marshall Islands	5.7		Slovenia	6.4	6.4
Bahrain	8		Fiji	5.8	9.6	Mauritania	24.5	24.7	Solomon Islands	19.2	17.4
Bangladesh	13.6	15.3	Finland	4.8	4.7	Mauritius	12.2	13.7	Somalia	25.4	27.1
Barbados	6.7	5.6	France	5.1	5.5	Mexico	12.3	13.1	South Africa	25.1	25.9
Belarus	13.7	8.9	Gabon	22.9	23.2	Micronesia	1.9	1.9	South Sudan	27.9	29.9
Belgium	6.7	5.8	Gambia	29.4	29.7	Monaco	0		Spain	3.7	4.1
Belize	24.4	28.3	Georgia	11.8	15.3	Mongolia	21	16.5	Sri Lanka	17.4	14.9
Benin	27.7	27.5	Germany	4.3	4.1	Montenegro	11.9	10.7	Sudan	24.3	25.7
Bhutan	15.1	17.4	Ghana	26.2	24.9	Morocco	20.8	19.6	Suriname	19.1	14.5
Bolivia	23.2	15.5	Greece	9.1	9.2	Mozambique	31.6	30.1	Sweden	2.8	2.8
Bosnia and Herzegovina	17.7	15.7	Grenada	5.7	9.3	Myanmar	20.3	19.9	Switzerland	3.3	2.7

Botswana	23.6	23.8	Guatemala	19	16.6	Namibia	23.9	30.4	Syrian Arab Republic	20	26.5
Brazil	23.4	19.7	Guinea	27.3	28.2	Nepal	17	15.9	Tajikistan	18.8	18.1
Brunei Darussalam	8		Guinea-Bissau	27.5	31.1	Netherlands	3.4	3.8	Thailand	36.2	32.7
Bulgaria	8.3	10.2	Guyana	17.3	24.6	New Zealand	6	7.8	Timor-Leste	16.6	12.7
Burkina Faso	30	30.5	Haiti	15.1		Nicaragua	15.3		Togo	31.1	29.2
Burundi	31.3	34.7	Honduras	17.4	16.7	Niger	26.4	26.2	Tonga	7.6	16.8
Cabo Verde	26.1	25	Hungary	7.7	7.8	Nigeria	20.5	21.4	Trinidad and Tobago	14.1	12.1
Cambodia	17.4	17.8	Iceland	4.6	6.6	Norway	3.8	2.7	Tunisia	24.4	22.8
Cameroon	27.6	30.1	India	16.6	22.6	Oman	25.4	16.1	Turkey	8.9	12.3
Canada	6	5.8	Indonesia	15.3	12.2	Pakistan	14.2	14.3	Turkmenistan	17.4	14.5
Central African Republic	32.4	33.6	Iran	32.1	20.5	Palau	4.8		Uganda	27.4	29
Chad	24.1	27.6	Iraq	20.2	20.7	Panama	10	14.3	Ukraine	10.6	13.7
Chile	12.4	12.5	Ireland	4.1	4.1	Papua New Guinea	16.8	14.2	UAE	10.9	18.1
China	18.8	18.2	Israel	3.6	4.2	Paraguay	20.7	22.7	UK and Northern Ireland	2.9	3.1
Colombia	16.8	18.5	Italy	6.1	5.6	Peru	13.9	13.5	Tanzania	32.9	29.2
Comoros	28	26.5	Jamaica	11.5	13.6	Philippines	10.5	12.3	USA	10.6	12.4
Congo	26.4	27.4	Japan	4.7	4.1	Poland	10.3	9.7	Uruguay	16.6	13.4
Cook Islands	24.2	17.3	Jordan	26.3	24.4	Portugal	7.8	7.4	Uzbekistan	11.2	11.5
Costa Rica	13.9	16.7	Kazakhstan	24.2	17.6	Qatar	15.2	9.3	Vanuatu	16.6	15.9
Côte d’Ivoire	24.2	23.6	Kenya	29.1	27.8	Korea	12	9.8	Venezuela	45.1	33.7
Croatia	9.2	8.1	Kiribati	2.9	4.4	Republic of Moldova	12.5	9.7	Viet Nam	24.5	26.4

(continued)

Table 16.1 (continued)

Country	2013	2016	Country	2013	2016	Country	2013	2016	Country	2013	2016
Cuba	7.5	8.5	Kuwait	18.7	17.6	Republic of North Macedonia	9.4	6.4	Yemen	21.5	
Cyprus	5.2	5.1	Kyrgyzstan	22	15.4	Romania	8.7	10.3	Zambia	24.7	
Czechia	6.1	5.9	Lao People's Democratic Republic	14.3	16.6	Russian Federation	18.9	18	Zimbabwe	28.2	34.7
Democratic People's Republic of Korea	20.8		Latvia	10	9.3	Rwanda	32.1	29.7			
Democratic Republic of the Congo	33.2	33.7	Lebanon	22.6	18.1	Saint Lucia	18.1	35.4			

An accident, realistically, is a complex phenomenon that is not supposed to happen. Whenever an accident occurs, the possible reason behind it must be accurately determined. Forensic investigations of accident cases may conveniently be arranged by the responsible government agencies or private insurance companies themselves. The valuable perspectives of an official investigation ostensibly based on the accident case should voluntarily be reported to the legitimate agencies. It may be for an insurance claim, hit and run case, or crash cases. However, in an accident, the rare event could have happened due to contributory negligence. A reasonable person alleges to be arrested and prosecuted (Giummarra et al. 2020).

The results of an accident may be based on a single cause, or it will come by the combination of several causes or incidents in the sequence called the "domino effect" (Bohan 2009). For instance, the outside visibility is low due to excessive rain. Vehicles are running nimbly on the road at their possible speed, and suddenly an animal comes across. Although the driver tried to brake, the vehicle could not stop and collided with a road divider followed by some other vehicles due to a wet road. In this, the vehicle's speed (human negligence), the sudden appearance of the animal, and the rain resist the vehicle's driver visibility and braking system. Knowingly, all of these conditions came into sequence and made enough reasonable cause for the accident.

A vehicle accident gives the investigating officer and forensic fraternity formidable challenges to investigate and reconstruct the accident events aptly. Multiple vehicle crash makes an accident more heinous, and complicated to reconstruct the scene. Efficiently it is justifiable that the suggestion of forensic investigation and analysis of vehicle accident reconstruction narrow down the span of the event phrase. A comprehensive investigation of such vehicle crashes is usually pursued to channelize the human intension or contributory negligence or due to vehicle flaw or road error. Forensic accident investigation is correctly needed where effective techniques and styles are applied to reconstruct the accident scene accurately. The accident investigation process constitutes a necessary part performed by the forensic experts. Investigation of the scene is based on determining the possible causes that lead to the inauspicious event. Reconstruction of any accident event depends on the credibility and performance of an investigator in identifying and collecting physical evidence at the scene. The forensic engineer or investigating officer analyzes the fact and tells why, how, where, and when the accident happened.

Accident investigation has been popularly used for both civil and criminal litigation. Forensic experts opine the report of the event based on evidence found at the scene. Later on, the court will take as per the grant and render their verdict. Criminal action will be promptly taken toward active drivers intimately concerned about the accident. Possible charges may progressively reduce with ordinary negligence. Action may also be taken against the vehicular manufacturer for manufacturing defective vehicle designs. Insomuch, as the possible reconstruction of vehicles accident becomes acceptable, the cause of vehicle accident is precisely known by forensic analysis.

Investigating an accident-related scene should be thoroughly organized with essential elements. Essential elements like an immediate response, proper investigation planning, appropriate public handling during and after an accident occur. A comprehensive collection and documentation of physical evidence will generously help to believe in the causative factors, contributing causes, and reconstructing the gruesome accident scene. Accident investigation techniques may differ subtly from others due to accident types, places, and local conditions. Insomuch, as the possible reconstruction and understanding causation in vehicles accident become acceptable, it is precisely known by the forensic analysis of vehicle accidents.

16.2 Classification of Road Accidents

The accident is a vicious phenomenon whose probability and severity can be defined by the accident classification that helps to maintain valuable accident information. Knowledge of accident classification is essential for planning and establishing priorities in accident investigation. Accidents are classified in the following ways:

1. **Collision with objects**—usually, the collision of a motor vehicle with two types of objects (Struble and Struble 2020).
   (a) Collision with moving objects (another vehicle, pedestrians, animals).
   (b) Collision with stationary objects (road divider, tree, pole, and building on or near the road).
2. **Rigidity of colliding objects**—The object collision compatibility in the combination of momentum disproportion is one of the essential entities to understand the overall damage involved in a road accident. The relative rigidity of any two objects collided in a road accident is classified by three parameters (Jirovsky 2015).
   (a) Vehicle has higher rigidity and weight (momentum)—collision with human, cyclist, small animal, light road barricades, etc.
   (b) Both colliding objects are compatible—collision with same type of vehicle and large animal with similar weight.
   (c) Vehicle has lower rigidity and weight—collision with heavier and larger vehicle, tree, building, etc.
3. **Number of subsequent collisions**—Collisions in accidents carry consequential information. The subsequent collisions are classified into two types (Jirovsky 2015; Kirk 2001).
   (a) Single collision—collision between two object, i.e., vehicle-vehicle or vehicle to obstacles at the same time.
   (b) Multiple collisions—cumulative accident at the same time, i.e., multi-vehicular collision (3 or more vehicle) and multiple collision (2 or more vehicle with a fixed obstacle).
4. **Direction of principal impact force**—Generally, the collision in a road accident occurs between vehicle-vehicle and vehicle-object and vehicle-pedestrian. Collision-caused deformation on a vehicle may be utilized to understand the impact point and principal direction of force. Collision of the vehicle during an accident

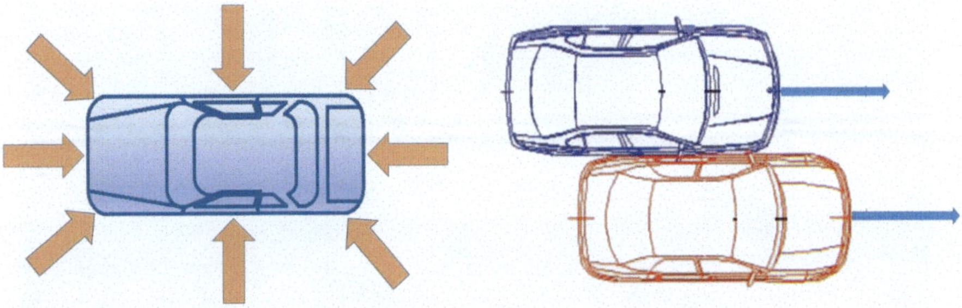

Fig. 16.2 Possible direction of principal impact force in vehicle accident. (**a**) Direct impact on vehicle body. (**b**) Side-to-side impact

is classified as follows (Fig. 16.2) (Eboli et al. 2020; Prentkovskis et al. 2010; Kirk 2001; Jones 1976):
   (a) Frontal impact or head-on collision
   (b) Frontal and side impact combination
   (c) Rear-end impact
   (d) Rear-end and side impact combination
   (e) Side impact (T-bone collision)
   (f) Side-to-side impact
5. **Possible accident condition**—to rate the accident severity and losses, accidents are typically categorized into four distinct conditions (Vincoli 1994):
   (a) **Major accident condition**—accident resulting in hazardous or catastrophic causes major loss of human and economic aspects; e.g., multiple collisions, vehicle pileup, vehicle catches fire after the collision, etc. cause multiple deaths, injury, and massive loss of property.
   (b) **Serious accident condition**—accident resulting in serious injury to humans and property; e.g., a collision between vehicle-vehicle, vehicle-object, vehicle-pedestrian, and vehicle rollover causes death and property loss to participants involved in the accident.
   (c) **Minor accident condition**—accident resulting in disability and damage to a vehicle that is compensable; e.g., breaking of vehicle lights, looking mirror, vehicle deformation, and any physical harm to participants, etc. (Fig. 16.3).
   (d) **"Near misses" accident condition**—an unplanned event that could happen without any detectable injury or resultant damage; e.g., the vehicle losses control, but it is manageable and stops without any damage to a person or property.
6. **Vehicle movement during the accident**—vehicle movement on the road during an accident is classified as follows (Jirovsky 2015):
   (a) Vehicle stays on the road without collision with another obstacle (stops after skidding without collision).
   (b) Vehicle stays on the road due to collision with another obstacle.

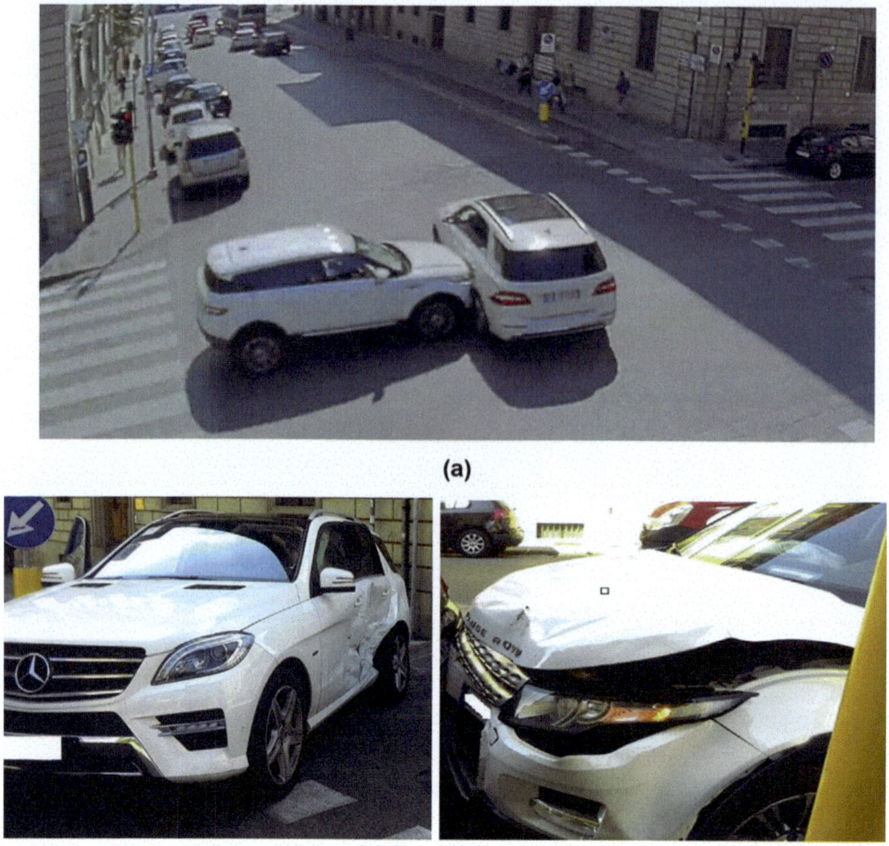

(a)

(b) (c)

Fig. 16.3 Minor accident between Mercedes and Range Rover. (**a**) Front of Range Rover impacts Mercedes' side (T-bone collision). (**b**) Mercedes side deformations: Analysis and Reconstruction. (**c**) Range Rover front deformation. (Reprinted from D. Vangi, Vehicle Collision Dynamics, Butterworth-Heinemann is an imprint of Elsevier (2020) ISBN: 978-0-12-812750-6. (Vangi 2020). Copyright 2021, with permission from Elsevier)

   (c) Vehicle leaves the road or free-fall without primary collision.
   (d) Vehicle leaves the road due to collision (single or multiple).
7. **Vehicle occupation**—vehicle occupants are discerned as load and its distribution in a vehicle influences vehicle movement. Knowledge of vehicle occupation to an investigating officer during an accident helps to understand possible causes and severity in an accident. Vehicle occupation is classified using the following parameters (Jirovsky 2015):
   Autonomous vehicle driving without any passenger (e.g. taxi).
   (a) Vehicle with only driver.
   (b) Vehicle's load is balanced.

(c) Vehicle liable to pitch due to unbalanced load.
(d) Vehicle liable to roll due to unbalanced load.

The only social characteristic among all types of accident classification is that the resulting event is undesirable. An accident can moreover remain a crime. At the initial stage of the official investigation, it is not apparent that the notable casualty is done due to contributory negligence or by criminal intention. Accidents and organized crimes are discriminated by the possible motive, favorable condition of willfulness, or whether the situation is addressed satisfactorily in the legal code. An investigation must be properly done to determine the cause of the accident and criminal motive liable to prosecution.

16.3 Why Investigation Need

"Why proper investigation needed?" Somehow, the question might have come in everyone's conscious mind. It may sound because of "Procedure of any Law agencies" or "To find evidence" that will help make an opinion for a forensic expert and judgment by the jurisprudence. As in earlier discussion, excessive causality due to accidents is a concern to the forensic fraternity. Where and why an accident happened, and proper investigation of the scene will generously help to understand. The investigation constitutes the initial step and the sole solution to any unfortunate event and incidental things (Horswell 2004). Carefully investigating an accident scene is essential. However, it does not immediately solve the probable cause and continuous sequence of events. But it helps to understand reasonably and develop linkages between pieces of evidence to reconstruct the scene possibly. Impartial investigation of the accident scene may help to develop the following things:

- Investigative leads to forensic expert/investigating officer.
- Specific information to enable a successful prosecution.
- Provide exculpatory, inculpatory, or probative evidence to ascertain the cause and sequence of events.
- Significant evidence that helps in the reconstruction of the event.
- Link intension (negligently, knowingly) of an accident.

Any accident scene is never similar to the previous one and another. Investigation of the accident scene always comes with new challenges. Before starting the investigation, an investigating officer, criminalist, police officer, or forensic expert are devoted to solving the unanticipated event, channelize the objectives, purpose, and investigative questions. Some of the investigative questions include "What happened? When did it happen? Where did it happen? How did it start? Who was involved? How was it performed? Why was it performed? These questions help expand the vision to the comprehensive investigation of the pre-crash, during the crash, and post-crash scenarios (Islam and Kanitpong 2008).

16.4 The Investigator: Role and Responsibilities

Whenever an accident, possible crime, or any unlawful activity happens, the law enforcement agencies assign a person or a team to investigate the event, which is known as an investigator or investigating unit. An investigating team could correctly be forensic experts, police officers, and the criminalist. Forensic scientists, investigators, and crime scene specialists are the individuals whose noble profession is to embrace applied science and modern technology to solve any unlawful act or crime. The function and responsibility of these teams toward investigation are helpful because they possess a certain degree of specialization (Fisher and Fisher 2012). An investigator personally involved in any investigation must have the potential to derive the maximum possible evidence from the scene, and use wisely to determining and accurately reconstructing the complex sequence of accident events. When any vehicle gets into an accident and causes damage to a person or property, it must investigate the scene to collect the possible information. Primarily, an investigator should understand the priority to deal with the accident scene. Evacuate the crowd around the scene to avoid further causality and send the person for medical treatment if needed. Carefully preserving an accident scene to the most significant possible degree is another task for the investigator. An investigator should not allow any private person other than their investigating team. The conviction of teamwork in an accident investigation is a crucial factor to the success of the case. Collecting physical evidence is not as easy because of the complexity of the accident event. The job of the accident investigator is to find the trace or physical evidence and to preserve them wisely. The investigator should keep in mind that "the analysis can be no better than the sample analyzed." Such physical evidence helps the investigator determine the cause of the accident (negligence or criminal intention), involved, sequence of events, etc. Any ignorance with evidence collection and its preservation undoubtedly results in fruitless investigation and often may never be rectified. An accident investigator should not come with a preconceived idea or deduce premature conclusions. Forensic investigation of any scene must proceed deliberately and calmly.

The investigator should objectively analyze every possible inch of the scene on their own for pertinent details. It is worth collecting more evidence than desired, which may not be necessary, but in a later investigation, it becomes imperative. Any bulky or compact body should not overlook any item. A proper investigation helps to collect all the valuable information that substantiates a confession or proves a defense contention raised during the trial. An investigator should not be biased or emotional and adroitly avoid a rush during the investigation that may cause evidence to be overlooked. Every accident scene is different from others; it may not be possible to apply the same absolute for every investigation. However, the leading investigator should figure out the local condition and make outlines to proceed accident scene.

16.5 The Investigation Planning

Pre-planning to fascinate any accident scene is essential that the investigation team make it familiar with the method and sequence of reporting an accident and receiving facts. While investigation planning, wide varieties of activities are involved. Numerous factors may influence the level of investigation planning, such as accident scene, scene distance, and size of investigating team. Nevertheless, the essential steps for investigation planning followed by the many experts were distributed into four quadrants (Vincoli 1994).

1. **Establishing objectives**: establishing clear objectives determines the course and direction of all activities in the investigation. The lack of goals potentially turns to the most significant threat and may divert the investigation.
2. **Understanding priorities**: planning for action priorities to the investigation of the accident scene is another essential step. A clear understanding of priorities will pronounce the methods to achieving the objectives established earlier. It is possibly impalpable to find the myriad facts and information to be collected and evaluated at the heat of investigation. Much of the information may escape that nevertheless turn out to be important for the reconstruction of accident scene later. Proper planning of priorities before the investigation will help to clear the path of objectives. Then the investigating team proceeds with the investigation in a more focused and direct manner instead of haphazard or trial-and-error methods. During the planning, the leading investigator identifies and prioritizes the resource used in the investigation. Knowledge of accident classification, as discussed above, will help to lead the investigator to establish the priorities and organize qualified team for investigation. People with the required skills for certain types of investigation, proper equipment, and materials are also included in the priorities. Investigation with inadequate or inappropriate people and equipment can liquidate the evidence.
3. **Development of actions and schedules**: in this planning process, plan the alternative (personal or equipment) and repetitive course of action following an investigation. As the action plan is versatile and flexible, the investigating officer will offer the greater option to perform the investigation. Continuous consideration of report scheduling and information transfer is also included in action planning to strengthen investigation and further action to be taken. However, the interested officer is provided accurate information that helps to perform suitable action and deduce adverse effect. At the same time, proper scheduling of investigation activities, somewhat, provides control and establishes such milestone. That, later on, must be helpful in adequately accomplishing the investigation promptly. The longer it takes to investigate an accident event, it increases the probability of losing evidence and affects the result.
4. **Preparation of corrective action procedures**: an additional thorough effort may also yield, i.e., the building of courses that will apply in the investigation by the investing team. The disciplinary process identifies the primary program deficiencies and prevents further accidents. Another attractive aspect of corrective

action procedure is flexibility. The course can be in the form of a placard, short and amplified checklists, instructional notebook or guide, detailed operating procedures, manual, or any other condition that facilitates an investigation. At the moment, procedures have been developed, and all the team members in an investigation should be thoroughly familiar with each procedure's contents.

Each of the four steps of the investigation planning process described above for successful accident investigation should exist in one form or another. Except for precise planning and systematic approach, the accident investigation and prevention for further loss of evidence is void.

16.6 Principle of Investigation Process

A forensic accident investigation is an endeavor of attentively examining the possible conditions around the accident scene. Before attempting the accident investigation process, an intuitive understanding of fundamental principles associated with the comprehensive analysis of such incidents is important. Proper reporting is essential to the entire investigation procedure of all the accidents. Therefore, one of the most overarching principles for any accident investigation process is a formal policy typically requiring the proper and consistent reporting of all accidents. The basic statute to a fruitful investigation is knowledge of accident background, properly forming an investigation parameter, securing a scene, frequently searching for physical evidence, proper collection of evidence, and identifying an accident source. It is reasonable that the general objective of investigating a scene is varied. Every crime scene is unique to others. A forensic investigating officer or team should be the empiricist and rationalist to adequately establish the hypothesis and instantly grasp the fundamental principle for the resulting investigation.

16.6.1 Background Understanding and Management

Whenever a massive accident happens, a mishap has undoubtedly resulted from one or a continuous sequence of events. Accidents may be hazardous (major), minor, or "near misses." Before accident investigation is processed, understanding an accident's type, condition, and surroundings is necessary. As accident types and their causes are different, management for investigating the scene is equally varied. The principal objectives of management are proper consideration of property damage, confirmed death or injury of a person, and the leading cause of the accident. Management for the scene investigation is an important factor that helps control the chances of further accidents or injuries. The four prominent management options for accident investigation are: (a) information management, (b) human resources management, (c) technology management, and (d) logistics management. Inadequacy, negligence, or overemphasis of any one of these managements will affect the investigation. Quantifying all these components is based on the background of the accident. The essential component of management has its advantage and disadvantage based on the allocation of personnel and resources, types of accidents, training and expertise, support service available, and jurisdictional issues. Without understanding of accident background, management decision turns to be subjective, which is itself and somewhat dangerous.

16.6.2 Establishing Investigation Parameters

Forensic experts ostensibly have to analyze the parameter within which the impartial investigation is to be followed for making a productive investigation. The successful establishment of necessary parameters through investigation is an important executive decision for reliable identification of the possible cause. Accident investigation is required to satisfactorily establish all possible parameters and a comparative analysis of all the possible reasons that help in decision making. For effective investigation, several fundamental parameters need to be considered such as types of the occurrence, establishing objectives to what to investigate at what extent, possible causes, etc. Factors that affect the establishment of effective accident investigation parameters are faulty communication, improper training, and lack of adequate information. A disciplined and methodological investigation of a scene can be fruitful and productive for the investigating officers. However, the establishment of investigating parameters is equally affected by the misguided and haphazard investigation of the reported accident.

16.6.3 Accident Sources

To understand the fundamental principles of accident investigation, a forensic investigator must also understand the sources of mishaps as it aid the investigating officer to identify the cause, the methods and techniques to be used and the type of evidences to be traced. An extensive collection of physical evidence is essential in any judicial investigation. In accident investigation, the undesired events are caused due to the source of error like human, material, mechanical equipment procedure, and environment. An accident may occur due to the single source of error or a combination of different sources of error in sequence, or may one source affect another source, also known as the "domino effect."

16.6.4 The Investigation Pyramid

The scientific investigation and analysis of an accident are structured like a pyramid. At the beginning of any case, available facts and information seem like scattered pieces of a puzzle. At first, facts and pieces of evidence are merely collected, gathered, and placed at the bottom of the table. These are the exclusive base

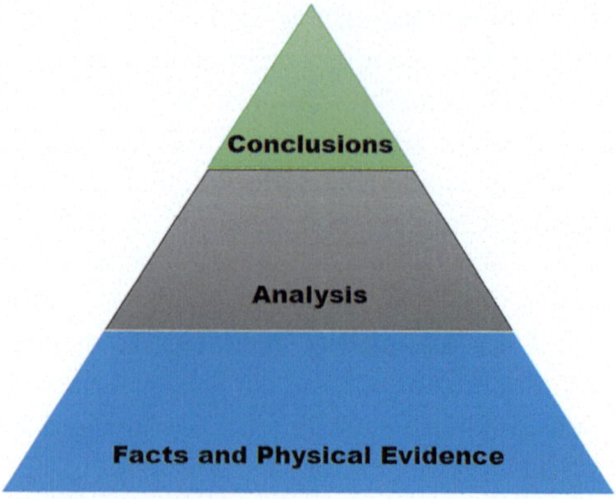

Fig. 16.4 Investigation pyramid

foundation for the conclusive pyramid. All the pieces of evidence are sorted and each piece is fitted to all the other evidence until the facts are proven. These facts are formed for the analysis which is proven by the scientific principle and methods. The facts and physical evidence and analysis are taken together that support the conclusion that is the apex of the pyramid (Fig. 16.4). Conclusions should completely be dependent on facts and analysis, and never be on a personal assumption, conclusions, or any other hypotheses that may collapse the logical construction. If the facts and physical evidence are logically and symmetrically arranged, the conclusion appears self-evident and stronger.

16.7 Tools and Techniques for Investigation

Considerable success or evident failure of any accident investigation may depend upon planning and elaborate preparation for the complete investigation. Addressing of proper accident investigation kit is another substantial part of preparation. Before reaching the occurrence, positively assuring of proper tools required for the investigation is essential. The adequacy of necessary tools in investigator suitcase may depend on the distinct type of accident, distance of the accident scene, etc.

The accident investigation toolkit, based on its use, may be divided into four types (Kirk 2001):

1. Basic tools (used in open, cut, or removing)
   - Allen wrench
   - Screwdrivers (different sizes and types)
   - Open and closed-end metric and English wrenches
   - Set of 1/4- and 3/8-in. drive sockets, metric and English
   - Jackknife
2. Special equipment (used in marking, documenting, and preserving)
   - Chalk
   - Pencils and pens (different color)

- Blank card (3 × 5)
- Contour gauge
- Measures (12, 15, and 100 ft)
- Cardboard play card
- Clay
- Graph and plain paper
- Stick-on tape measures
- Menu board
- Surveyor's pin
- Vehicle trajectory rods
- Handheld compass and magnifying glass
- Tags for label the evidence at the scene
- Accident investigation form
- Duct tape
- Evidence collecting bags

3. Photographic and videographic equipment (used for accurately detailed investigation)
   - SLR camera (35 mm) with 50- or 70- to 115-mm and wide-angle lens (25 mm, 1-in.)/UV filters
   - Motorized unit and data back for dates
   - Standard adjustable angle flash with the detachable hot shoe with a diffuser
   - Ring flash
   - Color film, 100 and 400 DIN, 24 and 36 exposures
   - Panoramic lens camera
   - Monopod or small tripod
   - Backup camera with all the above equipment
   - 8- or Super-8-mm camera with carrying case
   - Spare charged batteries and cassettes
4. Special safety gear or equipment (use by the investigator for his safety)
   - Orange road cones and vests
   - Gloves
   - Flasher for cars
   - Telephone (cellular)
   - Business card and authorization from the client
   - First aid box

16.8 Accident Scene Investigation

A vehicular accident investigation is complicated, outdoor, and generally found in high-traffic areas. Scene investigation and archiving of potential evidence to understand the cause and sequence of accidents have always been challenging. Forensic experts or forensic engineers remain the first individuals to investigate any accidents scene. Acquiring the knowledge of accidents type, vehicles and their dynamic motion, road, geographical area, etc., may help to channelize what they require to observe. Undoubtedly, the accident scene is customarily restricted with traffic, time, nearby construction, or frequent changes in climate (Dong et al. 2018; Topolšek et al. 2014). As discussed earlier in step 3 of investigation planning, they must maintain a backup plan as the situation changes. Perhaps, accident investigation begins at the end of the accident. It is at this point some questions are raised: how did this happen, who and what is responsible for the accident? With the chronological investigation, the investigator gathers, establishes, and assesses evidence to understand how and why the accidents occurred. The events that leading to an accident may be differentiated into pre-accident, during accident, and post-accident. In typical instances, information about pre and post-accident events is reasonably known. Nevertheless, information about the event between pre- and post-accidents is unclear, confusing, or even contradictory (Noon 2009). Assume car A and car B heading north and south and collide in the street and freeze at the same point. However, this pre-accident (heading of a car) and post-accident (point of rest) are clear. The investigator role is to fill the intermediate event sequence and its reason. The intermediate points are usually revealed by the evidence gathered and assessed. The investigators need to assess, sort, and sequence the evidence into a logical and coherent story. Like puzzles, some of the missing or few extra pieces are thrown in from other puzzles, and the investigator considers each piece of evidence with different perspectives and combinations to determine the perfect fit. Reconstruction of accident events depends on the quality of investigation, and that can be concluded by following the steps as in Fig. 16.5 (Cameron 2008). An investigation phase has started adequately after all the immediate rescue and providing medical treatment to any injured person.

The investigator typically collects evidence from accident scenes, which are generally fragile and important in reconstruction. Pieces of evidence at the accident scene may refer to the "four Ps" evidence (Ferry 1988). The "four Ps" are people, position, parts, and papers. Peoples are the wellspring of eyewitness testimony to the accident events. Eyewitness evidence is obviously based on their observation and memories that may conflict with others' stories and fade by the passage of time. Positions entrust to the physical relationship, placement, and sequence of events occur during pre - contact, contact and post contact duration of the accident. This includes, for example, location, weather, and roadways condition, physical evidence like scatter parts, tire marks, broken glass or mirror, dent on a vehicle, etc. Parts refer to internal parts of vehicles that can be potential evidence in understanding the cause of an accident. Parts evidence can include improper installation or use of faulty parts or materials or inadvertent abuse of parts, violation of manufacturing standards, etc. Paper evidence invokes as background information of any vehicle like operating instruction, maintenance record, etc. These are the evidence recorded on paper (i.e., "paper trail"), generally destroyed in an accident (Vincoli 1994). Recovery of paper makes it easy to understand the condition of the vehicle before getting in the accident.

While practicing an investigation and collecting physical evidence from the accident scene, the primary step is documentation. Documentation includes

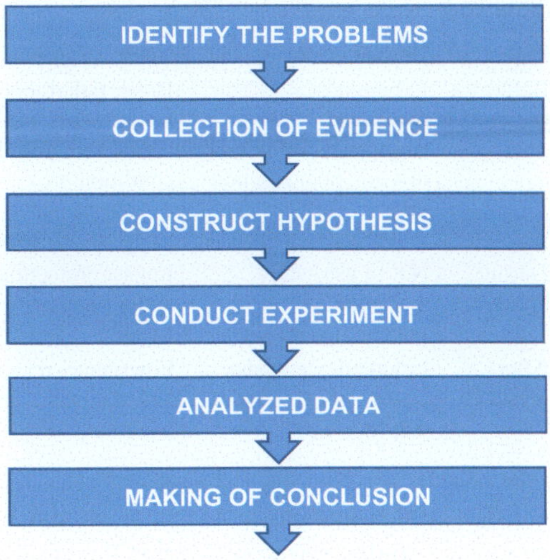

Fig. 16.5 Steps in accident scene investigation

statement recording, noting, sketching, photography, and videography of physical evidence with proper scaling and reference with other pieces of evidence. For example, tire and skid marks, depth and size of crush, paint and gauge marks, and position of all debris pieces are subjects of appropriate documentation or make a note with proper measurements. An aware investigator can primarily use the "Haddon matrix" for meticulously documenting credible evidence and the complex situation of the accident (Struble and Struble 2020). In 1970, Dr. William Haddon typically developed the grid on investigators who may record information before, during, and after an accident. Haddon matrix for accidents allows nine cells which efficiently formed by three columns and three rows. Rows show phases of events such as before the accident, during the accident, and after the accident. Columns recognize the causal factors of an accident in each period like human factors, vehicle and equipment factors, and physical environment factors (Table 16.2 Haddon matrix). The comprehensive forensic investigation of 'four Ps' prorates the evidence as subjective and objective evidence (Bohan 2009).

16.8.1 Subjective Evidence

Subjective evidence matters to the statement of a person physically present during an accident and claiming knowledge of the events (Wach 2013). They are persons apprehended as the witness or fact witness or eye witness. An eyewitness can represent any pedestrian, local passenger, or the drivers and participants themselves. It is the human tendency to remember precisely what they saw by their own eyes. Accounting of leading investigator with eyewitnesses could willingly have sources of valuable information. A valuable piece of evidence is concluded as what somebody was riding, direction, possible speed, and any mechanical failure before the

Table 16.2 Haddon matrix

Phase	Human error	Vehicle/equipment error	Physical environment
Before accident	Experience, overspeed, negligence, drink and driving, poor reaction time	Break failed, poor visibility, active safety vehicle system, vehicle control and technical condition	Road geometry, narrow shoulder, road surface condition, visibility and weather condition, pedestrian and cycling facility
During accident	Not to use safety measures	Impact protection (safety belt and air bag not properly fixed)	Road side safety (improper guardrails, shoulders, and clear zone)
After accident	Emergency response, control of behavior of culprit	Emergency response system "Era-Glonass," victim extraction, means of first aid	Restoration, unwell emergency communication system

collision. But a leading investigator should not rely on witness statements. Very convincing studies have proved that the ability of a human to recognize any events exactly as he/she saw is not permanent (Bohan 2009).

Any statement given by the eyewitness is taken as "corroborative evidence" because "circumstantial facts" of events may be un-followed with the statements. However, the oral testimony may also turn into hostile. They may draw their own story, conclusion, idea, and give incomplete information to the investigator. Statements of an eyewitness may be partial if he/she or any relative of the parties are involved in accidents. However, some important condition is absolutely unknown to any of the eyewitness and participants, though may come to light with a thorough and unbiased investigation. For example, instant or internal mechanical issue in any of vehicles involved in an accident unknown to the eyewitnesses could have increased the stopping distance, improper timing of traffic light, speed limit board, etc. Surprisingly many of "obvious" causes, which are not known to eyewitnesses, can be brought to light with modest investigation of physical evidence and facts.

The key elements in any vehicle accident are speed, skid distance, direction, and elapsed time, which may not be known to the eyewitnesses. They usually do not see or comprehend the latent deficiencies. Eyewitnesses focus on the immediate crash due to its noise and exclude other events and circumstances that existed at the incident site at the same time (Noon 2009). Eyewitness report is not direct, as often it is based on observations. They generally produce conclusions based on what they sensually observe. Sense-based conclusions are often formed by connecting the possible dots of disconnected events they observed. However, some of witness are "hearsay witness." Hearsay witnesses are persons who have not actually witnessed the event but they know what they heard from their friend or neighbors. Over time, they may forget the sequence of events and remember the things that they find interesting. Also it is obvious that some of the witnesses come out for attention who simply lie. With a proper scientific investigation of accidents and carefully analyzing physical evidence, investigators may arbitrate who is embellishing the truth, who is telling truth, and who is not.

16.8.2 Objective Evidence

The physical evidence moreover identifies a piece of objective evidence. A piece of physical evidence may the part or the vehicle itself and the marks formed due to friction between tires and the surface. The physical evidence in vehicular accidents ordinarily includes tire (skid) marks, paint chips, broken glasses and vehicle parts, and dents or sketches. Such credible evidence is examined directly at the scene or through photography and other documentation for later. Objective evidence present at the accident scene are reliable and and can be analyzed by using science and technology (Wach 2013). For example, assume a car caused skid marks of 165 ft (49.5 m) before the direct collision with a big stone and a dent of 15 in. deep created at the car's front end. Visible skid marks and dents on the car can give a clear and complete idea to understand that the car maintains enough velocity to crash by skidding tires after braking hard-to-wheel lockup. The source of the objective evidence in a vehicle accident is mainly two types. The first is the accident scene and surroundings, and the second is the exterior and interior surface of vehicles.

16.8.2.1 Accident Scene and Surrounding

Accident scenes and its surrounding are abundant sources of physical evidence. Evaluation of accident surroundings may turn more difficult due to scatterings of the fragmented particle, forest areas, traffic, etc. (Kirk 2001). Scene investigation is a preliminary step for understanding the direction, speed, and cause of an accident (Islam and Kanitpong 2008). The first logical step for an investigator is to carefully choose a reference point (RP) with all the sketches and accurate measurements satisfactorily performed. The reference point must be close and permanent with the accident scene.

Furthermore, it cannot be changed or moved for years to assist another investigator on a more recent day of the investigation. Reference points could represent a milestone, telephone or utility pole, tree, etc. Another is to identify the point of impact (POI) (vehicle-vehicle POI or vehicle-object POI) and point of rest (POR). POI may be considered the point of exchange, following Locard's exchange principle, where vehicle-vehicle or vehicle-objects impact and exchange their traces. The POI may turn to the point of rest (POR). Point of rest is the place where rolling or skidding of tire freezes. More often than not, the point of rest is one, but it may change in multiple collisions accidents. Tire marks of a vehicle involved in the accident constitute a substantial source of evidence. That wisely helps determine possible direction, wheels (rolling or stopped), and possible speed of the vehicle before the crash.

16.8.2.2 Tire Marks

Tire marks are generic evidence at the accident scene to assume the direction, speed, and load on vehicles on the road (O'Hara and Osterbug 1960). Investigators may search tire marks as per three types, which appear at distinct phases of the accident, such as "Yaw, Skid and Acceleration Marks," mainly in the patent form (2-dimensional impression). The problem with tire marks is it starts fading up within a day or even within hours or maybe messed up with the other vehicle tire marks. Fading of skid marks causes shortening in skid marks length, results in an underestimating of vehicle speed. Furthermore, whether associated with an accident or not, the mixed tire marks should be measured or at least photographed until it is not confirmed. Preservation of tire marks to be done by documentation (photography) with proper measurements (scaling) may assist the later investigator in the reconstruction process. The appearance of tire marks in a vehicular accident is classified into three forms, i.e., yaw marks, skid marks, and acceleration marks.

16.8.2.2.1 Acceleration Marks

The acceleration mark always appears before a collision phase. Sometimes, an investigator gets confused between the acceleration and skid marks made before, during, and after the potential collision. Acceleration marks may carefully be differentiated by their dark pattern. The skid marks start as light in color and turns in dark as the tire get hotter. In acceleration, marks are somehow opposite. Marks at the possible beginning are darker and lighten up as the vehicle moves forward. Acceleration marks depend on the rotating power of the axle and the coefficient of friction between the road surface and tire treads. From a forensic perspective, acceleration marks corroborate to understand the intention of the vehicle driver. The intentional frame did the accident, or it just happened in negligence.

16.8.2.2.2 Skid Marks

Skid marks are the unidirectional visible marks left by the sudden braking of the vehicle (Wang and Lin 2008). It appears due to friction between the road and vehicle tires. The wheel suddenly stops rolling and starts sliding at the road (Fig. 16.6). Skid marks are the most valuable trace evidence at the accident scene for forensic experts or investigating officers. Skids marks could occur before, during, and after a collision. Tire skid marks can appear in three phases, i.e., cleaning, tire heat up, and end with heavy black skid marks. In the cleaning phase, tires skid on the road, but no marks occur, only cleaning the road and tire surface. In the second phase, the tire surface experiences heat up, which makes marks as light to slightly darker. The first two, i.e., skid marks' cleaning and heating phase, are not easily visible unless it is evaluated from different directions. The heavy black mark phase is distinctly visible to the investigator. It forms due to the heating up of tires and sudden end under the tire at the point of rest. All three phases of skids help investigative officers investigate and understand the possible direction and speed of vehicles with more accuracy.

Skid marks appear due to sudden braking or sudden locking up of vehicle wheels. Sometimes more than one unique set of skid marks of the same vehicle that appear at

Fig. 16.6 Skid mark. (Reprinted from YW. Wang, A line-based skid mark segmentation system using image-processing methods, Transportation Research Part C 16 (2008) doi:10.1016/j.trc.2007.09.002. (Wang and Lin 2008). Copyright 2021, with permission from Elsevier)

the scene is difficult to determine resolutely. By a close analysis, an investigator can see that one set of marks usually grows lighter as pressure is released. The reasonable length of skid marks more often depends on the vehicle's kinetic energy (weight and speed), the pressure of the brake pad against the disk or drum, surface, and tire conditions. The vehicle's speed before skidding is calculated by measuring the length of skid marks.

16.8.2.2.3 Yaw Marks

The vehicle's tires rotating and turning simultaneously and leaving a mark are called scuff marks or yaw marks. It forms when a vehicle develops an angle of slip or disparity between its heading and velocity (Siegel and Mirakovits 2016). Striation in yaw marks is very distinctive from other striations. In the case of lockup or full braking, striation is situated by the tire marks and parallel to the direction of vehicle wheel hub movement (Fig. 16.7). Yaw marks can appear before, during, and after the accident. Striation marks of a vehicle can be at various points. It depends on the number of collisions and the amount of "rolling under" the tread while maneuvering. The rear as well front tires both can create the striation and skid marks. The skid marks are usually more dark than the striation marks. The Yaw mark's width, number, and striation angle are critically dependent on the vehicle speed and velocity direction (Franck and Franck 2010). An investigator may differentiate the yaw and side skid marks by measuring the width of the mark. The tire's pitch size appears double as the tires skid sideways. Change set in the position of a vehicle can instantly be recognized by the investigator by analyzing skid or yaw marks that end under the tires at a point of rest.

Fig. 16.7 A yaw or scruff mark. (Reprinted from EM. Robinson, Crime Scene Photography—2nd Edition, Academic Press is an imprint of Elsevier (2010) ISBN: 978-0-12-375728-9. (Robinson 2010). Copyright 2021, with permission from Elsevier)

16.8.2.2.4 Location of Debris

Locating debris of accidental crashes is vital for the investigator. Debris may be of a vehicle door, shattered glass pieces, screws, paint chips, shattered windshield, or any fragmented part of a vehicle. The point of impact and rest, road, shoulders, poles, trees, the vehicle itself, etc. are the most common places from where an investigator can unearth the evidence point of impact, point of rest, road, shoulders, poles, trees, the vehicle itself, etc. (Struble and Struble 2020). Location of debris helps to assume direction, point of impact, point of rest, and vehicle speed. Documentation (sketch) of debris may be performed on an overlay sheet of clean Mylar by framing of vehicle point of rest and reference point. Investigators may find any discrepancy later; they will place the overlay on measurements and reconstruct the scene. The sketch can be enlarged and used as court exhibits by placing overlay in a computer-aided designed (CAD) program or high-speed plotter.

16.8.2.3 Vehicle: Exterior and Interior Surface

An investigating officer often does not include the window of opportunity to evaluate vehicles at the scene. The traffic issue, climate changes, and complexity in the accident scene give trouble searching for necessary scene evidence for reconstruction. After making detailed vehicle documentation concerning the accident scene and other evidence, the vehicle towed away for a later examination.

Vehicles involved in any accidental scene are the considerable body having fundamentally significant evidence for the forensic investigation. An accidental vehicle, inside and outside, have various deformations and scratches. That can give some good sense of idea for accident causation and reconstruct the scene. However, the vehicle not in control and collided with any other vehicle, tree, road divider, pedestrian, etc., mutual exchange of empirical evidence took place (Locard's principle of exchange). The condition of marks, fracture or dent, and exchange of trace on the vehicles tell some story. The investigator may understand all the possible conditions of the accidents by making an effort and evaluating the vehicle's exterior surface and interior deformation. Evidence source at the exterior surface could be the metal fold, tires condition, paint transfer, scrape, scratches, gouges, wheel metal condition, fluid leaks, side marker light, taillights, and headlight and vehicle deterioration condition. Deformed vehicle could indicate the POI and direction of impact force (Fig. 16.8). Vehicle interior deformations include instrument panels, steering column, steering wheel rims, sun visors, sunroof, seat cushions and seatback, smear and blood pooling, windshield, rear window, etc.

Carefully noting, sketching, photography, and videography with proper measurements at every phase is necessary for preserving evidence at accident scenes. The frame of documentation (photography and videotaping) of the accident scene depends on carefully noting, sketching, photography, and videography with proper measurements at every phase necessary for preserving evidence at accident scenes. The frame of documentation (photography and videotaping) of the accident scene depends on the investigation's objectives, as in Tables 16.3 and 16.4 (Shaler 2012). Documentation helps in the more recent examination and reconstruction of the accident scene.

An investigating officer should be aware of the vehicle's extensive evaluation, either the interior or the exterior, and note down all the missing parts. While transporting vehicles to the garage or yard, unrelated damages and modifications may form, such as the door may be cut off to rescue the victim, tire place, axle where towing machine hooked, removing of paint, etc. These are the details investigator should always be aware of on both the crime scene and subsequent vehicle inspections. Instead of all, information of a specific vehicle, model, performance, traffic device and sign, roadways specification, traffic on the road, and date and time of the accident are equally notable.

16.9 Accident Reconstruction

Many people undertake that the accident investigation and accident reconstruction are the same subjects of a thing. Nevertheless, in the investigation, the investigator evaluates the scene strictly and also documents and preserves the evidence at the scene. Reconstruction is building up of accident as approximate with the help of remaining parts of vehicles, credible evidence, and documentation. A forensic examination of the accident scene may come with a qualitative and quantitative description. However, the primary objective of the reconstruction of an accident is to

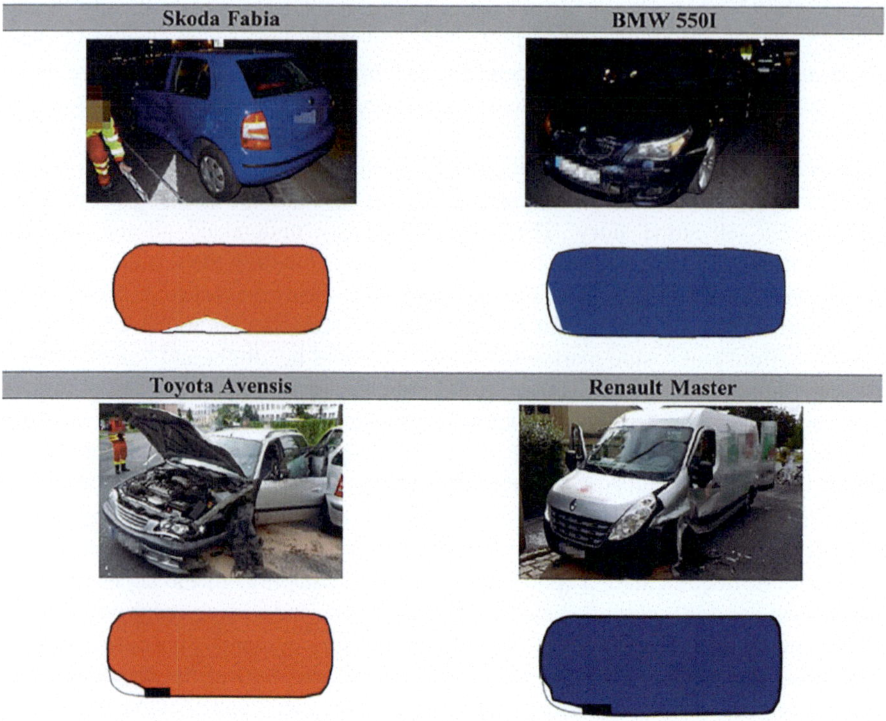

Fig. 16.8 Deformed shapes of vehicle involved in real accident utilized in reconstructing the POI and direction of impact force. (Reprinted from D. Vangi, Vehicle accident reconstruction by a reduced order impact model, Forensic Science International 298 (2019) https://doi.org/10.1016/j.forsciint.2019.02.042 (Vangi et al. 2019). Copyright 2021, with permission from Elsevier)

come by a numerical description (quantitative description) (Bohan 2009). For example, saying "the truck was skidded by the 110 ft and then collide with the street light (quantitative description)" is far worthy to saying that "the truck was skidded to some reasonable distance and then smashed into street light" (qualitative description).

In proceeding to a forensic reconstruction of the accident field the investigating officer requires specific grip in:

- Criminalistics (interpretation to traces)
- Vehicle dynamics and technology, particular reference to steering, rolling, braking, passive and active safety systems
- Basic knowledge of crash-worthiness
- Collision mechanics or collision theories
- Kinematic calculation (time-distance analysis)
- Human factors (individual and age differences, perception and information processing, driver perception-response time)

Table 16.3 Guideline for vehicle accident scenes photography and videography

Object to photograph/ videograph	Reason for photograph/videograph
Point of impact	To relate other aspects of scene and to identify where the hit took place
Traffic lights and board	Their location is important to know
Driver's viewpoint	To understand what the driver was able to saw
Skid marks	To understand the speed and momentum of the vehicle before and after the collision
Roadways condition	To understand aspect of road in accident
Roadways	To know road environment, i.e., slope, defect, distance of debris from impact site, and vehicle position
Tire tracks	Direction and location of tire tracks
Instructions board	To know if any banner, board, obstacle that would have come across the driver
Biological evidence	To know the place of biological evidence
Paint removed	To document possible paint transfer from vehicle, close-up photography
Trace and debris evidence	To understand the location of glass, fiber, plastic and metal or other fragmented particles from reference point and collision place
Interior and exterior photographs of vehicle	Scratches on vehicle surface, position of crush, length and depth of crush, seat position, gear lever position, etc.
Other shots	License plates, VIN number, previous welding place, etc.

Table 16.4 Photography and videography

Documentation must include markers (scale) to identify position of evidence and vehicle	
Overview	To record the story and relationship of evidence to the overall scene
Midrange	To relate the evidence to its nearby evidence, i.e., evidence-to-evidence relationships
Close	To record the proper detailing of evidence with and without scaling

- Computer simulation techniques
- Digital photography, imaging techniques, and photogrammetry
- Road infrastructure
- Basic knowledge regarding accident scene and complementary examination in road accident

Vehicular accident reconstruction represents the exploratory phase. The forensic investigator analyzes an accident and exploits their knowledge of physics, physical fact, and data collected from the accident scene. By utilizing extensive knowledge of the evidence, an investigator can determine the speed of vehicles involved, angle of impact (primary and secondary), mechanical failures, and environmental factors that may have caused and affected an accident's responsibility. Accident reconstruction comprises two types, i.e., damaged-based reconstruction and trajectory-based reconstruction (based on the principle of momentum is conserved). The reconstruction starts with the damaged vehicle and sufficient distance of its debris to skid and yaw marks and road condition. The conjunction of both reconstruction methods typically results in a more accurate reconstruction. The two vital tools for the reconstruction of accident events are the law of conservation of momentum and conservation of energy. With sufficient data, the law of conservation of energy and conservation of momentum makes it possible to determine the speed of vehicles after and before the accident (James and Nordby 2009). According to the law of conservation of energy, the system's energy at a beginning process is equal to the end of the process (Eq. 16.1). In any vehicle accident case scenario, the combined energy at the end is irreversible and cannot be returned into kinetic energy again. Such an example of irreversible work is braking, yawing, skidding, crushing, bending, and twisting vehicles.

$$E_{\text{start}} = E_{\text{end}} \tag{16.1}$$

where E is total energy of system.

Every moving vehicle possesses its own kinetic energy which is directly proportional to the speed and mass of vehicle (Eq. 16.2).

$$\text{KE} = (1/2)mv^2 \tag{16.2}$$

where KE is kinetic energy, m is the mass of vehicle, v is the velocity of the vehicle.

As the eq. 16.2 shows, KE increases to the four times as the velocity doubles. This is why a vehicle traveling at 60 mph requires four times more braking distance to stop than the exact vehicle traveling at 30 mph. As with the braking distance, the severity of accidents and injury is proportional to vehicles kinetic energy. Skid marks are one of the dissipated ways to calculate the initial kinetic energy before braking and how fast the vehicle was during striking with any pedestrian or any other obstacles.

The force applied through the irreversible frictional work done is calculated by the formula.

$$E_{\text{work}} = (mg)fd \tag{16.3}$$

where

E_{work} = work done by skidding
m = vehicle mass
g = gravitational constant
mg = mass of vehicle × acceleration of gravity

$f =$ frictional coefficient between tire and surface (road)
$d =$ distance of skid

As we discussed above, the kinetic energy of vehicle in motion is equal to the energy dissipated by vehicle skidding. By applying Eqs. 16.2 and 16.3 an investigator can simplify the results.

$$\begin{aligned} E_{\text{start}} &= E_{\text{end}} \\ \text{KE} &= E_{\text{work}} \\ (1/2)mv^2 &= mgfd \\ V &= [2gfd]^{1/2} \end{aligned} \tag{16.4}$$

Therefore, by precisely measuring the reasonable length of skid marks, the speed of a vehicle just before skidding can be calculated. This formula is moreover known as the skid formula (Eq. 16.4). During a collision with any pedestrian or object, the length of skid marks formed utilizes to calculate the pre-collision vehicle velocity. Although the vehicle continues to skid, the front end of a vehicle crashes into the wall. Crushing the vehicle's front end causes another way of dissipating the kinetic energy of the vehicle. As we know, the crush at the front end of a vehicle is directly proportional to the vehicle speed. Therefore, the speed and crush relationship varies with the make and model of the vehicle. Government and private organizations produce data of crush rates at different speeds every year. The reliable crush rate versus impact speed data may be directly utilized in determining the accident crush. After skidding some feet, it crashed into the wall and got some deformation if a vehicle is moving forward. It shows that the vehicle must have been going with much more kinetic energy than the skid formula alone would measure skid length. In this, the vehicle's kinetic energy dissipated in skidding and crushing the front end of the car to any wall without hitting any pedestrian, as we can see in Eq. 16.5.

$$\begin{aligned} \text{Kinetic energy} &= \text{Skid work} + \text{Crush work} \\ (1/2)mv^2 &= mgfd + Kx \end{aligned} \tag{16.5}$$

where

$K =$ crush coefficient
$x =$ average crush depth at the front end of vehicle

Solving Eq. 16.5 for the velocity (v) of vehicle gives the following:

$$V^2 = 2gfd + 2(K/m)x \tag{16.6}$$

Investigator can also estimate the deceleration rate of vehicle during collision with wall. By using basic kinematics, the deceleration rate can be computed as follows:

$$a = v^2/2x$$

where

$v =$ velocity
$x =$ crush distance
$a =$ deceleration

Understanding friction coefficient between tire and surface is another challenge for the investigator. To apply in skid formula, the determination of the friction coefficient is essential. Generally, the friction coefficient is untaken into the measure. The investigating officer may directly apply the predetermined friction coefficient to calculate the speed. The friction coefficient varies with place, climate, vehicle model, load on the vehicle, and the surface. The friction coefficient for regular vehicles at dry concrete, dry bricks, wet tar, wet concrete, and wet snow is 0.8, 0.7, 0.5, 0.4, and 0.2 (Sharma 2014).

Nevertheless, the friction coefficient of the vehicle varies with road and vehicle conditions. To establish the vehicle's speed more accurately at the accident time, the investigator performs experimental work for friction coefficient with possibly the same conditions. In most cases, the vehicle involved in the accident is not in the condition to experiment with determining the friction coefficient. If the vehicle tire is affected by the accident, the tire may be used for the experimental tests by shifting it to the test vehicle from the the accidental vehicle. As Newton's third law states, whenever two vehicles collide with each other, they exert equal and opposite force to each other. If the two vehicle has the same mass and velocity and collides with each other, the net force between the two vehicle turns to zero. As follows, the net momentum of a vehicle just before the collision is equal to the net momentum of a vehicle after the collision. The net momentum could be changed by applying external force or due to differences in mass and velocity in a vehicle. This law of conservation of momentum may help in formulating the velocity of a vehicle before the collision. The principle of the law of conservation of momentum is not only used in determining the speed of a vehicle, but it also helps to recognize the conservation of energy. By implementing the conservation of energy method, the "after impact" speed of the vehicle is calculated with the help of skid marks. Whereas the the speed of vehicle (before impact) can be calculated by using the conservation of momentum. To understand, a car of 2700-lb stands hand braked by the roadside and a driver with a mini-truck of 6000-lb not seen the car drives into the rear end at a speed of 36 mph. Before the potential collision, the mini-truck only had the initial energy and considerable momentum. The car was not in momentum before the collision gets pushed onward by a speed of 23 mph, and the mini-truck slows down by 17 mph. Both cars and mini-trucks come to a stop by skidding 31.7-ft and 25.3-ft. Consequently, the total momentum of the truck and car after the collision is the same as the momentum of the truck alone.

Conservation of energy and conservation of momentum more often are used collectively to formulate a mini-truck's speed in an accident more precisely and accurately. The speed (kinetic energy) of the mini-truck "before impact" is equally possible to be determined by measuring the rear and front crush depth of the car and mini-truck.

16.10 Advancement in Accidents Reconstruction Methods

Calculating the accident scene with accuracy is synonymous to the reconstruction of the accident scene. The relationship between reconstructed results and traces left at the accident scene is described best as suitable methodologies. Reconstruction of the accident scene includes five types of methods (Zou et al. 2018). The first method includes theories and empirical formulas that include models based on braking distance, vehicle deformation, the distance of the pedestrian, and injury to the human body. The second method is based on the true vehicle test. In the provision to know more information about the accident, true vehicle tests will be prosecuted evenly as information obtained from the accident scene. Third is allowed to use database based on the crash, injury, and vehicle model, provided by the National Highway Traffic Safety (NHTSA), Research Input for Computer Simulation of Automobiles Collisions (RICSAC), Insurance Institute for Highway Safety (IIHS), Energy Equivalent Speed (EES), Aggregated Homologation proposal for the Event data recorder for Automated Driving (AHEAD), NASS-CDS, Crash Injury Research Engineering Network (CIREN), German In-Depth Accident Study (GIDAS), Co-operative Crash Injury Study (CCIS), and Road Accident Sampling System-India (RASSAI) (Böhm et al. 2020; Pinter and Szalay 2018; Shannon et al. 2018; Vangi et al. 2018; Bhuvanesh et al. 2015; Prasad et al. 2014; Teoh and Lund 2011). The fourth method concludes computer simulation software which is accurate and more reliable to forensic experts. The computer simulation software commercially available includes PC-Crash, Virtual Crash, HVE-3D, V-SIM, MADYMO, Japan Automobile Research Institute (JARI's) car-pedestrian computer simulation model, CarMaker, Simpack, AnalyzerPro, PC-RECT (photogrammetry), MATLAB (based on Brach's model), Computer Reconstruction of Automobile Speed on the Highway (CRASH, CRASH2, or CRASH3) and SMAC (based on McHenry model), DPAM CRASH, Finite Element Method (LS DYNA, Abaqus FEA©, or Ansys©), and Computer-Aided Reconstruction of Accidents in Traffic (CARAT) (Woering et al. 2021; Vangi et al. 2019; Martínez et al. 2016; Gönczi 2013; Topolšek et al. 2014; Roberts et al. 2011; Xinguang et al. 2009; Konosu 2002). Computer simulation software officially produces kinematic and dynamic modeling of collision and vehicle trajectory. Simulation methods employ the rest positions of the vehicle and the traces examined during the accident scene investigation. This simulation software allows crash parameters (point of impact, pre-impact directions, vehicles' position, contact plane angle, contact plane coefficient of friction, and restitution coefficient) in the optimization process. The software allows for optimization and uses three methods, i.e., least square method, Gauss-Seidel (linear algorithm), and Monte Carlo method (Guzek and Lozia 2020; Vossou and Koulocheris 2018; Mozumder et al. 2015; Steffan 2009; Li 2003). The fifth method is based on information extracted from automobiles event data recorder or event data recorder (EDR) tools in vehicles involved in accidents (Nance et al. 2006). EDR records performance and system status data through electrical, audio and video systems. EDR of vehicles senses the pre-crash situation, acceleration during crash, safety restraint system data and driver control input, and post-crash facts such as automatic crash notification (Fay et al. 2002). Such recording tools are vehicle's airbag control module (ACM) (Oga et al. 2018), Black Box, Electronic Control Module (ECM), sensing and diagnostic modules (SDMs) (Singleton et al. 2008), GPS, Residual Speedometer (Chung and Chang 2015), Controller Area Network (CAN), and Tachographs (mainly used in heavy vehicles) (Zago et al. 2020; Baldini et al. 2018; Baek 2016). Some video systems such as DriveCam, MACBox, and BusWatch are installed during the vehicle manufacturing, and the CCTV installation is exterior to the vehicle (Wong et al. 2014; Fay et al. 2002). To reconstruct vehicle accidents, the EDR data is retrieved by a set of hardware and software such as Hexadecimal Translation Tools, Bosh crash data retrieval (CDR) (Singleton et al. 2008; Gazdag et al., 2018), and Vetronix Crash Data Retrieval System (Correia et al. 2001).

Case Study

In November 2004, Danny Hopkins was sentenced to second-degree manslaughter for causing the death of Lindsay Kyle in a car accident. The black box (event information recorder) already installed in Hopkins' vehicle indicated the vehicle was running at 106 miles/h just 4 s before it collided with the rear of Kyle's vehicle, which was halted at a red light. On the off chance that Hopkins' vehicle had not been furnished with an event information recorder, a measurable examination of the physical proof, for example, skid marks and crash harm, could have been utilized to evaluate the vehicle's speed. Nonetheless, the recorded information delivered better accuracy, progressively increasing the forensic investigators' considerable certainty that the vehicle speed was 106 miles/h at the moment of collision.

Accurate reconstruction of the accident scene is entirely dependent on the deformation of an accidental vehicle, skid or yaw marks, body injury of a pedestrian, and traces examined at the accident scene. The first and second methods discussed above are the conventional methods to reconstruct the accident scene. Nowadays, the plastic deformation of a vehicle body and the skid marks is a glimpse of reconstructing the accident scene through conventional methods. Documentation of skid marks cannot always be possible because of the anti-lock braking system in the modern vehicle, or in a case where a driver has not taken measures to make sudden brake or emergency stop, and wet or snowed roadways. In these conditions, vehicles usually do not leave any skid marks. However, performing a crash test to determine vehicle speed at the moment of impact by examining the vehicle's plastic deformation is eventually complicated and more challenging (Zeidler et al. 1985).

On viewing the different conditions and modernization in the vehicle, the field of forensic science is rapidly developing. Before 20–25 years ago, methods for reconstructing any accident scene used by forensic scientists are trivial to modern vehicles. Advancement in accident examination and its reconstruction utilizes advanced methods based on video and images, databases, computer simulation software, and vehicle recording tools (Nogayeva et al. 2020). The change in velocity is often defined in terms of delta-*V* (ΔV) and energy equivalent speed (EES) (Dima and Covaciu 2019; Smit et al. 2019; Vangi 2009). Delta-*V* ultimately depends on the deformation of the vehicle in a crash. NASS-CDS database contains all the delta-*V* estimates using damage-based (Calspan Reconstruction of Accident Speeds on the Highway (CRASH3)) program called Microsoft Windows version of Simulating Motor Vehicle Accident Speeds on the Highway (WinSMASH). Engineering Dynamics Corporation Reconstruction of Accident Speeds on the Highway (EDCRASH) and SLAM are updated version of CRASH3 program (Johnson and Gabler 2014; Iraeus and Lindquist 2013). The post-crash vehicle's Delta-*V* potentially is measured with the help of an event data recorder (EDR) (Nance et al. 2006). The methodology of collision analysis, like energy equivalent speed (EES), is firstly defined by Burg, Martin, and Zeidler (1980) to calculate delta-*V* and EES (Berg et al. 1998). The database as NHTSA, IIHS, EES, etc., provides vehicle types and crash types with images, which can also be maneuvers to calculate the pre-crash velocity of the vehicle (Pinter and Szalay 2018; Gabler and Hinch 2015). Finite Element Method (FEM) and Response Surface Models (RSM) calculate the deformation, but they will take high computational resources and simulation time for kinematic output for the vehicle. Reduced Order Dynamic Model (RODM) can be subsequently employed to reconstruct multiple vehicle accidents. RODM features of simulation of different. The impulse-momentum model combined with RODM assures more accurate and detailed information of velocity and acceleration of any vehicle at every instant (Macurová et al. 2020; Vangi et al. 2019). Mathematical tools of the fuzzy set theory, including general theoretical tasks, are generally used in the reconstruction of accident scene. The main advantage of the fuzzy set theory is to give the possibility of matching the qualitative and quantitative index even under inaccuracy and insufficiency of initial documentation (data) (Vasiliev et al. 2017). In a car-pedestrian accident, the analysis process utilizes the JARI's pedestrian model and validation using Postmortem Human Subject (PMHS) and ITARDA accident data and reconstruction process (Konosu 2002). Given the reconstruction of the vehicle's continuous collision in an accident, trajectory preview iterative algorithm, serial collision, contact position, reconstruction localization algorithm, trace inspection reconstruction algorithm, and vehicle serial collision accident reverse-phase combination algorithm are used (Lang et al. 2013). Other models, such as McHenry, Brach, and Ishikawa, define conservation of energy and conservation of linear or angular momentum. Brach's (Planer Impact Mechanics) collision model integrates with the least square method to calculate impact coefficient and unknown velocity components (Vossou and Koulocheris 2018).

Reconstruction of the accident scene predominantly depends on proper documentation of the accident scene. Conventional documentation methods are less prompt and two dimensionally reconstruct the scene since the measurements are taken along and offset either from road edge or centerline. Recent advancement uses complex total station, laser rangefinder (LRF), Global Positioning (GPS), tachymeters, CCTV, dash camera, prism, photogrammetry (a technique to measure 3D and represent using data stored in a 2D photo and video), and terrestrial laser scanner (TLS) methods for more accurate documentation of accident scene and damaged vehicles. Terrestrial laser scanning (LS) method and photogrammetry method allow 3D documentation of accident scene. Investigating officers can use laser scanners as the safest and fastest method in data collection that can operate in both direct sunlight and darkness (Verolme and Mieremet 2017; Osman and Tahar 2016; Topolšek et al. 2014; Buck et al. 2013; Oguchi et al. 2011, 2013; Lee 2009).

Documentation through sketching of crime scenes carries different significance for later examination. Conventional handheld sketching techniques required colossal time and man-force. Some advanced 3D sketching programs include SketchUp (SU) that is supported by Google Earth's (GE) Digital Elevation Model (DEM), 3D Warehouse (3DW), and Aerial Photography. This SU involves documenting accident scenes imported into HVE as a 3D environment (Roberts III et al. 2011). HVE also has some physics models, such as 2D and 3D total reconstruction solutions, such as SIMON, DyMESH, EDVAP, EDVSM, EDVDS, Engineering Dynamic Corporation Simulation Model of Automobile Collision (EDSMAC), or EDSMAC4 (Fittanto and Rodowicz 2012; Fay et al. 2001). Documentation of pedestrian or person involved in an accident carries significant evidence on their body. Injury inside and outside of the body can also be utilized to reconstruct impact velocity. Tools, such as multi-slice computed tomography (MSCT) and magnetic resonance imaging (MRI), are used for documentation and analysis of internal and external body (Buck et al. 2007). These accident reconstruction tools permit experts to analyze and reconstruct a wide range of accidents scene accurately.

The application of advanced simulated tools for accident reconstruction has significant advantages over conventional methods. The most important benefit is the result of accident reconstruction. The conventional approach is highly reliant on the theoretical and practical knowledge of a forensic expert. Still, advanced simulated tools ease reconstructing accident scenes with more accuracy with minimum human resources. These advanced tools may significantly reduce the overall time taken and the difficulties of accident reconstruction when utilizing conventional techniques (Nogayeva et al. 2020). Another advantage of utilizing advanced tools depends on the intricacy of some accidents. Demonstrating vehicle crush, applying momentum examination to a multivehicle pile-up impact, and three-dimensional models are very likely circumstances that cannot be tackled without a computer. Added intricacy to the code allows the end of certain suppositions, and in this way, makes a more remarkable precision in the reconstruction.

16.11 Conclusions

This chapter represents the introduction to vehicle accidents and techniques to investigate and reconstruct the accident scene. Road accident is as heinous and complicated to reconstruct. Multiple collision and vehicle pileup are even more complicated to reconstruct. Knowledge of accident types comes with essential factor in accident scene investigation. The investigating officer should know the accident background and planning for investigating process and its systematic implementation to succeed in accident investigation. Collecting evidence based on objectives and continuous communication between the investigation team prevent the investigation from diverting and saturating. Sense of four Ps evidence to the investigating officer eases evidence collection and understanding the vehicle situation.

Methods for reconstruction of the accident scene are split into conventional and advanced tools. Conventional methods conclude theories, empirical formulas, and methods based on true vehicle tests (Crash test). Theories and formulas like conservation of momentum, conservation of energy, and friction coefficient of vehicle tire collectively are used to reconstruct the vehicle's speed before, during, and after the collision. The friction coefficient of vehicle tires varies in reference to different surfaces, ages, and conditions published by the manufacturer routinely. Sometimes, the investigating officer performs a crash test by himself to find the friction coefficient of the vehicle. Manually performing any crash test to reconstruct requires the same environmental and vehicle condition, which voids and increases the chances of error in reconstruction. Advancement in technology is utilized in accident investigation to overcome the limitations of conventional methods. The utilization of advanced tools is classified into three classes, i.e., documentation, event data recorder (EDR) of vehicles, and computer simulation software. The pitfalls of applying advanced tools for documentation and computer simulation software for reconstruction work are that the investigating officer becomes less involved and may save money and resources. EDR is a tool installed during the vehicle manufacture that helps to understand the pre-crash, during the crash, and post-crash velocity, and vehicle conditions. Conventional methods only present 2D models but with advanced tools reconstruction can be possible in 2D and 3D models using software. The accident database produced by NHTSA, RICSAC, IIHS, NASS-CDS, etc., is based on accident type, deformation, and vehicle utilization as a reconstruction tool.

Dependency as a daily routine on vehicles increases accident cases around the world. The effectiveness of conventional methods used by investigating officers to investigate and reconstruct accidents is currently limited in its ability to keep with the increasing frequency of accident cases, which diminishes the pendency. Therefore, there is a need for investigators to incorporate advanced tools in accident investigations, enabling them to solve with great accuracy and improve the reconstruction of accident events.

References

Baek SH (2016) A reliable and fast data recovery in a digital tachograph. Adv Sci Lett 22:3511–3515. https://doi.org/10.1166/asl.2016.7861

Bailey LB (1960) 1891 Lambert a new claim for America's first gasoline automobile. Antique Automobile 24(5):340–400

Baldini G, Sportiello L, Chiaramello M, Mahieu V (2018) Regulated applications for the road transportation infrastructure: the case study of the smart tachograph in the European Union. Int J Crit Infrastruct Prot 21:3–21. https://doi.org/10.1016/j.ijcip.2018.02.001

Berg FA, Walz F, Muser M, Bürkle H, Epple J (1998) Implications of velocity change delta-V and energy equivalent speed EES for injury mechanism assessment in various collision configurations. JRCOBI Conference—Göteborg

Bhuvanesh M, Padmanaban J, Goldberger S (2015) Development of accident reconstruction using in-depth accident investigation data in India. IRCOBI Conference 2015

Bohan TL (2009) Essentials of forensic science—crash and collapses. Facts on File Inc.

Böhm K, Kubjatko T, Paula D, Schweiger HG (2020) New developments on EDR (event data recorder) for automated vehicles. Open Eng 10:140–146. https://doi.org/10.1515/eng-2020-0007

Buck U, Naether S, Braun M, Bolliger S, Friederich H, Jackowski C, Aghayev E, Christe A, Vock P, Dirnhofer R, Thali MJ (2007) Application of 3D documentation and geometric reconstruction methods in traffic accident analysis: with high resolution surface scanning, radiological MSCT/MRI scanning and real data based animation. Forensic Sci Int 170:20–28. https://doi.org/10.1016/j.forsciint.2006.08.024

Buck U, Naether S, Rass B, Jackowski C, Thali MJ (2013) Accident or homicide—virtual crime scene reconstruction using 3D methods. Forensic Sci Int 225:75–84. https://doi.org/10.1016/j.forsciint.2012.05.015

Cameron S (2008) Forensic investigations: using science to solve crime. Mark Twain Media, Inc.

Chung Y, Chang I (2015) How accurate is accident data in road safety research? An application of vehicle black box data regarding pedestrian-to-taxi accidents in Korea. Accid Anal Prev 84:1–8

Correia JT, Iliadis KA, McCarron ES, Smolej MA (2001) Utilizing data from automotive event data recorders. In: Proceeding of Canadian multidisciplinary road safety conference XII, London, Ontario

Dima DS, Covaciu D (2019) Vehicles frontal impact analysis using computer simulation and crash test. Int J Automot Technol 20(4):655–666. https://doi.org/10.1007/s12239-019-0062-3

Dong B, Ma X, Chen F, Chen S (2018) Investigating the differences of single-vehicle and multivehicle accident probability using mixed logit model. J Adv Transp 2018:1. https://doi.org/10.1155/2018/2702360

Eboli L, Forciniti C, Mazzulla G (2020) Factors influencing accident severity: an analysis by road accident type. Transp Res Procedia 47:449–456. https://doi.org/10.1016/j.trpro.2020.03.120

Fay R, Robinette R, Scott J, Fay P (2001) PC-crash and HVE, an overview of similarities and differences. SAE. ISSN 0148-7191

Fay R, Robinette R, Deering D, Scott J (2002) Using event data recorders in collision reconstruction. SAE. ISSN 0148-7191

Ferry TS (1988) Modern accident investigation and analysis, 2nd edn. Wiley

Fisher BAJ, Fisher DR (2012) Techniques of crime scene investigation, 8th edn. CRC Press/Taylor & Francis Group

Fittanto D, Rodowicz KA (2012) A comparison of 3D model dynamic simulation results with low-speed crash test data. SAE International. https://doi.org/10.4271/2012-01-0601

Franck H, Franck D (2010) Mathematical methods for accident reconstruction: a forensic engineering perspective. CRC Press/Taylor & Francis Group. ISBN: 978-1-4200-8897-7

Gabler H, Hinch J (2015) Evaluation of event data recorders in full systems crash tests. National Highway Traffic Safety Administration, Paper No: 05-0271

Gazdag A, Holczer T, Buttyan L, Zsolt S (2018) Vehicular Can Traffic Based Microtracking For Accident Reconstruction. Vehicle and Automobile Engineering 2:457–465. https://doi.org/10.1007/978-3-319-75677-6_39

Giummarra MJ, Lau G, Grant G, Gabbe BJ (2020) A systematic review of the association between fault or blame-related attributions and procedures after transport injury and health and work-related outcomes. Accid Anal Prev 135:105333. https://doi.org/10.1016/j.aap.2019.105333

Gönczi AL (2013) Reconstruction of an unusual road traffic accident using computer simulation. Int J Eng Tome XI. ISSN 1584-2665

Guzek M, Lozia Z (2020) Computing methods in the analysis of road accident reconstruction uncertainty. Arch Comput Methods Eng 28:2459–2476. https://doi.org/10.1007/s11831-020-09462-w

Horswell J (2004) The practice of crime scene investigation. CRC Press, Boca Raton

Iraeus J, Lindquist M (2013) Analysis of delta velocity and PDOF by means of collision partner and structural involvement in real life crash pulses with modern passenger cars. Traffic Inj Prev 15:56. https://doi.org/10.1080/15389588.2013.793796

Islam MB, Kanitpong K (2008) Identification of factors in road accidents through in-depth accident analysis. IATSS Res 32(2):58–67

James SH, Nordby JJ (2009) Forensic science—an introduction to scientific and investigative techniques, 3rd edn. CRC Press/Taylor & Francis Group

Jirovsky V (2015) Classification of road accidents from the perspective of vehicle safety systems. J Middle Eur Construct Design Cars 13:1–9. https://doi.org/10.1515/mecdc-2015-0005

Johnson N, Gabler HC (2014) Evaluation of NASS-CDS side crash delta-V estimates using event data recorders. Traffic Inj Prev 15:827–834. https://doi.org/10.1080/15389588.2014.881995

Jones IS (1976) The effect of vehicle characteristics on road accidents. Pergamon Press, ISBN 0-08-018963-6, pp 2–5

Kirk DJV (2001) Vehicular accident investigation and reconstruction. CRC Press, Boca Raton

Konosu A (2002) Reconstruction analysis for car–pedestrian accidents using a computer simulation model. JSAE Rev 23:357–363

Lang W, Biao G, Tao C (2013) Vehicle continuous collision accident reconstruction system development. Procedia Soc Behav Sci 96:1659–1669. https://doi.org/10.1016/j.sbspro.2013.08.188

Lee J (2009) Global positioning/GPS. In: International encyclopedia of human geography, pp 548–555. https://doi.org/10.1016/B978-008044910-4.00035-3

Li W (2003) The convergence of the modified Gauss–Seidel methods for consistent linear systems. J Comput Appl Math 154:97–105

Macurová Ľ, Kohút P, Čopiak M, Imrich L, Rédl M (2020) Determining the energy equivalent speed by using software based on the finite element method. Transp Res Procedia 44:219–225. https://doi.org/10.1016/j.trpro.2020.02.050

Mahata D, Narzary PK, Govil D (2019) Spatio-temporal analysis of road traffic accidents in Indian large cities. Clin Epidemiol Global Health 7:586. https://doi.org/10.1016/j.cegh.2019.01.005

Martínez F, Páez J, Furones A, Sánchez S (2016) Pedestrian-vehicle accidents reconstruction with PC-Crash®: sensibility analysis of factors variation. Transp Res Procedia 18:115–121

Mozumder S, Hossain ABMS, Tasnim S, Rahman A (2015) Numerical schemes and Monte Carlo method for black and Scholes partial differential equation: a comparative note. Univ J Comput Math 3(4):30–33. https://doi.org/10.13189/ujcmj.2015.030402

Nance ML, Elliott MR, Arbogast KB, Winston FK, Durbin DR (2006) Delta V as a predictor of significant injury for children involved in frontal motor vehicle crashes. Ann Surg 243:121–125. https://doi.org/10.1097/01.sla.0000193838.11102.56

Naurois CJD, Bourdin C, Stratulat A, Diaz E, Vercher J-L (2017) Detection and prediction of driver drowsiness using artificial neural network models. Accid Anal Prev 126:95. https://doi.org/10.1016/j.aap.2017.11.038

Nogayeva S, Gooch J, Frascione N (2020) The forensic investigation of vehicle–pedestrian collisions: a review. Sci Justice 61(2):112–118. https://doi.org/10.1016/j.scijus.2020.10.006

Noon RK (2009) Scientific method: applications in failure investigation and forensic science. CRC Press/Taylor & Francis Group. ISBN-13:978-1-4200-9280-6

Nyamwange J, Nyamwange M (2014) Major innovations in transportation: evolution of automobiles. Int J Humanit Soc Sci 4(5):1

O'Hara CE, Osterbug JW (1960) An introduction to criminalistics, the application of the physical sciences to detection of crime. The Macmillan Company, New York

Oga R, Takubo N, Kato K, Terashima T, Kida Y, Akita K, Ambe Y, Ishii A (2018) Accident reconstruction with data recorded by electronic control units in vehicles with a pre-crash safety system. SAE Technical. https://doi.org/10.4271/2018-01-1440

Oguchi T, Hayakawa YS, Wasklewicz T (2011) DATA sources. Dev Earth Surf Process 15:189–224. https://doi.org/10.1016/B978-0-444-53446-0.00007-0

Oguchi T, Wasklewicz T, Hayakawa YS (2013) Remote data in fluvial geomorphology: characteristics and applications. Treatise Geomorphol 9:711–729. https://doi.org/10.1016/B978-0-12-374739-6.00262-1

Osman MR, Tahar KN (2016) 3D accident reconstruction using low-cost imaging technique. Adv Eng Softw 100:231–237. https://doi.org/10.1016/j.advengsoft.2016.07.007

Pinter K, Szalay Z (2018) Comparison of data required for accident reconstruction based on crash test. In: LNME. Springer, pp 1–11. https://doi.org/10.1007/978-3-319-75677-6_41

Prasad P, Dalmotas D, German A (2014) An examination of crash and NASS data to evaluate the field relevance of IIHS small offset tests. SAE Int J Trans Safety 2(2):326–335. https://doi.org/10.4271/2014-01-1989

Prentkovskis O, Sokolovskij E, Bartulis V (2010) Investigating traffic accidents: a collision of two motor vehicles. Transport 25(2):105–115. https://doi.org/10.3846/transport.2010.14

Roberts RT, Cornetto AD III, Wahba R (2011) Introduction to HVE 3D environments with Google SketchUp. SAE Limited

Robinson EM (2010) Crime scene photography, 2nd edn. Academic Press is an imprint of Elsevier, pp 442–457. ISBN: 978-0-12-375728-9

Rolison JJ (2020) Identifying the causes of road traffic collisions: using police officers' expertise to improve the reporting of contributory factors data. Accid Anal Prev 135:105390. https://doi.org/10.1016/j.aap.2019.105390

Shaler RC (2012) Crime scene forensic—a scientific method approach. CRC Press/Taylor & Francis Group. ISBN-13: 978-1-4398-9773-7

Shannon D, Murphy F, Mullins M, Eggert J (2018) Applying crash data to injury claims—an investigation of determinant factors in severe motor vehicle accidents. Accid Anal Prev 113: 244–256. https://doi.org/10.1016/j.aap.2018.01.037

Sharma BR (2014) Forensic science in criminal investigation and trial, 5th edn. Universal Law Publishing Co. Pvt. Ltd

Siegel JA, Mirakovits K (2016) Forensic science: the basic, 3rd edn. CRC Press/Taylor & Francis Group. ISBN-13:978-1-4822-5337-5

Singleton N, Daily J, Manes G (2008) Automobile event data recorder forensics. Int Federation Inform Process 285:261–272

Smit S, Tomasch E, Kolk H, Plank MA, Gugler J, Glaser H (2019) Evaluation of a momentum based impact model in frontal car collisions for the prospective assessment of ADAS. Eur Transp Res Rev 11:2. https://doi.org/10.1186/s12544-018-0343-3

Steffan H (2009) Accident reconstruction methods. Veh Syst Dyn 47(8):1049–1073. https://doi.org/10.1080/00423110903100440

Struble DE, Struble JD (2020) Automotive accident reconstruction practices and principles, 2nd edn. CRC Press/Taylor & Francis Group. ISBN-13: 978-0-367-41583-9

Teoh ER, Lund AK (2011) IIHS side crash test ratings and occupant death risk in real-world crashes. Traffic Inj Prev 12:500–507. https://doi.org/10.1080/15389588.2011.585671

Topolšek D, Herbaj EA, Sternad M (2014) The accuracy analysis of measurement tools for traffic accident investigation. J Transp Technol 4:84–92

Vangi D (2009) Simplified method for evaluating energy loss in vehicle collisions. Accid Anal Prev 41:633–641. https://doi.org/10.1016/j.aap.2009.02.012

Vangi D (2020) Vehicle collision dynamics: analysis and reconstruction. Butterworth-Heinemann is an imprint of Elsevier, pp 157–191. ISBN: 978-0-12-812750-6

Vangi D, Cialdai C, Gulino M-S, Robbersmyr KG (2018) Vehicle accident databases: correctness checks for accident kinematic data. Designs 2:4. https://doi.org/10.3390/designs2010004

Vangi D, Begani F, Spitzhüttl F, Gulino M-S (2019) Vehicle accident reconstruction by a reduced order impact model. Forensic Sci Int 298:426.e1–426.e11. https://doi.org/10.1016/j.forsciint.2019.02.042

Vasiliev Y, Evtiukov S, Lukinskiy V (2017) Concept of quantitative assessment of knowledge uncertainty in accident reconstruction tasks. Transp Res Procedia 20:659–664. https://doi.org/10.1016/j.trpro.2017.01.107

Verolme K, Mieremet A (2017) Application of forensic image analysis in accident investigations. Forensic Sci Int 278:137. https://doi.org/10.1016/j.forsciint.2017.06.039

Vincoli JW (1994) Accident investigation and loss control. Wiley

Vossou C, Koulocheris D (2018) A computational model for the reconstruction of vehicle collisions. Mobil Veh Mech 44(3):27–42. https://doi.org/10.24874/mvm.2018.44.03.03

Wach W (2013) Structural reliability of road accidents reconstruction. Forensic Sci Int 228:83–93. https://doi.org/10.1016/j.forsciint.2013.02.026

Wang YW, Lin CN (2008) A line-based skid mark segmentation system using image-processing methods. Transp Res C 16:390–409. https://doi.org/10.1016/j.trc.2007.09.002

Woering MH, Depreitere B, Sloten JV (2021) Estimated and underreported parameters in report based vehicle-bicycle accident reconstructions have a significant influence. Accid Anal Prev 150:105903. https://doi.org/10.1016/j.aap.2020.105903

Wong TW, Tao CH, Cheng YK, Wong KH, Tam CN (2014) Application of cross-ratio in traffic accident reconstruction. Forensic Sci Int 235:19–23. https://doi.org/10.1016/j.forsciint.2013.11.012

Xinguang D, Xianlong J, Xiaoyun Z, Jie S, Xinyi H (2009) Geometry features measurement of traffic accident for reconstruction based on close-range photogrammetry. Adv Eng Softw 40:497–505. https://doi.org/10.1016/j.advengsoft.2008.09.002

Zago M, Longari S, Tricarico A, Carminati M, Pérez MG, Pérez GM, Zanero S (2020) ReCAN e—dataset for reverse engineering of controller area networks. Data Brief 29:105149. https://doi.org/10.1016/j.dib.2020.105149

Zeidler F, Schreirer H, Stadelmann R (1985) Accident research and accident reconstruction by the EES—accident reconstruction method. SAE international congress and exposition. SAE Paper 850256

Zou T, He F, Cail M, Li Y (2018) Methods for describing different result obtained from different methods in accidents reconstruction. Forensic Sci Int 291:253–259. https://doi.org/10.1016/j.forsciint.2018.08.029

Forensic Biology

17

Pushpesh Kushwaha, Manisha Rana, Rajesh Singh, R. K. Kumawat, Ankit Srivastava, and Pankaj Shrivastava

Abstract

The field of forensic biology is an ever-evolving and constantly developing field. It utilizes knowledge of biological concepts and practical approaches that assists in a legal investigation. Forensic biology serves as a significant discipline dealing with multifarious sub-disciplines such as forensic genetics, forensic serology, forensic anthropology, forensic botany, forensic entomology, forensic microbiology, etc. For examination of different biological evidences, bodily fluids, and cellular components related to humans, animals plant or micro-organisms that are encountered at the crime scene or are relatable to the concerned crime. From the development of amthropometrical science in the 1870s by Alphonse Bertillon for personal identification to the currently emerging and developing field of DNA fingerprinting and microbial patterns, forensic biology has provided novel approaches and improved methodology for collection, preservation and analysis of compromised evidences encountered at the crime scene. This chapter deals with the basic introduction of various sub-branches of forensic biology and their utilization in the field of forensic science. The chapter also describes various bodily substances such as hairs, nails, seminal fluid, teeth and botanical evidences such as wood, leaves, pollens, etc., that are generally encountered at the crime scene along with the techniques of their identification and segregation and

P. Kushwaha · M. Rana · R. Singh · R. K. Kumawat (✉)
Serology and DNA Division, State Forensic Science Laboratory, Jaipur, Rajasthan, India

A. Srivastava
School of Forensic Sciences, The West Bengal National University of Juridical Sciences, Kolkata, West Bengal, India

P. Shrivastava
Biology and Serology Division, Regional Forensic Science Laboratory, Gwalior, Madhya Pradesh, India

P. Shrivastava et al. (eds.), *Textbook of Forensic Science*,
https://doi.org/10.1007/978-981-99-1377-0_17

application in the forensic context. A detailed approach of wildlife forensics, forensic entomology, forensic limnology and forensic mycology towards assistance in the criminal investigation has been elucidated in this chapter.

Keywords

Forensic palynology · Forensic entomology · Forensic dendrochronology · Forensic limnology · Forensic mycology · Wildlife forensics

17.1 Introduction

Forensic biology deals with the application of biology, various concepts and procedures involved in biological science in the law enforcement system. It is the outspreaded discipline of forensic science involving the examination of humans, animals and plants in a legal context with diverse sub-disciplines that include forensic anthropology, forensic serology, wildlife forensic, forensic botany, forensic entomology, and forensic mycology. Examination of materials like wood, diatoms, hair, nails, teeth, leaves, seeds, pollen and other biological evidences is done to link the crime scene to the victim and the assailant as well as to establish the identity also.

Human identification is one of the major demands resolved by the application of forensic biology. Anatomical, morphological, biochemical as well as molecular examination of various ranges of biological evidences serve the purpose. Besides, utilization of botanical and zoological evidences can help in linking a suspect to a victim or scene of crime. In addition to this, botanical and zoological evidences can also assist in solving wildlife crimes such as poaching, hunting, and illegal logging of timber. Entomological as well as mycological evidences can provide significant information related to a cadaver such as time since death, cause of death as well as the location of crime.

17.2 Hair

Hair is ubiquitous evidence that can be found at any crime scene in the form of shed hair or cut hair. Considered to be the defining feature for characterizing mammals, hair can be a useful evidence for developing a link between the victim, suspect and scene of crime following the Locard's principle of exchange. Hair evidences is generally encountered in cases involving vigorous combative contact between individuals, as in cases of homicide, sexual assault, etc. The basic process of analysis of hair is depended on hair growth, hair types, and care. The human hair is a vital biomaterial, that principally grows as follicles in the dermis comprises protein, particularly keratin. Hair properties vary broadly across different geographical locations and historical eras and thereby can be useful for the identification of a person's age, gender or ethnicity.

17.2.1 Structure of Hair Follicle

Hair follicle is a miniorgan found in mammalian skin located above the dermal layer of skin. It primarily functions in the differentiation of hair cells, growth of hair shaft and anchoring of hair shaft into the skin (Robertson 1999; Erdoğan 2017).

Development of hair follicle from the embryonic epidermis occurs in the form of an epithelial finger-like structure consisting of several cylindrical concentric cell layers (Fig. 17.1). The outermost cylindrical layer or **outer root sheath (ORS)** surrounds other cellular structure and separates them from the dermis. The middle cylindrical layer or **inner root sheath (IRS)** encases the hair shaft and directs its outward pathways. Innermost layer, the **hair shaft** has a complex arrangement containing various layers. Outermost layer is the cuticle, which comprises of layers of flat, thin overlapping one another as roof shingles followed by the middle region of cortex, which contains the keratin bundles in roughly rod like and cell structures and inner most layer of medulla that is unsystematic and exposed area in the fiber's center (Stenn and Paus 2001; Buffoli et al. 2014).

17.2.1.1 Cuticle

The outer layer of the human hair shaft is called cuticle. It consists of flattened, imbricated, translucent scales, laid one over the other with the open end pointing towards the end of the hair. About fifth-sixths of each scale is covered by the attached scale (Ryder 1963). The pattern of cuticle arrangements, also known as scale patterns can be examined microscopically and are useful in species

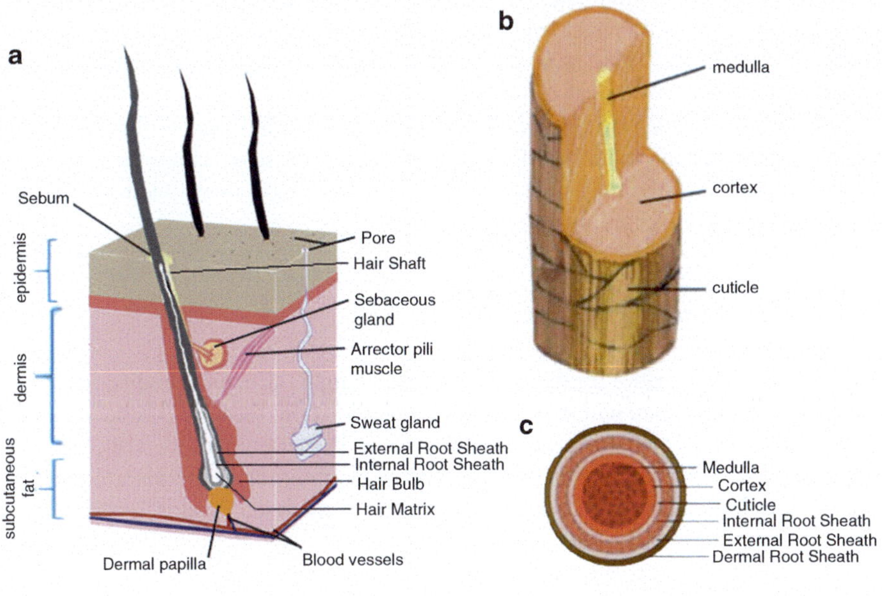

Fig. 17.1 Anatomy of anagen hair follicle (**a**) a cross-sectional anatomy of skin showing the parts of hair follicle; (**b**) longitudinal anatomy of hair shaft; (**c**) cross-sectional anatomy of hair shaft

identifications. Three categories of scale pattern include coronal, spinous and imbricate.

17.2.1.2 Cortex

Cortex is a hollow cylindrical composed of fine fibers of protein material composed of spindle-shaped cells aligned parallel to the axis of hair shaft forming cell membrane complex (CMC). CMCs are responsible for tensile strength of hair and also carry pigment material. The cortical cells also contain keratin micro-fibrils embedded in the sulfur-rich proteinous matrix that provides color to the hairs. Hair cortex also contains melanocytes that produces melanin—a pigment also present in skin and is responsible for providing hair color. The dispersal pattern of melanocyte is another characterizing feature useful in species identification. In humans, the pigments are dispersed more towards the cuticle while in animals they are dispersed more towards the medulla.

17.2.1.3 Medulla

Medulla is the innermost pith of hair shaft that originates lesser or more near the root. Its proteinous matrix differs from cortex and cuticle as it contains granules filled with an amino acid—citrulline. Cellular components of medulla are dispersed in a manner that it appears as a narrow canal with spaces filled with air. The pattern of cellular distribution in medulla are characterizing features in certain species, occupying more than half of hair's diameter, thereby are indicative of species origin (Saferstein 2007). The ratio of diameter of medulla to the diameter of hair shaft is termed as medullary index. In many animals, the medulla is very broad, occupying more than one-third of the shaft's diameter. In human medullary index is generally less than one-third (Zafarina and Panneerchelvam 2009). On the basis of level of modulation, human hair can be classified as no medulla or if present, continuous, interrupted and fragmented.

Arrector pili muscles are the bands of smooth muscle that connects the shaft with the dermis and aids in thermal regulation. Besides, one or more sebaceous glands are also associated with the hair shaft and secrete an oily substance called sebum that helps in lubrication of hair and skin.

17.2.2 Morphology of Hairs

Hair can be differentiated on the basis of color, length, structure, bodily source of origin. Dyed or bleached hair may delude the examination, therefore proper cleaning of hair evidence is a major prerequisite prior to the examination. Also, the root portion of hair must be examined in such cases as roots retain the natural color of hair. Morphological characteristics of hairs such as medullary index, scale pattern, pigment distribution pattern can be employed in the examination. Characteristics features of hair that can be used for identification are tabulated below (Table 17.1):

Table 17.1 Various characteristic features of hairs

S no	Characteristics	Types of hairs
1	Color	White, blonde, light brown, gray brown, dark brown, grey, black, auburn, red.
2	Length	Fragment, 1″, 1–3″, 3–5″, 5–8″, 8–12″, 12–18″, 18–30″, segment.
3	Spatial configuration	Undulating, kinky, curly, wavy, curved, straight, sinuous.
4	Site of location	Scalp, pubic, vulvar, anal, chest, beard, axillary, eyebrow, eyelash, limb, ear, nose.
5	Tip	Singed, uncut, tapered, rounded, sharp cut, cut at angle, frayed, split, crushed, broken.
6	Root	Stretched, absent, bulbous, sheathed, atrophied, follicular, wrenched.
7	Pigment	Absent, non-granular, granular, multicolor, chain, massive (clumped), dense, streaked, opaque.
8	Medulla	Absent, sparse, scanty, fractional, broken, globular continuous, irregular, double, cellular.
9	Cosmetic treatment	Bleached, rinsed, natural, dyed, damaged.
10	Cuticle	Ragged, serrated, looped, narrow, layered, wide, cracked, absent, clear, dyed.
11	Scales	Flattened, smooth, level, arched, prominent, and serrated.

17.2.3 Human Hairs vs. Non-human Hairs

Differentiation of human hair and non-human hair is significant in forensic caseworks. Variations in characters of the above-mentioned anatomical regions of hairs such as scale patterns and medullary index are useful in distinguishing human and non-human hairs. Macroscopic as well as microscopic examination of fine details of hair structure is essential for accurate comparison (Zafarina and Panneerchelvam 2009). Hair-based difference between humans and animals are described in Table 17.2.

Non-human hairs have primary function of thermal regulation. Three types of non-human hairs can be observed namely—vibrissae, bristle and wool. Vibrissae are the long, coarse hairs present in the muzzle area of animals and helps in sensation. Bristles are the short coarse hairs that act as guard hairs. Color of bristle hair is an important criterion for species identification. Wools are the fine hairs that aids in insulation.

Human hairs grow throughout the body except mucus membranes and glabrous skin such as lips palms, feet, labia minora and penis. The human hair is of four types—primordial, lanugo, vellus and terminal. Primordial hairs are formed in the beginning of 3 months after conception. Lanugo hairs are the fetal hairs generally fine and soft in nature and are shed before birth. Vellus hairs are short and fine hair covering entire body except the palms and soles of feet. Terminal hairs are longer and thicker, sex-limited hairs that replaces the vellus hairs. These are produced by hair follicles with sebaceous glands (Robertson 1999).

Table 17.2 Microscopic difference between human and animal hair

Characteristic	Human hair	Animal hair
Hair length	Longer	Generally shorter
Hair color distribution	Consistent throughout the shaft	Shows banding, a radical color change at shorter distance
Cuticle	Scale is small, flattened or imbricate and surrounds the shaft uniformly	Scales are large, polyhedral, wavy and their structure varies throughout the shaft
Medulla	Narrow, may be absent, fragmented, amorphous or discontinuous	Broad, always present and continuous with defined structure
Cortex	Thick, 4–10 times broad as medulla	Thin, rarely more than twice the breath of medulla
Medullary index	Less than 0.3	More than 0.5
Pigment	More towards the periphery of cortex	Uniform, peripheral or central

Hair shape is one of the characterizing features that helps in determining bodily origin as well as aids in racial identification. Human hairs generally lack medulla, and if present, they are of fragmented types. Mongoloids race exceptionally have scalp hairs with continuous medulla. Mongoloids have auburn hairs with thick cuticle and round cross-section. Caucasoids have hairs with oval cross-section, evenly distributed pigmentation and moderate cuticle. Negroids hairs are dense and clumped with flat cross-section and extremely thin or no cuticle.

Hairs can also be distinguished on the basis of their body origin. Scalp hairs are generally long and soft textured with thin medulla as compared to hairs from other body parts. Medulla may range from being continuous to absent. Pubic hairs are coarser hairs with stiff wiry or buckled texture. The medulla if present is broad and continuous. Auxillary hairs have appearance similar to pubic hairs with less extent of buckling. Limb hairs appear in arc-like shape. They have fine diameter with soft texture and have wide medulla with granular appearance. Beard or moustache hairs have triangular cross-section with wide and continuous medulla.

Besides species identification, medullary index can be employed for gender differentiation. Medullary index varies somewhat in male and female hairs and in the hairs from different parts of the body. Ordinarily, the medullary index is greater in woman when hairs from the corresponding parts of the body are compared. The male beard hairs have greater medullary index than hairs from other parts (Srettabunjong et al. 2016).

Biological examination of hair includes techniques such as scale casting, cross-sectioning and micrometrical analysis such as determination of scale count, scale count index, medullary index, hair index etc. Besides these, molecular examination of hair can be useful in sex-determination and individualization of the hair. Hairs in the anagen phase that have sheath cells are most preferable material for molecular examination. Mitochondrial DNA analysis is the most approachable type of DNA typing technique. Elemental analysis of hair using techniques such as emission spectroscopy (ES), X-ray fluorescence (XRF), energy dispersive X-ray microanalysis (EDX), inductively coupled plasma arc mass spectrometry (ICP-MS), and the nuclear-based analyses of neutron activation analysis (NAA) are informative regarding presence of atypical elements or abnormal concentration of any common element in cases of deliberate poisoning or intake from polluted environment.

17.3 Nails

Nail as physical evidence is easily encountered in homicide and sexual assault cases and can aid in linking the criminal with victim and the crime scene. In cases of assaults, if the victim scratches the perpetrator, cells (skin) or hairs can be trapped under fingernails. Then during examination, the accused can be linked to crime. The study about fingernails and toenails is known as 'Onychology' (Onuks-nails and Logia-study). A nail is envelope like tough keratinized covering that protects the fingertips and the adjacent tissues from injuries. The epithelial matrix beneath the nail plate cells aids in the formation of a nail by pushing older nail plate cells forward. The only living part of the nail lies at the proximal end below the epidermis. White crescent-shaped lanula can be seen clearly in the thumb while it may not be visible in the little finger. A healthy nail generally gives slight pinkish hard but flexible smooth, shiny appearance and unspotted without any ridges, pits or splits. The average growth rate of nails is 3 mm in a month and is more in children than adults (Devi and Banu 2015; Kumar et al. 2017) (Fig. 17.2).

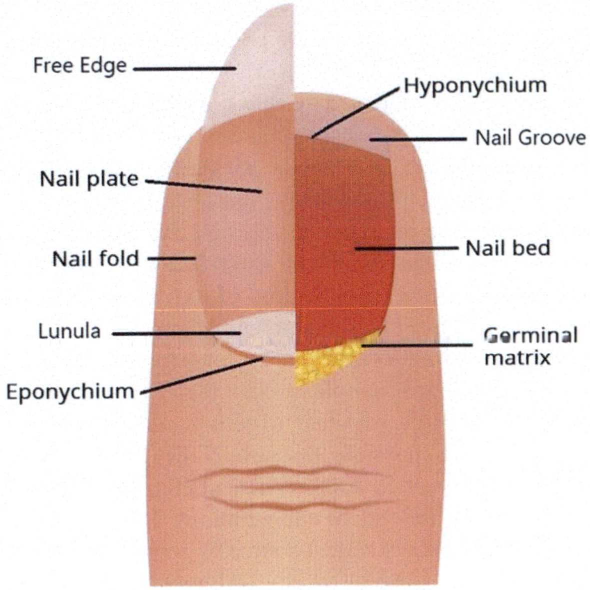

Fig. 17.2 Structural representation of human nail

The major advantage of this evidence is that it is unaffected of most of the external conditions (environmental conditions) and unlike other biological evidence, does not break down easily and can remain at the crime scene for longer time even at a decomposed environment. In addition it is relatively unnoticeable to the untrained eye; therefore a criminal is not likely to make special efforts to destroy the nail evidence, as it is not known to many people that this small nail clipping can also play important role in linking the criminal to either to crime scene or a victim. Its successful evaluation can help in providing useful information in individualization and personal identification. Thus taking this point as a major advantage of using nails for identification purpose in contrast to other body tissues is that the sample size does not matter and sample processing is generally non-destructive and non-invasive and yet each nail retains a discrete record of detailed information on genetic inheritance and individualization. Also, in contrast to other tissues like bones, nails can be easily decontaminated from effect of external environment. The important thing to be kept in mind is that they must be collected carefully in a container (clear micro-centrifuge tube or similar) where dislodged exogenous material would not be lost and medium size clippings should be used. The evidence should be dry in order to prevent degradation of DNA (Hebda et al. 2014). The common methods to collect fingernail evidence are clipping the nail, swabbing beneath the nail using a small, moistened swab, or scraping beneath the nail, generally using a wooden applicator and collecting the debris. While collecting it from the body, hyponychium, the area below the free edge of the fingernail should be thoroughly checked for accumulation of biological and non-biological foreign materials (Bozzo et al. 2015; Devi and Banu 2015). Samples can be collected on a plain sheet of paper or in sterile micro-centrifuge tubes (for DNA analysis). No nail cosmetic or nail treatment should have been done and hands should be thoroughly wash with soap and warm water and then allowed to dry. Conventional and sterilized metallic nail clippers should be used. The samples can easily be stored at room temperature (Grover and Bansal 2017).

Once the nail evidence reaches the laboratory, its examination can be done using scanning electron microscopy and atomic force microscopy for obtaining discrete information (Devi and Banu 2015). Microscopic examination looking for any external material (blood, skin, hairs etc.) can be done (Foran et al. 2015). Nail surface can also be examined using compound microscope in order to determine any possible difference in color. FT-IR (ATR) spectroscopy technique can be used for non-destructive identification of molecular species. The “fingerprint region” of the keratin fiber (FTIR spectral region between 1750 and 750 cm^{-1}) can be analyzed as it mainly consists of the major amide bands, CH deformations cysteine oxides. In cases where control samples are not readily available or in cases where the unknown samples cannot be matched to either nail from the particular animal or suspect animal, it is then possible, through FT-IR microscopy to establish the characteristics of a nail (Italiya et al. 2009). The nail clippings can be compared using comparison microscope for individual nail striations (Loveleen 2017).

Nails can be an excellent source of germline DNA for genetic analyses in almost all forensic and clinical aspects. Although, the special structure of nails (DNA in keratinized cells) makes DNA extraction more complex but it can yield a high amount of DNA if standard and well-defined protocols and reagents are used for lysing keratin, without compromising the quality of DNA.

17.4 Teeth

Teeth as a forensic evidences are the most commonly traced and sometimes, the only evidences left for forensic human identification in cases of mass disasters, mutilated, decomposed and burnt body remains (Shah et al. 2019). The persistence and longevity of teeth in extremely harsh condition of extreme heat and pressure is attributable to their structural composition comprising of calcified minerals (Yukseloglu et al. 2019). Biologically, a tooth is composed of four dental tissues, comprising of three calcified hard tissue namely enamel, dentine and cementum and a non-calcified soft tissue—pulp. Enamel of a tooth made up of calcium phosphate is considered as the hardest part of human body that protects the internal components of tooth. Dentin is a hard tissue similar to bone but is sensitive to touch and thermal variation. Cementum helps in cushioning the tooth firmly to the jaw bone. Pulp is the central part of tooth that holds the nerves and blood vessels. An adult human dentition comprises of 32 teeth categorized into 4 types of teeth namely incisors, canines, pre-molar and molar (Arola et al. 2017) (Fig. 17.3).

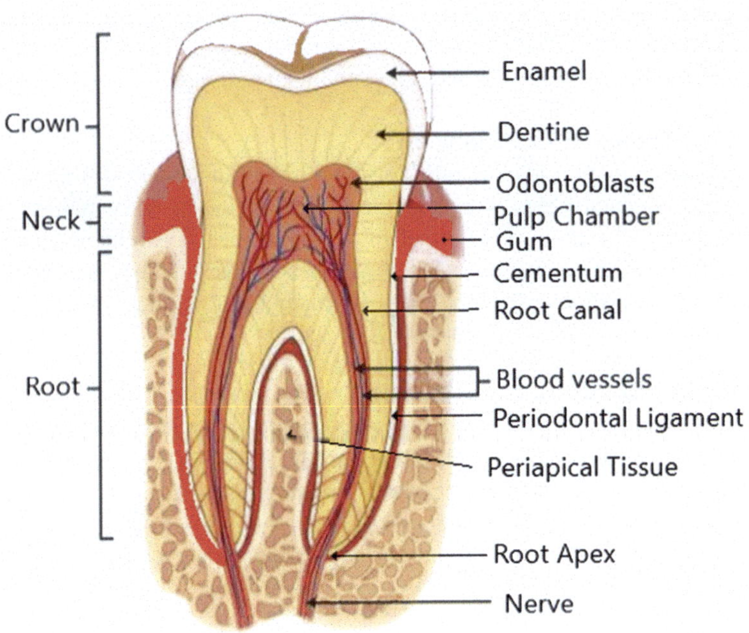

Fig. 17.3 Structure of human tooth

Forensic dentistry aids in human identification by determining age, gender and race based on the variation in dental pattern that includes inter-space between teeth, tooth's individual unique characteristics, dental anomalies etc. Also, forensic dentistry plays an important role in cases of sexual abuses, criminal deaths etc. involving bite mark patterns left in the form of defensive wounds. The field of forensic dentistry encompasses examination of bite-mark patterns, tooth prints, radiographic and photographic examination, dental DNA analysis as well as rugoscopy, and cheiloscopy (Adler et al. 2011; Krishan et al. 2015; Divakar 2017).

17.4.1 Age Estimation

Assessment of dental age is one of the accurate methods for estimation of chronological age as it is least affected by nutritional and endocrinal activities. Development of tooth is a continual process that initiates at embryonic stage, progressing till early adult life and is reliable on various factors such as inter-spacing, and other local as well as systemic factors (Divakar 2017; Shah et al. 2019) . Chronological sequence of mineralization and eruption sequences of both deciduous and permanent set of teeth has been described in the Table 17.3.

Various methods for estimation of dental age have been proposed under the following categories.

17.4.1.1 Visual Examination

Assessment of eruption condition of tooth, dental anomalies and degenerative changes in teeth such as subsequent wear and tear, attrition etc. are some of the reliable criteria that provide information related with individual's chronological age.

17.4.1.2 Histological Examination

Histological examination is evidential for determining the extent of mineralization especially in neonatal cases where the teeth are not sufficiently radiopaque for radiographic visualization. Assessment of neonatal lines is a reliable method for determining age of babies in days. Also, the increment lines in the cementum, known as cementum annulations, cross striation in enamel due to gradual deposition of enamel are also informative for estimation of age.

17.4.1.3 Morphological Examination

Conditions of completion of dental development stages, i.e. in case of elderly adults, require alternate method for age determination. Morphological examinations of teeth for age determination fits well in such cases and rely on the subsequent variation in the dental structures throughout one's life. Generally, morphological assessment is applicable to teeth from body remains of dead adults and involves assessment of mineralization extent of adult teeth.

Table 17.3 Chronology of mineralization and eruption sequences of Human Dentition Set

Jaw	Tooth	Eruption sequence	Initiation of calcification	Completion of crown	Completion of root
Permanent set of dentition					
Maxillary	Central incisor	4	3–4 months	4–5 years	10 years
	Lateral incisor	6	10–12 months	4–5 years	10–11 years
	Canine	12	4–5 months	6–7 years	14–15 years
	First premolar	8	1.5–1.75 years	6–7 years	12–14 years
	Second premolar	10	2–2.5 years	7–8 years	13–14 years
	First molar	2	At birth	4–5 years	9–10 years
	Second molar	14	2.5–3 years	7–8 years	15–16 years
	Third molar	16	7–9 years	12–16 years	18–25 years
Mandible	Central incisor	3	3–4 months	3–4 years	9 years
	Lateral incisor	5	3–4 months	4–5 years	9–10 years
	Canine	7	4–5 months	5–6 years	12–13 years
	First premolar	9	1–2 years	6–7 years	12–14 years
	Second premolar	11	2–3 years	7 years	14–15 years
	First molar	1	At birth	3–4 years	9–10 years
	Second molar	13	2–3 years	7–8 years	14–15 years
	Third molar	15	8–10 years	12–16 years	18–25 years
Deciduous set of dentition					
Maxillary	Central incisor	2	3–4 months in utero	2 months	2.5 years
	Lateral incisor	3	4 months in utero	2–3 months	2.5 years
	Canine	7	4–5 months in utero	9 months	3.5 years
	First molar	5	4 months in utero	6 months	3 years
	Second molar	10	5 months in utero	11 months	4 years
Mandible	Central incisor	1	3–4 months in utero	2–3 months	2.5 years
	Lateral incisor	4	4 months in utero	3 months	2.5 years

(continued)

Table 17.3 (continued)

Jaw	Tooth	Eruption sequence	Initiation of calcification	Completion of crown	Completion of root
	Canine	8	4–5 months in utero	9 months	3.5 years
	First molar	6	4 months in utero	6 months	3 years
	Second molar	9	5 months in utero	10 months	3.5 years

17.4.1.4 Radiological Examination

Radiological examination provides graphical visualization of teeth structure and helps in determining dental age in two approaches, i.e. by tooth eruption pattern and dental maturity based on their extent of mineralization. Advanced imaging technologies offer visualization of radiopaque spots on teeth that extends from the period prior to teeth calcification till the closure of teeth apex. In, simpler words, radiographic examination of teeth provide information regarding dental age for age group of children to adolescents. Atlas method and scoring method are the commonly used radiographic methods for assessment of chronological age.

17.4.1.5 Bio-chemical Examination

Bio-chemical examinations are beneficial in cases of pre-natal ages ranging up to 6 months, in which the radiographic examinations are unable to provide accurate age due to radiolucent conditions of teeth. Bio-chemical examinations in such conditions involve correlation of dry weights and heights of tooth's crown with chronological age. Racemization of amino acids is another bio-chemical marker of age determination in cases of adults.

17.4.2 Gender Determination

Gender of the unknown deceased is another criterion for narrowing down the range of persons to be identified for positive identification of such deceased. Like skeletons, teeth possess the characteristics of sexual dimorphism, i.e. different morphological features depending upon the gender of an individual. Morphological as well as molecular examination of teeth assists in determining gender of an individual.

17.4.2.1 Morphological Examination

Morphological measurements of dental indices such as mandibular inter-canine arch widths, distances of molar cusps, canine dimorphism, root length and crown diameter are the common grounds for gender determination. However, ratio of enamel, dentin and pulp tissue play a major role in describing the sexual dimorphism in crown morphology and size of the permanent dentition (Khangura et al. 2011; Krishan et al. 2015).

17.4.2.1.1 Root Length and Crown Diameter

Mesiodistal crown diameter of incisors and canines, bucco-lingual crown diameter along with the length of root region are useful morphological criteria for distinction of gender.

17.4.2.1.2 Canine Dimorphism

Variation in measurements of canine parameters such as mesiodistal arch width, buccolingual width, canine size, height etc. between males and females can be employed for gender determination of any evidence.

Besides other canine dimorphic features, inter canine arch width can also be an useful parameter for differentiating males and females. Inter canine arch width is the distance between the cusp tips of both the canines and are found to be higher in males than in females.

17.4.2.2 Molecular Examination

Molecular analysis of teeth for sex determination involves examination of barr bodies, F-bodies, Sex determining regions of Y (SRY) gene, enamel protein-amelogenin gene.

17.4.2.2.1 Barr Bodies

Sex chromatins found in the nuclei of cells are found to be highly stained by nuclear dyes in females and are often termed as Barr bodies. These are indicative of the inactive X chromosome present in the somatic cells of females, thereby can be useful in gender determination.

17.4.2.2.2 F-Bodies

Y-chromosomes (found in males) possess a binding fluorescent dye, quinacrine, creating a bright fluorescent spot (F body) visible in ultraviolet light.

17.4.2.2.3 Sex Determining Regions of Y (SRY) Gene

The sex-determining region Y (SRY) gene is responsible for generation of HMG box protein that assists in testis formation by means of specific DNA-binding activity. SRY gene is located on the short arm of the Y-chromosome at p11-31. Detection of SRY gene in odontological evidence may point to a male (but not female) genotype.

17.4.2.2.4 Amelogenin Gene

Amelogenin (AMEL) is a componential protein essential for development of tooth enamel. The AMEL gene is located on both X and Y chromosome. AMEL-X allele is 2872 base pair long and located at the Xp22.1–Xp22.3 area of X-chromosome, while the human AMEL Y-allele is a 3272 base pair component situated at Yp11.2 section of Y-chromosome.

17.5 Botanical Evidences and Their Forensic Examinations

Evidences originated from plants and plant materials that are informative in forensic cases are categorized under botanical evidences. These botanical materials can be unique and specific to a location and thereby can be useful in linking a perpetrator, victim and crime scene. Plants can provide information such as seasonal duration, geographical location of crime as well as identification and location of primary and secondary crime scene. The botanical aspects deals with the study of anatomy, morphology, development, taxonomy of plant and the forensic aspects deals with the recognition, collection, preservation and admissibility of botanical evidence in court of law. These evidences can be found on the dead-bodies, on cloths, footwear, nails or hairs of victim and/or accused. Forensic botany is classified into sub-categories such as dendrochronology, palynology, limnology, ecology etc. These sub-disciplines are engrossed with the analysis of plant materials and their relation with the environment in which they are found. Some of the important botanical evidences and their forensic examination techniques are discussed hereunder.

17.5.1 Forensic Examination of Woods

Woods can be related to a crime in various forms ranging from large logs or sticks as a weapon of crime, or tiny twigs as a trace evidence that can aid in linking victim-perpetrator-crime scene. Besides, illicit trade of wood and timber is another condition that requires forensic identification of wood (Wiedenhoeft 2006). The contemporary techniques of identification are much useful in identification of wood. Physical examination of wood involves assessment of color, texture, hardness, weight, lustre (Barbour 2004).

17.5.1.1 Color

Color distinction between the light-colored outer sapwood and dark-colored inner heartwood is well defined is many woods and thereby helps in distinct identification of wood. Sapwood is involved in conduction of minerals from roots to stem. Heartwood is deposition of tannins, resins, oils, gums and helps in mechanical support to the stem. Size of sapwood differs largely across a variety of species from the wide sapwood as seen in black cherry to the narrow sapwood as in locust. The color darkness and the odor of heartwood in tree species such as red cedar, black walnut is distinct and individualized feature of these species.

17.5.1.2 Florescence

Florescence is a distinct character in woods such as Staghorn sumac (*Rhus typhina*), Bijasal (*Pterocarpus marsupium*), Black Locust (*Robinia pseudoacacia*), and Padauk (*Pterrocarpus dalbergioides*). Black Locust (*Robinia pseudoacacia*) and Mulberry (*Morus* spp.) are identical woods in terms of appearance and weight. They can be differentiated on the basis of florescence. Black locust emits a strong yellow green light while Mulberry shows no florescence when exposed to a black light or UV-light (Davies 2017).

17.5.1.3 Odor

Odor is a subtle but sometimes very useful characteristic in examination of woods. Woods such as teak, deodar, chir, rosewood and ton can be identified by means of their characteristic odors.

17.5.1.4 Hardness

Hardness of wood can be related to its density, strength and weight. It is the characteristics of wood to resist the penetration by any foreign body. Soft woods are readily indented by fingernails while moderately harder woods can be dented with sharp knife. Hard woods are difficult to be penetrated by means of sharp objects.

Visual analysis of anatomical characteristics of woods at both macroscopic and microscopic level is beneficial for wood identification. Heartwood and sapwood can also be classified on the basis of vessel elements or pores that are present only in heartwoods. Classification of woods into porous and non-porous, pore size, pore number and pore arrangement in case of porous woods (heartwoods), presence of parenchyma, rays and fibers are some of the common anatomical grounds essential for identification of woods (Miller 1991).

17.5.1.5 Pore Size and Pore Arrangements

Pore size can vary from large (observable through naked eye) to small (not visible to naked eye). Pore or vessel arrangement can be categorized on the basis of their position relative to each other into the following.

17.5.1.5.1 Solitary Pores

Solitary pores are the single pores that do not posses any contact with the nearby pores.

17.5.1.5.2 Pore Multiples

Pore multiples is the arrangement of pores that involves clumping of two to five pores.

17.5.1.5.3 Pore Chains

Pore chains are the radial arrangement of multiple pores.

17.5.1.5.4 Nested Pores

Nested pores includes multiple pores clustered together in radial as well as tangential directions.

17.5.1.5.5 Wavy Band

Wavy band is the arrangement of pores in the manner of irregular concentric bands.

17.5.1.6 Parenchyma

Wood or xylem parenchyma cells are vertically and axially arranged elements of a complex tissue and are concerned with the storage of food in form of carbohydrates, fats and conduction of water. Parenchyma cells are characteristic elements of hardwoods and are scarcely found in softwoods. Based upon the location of parechyma with respect to the pores, it can be categorized into two broad types—paratracheal and apitracheal and therefore, are counted upon as one of the useful features in wood identification. Paratracheal parenchyma is the one that is located in close proximity of the pores whereas apitracheal parenchyma are separated from pores by means of rays and fibers.

17.5.1.7 Wood Rays

Wood rays or medullary rays are narrow strips or ribbon-like structure running perpendicular to the growth rings running from inner to outward directions. They are involved in transportation of food and water across the wood's diameter. Woods of different species can be distinguished on the basis of size and distribution of rays across the specimen.

17.5.1.8 Tyloses

Tyloses are the balloon-like ingrowths of parenchyma protruding into the lumen of adjacent vessels obstructing the opening of vessel elements. Presence or absence and distribution of tyloses (if present) is a ground useful for distinguishing wood species (Fig. 17.4).

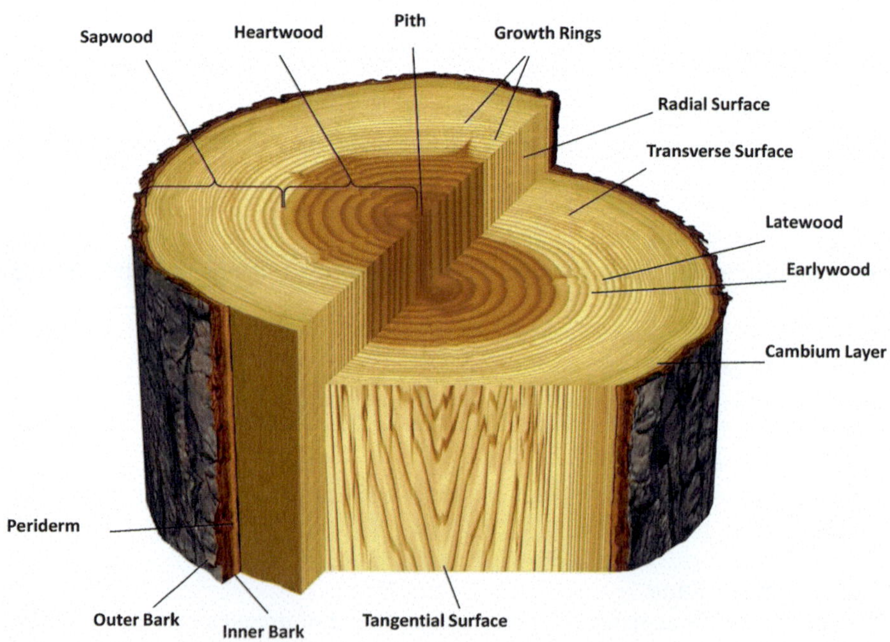

Fig. 17.4 Cross-sectional diagram of wood

17.5.1.9 Dendrochronology

It is a well characterized discipline that is useful for wood identification. It involves the determining age of wood by examining the tree growth increments. Growth rings are concentric annular rings layer seen in secondary xylem in a cross-section of wood formed during one growth season. Spring wood or early wood is formed during spring season in which cambium is in highly active state and produces ample number of xylem substances. On the contrary, autumn wood or late wood is produced during winter season in which the activity of cambium is suspended thereby producing few number of xylem substances. Counting the number of annual tree growth rings can provide details regarding the minimum age of wood. Also, the comparison of pattern of the rings on a wood to that of a parent tree can help in individualization of the wood and its identification (Dormontt et al. 2015). But, application of dendrochronology is confined to a limited group of timbers from tropical region that produces growth rings.

Radio-carbon dating is more promising technique for determining the age of wood. It involves estimating the ratio of C_{14}-C_{12} isotope of carbon and comparing with the standard value that provides the radio-carbon age of that particular wood. Similarly, ratio of stable isotopes of several chemicals synthesized from the trees such as Sulphur, Strontium can provides information regarding the geological area of origin of plant and its climatic conditions (Allen and Huebert 2014). Near Infrared spectroscopy (NIRS) technique that involves exposure of sample to near infrared light can reveal information regarding physical and chemical components of the wood and helps in distinguishing different species of same genus as well as same species found in different location (Ma et al. 2019). Phytochemicals present within the heartwood of timber in form of exudates and extractives can be traced by means of mass spectrometry (MS) technique that involves ionization of chemical substances into charged molecules and measurement of the mass-charge ratio (Altemimi et al. 2017).

Anatomical evaluation of woods is well-to-do for identification of woods, however, the accuracy of identification decreases with decreasing size of wood. Molecular examination of wood can successfully aid in identification of trace samples of wood.

At molecular level, the technique of DNA barcoding is a promising technique for identification of plant species. The range of samples for DNA barcoding extends to all stages of a plant's life, i.e. from flowering, seedling condition to mature plants as well as decomposing plant specimens under environment condition and in the gut and fecal remnants of animals (Kress—plant DNA barcodes) applications today and in the future. Frequently used barcoding region of plants include rbcL gene, trnH-psbA gene, matK gene and internal transcribed spacer (ITS) region of ribosomal cistrons (Kang et al. 2017).

17.5.2 Leaves

Leaves are one of the easiest parts of a plant that aids in identifying the specific plant, its growth conditions, soil type and thereby can help in identifying the location of primary and secondary scene of crime. Such evidences can easily be located clutched in victim's hands or stuck in hairs; trapped in wheels of vehicles used in crime or at the bottom soles of shoes of victim/suspect. A leaf is defined as an expanded lamina attached to the plant's stem by means of stalk or petiolate.

17.5.2.1 Structure of a Leaf

Leaf is a bilateral, flattened part on the stem developing from the bud and comprises three basic structures—leaf-base, petiole and lamina. Leaf base helps in attachment of leaf to the stem. Petiole is a stalk-like structure that extends from the leaf lamina to leaf base and helps in holding the leaf as per desired exposure to sunlight. A leaf with no petiole is known as sessile leaf and the one with petiole is known as petiolate leaf. Lamina is a broad, flattened and expanded structure of leaf consisting of meshy network of midrib, veins and veinlets. These veins help in providing rigidity to the lamina and act as network of water and nutrients for the leaf (Fig. 17.5).

Microscopic examination of morphological and anatomical structure of non-degraded and dried leaves helps in distinguishing them and identifying their origin plants (Thyagharajan and Raji 2019). The shape, margin and surface of lamina vary in different leaves and therefore can be used for identification of a leaf. Presence or absence of incision on leaf lamina is another useful criterion for distinguishing leaves. If the incisions do not touch the midrib, the leaves can be classified as **simple** leaves. In case of incisions reaching the midrib and dividing the lamina into

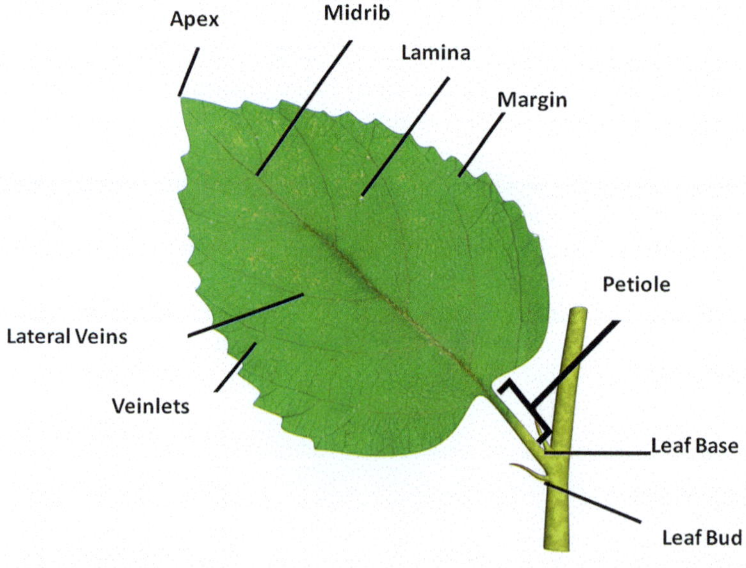

Fig. 17.5 Anatomy of a leaf

numerous leaflets, the leaves are said to be **compound** leaves. Compound leaves with common axis are said to be **pinnately compounded** leaves while the leaflets attached at the tip of petiole, at a common point, the leaves are said to be **palmately compounded** leaves (Oguchi et al. 2018). Various other grounds such as vein counts, stomata index, palisade ratio, types of trichomes, nature of epidermal cells and stomata, that can can be utilized for morphologically distinguishing the leaves are discussed below (Bhatia et al. 1973).

17.5.2.2 Vein Counts and Venation

The arrangement of veins and veinlets on the lamina of leaves is known as venation. The hierarchy of veins forms a complex reticulate mesh. The first-order veins or major veins are one or more in number, ribbed with vascular tissue and schlerenchyma that stretches from the petiole to leaf apex. Second-order veins split off from major veins at certain intervals and the third-order veins branches between the second-order veins, connecting them. Angiosperms have wide diversity in venation extending upto four orders of veins that can be distinguished on the basis of time of formation, size and branching (Sack and Scoffoni 2013).

17.5.2.3 Stomatal Index

Stomatal index can be defined as the ratio of number of stomata to the total number of stomata and epidermal cells present in a given area of leaf. It can be formulated by the equation: Stomatal index $= S * 100/(E + S)$, where, S is the number of stomatal cells and E is the number of epidermal cells in a specified area of leaf (Rowson 1946). Stomatal density can be described as number of stomata cells present in unit area of leaf. Stomata cells are concerned with exchange of gases in plants and therefore, the pattern of their distribution can be useful differential marker for identifying a plant species (Khan et al. 2014).

17.5.2.4 Palisade Ratio

Palisade ratio can be described as the average number of palisade cells that contains maximum number of chloroplast and are prime site of photosynthesis, present under each upper epidermal cell. Palisade ratio has paramountcy over other features as it remains constant despite of the varying environment and location of plant. However, it is less used in monocot leaves as mesophylls cannot be differentiated into palisade and spongy cells in such leaves.

17.5.2.5 Types of Trichomes

Trichomes are outgrowth appendages of epidermal layer present in the form of epidermal hairs that does the function of preventing water loss during transpiration, protection from UV rays, stress-resistance. Trichomes may be unicellular or multicelluar; glandular or non-grandular; branched or unbranched. They are found with diverse structure as per function in the form of hairs, thorns, scales etc.

Several climatic factors such as temperature, pressure, humidity, amount of available sunlight, etc. influence the structure of leaves (Sharma et al. 2020b). Morphological and physiological variations among the leaves depending upon the climatic factor have been described in Table 17.4. In case of leaves with initial

Table 17.4 Effect of different climates on the structure of leaves

Climate	Effect on leaves
Tropical cold climate	Leaves are large and typically hunter-green and have the capacity to absorb sunlight because the sun is visible for a very short period of time. These kinds of leaves are present mainly towards the pole.
Tropical dry climate	Leaves are much more variable including many compound-leaved legumes and more species with thorns.
Subtropical humid climate	The leaves present in this region are mostly wax coated because of the regular rainfall in the area and the plant and leaves are well nourished because of all the nutrients available.
Temperate climate	All size of leaves is present in this kind of climate because in this type of climate, winters are mild and rainfall is moderate.

degradation stage, molecular examination of leaves can help in tracing the plant source.

17.5.3 Pollen Grains

Forensic palynology was used as a crime-solving tool (murder case) for the first time in 1959 in Sweden. Forensic palynology is the utilization and analysis of pollens and spores in criminal and civil cases (Alotaibi et al. 2020). Due to its morphology and microscopic size, protection from mechanical and chemical destruction and its endurance in the intestine for 21 days, pollen analysis has become an advancing scope for establishing a link between victim(s), suspect(s) and crime-scene(s) and is considered among the best application of Locard's principle of exchange (Bennett and Willis 2002; Arguelles et al. 2015; Boi 2018; Alotaibi et al. 2020). Pollens are an ideal material for investigation as they are microscopic, highly variable and can be found on things which are exposed to or interact with the air (Alotaibi et al. 2020). Pollens, often considered as trace evidences are one of the least destroyable evidence that easily gets attached to any surfaces, skins, and cloths and can remain at a location for a long interval of time. Also, the bi-layered walls of pollens are tough and resistant to the adverse environmental conditions due to the presence of sporopollenin in the outer exine layer, thereby enhancing the retrieval rate of such trace evidences even after a long span of time. Any geographical region can be distinguished from the other in terms of pollen prints of that location. Pollen prints are clusters of pollens from different plants of a location that gets shed due to air current and settle down on the ground in a form of a thin layer. Soil, dirt, dust, ropes and twines, clothing and fabrics, drugs, air filters, plant material, and animal and human material, such as fur, hair and stomach contents are common elements at almost every crime scene (Hirapure et al. 2014; Alotaibi et al. 2020). They are held firmly by their surface due to static charges and are not effectively shed, making them highly valuable as evidence. The structure and outer surface of pollens and spores is highly resistance to environmental factors like heat, cold, washing, smudging and degradation etc. and may remain preserved for many years. Pollen is the male gametophyte of gymnosperms and angiosperms. Its size ranges from 15 to 200 mm; its shape, when dry, is generally oval or spherical. Pollination is the

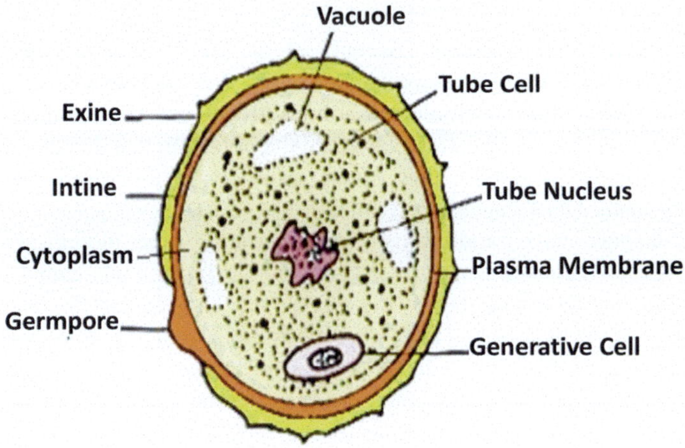

Fig. 17.6 Structural anatomy of pollen grain (microspore)

transport of pollen from its site of production to the female landing site. Analysis of pollen helps in the identification of plants which can determine the geographical origin of a specimen. This creates a link between crime scene and individuals and can determine possession of prohibited or endangered species (Alotaibi et al. 2020) (Fig. 17.6).

Production and dispersion of pollens and spores are important considerations in forensic analysis. If one can guess the expected pattern of production and dispersion of spores and pollens, one can easily know the type of pollen fingerprint of the area (Kumari et al. 2017). Sample collection and recovering pollen from the samples is the crucial step for the identification of pollens (Mildenhall 2006). Soil, dirt, and dust are the most common elements one can find at every crime scene. They should be collected thoroughly and carefully because these elements contain abundant pollen and spores (Kumari et al. 2017). Methods such as tape-lifting for the collection of the microscopic samples, chemical treatments for removal of debris, minerals and other organic substrates, sieving for obtaining the desired size ratio, grain preparation by acetolysis for constant sizing, staining for enhanced visualization are the chronological steps to be performed prior to visual analysis under a microscope. The mounted slide containing the pollen specimen is analyzed using a transmitting light microscope that basically involves the transmission of light through the sample and visualization of the sample through a lens. Quantitative Evaluations of Minerals using a Scanning Electron Microscope (QEMSCAN) is an advanced microscopic technique that involves simultaneous assessment of minerals and other substances as it gives greater pictures and diminutions for pollen grains and has been used in routine analysis since the 1970s. The imaging of pollen grains can also be done due to its increased accuracy, time-saving method, clarity of pictures and decreased human effort. There are three methods for obtaining useful pollen grains images, including transmitted-light microscopy (TLM), the wide field fluorescent method and the structured illumination (Apotome) method. The highest recall is shown by transmitted-light microscopy (TLM) for all types of imaging. All these analyses depend on the role of dispersal (Alotaibi et al. 2020). Recently, using DNA barcoding, it has recently been demonstrated that DNA analysis can be done from even a single pollen grain. Multiple taxonomies groups can be identified using this method along with the identification of parts of the organism that do not appear in the morphology (Bell et al. 2016). One of the fastest ways to differentiate between pollens is by using DNA barcoding (Alotaibi et al. 2020).

Pollen and spores have various advantages over many other biological sources of evidence. Due to their smaller size (avg. 20–60 μm), criminals cannot clean the crime scene as they cannot be seen by the naked eyes. They can adhere to any surface and may become firmly attached even after washing in domestic detergent. Another advantage is that pollens don't decompose. Due to their multi-layered cell wall (composed of cellulose and sporopollenin), they can be preserved for hundreds of millions years as sporopollenin is one of the most chemically resistant organic molecules (Mildenhall 2008). Palynology can be helpful in various aspects such as: relate materials at the disclosure scene or crime scene with a suspect, reduce potential suspects list, determine the movement of things and their origin including their geographic location, helps to decide the perimortem destiny of an unfortunate casualty and finally, help to determine the age of human remains. It can be a profoundly significant precise and powerful method of forensic analysis in cases of rape, murder and other types of crimes, particularly in open areas, but even if they occur in closed premises (Mildenhall 2006; Alotaibi et al. 2020).

17.6 Diatoms

Diatoms are considered to be the most effective and reliable evidence in forensic cases of drowning deaths due to their large diversity of species, expressed morphologically as the difference in size and shape of frustules (Bogusz and Bogusz 2018; Calder 1984). Forensic application of diatoms is studied under Forensic limnology. Diatoms (Bacillariophyta) are microscopic, photosynthetic, uniflagellete alga with a siliceous cell wall found in all varieties of water bodies including fresh water and salt water (springs, rivers, ponds, lakes, ditches) that have been recorded and classified for over 200 years (Horton et al. 2006; Levkov et al. 2017; Vinayak and Gautam 2019). It consists of two overlapping valves: the top called the lid (epitheca) and the bottom valve, called the bottom (hypotheca). The hard cell wall of diatoms impregnated with silica (over 60% of dry weight of diatom), called as frustules which makes it resistant to most chemicals, including strong inorganic acids, hydrogen peroxide and high temperature, making it a specific protective cover for the protoplast (Bogusz and Bogusz 2018; Cameron 2004). The basic principle behind employing diatom analysis in drowning deaths is the potential of diatoms to exist in the organs of the drowned person in case of ante-mortem aspiration of diatom-rich water into the lungs. The smaller size of diatoms ranging between 20 and 200 μm and their morphological structure allow them to seep through the alveolo-capillary barrier and subsequently enter into the blood flow and thereby entering other vital organs such as the spleen, brain, liver, kidneys and bone marrow

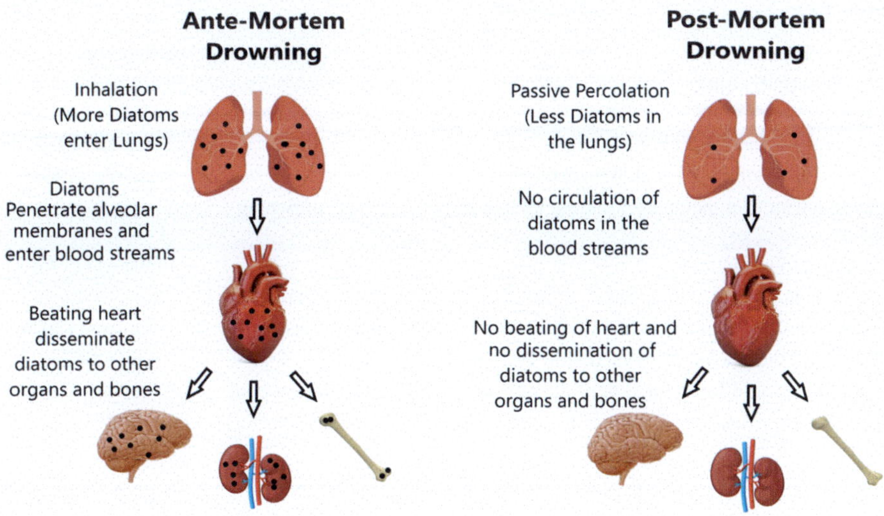

Fig. 17.7 Principle of utilizing diatoms for differentiation of ante-mortem and post-mortem drowning

prior to the death of the person. This forms a major ground to distinguish ante-mortem and post-mortem drowning of a person. Also, the category of diatoms (such as freshwater diatoms, and marine diatoms) detected in a body during autopsy can give an idea about the location of death (Bogusz and Bogusz 2018; Anand and Unmesh 2016; Kaushik et al. 2017). Identifying the provenance of individuals, clothing or materials using diatom analysis can be of further use in forensic science (Horton et al. 2018) (Fig. 17.7).

As per Bogusz and Bogusz (2018), the process of drowning consists of several stages-periods:

1. Fast breathing period (few to several seconds).
2. Resistance period (half a minute to several minutes)—submersion under water.
3. Significant respiratory movement's period (one to two and a half minute)—water entering the respiratory tract.
4. Mortification period (one to one and a half minute)—loss of sensation and unconsciousness.
5. Final breathing period (around 1 min)—tonic convulsions and body strain occur.

Prior to diatoms analysis, the samples to be processed must be thoroughly cleaned from substances such as pigments, cells, sand, mud etc. that might interfere with the visual examination of diatoms. A small section of the sample (~10 g), preferably femoral or sterna bone marrow is taken in a tube and acid digestion is carried out by treating it with concentrated nitric acid (conc. HNO_3) and heating it till a clear solution is obtained. This is followed by the addition of hydrogen peroxidase and boiling of the fluid. The fluid once cooled is then centrifuged, the supernatant is decanted off and the sediment is examined under the microscope. The fluid

Table 17.5 Advancements in diatom analysis

Advancements	References
Detection of diatoms	Timperman (1972)
Detection of diatoms in bone marrow	Tamaska (1949)
Diatoms indicative of antimortem drowning	Porawski (1966)
Development of a method for diatom test for direct screening drowning deaths	Timperman (1972)
Acid digestion method	Pollanen (1998)
Use of a mixture of HNO_3 and H_2O_2 for the digestion of tissue samples	Auer (1988)
Use of nitric acid for extraction of diatoms from bone marrow tissue	Hurlimann (2000)
Use of sulphuric acid for extraction of diatoms	Krstic (2002)
Use of nitric acid for extraction of diatoms from lungs and sternum bone	Bortolotti (2011)
Use of H_2O_2 extraction technique for diatom samples from clothes	Scott (2014)

containing the diatoms is dropped on a glass slide, thermally fixed on a hot plate and mounted using Naphrax before visualizing it under the microscope. Comparison of all the species of diatoms recovered from the specimen and the suspected site of drowning can help in correlating the events. In absence of a reference or control water sample, the presence of a preset minimal number of diatoms in different vital organs can help in the establishment of ante-mortem drowning. By using Fluorimetry (luminescent properties), diatom samples can be located in the bone marrow and then can be differentiated from other diatoms found in nature by incorporating specific fluorescent tags. Using electric impedance spectroscopy, diagnosis of putrefactive corpses can also be done.

Advanced technique for diatom test includes visualization through scanning electron microscope and molecular analysis including PCR-based DNA sequencing. Molecular biology-based technique can be used for the detection of 16S rRNA subunits of ribosomal RNA (Rana and Manhas 2018; Zhou et al. 2020) (Table 17.5).

In cases of drowning, the identification of diatoms has been considered to be the "gold standard" (Khurshid et al. 2021). The diatoms can also be significant even occasionally if they have been recovered from the internal organs of non-drowning bodies. In the near future, Advanced technologies such as Nuclear Magnetic Resonance (NMR), Fluorimetry, Molecular biological techniques, Automatic Diatom Identification and Classification (ADIAC) etc. can be used for the detection of diatoms (Rana and Manhas 2018).

17.7 Wildlife Forensics

Wildlife forensics is an advancing field of criminal investigation which aims at using scientific procedures to examine, identify, and compare evidence from crime scenes related to plants and animals but also in monitoring the health and impact of environmental factors on the well-being of wildlife populations. Poaching is one of the most serious crimes investigated by wildlife forensic scientists. Other crime

Fig. 17.8 Types of offences related to wildlife

against wildlife includes the illegal trade of protected animals and products made from protected animals (Bell 2011; Gouda et al. 2020).

Major types of evidence encountered and analyzed in a wildlife crime include any part of an animal such as whole animals (live or dead), skins or skeletons of vertebrate species, exoskeletons and shells of invertebrate species (such as butterflies, rhinoceros beetles and mollusc shells) and animal body parts (intact or processed, such as internal organs, whole feet/legs/wings/heads/fins, furs, feathers, scales, teeth, beaks, claws, muscle fillets, powdered shells/skeletons/skins and blood samples), carcasses, hair, teeth, claws, talons, tusks, hides, stomach contents etc. Wildlife forensic scientists may also investigate materials used to kill or harm animals, such as poisons, pesticides, projectiles, and weapons. Identification and individualization of products that are made from animals such as leather goods and medicines are also of interest (Fig. 17.8).

Variety of biological disciplines such as hair and fiber analysis, blood splatter analysis, DNA analysis; chemical, pathological as well as physical examination of various evidences can together be employed in wildlife caseworks as demonstrative evidences for linking the suspect with the crime.

17.7.1 Morphological Analysis

The morphological or physical characteristics are the simplest way of wildlife forensic method in the identification process of evidences and the least expensive forensic analysis. The identification of species based on morphological characteristics of wildlife flora and fauna provides important clues based on external appearance. Different species generally possess distinct physical appearances like skin coat color, pattern of coloration, eyes, pinna, tails, ivory etc. (Burnham-Curtis et al. 2015).

17.7.2 Footprints Analysis

Footprints of wildlife species are one of the commonly encountered evidence in the forensic analysis of species. Structural and dimensional analysis of footprint impressions on the surface can be useful for determining the species of the animal as well as confirming the presence of the specific animal at the location.

17.7.3 Osteology

It is the use of the morphology of bones of the skeleton to make identifications. The first question that always arises is whether it is human or not and if it is an animal then what animal is it. Identification of animals is really difficult because of the possibilities of various inter and intra-species. In cases when dentition is present, chances of identification become more (Bell 2011).

17.7.4 Microscopic Examination

It includes the morphological, structural as well as elemental analysis of evidences to identify the species of origin. Analysis of hair, fur, skins, and ivory can provide leading information in case of metallic poisoning or other cause of death. Microscopy can be one of the most useful tools in wildlife forensics, especially while dealing with hair evidence. Scanning electron microscopy (SEM) can also be used in the study of surface morphology hairs. Scale patterns of wool fibers can be analyzed for species characterization (Sahajpal et al. 2021).

17.7.5 Molecular Examination

In the past decades, advancements in molecular techniques had allowed forensic researchers to extract genomic DNA from different evidences encountered at the crime scene which may provide evidential link related to the individualization of any animal. DNA analysis of trace evidences generally exchanged during the crime can successfully link the suspect with the victim as well as the crime. Similar to human forensic analysis, molecular examination in wildlife crime can be useful in the identification of species, individualization of animal, age determination, gender determination, and paternity testing as well as in population studies such as phylogenetic evolution of animals (Sahajpal et al. 2021).

17.7.6 Isotopic Examination

The geographic origin of the unknown wildlife samples can also be identified using the study of elemental analysis. This becomes important in the cases where a particular species is endangered in one region and not in other. In this method, a comparison of the ratios of different isotopes can be done using inductively coupled plasma mass spectrometry (ICP-MS) and isotope ratio mass spectrometry (IRMS). The relative abundance of isotopes of various elements can also be measured using mass spectrometry and laser ablation–inductively coupled plasma–mass spectrometry (LA-ICP-MS) (Sahajpal et al. 2021).

17.8 Forensic Entomology

Forensic entomology is another interesting branch of forensic biology that incorporates the study of arthropods and other insects, their anatomy, life cycle, and other information to infer conclusions in legal caseworks. It particularly deals with the estimation of time since death or post-mortem interval (PMI), differentiation of primary and secondary crime-scene, determination of the cause of death, and an indication of physical abuse and illicit drug ingestions (Sharma et al. 2015; Harvey et al. 2016) Forensically significant group of insects includes flies (Order—Diptera) such as blowflies (Calliphoridae), flesh flies (Sarcophagidae), and beetles (Order—Coleoptera) such as rove beetles (Staphylinidae), Carrion Beetles (Silphidae) along with wasps, ants moths and other insects. Infestation and relative progression of these arthropods on cadavers at different stages of decomposition form the basis of forensic entomology (Rivers and Dahlem 2014). The famous 'Ruxton' case (1935) involved the application of forensic entomology for linking crime with the suspect. The third-instar larvae of blowflies on the body remains indicated disposal of bodies 12–14 days before their discovery that matched with the time-period of Mrs Ruxton and her nursemaid's disappearance (Sharma and Singh 2015). For successful inference, detailed knowledge related to the colonization of insect, developmental phases and time along with the impact of insects on the decomposition of the corpse is essential.

17.8.1 Necrophagous Insects

Insects/arthropods that feed directly on the body remains, or the fluids released from the remains during the decomposition process are classified as Necrophagous species that include many species of the order Diptera from the families—Calliphoridae and Sarcophagidae.

Calliphoridae, also known as blowflies, carrion flies or cluster flies are the primary agent involved in the process of decomposition of organic matters. These are typically metallic blue, black, or green in color and possess antennae covered in fine filaments or branches. A fully grown calliphoridae ranges in size from approximately 6–10 mm.

Sarcophagidae or flesh flies differ from most of the flies as they are ovoviviparous. They lay hatched or hatching maggots instead of eggs upon the carrion. An adult flesh fly range in size from 4 to 23 mm and has black and gray longitudinal stripes on the thorax and checkering on the stomach (Gennard 2012; Sharma et al. 2015).

17.8.2 Life Cycle of Blowflies

Flies, particularly Calliphoridae are among the pioneering insects to infest a corpse. The flies lay eggs usually in clumps on the surface of a cadaver that is white and slightly elongated, similar to a grain of rice in size, shape and color. On a fresh cadaver, these clumps are usually found on the area where the body's mucus membranes come into contact with the outside. The eggs hatch into larvae (maggots) in the duration of 8–23 h, depending upon the climate. The larvae undergo three instars or stages and develop through by feeding on the corpse, with a moulting event at the end of each one. The larvae at the first instar stage are typically around 2 mm long after nearly 2 days. The second instar stage is relatively quick, lasting only half a day and the larvae grow around 10 mm. Finally, the third instar lasts around 2.5 days and the larvae measure upto 17 mm. At the end of the third instar, the larvae undergo the pupal stage and will become mobile. The larvae moult again but do not shed their skin. Instead, the skin shrinks to form a cocoon which is hard and protective. During this stage, the larvae cannot move, feed, or defend themselves. It finds a safe place to shed its skin for the third time. At this stage, the larva forms rudimentary legs and wings, and an adult fly emerges out from hard cover on completion of the pupal stage, typically around 18–20 days from when the eggs are first laid. The adult that emerges from the pupa is pale and soft with crumbled wings and it takes around 2 days until its wings expand and its body color changes (Higley et al. 2001; Szpila 2009; Gennard 2012) (Fig. 17.9).

Life-cycle and age of an insect are useful for estimating PMI up to a week, before the completion of the whole cycle as identification of generations would become difficult in case of multiple generations infesting upon the cadaver. For such a situation, in which the dead bodies were disposed for a longer time, the technique of identifying insect succession must be employed. This involves information related to the succession of different orders of insects at different stages of body decompositions(Anderson and Byrd 2010).

Besides the morphological characterization of various insects, molecular analysis of these insects can be of great importance. In cases like Sarcophaga, microscopic examination of insects cannot infer the difference between the insects. Molecular examination of PCR-based DNA analysis makes use of cytochorme oxidase (CO-I) to differentiate two individual insects from the same colonies (Wells et al. 2009; Tarone et al. 2015). Entomotoxicology is an advancing field of entomology that deals with ante-mortem consumption of drugs and absorption of drugs by the insects

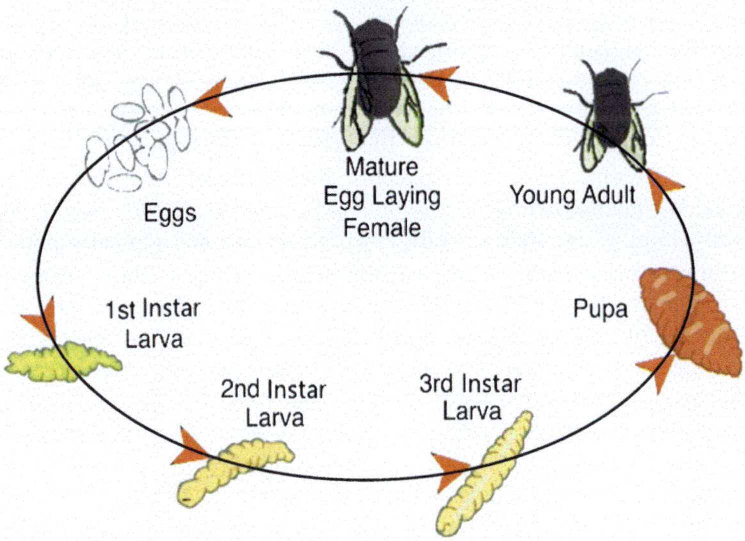

Fig. 17.9 Life cycle of Calliphoridae

infesting on the corpse. These absorbed drugs may have an accelerating or degenerating impact on the development of insects thereby hampering the correlation of the insect's developmental stage and the actual post-mortem interval. Therefore, precise knowledge about ecology, distribution pattern and the developmental pattern is essential for the successful employment of entomology in forensic caseworks (Goff and Lord 2001; Vasudeva Murthy and Mohanty 2010).

17.9 Forensic Mycology

Besides insects, fungal species infesting upon a cadaver can be potentially employed to estimate the source of information about post-mortem interval (PMI), cause of toxicity or poisoning and death, determining time since deposition. In addition, the small size of fungal spores and their abundance assists in linking the suspect with crime-scene and/or victim in the form of trace evidence. The application of fungi in the legal context is dealt under the subject of forensic mycology.

17.9.1 Structure of a Fungus

Fungi (singular—Fungus) are filamentous multicellular eukaryotic organisms that are heterotrophic in nature with cell walls composed of chitin and polysaccharides. The body of a fungus known as thallus is formed of small tube-like cells interconnected to each other that are known as hyphae. The bulk of such tubular hyphae is called mycelium. Some fungi have septae or cross walls in their hyphae

(Webster and Weber 2007; Raghukumar 2017). On the basis of their roles in the ecosystem, the fungi can be categorized into three- pathogens or the disease-causing fungi; symbionts or the mutualistic beneficial fungi such as lichen, mycorrhiza, etc., and the saprobes or the decomposing fungi that decay the organic matter from the ecosystem. Based on their morphology, life cycle, and physiology, the major groups of fungi are Phycomycetes, Asscomycetes, Basidiomycetes and Deuteromycetes (Brandt and Warnock 2015).

Cells of a fungus are similar to those of eukaryotes and typically possess cell walls, cell membranes, endoplasmic reticulum, mitochondria, ribosomes, vacuoles, and microtubules. Besides a membranous structure, lomasomes are presently attached to the plasma membrane that facilitates vesicular transport and enlarge the surface area (Zadworny and Eissenstat 2011). Cells of fungus may be uninucleate or multinucleate. Hyphae that are continuous and filled with multinucleated cytoplasm are called coenocytic hyphae. A variety of decay fungi possess binucleate cells. The stage of cells in binucleate condition can be termed as dikaryon stage on the condition of the nuclei being genetically different and can result from the fusion of two hyphae cells with an incomplete fusion of their nuclei. Cross walls or septae in the hyphae are present in higher orders of fungi and help in strengthening the cells as well as maintaining turgor pressure (Clark and Anderson 2004).

17.9.2 Life Cycles of Fungi

The life cycle of fungi has many different patterns based on the species of the fungi. They may reproduce vegetatively, sexually or asexually. Vegetative reproduction can be of three types—fragmentation, budding and fission. Asexual reproduction is the most common method of reproduction and ensures the dispersal of species to different locations. Sexual reproduction is beneficial in the condition of extreme environments with limited resources. The life cycle of fungi consists of three stages—Spores, Mycelium and Germ cells. Life of all fungi begins with the spore stage which is in haploid condition and genetically identical to their parent fungus. They may be motile or non-motile, thin or thick-walled propagules that separate from parent bodies when ready for dispersal. After reaching a suitable location, mass of spores club together and forms a bunch of root-like structure known as mycelium. At the mycelium stage, the fungi can opt for reproducing sexually or asexually. For asexual reproduction, the mycelium grows into spore-producing bodies. For sexual reproduction, the mycelium undergoes meiotic phase. Meiotic phase involves two steps—plasmogamy or the fusion of cytoplasm and karyogamy or the fusion of nuclei. Haploid gametangia conjugate to form diploid zygospores. The zygospores are genetically different from the parent fungi due to the phenomenon of crossing over during meiosis. Sexual reproduction occurs by different methods, namely planogametic copulation, gametangial contact, gametangial copulation, spermatogamy, somatogamy (Moore-Landecker 1972; Bridge and Spooner 2001; Gruninger et al. 2014) (Fig. 17.10).

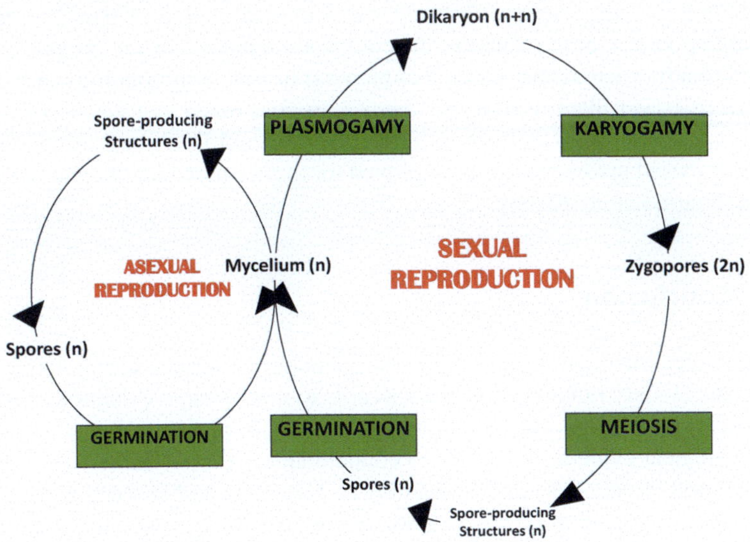

Fig. 17.10 Schematic diagram demonstrating the life cycle of fungi

17.9.3 Roles of Fungi in Forensic Sciences

There are more than 1.5 million of fungal species known worldwide. A small locality may possess thousands of fungal species generating a unique microbiota of that location. Identification and differentiation of multiple crime scenes can be relied on the unique pattern of fungal distribution or particular pattern of microbiota belonging to a specific location. As fungal spores are produced in abundance and are lightweight, they can easily be dispersed by wind. Also, the anatomical structure of fungal spores reveals the presence of spike-like structure on the outer wall that helps the spore in adhering to the clothes, hair, or body of an individual. As per Locard's principle of exchange, the spores may get picked up from the surface of an object by another object that comes in contact with it, thereby forming a link between both objects (Menezes et al. 2007; Hawksworth and Wiltshire 2015).

Information related to the fungal life cycle and development pattern can be useful in taphonomical study of a cadaver, particularly in determining the time since death, cause of death, etc. Fungal colonies infesting on dead bodies are different from the ones found in living tissues, often pathogenic in nature. Studies reveal accession of soil fungi on the surface of cadavers deposited on the soil upon reaching the stage of decomposition. These fungi found on cadavers are medically-insignificant but include the majority of decomposer or spoilage fungi. Details related to the growth rate of such fungal colonies found on the cadaver, along with the impact of various environmental factors are essential for determining the postmortem interval (Bridge and Spooner 2001; Tranchida et al. 2014). However, precise identification of the fungus, knowledge of biotic and abiotic factors around the cadaver, storage conditions etc. are crucial criteria for counting on such methods. Time and location of deposition of any biotic substance can be identified in a similar manner, depending upon the study related to the colonization pattern of the fungus.

In addition to microscopic-based examination of fungal morphology and colonization, DNA-based identification of fungus can be utilized in forensic mycology. Singleplex and multiplex PCR-based DNA profiling and DNA barcoding are some of the DNA-based taxonomic tools employed for the accurate identification of fungal colonies (Sharma et al. 2020a).

17.10 Conclusion

Biological specimens are one of the most valuable evidences encountered at the crime scene. Widely ranging from macroscopic to microscopic evidences, these can significantly help in linking perpetrator-victim-scene of crime. Being organic in nature, biological evidences is prone to contamination, deterioration and decomposition, therefore proper handling, collection, and storage condition are demanded for the successful application of such samples. Forensic biology is one of the highly recognized disciplines of forensic science and is thriving day by day with the introduction of molecular biology and instrumental advancements. Further advancement in these techniques is highly expected for fulfilling future demands.

References

Adler CJ, Haak W, Donlon D et al (2011) Survival and recovery of DNA from ancient teeth and bones. J Archaeol Sci 38:956–964

Allen MS, Huebert JM (2014) Short-lived plant materials, long-lived trees, and polynesian 14C dating: considerations for 14C sample selection and documentation. Radiocarbon 56:257–276. https://doi.org/10.2458/56.16784

Alotaibi SS, Sayed SM, Alosaimi M et al (2020) Pollen molecular biology: applications in the forensic palynology and future prospects: a review. Saudi J Biol Sci 27:1185–1190

Altemimi A, Lakhssassi N, Baharlouei A et al (2017) Phytochemicals: extraction, isolation, and identification of bioactive compounds from plant extracts. Plants (Basel, Switzerland) 6:42. https://doi.org/10.3390/plants6040042

Anand TP, Unmesh AK (2016) Diatom test: a reliable tool to assess death by drowning? Int J Res Med Sci 4:1479–1484

Anderson GS, Byrd JH (2010) Factors that influence insect succession on carrion. In: Forensic entomology: the utility of arthropods in legal investigations, vol 2. CRC Press, Boca Raton

Arguelles P, Reinhard K, Shin DH (2015) Forensic palynological analysis of intestinal contents of a Korean mummy. Anat Rec 298:1182–1190

Arola DD, Gao S, Zhang H, Masri R (2017) The tooth: its structure and properties. Dent Clin 61: 651–668

Auer AMM (1988) Diatoms and drowning. Zeitschrift fur Rechtsmedizin 101:87–98

Barbour J (2004) Wood formation and properties | WOOD quality. In: Burley JBT-E of FS (ed) Encyclopedia of forest sciences. Elsevier, Oxford, pp 1840–1846

Bell LS (2011) Forensic science in support of wildlife conservation efforts. Morphological and chemical approaches (global trends). Forensic Sci Rev 23:31–36

Bell KL, Burgess KS, Okamoto KC et al (2016) Review and future prospects for DNA barcoding methods in forensic palynology. Forensic Sci Int Genet 21:110–116

Bennett KD, Willis KJ (2002) Pollen. In: Tracking environmental change using lake sediments. Springer, Berlin, pp 5–32

Bhatia RYP, Raghavan S, Rao KVS, Prasad VN (1973) Forensic examination of leaf and leaf fragments in fresh and dried conditions. J Forensic Sci Soc 13:183–190. https://doi.org/10.1016/S0015-7368(73)70794-5

Bogusz I, Bogusz M (2018) Use of diatoms in forensics

Boi M (2018) The importance of palynology in forensic investigations. Forensic Sci Int 163:231–235

Bortolotti F, Del Balzo G, Calza R, Valerio FTF (2011) Testing the specificity of diatom test: search for false positives. Med Sci Law 21:7–10

Bozzo WR, Colussi AG, Ortíz MI et al (2015) Analysis of DNA from fingernail samples in criminal cases. Forensic Sci Int Genet Suppl Ser 5:e601–e602

Brandt ME, Warnock DW (2015) Taxonomy and classification of fungi. In: Manual of clinical microbiology, 11th edn. American Society for Microbiology, Washington, DC, pp 1935–1943

Bridge P, Spooner B (2001) Soil fungi: diversity and detection. Plant Soil 232:147–154

Buffoli B, Rinaldi F, Labanca M et al (2014) The human hair: from anatomy to physiology. Int J Dermatol 53:331–341

Burnham-Curtis MK, Trail PW, Kagan R, Moore MK (2015) Wildlife forensics: an overview and update for the prosecutor. US Att'ys Bull 63:53

Calder IM (1984) An evaluation of the diatom test in deaths of professional divers. Med Sci Law 24:41–46

Cameron NG (2004) The use of diatom analysis in forensic geoscience. Geol Soc London Spec Publ 232:277–280

Clark TA, Anderson JB (2004) Dikaryons of the basidiomycete fungus Schizophyllum commune: evolution in long-term culture. Genetics 167:1663–1675

Davies A (2017) Digital ultraviolet and infrared photography. Routledge, Milton Park

Devi MR, Banu VT (2015) Study of nail unit using image processing methods. In: 2015 international conference on computer communication and informatics (ICCCI), IEEE, pp 1–6

Divakar KP (2017) Forensic odontology: the new dimension in dental analysis. Int J Biomed Sci 13:1–5

Dormontt EE, Boner M, Braun B et al (2015) Forensic timber identification: it's time to integrate disciplines to combat illegal logging. Biol Conserv 191:790–798

Erdoğan B (2017) Anatomy and physiology of hair. In: Hair and scalp disorders, vol 13. IntechOpen, London

Foran D, Lisa Hebda MS, Doran A, n.d. (2015) Document title: trace dna from fingernails: increasing the success rate of widely collected forensic evidence:49534

Gennard D (2012) Forensic entomology: an introduction. Wiley, Chichester

Goff ML, Lord WD (2001) Entomotoxicology: insects as toxicological indicators and the impact of drugs and toxins on insect development. In: Forensic entomology: the utility of arthropods in legal investigations. CRC Press, Boca Raton, pp 331–340

Gouda S, Kerry RG, Das A, Chauhan NS (2020) Wildlife forensics: a boon for species identification and conservation implications. Forensic Sci Int 317:110530

Grover C, Bansal S (2017) The nail as an investigative tool in medicine: what a dermatologist ought to know. Indian J Dermatol Venereol Leprol 83:635–643

Gruninger RJ, Puniya AK, Callaghan TM et al (2014) Anaerobic fungi (phylum Neocallimastigomycota): advances in understanding their taxonomy, life cycle, ecology, role and biotechnological potential. FEMS Microbiol Ecol 90:1–17

Harvey ML, Gasz NE, Voss SC (2016) Entomology-based methods for estimation of postmortem interval. Res Rep Forensic Med Sci 6:1–9

Hawksworth DL, Wiltshire PEJ (2015) Forensic mycology: current perspectives. Res Rep Forensic Med Sci 5:75–83

Hebda LM, Doran AE, Foran DR (2014) Collecting and analyzing DNA evidence from fingernails: a comparative study. J Forensic Sci 59:1343–1350

Higley LG, Haskell NH, Byrd JH, Castner JL (2001) Insect development and forensic entomology. In: Forensic entomology: the utility of arthropods in legal investigations. CRC Press, Boca Raton, pp 287–302

Hirapure P, Jagtap S, Jabadurai NER (2014) Research article morphological study of pollen as an aid in criminal investigation. Sch Acad J Biosci 2(3):187–192

Horton BP, Boreham S, Hillier C (2006) The development and application of a diatom-based quantitative reconstruction technique in forensic science. J Forensic Sci 51:643–650

Horton MD, Vital D, Defino P, Spaulding S, Albarelli G (2018) Enhancing percolation in phosphatic clay using diatoms under laboratory conditions. bioRxiv 357889

Hurlimann J, Feer P, Elber F, Niederberger K, Dirnhofer R et al (2000) Diatom detection in the diagnosis of death by drowning. Int J Leg 114:6–14

Italiya AH, Ansari N, Menon SK (2009) Non-destructive technique for individualizing trace evidence analysis of tiger nail.

Kang Y, Deng Z, Zang R, Long W (2017) DNA barcoding analysis and phylogenetic relationships of tree species in tropical cloud forests. Sci Rep 7:1–9

Kaushik N, Pal KS, Sharma A, Thakur G (2017) Role of diatoms in diagnosis of death due to drowning: case studies. Medicine (Baltimore) 7:59–65

Khan F, Yousaf Z, Ahmed H et al (2014) Stomatal patterning: an important taxonomic tool for systematical studies of tree species of angiosperm. Annu Res Rev Biol 4:4034–4053. https://doi.org/10.9734/ARRB/2014/10073

Khangura RK, Sircar K, Singh S, Rastogi V (2011) Sex determination using mesiodistal dimension of permanent maxillary incisors and canines. J Forensic Dent Sci 3:81–85. https://doi.org/10.4103/0975-1475.92152

Khurshid A, Shah MU, Khurshid M et al (2021) Diatom-positive cadaver: drowning or homicide? Cureus 13(9):e18312

Krishan K, Kanchan T, Garg AK (2015) Dental evidence in forensic identification—an overview, methodology and present status. Open Dent J 9:250–256. https://doi.org/10.2174/1874210601509010250

Krstic S, Duma A, Janevska B, Levkov Z, Nikolova K et al (2002) Diatom in forensic expertise of drowning. A Macedonian experience. Forensic Sci Int 127:198–203

Kumar V, Sharma S, Jalwal P (2017) A comprehensive review on human nail. Int J Med Heal Res 3: 72–74. wwwmedicalsciencejournalcom

Kumari M, Sankhla MS, Nandan M et al (2017) Role of forensic palynology in crime investigation. IJournals Int J Soc Relev Concern 5:1–13

Levkov Z, Williams DM, Nikolovska D et al (2017) The use of diatoms in forensic science: advantages and limitations of the diatom test in cases of drowning. In: The archaeological and forensic applications of microfossils: a deeper understanding of human history. Geological Society of London, London, pp 261–277

Loveleen (2017) Role of nail striation in forensic identification. Int J Res Cult Soc 1:12–16

Ma T, Inagaki T, Ban M, Tsuchikawa S (2019) Rapid identification of wood species by near-infrared spatially resolved spectroscopy (NIR-SRS) based on hyperspectral imaging (HSI). Holzforschung 73:323–330. https://doi.org/10.1515/hf-2018-0128

Menezes RG, Jain A, Kanchan T et al (2007) Forensic mycology. Leg Med 9:48

Mildenhall DC (2006) An unusual appearance of a common pollen type indicates the scene of the crime. Forensic Sci Int 163:236–240

Mildenhall DC (2008) Civil and criminal investigations. Use spores pollen. SIAK J 4:35–52

Miller RB (1991) Identification of wood fragments in trace evidence. In: Proceedings of the international symposium on the forensic aspects of trace evidence. FBI Academy US Department of Justice Quantico, pp 91–111

Moore-Landecker E (1972) Fundamentals of the fungi. Prentice-Hall, Englewood Cliffs, NJ

Oguchi R, Onoda Y, Terashima I, Tholen D (2018) Leaf anatomy and function. In: The leaf: a platform for performing photosynthesis. Springer, Berlin, pp 97–139

Pollanen M (1998) Forensic diatomology and drowning. Elsevier, Amsterdam

Porawski R (1966) Investigation of occurrence of diatoms in organs in death from various causes. J Forensic Med 13:134–137
Raghukumar S (2017) Fungi: characteristics and classification. In: Fungi in coastal and oceanic marine ecosystems. Springer, Berlin, pp 1–15
Rana AS, Manhas S (2018) Significance of diatoms in diagnosis of drowning deaths: a review. J Forensic Genet Sci 5:77–81
Rivers DB, Dahlem GA (2014) The science of forensic entomology. Wiley, Chichester
Robertson JR (1999) Forensic examination of hair. CRC Press, Boca Raton
Rowson JM (1946) The significance of stomatal index as a differential character; studies in the genera Atropa, Datura, digitalis, Phytolacca and in polyploid leaves. Q J Pharm Pharmacol 19: 136–143
Ryder ML (1963) A survey of the gross structural features of protein fibres. In: Fibre structure. Elsevier, Amsterdam, pp 534–566
Sack L, Scoffoni C (2013) Leaf venation: structure, function, development, evolution, ecology and applications in the past, present and future. New Phytol 198:983–1000. https://doi.org/10.1111/nph.12253
Saferstein R (2007) Criminalistics: an introduction to forensic science. Pearson Prentice Hall, Upper Saddle River, NJ
Sahajpal V, Mishra S, Bhandari D (2021) Forensic analysis in wildlife crime cases: microscopy, DNA profiling and isotope analysis. In: Forensic analysis—scientific and medical techniques and evidence under the microscope. IntechOpen, London
Scott KR, Morgan RM, Jones VJ, Cameron NG (2014) The transferability of diatoms to clothing and the methods appropriate for their collection and analysis in forensic geosciences. Forensic Sci Int 241:127–137
Shah P, Velani P, Lakade L, Dukle S (2019) Teeth in forensics: a review. Indian J Dent Res 30:291–299. https://doi.org/10.4103/ijdr.IJDR_9_17
Sharma M, Singh D (2015) Historical approach of forensic entomology: a review. Int J Adv Res Sci Eng Technol 9:838–845
Sharma R, Garg RK, Gaur JR (2015) Various methods for the estimation of the post mortem interval from Calliphoridae: a review. Egypt J Forensic Sci 5:1–12
Sharma S, Jossan JK, Singh R (2020a) DNA barcoding in forensic mycology: concepts, limitations, and future prospects. In: Forensic DNA typing: principles, applications and advancements. Springer, Berlin, pp 431–448
Sharma S, Rohatgi S, Singla P (2020b) Forensic analysis of leaf as a botanical evidence
Srettabunjong S, Patompakdeesakul P, Limawongpranee S (2016) Relative studies between hair index, hair area, and medullary index with age and sex in Thai scalp hair. Forensic Sci Int 267: 196–203. https://doi.org/10.1016/j.forsciint.2016.08.030
Stenn KS, Paus R (2001) Controls of hair follicle cycling. Physiol Rev 81:449
Szpila K (2009) Key for the identification of third instars of European blowflies (Diptera: Calliphoridae) of forensic importance. In: Current concepts in forensic entomology. Springer, Berlin, pp 43–56
Tamaska L (1949) Diatom content of bone marrow in corpses in water. Orv Hetil 16:509–511
Tarone AM, Singh B, Picard CJ (2015) Molecular biology in forensic entomology. In: Forensic entomology: international dimensions and frontiers. CRC Press, Boca Raton, pp 297–316
Thyagharajan KK, Raji IK (2019) A review of visual descriptors and classification techniques used in leaf species identification. Arch Comput Methods Eng 26:933–960
Timperman J (1972) The diagnosis of drowning—a review. J Forensic Sci 1:397–409
Tranchida MC, Centeno ND, Cabello MN (2014) Soil fungi: their potential use as a forensic tool. J Forensic Sci 59:785–789
Vasudeva Murthy CR, Mohanty M (2010) Entomotoxicology: a review. J Indian Acad Forensic Med 32:82–84
Vinayak V, Gautam S (2019) Diatoms in forensics: a molecular approach to diatom testing in forensic science. In: Diatoms: fundamentals and applications. Wiley, Chichester, pp 435–470

Webster J, Weber R (2007) Introduction to fungi. Cambridge University Press, Cambridge
Wells JD, Stevens JR, Byrd JH, Castner JL (2009) Molecular methods for forensic entomology. In: Castner JH, Byrd JL (eds) Forensic entomology: the utility of arthropods in legal investigations, vol 2. CRC Press, Boca Raton, pp 437–452
Wiedenhoeft A (2006) Wood evidence: proper collection, documentation, and storage of wood evidence from a crime scene. Evid Technol Mag 4(3):30–32, 36–37
Yukseloglu EH, Dastan K, Yonar FC et al (2019) The comparison of DNA extraction techniques in human bone and tooth samples exposed to high heat. Medicine (Baltimore) 8:489–495
Zadworny M, Eissenstat DM (2011) Contrasting the morphology, anatomy and fungal colonization of new pioneer and fibrous roots. New Phytol 190:213–221
Zafarina Z, Panneerchelvam S (2009) Analysis of hair samples using microscopical and molecular techniques to ascertain claims of rare animal species. Malaysian J Med Sci MJMS 16:35
Zhou Y, Cao Y, Huang J et al (2020) Research advances in forensic diatom testing. Forensic Sci Res 5:98–105

Forensic Serology

18

Manisha Rana, Pankaj Shrivastava, Ankit Srivastava,
Pushpesh Kushwaha, and R. K. Kumawat

Abstract

Biological evidences, e.g. blood, semen, vaginal secretion, saliva, urine, and sweat encountered at the crime scene, are the most pervasive in surroundings. Their existence helps in associating the assassin with the victim as well as with the crime scene. Moreover, a lot depends on their collection methods and preservation conditions in identifying the source of such materials. Forensic serology is a sub-discipline of forensic biology concerned with the analytical knowledge of bodily fluid evidences encountered at the crime scene. Identification of such body fluids and their segregation from physically and chemically similar substances is essential for linking the evidences to the crime. Sets of physical observation, preliminary examination and confirmatory examinations have been described for the identification of various bodily fluids. Physical and preliminary tests are essential for excluding or eliminating a stain as a bodily fluid, while the confirmatory examination is the conclusive method of identifying a biological fluid. The chapter focuses on various types of bodily fluids encountered in relation to the crime, physical properties specific to each bodily fluid as well as preliminary and confirmatory tests for their identification. The chapter also provides an insight into the method of crime scene reconstruction methods by means of bloodstain patterns. Different types of blood grouping methods as

M. Rana · P. Kushwaha · R. K. Kumawat (✉)
Serology and DNA Division, State Forensic Science Laboratory, Jaipur, Rajasthan, India

P. Shrivastava
Biology and Serology Division, Regional Forensic Science Laboratory, Gwalior, Madhya Pradesh, India

A. Srivastava
School of Forensic Sciences, The West Bengal National University of Juridical Sciences, Kolkata, West Bengal, India

P. Shrivastava et al. (eds.), *Textbook of Forensic Science*,
https://doi.org/10.1007/978-981-99-1377-0_18

well as techniques of species identification have also been described in the chapter.

Keywords

ELISA · Immunochromatographic assays · Bloodstain pattern analysis (BPA) · Blood grouping · Species identification

18.1 Introduction

Forensic serology is a branch of forensic biology that mainly deals with the examination, identification and classification of bodily fluids such as blood, semen, sweat, saliva, urine, fecal matter, vomit etc. that are majorly associated with violent criminal cases. For example, the identification of blood is crucial in the investigation of the cases involving homicide, sexual assault, burglary etc. Confirming the existence of blood has an empirical value or can support allegations of violent acts and then this information can be used in further investigation. For instance, in crimes related to murder, the presence of the victim's blood on a suspect's weapon can link the victim and the suspect. Same way, the identification of semen, saliva, and vaginal stains becomes important in crimes related to sexual assaults. The stain from these fluids on the victim's and/or perpetrator's body parts, clothing could be helpful in linking the victim with the alleged suspect. This chapter deals with the examination and identification of various biological fluids commonly encountered at crime scene and their evidential value along with various factors and conditions affecting the forensic analysis of such samples (Fig. 18.1).

Analyses of forensic samples encountered at the crime scene are performed at several stages using different techniques. Classification of such examination includes physical examination, preliminary examinations, and confirmatory examinations. Physical examination defines in identifying physical characteristics such as color, density, odour, etc., that are specific to certain kind of bodily fluid. Preliminary examination or assays provides a direction towards establishing the chances of the presence of the expected bodily fluid. Chances of positive reaction are also possible with other substances that have a similar molecular structure. In simpler terms, many substances often give a false positive result with presumptive assays. Therefore, a positive result with preliminary examinations denotes a probability of the presence of expected bodily fluid. However, negative results of such examinations are confirmed indicative of the absence of the bodily fluid being tested. Confirmatory examinations are conclusive and substance-specific method of identifying the bodily fluids.

Advantages		Disadvantages
• Detection by emission or absorption of light • Observable Biological Evidences on any type of surfaces • Non destructive • Test Reproducibility	**Light Source** 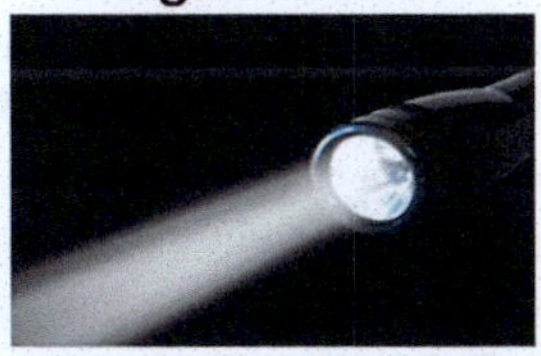 Blood, Semen, Saliva, Urine (300-700 nm wavelength)	• Non specificity for Biological Evidences • Requires preciseness • Masked reaction in certain surfaces
• Rapid Testing • Ease of handling and cost effective • Can be utilized in crime scene • Identification of Semen in cases of azoospermia • Non destructive	**Chemical**  Blood, Semen (Acid phosphatase), Saliva, Vaginal fluid, Urine	• Non specificity to human • Analyte concentration is essential prerequisite • May infer false positive results with similar substances
• Direct identification of sperm cells • Low Cost • Use of different staining methods	**Microscopy**  Brightfield, Phase-contrast and Fluorescence microscopy	• Sample loss during slide preparation • Requires preciseness • Not suitable for cases of azoospermia or vasectomy • Observation of unstained cells requires contrasts
• Requires less sample • Low cost • Rapid testing • Specificity to Humans • High sensitivity	**Immunological** 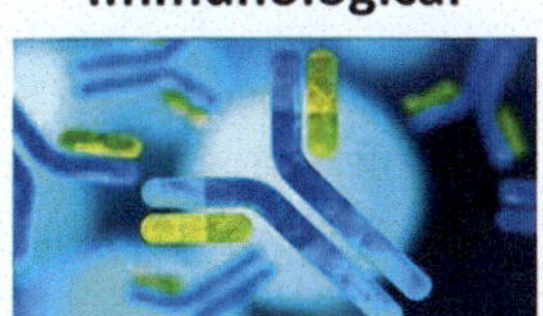 Blood, Semen (Prostate Specific Antigen, Semenogelin), Saliva, Vaginal fluid, Urea	• Hook's effect • Destructive • External environment may affect the sensitivity • Chances of false positive results

Fig. 18.1 Advantages and disadvantages of presumptive and confirmatory examinations

18.2 Blood

Blood is one of the most prevalent evidences to be found at a crime scene in various cases like homicide, sexual assault, suicide, accidents etc. Blood is a complex viscous red fluid with a pH of about 7.4, mainly composed of cells and plasma and constitutes about 8% of the human body weight. The liquid part is called plasma and the solids are red cells (erythrocytes), white cells (leukocytes) and thrombocytes (platelets). The cells are also known as corpuscles. When the blood flows out of the body, a part separates out as blood clots consisting of blood cells, discs and fibrin. Fibrin comes out of plasma and is responsible for the clotting of blood. The liquid left is called serum. It is the plasma without fibrinogen which turns into fibrin. Plasma and serum are complex mixtures of proteins, minerals and organic compounds dissolved in water (Hardwick 2008; Basu and Kulkarni 2014).

The presence of blood on evidentiary items is very crucial in arbitrating innocence or guilt during legal proceedings. Interpretation of blood spatter can be relevant in adjudicating how blood was stashed at the crime scene or on an item, helping in the reconstruction of the crime scene. From the collection of samples to examination, every step is crucial in analysis. One of the most important considerations is the collection of the sample with zero or minimal contamination. One must take care of essential precautionary measures during the collection of blood samples such as wearing of surgical mask, latex gloves, and aprons during collection, label all the samples accurately, decontaminate all non-disposable items and dispose-off the disposable items, and clean up the hands with bleach. A sterilized syringe should be used for control sample collection. A note of precaution must be added if biohazards like AIDS, COVID, or hepatitis are suspected. Wet blood-stained objects need to be air-dried after collection. The stains can also be collected on cotton swabs and then air-dried or collected in containers with the help of a syringe. In case of dried blood stains, tape-lifting or scrapping is used (Lee and Ladd 2001; Castro and Coyle 2013). Preservation of blood samples is another important criterion that must be taken care of. The stability of blood is influenced by factors such as the use of stabilizing agents such as heparin or anticoagulant agents such as EDTA used for sample storage, Storage period, storage conditions such as temperature, exposure to ultraviolet radiations, heat, light, humidity and soil contaminations (McNally et al. 1989; Vaught 2006).

18.2.1 Physical Examination

Examination of exhibits in natural light for red, brown or reddish brown stains, crystals or fine powder of reddish brown color, particular areas should be separated for sampling. In cases of washed stains or when stains are not visible, UV light of 230–269 nm frequency should be used for examination. Hemoglobin on treatment with acids, alkalis, reducing agents or oxidizing agents gives a variety of products which have characteristics absorption spectra. They help to identify the blood. The absorption bands are seen in length which is characteristic of blood. Spectroscopic examination of the blood is very useful as well as convenient. The test is usually carried out microscopically. The blood hemoglobin is changed in two or three forms on the slide itself and characteristic absorption is observed. Usually, alkali hematin and cyanhemochromogen are studied for their characteristic spectra. Ascending paper chromatography using acetic acid, methanol and water solvent system has been employed to study the Rf values. Electrophoresis is used for the separation of various enzyme systems. It is being adopted to study the body's proteins. This technique is becoming important to distinguish between blood samples.

18.2.2 Presumptive Examinations

These tests are the first series of tests that are qualitative in nature and are employed for the identification of a specific substance after a visual study of stains. If a stain gives positive color or luminescent reactions, the stain is possibly a blood stain. If it fails to give a positive reaction, in all probability it is not a bloodstain. However, certain substances similar to blood in molecular structure can give false positive results.

18.2.2.1 Colorimetric Tests

18.2.2.1.1 Guaiacum Test

It is the oldest known forensic assay used for the preliminary examination of blood. Guaiacum is a resin isolated from Guaiacum officinale and Guaiacum sanctum and gives deep blue color.

18.2.2.1.2 Benzidine Reaction

Benzidine (0.1 g) and dry sodium perborate (0.1 g) are dissolved in glacial acetic acid (10 mL) and sprayed over the stain. A strong blue color indicates blood.

18.2.2.1.3 Leucomalachite Green Reaction

The reagent is prepared by dissolving leucomalachite green (0.1 g), sodium perborate (0.3 g) in 65% glacial acetic acid. The reagent is applied to the stain. Intense green color indicates blood.

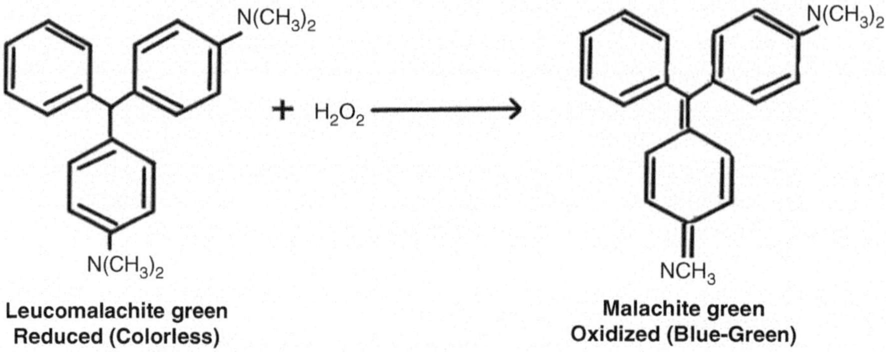

18.2.2.1.4 Phenolphthalein Reaction

Phenolphthalein (1 g) is reduced and dissolved in acetic acid (100 mL). Sodium perborate (1.4 g) is dissolved in the solution and applied to the blood stain. Pink coloration indicates blood.

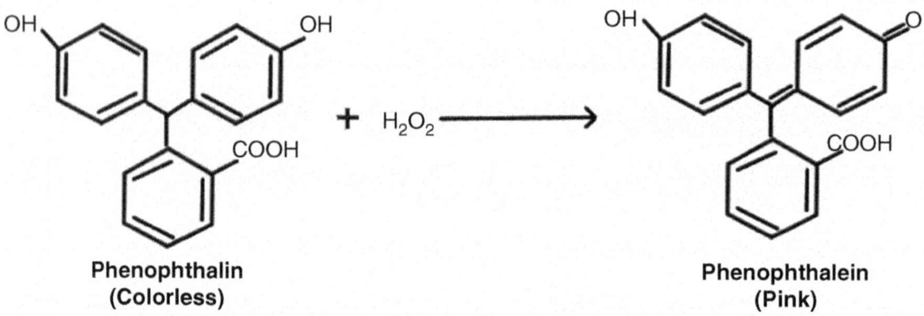

18.2.2.1.5 Aloin Test

Aloin is a mixture of pentosides of aloe plants that gives a bright red color on reacting with blood.

18.2.2.2 Chemiluminescence and Fluorescence Tests

18.2.2.2.1 Luminol Test

Luminol is a chemical which has been used to locate bloodstains. The articles suspected to bear stains are sprayed with luminol. It reacts with haeme of blood to give luminescence thereby visualizing the bloodstains are thus made visible. Even decomposed blood reacts with the reagent. The reagent does not interfere with subsequent blood tests. It is prepared by dissolving sodium perborate (0.7 g) in water (100 mL) and adding 3-arninophthalhydrazide (0.1 g) and sodium carbonate (5.0 g) to the solution. The solution is sprayed upon the article with glass sprayers in a dark room. Blood gives strong luminescence.

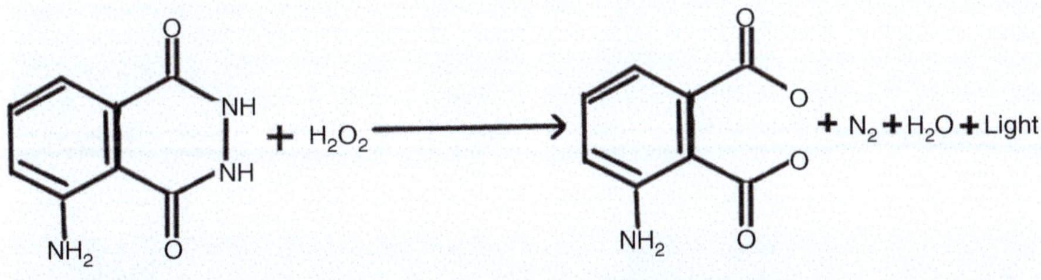

18.2.2.2.2 Fluorescin Reaction

Fluorescin is another reagent that is employed to test for the presence of bloodstains at a crime scene by means of fluorescence. Oxidation and catalysis by heme followed by exposure to light in the range of 425–485 nm using an alternate light source device results in an intense yellowish-green fluorescent light, which indicates the presence of a bloodstain. The light emitted from fluorescin-sprayed stains lasts longer than that of luminol.

18.2.3 Confirmatory Examinations

18.2.3.1 Micro-Crystal Test

Two crystal tests are commonly employed. They are specific for blood but they are not sensitive. They often fail if the conditions are not rigidly controlled or if the blood is disintegrated or contaminated.

18.2.3.1.1 Teichmann Test

The Teichmann test is much older, having been developed or invented in 1853 by Polish anatomist Ludwig Karl Teichmann. Take a dry crust or smear of blood on a slide. Put a drop of potassium iodide, bromide or chloride (0.1 g) solution in 100 mL glacial acetic acid over the blood and cover it with a cover slip. Warm the slide gently till it gives out bubbles. The reagent causes hemoglobin molecules to cleave, producing brownish crystals of pure hemin that have a violet, almost black, sheen (Hemin is the form of heme that contains the Fe^{3+} ion).

18.2.3.1.2 Takayama Test

One of the best-known crystal tests was developed in 1912 by Masaeo Takayama, a Japanese criminologist. A bloodstain is treated with pyridine and glucose (a reducing sugar that is capable of reducing ferric ions) under alkaline conditions to form pink needle-shaped crystals of pyridine ferroprotoporphyrin. Hemochromagens are heme derivatives in which the ferrous iron of the heme forms two bonds with nitrogenous bases (Fig. 18.2).

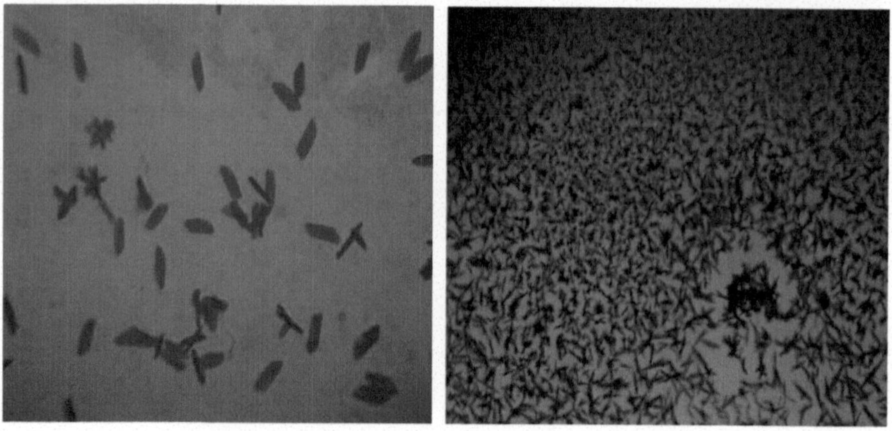

Fig. 18.2 Microscopic examination of blood demonstrating (**a**) hemin crystals in Teichmann test and (**b**) pyridine ferroprotoporphyrin crystals in Takayama test

18.2.3.2 Immunological Tests

Immunological methods utilize antihuman hemoglobin antibodies to detect human hemoglobin and therefore indicate the presence of human blood. These are rapid and sensitive as well as species-specific and can be used in both laboratory and field tests for species identification.

18.2.3.2.1 Tests Based on Haemoglobin Proteins

Bluestar® OBTI (Human Gesellschaft für Biochemica und Diagnostica mbH, Wiesbaden) and the ABAcard HemaTraceR (Abacus Diagnostics, California) are commercially available kits that utilize the antibody–antigen–antibody sandwich method by using antibodies that recognize human hemoglobin. These are two-part test that includes a collection tube for the blood sample, and a test bar. The test bar contains a labeled monoclonal antihuman hemoglobin antibody contained in a sample well; a polyclonal antihuman hemoglobin antibody immobilized at a test zone of a nitrocellulose membrane as well as an antiglobulin that recognizes the antibody is immobilized onto a control zone. A sample of the presumed human blood trace is transferred into the tube with a transport medium. This mixture is added drop by drop to the sample well. A positive sample is typically detected within 2–5 min. A single red line at the control zone means the testing liquid is working fine but no human blood has been detected, two red/pink lines, one at the test zone and other at the control zone mean the test has detected human blood.

18.2.3.2.2 Tests Based on Glycophorin-A Protein

Commercial kits like RSID™-Blood (Independent Forensics, Hillside, IL) utilizes antibodies that recognize human Glycophorin-A proteins (GPA). The kit works on the same principle as other immunological assays, making use of monoclonal antihuman GPA antibody contained in a sample well. A second monoclonal antihuman GPA antibody adhered to a different epitope of GPA, is immobilized onto a test zone of the membrane. An antiglobulin that recognizes the antibody is immobilized in a control zone.

18.3 Menstrual Blood

Menstruation is a periodic biological phenomenon that involves the shedding of the uterus lining of women along with the discharge of blood. Identification of the biological source of any stain can provide important hints in the investigation. Especially in cases of sexual assault, it may be relevant to distinguish the bloodstain of menstrual origin to that of the peripheral origin. The presence of peripheral blood (flowing through arteries and veins) stains indicates the possibility of a traumatic cause while the presence of menstrual blood points to a natural cause. The composition of menstrual blood can be an important criterion to distinguish it from peripheral blood. Menstrual blood comprises vaginal and cervical secretion or mucus, epithelial cells from endometrial linings and blood along with fibrinolytic components. These fibrinolytic components prevent the clotting of blood. On the contrary, the peripheral blood possesses the tendency of clotting due to the presence of thrombocytes and clotting factors or proteins such as fibrinogen, prothrombin, etc. The physical appearance of menstrual bloodstain is another factor useful for its identification. Menstrual blood does not splash instead it is found in the form of trickling descent.

18.3.1 Microscopic Examination

Along with endometrial cells, vaginal epithelium cells and residual cells are generally present in menstrual bloodstains and microscopical identification of these cells can confirm a bloodstain to be of menstrual origin. Staining tests such as Lugol's iodine test and Dane's staining test are some preliminary tests used for the identification of menstrual blood. Both Lugol's iodine test and Dane's staining test are based on the detection of vaginal epithelial cells in the menstrual blood. Lugol's test is based on iodine-staining and microscopical detection of the glycogens present in the nucleated squamous epithelial cells, which are found in considerably high concentrations in the vaginal cells as compared to buccal cells. However, the test is not specific for vaginal epithelial cells, as epithelial cells present in the buccal area and male urinary tract also consists of traces of glycogen and therefore can give a false positive test. Dane's staining method is considered to be more specific than Lugol's test or Schiff's test. The test is based on the difference in color and morphology of the stained epithelial cells (Bagwe 2018).

18.3.1.1 Lactate Dehydrogenase Immunoassay

Lactate dehydrogenase (LDH) is a tetrameric enzyme, beneficial in glycolysis that catalyzes the reduction reaction of pyruvate into lactate in scarcity of oxygen. LDH

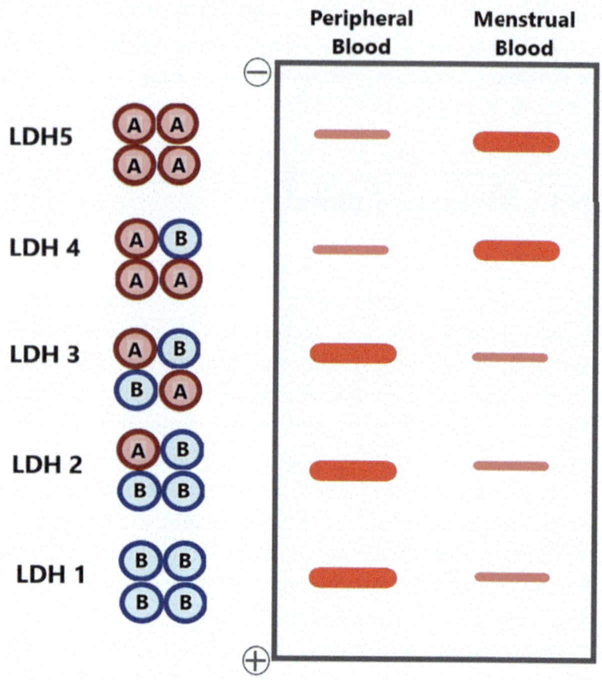

Fig. 18.3 Lactate Dehydrogenase Immunoassay

is present in human blood in the form of five isoenzymes that differ in the structural composition of their subunits. These isoenzymes function in the same catalytic reaction inspite of the difference in their molecular structure and can be separated by means of electrophoretic mobility and colorimetric assay (Fig. 18.3).

LDH1 has the highest electrophoretic mobility and LDH5 has the lowest electrophoretic mobility. Isoenzyme LDH4 and LDH5 are predominant in menstrual blood, while LDH1, LDH2 and LDH3 are predominant in peripheral blood (Li 2015; Holtkötter et al. 2018). This difference in concentration of isoenzymes can distinguish menstrual blood from peripheral blood.

18.3.1.2 D-dimer Identification

Detection of fibrinolysis degradation products (FDPs) that are specific to menstrual blood is another important aspect for distinguishing menstrual blood from peripheral blood. Cleaving of cross-linked fibrin by plasmin during the process of fibrinolysis, results in the formation of these FDPs. D-dimer, a subunit of FDPs is a fibrinolysis-specific fragment of the protein, therefore this assay is also known as D-dimer assay (Holtkötter et al. 2018; Kaur et al. 2018). The application of D-dimer assay for the identification of menstrual blood was suggested by Miyaishi et al. in 1996 (Miyaishi et al. 1996). They reported an extensively higher concentration of D-dimer approximately 200-fold in menstrual blood than that of peripheral blood. Baker et al. later

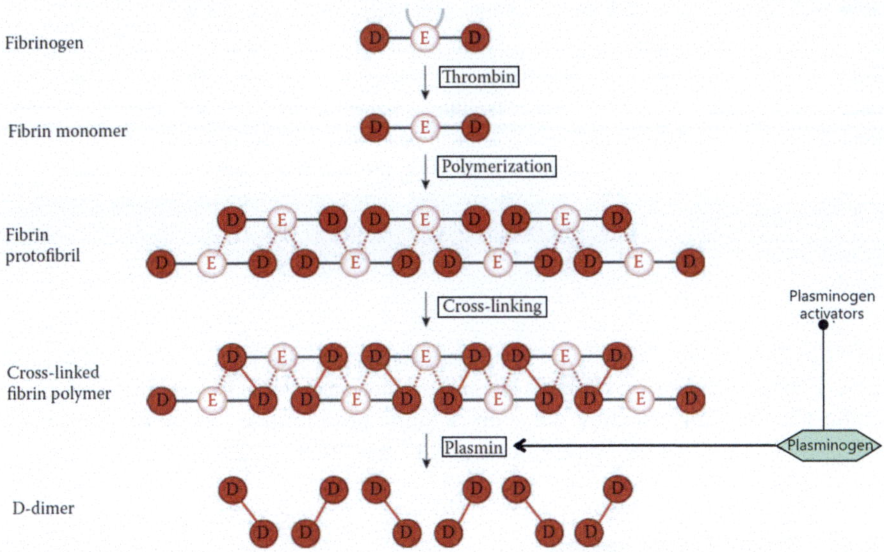

Fig. 18.4 Mechanism of d-dimer formation

identified four assays based on D-dimer detection for the identification of menstrual blood (Fig. 18.4) (Baker et al. 2011).

Immunological assays such as enzyme-linked immunosorbent assay (ELISA), agglutination assays, and immunochromatographic assays make use of D-dimer specific antibodies for the detection of D-dimer in the sample (Bagwe 2018). These techniques are highly sensitive in nature, thereby aid in distinguishing menstrual blood from peripheral blood. However, an adequate quantity of D-dimer subunit is also found in postmortem blood which may pose complications in the interpretation of the result. But at the same time, PM blood is not frequently encountered in cases of sexual assaults; therefore, the assay can be reliably applied in such cases.

18.4 Semen

Majority of cases received in the Forensic Laboratories are sexual assault cases, in which semen is one of the commonly encountered evidences. So, the analysis of semen plays an important role in solving sexual assault crimes. Semen is a viscous, slightly yellowish or grayish, and opalescent secretion having a characteristic odor known as seminal odor. It basically comprises seminal fluid and sperm cells. Seminal fluid is generally made up of water, sugar, protein, vitamins and minerals while the sperm cells comprises spermatozoa (Table 18.1) (Gill et al. 1985; Li 2015).

General exhibits collected for semen examination are swabs, vaginal slides, clothing, bedding items, condoms, etc. Stains from semen are readily visible on

Table 18.1 Percentage contribution of various gland secretions in seminal fluid

Gland	Percentage (approx.)	Description
Testes	2–5%	200–500 million spermatozoa released per ejaculation
Seminal vesicle	65–75%	Amino acids, citrate, enzymes, flavins, fructose, phosphorylcholine, prostaglandins, proteins, vitamin C
Prostate	25–30%	Acid phosphatase, citric acid, fibrinolysin, prostate specific antigen, proteolytic enzymes, zinc
Bulbourethral glands	<1%	Galactose, mucus, pre-ejaculate, sialic acid

fabrics as they exhibit a stiff and crusty appearance. Generally, in many cases, the fabric is been washed or contains a very minute stain, visual examination of the exhibit may help in detecting the stain or some presumptive or confirmatory tests may also be done (Butler 2007; Cotton and Fisher 2015; Li 2015).

18.4.1 Visual Examination

18.4.1.1 Color

Thick, yellowish-white, glary, and opalescent secretion having a characteristic odor known as seminal odor.

18.4.1.2 Texture

On touch, seminal stains are starchy and after drying, they become hard and rough.

18.4.1.3 Smell

The faint smell of fresh or wet seminal stains is characteristic due to a mixture of chemicals.

18.4.1.4 Appearance

In natural light, some stains are reddish colored, while others are brown, yellow or faint grey in color.

18.4.1.5 Peel

Dry stains have a rough feel like dried starch solution and have uneven surface (Stefanidou et al. 2010).

18.4.2 Examination Under UV Rays

The exhibit/article suspected to bear seminal stains gives bluish-white color fluorescence when examined under ultraviolet rays in darkness. It depends a lot upon the quantity and freshness of the semen (Kobus et al. 2002).

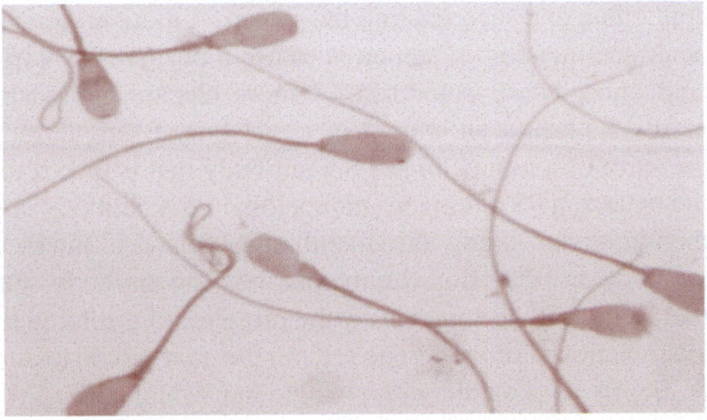

Fig. 18.5 Microscopic examination of sperm cells

18.4.3 Microscopic Examination

It is considered as a confirmatory technique for the presence of semen in the suspected exhibit. By extracting a small portion of a stain with water, followed by gentle vortexing, the cells from a suspected stain on an absorbent material can be transferred to a microscope slide and then heated. Then the slide is observed under microscope. Spermatozoa are slender, elongated structures 50–70 µm long, each with a head and a thin flagellate tail. Microscopic identification of spermatozoa provides the proof of a seminal stain. Histological staining can facilitate microscopic examination. The most common staining technique is the Christmas tree stain. Since spermatozoa holds gram-positive protein, the appearance of purple bodies will confirm the presence of spermatozoa (Fig. 18.5) (Stefanidou et al. 2010; Li 2015).

18.4.4 Phosphatase Method

The Acid phosphate test is one of the best-known and most commonly used techniques for the purpose of identification of semen. Acid phosphatase is an enzyme that is secreted into a seminal fluid by the prostate gland. When it comes in contact with an acidic solution of sodium alpha naphthylphosphate and Fast Blue B dye, its presence can easily be detected. The presence of acid phosphatase in semen helps to search large areas and garments for semen stains.

If a moistened filter paper is rubbed on the suspected area, acid phosphatase may be transferred to the filter paper. Now, on adding alpha naphthylphosphate and Fast Blue B solution, purple color will appear, indicating the presence of acid phosphatase (Romero-Montoya et al. 2011; Li 2015).

18.4.5 Prostate-Specific Antigen

In 1970s, a protein called p30 or prostate-specific antigen (PSA) was discovered which was thought to be prostate-specific. PSA is produced in the prostate epithelium and secreted into the semen. A more reasonable approach to the unequivocal identification of semen is to use a positive PSA (p30) in combination with an acid phosphatase color test. A more elegant approach to identifying PSA (p30) involves placing an extract of a questioned sample on a porous membrane in the presence of a monoclonal PSA antibody that is linked to a dye. If PSA is present in the extract, a PSA antigen–monoclonal PSA antibody complex forms. This complex then migrates along the membrane, where it interacts with a polyclonal PSA antibody embedded in the membrane. The antibody–antigen–antibody "sandwich" that forms will be apparent by the presence of a colored line. Once the material under examination is proven to be semen, the next task is to attempt to associate the semen as closely as possible with a single individual (Laux 2003; Li 2015).

18.4.6 Biological Tests

Precipitin reaction with anti-human semen serum and specific blood group anti sera are employed. The former determines whether it is human semen and the latter determines the blood group of the secretor. The techniques employed are similar to those applied for blood grouping.

18.4.7 Chemical Tests

The following chemical tests are performed for the detection of semen:

18.4.7.1 Barberio's Test

Barberio's test was discovered by Barberio in the year 1905. A small amount of semen is taken and treated with a saturated aqueous solution of picric acid. Needle-shaped spermine picrate crystals having yellow color with characteristic structure, separate out.

18.4.7.2 Florence Test

This test was discovered by Dr. Florence in the year 1886. A small amount of semen is treated with iodine in a potassium iodide solution (Potassium Iodide + Iodine + Water). Characteristic dark crystals of choline iodide having rhomboidal shape are formed (Table 18.2) (Yudianto and Sispitasari 2016).

Table 18.2 Time duration for the presence of motile and non-motile sperms in the body cavities

	Motile sperms	Non-motile sperms
Vagina	6–28 h	14 h to 10 days
Cervix	3–7.5 days	7.5–19 days
Mouth	–	2–31 h
Rectum	–	4–113 h
Anus	–	2–44 h

18.5 Vaginal Fluid

Vaginal fluid is crucial evidence found in cases of sexual assault as these evidences can support in verifying the allegations of sexual assault. If the stain is originating from the victim, it creates a link between the victim and the perpetrator. But, it may be questioned whether the stain is originated from sweat or vaginal secretion. So, the value of evidence may increase if it is found to be a vaginal stain. A mixture of vaginal secretion and semen stain is generally found and the presence of vaginal secretion confirms the incidence of sexual assault. When these are on clothing, vaginal Secretions appear to be rough and stiff on feeling. If observed under UV light examination, these show fluorescence (Li 2015).

The human vagina is mainly composed of squamous mucosa, submucosa, and muscularis. The vaginal fluid generally is a mixture of miscellaneous proteins from the upper genital tract, cervical mucus, transudate, desquamated cellular debris, leukocytes, epithelial residue, lactic acid and electrolytes (Shrivastava et al. 2020). Cotton swabs can be used for sample collection from a suspect's pubic area or fingers or by cutting or scraping the stain from the suspected item. Stains can be detected by fluorescence of vaginal fluid constituents using the alternate light source (ALS) method. One of the most commonly used methods of vaginal fluid identification is based on immunological assays. Some characteristics used in female hormone markers are 17b-estradiol (E2-17b), estrogen receptors, mucin 4 (MUC4) and human b-defensin 1 (HBD-1) etc.

18.5.1 Lugol's Iodine Test

Lugol's iodine solution is a color test that is utilized for the identification of glycogenated vaginal epithelial cells. The technique is based on the principle that iodine reacts with intracellular glycogen to exhibit a dark brown color. In cases of evidences containing skin, buccal and vaginal epithelial cells, it is necessary to distinguish between these cells. Dane's staining method has been developed to distinguish all three types of cells. Skin cells are stained red and orange; buccal cells are stained predominantly orange-pink with red nuclei; and vaginal cells are stained bright orange with orange nuclei (Rothwell and Harvey 1978).

18.5.2 Vaginal Acid Phosphatase

Very small amounts of acid phosphatase which is produced in normal cervical epithelial cells can be detected in vaginal fluid. But, molecular characteristics of vaginal acid phosphatase are still not known. Earlier, using acid phosphatase catalytic assays vaginal acid phosphatase was used as a biomarker for the identification of vaginal secretions. Using agarose electrophoresis, vaginal and prostate acid phosphatases can also be distinguished on the basis of their electrophoretic mobility. Prostate acid phosphatase has higher electrophoretic mobility toward an anode (a positively charged electrode) than vaginal acid phosphatase. Thus, the presence of vaginal acid phosphatase can be determined (Adams and Wraxall 1974).

18.6 Saliva

Saliva as an evidence is generally recovered from crime scenes involving oral activities, often in relation with bite marks on the skin as in cases of violent crimes and sexual assaults, on eatables, clothing, cigarette butts, chewing gums, documents, postage stamps etc (Houck and Siegel 2015). Saliva is an extracellular fluid mixture of various secretions from acinar cells of salivary glands, together with secretion from non-salivary sources like nasal secretion, gingival fluid, bronchial mucus, buccal cells, bacterial products and food remains (Tanaka et al. 2017). The colorless and quick-drying nature of saliva stains as well as its presence in trace amounts makes identification and collection of these stains difficult. A double swab technique is preferred for the collection of such samples. In this technique, the surface (skin, clothing etc) should be swabbed twice, firstly, using a wet swab and then followed by second swabbing with a dry swab (Rutty et al. 2003; John et al. 2018).

18.6.1 Characteristics of Saliva

The human salivary glands contribute about 1.0–1.5 L of saliva daily out of which 70% of saliva is released from the submandibular 25% from the parotids, and 5% from the sublingual salivary glands (Li 2015). Besides fluid contents, saliva also contains small amounts of antibodies, electrolytes and enzymes. The enzymes present in the saliva, particularly amylase is the prime factors for the readily digestion of complex carbohydrates or polysaccharides such as starch in the oral cavity. Besides saliva, amylase is also, localized in other body fluids such as blood, urine, sweat, tears, semen, breast milk, feces, and vaginal secretions but is in trace concentration as compared to the salivary fluid. Thus, determining the presence of amylase in the evidences indicates the existence of saliva (Gefrides and Welch 2011; Gunn 2019).

18.6.2 Visual Examination

The colorless nature of dried saliva stains makes them difficult to be identified in normal lights. Application of alternating sources of light in the range of 470 nm excitation wavelength (using red goggles), UV lights, and argon laser lights helps in identifying and locating saliva easily. Microscopic examination with proper histological staining can also be performed to identify the buccal epithelial cells, indicating the presence of a saliva stain.

18.6.3 Preliminary Test

18.6.3.1 Iodine Assay

The enzymatic activity of amylase can be determined by observing the reaction of iodine with the starch. The glucose polymers of starch, namely amylose and amylopectin react with iodine to form dark blue and reddish purple color respectively. In presence of amylase within the sample, the starch breaks down into simpler disaccharides and mono-saccharides, thereby no color appears on adding iodine to the sample.

The iodine assay must be performed on the test sample along with positive and negative control samples. All three samples namely the test sample, positive control, and negative control must be taken in equal quantity or dimension. Two to three drops of 0.5% soluble starch solution are added to each of the three samples and incubated at 37 °C for 1 h. Two drops of Lugol's iodine solution (composed of 1 g Iodine and 2 g Potassium iodide dissolved in 200 mL of distilled water) are added to these samples and observed for notable color change. The appearance of blue color indicates the absence of amylase thereby pointing the absence of saliva in the sample. Discolored reaction or absence of blue color after the reaction indicates a positive amylase reaction and the presence of saliva in the sample.

18.6.3.2 Phadebas Test

This test is based on the fact that amylase digests starch. Phadebas reagent consists of a dye cross-linked with starch. The presence of saliva digests the starch and releases the dye from the complex. The solution thus becomes blue in color. This indicates the presence of saliva. The test can be used as a quantitative test by measuring the intensity of the developed color at 620 nm wavelength. A standard concentration curve of known concentration of colored dye may be prepared and used for quantitative data.

18.6.3.3 Radial Diffusion Assay

An agar gel containing starch is prepared. A sample well is created by punching a hole in the gel and an extract of the questioned sample is placed into the well. If amylase is present in the sample, it diffuses from the sample well and hydrolyzes the starch in the gel. The gel is then stained using an iodine solution. A clear area in the gel indicates amylase activity, and the size of the clear area is proportional to the amount of amylase in the sample. A linear standard curve can be prepared using a series of standard amylases with known concentrations. The amount of amylase can be quantified by comparing the results with the standard curve.

18.6.4 Confirmatory Test

18.6.4.1 Immuno-Chromatographic Assays

Various commercially produced immuno-chromatographic kits are used for the identification of Human *salivary α-amylase* (HSA). RSID®-Saliva kit (Independent

Forensics, Hillside, IL) utilizes a labeled monoclonal anti-HSA antibody is contained in a sample well. A second monoclonal anti-HSA antibody is immobilized onto a test zone of a membrane, and an antiglobulin that recognizes the antibody is immobilized onto a control zone.

18.6.4.2 Enzyme-Linked Immunosorbent Assay (ELISA)

Enzyme-Linked Immunosorbent Assay (ELISA) is an immunoenzymatic test used for the quantitation of species-specific antigens or antibodies. For the identification of saliva, ELISA can be employed to quantify the human-specific amylase antigen present in the sample. The method utilizes reporting enzymes that produce colorimetric or fluorometric signals of intensities that are proportional to the amount of binding antigens with the use of an anti-HSA antibody. Antibody-antigen-antibody sandwich is one of the most common configurations in forensic serology. The intensity of the signals can be detected by means of spectrophotometers and the total quantity of HSA can be calculated using a standard of known concentration. ELISA is a species-specific and highly sensitive assay but, it is time-consuming.

18.7 Urine

In cases of violent crimes, hanging, illicit drug screening tests, sexual assault and harassment involving urination, urine may be submitted as important forensic evidence. The location of the stains of urine at the crime scene may provide vital information to determine the site of violence occurred.

The formation of urine takes place in the nephrons in the kidneys. Urine is an aqueous solution, yellow in color, consisting largely of water having urea in the most abundant quantity, which is resulted from the elimination of ammonia, also providing it a unique odor. The average urea concentration in human urine is approximately 9 g/L. Other major components of urine are creatinine, uric acid, and ions such as phosphate, sulfate, chloride, sodium, and potassium. In cases of urine stains, the sample should always be collected from the largest stains that are available. The collection and storage of samples should be properly done in order to avoid degradation. Medicines and foods such as penicillin and red beets, asparagus may affect the odor and color of urine. The ph of urine ranges between 4.6 and 8.0 and a specific gravity between 1.005 and 1.030 (Jones et al. 2012; Li 2015; Joki-Erkkilä et al. 2016; Vyas et al. 2020).

18.7.1 Visual Examination

Urine stains can be located by visual examination based on the characteristic yellow color of urine and the detection of the distinctive odor of urine stains. A suspected urine stain may show fluorescence of pale yellow or pale blue color when viewed under UV light. Medicines, foods and drugs may affect the color of urine.

18.7.2 Odor Test

The characteristic odor of urine may be detected by placing a small sample of the stain in a test tube and heating it gently over the flame.

18.7.3 Presumptive Test

18.7.3.1 Creatinine Test

This presumptive test for the detection of creatinine in urine was developed by a German biochemist Jaffe in 1886. Therefore, it is also known as Jaffe's test. To a drop of stain extract on filter paper, add one drop of picric acid followed by one drop of 5% Sodium hydroxide (weak base) to form a deep yellow-orange color.

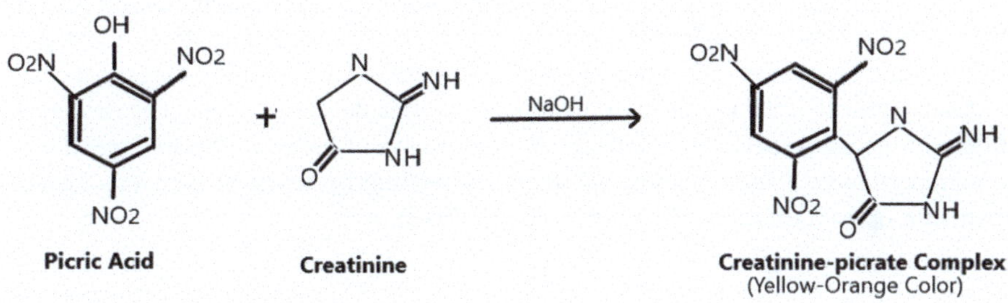

18.7.4 Confirmatory Test

18.7.4.1 Urea Nitrate Crystal Test

An aqueous extract of stain is made with acetone and then the acetone extract is concentrated by evaporation and then dried, after filtration. The residue, after dissolving in acetone is again evaporated. A thin film is made on a microscopic slide by adding one drop of conc. Nitric acid. In the presence of urea, hexagonal stacked crystals of Urea nitrate can be observed. The crystals are long colorless, four or six-sided rhombic crystals (Desroches et al. 2009).

18.7.4.2 Detection of Indican

In this test, the extracted stain is treated with resorcinol reagent and cupric bromide ($CuBr_2$) solution. Red color crystals are observed, indicating the presence of Indican (Desroches et al. 2009; Li 2015).

18.8 Sweat

Sweat, deposited unconsciously at various surfaces, rarely engages one's attention during the deliberate cleaning of other evidences. Biologically, sweat is a transparent bio-fluid secreted from eccrine and apocrine sweat glands, with low tonicity and a slightly acidic nature with mean pH of 6.3, that is, more acidic than blood. The majority of sweat evidence that is analyzed in forensic laboratories is sweat stains secreted from eccrine glands. Sweat contains water, minerals, lactate, and urea. Its biochemical composition varies among individuals and their physical activities. Sweat contains low levels of constituents that are also present in other bodily fluids such as urine such as amino acids and urea, potassium, sodium, chloride ions, lactate, pyruvate and xenobiotics. Thus, it has been considered a difficult bodily fluid to identify. Around 650 sweat glands are present in an average square inch of the skin resulting in primary transfer, i.e., deposition of a trace amount of sweat on surfaces that come in contact with the skin (Jadoon et al. 2015).

Sweat as evidence can be analyzed using various presumptive assays. The quality of sweat analysis depends on the efficiency of sample collection and the accuracy and sensitivity of analytical methods. Elemental analysis using scanning electron microscopes coupled with energy-dispersive X-ray spectroscopy in the detection of lactic acid is generally used. Raman micro-spectroscopy is potentially useful for the identification of sweat for forensic purposes. Another technique has been identified as a potential biomarker of human sweat i.e. dermcidin. Dermcidin belongs to a class of human antimicrobial peptides of the innate immune defense system. The detection of dermcidin can be performed through ELISA assays utilizing antibodies specific to human dermcidin. This method of detection is highly sensitive and can detect dermcidin up to a dilution of 10,000-fold (Li 2015).

18.9 Tears

Tears, secreted in very less volume, can be a potential tool to establish the identity. Tears can be found as stains deposited on tissue papers, handkerchiefs, pillows, bedding, etc. Traditionally, investigators have been trained to identify the presence of blood, saliva, semen, urine, etc. but generally, they fail to endorse the possibility of finding tears as evidence. Tears can offer important clues both qualitatively and quantitatively as they may help in personal identification (Aparna and Iyer 2021).

Lacrimation is generally classified into three categories based on their composition—basal tears, biochemical substances such as proteins, lipids, organic molecules, metabolites, and electrolytes. Tears contain a high concentration of proteins, ions and antioxidant compounds such as tear albumin, lysozymes, lactoferrin, transferrin, ceruloplasmin, lipocalin, prealbumin, lipophilin, IgA, IgG, secretory IgA, IgE, Glycoproteins, antiproteinases, Enzymes such as lactate dehydrogenase, Lysosomal enzymes, amylase, peroxidase, plasminogen activators, collagenase, Lipids such as cholesterol, Metabolites as glucose, lactate, urea, catecholamine, histamine, prostaglandins, Electrolytes such as hydrogen ions, potassium, calcium and magnesium.

Cloth or paper material, tissue paper or a handkerchief, and bedding material can be potential sources for finding the presence of tears. The use of Alternate Light Sources (ALS) can help in locating their presence on various surfaces since body fluids are known to fluoresce when exposed to varying wavelengths of light. It is also possible to perform ABO typing and DNA profiling from tears deposited on various substrates (Shrivastava et al. 2020; Aparna and Iyer 2021).

18.10 Bloodstain Pattern Analysis

Bloodstain Pattern Analysis plays a major role in crime scene analysis and reconstruction of crime scene. In violent crimes, it is very usual for the participants to be injured. In general, these injuries are accompanied by blood flow in different blood stain patterns may result which can provide crucial information about the crime. Bloodstain Pattern Analysis (BPA) may be termed as the study of the shapes, sizes, distribution, and locations of bloodstains and may provide information about the events that have taken place during the crime (Wideman 2009). It is principally based on the physical science (cohesion, capillary action and velocity) in addition to chemical, biological (behavior of blood), and medical knowledge. The history of BPA can be traced back to the 1500s as Herbert Leon MacDonnellhas found literature references to bloodshed characteristics. In 1895, an article based on experiments to examine bloodstain patterns resulting from head wounds was published by Dr. Eduard Piotrowski (James et al. 2005). Characteristics of blood in terms of physical laws are essential factors affecting blood stain patterns. This includes:

1. **Surface Tension**: The spherical shape of blood drops is maintained by the phenomenon of surface tension that results in the inward pull of blood drop in horizontal and vertical direction thereby maintaining the shape of blood drop.
2. **Viscosity**: The resisting characteristic of blood towards the flow is called its viscosity
3. **Density**: The mass of blood per unit volume of surface is known as the density of bloodstain.

18.10.1 Categories of Bloodstains on the Basis of Velocity

The abovementioned phenomenon of fluid dynamics plays an important role in retaining the shape of blood stain. Besides, velocity related to the force applied on the blood source also directs the size, shape, and characteristics of blood stain. The diameter of blood stain formed due to a certain force is inversely related to the velocity (Boos et al. 2019; Faiz 2021). Based on this concept, blood stains can be classified into three categories:

18.10.1.1 Low-Velocity Blood Spatter

The blood spatter formed as a result of force with a velocity up to 5 ft/s is said to be a Low-velocity blood spatter. The diameter of such spatter measures more than 4 mm. Free-falling blood drops under gravity, splashing blood, and stepping into the blood pool are examples of low-velocity blood spatter.

18.10.1.2 Medium-Velocity Blood Spatter

The blood spatters with diameter ranging between 1 and 3 mm are produced from the force with a velocity between 5 and 25 ft/s. The wound caused by blunt objects such as fist, hammer, etc and stabbing wound create medium-velocity blood spatter.

18.10.1.3 High-Velocity Blood Spatter

When force of velocity greater than 100 ft/s is applied to a blood source, the spatter formed is called a high-velocity blood spatter. The stains so formed are with a diameter less than 1 mm. High-speed trauma such as gunshot, explosive, or machinery injury causes the formation of high-velocity blood spatter.

18.10.2 Types of Bloodstain Patterns

Bloodstain patterns can be mainly categorized into three types: passive, transfer and projected patterns. Passive patterns are formed due to gravity and include patterns like drip stain, flow stain, blood pool, and serum stain. The blood stain patterns formed due to contact of a blood-bearing surface and non-blood-bearing surface, the pattern is said to be of pattern bloodstains. Projected bloodstain patterns result from excessive pressure or force. Besides the three categories, some of the unusually modified bloodstains can also be observed at the crime scene. In case of physical alteration or change occurs to the bloodstain pattern by means of physical activity, diffusion, dilution, or insects, the pattern is said to be an altered pattern (Fig. 18.6) (Griffin 2006; Houck and Siegel 2015; Li 2015).

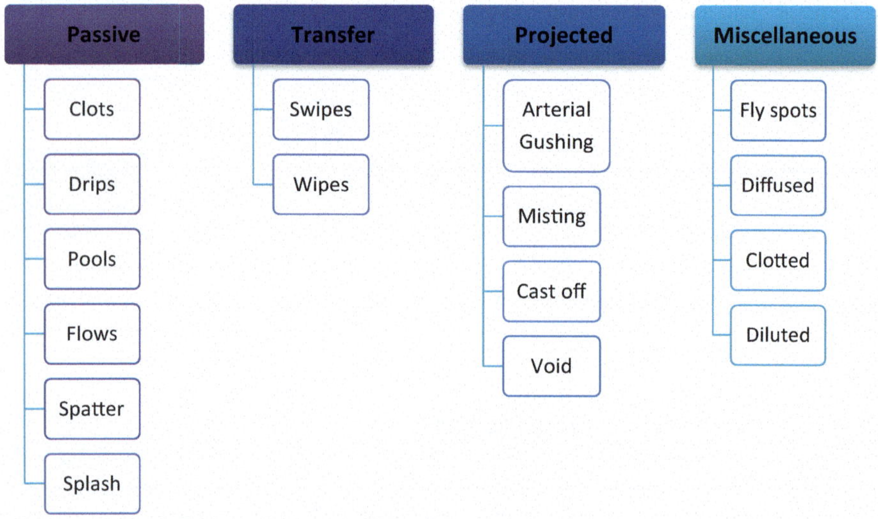

Fig. 18.6 Classification of bloodstain patterns

18.10.2.1 Passive Bloodstain Patterns

Passive bloodstain results from the flow of liquid blood in the form of bleeding generally deposited onto the surface under the influence of gravitational force alone.

18.10.2.1.1 Clots

A clot is can be described as the mass of blood cells trapped with fibrin. The phenomenon of serum separation is often seen in the clotted bloodstain patterns.

18.10.2.1.2 Drips

When drops of blood from any wound or blood source fall on the surface, they are said to be blood drip stains. If the blood source is in motion, the pattern of bloodstain is known as a drip trail. If a liquid falls on other liquid surfaces, with the circumstance of one or both the liquids being blood, a drip pattern is formed. Drip pattern is different from drip stains and results in the formation of secondary spatter.

18.10.2.1.3 Pools

The accumulation of liquid blood on the surface is called a blood pool.

18.10.2.1.4 Flows

Movement or disturbance in the large volume of blood pool on the surface due to some external force, such as gravity or post-mortem disturbance results in the formation of blood flows.

18.10.2.1.5 Spatter

When hard objects are used to strike the blood source, the force applied results in the dispersal of blood drops in the air. The patterns so formed are called spatter.

18.10.2.1.6 Splash

A large volume of blood spilling onto the surface is known as a blood splash.

18.10.2.2 Transfer Bloodstain Patterns

18.10.2.2.1 Swipe

The transfer of blood from any blood-bearing surface to another surface, characterizing the relativity of both surfaces is called a swipe pattern. The impressions probably provide information such as the shape and size of the object.

18.10.2.2.2 Wipe

It is a type of altered or disturbed pattern created by a moving object sliding onto the blood-bearing surface before it is dried and disturbing the patterns of the original stain.

18.10.2.3 Projected Bloodstain Patterns

18.10.2.3.1 Arterial Gushing and Spurts

Expulsion of blood in the form of gush and spurts under pressure fluctuation caused due to any injury to the artery or heart. Arterial gush is large-volume blood stain patterns while spurts refer to lesser-volume bloodstain patterns.

18.10.2.3.2 Misting

Explosive forces such as gunshot spatter result in blood stains formed in the pattern of mist or fine spray. This is known as atomized misting of blood. The blood stain patterns consist of multiple circular stains often microscopic in size. The size of individual stains is inversely proportional to the force implied to the blood source. As the force to the source of blood increases, the size of each stain decreases considerably.

18.10.2.3.3 Cast Off

When a stain is created as a result of blood, being projected from a secondary object in motion or suddenly coming to rest after some motion. The cast-off stain forms a linear pattern that provides information related to the general position of the secondary carrier, the number of blows struck and motions as well as directions.

18.10.2.3.4 Void Pattern

A void pattern is found when an object is placed between the blood source and projection area, it is likely to receive some of the stains, which consequently leads to an absence of stains in an otherwise continuous bloodstain pattern (Fig. 18.7).

18.10.3 Interpretation of Bloodstain Patterns

Bloodstain patterns play an important role in the reconstruction of crime scene. They provide vital information which may be helpful in the investigation and includes:

- Origin or source of bloodstain
- Direction of impact
- Number of blows or strikes
- Relative position and movement of victim, perpetrator or object in the crime scene
- Object or weapon used for the attack that produce particular bloodstain

Physical characteristics such as angle of impact, area of convergence, velocity of strike or spatter, relative distance between object and victim, surface type, and others are often useful parameters that help in the interpretation of bloodstain patterns (Table 18.3) (Damelio and Gardner 2001; Faiz 2021).

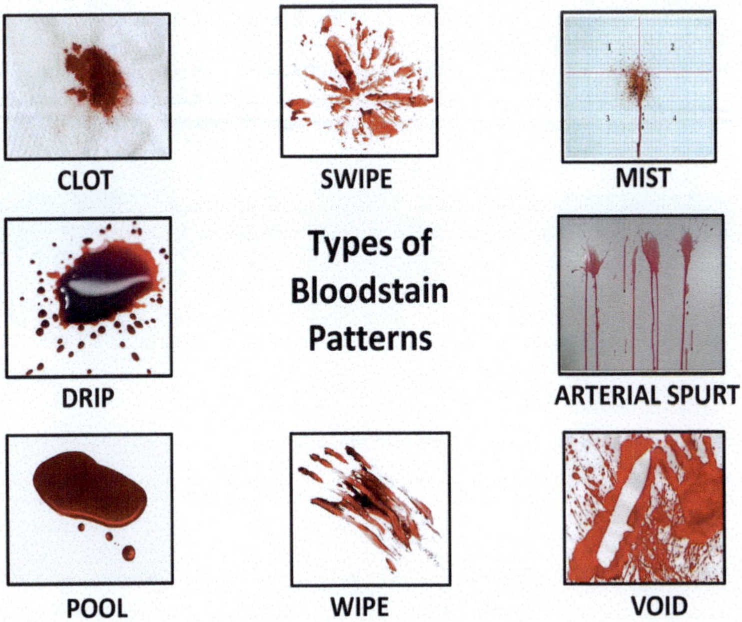

Fig. 18.7 Various types of bloodstain patterns commonly encountered at crime scenes

Table 18.3 Variation in the shape of bloodstains with changes in height

Shape of bloodstains	Height (in cm)
Round sharp edges	Up to 50
Spike like projections along edges	50–150
Corrugated edges	Over 150

18.11 Blood Grouping

The most widespread application of serology is the grouping of whole blood for its A-B-O identity. Blood group refers to the complete vast blood group system which is controlled genetically for specificity while blood type refers to a unique pattern of reaction to testing antisera within a given system. The earlier different blood types were recognized in 1875, but in 1901, Karl Landsteiner named and standardized the groups (Fig. 18.8).

The International Society of Blood Transfusion currently recognizes 43 blood group systems representing over 300 antigen polymorphisms. The ABO system of antigens in human erythrocytes is the most commonly used blood grouping system, which is used for its forensic applications. Other systems like Rh, MNS, Kell, Duffy, and Kidd systems are also used by Forensic laboratories (Rous 1947; Khan et al. 2013; St-Louis 2014; Li 2015; Minari and Mgbada 2017).

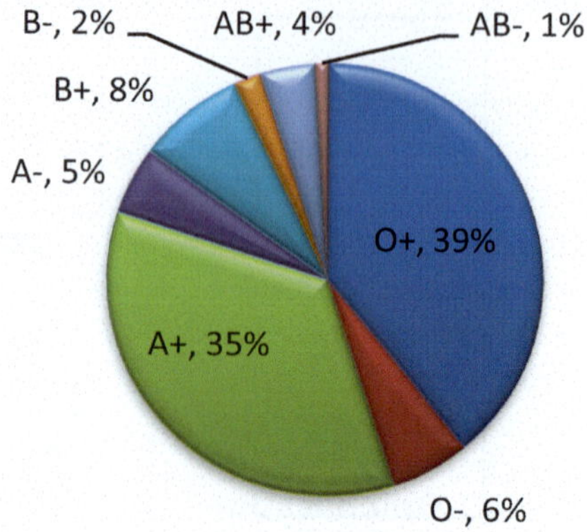

Fig. 18.8 Distribution of different blood-groups among world population

Table 18.4 Antigens and antibodies in different blood types

Blood types	Antigens on red cells	Antibodies in serum
A	A	Anti-B
B	B	Anti-A
AB	AB	Neither anti-A or anti-B
O	Neither A nor B	Both anti-A and anti-B

18.11.1 ABO System

It is of the most important and oldest transfusion and transplantation system. Any person above the age of 6 months possess clinically significant anti-A and/or anti-B antibodies in their serum. Blood group A contains antibody against blood group B in serum and vice-versa and blood group O contains both the antibodies in the serum but no A/B antigen. H-antigen is present in the entire RBC's irrespective of what the blood group system is. The only exception is the rare Bombay phenotype (homozygous for the H gene HH) where antigen A and B are absent. However, iso-antibodies to H-antigen as well as to antigens A and B are produced by these individuals (Table 18.4) (Olsson and Chester 2001; Storry and Olsson 2009; Khan et al. 2013; Landsteiner 2013; Li 2015).

- The "O" type is most common among indigenous people (like Aborigines and Native Americans) and Latin Americans.
- The "A" type is most common among Caucasians and those of European desert.
- The "B" type is most common among African-Americans and certain Asians (eg: Thai).
- The "AB" type is most common among the Japanese and certain Asians (eg: Chinese).

18.11.2 Rhesus System

After the ABO system, Rhesus-system (Rh-system) is the second most important blood group system. Around 50 defined blood group antigens are present in Rh-system out of which only five are important. Landsteiner and Wiener in 1940 discovered the human blood factor. The RBC surface of an individual may or may not have Rh factor or immunogenic D-antigen. Accordingly, the status is indicated as either Rh-positive (D-antigen present) or Rh-negative (D-antigen absent) (BOWMAN 1978; Gaensslen et al. 1985; Sinor et al. 1985).

18.11.3 MNS Antigen System

This system was first described by Landsteiner and Levine in 1927. It is generally based on two genes: Glycophorin A and Glycophorin B. Two antibodies called anti-M and anti-N were identified. These two antigens were derived from a single pair of genes which are allomorphic and co-dominant. The frequency for these groups in the human population for Group M is 20%, for Group N is 22% and for Group MN is 50%. Anti-M and anti-N antibodies are usually IgM types and rarely, associated with transfusion reactions (Gaensslen et al. 1985; Reid 2009).

18.11.4 Lutheran System

It basically comprises four pairs of allelic antigens which represent single amino acid substitution at chromosome 19 in Lutheran glycoprotein. The finding of a Lu (a+) child with Lu (a−) mother and putative father can be regarded as evidence of an exclusion based on another blood-group system. Anti-Lub is too rare for regular use and furthermore is of small value as it reacts with over 99% of samples (Gaensslen et al. 1985; Schenkel-Brunner 2000; Daniels 2009).

18.11.5 Kell System

After ABO and Rh system, these erythrocyte antigens are the third most important immunogenic antigen. These are defined by anti-K, an immune antibody. Rarely there is a presence of anti-K and this is sometimes helpful in paternity cases. The finding of a K-positive child with a K-negative mother and putative father would constitute an exclusion of paternity. Around 25 Kell antigens have been discovered so far (Lee et al. 2000; Dean 2005).

18.11.6 Duffy System

First isolated in a patient named Duffy having haemophilia, that's why this system is known as the Duffy system. It is present on the surface of RBCs and is also known as Fy glycoprotein. This system employs the use of two sera anti-Fya and anti-Fyb. Anti-Fya provides evidence of non-paternity when the putative father and mother are Fya− and the child Fya+. Anti-Fyb is a rare serum but if obtainable in sufficient quantity and strength could be usefully used with anti-Fya in the testing of white races (Meny 2010; Howes et al. 2011).

18.11.7 Kidd System

It comprises Kidd antigen (also known as Jk antigen), is a glycoprotein which is present on RBC's membrane and acts as a urea transporter in RBCs and renal endothelial cells. Although, being rare they can still cause severe transfusion reactions. Jka was the first antigen to be discovered by the Kidd blood group system, subsequently, two other antigens Jkb and Jk3 were found (Table 18.5) (Lundevall 1956; Hamilton 2015; Lawicki et al. 2017).

The application and usefulness of blood typing in forensic Science is the identification of individuals. Like, if at a crime scene, the blood found is type A, and the suspect is having type B, then the crime scene sample must have a different origin. And if both are having same blood group, then the sample may have come from the same origin or from a different origin that happened to be type A. Even in dried blood, A and B antigens can be identified after many years. They can also be identified in semen and other bodily fluids (Fig. 18.9).

18.12 Species Identification

After the identification of biological evidence, it becomes necessary to determine whether or not it is of human origin; and if of non-human origin, then to what species it belongs. The specific proteins of species in the bloodstains or any other biological fluid or any tissue of species can be identified with the aid of species-specific antibodies. Before the era of DNA technology, species identification was a common serological method. Currently, most forensic laboratories perform DNA quantitation prior to DNA profile analysis. To eliminate the possibility of nonhuman samples unrelated to an investigation, species identification methods can be vital.

The most common primary binding assays are immune-chromatographic assays. The most commonly used secondary binding assays are precipitation-based assays that rely on the binding of an antigen to an antibody, causing the formation of visible precipitation. These precipitation-based assays include the precipitin tube method, double diffusion (ring assays, Ouchterlony assays) and crossed-over immune-electrophoresis. These assays utilize antihuman and anti-animal antibodies to identify human and animal species, respectively. An antihuman antibody can be made by

Table 18.5 Globally recognized blood group systems

S. No.	System name	System symbol	Gene name(s)	Chromosomal location
1.	ABO	ABO	*ABO*	9q34.2
2.	MNS	MNS	*GYPA*, *GYPB*, (*GYPE*)	4q31.21
3.	P	P1PK	*A4GALT*	22q13.2
4.	Rh	RH	*RHD*, *RHCE*	1p36.11
5.	Lutheran	LU	*LU*	19q13.32
6.	Kell	KEL	*KEL*	7q34
7.	Lewis	LE	*FUT3*	19p13.3
8.	Duffy	FY	*DARC*	1q23.2
9.	Kidd	JK	*SLC14A1*	18q12.3
10.	Diego	DI	*SLC4A1*	17q21.31
11.	Yt	YT	*ACHE*	7q22.1
12.	Xg	XG	*XG*, *MIC2*	Xp22.33
13.	Scianna	SC	*ERMAP*	1p34.2
14.	Dombrock	DO	*ART4*	12p12.3
15.	Colton	CO	*AQP1*	7p14.3
16.	Landsteiner-Weiner	LW	*ICAM4*	19p13.2
17.	Chido/Rodgers	CH/RG	*C4A*, *C4B*	6p21.3
18.	Hh	H	*FUT1*	19q13.33
19.	Xk	XK	*XK*	Xp21.1
20.	Gerbich	GE	*GYPC*	2q14.3
21.	Cromer	CROM	*CD55*	1q32.2
22.	Knops	KN	*CR1*	1q32.2
23.	Indian	IN	*CD44*	11p13
24.	Ok	OK	*BSG*	19p13.3
25.	Raph	RAPH	*CD151*	11p15.5
26.	John Milton Hagen	JMH	*SEMA7A*	15q24.1
27.	I	I	*GCNT2*	6p24.2
28.	Globoside	GLOB	*B3GALT3*	3q26.1
29.	Gill	GIL	*AQP3*	9p13.3
30.	Rh-associated glycoprotein	RHAG	*RHAG*	6p21-qter
31.	Forssman	FORS	*GBGT1*	9q34.13
32.	Junior	JR	*ABCG2*	4q22
33.	Langereis	LAN	*ABCB6*	2q36
34.	VEL	VEL	*SMIM1*	1p36.32
35.	CD59	CD59	*CD59*	11p13
36.	Augustine	AUG	*SLC29A1*	6p21.1
37.	KANNO	PRNP	*PRNP*	20p13
38.	SID	SID	*B4GALNT2*	17q21.32
39.	CTL2	CTL2	*SLC44A2*	19p13.2
40.	PEL	PEL	*MRP4/ABCC4*	13q32.1

(continued)

Table 18.5 (continued)

S. No.	System name	System symbol	Gene name(s)	Chromosomal location
41.	MAM	MAM	*EMP3*	19q13.33
42.	EMM	EMM	*PIGG*	4p16.3
43.	ABCC1	ABCC1	*MRP1/ABCC1*	16p13.11

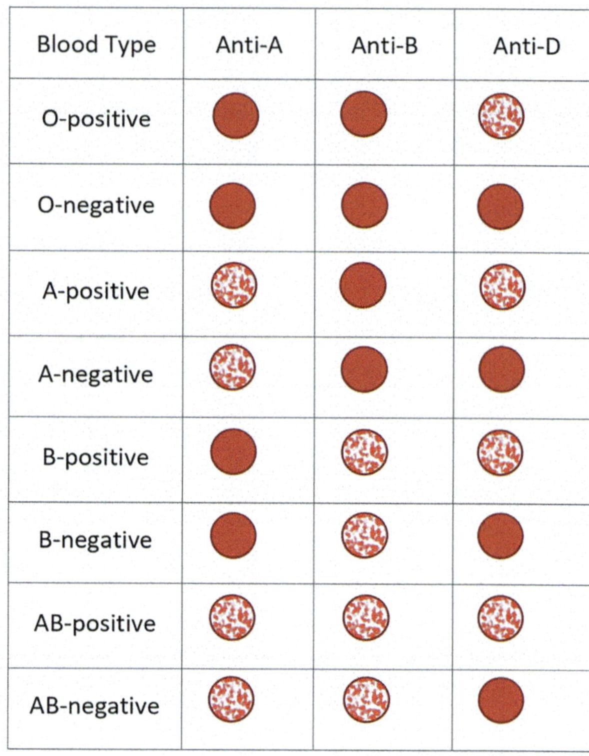

Fig. 18.9 Commonly employed kit for Human Blood Grouping and its agglutination reaction with different types of blood groups

introducing human serum into a host animal, for which specific antibodies are produced against the human serum proteins. The antihuman antibody reacts highly with human albumin. Then the serum part is collected from the blood drawn from the host and this serum is a polyclonal antihuman antiserum. Commercially produced immune-chromatographic kits such as the Hexagon OBTI and the ABAcard HemaTrace® are available to utilize the antibody–antigen–antibody sandwich method by using antibodies that recognize human Hb. Commercially produced immunochromatographic kits such as RSID™-Blood (Independent Forensics, Hillside, IL) use antibodies that recognize human GPA.

18.12.1 Precipitin Tube Method

Take six precipitin tubes (the number can vary on the number of anti-sera used) and place them vertically in a precipitin tube stand and label them. Put a drop of the bloodstain/tissue extract in the tubes. Carefully add one drop of antiserum for species origin (anti-Human serum, anti-Fowl serum, anti-Dog serum, anti-Cow Serum, anti-Goat serum, etc.) along the walls of the tube. Leave undisturbed for 30 min at room temperature. Carefully examine the white ring at the interface of the two solutions. If a precipitate is formed, it belongs to that specific anti-serum.

18.12.2 Double Diffusion Methods

In this method, both of the reactants, antigen and antibody diffuse towards each other in an agar gel plate, and when an antigen combines with its specific antibody at optimum proportions, precipitin is formed. Fill the central well with tissue extract and peripheral wells with different anti-sera for species origin (anti-Human serum, anti-Fowl serum, anti-Dog serum, anti-Cow Serum, anti-Goat serum, etc.). Cover the petri dish and keep the gel in a moist chamber overnight. Examine the gel for the presence of a precipitin band formed.

18.12.3 Crossed-Over Electrophoresis

Crossed-over electrophoretic technique is a fusion of immunodiffusion assay and electrophoresis. Two sets of wells are created in the agarose gel by punching holes arranged opposite to one another, the one proximal to anode is used for loading antibody and other proximal to the cathode is filled with samples. Electrophoresis is operated by the application of current to the gel plate that drives antigen (or samples) and antibody toward one another. Antigens being negatively charged migrate toward anode while antibodies being positively charged migrated due to the process of endo-osmosis or migrate under fluid flow. Observation of a sharp precipitate band indicates a positive result.

18.13 Polymorphic Enzyme Typing

Forensic Serologist uses multiple enzymes PGM, GLO I, EsD, EAP, AK, ADA, etc., for individualization purposes. The choice of markers employed completely depends upon the degree of polymorphism of the marker in the given population and its stability in aged bloodstains and tissues. Polymorphism in enzymes may be defined as the variant or allele of an enzyme encoded by one locus. Due to limitations in the blood grouping system, genetic protein polymorphic markers have been used to minimize the chance of matching among two unrelated individuals. The sequences of amino acids in proteins vary in the human population. Around 20–30% of human proteins are polymorphic and individuals can be divided on the basis of this polymorphism. For parentage testing and in analysis of criminal cases, a combination of blood grouping system and enzyme typing can be employed in order to decrease the possibility of match between two unrelated persons. Protein polymorphism identification process is based on electrophoretic separation which depends on molecular weight of proteins and charge on its variants.

18.13.1 Matrices Supporting Protein Electrophoresis

To separate various macromolecules, Electrophoresis of proteins is generally carried out in a support material called the matrix. Conventionally, two types of matrices for protein profiling were used: papers such as cellulose acetate; and gels composed of starch, agar, agarose, or polyacrylamide. The oldest polymorphic protein marker was phosphor-glucomutase which was used on starch-gel electrophoresis. But, agarose and polyacrylamide became more popular due to better reproducibility and reliability.

18.13.2 Separation by Molecular Weight

This separation is completely based on the molecular weights of the proteins. Non-denaturing electrophoresis (Native electrophoresis) was used to isolate proteins for studying their functions.

18.13.3 Separation by Isoelectric Point

This separation method, generally known as isoelectric focusing (IEF) technique is based on the isoelectric points (pI) of the proteins. The pI is the pH value when the net electric charge of an amino acid is zero and each amino acid has its own characteristic pI and is unable to migrate under electric charge.

18.13.4 Erythrocyte Protein Polymorphisms

Isoenzymes are multiple forms of an enzyme which vary in their amino acid sequences but catalyze the same reaction. The individuals can also be divided into units or groups based on different isoenzymes present in their erythrocytes according to Mendelian principles. Around 200 Hb variants have been identified of which Adult human consists of two α chains and two β chains. In cases of infanticide and concealed birth, the detection of fetal Hb in a bloodstain via electrophoresis process can provide important evidence. The ethnic origin of a perpetrator can be identified using a protein polymorphic marker e.g. Hb S polymorphism.

18.13.5 Serum Protein Polymorphisms

One of the most widely used polymorphic serum proteins in the forensic scenario was Haptoglobin (Hp). This method is based on the net charge, size, and shape of the protein and can be determined by electrophoresis or serological methods.

18.14 Conclusion

Advanced technologies and methods have revolutionized the use of biological evidences even collected decades ago in the hopes of linking criminals with the victim and the crime scene. Collection and preservation methods must be taken into consideration while collecting these evidences (serological evidences) as the condition of the exhibit during examination endures to be a critical element for its successful detection and analysis. Hence, pertinent handling standards during identifying, collecting, packaging, storing, and transporting samples are the elemental prerequisites.

References

Adams EG, Wraxall BG (1974) Phosphatases in body fluids: the differentiation of semen and vaginal secretion. Forens Sci 3:57–62

Aparna R, Iyer RS (2021) Detection and visualization of human tears using alternate light sources for forensic purposes. Sci Justice 61:771–778

Bagwe K (2018) Evaluation of recently developed methods for the forensic detection of menstrual blood

Baker DJ, Grimes EA, Hopwood AJ (2011) D-dimer assays for the identification of menstrual blood. Forensic Sci Int 212:210–214

Basu D, Kulkarni R (2014) Overview of blood components and their preparation. Indian J Anaesth 58:529

Boos K, Orr A, Illes M, Stotesbury T (2019) Characterizing drip patterns in bloodstain pattern analysis: an investigation of the influence of droplet impact velocity and number of droplets on static pattern features. Forensic Sci Int 301:55–66

Bowman JM (1978) The management of Rh-isoimmunization. Obstet Gynecol 52:1–16

Butler JM (2007) Short tandem repeat typing technologies used in human identity testing. BioTechniques 43:Sii–SSv

Castro DM, Coyle HM (2013) Biological evidence collection and forensic blood identification. Forensic Sci Dep Henry C Lee Coll Crim Justice Forensic Sci Univ New Haven, p 300

Cotton RW, Fisher MB (2015) Properties of sperm and seminal fluid, informed by research on reproduction and contraception. Forens Sci Int Genet 18:66–77

Damelio R, Gardner RM (2001) Bloodstain pattern analysis: with an introduction to crime scene reconstruction. CRC Press, Boca Raton, FL

Daniels G (2009) Lutheran. Immunohematology 25:152–159

Dean L (2005) The Kell blood group. In: Blood groups and red cell antigens. National Center for Biotechnology Information (US), Bethesda, MD

Desroches AN, Buckle JL, Fourney RM (2009) Forensic biology evidence screening past and present. Can Soc Forens Sci J 42:101–120

Faiz KHMA (2021) Bloodstain pattern analysis and its dynamics

Gaensslen RE, Lee HC, Pagliaro EM, Bremser JK (1985) Evaluation of antisera for bloodstain grouping I. ABH, MN, and Rh. J Forensic Sci 30:632–654

Gefrides L, Welch K (2011) Forensic biology: serology and DNA. In: The forensic laboratory handbook procedures and practice. Springer, New York, NY, pp 15–50

Gill P, Jeffreys AJ, Werrett DJ (1985) Forensic application of DNA 'fingerprints'. Nature 318:577–579

Griffin TJ (2006) Principles of bloodstain pattern analysis: theory and practice. J Forens Identif 56: 435

Gunn A (2019) Essential forensic biology. John Wiley & Sons, New York, NY

Hamilton JR (2015) Kidd blood group system: a review. Immunohematology 31:29–35

Hardwick J (2008) Blood processing. ISBT Sci Ser 3:148–176

Holtkötter H, Dias Filho CR, Schwender K et al (2018) Forensic differentiation between peripheral and menstrual blood in cases of alleged sexual assault—validating an immunochromatographic multiplex assay for simultaneous detection of human hemoglobin and D-dimer. Int J Legal Med 132:683–690

Houck MM, Siegel JA (2015) Chapter 10 - Serology and bloodstain pattern analysis. In: Houck MM, Siegel JA (eds) Fundamentals of forensic science. Academic Press, San Diego, CA, pp 235–260

Howes RE, Patil AP, Piel FB et al (2011) The global distribution of the Duffy blood group. Nat Commun 2:1–10

Jadoon S, Karim S, Akram MR et al (2015) Recent developments in sweat analysis and its applications. Int J Anal Chem 2015:164974. https://doi.org/10.1155/2015/164974

James SH, Kish PE, Sutton TP (2005) Principles of bloodstain pattern analysis: theory and practice. CRC Press, Boca Raton, FL

John SJ, Rajaji D, Jaleel D et al (2018) Application of saliva in forensics. Oral Maxillofac Pathol J 9:85

Joki-Erkkilä M, Tuomisto S, Seppänen M et al (2016) Urine specimen collection following consensual intercourse–a forensic evidence collection method for Y-DNA and spermatozoa. J Forensic Legal Med 37:50–54

Jones AW, Holmgren A, Ahlner J (2012) Toxicological analysis of blood and urine samples from female victims of alleged sexual assault. Clin Toxicol 50:555–561

Kaur H, Verma DP, Bhatia D (2018) Detection and comparison of Normal and Menstrual blood samples found at crime scene. Int J Curr Res Life Sci 7:2233–2236

Khan MN, Khan TA, Ahmed Z (2013) Discrepancy in ABO blood grouping. J Coll Physicians Surg Pak 23:590–592

Kobus HJ, Silenieks E, Scharnberg J (2002) Improving the effectiveness of fluorescence for the detection of semen stains on fabrics. J Forensic Sci 47:1–5

Landsteiner K (2013) The specificity of serological reactions. Courier Corporation, Chelmsford, MA

Laux DL (2003) Forensic detection of Semen I: the acid phosphatase test. Midw Assoc For Sci Newsl 32:6–10

Lawicki S, Covin RB, Powers AA (2017) The Kidd (JK) blood group system. Transfus Med Rev 31:165–172

Lee HC, Ladd C (2001) Preservation and collection of biological evidence. Croat Med J 42:225–228

Lee S, Russo D, Redman CM (2000) The Kell blood group system: Kell and XK membrane proteins. In: Seminars in hematology. Elsevier, London, pp 113–121

Li R (2015) Forensic biology. CRC Press, Boca Raton, FL

Lundevall J (1956) The Kidd Blood Group System. Acta Pathol Microbiol Scand 38:39–42

McNally L, Shaler RC, Baird M et al (1989) Evaluation of deoxyribonucleic acid (DNA) isolated from human bloodstains exposed to ultraviolet light, heat, humidity, and soil contamination. J Forensic Sci 34:1059–1069

Meny G (2010) The Duffy blood group system: a review. Immunohematology 26:51–56

Minari JB, Mgbada NM (2017) Forensic analysis of the correlation of ABO blood group frequency and criminalities among female inmates in a typical Nigerian Prison. Afr Sci 18:99–106
Miyaishi S, Kitao T, Yamamoto Y et al (1996) Identification of menstrual blood by the simultaneous determination of FDP-D dimer and myoglobin contents. Nihon Hoigaku Zasshi 50:400–403
Olsson ML, Chester MA (2001) Polymorphism and recombination events at the ABO locus: a major challenge for genomic ABO blood grouping strategies. Transfus Med 11:295–313
Reid ME (2009) MNS blood group system: a review. Immunohematology 25:95
Romero-Montoya L, Martínez-Rodríguez H, Pérez MA, Argüello-García R (2011) Relationship of spermatoscopy, prostatic acid phosphatase activity and prostate-specific antigen (p30) assays with further DNA typing in forensic samples from rape cases. Forensic Sci Int 206:111–118
Rothwell TJ, Harvey KJ (1978) The limitations of the Lugol's iodine staining technique for the identification of vaginal epithelial cells. J Forens Sci Soc 18:181–184
Rous FP (1947) Karl Landsteiner, 1868–1943
Rutty GN, Hopwood A, Tucker V (2003) The effectiveness of protective clothing in the reduction of potential DNA contamination of the scene of crime. Int J Legal Med 117:170–174
Schenkel-Brunner H (2000) Lutheran system. In: Human blood groups. Springer, New York, NY, pp 518–526
Shrivastava P, Kumawat RK, Kushwaha P, Rana M (2020) Biological sources of DNA: the target materials for forensic DNA typing. In: Dash HR, Shrivastava P, Lorente JA (eds) Handbook of DNA profiling. Springer, Singapore, pp 1–17
Sinor LT, Rachel JM, Beck ML et al (1985) Solid-phase ABO grouping and Rh typing. Transfusion 25:21–23
Stefanidou M, Alevisopoulos G, Spiliopoulou C (2010) Fundamental issues in forensic semen detection. West Indian Med J 59:280
St-Louis M (2014) Molecular blood grouping of donors. Transfus Apher Sci 50:175–182
Storry JR, Olsson ML (2009) The ABO blood group system revisited: a review and update. Immunohematology 25:48
Tanaka MH, Lima GMG, Ito CYK (2017) Biology of the oral environment and its impact on the stability of dental and craniofacial reconstructions. In: Material-tissue interfacial phenomena. Elsevier, London, pp 181–202
Vaught JB (2006) Blood collection, shipment, processing, and storage. Cancer Epidemiol Prev Biomark 15:1582–1584
Vyas B, Halamkova L, Lednev IK (2020) A universal test for the forensic identification of all main body fluids including urine. Forens Chem 20:100247
Wideman DA (2009) Tom Bevel, Ross Gardner: bloodstain pattern analysis. Forens Sci Med Pathol 5:56
Yudianto A, Sispitasari YE (2016) DNA isolation from human urine stain as an alternative material for personal identification examination. Folia Medica Indones 52:277–284

DNA and Its Significance in Forensic Science 19

Shivani Dixit, Manisha Rana, Pushpesh Kushwaha, Akash Kumar, Kapil Dev, and Pankaj Shrivastava

Abstract

The technique of DNA fingerprinting is considered as one of the enthralling innovations of the scientific era. The massive potential of the technique and its great evidentiary value has made it a boon for the world of forensic science and the criminal justice system. In the meantime, this particular DNA science has crossed significant milestones and hence assists in providing resolutions to various criminal offenses. The capability of discovering the polymorphism of human DNA in non-coding regions has been a great achievement for forensic DNA science. DNA typing is just like a miracle to the judiciary since it is a highly sensitive, specific, advanced, accurate and reliable technique whose outcomes can be easily trusted. There are various commercial STR kits available in the market

S. Dixit
Department of Forensic Science, DNA Division, UP State Institute of Forensic Sciences, Lucknow, UP, India

M. Rana
Biology and DNA Division, State Forensic Science Laboratory, Jaipur, India

P. Kushwaha
Serology and DNA Division, State Forensic Science Laboratory, Jaipur, Rajasthan, India

A. Kumar
Dr. A.P.J. Abdul Kalam Institute of Forensic Science and Criminology, Bundelkhand University, Jhansi, India

K. Dev
Biology, Serology and DNA Division, Forensic Science Laboratory, Moradabad, Uttar Pradesh, India

P. Shrivastava (✉)
Biology and Serology Division, Regional Forensic Science Laboratory, Gwalior, Madhya Pradesh, India

P. Shrivastava et al. (eds.), *Textbook of Forensic Science*,
https://doi.org/10.1007/978-981-99-1377-0_19

which have made recent advancements in the procedure and improvised the automation procedure. The progression of DNA typing methods from RFLP to STRs has escalated the sensitivity of the outcomes. Non-human DNA analysis stands as a fairly recent but powerful field. The latest practice in DNA fingerprinting is NGS which provides rapid evolution of results with high discrimination power. Further, there are several other prospective innovations in this science such as the development of different STR kits, i.e., autosomal STRs, Y-STRs, X-STRs, mini-STRs, etc., for forensic applications. The main focus of this chapter is to describe the applications of DNA fingerprinting techniques in the analysis of individuals in cases of mass fatalities or natural disasters where the family members do not even receive the dead body of their loved ones which leaves an indelible remark on them. Hence this efficacious science of DNA typing can help in evaluating the identity of those folks with the generation of links between them and their biological family members. The procedure of sample collection from the subsequent locations where these types of calamities take place is also demonstrated in this chapter for reference.

Keywords

Polymorphism · Short tandem repeats (STRs) · Genetic identification · Markers · Mitochondrial · Next generation sequencing (NGS)

19.1 DNA: The Genetic Molecule

The formation of genetic polymer molecule DNA or Deoxyribonucleic acid is based on four elementary nucleotides namely Adenine (A), thymine (T), Guanine (G) and Cytosine (C) which are organized in such a sequential manner that they symbolize the hereditary representation of all living organisms. The nucleus present inside the cell is comprised of DNA molecules where the exception is only observed in Red Blood Cells, it is structured with 46 diverse chromosomes which are inclusive of 22 pairs of Autosomes and one pair of sex chromosomes. The length of haploid DNA is approximately three billion pairs (Shewale et al. 2013; Li 2015) (Fig.19.1).

Each and every individual is inhabited with significant discriminations which individualize the person with respect to the inherited traits present inside the other individual. Further, the probability that the DNA sequences are similar between two individuals is about 99.9% and the 0.1% variations in the DNA sequence are found existing along the non-coding regions of DNA. The incongruities of the DNA sequences are specifically being kept under consideration to discriminate the traits amongst individuals which are made possible via DNA profiling (Venter et al. 2015). The discrepancy in the DNA sequences arises in the form of polymorphism, which accounts for diverse phenotypes and is significantly used in criminal investigations in the form of genetic markers. These polymorphisms are heritable and selectable and are transmitted from the parents to their offspring during the process of meiosis. Restriction Fragment Length Polymoprhism (RFLP), Variable Number of Tandem Repeats (VNTR), Random Amplification of Polymorphic DNA (RAPD) and

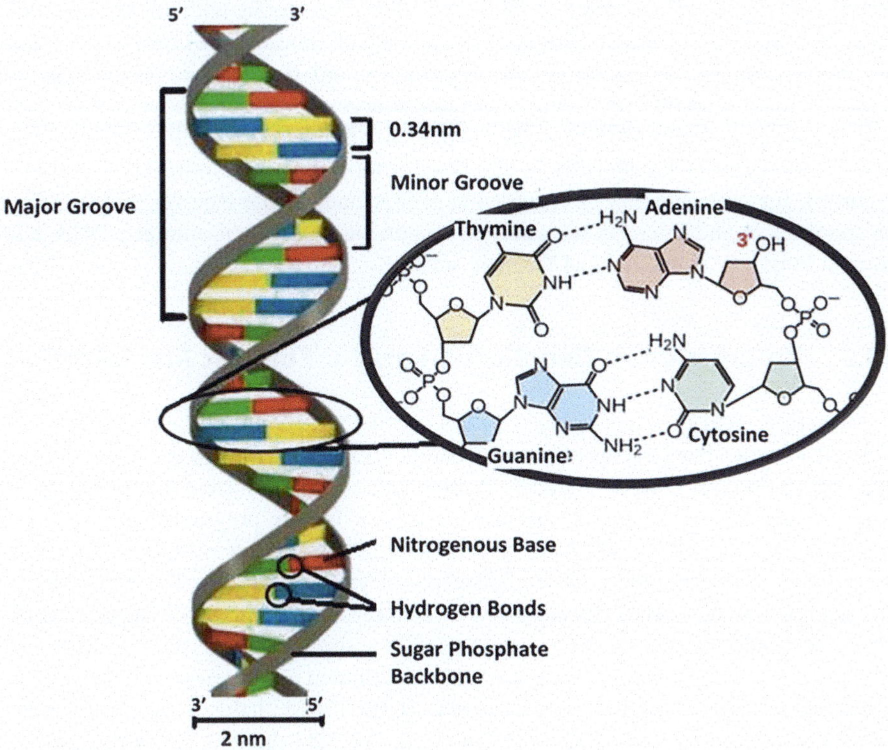

Fig. 19.1 Structure of DNA molecule and its elementary nucleotides

Amplified Fragment Length Polymorphism (AFLP) are some of the popular genetic polymorphisms used as a genetic marker in forensic science (Li 2015).

19.2 Commencement of Genetic Identification

The science of DNA Profiling was primarily used to detect the inherited diseases which are being transferred from the ancestors to the progenies. The analysis was carried out by the alliance of respective DNA sequences in context with the integrated markers which were found adjacent to each other inside the chromosome. The admissibility of the DNA profiling technique as new factual evidence began when a confident Ph.D. scholar Alec J. Jeffrey's from Leicester University, UK, described the existence of individual-specific fragments of cluttered DNA and their significance in individual identification and paternity testing (Jeffreys et al. 1985). The very first case involving the emergence of genetic evidence was not specifically a forensic case but a case of immigration disputes with the association of inherited components between the folks. The technique came to prominence in the field of criminal investigation in 1987 with a double murder case. Two 15-year-old girls were found raped and murdered in 1983 and 1986 respectively with the same modus operandi. Analysis of tissue samples & semen stains found at the crime scenes and the blood sample collected from the suspect Richard Buckland revealed that the semen stains at both the scenes had a common source of origin and they do not match with the blood samples of Richard Buckland. Six months later, Colin Pitchfork was apprehended and DNA analysis of his blood samples resulted in the conviction of Pitchfork for both murders (Jeffreys et al. 1985; Saad 2005; Roewer 2013). From morphological and microscopic analysis to genetic analysis of animals, DNA has come a long way in the field of forensic science.

19.3 Progression of Genetic Markers for Forensic Identification

From various RFLP-based markers to advanced PCR-based markers, the field of forensic genetics has undergone several technical advancements in the development and applications of genetic markers documented since the decade of 80s which is still progressing till date. Restriction fragment length polymorphism (RFLP) involves the cleavage of DNA strands at specific sites using restriction enzymes resulting in the formation of DNA fragments of variable lengths. These fragments are processed with southern blotting and detected using radiography (Vajpayee et al. 2020). Variable number tandem repeats (VNTR), also termed as mini-satellites are one of the classes of tandemly repeated DNA distributed in the genome. Every unit is consisted of around 6–16 base pair sequences (Li 2015). With the usage of restriction enzymes specifically for spots adjoining the VNTR, there is a probability of obtaining fragments of variable lengths in distinct individuals as there is an availability of various repeats in the subject. Due to their high polymorphic content and multi-allelic nature, VNTR serves as a useful tool in linkage analysis, forensic identification, paternity testing and population genetic studies (Pakzad et al. 2014). However, high time consumption, requirement of good quality DNA and inefficiency in the analysis of degraded samples resulted in superseding of RFLP-based markers by PCR-based multiplex markers (Li 2015; Imam et al. 2018a).

The second generation of molecular markers comprised polymerase chain reaction (PCR) based markers which involved the detection of polymorphisms in the amplified products of targeted DNA samples (Ma 1995; Benschop et al. 2012; Lorenz 2012). These markers can be classified on the basis of the sequence of DNA primers as (a) arbitrary sequence primer-based markers such as Randomly Amplified Polymorphic DNAs (RAPD), Inter Simple Sequence Repeats (ISSR), Arbitrarily Primed PCR (AP-PCR), (b) specific sequence primer based markers such as Sequence-Tagged Sites (STS), Short Tandem Repeats (STR), Sequence Characterized Amplified Region (SCAR), (c) intermediate or combined sequence-based markers such as Sequence Related Amplified Polymorphism (SRAP), Target Region Amplification Polymorphism (TRAP) and (d) restriction digestion based PCR markers such as Amplified Fragment Length Polymorphism (AFLP), Cleaved Amplified Polymorphic Sequence (CAPS) (Stone et al. 1993; Singh and Singh 2015). Short Tandem Repeat (STR), also known as Simple Sequence Repeats (SSRs) is a preponderant standard marker used in forensic caseworks.

19.3.1 Variable Number of Tandem Repeats (VNTRs)

Variable Number of Tandem Repeat (VNTR) loci are defined as genetic markers that are characterized by the repetition of a short DNA sequence motif at a single location multiple times (tandem repeat). In humans, these repeats are typically 1–5 kb long. VNTRs, commonly referred to as Minisatellites or Hyper Variable Regions (HVR) were the first polymorphisms used in DNA profiling (Jeffreys et al. 1985). These repeats comprise 10–60 bp and are prominently located in the centromeres and telomeres of chromosomes. The core of the fragment comprises a variable number of repeats linked in tandem that essentially comprise fixed-length repeats. The number of repeated motifs in a VNTR and the length of the sequence formed by VNTRs vary between individuals and therefore forms the basis of human identification based on VNTRs. Due to their high polymorphic content and multi-allelic nature, VNTR successfully aids in linkage analysis, forensic identification, paternity testing and population genetic studies (Pakzad et al. 2014). However, the requirement of a relatively large amount of DNA, complexity while working with degraded DNA and time-consuming procedure limits the use of VNTR analysis.

19.3.2 Single Nucleotide Polymorphism (SNPs)

Single nucleotide polymorphisms (SNPs) are the genetic loci consisting of alleles differing at a single base. These are the most abundant form of genetic variation in humans, accounting for more than 90% of all differences between unrelated people. Transition or transversion type of mutation is the possible cause for such polymorphisms (Budowle and Van Daal 2008). SNPs are widely distributed throughout the genome and can be present both in the coding region and in the non-coding region of the genome at a frequency of about one in thousand base pairs. The abundance of SNPs in the human genome, their low mutation rate, and the criteria for analyzing smaller fragments of DNA are the reason for their emergence as markers of interest in the field of forensic science (Sobrino et al. 2005). Multiplexing and automation of these markers assures their utility in cases of degraded DNA. Careful selection of SNP markers can also be applied for the prediction of ethnic origin and certain physical traits, defined as DNA phenotyping. Despite such advantages, SNPs are not ready to replace STRs as they are not polymorphic. A higher number of SNPs is required to reach equivalent powers of discrimination or random match probabilities. Also, the limited number of alleles (typically two) for each SNP locus limits the reliability of SNPs in mixture interpretation (Butler et al. 2007).

19.3.3 Short Tandem Repeats (STRs)

STRs are the microsatellites that consist of repetitive stretches of core repeat units formed of two to six nucleotides, tandemly repeated multiple times characterizing

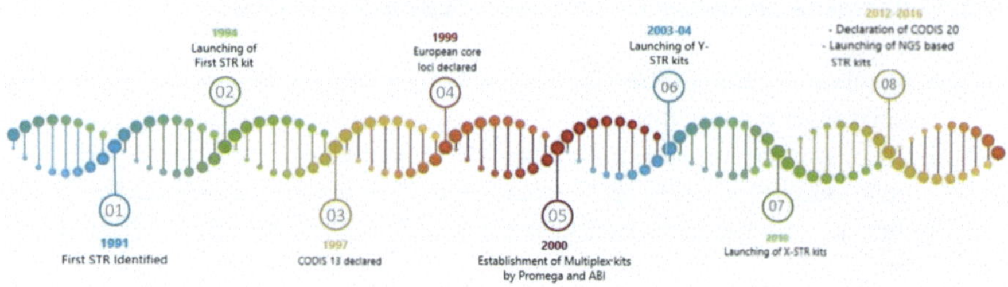

Fig. 19.2 Sequential Progression in the development of STR technique

intronic polymorphism among individuals (Tilanus 2006; Butler 2007). With the discovery in 1989 (Litt and Luty 1989), STRs became forensically important marker for individual identification due to their features such as multitude of occurrence within the genome with distant chromosomal location, short allelic lengths that make STR markers ideal for the analysis of compromised or degraded samples, high degree of polymorphisms and heterozygosity representing high discriminating power of loci, low stutter rate, low mutational rate and presence of less artefacts assuring the reproducibility of results (Somanathan and Mathur 2017; Barbaro 2020). Tetranucleotide STR loci are more prevalent in forensic DNA analysis over VNTRs and other types of STR systems. Penta and hexanucleotide loci are also employed along with tetranucleotide loci for enhanced forensic effectiveness in human identification (Butler 2011; Primorac et al. 2014). Progression in the development of STR markers for forensic purposes has been listed in Fig. 19.2.

On the basis of chromosomal location, STR can be categorized into three—(a) autosomal STRs, (b) Y-STRs and (c) X-STRs. Besides nuclear chromosomal STRs, analysis of mitochondrial DNA (mt-DNA) is also employed in forensic caseworks.

19.3.3.1 Autosomal Short Tandem Repeats (Autosomal STRs)

Autosomal STRs are the class of repetitive DNA motifs present within the non-coding region of autosomal chromosomes. These are the most significant markers used in forensic DNA profiling and employed for paternity and maternity testing, one-sided sibling match, establishment of familial relation, missing person identification and linking of an individual (either victim or accused) with the scene of crime (Wyner et al. 2020). Inheritance of single copy STR allele from each parent and easy amplification by polymerase chain reaction make autosomal STR suitable for individual identification. Further, the expansion of the set of the STR loci used for identification is supposed to enhance the discrimination power of STR loci set and ameliorate forensic individualization purposes (Dash et al. 2018). The combined DNA Index system (CODIS) is a database that originated in the USA established in 1996 and is administered by *Federal Bureau of Investigation (FBI)*. It allies forensic science and computer science implemented together into an effective tool which initializes the interchange and assessment of DNA profiles electronically at federal, state and local forensic laboratories. The database integrates 13 autosomal core loci

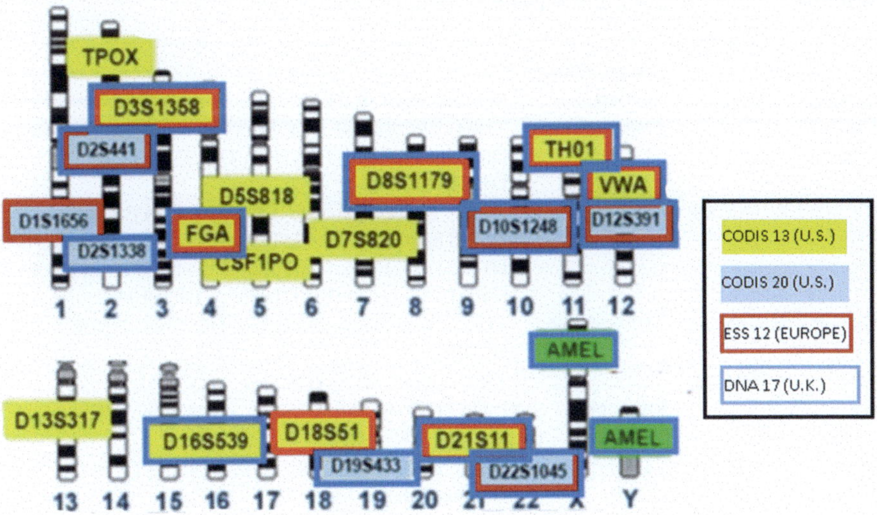

Fig. 19.3 Core loci included in different databases around the world and their chromosomal location. (Source- strbase.nist.gov)

along with the Amelogenin sex loci. National DNA Index System (NDIS), a national repository of DNA profile was later developed in October 1998 with around 190 participating public law enforcement laboratories in the USA and more than 90 forensic laboratories in around 50 countries that use CODIS software for their own database initiatives. Currently, with the addition of seven loci (namely D1S1656, D2S441, D2S1338, D10S1248, D12S391, D19S433 and D22S1045), the number of core loci in CODIS has increased to 20 resulting in the formation of expanded CODIS 20 set. In 1998, European DNA profiling (EDNAP) in collaboration with European National Forensic Science Institutes (ENFSI) established a similar national database across European countries known as European Standard Set (ESS) with seven core loci which was later extended to 12 loci (Butler 2011; Dash et al. 2018) (Fig. 19.3) (Table 19.1).

19.3.3.2 Y-Short Tandem Repeats (Y-STR)

The Y chromosome is one of the most informative loci for investigating genetic diversity and population substructure (Zhao et al. 2009). Y chromosomes transfer from father to son largely unchanged, except for the gradual accumulation of mutation. By examining the differences between modern Y chromosomes (as DNA polymorphisms) we can attempt to reconstruct a history of human paternal lineages (Bachtrog 2013). Y-STR examination is very useful in the identification of paternally associated male individuals. One of the major disadvantages associated with Y-STR is that it fails to discriminate between male relatives as the rate of genetic recombination in this region is negligible. So, unless any mutation occurs, it is difficult to differentiate male members within a family, using Y-STR markers

Table 19.1 Core loci set used in different countries

Country	Core Loci Set	Application period	Loci included in the set
United States	CODIS 13	1997–2017	TH01, TPOX, CSF1PO, FGA, vWA, D3S1358, D5S818, D7S820, D8S1179, D13S317, D16S539, D18S51, D21S11
	CODIS 20	2017-present	TH01, TPOX, CSF1PO, FGA, vWA, D3S1358, D5S818, D7S820, D8S1179, D13S317, D16S539, D18S51, D21S11, D1S1656, D2S441, D2S1338, D10S1248, D12S391, D19S433, D22S1045
Europe	ESS 7	1998–2009	TH01, FGA, vWA, D3S1358, D8S1179, D18S51, D21S11
	ESS 12	2009-present	TH01, FGA, vWA, D3S1358, D8S1179, D18S51, D21S11, D1S1656, D2S441, D10S1248, D12S391, D22S1045
United Kingdom	SGM	1995–1999	TH01, FGA, vWA, D8S1179, D18S51, D21S11, Amelogenin
	SGM plus	1994–2014	TH01, FGA, vWA, D8S1179, D18S51, D21S11, D2S1338, D3S1358, D16S539, D19S433, Amelogenin
	DNA 17	2014-present	TH01, FGA, vWA, D3S1358, D8S1179, D18S51, D21S11, D1S1656, D2S441, D10S1248, D12S391, D22S1045, D2S1338, D16S539, D19S433, SE33, Amelogenin

(Roewer 2009). STR's based haplotypes are mostly utilized in Forensic work. The first Y-STR locus was DYS19 in 1992 and after that, the interest in Y-STRs has led to the discovery of hundreds of YSTRs. Due to the development of Y-STR typing, multiplexes have been developed with high discriminating capacity. This interest in Y-STR loci has led to various research work and population studies to establish a global database. The Y Chromosome Haplotype Reference Database (YHRD) was established for this purpose. Minimal and extended haplotypes were defined to ensure accord among datasets (Shrivastava et al. 2018; Butler 2011). Y-STRs are suitable for use in forensic DNA analysis and paternity testing, especially when standard autosomal DNA profiling is not informative. The Y-STR markers are inherited along the paternal lineage (transmission without recombination from fathers to sons). The autosomal STR markers are commonly chosen due to their high discrimination potential; however, they are not ideal for rape cases where more than one male accused is involved. Y-chromosome DNA analysis is widely used in different human genetics cases for solving paternity disputes of male offspring or other paternal kinship questions. It is also suitable for male identification cases, which include historical cases, as well as missing person cases and disaster victim identification involving males, where only distant relatives are available. Mutation at specific loci on the Y chromosome is proposed to facilitate the identification of male individuals in Forensic investigations, but can also result in the incorrect exclusion of biological paternity. Therefore, reliable estimates of mutation rates are needed for the proper use of Y-STRs and accurate interpretation of genetic profiles (Butler 2011; Li 2015; Petrovic et al. 2019).

19.3.3.3 X-Short Tandem Repeats (X-STRs)

Short Tandem Repeats present within the X-chromosomes are considerable in forensic caseworks as well as population genetics. X-chromosome is considered as the physically most stable and tightly linked chromosome as compared to other nuclear chromosomes such as autosomes and Y-chromosomes (Kakkar et al. 2020). X-STR markers are effective for analyzing complex kinship cases due to the distinct inheritance pattern of X chromosome. Female offspring possess two X chromosomes one inherited from each parent whereas male offspring possess only one X chromosome transferred from the mother. X-STRs are efficiently employed in kinship cases that involve at least one female and are beneficial for caseworks such as missing person identification, incest, deficiency paternity, and immigration cases involving individual identification with limited sample source from close relatives (Butler 2011; Bara et al. 2018).

19.4 STR Multiplex Kit

A set of several tetra- and pentanucleotide alleles can successfully work on enhancing its discriminatory power as well as minimizing erroneous matches. Commercial multiplexing kits have become a choice of interest for forensic caseworks. These kits are a combination of pre-designed amplification buffers and primers along with compatible size standard and allelic ladders for yielding ideal STR profiles. Pre-validated aspect of such kits along with predefined and standardized workflow renders them as user-friendly. Promega, Applied Biosystem, and Qiagen are among the pioneering and prevailing companies engaged in manufacturing of STR systems useful in routine forensic caseworks (Butler 2005; Primorac et al. 2014; Shrivastava et al. 2018). Some of the prominent STR multiplex systems utilized for forensic analysis are described in Table 19.2.

19.5 Mitochondrial DNA (Mt-DNA) Analysis

There is a separate genome in mitochondria, which consists of double-stranded circular DNA of 16.6 Kb without any intronic sequence. Under the process of fertilization, mtDNA is accompanied by an egg and the inheritance takes place in both sexes (male and female) from their mother. Thereby mitochondrial DNA is specifically known for its usage in the form of matri-lineage marker for revealing the maternal ancestors of an individual (Ginther et al. 1992; Sullivan et al. 1992). In comparison with nuclear genome, a high copy number of mtDNA genome within a single mitochondrion and the presence of numerous mitochondria in a eukaryotic cell depending upon the energy requirement of that cell enables the extraction of adequate quantities of mtDNA even from the degraded samples (Holland and Lauc 2014). The mitochondrial genome contains two hypervariable regions namely HV1 and HV2 that are highly polymorphic non-coding, mutation-bearing portions and are

Table 19.2 Various commercial multiplex STR kits used in forensic caseworks

Commericial mutliplex kit	Production year	No. of markers	Type of markers	Developer
Profiler	1997	9	Autosomal	Applied biosystem
Identifiler	2001	16	Autosomal	Applied biosystem
PowerPlex Y	2003	12	Y-STR	Promega
Y filer	2004	17	Y-STR	Applied biosystem
NGM	2009	16	Autosomal	Applied biosystem
PowerPlex 16 HS	2009	16	Autosomal	Promega
Argus X-12 QS	2010	12	X-STR	Qiagen
GlobalFiler	2012	24	21 autosomal + Amelogenin + 1 Y-Indel +1 Y-STR	Applied biosystem
PowerPlex Y23	2012	23	Y-STR	Promega
PowerPlex Fusion6C	2015	27	23 autosomal+ Amelogenin +3Y-STR	Promega
Investigator 24plex QS	2015	24	22 autosomal+ Amelogenin +1 Y-STR	Qiagen
SureID 27Y	2015	27	Y-STR	Health Gene Technologies
VeriFiler express	2016	25	23 autosomal + Amelogenin +1 Y-Indel	Applied biosystem
SureID PanGlobal	2018	27	24 autosomal + Amelogenin +1 Y-Indel+1Y-STR	Health Gene Technologies

significant in forensic perspectives. Unlike the nuclear DNA, the independent replication of mtDNA is responsible for the absence of recombination of mtDNA strands and mutation within the sequence is the only source of variability and differentiation in the mitochondrial genome (Primorac et al. 2014). mtDNA analysis is applicable in forensic caseworks such as maternal dispute cases, baby swapping, phylogenetic analysis, identification of ancient DNA or highly degraded body remains etc. (Sinha et al. 2020).

19.6 Present Context of Routine DNA Analysis

19.6.1 Handling of Biological Evidence for DNA Analysis

An extremely small amount of evidence samples can be used to yield a sufficient amount of DNA, significant attention should be paid while the collection, packaging, and preservation of the evidence. Biological pieces of evidence are subject to degradation (Cătălin et al. 2011). Good evidence management must be properly followed in the selection, collection, packaging, sealing, labeling, preservation, storage, and transportation of the evidence ensuring conformity with the chain of custody (Magalhães et al. 2015). If good evidence management is not followed then the samples may get contaminated and which will subsequently lead to a decrease in sensitivity. In general, samples from crime scene contains a considerably low amount of DNA depending on various factors. And, it becomes difficult to get results in these conditions due to degradation as the contaminants can affect the DNA typing process. The collection method generally depends on the condition of evidence present at the scene of crime as it should be ensured that a sufficient amount of DNA should be recovered and the additional contaminants (like dirt, dust, and other fluids) should be limited. Each sample should be packed in paper bags or envelopes after air drying or as per the norms of the forensic laboratory and then sealed and labeled before transportation. It is to be remembered that evidence samples should never be packed in plastic bags. To mitigate degradation, the sample should be stored in a cool and dry environment. Questioned and control samples must be handled and packaged independently (van Oorschot et al. 1996; Chisum and Turvey 2000; Tan et al. 2010; Cătălin et al. 2011; Magalhães et al. 2015).

Laboratory personnel and investigators need to work together to focus on good evidence management. And to perform successful DNA analysis, a lot depends on the collection, packaging and preservation of the specimen. Therefore, the methodologies used to collect and preserve biological pieces of evidence, the quantity of the sample collected, and the handling and packaging procedure are a few important points for successful DNA analysis (Cătălin et al. 2011; Magalhães et al. 2015).

19.6.2 Laboratory Analysis of DNA

Subsequently, after the collection and preservation of biological pieces of evidence, the major steps in DNA analysis include- DNA extraction (or isolation), Quantitation of extracted DNA, multiplex amplification using Polymerase Chain Reaction (PCR) and data processing or sequencing using capillary electrophoresis. A computer-based software linked with the capillary electrophoresis instrument assists in the generation of a DNA profile (Shrivastava et al. 2020; Vajpayee et al. 2020). The process in detail has been described below:

19.6.2.1 DNA Extraction

Extraction of a high yield of DNA with minimal contamination is essential for the generation of a balanced DNA profile. Several DNA extraction protocols such as Organic Phenol-Chloroform-Isoamyl Alcohol (PCIA) method, Chelex method, and Salting Out method have been developed. Several semi-automatic and automatic instruments have also been introduced for better yield in lesser time and reduction in possible contaminations.

19.6.2.1.1 Phenol-Chloroform Isoamyl Extraction Method

It is the most common and ancient method for DNA extraction. This method basically comprises cell and protein lysis followed by extraction of genetic material using organic reagents and then concentrating and storing DNA. Reagents like proteinase K (Protein digestion) and the mixture of phenol:chloroform:isoamyl alcohol (for protein removal) in the ratio of 25:24:1 are used (Butler 2005; Li 2015; Dash et al. 2018; Vajpayee et al. 2020).

19.6.2.1.2 Silica-Based Extraction Method

It is an easy, simple and less time-consuming method when compared to other extraction methods. In this method, silica solid surfaces adsorb DNA molecules using chaotropic salts which denature proteins and result in cell lysis (Butler 2012).

19.6.2.1.3 Salting Out Method for DNA Extraction

In this method, saturated NaCl solution is used for salting out cellular proteins by dehydration and precipitation. SDS and proteinase K reagents are used for cell digestion by overnight incubation at 37 °C. And then the DNA is precipitated (Butler 2012; Vajpayee et al. 2020).

19.6.2.1.4 Chelex Extraction Method

It is a fast but harsh method due to high pH and high temperature and may degrade DNA if stored for a longer term. This method involves three steps: washing (contaminants and PCR inhibitors are removed), boiling (denatures cell proteins and releases the DNA using 5% of Chelex—100) and centrifugation (separating resin and cellular debris) (Butler 2005; Vajpayee et al. 2020).

19.6.2.1.5 Column-Based Isolation of DNA

In this method, silica (positively charged) and some salt ions are present at the bottom in a typically designed spin column. The sample and the lysis buffer are injected into these columns. Once, the cells are lysed the DNA will bind to the silica and the debris will drain out. In the end, the column is washed with wash buffer and DNA is eluted (Mohapatra 2018).

19.6.2.1.6 Magnetic Bead-Based Isolation

This is a highly advanced method of isolation. It is quick, reliable, easy to use method which is commonly used by laboratories these days. Automated DNA extraction instruments are majorly based on magnetic bead-based separation which generally contains already filled cartridges consisting of all the reagents in different wells. Once, the cells are lysed, magnetic beads are added and introduced to the electric field. Now, due to charge and affinity, DNA binds to the magnetic beads. And, then the DNA is eluted after eliminating the electric field (Butler 2005; Mohapatra 2018) (Fig. 19.4)

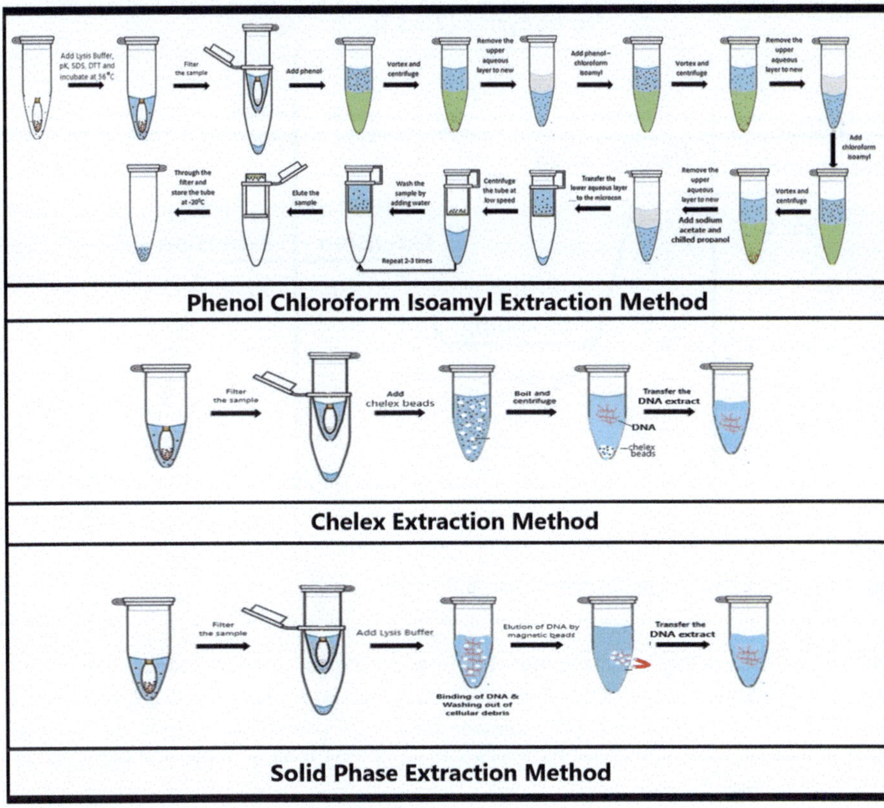

Fig. 19.4 Different DNA extraction methods

19.6.2.2 Quantitation

Knowledge about the amount of DNA extracted is necessary so as to supply the required DNA input for the amplification process based on polymerase chain reaction (PCR) technology. Adding exact quantity for amplification will give the best results. UV absorbance-based NanoDrop spectrophotometer; Agarose Gel Electrophoresis, Hybridization and Real-time PCR are some of the commonly employed methods for DNA Quantitation (Butler 2005; Mohapatra 2018; Vajpayee et al. 2020).

19.6.2.3 Amplification

Amplification of DNA is carried out using Polymerase Chain Reaction (PCR). Amplification is essential for DNA analysis in forensic caseworks as the evidence found at crime scenes generally have limited DNA in term of quantity and quality (Shewale et al. 2013; Li 2015). The procedure involves an enzymatic activity where nucleic acid is multiplied continuously depending on the temperature provided in each cycle. The PCR process involves three steps: denaturation (double-stranded

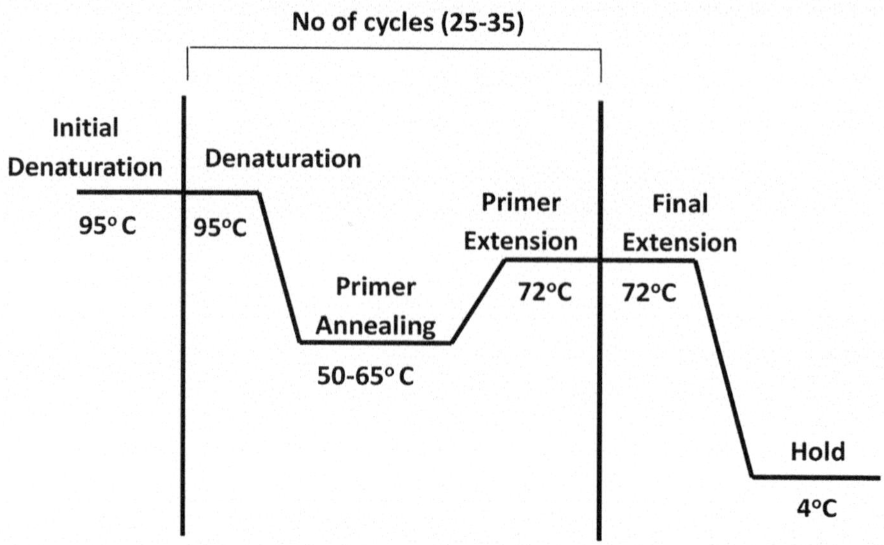

Fig. 19.5 Steps involved in Polymerase Chain Reaction

DNA denatures at high temperature to form the single-stranded form), annealing (binding of primers to the DNA sequence) and extension (using the deoxynucleotide triphosphate building blocks, polymerase extends the primers by coping the complimentary target region) (Butler 2012; Shewale et al. 2013; Mohapatra 2018; Vajpayee et al. 2020) (Fig. 19.5).

19.6.2.4 Genotyping

Genotyping or sequencing of amplified DNA fragments that determines the order of the aligned nucleotide within the genome is important so as to picturize a complete profile of an individual. Capillary Electrophoresis involves the flow of electric current through the samples contained within a thin glass capillary to separate the fragments on the basis of their size. A computer attached to the instrument then collects the data and a software program is used to generate a DNA profile. Next Generation Sequencing platforms are the future scope for DNA sequencing procedures (Li 2015; Vajpayee et al. 2020).

19.6.3 Recent Advancements in Forensic DNA

There are various practices which have provided a new approach to deal with forensic DNA applications and have proved to be of great evidentiary value even in extremely typical cases. Some of the techniques are discussed here:

19.6.3.1 Development of Capillary Electrophoresis (CE) Based STR Analysis

During the start-up phase of STR analysis, DNA fragments were detected by virtue of their separation using slab gel-electrophoresis. The development of fluorescence detection and the emergence of instrumentation technique Capillary Electrophoresis (CE) has been proven to be a proficient advancement in DNA profiling. As compared to traditional slab gel-based electrophoresis, CE allows multiplexing for the simultaneous separation of multiple amplified fragments in one go. Further, the attribute of CE for producing single base resolution due to plug flow mechanism and marginal diffusion is responsible for delivering accurate and reliable results in human identification based on fragment analysis (Buel et al. 1998; Shewale et al. 2013).

Fundamental instrumental component of CE includes a laser excitation source, slender glass capillary filled with polymer having an average internal diameter of 50 μm, two buffer chambers, positive and negative electrodes connected to an external high-voltage power supply, and fluorescence detector (Butler 2011).

There are various capillary electrophoresis systems which are rapidly in usage for forensic DNA analysis which includes ABI PRISM® 310, 3100, 3100 Avant, 3130 3130xL, 3500 and 3500xL genetic analyzers. The latest versions of automated capillary electrophoresis are applied with various advanced features like standardization of peak height, accurate sizing of fragments, injection of samples, single-base resolution, high run-to-run precision, upright temperature control, high sensitivity, user-friendly, cost-effective and abided with easy software features to analyze the raw data with exact outputs hence with all these in-built efficiencies capillary electrophoresis can be stated to be a revolutionary invention for the scientific world. The automation in the procedure and encrypted software for the collection of data has attained its worldwide acceptability (Imam et al. 2018a).

19.6.3.2 Next Generation Sequencing (NGS)

Next generation sequencing (NGS), also known as Massive Parallel Sequencing (MPS) is a highly advanced method for the analysis of DNA. NGS has emerged as a leading technology in the field of genetic research within no time (Imam et al. 2018b). NGS was first employed by Peter de Knijff in 2011 in a sexual assault case which set a landmark in the field of forensic genetics (de Knijff 2019). NGS is generally helpful in resolving the issue when there is a very low amount of sample or mixed samples which we generally encounter in forensic casework (Masoudi-Nejad et al. 2013; Kulski 2016). This advancement in technology has provided a wide range of platforms in terms of run time, read length, cost, accuracy, etc., to be used in the genetic analysis that outperforms the conventional method. Currently, Sanger sequencing is generally used through individual PCR amplification for autosomal, STRs, and SNPs. The basic advantage of NGS is that it can perform all the above-mentioned processes in a single assay of up to 96 samples by simultaneous amplification (Aly and Sabri 2015; Børsting and Morling 2015; Iozzi et al. 2015). It can sequence much larger pieces of DNA or even a whole genome. Every time, a base is added during a DNA synthesis reaction, the new sequence information is read and simultaneously thousands of reactions are sequenced (https://www.news-medical.net/life-sciences/Sanger-and-next-generation-compared.aspxP). It not only analyses STR markers but also phenotypes and ancestry can be determined. Apart from this, NGS can analyze autosomal DNA, mtDNA and methylation. Currently, there are few NGS sequencers that dominate the forensics: Illumina's MiSeq FGx (cycle-based sequencing technology), ThermoFisher's Ion Torrent PGM (semi-conductor sequencer), and Ion S5 (Yang et al. 2014; Bruijns et al. 2018; Ballard et al. 2020).

19.6.3.2.1 Sequencing by Synthesis

In the mould of Sanger's dideoxy sequencing technique, the earliest techniques of Next Generation Sequencing were attributed to the principle of 'Sequence by Synthesis' (SBS). The approach to sequencing-by-synthesis was pioneered by Robert Melamede in 1985 (Kayser et al. 2000). The term was designated as these techniques involved synthesis activity of DNA polymerase for a primer-directed extension that forms a complementary strand by incorporation of dNTPs and leads to the production of observable result (Gharizadeh et al. 2003; Heather and Chain 2016). SBS techniques have been incorporated in various platforms with modified sequencing chemistry such as Roche 454 pyrosequencing, Illumina which is based on the sequencing chemistry of reversible terminator and Ion Torrent which involves sequencing by semiconductors through the analysis of hydrogen ions.

19.6.3.2.2 Pyrosequencing

Pyrosequencing is another modification of 'sequencing by synthesis' that involves a non-electrophoretic bioluminometric method of detecting nucleotide incorporation. It utilizes the real-time monitoring method to measure the intensity of light corresponding to inorganic pyrophosphates (PPi) that are proportionally liberated on nucleotide incorporation during DNA synthesis (Ronaghi and Elahi 2002). Successful incorporation of nucleotide initiates various enzymatic and chemical reactions including the activity of ATP sulfurylase for conversion of PPi to adenosine triphosphate (ATP) which cofactors in the luciferase-mediated oxidization accompanied by the liberation of visible light energy that is detected by a charge-coupled device (CCD) and recognized as the peak signal in flow grams (Harrington et al. 2013; Kreutz et al. 2013; Bruijns et al. 2018). The remaining ATP and unincorporated nucleotides are degenerated by the action of a nucleotide degrading enzyme—Apyrase (Ronaghi and Elahi 2002; Kreutz et al. 2013).

The method was described as a sequencing method implementing sensitivity of enzymatic analysis of PPi (Nyrén 1987; Hyman 1988). Later Nyren along with his colleagues expanded the work that lead to the development of a non-electrophoretic solid-phase DNA mini-sequencing method using immobilization and washing techniques (Nyrén et al. 1993) and liquid phase pyrosequencing by utilizing activity of apyrase (Nyrén 1994). Pyrosequencing was commercialized as microfluidic assay in the name of GS FLX by 454 Life Sciences Corporation (later acquired by Roche).

19.6.3.2.3 Sequencing by Cyclic Reversible Terminator

Sequencing by cyclic reversible terminator is the most acceptable and widely employed sequencing approach to the sequencing by synthesis (SBS) technique. The method utilizes polymerase activity on cleavable fluorophore-linked nucleotides that acts as reversible terminators enabling the incorporation of single base at a time (Ju et al. 2006). The process involves continuous cycles of incorporation, tag imaging tag removal/cleavage and re-incorporation (Canard and Sarfati 1994). The reaction occurs on the surface of flow cells where millions of nucleotides are ligated to the complementary strand. Upon attachment of each nucleotide, chemical reaction at 3′- OH end results is released from the bases which are traced by laser in form of different color channels forming a distinct image and aiding base call to the peaks in the chromatogram. Illumina/Solexa Genome analyzer uses a combination of the Bridge PCR method with four-color cyclic reversible terminator method of the SBS technique using 3′-O-allyl reversible terminator (Chen et al. 2013).

19.6.3.2.4 Semiconductor Sequencing

The technique of semiconductor sequencing is based on the direct conversion of nucleotide sequencing into digital outputs on a semiconductor device, generally in the form of silica chips. It utilizes an electronic detection method unlike the optical detection principles as used in other platforms, thus, offering high-speed runs and cost-effectiveness (Stranneheim and Lundeberg 2012; Reuter et al. 2015). Working mechanism of semiconductor sequencing is conceptually in imitation of pyrosequencing technique with similar library construction and clonal amplification method. But it involves the detection of liberated protons (H^+ ions) and variation in pH in contrast with the luciferase-based optical detection of released PPi during the incorporation of nucleotides (Kchouk et al. 2017).

19.6.3.2.5 Sequencing by Hybridization and Ligation

SOLiD (Supported Oligonucleotide Ligation Detection) is a sequencer platform based on the principle of two-base sequencing by ligation (SBL) (Liu et al. 2012; Kulski 2016; Alvarez-Cubero et al. 2017). The system was developed by McKernan from Agencourt Personal Genomics (APG) in 2006 and later acquired by Applied Biosystems (Bruijns et al. 2018). SBL method involves the enzymatic activity of DNA ligase for the extension of oligonucleotide template, contrary to the synthesizing activity of polymerase in SBS techniques (Liu et al. 2012; Alvarez-Cubero et al. 2017). The concept of SBL includes primer-directed hybridization and ligation of fluorophore-hybridized one/two base oligonucleotide probe onto the complementary DNA template that generates a sequence of some of the bases. The oligonucleotide probes embody a dissociative ligated octamer with a ligation site (first base), cleavage site at the fifth base and 4 distinct fluorophore attached to the last base. These fluorophores are liberated during the cleavage of the probe to prepare for the next round of ligation. Thus sequencing of a complete DNA strand can be processed in several sets of cycles (Hert et al. 2008; Liu et al. 2012; Ambardar et al. 2016; Bruijns et al. 2018).

19.7 Case Studies

19.7.1 Rajiv Gandhi Assassination Case

During a General Election Campaign in Tamil Nadu in 1991, Rajiv Gandhi, former Prime Minister of India was assassinated with the help of a suicide bomb. DNA fingerprinting not only aided in identifying victims who were shattered into pieces but also assisted in establishing the identity of the assassin (or the suicide bomber)-Dhanu, by matching the genetic pattern of charred muscles on the bomber's belt to the genetic pattern found in a skull. The murder of Rajiv Gandhi was linked with LTTE on basis of the identification of LTTE mastermind Sivarasan, effectuated by DNA analysis of his parents for establishing paternity.

19.7.2 Naina Sahani (Tandoor Murder Case)

In 1995, a burnt body was found in a tandoor (clay oven) of an open-air restaurant. DNA analysis and a second autopsy of dismembered, half-burnt dead body proved to be effective in establishing the guilt of the accused. Sushil Kumar Sharma fatally shot Naina out of rage and tried to dispose of the body by chopping it off into pieces and burning it in the clay oven.

19.7.3 Nirbhaya Case

The Delhi Rape Case popularly called 'Nirbhaya Rape Case' involved brutal assaults and gang rape of a 23 year old woman in a moving bus. The DNA profiles generated from blood stains present on the clothes of the accused, recovered iron rod and articles of the bus corroborated the medical evidence, evidence of injured eye-witness and dying declaration of the victim. The Court stated 'If the sampling is proper and if there is no evidence as to tampering of samples, the DNA test report is to be accepted. Further, the Court observed—'The prosecution has established the presence of the accused in the bus and the heinous act of gang rape committed on the prosecutrix by the accused. The scientific evidence in particular the DNA analysis report clearly brings home the guilt of the accused.

19.8 Conclusion

DNA analysis plays an important role in the identification of highly degraded and contaminated samples. The recent advancements in molecular techniques have allowed solving criminal cases very efficiently and accurately and have allowed us to better understand the work and reduce the limitations in the way to restrict crime. However, more work is required to fulfill this objective. As the sensitivity of DNA techniques increases, so does the risk of contamination during every step also increases. If the analysis of DNA should be taken care of with practice, precaution and precision, from the inception to the end, one would easily utilize the maximum prospects of DNA evidence.

References

Alvarez-Cubero M, Saiz M, Martínez-García B et al (2017) Next generation sequencing: an application in forensic sciences? Ann Hum Biol 44:1–12. https://doi.org/10.1080/03014460.2017.1375155

Aly SM, Sabri DM (2015) Next generation sequencing (NGS): a golden tool in forensic toolkit. Arch Med Sądowej Kryminol 65:260–271

Ambardar S, Gupta R, Trakroo D et al (2016) High throughput sequencing: an overview of sequencing chemistry. Indian J Microbiol 56:394–404

Bachtrog D (2013) Y-chromosome evolution: emerging insights into processes of Y-chromosome degeneration. Nat Rev Genet 14:113–124

Ballard D, Winkler-Galicki J, Wesoły J (2020) Massive parallel sequencing in forensics: advantages, issues, technicalities, and prospects. Int J Legal Med 134:1291–1303

Bara N, Kumawat R, Imam J (2018) DNA fingerprinting techniques for forensic application: past, present, and future. In: DNA fingerprinting: advancements and future endeavors. Springer, Cham, pp 25–33

Barbaro A (2020) STR typing and available multiplex kits including validation methods. In: Forensic DNA typing: principles, applications and advancements. Springer, Cham, pp 27–43

Benschop CCG, Haned H, de Blaeij TJP et al (2012) Assessment of mock cases involving complex low template DNA mixtures: a descriptive study. Forensic Sci Int Genet 6:697–707

Børsting C, Morling N (2015) Next generation sequencing and its applications in forensic genetics. Forensic Sci Int Genet 18:78–89

Bruijns B, Tiggelaar R, Gardeniers H (2018) Massively parallel sequencing techniques for forensics: a review. Electrophoresis 39:2642–2654

Budowle B, Van Daal A (2008) Forensically relevant SNP classes. BioTechniques 44:603–610

Buel E, Schwartz MB, LaFountain MJ (1998) Capillary electrophoresis STR analysis: comparison to gel-based systems. J Forensic Sci 43:164–170

Butler JM (2005) Forensic DNA typing: biology, technology, and genetics of STR markers. Elsevier, Amsterdam

Butler JM (2007) Short tandem repeat typing technologies used in human identity testing. Biotechniques 43:Sii–SSv

Butler JM (2011) Advanced topics in forensic DNA typing: methodology. Academic, Cambridge, MA

Butler JM (2012) Advanced topics in forensic DNA typing: methodology. Elsevier, Amsterdam

Butler JM, Coble MD, Vallone PM (2007) STRs vs. SNPs: thoughts on the future of forensic DNA testing. Forensic Sci Med Pathol 3:200–205

Canard B, Sarfati RS (1994) DNA polymerase fluorescent substrates with reversible 3′-tags. Gene 148:1–6

Cătălin M, Andrei A, Mitraşca O (2011) Modern methods of collection and preservation of biological evidence for human identification by DNA analysis. Abacus Diagnostics, West Hills, CA

Chen F, Dong M, Ge M et al (2013) The history and advances of reversible terminators used in new generations of sequencing technology. Genom Proteom Bioinform 11:34–40. https://doi.org/10.1016/j.gpb.2013.01.003

Chisum WJ, Turvey B (2000) Evidence dynamics: Locard's exchange principle & crime reconstruction. J Behav Profiling 1:1–15

Dash HR, Rawat N, Kakkar S, Swain AK (2018) Fundamentals of autosomal STR typing for forensic applications: case studies. In: DNA fingerprinting: advancements and future endeavors. Springer, Cham, pp 209–221
de Knijff P (2019) From next generation sequencing to now generation sequencing in forensics. Forensic Sci Int Genet 38:175–180
Gharizadeh B, Ghaderi M, Donnelly D et al (2003) Multiple-primer DNA sequencing method. Electrophoresis 24:1145–1151
Ginther C, Issel-Tarver L, King M-C (1992) Identifying individuals by sequencing mitochondrial DNA from teeth. Nat Genet 2:135–138
Harrington CT, Lin EI, Olson MT, Eshleman JR (2013) Fundamentals of pyrosequencing. Arch Pathol Lab Med 137:1296–1303
Heather JM, Chain B (2016) The sequence of sequencers: the history of sequencing DNA. Genomics 107:1–8
Hert D, Fredlake C, Barron A (2008) Advantages and limitations of next-generation sequencing technologies: a comparison of electrophoresis and non-electrophoresis methods. Electrophoresis 29:4618–4626. https://doi.org/10.1002/elps.200800456
Holland MM, LAUC G (2014) Forensic aspects of mtDNA analysis. In: Forensic DNA applications: an interdisciplinary perspective, vol 85. CRC, Boca Raton, FL
Hyman ED (1988) A new method of sequencing DNA. Anal Biochem 174:423–436
Imam J, Reyaz R, Rana AK, Yadav VK (2018a) DNA fingerprinting: discovery, advancements, and milestones. In: DNA fingerprinting: advancements and future endeavors. Springer, Cham, pp 3–24
Imam J, Shrivastava P, Dixit S, Shrivastava A (2018b) Future of DNA fingerprinting: application of NGS in forensic science. In: DNA fingerprinting advancements and future endeavors. Springer, Singapore, pp 259–275
Iozzi S, Carboni I, Contini E et al (2015) Forensic genetics in NGS era: new frontiers for massively parallel typing. Forensic Sci Int Genet Suppl Ser 5:e418–e419
Jeffreys AJ, Wilson V, Thein SL (1985) Hypervariable 'minisatellite'regions in human DNA. Nature 314:67–73
Ju J, Kim DH, Bi L et al (2006) Four-color DNA sequencing by synthesis using cleavable fluorescent nucleotide reversible terminators. Proc Natl Acad Sci 103:19635–19640
Kakkar S, Kumawat RK, Shrivastava P (2020) X-STRs: potentials and applications. In: Forensic DNA typing: principles, applications and advancements. Springer, Cham, pp 301–327
Kayser M, Brauer S, Weiss G et al (2000) Melanesian origin of polynesian Y chromosomes. Curr Biol 10:1237–1246
Kchouk M, Gibrat J-F, Elloumi M (2017) Generations of sequencing technologies: from first to next generation. Biol Med 09:8. https://doi.org/10.4172/0974-8369.1000395
Kreutz M, Hochstein N, Kaiser J et al (2013) Pyrosequencing: powerful and quantitative sequencing technology. Curr Protoc Mol Biol 104:7–15
Kulski JK (2016) Next-generation sequencing—an overview of the history, tools, and "omic" applications. In: Next generation sequencing—advances, applications and challenges. IntechOpen, London, pp 3–60
Li R (2015) Forensic biology. CRC, Boca Raton, FL
Litt M, Luty JA (1989) A hypervariable microsatellite revealed by in vitro amplification of a dinucleotide repeat within the cardiac muscle actin gene. Am J Hum Genet 44:397
Liu L, Li Y, Li S et al (2012) Comparison of next-generation sequencing systems. J Biomed Biotechnol 2012:251364. https://doi.org/10.1155/2012/251364
Lorenz TC (2012) Polymerase chain reaction: basic protocol plus troubleshooting and optimization strategies. J Vis Exp 63:e3998
Ma TS (1995) Applications and limitations of polymerase chain reaction amplification. Chest 108: 1393–1404
Magalhães T, Dinis-Oliveira RJ, Silva B et al (2015) Biological evidence management for DNA analysis in cases of sexual assault. Sci World J 2015:1

Masoudi-Nejad A, Narimani Z, Hosseinkhan N (2013) Next generation sequencing and sequence assembly: methodologies and algorithms. Springer, Cham

Mohapatra BK (2018) Techniques involved in DNA fingerprinting: isolation, quantification, PCR, genotyping, and analysis BT—DNA fingerprinting: advancements and future endeavors. In: Dash HR, Shrivastava P, Mohapatra BK, Das S (eds). Springer, Singapore, pp. 35–59

Nyrén P (1987) Enzymatic method for continuous monitoring of DNA polymerase activity. Anal Biochem 167:235–238

Nyrén P (1994) Apyrase immobilized on paramagnetic beads used to improve detection limits in bioluminometric ATP monitoring. J Biolumin Chemilumin 9:29–34. https://doi.org/10.1002/bio.1170090106

Nyrén P, Pettersson B, Uhlén M (1993) Solid phase DNA minisequencing by an enzymatic luminometric inorganic pyrophosphate detection assay. Anal Biochem 208:171–175

Pakzad Z, Mozdarani H, Izadi-Mood N, Niromanesh S (2014) Variable number tandem repeat (VNTR) genotyping of hydatidiform mole in Iranian patients. Avicenna J Med Biotechnol 6:246

Petrovic V, Kecmanovic M, Markovic MK, Keckarevic D (2019) Assessment of mutation rates for PPY23 Y chromosome STR loci in Serbian father-son pairs. Forensic Sci Int Genet 39:e5–e9

Primorac D, Schanfield MS, Marjanović D (2014) Basic genetics and human genetic variation. In: Forensic DNA applications an interdisciplinary perspective, vol 1. CRC, Boca Raton, FL, pp 3–51

Reuter JA, Spacek DV, Snyder MP (2015) High-throughput sequencing technologies. Mol Cell 58: 586–597. https://doi.org/10.1016/j.molcel.2015.05.004

Roewer L (2009) Y chromosome STR typing in crime casework. Forensic Sci Med Pathol 5:77–84

Roewer L (2013) DNA fingerprinting in forensics: past, present, future. Investig Genet 4:1–10

Ronaghi M, Elahi E (2002) Pyrosequencing for microbial typing. J Chromatogr B 782:67–72

Saad R (2005) Discovery, development, and current applications of DNA identity testing. In: Baylor University medical center proceedings, vol 18. Taylor & Francis, Abingdon, pp 130–133

Shewale JG, Qi L, Calandro L (2013) Principles, practice, and evolution of capillary electrophoresis, as a tool for forensic DNA analysis. In: Forensic DNA analysis current practices emerging technologies. CRC, Boca Raton, FL, pp 131–162

Shrivastava P, Dash HR, Kumawat RK et al (2018) STR typing and available kits. In: DNA fingerprinting: advancements and future endeavors. Springer, Cham, pp 61–74

Shrivastava P, Ranjan H, Jose D, Jahangir AL, Forensic DNA (2020) Typing: principles, applications and advancements. Springer, Cham

Singh BD, Singh AK (2015) Polymerase chain reaction-based markers. In: Marker-assisted plant breeding: principles and practices. Springer, Cham, pp 47–75

Sinha M, Rana M, Kushwaha P (2020) Applications of mitochondrial DNA in forensic science. In: Forensic DNA typing: principles, applications and advancements. Springer, Cham, pp 329–343

Sobrino B, Brión M, Carracedo A (2005) SNPs in forensic genetics: a review on SNP typing methodologies. Forensic Sci Int 154:181–194

Somanathan A, Mathur K (2017) Application of STR markers in forensics. Int J Adv Res Sci Eng 6: 61–79

Stone WH, Ely JJ, Manis GS, VandeBerg JL (1993) Classical genetic markers and DNA markers: a commensal marriage. Primates 34:365–376

Stranneheim H, Lundeberg J (2012) Stepping stones in DNA sequencing. Biotechnol J 7:1063–1073. https://doi.org/10.1002/biot.201200153

Sullivan KM, Hopgood R, Gill P (1992) Identification of human remains by amplification and automated sequencing of mitochondrial DNA. Int J Legal Med 105:83–86

Tan E, Inc. N, America US (2010) Sample collection system for DNA analysis of forensic evidence: towards practical, fully-integrated STR analysis. NetBio Inc, Waltham, MA, pp 1–45

Tilanus MGJ (2006) Short tandem repeat markers in diagnostics: what's in a repeat? Leukemia 20: 1353–1355

Vajpayee K, Sagar DC, Dash HR (2020) Forensic DNA typing: inception, methodology, and technical advancements. In: Forensic DNA typing: principles, applications and advancements. Springer, Cham, pp 3–26

van Oorschot RAH, Gutowski SJ, Robinson SL et al (1996) HUMTH01 validation studies: effect of substrate, environment, and mixtures. J Forensic Sci 41:142–145

Venter JC, Smith HO, Adams MD (2015) The sequence of the human genome. Clin Chem 61: 1207–1208

Wyner N, Barash M, McNevin D (2020) Forensic autosomal short tandem repeats and their potential association with phenotype. Front Genet 11:884

Yang Y, Xie B, Yan J (2014) Application of next-generation sequencing technology in forensic science. Genom Proteom Bioinform 12:190–197

Zhao Z, Khan F, Borkar M et al (2009) Presence of three different paternal lineages among north Indians: a study of 560 Y chromosomes. Ann Hum Biol 36:46–59

Introduction to Forensic Medicine and Pathology

20

Mandar R. Sane, Neeti Kapoor, and Ashish Badiye

Abstract

Forensic medicine is a broader field that encompasses various disciplines within medicine applied to legal matters, while forensic pathology is a specialized branch of forensic medicine that focuses specifically on the examination and analysis of deceased individuals to determine the cause and manner of death. Both disciplines are integral to the field of forensic science and contribute to the investigation of crimes and the administration of justice. This chapter provides an introductory overview of the field of forensic medicine and pathology, encompassing various aspects essential to the understanding and practice of this specialized discipline. It provides an introduction to the multifaceted field of forensic medicine, acquainting readers with key topics such as autopsies, identification, pathology of wounds, asphyxia, sexual offenses, and toxicology. It serves as a foundation for further exploration into the fascinating world of forensic medicine, highlighting its vital role in the pursuit of justice.

Keywords

Autopsy · Identification · Pathology of wounds · Asphyxia · Sexual offences

M. R. Sane
Department of Forensic Medicine and Toxicology, All India Institute of Medical Sciences (AIIMS), Nagpur, India

N. Kapoor · A. Badiye (✉)
Department of Forensic Science, Government Institute of Forensic Science, Nagpur, Maharashtra, India
e-mail: ashishbadiye@ifscnagpur.in

P. Shrivastava et al. (eds.), *Textbook of Forensic Science*,
https://doi.org/10.1007/978-981-99-1377-0_20

Forensic medicine, also known as legal medicine or forensic medical science, is a broader field that encompasses various aspects of medicine applied to legal and criminal matters. It includes not only the examination of deceased individuals (post-mortem examinations) but also the evaluation and interpretation of medical evidence in living individuals. Forensic pathology, on the other hand, is a specialized branch of forensic medicine that specifically focuses on the examination and analysis of deceased individuals to determine the cause and manner of death. Forensic Medicine and Pathology per se deals with medicolegal issues related to the human body. These issues may arise when any kind of trauma is inflicted by mechanical means or by any poison introduced into the body. Medicolegal issues may also arise when a human corpse remains unidentified, or only fragments of the corpse or skeletal remains are recovered. The services of a Doctor are called upon to examine such a corpse or an injured person. They need to examine, collect evidence, interpret the facts on scientific merits and testify in a court of law. Hence, the discipline of Forensic Medicine and Pathology can be sectioned into:

1. Autopsy.
2. Identification.
3. Pathology of wounds.
4. Asphyxia.
5. Sexual offences.
6. Toxicology.

A detailed description of each of the above sections is beyond the scope of this venture. Dedicated Forensic Medicine and Pathology textbooks can be referred to for further reading. However, an overview of the above sections is discussed to comprehend the applicability of medical knowledge to aid in administering justice. These sections represent key areas within the discipline of Forensic Medicine and Pathology, where forensic doctors apply their knowledge and expertise to investigate and provide evidence in medicolegal cases. It's important to note that specific procedures and protocols may vary depending on the legal norms and practices of different countries.

20.1 Autopsy

An autopsy may be a clinical autopsy or a medicolegal autopsy. A clinical autopsy is primarily done to establish the cause of death, study the progress of the disease, or detect any anomalies. Consent from relatives of the decedent is mandatorily in such cases. However, a medicolegal autopsy may have objectives other than just ascertaining 'cause of the death'. It may be establishing the identity of the body, to determine the probable manner of death, probable time since death, conducting investigations like histopathology or microbiological tests, establishing live birth and viability in a newborn, to collect samples for analysis like a toxicology screen, etc. (Saukko and Knight 2016). Consent from the relatives of the decedent is not relevant, as investigation of crime mandates such autopsy. Nevertheless, relatives of the decedent should be communicated about the requirement of such an autopsy and their involvement may be necessary for establishing the identity of the person.

Usually, Police are authorized to request an autopsy as per Section 174 CrPC. The coroner system is not prevalent in India. However, in special circumstances like Dowry deaths, Custodial deaths, deaths in Police firing or in cases of exhumation, authorization for autopsy has to come from a Magistrate (U/s 176 CrPC). Protocols like videography during autopsy in such cases are mandated by National Human Rights Commission (NHRC) (Modi 2016). Pre-requisites for autopsy authorization and other documentation may vary as per legal norms of different countries.

Before one proceeds for an autopsy, a crime scene or place of incidence should be visited. Such a visit is vital in some cases as it may offer some clues regarding the position of the body in relation to its surrounding objects, environmental conditions, corroboration of findings with the history narrated by witnesses and avoidance of introduction of transportation artefacts in the body. Scientific techniques for crime scene visits are elaborated in the concerned chapter of the book. Medical Examiners system followed in some countries gives a tactical advantage to Forensic Pathologist before they proceeds with the autopsy. In India, this system is not prevalent; however, Police agencies cooperate with the crime visits of the Doctor if they insists so.

Before proceeding to an autopsy, an examination of clothes should be done as it will help in correlating with external injuries/lesions/artefacts present on the body. It may occasionally also help in the identification of the body. Clothing must be properly removed without extending the tears or soiling them further. If blood stains or otherwise are present on clothes, then they should be air-dried before they are packed for further investigations. Radiological examination of the body is warranted in unknown bodies, decomposed bodies, deaths due to firearms or bomb blasts, skeletal remains and in cases of death with suspicion of child abuse. Any other procedure other than routine dissection e.g. vitreous humour collection, CSF collection or nail clippings is required, such has to be done before the start of the conventional autopsy.

Autopsy connotes external and internal examination of the body. The external examination includes steps for determining of time since death, establishing the identity of the deceased, injury documentation and collection of trace evidence. Time since death can be estimated by observation of rigour mortis, postmortem lividity, and algor mortis. Once the putrefaction sets in, the time since death can be determined by changes that occur due to putrefaction. Similarly, it can be determined by studying the progressive invasion of the body by insects (Forensic Entomology).

Establishing the identity of a deceased becomes necessary in unknown bodies, exhumed bodies, skeletal remains, fragmentary remains or decomposed bodies. Identity can be ascertained by determining sex, age, race and stature. Comparative techniques like DNA analysis, Blood groups, fingerprints, dental study (including teeth eruption and Gustafson's technique), anthropometry, superimposition, facial reconstruction, etc. are also used for fixing the identity of a person (Vij 2011).

Detailed elaboration of the above steps for determining the time since death and establishing the identity of a person is beyond scope of this section.

Injuries can be caused by blunt force or sharp force or thermal effect. Injuries caused by blunt force are abrasions, contusions, lacerations or fractures. While, injuries caused by sharp force are incised wounds, chop wounds, and stab wounds. Thermal effects are either by cold i.e. frostbite/trench foot, while effects due to heat are burns or scalds. For obvious reasons, injuries inflicted by critical severe force or at a vital location will lead to the death of a person. Injuries should be photographed. Representative marking should be done on body outline diagrams (Fig 20.1 A, B).

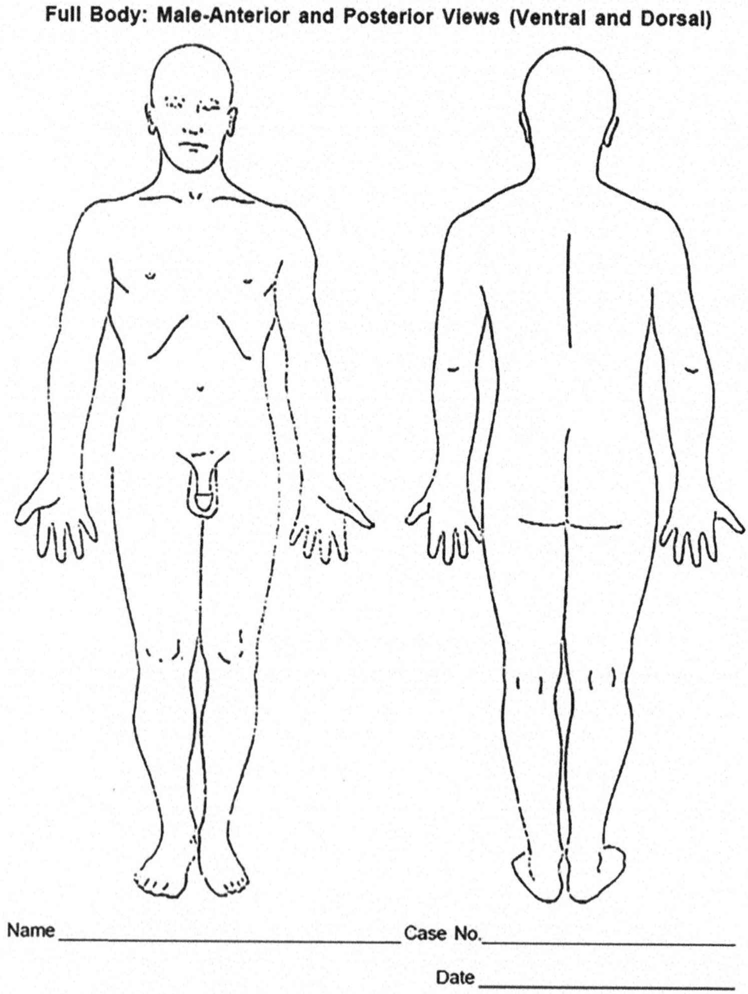

Fig. 20.1 Body diagrams for marking injuries (Commission NHR n.d.)

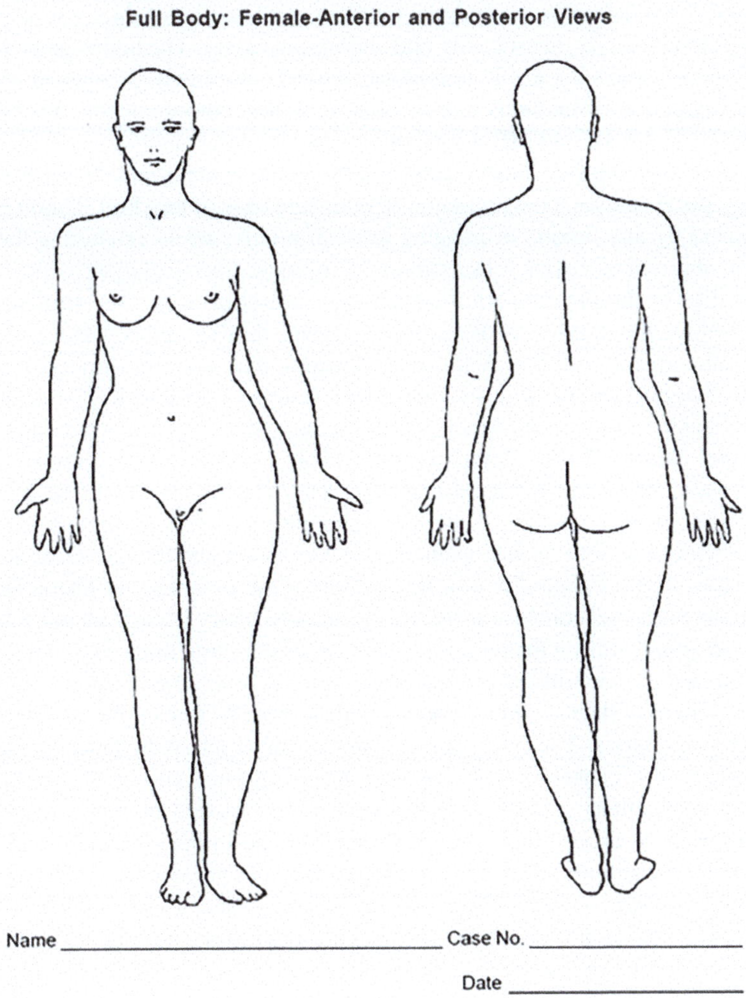

Fig. 20.1 (continued)

Injuries need to be described in their size, site, shape, orientation, age of injury and about its antemortem status.

The collection of biological trace evidence is an important step during an autopsy. These trace evidence may include blood stains in case of assault for blood grouping and DNA typing. It may include the collection of vaginal/cervical swabs for the detection of seminal stains. Nail clippings may provide a piece of vital evidence for DNA typing. Similarly, other trace evidence like hair, saliva stains, microbiological tests, etc. may provide leading clues in crime investigation.

Internal examination of the body includes an examination of three cavities of the body, i.e. cranial cavity, chest cavity and abdominal cavity. The body can be opened by a ‘Y’ shaped incision, an ‘I’ shaped incision or a modified ‘Y’ shaped incision. Minimal dissection of the body can be done in highly communicable diseases like rabies, COVID-19, HIV or HBsAg-positive cases. Cranial cavity examination shall include noting of injuries, haemorrhages, infections or abnormalities of the skull, meninges, dural sinuses, brain, vascular of brain and base of the skull. This should be corroborated by any reports of imaging tests. Similarly, while examining the chest cavity or abdominal cavity, observation of injuries, haemorrhages, infections or abnormalities of the pleural/peritoneal cavity, visceral organs, bony structures and vessels. Before, the removal or dissection of organs, they should be examined in-situ in their anatomical location. Various techniques that can be employed for the removal of organs are *Rokitansky's technique* (en block removal), *Lettulle's technique* (en masse removal) and *Virchow's technique* (organs are removed one by one) (Reddy and Murthy 2017). After the removal of visceral organs, they should be photographed, weighed, inspected and dissected. The organ should be described with regard to its size, surface, consistency and cut section. Representative sections of organs should be sent for histopathology examination and toxicological analysis.

An autopsy report should have a description of the external and internal examination of the body and conclusions drawn thereupon. Injury documentation has to be done meticulously during the autopsy; however, at the same time, such documentation should not be scientific jargon. The document is generated for the investigating agency or judiciary. Hence, injury documentation must be a scientific and simplified description of injuries. The cause of death should be based on the facts described in the report. If the cause of death is kept reserved for want of histopathology, toxicology or ancillary reports, then it should be mentioned likewise. If no cause of death could be ascertained from gross findings at autopsy and after obtaining reports of investigations, then one should not hesitate to conclude that ‘Cause of death could not be ascertained. This may occur when the cause of death is having a physiological basis e.g. in death due to vasovagal inhibition or primary neurogenic shock. Inference about the cause of death has to be in light of the circumstances of death.

Manner of death i.e. suicidal, homicidal or accidental is the primary domain of the Police or investigating agency. Unless there is strong evidence suggesting a particular manner of death, the Doctor should avoid commenting regarding it. The autopsy report should also mention the probable time since death and whether the injuries described are antemortem or postmortem in nature. It is also expected to comment upon the role of injuries sustained in causing the death of a person. In obvious cases, injuries are severe enough to cause death in the ordinary course of nature, or whether injuries are individually or collectively responsible for the death. The autopsy report has to be handed over to the Police in cases of 174 CrPC, while it has to be handed over to the Magistrate in cases of 176 CrPC.

20.2 Identification

Fixing the identity of an individual becomes important in cases of unknown bodies, skeletal remains, fragmented remains or decomposed bodies. It is briefly discussed vide supra. However, the fixing of identification also indicates the age of a person (victim or accused) or establishes the precise sex of a person. These issues arise in living individuals or criminal cases where age estimation is required to be done in sexual offence cases. Offence done on a minor victim is having aggravated punishment, while an offence committed by a minor accused person will be treated as a juvenile offender. While in civil cases, age estimation may be required to be done in cases of marriage, the age for employment/retirement, participation in various age categories of sports, etc. Establishing the gender of a person may be important when the victim/accused person is involved in gender-specific offences or want to participate in gender-specific sports events. Tattoo marks on the body play a significant role in the identification of individuals. They are unique, permanent, and hold personal meaning, making them valuable markers for establishing identity. Tattoos can provide distinctive features that set individuals apart and serve as a reference for matching information provided by the person or their acquaintances. Additionally, certain tattoo designs or symbols may indicate cultural or group associations, offering clues about a person's background. (Fig. 20.2).

Age estimation can be done by morphological examination, radiological examination and dental examination. Morphological features that occur in the body are studied by Tanner's staging, which has stages according to the development of breast and body hair in both sexes. The radiological method of age estimation involves the examination of the epiphysis of long bones. Epiphyses of long bones

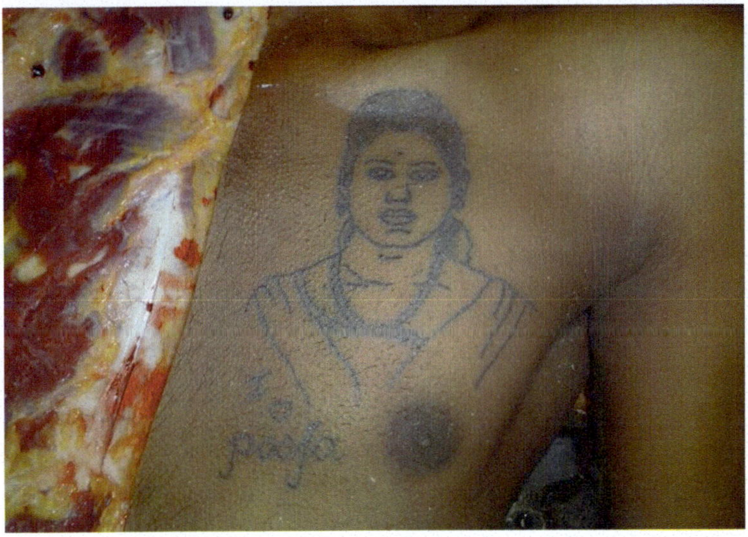

Fig. 20.2 Tattoo mark on the body

appear at a specific age and fuse with the shaft at a specific age. Bones which can be examined are the upper end of the humerus, elbow joint (lower end of humerus, the upper end of radius and ulna), the lower end of radius and ulna, carpal bones, the base of the first metacarpal, and hip joint (upper end of femur, iliac crest, ischial tuberosity and ischial rami). A dental examination has to be done by examining the eruption of teeth. Teeth erupt in a temporal sequence. The first permanent molar erupts at around the age of 6 years; thereafter permanent teeth gradually replace temporary teeth up to 12 years of age. Hence, mixed dentition will be present between 6 and 12 years. The third molar erupts at age of 17–25 years. The sequence of teeth eruption is considered more consistent as compared to the temporal sequence of fusion of epiphysis of bones.

Gender determination of an individual arises when there is intermixing of features of both sexes in an individual. External/internal sex organs may not be fully differentiated into male or female. Examination of 'Barr bodies' in buccal epithelial cells or nucleated cells is considered a standard for establishing the biological sex of an individual.

20.3 Pathology of Wounds

Section 44 of the Indian Penal Code defines injury as any harm whatever illegally caused to any person, in body, mind, reputation or property. Section 319 IPC and 320 IPC deal with hurt and grievous hurt respectively. Section 319 IPC defines hurt as 'Whoever causes bodily pain, disease or infirmity to any person is said to cause hurt'. While following kinds of hurt only are designated as "grievous" (Government of India 1860):

1. Emasculation.
2. Permanent privation of the sight of either eye.
3. Permanent privation of the hearing of either ear.
4. Privation of any member or joint.
5. Destruction or permanent impairing of the powers of any member or joint.
6. Permanent disfiguration of the head or face.
7. Fracture or dislocation of a bone or tooth.
8. Any hurt which endangers life or which causes the sufferer to be during the space of 20 days in severe bodily pain, or unable to follow his ordinary pursuits.

However, Forensic Pathology restricts the harm caused to a person in his body. It studies the effect of various kinds of weapons on the infliction of wounds, differentiation of wounds, effects of wounds based on severity and ageing of wounds in relation to medico-legal aspects. Based on the means of infliction, wounds can be classified as-

1. Mechanical injuries.
   (a) Blunt force injuries: Abrasion, contusion, laceration, fracture.
   (b) Sharp force injuries: Incision, chop wound, stab wound.
2. Thermal injuries.
   (a) Cold: Frostbite, trench foot.
   (b) Heat: Burns, scalds.
3. Firearm injuries.

Abrasions are injuries limited to the skin. They can be scratch abrasions, graze or pressure abrasions. Contusions are injuries caused due to rupture of vessels leading to extravasation of blood, with skin remaining intact. While, when the force which can cause the contusion exceeds a critical limit, it will cause a breach in the continuation of skin/tissue leading to laceration. Lacerations can be tears, split lacerations, avulsion lacerations and cut lacerations. Lacerations will have contused margins of skin, with tissue bridges at the floor of the wound.

As against lacerations which are caused by blunt force, incised wounds are caused by the sharp cutting edge. Margins will be regular, and free from contusions. Underlying tissues will be clean-cut. Tailing may be present at one of the ends which indicates the withdrawal of the weapon. Length is the largest dimension of the incised wound. A stab wound is caused by a pointed weapon with the direction of the force along the long axis of the weapon. Penetrating or perforating wounds can be caused by such force. Depth is the largest dimension of stab wounds. A stab wound will be 'spindle shaped' if inflicting weapon is having two sharp cutting edges, while it will be 'wedge shaped' if inflicting weapon is having a single sharp cutting edge.

Fractures over the skull can be of different types like linear fracture, depressed fracture, comminuted fracture, pond fracture, hinge fracture and ring fracture (around the foramen magnum). The Squamous part of the temporal bone is a common area of skull fracture which may also lead to extradural haemorrhage. Fractures of the cervical region may occur due to sudden hyperflexion or hyperextension as may be seen in the acceleration-deceleration mechanism. A cervical fracture is also seen in long drop suspension (Hangman's fracture). Fracture in the chest is also common with fracture line along the anterior axillary line or along the paravertebral line. These fractures may lacerate the underlying pleura leading to haemothorax. Multiple fractures of ribs at different stages of healing may indicate child abuse. Fractures are also common over long bones of libs, which may be sustained due to road traffic accidents, sometimes termed as '*bumper fractures*'. Multiple long bone fractures may lead to extensive haemorrhage causing death due to haemorrhagic shock.

Thermal injuries are usually caused by heat leading to burns. Burns may be superficial or deep in nature. However, surface area involvement is considered the most important indicator for prognosis and treatment strategy. Hence, body areas are divided with each area assigned 9% for calculation of the extent of surface area involved by burns. Areas divided are the head, neck face, each upper limb, each lower limb, the front of the chest and abdomen, the back of the chest and abdomen, and, 1% for genitals. Area involvement of more than 30–40% is considered a poor prognosis. Burns heal with scar formation and may lead to extensive deformities. Burns may also lead to deaths, with causes of death varying from primary neurogenic shock, hypovolemic shock or septicemic shock.

Forensic Pathology also deals with terminal ballistics or wound ballistics, i.e. injuries caused by firearm projectiles/missiles. Firearms are of two types i.e. rifled firearms or smoothbore firearms, with a bullet or pellets as their projectiles respectively. Firearms fired from contact or close range will have effects produced by flame and hot expansile gases, apart from the effects of their missiles. However, beyond the range of flame, injuries are primarily caused by missiles i.e. bullets or pellets. As the distance between the muzzle end and the target increases, the kinetic energy of missiles decreases leading to lesser severity of injuries. Distance/range of firing can be estimated by observation of smoke, flame effects (burns), tattooing, the extent of spread of pellets, and injuries caused by wads/cards. Recovery of missiles from the body is essential in such cases for comparative analysis with test-fired missiles. Radiology of the body before the commencement of autopsy is mandatory in such cases.

20.4 Asphyxia

Anoxia is a state characterized by the failure of oxygen to reach the cells or tissues. There are various types of anoxia, including anoxic anoxia (caused by a lack of oxygen in the environment), stagnant anoxia (caused by reduced blood flow), anaemic anoxia (caused by a decreased oxygen-carrying capacity of the blood) and histotoxic anoxia (caused by the inability of cells to use oxygen). Asphyxia, which is a commonly used term in a medico-legal context is not synonymous with anoxia. Asphyxia is a condition in which the supply of oxygen to the body has been reduced below working level, for maintenance of life, by any means of mechanical interference with respiration. Different types of asphyxia are mentioned in Chart 20.1 (Karmakar 2007).

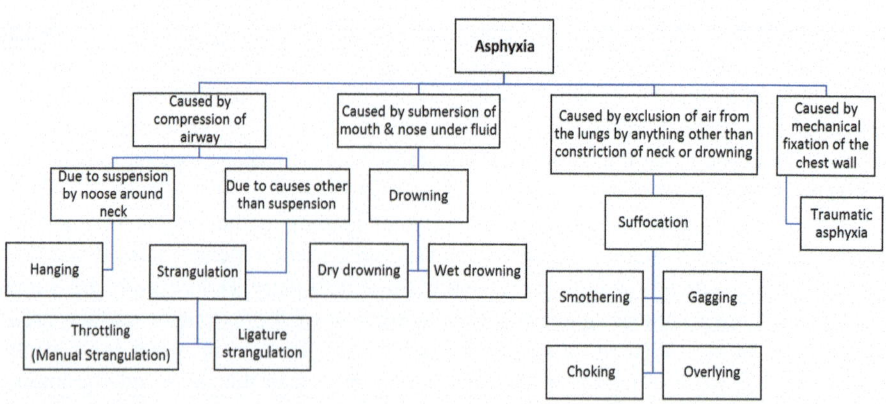

Chart 20.1 Classification of Asphyxial deaths

Classical triad of asphyxia is (Pillay 2019):

1. Cyanosis: Cyanosis is bluish discolouration of lips, fingernails, earlobes and tongue. Cyanosis is more marked in cases of slow asphyxia e.g. in partial hanging, while it will be minimally present in death in hanging due to vagal inhibition. Similarly, cyanosis is uncommon in death due to drowning.
2. Petechial haemorrhages: They are pinpoint collections of blood due to the rupture of small venules. They are usually seen over the conjunctiva, pleural surface, pericardial surface and white matter of the brain.
3. Congestion of organs: As against cyanosis or petechial haemorrhages which are seen in living victims too, congestion of organs can be noticed only during autopsy.

The above signs of asphyxia may not be prominent in asphyxial deaths due to carbon monoxide or other asphyxiants. There are other signs of asphyxia which are described in literature like the fluidity of blood or dilatation of blood. However, these signs are obsolete and atypical. They can also be found in deaths due to other causes.

20.4.1 Hanging

Hanging is a form of asphyxia death, where air entry is prevented by constriction of air passage at the level of the neck, as a result of the suspension of the body by a ligature in the form of a noose, applied in such a manner that the weight of the body acts as a constricting force.

Depending on the position of the knot, it will be typical hanging (knot at the occiput) and atypical hanging (the knot at a position other than the occiput). Similarly, depending on the degree of suspension, it will be complete hanging (the body is in a completely suspended position) and partial hanging (when some part of the body touches the ground in a suspended position) (Fig. 20.3 A, B). Hanging victims will typically have a ligature mark around the neck, which is 'V-shaped', oblique, above the thyroid cartilage and discontinuous in nature. The width and pattern of the ligature marks will depend on the type of ligature material used. There are usually no injuries to the underlying structures of the neck.

20.4.2 Strangulation

It is a form of asphyxia death caused by constriction of air passage at the neck by means of a ligature or by any means other than suspension of the body. There are two main types of strangulation: ligature strangulation and throttling. Ligature strangulation refers to the use of a ligature, such as a rope, cord, or belt, to constrict the neck. Throttling, on the other hand, involves the use of hands or manual force to compress the neck. As against hanging, the ligature mark of ligature strangulation will be

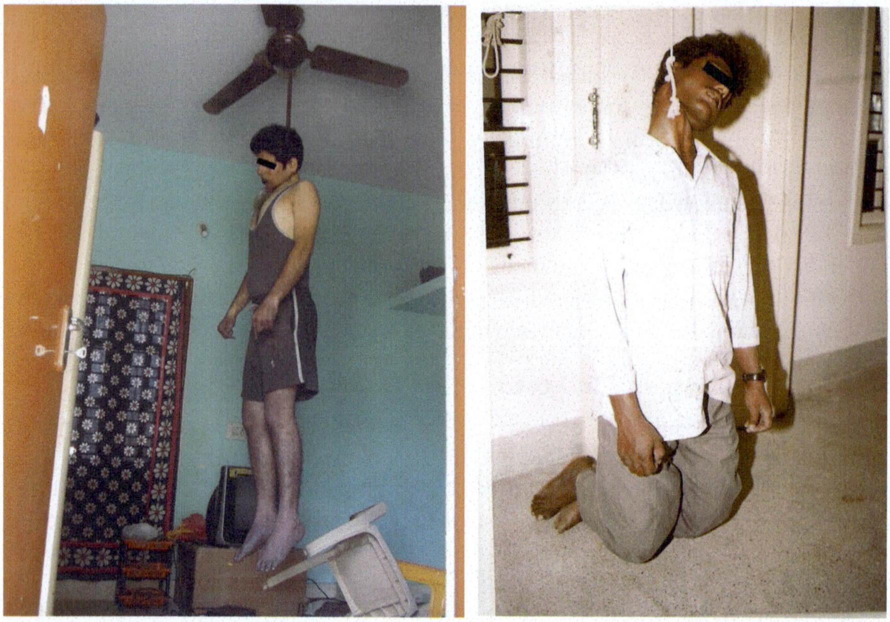

Fig. 20.3 A. Complete hanging; B. Partial hanging

horizontal most of the time, continuous and placed below the thyroid cartilage. There shall be injuries to the internal structures of the neck.

20.4.3 Smothering

It is a type of asphyxia or suffocation that occurs when an individual's airway is blocked, and they are unable to breathe properly. It typically involves the restriction of airflow by covering the nose and mouth, either by hands or any clothing or other substance or by compressing the chest, preventing the person from getting sufficient oxygen. Smothering is usually homicidal in nature; however, accidental smothering may be seen in infants (when they are covered by the weight of bedclothes) or in workers who fall accidentally in a large amount of semisolid material like pulp or sand. Smothering in an adult may be characterized by injuries to the side ala of the nose, contusions or tears over the mucosal aspect of lips and congested face with petechial haemorrhages, which are tiny red or purple spots caused by capillary rupture. These findings are indicative of the obstruction of airflow and the resultant struggle for breath that occurs during smothering.

Gagging is suffocation caused by the closure of the glottis of the mouth. Overlying (compression suffocation) results due to compression of the chest, so as

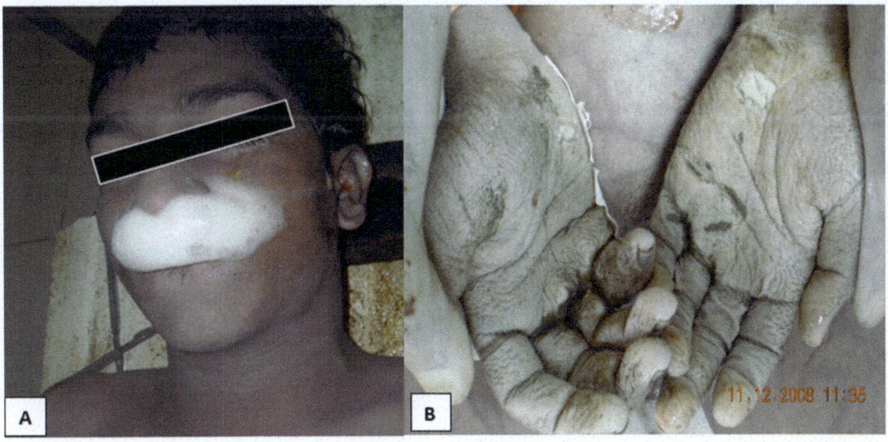

Fig. 20.4 A. Froth in case of drowning; B Washerwoman's hands

to prevent breathing. Smothering is distinct from choking, as it involves the obstruction of airflow rather than the obstruction of the airway itself. Choking is a form of suffocation caused by the impact of a foreign body in the glottis.

20.4.4 Drowning

It is a form of asphyxia death where air entry into the lungs is prevented due to submersion of the mouth and nostrils into water or any fluid medium. Classical drowning where air entry is prevented by a column of water in the airways is called wet drowning, while in dry drowning, death is because of a laryngeal spasm induced by a small amount of water entering the larynx. Froth is a characteristic feature of death due to drowning. It is produced due to the churning of air, mucous, water and surfactant in airways. It is white, lathery, fine and persistent froth filling the airways (Fig. 20.4 A, B). Other signs of drowning like cutis anserine and washerwoman's hands are non-specific and are signs of submersion and not drowning. In decomposed bodies recovered from the water, middle ear haemorrhages and diatoms tests are useful for diagnosing death due to drowning.

20.4.5 Traumatic Asphyxia

It is asphyxia caused by fixation of the chest preventing normal excursion of the chest wall. Signs of asphyxia are found to be localized. Below the level of compression, the skin will be pale. It is mostly accidental in nature.

20.5 Sexual Offences

Sexual offences can be divided into natural sexual offences (e.g. rape) and unnatural sexual offences (e.g. bestiality, etc.). The definition of sexual assault/rape varies in different countries. In India, post-Nirbhaya case, Criminal Amendment Act, 2013, (Government of India 2013) redefined sexual assault, and it is as follows (Section 375 IPC).

A man is said to commit "rape" if he

(a) Penetrates his penis, to any extent, into the vagina, mouth, urethra or anus of a woman or makes her to do so with him or any other person; or,
(b) Inserts, to any extent, any object or a part of the body, not being the penis, into the vagina, the urethra or anus of a woman or makes her to do so with him or any other person; or,
(c) Manipulates any part of the body of a woman so as to cause penetration into the vagina, urethra, anus or any part of the body of such woman or makes her to do so with him or any other person; or,
(d) Applies his mouth to the vagina, anus, or urethra of a woman or makes her do so with him or any other person, under the circumstances falling under any of the following seven descriptions.
    - **First**-Against her will.
    - **Secondly**-Without her consent.
    - **Thirdly**-With her consent, when her consent has been obtained by putting her or any person in whom she is interested, in fear of death or of hurt.
    - **Fourthly**-With her consent, when the man knows that he is not her husband and that her consent is given because she believes that he is another man to whom she is or believes herself to be lawfully married.
    - **Fifthly**-With her consent when, at the time of giving such consent, by reason of unsoundness of mind or intoxication or the administration by him personally or through another of any stupefying or unwholesome Substance, she is unable to understand the nature and consequences of that to which she gives consent.
    - **Sixthly** -With or without her consent, when she is under 18 years of age.
    - **Seventhly** -When she is unable to communicate consent.
    - **Explanation 1-** For the purposes of this section, "vagina" shall also include labia majora.
    - **Explanation 2-** Consent means an unequivocal voluntary agreement when the woman by words, gestures or any form of verbal or non-verbal communication, communicates a willingness to participate in the specific sexual act:
    - Provided that a woman who does not physically resist to the act of penetration shall not by the reason only of that fact, be regarded as consenting to the sexual activity.
    - **Exception 1-** A medical procedure or intervention shall not constitute rape.
    - **Exception 2-** Sexual intercourse or sexual acts by a man with his own wife, the wife not being under 15 years of age, is not rape.'

Aggravated punishment is given for rape on a pregnant woman, mentally challenged woman or a child less than 12 years of age, causing grievous injury during offence of rape, when rape is committed by a person with a fiduciary relationship and in case of gang rape.

Due to reforms in rape laws, the focus of the management of sexual assault survivors has shifted from examination to treatment. Lack of consent for treatment should not hamper in any way treatment of a survivor of a sexual assault survivor.

As per the law, the hospital/examining doctor must inform the police about the sexual offence (Section 357C CrPC and Section 19 POCSO Act). However, the survivor may refuse to register a complaint.

Evidence which is required in sexual assault cases is related to the age of the victim, marks of resistance, violence on genitals, stains of blood and sperms on clothing, detection of semen in the vagina, the status of hymen, the indication of penetration, the indication of communication of any venereal diseases. This may involve an examination of the mouth, breasts, vagina, anus and rectum. The medico-legal examination assists in the investigation, arrest and prosecution of those who committed the sexual offence.

Elaborate consent should be taken before Doctor proceeds with the examination. Steps in the examination for which consent should be sought can include external examination of the body, local examination of genitals, examination for age estimation, USG/Urinary pregnancy test for detection of pregnancy, retention of products of conception for DNA examination, collection of blood for blood grouping or DNA analysis, detection of intoxicating drugs, photography or police intimation.

Examine the body parts for sexual violence-related findings (such as injuries, bleeding, swelling, tenderness, and discharge). It will include the detection of general violence and local violence. General violence injuries may be over the face, inner aspect of arms, inner aspect of thighs, shoulder blades and sacral region. Assistance may be sought from a Forensic Medicine consultant for correct documentation and interpretation of injuries. The local genital examination includes both micro-mucosal injuries, which may heal within a short period, and those severe injuries which would take longer to heal. Injuries must be recorded with detailssuch as size, site, shape and colour. The presence of injuries is only observed in one-third of cases of forced sexual intercourse. The absence of injuries does not mean the survivor has consented to sexual activity. The lack of injuries may be due to the inability of the survivor to offer resistance because of intoxication or threats.

20.5.1 Opinion

The issue of whether an incident of rape/sexual assault occurred is a legal issue and not a medical diagnosis. Consequently, doctors should not use terminology like ‘rape’ or ‘sexual assault’ in his opinion, as they are legal terminologies. Only medical findings should be recorded in the report. It should always be kept in mind that normal examination findings neither refute nor confirm sexual violence.

Sympathetic response to the victim, informed consent for various steps in the examination, adequate evidence collection, prudent opinion framing and testifying in a court of law is the cornerstone for effective evidence deposition. The doctor must be aware of recent updates in law related to sexual assault examinations.

20.6 Toxicology

Toxicology in Forensic Medicine comes into play when a patient presents to the Casualty/Emergency area with a history of consumption of some poison and/or symptoms suggestive of it. A person may succumb to such poison and be subject to an autopsy. The autopsy findings, in their correct perspective, are only one of the special investigations which must be considered in the differential diagnosis to reach a conclusion.

Various poisons which find a mention in the literature are classified as corrosives (acids and alkalis), irritant poisons (inorganic and organic irritants), agricultural poisons, rodenticides, alcohol, inebriants, narcotics, cardiac poisons, spinal poisons, asphyxiants, war gases and food poisons. In the Indian context, agricultural poisons and alcohol form the majority of the cases. Organophosphorus compounds and Aluminum Phosphide are the most commonly used agricultural poisons (Mishra et al. 2016). Salivation, lachrymation, urination, miosis, bronchial secretions and kerosene-like smell strongly indicates consumption of organophosphorus compound. Gastric lavage, securing airways, and administration of atropine and oximes form the mainstay in the treatment of organophosphorus compound.

Sporadic incidences of deaths due to methyl alcohol intoxication are reported (*'Hooch tragedy'*). Isolated cases of death due to ethyl alcohol intoxication are rare; however, ethyl alcohol intoxication is notoriously associated with offences like road traffic fatalities, assault, causing a public nuisance while under intoxication, etc. 'Drink and Drive' with blood alcohol concentration above 30 mg% is punishable under Motor Vehicle Act, 1988. Stage of excitement, stage of incoordination and stage of stupor are stages of alcohol intoxication.

In deaths due to suspected poisoning, viscera is required to be preserved for chemical analysis. Various guidelines for viscera preservation exist in different regions of the country.

Generally, viscera is preserved in the following containers-

1. Bottle 1: Whole of the stomach, with its contents and proximal part of the small intestine.
2. Bottle 2: Half of each kidney, a portion of the spleen, and a portion of the liver.
3. Bottle 3: 100 ml of blood.
4. Bottle 4: Sample of preservative (acts as control).

The Preservative used is usually a saturated solution of common salt. Cause of death in poisoning cases is to be diagnosed by the history, the clinical record (clinical signs and symptoms observed by the physician), autopsy findings and the discovery of poison in the viscera and blood by chemical analysis. The detailed aspects of Forensic Toxicology are discussed in the relevant chapter(s) of this book.

20.7 Conclusion

To sum up, the chapter titled "Introduction to Forensic Medicine and pathology" provides a brief yet comprehensive overview of the fundamental aspects of this field. It highlights the importance of autopsies in determining the cause and manner of death, which is crucial in solving the mysteries surrounding suspicious deaths. The chapter also emphasizes the significance of accurate identification methods and showcases various techniques used in forensic investigations to establish the identity of individuals. Besides, the chapter delves into the pathology of wounds, discusses their classification and healing processes, and explores the forensic implications of asphyxia and sexual offences. Lastly, the chapter underscores the importance of toxicology in identifying the presence of drugs and toxins in the human body, contributing to understanding drug-related crimes and fatalities. By covering these topics, this chapter serves as a sturdy foundation for further exploration and study of forensic medicine, highlighting its pivotal role in the fields of law and medicine.

References

Commission NHR (n.d.) On custodial deaths/rapes [Internet]. https://nhrc.nic.in/sites/default/files/sec-1.pdf

Government of India (1860) Indian Penal Code [Internet]. https://www.indiacode.nic.in/show-data?actid=AC_CEN_5_23_00037_186045_1523266765688&sectionId=46085&sectionno=320&orderno=358

Government of India (2013) The criminal law (Amendment) act [Internet]. https://www.mha.gov.in/sites/default/files/CSdivTheCriminalLawAct_14082018_2.pdf

Karmakar RN (2007) J B Mukherjee's forensic medicine and toxicology, 3rd edn. Academic, Kolkata, p 576

Mishra PK, Kulkarni R, Sane MR, Deshpande A, Kushwah M (2016) Prospects of poisoning—a multi facet study. Arch Med Sadowej Kryminol 66(4):235–243

Modi JP (2016) In: Kannan K (ed) Modi a textbook of medical jurisprudence and toxicology, 25th edn. Lexis Nexis, Gurgaon, p 301

Pillay VV (2019) NACPFMT's practical medicolegal manual. Paras Medical Publishers, New Delhi, p 166

Reddy KSN, Murthy OP (2017) The essentials of forensic medicine & toxicology, 34th edn. Jaypee Brothers Medical Publishers, New Delhi, pp 104–105

Saukko P, Knight B (2016) Knight's forensic pathology, 4th edn. CRC, Boca Raton, FL, p 4

Vij K (2011) Textbook of forensic medicine and toxicology, 5th edn. Elsevier, New Delhi, p 37

Forensic Anthropology 21

Muktikanta Panda, Karan Sharma, A. N. Sharma, Pankaj Shrivastava, and Ankit Srivastava

Abstract

Forensic Anthropology, a subdiscipline of Physical Anthropology, practices various methodological aspects for the welfare of society, especially for law and authority. In the modern era, medico-legal aspects use the old age features and concurrently realise the shift towards state-of-the-art. Forensic anthropologists, like other forensic professionals, share their knowledge and views and gather physical evidence for cadavers, associate pieces or matters and identify living ones. This chapter depicts the meaning, scope, and some application of forensic anthropology systematically. Here the growing concern of Forensic Anthropology is also discussed.

Keywords

Forensic anthropology · Forensic anthropologist · Human identification · Skeletal remains

M. Panda · A. N. Sharma
Department of Anthropology, Dr. Harisingh Gour Vishwavidyalaya, Sagar, India

K. Sharma
Jaipur National University, Jaipur, Rajasthan, India

P. Shrivastava
Biology and Serology Division, Regional Forensic Science Laboratory, Gwalior, Madhya Pradesh, India

A. Srivastava (✉)
School of Forensic Sciences, The West Bengal National University of Juridical Sciences, Kolkata, West Bengal, India
e-mail: ankitsrivastava@nujs.edu

P. Shrivastava et al. (eds.), *Textbook of Forensic Science*,
https://doi.org/10.1007/978-981-99-1377-0_21

21.1 Introduction

Anthropology is the study of human kind in every space and time through applying knowledge for the welfare of humankind. Its holistic stance is unique as it studies about the bodily features, ecological behaviour/responses, societal aspects, historical occurrence, and cognitive aspects of human being, as well as treat human as whole; physically like a biological being and intellectually as a social creature (Kehoe 2013). Broadly speaking it gathers the evidence about variation, evolution and facts linked to the human and its society. Though an interdisciplinary science it synthesizes the knowledge with both theoretical and application perspective for the welfare of humanity. The term Anthropology came from the Greek words *'anthropos'* which means 'human' and the word *'logos'* which means 'thought' (Britannica 2021). Physiques of Anthropology are built with the platform of knowledge with different dimensions encircling a number of subjects and their tributaries. Its identity as a major discipline, can broadly be categorized into subsequent subdivisions or branches (Fig. 21.1).

21.2 Forensic Anthropology

As a sub discipline, Forensic Anthropology is classified under Physical or Biological anthropology. The American Board of Forensic Anthropology (ABFA) describes the discipline by the definition- 'the application of the science of physical or biological anthropology to the legal process' (American Board of Forensic Anthropology 2021). Forensic anthropology is an inter-disciplinary arena that pleats evidences of human remnants for the purpose of medico-legal exploration, especially for an

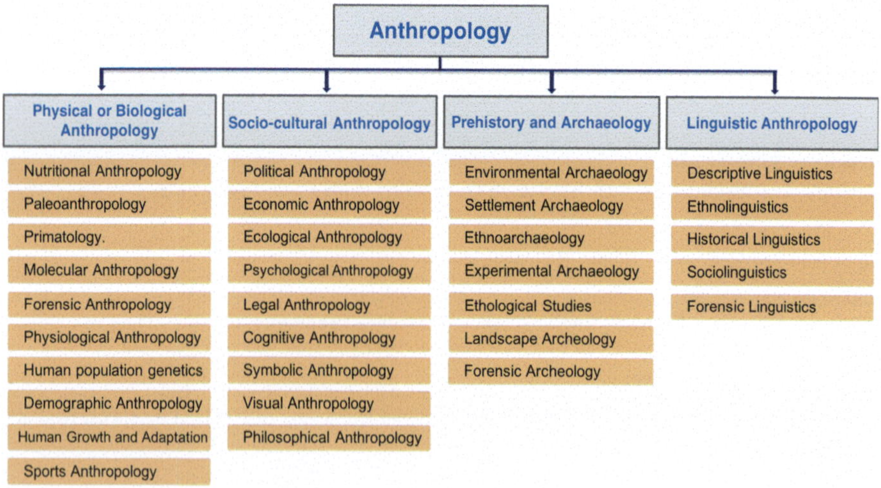

Fig. 21.1 Different specialized areas of study in Anthropology

identification perspective. From the goal point of view, forensic anthropology is a discipline comparable with forensic pathology and considered as more multidisciplinary (Cattaneo 2007). Similarly from the methodological point of view, the discipline of forensic anthropology enriches itself from different slants of biological anthropology, forensic sciences and medicine. Forensic anthropologists are professional experts in the skeletal morphology of human beings, proficient in human anatomy, osteoarchaeology, and in biological anthropology (OBE 2003). This multidisciplinary field working in corresponding with other disciplines like taphonomy, archaeology, anatomy, odontology, pathology, biology, osteology, entomology and botany (James and Nordby 2002).

21.2.1 Sub-Fields of Forensic Anthropology

The major sub-fields of Forensic Anthropology are mentioned in Fig. 21.2.

21.2.1.1 Forensic Osteology

Forensic Osteology is a sub-branch of forensic anthropology that deals with different issues like the facial reconstruction and superimposition, bone pathology, and archaeological investigations; provide evidences that either confirm, or support in determining the identity from the skeletal remains of an individual associated to different mysterious or natural death cases, a suicide, homicide victims, and remains of a mass disaster (Scheuer 2002). As, all the matters associated to the legal arena, levels of accuracy need to be greater than comparable to other disciplines. The word osteology is derived from the Greek words *"osteon"*, which means bone and *"logos"*, which means knowledge. It is the scientific study including structure, function, development and variation of bones of the skeleton. Human Osteology focuses on the morphology of the human skeleton and incorporates information about the names, placement, visible features of bones and articulations of bones with other bones etc.

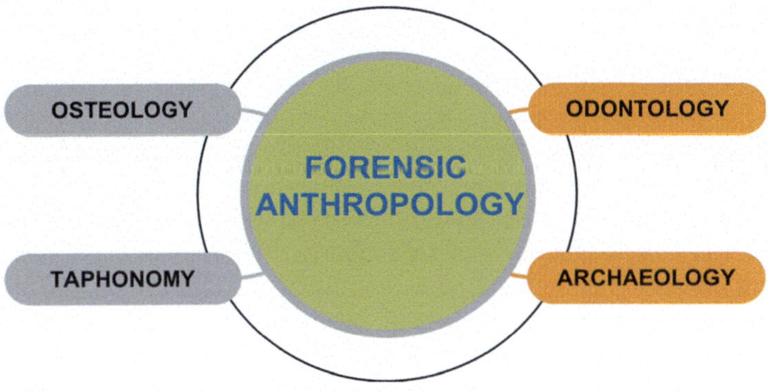

Fig. 21.2 Sub-fields of Forensic Anthropology

There is always a challenge for the forensic scientist in identification of deceased through their skeletal remains. Hence having knowledge of human osteology is important in positive identification of the individual from its skeletal remains. An expert forensic anthropologist identify a human skeleton as whole or in fragmentary remains. Skeletal remains are used for determining the demographic characters of the deceased including race, age, sex and stature. Study of human osteology also helps in understanding what is called normal in the human skeleton, and by knowing these standards, differences can be identified which help in positive identification of the deceased and also give information relating to the cause and manner of death.

21.2.1.2 Forensic Odontology

Forensic Odontology is the application of the science of dentistry in legal matters. The examination, assessment, management and demonstration of dental evidences are done by Forensic odontologists for civil or criminal proceedings for legal perspective (Avon 2004). Roughly speaking the sub-discipline alienated into 3 major fields based upon the activities, i.e. criminal, noncriminal or civil and research (Cameron et al. 1974; Neville et al. 2002). It is the science behind the practice of dentistry. Forensic odontology basically uses the science of dentistry to identify a person from the dental evidences left by him/her (i.e. bite marks, dental remains etc.).The forensic anthropologist is the first person to see the dental evidence, chart them, and report the evidence but for accurate results, the final analysis is done by an expert odontologist.

The importance of dental evidence in a forensic analysis is very high. The teeth have an outer layer of enamel that makes it the hardest and most durable substance of the human body. Hence they are highly resistant to physical and chemical influences such as high temperature, decomposition, desiccation, or long-term submersion in water etc. Having almost similar composition, teeth are more resilient then bones, thus sometimes dental evidences are the only human remains recovered from forensic scenes. Another important aspect is the pattern of dentition which is unique in every human being exactly like the fingerprints. This unique character of human dentition makes it important evidence when it comes to identification of a person. Apart from identification, dental evidence can also help in the determination of age, race and medical history of an individual.

21.2.1.3 Forensic Taphonomy

The word Taphonomy comes from the Greek word *"taphos"* which means burial or grave and *"anomy"* which means law. Taphonomy is a sub-field of forensic anthropology basically studied under the science of paleontology. The procedures linked with decay of cadaver are study in Forensic taphonomy (Tibbett and Carter 2009). Or it can be said that Forensic taphonomy is the study of the events (such as postmortem changes and interval, decomposition, mummification, saponification etc.) that happens to an organism after its death to the point of its recovery. The postmortem changes, decomposition of the body and the factors affecting such changes are studied in this discipline. Most of the changes occur to the body after death is due to natural factors such as temperature, plant, animals, soils, weather,

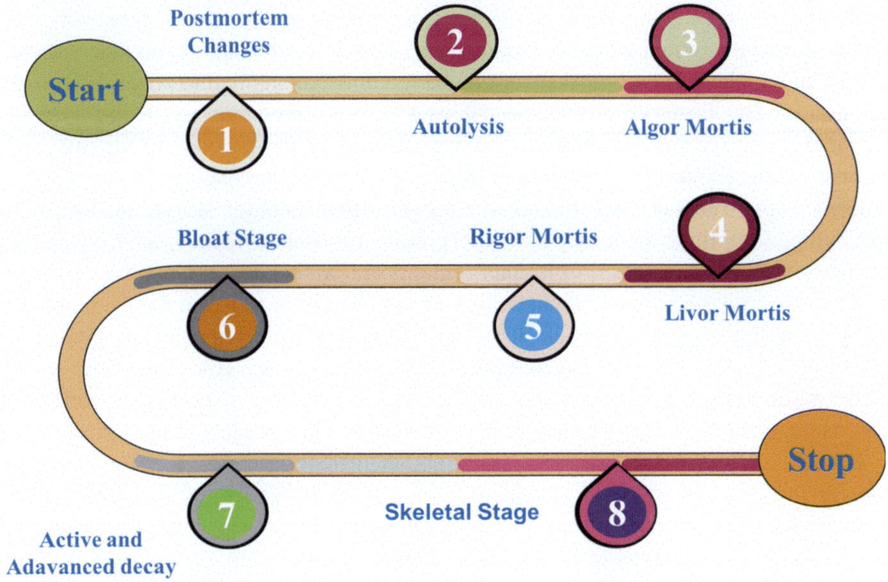

Fig. 21.3 Stages of Decomposition

gravity etc. Studying the specific role played by each of these natural factors is important in understanding and establishing the present state of the collected skeletal evidence. This also helps to focus on unusual patterns of dispersal or removal of evidence that indicates any human intervention (i.e. removing/moving remains to hide evidence). Taphonomy, on the basis of studying the condition of skeletal remains at the time of its recovery help to determine the circumstances surrounding the death, assessment of post-mortem interval and how long the body remains has been at the location of its recovery.

Taphonomy involves the study of all peri- and post-mortem processes including stages of decomposition mentioned below (Fig. 21.3).

The difficulties in estimating the postmortem interval (PMI) increase with the older human remnants. Particularly in the case of PMI the knowledge of forensic anthropologist is very limited, only confined to the dry bone; whether the bones belong to archaeological period, old, or very recent. It is a very difficult question for forensic anthropologists that 'time since death' is to be answered due to the lack of effective methods for the evaluation of the PMI. Even in some cases, it is impossible to say whether it is a forensic case or from earlier populations.

21.2.1.4 Forensic Archaeology

An essential set of methodologies in the discipline of Archaeology dealing with different buried remnants, evaluating and recording a graveyard and the close surrounding setting associated to them (Haglund 2001; Schmitt 2001; Tuller 2012; Wright et al. 2005). Forensic archaeology is placed at the juncture of various evidential regimes that articulate diverse and often contradictory prospects for different archaeological works (Crossland 2013). It is a sub-field of forensic anthropology in which archaeological theories and methods are applied to solve medicolegal issues. The Forensic Archaeologist uses various methods and techniques of archaeology in the investigation of a crime scene with the purpose to identify and reconstruct the crime scene. The major duties of a Forensic archaeologist are to assist in crime scene recovery and evidence collection that includes searching, locating, surveying, sampling, recording and interpreting relevant evidence, as well as the recovery and documentation of human remains and associated evidence.

The objective of Forensic archaeology is to properly investigate the crime scene using an archaeological approach. It includes selecting a precise detection or recovery strategy which will provide maximum data and evidence from the crime scene while minimizing the alterations of the scene and evidence. Another objective of Forensic archaeology is the proper recovery, systematic storage and recording of all evidences (such as human remains and associated materials) which helps in determining the manner of death, reconstructing the scene and identifying the post-depositional taphonomic processes and ultimately identifying the deceased. A proper chain of custody is to be maintained from point of recovery to accession by the appropriate agency. Diverse studies of the recent past have encouraged different new scenarios by the growth of forensic archaeology (Buchli and Lucas 2002).

21.3 Need of Forensic Anthropologist

Forensic anthropology has emerged extensively as an important field of study in last several decades. Different cases related to individual identification like the severely decayed body remnants, burned, maimed and disrupted are solved or assisted with the help of forensic anthropologist. Conventionally speaking the forensic anthropologist investigates the recovered human remnants to examine the bones associated with human or not, species recognition, time intervals from death and age at death, taphonomic history, sex, ancestry, height and not least to other sorts clues to identification and to spot the foul plays (Blau and Ubelaker 2016; Stewart 1951; Ubelaker 2018). The major concerning areas called upon the forensic anthropologist are the inquiries associated with criminal cases, like homicide, natural deaths with unknown causes, mass fatalities and different accidents; issues linked with non-criminal events i.e. numerous deaths in natural calamities; an inquiry into genocide and war crimes (Randolph-Quinney et al. 2011); estimate the age of a living individual related to immigration cases or asylum status and matter with legal accountability (Scheuer and Black 2007). As the present century expects a high perception of risks associated with mass fatality, accidents, terror outbreaks and different natural calamities (Thompson and Black 2006), which needs more methodological inventions and collaborations with forensic anthropologists. Different other methods like the techniques of facial approximation and/or photographic superimposition are used by the forensic anthropologists in different circumstances (Stephan 2016; Ubelaker 2015, 2018) for facial recognition. The expanded theoretical concept and their practicality in medico-legal field encourage the forensic anthropologist to solve issues like age determination and identification of living being (Black et al. 2010; Fenger et al. 1996; Sauer et al. 2012).

21.4 Historical Background: Development of the Forensic Anthropology as Discipline (World and India)

The field of Forensic Anthropology, which is an application of skeletal biology to medicolegal investigation, first emerged in the late eighteenth century in the European continent. Forensic anthropology is a relatively young subfield of biological anthropology, which is said to have its roots in the American continent during the nineteenth century. The development in the field of Forensic Anthropology majorly occurred in these two subcontinents. Academically the development of forensic anthropology rooted back to European centres of comparative anatomy closely linked to physical anthropology (Spencer 1982; Stewart 1979; Ubelaker 2009). Among key early scholars, Jeffries Wyman (1814–1874) known for forensic anthropology testimony (Ubelaker 2018) (Table 21.1).

21.5 What a Forensic Anthropologist Do

The ultimate aim is to establish or rebutting the personal identification with the confirmation through specifics knowledge of morphological characteristics, development and variation in human bodies (Randolph-Quinney et al. 2011). This is not a single task undertaken by the forensic anthropologist but must recognize the cause of the death along with the personal identification (Cattaneo 2007) wherever necessary. All these purpose are fulfilled with four elementary biological principles, i.e. biological sex determination, developmental or skeletal age estimation, assessment of living stature and establish the ethnic or racial affiliation (Klepinger 2006); followed by secondary examinations wherever applicable. The secondary investigation deals with identification of different macroscopic and microscopic marks like the trauma, scar marks, chronic pathological alterations in soft and hard tissue, modification found in human body and proof of surgical intercessions (Black and Thompson 2007; Clarkson and Schaefer 2007; Eugænia Cunha 2006). Broadly speaking the present day forensic anthropologist not only deal with the dead but also to identify and age approximation of a living one, hence become a crucial in medico-legal investigation.

Here we try to discuss the work of a forensic anthropologist with reference to explain three broad aspects, i.e. A. Identification/investigation associated with dead individuals/scattered remains and B. Identification/investigation associated with the living one C. New emerging trends in forensic anthropology.

Table 21.1 shows a timeline view of developments and personalities behind the major contribution to literature and developments in the field of Forensic Anthropology from world context

S. No.	Year/time	Personality/ organization/ region	Description of work	References
1	1684	François Bernier	François Bernier's ''new division of earth by the different species or races which inhabit it". Classified world population into 4 races-considered as first racial classification	Stuurman (2000)
2	17th centurt	J. Sigismund Elshwltz (1623–88 AD)	The word anthropometry was first used in the seventeenth century by him for his graduation thesis entitled "Authropometria"	Venkatachalam (2008)
3	1775–1899	European scholars	Foundation work related to forensic anthropology by estimation of living stature	Beddoe (1888), Manouvrier (1893), Orfila and Lesueur (1831), Pearson (1899), Rollet (1888), Sue (1755) and Topinard (1885)
4	1859	Paul Broca (1824–1880)	Founded world's first official organization of physical anthropology in Paris, the *"Société d'Anthropologie de Paris"*. Initiated study and training in comparative skeletal anatomy and developed instruments (e.g., the stereograph, osteometric board and goniometer) for the quantification of skeletal measurements	Sapweb (n.d.)
5	1878-1905	Dwight (1843 AD–1911 AD)	Father of American forensic anthropology. He published many literatures that build an initial foundation for forensic anthropology and skeletal biology	Stewart (1979b) and Dwight, (1878a, b, 1881, 1890a, b, 1894a, b, 1905)
6	1883	Alphonse Bertillon (1853–1914)	Known as Father of Criminal Identification, Devised a criminal identification system based on measurement of	Bertillon (1853–1914)

(continued)

Table 21.1 (continued)

S. No.	Year/time	Personality/ organization/ region	Description of work	References
			physical dimensions of the body such as arm, foot length etc. In 1884, Bertillon's Anthropometric Identification System which later called as Bertillonage is announced to be used in all of the french prisons and accepted as a popular criminal identification technique	
7	1897–1903	Wilder (1864 AD–1928 AD)	Trying to establish academic bridge between American and European scholar with respect to forensic anthropology. Published literature on dermatoglyphics and facial approximation techniques	Wilder (1897, 1902, 1903) and Ubelaker (2018)
8	1918	Wilder and Wentworth	Published manual on personal identification (fingerprint analysis and facial approximation)	Wilder and Wentworth (1918)
9	1924	N. Pan	An Indian anatomist was first to study the length of long bones and their proportions to body height in Indian population and observed that males have larger length of long bones as compared to females	Pan (1924)
10	1932	Ales Hrdlička	First attempt on cranial/ photograph comparison in a legal context was done	Ubelaker (1999)
11	1939	Krogman (1903–1987)	Published "guide to the identification of human skeletal material"	Krogman (1939)
12	1972	American Academy of forensic sciences (AAFS)	Newly section named "physical anthropology" was formed by AAFS	Pickering and Bach (2009)

(continued)

Table 21.1 (continued)

S. No.	Year/time	Personality/ organization/ region	Description of work	References
13	1989	Surinder Nath	Indian anthropologist published an book "an introduction to forensic anthropology"	Nath (1989)
14	2003	Establishment of forensic anthropological Society of Europe (FASE)	FASE was established as a subsection of the international academy of legal medicine	Forensic Anthropology Society of Europe (n.d.)
15	2005-2009	L'Abbe et al. Hunt and Albanese; Dayal et al.	World-wide skeletal collections from different geography and people	L'Abbe et al. (2005), Hunt and Albanese (2005) and Dayal et al. (2009)
16	2008	SWAGANTH establishment	Scientific working Group for Forensic Anthropology (SWGANTH), was formed under joint sponsorship of FBI laboratory and Department of Defense Identification Laboratory (DDIL) with the objective to develop and spread best practice guidelines and standards for forensic anthropological investigations	Forensic-Science Anthropology-Subcommittee (n.d.)

21.5.1 The Stages/Scenario of Forensic Human Identification Process Conducted by a Physical Anthropologist: A Brief View

21.5.1.1 Initial Assessment of Skeletons

Some are the general question arise after collection of Skeletal Evidence from different areas:

- Whether the collected evidence is a skeletal material (i.e. bone or tooth) or some other material?
- Whether the collected evidence belongs to human or non-human decedent?
- Whether the collected evidence belong to a single or more persons (i.e. what is the number of victims)?

21.5.1.1.1 Is the Evidence, Skeletal Material or Not?

Ans: For a forensic anthropologist, the determination of skeleton remains during evidence collection is not considered as easy in every cases. Identification of skeleton remains can be done on the basis of thorough visual examination of different morphological features. But sometimes it is difficult to recognize skeleton remains when the bones are found in fragments or due to taphonomic processes which may degenerate the recognizable morphological features of the bones. Also in cases of burning, especially within a confined space (e.g. house fires) it is difficult to distinguish skeleton material from other materials (such as wood, plastic, mineral, shell or metal) due to intermixing of bone fragments with other burned materials (such as furniture, appliances, building material etc.).

In cases where the determination of skeleton material is not possible by thorough visual examination following techniques could be used,

- **Radiography:** Skeleton remains due to their high mineral content are more radiopaque, which can differentiate them from commonly encountered non-mineralized materials.
- **Microscopic Analysis**: Using a high magnification microscope identification of skeleton material can be done by locating microstructures such as trabecular bone, Haversian system, layers of bones etc.
- **Elemental Analysis:** Most accurate but destructive technique. Skeleton remains can be identified by their elemental analysis using techniques like SEM/EDS, XRF(non-destructive analysis).
- **Alternative Light Source (ALS):** Due to the fluorescence property of the collagen protein of the bones, identification of the bones can be done using a short wavelength alternate light source.

21.5.1.1.2 Is the Skeletal Evidence Belongs to Human Skeleton or Not?

Ans: After identification of the collected evidence as skeleton material the next question arises is what the origin is? Is it belonging to a human or some other animal? Again answering such questions is easy for an expert anthropologist on the basis of gross visual examination of the morphological features. Due to differences in locomotion, growth and development, there are numerous differences exist between a human and animal skeleton (Table 21.2). But, certain taxa may be difficult to discriminate because of resemblances in structure, size, or quality; particularly the mammalian species such as cows, bears, deer, large dogs and pigs (Randolph-Quinney et al. 2011). But still certain exceptions are there where some animal bones resemble to humans and hence difficulty arises in differentiation (Table 21.3). Another problem in differentiation comes when scattered/ fragments of bones are found which lack the presence of diagnostic morphology.

Determination of origin of the skeleton (i.e. human or non-human) can be assessed by following methods:

- **Macroscopic Method**: Includes visual and radiographic examination of the skeleton, with attention to the shape, size as well as stage of growth and development of the skeleton. E.g. at macrostructural level cancellous bone of

Table 21.2 Differences between human and non-human skeleton

Bone	Human	Non-human
Skull	Rounded, globular, non-projecting face, anterior foramen magnum	Elongated front to back, projecting snout, posterior foramen magnum
Vertebral column	S-shaped curve, bifurcated spinous process in cervical vertebrae, sharp, point inferior in thoracic vertebrae	Little variation in vertebrae size, some have elongated spinous process which forms shoulder hump
Thorax	Broad and shallow, high degree of curvature, well defined costal groove on internal and inferior aspect of human ribs	Narrow and deeper, costal grooves are absent in non-human mammalian skeleton
Pectoral girdle	Clavicle is elongated, scapula is triangular and elongated supero-inferiorly	Clavicle is reduced or absent, scapula is longest Medio-laterally
Pelvic girdle	Pelvis is wide and broad, illium is short and flaring,	Narrow and elongated illium, pelvis is fused along pubic symphysis
Long bones	Long bones are more gracile and smoother, less complex joint surface, rounded and large femoral and humoral heads	More defined morphology of non-human mammal joint surfaces, smaller size of head of femur and humerus

Table 21.3 Bones of human and non-human origin that resembles each other

Non-human bone	Human bone
Raccoon baculum (penis bone)	Clavicle bone (young child)
Long bones of the birds	Metacarpals/metatarsals (adult), long bones (infant)
Tortoise carapace (dorsal shell) and plastron (ventral shell)	Cranial bone (infant or child)
Bones of Hindpaw of bear	Bones of human foot

non-human origin is more homogeneously distributed then the bone of human origin.

- **Microscopic or Histologic Method**: Such method help in case of burned, fragmented or weathered bones. In these methods microscopy (Cuijpers 2006) is used to compare the microstructures of the bones. E.g. at microstructural level human bones contain Haversian system of arrangement (i.e. concentric rings oriented around the long axis of the bone) whereas non-human bones are arranged in more linear form (i.e. non-Haversian system).
- **Biochemical/immunological Method**: Includes protein based methods (e.g. protein based RIA and solid-phase double antibody RIA) (Lowenstein et al. 2006; Ubelaker et al. 2004) where protein is extracted from bone's organic matter and combined with rabbit antisera pre-exposed with sera of selected animal species (e.g. human, bear, goat, dog etc.). Species-specific antibodies are then combined with protein-antisera and show precipitin reaction and thus species can be determined.
- **DNA Analysis**: This method gives the most accurate result (Guglich et al. 1994) but is comprised of a complex procedure and also not so economical and hence is

used when other methods are not effective. mtDNA cyt-b gene (the specific coding regions) is also useful for taxa differentiation (Linacre and Lee 2016; Matsuda et al. 2005).

21.5.1.1.3 Is the Skeletal Evidence Belongs to a Single or More Persons?

Ans: Once the origin of the skeletal material is determined, the next problem that a Forensic anthropologist faces is the determination of the number of deceased from whom the skeletal material comes from or in other words identifying the number of victims. The process of identifying the number of individuals from the commingled skeletal remains is called the determination of a minimum number of individuals (MNI). The process involves the following steps.

- The first step of analysis involves the arrangement of collected skeletal remains or fragments in anatomical order (i.e. arrange remains into left side and right side elements into complete skeleton).
- The next step is identifying duplicates or duplicating segments of bone. E.g. if two right femur bones are present it means the remains belong to two individuals as no single human has two right femur bones.
- Differentiation can also be made by visual analysis of the remains by checking the size of the elements with each other. E.g. if two complete femur bones are identified, both are different in size. Then it's indicative of the presence of more than one person.
- Another way of segregation between remains is done by checking the compatibility of the bones with each other on the basis of age, sex, robusticity, or configuration.

In 2001, a formula was developed to determine the probable number of individuals (PNI) from commingled skeletal remains by West and Giles (Klepinger 2006). They create the formula by taking the Lincoln Index approach in mind.

$$\text{PNI} = (R \times L)/P$$

where 'R' = Number of right side elements, 'L' = Number of left side elements and 'P' = Number of matched pair of elements.

Formula for small samples and small number of pairs:

$$\text{PNI} = (L + 1)(R + 1)/(P + 1) - 1$$

Formula if no right-left pairs are found.

$$\text{PNI} = (R + 1)(L + 1)$$

Besides this, other new methodologies, like the use of pair-wise maximum likelihood models, recording of distinct anatomical sutures, DNA analysis and Geographical Information System (GIS) -based statistical models will be useful to mentioned above matter (Adams and Byrd 2006; Adams and Konigsberg 2004, 2008; Outram et al. 2005).

21.6 Determination of Demographic Characteristics

Forensic anthropologists have an important role to provide enough information regarding the human skeletal remains. The law enforcement agency by using that information and matching it with a missing persons file, can lead to a positive identification of a person. The information or data required for positive identification of individual from skeletal remains include determination of the four principle components that together makes up the biological profile of an individual. These basic demographics are

1. Ancestry.
2. Sex.
3. Age.
4. Stature.

This text provides in depth knowledge regarding determination of the above mentioned components of the biological profile which leads to the positive identification of an individual from its skeletal remains.

21.6.1 Determination of Ancestry

Classification of a population is done on the basis of geographical region of origin. People of different geographic location have significant morphological as well as cultural differences between them and it is due to the climate and environment where they lived for ages. People get these different morphological traits from their ancestors. These ancestral traits provide a means to classify people for identification purposes in forensic anthropology. Groups of physical traits differ in frequency from one major region of the world to another and help to determine ancestry. Variation in genotype and phenotypic characters among human population group are shaped by the geography and culture (Klepinger 2006). The genetic variation among inter-individuals inside a population account for about 93–95% of and that differences between major population groups (inter-population) account for only 3–5% (Rosenberg et al. 2002).

Forensic Anthropologist, tend to classify individuals into three major groups:

1. **Caucasoid:** It includes Europeans, inhabitants of South-Western Asia and North Africa.
2. **Mongoloid:** It includes rest of inhabitants of Asia (i.e. Chinese, Japanese, and Koreans etc.).
3. **Negroid:** It includes rest of inhabitants of the continent of Africa.

Ancestry can be traced by different indicators, which are discussed below.

21.6.1.1 Skeletal Indicators

Racial/ancestral association in forensic investigation are conceded out using metric and morphological methods both, on the cranial and postcranial skeletons (Barker et al. 2008; Craig 1995; Gilbert 1976; St Hoyme and Iscan 1989; Walker 2005). The differences are associated to the morphology of the human skeleton as well and hence classifying an individual on the basis of these morphological variations at the skeletal level plays an important role in the identification of individual's ancestry. The variations can be studied under following types:

(a) **Nonmetric Variation in Skeletal Morphology**: It includes morphological variation in various part of the skeleton (i.e. skull, dentition, postcranial bones etc.) that can be visually identified. Table 21.4 shows Non-metric racial traits.

Table 21.4 Morphological variations in skeleton of different race

Elements of difference	Caucasoid	Mongoloid	Negroid
Skull			
Facial profile	Orthognathic	Orthognathic	Prognathic
Nasal spine	Large, long	Medium, tilted	Little or none
Nasal aperture	Narrow, elongated	Medium, rounded	Broad
Nasal sill	Single, sharp	Single, sharp	Double, guttered
Skull shape	Rounded	Square	Narrow, elongated
Forehead	Raised	Inclined	Small, compressed
Orbits	Triangular	Small, round	Square
Palatal shape	Parabolic, triangular	Elliptical, rounded	U-shaped, square
Palatal suture	Not straight	Straight	Not straight
Cranial sutures	Simple	Complex	Simple
Chin	Square, projecting	Blunt	Retreating
Skull length	Short	Long	Long
Skull breadth	Broad	Board	Narrow
Skull height	High	Middle	Low
Sagittal contour	Arched	Arched	Flat
Dentition			
Maxillary incisors	Blade shaped	Shovel shaped	Blade shaped
Maxillary molars	Carabelli's cusp	Simple, 4 cusps	Simple, 4 cusps
Dentition	Crowded	Not crowded	Not crowded
Postcranial bones (femur)			
Anterior curvature	More curved	Straight	Straight
Proximal diaphysis shape	Round	Anteroposterior flattening	Round
Intercondylar notch depth	Shallow	Undetermined	Deep

Table 21.5 Metric indexes to differentiate between skeleton of various races

Index	Formula	Caucasoid	Mongoloid	Negroid
Cephalic index (CI)	(maximum transverse breadth of skull)/(maximum anteroposterior length of skull) × 100	75–79.99	80–84.99	70–74.99
Skull height index (HI)	(height of the skull)/(length of the skull) × 100	71	75	72
Nasal index (NI)	(width of nasal aperture)/(height of nasal aperture) × 100	46	50	55
Brachial index	(length of radius)/(length of Humerus) × 100	74.5	–	78.5
Crural index	(length of tibia)/(length of femur) × 100	83.3	86.5 (Indians)	86.2
Humero-femoral index	(length of Humerus)/(length of femur) × 100	69	–	72.4
Intermembral index	(length of Humerus + radius)/(length of femur + tibia) × 100	More than 72	–	Less than 70.5

Other than the above-mentioned variation, few differences are also there such as,

- Mongoloids have the largest teeth among the three races.
- Third upper molar is absent in Mongoloids.
- Mongoloids have an extra tubercle on mandibular premolars (i.e. Dens Evaginatus).
- Negroids have extra lingual cusp in the mandibular molars (i.e. Tuberculum intermedium).
- Mongoloids have long pointed canines and also have a condition of Taurodontism (i.e. Bull tooth).
- Caucasoid population has a small additional cusp at the mesiopalatal line angle of maxillary molars (i.e. Carabelli's cusp).

(b) **Metric Variation in Skeletal Morphology**: Metric variations are the differences related to measurements. People of different races have different body measurements (i.e. height, length, breadth and width) using these variations multiple indexes (i.e. cephalic index, brachial index, nasal index etc.) are formed which help to differentiate between races of individuals. Some of the indexes use to differentiate between races along with their formula and approximate values are mentioned in (Table 21.5).

Skull can be classified into three categories on the basis of Cephalic Index,

1. **Dolicho-cephalic:** When the CI is 70–74.99, then they are long, narrow-headed person or dolichocranic. E.g. Negroid, Aborigines, Aryans etc.
2. **Mesati-cephalic:** When the CI is 75–79.99, then they are medium or average headed person or mesocranic. E.g. Caucasoid, Indians etc.

3. **Brachy-cephalic:** When the CI is 80–84.99, then they are short, broad, round headed person or brachycranic. E.g. Mongoloids.

Below the Table 21.5 shows various indexes related to person of different racial backgrounds.

21.6.1.2 Cultural Indicators

The forensic anthropologist always seeks for the cultural indicators associated with the body remains of also with living individuals and connect them to their ancestry/ race. These indicators are the customs, jewelleries, different body modification (as that practises by specified groups all over the world) and materials with religious significances. E.g. hole in ear lobe is common among adult Brahmins and Kshatriyas in Hindu community. Other cultural Modification marks are imprinted on skin includes permanent and semipermanent tattoos, cutting marks, beads and rings implant sub-dermally and piercing trans-dermally respectively and also scarifications has significance potentiality for personal identification purpose. Also surgical inventions or modifications were performed as a part of cultural or religious/ aesthetic and cosmetic purpose either by trained medical practitioner or by non-medically trained persons. E.g. penis circumcision by the Jews and Muslims all over the world. These kind of crucial indicators are comparable to different ethnic groups of different geography during the legal investigation. The major issues/ drawbacks associated to these practises are seen due to the availability of these crucial witnesses due to preservation point of view. Also in present globalised world the modern lifestyle promote/distribute different ethnic wears and practises among the natives, hence creates misconception to the investigation agency if they found any such evidences.

21.6.1.3 Molecular Indicators

With the advancement in DNA based identification methods, allows forensic anthropologist to adopt such techniques where the traditional methods (osteological investigation) are not suited to identification confirmation of evidential remains. The cases like the identification of mass disaster victims, totally burnt individuals with limited body residues fragmented body parts of skeletons and ancestry of an orphan can be solved by DNA analysis. The drawback is associated with the biological samples, which immediately start the degradation after the death of an individuals. To compare the ancestry a proper sophisticated DNA data base is needed, which now lacks to even in different developed nations.

21.6.1.4 Somatoscopic Indicators

These indicators are different somatic features that can be seen to the naked eyes. Those are the skin tone type, eye-fold pattern, hair pattern and colour etc. These characters helps the physical anthropologist to trace the ancestry to the respective family or with an ethnic group or to conclude in personal identification.

21.6.2 Determination of Sex

After estimation of ancestry of an unidentified skeleton the next step is the determination of its sex. The skeleton remains serves best in the estimation of sex until most of the bones are available for analysis. Sexual dimorphism or expression of phenotypic differences between male and female of the same species have the ability to differentiate between male and female skeleton. Due to this condition of sexual dimorphism male and female skeleton have prominent morphological differences (i.e. in size and architecture).

Estimation of sex from bone morphology is not so reliable in immature skeletal cases, where the molecular analysis, i.e. amelogenin marker testing consider as reliable alternative irrespective of age and where the skeletal remains are fragmentary or incomplete (Baker 2016; Ostrofsky and Churchill 2015; Ubelaker 2019). Sex is an important component of the biological profile of a missing person. In most of the cases the sex can be reliably estimated from pelvis and found difficult in cases where the pelvis is damaged or completely absent (Abdel Fatah et al. 2014; Michel et al. 2015). Different researches established substantial population variation in appearance of sexual dimorphism seen in human skeleton (Brzobohatá et al. 2015), and published literature for specific data based on the sex differences (Spradley et al. 2015).

In general speaking, an adult male human skeleton is larger in size and more strongly built than female skeleton. The difference in size between male and female skeleton is about 8% i.e. female skeleton is about 92% the size of male skeleton. Male skeleton exceeds the female skeleton in height, weight and breadth. The bones of male skeleton are longer, thicker and have more prominent attachment of muscles. On the other hand the architecture of both male and female skeleton also varies greatly. One of the reason of difference in architecture is that female gave birth due to which they have wider pelvis (i.e. to accommodate passage of infants) than males of comparable size.

A forensic anthropologist, classify two categories of methods to differentiate between male and female skeleton,

Non-metric (microscopic or visual analysis) Methods**,** involve examination of morphological features of bones that vary between male and female (i.e. pelvis, skull, long bones etc.). These methods are more accurate to identify the sex of the skeleton. The entire skeleton can be used to assess the sex, but some of the major bones like skull, pelvis, long bones play major role in establishment of sex because they show prominent difference in male and female skeleton. Table 21.6 shows accuracy of sex determination based on skeletal remains.

According to the above data, pelvis is the best single bone which gives 95% accuracy in sex determination. Table 21.7 shows features of pelvis that are diagnostic of sex.

After pelvis, another sex differentiating bone is the skull that gives around 92% accuracy in sex estimation. Table 21.8 shows various differentiating feature of male and female skull.

Table 21.6 Accuracy in sex determination based on skeletal remains

Skeletal remains	Accuracy in sex determination
Pelvis	95%
Skull	92%
Long bones	80–85%
Skull + pelvis	98%
Long bones + pelvis	98%
Entire skeleton	100%

Table 21.7 Differentiating features of male and female pelvis

Features	Male pelvis	Female pelvis
General appearance	Massive, rougher, prominent muscular markings	Less massive, slender, smoother, muscular markings are not prominent
Shape	Deep funnel	Flat bowl
Body of pubis	Narrow, triangular	Broad, square, pits on posterior surface
Acetabulam	Large (52 mm diameter), more forwardly directed	Small (46 mm diameter), more laterally directed
Preauricular sulcus	Generally absent, if present narrow, shallow	Better developed, broad, deep
Iliac auricular surface	That is not elevated from the surrounding bone	That partially or completely elevated
Ischio-pubic ramus	Broader and less everted	Sharp, often everted with ridge
Greater sciatic notch	Deep, small, narrow	Shallow, large, wide
Obturator foramen	Large, oval, base upwards	Small, triangular, apex forwards
Ischial tuberosity	Inverted	Everted
Ilium	High and vertical	Low and flaring
Subpubic angle	V-shaped, sharp angle (70^0–75^0)	U-shaped, rounded, broader angle (90^0–100^0)
Pelvic inlet	Heart shaped	Circular or elliptical shaped
Pelvic outlet	Smaller	Larger
Pelvic cavity	Conical, funnel shaped	Broad, round
Subpubic contour	Straight	Concave
Auricular surface	Raised	Flat

Other bones such as mandible, sacrum, scapula, clavicle, long bones (i.e. humerus, radius, ulna, femur, tibia) also have differentiating features in male and female skeleton that can also be used for the assessment of sex from the skeletal remains.

Metric Methods**,** involve estimation of sex on the basis of measurement of bone lengths, width and breadth. Table 21.9 contains certain indexes that tell about the sex from the skeletal remains.

Table 21.8 Differentiating features of male and female skull

Features	Male skull	Female skull
General appearance	Large, heavy, rugged, marked muscular ridges	Small, light, thin walls, smooth
Forehead	More retreating, irregular, rough, less rounded	Vertical, rounded, full, infantile, smooth
Mastoid process	Large, round, blunt	Small, smooth, pointed
Cranial capacity	1450–1550 cc	1300–1350 cc
Orbits	Square, small	Rounded, large
Frontal and parietal eminence	Less prominent	Prominent
Zygomatic arch	Prominent	Not prominent
Supraorbital ridges	Thick, rounded, more pronounced	Sharp and less pronounced
Suprameatal crest	Present (extends)	Absent (no extension)
Nasal aperture	High, thin,sharp margins	Lower, wider, rounded margins
Palate	Large, U-shaped, broad	Small, parabolic
Foramen magnum	Relatively large, long	Small, round
Mental eminence	Large projection	Small or no projection
Glabella	Prominent	Less prominent

Table 21.9 Diagnostic Indexes for determination of sex

Index	Formula	Average value in male	Average value in female
Ischiopubic index	Length of pubis/length of ischium × 100	73–94 (average 75)	91–115 (average 100)
Sciatic notch index	Width of sciatic notch/depth of sciatic notch × 100	145	166
Sternal index	Length of manubrium/length of body × 100	46.2	54.3
Chilotic line index	Sacral part of chilotic line/pelvic part of chilotic line × 100	More than 100	Less than 100
Sacral index	Transverse diameter of base of sacrum/ anterior length of sacrum × 100	Less than 114	More than 114
Kimura's base wing index (alar index)	Width of wing (ala of sacrum)/width of base (transverse diameter of body of S1) × 100	65	80
Corporobasal index	Breadth of body of first sacral vertebra/ breadth of base of sacrum × 100	More than 42	Less than 42

21.6.3 Determination of Age/Age at Death

Human skeleton can also be used to estimate the age of the deceased at the time of death. In case of unidentified skeletal remains, once the age is determined, the law enforcement agency can narrow down their search and this information will limit the pool of potential matches with missing individuals and identification of the individual can be done.

Forensic anthropologist can determine the age from skeletal remains by in-depth understanding of the nature, sequence and timing of skeletal changes throughout a lifetime. A Forensic anthropologist provides the estimated age in a range, because there is no method or clue present which allows the determination of exact age from the skeletal remain. The age range will be narrow (i.e. 1–3 years) in case of younger person (i.e. 15–25 years) and will widen (i.e. 5–10 years) as the age of the person increases or in case of an older (i.e. 40 years and above) person. The most accurate age determination is done for infants and children.

Until the sub-adult age (i.e. from infant to children to adolescents) there are many biological changes going on the body including in the bones that are occurring at regular times and rates and hence estimation of age in subadults is quite precise (i.e. Age range is narrower). At the age of biological maturity the number and rate of developmental changes in the body decreases as during this age (25–35 years) the body is in maintenance phase. After the age of 40 years, the developmental change ceases. Estimation of age in adults (i.e 40 years and above) are based basically on the degenerative changes (i.e. breakdown, wear and tear of skeleton) that vary person to person and hence age range is broader (i.e. 5–10 years) in adults as compared to subadults (i.e. 1–3 years).

Determination of Age from skeletal remains in subadults, depends upon growing characteristics of the bones and teeth whereas in adults (i.e. 40 years or more) it depends upon the degenerative changes in the bones. The features that are used to establish the age from skeletal remains are mentioned below,

21.6.3.1 Determination of Age from Dentition

Age of an individual can be determined from its dentition. The stages of dental development (i.e. formation, mineralization, and eruption of the deciduous and permanent dentition) are the most relevant processes for age estimation. Eruption of teeth and dental ageing are said to be the most precise method of age estimation upto the juvenile period (i.e. 15 years) because dental development starts early in the sixth fetal week and does not complete until the early adulthood. Tables 21.10 and 21.11 shows time of eruption of deciduous and permanent dentition respectively.

Period of mixed dentition, is the time when both the deciduous and permanent teeth are present in the jaw and this is the most informative period for determination of the age, usually it is between 6–11 years, but may persist until 12–13 years. Table 21.12 represents the number of teeth with age.

By following the information given in Table 21.9, estimation of age can be done on the basis of presence of different numbers and types of teeth in the dental evidence of the skeletal remains.

Other methods of estimation of age from dental evidence include,

1. **Stack's Method:** This method helps in estimating the age of the fetus and infants from the weight of erupting teeth. Stack derived a regression line of weight of

Table 21.10 Eruption time of deciduous teeth

S. No.	Tooth	Eruption time	No. of teeth
1.	*Central incisor*		
	• Lower	6–8 months	2
	• Upper	7–9 months	4
2.	*Lateral incisor*		
	• Upper	7–9 months	6
	• Lower	10–12 months	8
3.	First molar	12–14 months	12
4.	Canine	17–18 months	16
5.	Second molar	20–30 months	20

Table 21.11 Eruption time of permanent teeth

			No. of teeth	
S. No.	Tooth	Eruption time	Permanent	Deciduous
1.	First molar	6–7 years	4	20
2.	Central incisor	6–8 years	8	16
3.	Lateral incisor	8–9 years	12	12
4.	First pre-molar	9–10 years	16	8
5.	Second pre-molar	10–11 years	20	4
6.	Canine	11–12 years	24	0
7.	Second molar	12–14 years	28	0
8.	Third molar	17–25 years	32	0

Table 21.12 Number and types of teeth present at various age

Age (in years)	No. of teeth	Type of teeth
2–5	20	All deciduous
6	21–24	20 deciduous, 1–4 first permanent molars
7–9	24	12 permanent—8 incisors, 4 molars 12 deciduous—8 molars, 4 canines
10	24	16 permanent—8 incisors, 4 molars, 4 premolars 8 deciduous—4 second molars, 4 canines
11	24	20 permanent—8 incisors, 4 molars, 8 premolars 4 deciduous—4 canines
12–14	25–28	Eruption of second permanent molars
14–17	28	All permanent
17–25	29–32	Eruption of third permanent molars

growing dental tissues with respect to age. Table 21.13 shows the weight of dental tissues with respect to age.

2. **Boyde's Method:** This method is basically used to determine the age of dead infants. This method estimates the age of the dead infant on the basis of counting the number of cross striations (i.e. incremental lines) in the enamel of the teeth.
3. **Gustafson's Method:** A method for estimation of age between 25–60 years using dental evidence. By microscopically examining the physiological age changes

Table 21.13 Weight of dental tissue with respect to age

Age (in weeks)	Sum of teeth weight (in mg)
28 (prenatal)	60
40 (prenatal)	460
2 (postnatal)	530
30 (postnatal)	1840

(i.e. wear and tear) in each of the dental tissue, age of an individual is determined. This method is useful in determining the age from a dead body or skeletal remains because the methodology requires extraction of tooth from the jaw. After extraction, the longitudinal section of central part of the tooth is taken for assessing following physiological changes,

(a) Secondary dentin.
(b) Cementum Apposition.
(c) Root Resorption.
(d) Attrition.
(e) Periodontosis.
(f) Root transparency.

By assessing the above given changes, age of the deceased is determined (Table 21.14).

1. **Miles Method:** He derived a method of estimation of age at death from the dental remains. The method involves measuring the thickness of enamel and dentin from neonatal line and divided it by appropriate daily rate of formation.
2. **Radiocarbon Analysis of Tooth enamel:** On the basis of levels of radiocarbon present in tooth enamel, the year of tooth formation can be determined.
3. **Chemical Analysis:** Chemical methods are also useful for determination of age from skeletal remains. These methods are destructive but can produce precise results. Some of the chemical method includes,
   (a) **Estimation of Nitrogen content in tooth enamel** (Increase with age).
   (b) **Estimation of Carbonate content** (Decreases with age).
   (c) **Estimation of Copper, selenium, lead and iron ions** (Increases with age).
   (d) **Amino Acid Racemization:** Most reliable destructive method for dental age estimation. With age the L-form of amino acid transformed to D-form by racemization. By estimation of extent of racemization of amino acid in the tooth enamel and crown dentin, age can be estimated. Out of all amino acid Aspartic acid has one of the fastest racemization and hence used to estimate age from dental tissues.

21.6.3.2 Determination of Age from Ossification of Bones

Ossification is the process where soft bone tissues become hard and calcified. The process of ossification starts around the sixth and seventh week of embryonic development and continues until 25 years of age (except in case of ossification of

Table 21.14 Ossification of bones with age in human male

Bone	Ossification centres	Age of appearance of ossification	Age of complete ossification
1. Sternum	Manubrium	5th month of IUL	60–70 years
	1st sternebrae	5th month of IUL	14–25 years
	Second and third sternebrae	7th month of IUL	14–25 years
	4th sternbrae	10th month of IUL	14–25 years
	Xiphisternum	3rd year (after birth)	40–45 years
2. Clavicle	Medial end	15–17 years	20–22 years
3. Scapula	Coracoid base	10–11 years	14–15 years
4. Hyiod	Greater cornu	–	40–60 years
5. Sacrum	–	–	20–25 years
Upper limb	Head	1 year	Conjoint epiphysis in three bones at age of 5–6 years and union with shaft at 17–18 years.
6. Humerus	Greater tubercle	3 years	
	Lesser tubercle	5 years	
	Capitulum	1 year	At 14–15 years, all three fuses with the shaft.
	Trochlea	9–10 years	
	Lateral epicondyle	10–11 years	
	Medial epicondyle	5–6 years	16 years
7. Radius	Upper end	5–6 years	15–17 years
	Lower end	1–2 years	17–19 years
8. Ulna	Upper end	8–9 years	15–17 years
	Lower end	5–6 years	17–19 years
9. Carpals	Capitate	At birth	2 month
	Hamate	3 month	14–16 years
	Triquetrum	3 years	6–7 years
	Lunate	4 years	6–7 years
	Scaphoid	4 years	5 years
	Trapezium	4–5 years	6 years
	Trapezoid	5 years	7 years
	Pisiform	9–12 years	–
Lower limb	Ischiopubic rami	–	7 years

Table 21.14 (continued)

Bone	Ossification centres	Age of appearance of ossification	Age of complete ossification
10. Hip bone	Triradiate cartilage	–	12–14 years
	Iliac crest	15–16 years	19–21 years
	Ischial tuberosity	16–17 years	20–22 years
11. Femur	Head	1 year	17–18 years
	Greater trochanter	4 years	14–15 years
	Lesser trochanter	14 years	15–17 years
	Lower end	At birth	17–18 years
12. Tibia	Upper end	At birth	17–18 years
	Lower end	1 year	16–17 years
13. Fibula	Upper end	4 years	17–18 years
	Lower end	2 years	16–17 years
14. Tarsals	Calcaneum	5th month of IUL	17–18 years
	Talus	7th month of IUL	–
	Cuboid	9th month of IUL	–

cranial sutures, sternum and hyoid bone). Ossification starts centrally in an epiphysis and spread peripherally. The centre of ossification in most of the bones appears during the seventh to 12th week of embryonic development. At about 11th to 12th week of embryonic development there are around 806 centres of ossification which decreases to 450 during the birth. The disappearance of ossification centres shows that ossification centres unites with adjacent centres and forms an adult bone and finally an adult human skeleton consists of 206 bones.

Ossification of bones is a relevant method to estimate the age in the subadults as this process continues until the age of 25 years. Table 21.16 shows the age at which these ossification centres appear and unite to complete the ossification in a human male. In females the union of epiphyses occurs 1 year earlier.

Fusion of joints can also be used for age estimation before 25 years of age, because all the joint get fused in 25 years. Table 21.15 shows the approximate age of fusion of various joints.

21.6.4 Determination of Age from Skull Suture Closure

The human skull is not a single bone but it is composed of several major bones which are joined together with the help of fibrous joints known as the suture. These sutures help the skull bones in movement during the birth process and act as expansion joints. Closure of cranial sutures is said to be a reliable method of age estimation

Table 21.15 Age of fusion of various joints

Joint	Approximate age of fusion
Elbow joint	16 years
Ankle joint	16–17 years
Hip joint	17–18 years
Shoulder joint	18 years
Knee joint	18 years
Wrist joint	18 years

Table 21.16 Closure age of various sutures of the skull

Suture	Age of closure
Posterior Fontanelle (occipital)	At birth to 6 months
Anterior Fontanelle (bregma)	1 ½–2 years
Two halves of mendible	1–2 years
Metopic suture (between frontal bones)	2–4 years, may extend to 6 years or remain unfused
Bassiocciput and basisphenoid	18–20 years in female, 20–22 years in male
Coronal suture (between frontal and parietal bones)	Lower half in 40–50 years, upper half in 50–60 years
Lambdoid suture (between occipital and parietal bones)	45–50 years
Sagittal suture (between right and left parietals) Posterior one third in 30–40 years, anterior one third in 40–50 years, middle part in 50–60 years	
Parieto-temporal	60–70 years

between 25–40 years of age. The human skull contains sutures on the inner and outer surfaces known as **endocranial** and **ectocranial** sutures respectively. Closure of sutures on the outer surface (i.e ectocranial sutures) is useful in estimation of age at death whereas the inner sutures (i.e. endocranial sutures) are said to give a rough estimate of age at death. Closure of endocranial sutures begin 5–10 years earlier than the ectocranial sutures. The palate also contains sutures known as the palatal sutures which are also used in age estimation. Table 21.16 shows the ages at which different sutures closes.

The above given information is utilized to estimate the age at death and the most precise age estimation is done from sagittal suture followed by lambdoid suture and then from coronal suture. Closure of all sutures indicates that the age is above 60 years.

Other method of age estimation from skeletal remains include,

21.6.5 Determination of Age Based on Changes in Pubic Symphyseal Surface

The pubic symphyseal surface starts changing from 18 years of age. This surface at young age is an undulating surface, at 25–40 years the surface become granular and become eroded around 60 years. These alterations in the pubic symphyseal surface with ageing are the best single criteria to determine the age at death for the individuals of 30—50 years of age.

21.6.6 Determination of Age Based on Changes in Morphology of Mendible

Morphological features of the mendible bone can be utilized to estimate a rough outline regarding the age group (i.e. infant, adult and oldage) of the individual. Mendible bone's morphology changes with time like the body is shallow at infancy which become thick and long during the adulthood and in old age again become shallow. The angle of Ramus with the body is obtuse (about 140°) at infancy which become less obtuse during adulthood and again become obtuse at oldage. The mental foramen moves towards the alveolar margin with age.

21.6.7 Determination of Stature from Skeletal Remains

From the four principle components of a person's biological profile or demographics (i.e. ancestry, sex, age, stature) stature is the fourth component of importance. Estimation of stature along with other demographics from the skeletal remains will help the law enforcement agency to identify the person. The word stature is derived from Latin word "*statura*" which means height or size of the body and the Latin verb "*stare*" which means to stand. Stature of a person relates to its standing height.

Estimation of stature from skeletal remains can be done by following methods,

(a) **Anatomical or full skeleton method**: It is a rarely used method also known as full skeleton method. This method involves taking vertical measurements of all the bones that contribute to stature (i.e skull, vertebrae, scapula, long bones, tarsals etc.) using calipers and osteometric boards. After taking the measurements, stature is estimated by adding the measurements of all bones along with a correction factor for soft tissue. This method gives high accuracy but from a forensic point of view it is bit impractical. As this method requires measurements of all bones and it is quite difficult to recover a full skeleton because usually incomplete skeletons and fragmentary remains are recovered from the scene.
(b) **Mathematical or Regression method:** This is the most commonly used method for stature estimation. Based on the principle that components of the skeleton grow in an orderly manner along with the growing human body and hence have a specific relationship with the increasing height of the body. The mathematical relationship between body height and various bones that contributes to the stature (i.e humerus, radius, ulna etc.) is devised in the form of regression formula. This formula consists of a multiplication factor which is different for different bone along with correction factor for soft tissues and is

Table 21.17 Long bones with their respective multiplication factors for stature estimation

Bone	Multiplication factor (approx.)
Femur	3.6–3.8 (3.7)
Tibia/fibula	4.48
Humerus	5.30
Radius	6.7–6.9
Ulna	6.0–6.3 (6.1)

used to estimate the stature from different bones. From the forensic perspective the regression method is better as single bone is sufficient to estimate the stature but it is better to have combination of bones as they provide more accurate results than single bone. Regression formulas are derived for various long bones as they give better results. **Karl Pearson's regression formula** is the most commonly used method for estimation of stature from long bones. For e.g. the formula for stature estimation from femur is,

$$\text{Stature} = 81.306 + 1.88 \times F \text{ (Length of femur in males)}$$

Table 21.17 shows multiplication factors for calculation of stature from various long bones.

Sex and race of individuals should be taken into account while applying these methods. Long bones of lower limb gave more accurate result than long bones of upper limb. Apart from long bones studies have been done for the estimation of stature from non-long bones such as calcaneus bones, metatarsals, size and shape of foot and hand, parts of vertebral column etc.

Other methods used for Stature estimation include,

- Radiographs to study stature and bone lengths of living and recently deceased person.
- Multislice CT scans to determine regression formula between stature and bone (i.e. sacrum) length.
- Magnetic resonance imaging (MRI) also been used in few studies.

21.7 Identity Markers Related to Individual and Its Life History

Personal identity of the deceased may judge more appropriately by difference skeletal marks acquires by live events. Certain type of erosions like the depressions, scars and pits on the dorsal surface of the pubic bones that adjacent to the pubic symphyses portion observed more often in female's pelvis than the opposite sex. Radiographic examination are carried out during forensic post-mortem to examine the pathological and non-pathological marks acquired by the deceased and the ante mortem radiographic report should compare to the previous one in case of availability, either confirm or exclude in identification point of view (Murphy and Gantner 1982). Some characters are unique to a single individual. Some of them are secure characteristics as they control by genetics itself, or acquired due to the addition, removal, or alteration of bodily tissues i.e. in ontogeny and phenotypically become plastic/fix (Randolph-Quinney et al. 2011). Such type of individualities are ascend upon intervention in development naturally or intesionally, through accident, or intended alteration, with the aim that those are suitably becomes a mark of identity to an individual. These are the pathological effects of any disease or trauma, surgical mediation for therapeutic or cosmetic tenacities and uniqueness in soft tissue or in bones; and such signs should provide a resilient evident for establish discrete identity. Joint replacement surgery/ orthopedic plating, breast augmentation in female, use of cardiac pacemakers, or other life supporting surgical maneuvers (having manufactures mark/number) are certain types of surgical interventions that left some imprints permanently, useful as personal identification purpose.

21.8 Trauma Analysis

Forensic anthropologist are expert to access the bone's response with respect to any type of trauma. Systematic analysis of skeletal remains for knew the timing and mechanism of skeletal trauma give clues to relevant forensic questions. That involve careful observation, documentation and interpretation with proper scientific methods and principles. For trauma analysis forensic anthropologist through assessing the timing of occurrence of the trauma (antemortem, post-mortem/perimortem) and the mechanism responsible for the occurrence of the trauma (like the projectile, blunt, sharp and thermal) (SWGANTH 2011). This needs an interdisciplinary approach and brings methodologies from disciplines like osteology, taphonomy, anatomy, physics, materials engineering, biomechanics and ballistics. Not only the trauma associated with the bones but with the cartilages are recruited to forensic anthropologists. They carefully restructure the fragmented bone, study the pattern of any fracture, characteristics of the wound, and lastly the nature of tool as well as the minimal force that should responsible for the trauma (Love and Wiersema 2016).

21.9 Craniofacial Reconstruction

When the other methods are failed to identify the unknown human remnant Forensic facial reconstruction can be useful to identification purpose. Forensic facial reconstruction is a quick, non-invasive as well as effectual method that made facial reconstruction, useful for individual identification from skeletal remains and also in archaeological research (Gupta et al. 2015). The techniques are varied from two dimensional (2D) drawings to three dimensional (3D) clay models (Abate et al. 2004; Yadav et al. 2010). Based on antemortem snaps and the skull the former model requires an artist and a forensic anthropologist to work on the facial reconstruction (Yadav et al. 2010). Accurate identification allows the legal agencies to make a list of alleged victims'. A 3D techniques called as Anatomical Russian Method used for reconstruction of face of fossilized skulls (Kähler et al. 2003). For facial recognition of an individual the combination Manchester method has been considered as the best and most precise one (Short et al. 2014).

21.10 Identifying Living Individuals

Forensic anthropologist also involve in the matter of identifying the living being, but facial identification is quite difficult (Fraser et al. 2003). It is quite a different aspect in the field of forensic identification, which study the human diversity and attempt to construct and verify morphological characteristics to understand the differences in physiognomy of one from other. They collect the CCTV footages and reconstruct the face of the suspects who involves in crimes like robberies and assaults etc. proper attention should be given to verify the falsification arises by projective geometry during the measurement of the dimension of the real items seen at crime surroundings (Criminisi et al. 1999). Traditional literature use conventional anthropometry (i.e. indices and facial characters) in for verify the resemblance in between the two individuals (Halberstein 2001). The 3D models of the person are examined to check matching of different facial landmarks and outlines, for an efficient analysis on 2D image (Fraser et al. 2003; Yoshino et al. 2001). Most recently the with technological shift improvement in 3D image acquisition technology will enable the researcher to achieve 3D-3D facial superimposition goal (Gibelli et al. 2017).

21.11 Determining the Age of Living Individuals (Imputability, Migration Issues and Pedo-Pornography)

The issues related to the individual's identification arises, when there is no documental evidence present near the person. This kind of concerns related to the victims of war survivals, persons associated with illegal migration and children survived in mass disaster cases. Other issues arises with the culprit, whose age is not known to the law enforcement agencies, hence issue arises with the type of court proceedings either for underage or adults. Forensic anthropologist with radiological, anthropological, and odontological investigations determine whether they belongs to underage or adult after the ancestry tracing, as the somatic growth differ with the geographical areas and ethnicity (Cattaneo 2007; Eugénia Cunha and Cattaneo 2006). Where the person ≥18 years old then CT examination of collar bones is necessary to construct the accurate age (Schmeling et al. 2006). A recent method is called as exfoliative cytology (EC) is considered as unique, use noninvasive technique, that involving simple, and based on the pain-free collection of intact cells from the oral cavity for different microscopic examination (Nallamala et al. 2017).

Child pornography is a type sexual exploitation, where the victims are the children/ underages. The issue associated to the pedoponography is quite difference, where the age calculation are performed with the help of 2D images over anthropological assessment. The facial and secondary sexual characteristics are extremely variable and do not represent chronological age, even the rate of sexual maturation is vary with geography, hence considered as a novel and very tough aspect of age estimation (Gehlen et al. 2005; Greil and Kahl 2005; Parent et al. 2003). Now other new methods of age estimation used 'Iris Ratio' (Machado et al. 2017) and face (Ratnayake et al. 2014) as indicator that capable with the potentiality for forensic applications, especially to the crimes like the child pornography and child abuse issues.

21.12 Positive or Confirmed Identity and Exclusion

The important step of any forensic investigation is to conclude its own way. Proper identification in the forensic anthropological investigation complete with the two-step procedure. Formerly, the features which are found are match in between the recovered remains and the antemortem feature/evidences of the missing person. The later step must clarify any differences which exists and explain the uniqueness of the common attributes. When the commonly found features are properly umpired as unique and the differences are reconciled successfully, a positive identification result will be established, otherwise exclusion is concluded.

21.12.1 Human Right Issues and Forensic Anthropologist

Forensic anthropology apply scientific knowledge as well as methodologies to solve law and justice related issues. The problem not only associated with the individual identification and identify the foul play in crimes but also with humanitarian and issues with human right. Forensic anthropologists identify the missing persons and helps in detect crime and take part to give justice against the culprit for of any crimes. Human rights in forensic anthropology is the specific application of forensic anthropology to the cases with mass killing or genocide has occurred intensively in a large scale. Forensic anthropologists associated to the human rights work are recruited by federal agency to gather precise evidence related to any war, genocide, human trafficking and child abuse. The first ever involvement of international forensic anthropologist into human rights inquiries started in 1984 by the American Association for the Advancement of Science (AAAS) sponsored forensic anthropology experts responded to Argentina's request regarding the support of forensic experts in unearthing and identifying thousands of individuals who missed during the period of 1976 and 1983.

21.12.2 Case Studies/Famous Case Histories

- In 1849, The Parkman Murder (Killgrove 2016), known to be the first case that originates Forensic anthropology in America. Two anatomists Oliver Wendell Holmes and Jeffries Wyman at Harvard University investigate the Murder of the prominent physician Dr. George Parkman who was killed by a chemistry professor at Harvard named John W. Webster. The conviction was done on the basis of investigation done by the two anatomists by examining the segmented body parts for stature estimation and comparing the dentures found in the furnace.

- In 1897, The Luetgert Case (Murderpedia n.d.), become another famous case in which Adolph Luetgert, a Chicago based sausage producer was accused of killing his wife and attempting to dispose of the remains by cooking them in a potash vat in the factory. George A. Dorsey, an anthropologist, investigated the case and recovered small fragments of bones and a ring (belongs to Luetgert's wife) from the vat. On examination he found that the small fragments were from a human hand, foot and rib, hence stated Luetgert as guilty and gave testimony in court which helped in conviction of Adolph Luetgert. His testimony was sternly challenged by other specialists, and Dorsey left his contribute further to the study of forensic anthropology.
- In April 1997, The Marty Miller Case(Casto 2016), is an incident that happen in a quite rural area of upstate of New York. Marty Miller shot his daughter with a shotgun which fatally wounded her. After this incident Marty ran into the woods behind his house, in spite of a massive manhunt, he was not seen again. This incident became something of a legend in the community due to the notoriety of the missing suspect. Marty was an enthusiastic outdoorsman and know the survival techniques in the forest. As a fugitive, he could be quite dangerous and people feared of his reappearance. After 4 years in December 8, 2001, a hunter found a human skeleton at a remote place into the woods and called to the police. The New York Police investigated the scene and recover the skeletal remains along with other important evidences (such as clothes, wallet, eye glasses, wrist watch, shotgun etc.) and send the evidences to Forensic Anthropology Lab at Binghamton University where anthropologist using methods of identification through skeletal remains helped in positive identification of the deceased as Marty Miller.

Case Study 1: Ancestry Estimation

In 2012, a scattered human remain was found along a hill side in Northern California. The skeletal remains found were highly fragmentary and incomplete. Due to carnivore scavenging the pelvic features are not clear but the intact skull was located which is then used for assessment of ancestry. Although the age estimation was not easy task due to scavenging but cranial sutures and osteophytic lipping on vertebral column gave an idea that the decedent was of 40+ years and on the basis of maximum length of ulna, the stature was estimated as 6 ft. $\pm$4.5 in. Apart from these findings law was interested in ancestry of the decedent to narrow down the search from the pool of missing persons hence they compared 16 measurement of cranium with the sample group of male and found the results as:

- Fordisc 3.0 classified it as white male.
- High posterior probability value $p = 0.984$ indicated it as white male.
- Typical value $p = 0.366$ indicated the skull as white male.

After all the above mentioned findings it was identified by DNA analysis that the remains was of a 54 year old white male with a stature of 6 ft. 3 in. and the result is consistent with the above findings.

Case Study 2: Sex Estimation

In 2006, a nearly complete human skeleton is recovered from grave in Northern California. The deceased remains showed male pelvic traits such as a narrow sub-pubic angle, absence of a ventral arc, a narrow sciatic notch etc. The cranial features like mastoid process temporal lines, supraorbital region indicated the skeleton to be of male sex. On comparing the postcranial measurement with statistics of Forensic Anthropology Databank (i.e. Fordisc 3.0) it was suggested that the skeleton was of human male. It was later identified that the remains were of a 26 year old white male with living stature of 5 ft. 8 in.

Case Study 3: Age Estimation

In 2008, human remains from a cemetery in Northern California were exhumed; the decedent's age was estimated to be of 6.0 ± 2 years. This age was estimated by seeing the dental eruption, dental development and epiphyseal union in the skeletal elements which were surprisingly in a good preserved state with clearly visible features even after 30 years of the body being buried. The maxillary and mandibular first molars were almost erupted and permanent central incisors were in process of eruption. Apart from this even the degree of fusion of vertebral column, early stage development of several epiphyses and length of limb bones indicated the age of the decedent to be approx. 6–8 years. Later the individual was identified as 6 year old child from American Ancestry.

Case Study 4: Stature Estimation

A different case of carnivorous scavenging of human skeleton was discovered in Northern California in 2008. The estimated biological profile said, descendent was an adult male of European ancestry and was of about 50–80 years of age. The skeleton was heavily degraded but the case was solved on the basis of postcranial elements. Osteometric data was collected from left long bones of upper and lower limbs, clavicle, and scapula. The data then entered into Fordisc. Using the formula derived for twentieth century white males the stature is estimated. The result concluded that the stature is best estimated using the maximum lengths of bones like clavicle, femur and tibia.

The combination of the measurements of these bones was used in regression formula which generated the stature as 67 ± 3.3 in. with 95% confidence level. Later the profile matched closely with a missing individual's file and descendent was identified as 70 years old white male with a stature of 68 in.

Case Study 5: Human or Non-human

In this case, a partly skeletonized leg was discovered in a river in Northern California. Local law enforcement sent it to an archeologist, pathologist and veterinarian for identification to which the archeologist and pathologist identified it as human right leg but the veterinarian identified it from a non-human origin. The leg was attacked by a saw which caused dismemberment of the bone. The law enforcement searched for the other remains of the skeleton for 3 days considering the skeleton to be of a human. On searching a complete left femur and proximal two thirds of a tibia and fibula were found which is then identified to be of a black bear. In this case much time and money would have been saved if the case was handed to the forensic anthropologist and not to the experts of three different streams who had the conflicting opinion.

21.12.3 Concluding Remarks and Future Prospects

Forensic anthropologists work in humanitarian and medico-legal issues with the primary aim of establishing the identity. Traditionally, the forensic anthropology begins from human anatomy and focuses majorly on osteological evidences. With the ongoing research and increasing need of forensic anthropologists in world scenario the branch become more liberal in accepting methodological collaborations and make the investigation effective. Over time forensic anthropologist makes the discipline as a unique one, at its standpoint. In the present scenario, new experimental trends in forensic sciences focus on trauma analysis, taphonomy, examination of isotopes, time since death and visual interpretation are going on to meet the demand in the identification process. The current trend of forensic anthropological research and teaching progressively attracts the best and dedicated students through graduate and post-graduate studies as an applied discipline with problem-oriented interdisciplinary approaches. During the investigation by the forensic anthropologist number of ethical issues faces by them, brings a challenge when establish the study conclusion. The future perspective will focus on, but not least to utilization of interdisciplinary techniques, expansion of new centres and laboratories, introduce new school programs, and enhanced understanding on the variation of global population Lastly it can be said that in this age of 'necronominalism' the personal identification of deceased is important as much as like the identity of a living.

References

Abate AF, Nappi M, Ricciardi S, Tortora G (2004) FACES: 3D FAcial reConstruction from anciEnt skulls using content based image retrieval. J Visual Lang Comput 15(5):373–389

Abdel Fatah EE, Shirley NR, Jantz RL, Mahfouz MR (2014) Improving sex estimation from crania using a novel three-dimensional quantitative method. J Forensic Sci 59(3):590–600

Adams BJ, Byrd JE (2006) Resolution of small-scale commingling: a case report from the Vietnam war. Forensic Sci Int 156(1):63–69

Adams BJ, Konigsberg LW (2004) Estimation of the most likely number of individuals from commingled human skeletal remains. Am J Phys Anthropol 125(2):138–151

Adams BJ, Konigsberg LW (2008) How many people? Determining the number of individuals represented by commingled human remains. In: Recovery, analysis, and identification of commingled human remains. Springer, Berlin, pp 241–255

American Board of Forensic Anthropology (2021). http://theabfa.org/

Avon SL (2004) Forensic odontology: the roles and responsibilities of the dentist. J Canad Dental Assoc 70(7):453–458
Baker L (2016) Biomolecular applications. In: Handbook of forensic anthropology and archaeology. Routledge, London, pp 458–471. https://doi.org/10.4324/9781315528939-38
Barker C, Cox M, Flavel A, Laver J, Loe L (2008) Mortuary procedures II—skeletal analysis I: basic procedures and demographic assessment. In: The Scientific Investigation of Mass Graves: Towards Protocols and Standard Operating Procedures. Cambridge University Press, Cambridge, MA, pp 295–382
Beddoe J (1888) On the stature of the older races of England, as estimated from the long bones. J.R Anthropol Inst G. B. Irel 17:201–209
A Bertillon (1853–1914) Visible proofs: Forensic views of thn.d.e Body: Galleries: Biographies: [Exhibitions]. U.S. National Library of Medicine. https://www.nlm.nih.gov/exhibition/visibleproofs/galleries/biographies/bertillon.html. Accessed 27 Feb 2021
Black S, Thompson T (2007) Body modification. In: Forensic human identification. CRC, Boca Raton, pp 379–399
Black S, Aggrawal A, Payne-James J (2010) Age estimation in the living: the practitioner's guide. Wiley, Hoboken, NJ
Blau S, Ubelaker DH (2016) Handbook of forensic anthropology and archeology, 2nd edn. Routledge, London
Britannica (2021) Anthropology. https://kids.britannica.com/students/article/anthropology/272896
Brzobohatá H, Krajíček V, Horák Z, Velemínská J (2015) Sex classification using the three-dimensional tibia form or shape including population specificity approach. J Forensic Sci 60(1):29–40
Buchli V, Lucas G (2002) Archaeologies of the contemporary past. Routledge, London
Cameron JM, Sims BG, Simpson KC (1974) Forensic dentistry. Churchill Livingstone, Edinburgh
Casto M (2016) The Marty miller case. https://prezi.com/ojkwwf8ndx1m/the-marty-miller-case/
Cattaneo C (2007) Forensic anthropology: developments of a classical discipline in the new millennium. Forensic Sci Int 165(2–3):185–193
Clarkson J, Schaefer M (2007) Surgical intervention. In: Forensic human identification. CRC, Boca Raton, FL, pp 127–146
Craig EA (1995) Intercondylar shelf angle: a new method to determine race from the distal femur. J Forensic Sci 40(5):777–782
Criminisi A, Zisserman A, Van Gool LJ, Bramble SK, Compton D (1999) New approach to obtain height measurements from video. Proceedings of SPIE 3576:227–238
Crossland Z (2013) Evidential regimes of forensic archaeology. Annu Rev Anthropol 42:121–137
Cuijpers A (2006) Histological identification of bone fragments in archaeology: telling humans apart from horses and cattle. Int J Osteoarchaeol 16(6):465–480
Cunha E (2006) Pathology as a factor of personal identity in forensic anthropology. In: Forensic anthropology and medicine. Springer, Berlin, pp 333–358
Cunha E, Cattaneo C (2006) Forensic anthropology and forensic pathology. In: Forensic anthropology and medicine. Springer, Berlin, pp 39–53
Dayal MR, Kegley AD, Strkalj G et al (2009) The history and composition of the Raymond A. Dart collection of human skeletons at the University of the Witwatersrand, Johannesburg, South Africa. Am J Phys Anthropol 140:324–335
Dwight T (1878a) The identification of the human skeleton: a medico-legal study. David Clapp & Son, Boston, MA
Dwight T (1878b) In: Clapp D (ed) The identification of the human skeleton: a medico-legal study: to which was awarded the prize of the Massachusetts medical society for 1878, vol 153. Kessinger Publishing, Whitefish, p 201
Dwight T (1881) The sternum as an index of sex, height, and age. J Anat Physiol 15:327–330
Dwight T (1890a) The closure of the cranial sutures as a sign of age. Boston Med Surg J 122:389–392
Dwight T (1890b) The sternum as an index of sex, height and age. J Anat Physiol 24:527–535

Dwight T (1894a) Methods of estimating the height from parts of the skeleton, medical records in New York, vol 46. Trow Directory, New York, NY, pp 293–296

Dwight T (1894b) The range and significance of variations in the human skeleton. Boston Med Surg J 1:73–76

Dwight T (1905) The size of the auricular surfaces of the long bones as a characteristic of sex: an anthropological study. Am J Anat 4:19–31

Fenger S, Ubelaker D, Rubinstein D (1996) Identification of workers' compensation fraud through radiographic comparison. JFI 46:418–431

Forensic Anthropology Society of Europe (n.d.). http://forensicanthropology.eu/

Forensic-Science Anthropology-Subcommittee (n.d.). https://www.nist.gov/topics/forensic-science/anthropology-subcommittee

Fraser NL, Yoshino M, Imaizumi K, Blackwell SA, Thomas CDL, Clement JG (2003) A Japanese computer-assisted facial identification system successfully identifies non-Japanese faces. Forensic Sci Int 135(2):122–128

Gehlen S, Broker H, Ritz-Timme S, Tuktuviene J, Cattaneo C (2005) Child pornography: development of a method for identification of faces as childish. Second international conference on reconstruction of soft facial parts, RheinAhrCampus Remagen

Gibelli D, De Angelis D, Poppa P, Sforza C, Cattaneo C (2017) A view to the future: a novel approach for 3D–3D superimposition and quantification of differences for identification from next-generation video surveillance systems. J Forensic Sci 62(2):457–461

Gilbert BM (1976) Anterior femoral curvature: its probable basis and utility as a criterion of racial assessment. Am J Phys Anthropol 45(3):601–604

Greil H, Kahl H (2005) Assessment of developmental age: cross-sectional analysis of secondary sexual characteristics. Anthropol Anz 63:63–75

Guglich EA, Wilson PJ, White B (1994) Forensic application of repetitive DNA markers to the species identification of animal tissues. J Forensic Sci 39(2):353–361

Gupta S, Gupta V, Vij H, Vij R, Tyagi N (2015) Forensic facial reconstruction: the final frontier. J Clin Diagn Res 9(9):ZE26–ZE28. https://doi.org/10.7860/JCDR/2015/14621.6568

Haglund WD (2001) Archaeology and forensic death investigations. Hist Archaeol 35(1):26–34

Halberstein R (2001) The application of anthropometric indices in forensic photography: three case studies. J Forensic Sci 46(6):1438–1441

Hunt DR, Albanese J (2005) History and demographic composition of the Robert J. Terry anatomical colletion. Am J Phys Anthropol 127:406–417

James SH, Nordby JJ (2002) Forensic science: an introduction to scientific and investigative techniques. CRC, Boca Raton, FL

Kähler K, Haber J, Seidel H-P (2003) Reanimating the dead: reconstruction of expressive faces from skull data. ACM Transactions on Graphics (TOG) 22(3):554–561

Kehoe AB (2013) Humans: an introduction to four-field anthropology. Routledge, London

Killgrove K (2016) How a Harvard doctor's sordid murder launched modern forensic anthropology. Forbes. https://www.forbes.com/sites/kristinakillgrove/2016/08/26/how-a-harvard-doctors-sordid-murder-launched-modern-forensic-anthropology/

Klepinger LL (2006) Deciphering ancestral background. In: Fundamentals of forensic anthropology. Wiley, Hoboken, NJ, pp 64–76. https://doi.org/10.1002/0470007729.ch6

Krogman WM (1939) A guide to the identification of human skeletal material. United States Federal Bureau of Investigation, Washington, DC

L'Abbe EN, Loots M, Meiring JH (2005) The pretoria bone collection: a modern south African skeletal sample. Homo 56:197–205

Linacre A, Lee JC-I (2016) Species determination: the role and use of the cytochrome b gene. In: Forensic DNA typing protocols. Springer, Berlin, pp 287–296

Love JC, Wiersema JM (2016) Skeletal trauma: an anthropological review. Acad Forensic Pathol 6(3):463–477

Lowenstein JM, Reuther JD, Hood DG, Scheuenstuhl G, Gerlach SC, Ubelaker DH (2006) Identification of animal species by protein radioimmunoassay of bone fragments and blood-stained stone tools. Forensic Sci Int 159(2–3):182–188

Machado CEP, Flores MRP, Lima LNC, Tinoco RLR, Franco A, Bezerra ACB, Evison MP, Guimarães MA (2017) A new approach for the analysis of facial growth and age estimation: iris ratio. PLoS One 12(7):e0180330. https://doi.org/10.1371/journal.pone.0180330

Manouvrier L (1893) La determination de la taille d'après les grands os des membres. Memoires de la Societe Anthropologie de Paris 4:347–402

Matsuda H, Seo Y, Kakizaki E, Kozawa S, Muraoka E, Yukawa N (2005) Identification of DNA of human origin based on amplification of human-specific mitochondrial cytochrome b region. Forensic Sci Int 152(2–3):109–114

Michel J, Paganelli A, Varoquaux A, Piercecchi-Marti M, Adalian P, Leonetti G, Dessi P (2015) Determination of sex: interest of frontal sinus 3 D reconstructions. J Forensic Sci 60(2):269–273

Murderpedia (n.d.) Adolph Luetgert|Murderpedia, the encyclopedia of murderers. https://murderpedia.org/male.L/l/luetgert-dolph.htm. Accessed 1 Mar 2021

Murphy W, Gantner G (1982) Radiologic examination of anatomic parts and skeletonized remains. J Forensic Sci 27(1):9–18

Nallamala S, Guttikonda VR, Manchikatla PK, Taneeru S (2017) Age estimation using exfoliative cytology and radiovisiography: a comparative study. J Forensic Dent Sci 9(3):144–148. https://doi.org/10.4103/jfo.jfds_39_16

Nath S (1989) An introduction to forensic anthropology. Gian Publishing House, New Delhi

Neville B, Douglas D, Allen C, Bouquot J (2002) Forensic dentistry. In: Oral and maxillofacial pathology, 2nd edn. W.B. Saunders Co., Philadelphia, PA

OBE SMB (2003) Forensic anthropology–regulation in the United Kingdom. Sci Justice 43(4): 187–192

Orfila MJB, Lesueur O (1831) Traite des exhumation juridique. considerations Sur les changemens physiques que les cadavres eprouvent en se pourrissant dans la terre, dans l'eau, dans lesfossesd'aisance et dans le fumier, vol 2. Bechet Jeune, Paris

Ostrofsky KR, Churchill SE (2015) Sex determination by discriminant function analysis of lumbar vertebrae. J Forensic Sci 60(1):21–28

Outram AK, Knüsel CJ, Knight S, Harding AF (2005) Understanding complex fragmented assemblages of human and animal remains: a fully integrated approach. J Archaeol Sci 32(12):1699–1710

Pan N (1924) Length of long bones and their proportion to body height in Hindus. J Anat 58(Pt 4): 374

Parent A-S, Teilmann G, Juul A, Skakkebaek NE, Toppari J, Bourguignon J-P (2003) The timing of normal puberty and the age limits of sexual precocity: variations around the world, secular trends, and changes after migration. Endocr Rev 24(5):668–693

Pearson K (1899) Mathematical contributions to the theory of evolution. V. on the reconstruction of the stature of prehistoric races. Series a. containing papers of a mathematical or physical character, vol 192. Philosophical Transactions of the Royal Society of London, London, pp 169–244

Pickering R, Bach D (2009) The use of forensic anthropology, 2nd edn. CRC, Boca Raton, FL

Randolph-Quinney P, Mallett X, Black S (2011) Forensic anthropology. Wiley, Hoboken, NJ, pp 152–178

Ratnayake M, Obertová Z, Dose M, Gabriel P, Bröker H, Brauckmann M, Barkus A, Rizgeliene R, Tutkuviene J, Ritz-Timme S (2014) The juvenile face as a suitable age indicator in child pornography cases: a pilot study on the reliability of automated and visual estimation approaches. Int J Legal Med 128(5):803–808

Rollet E (1888) De la mensuration des os longs des membres dans sesrapportsavec l'anthropologie, la clinique et la medecine judici- aire. D'Anthropologie Criminelle Et Des Sciences Penales, Paris, France

Rosenberg NA, Pritchard JK, Weber JL, Cann HM, Kidd KK, Zhivotovsky LA, Feldman MW (2002) Genetic structure of human populations. Science 298(5602):2381–2385

Sapweb (n.d.). https://Sapweb.Fr/

Sauer NJ, Michael AR, Fenton TW (2012) Human identification using skull–photo superimposition and forensic image comparison. In: A companion to forensic anthropology. Wiley, Hoboken, NJ, pp 432–446

Scheuer L (2002) Application of osteology to forensic medicine. Clin Anat 15(4):297–312

Scheuer L, Black S (2007) Osteology. In: Forensic human identification: an introduction. CRC, Boca Raton, FL, pp 199–219

Schmeling A, Reisinger W, Geserick G, Olze A (2006) Age estimation of unaccompanied minors: part I. General considerations. Forensic Sci Int 159:S61–S64

Schmitt S (2001) Mass graves and the collection of forensic evidence: genocide, war crimes, and crimes against humanity. In: Advances in forensic taphonomy: method, theory, and archaeological perspectives, vol 277. CRC, Boca Raton, FL

Short LJ, Khambay B, Ayoub A, Erolin C, Rynn C, Wilkinson C (2014) Validation of a computer modelled forensic facial reconstruction technique using CT data from live subjects: a pilot study. Forensic Sci Int 237:147–1e1

Spencer F (1982) A history of American physical anthropology 1930–1980. Academic, Cambridge, MA

Spradley MK, Anderson BE, Tise ML (2015) Postcranial sex estimation criteria for Mexican Hispanics. J Forensic Sci 60:S27–S31

St Hoyme LE, Iscan MY (1989) Determination of sex and race: accuracy and assumptions. In: Reconstruction of Life from the Skeleton. Wiley, Hoboken, NJ, pp 53–93

Stephan CN (2016) Craniofacial identification: techniques of facial approximation and craniofacial superimposition. In: Handbook of forensic anthropology and archaeology, vol 25. CRC, Boca Raton, FL, pp 304–321

Stewart T (1951) What the bone tell. FBI L Enforcement Bull 20:2–5

Stewart TD (1979) Essentials of forensic anthropology: especially as developed in the United States. Charles C. Thomas, Springfield, IL

Stewart TD (1979b) A tribute to the French forensic anthropologist georges fully (1926–1973). J Forensic Sci 24:916–924

Stuurman S (2000) François Bernier and the invention of racial classification. Hist Workshop J 50(1):1–21

Sue M (1755) Sur les proportions des squelette de homme, examine depuis lage le plus tendre, jusqu' a celui de vingt-cinq, soixante ans, & au dela. In: Academie des sciences, vol 2. Memoires de Mathematique, et de Physique, Presentes par Divers Savants et lus dan ses Assemblees, Paris, pp 572–585

SWGANTH (2011) In: Trauma analysis. Scientific Working Group for Forensic Anthropology (SWGANTH)

Thompson T, Black S (2006) Forensic human identification: an introduction. CRC, Boca Raton, FL

Tibbett M, Carter DO (2009) Research in forensic taphonomy: a soil-based perspective. In: Criminal and environmental soil forensics. Springer, Berlin, pp 317–331

Topinard P (1885) Procede de mensuration des os longs, dans le but de reconstituer la taille. Bull de la Soc Anthropol de Paris 8:73–83

Tuller HH (2012) Mass graves and human rights: latest developments, methods, and lessons learned. In: A companion to forensic anthropology. Wiley, Hoboken, NJ, pp 157–174

Ubelaker DH (1999) Ales Hrdlička's role in the history of forensic anthropology. J For Sci 44:724–730

Ubelaker DH (2009) Historical development of forensic anthropology: perspective from the United States. In: Handbook of forensic anthropology and archaeology. CRC, Boca Raton, FL, pp 76–86

Ubelaker DH (2015) Craniofacial superimposition: historical review and current issues. J Forensic Sci 60(6):1412–1419

Ubelaker DH (2018) A history of forensic anthropology. Am J Phys Anthropol 165:915
Ubelaker DH (2019) New directions in forensic anthropology. In: Martell DA (ed) The future of forensic science. Wiley, Hoboken, NJ, pp 1–18. https://doi.org/10.1002/9781119226703.ch1
Ubelaker DH, Lowenstein JM, Hood DG (2004) Use of solid-phase double-antibody radioimmunoassay to identify species from small skeletal fragments. J Forensic Sci 49(5):924
Venkatachalam KSM (2008) Stature estimation from hand length and foot length in adults—a regional study in Chennai, Tamilnadu
Walker PL (2005) Greater sciatic notch morphology: sex, age, and population differences. Am J Phys Anthropol 127(4):385–391
Wilder HH (1897) On the disposition of the epidermic folds upon the palms and soles of primates. Anat Anz 13:250–256
Wilder HH (1902) Scientific palmistry. Pop Sci Mon 62:41–54
Wilder HH (1903) Palm and sole impressions and their use for purposes of personal identification. Pop Sci Mon 63:385–410
Wilder HH, Wentworth B (1918) Personal identification: methods for the identification of individuals, living or dead. The Gorham Press, Boston, MA, pp 96–110
Wright R, Hanson I, Sterenberg J (2005) The archaeology of mass graves. In: Forensic archaeology: advances in theory and practice, vol 137. Routledge, London, p 58
Yadav N, Panat R, Aggarwal A (2010) CT scans- a compelling tool in forensic facial reconstruction 1(39):42
Yoshino M, Matsuda H, Kubota S, Imaizumi K, Miyasaka S (2001) Computer-assisted facial image identification system. Forensic Sci Commun 3(1):225–237

Forensic Chemistry 22

Vijay Kumar Yadav, Alok Kumar, Shaesta Shahid, Kriti Nigam, and Ankit Srivastava

Abstract

Forensic Chemistry applies the principles and techniques of chemical science to forensic analysis of evidences. This includes, but not limited to, seized drug analysis, alcohol analysis, fire debris, and post-blast residue analysis and other analysis wherein the chemical identity of material is explored to strengthen its evidentiary significance. Though the field of Forensic is fascinating, it is challenging as well. For instance, changes and destruction brought by fire and explosion incidents often make it difficult for an investigator to classify whether the cause of the incident was accidental or intentional. However, by applying thoughtful analytical processes and using science involved in the fire and explosion process, origin and cause of incident can be apprehended. Accordingly, this chapter focuses on investigative aspects of fire and explosion scenes and analytical approaches followed by an investigation. In addition, testing for drugs and alcohol has become a routine part of forensic chemists over the past few decades as their abuse has been the cause of many violent as well as non-violent crimes. Therefore, the fundamentals of the analytical approach applied in their detection and identification have also been discussed in this chapter.

V. K. Yadav · A. Kumar · S. Shahid
Dr. APJ Abdul Kalam Institute of Forensic Science & Criminology, Bundelkhand University, Jhansi, Uttar Pradesh, India

K. Nigam
Department of Forensic Science, Jharkhand Raksha Shakti University, Ranchi, Jharkhand, India

A. Srivastava (✉)
School of Forensic Sciences, The West Bengal National University of Juridical Sciences, Kolkata, West Bengal, India
e-mail: ankitsrivastava@nujs.edu

P. Shrivastava et al. (eds.), *Textbook of Forensic Science*,
https://doi.org/10.1007/978-981-99-1377-0_22

Keywords

Forensic · Fire · Explosion · Investigation · Drug · Alcohol

22.1 Introduction

In the domain of science and technology, chemistry plays a central role. Every single tangible entity known to the human being is composed of *fundamental particles* i.e., electron, proton and neutron which in turn makes atoms, molecules and ultimately called as matter. Chemistry is the study of the composition of matter and the associated changes it undergoes. Forensic chemistry is a subdiscipline of forensic science wherein principles and techniques of chemistry, especially analytical chemistry, are applied to the field of forensic investigation. From the methods and techniques used to collect and preserve the physical evidences to qualitative and quantitative characterization of physical evidences, all rely on principles of chemistry (Khan et al. 2012; Bell 2014). Using characterizing parameters of material identification, forensic scientist associates the physical evidence collected from the scene of an incident with the suspect(s). However, if the suspect can't be linked with the resultant analytical data, it will be helpful in exonerating him. This entails how important role forensic chemistry plays in the dissemination of justice.

In the context of forensic analysis, evidences requiring analysis based on chemical properties of substances are sent to the forensic chemistry division of Forensic Science Laboratory. The range of evidences being analyzed is vast. However, commonly encountered evidences in the chemistry division of forensic science laboratory are *fire debris* to detect and identify ignitable liquid, *post-blast debris* to detect and identify explosive material, *drugs and other substances* used to spike controlled substances and *alcohol* for their qualitative and quantitative characterization (Fig. 22.1).

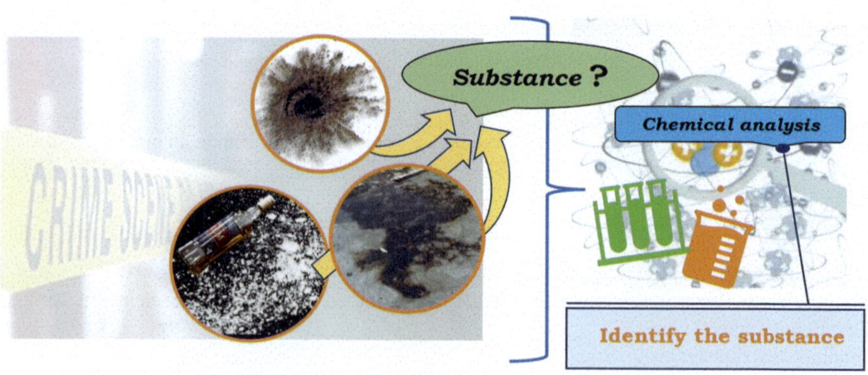

Fig. 22.1 Role of Forensic Chemistry in identification of unknown substance

The present chapter deals with the fundamentals of fire and explosion investigation and analysis of associated debris. In addition to that focus has also been made on the analytical aspects of commonly encountered drugs and alcohol in the forensic laboratory. Important to note that these fields are large and dynamic and, in this chapter, the basic and introductory aspect is presented.

22.2 Fire and Arson

There are well-known evidences of fire incidents since ancient times as the reach and execution of the crime is simple and unchallenging but brings a huge amount of damage. It is liable for causing harm to a person as well as property. Examples of these cases include bride burning (highly prevalent in India) (Kaur and Byard 2020), property burning, crime concealment, profit, and cases of negligence, rivalry, revenge, and terrorism. Arson is one of the most recurrently committed crimes all over the world. These types of cases pose great challenges for forensic investigator as the complexity in such scenes is much higher (Figs. 22.2 and 22.3). Its complexity may result in an advantage to the perpetrator and makes the investigation challenging since fire often destroys the potential evidences of its origin and cause. A fire and explosion/bomb scene investigator tries to obtain information to reconstruct the sequence of events leading up to fire by observing the fire and post-blast patterns/residues. However, this task involves individuals with expertise in fire chemistry.

Fig. 22.2 Scene of fire

(a) (b)

Fig. 22.3 (**a**) Presence of smoke and (**b**) destruction caused by fire

The word *arson* originated from the Latin word *ardere*, meaning "to burn" (Stauffer et al. 2008). It is a process of initiating a fire (DeTata 2018). The fire is considered as an arson only when the intention for destruction and destroying is reflected through the scene. The investigation is proceeded in order to get answers to the questions such as, where was the origin of fire? What was the source of ignition? If the fire was an accidental or intentional incident?

22.2.1 Chemistry of Fire

From early dictation of fire as substance unto itself i.e., an element in *Panchbhoot* concept of Hindu mythology (Jaiswal and Williams 2016) or one element of four fundamental elements according to Greek mythology to current explanations, it also has taken a long route of journey. Johann Becher and Georg Stahl came up with the '***phlogiston theory***'. Theory envisaged the existence of a weightless substance (phlogiston) in materials/substances which are released in the environment during a fire and so combustible and lose weight after being burned. In case of closed fire, phlogiston gets saturated with the inner environment and hence fire is extinguished. Some criticized whereas others defended this theory and presented it in a new form. By conclusions of Priestley's experiment on the discovery of oxygen (erstwhile dephlogisticated air), Lavoisier dictated the role that oxygen plays in the fire process. Consequently, answers to questions not explained by earlier theories were provided (Lentini 2018). This paved the way for modern explanations of fire.

Fire is the manifestation of combustion. But all combustion reactions do not result in fire. For a fire to occur, combustible substance, oxidant and activation energy (that can be generated from mechanical, chemical, electrical or nuclear sources) must be interacting together and the resulting exothermic reaction must occur at a rate high enough to produce both heat and light. These three elements constitute arms in the '**fire triangle**' (Fig. 22.4) illustrating the requirements for fire initiation graphically. The absence of any element will lead to the decay of fire and extinguishment. Another model to describe fire is **tetrahedron** (Fig. 22.5). It conditions the presence

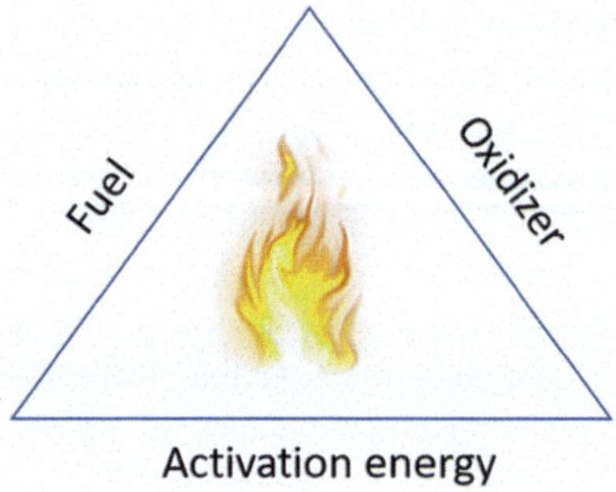

Fig. 22.4 Fire triangle

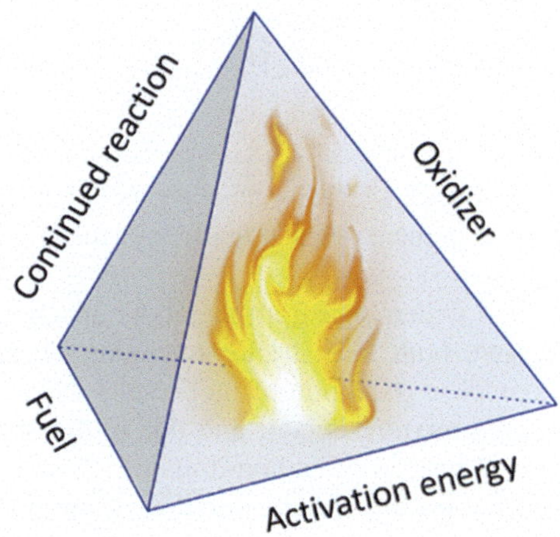

Fig. 22.5 Fire tetrahedron

of a continuous chain of chemical reactions in addition to requirements set by the fire triangle model. Thus, the tetrahedron model is focused on the sustainability of fire while the former one describes the start of fire process (Stauffer et al. 2008).

Oxidizer It is the atmospheric oxygen present in air that act as an oxidizing agent in the chain reaction of fire. The spread and intensity of fire are highly dependent on the amount of oxygen available. In some cases, oxygen can be supplied to fire by other oxidizing agents such as $KClO_3$ and $NaNO_3$, under favorable conditions.

Fuel It is regarded as any substance in a chemical state which can be oxidized by oxygen. This phenomenon takes place in the presence of a suitable ignition source. Wood, paper, cloth or petroleum distillates are common fuels. It is not necessary that only one type of combustible would participate in the combustion reaction, there could be a combination thereof. Refined fuels and solvents such as petrol, diesel, kerosene and methylated spirits, etc. are often used as accelerants. Most of them are hydrocarbons usually containing 50% and higher ratios of carbon.

Activation Energy To initiate the chemical reaction, heat acts as energy to activate the molecules of oxygen and the fuel. The heat required in a fire can also be referred to as "ignition temperature of the fuel" which is the minimum temperature required to initiate a self-sustaining chemical reaction (Thatcher 2000). Activation energy may be got from electrical, chemical, mechanical or nuclear sources. Identification of ignition sources is a key part of arson investigation.

Chemical reaction that leads to the phenomenon of fire is basically a redox reaction (Reaction 22.1), in which an oxidant (commonly oxygen) oxidizes the fuel while being reduced itself.

$$\underset{(\text{Fuel})}{2\overset{-3}{C}_2H_6} + \underset{(\text{Oxygen})}{7\overset{0}{O}_2} \rightarrow 4\overset{+4}{C}\overset{-2}{O}_2 + 6H_2O + \text{Energy} \tag{22.1}$$

Reaction 22.1 Redox reaction; Number above the chemical formula indicates the change in the oxidation number of respective elements.

It is understood from the above reaction that for complete oxidation of fuel by oxygen, both must be in stoichiometric ratio which is seldom a case in reality. Incomplete oxidation of fuel results when oxygen is not in ample amount or fuel-oxygen mixture is poor and due to this carbon mono oxide and/or carbon soot is formed instead of carbon-di-oxide. Products formed will also be dependent on the material on fire and the duration of fire. Orange/yellow color flame reflects visibly this incomplete oxidation of fuel which would otherwise have been blue if oxidation was complete (Stauffer et al. 2008).

As fire is a result of an exothermic reaction, the energy liberated here is in form of heat and light. Liberated heat gets transferred from one place to another through convection, conduction and radiation. Interaction of it with other materials present in the surrounding environment may serve as activation energy, raising the temperature to ignition temperature and causing combustion. In this way, fire propagates from one substance to another (Stauffer et al. 2008).

22.2.2 Ignitable Liquids

Ignitable liquids (ILs) are defined as any liquid capable of fueling a fire. These may include combustible liquid, flammable liquid, or any other material which in its liquid phase can cause a fire on ignition. The fire debris collected from a fire scene as evidences are subjected for examination in the laboratory for the detection of ignitable liquid residue (**hereinafter ILR**), if any. The presence of an ILR is a crucial element in establishing that fire was set forth intentionally i.e., arson (Sampat et al. 2018). The ILs generally found at fire scenes are gasoline, diesel, and lighter fluids. In addition, other types of ignitable liquids may be encountered at fire scenes.

Ignitable liquids are identified and classified based on their chemical composition, carbon numbers, and boiling point range. Hence, ignitable liquids residues are important evidence left behind at the scene of fire and provide fingerprint of the ignitable liquid that had been used to start a fire. This ILR fingerprint is used to determine what type of IL was used. Table 22.1 illustrates the classification scheme of Ignitable liquids according to ASTM standard (1618-06).

22.2.3 Forensic Investigation of Fire Scene

The complexity in a fire scene is much higher. Its complexity may result in an advantage to the perpetrator and make the investigation difficult by misguiding the investigator (Sadler 1950). However, by applying a logical investigative and analytical approach using science involved in fire evolvement, conclusions with regard to an incident can be drawn.

A fire investigation is carried out in a two-step procedure. First, the examination of the scene of fire to determine the cause, origin and spread of fire while the second involves the laboratory analysis of fire debris obtained from the scene as evidences (Daeid 2004). Unlike other scene investigations, witness interviews should be the first priority in fire investigation as these are helpful in determining the line of the investigation procedure. It is followed by scene observation and thorough searching for physical evidences as these may be helpful in associating the arsonist with the scene of offence. Though very nature of fire is causing destruction and turning evidences into ash, it often leaves some characteristic pattern about how it may have been started or set forth. These patterns are called as *fire patterns or burn patterns*. Fire investigator often looks for these patterns as the point of origin determination is mainly based on the study of fire pattern. As fire develops, hot gases are released that move upward and outward direction. This often leaves a 'V-shaped pattern on the surrounding vertical surface. Characteristic V pattern may deviate from its geometric shape subjected to the distance of fire from the vertical surface or flame distance from the ceiling in case of building fires. It may be inverted or everted shaped V and interpretation requires careful observation of the scene. But depending upon the intensity and duration of fire, a pattern could not be apparently visible, thus, incomprehensible or may be absent in outdoor fires. Many times patterns could be made visible after the removal of fire debris. In the advanced stage of fire where fire has completely involved the surrounding area, pattern recognition could not be possible (Hine 2004; Bell 2014; Lentini 2013).

Like every scene investigation, documentation should be completed and samples must be collected in an appropriate container and must be entrusted to the scientific crew. Typical steps involved in an investigation of fire are presented briefly as in Fig. 22.6 (Stauffer et al. 2008).

Though a meticulous examination of the scene is at the apex to trace fire back to its origin, Laboratory findings are also equally important for the detection and identification of ignitable liquid in samples collected from the scene. But it is an investigator who concludes fire as arson and not the analyst. However, to conclude

Table 22.1 Classification of Ignitable liquids

Class	Light (C_{4-9})	Medium (C_{8-13})	Heavy (C_{8-20+})
Gasoline-all brands, including gasohol	Fresh gasoline is typically in the range C_4–C_{12}		
Petroleum distillates (including de-aromatized)	Petroleum ether	Some charcoal starters *B*	Kerosene
	Some cigarette lighter fluids	Some paint thinners	Diesel fuel
	Some camping fuels	Some dry-cleaning solvents	Some jet fuels
			Some charcoal starters
Isoparaffinic products	Aviation gas	Some charcoal starters	Some commercial specialty
	Some specialty solvents	Some paint thinners	Solvents
		Some copier toners	
Aromatic products	Some paint and varnish	Some automotive parts cleaners	Some insecticide
	Removers	Specialty cleaning solvents	Vehicles
	Some automotive parts cleaners	Some insecticide vehicles	Industrial cleaning
	Xylenes, toluene-based products	Fuel additives	Solvents
Naphthenic paraffinic products	Cyclohexane based	Some charcoal starters	Some insecticide
	Solvents/products	Some insecticide vehicles	Vehicles
		Some lamp oils	Some lamp oils
			Industrial solvents
Normal-alkanes products	Solvents	Some candle oils	Some candle oils
	Pentane	Some copier toners	Carbonless forms
	Hexane		Some copier toners
	Heptane		
Oxygenated solvents	Alcohols	Some lacquer thinners	
	Ketones, lacquer thinners	Some industrial solvents	
	Fuel additives	Metal cleaners/ gloss removers	
	Surface preparation solvents		

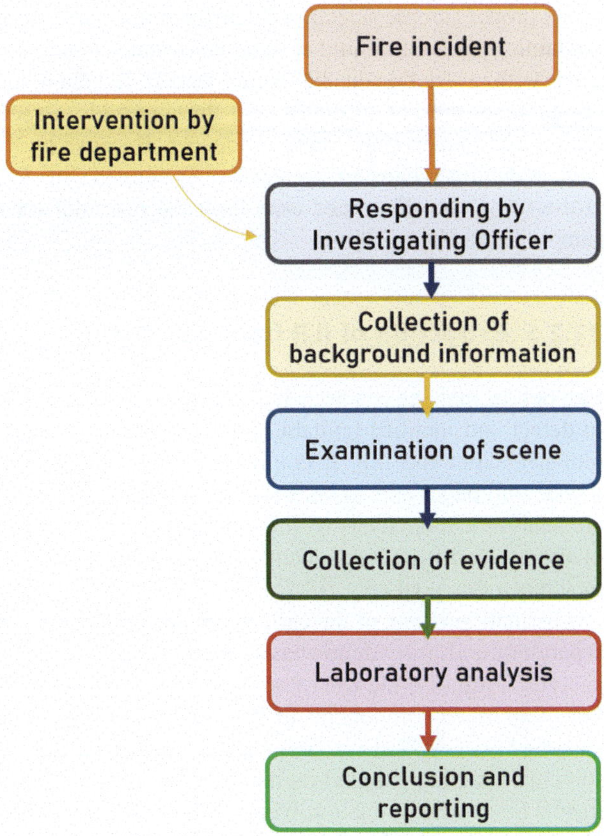

Fig. 22.6 Steps involved in fire investigation

the same, an investigator must evince that tampering has been done in at least one factor of the fire triangle, for example, the introduction of flammable material. In this regard, multiple points of ignition, the presence of ignitable liquid or pour patterns serve the purpose as these indicate a case of arson (Sturaro et al. 2013).

In an approach to systemize and standardize the investigation of fire scenes, National Fire Protection Association (**NFPA**) has set certain guidelines and published its first edition NFPA 921 (Hine 2004; Stauffer et al. 2008; Lentini 2018) '*Guide for fire and explosion investigations*' in 1992. It is regularly updated by NFPA and the latest version was released in 2017 (Lentini 2018).

22.2.4 Sample Collection and Packaging

"Analysis can be no better than appropriate sample submitted" is a guiding principle for every analysis. Hence, debris must be carefully collected and packaged as analytical results will be based on it. Use of e-sniffers based on catalytic combustion or photoionization, colorimetric tube, UV light and portable Gas Chromatography aid in proper sample selection (Stauffer et al. 2008). Samples of debris suspected of containing ignitable liquid residue are usually placed in clean and unused metallic cans with a friction-fit lid (often called a "paint can"). These retain volatile components present in debris and thus, provide a secure and convenient way to collect and preserve fire scene evidences. Because by nature fire debris tends to be wet, Teflon lined cans are preferred over unlined cans for the collection of fire debris at the fire scene. The lined cans limit the potential for rust, therefore, keeping the sample intact (Hine 2004).

22.2.5 Extraction of ILR from Fire Debris

Fire debris analysis is a branch of forensic chemistry that deals with its examination to detect and identify ignitable liquid residues. Broadly, Fire Debris is defined as remanent after the fire. It could be partially or completely burnt clothes, carpet, wood, soil, paper and so on. From the collected fire debris, Ignitable liquid residues are analyzed. In analysis of ILR, the first step is its extraction from debris. Several methods viz. distillation, solvent extraction, headspace, adsorption, etc. are available to achieve this goal (Fig. 22.7).

Distillation is one of the earliest methods applied to extract IL from debris which separates the IL from debris based on the vapor pressure of components present in an analyte. Similarly, the use of activated charcoal strips (ACS) is based on vaporization. Vaporized components of ILR, instead of being collected as in distillation, get adsorbed over ACS strips, and further, these strips are used for analysis. In contrast, solvent extraction is based on the principle of 'like dissolves like' wherein debris is treated first with a suitable solvent (commonly used are hexane, diethyl ether, carbon di-sulphide) to dissolve ILR components and filtered. Filtrate is used for subsequent analysis (Fig. 22.8). However, each method has its own advantages and limitations to which it can extract the ILR (Stauffer et al. 2008).

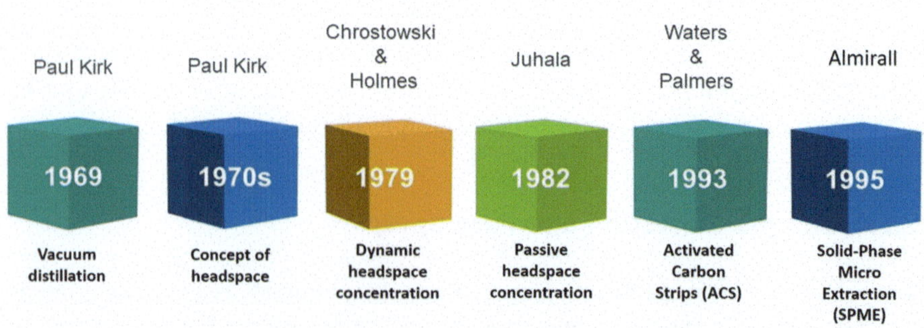

Fig. 22.7 Timeline of extraction techniques in which they were first applied in ILR analysis (Almirall et al. 1995; Lentini 2012)

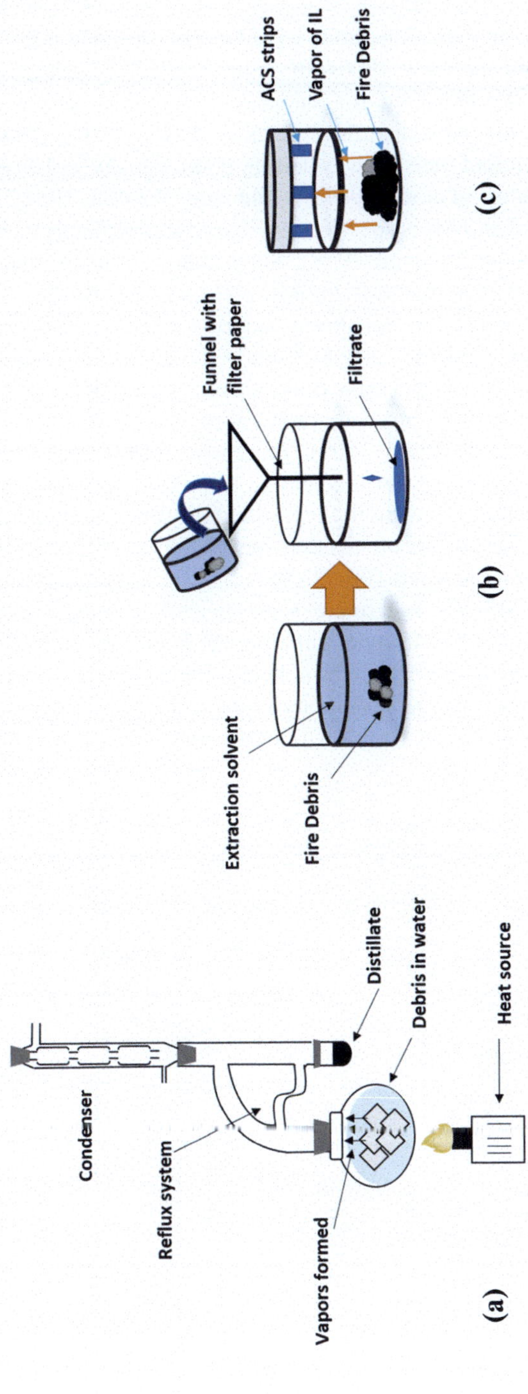

Fig. 22.8 Commonly used extraction techniques (**a**) Distillation (**b**) Solvent extraction (**c**) Passive headspace extraction using ACS strips

22.2.6 Analysis of Extracted ILR

At the inception, the analytical methods were largely primitive with a huge number of error rates. During the early 1900s, the human olfactory sense was the solitary way of identifying the extracted ILs samples (Reiss 1911; Bischoff 1938). This technique sustained for more than three decades. In the 1940s, additional physical characteristics of different fuels such as boiling point, density, color, etc. were added as analytical measures (Turner 1949; Battle and Weston 1954; Myren 1954). Surprisingly, Infrared and Mass spectrometry-based sample analysis was introduced during this decade only (Bennett 1958). Since then, chromatographic techniques have spearheaded the analytical task until now (Inman and Rudin 2001; Rudin and Inman 2002). Due to simplicity, sensitivity, rapidity and cost-effectiveness, chromatography methods are preferred analytical tools to detect the presence of ignitable liquid residues. During the initial stage of the chromatographic techniques, thin-layer chromatography and paper chromatography were used for screening as well as confirmation (Inman and Rudin 2001). Presently, sophisticated techniques, i.e., GC, GC-GC, GC-MS are key instrumentation techniques that are applied for arson debris analysis. Selectivity, sensitivity, reproducibility and pin point identification of the ignitable liquid or accelerant residue makes GC-MS the most widely used technique for fire debris analysis (Fig. 22.9).

In addition, GC-MS-MS is a more sophisticated technique that offers some advantages over regular GC-MS by eliminating the interference of other substances. In addition, the hyphenation of the chromatographic techniques with spectroscopic methods adds the selectivity and specificity of the technique along with the sensitivity to the investigation. In the trend of portable and field-deployable devices, the

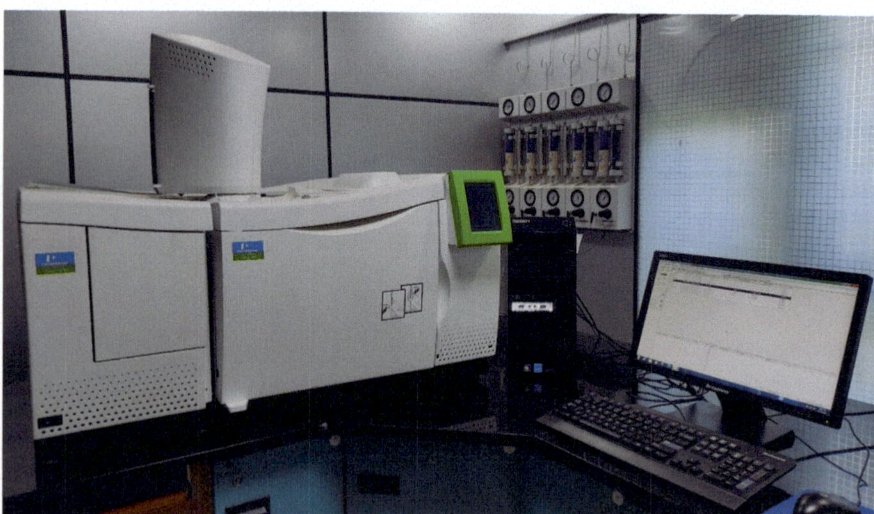

Fig. 22.9 GC-MS instrument

development of sensors, namely E-NOSE and the vibrational spectroscopic technique (namely Raman spectroscopy and ATR-FTIR) devices for fire debris analysis is also a current perspective (Yadav et al. 2020). Derivative UV spectrophotometry is another very useful technique in the identification of IL residues. The higher derivative shows minute absorption peaks not visible in the basic zero-order spectra of different ILs. These minute peaks help to distinguish between these fuels (Rojas and Bosch Ojeda 2008; Bumbrah et al. 2016).

22.3 Explosion

An explosion can be defined as the sudden expansion of gases accompanied by high pressure, heat and noise. The kinetic energy produced in this way may get conferred to surrounding materials including decomposition products that come in contact with these expanding gases and cause damage to them. In other words, it is extremely rapid combustion.

Materials that undergo this type of phenomenon on the application of suitable stimuli are called explosive substances. Some materials undergo such rapid reactions either alone or in combination with other materials. These materials are listed as explosive materials viz. TNT, PETN, Black powder and Cyclotol (RDX + TNT), etc. However, several other materials and combinations that may be in existence and not characterized as explosive may be used in causing explosions intentionally or occur accidentally due to non-awareness (Fisher and Fisher 2012).

Based on the velocity at which waves produce after initiation, an explosion could be classified into deflagration and detonation. If the wave travels at a speed that is less than the speed of sound (331 m/s, subsonic), the explosion is categorized as deflagration. Herein, layer to layer burning takes place. Deflagrating explosives burn faster with sparks, hissing noise and more violently than ordinary combustible materials. On the other hand, explosive substances which on initiation decompose via the passage of a shockwave rather than a thermal mechanism are called detonating explosives. In detonation, shock waves travel faster than the speed of sound. A deflagration can be transitioned to detonation if initiated in a confined space (Figs. 22.10 and 22.11) (Akhavan 2011; Mohanty 2012; Bell 2014).

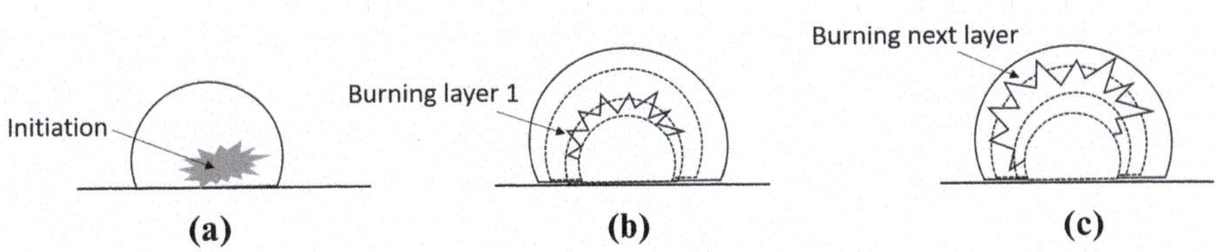

Fig. 22.10 (**a**) Initiation of explosion and subsequent Layer by layer burning (**b**) and (**c**) in deflagrating explosive

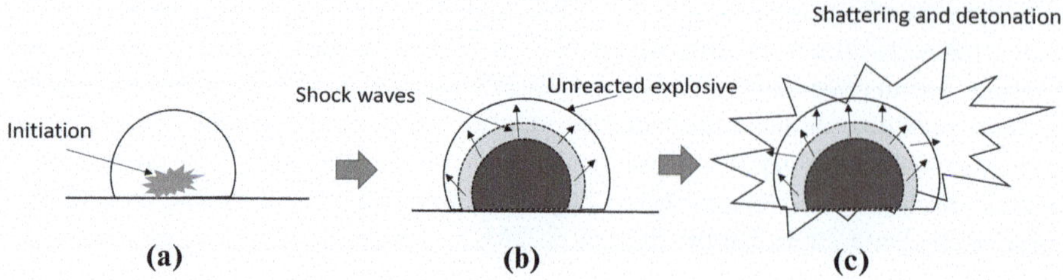

Fig. 22.11 (**a**) Initiation of explosion and propagation of generated shock waves (**b**) and (**c**) in detonating explosive

22.3.1 Classification of Explosives

Broadly, explosives could be classified into two groups: low explosives and high explosives. This classification is based on the process and speed they explode.

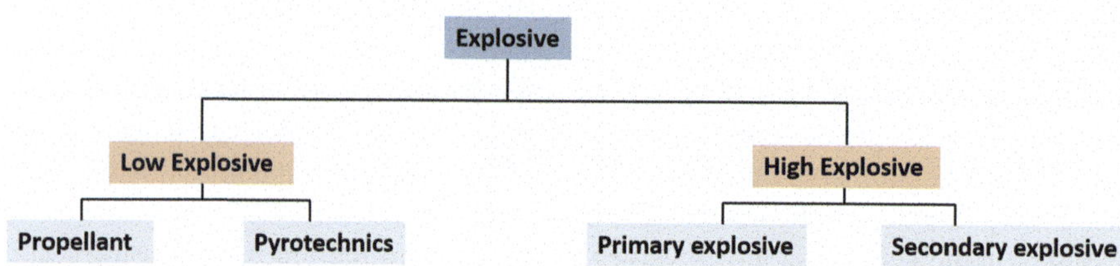

Nitrogen is a ubiquitous constituent of almost all explosives except a few such as peroxides (Kumar and Elias 2019). Nitration reaction is the process through which nitrogen in form of nitro-group is introduced to organic material. The role of nitration in the world of explosive chemistry is fascinating in determining explosive properties. On the basis of nitration reaction, explosives can be classified (Akhavan 2011) as:

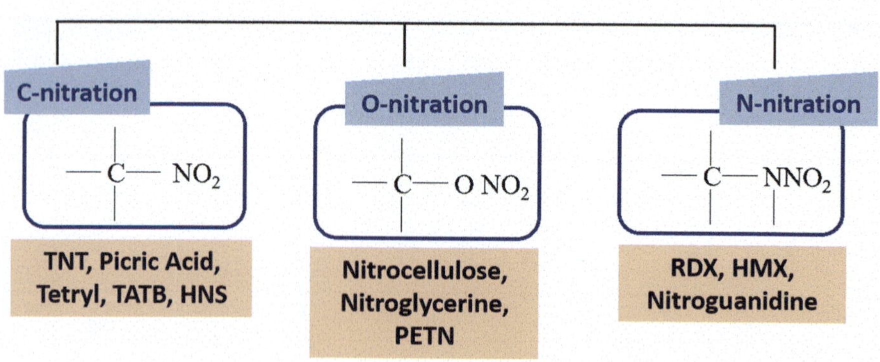

22.3.1.1 Low Explosives

Low explosives which are solid flammable materials undergo deflagration and the gas formed expand rapidly causing damage. However, for an explosion, they need to be confined. Low explosives are further classified into two groups.

22.3.1.1.1 Propellant

Propellants are such explosive materials that generate energy through chemical reaction and the resultant energy is subsequently used in the propulsion of projectiles or other objects.

The earliest known explosive is black powder. In 1267 for the first time, Roger Bacon in his book '*Opus Majus*' recorded its composition as a mixture of potassium nitrate (saltpetre), charcoal and sulphur (Heard 2008). Over the years, several variations and formulations to the ratio in which these chemicals are mixed appeared. However, its typical composition is 75% potassium nitrate, 15% charcoal and 10% sulfur (Wallace 2018). The most common use of black powder was in the propulsion of projectiles from a firearm. Nowadays, smokeless powders are used for that purpose. Another common use is in safety fuses and pipe bombs (Fisher and Fisher 2012).

With the discovery of nitrocellulose by Schonbein (Kumar and Elias 2019), smokeless powders came into existence because they didn't produce smoke as in the case of black powder. French chemist Villie in 1886, rolled out nitrocellulose with ether into thin sheets, cut and dried. This was used as a propellant for the rifle. Because this type of formulation contains only one type of oxidizer i.e., nitrocellulose, these are called single-base propellants. On the other hand, double-base propellant contains nitrocellulose as well as nitro-glycerine. The triple-base propellant is also used in the military formulation that is composed of nitroguanidine incorporated into double-base powder (Holper 2012; Wallace 2018).

22.3.1.1.2 Pyrotechnics

Like propellants, pyrotechnics also produce a lot of energy but differ in that rate of reaction in pyrotechnics is at visibly observable rates. The name pyrotechnic is originated from the Greek 'pyre' meaning 'fire' and 'techne' meaning 'an art'. In this way, pyrotechnics describes the effect observed from burning and thus include colored smoke, bright light and noise also. Flash powders are a typical example of pyrotechnics. It is comprised of a binder, an oxidizer (Chlorates, nitrates etc.) fuel like sulfur, charcoal, and metallic ions (aluminium, magnesium, boron etc.) to display colors (Agrawal 2010; Akhavan 2011).

22.3.1.2 High Explosives

High explosives undergo detonation and have a shattering effect on their surroundings. They do not need not to be confined to explode. These are further categorized as follows.

22.3.1.2.1 Primary Explosives

These are sensitive to shock or heat and are therefore used as initiators to detonate main charges (secondary explosives), in blasting caps and primers of ammunition.

Priming compositions commonly used in ammunitions such as mercury fulminate ($Hg(CNO)_2$), Lead Azide (PbN_6), Lead Styphnate ($C_6HN_3O_8Pb$), Tetrazene ($C_2H_6N_{10}.H_2O$) Tri-Acetone Triperoxide (TATP, $C_9H_{18}O_6$) etc. are examples of primary explosives. In comparison to mercury fulminate, Lead azide is more sensitive to impact but both are hygroscopic in nature. Therefore, they have a good shelf life in dry conditions. A similar case is with tetrazene, but it is not hygroscopic to the extent the previous two are. Due to its high metal content (44.5%), lead styphnate is a weak primary explosive and hence, is not used in fillings of detonators but is non-hygroscopic (Akhavan 2011). In contrast to these metallic explosives, TATP is a metal-free primary explosive that has gained wider attention in recent years. Richard Reid had used TATP in *shoe bomb* and attempted to detonate on American airlines flight on December 22, 2001 (Fisher and Fisher 2012).

22.3.1.2.2 Secondary Explosives

These are mainly used as the main charge and are less sensitive to shock or heat in comparison to primary explosives. The energy produced from deflagration of primary explosives initiates the detonation of these explosives. Examples of common secondary explosives and their structural formula are appended in Table 22.2 (Bell 2014).

Although detonating explosives have great detonation velocity and shattering effect, many formulations have been designed by combining these explosives with others in different proportions. Such explosives are also called as composite explosives (Agrawal 2010; Akhavan 2011). Brief to such a combination is tabulated in Table 22.3.

The use of these explosives is not limited to deployment by military or mining workers. Criminals often use these explosives and make homemade bombs also called Improvized explosive devices (**IED**).

22.3.2 Investigation of the Explosion Scene

An explosion occurs when a chemical substance is subjected to suitable stimuli. After the scene investigation, it is the role of an investigator to determine how and why these factors came together that resulted in the incident. By gathering the evidences from the scene of offence, the investigator provides answers to whether the act was intentional or accidental (Fisher and Fisher 2012; Vermette 2012).

First, the crime scene must be protected from any unauthorized person so that physical evidences are not tampered with. If a burnt/injured body shows any sign of life, it should be provided medical assistance immediately. The witness should be interviewed as these are helpful in determining the line of investigation. Before entering the scene, the investigator should assess potential hazards. If an unexploded IED/bomb is found, it is necessary to call a technician to diffuse the device (Fisher and Fisher 2012; Vermette 2012).

The scene should be thoroughly searched to determine the nature of the explosive and the extent of the crime scene must be identified. Due to the shattering effect

Table 22.2 Common secondary explosives

Explosive	Detonation velocity (in m/s)	Structure
TNT (trinitro toluene)	6850	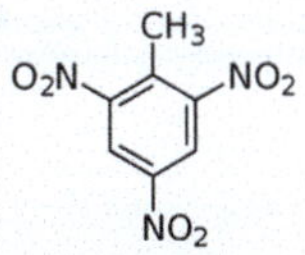
PETN (pentaerythritol tetranitrate)	7920	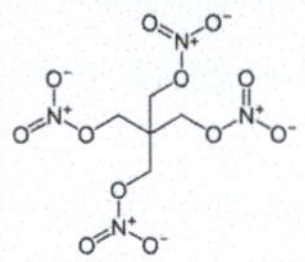
RDX (research department explosive/hexogen/ cyclonite/cyclotrimethylenetrinitramine)	8440	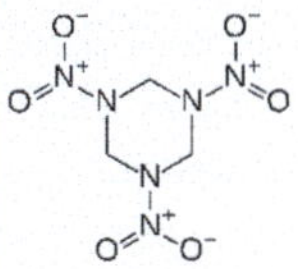
HMX (high melting explosive/octogen/ Cyclotetramethylenetetranitramine)	9100	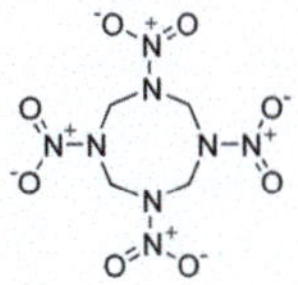
TATB (1,3,5-triamino-2,4,6-trinitrobenzene)	7760	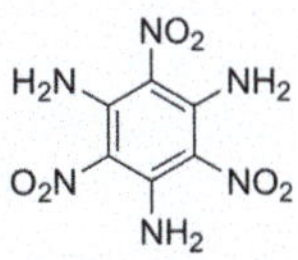
Tetryl (2,4,6-trinitrophenylmethylnitramine)	7080	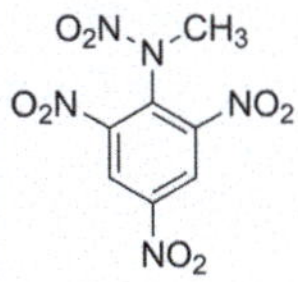

Table 22.3 Examples of composite explosives

Composite explosive	Components
Amatol	TNT + ammonium nitrate
Cyclotol/ composition B	RDX + TNT
Octol	HMX + TNT
Minol	Ammonium nitrate + aluminium + TNT
Tritonal	TNT + aluminium powder
Pentolite	TNT + PETN
Semtex	RDX + PETN
Amatex	Ammonium nitrate + TNT + RDX
Debrix	RDX + wax
ANFO	Ammonium nitrate + fuel oil

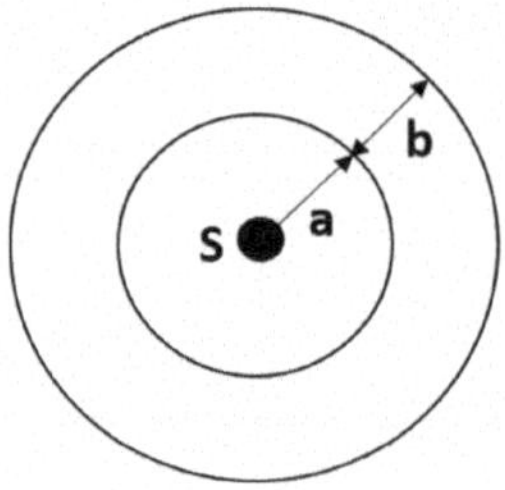

S = seat of explosion

a = farthest location from seat where fragments are found.

b = half of the a

a+b = total area to be secured

Fig. 22.12 Total area that should be secured and searched where explosion takes place in outdoor

produced by the detonation of high explosive, physical evidences, partially or completely burnt, are scattered around the scene. Therefore, fragmented containers, pieces of IEDs, wrappers used to carry explosives, partially burnt explosives, pieces of wires, etc. should be looked for during the search. In this regard, the seat of the explosion can be a focal point, and the location farthest from the seat where fragments from the explosion are located will define the outer perimeter of the scene. This area with the addition of an area equal to half of the farthest location from the seat of fire represents the total area that should be secured and searched (Fig. 22.12) (Fisher and Fisher 2012; Vermette 2012).

In addition, anything that does not appear to belong in the area must be properly examined. Items such as tire tracks, tool marks, and the like are valuable and must not be overlooked. During the search, the location and description scene such as smoke, description of the crater, damage to structure etc. must duly be documented, photographed and videotaped.

Physical evidences found at the crime scene must be collected and entrusted to the scientific crew for the detection and identification of the type of explosive involved in an incident. If a suspect is located shortly after the incident, their clothing and hand washings/swabs in cotton moistened with acetone should be collected and forwarded to the scientific crew for examination of traces of explosives. Similarly, if a vehicle of the suspect is apprehended, careful searching and trace evidence collection should also be done (Fisher and Fisher 2012).

22.3.3 Laboratory Analysis of Post-blast Residue

Whenever an unknown substance is submitted to the Forensic Science Laboratory for material identification, forensic scientist proceeds with a preliminary/color/spot test for possible identification of suspected material. If a positive reaction is observed during spot testing, further tests or instrument-based methods are applied for its confirmation.

Table 22.4 List of commonly used spot test for explosive identification

Test	Reagent	Observation	Possible explosive
Test for polynitroaromatics	30% aqueous/ethanolic KOH	Red/purple	TNT, TNB, etc.
Griess test or test for nitrite ion	Aniline derivative and coupling agent such as *N*-1-naphthyl ethylenediamine in acidic medium	Pink-purple color	Nitrocellulose, Nitro-glycerine, PETN, RDX, HMX, etc.
Test for chlorate	Aniline sulphate and sulfuric acid	Blue color	Sodium/potassium chlorate
Test for barium	Sodium rhodizonate and hydrochloric acid	Reddish brown color	Barium nitrate
Test for ammonium ion	Nessler reagent (HgI_2, KI and KOH in water)	Orange brown precipitate	Ammonium nitrate, ANFO, etc.

22.3.3.1 Preliminary Tests

Spot tests are mainly based on ionic moiety present in explosives which may include as listed in Table 22.4 but are not limited to this (Table 22.4) (Almog and Zitrin 2009; Stuart 2013; Tamiri and Zitrin 2013).

Number of kits for field testing have been developed are being developed for spot testing. All of these rely on the basic principle of color chemistry. For example, ETK (Explosive Testing Kit) developed by Israel (Tamiri and Zitrin 2013) and EDK (Explosive Detection Kit) developed by DRDO (India), can detect the poly-nitroaromatic compounds, nitrate esters, nitramines, inorganic nitrate salts, and peroxides.

22.3.3.2 Confirmatory Tests/Techniques

Conventionally, Thin layer chromatography was used to confirm the presence of explosive residue using at least two solvent systems. But nowadays, more sophisticated instruments are available by which more accurate results are obtained.

Like in ILR analysis, extraction of explosive residue from debris is an important step. It can be achieved through aqueous (for inorganic) and organic extraction. Further, it is subjected to instrumental analysis like Capillary electrophoresis, Immunoassays, Ion chromatography, GC-MS/Headspace GC-MS, LC-MS and Spectroscopic techniques like FTIR, Raman and NMR (Tamiri and Zitrin 2013).

22.4 Drugs as Physical Evidence

Drugs can be defined as any foreign substances natural or synthetic that are administered in an organism to bring physiological or psychological changes in the body. But why are drugs a matter of concern and a part of Forensic Chemistry? Not every drug out in the market is concerning, however, a few of them are reported for their "illicit use". These are well known for their intoxicating effects. The term

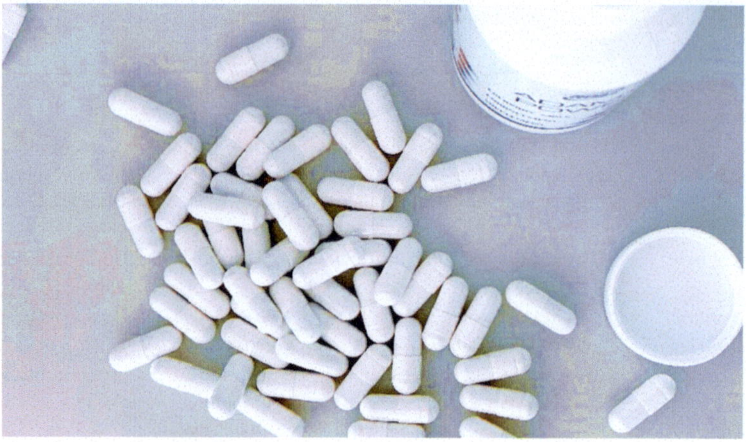

Fig. 22.13 Drugs in the form of capsules

illicit must not be confused with illegal drugs as these are substances that may be otherwise legal but are used in an inappropriate context such as manufacturing them without a license. Examples include marijuana, benzodiazepine, morphine and other scheduled drugs. Illicit drugs are classified under "controlled substances", of which, use, sale, and distribution are regulated by a government entity. The government produces a specific list of drugs that falls under the controlled substance category. These substances are more appropriately referred to as "drugs of abuse" (Fig. 22.13) (Siegel et al. 2013a, b).

The purpose behind this legislation is to limit the quantity of these substances as they are more likely to get abused and also to provide the legitimate medical, scientific and industrial requirements of these substances. Hence, a legal and scientific validation of a drug is required. Failing to do that will be subjected to enquiry, analysis and justification (Karch 1998). To accomplish this task a Forensic chemist must be well acquainted with the nature and relevant pharmacological behavior of different drugs encountered and reported often for their abuse. In addition, prior knowledge of the analytical method for the examination and identification will aid in finding accurate results.

There have been much evidences for the use of psychoactive substances by humans since the earliest recorded times and being abused by some, creating problems. There has been a dramatic upswing in the number of use and abuse during the period of a decade. According to a report of the United Nations Office on Drugs and Crime (UNODC), an estimated 275 million people aged between 15 and 64 had used drugs at least once in 2018 and out of which 36 million people suffered from drug use disorders, meaning abused some type of drug to an extent where they experienced drug dependence or required treatment (UNODC 2021). The report also demonstrates the increasing trend of drugs use and their trafficking through different mediums as well such as over the internet, clear web and dark web. The increasing trend observed in drug abuse requires a deep understanding of the diversification of drugs and legitimate procedures to control and determine them for their potential. This chapter dives deep into the classification of drugs, their mechanism, use and analytical methods of forensic relevance.

22.4.1 Classification of Drugs

Drugs can be broadly classified under three main categories (Fig. 22.14) (Siegel et al. 2013a, b):

1. Form and Origin—Natural plant materials, derived plant materials or semisynthetic drugs, synthetic drugs
2. Pharmacological classification—depressants, stimulants, analgesics, psychomimetics
3. Legislative control-scheduled and non-scheduled drugs (Fig. 22.14) (Siegel et al. 2013a, b).

22.4.1.1 Form and Origin

Drugs of abuse are classified on the basis of their source and the form it is consumed.

Natural plant materials such as *Cannabis indica* and related species whose dried female flowering tops and dried leaves are usually smoked with tobacco for its hallucinogenic effects but can also be ingested. The active principle of cannabis is tetrahydrocannabinol (THC). The average THC content in herbal cannabis ranges between 5% and 20% (20% of THC content is observed under ideal conditions provided in intensive indoor cultivation). Similarly, leaves of *Erythroxylum Coca* are chewed as a stimulant and opium, the milky latex of *Papaver Somniferum*, is used to derive morphine, codeine and heroin (Siegel et al. 2013a, b).

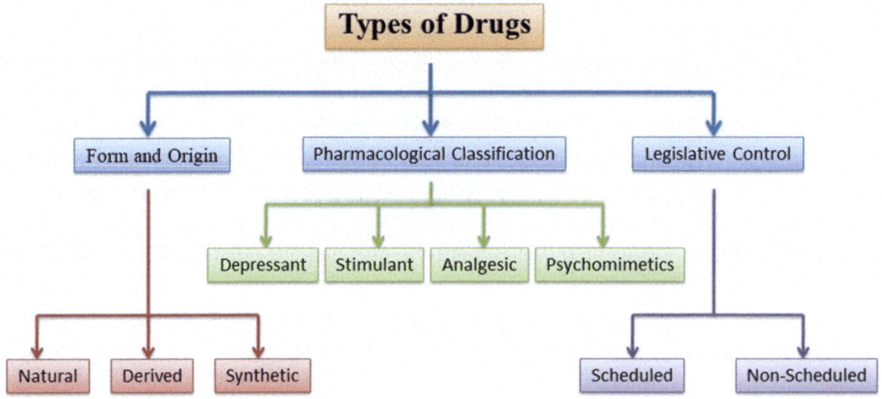

Fig. 22.14 Types of drugs

Derived plant materials or semisynthetic drugs can be abused in different forms. For instance, coca leaves are used to manufacture cocaine which comprises 1% of coca, converted into a white powder of cocaine hydrochloride and snorted which produces a stimulant effect triggering the CNS. Cocaine can be reconverted into "crack", a highly addictive substance obtained through its free base. Cannabis resin and hash oil, likewise, is a derivative of herbal cannabis containing 5% and 30–40% THC content respectively. Dried latex exuding from the capsules of opium poppy is smoked which contains 10% morphine as its principal content. Semisynthetic drugs are made by the synthesis of natural plant materials to isolate their active ingredient or to modify them and the most common example includes heroin. Heroin is produced by the acetylation of crude morphine. It consists of dimorphine and other opium alkaloids such as monoacetylmorphine, papaverine etc. Other semisynthetic drug examples include codeine, morphine and cocaine.

Synthetic drugs are complete chemically synthesized drugs, amphetamine reported to be first synthesized over 100 years ago. It is synthesized from phenyl 2-propanone/benzyl methyl ketone found in the form of white powder. Other common examples include methamphetamines, ecstasy drugs (MDMA), diazepam, methaqualone commonly known as mandrax, Lysergic acid diethylamide (LSD), dimethyltryptamine (DMTA) (Siegel et al. 2013a, b).

22.4.1.2 Pharmacological Classification

Most abused drugs fall into these categories which are classified based on their pharmacological properties, toxicity and ability to produce dependence. It actually emphasizes on the different kinds of effects the drugs produce on the biological systems of the body and alter its ordinary functioning. This classification has legal significance because the abused drug is determined according to the tendency to harm individual health or risk to society.

CNS Depressants also known as sedatives and the drugs referred to as hypnotics or tranquillizers are among the most common type to be abused around the globe. The primary uses of these drugs are as a treatment for insomnia, muscle pain, anxiety and panic disorders. The drugs are purported to be abused when an individual self-administer a high dosage of tranquillizer or continue to have them even after the treatment is over. This can be done for their personal pleasure or to avoid the sense of mental agony. Most of the time individuals are unaware of abuse potential of these drugs and become reliant to cope with life. Tranquillizers may be recreationally abused along with other forms of drugs to enhance their potential and for their intoxicating effects. Drugs also cause memory-impairment effects and facilitates the use in sexual abuse and most of them are known as date-rape drugs. The drugs used as hypnotics include benzodiazepines, non-benzodiazepine sedative-hypnotic (zolpidem, zaleplon, zopiclone, and eszopiclone) barbiturates, first-generation antihistamines, dextromethorphan in high doses, trazodone, methaqualone and alcohol (Couper 2016).

Stimulants are the most widely abused kind of drugs known for their euphoric effects. A close structural relationship is observed with the neurotransmitters such as dopamine and noradrenaline in this class. Stimulants act on the receptors in the brain causing an increase in the levels of neurotransmitters leading to high blood pressure, mental alertness and wakefulness, decreased sense of physical pain, fatigue and appetite and anorexia in some cases. Prolonged use may lead to psychosis. Drugs such as cocaine, caffeine, phenmetrazine, amphetamine and methamphetamine are the most common examples of CNS stimulants (Siegel et al. 2013a, b).

Analgesics are drugs that are known to relieve pain. These may be narcotic or non-narcotic. Narcotic analgesics include opioids and its semi-synthetic derivatives. Others include aspirin, acetaminophen, Nonsteroidal anti-inflammatory drugs (NSAIDs). Analgesics interact with receptors in the brain, responsible for the transmission of and response to pain (Smith 2005).

Psychomimetics commonly referred as hallucinogens comprise a diverse collection of chemicals and numerous receptor actions in the central nervous system. There is a close relationship between these drugs and serotonin. It causes the perception of senses (object, smell, sound, touch) or hallucination which has no basis in reality. Most common examples include LSD and marijuana. Psilocin is a known naturally derived hallucinogen obtained from Psilocybe mushrooms. Other examples include DOB (2,5-dimethoxy-4-bromoamphetamine) and phenetylamines (Smith 2005).

4.1.3 Legislative classification *Scheduled* and *non-scheduled* drugs are classified in legal terms when the former is controlled and listed in one of the schedules and the latter refer to the ones not listed in any of them (Saferstein 2013).

22.4.2 Commonly Encountered Drugs in Forensic Laboratories

22.4.2.1 Opium

Opium belongs to the category of narcotic drugs that are found universally and has been ruling the market since time immortal (Lauren 2013). The first found evidence of opium as a drug has been dated back to the late Stone Age. The consumption and medicinal use are till date in practice through Neolithic, Bronze, and Iron Age (Figs. 22.15, 22.16, and 22.17) (Martinez and Ballesteros 2019).

Opium is the resin obtained after lancing the seed capsules of the plant *Papaver Somniferum*, commonly known as the poppy plant. Morphine, Codeine, Thebaine, Noscapine are major alkaloids. When opium is in its natural form they are termed as opiates. From these alkaloids, other drugs are also synthesized that are called opioids.

Synthetically modified forms also rule the market which includes drugs such as heroin, methadone, and hydromorphone. In the medical field, they serve as proper analgesics. When it comes to its dependency nature, they have high potential and hence are abused at a high rate. Depending on the variation in the chemical structure

Fig. 22.15 (**a**) Opium plant and (**b**) how it is used. (Reprinted from Decuyper et al. 2021 with permission from Elsevier)

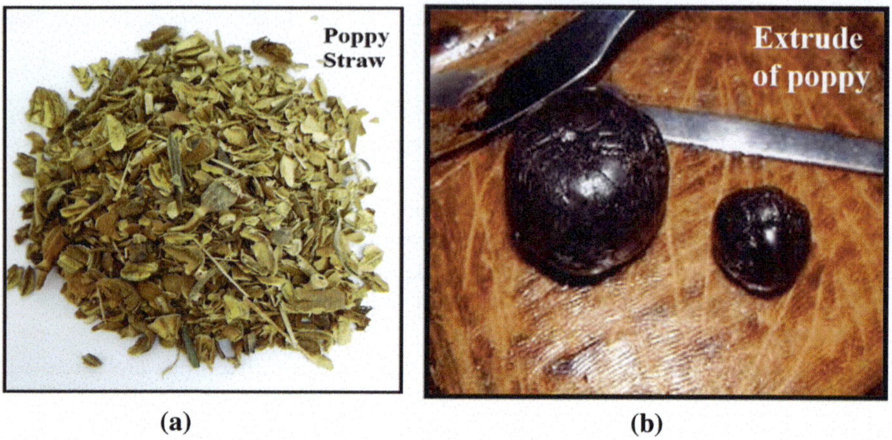

Fig. 22.16 (**a**) Poppy straw and (**b**) extrude of poppy turned into brown color

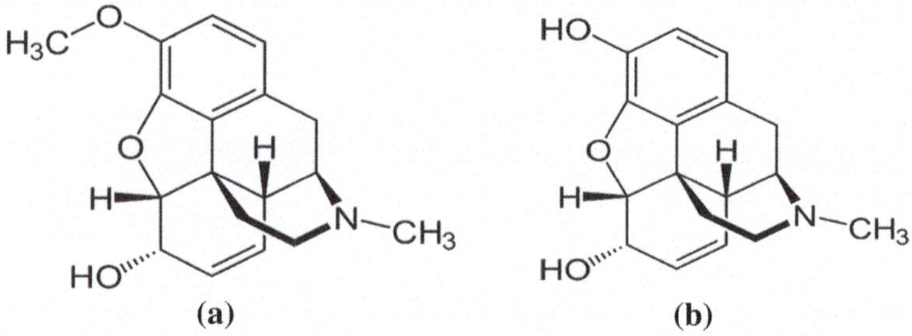

Fig. 22.17 Chemical structure of (**a**) Codeine and (**b**) morphine

opium related drugs can be classified into a class generally called as opium alkaloids. The opiates mentioned above fall under this category. Other members include semi-synthetic derivatives of natural alkaloids and synthetic derivatives.

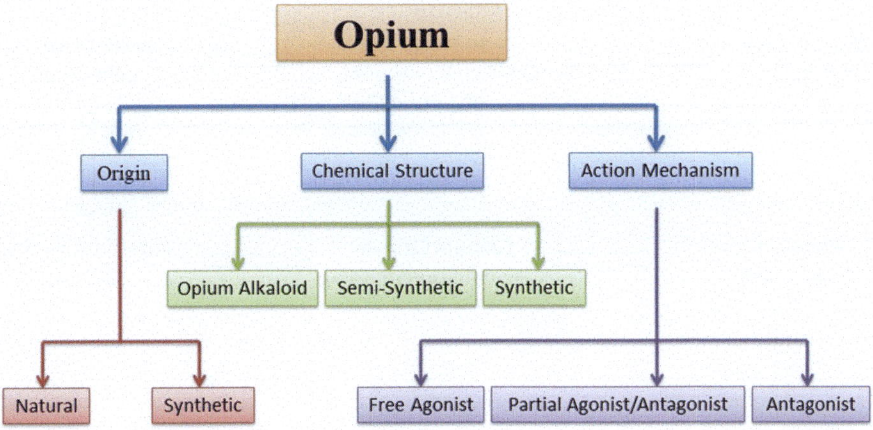

Fig. 22.18 Classification scheme of opium drugs

The former include hydromorphone and oxycodone whereas sufentanil and fentanyl falls under the latter. The opium alkaloids also include diphenylpropylamine derivatives like propoxyphene, methadone, and loperamide. When the action mechanism of the drug is considered, it can be classified into full agonists, partial or mixed agonist/antagonist and antagonist. They are classified taking into consideration the receptors of the opioid drugs (Fig. 22.18).

Opioid drugs are bound to engage with the opiate receptors which are located in the central nervous system (CNS), spinal cord, and brain. These receptors are named mu (μ), kappa (κ), or delta (δ) and are found on the surface of specific cells. Certain areas such as lungs, heart, vessels, gastro-intestinal, and mononuclear cells of the peripheral blood also include the receptors for the drug. When the drug interacts with such receptors a series of signals are generated. The adenylate cyclase enzyme gets inhibited, the calcium channel opening drastically decreases, potassium level increases, and at the same time the prominent activation of protein kinase C (PKC) also takes place. This reduces the neurotransmission thereby cells become less excitable. Figure 22.19 below illustrates the action mechanism of opium.

The continued use of the drug leads to a state of unconsciousness, lung collapse, hypotension, vomiting, tachycardia, hyperthermia, mild metabolic acidosis, dyspnea, gastric content aspiration, anoxia (acute) and may lead to death (NIH 2020).

22.4.2.2 Marijuana

Marijuana has been used as a psychoactive material since ancient times (Fitzgerald et al. 2013). They are derived from the resin of the plant *Cannabis sativa* and are potent hallucinogens. The word implies a meaning of materials like tobacco prepared from the flowers and leaves of the plant. Figure 22.20a below shows marijuana plant leaves. The plant act as a reservoir of about 500 chemicals (120 identified cannabinoids) (Cohen et al. 2019). But when it comes to substances of psychoactive importance cannabinol, cannabidiol and tetrahydrocannabinol

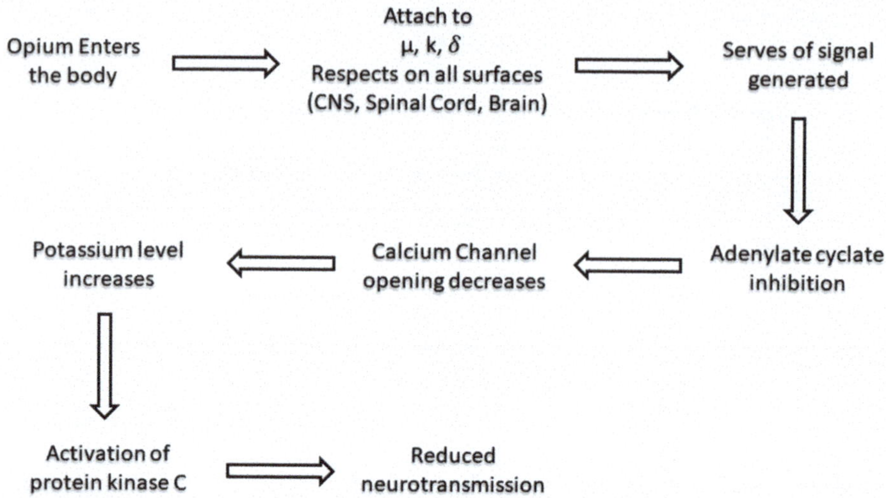

Fig. 22.19 Action mechanism of Opium

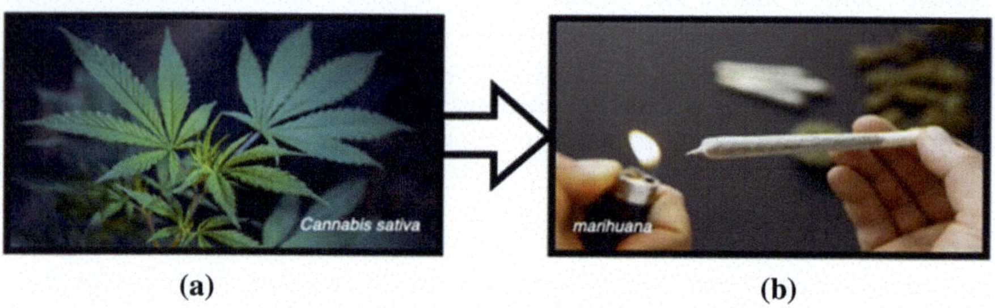

Fig. 22.20 (**a**) Cannabis plant and (**b**) how it is used. (Reprinted from Decuyper et al. 2021 with permission from Elsevier)

(THC) are considered (Fig. 22.21). The potential of THC weights ten times that of the other two components. Depending on how the plant is cultivated the concentration of THC varies within the range of 0.4–20%.

The drug is commonly known as herb, pot, weed, grass, reefer, hemp, MJ, and Mary Jane in the street. Of the most active marijuana, a seedless form named sinsemilla has a high THC concentration (Fitzgerald et al. 2013). The stem of the plant is collected and chopped and dried along with the leaves and seed to get the raw marijuana. The drug can be ingested by inhalation (cigarettes, and bongs), or orally by adding it along with food items like cookies and brownies. Cigarettes of marijuana contain crude plant content in a concentration range of 500–1000 mg and a THC concentration of 15–30 mg (Fig. 22.22) (Martin and Szara 1998).

Certain cannabinoids which are endogenous including anandamide act as neurotransmitters due to their ability to communicate between cells of the nervous system. They have a high potential to influence memory, control and coordination,

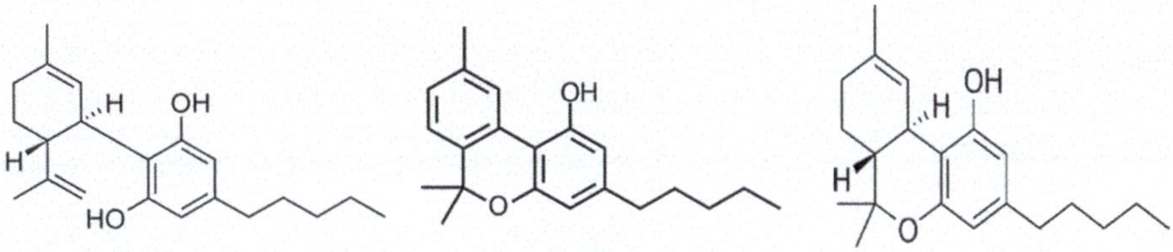

(a) (b) (c)

Fig. 22.21 Chemical structure of (**a**) Cannabidiol, (**b**) Cannabinol and (**c**) THC

(a) (b)

Fig. 22.22 Forms of cannabis use (**a**) Ganja and (**b**) Charas

thinking, and other sensory perceptions. Since THC is similar to these compounds, they bind itself to the cannabinoid receptors of the brain cells or neurons. This causes both physical and chemical imbalance of brain activity. The effect of THC on areas such as the hippocampus and orbitofrontal cortex is potential enough to change the focus of an individual and even create fresh memories. The cerebellum and basal ganglia are also affected by the compound which leads to an imbalance in control, coordination, movement, and posture (Green et al. 2003). They also increase the flow of dopamine which gives a profound feeling of wellbeing and pleasure. This activates the natural rewarding system which leads to the repeated use of the material.

Abuse of the drug leads to anxiety and panic attacks, depression, mania, tachycardia, hypotension, acute myocardial infarction, cardiomyopathy, and cardiac death. Chronic use of the same may lead to lung cancer. Acute use results in the resistance of the airway, a higher chance of emphysema, and puts a high workload on the heart (Table 22.5) (Sachs et al. 2015).

22.4.2.3 Lysergic Acid Diethylamide (LSD)

LSD is a well-known hallucinogen synthesized first in 1938 by Switzerland-based chemist Albert Hofmann. The potential of the drug as a psychoactive substance was discovered in 1943. Lysergic acid is derived from the fungus *Claviceps purpurea* and is further underwent processing to generate the semi-synthetic product called as LSD. The chemical structure of LSD incorporates a tetracyclic ring within an indole

Table 22.5 Forms of cannabis and their % THC content

Forms of cannabis					
Form	Bhang	Ganja	Charas	Hash oil	Marijuana
Source	Dried leaves and shoot	Flowering top of female plant	Resinous exudates from leaves flower and stem	Liquid soluble plant extract	Dried leaves and flowers
THC content	2–5%	5–8%	10–20%	25–50%	5–8%

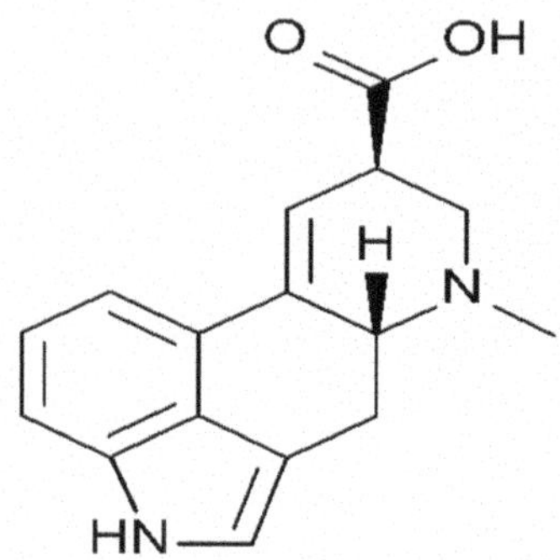

Fig. 22.23 Chemical structure of Lysergic acid diethylamide

system. Various isomers of LSD are formed as an asymmetry exists in the carbon positioned fifth and eighth in the parent structure. This results in the formation of D-LSD, L-LSD, L-isolysergic acid diethylamide and D-isolysergic acid diethylamide. But when it comes to the psychoactive property only D-LSD is active (Passie et al. 2008).

LSD falls under the classification of tryptamines which belong to one of the two broad classifications of hallucinogens (phenethylamines and tryptamines) as per its chemical structure (Fig. 22.23). Within tryptamines, they can further be classified under ergolines.

The major receptors upon which LSD acts are serotonin receptors 5hydroxytryptamine 2A (5HT2A). Researches are still being done in the field to completely understand the mechanism of LSD action. One prominent theory suggests that the LSD bind with the receptor to initiate the breakdown of hippocampal prefrontal cortex inhibition. The activity of various regions of the brain is reduced drastically. The part affected includes various gyrus (right middle temporal, superior/middle/inferior frontal, postcentral, and superior frontal) and cerebellum. The drug also enables the altered activity of the paralimbic system by activating the right brain hemisphere and thereby inducing visual images which are not real. Repeated use affects the neuroglial cell lines and leads to degeneration of the neuron and in turn leads to learning disability and memory loss (Hwang and Saadabadi 2021).

When LSD is provided in a moderate dosage (75–150 μg) orally they induce a state of unconsciousness. LSD is also considered a prominent drug that impairs the psychomotor function of the body. Mild to moderate doses also produce tachycardia, tachypnea, and mydriasis (Baquiran and Khalilili 2021).

22.4.2.4 Barbiturates

Barbiturates were introduced into the clinical setting during the initiation of the twentieth century. Shortly, it was found that its chronic use led to physical dependence which in turn may lead to its abuse. One of the major facts about barbiturates is their difficulty in diagnosing abuse during the early stages of use. When the dependency reaches a severe stage and the individual is treated under a medical system only their abuse is diagnosed. This condition of abuse of the drug may either be accidental or intentional. Barbituric Acid, synthesized by condensation of malonic acid and urea in 1864 by Adolf Von Baeyer, is precursor to barbiturates. This potent hypnotic and sedative drug holds several street names such as downers, gorilla pills, goofballs, and courage pills. Phenobarbital, amobarbital sodium, secobarbital sodium, and pentobarbital sodium are commonly used barbiturates drugs (Fig. 22.24).

The receptor upon which the drug acts is the GABA receptor. GABA-A receptor contains two subunits to which barbiturates are sensitive. This includes the alpha and beta subunits. The intake of barbiturates increases the flux of chloride ions. This leads to the post-synaptic inhibition of the GABA receptor. When the drug is ingested in a concentration range higher than normal, they directly affect the chloride channel by activating them. The effects of barbiturates generally last from 2 to 6 h depending on their potential and concentration. When barbital and phenobarbital are considered, they hold an effect duration of 6 h.

Phenobarbitals induce the cytochrome system especially CYP1A2, 2C9, 3A4/5, and 2B6. Inducing such a system reduces the effect various other medications have on the body. The intake of barbiturates regularly decreases the effect of steroids, oral contraceptives, and various immunosuppressants. They also lead to the reduced concentration of antiepileptic drugs by decreasing the plasma concentration of the drugs. Continuous use can also lead to congenital birth defects while used during the gestational period. Other effects of barbiturates include increased heartbeat, respiratory depression, apnea, reduced blood pressure, and neonatal depression (Matthew 1975; Ho and Harris 1981).

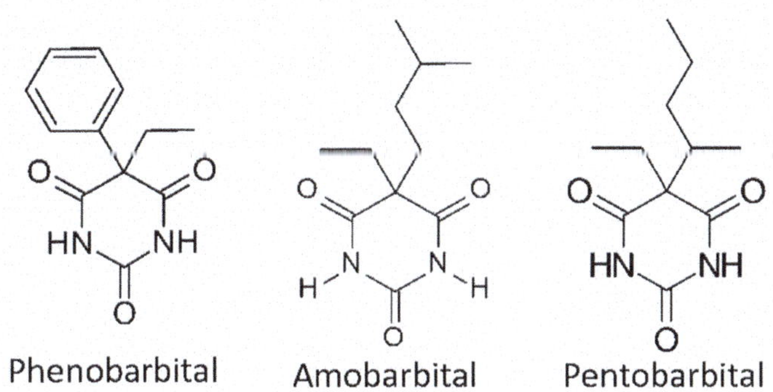

Fig. 22.24 Chemical structure of common barbiturates

22.4.2.5 Amphetamines

Amphetamine or α-methylphenethylamine was initially discovered in 1910 by the British chemist George Barger, and English pharmacologist and physiologist Henry Dale. Even after its discovery, it was not synthesized until 1927 as part of the research done to make a cost-effective ephedrine substitute by G. A. Alles. The trade name given to amphetamines is Benzedrine. The commonly known name 'Amphetamine' was proposed by the Council on Pharmacy and Chemistry of the American Medical Association (Fleckenstein et al. 2007).

Amphetamine generally exists in two different forms that are optically active. This includes the dextro and levo isomers or enantiomers. Amphetamine acts both as a stimulant and a stress reducer. The ability of amphetamine in increasing concentration and intellectual performance has been noted by various researchers. The drug is generally known by various names viz. jelly babies, chunk, speed, up, and morning shots. Commonly used amphetamine is dexamphetamine, amphetamine sulfate, methamphetamine and so on (Fig. 22.25) (Heal et al. 2013).

The major molecules upon which amphetamine acts are dopamine, serotonin, and norepinephrine. The drug inhibits the transportation of these molecules at the presynaptic nerve terminal. Hence, the molecular release increase and thereby stimulates the alpha and beta receptors. At certain times amphetamine can also defend the breakdown of catecholamines by inhibiting the monoamine oxidase. These effects altogether affect the sympathomimetic and central nervous systems.

Acute toxicity of the drug leads to hypervigilance, decrease in appetite, agitation, restlessness, insomnia, and irritability. In higher doses, panic reactions along with confusion may result. This is aided with hallucination, aggressive behavior, coma, and death. Fatigue, depression, and paranoia result due to frequent use of the drug. Chronic amphetamine usage leads to cardiomyopathy, paranoia, bruxism, psychosis, and compulsive behavior. Along with these certain other effects like tachycardia, elevated respiratory rate, pupillary dilation, rhabdomyolysis, flushing, and cardiovascular collapse (Fleckenstein et al. 2007).

22.4.2.6 Cocaine

Cocaine from the coca leaf of *Erythroxylum coca* was first isolated by German chemist Friedrich Gaedcke in the year 1855. The alkaloid extracted was initially named erythroxyline. The alkaloid was later named cocaine by Albert Niemann deriving it from a Quechua word 'cuca'. Treating cocaine with hydrochloric acid generates cocaine hydrochloride salt. This salt is water-soluble which enables the

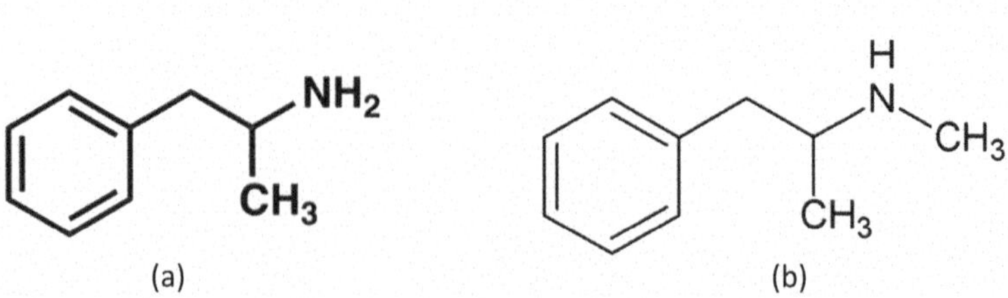

Fig. 22.25 Chemical structure of (**a**) amphetamine and (**b**) methamphetamine

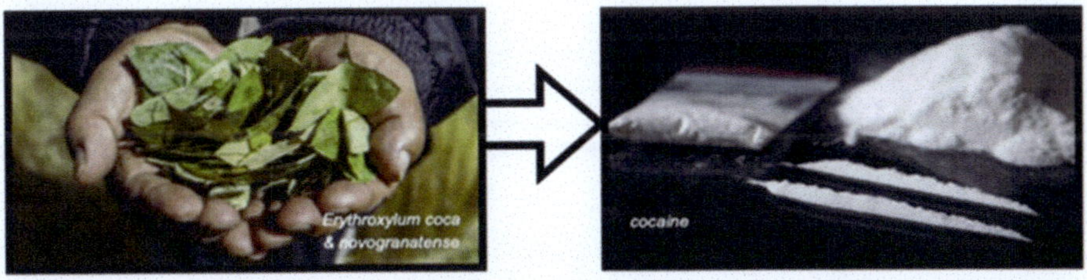

(a) (b)

Fig. 22.26 (**a**) Coca plant and (**b**) how it is used. (Reprinted from Decuyper et al. 2021 with permission from Elsevier)

intake of the drug intravenously. The insoluble and colorless form of cocaine is called crack or crack cocaine. The hydrochloride salt of cocaine has street names such as coke, coconut, devils' dandruff, flake, lady and so on. Crack is also called black rock, base, gravel, Scotty, twinkie, yam, window pane and so on (Fig. 22.26) (Boghdadi and Henning 1997).

Cocaine has been shown to affect the sympathetic nervous system, nerve conduction and the central nervous system. The drug inhibits the reuptake of catecholamines and leads to the accumulation of the same. Catecholamines get accumulated in the synaptic cleft thereby enhancing cell receptor stimulation. Cocaine has also been shown to produce local anaesthetic effects. This is achieved by blocking the sodium channels in the neurons. Various effects of cocaine include cardiac dysrhythmias, sudden cardiac death, and acute massive myocardial infarction. They have a direct effect on the neurotransmitters such as dopamine, norepinephrine, and serotonin. Cocaine also produces euphoria.

The major effects of cocaine other than the above-mentioned include antianxiety effects, seizures, haemorrhage, and excited delirium. Acute cocaine intake leads to acute ischemic stroke, subarachnoid haemorrhage, and intracranial haemorrhage. The gradual progress of cocaine toxicity produces bradycardia, dysrhythmias, and hypotension (Siegrist and Wiegand 2014).

22.4.2.7 Club Drugs

Club drugs can be defined as a pharmacologically heterogeneous group of psychoactive substances that are intended to be abused at bars, nightclubs, and parties by individuals. In cases of sexual assault, these drugs are usually found to be given to victims by adding these to their drinks as most of these drugs are tasteless, odourless, and colorless. Some of the frequently used club drugs along with their mechanism and effects are listed below (Table 22.6).

22.4.3 Analysis of Drugs in Forensic Laboratories

To meet the legal requirements, it is obligatory to follow systematic and organized procedures while analyzing a suspected drug. This proceeds from screening or

Table 22.6 Common club drugs

S. No.	Drugs	Nature	Mechanism	Effects	References
1.	3,4-Methylenedioxymethamphetamine (MDMA)	Stimulant (Causes hallucination)	To increased levels of serotonin, dopamine, and norepinephrine from presynaptic neurons and prevents their metabolism by inhibiting monoamine oxidase	Sense of well-being, increased social and physical activities, empathy, high blood pressure, panic attack, seizure	Gahlinger (2004)
2.	Gamma-Hydroxybutyrate (GHB)	CNS depressant	GHB is said to interact and bind to the GABA receptors and thus, they pharmacologically affect the central nervous system	Headache, nausea, dizziness, sedation, relaxation, euphoria, increased libido, disinhibition	Singh (2020)
3.	Flunitrazepam (Rophynol)	CNS depressant	A selective effect on GABA receptors which inhibits the neurotransmission in the brain and medial spinal	Unconsciousness, short-term memory loss, muscle relaxation, disinhibition, blackouts	Singh (2020)
4.	Ketamine	Hallucinogen	Produces a "dissociative anaesthesia" state, caused due to the inhibition of NDMAR (*N*-methyl-D-aspartate receptor) as ketamine act as an NDMAR agonist	Amnesia, increased blood pressure, mild respiratory depression, motor function impairment, euphoria	Sleigh et al. (2014), Zanos and Gould (2018)

Table 22.7 Preliminary and confirmatory tests for drugs

Drugs	Physical properties	Preliminary tests	Confirmatory tests
Opium	(a) Raw-sticky, brown, characteristic smell (b) Prepared-characteristic odour absent	Marquis Test, Mecke test, Frohde test, Microcrystalline test	Thin-layer chromatography (TLC), Gas chromatography (GC), High-performance liquid chromatography (HPLC), Gas chromatography-Mass spectrometry (GC-MS), Infrared spectrophotometry, Liquid chromatography-Mass spectrophotometry (LC-MS), Immunoassays, Electrophoresis
Marijuana	Greenish-grey mixture of the dried flowers of Cannabis Sativa	Dilli-Koppanyi test, Fast-Blue test Microcrystalline test	
LSD	Clear or white, odourless, water-soluble material	Van Urk test, Microcrystalline test	
Barbiturates	White, crystalline, odourless, bitter	Dilli-Koppanyi test, Zwikkwer's test	
Amphetamines	Colorless, volatile liquid, characteristic strong amine odour, acid, burning taste	Marquis test, Simon's reagent test, Libermann's test, Mandelin's test, Microcrystal test	
Cocaine	Solid, colorless to white crystals/ powder	Scott test, Microcrystal test	
MDMA	Colorless oil insoluble in water.	Marquis test, Chen test, Mandelin test, Mecke test, Frohde test	
GHB	Solid, viscid yellow mass, extremely soluble in water, alcohol and ether	Ferric hydroxamate test	
Rophynol	Solid, pale yellow needles or crystals, soluble in water		
Ketamine	White crystals	Modified Scott test	

Sources: Baker and Phillips (1983), Darsigny et al. (2018)

preliminary examinations towards more specific confirmatory tests. This is necessary because a forensic chemist receives the drugs in forms that may be submitted for its identification. For instance, it may be presented in the form of powder, tablets, mixtures, capsules, and traces in clothing, vehicles, syringes or any kind of smuggling concealments. The amount received for the suspected substances must also be handled cautiously, it may be sometimes in traces or also can be received in tons. Another key point includes the wide range of drugs present in the market that are prone to abuse. Thus, common sense plays a vital role in carrying out a forensic analysis of drugs. Table 22.7 shows a summarized preliminary and confirmatory test applicable for the identification of different drugs.

22.5 Alcohol as Physical Evidence

For ages, alcohol has been consumed in social settings and for recreational purposes. Drinking usually occurs in discos, bars and parties. Young adults living in such surroundings are influenced and this triggers them to consume alcohol also. Alcohol affects physiological behavior and is the reason for many road accidents. In addition, the death of the imbiber may also result if he has consumed large quantities of alcohol. The government regulates the maximum concentration of alcohol in a beverage but alcohol production in the clandestine laboratory is not a surprise where the method to assess concentration is the individual perspective of the operator. There may be a sufficient quantity of deadly methanol.

A great number of cases are received in Forensic Science Laboratories in which either an alcoholic beverage is submitted as a sample to determine its alcoholic content or biological matrices are submitted to determine alcohol and alcohol concentration in suspected cases of alcohol intoxication.

22.5.1 Chemistry of Alcohols

Chemically, alcohols are hydroxy derivatives of hydrocarbons that are formed by the replacement of hydrogen atom(s) by a hydroxyl group. According to the International Union of Pure and Applied Chemistry (IUPAC) system of nomenclature, alcohols are referred as *alkanols* where alkan- signifies hydrocarbon from which hydrogen atom has been replaced and -ol connotes the presence of hydroxyl group. However, the term alkanol is reserved for aliphatic alcohols due to the linkage of a hydroxyl group with an aliphatic hydrocarbon. If the hydrocarbon chain is aromatic, it will be aromatic alcohol (Rabinowitz and Vogel 2009). Compounds having –OH group are regarded as alcohols but every compound containing a hydroxyl group is not alcohol. For alcohols, carbon attached to a hydroxy group must satisfy its valency by hydrogen and/or carbon only. For example, in the case of acetic acid carbon attached to the hydroxy group satisfies its valency with oxygen, therefore, it is not considered as alcohol (Fig. 22.27).

Given the condition to be called as alcohol, the maximum number of hydroxyl groups that could replace hydrogen atoms from the carbon of hydrocarbon chain is three. Thus, alcohols could be monohydric, dihydric or trihydric. Further, on monohydric alcohols, hydroxyl group could be attached to primary (1^0), secondary (2^0) or

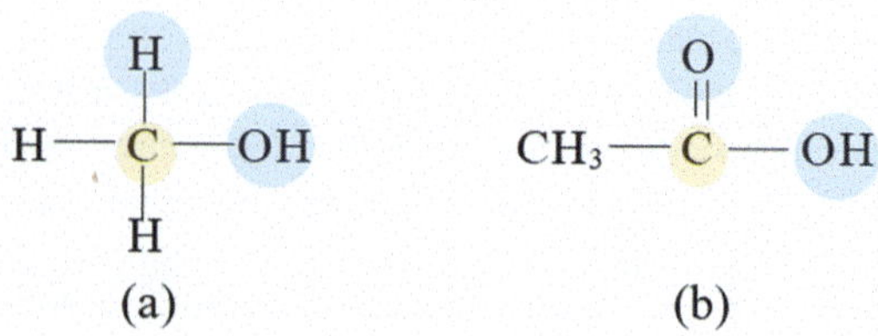

Fig. 22.27 Chemical structure of (**a**) Methyl Alcohol (**b**) Acetic Acid

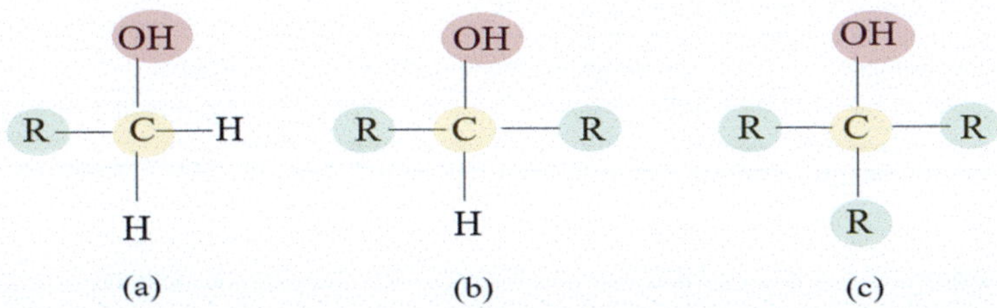

Fig. 22.28 General chemical structure of (**a**) Primary Alcohol (**b**) Secondary Alcohol and (**c**) Tertiary Alcohol where 'R' refers to alkyl group that may or may not be same

tertiary (3^0) carbon which is referred as primary, secondary and tertiary alcohol (Fig. 22.28).

In alcohols, the –OH group is hydrophilic while the hydrocarbon chain is hydrophobic in nature. This makes lower members of the alcohol family more water-soluble than higher ones because a hydrophobic character will increase with the increase in the chain length. In a similar way, boiling points of alcohols increase gradually with an increase in the carbon chain and decrease with branching. Therefore, it will follow the trend given as:

Methyl alcohol < Ethyl alcohol < Propyl alcohol . . . (Effect of carbon chain)
Primary alcohol > Secondary alcohol > tertiary alcohol (Effect of branching)

22.5.2 Alcoholic Beverages

Except for water, any liquid prepared for human consumption is a beverage (Day and McSweeney 2016). Diverse group of sources exist from which beverages can be prepared which in turn affects the color, taste, and nutritional value of the beverage. Consequently, beverages are classified in many ways i.e., alcoholic and non-alcoholic (Day and McSweeney 2016), natural and synthetic, carbonated and non-carbonated, hot and cold, stimulating and non-stimulating beverages.

In alcoholic beverages, ethyl alcohol is the main ingredient and have a concentration greater than 0.5% by volume. Sugar-containing raw materials like molasses, grapes and other fruit juices are subjected to processing. Processing results in simple sugars that are subjected to fermentation by yeast, *Saccharomyces cerevisiae* also called as baker's yeast (Walker 2009) *or* one of its close relatives, *S. uvarum* or *S. pastorianus*, producing alcohol (Belitz et al. 2009; Barth and Benvenuto 2015). This transformation is brought by the action of enzymes, invertase and zymase, present in yeast (Walker 2009). Besides alcohol, these contain large amounts of water, organic acids, coloring and flavoring materials.

Some fermented liquids after clarification were used as such i.e., without distillation and thus categorized as undistilled beverages. Beer, Cider, Wine, Claret dominates in this category. Wines made stronger by the addition of rectified alcohol are known as fortified wines/appetizer/Dessert wines (Kunkee 2002).

Table 22.8 Alcohol content of common undistilled beverages

Undistilled beverages	Percentage[a] of alcohol (v/v)	Source
Beer	4–7	Germinated barley (Malt)
Cider	4–8	Apple
Wine	8–17	Grape
Claret	7–13	Grape juice
Port and sherry	15–22	Grape juice

[a] Given percentage is not absolute, it may vary from brand to brand of beverage

Table 22.9 Alcohol content of common distilled beverages

Distilled beverages	Percentage[a] of alcohol (v/v)	Source
Whisky	40–50	Malt
Rum	35–54	Molasses
Gin	40–50	Maize
Vodka	40–50	Potatoes/cereal grains
Brandy	40–45	Grape juice

[a] Given percentage is not absolute, it may vary from brand to brand of beverage

Alcohol content of undistilled beverages is appended in Table 22.8 (Dasgupta 2019).

Much later, the distillation process was introduced in the beverage industry. Owing to the separation and purification of substances as the main function of distillation, it resulted in the production of beverages containing a higher percentage of alcohol (Belitz et al. 2009). Examples of distilled beverages with their alcohol content is appended in Table 22.9 (Jacobsen and McMartin 1996; Granados et al. 2016).

French people were the first to distillate the wine. They called it 'Eau-de-vie' which is obsolete now. Brandy derived its present name from French word 'brandevin' meaning 'burnt' wine (Wiley et al. 1910).

Alcoholic-free beverages, also called as non-alcoholic beverages, have alcoholic content of less than 0.5% by volume. By reverse osmosis or vacuum distillation alcohol is removed from normal alcoholic beverages (Belitz et al. 2009). Non-alcoholic drinks which may be carbonated or non-carbonated are also called as soft drinks (Rao and Ramalakshmi 2011). In India, Alcohol is state subject, meaning its sale and purchase will be regulated by the state government. Specific days notified by the government, to which the sale and purchase of alcohol are not permitted are called dry days (Reddy 2016).

22.5.3 Fate of Alcohol in the Body

Unlike food materials ingested orally requiring digestion, alcohol gets absorbed by the way of diffusion in the stomach following Fick's law. But, much of the absorption takes place in the proximal intestine. The type and quantity of alcoholic

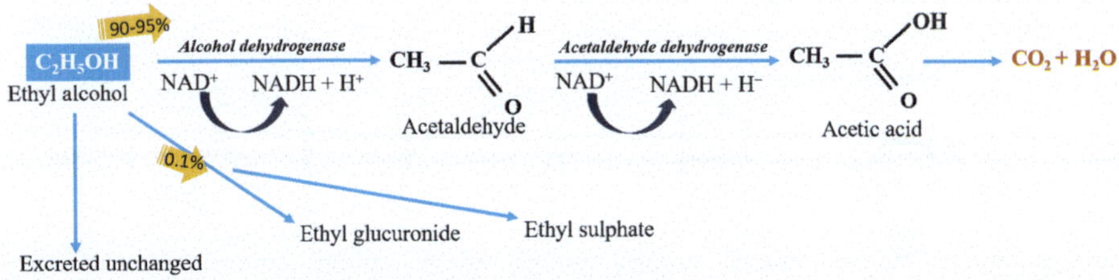

Fig. 22.29 Metabolism of alcohol in human body

beverage consumed, duration within which it is taken, food and type of food content present in the stomach or consumption of alcohol with food, imbiber's age and fitness, gene, all affects the process of absorption. So, it is not easy to answer how long the absorption process will be. But it influences the blood–alcohol peak concentration (BAC). The longer the absorption process, the lower will be blood-alcohol peak and vice versa (White and Emerson 2004).

Once absorbed, it is gradually distributed to the watery portion of the body given the water solubility of ethanol. Because of significant differences in the water present in the tissues of male and female's body, BAC will also be different to both sexes of the same weight and consuming an equal amount of alcohol. Consequently, BAC for the female is higher due to low water content in their body than males.

With the circulation of alcohol in the blood, the body also starts to eliminate it through its metabolism in the liver and excretion. But if the amount consumed is much high it bypasses the liver and gets distributed to the body. There are four enzymes viz, alcohol dehydrogenase (ADH), Cytochrome P450 (CYP2E1), catalase (active in chronic poisoning) and acetaldehyde dehydrogenase (ALDH) that takes part in metabolizing the alcohol into carbon dioxide and water through oxidation (Fig. 22.29) (Bell 2014; Dasgupta 2019). In the process, the linings of the liver are damaged by alcohol otherwise known as alcohol cirrhosis.

The remaining alcohol is excreted unchanged through sweat, breast milk, saliva, urine and breath (Saferstein 2013; Wigmore 2013; Bell 2014). Though much less amount of alcohol is excreted through urine, it is noted that alcohol increases urine output. This is because of the depression of the pituitary gland's production of vasopressin, an antidiuretic.

22.5.4 Field Test (Breath Analyzer)

In suspected drunk and driving cases, police often ask the driver to exhale their breath and assess whether the driver is under influence of alcohol over the legal limit. The basis of it is the excretion of alcohol with exhaled air. The ratio of alcohol in blood to alcohol in breath is approximately 2100:1 (Saferstein 2013).

An instrument by which alcohol is tested is called breath analyzer. Robert Brokenstein developed such breath analyzer in 1954. Breath analyzer draws a fixed volume of the driver's breath where it is subjected to the action of an acidic

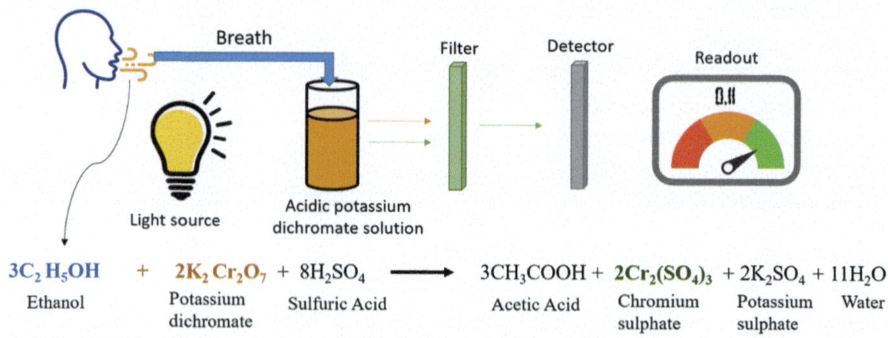

Fig. 22.30 Schematic representation of working of breath analyzer

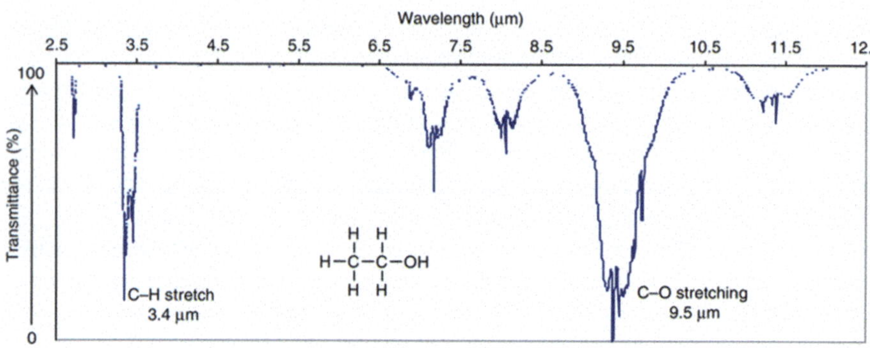

Fig. 22.31 Infrared absorption spectrum of ethyl alcohol. (Reprinted from Jones 2016 with permission from Elsevier)

potassium dichromate solution. If alcohol is present in the breath, it will be oxidized into acetic acid and orange-yellow dichromate will be reduced into green chromium sulphate (Fig. 22.30). The instrument is programmed and calibrated to give blood alcohol concentration by assessing the degree of color change (Wigmore 2013). In India, the legal limit of blood alcohol concentration is 0.3%.

However, instrumental design has gone several modifications. Currently, such devices are available whose basis is not redox reaction but are chemical-free and work on the principle of absorption of InfraRed radiation. Due to the presence of C-H stretching, C-O stretching and O-H stretching vibrations in ethanol, it shows its corresponding absorption peaks at 3.4 μm (2941 cm^{-1}), 9.5 μm (1055 cm^{-1}) and 2.95 μm (3391 cm^{-1}). Accordingly, optical filters are used in breath analyzer to detect ethanol in a breath sample (Fig. 22.31) (Jones 2016).

22.5.5 Laboratory Analysis

Blood and urine are frequently encountered biological matrices in suspected cases of alcohol intoxication although viscera may also be encountered. Analysis of alcohol from biological matrices requires its extraction from the matrix. Distillation is a widely used method to extract alcohol from the biological matrix because of the volatile nature of alcohol. The distillate is collected and further tests are applied.

22.5.5.1 Chemical Analysis

22.5.5.1.1 Preliminary Tests (Functional Group Test)

As alcohols contain hydroxyl groups, tests given in Table 22.10 (Duke and Smith 1940) are applied first to detect this group in a given sample. If a positive reaction is observed, further tests are carried out.

22.5.5.1.2 Test for Specific Alcohols

The following tests (Davy 1876; Schaeffer 1942; Gracia et al. 2016; Saadat and Rafizadeh 2019) are to be carried out for the detection of specific alcohol in the exhibits (Tables 22.11 and 22.12):

22.5.5.2 Determination of Alcohol Concentration

It is the quantity of alcohol consumed affecting the behavior of imbiber and depressing the brain to such an extent that death could also have resulted. To establish alcoholic influence in such cases, the concentration of alcohol must be

Table 22.10 Preliminary tests for alcohol

Test	Observation
Litmus paper test	No response
Ceric ammonium nitrate test	Color change from yellow to orange
Phosphorous pentachloride test	Solution becomes warm due to evolution of HCl

Table 22.11 Tests for ethanol

Test	Reagents	Observation	Remark
Iodoform test/ haloform test	10% solution of sodium hydroxide and iodine solution	Yellow precipitate which after some time forms crystals resembling six-pointed 'snow star'	Acetaldehyde, methyl ketones and isopropanol show a *positive color* reaction
Sulpho-molybdic acid test/oil of winter green test	Sulfuric acid and molybdic acid	Blue ring at the junction of liquids which renders whole mixture deep blue on shaking.	Very sensitive
Ethyl benzoate test	Benzyl chloride and 10% sodium hydroxide	Fruity smell	Methyl alcohol also shows a positive reaction

Table 22.12 Test for methanol

Test	Reagent	Observation
Schiff reagent test	Potassium permanganate, phosphoric acid, oxalic acid and Schiff reagent	Purple color
Chromotropic acid test	Potassium permanganate, Sulfuric acid, Sodium bisulfite and Chromotropic acid	Violet color

determined. Conventionally, the alcohol concentration is determined by *Kozelka and Hine Method (1941)*. It requires the steam distillation of blood or urine samples in presence of alkaline mercuric chloride. Mercuric chloride traps the ketones, aldehydes and other volatile acids. Following that potassium dichromate and sulfuric acid are added in distillate to oxidize the alcohol. It is then titrated iodometrically against sodium thiosulphate (Sunshine and Hodnett 1971; White and Emerson 2004).

Alternatively, concentration is determined by enzymatic oxidation which is more sensitive than chemical oxidation described above. Similar to metabolism taking place inside the body, in this method, alcohol is oxidized to acetaldehyde by exogenous ADH, often yeast-ADH, and co-enzyme nicotinamide adenine dinucleotide (NAD+). Alcohol reduces NAD+ to NADH which is assayed by spectrophotometer giving absorbance at 340 nm. Because NAD+ exhibits no absorption at 340 nm, absorbance due to NADH is directly correlated with alcohol concentration present in a sample (Walker 1992; Dasgupta and Wahed 2014). However, interference may arise in the case of postmortem blood samples due to the presence of LDH and lactate (Dasgupta and Wahed 2014).

22.5.5.3 Instrumental Analysis

Gas Chromatography (GC) is the widely used method to determine the alcohol and its concentration in a given matrix. The use of Head-space with GC (GC-HS) has simplified the procedure as there is no requirement for distillation to be carried out. In GC-HS, alcohol is vaporized and vapour is then injected into the GC column automatically. The resultant chromatogram is then assayed by peak area with standard *N*-propanol, and alcohol concentration is determined.

In the current scenario, GC is hyphenated with a mass spectrometer which gives a more definitive identification of unknown compounds (Stowell 2013). Besides, Liquid Chromatography (LC) and Spectroscopic analysis (namely UV-Visible Spectroscopy, NIR spectroscopy, ATR-FTIR) are also carried out to identify alcohol present in a sample (Gallignani et al. 1993; Cacho and Lopez 2005; Yadav and Sharma 2019).

22.5.6 Alcoholic Content and Its Determination in Alcoholic Beverage

Historically, alcoholic content was expressed as 'proof'. This term has its roots in the eighteenth century when rum was given to British sailors in addition to their wages. To ensure the concentration of alcohol in rum, rum was doused with gunpowder and ignited. Ignition with steady flame was 'proof' that it is not diluted with water while non-ignition was evidence for 'underproof' meaning rum is diluted with much amount of water. In a similar way, if the flame was too yellowish, it indicated the higher alcoholic content and was considered as 'overproof' (Dasgupta 2019; Wallace 2018). The minimum concentration of alcohol to ignite the mixture of gunpowder with alcohol is 57.06% by volume. In the USA, 'proof' is the twice concentration of alcohol by volume. So, 50% alcohol by volume is 100 proof while in the United Kingdom proof is 1.75 times the concentration of alcohol by volume (Dasgupta 2019).

Measurement of alcohol content in the beverage is a two-step process. The first step is the distillation and the second step involves the measurement of alcohol content through the density of the distillate. Pycnometer, electronic densitometer and densitometer based on hydrostatic balances are an example of instruments used to measure density (Cacho and Lopez 2005). Density measurement is affected by temperature, therefore, it should be taken into account in calculating the alcohol content of the beverage.

References

Agrawal JP (2010) High energy materials: propellants, explosives and pyrotechnics. Wiley-VCH, Weinheim

Akhavan J (2011) The chemistry of explosives. Royal Society of Chemistry, London. https://doi.org/10.1007/978-1-4612-0589-0_5

Almirall JR, Furton KG, Bruna JC (1995) A novel method for the analysis of gasoline from fire debris using headspace solid-phase microextraction. J Forens Sci 41(1):12–22

Almog J, Zitrin S (2009) Colorimetric detection of explosives. In: Aspects of explosives detection. Elsevier, Amsterdam, pp 41–58. https://doi.org/10.1016/B978-0-12-374533-0.00004-0

Baker PB, Phillips GF (1983) The forensic analysis of drugs of abuse. Analyst 108:777

Baquiran M, Khalilili A (2021) Lysergic acid diethylamide toxicity. StarPearls Publishing, Treasure Island, FL

Barth R, Benvenuto MA (2015) Ethanol and education: alcohol as a theme for teaching chemistry. American Chemical Society, Washington, DC. https://doi.org/10.1021/bk-2015-1189.ch001

Battle BP, Weston PB (1954) Arson: a handbook of detection and investigation. Arco Publishing Co, New York, NY

Belitz HD, Grosch W, Schieberle P (2009) Alcoholic beverages. In: Food chemistry. Springer, New York, NY, pp 892–937

Bell S (2014) Forensic chemistry. Pearson, London

Bennett GD (1958) The arson investigation and technical aids. J Crim Law Criminol Police Sci 49: 172–177

Bischoff M (1938) La police scientifique. Payot, Paris

Boghdadi MS, Henning RJ (1997) Cocaine: pathophysiology and clinical toxicology. Heart Lung J Acute Crit Care 26(6):466–483. https://doi.org/10.1016/S0147-9563(97)90040-6
Bumbrah GS, Sarin RK, Sharma RM (2016) Derivative ultraviolet spectrophotometry: a rapid, screening tool for the detection of petroleum products residues in fire debris samples. Malay J Forens Sci 7(1):17–26
Cacho JF, Lopez R (2005) Food and nutritional analysis: alcoholic beverages. In: Encyclopedia of analytical science. Elsevier, London, pp 285–291. https://doi.org/10.1016/B0-12-369397-7/00181-3
Cohen K, Weizman A, Weinstein A (2019) Positive and negative effects of cannabis and cannabinoids on health. Clin Pharmacol Ther 105(5):1139–1147. https://doi.org/10.1002/cpt.1381
Couper FJ (2016) Substance misuse. Encycl Forens Legal Med 4:418–421. https://doi.org/10.1016/B978-0-12-800034-2.00358-X
Daeid NN (2004) Fire investigation. CRC Press, Boca Raton, FL
Darsigny C, Leblanc-Couture M, Desgagne-Penix I (2018) Forensic chemistry of alkaloids: presumptive color test. Austin J Forens Sci Criminol 5(1):1–9
Dasgupta A (2019) Alcohol: pharmacokinetics, health benefits with moderate consumption and toxicity. In: Critical issues in alcohol and drugs of abuse testing, 2nd edn. Elsevier, London, pp 1–16. https://doi.org/10.1016/B978-0-12-815607-0.00001-0
Dasgupta A, Wahed A (2014) Testing for ethyl alcohol(alcohol) and other volatiles. In: Clinical chemistry, immunology and laboratory quality control. Elsevier, London, pp 317–335. https://doi.org/10.1016/B978-0-12-407821-5.00018-8
Davy EW (1876) On a new chemical test for alcohol. Proc Roy Irish Acad Sci 2:579–582. https://www.jstor.org/stable/20490026
Day L, McSweeney PLH (2016) Beverages. Reference module in food science. Elsevier, London, pp 1–5. https://doi.org/10.1016/b978-0-08-100596-5.03409-0
Decuyper II, Armentia A, Martín-Armentia B, Almuzara AC, Ebo DG, Brucker HA (2021) Adverse reactions to illicit drugs (marijuana, opioids, cocaine) and alcohol. J Allergy Clin Immunol Pract 9(8):3006–3014. https://doi.org/10.1016/j.jaip.2021.04.061
DeTata D (2018) Forensic sciences - arson residues. In: Encyclopedia of analytical science, 3rd edn. Elsevier Inc, London. https://doi.org/10.1016/B978-0-12-409547-2.14450-6
Duke FR, Smith GF (1940) Rapid qualitative test for alcoholic hydroxyl group: use of nitrato and perchlorato cerate anions as test reagents. Ind Eng Chem Anal Ed 12(4):201–203. https://doi.org/10.1021/ac50144a008
Fisher BAJ, Fisher DR (2012) Techniques of crime scene investigation, 8th edn. CRC Press, Boca Raton, FL
Fitzgerald KT, Bronstein AC, Newquist KL (2013) Marijuana poisoning. Top Compan Anim Med 28(1):8–12. https://doi.org/10.1053/j.tcam.2013.03.004
Fleckenstein AE, Volz TJ, Riddle EL, Gibb JW, Hanson GR (2007) New insights into the mechanism of action of amphetamines. Annu Rev Pharmacol Toxicol 47:681–698. https://doi.org/10.1146/annurev.pharmtox.47.120505.105140
Gahlinger P (2004) Club drugs: MDMA, gamma-hydroxybutyrate (GHB), Rohypnol, and ketamine. Am Fam Physician 69:2619–2626
Gallignani M, Garrigues S, De La Guardia M (1993) Direct determination of ethanol in all types of alcoholic beverages by near-infrared derivative spectrometry. Analyst 118(9):1167–1173. https://doi.org/10.1039/AN9931801167
Gracia JI, Dobado JA, Flores C, Gracia HM (2016) Functional group analysis. In: Experimental organic chemistry: laboratory manual. Academic Press, London. https://doi.org/10.1016/B978-0-12-803893-2.50006-1
Granados JJQ, Samaniego-Sánchez C, Blanca-Herrera RM (2016) Rhum-Ron-Rum: technology and tradition. In: Encyclopaedia of food and health. Elsevier, London, pp 618–627. https://doi.org/10.1016/B978-0-12-384947-2.00598-5

Green B, Kavanagh D, Young R (2003) Being stoned: a review of self-reported cannabis effects. Drug Alcohol Rev 22(4):453–460. https://doi.org/10.1080/09595230310001613976

Heal DJ, Smith SL, Gosden J, Nutt DJ (2013) Amphetamine, past and present – a pharmacological and clinical perspective. J Psychopharmacol 27(6):479–496

Heard BJ (2008) Handbook of firearms and ballistics, 2nd edn. Wiley Blackwell, London

Hine G (2004) Fire scene investigation. CRC Press, Boca Raton, FL. https://doi.org/10.1201/9780203492727.ch2

Ho IK, Harris RA (1981) Mechanism of action of barbiturates. Annu Rev Pharmacol Toxicol 21: 83–111

Holper RB (2012) The history, development, and characteristics of explosives and propellants. In: Forensic investigation of explosion, 2nd edn. Routledge, London, pp 1–18

Hwang KAJ, Saadabadi A (2021) Lysergic acid diethylamide (LSD). StarPearls Publishing, Treasure Land, FL. https://www.ncbi.nlm.nih.gov/books/NBK482407/?report=classis

Inman K, Rudin N (2001) Principles and practice of criminalistics: the profession of forensic science. CRC Press, Boca Raton, FL

Jacobsen D, McMartin KE (1996) Alcohols and glycols. In: Descotes J (ed) Human toxicology. Elsevier Science, London. https://doi.org/10.1016/j.mpmed.2015.12.001

Jaiswal YS, Williams LL (2016) A glimpse of Ayurveda – the forgotten history and principles of Indian traditional medicine. J Tradit Complement Med 7(1):50–53. https://doi.org/10.1016/j.jtcme.2016.02.002

Jones AW (2016) Alcohol: breath analysis. In: Encyclopedia of forensic and legal medicine, vol 1. Elsevier, London, pp 119–137. https://doi.org/10.1016/B978-0-12-800034-2.00011-2

Karch SB (1998) Drug abuse handbook. CRC Press, Boca Raton, FL

Kaur N, Byard RW (2020) Bride burning: a unique and ongoing form of gender-based violence. J Forensic Legal Med 75(126):102035. https://doi.org/10.1016/j.jflm.2020.102035

Khan JI, Kennedy TJ, Christian DR (2012) Basic principles of Forensic Chemistry. Humana Press, Totowa, NJ

Kumar D, Elias AJ (2019) The explosive chemistry of nitrogen: a fascinating journey from 9th century to the present. Resonance 24(11):1253–1271. https://doi.org/10.1007/s12045-019-0893-2

Kunkee RE (2002) Wine. Wiley-VCH, Weinheim. https://doi.org/10.1002/14356007.a28269

Lauren J (2013) Opium. Postgrad Med J 89:491–492. https://doi.org/10.1136/postgradmedj-2013-132218

Lentini JJ (2012) Analysis of fire debris. In: Forensic chemistry handbook, 1st edn. Wiley-VCH, Weinheim, pp 41–108

Lentini JJ (2013) Fire patterns and their interpretation. In: Encyclopedia of forensic sciences. Elsevier, London. https://doi.org/10.1016/B978-0-12-382165-2.00213-0

Lentini JJ (2018) Scientific protocols for fire investigation. In: Scientific protocols for fire investigation, 3rd edn. Taylor and Francis, New York, NY. https://doi.org/10.4324/9781315178097

Martin B, Szara S (1998) Marijuana. In: Clinical management of poisoning and drug overdose, 3rd edn. Elsevier, London, pp 528–541

Martinez MA, Ballesteros S (2019) Opium poisoning in modern times: an overview. Forensic Sci Int 302:109848. https://doi.org/10.1016/jforsciint.2019.06006

Matthew H (1975) Barbiturates. Clin Toxicol 8(5):495–513

Mohanty B (2012) Physics of explosion hazard. In: Forensic investigation of explosion, 2nd edn. Routledge, London, pp 19–52

Myren RA (1954) Investigation of arson and other unlawful burnings. Institute of Government, The University of North Carolina

NIH (2020) Opioids. National Institute of Diabetes and Digestive and Kidney Diseases, Bethesda, MD. https://www.ncbi.nlm.nih.gov/books/

Passie T, Halpern JH, Stichtenoth DO, Emrich HM, Hintzen A (2008) The pharmacology of lysergic acid diethylamide: a review. CNS Neurosci Ther 14(4):295–314. https://doi.org/10.1111/j.1755-5949.2008.00059.x

Rabinowitz H, Vogel S (2009) Style and usage for organic chemistry. In: The manual of scientific style. Elsevier, London, pp 399–425. https://doi.org/10.1016/b978-012373980-3.50014-9
Rao LJM, Ramalakshmi K (2011) Introduction to soft drinks, Recent trends in soft drinks. Woodhead Publishing, New Delhi. https://doi.org/10.1533/9780857093653.3.177
Reddy VR (2016) Neuropathy of drug addiction and substance misuse, 2nd edn. Academic Press, London
Reiss RA (1911) Manuel de police scientifique (technique) - I Vols et homicides. Librairie Payot and Cie, Paris
Rojas SF, Bosch Ojeda C (2008) Recent development in derivative ultraviolet/visible absorption spectrophotometry: 2004–2008: a review. Anal Chim Acta 635(1):22–44. https://doi.org/10.1016/j.aca.2008.12.039
Rudin N, Inman K (2002) Forensic science timeline. http://www.forensicdna.com.Tiemline020702.pdf
Saadat F, Rafizadeh A (2019) Rapid determination of methanol in herbaceous distillates for their safety evaluation by a new modified chromotropic acid method. Iran J Pharmaceut Res 18(2): 696–703. https://doi.org/10.22037/ijpr.2019.1100661
Sachs J, McGlade E, Yurgelun-Todd D (2015) Safety and toxicology of cannabinoids. Neurotherapeutics 12(4):735–746. https://doi.org/10.1007/s13311-015-0380-8
Sadler PJ (1950) The crime of arson. J Crim Law Criminol 41(3):290–305
Saferstein R (2013) Forensic science - from crime scene to the crime lab, 2nd edn. Pearson, London
Sampat AAS, Van Daelen B, Lopatka M, Mol H, Van Derweg G, Truyols GV, Sjerps M, Schoenmakers PJ, Asten ACV (2018) Detection and characterization of ignitable liquid residues in forensic fire debris samples by comprehensive two-dimensional gas chromatography. Separations 5(3):1–27. https://doi.org/10.3390/separations5030043
Schaeffer HF (1942) The iodoform reaction by methods of microscopy. J Chem Educ 19(1):15–16. https://doi.org/10.1021/ed019p15
Siegel J, Knupfer G, Saukko P (2013a) Drugs of abuse. In: Encyclopedia of forensic science, 2nd edn. Academic Press, London, pp 598–626
Siegel J, Saukko PJ, Houck MM (2013b) Encyclopedia of forensic sciences, 2nd edn. Academic Press, London, pp 579–585
Siegrist M, Wiegand TJ (2014) Cocaine. Encyclopedia of toxicology, vol 1, 3rd edn. Academic Press, London, pp 999–1002. https://doi.org/10.1016/B978-0-12-386454-3.00715-6
Singh GPS (2020) Date rape drugs in sexual assault: a threat to Indian society. Eur J Mol Clin Med 7:4677
Sleigh J, Harvey M, Voss L, Denny B (2014) Ketamine - more mechanisms of action than just NMDA blockade. Trends Anaesth Crit Care 4(2–3):76–81. https://doi.org/10.1016/j.tacc.2014.03.002
Smith FP (2005) Forensic drug analysis. Academic Press, London
Stauffer E, Dolan JA, Newman R (2008) Fire debris analysis. Academic Press, London
Stowell A (2013) Blood-alcohol. In: Encyclopedia of forensic sciences, 2nd edn. Academic Press, London. https://doi.org/10.1016/B978-0-12-382165-2.00294-4
Stuart B (2013) Forensic analytical techniques. John Wiley and Sons, New York, NY
Sturaro A, Vianello A, Denti P, Rella R (2013) Fire debris analysis and scene reconstruction. Sci Justice 53:201–205. https://doi.org/10.1016/j.scijus.2012.08.002
Sunshine I, Hodnett N (1971) Methods for the determination of ethanol and acetaldehyde. The biology of alcoholism. Springer, New York, NY, pp 545–573. https://doi.org/10.1007/978-1-4615-6525-3_16
Tamiri T, Zitrin S (2013) Explosives: analysis. In: Encyclopaedia of forensic sciences, 2nd edn. Academic Press, London. https://doi.org/10.1016/B978-0-12-382165-2.00083-0
Thatcher PJ (2000) Chemistry of fire. In: Encyclopedia of forensic sciences, vol 1. Academic Press, London, pp 900–905
Turner RF (1949) Forensic science and laboratory technics. Charles C. Thomas, Springfield, IL

UNODC (2021) Pandemic effect ramp up drug risks, as youth underestimate cannabis dangers. World drug Report. UNODC, Vienna. https://wdr.unodc.org/

Vermette JY (2012) General protocols at the scene of an explosion. In: Forensic investigation of explosions, 2nd edn. Routledge, London, pp 80–95

Walker JRL (1992) Spectrophotometric determination of enzyme activity: alcohol dehydrogenase (ADH). Biochem Educ 20:42

Walker GM (2009) Yeasts. In: Encyclopedia of microbiology. Academic Press, London. https://doi.org/10.1016/B978-012373944-5.00335-7

Wallace JS (2018) Chemical analysis of firearms, ammunition, and Gunshot residue. CRC Press, Boca Raton, FL

White P, Emerson V (2004) Alcohol. In: From crime scene to court: the essential of forensic science, 2nd edn. RSC, London, pp 350–376. https://doi.org/10.1039/9781847550651-00350

Wigmore JG (2013) Breath alcohol. In: Encyclopedia of forensic sciences, 2nd edn. Academic Press, London, pp 313–317. https://doi.org/10.1016/B978-0-12-382165-2.00296-8

Wiley HW, Tolman LM, Bryan AH (1910) Manufacture of denatured alcohol. U.S. Govt. Printing Office, Washington, DC

Yadav PK, Sharma RM (2019) Classification of illicit liquors based on their geographic origin using Attenuated total reflectance (ATR) – Fourier transform infrared (FT-IR) spectroscopy and chemometrics. Forensic Sci Int 295:e1–e5. https://doi.org/10.1016/j.forsciint.2018.12.017

Yadav VK, Nigam K, Srivastava A (2020) Forensic investigation of arson residue by infrared and Raman spectroscopy: from conventional to non-destructive techniques. Med Sci Law 60(3): 206–215. https://doi.org/10.1177/0025802420914807

Zanos P, Gould TD (2018) Mechanisms of ketamine action as an antidepressant. Mol Psychiatry 23(4):801–811. https://doi.org/10.1038/mp.2017.255

Forensic Toxicology: An Overview

23

Neeti Kapoor, Ashish Badiye, Poonam Moon, and Ritesh K. Shukla

Abstract

Forensic Toxicology is a branch of Forensic Science that involves the application of various scientific principles, methods and techniques to aid in the clinical or legal investigation of death, poisoning, and drug abuse. The chapter provides a concise yet comprehensive overview of the field, focusing on the analysis and investigation of toxic substances in forensic contexts. It covers various aspects, including the classification of poisons based on their origin, mode of action, and medicolegal classification. The chapter explores the forms of poison, their sites of action, and factors influencing their effects. It delves into the detection and analysis of illicit drugs, alcohol, and frequently encountered poisons, highlighting the importance of analytical techniques in forensic toxicology laboratories. The collection and preservation of toxicological evidence are also discussed, ensuring proper procedures are followed for accurate results. Moreover, the chapter provides insights into alcohol intoxication stages, offering an understanding of the physiological and behavioral effects of alcohol consumption. It emphasizes the significance of identifying and quantifying toxic substances in various biological and non-biological samples to support evidence-based conclusions in forensic investigations. Overall, this chapter serves as a concise introduction to

N. Kapoor · A. Badiye
Department of Forensic Science, Government Institute of Forensic Science, Nagpur, Maharashtra, India

P. Moon
Karunya Institute of Technology and Sciences, Coimbatore, Tamil Nadu, India
e-mail: poonamanil@karunya.edu.in

R. K. Shukla (✉)
Biological and Life Sciences, School of Arts and Sciences, Ahmedabad University, Ahmedabad, Gujarat, India
e-mail: ritesh.shukla@ahduni.edu.in

P. Shrivastava et al. (eds.), *Textbook of Forensic Science*,
https://doi.org/10.1007/978-981-99-1377-0_23

the field of forensic toxicology, covering essential topics and methodologies necessary for the analysis, detection, and interpretation of toxic substances in forensic science.

Keywords

Poison · Drugs · Analytical techniques · Alcohol

23.1 Introduction

Toxicology is a diversified branch of science that can be defined in different ways. Toxicology originated from Greek words: "*Toxikon*" and "*logos*". Toxikon means "*poison in which arrow heads dipped*", and *logos* means "*study*". It is the branch of science that studies poisonous substances. "*Toxicology is a branch of science that deals with the adverse effects of chemicals/xenobiotics on living organisms and assesses the probability of their occurrence*" (Vij 2011; Anuj and Krishna 2017). "*Toxicology is the study of poisons, or, more comprehensively, the identification and quantification of adverse outcomes associated with exposures to physical agents, chemical substances and other conditions*".

Toxicology is a multidisciplinary field that expanded into different dimensions, namely the social, moral and legal aspects of exposure of xenobiotics to exposure to living organisms with unknown or uncertain hazards. Thus, toxicology is defined as "*a multidisciplinary science field encompassing the basic sciences (Physical, Chemical or Biological Sciences), medical disciplines, epidemiology and other allied branches of science for information, research designs and methods*".

It is well known that Xenobiotics is derived from Greek, meaning "***foreign substance taken into the body***". These Xenobiotics may produce beneficial effects *(such as pharmaceuticals) or* toxic *(such as Psychotropic drugs).* Thus, Toxicology can also be defined as

> *Toxicology is the study of the mode of action and mechanism by which xenobiotics produce an adverse effect in the living system. It deals with properties, actions, toxicity, fatal dose, detection estimation of, interpretation of the result of toxicological analysis and treatment of poison.*

23.2 A Brief Historical Perspective

Toxicology has undergone significant transformation from a practical approach employed by early human civilizations to a scientific discipline over the course of the past two centuries. In ancient times, cave dwellers relied on their observations to recognize poisonous plants and animals, utilizing their extracts for hunting, warfare, or even acts of murder and assassination. The Ebers Papyrus, a medical document prepared around 1550 BCE in Egypt, contained valuable references and formulas for the poisons used during that era. This historical record is currently preserved in the archives of the University of Leipzig in Germany.During the first century CE, Dioscorides, a Greek physician, made notable contributions to toxicology by classifying poisons into categories of plants, animals, and minerals. He also recognized the therapeutic value of emetics, substances that induce vomiting to counteract poisoning. In the twelfth century, Maimonides further advanced the knowledge of poisons by documenting their effects and proposing antidotes for treatment.However, the most significant advancements in toxicology came during the sixteenth century when Philippus Aureolus Theophrastus Bombastus von Hohenheim, commonly known as Paracelsus, introduced the concept of "similia similibus curantur" or "like cures like." Paracelsus proposed that substances with similar properties could be employed to counteract the effects of poisonous substances, but emphasized the crucial role of dosage in achieving the desired outcome. The famous phrase describes this concept of Paracelsus, "**All substances are poisons; there is none that is not a poison. The right dose differentiates a poison from a remedy**". This concept made a significant change in the field of Toxicology; hence, Paracelsus is acknowledged as the Father of Toxicology. In the nineteenth century, Mathieu Joseph Bonaventure Orfila, a Spanish toxicologist, chemist and physician, first elucidated the correlation between chemicals/ poisons and their mechanism of action in the biological system. He was the scientist who established Toxicology as a distinct scientific discipline and wrote the first book on General Toxicology. Thus, he is considered as Father of Modern Toxicology. In addition, Orfila was the first toxicologist to systematically utilize autopsy material and chemical analysis as legal evidence in case of poisoning. This contribution of Orfila serves as the basis of forensic toxicology. After this, in the twentieth century, Toxicology became more focused on the detection of poisons (screening and confirmatory tests) and treatment of poisoning (development of antidote) than the use of poisons (Vij 2011; Klaassen 2008, 2013).

23.3 Working Mechanism and the Subsequent Effect of Xenobiotics/Toxicants

Toxicokinetics and toxicodynamics are the two major areas on which the entire toxicological analysis is based. Toxicokinetics can be defined as the fate of toxicants/ xenobiotics inside the body. Toxicodynamic can be defined as what happens to the body/organs/tissues once toxicants/xenobiotics interact with them at the effective dose.

Toxicokinetics

Toxicokinetics can be described as how toxicants are administered into the body, moved and distributed inside the body and eventually eliminated from the body. The 'Half-life' of the toxicants plays a vital role in toxicokinetic, which means the time taken by toxicants to excrete ½ part of it from the body. Toxicokinetics depends on different factors, including gender, age, health, drug addiction, exercise, environmental conditions, etc.

Toxicodynamics

Toxicodynamics can be described as how a body responds (toxic effect)/internal organs get affected after exposure to toxicants. Toxicodynamics depends on the concept of the molecular target. According to this concept, toxicants can interact with the cellular system directly via covalent and non-covalent bonding or indirectly by electron transfer and enzymatic reaction. As a result, the target molecule is either destroyed or inactivated.

23.4 Forensic Toxicology

Forensic toxicology is a branch of forensic science that focuses on the analysis of drugs, chemicals, and other toxic substances in biological samples to determine their presence, concentration, and potential role in causing injury or death. It involves the application of scientific techniques and methodologies to identify and quantify toxic substances, such as drugs, alcohol, poisons, and environmental contaminants, in various biological specimens including blood, urine, hair, and tissues. Forensic toxicologists work closely with forensic pathologists, law enforcement agencies, and legal professionals to provide objective and scientifically sound evidence regarding the toxicological aspects of criminal investigations, post-mortem examinations, and cases involving substance abuse, impaired driving, workplace accidents, and other incidents where toxic substances may be involved. There are three main objectives to be kept in mind while investigating the death, poisoning, and/or drug abuse cases which play a crucial role in making the right decision to solve the mystery of these cases.

These objectives are to

- Establish the presence of toxicant and, if present, check whether or not it is capable of contributing to death.
- Establish the presence of toxicant and, if present, check whether or not it is capable of causing behavioural changes.
- Establish the presence of toxicant and, if present, check whether or not it represents legitimate use/exposure.

Besides medicolegal cases, Forensic Toxicology can also be applied to establish the presence of drugs used to enhance human performance in sports as "doping". In addition, Forensic toxicology can also be used for toxico-vigilance, which is a part of Preventive Forensics, where hazardous materials are monitored and assessed. This study can help prevent the nearby population from the potential risk that may be caused by the release/deposit of hazardous materials in the vicinity.

23.5 Poisons

The term "Poison" is derived from the Latin word "*Potion*", which means a drink, potion or poisonous draught. The most astute concept of poison was given by famous Scientist Philippus Theophrastus Aureolus Bombastus von Hohenheim, (1493–1541), who is more popular with the name of Paracelsus. He says, "*What is there that is not a poison? All things are poison and nothing without poison. Solely the dose determines that a thing is not a poison.*" (Deichmann et al. 1986). In a more simplified way, Paracelsus' definition of poison can be elucidated as "*All substances are poison; there is none which is not a poison. The right dose differentiates poison from remedy.*"

Some more definitions of poison have been cited in the literature, which is given ahead: "*Any substance, either taken internally or applied externally, that is injurious to health or dangerous to life.*" (Stedman's Medical Dictionary, 27th ed., 2000, p. 1416). "*Any substance that, when relatively small amounts are injected, inhaled, or absorbed, or applied to, injected into, or developed within the body, has chemical action that causes damage to structure or disturbance of function, producing symptoms, illness, or death.*" (Dorland' Illustrated Medical Dictionary, 29th ed., 2000, p. 1422).

In other words, poison can also be defined as "*a substance (solid, liquid or gases) which if introduced in the living body, or brought into contact with any part thereof, will produce ill health or death, by its constitutional or local effect or both*". A substance that is capable of causing the illness or death of a living organism when introduced or absorbed. There is a very fine difference between poisonous substances and medicines. According to famous British toxicologist Alfred Swaine Taylor "*A poison in a small dose is a medicine, and a medicine in a large dose is a poison.*" (Taylor 1859, p. 2). According to the law, *a therapeutic drug can be differentiated from a poisonous substance based on the intention with which it is given to an individual* (Trestrail 2007a, b).

Poison and Toxin

The terms "poison" and "toxin" are often used interchangeably, but there are subtle differences in their meanings. The term "poison" generally refers to any substance that can cause harm, illness, or death when it enters the body. Poisons can be natural or synthetic and can have a wide range of toxic effects. Poisons can be ingested, inhaled, injected, or absorbed through the skin. The term "poison" is often used in the context of intentional harm, such as poisoning someone intending to cause harm or death. A "toxin" specifically refers to a harmful substance produced by a living organism, such as bacteria, fungi, plants, or animals. Toxins are typically produced as defense mechanisms or for capturing prey. They can be found in various forms, including proteins, peptides, or small molecules. Toxins can cause a wide range of toxic effects in the body, including damage to cells, tissues, or organs. In summary, while all toxins can be considered poisons, not all poisons are toxins. Toxins are a specific type of poison that is derived from living organisms. Poison is a broader term encompassing both natural and synthetic substances with harmful effects on the body.

23.6 Classification of Poison

Poisons can be classified based on their origin, mode of action, medicolegal aspects, nature (form) of the poisons and site of action (Fig. 23.1).

23.6.1 Based on Origin

According to the origin, poisons are of Plant, Animal, Microbial or Synthetic origin.

1. Plant Poison—When a poisonous substance is extracted from plants. E.g., Belladonna from *Atropa belladonna*, Hyoscyamine alkaloids from *Datura stramonium*
2. Animal Poison—This type of poison is generally transferred through the bites and stings of terrestrial or marine animals. E.g., Venoms of snakes, scorpions, spiders
3. Microbial Poison—This type of poison is obtained from a microorganism. E.g., Botulinus toxin from *Clostridium botulinum*
4. Synthetic Poison—This type of poison is synthesized in the laboratory. E.g., Illicit drugs, Pesticides, hydrocarbons

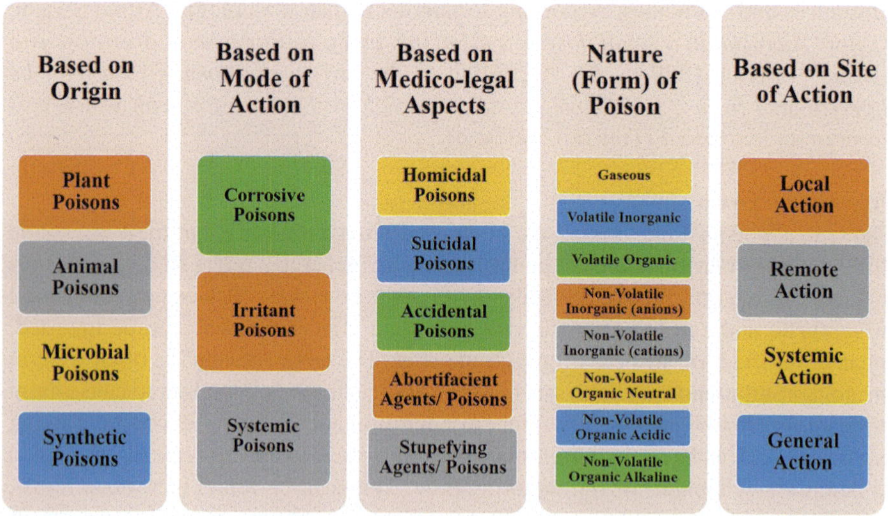

Fig. 23.1 Classification of Poisons

23.6.2 Based on the Mode of Action

Based on the mode of action, poison can be sub-classified into corrosive, irritant and systemic poisons.

23.6.2.1 Corrosive Poisons

The substances that act instantly on the surface with which they come in direct contact and consequently burn, destroy or erode the contacted surface are known as corrosive poisons. Strong acids and strong bases are the best examples of corrosive poisons. Typically, when the corrosive poison comes in contact with skin, they hydrolyze the fats, proteins and other biological contents by breaking down their hydrogen bonds. The poison of this category is comprised of Strong Acid (H_2SO_4, HNO_3, HCl), Strong Base (KOH, $Al_2(OH)_3$), Organic acid (Oxalic acid, Acetic Acid), and Metallic ($HgCl_2$).

23.6.2.2 Irritant Poisons

Corrosive poisons in diluted form act as irritant poisons. These poisons cause pain, irritation and inflammation in the area to which it was applied to. In postmortem appearance, irritant poisons show redness or ulcer in the GI tract, which unaided eyes can generally see. This category is further divided into Inorganic, Organic and Mechanical poisons.

- Inorganic poisons consist of metallic (Ar, Sn, Hg, Pb, Cu, Th, Zn, Mn, Ba etc) and non-metallic (Cl, P, Br, I etc.) poisons.
- Organic poisons are comprised of animal (snakes, insects, spiders) and plant (Poppy, Datura, war gases) poisons.
- Mechanical poisons include powdered glass, needles, chopped hairs, diamond dust etc.

23.6.2.3 Systemic Poisons

Systemic poisons directly affect the human body's target organs (physiological system). This class of poisons are further sub-divided into Neurotics, Cardiac and Asphyxiant poisons.

1. Neurotic Poison—The brain, nerves and spinal cord are the targeted organs by this group of poisons. This group of poison directly affect the nervous system. This group comprises Cerebral, Spinal and Peripheral poisons. Cerebral poisons are further divided into Narcotic (Opium), inebriant (Alcohol, anaesthetics) and deliriant (Datura, Cannabis). Spinal poison includes stimulants (nux vomica, Strychnine) and depressants (Gelsemium), while Peripheral poison includes curare and conium.
2. Cardiac poison—This class of poison directly affects the heart of the body. Digitalis, oleander, aconite, and nicotine are some examples of cardiac poison.

3. Asphyxiant poison—This class of poisons affects—the body's respiratory system. Carbon monoxide, sewer, and war gases are a few examples of asphyxiants.
4. Miscellaneous poisons—Besides all the poisons not classified in the group mentioned above of systemic poisons, they are categorized into miscellaneous poisons. E.g., Tranquilizers, Antidepressants, Antipyretics, Stimulants, Hallucinogens, street and designer drugs.

23.6.3 Based on Medico-Legal Aspects

1. Homicidal Poisons—These are the substances intentionally used to case harm or death to another person. These toxic agents are employed with the intent to commit murder or facilitate another criminal act; hence, are known as homicidal poisons. E.g., Aconite, *Abrus precatorius*, Arsenic, Strychnine, Antimony, etc.
2. Suicidal Poisons—Suicidal poisons refer to substances that individuals intentionally ingest or administer with the intent to cause harm to themselves, leading to self-inflicted injury or death. These toxic substances are used as a means of committing suicide, often driven by various underlying factors such as mental health issues, emotional distress, or personal circumstances. E.g., opium, barbiturate, KCN, Organophosphate, household chemicals, pesticides, household medications, etc.
3. Accidental Poisons—Accidental poisons are substances that are unintentionally ingested, inhaled, or absorbed by individuals, resulting in harmful effects or toxicity. These incidents typically occur due to accidental exposure or mishandling of toxic substances, often in the home, workplace, or environment. Accidental poisonings can affect people of all ages, but children are particularly vulnerable due to their curiosity and limited understanding of potential dangers. E.g., Copper Sulphate, insecticides, etc.
4. Abortifacient Agents/Poisons—Abortifacient agents or poisons refer to substances or medications that are used with the intent to induce abortion, the termination of a pregnancy. These agents are employed to cause the expulsion of the developing fetus from the uterus before it reaches full term. Abortifacients can be of various types, including pharmaceutical drugs, herbal remedies, or other chemical substances. E.g., Cantharides, Quinine (alkaloid), Calotropis, Croton, Oleander, Marking nut etc.
5. Stupefying Agents/Poisons—Stupefying agents or poisons are substances that are used to induce a state of stupor or unconsciousness in individuals. These agents affect the central nervous system, causing sedation, drowsiness, and loss of consciousness. Stupefying agents can be administered with the intent to incapacitate or immobilize someone for various purposes, including criminal activities. E.g., Dhatura, Chloral hydrate, diazepam, lorazepam, gamma-hydroxybutyric acid (GHB), Rohypnol (flunitrazepam), Cannabis etc.

23.6.4 Based on Nature (Form) of Poison

1. Gaseous Poisons: These groups of substances are gaseous. E.g., CO, CO_2, H_2S, SO_2, Cl_2, NO, tear gas, etc.
2. Volatile Inorganic Poisons: These are inorganic chemicals that usually spread slowly and intoxication occurs when a person is exposed to these chemicals for a long time. E.g., CN, PH_3, AsH_3, $COCl_2$, Cl_2, etc.
3. Volatile Organic Poisons: These organic chemicals generally spread rapidly, with high vapour pressure and a low boiling point at ordinary room temperature. Hence, a more significant number of molecules rapidly enter the surrounding air, and intoxication occurs if a person is exposed to these chemicals for even a short time. E.g., C_2H_5OH (ethanol), CH_3OH (methanol), HCHO (formaldehyde), CH_3CHO (acetaldehyde) etc.
4. Non-Volatile Inorganic (anions) Poisons: E.g., halides, hypochlorite, dichromate, chlorates, azides, nitrate, sulphate, phosphide, cyanide, etc.
5. Non-Volatile Inorganic (cations) Poisons: E.g., Hg, As, Ba, Th, Pb, Sb, Bi etc.
6. Non-Volatile Organic Neutral Poisons: E.g., Pesticide (Organophosphates, Organochlorates, Carbamates, Pyrethroids).
7. Non-Volatile Organic Acidic Compound: These compounds are acidic. These compounds readily react with alkali to form salts. E.g., Barbiturates, Phenolic compounds (Phenol, Cresols etc.), Salicylates, etc.
8. Non-Volatile Organic Alkaline Compounds: These compounds are alkaline in nature. E.g. Alkaloids, Benzodiazepine.

23.6.5 Based on Site of Action

Poison can also be classified based on the action of the poison. It includes local, remote, systemic and general.

1. Local— These substances cause adverse effects at the site or part of the body where they come into direct contact. Examples include corrosive substances that can damage tissues upon contact or irritant poisons that cause irritation and inflammation locally.
2. Remote—These substances produce adverse effects in specific or non-specific regions of the body that are not necessarily the direct site of contact. For example, substances like opium may have an effect on the cerebral cortex, while strychnine stimulates the spinal cord.
3. Systemic—These substances not only produce adverse effects at the site of contact but also affect specific sites or systems in the body. E.g., Carbolic acid, Oxalic acid, Phosphorus etc.
4. General—These substances have adverse effects that extend beyond a specific system or site of the body. These substances can affect multiple systems or the entire body. E.g., As, Hg, DDT etc. (Vij 2011; Biswas 2012).

23.7 Antidote (Treatment of Poison)

The term "Antidote" is derived from the Greek word "Antididonai" which means "given against". Antidotes are natural or synthesized substances that counteract poisons/toxicants. Antidotes usually act by altering the poison's chemical nature or function. In either case, the main aim of the antidote is to interfere with the poison to reduce its adverse effect. Antidotes can be derived from natural sources, such as certain plant extracts or animal products, or they can be synthesized in the laboratory. They work by various mechanisms, such as chemically binding to the poison to neutralize its toxicity, enhancing its elimination from the body, or blocking its interaction with target receptors or enzymes.

Although there is no widely accepted definition of the antidote, according to the Macquarie Dictionary, an antidote is "*a medicine or other remedy for counteracting the effects of poison, disease, etc.*,". The Oxford Dictionary defines the antidote explicitly as "A medicine taken or given to counteract a particular poison." This definition broadly covered all therapeutic/medicinal agents used to treat poison. According to WHO, "Antidote was defined as a therapeutic substance used to counteract the toxic action(s) of a specified xenobiotic."

An antidote can act on poison in various ways. It includes:

- Limited absorption: Antidotes can work by reducing the absorption of the poison from the site of exposure, thereby limiting its entry into the bloodstream and reducing its distribution throughout the body.
- The poison sequestering: Some antidotes can bind to the poison and form complexes that are less toxic or inactive. This sequestering action helps to prevent the poison from exerting its harmful effects.
- Metabolic inhibition of toxic metabolite: In certain cases, the toxic effects of a poison result from the formation of metabolites that are more toxic than the original substance. Antidotes can inhibit the metabolic pathways responsible for the formation of these toxic metabolites, thereby reducing their production and subsequent harm.
- Enhancing distribution from tissues: Antidotes can facilitate the movement of the poison out of target tissues and organs, promoting its elimination from the body.
- Receptor Antagonism (Poison substitution or competition for the receptor): Antidotes can compete with the poison for binding to specific receptors, thereby blocking the toxic effects caused by the poison's interaction with those receptors. This is sometimes referred to as "poison substitution" or "competition for the receptor."
- Altering the functions of the poison: Certain antidotes can directly modify the chemical properties or functions of the poison, rendering it less toxic or inert.
- Enhancing detoxification

The following are essential facts about antidotes that should always be kept in mind:

1. Antidote helps in supportive therapy and enhances the chances of survival, but an antidote alone cannot be used for supportive and symptomatic treatment.
2. Antidotes have been developed for some specific poisons, those with a specifically high mortality rate. But it doesn't mean those for which no antidote has been developed are less poisonous in nature.
3. Many Antidotes themselves have toxic properties and hence may elicit toxicity if either poison is misdiagnosed or given for a long time.

23.7.1 Classification of Antidote

Antidotes are classified into four classes.

23.7.1.1 Physical or Mechanical Antidote

The substances that interfere with poison and inhibit the action of poison without neutralizing it through physical properties (mechanically) are known as physical antidotes. These antidotes can work via three mechanisms.

1. **Adsorbent:** In this mechanism, the antidote adsorbs the poison on its surface by forming a film around the surface of the poison. E.g., Activated Charcoal.
2. **Demulcents:** In this mechanism, the antidote forms a preventive layer on the mucous membrane of the stomach. E.g., Egg albumin, starch, milk, barley.
3. **Diluents:** In this mechanism, the antidote delays the absorption of poison by diluting it. E.g., 10% alcohol or glycine, water, milk.

23.7.1.2 Chemical Antidote

The substance that inactivates or neutralizes the poison by undergoing chemical interaction with them is known as the chemical antidote. These antidotes work via two mechanisms.

Complex Formation

In this mechanism, the antidote is combined with toxicants and forms a complex that cannot cross the membrane or interact with receptors.

DMSA, a sulfhydryl compound, works as the antidote for Arsenic and lead poison by binding with the metal.

EDTA act as a metal chelator that combines metal and water-soluble complex. This complex can be eliminated efficiently from the body.

Metabolic Conversion

In this mechanism, the antidote interacts with the toxicant and converts it into a less toxic product.

For example, Nitrite interacts with haemoglobin and cyanide to form cyanomethaemoglobin, which is less toxic than cyanide and interferes with the cyanide access to the cytochrome oxidase system.

23.7.1.3 Physiological Antidote

The substances producing a countereffect on toxicants are known as physiological antidotes. They act by producing the opposite effect to that of poison. E.g., Atropine in organophosphate poisoning.

23.7.1.4 Universal Antidote

In the context of toxicology and medicine, the concept of a universal antidote is often discussed as an ideal solution that could be used to quickly neutralize the harmful effects of various substances, regardless of their chemical properties or mechanisms of action. However, in reality, the development of a true universal antidote is extremely challenging due to the diverse and complex nature of toxins and drugs. Different toxins and substances affect the body in different ways, targeting various organs and systems. Moreover, the mechanisms by which toxins exert their effects can vary widely, making it difficult to design a single treatment that can counteract them all effectively. Generally, this is a combination of physical and chemical antidotes used against unknown poison. E.g., Activated charcoal: 2 parts; Magnesium oxide: 1 part, Tannic acid: 1 part, British Anti-Lewisite (BAL) more commonly referred to as "dimercaprol".

23.8 Factors Affecting the Action of the Poison

Many factors can affect the action of the poison. Some of those factors are as follows:

23.8.1 Factors Pertaining to Poison

Quantity

A large quantity of the substance does not always cause poisoning. Sometimes, the body responds to many substances in the form of vomiting or frequent excretion, which may reduce the intensity of the poisoning.

Form of Poison

Poisons are found in three forms: physical, chemical and dilution or mechanical combination.

Physical State

Poisons are found in three different states of substance: solid, liquid and gas. Among three of these states, the gaseous state of poisons spreads faster than liquid, while poisonous liquids are absorbed faster than the poisons in solid-state.

The gaseous state of poison > liquid state of poison > solid-state of poison.

Chemical Combination

Some substances are non-poisonous in their pure form, but when combined with other substances, they turn into poisonous compounds. E.g., Metals like Hg and As are non-poisonous in their elemental form but, when associated with halides and oxide, turn into poisonous compounds such as $HgCl_2$, As_2O_3, etc.

A reverse action is also possible, where some substances having poisonous characteristics in their pure form become insoluble in combination, turning into non-poisonous. E.g., $AgNO_3$ and HCl are toxic in their pure form and become non-toxic when combined.

Dilution or Mechanical Combination

Poisonous substances' characteristics change when they are diluted or combined with non-toxic substances.

Synergism

When two substances with the same toxicity nature are combined, the cumulative effect is much higher than the sum of their individual effects. This process is known as the synergistic effect. E.g., CCl_4 and C_2H_5OH induced hepatoxicity individually but in combination, producing more liver injury than their effect.

Antagonism

When two substances with opposite action of toxicity mechanisms are combined, then they mutually nullify the effect of each other. This is opposite to the synergism process. E.g., Atropine blocks the cholinergic receptor and reduces the toxicity of Organophosphate.

23.8.2 Factors Pertaining to the Host

Body Weight

The toxicity of poison depends upon its dosage. Moreover, the dosage depends on the body weight and would decide whether it acts as a poison or as a remedy.

Age

Age plays a vital role in toxicity. For example, the microsomal enzyme system is not fully developed in neonatal and infants, so the metabolic rate is prolonged; hence, the dose prescribed for an adult is toxic to the neonatal and infants. Similarly, in old age, the liver size is reduced, which again affects the metabolic rate, so an average dose of medicine can be toxic to the person of this age group.

Sex

Physiological (endocrine system) differences in males and females also play a significant role in the appearance of toxicity. For example, females are more susceptible to alcohol than males because females have higher fat content and low water content, so the alcohol content becomes higher in the blood due to less water. It also metabolizes slowly because the enzyme alcohol dehydrogenase, which is responsible for metabolizing alcohol, is also less in females. Hence, alcohol persists for a long time in the female body compared to males if consumed equally. Due to the longer persistence of alcohol in the female body, the chances of toxicity are also higher.

State of Health

State of health is also an essential factor in poisoning, where the immune system of an ill or weak person becomes compromised, and this weak defence system causes poisoning even at low doses of a substance. In contrast, the tolerance level of a healthy person is better at the same dose due to an excellent immune system.

Tolerance

It is the extent of a person's ability not to exhibit any adverse effects, even when exposed to xenobiotics, that can usually cause toxicity in an average person. Two mechanisms can achieve tolerance. In the first mechanism, the toxicant reaches the site of action in a minimal amount; in the second mechanism, the site of action exhibits less response to the toxicants.

Sleep

During sleep, physiological activity and reflexes are in a relaxed state. Therefore, the metabolic reaction is slowed if a person is exposed to toxicants and immediately sleeps. The toxic substance persists for a longer time in the body without being metabolized, which may cause further toxicity (Vij 2011; Biswas 2012).

23.9 Illicit Drugs

To be devoid of hesitation, criminals prefer using certain drugs to carry out their crimes. Under the influence of intoxication, victims become unable to resist. The drugs involved in such offences are regulated (some are strictly prohibited for general use) by law or can be obtained only after the physician grants medical approval. Drugs are defined as natural or synthetic substances designed to affect a person psychologically or physiologically, and when such substances are regulated/ prohibited by the law of a nation, they are known as controlled drugs or illicit drugs.

Controlled Substances Act

These controlled drugs are categorically listed in the different schedules of the Controlled Substances Act, which was enacted in India in 1970. Besides, the lists of controlled drugs and their penalty for possession, sale or use are also mentioned in this act. A list of scheduled and controlled drugs is shown in the Table 23.1 below (Johnson et al. 2018; Duffy's Rehab 2023).

Table 23.1 List of the controlled drugs in the different schedules of the Controlled Substances Act, 1970

Schedule	Description	Drug
Schedule I	No approved medical use	Heroin, LSD
Schedule II	Medical use, only with "severe restrictions."	Morphine, cocaine, methadone
Schedule III	Medical use, somewhat addictive	Barbiturates, Opium, amphetamines
Schedule IV	Medical use, low addictive potential	Cough syrup, other stimulates and depressants
Schedule V	Medical use, lowest addictive potential	Codeine

The Working Mechanism of Controlled/Illicit Drug

When controlled drugs are administered, it causes a surge in levels of dopamine in the brain, which trigger feelings of pleasure. These drugs carry out specific changes in the brain while interfering with

- The clarity in thinking ability
- Judgment/Decision-making ability
- Ability to Self-Control
- Ability to feel normal without drugs

General Signs and Symptoms

- Rupture of blood vessels on the surface of the eye
- Unusual Pupils (Either large or small)
- Alteration in appetite or sleeping disorder
- Sudden gain/loss of body weight
- Degradation of physical appearance
- Unusual smells on breath
- Impaired/loss of coordination
- Poor Judgement
- Decline in performance
- Slowed reflection
- Secretive behaviors
- Alteration in social behaviors (Sudden self-isolation)
- Prone to Accident or trouble
- Lack of willpower
- Unexplained anxiety
- Memory loss
- Distorted vision

23.9.1 Classification of the Controlled/Illicit Drugs

Controlled/illicit drugs are classified into the following categories.

Stimulants
The drug under this category enhances the activity of the CNS (Central Nervous System). Stimulant drugs increase alertness, attention, blood pressure, breathing, and heart rate. At high doses, it may cause heart failure and seizures. E.g., Amphetamine, Cocaine, Nicotine, and Caffeine.

Depressants
The drugs that fall in this category impair CNS functions. These drugs are generally prescribed for sleep disorders, anxiety and stress. E.g., Alcohol, Tranquillisers, Benzodiazepine, Barbiturate, GHB.

Hallucinogens
The drugs alter the mind's perception and induce the consciousness of non-existing/unrealistic objects or events. Drug of this category affects the brain's serotonin level, which impacts cognition and memory. E.g., LSD, Psilocybin, Mescaline, Ketamine, MDMA.

Narcotics (Opioids)
The drugs that fall in this category act as pain relievers. These drugs are specifically prescribed for moderate to severe pain. These drugs block the sensation of pain in the brain. These drugs can cause intense sedation and euphoria and are often abused. E.g., Heroin, Codeine, Methadone, and Morphine.

Cannabinoids
The drug of this category binds with cannabinoid receptors in the body. Tetrahydrocannabinol (THC) and Cannabidiol (CBD) are two primary components of cannabinoids that are more often used in marijuana. THC makes feel the consumer high when smoked marijuana, while CBD induces sleep, makes the consumer feel calm and is used to treat anxiety. E.g., Marijuana.

Inhalants
When inhaled, the drugs of this category produce mind-altering or psychoactive effects. E.g., paint thinners, paint removers, gasoline, glue, and spray deodorant.

Steroids
These are synthetic drugs often used to treat the low level of steroid hormones. These drugs are, without prescription, used to enhance athletic and physical performance. E.g., Testosterone, Cypt, Parabolan, Anadrol (Houck and Siegel 2010).

23.9.2 Drugs of Abuse: Uses and Risk (Table 23.2)

Table 23.2 Classification of the controlled/illicit drugs, their uses, and risks

Class of drug	Example	Medical use	Antidote	Effect
Stimulant	Cocaine	Local Anaesthesia	None	Increased alertness, excitation, euphoria, Enhancing pulse rate and blood pressure, sleeping disorder, loss of appetite
	Amphetamine	Hyperactivity, Attention seeking disorder, narcolepsy, weight control	*N*-Acetylcysteine	
Depressant	Gamma Hydroxybutyric Acid (GHB)	Anaesthetic	Physostigmine	Slurred speech, disorientation, loss of coordination without the odour of alcohol, memory loss, interaction with alcohol, reduced anxiety, lack of concentration, physical and mental fatigue, confusion, poor judgment
	Benzodiazepines	Antianxiety, Sedative, Anti-convulsant, Hypnotic, Muscle Relaxant	Flumazenil	
	Barbiturate	Antianxiety, Sedative, Hypnotic	None	
Hallucinogens	MDMA, MDA	None	None	Heigh sensitivity, Bruxism and water loss, a mild hallucinogen
	LSD	None		Illusions and hallucinations, alteration in perception of time and distance, Poor motor function, impaired memory
	Ketamine	Anaesthetic	Naloxone	
Narcotic	Heroine	Analgesic	Naloxone	Euphoria, drowsiness, respiratory depression, Pupil constriction, nausea, pain reliever, confusion
	Morphine	Analgesic	Potassium Permanganate	
	Codeine	Analgesic	Naloxone	
Cannabinoids	Marijuana	Nausea and Pain relief	None	Euphoria, relaxed inhibitions, increased appetite, lack of coordination, anxiety, confusion, loss of memory and learning
	THC	Appetite stimulant	None	
	Hashish	None	None	

(continued)

Table 23.2 (continued)

Class of drug	Example	Medical use	Antidote	Effect
Inhalant	Adhesives, spray paint, hair spray, dry cleaning fluid, spot remover, lighter fluid	None	None	Memory loss, slurred speech, Alcoholic behaviour, slow onset of vitamin deficiency, organ damage
	Nicotine	None	None	Chronic lung disorder, cardiovascular disease, stroke, cancer, adverse pregnancy outcomes
Steroids	Testosterone, Cypt	Hypogonadism	None	Edema, testicular atrophy, gynecomastia, acne, aggression in behaviour, Clotting of blood, premature stoppage of developmental growth
	Parabolan, Anadrol	Anemia, Breast cancer	None	

23.9.3 Detection/Examination of the Controlled/Illicit Drugs

A colour spot test generally detects illicit drugs. Some colour spot tests for illicit drugs are shown in Table 23.3 below (Houck and Siegel 2010):

Table 23.3 List of Spot tests (Colorimetric chemical test) for the preliminary examination of Controlled/illicit drugs

Chemical test	Reagents	Name of drug	Colourimetric result
Marquis	H_2SO_4 and HCHO	Amphetamine	Red-orange-brown
		Opium	Greyish red-brown
		Mescaline	Strong orange
		Heroin	Purple
Dille-Koppanyi	Co $(CH_3COO)_2$ [Cobalt (II) acetate] solution, $(CH_3)_2CHNH_2$ [Isopropylamine] solution	Barbiturate	Violet-blue
Duquenois-Levine	CH_3COOH [Acetaldehyde] and vanillin in ethanol, HCl, $CHCl_3$	Marijuana	Purple
Ehrlich or Van Urk	Para-dimethylamino-benzaldehyde in ethanol, HCl	LSD	Blue purple

(continued)

Table 23.3 (continued)

Chemical test	Reagents	Name of drug	Colourimetric result
Scott	Co $(SCN)_2$ [Cobalt thiocyante] solution	Cocaine	Strong greenish blue
		Methadone	
Mandelin	Ammonium metavanadate + Conc H_2SO_4	MDMA and MDA	Bluish black
		Ketamine	Deep reddish-orange
		Morphine	Dark greyish reddish brown
		Cocaine	Deep orange yellow
		Codeine	Dark olive
		Psilocybin	Green

23.10 Alcohol

Alcohol (Ethanol and methanol) are widely used organic solvents. They are used in medicine, chemical industries, households, etc. Ethanol is more commonly used for drinking purposes. Alcohol is comprised of many chemicals, including Methanol, Ethanol, Propanol, Butanol, Ethylene Glycol, etc. Intake of Excessive alcohol is a primary concern of public health and, most of the time is the reason behind the crime being committed. In addition, various non-communicable diseases arise from excessive alcohol consumption. From a forensic point of view, there are two significant issues. First, to identify the role of ethanol in the commission of crime and death investigation due to alcohol intoxication and second, to detect methanol adulteration in the 'country-made liquor'.

Alcohol Properties

The chemical composition of ethanol is C_2H_5OH. It is a volatile, flammable, colourless liquid with a slight characteristic odour. Ethanol is water soluble and used in beverages, perfumes, paints, antifreeze and tinctures as a solvent. There is a variety of tastes in alcoholic drinks since various flavouring compounds are mixed in them during brewing. Ethanol solution (70–80%) is often used as a disinfectant that kllls the microorganism through protein denaturation and lipid disintegration. Ethanolic disinfectant is effective against most bacteria, fungi, and many viruses but is incompetent against bacterial spores. This unique disinfectant property of ethanol makes them suitable for long time storage.

23.10.1 Kinetics of Alcohol

Ethanol is rapidly absorbed and interacts with many neurotransmitters and other systems (influences GABA and NMDA receptors, and dissolves lipids in membranes) in the human body.

Absorption
Ethanol is rapidly absorbed from the stomach, small intestine, and colon when administered orally. Due to its volatile nature, ethanol can also be absorbed through the lungs.

Distribution
After rapid absorption, ethanol is uniformly distributed throughout tissues and body fluids as they are soluble in water. It can also cross the placental barrier easily; therefore, it may show adverse effects on the fetus in the form of Alcohol syndrome.

Metabolism
Ethanol is metabolized into acetaldehyde (toxic metabolite) in the presence of alcohol dehydrogenase enzyme, which is further metabolized into acetic acid in the presence of the enzyme aldehyde dehydrogenase.

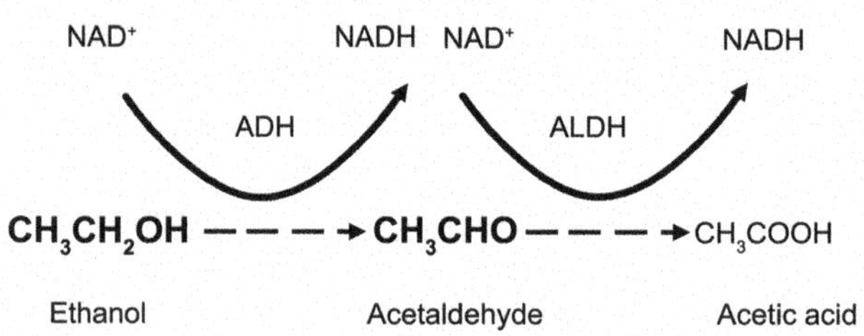

Elimination
Alcohol is a unique compound that is water-soluble and volatile; therefore, it can be excreted in different ways from the human body.

Urination—Intake of alcohol suppresses the brain area, which releases vasopressin chemicals. This chemical generally reabsorbs fluids that are filtered via the kidney. When vasopressin suppresses, the body does not reabsorb as much fluids from the kidney; hence kidney accumulates more fluids excreted in the form of urine.

Exhalation—When alcohol is administered, it dissolves in the mucous lining of the alveoli. When the ethanol vaporizes, it fills the open-air space of the mucous layer with the alveolar sac that exits from the body when exhaled.

Metabolism—Alcohol is metabolized into acetic acid and can be easily eliminated from the body.

23.10.2 Stages of Alcohol Intoxication

Alcohol intoxication occurs in three different stages. First excitation, then depression of CNS, causes hypoglycaemia, disturbs thermoregulation

- First Stage—In this stage, CNS get excited after the administration of alcohol, due to which initiates muscle coordination impairment, emotional instability and frequent urination.
- Second Stage—In this stage, due to strong inebriety, emotional outbursts and significant loss of muscle coordination occur. Extreme confusion in the brain can make a person unable to walk or even stand.
- Third and Fourth Stage—This stage can be perilous because breathing and gag reflexes are impaired. It becomes fatal if a person chokes on their vomit or is critically injured. In this stage, blood pressure and breathing rate become significantly slow, and body temperature drops which cumulatively initiates the condition of coma that may further lead to death.

Symptoms
- Slurred speech
- Unsteady walk
- Inability to react quickly
- Vomiting
- Frequent urination
- Difficulty awakening and
- Slow or shallow breathing

Acute Effect
- Suppress the specific part of the Central Nervous System
- Suppression of inhibitory control
- Warm and Reddish skin, Vasodilation
- Emotional outbursts
- Loss of memory and concentration (Blackout)
- Poor Decision-making ability
- Decreased reflexes
- Decreased sexual response

Chronic Effect
- Enhancement in digestive juices secretion,
- Vasoconstriction in GIT
- Ulcer in Stomach
- Steatosis (abnormal retention of fat (lipids) within a cell or organ)
- Liver cirrhosis
- Polyneuritis (Peripheral Neuropathy)
- Worse immune reactions
- Thiamine deficiency

23.10.3 Breath Analyzer Test

A Breath analyzer is an electrochemical device that measures how much alcohol is present when the subject exhales. With the help of a breath analyzer, blood alcohol content (BAC) is calculated. The breath analyzer works on the principle of ion mobility spectrometry (IMS). In this device, when expired air enters the system, the catalyst converts the alcohol in the air into acetic acid, which breaks down into CO_2 and water. During this oxidation process, chemical energy is released, converted into electrical voltage by the fuel cell and then measured by the detector. High voltage indicates a high concentration of alcohol in expired air (Vij 2011; Biswas 2012).

23.11 Collection and Preservation of Poison, Illicit Drugs and Alcohol

Toxicological evidence is collected (investigated and identified) from the crime scene and appropriately preserved per the guideline, labelled, sealed and then sent to the forensic science laboratory for toxicological testing. All evidence must be sealed separately in tamper-proof containers. Like other pieces of evidence, the chain of custody must be maintained from the crime scene to the court proceeding and further storage for re-testing (Badiye et al. 2021).

23.11.1 Collection of Toxicological Evidences

Some of the body organs, fluids and evidences used as toxicological evidence in cases such as suicide, homicide, accidental death, drugs or poisoning are briefed below.

23.11.1.1 Blood

Blood is most commonly found evidence at the crime scene, which may provide information to detect, quantify and interpret drugs and other poison/toxic materials. This information (concentrations of drugs and other toxicants) obtained from blood helps establish the drugs/toxicant administration and determine the adverse effect of the drugs/toxicants on the deceased at the time the blood was taken or at the time of death. Due to variable conditions, detecting drugs from postmortem blood is challenging. However, the degree of decomposition may also interfere with toxicological testing because analysis from the decomposed sample is also tricky.

EDTA vials may be used for preservation of blood. Ten milliliter of peripheral blood should be collected in a plastic/glass container with having screw cap with fluoride salt preservative (such as sodium or potassium; 1–5%). An aliquot should be collected without preservatives in case of suspected fluoride poisoning. Blood should be collected from the femoral artery or vein in the postmortem. Before collection, tie/clamp the vessels near the inguinal ligament to prevent siphoning blood down from the larger central vessels. To obtain more blood, the leg may be slightly elevated. Avoid doing massage or shaking to increase the flow. Blood should be collected from the cephalic vein in case of antemortem sample.

23.11.1.2 Urine

In the case of drug testing, urine is the most common sample used to collect. Drug testing from urine samples helps detect metabolites of the drugs when there is no sign of drug ingestion in the blood.

All available or 30 mL urine should be collected in a plastic/glass container without preservatives. During the postmortem, it is collected by inserting the needle directly above the pubic symphysis or by urethral catheterization (in the external examination only). If an internal examination is performed, urine can be collected directly from the bladder. If a very small amount of urine is present in the bladder, then the residual quantity is collected by opening the bladder. If urine is unavailable, the bladder could be washed with a saline solution to obtain any sample, and it must be assured that vitreous humour is provided.

23.11.1.3 Liver

The liver is a vital organ where drugs and other toxicants are metabolized; hence, it is used in forensic toxicology studies for drug/poison testing. Some xenobiotics are non-toxic in pure form, while they become toxic when metabolized. Therefore, liver screening plays a vital role in death investigations where information about poisons/drugs/toxins (detection, quantification) is obtained.

Thirty grams of the liver should be collected in a plastic/glass container with a screw cap—no need to add preservatives. The deep right lobe of the liver is preferably collected to avoid contamination with the diffusion of xenobiotics from gastric contents into the left lobe. Gall bladder should be collected separately.

23.11.1.4 Vitreous Humour

Vitreous humour (VH) is a clear gel-like substance that remains intact in the eyes even when various organs/tissues in the body get decomposed. This property of VH makes it useful for drug detection even long after death. VH is often used to analyze alcohol content in the blood.

The blood content in VH is slightly higher than blood (about 20% on average); however, other toxicological analyses are slightly more complex via VH, so it is also challenging to interpret.

It is collected from both eyes in separate vials of 10 mL sodium fluoride (10 mg/mL) is used as a preservative. It is useful for the analysis of psychotropic substances (e.g. alcohol). It is collected by ophthalmocentesis from each eye. The needle is inserted from the outer corner until its tip is placed centrally in the globe, and gentle aspiration is performed to avoid retinal detachment. An approximate amount of saline solution is injected into the eyes to restore cosmetic integrity.

23.11.1.5 Stomach Contents

In cases of acute poisoning or drug overdoses, drugs or poison may be detected depending on how much time elapsed between intake and death. Generally, Drugs and poisons are given orally, so stomach content may provide valuable information about the signs of drugs and poisons consumed. In many acute poisoning cases, insoluble tablets or powder may be recovered from the stomach contents, which may help to identify the poison or drugs present in it. The amount of drugs or poisons recovered from the stomach contents is enough to interpret the extent of the level of toxicity.

Collect 30 mL aliquot of the total homogenized in a plastic/glass container with the screw cap without preservatives. If gastric contents are unavailable, 30 g of the stomach wall should be collected without preservatives. To collect the stomach contents, clamp the distal Oesophagus and the pylorus and cut the wall to collect the content.

23.11.1.6 Bone and Bone Marrow

Bone and bone marrow may be helpful for toxicological testing in cases where only skeletal remains are found at the crime scene. In chronic poisoning cases, when poisons are insoluble, unable to excrete out from the body, deposited in soft tissues and bones that can be recovered from skeletal remains. Although drugs/poisons can be detected from bones and bone marrow, the time when these toxicants were ingested cannot be accurately determined.

Thirty grams of bone should be collected in a plastic/glass container with a screw cap. Larger bones (e.g. femur) can be cut into small pieces or crushed. No preservatives are added. All available bone marrow should be collected in a plastic container with a screw cap without preservatives. Usually, the ribs are cut approximately 5 cm from its distal end, i.e. near the Medio clavicular line where it is ossified. The red bone marrow can be aspirated by compressing or squeezing the remaining rib ends with the help of pliers. In antemortem cases, bone marrow can be obtained from vertebral bodies through trocar aspiration. In postmortem cases, it is collected from the femur after a section of the cortical bone (Dinis-Oliveria et al. 2016; Molina 2010).

23.11.1.7 Hair and Nails

Hair samples play a significant role in testing heavy metal poisons and drugs when they have been given for a period of weeks to a couple of months. Hair is mainly used to test illicit drugs, namely amphetamines, cocaine, marijuana (THC) and heroin. In addition, drugs or poisons can also be detected on fingers and nails, which may provide valuable information, especially in chronic poisoning cases. Contaminants on the hair surface can reduce its evidential value; hence, specific sample preparation is required for laboratory testing.

Hair should be collected from the posterior vertex region of the scalp. Approximately 150–200 hairs should be collected. Samples should be tightly tied together with ligature so as not to lose the orientation (the root end should be identified easily). If head hair are not available or excessively bleached or permed, then axillary, pubic, arms or beard hair can be collected as an alternative. In antemortem cases, nail clippings are collected from all the fingers and toes using Teflon®-coated stainless steel scissors to reduce contaminants. In postmortem cases, all the nails from the toes and fingers are collected (Dinis-Oliveria et al. 2016; Molina 2010).

23.11.1.8 Bile

All the available bile should be collected in a plastic/glass container with a screw cap without preservatives. For bile collection, the gallbladder is tied to reduce contamination and bile is collected by aspiration or directly from the common bile duct if cholecystectomy is performed. It should always be collected before the liver.

23.11.1.9 Brain

Whole-brain or 30 g should be collected in a plastic/glass container with a screw cap without any preservatives (Dinis-Oliveria et al. 2016; Molina 2010). The collected brain tissue samples are sent to a specialized laboratory for toxicological analysis. Advanced analytical techniques are used to detect and quantify the presence of toxic substances, such as drugs, alcohol, and poisons. The analysis provides insight into whether any toxic substances contributed to the person's death.

23.12 Detection of Some Frequently Used Poisons, Illicit Drugs and Alcohol

Extraction and Isolation

Extracting drugs and poisons from the biological matrix is the first step in a toxicological analysis. Generally, this is a time-consuming and tedious process, but it is indispensable for toxicology testing, as subsequent analytical methods are based on sample preparation, an integral part of the extraction process. A relevant extraction procedure allows for an adequate analysis of drugs and poisons. Some fundamental principles have been used to develop a successful extraction procedure. These extraction methods have been developed and optimized based on the efficiency of the extracted materials. It is well known that different drugs and poisons have different characteristics; hence, no universal standard extraction method exists for toxicological analysis.

Successful detection, identification and quantification of drugs/poisons solely depend on their extraction from the biological matrix. Proper sample preparation is a fundamental precondition for the success of the extraction process. Some frequently used extraction procedures for drugs and poisons are as follows:

23.12.1 Extraction of Volatile Poison

Acidic Steam Distillation

This method is used to extract acidic volatile poison.

Biological Material (Viscera)+ equal amount of H_2O + H_2SO_4

↓ Maceration

Distillation flask

↓ Add dil. H_2SO_4 (Make the solution acidic)

Steam transferred to the distillation flask

25 mL distillate is collected (used for the analysis of Ethanol, Methanol, Ether, CCl_4, $CHCl_3$ and other organic solvents)

Phosphide Test-	
Black precipitate in a porcelain basin	Remaining materials in the Distillation flask
↓ Conc. HNO_3 and heat	↓ NaOH (Make the solution alkaline)
↓ Add 1 mL of ammonium molybdate	Steam is passed ↓
Canary Yellow (Phosphide converted into Phosphate)	Distillate collected in 50 mL 1N HCl (ice cold)
	↓ Transferred into separating funnel
	Ether: $CHCl_3$ (3:1) twice
	Organic layer mixed after separation
	↓ Heat
	Concentrated residue (used to analyze for Amphetamine, Nicotine, Ephedrine, and Atropine)

23.12.2 Isolation of Toxic Anions (Dialysis Method)

10 g tissue taken in a cellophane bag

↓ Bag rotated in beaker by electric motor (100 mL distilled water for 1 h)

H_2O is replaced by 100 mL of fresh H_2O and again rotated for 30 min

Both water mixed

↓ Heat on water bath

Aqueous Concentrate

Analyzed for toxic anions

23.12.3 Isolation of Toxic Cations (Metallic Poison)

Dry Ashing Method

10 g tissue taken in a porcelain basin

↓ Heated on the burner to remove moisture

Now basin kept in a muffle furnace

↓ 550 °C for 1 h (organic material is incinerated {ash})

Basin is taken out

Residue

↓ Boiled with 10 mL 4N HCl and then filter

Filtrate

Analyzed for toxic cations

Wet Digestion Method

10 g chopped tissue in a porcelain basin

↓ Heated on a Water bath

Residue

↓ Add conc. H_2SO_4 and Conc. HNO_3

Heated on burner

Solution

↓ Cool and Transferred to Kjeldahl's flask with the help of dil. H_2O

Heat the solution until carbonized

Black residue due to C deposit

↓ Add conc. HNO_3 from the dropping funnel at the rate of 20 drop/min

Red fumes evolved until the organic material completely oxidized (indicated by the absence of charring and content of the flask becoming nearly colourless)

↓ Drop of HNO_3 is stop adding when material fully oxidized (heating continue to remove red fume)

After cooling Add saturated ammonium oxalate solution

Continue to boil till H_2SO_4 begin to reflex

↓ Flask content diluted with H_2O and filtered

Filtrate

Analyzed for As, Sb, Pb, Th, Bi, Cu, Zn, Sn, Mn, Ba, Mg etc.

23.12.4 Extraction of Non-volatile Organic Poison

This is the main class of poison which includes 90% of all poisons. Extraction of non-volatile organic poisons involves two steps:

23.12.4.1 Protein Precipitation

Tissues contain fats and proteins that can interfere with the poison extraction procedure. Therefore, to remove the protein, it is precipitated or coagulated first, and then fats are removed. The mixture is then filtered, and filtrate can be used for solvent extraction.

Protein can be precipitated by four different methods, which are as follows:

Modified Stass-Otto method

This is a general process used to extract various types of poisons. However, this method is not suitable for liquid samples and acidic drugs.

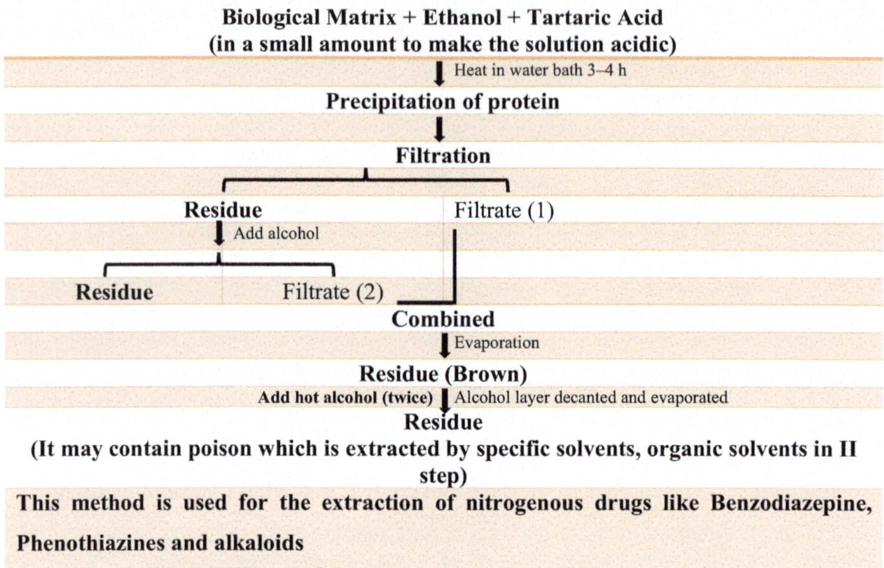

Acid Digestion Method

In this method, HCl hydrolyzes the protein-protein bond; as a result, the conjugated drug separates from the protein and comes into a solution, which is then extracted from solvent extraction.

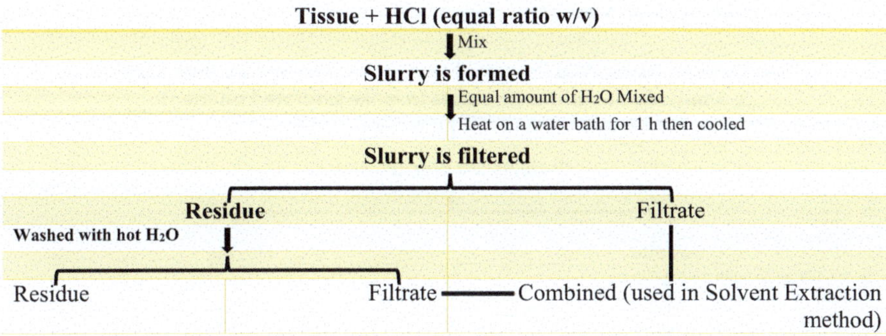

This method is most suitable for morphine, barbiturates, and cocaine and not for drugs readily hydrolyzed by HCl e.g., Paracetamol and Benzodiazepines.

Sodium Tungstate Method

This method is also known as the Valov method. This method is suitable for the extraction of acidic drugs. In this method, sodium tungstate is used as a de-proteinizing agent.

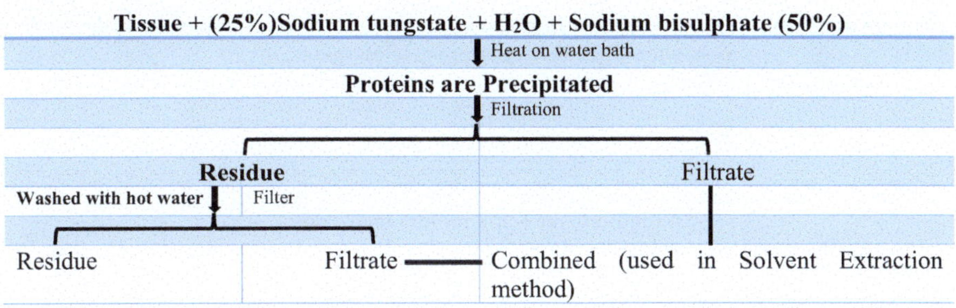

This method gives a good yield of acidic and neutral drugs but is unsuitable for basic drugs.

Ammonium Sulphate Method

This method is also known as the Daubney-Nicolls method.

➢ **Ammonium Sulphate Method:**

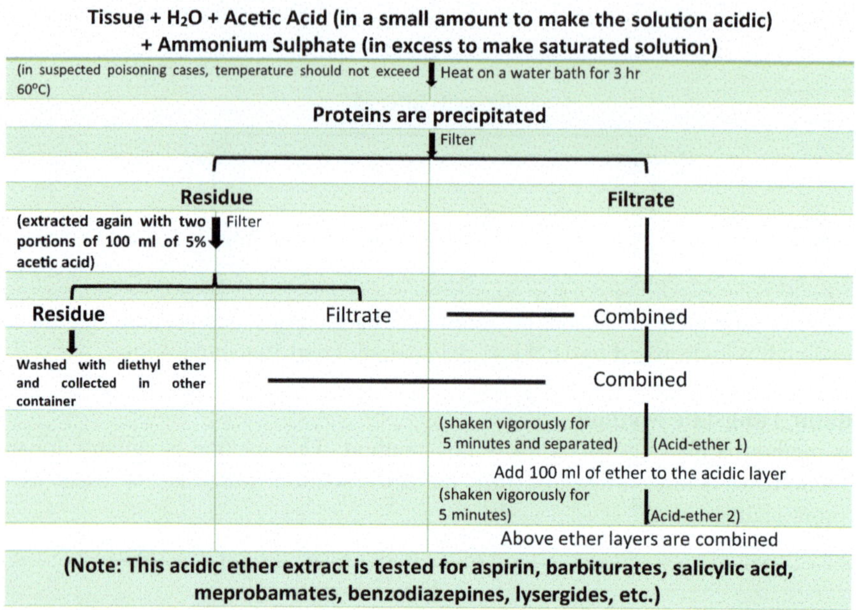

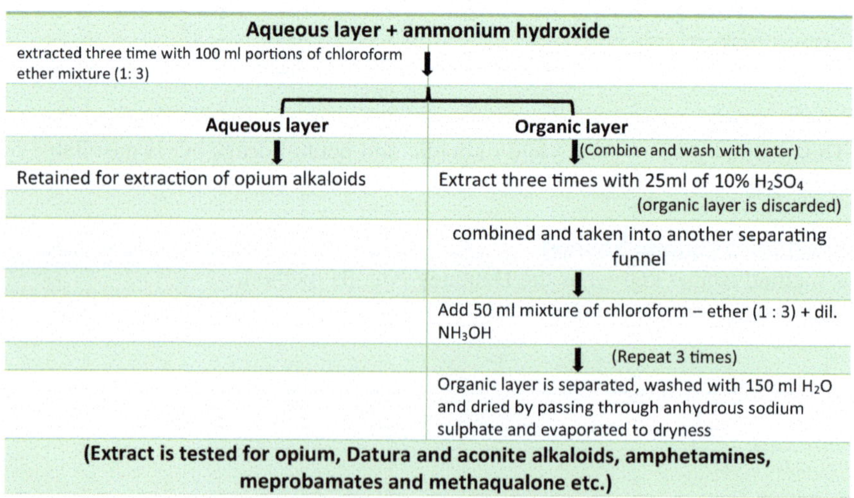

This method is helpful for the isolation of drugs and their metabolites from highly protein substances.

23.12.5 Extraction of Poison from Biological Matrices

The general isolation method provides filtrate in which the drug is generally not pure form so that these are purified by solvent extraction. Solvent extraction is based on distribution law; two immiscible solvents are used. It is well known that each substance's solubility varies in different solvents. For example, the same amount of CCl_4 and H_2O is taken in the test tube, and I_2 is added. It is observed that I_2 is more soluble in CCl_4 than H_2O.

Solvent Extraction Method

After protein precipitation, solvent extraction is a subsequent step for extracting non-volatile organic poison. Poisons can be extracted from a biological matrix using the solvent extraction method, which is as follows:

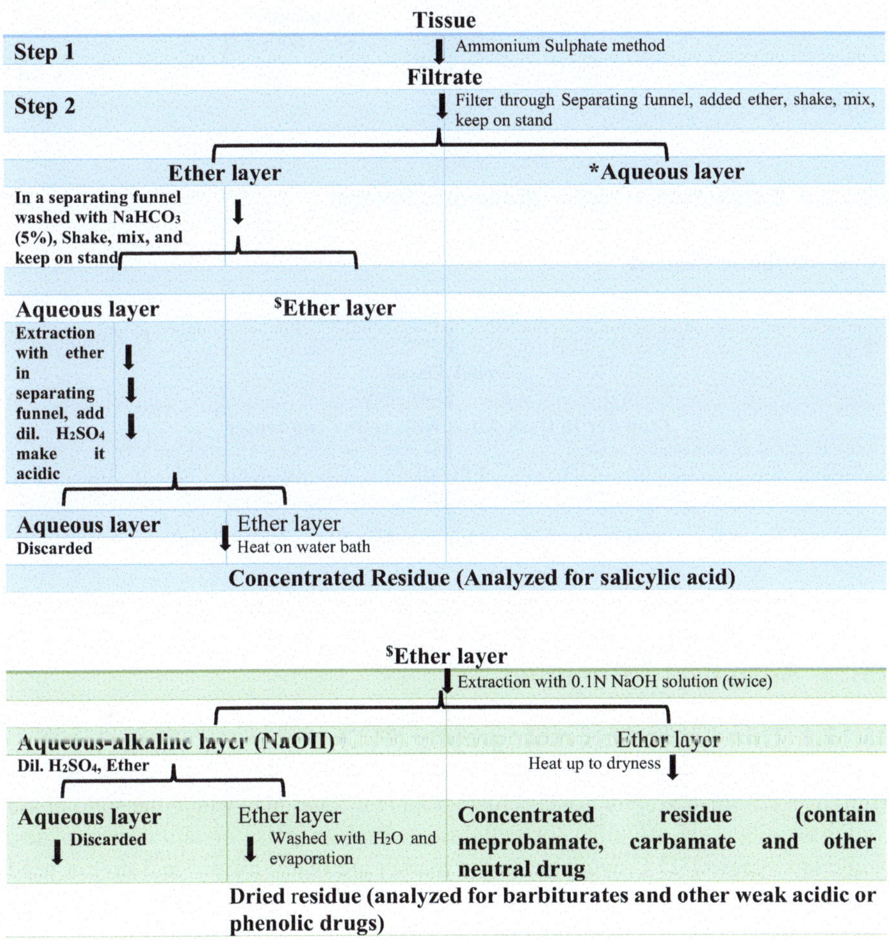

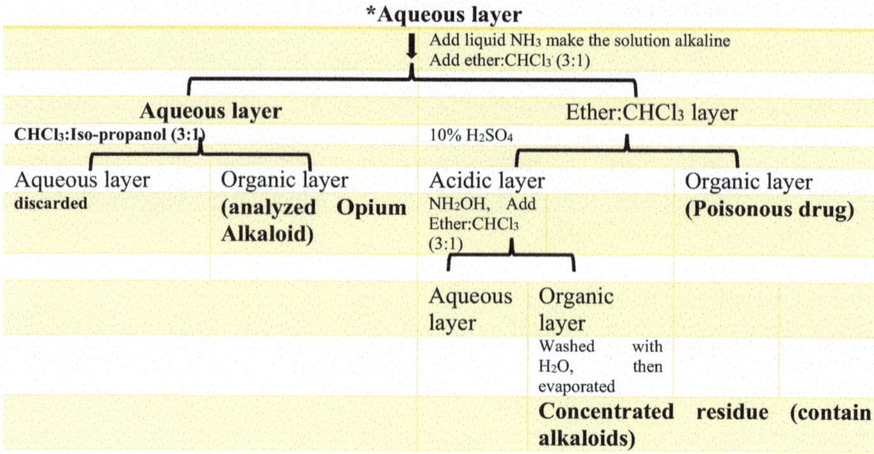

* and $ marked layers are kept aside for further testing of other drugs and metabolites.

23.12.6 Extraction of Miscellaneous Poison

Total Alcoholic Extract

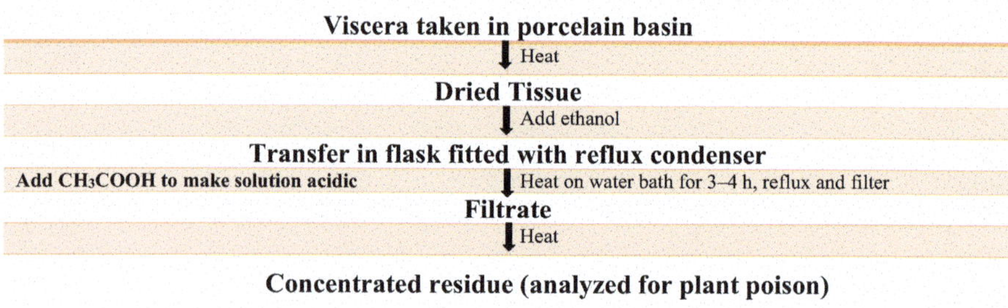

23.13 Analytical Techniques

23.13.1 Thin-Layer Chromatography (TLC)

Thin-layer chromatography is a chromatographic technique in which the solid phase comprises silica gel, alumina, or cellulose coated on glass or aluminium plates. Numerous types of TLC available in the market are ready for use and do not need pretreatment. The sample extract is spotted at the bottom of the TLC plate and allowed to dry. After drying the spot, the plate is kept in a beaker containing the mobile phase, a solution of various organic solvents, acids and/or water in various ratios. Along with the mobile phase, the compound spotted on the phase moves at a certain speed towards the top. The movement of various sample components is analyzed and expressed by retardation factor (Rf) values. This value represents how far a compound travels in a particular solvent. The following formula calculates it:

$$\text{Retardation Factor (Rf) value} = \frac{\text{Distance travelled by the solute(s) } \textit{or} \text{ component(s)}}{\text{Distance travelled by the solvent}}$$

Principle: Thin-layer chromatography works on the affinity of the analyte compound towards the mobile phase and stationary phase. The compounds with higher affinity towards the mobile phase will have higher speed and travel longer distances than those with a higher affinity toward the stationary phase (Branch 2004a, b).

Thin Layer Chromatography (TLC) is used to analyze non-volatile samples. It is used to identify components in a given mixture, determine the purity of the sample and can also be used to monitor the progress of a reaction. In forensic science, it is used to analyze the dye composition of the fabrics, qualitative analysis of gun powder and other suspected powders, and detect insecticides and pesticides in food and water samples. It can detect medicinal plants and their constituents or examine the radiopharmaceuticals' radiochemical purity (Namir et al. 2019; Kabera 2017). Various biological samples such as urine, blood, human serum, plasma, other body fluids, bacterial cultural broths, bacterial cell cultural media, etc. can be used for the detection of drugs by using TLC (Sherma and Fried 2005).

23.13.2 High-Performance Liquid Chromatography (HPLC)

It is a type of column chromatography in which the sample mixture or the analyte is pumped into a solvent at high pressure through a column with chromatographic packing material. Here the solvent is the mobile phase, and the column packing material acts as a stationary phase. Combined with a suitable detector, it can be used as a screening test for many drugs. The drugs are first dissolved in the liquid mobile phase and then are allowed to pass through a column of stationary phase under high pressure. The drug's components get separated and isolated inside the column and leave the column at different times. The time taken by different components to pass through the column is recorded by the detector and compared with the standard samples, allowing the detection of each component of the sample. There are three critical steps in HPLC, which are as follows:

1. *Injection of the sample*: The sample is injected into the column under high pressure. This is a straightforward and primarily automated step.

2. *Retention time is the time the component takes* to travel through the column to the detector. It depends on factors such as the particle size, column pressure and the nature of the stationary phase. Temperature and the composition of the solvent also affect the retention time.
3. *The Detector*: Different types of detectors are used in HPLC to detect components. The most commonly used is the ultra-violet detector, in which the output is recorded in the form of peaks.

Principle: HPLC is a type of column chromatography that works on the principle of separating analytes. The distribution of the analyte is based on the analyte's affinity toward the stationary and mobile phases. The components of the analyte are dissolved in the mobile phase. When the mobile phase passes through the stationary phase, the components are separated according to their affinity (or interaction) with the stationary phase. The retention time of each component of the analyte is different (Creative Proteomics 2022). HPLC can detect drugs from samples such as urine and plasma (Fernández et al. 1996). It also detects drugs, poisons and pesticides from body fluids and tissue samples (Pragst 2008).

23.13.3 Gas Chromatography (GC)

Gas Chromatography (GC) was previously known as gas-liquid chromatography. It is used to analyze gaseous, liquid and solid samples (which can be vaporized). The mobile phase in Gas chromatography is an inert gas (mostly nitrogen or helium). It is also called carrier gas. When the sample is injected inside the column, it is carried by the carrier gas towards the detector. This method cannot be used for non-volatile and thermolabile samples. The most commonly used detector in GC is a flame ionization detector or nitrogen phosphorous detector for identifying the components. Gas chromatography coupled with mass spectroscopy is widely used as a confirmatory test in forensic toxicology. This combined technique allows mass spectral analysis of analytes after they have been separated and isolated by chromatography. Mass spectrometry is accomplished by fragmenting a molecule with a barrage of electrons and then analyzing the relative abundance of the fragments (electron ionization) or by ionizing molecules and analyzing the charge transference (chemical ionization) (Kabera 2017).

Principle: The sample solution injected into the instrument enters the gas stream. The sample is then transported to the separation tube, which is known as the "column". The carrier gas used inside the column is helium or nitrogen. Various components of the sample solution are separated inside the column. Later the detector measures the quantity of the separated components that exit the column. The standard sample with known concentration is injected into the instrument to measure the sample with unknown concentration. The peak retention time of the sample and area are compared with the sample to calculate the concentration.

Drugs can be detected by using gas chromatography from the samples such as urine, plasma and blood, etc. (Bhoj et al. 2020). Gas chromatography is used to analyze the volatile samples. Samples such as human breath, blood, saliva, etc., containing volatile organic components can be analyzed with GC. It can analyze food products, cosmetics and even environmental toxins. It is also a preferred instrument for research work (Chemistry LibreTexts 2022)

23.13.4 Infrared Spectroscopy

The infrared spectrophotometers consist of three main components: radiation source, monochromator or interferometer, and detector. It includes the study of scattering, reflection, absorption or transmission of IR radiation in the spectral range of 800–1,000,000 nm (0.8–1000 μm). Fourier transform infrared spectrophotometer is analytical laboratories' most commonly used IR spectrophotometer. FTIR spectrometer is incorporated with an interferometer in the place of the monochromator. The IR spectrometer can measure relatively heterogeneous materials and poorly characterized samples, particularly in condensed phases (e.g. creams, powders, crystalline materials). IR spectra can be measured in the solid phase and liquid and gases. Most commonly, the samples analyzed under IR spectroscopy are solid at room temperature. IR spectra of samples as little as 1 μg can also be obtained.

Principle: In IR Spectroscopy, the analyte absorbs the infrared radiations and causes rotational changes and vibrational in the molecules. The vibrational energy levels within a molecule correspond to how the individual atoms or groups of atoms vibrate relative to the remainder of the molecule. Infrared spectroscopy can be used for organic qualitative analysis because the vibrational energy levels are dependent on the type of atoms and functional groups present in the analyte. It can also be used for quantitative analysis by monitoring the amount of radiation absorbed by the analyte at a given energy corresponding to one of the peaks in the spectrum of the molecule (Britannica 2023).

IR spectroscopy can be used for qualitative and quantitative analysis of different samples. Identification of functional groups and structure identification is also possible with IR spectroscopy. Identification of both organic and inorganic substances is possible through this technique. Almost any solid, liquid or gaseous sample can be analyzed. Blood, semen, saliva and other body fluids can be used to detect drugs by using IR spectroscopy (Mistek and Lednev 2018).

23.13.5 Immunoassays

Immunoassays are the routinely used methods for the detection of drugs in biological fluids. Smaller and larger laboratories use this technique for routine analysis. It has a wide range from single-use point-of-care tests for the analysis of a single sample to fully automated systems that can analyze thousands of samples daily. All the immunoassays are based on the principle of interaction of a specific target molecule with a corresponding antibody. For the testing of drugs, competitive immunoassays are mainly used. They use antibodies specific to a drug or a specific class of drugs. A labelled form of the same drug or a labelled form of the antibody is used for generating measurable signals. Immunoassays are also a method to detect the presence of drugs under study. Examples of such techniques are Radioimmunoassay (RIA) and enzyme-linked immunoassay (ELISA). RIA is very sensitive, and it can analyze a large number of samples rapidly. It does not require any preliminary extraction stages. The drug immunoassay technique involves a competition for binding the antibody with the antigen (drug) present in the sample and the fixed amount of antigen added as a part of the test system. The added antigen or the antibody is labelled with suitable markers, and The signals are measured and compared with calibrated curves obtained from the set of standard samples with a known amount of added drug (Fischer 2018; Jickells and Negrusz 2013).

Principle: The principle behind the immunoassays is that specific antibodies will bind to the antigen of interest. The antibodies used in this technique have a high affinity toward the antigen. They can be either monoclonal or polyclonal.

Toxicological analysis using immunoassays can be done from blood, plasma, serum, urine, milk, kidney extract, plant extract, etc. (Darwish 2006).

23.13.6 Nuclear Magnetic Resonance Spectroscopy (NMR)

Nuclear magnetic resonance spectroscopy is one of the most powerful techniques. This technique is used to retrieve detailed information about the structure, dynamics and interactions of organic and inorganic drugs. It is helpful for both qualitative and quantitative analysis. It is a non-destructive technique, thus allowing reanalysis of the sample by other methods. Different parameters are variable according to the temperature and pH of the solutions; therefore, NMR experiments should be carried out under the same physiochemical conditions. Each NMR signal is characterized by several magnitudes characteristic of the considered nucleus. These parameters give information about the number of nuclei, environment, and connectivity (Qriouet et al. 2019).

Principle: Nuclear Magnetic Resonance Spectroscopy works on the principle that many nuclei have a spin, and all nuclei are electrically charged. If we apply a magnetic external magnetic field, energy transfer is possible between the base energy to a higher energy level (generally a single energy gap). This energy transfer takes place at a wavelength corresponding to the radio frequencies, and when the spin returns to its base level, some amount of energy is emitted at the same frequency. The signal is then measured to match the transfer and processing to yield an NMR spectrum for the concerned nucleus.

It is mainly used to find out the purity of the sample and also its molecular structure. NMR is replacing X-ray crystallography for the determination of protein structure. NMR can be used for toxicological analysis through urine samples (Komoroski et al. 2000).

23.13.7 Atomic Absorption Spectroscopy (AAS)

It is one of the most frequently used tools in analytical chemistry. It is used for both quantitative and qualitative analysis of poisons in a sample. The quantity of a single poison can be determined even in a mixture of multiple poisons. AAS is used to measure quantities of chemical elements in the environmental samples by measuring the absorbed radiation of the chemical element of interest. The quantity of elements can be measured by reading the spectra produced by the sample when excited by the radiation. The atoms of the element absorb ultraviolet or visible light and transit to higher energy levels. AAS measured the Atomic amount of energy in the form of photons of light absorbed by the sample. The detector compared the wavelength transmitted by the sample with the wavelength which initially passed through the sample. A signal processor then integrates the changes in wavelength absorbed, which appear in the readout as energy absorption peaks at discrete wavelengths (Garcia and Baez 2012).

Principle: Atomic Absorption Spectroscopy is used for the analysis of liquid samples. It measures the concentrations of elements present in the given liquid sample. AAS works on the principle that elements in the gas phase absorb light at specific wavelengths. This provides the technique with excellent specificity and detection limits. Aqueous or organic solution and even the solid samples which are soluble in the solvent can be analyzed in this technique. The flame shows light specific to the appropriate wavelength of the element being analyzed. The absorption is directly proportional to the concentration of the element analyzed (Menzies 1960). AAS can be applied to various sample types, including serum, hair, liver, blood, urine, and other body fluids, provided they are properly prepared for analysis (De Groot et al. 1984; Afridi et al. 2006; Miksa et al. 2005).

23.13.8 Voltammetry/Polarography

Voltammetry denotes the study of intensity-potential curves of an electrochemical system. Variable potential difference is applied across two electrodes of a measuring cell, and the flowing current through the cell is recorded. The cell contains a solution with chemical species that can give an oxidation or reduction reaction. This technique can be used for the detection of traces of poisons with their physical and chemical properties. It is a prevalent technique for poison analysis due to its low cost, accuracy, precision and low quantification limit. This technique can be used alone and coupled with other techniques such as HPLC, GC, and TLC for the qualitative or quantitative determination of many organic substances (Qriouet et al. 2019).

Principle: Voltammetry is used for both qualitative and quantitative analysis. It involves the use of electrodes, typically consisting of an indicator electrode, a reference electrode, and sometimes an auxiliary or counter electrode. A varying potential difference is applied between the indicator electrode and the reference electrode, while the current flow is typically measured. The potential difference allows the electrochemical reaction of the analyte in the solution to occur at the indicator electrode. The reference electrode is used to maintain a constant potential difference throughout the measurement, regardless of changes in the solution. The auxiliary or counter electrode is often included to facilitate the flow of current in the solution, providing a path for the movement of electrons and compensating for any current imbalances. The current flowing between the indicator electrode and the auxiliary electrode is typically measured or controlled (Braun 2022).

23.13.9 Thermal or Chemical Sputtering Neutral Desorption

These techniques involve metastable and reactive ions. The metastable species are formed within the discharge-supporting gas, typically He or N_2, generating protonated water clusters. The species present reacts with the analyte directly or indirectly through proton or charge transfer reactions. DART (Direct analysis in real time) and LTP (Low-Temperature Plasma Probe) can be used for the analysis of drugs of abuse. Out of these two DART is most preferably used in the case of forensic toxicology. It uses a negatively biased point-to-plane atmospheric pressure glow discharge at lower currents, physically separated from the ionization region by one or several electrodes. The main advantage of this technique is that it can handle polar and non-polar analytes (of solid, liquid and gas) having masses below 1 kDa (Mogollón et al. 2018). Analyzing drugs using Thermal or Chemical Sputtering Neutral Desorption can be done from hair, urine and biological fluids extracts (Bianchi et al. 2018).

23.13.10 Capillary Electrophoresis (CE)

It is one of the new techniques which is receiving considerable attention in the field of toxicology. This is method is developed to analyze a diversity of compounds, including DNA adducts, drugs, small aromatic compounds and pesticides. The commercial capillary electrophoresis instrument includes an autosampler, high-voltage power supply, two buffer reservoirs, the capillary having a diameter of approximately 70 cm × 75 μm and a detector. Its versatile instrument can separate compounds of interest by several modes, including affinity, charge/mass ratios, chiral compounds, hydrophobicity, and size. The working principle of capillary electrophoresis is straightforward. It consists of a capillary made up of silica and silanol groups exposed on the internal surface, which can be ionized by increasing the pH of the eluting buffer. The ionization attracts cations to the silica surface, and when current is applied, these cations migrate toward the cathode, which causes a fluid migration through the capillary. The flow cations can be adjusted by changing the dielectric strength of the buffer, altering the pH, adjusting the voltage, or changing the viscosity (Fischer 2018; Leidy 2004).

Principle: Capillary electrophoresis is a separation technique in which elements are separated based on electrophoretic mobility and electro-osmosis when an electric field is applied. A defined volume of analyte solution is introduced in the capillary by replacing one of the buffer reservoirs with a sample vial (Rapley 2018). Capillary electrophoresis can be used for toxicological analysis from biological samples such as hair, skin, and all biological fluids (Tagliaro et al. 1995). It can also be used for ink and dye analysis (Cruces-Blanco et al. 2007).

23.13.11 Induced Coupled Plasma Spectrometry (ICP)

Induced coupled plasma spectrometry is another more sensitive technique developed for the simultaneous detection and quantification of all inorganic species enclosed with a sample matrix. One type of ICP is ICP-OES (optical emission spectrometer). In this method, a small sample is acid digested first and mixed with the gas (e.g. argon), forming a plasma (i.e. an ionized gas) channelled into a nebulizer. The atoms are excited by the applied energy, which is then converted by the optics of the instrument into individual wavelengths. Charged coupled device (CCD) captures the spectra and converts the light to measurable electrons at specific wavelengths. Wavelength coverage ranges from 175 to 785 nm. Other instruments use a mass spectrometer coupled with ICP (ICP-MS) to gather information on the analyte being sought within the sample matrix. These types of instruments are used for analysis, research and in industries.

Principle: ICP uses optical emission spectroscopy. The component elements of the analyte sample are excited when they are given plasma energy from outside. The excited atom returns to the lower energy position, emitting spectrum rays. The emission rays corresponding to the photon wavelength are measured. The type of element is thus determined based on the position of the photon rays, and the content of each element is determined based on the intensity of rays. Biological samples such as hair, bone, teeth, liver, urine and other biological fluids can be screened using induced coupled plasma spectroscopy for the presence of drugs and other toxicological substances (Hou et al. 2016; Miksa et al. 2005; Almirall and Trejos 2016; Trejos and Almirall 2010).

23.13.12 Mass Spectroscopy (MS)

Mass spectrometer is one of the outstanding instruments used to identify unknown samples. It is widely used in the toxicological analysis as a highly sensitive detection method along with GC, HPLC, CE and ICP. Chromatographic techniques such as GC, HPLC and CE separate the sample's components. Then the effluent from the column passes into the mass spectrometer, where the electron beam is bombarded. In this process, electrons and negative groups are removed, and the produced ions are accelerated. Accelerated ions pass through a magnetic field, separated by the different curvatures of their paths under gravity. The resulting pattern is the characteristics of every molecule under study. The two primarily used detectors in pollution analysis are the quadripole and the ion trap. Both detectors are reliable and produce reliable and reproducible data. Routine maintenance is required for proper working. Mass spectral data are available in computer libraries, and the database is expanding day by day as data are getting generated rapidly with current software (Fischer 2018).

Principle: The basic principle of mass spectroscopy is that it generates ions and multiple ions from the given sample (analyte) and then separates the ions based on their mass-to-charge ratio (m/z). It then records the relative abundance of each type of ions present in the sample. At first, electron ionization converts the compound under analysis to a gaseous phase. After that, molecular ions of the compounds undergo fragmentation and are converted into primary ions, which again undergo fragmentation and so on. These generated ions are then separated by the mass spectrometer according to their mass-to-charge ratios and are detected in proportion to their abundance (Hess and MacRae 2018) Blood, urine and other body fluids, serum, plasma, hair, nail, tissue and other forensic materials can be used for the toxicological analysis using mass spectroscopy (Mogollón et al. 2018; Mbughuni et al. 2016).

23.13.13 Bimolecular Interaction Analysis–Mass Spectrometry (BIA-MS)

It is a new field that utilizes mass spectrometry as a tool for toxicological and biological research to investigate protein interactions. This technique explores proteins within the cellular environment, their different forms, interacting factors (e.g. cofactors) and the processes that affect their regulation and processing. The BIS-MS technique can determine the kinetics of protein interactions and can selectively retrieve and concentrate specific proteins from the biological media. It can also quantitate proteins, identify protein: ligand interactions and recognize protein variants (e.g. point mutations). BIA-MS uses two technologies: Surface Plasma Resonance (SPR) sensing and Matrix-Assisted Laser Desorption Ionization—Time-of-flight Mass Spectroscopy (MALDI-TOF MS). First, the cells are fragmented, and then they come in contact with a gold-plated glass slide, known as a chip. This chip consists of highly defined sites containing many immobilized ligands. The proteins of interest bind to these ligands and are quantified by SPR, which monitors the interactions and thus quantifies the amount of protein localized at precise locations on the surface of the chip. This chip is then subjected to MALDI-TOF MS, yielding the masses of retained analyte and other bound biomolecules (Fischer 2018; Leidy 2004).

23.13.14 Cyclic Voltammetry and Pulsed Electrochemical Detectors (PED)

Cyclic voltammetric systems are used as LC detectors. These are not commonly used in forensic toxicology but are used to identify drugs from biological fluids and also have some advantages in particular applications. For example, some drugs and poisons which are poor chromophores can be amenable to electrochemical detection. In electrochemical detection, compounds are identified by measuring electric current as a function of the potential difference between electrodes in contact with the analyte solution. Every compound has its unique reduction potential. When an increasing potential difference between electrodes in solution reaches this voltage, the current will increase as the compound is reduced at the electrode's surface, thus providing detection. As the molecules are reduced, the compound in the solution must be filled at the electrode for continuous monitoring. In some systems, it can also be accomplished by stirring the solution. The problem of reduced compounds on the electrode surface by oxidizing can be solved by cyclic voltammetry. The entire testing cycle progresses as follows: first, the potential difference between the electrodes is increased; due to this, the compound is reduced on the cathode surface at its reduction potential, and thus an increase in current is observed. To a selected limit, the voltage continues to increase. After reaching the limit, the polarity is reversed, the cathode becomes the anode, and the voltage is again increased. As the voltage reaches the oxidation potential, the compound is oxidized (equal in magnitude to the reduction potential). The analyte is identified on the basis of the voltage that is required to oxidize and reduce it. The analyte concentration, which is proportional to the current recorded, is determined by comparison to standards (Smith et al. 2007).

23.14 Conclusion

The chapter covered various aspects of toxicology and its application in forensic investigations. It began by discussing poisons, including their classification based on origin, mode of action, medicolegal classification, forms, and site of action. Antidotes and factors influencing the action of poisons were also explored. The chapter further delves into illicit drugs, their classification, and the collection of toxicological evidence. The stages of alcohol intoxication are explained, and methods for detecting commonly used poisons, illicit drugs, and alcohol are outlined. The chapter concludes by highlighting different analytical techniques employed in forensic toxicology. Overall, this chapter provides a comprehensive introduction to the field, encompassing a range of important topics and methodologies in forensic toxicology.

References

Afridi HI, Kazi TG, Jamali MK et al (2006) Evaluation of toxic metals in biological samples (scalp hair, blood and urine) of steel mill workers by electrothermal atomic absorption spectrometry. Toxicol Ind Health 22:381. https://doi.org/10.1177/0748233706073420

Almirall JR, Trejos T (2016) Applications of LA-ICP-MS to forensic science. Elements 12:335–340. https://doi.org/10.2113/GSELEMENTS.12.5.335

Anuj A, Krishna G (2017) Principles of toxicology

Badiye A, Kapoor N, Menezes RG (2021) Chain of custody [updated 2021 Feb 21]. StatPearls [Internet]. StatPearls Publishing, Treasure Island. https://www.ncbi.nlm.nih.gov/books/NBK551677/

Bhoj Y, Tharmavaram M, Pandey G, Rawtani D, Mustansar Hussain C (2020) Chromatographic techniques for forensic investigations. In: Rawtani D, Hussain CM (eds) Technology in forensic science. https://doi.org/10.1002/9783527827688.ch7

Branch S (2004a) Chapter-Forensic and clinical toxicology (Thin layer chromatography (TLC) principle, procedure & applications). In: Hodgson E (ed) A textbook of modern toxicology, 3rd edn. Wiley, p 403. ISBN 0-471-26508-X

Branch S (2004b) Chapter-Forensic and clinical toxicology (Gas chromatography). In: Hodgson E (ed) A textbook of modern toxicology, 3rd edn. Wiley, p 404. ISBN 0-471-26508-X

Bianchi F, Ilag L, Termopoli V, Mendez L (2018) Advances in MS-based analytical methods: innovations and future trends. J Anal Methods Chem 2018:2084567

Biswas G (2012) Review of forensic medicine and toxicology: including clinical and pathological aspects, 2nd edn. Jaypee Brothers Medical Publishers, New Delhi

Britannica, T. Editors of Encyclopaedia (2023) Nuclear magnetic resonance. Encyclopedia Britannica. https://www.britannica.com/science/nuclear-magnetic-resonance

Braun RD (2022) Chemical analysis-electroanalysis. Encyclopedia Britannica. https://www.britannica.com/science/chemical-analysis

Chemistry LibreTexts (2022) Gas chromatography. https://chem.libretexts.org/Bookshelves/Analytical_Chemistry/Supplemental_Modules_(Analytical_Chemistry)/Instrumentation_and_Analysis/Chromatography/Gas_Chromatography

Creative Proteomics (2022) The principle of high-performance liquid chromatography (HPLC). https://www.creative-proteomics.com/pronalyse/the-principle-of-high-performance-liquid-chromatographyhplc.html

Cruces-Blanco C, Gámiz-Gracia L, García-Campaña AM (2007) Applications of capillary electrophoresis in forensic analytical chemistry. Trends Anal Chem 26:215. https://doi.org/10.1016/j.trac.2006.12.007

Deichmann WB, Henschler D, Holmstedt B, Keil G (1986) What is there that is not poison? A study of the Third Defense by Paracelsus. Arch Toxicol 58:207–213

Dorland WAN (2000) Dorland's illustrated medical dictionary, 29th edn. Saunders, Philadelphia

Darwish IA (2006) Immunoassay methods and their applications in pharmaceutical analysis: basic methodology and recent advances. Int J Biomed Sci 2:217

De Groot HJ, De Haas EJM, D'Haese P et al (1984) Determination by flameless atomic absorption of aluminium in serum and hair for toxicological monitoring of patients on chronic intermittent haemodialysis. Pharm Weekbl Sci Ed 6:11. https://doi.org/10.1007/BF01960191

Dinis-Oliveria RJ, Vieira ND, Magalhaes T (2016) Guidelines for collection of biological samples for clinical and forensic toxicological analysis. Forens Sci Res 1:42–51. https://doi.org/10.1080/20961790.2016.1271098

Duffy's Rehab (2023) Schedule I, II, III, IV, & V drugs. Drug classifications. https://www.duffysrehab.com/resources/articles/schedule-of-drugs/

Fernández P, Lafuente N, Bermejo AM et al (1996) HPLC determination of cocaine and benzoylecgonine in plasma and urine from drug abusers. J Anal Toxicol 20:224. https://doi.org/10.1093/jat/20.4.224

Fischer K (2018) Immunochemical techniques. In: Hofmann A, Clokie S (eds) Wilson and Walker's principles and techniques of biochemistry and molecular biology, 8th edn. Cambridge University Press, Cambridge, pp 253–285. https://doi.org/10.1017/9781316677056

Garcia R, Baez AP (2012) Atomic absorption spectroscopy. Elsevier, London, pp 1–13

Hess S, MacRae JI (2018) Mass spectrometric techniques. In: Hofmann A, Clokie S (eds) Wilson and Walker's principles and techniques of biochemistry and molecular biology, 8th edn. Cambridge University Press, Cambridge, pp 219–252. https://doi.org/10.1017/9781316677056

Hou X, Amais RS, Jones BT, Donati GL (2016) Inductively coupled plasma optical emission spectrometry, encyclopedia of analytical chemistry, online © 2006–2016. Wiley. https://doi.org/10.1002/9780470027318.a5110.pub3

Houck MM, Siegel JA (2010) Illicit drugs. Fundamentals of forensic science. Elsevier, London, pp 305–340. https://doi.org/10.1016/B978-0-12-374989-5.00013-2

Jickells S, Negrusz A (2013) Clarke's analytical forensic toxicology. Choice Rev Online 51:1520. https://doi.org/10.5860/choice.51-1520

Johnson MW, Griffiths RR, Hendricks PS, Henningfield JE (2018) The abuse potential of medical psilocybin according to the 8 factors of the controlled substances act. Neuropharmacology 142: 143–166. https://doi.org/10.1016/J.NEUROPHARM.2018.05.012

Kabera JN (2017) Analytical methods of compounds in biological specimens: applications in forensic toxicology. Int J Forens Sci 2:1

Klaassen CD (2008) Unit I Casarett and Doull's toxicology: the basic science of poisons, 7th edn. The McGraw-Hill Companies, Inc, pp 1–128. https://doi.org/10.1036/0071470514

Klaassen CD (2013) Casarett & Doull's toxicology: the basic science of poisons, 9th edn. McGraw Hill, New York, NY

Komoroski EM, Komoroski RA, Valentine JL et al (2000) The use of nuclear magnetic resonance spectroscopy in the detection of drug intoxication. J Anal Toxicol 24:180. https://doi.org/10.1093/jat/24.3.180

Leidy RB (2004) Analytical methods in toxicology. A textbook of modern toxicology. Wiley, New York, NY, pp 439–461. https://doi.org/10.1002/0471646776.CH25

Menzies AC (1960) A study of atomic absorption spectroscopy. Anal Chem 32(8):898–904. https://doi.org/10.1021/ac60164a001

Mbughuni MM, Jannetto PJ, Langman LJ (2016) Mass spectrometry applications for toxicology. EJIFCC 27:272

Miksa IR, Buckley CL, Carpenter NP, Poppenga RH (2005) Comparison of selenium determination in liver samples by atomic absorption spectroscopy and inductively coupled plasma–mass spectrometry. J Vet Diagn Investig 17:331–340. https://doi.org/10.1177/104063870501700405

Millo T, Jaiswal A, Prasad K (2017) The Indian laws relating to drugs and poisons. J Forens Chem Toxicol 3:17–21

Mistek E, Lednev IK (2018) FT-IR spectroscopy for identification of biological stains for forensic purposes. Spectroscopy (Santa Monica) 33:8

Mogollón NGS, Quiroz-Moreno CD, Prata PS et al (2018) New advances in toxicological forensic analysis using mass spectrometry techniques. J Anal Methods Chem 2018:4142527. https://doi.org/10.1155/2018/4142527

Molina DK (2010) Handbook of forensic toxicology for medical examiners, 4th edn. CRC Press, Boca Raton, FL

Namir H, Hadzic R, Malesevic I et al (2019) Application of thin layer chromatography for qualitative analysis of gunpowder in purpose of life prediction of ammunition. Int J Biosens Bioelectron 5:4. https://doi.org/10.15406/ijbsbe.2019.05.00144

Pragst F (2008) Chapter 13 High performance liquid chromatography in forensic toxicological analysis. In: Handbook of analytical separations. Elsevier, London

Pugh MB (ed) (2000) Stedman's medical dictionary, 27th edn. Lippincott Williams & Wilkins, Baltimore. ISBN 0-683-40008-8. 2098 pages

Qriouet Z, Qmichou Z, Bouchoutrouch N et al (2019) Analytical methods used for the detection and quantification of benzodiazepines. J Anal Methods Chem 2019:2035492. https://doi.org/10.1155/2019/2035492

Rapley R (2018) Electrophoretic techniques. In: Hofmann A, Clokie S (eds) Wilson and Walker's principles and techniques of biochemistry and molecular biology, 8th edn. Cambridge University Press, Cambridge, pp 219–252. https://doi.org/10.1017/9781316677056

Sherma J, Fried B (2005) Thin layer chromatographic analysis of biological samples. A review. J Liq Chromatogr Relat Technol 28:2297

Smith ML, Vorce SP, Holler JM et al (2007) Modern instrumental methods in forensic toxicology. J Anal Toxicol 31:237–253. https://doi.org/10.1093/JAT/31.5.237

Taylor (1859) On poisoning by nicotina, and detection of the poison. Pharm J 18:620–626

Tagliaro F, Smyth WF, Turrina S et al (1995) Capillary electrophoresis: a new tool in forensic toxicology. Applications and prospects in hair analysis for illicit drugs. Forensic Sci Int 70:93. https://doi.org/10.1016/0379-0738(94)01612-9

Trejos T, Almirall JR (2010) Laser ablation inductively coupled plasma mass spectrometry in forensic science. Encyclopedia of analytical chemistry. Wiley, New York, NY. https://doi.org/10.1002/9780470027318.A9103

Trestrail J (2007a) Criminal poisoning: investigational guide for law enforcement, toxicologists, forensic scientists and attorneys, 2nd edn. Humana Press, Totowa, NJ

Trestrail J (2007b) Types of poisons. In: Forensic science and medicine: criminal poisoning, 2nd edn. Humana Press, Totowa, NJ, pp 29–46

Vij K (2011) Textbook of forensic medicine and toxicology principles and practice, 5th edn. Elsevier, London

Drugs of Abuse: Trends and Advanced Analytical Methods

24

Sachil Kumar

Abstract

Abuse of drugs is correlated with various medical, behavioral, psychological, spiritual, financial, social, family, and legal concerns and profoundly impact the people involved, their families, and society. Drugs of abuse (DOA) testing in biological specimens may provide objective information on the usage or misuse of drugs by the person involved and thus it is considered as one of the main tasks in the different disciplines of forensic toxicology and related areas. Testing is carried out for two primary reasons. The first is to test for or prove an alleged acute drug effect or intoxication/poisoning. The second is monitoring abstinence from DOA, e.g., in workplace drug testing.

This chapter deals with the types and methods of analysis for DOA testing that focus on trends and developments in the last decade regarding relevant analytes and analytical methodology. The authors often rely on alternative matrices for monitoring DOAs.

Keywords

Drug of abuse · Forensic toxicology · Analytes · Bio-matrix · Urine · Blood · Oral-fluid · Hair · Immunoassay · LCMS · GC-MS

S. Kumar (✉)
Department of Forensic Sciences, College of Criminal Justice, Naif Arab University for Security Sciences, Riyadh, Saudi Arabia
e-mail: SKumar@nauss.edu.sa

P. Shrivastava et al. (eds.), *Textbook of Forensic Science*,
https://doi.org/10.1007/978-981-99-1377-0_24

24.1 Introduction

Drugs of Abuse (DOA) or Street Drugs are described as being mind-altering substances, typically taken on non-medicinal grounds. DOA may contribute to physical and mental damage and (with certain substances) dependence and addiction. DOA is linked to a wide range of medical, behavioral, social, interpersonal, financial, and legal problems.

The use of DOA has been a long-standing problem globally, a problem that has taken on a particular urgency in the last 30 years. The US has become the world's most industrialized drug-abusing country, but in other industrialized countries, illegal drugs also are an increasing concern. Approximately, 5% of people (230 million) used illegal drugs in 2010 (United Nations 2012; EMCDDA 2016). Substance use disorders culminated in 307,400 fatalities in 2015, an increase from 165,000 in 1990 (Wang et al. 2016; Abubakar et al. 2015). Drug abuse is documented in persons of all ages and from all walks of life and social backgrounds. Men are more likely to abuse drugs than females; single persons are far more likely than married individuals; and city inhabitants are more likely than rural ones. Detainees, homeless youths, and children are especially vulnerable to drug misuse. Throughout 2019, hospitals concerned with primary care, pain management or substance misuse problems reported significant spikes in urine samples testing positive for possibly lethal substances (Quest Diagnostics n.d.).

DOA testing is, therefore, a significant task in the fields of doping, forensic toxicology, clinical toxicology, and workplace drug testing. It is usually done to confirm the effect of acute drugs for example, in driving under the influence (DUI) or to monitor drug abstinence for instance, in workplace drug testing, drug withdrawal or substitution treatment, or drug-abstinence programs in the context of regranting for relicensing. In addition to conventional bio-matrices such as urine (abstinence testing) and blood (acute effects), oral fluid has emerged to be an extremely significant testing matrix for on-site samples using special collection equipment. In fact, hair has now proven itself as a well-established matrix for long-term DOA testing (Kumar et al. 2012). Several international associations of forensic toxicologists have assessed many alternate biological matrices as diagnostic tools for substance testing (Fucci et al. 2006).

Immunoassay technologies, such as counting immunoassay (CIA), radioimmunoassay (RIA), enzyme-linked immunosorbent assays (ELISA) or enzyme immunoassays (EIA), chemiluminescence immunoassay (CLIA), and fluoroimmnoassay (FIA) have been in practice to detect and presumptively measure the DOA samples in the targeted analysis. However, for positive screening results confirmation by more selective and sensitive techniques are required. Thus, analytical procedures are utilized for confirmatory and non-targeted DOA testing typically focused on specific chromatographic techniques that can involve GC or LC coupled with a single-stage (MS) or tandem mass spectrometry (MS^2 or MS/MS). These technologies are highly reactive and accurate, thus allowing for explicit recognition of compounds.

24.2 Drug Abuse Is Not a Victimless Crime

Drug users would like to assume that they will not hurt others, but it's simply not accurate. Drug abusers hurt their family members and the ones nearest to them the worst, but they have a cumulative impact. Substance misuse contributes to a variety of physical and psychological health issues. Withdrawal effects can also harm your well-being.

Drug dependency makes it harder for individuals to sustain stable personal relationships. The harmful aspect of drug addiction contributes to the breakdown of the family unit, which triggers a variety of psychological and behavioural issues for adolescents in their youth. There is also a link between drug abuse, societal issues, antisocial behavior and violence in certain countries. Those under the influence of drugs and alcohol have reduced inhibitions, rendering them more likely to commit offences or engage in antisocial behavior. Petty stealing to get money to purchase narcotics is even more prevalent in communities of heavy drug use. Drug addiction is recognized as a neurological condition by most medical practitioners, but it is often still misread by many individuals.

24.3 Drugs of Abuse: The Analytes

DOA is not a well-defined expression. In a limited context, it refers to controlled substances with psychoactive properties that are primarily consumed because of their mind-altering effects and may lead to drug dependence or addiction. However, a clear-cut differentiation between DOA and therapeutic drugs is not possible. On the one hand, many compounds such as amphetamine and cannabis generally considered as DOA also have therapeutic applications and have been utilized to treat narcolepsy, attention shortfall and pain, posttraumatic stress disorder, multiple sclerosis, nausea, cancer and epilepsy respectively (CDPHE (Colorado Department of Public Health and Environment) 2016). Hence, these drugs can only be considered as DOA when used without prescription or in doses exceeding those prescribed.

On the other hand, many drugs that are primarily used therapeutically have considerable abuse potentials, such as opioids, benzodiazepines, or ketamine. These drugs are frequently used in excess of the prescribed doses and often diverted to the illicit drug market and sold there as DOA. Over a few years, a new trend in the DOA market has become increasingly important, namely the availability of new psychoactive substances which are neither legally approved for medicinal usage nor regulated as restricted agents, when they initially emerge on the drug market as recreational/illicit. They are, therefore, also marketed as 'legal highs' and/or labeled as safe products, like bath salts, incense, or herbal nutrients (Table 24.1).

Table 24.1 Selected common drugs/metabolites and drug classes relevant in drugs of abuse analyses (Quest Diagnostics n.d.)

Drug class	Common drugs/metabolites
Amphetamines	Amphetamine, methamphetamine, MDMA
Cannabinoids	THC, HO-THC, THC-COOH
Cocaine	Cocaine, benzoylecgonine
Opiates	Heroin, morphine, codeine, Hydromorphone (Dilaudid®), Hydrocodone (Vicodin®, Lorcet®, Lortab® and Hycodan®), oxycodone (OxyContin®, Endocet®, Endodan®, Percoset®, Percodan®, OxyIR®, OxyFast®, Roxicet® and Tylox®), Oxymorphone (Opana® and Numorphan®), methadone, fentanyl
Opioids	Fentanyl, tramadol, lidine
Benzodiazepines	Nordiazepam, oxazepam (Serax®), temazepam (Restoril®), alprazolam (Xanax®), flurazepam (Dalmane®), lorazepam (Ativan®), diazepam (Valium®), chlordiazepoxide (Librium®), prazepam (Centrax®), clorazepate (Tranxene®), halazepam (Paxipam®), medazepam (Nobrium®), clonazepam (Klonopin®), flunitrazepam, and midazolam (Versed®)
Z-drugs	Zaleplon, zolpidem, and zopiclone
Anesthetics	Ketamine
Synthetic cannabinoids ("K2/Spice")	JWH-018, JWH-200, CP 47,497, RCS-4
Synthetic stimulants ("Bath Salts")	Alpha-PVP, flephedrone, butylone, methedrone, mephedrone, methylone, MDPV, pentylone, and pentedrone
Cathinones	Mephedrone, ephedrone, methylone, MDPV
Phenethylamines (2Cs)	2C-I, 2C-B, 2C-T-7
Substituted amphetamines	PMA, 4-FA, 4-MTA
Tryptamines	5-MeO-DIPT
Piperazines	BZP, mCPP and TFMPP

MDMA methylenedioxymethamphetamine, *THC* D^9-tetrahydrocannabinol, *HO-THC* 11-hydroxy-D^9-tetrahydrocannabinol, *THC-COOH* 11-nor-D^9-tetrahydrocannabinol-9-carboxylic acid, *MDPV* 3,4-methylenedioxypyrovalerone, *2C-B* 4-bromo-2,5-dimethoxyphenethylamine, *2C-I* 4-iodo-2,5-dimethoxyphenethylamine, *2C-T-7* 4-propylthio-2,5-dimethoxyphenetylamine, *PMA* 4-methylamphetamine, *4-FA* 4-uoroamphetamine, *4-MTA* 4-methlythioamphetamine, *5-MeO-DIPT* 5-methoxy-N,N-diisopropyltryptamine, *mCPP* meta-chlorophenylpiperazine, *TFMPP* tri uoromethylpiperazine, *BZP* N-benzylpiperazine

24.4 Bio-matrices for Drug Abuse Analysis

Depending on the purpose of the analysis, DOA testing can be carried out in various biological matrices. Different bodily fluids and tissues, like blood, urine, hair, sweat, saliva, nails, etc., are used for this screening, each with its pros and cons. Urine and blood (whole blood, plasma or serum) are the long-established conventional matrices for DOA testing.

Drug concentrations in whole blood or blood-derived matrices (serum, plasma) generally show the best correlation with drug effects during the sampling period. Blood samples can only be taken invasively and are generally only used when explicitly required by the law; such as in DUID cases in most countries and/or when drug concentrations are interpreted in terms of their consistency with observed or reported impairment either by symptomatology in clinical toxicology cases, or DOAs potential role in the cause of death in postmortem toxicology cases. Moreover, in blood samples, DOA has a relatively short half-life. Drugs with ester or amide groups, such as benzodiazepines and cocaine, are vulnerable to hydrolysis degradation (Drummer 2004). The instability of drugs in biological samples during transportation and storage makes interpreting analytical results difficult (Holmgren et al. 2004). Handling biological samples from suspected drug users is another important concern since it is frequently connected with the incidence of chronic disease infection and the likelihood of transmission of HIV, hepatitis, and other blood-borne viruses (World Health Organization 2004).

Dried blood spots (DBS) have gained significant attention in the past years. DBS, i.e., small amounts of blood spotted and dried on a special paper, are another blood-derived sample matrix. The usage of DBS (Guthrie Card) to monitor metabolic disorders in a broad neonate populace was first proposed by Dr. Robert Guthrie in the early 1960s (Guthrie and Susi 1963). They have been successfully used to screen for metabolic disorders in neonates and therapeutic drug monitoring and could become a promising alternative to conventional whole blood, serum, or plasma samples in DOA testing. Because a small prick in the fingertip or heel generally provides sufficient blood for collecting a DBS, qualified medical personnel is not necessarily needed for sampling. Moreover, handling and shipping of DBS is easier than for liquid samples. Two very recent studies reported good agreement for concentrations of 3,4-methylenedioxymethamphetamine (MDMA) and its metabolite 3,4-methylenedioxyamphetamine (MDA) (Jantos et al. 2011), amphetamine, the cocaine metabolite benzoylecgonine, and morphine (Saussereau et al. 2012) in whole blood and DBS. Nevertheless, additional research is required to establish DBS as a routine matrix for DOA analysis. Throughout postmortem toxicology, the lack of blood and urine is common; in this case, forensic matrices like postmortem blood, tissues and vitreous humor may be examined by the toxicologist.

Generally, urine has always been the most common matrix for drug testing when the presence rather than the acute influence of a drug is most relevant as in abstinence monitoring. In contrast to blood, urine can be taken noninvasively and in comparatively large volumes. Moreover, drugs and drug metabolites are concentrated in the urine, extending the detection windows for most drugs. However, it must be considered that many drugs are expelled in the urine in the form of metabolites and that drugs may be overlooked when only testing for the parent drugs. Another vital issue to be addressed in urine-based DOA analysis is adulteration. Unless the sampling process is directly observed by another person, which is considered unacceptable in some countries due to privacy issues, the sample's integrity must be checked to exclude dilution or the addition of chemicals that interfere with the applied analytical methodology (Jaffee et al. 2007).

Over the years, research has shown that new matrices like sweat, oral fluid, and hair samples have increased the prevalence for workplace drug testing and medico-legal sectors. Oral fluid, which comes from salivary glands and passively diffuse drugs in oral fluid, is the most popular and alternative sample for drug abuse testing. A significant benefit of oral fluid over blood and urine is the non-invasive selection of samples that another person can conveniently examine without violating the privacy of the study subject. Moreover, sampling can be performed directly on-site, which has made oral fluid testing particularly popular in roadside DOA testing. Due to the distasteful collection of oral fluid by expectoration or passive drooling and the low sample volumes obtained by these sampling methods, oral fluid collection is almost exclusively performed using collection devices specifically designed for this purpose. In some of the devices, the otherwise high variability of collected sample volumes is reduced by using a color indicator indicating a sufficient sample collection. A problem with such sampling devices is that the device may adsorb predominantly lipophilic drugs such as D9-tetrahydrocannabinol (THC; the active form of cannabis) increases the risk of false-negative results. Some of the collection devices contain elution buffers and preservatives to prevent the adsorption and degradation of analytes. However, these do not only dilute the collected oral fluid, but the additives may also interfere with the analysis of the oral fluid samples.

Sweat is yet another thoroughly researched drug abuse test specimen. Drugs passively diffuse from the blood to sweat glands and enter the sweat. Typically, high concentrations of the drugs are detected in the sweat compared to its metabolites (Bosker and Huestis 2009; Musshoff and Madea 2007).

Hair is another alternate and fundamental bio-matrix in the absence of blood and urine samples, which can also be collected noninvasively and is ideally suited for monitoring long-term exposure to drugs spanning from weeks or even months depending on the length of the sampled hair (Musshoff and Madea 2007). Circulating drugs or their metabolites are first accumulated in the hair follicle and later held in the middle of the hair shaft as the hair grows out of the hair follicle (Dolan et al. 2004; Garg and Ferguson 2012). Hair testing has a long detection window. The hair testing results can differ depending on the person in terms of the characteristics of their hair.

Strictly true, hair is no longer an alternate matrix, in forensic toxicology testing. There are still, however, a variety of uncertainties in the analysis of a hair sample. Cosmetic procedures, in particular, bleaching, permeating, or straightening and some medical conditions such as alopecia can degrade or remove the incorporated substances thus hair might have been removed for its application in Forensic Toxicity analysis. In the absence of appropriate matrix, keenness to use fingernails and toe nails as an alternative keratinized matrices has been suggested (Baumgartner 2014). Garside examined the usage of nails for the analysis of DOA (Garside 2008). Similarly, Krumbiegel et al., concluded that nail samples might serve as an alternative matrix for detecting the long-term activity of a wide range of drugs.

Meconium is the newborn's first stool, usually in the immediate days after birth. Meconium production begins between 12 and 16 weeks of fetal development, and deposits continue in the intestine of the fetus up until birth. It is a sticky, semi-solid,

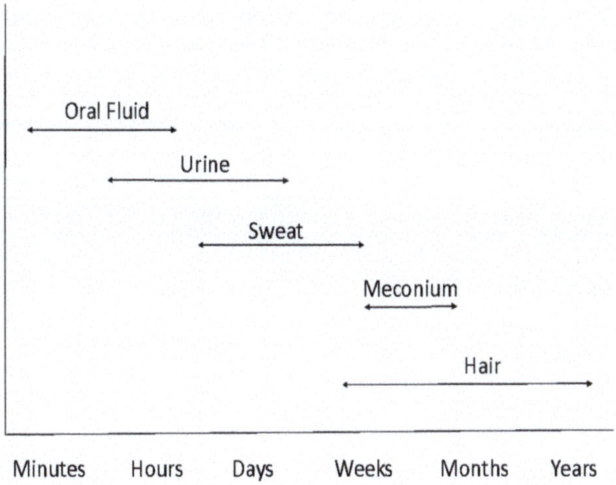

Fig. 24.1 Relative detection time for drugs of abuse in various sample types (Cone 1997; Dasgupta 2007)

tar-like excretory product composed of amniotic fluid, bile, mucus, and cells coming off from the intestinal tract. Meconium sampling is simple and completely non-invasive (Garg and Ferguson 2012). In DOA analysis, it is primarily used in long-term abstinence monitoring, such as in the context of regranting of driver's licenses. Apart from that, it may provide helpful information on the consumption pattern of a specific individual (for example, in cases of drug use during pregnancy or in opiate-related deaths in postmortem toxicology) (Fig. 24.1; Table 24.2).

24.5 Analytical Methods for Analysis of DOA in Biological Samples

24.5.1 Types of Analysis

Based on the goal of analysis, DOA testing may target a limited number of drugs/drug classes, usually classic DOA, or more comprehensively encompass a large number of compounds with abuse potential. The targeted approach is generally applied when the law requires testing for a defined list of drugs/drug classes as in workplace drug testing.

For example, Table 24.3 lists the drugs to be tested in US for workplace drug-testing programs, as mandated by Substance Abuse and Mental Health Services Administration (SAMSHA) (SAMHSA 2020). Another example is the schedule of drugs/drug classes listed in the annex to § 24a of the German Road Traffic Act ruling administrative offences regarding DUID. Similar laws exist around the world. Hence, analysts will need to be familiar with the appropriate inclusions of drugs in their jurisdiction.

The comprehensive approach is generally used, when the drugs/drug classes to be tested for are not scheduled by the law or guidelines for testing programs, and

Table 24.2 The approximate detection times for each drug in specific biological matrices (Hadland and Levy 2016; National Center on Substance Abuse and Child Welfare/Substance Abuse and Mental Health Services Administration 2015)

Substance	Hair	Urine	Sweat	Blood	Oral fluid/ saliva
Alcohol	Up to 90 days	10–12 h	n/a	Up to 6 h	Up to 24 h
Amphetamines	Up to 90 days	2–4 days	7–14 days	Up to 48 h	1–48 h
Methamphetamine	Up to 90 days	3–5 days	7–14 days	Up to 48 h	1–48 h
Barbiturates	Up to 90 days	Up to 7 days	n/a	Up to 48 h	n/a
Benzodiazepines	Up to 90 days	Up to 7 days	n/a	Varies	n/a
Marijuana	Up to 90 days	1–30 days	7–14 days	Up to 36 h	Up to 24 h
Cocaine	Up to 90 days	1–3 days	7–14 days	Up to 48 h	1–36 h
Codeine	Up to 90 days	2–3 days	7–14 days	n/a	1–36 h
Morphine	Up to 90 days	2–5 days	7–14 days	Up to 20 h	1–36 h
Heroin	Up to 90 days	2–3 days	7–14 days	Up to 20 h	1–36 h
Oxycodone	n/a	2–4 days	n/a	n/a	n/a
Hydromorphone	n/a	2–4 days	n/a	n/a	n/a
Methadone	n/a	3 days	n/a	n/a	n/a
Propoxyphene	n/a	6–48 h	n/a	n/a	n/a
PCP (Phencyclidine)	Up to 90 days	5–6 days	7–14 days	Up to 24 h	n/a
MDMA (Ecstacy)	n/a	Up to 48 h	n/a	Up to 24 h	Up to 24 h

Hours h, *n/a* not applicable

especially whenever relevant effects caused by DOA are to be confirmed or excluded as in postmortem toxicology or criminal offenses associated with DUID in some nations.

24.6 Analytical Methods for DOA Testing

24.6.1 Immunoassays

Methods for DOA testing have undergone significant changes in the past years. The DOA testing is a two-tier strategy. The laboratory must carry out a preliminary screening test, accompanied by a confirmatory test on the sample before the

Table 24.3 SAMSHA panel of drugs to be tested for in workplace drug testing (SAMHSA 2020)

Initial test analyte	Cutoff concentration (ng/mL)	Confirmatory test analyte	Cutoff concentrations (ng/mL)
Marijuana metabolites	50	THC-COOH	15
Cocaine metabolites	150	Benzoylecgonine	100
Opiate metabolites (codeine/ morphine)	2000	Codeine, morphine	2000 2000
6=AM (6-acetylmorphine)	10	6-AM	10
PCP (phencyclidine)	25	PCP	25
Amphetamines (AMP/MAMP)	500	AMP, MAMP	250, 250
MDMA (methylenedioxymethamphetamine)	500	MDMA, methylenedioxyamphetamine (MDA), methylenedioxyethylamphetamine (MDEA)	250, 250, 250
Vicodin®/Dilaudid® (new to SAMHSA)	300	Hydrocodone/hydromorphone	300
OxyContin® (new to SAMHSA)	100	Oxycodone/oxymorphone	100

specimen can be stated as positive. Immunoassay is a promising platform that can offer a simple, affordable and quick way to test large samples in a range of matrices. Based on the concept of immunological reaction, an immunoassay can identify the presence of drugs and their metabolites in a biological sample, hence reducing the need for further, more sophisticated and costly confirmatory tests. Whether in a forensic, clinical, doping, or workplace setting, immunoassay continues to be the most commonly used screening method for DOA samples.

Urine drug screening can be dated back to the 1970s and has been commonly used to screen troops coming back from combat during the Vietnam War. During that time, the techniques employed were EMIT and RIA. RIA has already been nearly outdated, and the most widely employed laboratory-based methods for urinary drug monitoring are ELISA, EMIT, and CEDIA (cloned enzyme donor immunoassay). Each of these technologies is now automated to fulfill the specifications of an advanced toxicology analysis laboratory. One of the most difficult procedures in forensic toxicology is to study autopsy samples. The techniques depend on ELISA has proven to be the most versatile one.

Modern automated immunoassays have advanced drug screening procedures further by providing precise results at fast speeds. Lab-on-a-chip technologies, that integrate and scale down laboratory operations and processes to a tiny chip format, have been introduced. Such multiplex immunoassays focused on ELISA principles can detect multiple DOA from a single undivided patient sample, resulting in more time- and labor-effective testing.

Instrumental immunological assays for DOA testing in urine and blood-derived matrices based on the enzyme immunoassay (EIA), ELISA or fluorescence polarization immunoassay (FPIA) principle are commercially available for the major classes of DOA (e.g., amphetamines, cannabinoids, cocaine, opiates, benzodiazepines, barbiturates) and for some individual drugs relevant in DOA testing, such as phencyclidine, methadone or buprenorphine.

These tests are well-established and widely used in routine DOA testing. Hence, only the likelihood of false-positive and false-negative results are highlighted here: typical reasons for false-negative results may be low cross-reactivity of a particular drug from a specific drug class with the antibody/antibodies from the respective group test or adulteration of the sample. A typical source for false-positive results is cross-reactivity of the antibody with other drugs or drug metabolites from different drug classes or unknown matrix compounds. Cross-reactivity with drugs from other drug classes is not always evident from the structure of the interfering compound (Moeller et al. 2008). Therefore, toxicologists must be familiar with the cross-reactivity profiles of the employed test and essential that all positive screening results are confirmed by more sensitive and selective methods (see below), at least in the forensic setting.

Only very recently, IAs targeting some of the new psychoactive compounds have become commercially available. They focus on synthetic cannabinoids and cathinone derivatives. However, the market for these legal highs is constantly changing, so it remains to be seen if these tests will prove helpful in routine drug testing. Likely, at least part of the particular drugs for which the tests have been

Table 24.4 MPA guidelines cut-offs for the most common drug classes of abuse in urine and hair

	Urine		Hair	
Substance class	Old cutoffs (ng/mL)	New cutoffs (ng/mL)[a]	Old cutoffs (ng/mg)	New cutoffs (ng/mg)[a]
Cannabinoids	50	10	0.1	0.02
Cocaine and metabolites	300	30	0.5	0.1
Amphetamines	500	25	0.2	0.1
Opiates	300	25	0.2	0.1
Benzodiazepines	200	50	–	0.05
Methadone and EDDP	300	50	–	0.1
Ethyl glucuronide	–	100	–	0.007

[a] New cut-offs adhere to the 2009 guidelines' 2nd edition (Schubert and Mattern 2009)

validated will soon lose relevance in the legal highs market and be replaced by the next generation of new psychoactive drugs.

The used cut-off values directly influence the false-positive and false-negative rates of the tests, and none of it can be optimized simultaneously. Workplace drug testing is generally performed with comparatively high cut-off values (Table 24.3) to avoid expensive confirmation testing of false-positive samples, whereas low cut-offs must be used if the primary goal is to avoid false-negative findings (e.g., in a zero-tolerance setting). In 2009, the screening cut-offs for DOA testing in urine were lowered considerably by the driving license regranting medical and psychological assessment (MPA) guidelines in Germany. The effect of the lowered cut-offs was evaluated by Agius et al., who compared the results of 3500 and 5000 urine samples and tested under the old and new MPA cut-offs respectively (Agius et al. 2012).

Table 24.4 shows the old and new DOA cut-offs. The actual positive rates for 11-nor-9-carboxy-THC (11-COOH-THC), morphine, benzoylecgonine and amphetamine were 1.6-, 2.3-, 3.3- and 7-times higher when using the new cut-off values (Agius et al. 2012). This clearly highlights how low cut-off values enhance the likelihood of detecting ongoing drug abuse in a population of supposedly abstinent subjects.

Laboratory-based IAs with adequate performance are also available for oral fluid testing. However, such instrumental IAs are generally not available on-site, and hence drug screening is often performed by so-called rapid tests. These are single-use testing devices, which are also based on immunochemical reactions and may be visually interpreted or with a particular reader. According to a recent study with eight different testing devices in the context of the European DUID, Alcohol and Medicines (DRUID) project, none of the tested devices showed acceptable diagnostic sensitivity, specificity and accuracy above 80% for all tested parameters (Blencowe et al. 2011) with particularly low sensitivity data for cannabinoids (≤59%) and cocaine/benzoylecgonine (≤59%).

Another issue that has not been resolved yet is that on-site screening tests are performed in oral fluid, whereas in most countries, whole blood or serum is the mandatory matrix for confirmation testing. Since there is no constant ratio between oral fluid and blood concentrations (Wille et al. 2009) definition of oral fluid cut-offs that adequately reflect relevant blood concentrations is not straightforward. However, recent studies indicate, that this goal may be achieved by using a combination of prevalence data and statistical tools (Gjerde and Verstraete 2011, 2010).

Recent studies have shown that hair samples can also be screened for major DOA utilizing commercially available products, either by combining a commercial sample preparation technique with commercial IA reagents (Baumgartner et al. 2012; Musshoff et al. 2012) or by using commercial ELISA kits (Musshoff et al. 2012; Pujol et al. 2007).

Owing to the shortcomings of IAs, several recent publications have discussed the potential replacement of IA-based DOA screening methods by LC-MS/MS-based systems employing simple dilute and shoot approaches (Eichhorst et al. 2009) or even flow injection analysis (Lua et al. 2012).

24.6.2 Hyphenated Chromatographic Techniques

The unprecedented advent of hyphenated methodology has demonstrated new analytical possibilities for forensic scientists. In 1980, Thomas Hirschfield defined "hyphenation" for the possible online merging of separation and spectroscopic analytical techniques in a single-run cycle (Wilson and Brinkman 2003). Hyphenated techniques range from the integration, or linking of chromatographic techniques (e.g., GC, LC, etc.) to spectral techniques (e.g., UV-Vis, PDA, MS, NMR, ICP etc.), using an effective interface, to maximize the benefits of both techniques (Patel et al. 2010). In hyphenation methodology, chromatography techniques are employed to obtain unblended forms of analytes, from complex chemical compounds, whereas spectral analysis provides standards, or the library spectrum required for selective identification information (Patel et al. 2010). Hyphenated methods have gained significant popularity in recent years as the primary tool to address complex theoretical challenges.

Hyphenation may sometimes include multiple separations or detection techniques, like LC/NMR/MS, LC/MS/MS, LC/PDA/MS, LC/PDA/NMR/MS, and so forth. During crucial trace analysis, the enrichment of analytes is accomplished with the online combination of SPE, SPME or LVI into a more efficient embedded system, such as (LVI)-GC-MS or (SPE)-LC-MS.

Hyphenated techniques mainly used in the DOA analysis include CE-MS, GC-MS, LC-NMR, and LC coupled to single-stage MS or tandem MS (MS/MS). One application of these techniques is quantitative confirmation of positive screening results, in which the MS/MS instruments are operated in the SIM or MRM mode, targeting only a limited number of analytes covered by the respective screening methods. Apart from such confirmation methods, SIM or MRM methods can also be employed for targeted screening, identification, and quantification of DOA not covered by IAs, exemplified for new psychoactive compounds (Wohlfarth et al. 2010; Peters et al. 2003).

In any case, it must be ensured that the mass spectrometric information recorded for each analyte is sufficient for unambiguous compound identification. The GTFCh (German-speaking Society of Toxicological and Forensic Chemistry) (Australian/New Zealand Specialist Advisory Group in Toxicology 2012) and the TOXSAG (Australian/New Zealand Specialist Advisory Group in Toxicology) (Eichhorst et al. 2009) have specified sets of identification criteria to be used in the forensic toxicology analysis. Both guidance documents require absolute retention times to be within ±2% and ±5%, and relative retention times to be within ±1% and ±2.5% for GC and LC, respectively. The GTFCh document requires monitoring at least three diagnostic ions when using SIM and at least two diagnostic ions (transitions) in MRM, whereas the TOXSAG document requires monitoring of three ions for both SIM and MRM.

GC-MS has long been the modus operandi model for confirmation testing in DOA analysis and is still widely used for this purpose. However, significant limitations of GC-MS are that it can only be utilized for analytes amenable to GC analysis (i.e., nonpolar, volatile and thermostable compounds). Moreover, sample preparation for GC-MS also requires an extraction step to isolate the analytes from the generally aqueous sample matrix. Pretreatment of samples using the cleavage of glucuronic acid conjugates of opiates and benzodiazepines in urine samples may be required before extraction. Finally, most DOA carries active functional groups such as primary or secondary amine moieties (e.g., amphetamines), phenolic hydroxyl moieties (e.g., opiates and THC) or carboxy groups (e.g., THC-COOH) that must be derivatized before GC-MS analysis to improve their gas chromatographic properties (Segura et al. 1998).

In the last decade, LC-MS and LC-MS/MS-based techniques have developed to be progressively prominent in DOA testing and partly replaced GC-MS in this field. Owing to the high selectivity of MS/MS detection volumes could be reduced to 100 μL for the determination of synthetic cannabinoids utilizing LC-MS/MS in MRM mode (Ammann et al. 2012). Moreover, analyzing samples with high water content has helped simplify sample preparation to rapid and simple dilution/protein precipitation of urine, oral fluid or blood samples in numerous applications. Alternatively, many LC-MS(/MS) applications for DOA testing have been developed in which extraction is performed online with an extraction column or cartridge being operated in line with the separation column allowing complete automation of the extraction process.

In most LC-MS(/MS) applications, reversed-phase stationary phases combine with volatile buffers like ammonium formate or acetate with acetonitrile or methanol as organic modifiers. More recently, the employment of stationary phases with sub-2-μm particle sizes resulted in the higher separation of multiple analytes in comparison to the short runtimes of the conventional LC columns. For example, Eichhorst et al. managed to isolate 42 compounds within 5 min. However, owing to the limited-run period, a single transformation per compound could be tracked. If not, the peak widths may have become very tiny to track a reasonable amount of data points per phase over the specified cycle time (Paul et al. 2009).

Little research has been published that relates to the LC/API-MS testing of drugs (opioids or cocaine) in urine (Drummer 2006). Drummer used the precipitation of proteins and fast LC/ESI-MS/MS to quantify opiates and cocaine in plasma, blood, and urine (Drummer 2006). Successfully, without sample preparation, LC/APCI-MS/MS conducted combined quantitative analyses of opioids, cocaine and urine metabolites (Dams et al. 2003). Nishikawa et al. (1994) demonstrated that the LC/APCI-MS hyphenated technique with dual SPE could be used effectively to analyze cocaine and its metabolites. Bogusz et al. (1997, 1998, 2001) published research papers on the adaptation of LC/APCI-MS to the analysis of opiate agonists, cocaine, benzodiazepines, amphetamines, and hallucinogens found in various biofluids, such as urine. Hyphenated LC–TOF-MS is also used to measure cocaine and ecgonine methyl ester in rat plasma (Jeanville et al. 2000). Pharmacokinetic and drug interaction studies (Schänzle et al. 1999) mainly focused on detecting morphine and its glucuronide, and normorphine, in various biofluids, by automated SPE and LC/ESI-MS/MS. In the case of urine drug abuse, an LC/ESI-MS in conjunction with non-automatic SPE or online SPE was used to identify amphetamine and heroin metabolites, specifically biomarkers of those substances (Katagi et al. 1998, 2000).

APCI–MS is used to identify cannabinoids in conjunction with supercritical fluid chromatography, while LC-PBI-MS is used to detect Hashish and its metabolites (THC, CBD, CBN) (Katagi et al. 2001). Amphetamines (Amphetamines, Methamphetamines, MDMA, MDE, and MDA) with different sources such as TSP, ESI, and APCI sources were identified by LC/MS (Bogusz 1999; Concheiro et al. 2007).

Lysergic acid diethylamide (LSD) is a highly effective and popular psychoactive drug among substance abusers and the most difficult to test due to poor detection of the parent drug in urine.

Jang et al. have validated two sensitive and effective methods that rely on LC-MS/MS for the synchronized identification of LSD and its metabolite, 2-oxo-3-hydroxy-LSD (O-H-LSD), in urine and hair samples. Hair is analyzed for trace elemental examination using methanol and evaluated with LC-MS/MS. Liquid extraction has been conducted for urine sampling (Jang et al. 2015). Dolder et al. demonstrated a responsive LC/MS/MS turbo-flow device for LSD, O-H-LSD, iso-LSD, and nor-LSD quantification and possible detection of LAE, LEO, 2-oxo-LSD, trioxylated LSD and 13/14 hydro hydrology in human plasma samples (Dolder et al. 2018). A group of researchers developed a new immunoassay for LSD screening in urine, and ESI for urinary LSD confirmation. In addition, this research group used methyesergide as an internal standard for urinary LSD determination in ESI, coupled with SPE. N-methyl–LSD was also detected in real samples (Bogusz 1999). An effective LC/MS/MS system has been established for the simultaneous identification of nicotine and cotinine in serum samples. LLE (Liquid-liquid extraction) with ethyl acetate, was used for serum sample preparation (Abdallah et al. 2016). LC/APCI/MS is also used to determine the nicotine concentration in smokers' and non-smokers' serums (Bogusz 1999).

Potential matrix effects led to the suppression or enhancement of analyte ionization by co-eluting compounds, are to be considered when performing DOA analysis by LC-MS (/MS), as they may compromise the sensitivity of detection as well as the quantitative performance parameters accuracy and precision, especially when no stable-isotope-labeled analogues of the analytes are available as internal standards. For these reasons, testing for matrix effects is acritical element in validating any LC-MS(/MS)-based method.

24.7 DOA in Alternative Matrices

24.7.1 Hair

Lately, hair has indeed been found to be a possible tool for drug detection in different contexts, such as forensic and occupational testing as well as monitoring enforcement in drug recovery and drug-facilitated crime (DFC), as any drug and its metabolites deposited in hair, tend to last longer than standard samples. The presence of standard reference material is required for hair testing in substance abuse cases (Rapinoja et al. 2005). DFC cases, including different categories of drugs, like benzodiazepines and hypnotics, methadone and buprenorphine, can be successfully solved with the help of hair samples (Hancock et al. 2005).

Kintz and his colleagues stated that "the sensitivity of LC/MS/MS is highly significant when detecting minimal concentrations of drugs deposited in hair (small pg/mg) in drug-facilitated sexual assault investigations". Nevertheless, they have introduced a clause in which hair analysis would be considered a complimentary blood and urine testing technique rather than an alternative technique. The LC-ESI/MS/MS is beneficial in cases where the concentration of the drug is minimal, as only one single therapeutic dose accumulates in the hair, such as benzodiazepines and benzodiazepine-like hypnotics (Chèze et al. 2005).

In a randomized trial to examine the detection window for lorazepam in semen, hair, and oral fluid, the value of this technique was discovered due to simultaneous examination of 26 benzodiazepines, zolpidem and zopiclone in blood, hair and urine (Caplan and Goldberger 2001). The LC-ESI-MS/MS system has also been introduced to actual samples of forensic and clinical cases, such as examining a woman's hair who had claimed to have been drugged and sexually assaulted for many years. Such findings showed the utility of hair in the sense of chronic drug use. Hair samples were screened for ethyl and fatty acid ethyl esters (FAEEsters), which were considered markers of chronic alcohol use. GC/MS and LC/MS/MS seemed to be the methodological approaches utilized for such determination (Janda et al. 2002).

24.7.2 Oral Fluids

Oral fluid (OF) can be exploited as anancillary matrix for the detection of abusive substances in occupational testing, clinical toxicological examinations, criminal enforcement cases, and DUI-cases (Aacc.org 2021). The OF matrix provides a fairly clean and secure way for sampling, thereby reducing the possibility of sample adulteration. LC/APCI-MS/MS, followed by protein precipitation (Dams et al. 2007), is utilized to determine and quantify cocaine, opiates, and its metabolites found in OF, investigated for drug abuse (Dams et al. 2007). Vindenes et al. utilized LC/MS/MS to perceive different drugs and their metabolites ($n = 32$), collected from the oral fluid of real-life patients undergoing a drug treatment program and the findings were compared to urine samples taken from the same patients simultaneously (Vindenes et al. 2011). In addition, Welch et al. identified a procedure for detecting methadone and other addictive substances and their metabolites in OF (Welch et al. 2003). PPT with acetonitrile, accompanied by LC/MS/MS analysis, was utilized in this protocol and was particularly effective for evaluating methadone concentrations in pregnant women. The US Food and Drugs Administration (FDA) has approved a screening tool used for large-scale workplace drug monitoring in the United States and is currently under review in a new EU-US roadside trial to identify DUID. As there is a lack of standard clean-up methods in ion suppression through LC/MS/MS, additive impurities of collected samples may increase the chance of contamination. Many researchers used LLE with hexane to process OF specimens for analysis (Concheiro et al. 2004); nowadays, the Salivette method is used for sample collection and the measurement of 9-THC in SPE and LC/MS OF samples. The hyphenated technique HPLC-MS/MS methods are used to quantify methadone enantiomers. Methadone enantiomers are significantly different in the contexts of receptor affinity, analgesic potency, and pharmacokinetic profiles and are also prescribed as a racemic combination that is a 50:50 enantiomer combination. This assay method utilized Salivette® (saliva collection device) for a simple, direct and validated extraction of the analytes, with a 100% recovery rate even in the minimal amount of sample volumes. After centrifugation, an immobilized α1-acid glycoprotein chiral stationary phase (AGP-CSP) combined with MS was used to distinguish analytes.

24.7.3 Meconium

Drug misuse is a significant concern during pregnancy and is linked with prenatal problems and elevated infant morbidity and mortality incidences. Many congenital disabilities are believed to be due to prenatal drug exposure. Urine drug testing has historically achieved the identification of drug exposure in the uterus. This, however, only indicates maternal drug usage within the last three-four days, and a mother's abstinence several days before delivery may produce a negative outcome. Alternative matrices, like neonatal meconium and hair, can be used to monitor exposure, including earlier gestational non-invasive collection and detection.

Meconium is the newborn's first stool, usually in the immediate days after birth. Meconium production begins between 12 and 16 weeks of fetal development, and deposits continue in the intestine of the fetus up until birth. The presence of this substance can considerably delay the drug detection period, which is up to about the last 20 weeks of pregnancy. Meconium sample testing is a steady and time-consuming process. Compared to liquid samples, meconium is a sticky, semi-solid, tar-like excretory product and should be weighed before extraction. Goggin et al. described a process by which ceramic homogenizers were used before the extraction of salt-assisted LLE and LC/MS/MS to analyze cocaine in meconium along with its metabolites and amphetamines (Goggin and Janis 2019).

Ristimaa et al. (2010) analyzed abused drugs in meconium within a routine examination, utilizing LC/MS/MS and TOF-MS technology. Jensen et al. (2019) demonstrated developing an LC/MS/MS system to classify and quantify four cannabinoid alkaloids in two neonatal matrices. Bogusz (1999) also used meconium to detect opiates, cocaine and amphetamine with the presence of their respective metabolites. In both instances, SPE was used in the sample preparation and the experiment was carried out utilizing LC–MS. This sensitivity to LC/MS/MS is precise in displaying concentrations of drugs in all ranges, as nanograms per gram, collected in meconium samples. In another study, LC/MS/MS was used for meconium for both methanol extractions accompanied by SPE and immediate quantification of methadone and its metabolites. This hyphenated technique can be used to detect methadone traces from meconium ingested continuously by the fetus's mother during pregnancy. Choo et al. (2005) employed LC-APCI-MS/MS for meconium drug testing.

24.7.4 Postmortem Alternative Specimens

Alternative specimens (e.g. muscle tissue rather than blood) are very useful in detecting ante-mortem substance addiction and being valid in postmortem procedures. Toxicological analyses of conventional postmortem specimens often pose problems such as the decomposition and putrefaction of specimens. The abstinence of any suitable biological substance or fluid is supplemented by valuable entomological evidence and is often utilized to confirm different drugs in the organism. Though insect tissues have proven to provide reliable samples, it is certainly impossible to claim that drugs were the cause of death. Wood et al. developed a system for quantifying benzodiazepines in larvae and puparia of Calliphora vicina (Diptera: Calliphoridae) through LC/MS/MS (Wood et al. 2006). Oxazepam is present in larvae or pupae as a compound or metabolite. Different stages of Larva can be used to determine the time after death. Throughout certain instances, drug presence has been found to affect insect development; consequently, such disruptions could have severe implications for the precise determination of postmortem interval.

Pelander et al. (2010) analyzed the usefulness of vitreous humor (VH) as an additional matrix for drug screening with LC/TOF/MS in 50 autopsy examination cases by comparing results in VH and urine. The comparative study revealed that VH is suitable for qualitative screening analysis, and not adequate for metabolite detection compared to urine. In all, 45 parent compounds and 24 metabolites were detected in VH and urine samples respectively with the mean and median cut-off values of 0.072 and 0.023 mg/L, each, acceptable for standard casework (Pelander et al. 2010).

24.8 Conclusion

Forensic toxicology testing for DOA is usually done either in the context of acute impairment/intoxication or to monitor abstinence from DOA. Classic illicit DOA, therapeutic drugs with potential for abuse, and so-called legal highs, new psychoactive substances that are neither approved for therapeutic use nor listed as controlled substances are relevant to the DOA analysis. Furthermore, in addition to the conventional drug-testing matrix urine and blood, the alternative matrices OF and hair have been more important in DOA analysis in recent years. Immunoassay-based approaches are commonly employed in targeted screening for major DOA but may yield false-positive results and require confirmation. OF collection is generally performed utilizing specifically developed collection devices that are supposed to ensure the collection of a sufficient amount of sample, but may adsorb considerable amounts of the drug. The performance of immunoassay-based DOA on-site testing devices for screening analysis in OF currently does not meet the requirements for an ideal testing device, while laboratory-based ELISA tests with adequate performance are available. LC-MS/MS methods have partially substituted GC-MS as the preferred analytical method for confirmation and multianalyte DOA testing and often require less sample volume, less sample preparation, and shorter runtimes. Matrix effects should be adequately evaluated during the validation of methods to avoid compromise in the performance of LC-MS/MS.

References

Aacc.org (2021) Developing standards for oral fluid as an alternative matrix for toxicology testing. AACC.org. Available https://www.aacc.org/cln/articles/2017/november/developing-standards-for-oral-fluid-as-an-alternative-matrix-for-toxicology-testing. Accessed 1 March 2021

Abdallah IA, Hammell DC, Stinchcomb AL, Hassan HE (2016) A fully validated LC–MS/MS method for simultaneous determination of nicotine and its metabolite cotinine in human serum and its application to a pharmacokinetic study after using nicotine transdermal delivery systems with standard heat application in adult smokers. J Chromatogr B 1020:67–77

Abubakar II, Tillmann T, Banerjee A (2015) Global, regional, and national age-sex specific all-cause and cause-specific mortality for 240 causes of death, 1990-2013: a systematic analysis for the Global Burden of Disease Study 2013. Lancet 385(9963):117–171

Agius R, Nadulski T, Kahl HG, Dufaux B (2012) Significantly increased detection rate of drugs of abuse in urine following the introduction of new German driving licence regranting guidelines. Forensic Sci Int 215(1-3):32–37

Ammann J, McLaren JM, Gerostamoulos D, Beyer J (2012) Detection and quantification of new designer drugs in human blood: part 1–synthetic cannabinoids. J Anal Toxicol 36(6):372–380

Australian/New Zealand Specialist Advisory Group in Toxicology (2012) MS identification guidelines in forensic toxicology – an Australian approach. TIAFT Bull 42(2):52–55

Baumgartner MR (2014) Nails: an adequate alternative matrix in forensic toxicology for drug analysis? Bioanalysis 6(17):2189–2191

Baumgartner MR, Guglielmello R, Fanger M, Kraemer T (2012) Analysis of drugs of abuse in hair: evaluation of the immunochemical method VMA-T vs. LC–MS/MS or GC–MS. Forensic Sci Int 215(1-3):56–59

Blencowe T, Pehrsson A, Lillsunde P, Vimpari K, Houwing S, Smink B, Verstraete A (2011) An analytical evaluation of eight on-site oral fluid drug screening devices using laboratory confirmation results from oral fluid. Forensic Sci Int 208(1-3):173–179

Bogusz MJ (1999) Hyphenated liquid chromatographic techniques in forensic toxicology. J Chromatogr B Biomed Sci Appl 733(1-2):65–91

Bogusz MJ, Maier RD, Erkens M, Driessen S (1997) Determination of morphine and its 3-and 6-glucuronides, codeine, codeine-glucuronide and 6-monoacetylmorphine in body fluids by liquid chromatography atmospheric pressure chemical ionization mass spectrometry. J Chromatogr B Biomed Sci Appl 703(1-2):115–127

Bogusz MJ, Maier RD, Krüger KD, Kohls U (1998) Determination of common drugs of abuse in body fluids using one isolation procedure and liquid chromatography-atmospheric-pressure chemical-ionization mass spectrometry. J Anal Toxicol 22(7):549–558

Bogusz MJ, Maier RD, Erkens M, Kohls U (2001) Detection of non-prescription heroin markers in urine with liquid chromatography—atmospheric pressure chemical ionization mass spectrometry. J Anal Toxicol 25(6):431–438

Bosker WM, Huestis MA (2009) Oral fluid testing for drugs of abuse. Clin Chem 55(11): 1910–1931

Caplan YH, Goldberger BA (2001) Alternative specimens for workplace drug testing. J Anal Toxicol 25(5):396–399

CDPHE (Colorado Department of Public Health and Environment) (2016) 2016 medical marijuana registry statistics. https://www.colorado.gov/pacific/cdphe/2016-medical-marijuana-registry-statistics

Chèze M, Duffort G, Deveaux M, Pépin G (2005) Hair analysis by liquid chromatography–tandem mass spectrometry in toxicological investigation of drug-facilitated crimes: report of 128 cases over the period June 2003–May 2004 in metropolitan Paris. Forensic Sci Int 153(1):3–10

Choo RE, Murphy CM, Jones HE, Huestis MA (2005) Determination of methadone, 2-ethylidene-1,5-dimethyl-3,3-diphenylpyrrolidine, 2-ethyl-5-methyl-3, 3-diphenylpyraline and methadol in meconium by liquid chromatography atmospheric pressure chemical ionization tandem mass spectrometry. J Chromatogr B 814(2):369–373

Concheiro M, de Castro A, Quintela O, Cruz A, Lopez-Rivadulla M (2004) Chromatogr B 810:319

Concheiro M, Simoes SMDSS, Quintela O, de Castro A, Dias MJR, Cruz A, López-Rivadulla M (2007) Fast LC–MS/MS method for the determination of amphetamine, methamphetamine, MDA, MDMA, MDEA, MBDB and PMA in urine. Forensic Sci Int 171(1):44–51

Cone EJ (1997) New developments in biological measures of drug prevalence. NIDA Res Monogr 167:108–129

Dams R, Murphy CM, Lambert WE, Huestis MA (2003) Urine drug testing for opioids, cocaine, and metabolites by direct injection liquid chromatography/tandem mass spectrometry. Rapid Commun Mass Spectrom 17(14):1665–1670

Dams R, Choo RE, Lambert WE, Jones H, Huestis MA (2007) Oral fluid as an alternative matrix to monitor opiate and cocaine use in substance-abuse treatment patients. Drug Alcohol Depend 87(2-3):258–267

Dasgupta A (2007) Handbook of drug monitoring methods: therapeutics and drugs of abuse. Springer, New York

Dolan K, Rouen D, Kimber JO (2004) An overview of the use of urine, hair, sweat and saliva to detect drug use. Drug Alcohol Rev 23(2):213–217

Dolder PC, Liechti ME, Rentsch KM (2018) Development and validation of an LC-MS/MS method to quantify lysergic acid diethylamide (LSD), iso-LSD, 2-oxo-3-hydroxy-LSD, and nor-LSD and identify novel metabolites in plasma samples in a controlled clinical trial. J Clin Lab Anal 32(2):e22265

Drummer OH (2004) Postmortem toxicology of drugs of abuse. Forensic Sci Int 142(2-3):101–113

Drummer OH (2006) Drug testing in oral fluid. Clin Biochem Rev 27(3):147

Eichhorst JC, Etter ML, Rousseaux N, Lehotay DC (2009) Drugs of abuse testing by tandem mass spectrometry: a rapid, simple method to replace immunoassays. Clin Biochem 42(15): 1531–1542

EMCDDA (2016) Information on the high-risk drug use (HRDU) (formerly 'problem drug use' (PDU)) key indicator. emcdda.europa.eu. Accessed 27 September 2016

Fucci N, De Giovanni N, De Giorgio F, Liddi R, Chiarotti M (2006) An evaluation of the Cozart® RapiScan system as an on-site screening tool for drugs of abuse in a non-conventional biological matrix: vitreous humor. Forensic Sci Int 156(2-3):102–105

Garg U, Ferguson AM (2012) Alternate specimens for drugs-of-abuse testing: preanalytical and interpretative considerations. In: Barbarajean M, Bissell MG, Kwong TC, Wu AHB (eds) Clinical toxicology testing: a guide for laboratory professionals. CAP Press, Durham, pp 71–80

Garside D (2008) Drugs-of-abuse in nails. In: Drug testing in alternate biological specimens. Humana Press, New York, pp 43–65

Gjerde H, Verstraete A (2010) Can the prevalence of high blood drug concentrations in a population be estimated by analyzing oral fluid? A study of tetrahydrocannabinol and amphetamine. Forensic Sci Int 195(1-3):153–159

Gjerde H, Verstraete AG (2011) Estimating equivalent cut-off thresholds for drugs in blood and oral fluid using prevalence regression: a study of tetrahydrocannabinol and amphetamine. Forensic Sci Int 212(1-3):e26–e30

Goggin MM, Janis GC (2019) Salt-assisted liquid-liquid extraction of meconium for analysis of cocaine and amphetamines by liquid chromatography-tandem mass spectrometry. In: LC-MS in drug analysis. Humana Press, New York

Guthrie R, Susi A (1963) A simple phenylalanine method for detecting phenylketonuria in large populations of newborn infants. Pediatrics 32(3):338–343

Hadland SE, Levy S (2016) Objective testing: urine and other drug tests. Child Adolesc Psychiatr Clin 25(3):549–565

Hancock JR, D'Agostino PA, Chenier CL (2005) Presented at the 3rd conference on mass spectrometry applied to chemical and biological warfare agents, Noordwijkerhout, The Netherlands, 17–20 April 2005

Holmgren P, Druid H, Holmgren A, Ahlner J (2004) Stability of drugs in stored postmortem femoral blood and vitreous humor. J For Sci 49(4):1–6

Jaffee WB, Trucco E, Levy S, Weiss RD (2007) Is this urine really negative? A systematic review of tampering methods in urine drug screening and testing. J Subst Abus Treat 33(1):33–42

Janda I, Weinmann W, Kuehnle T, Lahode M, Alt A (2002) Determination of ethyl glucuronide in human hair by SPE and LC–MS/MS. Forensic Sci Int 128(1-2):59–65

Jang M, Kim J, Han I, Yang W (2015) Simultaneous determination of LSD and 2-oxo-3-hydroxy LSD in hair and urine by LC–MS/MS and its application to forensic cases. J Pharm Biomed Anal 115:138–143

Jantos R, Veldstra JL, Mattern R, Brookhuis KA, Skopp G (2011) Analysis of 3,4-methylenedioxymetamphetamine: whole blood versus dried blood spots. J Anal Toxicol 35(5):269–273

Jeanville PM, Woods JH, Baird TJ III, Estapé ES (2000) Direct determination of ecgonine methyl ester and cocaine in rat plasma, utilizing online sample extraction coupled with rapid chromatography/quadrupole orthogonal acceleration time-of-flight detection. J Pharm Biomed Anal 23(5):897–907

Jensen TL, Wu F, McMillin GA (2019) Detection of in utero exposure to Cannabis in paired umbilical cord tissue and meconium by liquid chromatography-tandem mass spectrometry. Clin Mass Spectrometry 14:115–123

Katagi M, Nishikawa M, Tatsuno M, Miyazawa T, Tsuchihashi H, Suzuki A, Shirota O (1998) Direct analysis of methamphetamine and amphatamine enantiomers in human urine by semi-microcolumn HPLC: electrospray ionization mass spectrometry. Eisei Kagaku 44(2):107–115

Katagi M, Tatsuno M, Miki A, Nishikawa M, Tsuchihashi H (2000) Discrimination of dimethylamphetamine and methamphetamine use: simultaneous determination of dimethylamphetamine-N-oxide and other metabolites in urine by high-performance liquid chromatography-electrospray ionization mass spectrometry. J Anal Toxicol 24(5):354–358

Katagi M, Nishikawa M, Tatsuno M, Miki A, Tsuchihashi H (2001) Column-switching high-performance liquid chromatography–electrospray ionization mass spectrometry for identification of heroin metabolites in human urine. J Chromatogr B Biomed Sci Appl 751(1):177–185

Kumar S, Wahid A, Anoop KV (2012) Physiology and anatomy of hair in drug abusing cases. IJMTFM 2:153–159

Lua IA, Lin SL, Lin HR, Lua AC (2012) Replacing immunoassays for mephedrone, ketamines and six amphetamine-type stimulants with flow injection analysis tandem mass spectrometry. J Anal Toxicol 36(8):575–581

Moeller KE, Lee KC, Kissack JC (2008) Urine drug screening: practical guide for clinicians. In: Mayo clinic proceedings, vol 83. Elsevier, Amsterdam, pp 66–76

Musshoff F, Madea B (2007) Analytical pitfalls in hair testing. Anal Bioanal Chem 388(7): 1475–1494

Musshoff F, Kirschbaum KM, Graumann K, Herzfeld C, Sachs H, Madea B (2012) Evaluation of two immunoassay procedures for drug testing in hair samples. Forensic Sci Int 215(1-3):60–63

National Center on Substance Abuse and Child Welfare/Substance Abuse and Mental Health Services Administration (2015) Drug testing practice guidelines. Available https://ncsacw.samhsa.gov/files/IA_Drug_Testing_Bench_Card_508.pdf

Nishikawa M, Nakajima K, Tatsuno M, Kasuya F, Igarashi K, Fukui M, Tsuchihashi H (1994) The analysis of cocaine and its metabolites by liquid chromatography/atmospheric pressure chemical ionization-mass spectrometry (LC/APCI-MS). Forensic Sci Int 66(3):149–158

Patel KN, Patel JK, Patel MP, Rajput GC, Patel HA (2010) Introduction to hyphenated techniques and their applications in pharmacy. Pharm Methods 1(1):2–13

Paul LD, Musshoff F, Aebi B, Auwärter V, Krämer T, Peters F, Schmitt G (2009) Richtlinie der GTFCh zur Qualitätssicherung bei forensisch-toxikologischen Untersuchungen. Toxichem Krimtech 76(3):142–176

Pelander A, Ristimaa J, Ojanperä I (2010) Vitreous humor as an alternative matrix for comprehensive drug screening in postmortem toxicology by liquid chromatography-time-of-flight mass spectrometry. J Anal Toxicol 34(6):312–318

Peters FT, Schaefer S, Staack RF, Kraemer T, Maurer HH (2003) Screening for and validated quantification of amphetamines and of amphetamine-and piperazine-derived designer drugs in human blood plasma by gas chromatography/mass spectrometry. J Mass Spectrom 38(6): 659–676

Pujol ML, Cirimele V, Tritsch PJ, Villain M, Kintz P (2007) Evaluation of the IDS One-Step™ ELISA kits for the detection of illicit drugs in hair. Forensic Sci Int 170(2-3):189–192

Quest Diagnostics (n.d.) Common drugs of abuse. https://www.questdiagnostics.com/home/companies/employer/drug-screening/drugs-tested/

Rapinoja M-L, Kuitunen M-L, Bjork H, Rosendahl K, Vanninen P (2005) Presented at the 3rd conference on mass spectrometry applied to chemical and biological warfare agents, Noordwijkerhout, The Netherlands, 17–20 April 2005

Ristimaa J, Gergov M, Pelander A, Halmesmäki E, Ojanperä I (2010) Broad-spectrum drug screening of meconium by liquid chromatography with tandem mass spectrometry and time-of-flight mass spectrometry. Anal Bioanal Chem 398(2):925–935

SAMHSA (2020) Retrieved 24 June 2020. https://www.samhsa.gov/sites/default/files/workplace/2010GuidelinesAnalytesCutoffs.pdf

Saussereau E, Lacroix C, Gaulier JM, Goulle JP (2012) Online liquid chromatography/tandem mass spectrometry simultaneous determination of opiates, cocainics and amphetamines in dried blood spots. J Chromatogr B 885:1–7

Schänzle G, Li S, Mikus G, Hofmann U (1999) Rapid, highly sensitive method for the determination of morphine and its metabolites in body fluids by liquid chromatography–mass spectrometry. J Chromatogr B Biomed Sci Appl 721(1):55–65

Schubert W, Mattern R (2009) Urteilsbildung in der medizinisch-psychologischen Fahreignungsdiagnostik–Beurteilungskriterien. Kirschbaum, Bonn

Segura J, Ventura R, Jurado C (1998) Derivatization procedures for gas chromatographic–mass spectrometric determination of xenobiotics in biological samples, with special attention to drugs of abuse and doping agents. J Chromatogr B Biomed Sci Appl 713(1):61–90

United Nations (2012) World drug report 2012 (PDF). Retrieved 27 September 2016.

Vindenes V, Yttredal B, Øiestad EL, Waal H, Bernard JP, Mørland JG, Christophersen AS (2011) Oral fluid is a viable alternative for monitoring drug abuse: detection of drugs in oral fluid by liquid chromatography-tandem mass spectrometry and comparison to the results from urine samples from patients treated with methadone or buprenorphine. J Anal Toxicol 35(1):32–39

Wang H, Naghavi M, Allen C, Barber RM, Bhutta ZA, Carter A, Coggeshall M (2016) Global, regional, and national life expectancy, all-cause mortality, and cause-specific mortality for 249 causes of death, 1980–2015: a systematic analysis for the Global Burden of Disease Study 2015. Lancet 388(10053):1459–1544

Welch MJ, Sniegoski LT, Tai S (2003) Two new standard reference materials for the determination of drugs of abuse in human hair. Anal Bioanal Chem 376(8):1205–1211

Wille SM, Raes E, Lillsunde P, Gunnar T, Laloup M, Samyn N, Verstraete AG (2009) Relationship between oral fluid and blood concentrations of drugs of abuse in drivers suspected of driving under the influence of drugs. Ther Drug Monit 31(4):511–519

Wilson ID, Brinkman UT (2003) Hyphenation and hypernation: the practice and prospects of multiple hyphenation. J Chromatogr A 1000(1-2):325–356

Wohlfarth A, Weinmann W, Dresen S (2010) LC-MS/MS screening method for designer amphetamines, tryptamines, and piperazines in serum. Anal Bioanal Chem 396(7):2403–2414

Wood M, Laloup M, Samyn N, Fernandez MDMR, de Bruijn EA, Maes RA, De Boeck G (2006) Recent applications of liquid chromatography–mass spectrometry in forensic science. J Chromatogr A 1130(1):3–15

World Health Organization (2004) Substitution maintenance therapy in the management of opioid dependence and HIV/AIDS prevention: WHO/UNODC/UNAIDS position paper. WHO, Geneva

Cyber and Digital Forensic 25

Neelesh Tiwari, Yash Baroniya, Vishwas Bharadwaj, Akash Kumar, and Ankit Srivastava

Abstract

Digital forensic includes a wide variety of spectrum, which deals with the mobile forensic, computer forensic, network forensic or other types of different devices related to the digital evidence. The main goal of digital forensic is to focus on the recovery and investigation of artifacts found in digital evidences related to cyber-crimes. In comparison to various other domains of forensics digital forensics has evolved faster as simple because technology changes rapidly. The advancement and upgradation of forensic software's are needed with each new version of an operating system, digital forensic must keep up with advances in technology. It is withal important to maintain the chain of custody from proper collection, seizing and transportation. In the forensic laboratories there are various forensically sound software which are used for examination in which extraction and interpretation is done. This needs a well sound scientist having a great knowledge. Also, there are different types of certifications available by many of the renowned organizations.

Keywords

Digital forensic · Mobile forensic · Network forensic · Collection · Seizing · Software and certifications

N. Tiwari · Y. Baroniya · V. Bharadwaj
Cyber Division, State Forensic Science Laboratory, Jaipur, Rajasthan, India

A. Kumar
Department of Anthropology, Lucknow University, Lucknow, Uttar Pradesh, India

A. Srivastava (✉)
School of Forensic Sciences, The West Bengal National University of Juridical Sciences, Kolkata, West Bengal, India
e-mail: ankitsrivastava@nujs.edu

P. Shrivastava et al. (eds.), *Textbook of Forensic Science*,
https://doi.org/10.1007/978-981-99-1377-0_25

25.1 Introduction

Nowadays, as we are moving toward digitalization, computer is being used at almost all ends in common men's life such as digital transaction, social media, online exam, and so on. When the computer is connected to the network, it acts like the ubiquitous, so the data can be transferred between two or more points in different ways. Digital means any storage or transmitting data by using a computer having a proper number of combinations that represent information related to text, image, audio, video, etc. Undoubtfully, the advents in information technology have greatly impacted the world. In addition to benefits achieved due to the digitalization and IT revolution, the digital world has also created new possibilities for crime and unlawful acts. As a basic rule of exchange, physical contact between two or more objects is recorded in terms of mutually exchanged traces. Similarly, all the events in the digital modes are also recorded and possess distinguished evidential significance.

Digital crimes are increasing exponentially and posing several challenges and concerns to law enforcement agencies. In fact, a variety of digital crimes have been reported. Digital crimes have caused the emergence of digital forensics to strengthen the investigation with information and clues on scientific grounds. In fact, the term digital forensic is the notion of scientific methods for the investigation of digital crimes. Over the decades, digital forensic has created new maxims and has now emerged as one of the most interesting, developing, and challenging arena. The complexity of these crimes requires adequate knowledge and expertise, in concern domains, for the forensic analysis. Several countries have constituted legal frameworks work ethical implementation of IT. Legal perspectives of digitalization are another interesting topic of discussion for scholars and experts of law fraternity from across the globe. Here, it is worthy to note that like other physical evidence, pre-processing, collection, and packaging of digital evidence is equally important. Intact chain of custody and practicing of standard protocols for collection and packaging provides an escape from the allegation of evidence tempering and altering as well as increases the probative value of evidence.

In this chapter, several perspectives of digital crimes and digital forensics are discussed along with basic fundamentals for a better understanding of the topic to the readers. Digital crimes and their wide plethora are discussed to understand the nature of these types of crimes in subsequent sections. Forensic analytical tools and analytical procedures are also discussed. Indeed, this chapter is aimed to cover all significant perspectives on one plane.

25.2 Digital Crimes

Digital crime has many synonymies for example cybercrime, electronic crime, and computer crime are changeable words. Firstly, computer crime term was used to denote any criminal activity that was done against computers and networks or using computer as a tool to do that activity.

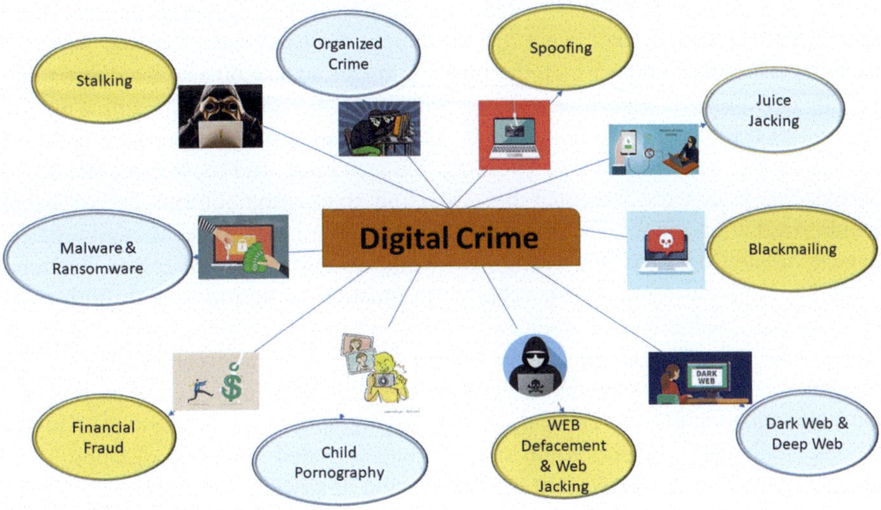

Fig. 25.1 Types of digital crimes

But in the last few years, these crimes extend to encompass other digital devices like cell phones, so the term was extended to digital crime. There is not one definition for digital crime till now and it is difficult to form a standard one. However, what can be said is that digital crime is focused on digital crime that has many synonymies for example cybercrime, electronic crime, and computer crime are changeable words. Firstly, computer crime term was used to denote any criminal activity that was done against computers and networks or using computer as a tool to do that activity.

Earlier only computer-related crimes were majorly considered as digital crimes. However, the advent of new digital gadgets extended the concept of digital crimes. There is no specific or standard definition for the term digital crime but on the basis of a basic understanding of law and forensics, a definition may be coined as any digitally performed act or omission that causes or tends to cause damage or harm to an individual are simply referred as digital crimes. Several types of digital crimes have emerged with technological upgradations as graphically presented in Fig. 25.1. Several terms such as cybercrimes, computer crimes, etc., are often encountered while discussing about digital crimes. The discussion provided below provides differences among these terms.

25.3 Cybercrime

Cybercrime covers a large domain of illegal activities, which includes the computer system, networks, storage, wireless communication, or done using some computer resources/tools (Sammons 2012, 2014; Cybercrimes Training Materials for

Investigators 2011; NFSTC 2009). There are various types of cybercrimes that often occurr. Malware and ransomware are the types of attachments, that are used for executing a specific task in which the instructions are sent or provided to the remote user. In ransomware, attackers hold some important data of the victim with the intention to bribe money or demands to release an important property. It includes different types such as Phishing, Spoofing, Virus, Trojan, BOTS, Worm, etc.

Financial frauds are executed by collecting transaction information or some unauthorized transaction which is providing or promising some attractive offer, business related deals to the wrongdoer. Some examples related to the financial frauds are Nigerian fraud, Ponzi scheme (promising for returning with high rates with little risk), Salami attack, illegal online transaction, job-related fraud, etc. Child Pornography is an atrocious crime against child rights and subject of serious concerns for all the law enforcement agencies. It includes to view, create, publish, distribute, and import obscene materials or pornography in the cyberspace. United Nations child right convention has outlined and included child pornography in its agenda. In addition, the projection or transmission of any kind of obscene content is strictly tabooed under the law.

Defacement attack involves the change in the visual appearance and the placing of unwanted files on the website page, to make a wrongful intention. In the cases of organized crime (murder, shooting incident, hit and run cases, and other crimes), where the digital evidence is not used as a tool, but is being carried with the delinquent, it may provide crucial information related to crime. The Web jacking attack is a technique where the attackers prepare a clone of the websites and sends the malicious link to them. This type of attack is used to gather information about passwords, usernames, card numbers, etc. from the preparator.

The dark web contents overlays on the network which uses the internet, but it is carried out with specific software, configuration and authorization to access the data. In the dark web, there is a small area which constitutes the deep web, where the web is not indexed by web search engines.

Blackmailing and Stalking The attacker steals other's identity or some important electronic information and blackmails the victim. This is technically referred in the literature as blackmailing. Stalking in terms of cyber is the access of information or data, such as mobile number, email, text messages, social media posts, etc., which are used by an unauthorized person for the personal benefit or to harass the victim.

Juice Jacking In these types of attacks, generally, the charging port (USB port) is provided for the mobile phone/tablet and other electronic gadgets, through which they copy the sensitive user data or install and execute other malware activities.

Spoofing The attacks in which the perpetrator or attacker used the technique of men in the middle attack which is done by the email/caller id/website/IP/ARP (Address Resolution Protocol) and DNS (Domain Name Server).

25.4 Digital Evidence and Digital Forensics

Digital evidence provides significant information and associative hints regarding the offense that occurred on digital platform. Digital evidences store the data by using magnetic or electric fields. Elements of the Computer system (open and embedded) and Communication system e.g. Laptop, C.P.U., Hard disk, Pen drive, DVR, CD, DVD, Mobile, SIM, Modem, Drone, GPS devices, Router, etc. often serve as digital evidence. However, some of the other definitions are also given by Standard Working Group on Digital Evidence (SWGDE) that, any crucial information is transmitted or stored digitally. International Organization of Computer Evidence (IOCE) proposed that the information that is stored or transmitted in a binary form is used for the purpose of the law which is finally used in the court (Cybercrimes Training Materials for Investigators 2011). Digital evidences significantly contribute to the investigation and adjudication of justice in several criminal and civil cases.

Digital forensic mainly deals with the examination and analysis of digital evidences. Obviously, it is the application of principles and technological modus operandi from computer science and IT domain to provide information of evidential significance. Interpretation of this extracted information enormously aids the forensic quest. Digital forensic has a long history. Over the decades, technological advancement in digital forensics also extended its dimensions. If we review the history, first offense related to the computer crimes found to be reported in the 1960s. In this incident, large number of computer systems were physically damaged at Concordia university, Canada as a consequence of student riots (Shaaban and Sapronov 2016).

Further in 1978, with the aim to address the intrusion, fraud and all unauthorized access to the computer systems, the first computer crime act (Florida Computer Crime Act) was formulated. It means computer-based fraud and unauthorized encroachment would come into existence. In due course, some new terms such as forensic computing, computer forensic, forensic computer analysis were coming into existence.

In the 1980s, several countries constituted legal framework to deal with computer-related offenses. In this regard, the U.S. Federal Computer Fraud and Abuse Act, 1984; Australian Crimes Act to Include Offenses Relating to Computers, 1989; British Computer Abuse Act, 1990; are noteworthy. In addition, several software developers also developed different applications competent for computer forensics-specific tasks.

In the first Digital Forensic Research Workshop (DFRWS) held in 2001, the term digital forensic was proposed. Further, the consideration was also extended to cellular and network forensic. At the end of the twentieth century, Scientific Working Group of Digital Evidence (SWGDE), G-8 high tec crime subcommittee, and international organization on computer evidence jointly published the principles of computer digital forensics. American Academy of forensic sciences initiated new forensic disciplines in connection with digital and multimedia sciences. In the view of newly emerged digital crimes, digital forensic may be branched into several

Table 25.1 Domains of digital forensics

Computer forensics	Gathering and analysis of digital information as digital evidence on computer systems and electronic storage medium
Network forensics	Monitoring and analysis of network traffic for the purposes of information gathering or intrusion detection
Memory forensics	Gathering and analysis of digital information contained within a system RAM or its associated memory
Cloud forensics	Related to the gathering and analysis of digital information from cloud computing systems
Electronic discovery (e-discovery)	Discovery, preservation, processing, and production of electronically stored information (ESI) in support, of legal or regulatory litigation matters
Incident response	Reducing business impact by managing the occurrence of computer security events

categories. The terms denoting the branches of digital forensics are as defined and summarized in Table 25.1 (Norris 2011).

25.5 Collection and Packaging of Digital Evidences

Proper collection and packaging of evidence enhance the probative value. Some procedures and precautions, which are followed to transport the evidence without any damage, are discussed in this section.

Computer, laptop, server tray, DVR, NVR, and other related digital evidence were found at the crime scene. Integrity is maintained by generating the Hash values of the particular evidence. Hash value is fixed sized of the unique alphanumeric set, that is calculated by different hash functions and represents the original data. There are different types of hash functions such as MD5, SHA 1, SHA 256, etc. These generated hash values are also mentioned in the seizure memo of the individual evidence. Computer, laptop, server tray or other related digital evidence, may be found in the three different conditions i.e., ON condition, OFF condition and connected to any network.

If the computer is found in the ON condition at the crime scene, "RAM Dump" of the exhibit should be performed by using the forensically sound software. The computer should be directly plug-OFF from the power plug. All the necessary details of the C.P.U., server-related details and hard disk should be seized by mentioning detailed information of the hard disk like brand, model/product number, firmware number and capacity of hard disk in the seizure memo. In case the computer is found in off condition, then detailed information of its hard disk like brand, model/product number, firmware number and capacity should be mentioned in the recovery memo. It is also provided that the signature of the accused and investigating officers should also be taken on a hard disk before sealing. If the Computers/Laptops are connected in the network during recovery, information of network topology should be mentioned in seizure memo.

During the seizing of DVR or NVR, detailed information of DVR and its hard disk like brand, model/product number, serial number, firmware number, and capacity should be mentioned in the recovery memo. After the proper ratification of the system lock or password, it should be mentioned in the seizure memo. It is also a notable parameter that the original time and display time of the DVR/NVR must be recorded at the time of seizure.

While collecting the mobile phone, Tablet, SIM, or other related devices, initially put the smart mobile phone on Flight/Airplane mode, as the network connectivity breaks down from the device. If the facility of flight mode option is not available in the mobile phone, then remove the SIM card from the mobile device before packing. Describe all the details of the mobile device like mobile phone body, SIM, memory card etc. (Model of mobile phone, IMEI/MIED, service provider of SIM, ICCID, capacity of memory card, brand etc.) should be mentioned in seizure memo during the seizing of mobile phone. It is also advised to mention the type and details of the system and application lock of the mobile phone (password, passcode, pattern lock, etc.). The verified PIN of SIM/PUK should be mentioned in the recovery memo for the retrieval of all types of desired data.

Computer, Laptop, DVR, NVR, and other digital evidence should be sent properly along with their power adapter. Keyboard and mouse are no longer needed in Forensic Laboratory. In case of seizure of the hard disk only, it must be packed into the anti-static bag and then further into another bag. Mobile phones should be wrapped into Faraday bag followed by bubble wrapping.

The investigation and forensic analysis of digital crimes as well its associated evidences is a challenging task for the investigator. The most important thing is to maintain the chain of custody, and the practice of standard protocol is necessary. Digital crimes are versatile in nature and therefore require specific approaches for forensic proceedings. Over the period, various domain experts proposed some standard protocol or model for forensic proceedings in digital crime cases. Some of the models are provided in Table 25.2.

25.6 Forensic Investigation in Digital Crimes

Communication devices such as cellular phones and digital assistant, which is used to communicate and transmit any information in the form of text, image, audio, video, etc., by using cellular networks. Cellular network covers a large geographical area to provide services and further it divides into smaller geographical areas that are called cells. These chain of cells are used in mobile phones to maintain the network system. In order to maintain the chain of cells, radio transceiver is the main component which performs specific channel assignment and switching system. Each mobile Switching centre controls radio frequency and manages all the communications such as cellular network, authentication, call routing, and location. There are two types of the location register: Home location and Visitor location which helps to identify the roaming service about the mobile device. Other associated information like subscriber information, CDR (Call Detail Record),

Table 25.2 Different model for investigation of computer forensic

Name of different model	References
Computer forensic investigative process	Pollitt (1995)
Computer forensic process model	US Department of Justice (2001)
Digital forensic research workshop investigative model (generic investigation process)	Palmer (2001)
Scientific crime scene investigation model	Lee et al. (2001)
Abstract model of the digital forensic procedures	Reith et al. (2002)
Integrated digital investigation process	Carrier and Spafford (2003)
End to end digital investigation	Stephenson (2003)
Enhanced integrated digital investigation process	Baryamureeba and Tushabe (2004)
Extended model of cyber crime investigation	Ciardhuain (2004)
A hierarchical, objective-based framework for the digital investigations process	Beebe and Clark (2005)
Event-based digital forensic investigation framework	Carrier and Spafford (2004)
Four step forensic process	Kent et al. (2006)
Framework for a digital forensic investigation	Kohn et al. (2006)
Computer forensic field triage process model	Rogers et al. (2006)
FORZA—digital forensics investigation framework	Leong (2006)
Common process model for incident and computer forensics	Freiling and Schwittay (2007)
Dual data analysis process	Bem and Huebner (2007)
Digital forensic model based on Malaysian investigation process	Perumal (2009)
Generic framework for network forensics	Pilli et al. (2010)
Generic computer forensic investigation model	Yusoff and Ismail (2011)
Systematic digital forensic investigation model	Agrawal et al. (2011)

phone number associated with SIM, ICCID (Integrated Circuit Cell-ID), IMSI (International Mobile Subscriber Identity), PUK (Personal Unlocking Key), Tower location, etc. are also examined. Nowadays, most of the people are using the social media and also this is used for the business perspective such as WhatsApp business, Facebook market and other applications. Some of them make fraud with the buyers, either they do not ship order, gather some bank-related information, or personal data. Some of the key points of the forensic investigation are graphically presented in Fig. 25.2.

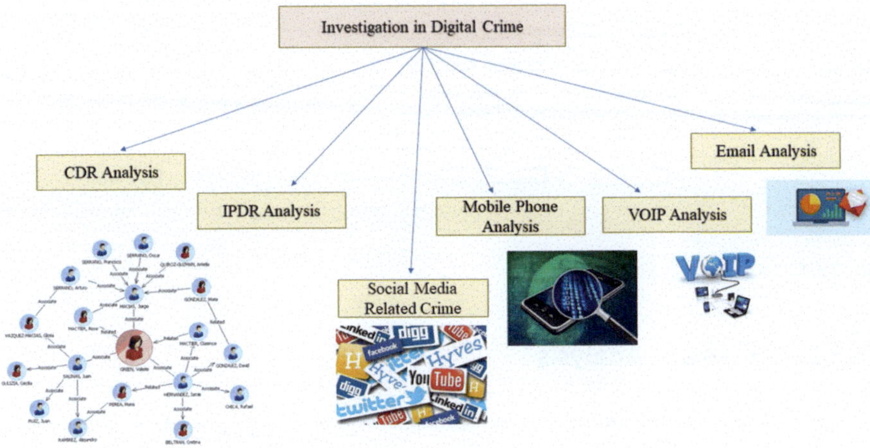

Fig. 25.2 Types of investigation related to digital crimes

Calling No	Called No	Date	Time	Dur(s)	Cell1	Cell2	Call Type	IMEI	IMSI No	Type	SMSC	Roam Nw
[redacted]	[redacted]	01-Nov-16	00:09:58	45	[redacted]	[redacted]	OUT	8.69E+14	4.04E+14	PRE	-	KK-0
[redacted]	[redacted]	01-Nov-16	08:32:41	45	[redacted]	[redacted]	IN	8.69E+14	4.04E+14	PRE	-	KK-0
[redacted]	[redacted]	01-Nov-16	09:10:21	20	[redacted]	[redacted]	OUT	8.69E+14	4.04E+14	PRE	-	KK-0
[redacted]	[redacted]	01-Nov-16	09:11:24	180	[redacted]	[redacted]	OUT	8.69E+14	4.04E+14	PRE	-	KK-0
[redacted]	[redacted]	01-Nov-16	10:30:20	70	[redacted]	[redacted]	IN	8.69E+14	4.04E+14	PRE	-	KK-0
[redacted]	[redacted]	01-Nov-16	10:32:49	0	[redacted]	[redacted]	SMT	8.69E+14	4.04E+14	PRE	9.85E+09	KK-0
[redacted]	[redacted]	01-Nov-16	10:37:29	9	[redacted]	[redacted]	IN	8.69E+14	4.04E+14	PRE	-	KK-0

Fig. 25.3 CDR analysis

25.6.1 Call Detail Record (CDR) and Internet Protocol Detailed Record (IPDR) Analysis

Under the Telecom Regulatory Authority of India (TRAI) guidelines, the service provider has to store the data for a limited extent of time. The service provider stores the details related to a subscriber, and they help to the law enforcement agencies to solve the crime issues. They provide the CDR file which contains information about the mobile details, date, time, tower location, etc. The analysis of the CDR related to the specific number is done by doing some logical operations on the Excel sheet or CDR software. CDR report can be exported in different formats such as text, HTML, .csv, .xls, and pdf.

Internet Protocol Detailed Record (IPDR) is needed when digital crime is done with the help of the internet. IPDR record the activity on internet, for the questioned IP addresses. IPDR analysis provides different details such as IP address of the source and destination, Ports, and time of access (Cybercrimes Training Materials for Investigators 2011; Norris 2011) (Fig. 25.3).

From	Pr[redacted]va <p[redacted]4@gmail.com>
Date	Mon, 25 Jan 2021 23:14:39 +0530
Message-ID	<CAP5vEV0U2ibLrmgQ+[redacted]1DSWhhoN=GxFhB=7w@mail.gmail.com>
Subject	Emailing 0_160363685[redacted]va.pdf
To	N[redacted]ari <n[redacted]@gmail.com>
Content-Type	multipart/mixed; boundary="000000000000633b1d05b9bd18cc"

Fig. 25.4 Email header analysis

25.6.2 Cell Tower Analysis

These types of analyses are performed for a specific investigation when there is very less information available about the victim or unknown place. It takes the dump from the tower and analyses the information. It is used at the crime scene or the suspected area. There are some portable hardware and software (Cell Site Analyzer) which is used for providing the cell tower analysis such as cell ID, tower ID, date and time.

25.6.3 Voice Over IP-Related Analysis

Voice Over IP (VOIP) technology makes communication cheaper and easier at a low cost. Voice and other multi-media content transfer through the internet can be done by using VOIP technology. In the investigation of the VOIP, first analyze the CDR of the victim, then take records from the respective service provider, and then check the gateway by which these calls were originated through the trunk information. Route-the-call process can be performed through the gateway such as skype and other social media platforms. From these social media, Law Enforcement agencies can request to provide detailed information about the particular account.

25.6.4 Email Analysis

Electronic mail is used to send or receive information in the form of text or media files. Three important protocols namely SMTP (Simple Mail Transfer Protocol), IMAP (Internet Message Access Protocol) and POP (Post Office Protocol) are used to transfer the information. SMTP is used when mail is transferred from one server to another server. IMAP and POP manage user mailbox to download and transmit mail in the application.

Email also gives rich information about the senders and receivers. It relays email on the simple Mail transfer protocol to its domain and the user connects through the HELO/EHLO to connect or send the email. The header of an email provides us information i.e., senders information, receivers information, Time zone (GMT or

CST in numerical value), date, and time, regarding IP (receiver's and senders) as shown in Fig. 25.4.

25.7 Forensic Analysis of Mobile Phone

Mobile phone forensics is one of the extremely complicated domains of digital forensics. Data extraction from the mobile phone depends on various factors such as its make and model, encryption, operating system version, security patch level version as well as many internal settings in the mobile phone like enabling USB-debugging, allowing other apps, etc., as well as the version of various applications like WhatsApp, Facebook, Messenger, etc.

Acquisition or Extraction, Examination and Report formation are major steps in the forensic examination of mobiles. There are various extractions or acquisition process for the mobile phone that depends on its Make/Model, operating system version. Extraction of mobile phone provides a wide spectrum of information that primarily involves device information, user data (Existing, Deleted, cached, encrypted, hidden data), files (document, picture, audio, video, database files), system details, application details, security accounts, and data, (messages, chat, internet details, call log, location details, network details etc. (Ligh et al. 2014). Different types of extraction strategies targeting specific objectives are there (Fig. 25.5).

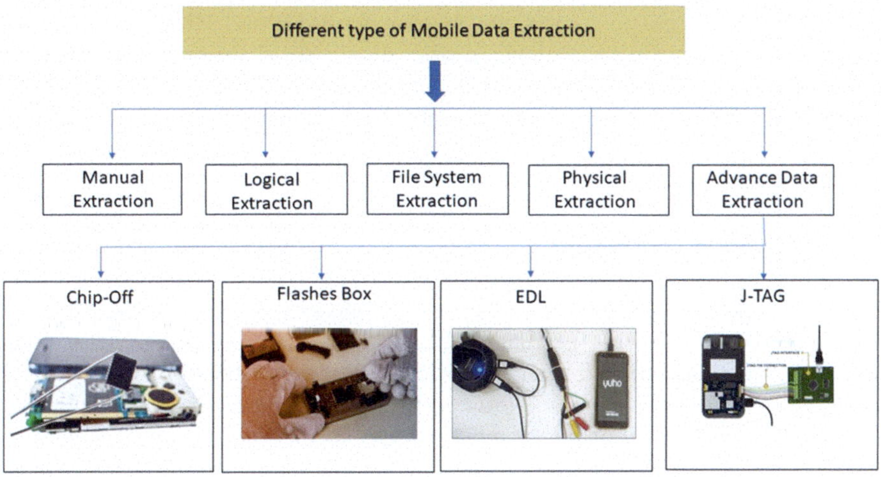

Fig. 25.5 Different types of mobile data extraction

25.7.1 Manual Extraction

Manual extraction is capturing stored data information through manual examination or photography. If mobile forensic software is not able to extract the data either from a certain directory like SMS, Contact, call log, etc., or any apps like WhatsApp, Messenger, etc., then a manual extraction procedure is used through software-based photo capturing process. Mobile forensic guidelines are followed in this process and reports may be generated in an appropriate manner (Tamma et al. 2020).

25.7.2 Logical Extraction

Logical extraction is capturing a copy of logical storage (such as directories and files) that resides on a logical storage (such as file system partition) using a data transfer method, whereby the software can communicate using mobile device protocols to extract data using commands comprehended by the mobile device. In its simplest form, logical extraction is used to extract the live data, which is present on the device like contacts, call logs, application and their data, SMS, MMS, photos, movies, audio files, etc.

25.7.3 File System Extraction

File system extraction is type of logical extraction, instead of treating every item of content separately, smart phones generally store many types of data within a file system. Mobile device having OS like Android, iOS, Blackberry and today's feature phone allow to access to logical file system via MTP and PTP. These modes recognise the mobile phone as device, rather than a drive, when mobile phone is connected to PC. File system acquisition can sometimes help in recovering deleted contents (stored in SQLite files) that are deleted from the device at logical file system level.

25.7.4 Physical Extraction

Physical extraction is capturing bit by bit of physical memory chip. Physical extraction is used to extract user data, application data and system data as well as deleted data may be retrieved from the device. Physical extraction involves reading through data cable, service ports, JTAG ports or Chip-off method with appropriate software. Physical extraction has many advantages in various ways since in extracts deleted data, Bluetooth pairing, security code, previous IMSI/ICCIDs. Other non-visible data, earlier version of file. However, interpretation of the data is typical and requires care and experience.

25.7.5 Advanced Data Extraction Tools

Besides afore discussed extraction methods, there are few more state-of-the-art tools and methods that have facilitated enhanced extraction of the data.

Flasher Box In mobile forensic field, flasher boxes have been used to read from the mobile device instead of writing. Flasher boxes allow for the extraction of data from damaged devices, dead device, or locked devices. It can provide the ability to reset passcodes and turn-off Factory reset Protection (FRP). If flasher box is handled improperly data can be destroyed (Fig. 25.6). Flasher boxes can write over device memory and content which is further flashed, and it is not in any documented way. It requires utmost care while operation. There are many flasher box solutions available that support a wide range of variety of featured mobile phones, as shown in Fig. 25.6.

Emergency Download Mode (EDL) The EDL is an emergency door to transfer the Android OS from a computer to the internal memory chip when the device is in a boot loop, hard brick, or dead boot. Emergency Download is a way to capture data from the mobile phone by using the EDL cable which has an inbuilt toggle switch through which we can sort the correct pin to make it successful, as shown in Fig. 25.7.

Joint Test Action Group (JTAG) JTAG points are printed on mother boards of the mobile during their manufacturing process, which are used to extract data. In mobile

Fig. 25.6 Flasher box

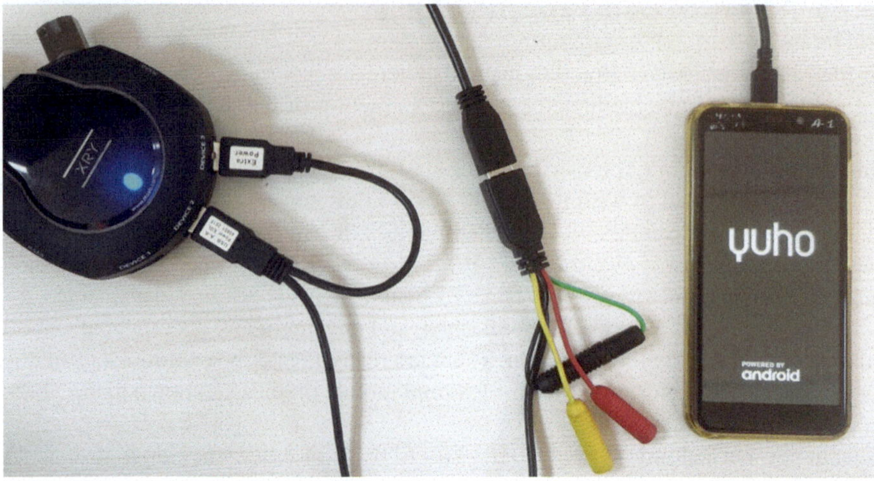

Fig. 25.7 EDL cable used for sorting pin

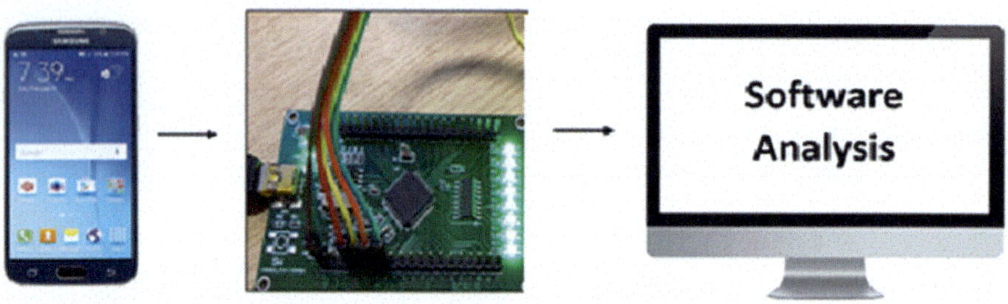

Fig. 25.8 JTAG Process

forensics, JTAG allows for the reading of memory and extraction of data from the locked or damaged device. These TAPs connect to the controller chip via a bus and allow communication to occur between the controller and other chips on the circuit board. JTAG ports are used to send and read commands through the controller to instruct it to read the content of the memory chip found on the circuit board, and output to the PC.

Several JTAG solutions are available in the market. Each brand has supported for a limited number of mobile phones. In JTAG process, the mobile device is connected to the JTAG box via wires soldered to test access points. JTAG box is connected to the computer via cable. JTAG manager software communicates with JTAG box, sending commands to the TAPs on the circuit board and ultimately acquires a read of the memory chip (Breeuwsma 2006) (Fig. 25.8).

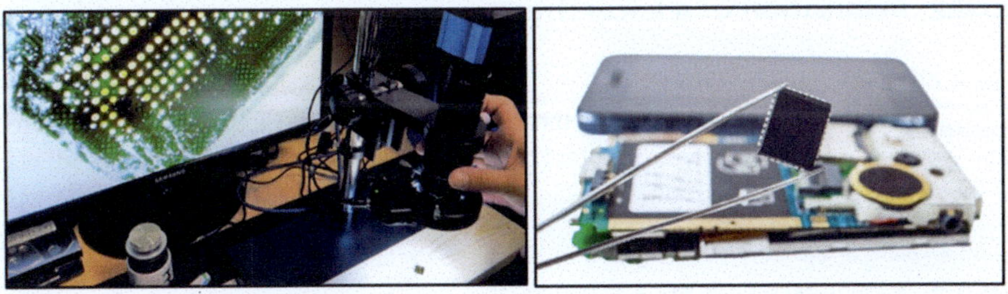

Fig. 25.9 Chip-off examination

Chip-off The chip-off examination is the physical removal of the mobile device flash memory by using specialised tools, technique. Examiner disassembles the mobile phone and removes the flash memory/eMNC from mother board by providing some heat and other systematic protocol. Now flash memory is placed over memory chip reader, and physical dump is prepared using any mobile forensic software, then after decoding data can be interpreted. This Memory chip-off method is used for either damaged mobile device or other mobile forensic software which does not support the mobile device. However, an encrypted memory chip limits the utility of Chip-off (Coert 2010) (Fig. 25.9).

25.8 Computer Forensic Examination

Computer forensics includes forensic data extraction from various types of memory devices like hard disk (SATA, SAS, SCSI, SSD), pen drive, memory card inserted in the computer, laptop, camera or internal memory chip/device of any electronic device having memory.

Existing /deleted/cached/encrypted/hidden data/user data, system details, software details and their data, windows registry, web access related artifact, network details, windows event logs, log details, file slack, RAM slack space of the memory device may be retrieved from file system.

25.8.1 Acquisition

Acquisition is the process in which forensic image of memory device is prepared and data of original memory devices is kept preserved. Generally, write blocker (either in hardware or software form) is used during preparation of forensic image so that data of the original is kept preserved as in original form.

25.8.2 Acquisition of a Local Drive

Local drive is connected directly to the computer system, where computer forensic software installed via, write blockers through local drive to be acquired was added to the case. Write blockers used to protect the local machine from altering the contents of the drive during acquisition.

25.8.3 Acquisition of Non-local Drive

The Linux-based utility acquires non-local drives by performing a network crossover acquisition. This type of acquisition is done when the system is found in on-condition. Linux-based utility is also used to acquire a disk through a disk-to-disk acquisition (Shaaban and Sapronov 2016; Lin 2018).

Forensic image is processed through forensic software in E01, EX01, DD, AFF3, AFF4, AFM, AFD, L01, LX01 format. Desired data may be searched, saved, documented and exported through various tools available in the software as well as by applying technical skills of cyber forensic experts. Hence, examination and analysis require a sound knowledge of various OS, file systems, metadata of various files, detailed knowledge of various social site applications as well as the location of data stored of various applications in memory, metadata analysis, database analysis, encryption technique analysis, and so on.

Report of examination should be written in presentable form, in the court of law and should contain details of the software used. The data provided in the report should be properly documented along with meta data and their hash value, kept as an internal record. Acquisition summary, log of the examination process, etc., should be documented and kept in the internal record.

25.9 DVR and NVR Forensic

In the present crime scenario, CCTV camera footage is playing an important role. CCTV footage of crime spot or nearby spot, offers a good deal to identify the suspect or vehicle used in the crime. Device details, Existing and Deleted data, Number of channels, State of setting of various camera, System Log, etc., may be retrieved by using DVR and NVR Forensic Software. DVR Forensic software is different from computer forensic software. Data extraction and functionality of software depend on the make, model, and manufacturer brand of DVR as they have their own operating system (Aarnes 2018; Robinson 2015).

25.10 Software and Tools for Digital Forensic

A wide variety of digital evidence has been used in the present scenario. Data extraction depends upon types of devices, OS, file system, types of encryptions and various software/App installed in the digital device. The software creates acquisition summary; examination logs and generates the forensic report of desired data. Cyber forensic software used for digital evidence may be classified broadly into three categories: Mobile Phone Forensic, Computer Forensic and DVR Forensics (Fig. 25.10).

25.10.1 Mobile Phone Forensic Toolkits

XRY, the product of Micro Systemation (MSAB),[1] Sweden and UFED, product of Cellebrite, Israel are mobile device forensics toolkits. These mobile forensic toolkits are used to analyse and recover information from mobile phone, tablet, drone, etc., as well as also possess capability of cloud data analysis and Link analysis. Hancom, Oxygen and MOBILedit are some other mobile phones forensic software (Fig. 25.11).

25.10.2 Computer Forensics Software

Encase,[2] FTK,[3] Magnet Axiom,[4] Nuix are computer forensic software. These softwares are capable to acquire image of various memory disks, computer or Laptop. Devices are connected through suitable write blocker. Each step is properly documented through acquisition summary, process logs and proper report may be generated of desired data stored/retrieved from the device through the computer forensic software (Shinder 2002) (Fig. 25.12).

25.10.3 DVR Forensic Software

DVR Examiner, VIP are DVR forensic software. As DVR have capability to store recent videos captured from various cameras by continuously overwriting the oldest recorded videos. Ergo, there is less possibility to retrieve overwritten video.

---

[1] XRY (MSAB), https://www.msab.com/products/.

[2] EnCase certificate. https://www.opentext.com/products-and-solutions/services/training-and-learning-services/encase-training/examiner-certification.

[3] Accessdata certificate, https://training.accessdata.com/exams.

[4] Magnet Forensic, https://www.magnetforensics.com/products/magnet-axiom/.

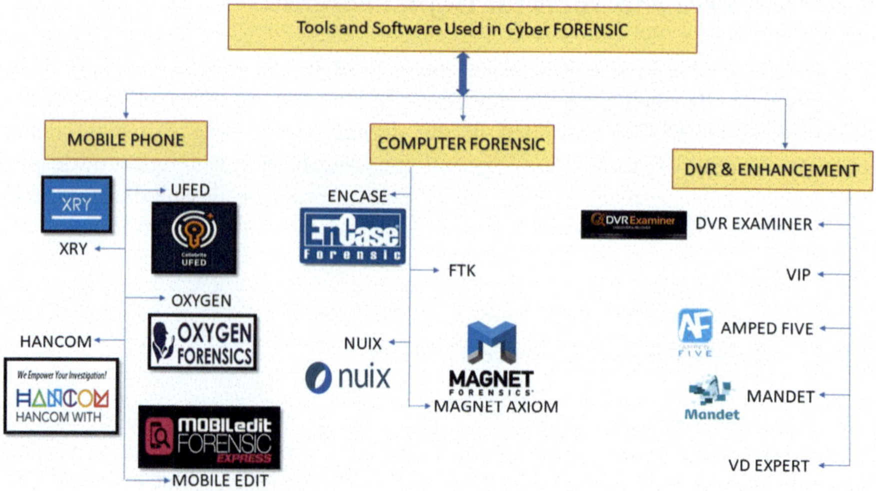

Fig. 25.10 Different tools used in digital forensic

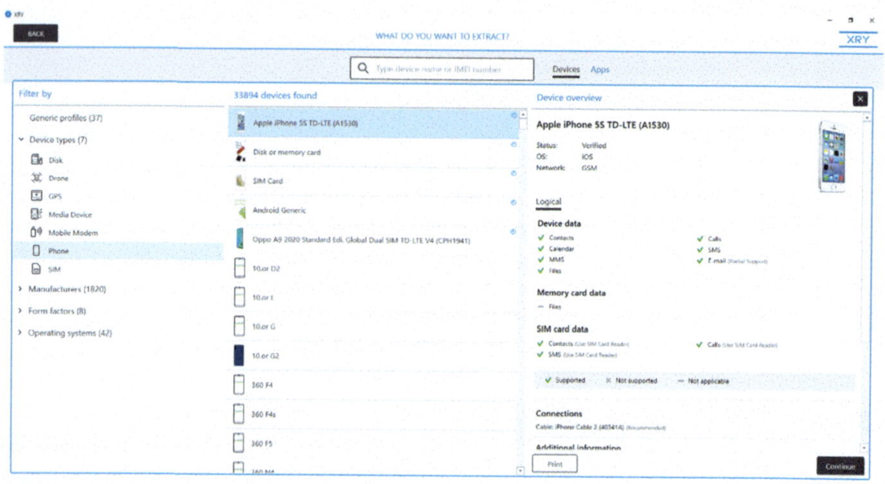

Fig. 25.11 Interface of the XRY

Retrieved videos from DVR/NVR requires further enhancement and authentication of suspects face, registration number plate of vehicle, etc.by using some video enhancement softwares such as Amped FIVE, Impress, etc. A proper documentation of all the steps of analysis and used filters must be done for the justification of report in the court of the Law. Various Video authentication software are also used to find out any kind of tempering in the picture or videos. Amped Authenticate, Mandet and VD-Expert are some video authentication software (Fig. 25.13).

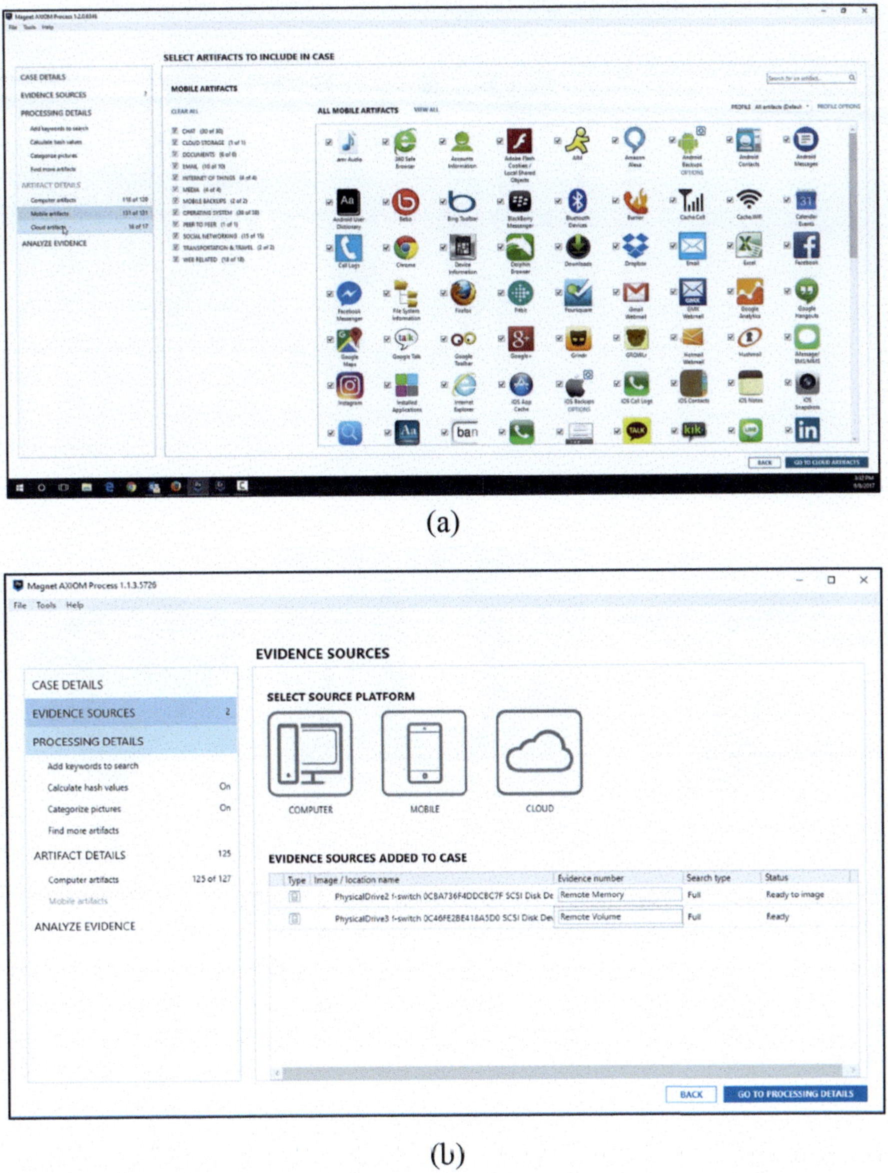

Fig. 25.12 (**a**, **b**) Shows the different interface of the Magnet Axiom software for the mobile related (**a**) and processing (**b**)

Fig. 25.13 Impress software interface

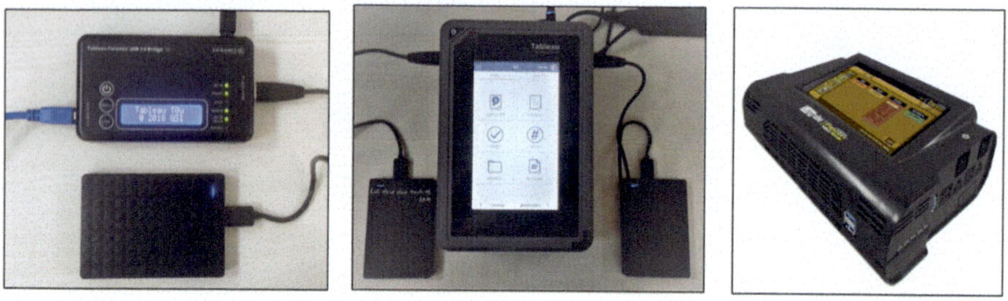

Fig. 25.14 Tableau USB write blocker, Tableau TX1 and Falcon devices (left to right)

25.10.4 Imaging Devices and Write Blockers Tools

Tableau Forensic Imager: Tx1 and Tx3, Falcon Neo,[5] dossier are various high speed imaging device solution, from which image of hard disks may be prepared in another hard disk or memory device without connecting the computer. These high-speed imaging devices are extremely useful during collection and seizing of computer or Laptop or any memory device.

There are various types of write blockers available (shown in Fig. 25.14), which are used to connect between the source or suspects hard disks and the examiners laptop/computer. Write blockers are used to protect any kind of tempering/modification in suspect's hard disk.

[5]Tableau, https://www.tableau.com.

25.11 Encryption and Decryption

Encryption and decryption of the data is just like the lock and key method. Data can be decrypted by the appropriate key only. Earlier encryption and decryption were based on the addition, substitution, other mathematical calculation. With the passage of time, the method of encryption and its associated algorithm also changed.

The encryption of the data standard called Data Encryption Standard (DES) was developed in the early seventies. DES provides the strengthened the encryption and it was supposed to be time being strongest encryption. It uses the series of 64-bit block size for encryption. In the 64-bit block size, the 8-bit are used for the parity checking and rest 56-bit are used for the usable block. Further, Triple Data Encryption Standard (3DES) with triple protection of the 56-bit key was introduced.

The introduction of the Advanced Encryption Standard (AES) overcame the DES. DES involved 64-bit encryption, but AES expended the encryption to three different sizes of key length i.e.,128-bit, 192-bit, and 256-bit. In the AES, more advanced algorithms were introduced that is also used by Government and Law Enforcement agencies. The count of the repetition cycles is chosen by the AES. This repetition makes the encrypted text or cipher text more protected, and it depends on the size of the encryption. AES has been using till date and also considered as the most secure encryption method. Now days, Rivest-Shamir-Adlmen (RSA) method of encryption is also popular. It includes the the public key for the encryption of data. Without the private key the decryption process remains undone. It is also used in the verification of the digitally signed document.

Moreover, some more tools such as Magma, Carmellia, Kyznyechik, Blowfish, Threefish, Twofish, 7-Zip, etc. are also available for the data encryption. Operating system also possess its own encryption e.g. File vault is used in Mac. Development of the technology to decrypt the message by using the voice over internet protocol is important future perspective in this thread.

25.12 Public and Private Key

Private Key or Symmetric Key is used for the purpose of encryption and decryption. It is a single key which can be send to other to decrypt the cipher text. It is comparatively faster than public key.

Public Key or Asymmetric Key have the two keys of which one is used for the purpose of the encryption and other is used for the purpose of decryption. In this one can encrypt his data by using the public key but receiver needs the private key to decrypt the ciphered text. This process needs the public key (by which encryption done) and Private key (by which the decryption done). Public key is known to everyone, but the private key is only known by only the receiver.

Some forensic tools are also available to decrypt the ciphered files for e.g. Password Kit Forensic. Decryptum tool is dedicated made to decrypt the data. The recovery rate depends on the computing power of the system as well as types of encryptions. It may take long time for the lengthy password as compared to small string password. Some browser saves the password and username. These passwords are recovered by using software e.g. PasswordFox (Nirsoft's), etc. There are the many ways to decrypt the data as discussed below.

1. *Dictionary method*: In this method the pre-existing words present in the library of the software are used in hit and trial mode in attempt to decrypt the data.
2. *Brute-force attack*: In this method the decryption of file is done by using all possible systematic combinations.
3. *Rainbow tables*: These tables are also used to decrypt the files by using their per-calculated library of the hash files and its database.

The encryption is a term which can make the text of the files in the cipher form, which means no other person can access these files without the decryption. The encryption may be done as single file (document, image, and other formats), partition encryption, and whole hard disk encryption. It can act over the mobile also. Different types of encryption are available by the manufacturer or third-party software. For the Forensic purpose the software also decrypts the password in the conditions as given below.

1. In Windows OS, an inbuilt feature of BitLocker is decrypted by the number of lists of the password related to it.
2. An encrypted McAfee is decrypted by using the machine key which is based on 64 strings and contains 44 characters long which are unique to each computer. McAfee administrator provides a key to decrypt the data.
3. FileVault encrypted files are created in the MacOS, and requires a password key and wipe key. The wipe key is usually stored in the \Recovery\HD\-com.apple.boot.P\System\Library\Caches\com.apple.corestorage\EncryptedRoot.plist.wipekey.
4. In the Cases of VeraCrypt-encryption, password and a Personal Iterations Multiplier (PIM) is required to decrypt these partitions.
5. Encryptions like GuardianEdge, Sophos (SafeGaurd Easy and Enterprise), Symantec (whole disk encryption and point-to-point encryption) and WinMagic, are decrypted by the forensically software such as the Encase Forensic, Magnet Axiom and FTK.
6. In the Cloud data, decryption also performed and which is related to the cloud based services (Apple iCloud, Dropbox, OneDrive, from iCloud keychains).
7. Mobile passwords, android backup, AppLock, FileLocker, Norton app lock, etc. are some examples of mobile phone encryptions. These files are also decrypt by using the mobile tools like XRY and UFED and other mobile forensic tools.

25.13 Network Forensic

There are the wide varieties of crimes encountered in the regular schedule. In which one of the crime is executed remotely through a network infrastructure. A branch of digital forensics that deals with network associated issues is called as the network forensic. Network is used to connect two or more devices across the globally or some defined area.

The computer connects to a network through an address often called as Internet Protocol. Data and information are transmitted by using hubs, switches and routers. 'Legs' are called as the number of connections is provided into the device. When the data is transmitted through the routers and it searches for the best most suitable leg for carrying this further, called as hop. The connection can be established into three different ways Peer to peer (the process through which both can receive and send information); client to server (where a server provides some information to client for example web pages); server to server (where two servers share the information).

The Open Systems Interconnection (OSI) conceptual model of network topology explains the assigned work for each level layer such as physical layer, data link layer, network layer, transport layer, session layer, presentation layer and application layer. There are some protocols on which the internet connection and application are depends, such as Border Gateway Protocol (BGP), Autonomous system and Internet Service Provider (ISP).

BGP is the type of network connection which uses routing table to determine the shortest route for the destination network. However, an autonomous system provides a set of IP prefixes which identifies the unique and globally recognised network under a single administrative control. Further, it is managed by the Regional Internet Registry (RIR) which has a specific range of the ASN that is assigned through the Internet Assigned Number Authority (IANA). IANA manages the global pool of the Internet Protocol address, as well as the authority of the root for DNS (Domain Name System). Domain name gathers the alphanumeric strings which are separated by dots. Additionally, *Internet Service Provider* is an organization which provides the access of internet to the consumer. Further, it is divided into three different tiers (Tier 1, Tier 2 and Tier 3) according to their geographical area. Tier 3 is the smallest area covered as compared to tier 2 and tier 1. Tier 2 covers a large area network and maintains the national network infrastructure. Tier 1 maintains the network infrastructure globally and the agreements with the tier 2 and tier 3 to sell their transit to gain access from any part of the world.

25.14 Ethical Hacking

Ethical hackers took the challenge to secure the computer or network system by searching the weak points, vulnerabilities which can be used by others to bypass the computer or network system. They are the authorized hacker which is appointed by the organization to secure the defence system. Sometimes they are also called the pen tester. Since all the files and important database are mostly stored in the computer or

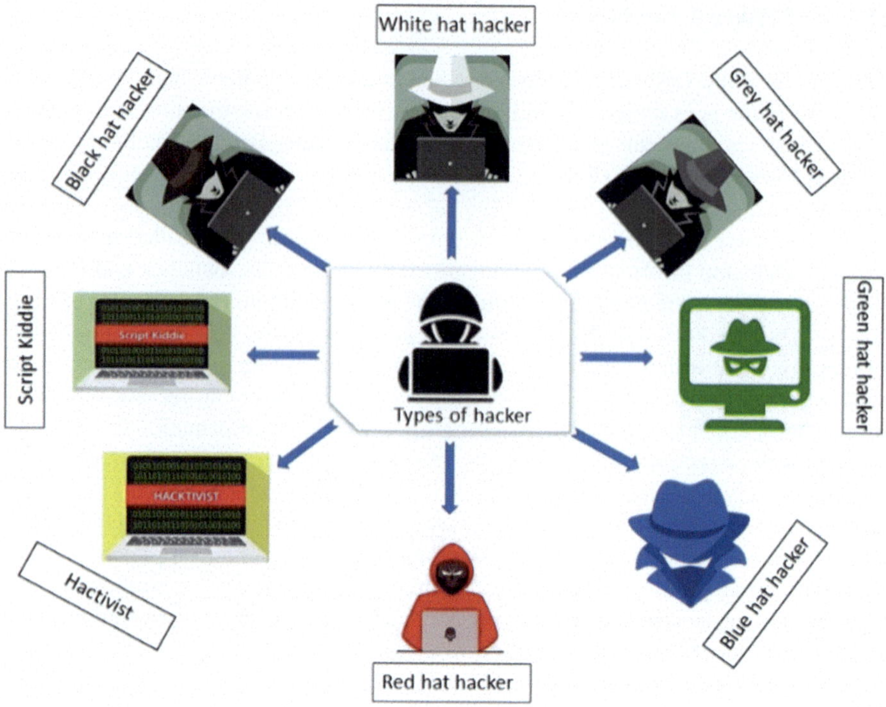

Fig. 25.15 Different types of hackers

cloud, therefore, amid the increasing rate of cybercrime, data breech, malware attack, etc. role of ethical hacker becomes important for security purposes. In the world of hacking variety of hackers are there with the distinguished aim as shown in Fig. 25.15. Table 25.3 consist of some terminologies frequently used in ethical hacking.

25.15 Certification

Certification are the additional qualification which ensures the particular person about the specific knowledge. There are various certification courses offered by different organizations which can enhance the knowledge. Some of the top hierarchy certification courses of different organizations are as discussed below.

Table 25.3 Terminologies related to ethical hacking

Term	Elaboration
Authorization	Grant of access to a person towards the computer system or network system
Authentication	Confirmation of the identity of user accessing the system
Vulnerability assessment	Checking the loopholes of the system to ensure secure platform for work
Penetration testing	Finding of maximum vulnerabilities and securing network from hackers
White hat hacker	Those which are authorized by the organization to test the vulnerability or the loopholes to provide more secure platform
Black hat hacker	Those who get unauthorized access with malicious intent to steal the important information for financial benefits. They are also called as crackers
Grey hat hacker	Those which are also unauthorized hackers, used their skills to access the data. They are lies between the white and black hat hacker and depending upon the intention by which they shifted from the grey to black. Also, the difference between the white and grey hat hackers, white hat hackers do not publicly exploit vulnerability
Script kiddies	Person who uses the script or downloaded tools available for hacking. They aim to prove himself superior in their society
Green hat hackers	These use scripts and assisted by hackers to resolve their query
Blue hat hackers	Beginners in the sky of hacking
Hacktivist	Hacktivist are the group of anonymous hackers who had accessed the unauthorized access to the computer or network system

25.15.1 EC-Council

The International council of E-commerce (EC-council)[6] is an organization that run many of the certification courses in the different specialization areas of the digital forensic, penetration testing and anti-hacking. Some of the certification courses offered by the EC-Council are listed below.

(a) *CHFI*: Computer Hacking Forensic Investigator
(b) *CEH*: Certified Ethical Hacker
(c) *ECSA*: EC-Council Certified Security Analyst
(d) *CND*: Certified Network Defender
(e) *LPT*: Licensed Penetration Tester
(f) *CASE*: Certified Application Security Engineer
(g) *CCISO*: Certified Chief Information Security Officer

[6] E-commerce (EC council) Certificate. https://www.eccouncil.org/programs/.

25.15.2 IACIS

The group namely International Association of Computer Investigative Specialists (IACIS)[7] provides the membership to the law enforcement, Retd. Enforcement officials, and associated practitioners. It is a non-profit organization which provide certification course such as Certified Forensic Computer Examiner (CFCE).

25.15.3 ISFCE

International Society of Forensic Computer Examiners (ISFCE)[8] organization offers the certification program for the forensic professionals, consultants, etc. It includes different modules such as digital investigation, computer forensic, etc., to prosecute the cases related to the cybercrime. ISFCE is also a member of the "The Alliance Group of Associations". It also runs the certification course i.e. Certified Computer Examiner (CCE).

25.15.4 SANS

SysAdmin, Audit, Network, Security (SANS official name is Escal Institute of Advanced Technologies)[9] is the company which is providing the certifications programme to the different domains in the digital forensic. It also provides information alerts, job information, and business organization-related suggestion. It provides thirty certification courses under the GIAC programme module out of which eleven certifications are accredited by ANSI/ISO/IEC 17024. It is also recognized by the government organization including the different law enforcement agencies. Some of the lists of the certificates are shown below.

(a) *GCFA*: GIAC Certified Forensic Analyst
(b) *GASF*: GIAC Advanced Smartphone Forensics
(c) *GCFE*: GIAC Certified Forensic Examiner
(d) *GNFA*: GIAC Network Forensic Analyst
(e) *GREM*: GIAC Reverse Engineering Malware
(f) *GCTI*: GIAC Cyber Threat Intelligence
(g) *GMOB*: GIAC Mobile Device Security Analyst
(h) *GCDA*: GIAC Certified Detection Analyst

---

[7] International Association of Computer Investigative Specialists (IACIS) certificate. https://www.iacis.com/certification/.

[8] International Society of Forensic Computer Examiners (ISFCE) certificate. https://www.isfce.com/certification.htm.

[9] SysAdmin, Audit, Network, Security (SANS) certificate, https://www.sans.org/cyber-security-courses/?msc=main-nav.

(i) *GCSA*: GIAC Cloud Security Automation
(j) *GDSA*: GIAC Defensible Security Architecture
(k) *GICSP*: GIAC Global Industrial Cyber Security Professional
(l) *GCTI*: GIAC Cyber Threat Intelligence
(m) *GNFA*: GIAC Network Forensic Analyst
(n) *GCFA*: GIAC Certified Forensic Analyst
(o) *GCFE*: GIAC Certified Forensic Examiner
(p) *GBFA*: GIAC Battlefield Forensics and Acquisition

25.15.5 HTCI

High Tech Crime Institute[10] provides different courses related to the computer forensic as given below.

(a) *CCST*: Computer Crime Scene Technician Certification
(b) *CCNI*: Certified Computer Network Investigation
(c) *CCFT*: Certified Computer Forensic Technician
(d) *FOSS*: Forensic Operating System Specialist

25.15.6 LEVA

The Law Enforcement and Emergency Services Video Association[11] is a non-profit organization that provides the certificate related to the video enhancement namely "Forensic Video Analyst". Some other educational and professional certifications are given below.

(a) *IACRB*: Information Assurance Certification Review Board
(b) *CCFE*: Certified Computer Forensics Examiner
(c) *CFCE*: Certified Forensic Computer Examiner
(d) *CAWFE*: Certified Advanced Windows Forensic Examiner
(e) *CMFS*: Certified MAC Forensics Specialist
(f) *CFIP*: Certified Forensic Investigation Practitioner
(g) *CFIS*: Certified Forensic Investigation Specialist
(h) *PCI*: Professional Certified Investigator
(i) *HTCN*: High Tech Crime Network
(j) *CCCI*: Certified Computer Crime Investigator
(k) *IISFA*: International Information Systems Forensic Association

[10] High Tech Crime Institute (HTCI) Certificate. https://www.gohtci.com/eb-my-courses/?v=1d20b5ff1ee9.

[11] Law Enforcement & Emergency Services Video Association (LEVA) certificate. https://www.leva.org/certification/.

(l) *CIFI*: Certified Information Forensics Investigator
(m) *(ISC)2*: International Information Systems Security Certification Consortium
(n) *CCFP*: Certified Cyber Forensics Professional
(o) *CCE*: Certified Computer Examiner

25.15.7 Vendor Certification

Many of the companies provide their certification courses for the professional's. In this certificate the information about the different modules of data is provided. Some of them are as discussed below.

25.15.7.1 Guidance Software

It provides the certificates to the forensic professionals who are using the Guidance software (EnCase computer forensic application), EnCase Endpoint Investigator, eDiscovery, Risk Management, Mobile Investigation, Endpoint security. They provide the tutorials to use different tools while doing the investigation. They also provide the different certification which are mentioned below.

(a) *CFSR*: Certified Forensic Security Responder
(b) *EnCE*: EnCase Certified Examiner
(c) *EnCep*: Encase Certified eDiscovery Practitioner

25.15.7.2 AccessData

The AccessData provides the forensic software like Forensic Toolkit (FTK), AccessData Lab, AccessData eDiscovery, AccessData Enterprise and AccessData Triage. Like the other vendor it also provides the certification in which different modules such as Imaging, Registry viewer, Password Recovery Toolkit (PRTK) are covered. It provides the certificates are shown below.

(a) *ACE*: AccessData Certified Examiner
(b) *AME*: AccessData Mobile Phone Examiner
(c) *ACI*: AccessData Certified Investigator
(d) *SCA*: AccessData Summation Certified Administrator
(e) *SCCM*: AccessData Summation Certified Case Manager
(f) *SCE*: AccessData Summation Certified Case End-user
(g) *eDCA*: AccessData eDiscovery Certified Administrator

MSAB certification, oxygen forensic, cellebrite, BlackBag Technologies, Certified Black Light Examiner, Macintosh and iOS Certified Forensic Examiner (MiCFE) etc are some other certification examples.

25.16 Conclusion

This chapter is a summary of knowledge of digital forensics. In this chapter, we have studied the basic knowledge of digital forensics, digital crimes, certification and various forensically sound methods used in the examination of digital evidence e.g., CDR, IPDR, VOIP, Mobile forensic tools, Computer forensic tools, Imaging devices, Write blockers, DVR and NVR forensic etc. Digital forensics concludes the process of identifying, collecting, acquiring, preserving, analysing and presenting digital evidence which must be authenticated to ensure its admissibility in a court of law. Ultimately, the investigation and examination of a digital artifacts depend on the forensic method used, it also depends on the security features of digital evidence. The emerging technology clusters like Artificial intelligence, Machine learning, Autonomous Devices and systems, Computing and data storage technologies, IOT, PETs, DLTs etc. are the near future concern for forensic professionals. The digitalization and exponential technological growth in the use of mobile phones, computers and other digital tools which are linked through networks have increased crime execution virtually. Thus, the role of digital forensics is very important to be understood as the challenges faced in this field of forensic science are increasing day by day.

References

Aarnes A (2018) Digital forensic, 1st edn. Wiley, Hoboken

Agrawal A, Gupta M, Gupta S, Gupta C (2011) Systematic digital forensic investigation model. Int J Comput Sci Secur 5(1):118–131

Baryamureeba V, Tushabe F (2004) The enhanced digital investigation process model. Proceeding of Digital Forensic Research Workshop, Baltimore

Beebe NL, Clark JG (2005) A hierarchical, objectives based framework for the digital investigations process. Digit Investig 2(2):147–167

Bem D, Huebner E (2007) Computer forensic analysis in a virtual environment. Int J Digit Evid 6 (2):1–13

Breeuwsma MF (2006) Forensic imaging of embedded systems using JTAG (boundary-scan). Digital Invest 2(1):3. https://doi.org/10.1016/j.diin.2006.01.003

Carrier B, Spafford EH (2003) Getting physical with the digital investigation process. Int J Digit Evid 2(2):1–20

Carrier BD, Spafford EH (2004) An event-based digital forensic investigation framework. Digital Investigation

Ciardhuain SO (2004) An extended model of cybercrime investigations. Int J Digit Evid 3(1):1–22

Coert K (2010) Windows mobile advance forensic. Digital Invest 6(3-4):1. https://doi.org/10.1016/j.diin.2010.02.001

Cybercrimes Training Materials for Investigators (2011) Data Security Council of India (DSCI). Niryat Bhawan, New Delhi

Freiling FC, Schwittay B (2007) A common process model for incident response and computer forensics, 3rd International Conference on IT-Incident Management and IT-Forensic

Kent K, Chevalier S, Grance T, Dang H (2006) Guide to integrating forensic techniques into incident response: recommendations of the national institute of standards and technology, National Institute of Standards and Technology (NIST), Tech Rep 800-886

Kohn M, Olivier MS, Eloff JHP (2006) Framework for a digital forensic investigation. In: Proceedings of the ISSA 2006 from Insight to Foresight Conference, Sandton, South Africa, pp 1–77

Lee HC, Palmbach TM, Miller MT (2001) Henry Lee's Crime Scene Handbook. Academic Press, San Diego

Leong RSC (2006) FROZA- Digitak forensic investigation framework that incorporate legal issues. Digit Investig 3:19–36

Ligh MH, Case A, Levy J, Walters A (2014) The art of memory forensics: detecting malware and threats in Windows, Linux and Mac memory. Wiley, Hoboken

Lin X (2018) Introduction computer forensic. Springer, Cham. https://doi.org/10.1007/978-3-030-00581-8

NFSTC (2009) A simplified guide to digital evidence. National Forensic Science Technology, Largo

Norris S (2011) Digital evidence and computer crime instructor manual. Elsevier, Amsterdam

Office of Legal Education Executive Office for United States Attorneys, Department of Justice (2001) Searching and Seizing Computers and Obtaining Electronic Evidence in Criminal Investigations

Palmer G (2001) Dtr-t001-01 technical report. A road map for digital forensic research. Digital Forensics Workshop, Utica

Perumal S (2009) Digital forensic model based on Malaysian investigation process. Int J Comput Sci Netw Secur 9(8):38–44

Pilli ES, Joshi RC, Niyogi R (2010) Network forensic frameworks: survey and research challenges. Digit Investig 7(1–2):14–27

Pollitt MM (1995) Computer forensics: an approach to evidence in cyberspace. In: Proceeding of the National Information Systems Security Conference, vol 2, Baltimore, pp 487–491

Reith M, Carr C, Gunsch G (2002) An examination of digital forensics models. Int J Digit Evid 1 (3):1–12

Robinson MK (2015) Digital forensic workbook. CreateSpace Independent Publishing Platform, Scotts Valley

Rogers MK, Goldman J, Mislan R, Wedge T, Debrota S (2006) Computer forensics field triage process model. J Digit Forensic Secur Law 1(2):2

Sammons J (2012) The basics of digital forensic the primer for getting started in digital forensic. Elsevier, Amsterdam

Sammons J (2014) The basics of digital forensics, 2nd edn. Elsevier, Amsterdam

Shaaban A, Sapronov K (2016) Practical windows forensics, 1st edn. Packt Publishing, Birmingham

Shinder DL (2002) Scene of the cybercrime computer forensic handbook. Elsevier, Amsterdam

Stephenson P (2003) A comprehensive approach to digital incident investigation. Inf Secur Tech Rep 8(2):42–54

Tamma R, Skulkin O, Mahalik H, Bommisetty S (2020) Practical mobile forensic, 4th edn. Packt Publishing, Birmingham

Yusoff Y, Ismail R (2011) Common phases of computer forensic investigation models. Int J Comput Sci Inf Technol 3(3):17–31

Useful Links

Accessdata certificate, https://training.accessdata.com/exams

E-commerce (EC council) Certificate. https://www.eccouncil.org/programs/

EnCase certificate. https://www.opentext.com/products-and-solutions/services/training-and-learning-services/encase-training/examiner-certification

High Tech Crime Institute (HTCI) Certificate. https://www.gohtci.com/eb-my-courses/?v=1d20b5ff1ee9

International Association of Computer Investigative Specialists (IACIS) certificate. https://www.iacis.com/certification/
International Society of Forensic Computer Examiners (ISFCE) certificate. https://www.isfce.com/certification.htm
Law Enforcement and Emergency Services Video Association (LEVA) certificate. https://www.leva.org/certification/
Magnet Forensic, https://www.magnetforensics.com/products/magnet-axiom/
SysAdmin, Audit, Network, Security (SANS) certificate, https://www.sans.org/cyber-security-courses/?msc=main-nav
Tableau, https://www.tableau.com
XRY (MSAB), https://www.msab.com/products/

An Introduction to Biometric Authentication Systems

26

Tanurup Das, Abhimanyu Harshey, Vindresh Mishra, and Ankit Srivastava

Abstract

The science of biometric exponentially evolved since its inception. From human identification to attendance verification in organizations, biometrics have expanded a very wide range of applicability in the modern era. It is divided into two categories based on the nature of the trait of the human being viz. physiological and behavioral. Fingerprint records during the medieval and early modern era built up the foundation stone of biometrics as a distinguished field of study. During the late twentieth century and especially since the new millennium, the technology behind biometrics exponentially evolved. The addition of several physiological features like; face, retina, iris, ear, vein pattern, and behavioral features like; voice, handwriting, keystroke, gait pattern, etc. strengthen the identification and verification systems. Recently, multimodal biometric setups, consisting of more than one feature, enhanced the security systems and identification process related to forensic investigation. Notwithstanding the advantages, not a single system has 100 percent accuracy due to several errors viz. FRR, FAR, FTE, ATV, etc. These limitations are needed to be rectified for optimum results in upcoming years.

T. Das · A. Srivastava (✉)
School of Forensic Sciences, The West Bengal National University of Juridical Sciences, Kolkata, West Bengal, India
e-mail: ankitsrivastava@nujs.edu

A. Harshey
Department of Anthropology, Lucknow University, Lucknow, Uttar Pradesh, India

V. Mishra
Central Forensic Science Laboratory, Kolkata, India

P. Shrivastava et al. (eds.), *Textbook of Forensic Science*,
https://doi.org/10.1007/978-981-99-1377-0_26

Keywords

Biometrics · Human identification · Physiological trait · Behavioral trait · Multimodal biometric systems

26.1 Introduction

The accurate identification of living or dead individual(s) is frequently encountered in forensic investigations. In a diverse scenario, personal identification is efficiently implemented to trace natural and man-made disaster victims, mass and individual murder victims, decomposed bodies, and perpetrators. In addition, the recognition of a dead body is obvious for medicolegal and social purposes (Saferstein 2011). Physiological and behavioral traits are widely used for the identification of individuals in the forensic analysis since the last century. The statistical measurements of these physiological and behavioral traits are considered biometric, and the identification and verification of the identity of a person by using these measurements are known as biometric recognition (Jain and Ross 2015). In its early days, biometric identification was a manual and cumbersome process to perform (Miller 1994). Fingerprint was used as the trait for the first biometric recognition at the beginning of the twentieth century. Since then, a drastic evolutionary pathway has modified the gradual process to the present time of handheld automated systems (Jain et al. 2011).

26.1.1 Biometric Recognition System

A manual, semi-automated, or automated setup typically comprise multiple hardware, software, or a combination of both, to capture, process, store and verify or identify a physiological or behavioral trait of an individual and is recognized as a biometric recognition system (Miller 1994). All the fundamental traits in each human are more or less distinct in nature. But all these cannot be used in biometrics systems. A specific trait should typically possess certain unique features to be carefully considered for the recognition system. Principally, seven fundamental features (Fig. 26.1) accurately determine the suitability of the trait for biometric applications.

Uniqueness: A trait must be sufficiently distinct in each individual throughout the diverse populations around the globe. In addition, the distinctiveness should be statistically proven and acceptable (Jain et al. 2011).

Universality: Every individual irrespective of race, country, population, caste, creed, etc. should possess the trait.

Permanence: All the measurable and comparable features and appearance must remain for the whole or majority of the lifetime.

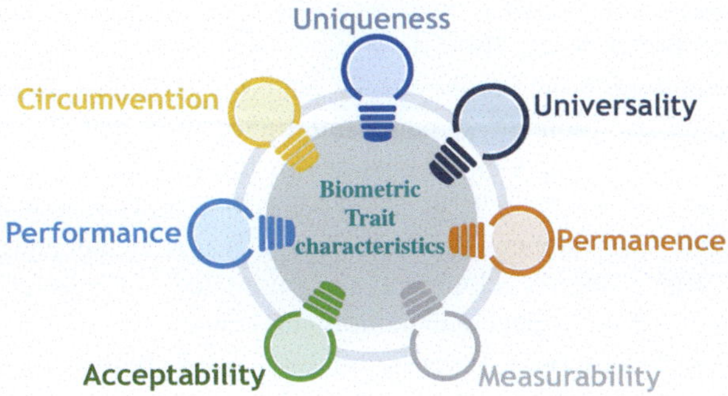

Fig. 26.1 Fundamental features of a physiological or behavioral biometric trait

Measurability: The trait should be easily measurable and transformable into digitized form without causing any inconvenience to the person during the acquisition process.

Acceptability: Individuals must be easily willing to present the trait to the acquisition system.

Performance: False acceptance and false rejection rates should be significantly low so that the person can be verified or identified with adequate accuracy.

Circumvention: The trait should be sufficiently complex so that a person cannot imitate or reproduce it for wrongful implementation (Miller 1994; Jain et al. 2011).

26.1.2 Biometrics and Forensic Science

Forensic science is a branch of applied science that is predominantly based on the comparison between a known and unknown material or source. Biometric systems accomplish a similar function in personal identification. Either in the authentication or identification of victims and criminals, biometrics always remain a key investigative tool in civil and criminal cases. Biometric systems overcome the difficulty of the memory-based identification of individuals by witnesses. This technique analyzes the evidences by using scientific principles that enhance the reliability and admissibility of the matching report. Except for this, the advanced automated biometric systems reduced the time consumption for the comparison of a huge amount of data in forensic analysis of mass identification circumstances (Jain and Ross 2015). Handwriting and signature comparison are the earliest used biometric trait in forensic investigation. Between the end of the nineteenth century and the beginning of the twentieth century, fingerprint comparison emerged as the flagship biometric tool in forensic science. Except for fingerprint-based identification, other biometric features, viz. barefoot impression, earmarks, bite marks, facial recognition, and DNA profiling are used for the same purpose since its early days. While the exceptional advancements in the field of DNA profiling separate it as an individual specialized branch of forensic science, the identification of a person based on different physiological features has been used for more than a century around the globe. On the contrary, handwriting and signature comparison are the earliest behavioral biometric features to be used in forensic investigation. Along with the traditional traits, forensic experts are exploring several new physiological and behavioral traits i.e., keystroke pattern, voice recognition, gait pattern, and image-based ear biometrics, hand and finger vein pattern matching in recent years to counter the exponential changes in the pattern of crimes. Except for the iris and retina, all the physiological and behavioral traits are potentially discoverable at crime scenes as evidences (Jain and Ross 2015; Kanchan and Krishan 2013).

Since the development of automated recognition systems, biometrics has emerged as a personal identity authentication tool in corporate sectors and for security purposes. Forensic analysis needs biometrics after the commitment of a crime, while biometrics exclusively work as a pre-accessing tool for registration, entrance, or login to any system. The quality of any impression or record of a biometric trait found as evidence in forensic investigation is inconsistent. The fundamental limitation is a questioned material obtained from an uncontrolled scenario. Additionally, the source of the material naturally goes through several transformational factors like deformities, aging, etc. The lack of sufficient comparative features hinders a convenient match. While biometric authentication always uses the standard quality of impressions for verification (Jain et al. 2011).

26.2 Historical Background

26.2.1 The Inception of Biometric Identification

Several decades before the invention of an automated biometric recognition system for security purposes, few significant biometric traits have been adequately explored for forensic purposes around the globe. The Argentinian police department remains arguably the first organization to conventionally use fingerprints in the forensic analysis of a homicide case in 1892. The use of fingerprints as a personal identification tool was steadily gaining popularity in the European continent since the early 1900s (Tistarelli and Champod 2017). Scotland yard was the first law enforcement authority in Europe to use fingerprints for identification purposes. In 1905, fingerprint was first accepted as an evidence in a British criminal case. Almost two decades later in 1924, the collection of fingerprints along with arrest information was authorized by the Department of Justice by the United States Congress. This step pioneered the successful establishment of the fingerprint-based identification system by the Federal Bureau of Investigation (FBI) in the United States (Jain et al. 2011; Jain and Ross 2015; Tistarelli and Champod 2017). In the beginning, the FBI used to collect fingerprints manually through tenprint cards until the automated fingerprint identification system (AFIS) came to the scene in the 1970s. Despite the term 'automated', the entire identification process still has human intervention as the system shortlists few possible matches. An expert analyzes these prints and ultimately establishes a positive match.

26.2.2 The Transition from Manual to Automated Systems

Since the mid-1960s, automated biometric authentication systems emerged as an advanced aid to manual biometric matching, previously used in forensic sciences. Fingerprint-based AFIS was the first one of its kind. In the initial stages, the system was not as accurate as its further updates and other future counterparts, but it was significantly effective to reduce the list of suspects to a large extent. The system gradually modified and included more features than only ridge minutiae and use all ten fingers for matching (Tistarelli and Champod 2017). Almost two and a half decades later Daugman proposed an iris-based personal identification that is more robust and accurate than a fingerprint and less vulnerable to forgery. Face recognition was the next big thing in automated biometric systems. Despite promising aspects, several practical limitations regarding imaging and data processing inhibited the large-scale application of facial recognition systems (Tistarelli and Champod 2017). As a consequence of recent developments in the algorithms for artificial intelligence, facial recognition becomes one of the vital features in automated security systems, authorization, and forensic analysis of close-circuit television (CCTV) footage. Analysis of the whole face is not always possible in erratic movements captured through CCTV. In those circumstances ear, biometric recognition can remain a vital aspect. Since the early 2000s, forensic sciences have seen a drastic uprising in ear biometric applications (Tistarelli and Champod 2017; Jain et al. 2011). The global development of biometrics hugely triggered during the last two decades with recent initiatives by the governments of several countries for their national security concerns, various sensitive sector and citizen identification protocols. In 2002, the government of the USA enacted the 'Visa Entry Reform Act' which enables the use of biometrics to issue a U.S. visa. Additionally, a fingerprint-based United States Visitor and Immigration Status Indicator.

Technology (US-VISIT) validates the entry of foreign visitors to the USA. The government of India established the Unique Identification Authority of India (UIDAI) and launched AADHAR in 2009, a multibiometric personal identification card including ten fingerprints, face, and iris scans as security features. This card also consists of a 12-digit unique identification number for each individual. Figure 26.2 elaborates on the brief timeline of historical development in biometric technology around the globe (Saini and Kapoor 2016).

26.3 Biometric Identification Process

In its early days, the biometric recognition process comprises a combination of multiple manual comparisons between several features of the trait by one or more expert individuals. In the initial phase of the twentieth century, fingerprints and numerous facial features were compared for inclusive and exclusive decisions by following the aforesaid steps (Kataria et al. 2013; Saini and Kapoor 2016). The inception of an automated biometric recognition system during the 1960s brought a revolution in the field as it is free from any human error, biasness, and time

Fig. 26.2 Brief timeline of biometric technology

consumption problem. An automated biometric recognition system is the systematic arrangement of multiple hardware and software. On the hardware front, a biometric system requires one or more data acquisition devices. While it requires software to preprocess, enhance, compare and carry out decisions based on the existing database. The types of devices and authentication processes largely vary between physiological and behavioral traits. Additionally, the system naturally differs for every individual biometric trait authentication system. For example, a fingerprint authentication identification system utilizes a camera as the main hardware component, while a voice authentication system consists of a microphone for data acquisition (Jain et al. 2011; Jain and Ross 2015; Kataria et al. 2013). Irrespective of the diversity in device setups, all the biometric systems operate in more or less similar steps (Fig. 26.3a).

26.3.1 Data Acquisition

Capture the data of the biometric feature and store it in the database for further comparison. A sensor carefully collects the data and sends it to the data acquisition module. Camera (NIR), Digital specific wavelength, microphone.

26.3.2 Data Preprocessing

Enhance, correct (corrupt or inaccurate data), and normalize a specific part of the data necessary for further use. E.g., in voice recognition, the background noise is carefully removed (Arneodo et al. 2000).

26.3.3 Feature Extraction

Identify the patterns or information hidden in the collected data from the trait by implementing mathematical algorithms. It reduces the dimensionality of the captured data and represents it as a compact set of features that correspond to the entire data. E.g., in a retina scan the algorithm judge the inter-distance between muscle fibers in the eye. In the fingerprint scanner, the algorithm detects different ridge minutiae like bifurcation, ridge ending, islets, etc. (Dash and Liu 1997; Kohavi and John 1997; Liu and Motoda 1998; Hall 1999).

26.3.4 Encoding

A template will be efficiently generated from the extracted feature and stored in the comprehensive database. All the stored files are encrypted to secure them from any external or internal breach.

26.3.5 Verification and Identification

There is a significant difference between the processes of both terms. Verification is a one-to-one comparison where the captured biometric data are compared with

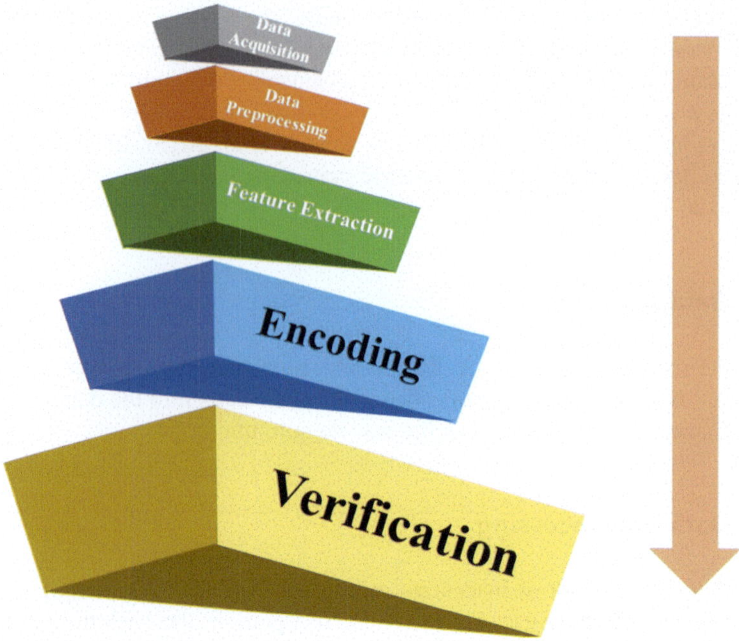

Fig. 26.3 (**a**) Fundamental operating steps of biometric systems. (**b**) Detailed processing of a biometric system

specific stored data for confirmation. While for identification purposes, the credible source of the biometric trait is unknown. Hence, the captured data are carefully searched in the database for a possible match. During the verification or identification process, the primary steps are identical as performed for database creation up to the feature extraction step. As soon as the feature extraction process ends the data is compared with pre-existing information corresponding to different individuals' biometric traits (Jain et al. 2011).

The aforesaid basic processing steps alone cannot explain the actual biometric processing. In the practical scenario, the process is much more complicated (Fig. 26.3b). The first step is the training phase in which, a database of standard samples from individuals is prepared for further verification or identification. In the next step, biometric data are collected from the suspect(s) and a similar process is applied for verification and identification as used for the database preparation. This step is known as the testing phase (Jain et al. 2011).

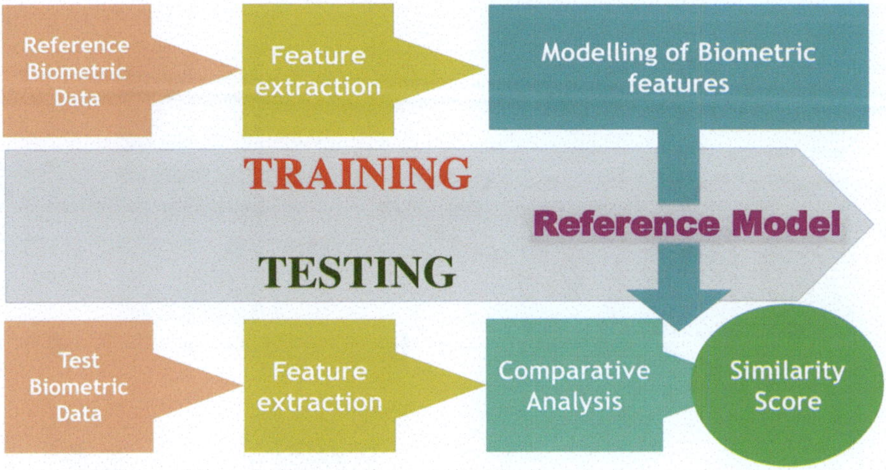

Fig. 26.3 (continued)

26.4 Biometric Systems

As a consequence of a large variety, all the biometric traits can be majorly classified into two categories i.e., physiological biometrics and behavioral biometrics (Tistarelli and Champod 2017; Jain et al. 2011; Pahuja and Nagabhushan 2015). Physiological traits are predominantly inherited and remain constant up to death. These are relatively more reliable in personal identification. Behavioral traits are a combination of inherited and acquired characters. Different factors present surrounding us largely affect these traits. Figure 26.4 shows different physiological and behavioral biometric traits.

26.4.1 Physiological Biometric Traits

As mentioned above, physiological biometric traits are predominantly inherited and remain constant throughout the whole lifetime. These biometric traits are largely controlled by genetic inheritance and most of the features develop during intrauterine life. Although these traits tend to grow after birth until a certain age. After attaining a certain age, the size, shape, and other dimensionality features remain relatively constant throughout life. Physiological biometric traits consist of fingerprint, iris, retina capillary structures, hand vein pattern, finger vein pattern, and face recognition (Tistarelli and Champod 2017). Among these traits, fingerprint, iris, retina, and vein patterns are mostly used around the world as personal identification and individual authentication tool (Jain et al. 2011; Kataria et al. 2013).

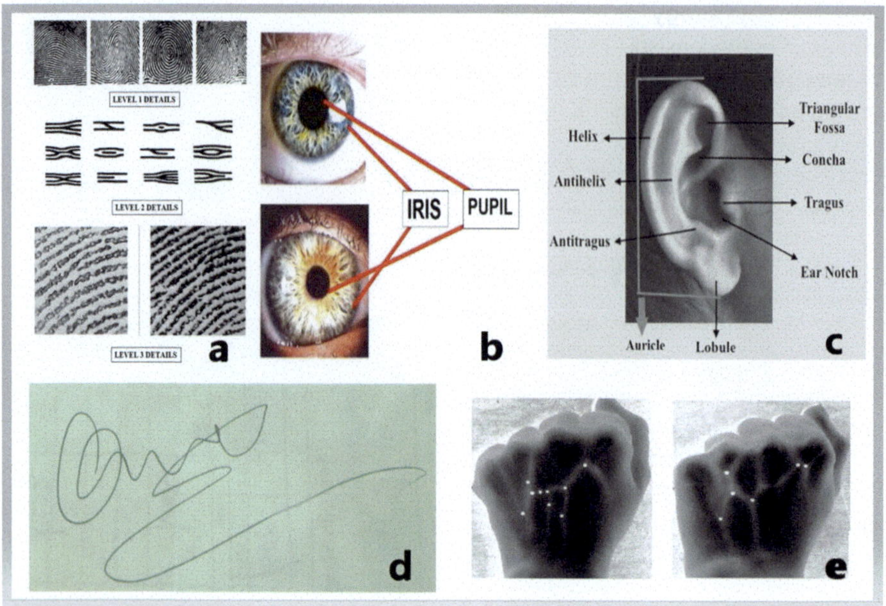

Fig. 26.4 Commonly used biometric traits in forensic sciences (**a**) fingerprint, (**b**) iris, (**c**) ear, (**d**) signature, and (**e**) vein pattern

26.4.1.1 Fingerprint

26.4.1.1.1 Background

The fingerprint is the first and most used biometric trait for verification and identification purpose in forensic investigations. Historically it is widely used around the globe for the last several centuries for various purposes like land and property-related issues, personal identification, substitute for personal signature, etc. Fingerprints are one of the major evidence for personal identification in forensic sciences. Latent or visible prints are mostly found in the scenes of every kind of offense. As evidence fingerprint is highly dynamic in quality. A complete and clear latent or visible print is very rare in a real scenario. Partial, smeared, overlapped prints are the most commonly discovered at crime scenes (Jain and Ross 2015; Tistarelli and Champod 2017). In recent years portable sensor-based automated identification and verification systems with additional human expertise enhanced the quality of fingerprint analysis in the aforesaid circumstances. The automation and miniaturization of the system enable its use in residential, commercial, and corporate sectors for verification purposes. Nowadays law enforcement agencies systematically record plain and rolled fingerprints of offenders on tenprint cards for further use in the identity verification of a suspect by matching the recovered from the crime scene with an existing record. Since the last half of the twentieth century, automated fingerprint identification systems emerged as a fast and reliable method for more efficient and accurate matching (Jain and Ross 2015).

26.4.1.1.2 Physiology

The human body consists of two kinds of external skin surfaces. The majority of the skin covering appears smooth with little to a significant amount of coverage of hairs. The remaining a few parts like palm, sole, and fingers consist of a flow of ridge (mounted) and furrows (indented). These ridges help in grasping any object by enhancing the friction between the fingers and the object's outer surface, hence these are known as 'frictional ridge'. The friction ridge is composed of two layers i.e., the outer epidermis and inner dermis. Finger ridges completely develop around the age of 6 months intrauterine. Every finger composed of these friction ridges creates a unique pattern. Even identical twins also possess different fingerprint patterns. These patterns are divided into three levels as level 1 details, level 2 details, and level 3 details. Fingerprint comparison based on these three levels can be done by manual or automated processes. In manual comparison, the detail of level 1 is a little different than the automated comparison. Level 1 details in manual matching consist of three fundamental fingerprint patterns i.e., loop, whorl, and arch. While in automated matching the level 1 details consist of ridge flow, ridge density at all locations of a fingerprint, and presence or absence of core and delta. As an example, the arch is an exclusive core and delta-less pattern. On the contrary loop and whorl contains one core and one or more delta in them. Level 2 and 3 details are similar in both matching processes. Level 2 details consist of individual minutiae created due to the complex arrangement of ridges. A large number of ridge-minutiae are compared during the manual matching but only bifurcation and ridge endings are considered in an automated matching system since these two are the most frequently distributed. Level 3 details consist of the finest details such as pores and edges of the ridges. Additionally, immature ridges and dot ridges are also included (Jain et al. 2011; Jain and Ross 2015; Kataria et al. 2013).

26.4.1.1.3 Recognition Process

Initially, a digitized version of the fingerprint is created. It can be made by two methods. A fingerprint present on paper or any other similar surface is scanned and converted to a digitized form. On the contrary, fingerprints can be directly scanned by digital imaging technologies like Optical Frustrated Total Internal Reflection (OFTIR), capacitance, ultrasound reflection, piezoelectric effect, and temperature differential (Tistarelli and Champod 2017; Jain et al. 2011; Jain and Ross 2015).

OFTIR digitizes a print by capturing the image of the finger by the reflection of light through a glass platen on which it is placed.

A capacitance-based scanner uses thousands of electrodes under the scanner. A finger placed on the scanner works as the other electrode and creates a small capacitance that is different for every ridge and furrow. This variable capacitance all over the area of the placed finger creates a digitized image. Capacitance-based scanners are the cheapest and most frequently used around the globe (Jain et al. 2011; Jain and Ross 2015).

The ultrasound method captures the acoustic signal echoed from the finger placed on the scanner surface. This method inhibits several interventions like dirt, sweat, etc. during the scanning process, but due to its high cost, it is used in limited sectors like sensitive security systems.

Differential temperature is created when the fingerprint ridges come in contact with the scanning surface. The high temperature under the scanning surface is constantly maintained by electrical heating.

The piezoelectric effect is observed when a finger is pressed over a non-conducting surface made up of dielectric material. An electric signal of a small amount is generated which in turn is converted into a digitized image of the ridges and furrows. This technique is not sufficiently sensitive as the variability of pressure affects the result (Jain et al. 2011; Jain and Ross 2015).

A minimum of 500 ppi resolution is necessary for good recognition. But level 3 details are only comparable above 1000 ppi. Commercial fingerprint recognition systems for identity verification are mostly limited to the comparison of level 1 and 2 details while level 3 details are included in the forensic analysis and highly sensitive security sectors. Different algorithms extract information like ridge orientation, ridge frequency, presence and absence of core and delta, ridge minutiae (Fig. 26.5), edges, and pores to convert them into binary form (Tistarelli and Champod 2017; Jain et al. 2011). This binary information is stored in the database for further comparison with suspected print or verification. The matching is divided into three steps i.e., alignment, correspondence, and score generation. By comparing the ridge orientation and frequency, the geometrical alignment is set between the two sets (stored and under verification) of fingerprints. A large number of comparisons are stopped in this step only. After the successful completion of step 1, corresponding minutiae pairs are formed between the two prints. Finally, a match score decides whether the prints are the same not by comparing the score with a predefined threshold value for a match (Jain et al. 2011; Jain and Ross 2015).

26.4.1.2 Palmprint

26.4.1.2.1 Background

Palmprints also possess a similar uniqueness as fingerprints. The significance of palmprint matching is that it has been found in approximately 30% of the latent prints found at crime scenes. Hence, the next-generation identification system of the FBI includes palmprints with fingerprints (Jain et al. 2011).

26.4.1.2.2 Physiology

The structure and appearance of palmprints are relatively more complex than fingerprints. Although palmprints consist of frictional ridge patterns like fingerprints, the number of minutiae is comparatively greater. Palmprints consist of palmer friction and flexion ridges. Flexion ridges are the earliest to appear during the embryonic stage. Both the friction and flexion ridges possess all the necessary features of a biometric trait. Flexion ridges are further divided into three categories, namely, distal, proximal, and radial transverse creases. The large area and rich ridge details are the advantages of palmprint as an identification tool in forensics. The probability of finding a complete latent print of a finger or palm is highly

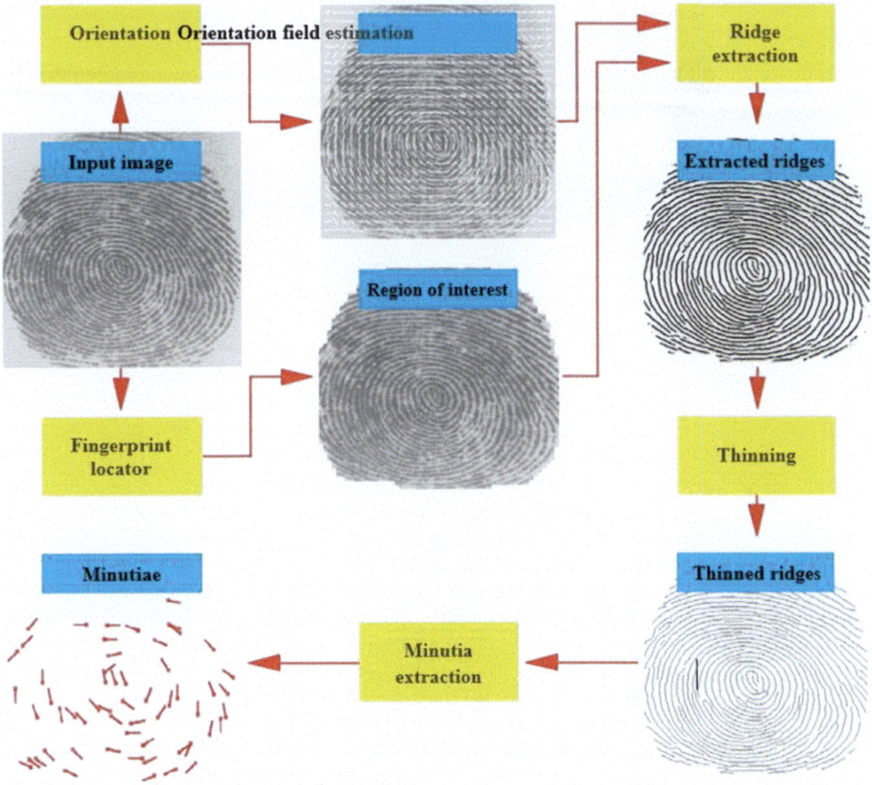

Fig. 26.5 Flowchart of the procedural steps for minutiae extraction algorithm. Reprinted from Jain A., Pankanti S., Fingerprint recognition in Bovik A (2009) The Essential Guide to Image Processing, Academic Press. https://doi.org/10.1016/B978-0-12-374457-9.00023-8. (Jain and Pankanti 2009). Copyright 2021, with permission from Elsevier

inconsistent. Hence, a partial latent palmprint possesses a sufficient number of ridge minutiae than a partial fingerprint (Jain et al. 2011).

26.4.1.2.3 Recognition Process

The palmprint recognition process is similar to that of fingerprints with some additional modifications. The major and minor minutiae details can be collectively captured by a resolution of 500 ppi or higher (Fig. 26.6). Ridge orientation and ridge flow extraction technique applied to fingerprints cannot be applied directly for the palmprints since it consists of several large creases. A modified algorithm extracts the aforesaid information from the palmprint. Further steps are the same as those used in fingerprints (Jain et al. 2011).

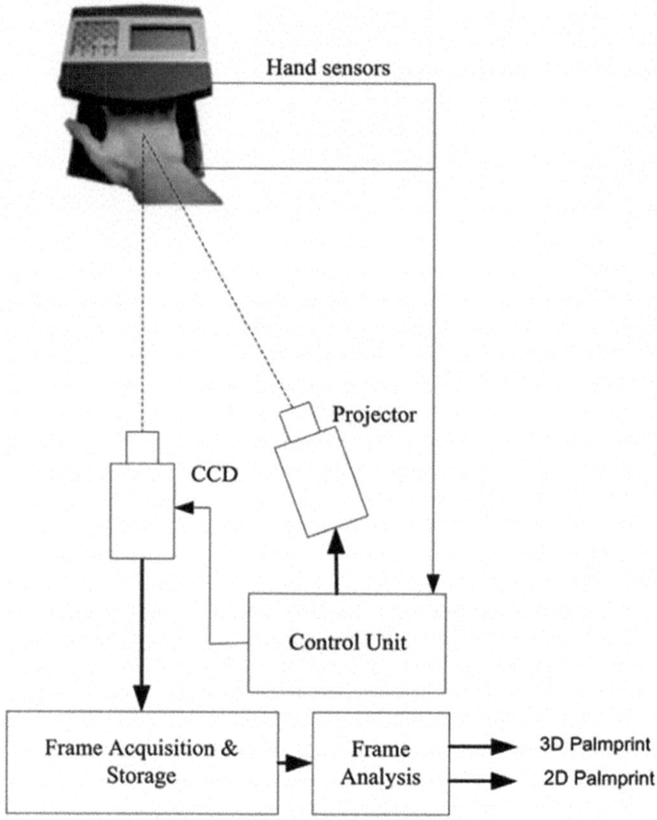

Fig. 26.6 The block diagram of the image acquisition model. Reprinted from Zhang, D., Kanhangad, V., Luo, N., Kumar, A., Robust palmprint verification using 2D and 3D features. Pattern Recognition, Pattern recognition. https://doi.org/10.1016/j.patcog.2009.04.026 (Zhang et al. 2010). Copyright 2021, with permission from Elsevier

26.4.1.3 Facial Recognition

26.4.1.3.1 Background

The face is the most frequently used biometric trait for personal identity by humans for several centuries. It has become a constant feature in personalized documents like Identity cards, driving license passports, etc. The face is the most commonly used biometric trait for identification by humans through their cognitive senses (Kanchan and Krishan 2013). Humans have the natural ability to overcome the problem of identifying a face under different circumstances and changes due to their complex neural structure and high-end cognitive ability. But to train a machine to identify several changing factors affecting the appearance of a face is a very difficult job. Fundamental problems occur when the faces of genetically related persons are scanned by the system or variations occur due to age. In forensic analysis, CCTV footages are the major source of the face as evidence in several cases like hit and run, burglary, murder, etc. Video-based face identification algorithms are most likely used in facial recognition for forensic purposes (Tistarelli and Champod 2017).

26.4.1.3.2 Physiology

The face is the frontal part of the human head. It consists of a forehead, eyes, nose, cheeks, mouth, and chin. Except for these prominent features, the human face consists of several significant landmarks. These landmarks are important to recognize a person in forensic analysis. Similar to fingerprints, facial recognition is also based on three-level details. Level 1 is the overall geometry, hue, fundamental distinctive gender-specific characters, and race-specific characters. Level 2 details include the geometry of specific parts of a face like eyes, nose, lips, etc., and their inter-relation. Level 3 details are more specific and unique features of a face like a scar, moles, discoloration, and freckles. Despite all these features, the discrimination of the faces of an identical twin is a highly difficult assignment (Jain et al. 2011).

26.4.1.3.3 Recognition System

Face detection is the primary step in the recognition system. This step includes face recognition, expression, face modelling, gender, age, and ethnicity. Fundamentally, a binary algorithm is used to detect a face that discriminates between a face and a non-face object. Although these algorithms are very sensitive to faces, still the false acceptance and false rejection rates are significant that need further research for rectification (Jain et al. 2011; Tistarelli and Champod 2017).

Image acquisition is the next step after facial detection. It can be classified in two ways i.e., based on the spectral region and based on the image rendering method. An image can be captured in visible or infrared region for biometric system and in a 2 or 3-dimensional form. Additionally, images can be automatically detected and captured from a dynamic framework (video) (Jain et al. 2011).

2-D is the most frequently used imaging system in facial recognition. These facial recognition systems capture the image in 2-dimension under the visible spectral region. But several minute characters occlude in an image captured in 2-D. Still, the majority of the significant features remain in the frontal 2-D image of a face. A multi-camera setup captures the image of a face from different angles and poses of a face to solve the pose variation problem. Low illumination problems can be addressed by using high-resolution and infrared cameras. Infrared illumination is predominantly designed for low natural light photography as it creates a different illumination for any object other than the visible spectrum. 1–2 m is the standard distance for capturing the facial image (Jain et al. 2011).

3-D imaging can overcome several fundamental drawbacks possess by a 2-D capturing system. Hence, an advanced image-capturing method including 3-D details took over the 2-D system. Laser scanning and stereographic methods are generally used to capture the image in this system. Typically, a 3-D scanner is known as 2.5-D as it captures approximately 1200 of a human face. The captured face models are represented as polygonal mesh. This model predominantly poses and is angle-independent (Jain et al. 2011).

The video sequencing technique for image capturing is used in a real-life scenario of forensic investigation. The facial features of a suspected person can be extracted from CCTV footage by this method. Although the quality of the extracted image is relatively worse than 2-D and 3-D capturing, still in criminal investigation cases this information has a very significant contribution (Tistarelli and Champod 2017; Jain et al. 2011).

Feature extraction and matching progress simultaneously after the image acquisition. Three different approaches are used in this process. In the *appearance-based technique*, the captured image is converted into multiple vector values by specific algorithms. Several statistical machine learning models like principal component analysis (PCA), linear discriminant analysis (LDA) independent component analysis (ICA) was used to build a model based on representative vector values of a person's face for further comparison. The extracted vector values from the captured image are compared with the trained representative vectors for a possible match (Tistarelli and Champod 2017; Jain et al. 2011). *The model-based technique* uses 2 and 3-dimensional facial models in different poses. The bunch graph matching scheme represents the whole face as a labeled image graph. The lines of the graph connect with each other by facial landmark points. The rich and minute information included in this method makes it more complex and sensitive than the appearance-based technique. The *texture-based technique* targets pose angle and lighting-independent features of the face. This method searches the pixels, independent of any random variation, and extracts those, and saves them in the form of data for further comparison and matching. Due to its robustness, this method becomes helpful in the comparison of images extracted from video footage (Tistarelli and Champod 2017; Jain et al. 2011).

Some advanced techniques are recently applied in the comparison of images captured in different models. For example, matching an image, captured in visible illumination with the image of the same person captured in infrared. Techniques like the synthesis method and feature-based methods are used for this purpose. *The synthesis method* creates a synthetic visible image from both formats. Now standard face recognition algorithms can match the images. While the feature-based method is similar to the texture-based method. Additionally, facial aging models detect age-related changes. This model strengthens the recognition system by adding a feature. Age-related changes like wrinkles, weight variation, sagged eyes, mouth, and cheeks (Jain et al. 2011).

26.4.1.4 Retina

26.4.1.4.1 Background

In the year 1935, Dr. Isodore Goldstein introduced the unique patterns present inside the retina. Fifteen years later, Dr. Paul Tower discovered that identical twins also possess unique patterns in the retina. In 1976, the company EyeDentify first manufactured a commercially available retina-based identification system. Later, the same company manufactured an advanced retina-based identification system with high storage capacity called ICAM 2001 (Mazumdar and Nirmala 2018).

Retina showed good potential as a biometric identification trait with the unique appearance of its capillaries. The features present in the retina are difficult to forge as it presents in the rear side of the eye and are also very difficult to attain (Mazumdar and Nirmala 2018).

26.4.1.4.2 Physiology

The human retina is composed of neural cells placed on the posterior portion of the eye. Capillaries for blood supply to the eye form a complex unique structure. The uniqueness is significant for the discrimination of two different persons. Even identical twins also do not possess identical capillary networks similar to fingerprints. The retina is an age-independent feature as the capillaries fully developed during intrauterine life (Mazumdar and Nirmala 2018).

26.4.1.4.3 Recognition System

The retina-based recognition system can be divided into two categories i.e., vascular pattern-based and nonvascular feature-based recognition systems.

The vascular pattern-based recognition system uses the unique feature of a complex branch of retinal blood vessels. The steps followed in this authentication system are similar to the process of fingerprint authentication with an additional step as image segmentation (Akram et al. 2011; Condurache et al. 2012; Hussain et al. 2013; Kose et al. 2011). A person is instructed to place his/her eye close contact with a scanner without any movement. The scanner captures the image of the retina. Following this the is converted into a greyscale format. Different image enhancement algorithms reduce the background noise and other deformities during image capture. The image segmentation algorithm removes the background of the vascular patterns and a branchlike complex network of retinal blood vessels remains (Fatima et al. 2013; Khakzar and Pourghassem 2014; Lajevardi et al. 2013). For ease of feature extraction, the segmented image is further converted into a one-pixel wide skeletonized (thinned) image. Bifurcation and corresponding joints of the vascular branches are the main unique patterns present in the retinal blood vessels. These vessel joints and bifurcations are converted into their corresponding vector values and saved in the database. For matching purposes, the same steps are followed up to feature extraction and a separate algorithm compares the vector values to reach a decision (Zahedi et al. 2010; Oinonen et al. 2010; Qamber et al. 2012).

The nonvascular feature-based recognition system compares different structural variabilities like luminance, relative contrast, edge dissimilarity, etc. inside a retina. Luminance is the result of mean intensity (Waheed et al. 2016; Dehghani et al. 2013; Ong et al. 2015; Sabaghi et al. 2011). While contrast is the measure of the standard deviation of two images of the same retina. A similarity score is generated to compare the retinal images of two persons. Except for the structural features, spectral variation of retinal images of different persons is used as an identification feature (Sabaghi et al. 2012).

26.4.1.5 Iris

26.4.1.5.1 Background

In the 1950s, British ophthalmologist J.H. Doggart first documented the importance and similar uniqueness of the iris as compared to fingerprints. A few decades later in 1985, the use of iris as a biometric identification trait has become popular in the early 1990s. Although several components of the eye have the potential to be a successful biometric trait, the large-scale uniqueness and ease of image acquisition make it the best choice. Purposefully, it largely replaced the retina-based biometric authentication system due to its efficiency in law enforcement and security organizations (Jain et al. 2011). The United Kingdom government began a new identification system namely, Iris Recognition Immigration System (IRIS) in 2002 across the international airports in the country for security measures. FBI is preparing for an additional automated identification system based on the iris. Iris is seldom found as evidence in a crime scene as it has a limited scope in personal identification in forensic analysis. In rare circumstances, video footage recorded by infrared or high-resolution visible light-based handheld cameras can accidentally record very close to the iris. But the quality of that frame containing the iris is very poor as it is a part of dynamic footage. The extraction and matching of the image of an iris with a standard sample from a suspect is a task of a lifetime. Besides the rarity of the iris as evidence in forensic analysis, it is a comprehensive tool to keep criminal records for verification purposes (Jain et al. 2011; Jain and Ross 2015).

26.4.1.5.2 Physiology

Iris is located between the cornea and the lens of an eye. It works as a quantitative regulator for lights entering the eye periodic contraction and dilation of a small opening pupil. Iris consists of four layers i.e., the posterior layer, the muscle layer, stromal layer, and anterior border layer. The *posterior layer* contains two layers of pigmented epithelial cells. The pigmentation makes it an illumination-impermeable layer. The *muscle layer* is made up of a dilator and sphincter muscle to dilate and contract the pupil. The *stromal layer* is located above the posterior and muscle layer. Blood vessels and collagen connective tissues are arranged along the radial direction in this layer (Jain et al. 2011). The *anterior border layer* is the topmost and the concerning layer for biometric measurements. It is composed of a rich layer of chromatophores. The external appearance of the iris is just like an annular object bound by the pupillary and limbus boundary. An image of the iris is divided into two zones: the central papillary and the surrounding ciliary zone. These two zones are separated by a circular ridgeline known as the collarette. Pit-like entities around the collarette are known as the crypts that permit the entry of fluids during the contraction and dilation process. Concentric lines and radial furrows are found near the outer ciliary zone and pupillary zone, respectively. The agglomeration and other typical textures present in the iris make it a unique feature. The diversity of the texture is huge around different populations. Melanin-controlled pigmentation defines the color of the iris. Pigmentation is a genetically controlled factor and is distributed in diverse variants (Jain et al. 2011).

26.4.1.5.3 Recognition Process

Iris-based identification is a matching system similar to fingerprint and retina. It consists of image acquisition, segmentation, normalization, and encoding or matching units.

The *image acquisition* unit captures a 2-dimensional image of the eye by using a monochromatic IR illuminated camera. The imaging of the iris under IR illumination provides several advantages over the visible range. The minute details of the dark-colored iris can only be observed under IR illumination. IR illumination is invisible to human eyes; hence it enables non-intrusive image acquisition. Approximately, 200 pixels around the iris region is a good quality image for further processing. A person needs to be cooperative during the image capture as he/she should stop any movement of their eyes (Jain et al. 2011).

The *image segmentation* unit isolates only the iris from the image of a whole eye by detecting the inner and outer boundary of the iris. In the case of poorly visible boundaries, a predefined active contour algorithm is used to extract the iris. Iris has a diverse inter-variation in its appearance and structure. Appearance-based models as discussed in the facial recognition section are used for automatic recognition of the iris. Distinct pupillary boundary works as a good discriminating factor in iris segmentation (Jain et al. 2011).

The *image normalization* converts the segmented image from the standard cartesian coordinate system with one set of coordinates for one point to a pseudo-polar coordinate with an infinite number of coordinates for one point. During this process, the iris is represented as a rectangle which is known as the Daugmanns rubber sheet model. The rows of the rectangle show the concentric regions of the iris (Jain et al. 2011).

Iris encoding is used to create a database or add a piece of new information to it. While the *matching* process follows the steps up to the normalization and processes the comparison algorithm for matching instead of the encoding algorithm. The encoding process extracts numerical information corresponding to the image of the iris (Jain et al. 2011).

26.4.1.6 Vein Pattern Recognition

26.4.1.6.1 Background

The venous networks beneath the human skin form a complex pattern that is unique in every individual. Since venous networks are safely placed in the human body, it is very difficult to forge the venous pattern to hide the identity. The thickness of the skin is irregular in different parts of the body (Revol 2010). Since the thickness of the skin over the venous network on the dorsal part of the hand and feet are relatively thinner than other parts of the body, visualization and imaging for biometric authentication are best suited at these two parts of the body. Most of the vein pattern-based recognition systems use the fingers, dorsal, and palmar parts of the hand as the image of a hand can be more easily captured than feet. In 1991, McGregor and Weldford proposed a hand vein pattern-based personal identification approach. In the early 2000s, the Japanese company Fujitsu experimented with the uniqueness of vein-based techniques and found that six persons possess similar vein patterns per one million population. Despite some similarities, there were significant distinctive characters to discriminate between them. Since then, vein hand vein patterns have been used for security purposes (Kommini et al. 2011). In 2006, vein pattern-based personal identification came into the limelight when a child sexual abuse case was solved through the comparison of the image of a hand from a video with the suspected person. It revolutionized the application of the vein pattern-based authentication process in forensic sciences in a large number of sexual abuse cases during the next few years in Europe (Al-Tamini 2019).

26.4.1.6.2 Physiology

Veins are present beneath the subcutaneous layer of the skin. The venous distribution of the upper limb of the body consists of superficial and deep vessels. The deep veins are accompanied by the arteries. They are connected to the superficial veins. These veins start on the back of the hand as a dorsal arch. Three major veins cephalic, basilic, and median cubital comprise the venous network around the wrist, palm, and fingers (Revol 2010; Valavan and Kalaivani 2014). All the veins inside the human body develop during intrauterine life and grow up to approximately eighteen years of age. Till then the branched structure remains relatively constant throughout life except for any venous disease or accidental repairing processes. The cephalic vein begins at the radial extremity of the arch and further ascends along the lateral aspect of the arm, and then it pierces the deep fascia to enter the axillary vein just distal to the clavicle. The basilic vein passes along the medial aspect of the forearm, pierces the deep fascia at the elbow, and joins the venae comitantes of the brachial artery. The median cubital vein links the cephalic and basilic veins in front of the elbow. All these three major veins collectively have a network-like structure on the hand (Revol 2010).

26.4.1.6.3 Recognition Process

The recognition consists of a similar setup as used for retinal vascular pattern authentication. An image acquisition unit captures the image of the venous structure present inside the fingers, palm, or the dorsal part of the hand (Hillerström et al. 2014). Veins are not identifiable under the visible spectrum of electromagnetic radiation (EMR). Since the near IR region of the EMR has the most penetration potential for the subcutaneous layer of the skin, an IR illumination source requires in this process (Kommini et al. 2011). The image acquisition process in the vein pattern recognition system is not yet standardized as it is a new field and requires more extensive experiments. Some systems capture the image by illuminating from the above and the remaining systems capture by illuminating the veins of the skin penetration. After the image acquisition, it is converted to greyscale form or the acquisition system pre-set in the greyscale (Kommini et al. 2011). Following the greyscale conversion several image processing algorithms enhance the image quality and remove the background noise by using different filters. Image segmentation is applied to the image to separate the venous network and it is further skeletonized to get a one-pixel-wide structure that can be easily converted to corresponding vector

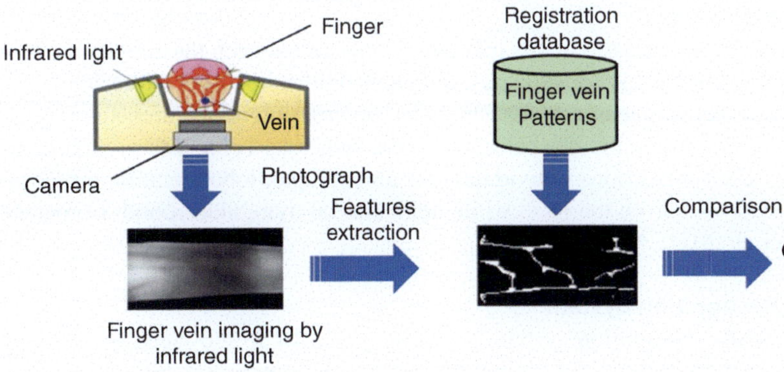

Fig. 26.7 Representation of a conventional finger vein pattern matching system. Reprinted from Mohsin A.H., Zaidan A.A., Zaidan B.B., Albahri O.S., Albahri A.S., Alsalem M.A., Mohammed K. I., Based blockchain-PSO-AES techniques in finger vein biometrics: A novel verification secure framework for patient authentication, Computer Standards & Interfaces, 66 (2019). https://doi.org/10.1016/j.csi.2019.04.002. (Mohsin et al. 2019). Copyright 2021, with permission from Elsevier

values (Al-Tamini 2019). Figure 26.7 represents the steps of a standard finger vein biometric system. Vein patterns consist of similar vascular features: bifurcation and vein joints as described in vascular biometric authentication of the retina. The position, inter distance, and inter-angles are unique in different individuals and even in the two different hands of the same individual. Despite the efficiency of this technique, several problems still need to be addressed for a worldwide standardized prototype (Al-Tamini 2019).

26.4.1.7 Ear Biometrics

26.4.1.7.1 Background

Earmarks are used for more than a century as a personal identification tool. But the authenticity of earmarks found on doors, windows, or walls is not up to the mark, and identification biases were always there until an image-based biometric authentication system was invented. This method was more reliable as it includes a clear image of the whole external ear for a reliable comparison (Alva et al. 2019). In 1890, French criminologist Alphonse Bertillon first proposed the external ear as a biometrics tool (Saferstein 2011). Burge and Burger first proposed an automated ear-based biometric identification system. CCTVs often capture the movements of suspected persons or perpetrators. In a practical scenario, the face of a suspected person or any perpetrator is not always clearly recognizable in the video footage and sometimes the side view of the person is captured with it. In those circumstances, ear-based biometric authentication arrives. The external ear (pinna) consists of several peculiar characteristics that are unique in nature. Manual or automatic comparison of these features can successfully identify an individual (Alva et al. 2019; Jain et al. 2011).

26.4.1.7.2 Physiology

The overall shape of the ear remains relatively constant between the age of approximately 8–70 years except for any physiological deformities due to accidents or diseases. The external ear of a human includes several unique features i.e., tragus, concha, triangular fossa, lobule, helix, antihelix, and crus helix. Every individual feature also differs in various individuals. As an example, lobule can be presently attached or detached from the face, while helix can be triangular, round, or rectangular (Jain et al. 2011; Alva et al. 2019).

26.4.1.7.3 Recognition System

The ear biometric recognition system is relatively similar to the facial recognition system. The system captures the image of the ear and preprocesses it to produce an enhanced and desired format. The enhanced image is then processed for feature extraction. Extracted features are mathematically converted and saved for further matching process (Jain et al. 2011).

Preprocessing enhances the overall quality of an image by removing the background noise and illumination problems. Different filters like a fuzzy filter, Gaussian filter, and wavelet transform are used for the preprocessing. Additionally, the conversion of an image from multichannel RGB (red green blue) to single-channel greyscale reduces the complexity. Histogram equalization can also fulfil the purpose (Alva et al. 2019).

Feature extraction predominantly identifies and separates the identifiable properties embedded in an image. Geometry-based techniques extract the features related to shapes like helix, tragus, concha, etc. It establishes the inter-distances and angles between them and converts them into mathematical data. Except for structural features, edge and contour detection methods are also used in the geometrical method. Appearance-based extract texture and intensity-based features by using the histogram. The force-field transformation method uses each pixel of the image and extracts its corresponding energy lines and channels (Jain et al. 2011; Alva et al. 2019).

The encoding process encrypts the extracted features, and *the authentication* step follows all the steps up to the feature extraction and then uses specific algorithms to compare and match the ear. Trained neural networks are used to compare the features. All the features are saved in the network as a training dataset. The network consists of several nodes that represent the features added to it. If the features of a test image are entered into the network, then it generates a comparative score. A threshold value of the score for a positive match is already set in the algorithm. Normalized cross-correlation, support vector machine, K-nearest neighbor methods use a similar process for authentication (Jain et al. 2011).

26.4.1.8 Hand Geometry

26.4.1.8.1 Background

Hand geometry is among the less frequently used biometric feature. In the early 1970s, hand geometry-based biometric systems were first commercially available.

Sidlauskas first introduced a 3-dimensional hand profile identification apparatus which was efficiently used for hand geometry-based personal identification. In the commercial front, hand geometry-based verification systems are implemented in several airports e.g., Ben Gurion Airport (Tel Aviv, Israel) and industrial sectors e.g., Nuclear power plants in United States (Jain et al. 2011).

26.4.1.8.2 Physiology

The hand geometry-based recognition emphasizes the fact that each human hand is unique. Finger width, length, curvatures, thickness and their relative location are different for each person (Varchol and Levicky 2007).

26.4.1.8.3 Recognition System

A hand geometry-based system consists of four main steps i.e., image capture/ acquisition, hand segmentation and alignment, feature extraction, and feature comparison/matching.

The *image capture* step is either contactless or contact-based. The image capture accessory acquires the image of the back of the hand. Generally, the system captures in-contact images, while, contactless systems are under development (Jain et al. 1999, 2011).

Hand segmentation is the next step after image capture. The hand boundary is extracted to determine the region of interest, followed by the extraction of the silhouette of the hand by using numerous morphological operators. Multiple image processing techniques remove remaining artefacts and noises from the images. Due to the variation in the placement of hands by different individuals, the silhouette of the hand from multiple captures are not correctly aligned. To counter this problem, individual finger-based small segmentations are performed. Each segmentation is sufficient for the feature extraction (Jain et al. 2011).

Hand segmentation is followed by *feature extraction*. Basically, two types of features are extracted from the segmented silhouette of the hand i.e., 1-D geometric measurements (finger and palm length, finger and palm width and finger thickness) and 2-D shape-based features. Other than these two major features, several points along the contours of the hand silhouette are also considered as features. Dimensionality of these features are reduced to achieve more discrimination potential (Varchol and Levicky 2007; Mohammad et al. 2021).

Feature matching is the final step in the system. Distance based comparison and matching are performed by using the extracted features. Generally, euclidean distance measurement is the most commonly used matching algorithm. Machine learning methods like, support vector machine (SVM) can be used for better precision (Jain et al. 1999, 2011; Varchol and Levicky 2007; Mohammad et al. 2021).

26.4.2 Behavioral Biometric Traits

Behavioral traits are predominantly fundamentally different from physiological features. These traits are acquired after birth and the appearance of the trait potentially changes throughout life. Behavioral biometric traits consist of handwriting and signature, keystroke pattern, voice authentication, and gait pattern. Behavioral biometrics do not need any additional scanning or image acquisition tool used in physiological systems (Purgason and Hibler 2012). Among all these four traits voice is the most consistent biometric tool for comparison as it shows relatively low variation throughout the lifetime. Behavioral patterns Several factors around us affect the behavior of a human being. Notwithstanding. the behavioral patterns of the aforesaid features change with time and due to some surrounding factors, the changes are relatively superficial as the core behavior remains consistent (Purgason and Hibler 2012).

26.4.2.1 Handwriting and Signature

26.4.2.1.1 Background

Signature and handwriting were used as personal identification tools way before fingerprints came into the act. Signature has been used as a personal identity for so many centuries around the world. Till now forensic experts perform a manual comparison of handwritten and signed documents in several properties related to forgeries, letters related to extortion, and suicide (Padmajadevi and Aprameya 2016). The dynamics of handwriting and signature are so diverse that creating an automated matching system was very difficult. In 1965, the North American Aviation department was the first organization to develop a signature recognition system. Since then, a lot changed in the way the recognition process works. But the fundamental principles behind the authentication remain consistent (Padmajadevi and Aprameya 2016).

26.4.2.1.2 Behavioral Features

Handwriting and signature both are combinations of an acquired neuro-muscular activity. It is an acquired skill that needs rigorous and regular practice. Class and individual characteristics affect the appearance of handwriting and signatures. Since class characteristics are relatively more dynamic (tends to change) than the individual characteristics with time and other factors, biometric systems mostly record the later ones (Padmajadevi and Aprameya 2016; Diaz et al. 2019). In handwriting samples, connecting strokes of certain words, letters, or inter-word connections are individual specific. The relative distance between the letters, words, sentences, and paragraphs is also unique. Typical features of some alphabets show a wide range of variability between individuals. The considerable features are significantly different in signatures than handwriting. More minute details are observed in it. The average angle between the baseline and the slant, connections, pen lifts, blind or complete loops, and several diacritics are the unique features. Besides these visible features, some latent features like whole signing time, pen lift timing between two different strokes, time to create a particular loop, etc. are used in a few systems (Padmajadevi and Aprameya 2016; Diaz et al. 2019).

26.4.2.1.3 Recognition System

Most of the recognition systems use a signature instead of handwriting because signature-based systems are relatively more robust than handwriting-based systems. Handwriting samples consist of larger dimensions in comparison to the signature. Hence, in this section, we will discuss the signature-based recognition system. Signature recognition techniques are either offline or online. Offline techniques use the visible features of the signature, while the online feature can use visible as well as latent features of the signature. Cameras, scanners, or mobile phones are used for offline data collection and tablets or similar touch panels. The authentication system typically consists of six steps (Padmajadevi and Aprameya 2016).

Registration of the written or signed sample is the first step in the system. A person is dictated a certain amount of writing material or directed to several signatures. A sensor digitizes the written sample for further processing. Different scanners, digital tablets, mobile phones, etc. are used for this purpose.

Pre-processing removes any kind of virtual pen-up strokes from the test signature. Now from the processed signature, several model signatures are produced. This step also removes other background noises during scanning or image capture. The enhanced image is further normalized by area normalization or histogram normalization. Normalized image is skeletonized similarly as performed in fingerprint, retina, and vein pattern analysis.

Handwritten signature analysis systems are either online (dynamic) or offline (static) depending on data acquisition method: Online devices like tablet PCs or graphic tablets generate position, velocity, acceleration, and force signal as the signature representative. Off-line data acquisition devices like cameras, scanners perform the data acquisition after the writing process has been completed. After the data acquisition, preprocessing of the signal is carried out to remove the noise or spurious signals, then normalization, skeletonization, and smoothing techniques are employed if required. Then segmentation is carried out. Different segmentation techniques are proposed based on various criteria like pen down/pen up signals, the velocity of signal, perceptually relevant point, connected components, tree structure analysis, statistics of directional data, etc. Two types of features are used for signature analysis: functions or parameters. Some of the most diffuse functions used are position, velocity, and acceleration, the direction of pen movement, pressure, and forces. Some of the most diffuse parameters used in the signature analysis are position, X-Y correlation of position, displacement, speed, acceleration. Fourier Transform. Hadamard Transform, Wavelet Transform total signature time duration, pen-down time ratio, number of pen-ups/pen-downs, and several parameters based on projections, geometry, slant, orientation, contour, grid, texture, etc. More than hundreds of parameters are reported in the literature (Padmajadevi and Aprameya 2016).

Feature extraction processes include two types of extraction. One is functional and the other is parametric. Functional features are extracted in offline mode, while parametric features are extracted in online mode. Position, velocity, direction, pen movement, etc. are major functional features. Displacement, speed, acceleration, etc. are major parametric features. Feature extraction is far more difficult in comparison to physiological biometric systems. Since the range of variations is wider in the mathematical dimensions of different features in signature samples, the system is more focused on the functional features.

The classification model is created by using several statistical tools. Extracted features are fed into the algorithms which create a training model for comparison.

The model validation process compares a controlled test signature with the pre-set training values corresponding to the extracted features. The matching score is compared with the previously decided threshold for a positive match.

Efficiency check is an additional process that needs to be performed during the system calibration for false acceptance and false rejection rates by using randomly collected forged or copied signature samples (Padmajadevi and Aprameya 2016; Diaz et al. 2019).

26.4.2.2 Keystroke Pattern

26.4.2.2.1 Background

Technological developments simultaneously change the way of security and crime investigation processes. The keystroke authentication system is one of these new realms of investigative tools in forensic sciences. Like other activities, a person has a distinctive keystroke pattern. Despite an acquired character, this activity builds uniqueness within an individual due to inter-personal differences of the brain. As an advantage. keystroke patterns can be observed continuously and clearly for several sessions. In 1975, R.J. Spillane first proposed a keystroke-based identification system. He described the unique characteristics associated with the keystroke of an individual (Teh et al. 2013).

26.4.2.2.2 Behavioral Features

The central concept of the keystroke pattern depends upon the timing of pressing and releasing the key and shifting from one key to another. Besides these two main features, some repetitive habits are also included. Keystroke authentication is all about how a person types instead of what he/she types (Karnan et al. 2011). The time between a 'key up' and the next 'key down' is called the flight time. From this data three-timing features i.e., press-to-press, release-to-release, and press-to-release can be extracted. Timing to type a single word, two letters (digraph), or three letters (trigraph) is also a significant feature. Diagraph and trigraph come under the press-to-press category. Different systems subdivide these superficial features into their sub-features as key interval time, internet time, up-up or down-down time, hold time, etc (Karnan et al. 2011; Teh et al. 2013).

26.4.2.2.3 Recognition System

The development of a keystroke authentication system involves four steps. Collection of typing characteristics data, feature extraction, set up a training dataset, and validation of the training dataset (Karnan et al. 2011). The data collection, training dataset creation, and validation steps are almost similar in different keystroke-based systems. While individual systems use a single or a combination of different features. The keystroke data is collected through different input devices like pressure-sensitive keyboards, num-pad, smartphones, etc. After feature extraction, several classification algorithms like PCA, LDA, HCA are used to create training models for data comparison (Balagani et al. 2011; Teh et al. 2013). Finally, the efficiency of the system is checked through validation. It is of two types for the keystroke recognition system. The efficiency of the system is first validated by the data set of known typing samples and further with the unknown random typing samples from the same individual. The latter decides the accuracy and applicability of the system (Khanna and Sasikumar 2010; Nauman and Ali 2010).

26.4.2.3 Voice Authentication

26.4.2.3.1 Background

The voice of every individual is unique like other biometric traits. It has been used as a biometric tool since the 1970s. A voice-based identification system deals with the authentication of a speaker through the typical characteristics included in it. Voice as evidence is often encountered in extortion, blackmailing, threat, or kidnapping cases. Perpetrators use several manuals or digital voice manipulation mediums like modulation software, handkerchief, or deliberate imitation of someone's voice. In these circumstances, voice-based authentication becomes highly significant to not only find out the original speaker but also to prove the innocence of a person.

26.4.2.3.2 Behavioral and Physiological Features

Various text pronunciation patterns are the majority of the voice-associated behavioral features. The utterance patterns of individual alphabets and words are different in different individuals. Even the pattern of the utterance of a person can change over time due to several factors like education, surrounding environment, physiological deformity, age, emotional state, etc. The physiological features of the voice are relatively consistent (Singh et al. 2018). The physiology of voice is controlled by inherited genetic features. It is expressed through the structure of the voice box, throat, and mouth. The exact shape, size, and other dimensions of these three parts are different among all the individuals. But the voice tends to change up to a certain age till these boy parts grow. Approximately, after 18 years of age, the pitch and frequency of the voice remain constant except for any physical deformity or accident of the voice-producing organs. Now, it is clearly understood that the produced voice is a collective result of physiological as well as behavioral features (Singh et al. 2018).

26.4.2.3.3 Recognition System

As it is observed that voice is a collection of physiological and behavioral features, the recognition systems are divided into text-dependent and text-independent methods. Text-dependent systems use the utterance pattern of predetermined alphabets, words, or phrases. On the contrary, text-independent methods use the pitch, frequency, intervals between words or alphabets, and utterance duration of the speaker (Singh et al. 2018). Although the text-independent method needs relatively more complex algorithms, it offers more secure identification against fraud and errors. Both methods consist of a similar recognition process as used for the majority of the biometric traits. The preprocessing algorithm removes background noise and any other interferences during the recording of the voice (Singh et al. 2018). Voice samples are represented in the form of a spectrum. Specific text-dependent and independent features are extracted from this spectrum and stored in the database for comparison. Statistical modelling is used in speaker identification. After the generation of a match score by comparing the test and training sample, a likelihood ratio approach is applied for decision making. The similarity score is converted into two univariate distributions represented by the probability density function (distribution of random variables). The values of these functions express the likelihood scores that can accept or reject a hypothesis (Singh et al. 2018). In this case, a hypothesis is a binary decision-making tool. A hypothesis either accepts that training and test samples are the same or different. The likelihood ratio approach is highly significant because it largely removes decision bias by comparing the values with the training sample as well as with the mean values for the same features calculated in a specific population (Singh et al. 2018).

26.4.2.4 Gait Pattern

26.4.2.4.1 Background

Human identification from a significant distance has emerged as an important aspect of forensic sciences as well as security sectors. All the biometric traits discussed above need a physical connection with the authentication system or should be present at a close distance for scanning. In real life, it does not happen always. CCTV footages very often capture distant human activity, that cannot be used for iris, ear, or facial identification (Jain et al. 2011). In this situation, gait analysis can be the rescuer (Fig. 26.5). Gait is the pattern of locomotion in bipedal or tetrapedal animals. It has a certain level of interpersonal uniqueness that can be a useful biometric trait for identification. Aristotle first described animal gait patterns. In 1890, Christian Wilhelm Braune, a German anatomist reported several research articles on human gait analysis. Since the early 1970s, individual gait pattern analysis has frequently been applied for personal identification purposes. As a distant recognition method, it can be analyzed without any direct subject interaction and it can be recorded in low illuminations without using any specialized imaging devices (Jain et al. 2011).

26.4.2.4.2 Behavioral Features

Gait is the locomotion patterns in all pedal animals. In human beings it is a bipedal activity combines with the changes in the body shape. It is a resultant of both statis and dynamic features. The variability in the musculo-skeletal structure of the body directly affect the gait pattern of a person (Jain et al. 2011).

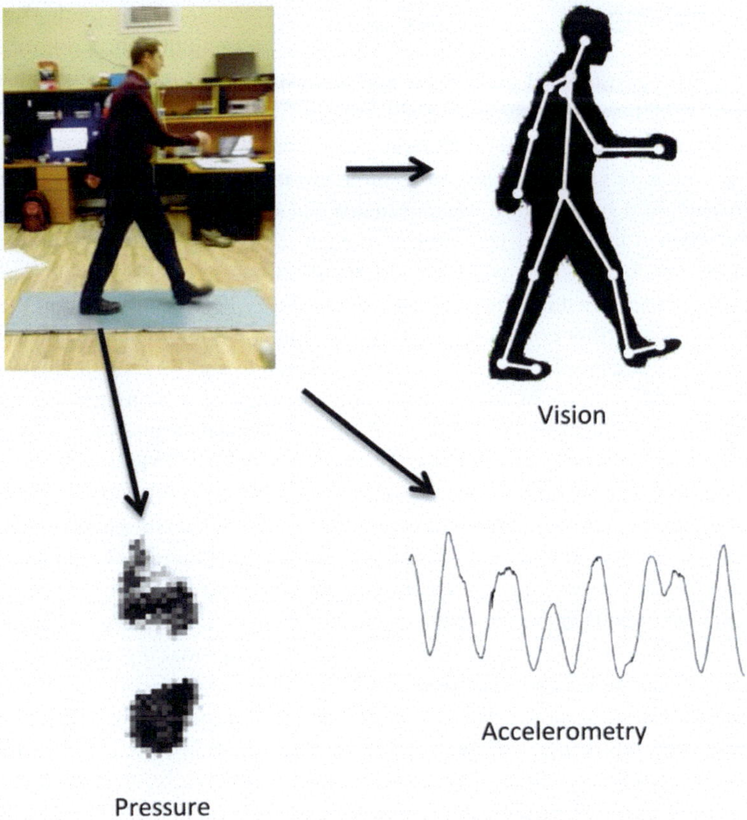

Fig. 26.8 The gait feature extraction from a video footage of a person. Reprinted from Connor P., Ross A., Biometric recognition by gait: A survey of modalities and features, Computer Vision and Image Understanding, 167 (2018). https://doi.org/10.1016/j.cviu.2018.01.007 (Connor and Ross 2018). Copyright 2021, with permission from Elsevier

26.4.2.4.3 Recognition System

The silhouette extraction algorithm is a contour isolation algorithm used in the gait analysis for the feature extraction (Fig. 26.8). It isolates the edges (contour) of the human body from a video frame. This algorithm uses the background subtraction process to achieve this feat. Now model-based or model-free approaches extract relevant gait-related features. Model-based methods extract structural information by using previous data or training data (Jain et al. 2011). It allows a robust feature extraction. Structural information keeps the silhouette shape relatively constant which tends to less error. Model-free extraction uses movement-based information. It extracts the time interval data between steps. Data computation is comparatively easier in model-free approaches. But silhouette distortion cannot be inhibited in this method. Statistical modelling and classification algorithms like PCA, HCA, LDA are used for feature matching and decision-making (Jain et al. 2011).

26.5 Challenges

Instead of a broad range of successful applications in forensic sciences, biometric recognition systems still possess several limitations. Physiological traits are comparatively more robust and reliable than behavioral ones. Positioning differences on the data acquisition device, variable user interaction, deformities, variable imaging environments, and background noise remains the major factors affecting the exact match between training and test samples (Xiao 2007). As a consequence, match score-based approaches are widely used in all modern biometric authentication systems. Match score establishes a degree of similarity between the test and training samples which is further compared with a predefined threshold value. A match score greater than the threshold value shows a positive match and vice versa. The genuine accept rate (GAR) is one of the measures of accuracy of a biometric system as it represents the ratio between the number of correctly classified input samples and the total number of positive input samples. The higher value of GAR is indicative of an efficient biometric recognition system (Manju and Rajendran 2012; Bharathiraja and Sumathi 2014). In addition, ability to verify (ATV) is another measure of efficiency of a biometric system. It is the combination of false rejection rate (FRR) and failure to enroll (FTE). The low values of FRR and FTE represent a high ATV value which in turn indicates good efficiency of the system (Nanavati and Thieme 2002). Several errors occur while implementing the aforesaid decision-making algorithm. False acceptance (FA) and false rejection (FR) are the most encountered errors in automated biometric systems. FA occurs when two samples are mistaken as from the same person but actually, those are from various persons. FR occurs when two samples are mistaken as from numerous persons but actually, those are from the person (Manju and Rajendran 2012; Bharathiraja and Sumathi 2014). FA and FR represent the functions of the threshold value. A reduced threshold value can make the system more tolerant of input variabilities but increases the false acceptance rate (FAR) and an increased threshold simultaneously enhance the FRR. There are some circumstances when a biometric system fails to automatically capture biometric data due to insufficient signal quality. It is comprehended as a failure to capture (FTC) or failure to acquire (FTA) (Manju and Rajendran 2012; Bharathiraja and Sumathi 2014). On the other side, an individual sometimes fails to enroll (FTE) the data in the recognition system due to physical deformities, or lack of training. Except for the limitation of the system itself, external factors also inhibit the optimum usability of the recognition systems. A person can easily fool the authentication system by using an artificial silicon finger consist of an individuals' fingerprint. The fingerprint can be collected from any surface touched by that particular individual. Facial recognition systems are more vulnerable than fingerprints as the rate of false acceptance is very high and by editing the lighting conditions, viewpoints, and artificial makeup someone can easily fool any automated face identifier. Printed iris images can successfully bypass the scanning sensor up to a large extent. Behavioral trait-based biometric systems are more vulnerable than physiological traits. A person can bypass a behavioral biometric system with extended and rigorous practice of that specific behavior. Additionally, similar to physiological system circumventions are

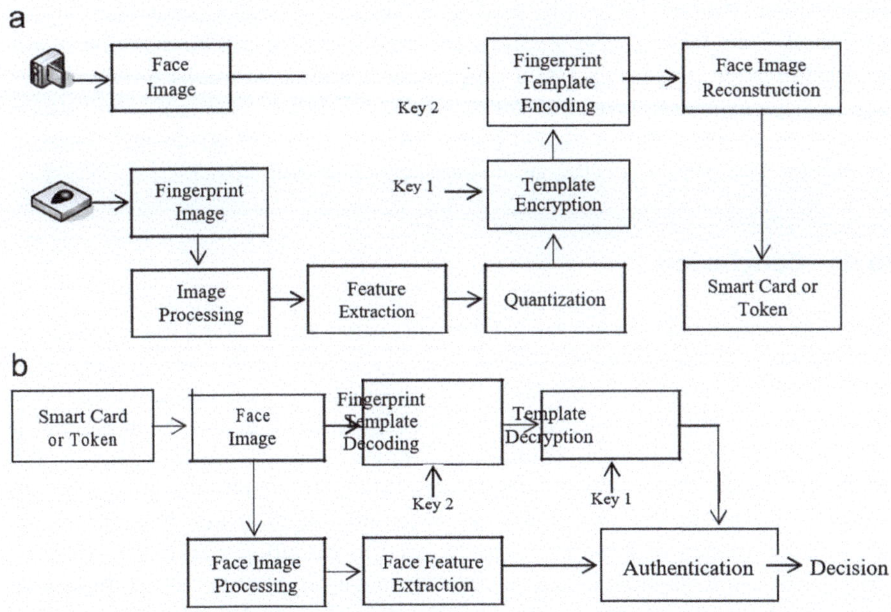

Fig. 26.9 Schematic diagram of the proposed system: (**a**) fingerprint template encoding into face image and (**b**) fingerprint template decoding from the face image. Reprinted from Khan M.K., Zhang J. Multimodal face and fingerprint biometrics authentication on space-limited tokens, Neurocomputing, 71 (2008). https://doi.org/10.1016/j.neucom.2007.12.017. Copyright 2021, with permission from Elsevier

also practiced in behavioral systems. Playback of recorded speech in voice authentication and Input modifications are reported in signature authentication. Instead of these vulnerabilities, a biometric system-based forensic analysis is relatively free from these circumventions as the test samples are recorded under controlled circumstances and in the presence of experts.

The aforesaid vulnerabilities of the biometric systems require a reasonable and effective solution. Therefore, multibiometric devices are the future of this field (Fig. 26.9). These systems are more secure and accurate than a single system. It integrates two or more biometric traits to enhance system performance. It can be made of any combination such as fingerprint and face, fingerprint and voice, face and iris, retina, iris, and face, or any other. Potential forger experiences more difficulties to bypass these kinds of authentication systems. Generally, multimodal systems integrate the match score that rectifies the FAR and FRR for a positive match to a large extent (Manju and Rajendran 2012; Bharathiraja and Sumathi 2014). Unavailability of the primary biometric data due to some system error or any other reasons, soft biometrics are the solitary solution. For example, instead of the whole facial features, some parts of the face can be useful to identify race, sex or even an individual if the section under comparison consists of any particular feature like a scar. Birthmarks, tattoos and accidental marks are other soft biometric features under consideration. Among frequently used soft biometric features periocular region, facial marks, and tattoo marks are most commonly used in soft biometric systems. The identification procedures based on periocular and facial marks follow similar steps as implemented in facial and ear recognition. While tattoo mark identification is analogous to fingerprint, vein and retinal identification methods as well as facial recognition methods for specific large characters (Jain et al. 2011).

26.6 Conclusion

Crimes are committed by humans, and they inevitably leave several traces related to their identity. On the contrary, criminals also try to hide or imitate the identity of someone else to commit a crime. In both these situations, personal identification is the only way to identify that person. Since every forensic investigation reaches a person or group person who committed a crime, personal identification is the principal purpose of the criminal justice system. Biometric traits either physiological or behavioral, are the true representatives of an individual. Traces, impressions, or any other expression of these traits can be used to identify a particular person by using a biometric identification system. The fingerprint is the oldest biometric feature used for identification purposes. The last six decades saw an enormous revolution in the field of biometric authentication based on automated devices. Most of these systems capture an image or scan the expression of the biometric trait, process it, extract relevant features corresponding to the collected data and save it in the database. The saved data of the trait are compared with a test sample to generate a match score. The generated match score is compared with a predefined threshold value. Automation always comes up with pros and cons. Similarly, automated biometric systems have several limitations. FAR, FRR, FTE, and FTC are the major limitations of these systems. While these systems are also vulnerable to human forging abilities. Bypassing a scanning system through artificial fingerprints, face or iris is a very common instance nowadays. To inhibit these attacks and other system limitations further researches are going around the globe with a more secure, robust, sensitive system set-up.

References

Akram MU, Tariq A, Khan SA (2011) Retinal recognition: personal identification using blood vessels. In: Internet technology and secured transactions (ICITST), international conference. IEEE, Manhattan, pp 180–184

Al-Tamini M (2019) A survey on the vein biometric recognition systems: trends and challenges. J Theor Appl Inf Technol 2019:11

Alva M, Srinivasaraghavan A, Sonawane K (2019) A review on techniques for ear biometrics. In: 2019 IEEE international conference on electrical, computer and communication technologies (ICECCT). IEEE, Manhattan

Arneodo A, Decoster N, Roux S (2000) A wavelet-based method for multifractal image analysis. I. Methodology and test applications on isotropic and anisotropic random rough surfaces. Eur Phys J B Condens Matter Complex Syst 15(3):567–600

Balagani KS, Phoh VV, Ray A, Phoha S (2011) On the discriminability of keystroke feature vectors used in fixed text keystroke authentication. Pattern Recogn Lett 32:1070–1080

Bharathiraja E, Sumathi S (2014) Person recognition using multimodal biometrics. Int J Eng Res Technol (IJERT) NCACCT-2014 2(12)

Condurache AP, Kotzerke J, Mertins A (2012) Robust retina-based person authentication using the sparse classifier. In: Signal processing conference (EUSIPCO) proceedings of the 20th European. IEEE, Manhattan, pp 1514–1518

Connor P, Ross A (2018) Biometric recognition by gait: a survey of modalities and features. Comput Vis Image Underst 167:1–27. https://doi.org/10.1016/j.cviu.2018.01.007

Dash M, Liu H (1997) Feature selection for classification. Intell Data Anal 1:131–156

Dehghani A, Ghassabi Z, Moghddam HA, Moin MS (2013) Human recognition based on retinal images and using new similarity function. EURASIP J Image Video Process 1:1–10

Diaz M, Ferrer MA, Impedovo D, Malik MI, Pirlo G, Plamondon R (2019) A perspective analysis of handwritten signature technology. ACM Comput Surv 51:6

Fatima J, Syed AM, Akram MU (2013) A secure personal identification system based on human retina. In: Industrial electronics and applications (ISIEA), IEEE symposium on IEEE. IEEE, Manhattan, pp 90–95

Hall M (1999) Correlation based feature selection for machine learning. Doctoral dissertation. University of Waikato

Hillerström F, Kumar A, Veldhuis R (2014) Generating and analyzing synthetic finger vein images. Biosig. IEEE, Manhattan

Hussain A, Bhuiyan A, Mian A, Ramamohanarao K (2013) Biometric security application for person authentication using retinal vessel feature. In: Digital image computing: techniques and applications (DICTA), international conference on IEEE. IEEE, Manhattan, pp 1–8

Jain A, Pankanti S (2009) The essential guide to image processing fingerprint recognition. Elsevier, pp 649–676

Jain AK, Ross A (2015) Bridging the gap: from biometrics to forensics. Philos Trans R Soc B 370: 20140254

Jain AK, Ross AA, Pankanti S (1999) A prototype hand geometry-based verification system. In: Proceedings of 2nd international conference on audio- and video-based biometric person authentication, Washington, DC

Jain AK, Ross AA, Nandakumar K (2011) Introduction to biometrics. Springer, Cham

Kanchan T, Krishan K (2013) Personal identification in forensic examinations. Anthropologie 2: 114

Karnan M, Akila M, Krishnaraj N (2011) Biometric personal authentication using keystroke dynamics: a review. Appl Soft Comput 11:1565–1573

Kataria AN, Adhyaru DM, Sharma AK, Zaveri TH (2013) A survey of automated biometric authentication technique (Member IEEE) 2, Nirma University International Conference on Engineering (NUiCONE)

Khakzar M, Pourghassem H (2014) A rotation invariant retina identification algorithm using tessellation-based spectral feature. In: Biomedical engineering (ICBME), 2014 21th Iranian conference. IEEE, Manhattan, pp 309–314

Khanna P, Sasikumar M (2010) Recognising emotions from keyboard stroke pattern. Int J Comput Appl 11(9):1–5

Kohavi R, John GH (1997) Wrappers for feature subset selection. Artif Intell 97:273–324

Kommini C, Ellanti K, Ellanti H (2011) Hand dorsal veins and knuckle shape based authentication system. Int J Comp Sci Inf Technol 2(4):1633–1638

Kose C, Iki C et al (2011) A personal identification system using retinal vasculature in retinal fundus images. Expert Syst Appl 38(11):13670–13681

Lajevardi SM, Arakala A, Davis SA, Horadam KJ (2013) Retina verification system based on biometric graph matching. IEEE Trans Image Process 22(9):3625–3635
Liu H, Motoda H (1998) Feature selection for knowledge discovery and data mining. Kluwer Academic, Boston
Manju R, Rajendran A (2012) Performance analysis of multimodal biometric based authentication system. Int J Eng Res Technol 1:7
Mazumdar JB, Nirmala SR (2018) Retina based biometric authentication system: a review. Int J Adv Res Comput Sci 9(1):711–718
Miller B (1994) Vital signs of identity. IEEE Spectr 31:22–30
Mohammad HH, Baker SA, Nori AS (2021) Biometric identity authentication system using hand geometry measurements. J Phys Conf Ser 1804:012144
Mohsin AH, Zaidan AA, Zaidan BB, Albahri OS, Albahri AS, Alsalem MA, Mohammed KI (2019) Based blockchain-PSO-AES techniques in finger vein biometrics: a novel verification secure framework for patient authentication. Comput Stand Interfaces 66. https://doi.org/10.1016/j.csi.2019.04.002
Nanavati S, Thieme M (2002) Ability to verify: a metric for system performance in real-world comparative biometric testing. In: Zhang D (ed) Biometric solutions, the Springer international series in engineering and computer science, vol 697. Springer, Boston
Nauman M, Ali T (2010) TOKEN: trustable keystroke-based authentication for web-based applications on smartphones. Springer, Berlin, pp 286–297
Oinonen H, Forsvik H, Ruusuvuori P, Yli-Harja O, Voipio V, Huttunen H (2010) Identity verification based on vessel matching from fundus images. In: 2010 IEEE international conference on image processing. IEEE, Manhattan, pp 4089–4092
Ong EP, Xu Y, Wong DWK, Liu J (2015) Retina verification using a combined points and edges approach. In: Image processing (ICIP), 2015 IEEE international conference. IEEE, Manhattan, pp 2720–2724
Padmajadevi G, Aprameya KS (2016) A review of handwritten signature verification systems and methodologies. In: International conference on electrical, electronics, and optimization techniques (ICEEOT)
Pahuja G, Nagabhushan TN (2015) Biometric authentication & identification through behavioral biometrics: a survey. In: International conference on cognitive computing and information processing (CCIP)
Purgason B, Hibler D (2012) Security through behavioral biometrics and artificial intelligence. Proc Comput Sci 12:398–403
Qamber S, Waheed Z, Akram MU (2012) Personal identification system based on vascular pattern of human retina. In: Biomedical engineering conference (CIBEC), Cairo international. IEEE, Manhattan, pp 64–67
Revol M (2010) Arteries and veins of the upper limb. http://www.anato.info/fiches/Upperlimb_vessels.pdf
Sabaghi M, Hadianamrei SR, Zahedi A, Lahiji MN (2011) A new partitioning method in frequency analysis of the retinal images for human identification. J Signal Inf Process 2(4):274
Sabaghi M, Hadianamrei SR, Fattahi M, Kouchaki MR, Zahedi A (2012) Retinal identification system based on the combination of Fourier and wavelet transform. J Signal Inf Process 3:1
Saferstein R (2011) Criminalistics an introduction to forensic science. Springer, New York
Saini M, Kapoor AK (2016) Biometrics in forensic identification: applications and challenges. J Forensic Med 1:2
Singh N, Agrawal A, Khan RA (2018) Voice biometric: a technology for voice based authentication. Adv Sci Eng Med 10(7):754
Teh PS, Teoh ABJ, Yue S (2013) A survey of keystroke dynamics biometrics. Sci World J 2013:408280
Tistarelli M, Champod C (2017) Handbook of biometrics for forensic science. Springer, Cham
Valavan TT, Kalaivani MR (2014) Biometric authentication system using finger vein. Piscataway, IEEE, pp 50–55

Varchol P, Levicky D (2007) Using of hand geometry in biometric security systems. Radioengineering 16(4):82–87

Waheed Z, Waheed A, Akram MU (2016) A robust nonvascular retina recognition system using structural features of retinal image. In: 2016 13th international Bhuban conference on applied sciences and technology. IEEE, Piscataway, pp 101–105

Xiao Q (2007) Biometrics—technology, application, challenge and computational intelligence solutions. In: IEEE computational intelligence magazine. IEEE, Piscataway

Zahedi A, Sadjedi H, Behrad A (2010) A new retinal image processing method for human identification using radon transform. In: 6th Iranian conference on machine vision and image processing. IEEE, Piscataway, pp 1–4

Zhang D, Kanhangad V, Luo N, Kumar A (2010) Robust palmprint verification using 2D and 3D features. Pattern Recogn 43(1):358–368. https://doi.org/10.1016/j.patcog.2009.04.026

SPRINGER NATURE

GPSR Compliance

The European Union's (EU) General Product Safety Regulation (GPSR) is a set of rules that requires consumer products to be safe and our obligations to ensure this.

If you have any concerns about our products, you can contact us on ProductSafety@springernature.com

In case Publisher is established outside the EU, the EU authorized representative is:

Springer Nature Customer Service Center GmbH
Europaplatz 3
69115 Heidelberg, Germany

The manufacturer's authorised representative in the EU is Springer Nature Customer Service Centre GmbH, Europaplatz 3, 69115 Heidelberg, Germany. If you have any concerns regarding our products, please contact ProductSafety@springernature.com

Printed and bound by CPI Group (UK) Ltd, Croydon, CR0 4YY
30/09/2026
02225317-0019